October 23–25, 2013
Barcelona, Spain

Association for Computing Machinery

Advancing Computing as a Science & Profession

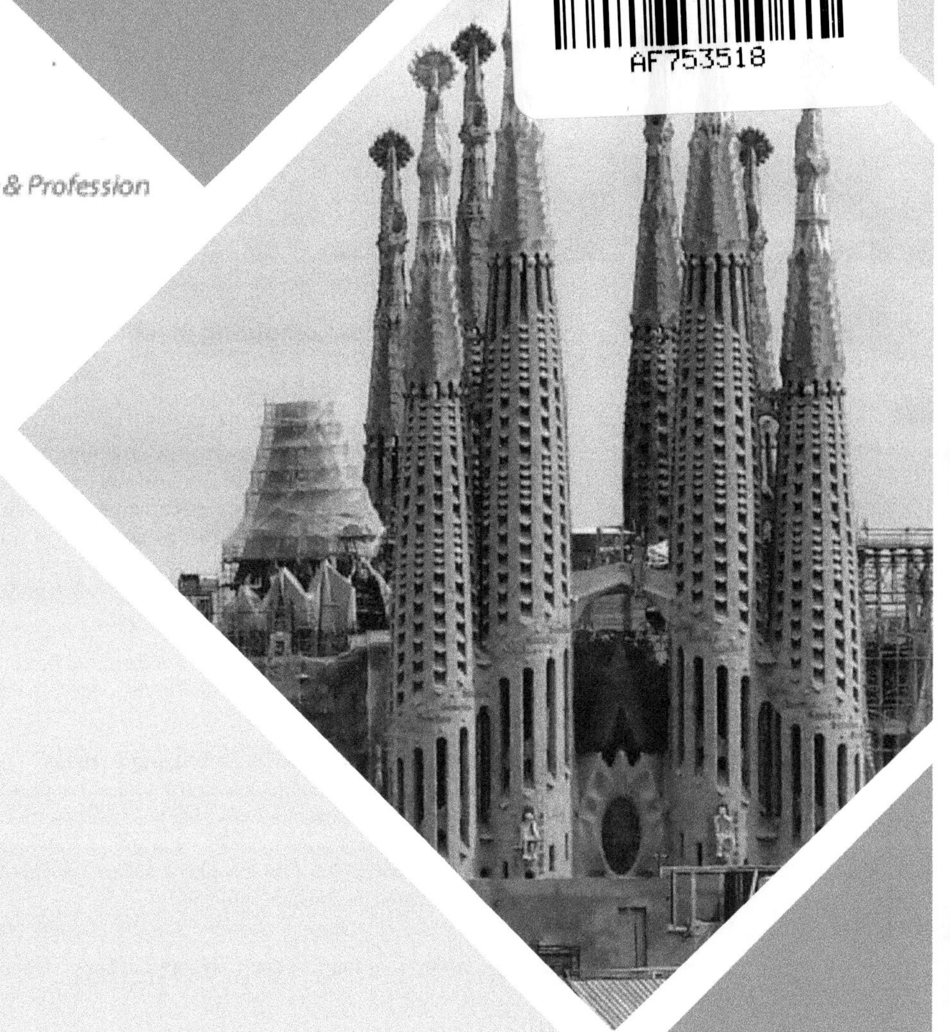

IMC'13

Proceedings of the 13th ACM
Internet Measurement Conference

Sponsored by:

ACM SIGCOMM and ACM SIGMETRICS

Supported by:

NSF, Akamai, Telefonica, mPlane, MLAB, ThousandEyes and technicolor

Association for
Computing Machinery

Advancing Computing as a Science & Profession

The Association for Computing Machinery
2 Penn Plaza, Suite 701
New York, New York 10121-0701

Notice to Past Authors of ACM-Published Articles
ACM intends to create a complete electronic archive of all articles and/or other material previously published by ACM. If you have written a work that has been previously published by ACM in any journal or conference proceedings prior to 1978, or any SIG Newsletter at any time, and you do NOT want this work to appear in the ACM Digital Library, please inform permissions@acm.org, stating the title of the work, the author(s), and where and when published.

ISBN: 978-1-4503-1953-9 (Digital)

ISBN: 978-1-4503-2679-7 (Print)

Additional copies may be ordered prepaid from:

ACM Order Department
PO Box 30777
New York, NY 10087-0777, USA

Phone: 1-800-342-6626 (USA and Canada)
+1-212-626-0500 (Global)
Fax: +1-212-944-1318
E-mail: acmhelp@acm.org
Hours of Operation: 8:30 am – 4:30 pm ET

Printed in the USA

General Chair's Welcome

It is our great pleasure to welcome you to Barcelona, Spain, for the 13th ACM Internet Measurement Conference.

This year's conference continues the tradition of a strong technical program, selected by a world renowned technical program committee, led by Dr. Krishna Gummadi, from MPI-SWS, and Dr. Craig Partirdge, from BBN. The program features 42 papers in total – 25 long and 17 short, as well as a keynote speech by Dr. Pablo Rodriguez Rodriguez, research and innovation director at Telefonica Digital.

Barcelona itself probably does not need a lot of introduction. It has been described as one of the most vibrant Mediterranean cities, with architectural works by Antoni Gaudí and Lluís Domènech i Montaner, designated as UNESCO World Heritage Sites, and has been designated as the world mobile capital until the year 2018. The conference will take place in the Telefonica Tower ZeroZero, that was built in 2011, and won the "best commercial building of the year" award in the architectural LEAF International Awards 2011.

As with every year, this conference would not have been possible without the generous support of our sponsors. We would like to sincerely thank the following organizations and companies for their continuous support: NSF (platinum sponsor), Akamai, Telefonica, MLAB, and mPlane (gold sponsors), and ThousandEyes, and Technicolor (silver sponsors). Thanks to them we were able to fund 27 students (including partial support) from North America, Europe, and Asia, that may not have been able to attend the conference otherwise.

Finally, this is the second time that the conference is organized by a general chair. I would like to personally thank the IMC Steering Committee for their continuous support throughout the conference organization. Not just for answering my questions, but for their wonderful attitude towards new ideas and for ensuring that our community keeps maturing and focusing on having an impact on society.

Konstantina (Dina) Papagiannaki
Telefonica Research, Telefonica Digital

Welcome from the Program Co-Chairs

Welcome to the 2013 edition of the Internet Measurement Conference. The 42 papers you will hear presented over the next three days represent some of the year's best work in network measurement and we hope you enjoy their contributions!

This year the conference received 178 submissions of which 92 were long papers and 86 were short papers. During an initial round of reviewing, each paper received 3 reviews. After assessing these reviews, 100 papers (63 long and 37 short) proceeded to a second round of additional reviewing. From these 100 papers, 72 papers (45 long, 27 short) were selected for discussion at the program committee meeting. The typical PC member reviewed between 20 and 22 papers and read several more.

The program committee met in Cambridge, Massachusetts, on July 10th. Almost the entire program committee was present. We are grateful for the effort they made (in some cases taking international and red-eye flights) to attend and for their insightful discussion.

Reviewing was single blind. The reviewers knew who the authors were, but the authors will not know who the reviewers are. We were careful to ensure reviewers did not review papers for which they were conflicted. We did catch a couple of cases where conflicts were inappropriately claimed to try to exclude a reviewer, a practice we resisted.

As Program Co-Chairs our job was largely that of orchestrating the hard work of others. Our greatest thanks are due to the members of the Program Committee. Their effort and insight can be seen in the review summaries that accompany each paper in the program. We would also like to thank the Steering Committee (Mark Allman, Chen-Nee Chuah, Jim Kurose and Renata Teixeira) for freely offering advice when asked and largely refraining from providing advice when we didn't want (and hopefully, did not need) it.

We would like to thank Dina Papagiannaki, our general chair; Blerim Cici, the IMC'13 website manager, and Bimal Viswanath, the IMC'13 submission site manager for helping with logistics. Finally, we want to thank ACM SIGCOMM and our corporate sponsors for making IMC'13 possible.

Krishna Gummadi
Max Planck Institute for Software Systems
gummadi@mpi-sws.org

Craig Partridge
Raytheon BBN Technologies
craig@aland.bbn.com

Table of Contents

Session Order 4: Money and Madison Avenue

Session Order 5: Weather in the Clouds

Session Order 6: Routing

Session Order 7: Fun with Phones

Session Order 8: Web

Session Order 9: Big or Fast

Session Order 10: Detective Stories

Session Order 11: Intriguing Results

Session Order 12: Paths and Flows

2013 Internet Measurement Conference Organization

General Chair

Konstantina (Dina) Papagiannaki, *Telefonica Research*

Technical Program Co-Chairs

Krishna Gummadi, *MPI-SWS*
Craig Partridge, *Raytheon BBN Technologies*

Technical Program Committee

Aditya Akella, *University of Wisconsin*
Mark Allman, *ICSI*
Lachlan Andrew, *Swinburne University of Technology*
Katerina Argyraki, *EPFL*
Aruna Balasubramanian, *University of Washington*
Theophilus Benson, *Duke University*
Meeyoung Cha, *KAIST*
Chen-Nee Chuah, *University of California Davis*
KC Claffy, *CAIDA/UCSD*
Alberto Dainotti, *CAIDA/UCSD*
Nick Feamster, *Georgia Tech*
Anja Feldman, *TU Berlin*
Yashar Ganjali, *University of Toronto*
Saikat Guha, *Microsoft Research*
John Heidemann, *USC/ISI*
Alefiya Hussain, *USC/ISI*
Ethan Katz-Bassett, *USC*
Haewoon Kwak, *Telefonica Research*
Vicky Manfredi, *Raytheon BBN Technologies*
Z. Morley Mao, *University of Michigan*
Cecilia Mascolo, *University of Cambridge*
Thyaga Nandagopal, *US National Science Foundation*
Jeffrey Pang, *AT&T Labs - Research*
Joel Sommers, *Colgate University*
Jia Wang, *AT&T Labs - Research*
Udi Weinsberg, *Technicolor*
Kuai Xu, *Arizona State University*
Ben Zhao, *University of California Santa Barbara*

Additional Reviewers

Hugh Cannon, *Wayne State University*
David D. Clark, *MIT LCS*
Jeffrey Erman, *AT&T Labs - Research*
Emir Halepovic, *AT&T Labs - Research*
Vikas Kawadia, *Raytheon BBN Technologies*
Robert Moskowitz, *Verizon*
Sam Nelson, *Raytheon BBN Technologies*
Aman Shaikh, *AT&T Labs - Research*
Narseo Vallina-Rodriguez, *University of Cambridge*
Shobha Venkataraman, *AT&T Labs - Research*

Website Manager

Blerim Cici, *University of California Irvine*

IMC Steering Committee

Mark Allman, *ICSI*
Chen-Nee Chuah, *University of California Davis*
Jim Kurose, *University of Massachusetts Amherst*
Renata Teixeira, *CNRS and UPMC Sorbonne Universités*

2013 Internet Measurement Conference Sponsors

The Steering Committee, Organizing Committee, attendees, and friends of the 2013 ACM Internet Measurement Conference are grateful to the sponsors and supporters of this conference. These supporters' generosity and investment in the network measurement research community has helped make this conference possible.

2013 IMC Sponsors

acm sigcomm

2013 IMC Platinum Supporter

NSF

2013 IMC Gold Supporters

Akamai

Telefónica
Telefónica
Investigación y Desarrollo

mPlane

MLAB

2013 IMC Silver Supporters

ThousandEyes

technicolor

Revealing Middlebox Interference with Tracebox

Gregory Detal, Benjamin Hesmans, Olivier Bonaventure
Université catholique de Louvain
Louvain-la-Neuve – Belgium
firstname.name@uclouvain.be

Yves Vanaubel, Benoit Donnet
Université de Liège
Liège – Belgium
firstname.name@ulg.ac.be

ABSTRACT

Middleboxes such as firewalls, NAT, proxies, or Deep Packet Inspection play an increasingly important role in various types of IP networks, including enterprise and cellular networks. Recent studies have shed the light on their impact on real traffic and the complexity of managing them. Network operators and researchers have few tools to understand the impact of those boxes on any path. In this paper, we propose `tracebox`, an extension to the widely used `traceroute` tool, that is capable of detecting various types of middlebox interference over almost any path. `tracebox` sends IP packets containing TCP segments with different TTL values and analyses the packet encapsulated in the returned ICMP messages. Further, as recent routers quote, in the ICMP message, the entire IP packet that they received, `tracebox` is able to detect any modification performed by upstream middleboxes. In addition, `tracebox` can often pinpoint the network hop where the middlebox interference occurs. We evaluate `tracebox` with measurements performed on PlanetLab nodes. Our analysis reveals various types of middleboxes that were not expected on such an experimental testbed supposed to be connected to the Internet without any restriction.

Categories and Subject Descriptors

C.2.3 [**Network Operations**]: Network Monitoring

Keywords

Network Discovery, Middleboxes, tracebox

1. INTRODUCTION

The TCP/IP architecture was designed to follow the end-to-end principle. A network is assumed to contain hosts implementing the transport and application protocols, routers implementing the network layer and processing packets, switches operating in the datalink layer, etc. This textbook description does not apply anymore to a wide range of networks. Enterprise networks, WiFi hotspots, and cellular networks often include various types of middleboxes in addition to traditional routers and switches [1]. A *middlebox*, defined as "any intermediary box performing functions apart from normal, standard functions of an IP router on the data path between a source host and destination host" [2], manipulates traffic for purposes other than simple packet forwarding. Middleboxes are often deployed for performance or security reasons. Typical middleboxes include Network Address Translators, firewalls, Deep Packet Inspection boxes, transparent proxies, Intrusion Prevention/Detection Systems, etc.

Recent papers have shed the light on the deployment of those middleboxes. For instance, Sherry et al. [1] obtained configurations from 57 enterprise networks and revealed that they can contain as many middleboxes as routers. Wang et al. [3] surveyed 107 cellular networks and found that 82 of them used NATs. Although these middleboxes are supposed to be transparent to the end-user, experience shows that they have a negative impact on the evolvability of the TCP/IP protocol suite [4]. For example, after more that ten years of existence, SCTP [5] is still not widely deployed, partially because many firewalls and NAT may consider SCTP as an unknown protocol and block the corresponding packets. Middleboxes have also heavily influenced the design of Multipath TCP [4, 6].

Despite of their growing importance in handling operational traffic, middleboxes are notoriously difficult and complex to manage [1]. One of the causes of this complexity is the lack of debugging tools that enable operators to understand where and how middleboxes interfere with packets. Many operators rely on `ping`, `traceroute`, and various types of `show` commands to monitor their networks.

In this paper, we propose, validate, and evaluate `tracebox`. `tracebox` is a `traceroute` [7] successor that enables network operators to detect which middleboxes modify packets on almost any path. `tracebox` allows one to easily generate complex probes to send to any destination. By using the quoted packet inside of ICMP replies, it allows to identify various types of packet modifications and can be used to pinpoint where a given modification takes place.

The remainder of this paper is organized as follows: Sec. 2 describes how `tracebox` works and how it is able to identify middleboxes along a path. Sec. 3 analyses three use cases from a deployment of `tracebox` on PlanetLab. Sec. 4 shows how `tracebox` can be used to debug networking issues. Sec. 5 compares `tracebox` regarding state of the art. Finally, Sec. 6 concludes and discusses further work.

IMC'13, October 23–25, 2013, Barcelona, Spain.
Copyright 2013 ACM 978-1-4503-1953-9/13/10 ...$15.00.
http://dx.doi.org/10.1145/2504730.2504757.

2. TRACEBOX

To detect middleboxes, `tracebox` uses the same incremental approach as `traceroute`, i.e., sending probes with increasing TTL values and waiting for ICMP `time-exceeded` replies. While `traceroute` uses this information to detect intermediate routers, `tracebox` uses it to infer the modification applied on a probe by an intermediate middlebox.

`tracebox` brings two important features.

Middleboxes Detection `tracebox` allows one to easily and precisely control all probes sent (IP header, TCP or UDP header, TCP options, payload, etc.). Further, `tracebox` keeps track of each transmitted packet. This permits to compare the quoted packet sent back in an ICMP `time-exceeded` by an intermediate router with the original one. By correlating the different modifications, `tracebox` is able to infer the presence of middleboxes.

Middleboxes Location Using an iterative technique (in the fashion of `traceroute`) to discover middleboxes also allows `tracebox` to approximately locate, on the path, where modifications occurred and so the approximate middleboxes position.

When an IPv4 router receives an IPv4 packet whose TTL is going to expire, it returns an ICMPv4 `time-exceeded` message that contains the offending packet. According to RFC792, the returned ICMP packet should quote the IP header of the original packet and the first 64 bits of the payload of this packet [8]. When the packet contains a TCP segment, these first 64 bits correspond to the source and destination ports and the sequence number. RFC1812 [9] recommended to quote the entire IP packet in the returned ICMP, but this recommendation has only been recently implemented on several major vendors' routers. Discussions with network operators showed that recent routers from Cisco (running IOX), Alcatel Lucent, HP, Linux, and Palo-Alto firewalls return the full IP packet. In the remainder of this paper, we use the term *Full ICMP* to indicate an ICMP message quoting the entire IP packet. We use the term RFC1812-compliant router to indicate a router that returns a *Full ICMP*.

By analyzing the returned quoted packet, `tracebox` is able to detect various modifications performed by middleboxes and routers. This includes changes in the Differentiated Service field and/or the Explicit Congestion Notification bits in the IP header, changes in the IP identification field, packet fragmentation, and changes in the TCP sequence numbers. Further, when `tracebox` receives a *Full ICMP*, it is able to detect more changes such as the TCP acknowledgement number, TCP window, removal/addition of TCP options, payload modifications, etc.

`tracebox` also allows for more complex probing techniques requiring to establish a connection and so multiple probes to be sent, e.g., to detect segment coalescing/splitting, Application-level Gateways, etc. In this case `tracebox` works in two phases: the *detection* and the *probing* phases. During the detection phase, `tracebox` sends probes by iteratively increasing the TTL until it reaches the destination. This phase allows `tracebox` to identify RFC1812-compliant routers. During the probing phase, `tracebox` sends additional probes with TTL values corresponding to the previously discovered RFC1812-compliant routers. This strategy allows `tracebox` to reduce its overhead by limiting the number of probes sent.

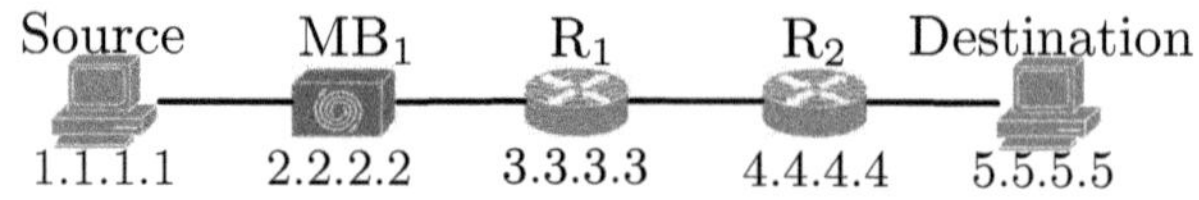

(a) topology

```
# tracebox -p 'IP / TCP / mss(9000)' -n 5.5.5.5
tracebox to 5.5.5.5 (5.5.5.5): 30 hops max
1: 3.3.3.3 TCP::SequenceNumber
2: 4.4.4.4 IP::TTL IP::CheckSum TCP::CheckSum TCP::SequenceNumber
           TCPOptionMaxSegSize::MaxSegSize
3: 5.5.5.5
```

(b) output

Figure 1: `tracebox` example

Fig. 1(a) shows a simple network, where MB_1 is a middlebox that changes the TCP sequence number and the MSS size in the TCP MSS option but that does not decrement the TTL. R_1 is an old router while R_2 is a RFC1812-compliant router. The server always answer with a TCP reset. The output of running `tracebox` between "Source" and "Destination" is given by Fig. 1(b). The output shows that `tracebox` is able to effectively detect the middlebox interference but it may occur at a downstream hop. Indeed, as R_1 does not reply with a *Full ICMP*, `tracebox` can only detect the TCP sequence change when analyzing the reply of R_1. Nevertheless, when receiving the *Full ICMP* message from R_2, that contains the complete IP and TCP header, `tracebox` is able to detect that a TCP option has been changed upstream of R_2. At the second hop, `tracebox` shows additional modifications on top of the expected ones. The TTL and IP checksum are modified by each router and the TCP checksum modification results from the modification of the header.

The detection of middleboxes depends on the reception of ICMP messages. If the router downstream of a middlebox does not reply with an ICMP message, `tracebox` will only be able to detect the change at a downstream hop similarly as the above example. Another limitation is that if the server does not reply with an ICMP (as in Fig. 1), then the detection of middleboxes in front of it is impossible.

`tracebox` is implemented in C++ in about 2,000 lines of code and embeds LUA [10] bindings to allow a flexible description of the probes as well to ease the development of more complex middlebox detection scripts. `tracebox` aims at providing the user with a simple and flexible way of defining probes without requiring a lot of lines of code. `tracebox` indeed allows to use a single line to define a probe (see as example the argument `-p` of `tracebox` in Fig. 1(b)) similarly to Scapy [11]. `tracebox` provides a complete API to easily define IPv4/IPv6 as well as TCP, UDP, ICMP headers and options on top of a raw payload. Several LUA scripts are already available and allows one to detect various types of middleboxes from Application-level Gateways to HTTP proxies. It is open-source and publicly available [12].

To verify the ability of `tracebox` to detect various types of middlebox interference, we developed several Click elements [13] modeling middleboxes. We wrote Click elements that modify various fields of the IP or TCP header, elements that add/remove/modify TCP options and elements that coalesce or split TCP segments. These elements have been included in a python library [14] that allows to easily describe a set of middleboxes and that generates the corresponding Click configuration. This library is used as unit tests to validate each new version of `tracebox`.

3. VALIDATION & USE CASES

In this section, we validate and demonstrate the usefulness of `tracebox` based on three use cases. We first explain how we deploy `tracebox` on the PlanetLab testbed (Sec. 3.1), next we asses the coverage of `tracebox` (Sec. 3.2) and finally discuss our use cases (Sec. 3.3, and 3.4).

3.1 PlanetLab Deployment

We deployed `tracebox` on PlanetLab, using 72 machines as vantage points (VPs). Each VP had a target list of 5,000 items build with the top 5,000 Alexa web sites. Each VP used a shuffled version of the target list. DNS resolution was not done before running `tracebox`. This means that, if each VP uses the same list of destination names, each VP potentially contacted a different IP address for a given web site due to the presence of load balancing or Content Distribution Networks. Our dataset was collected during one week starting on April 17th, 2013.

In this short paper, we focus on analyzing some interferences between middleboxes and TCP. In theory, PlanetLab is not the best place to study middleboxes because PlanetLab nodes are mainly installed in research labs with unrestricted Internet access. Surprisingly, we noticed that seven VPs, from the 72 considered for the use cases, automatically removed or changed TCP options at the very first hop. They replaced the Multipath TCP [6], MD5 [15], and Window Scale [16] options with NOP and changed the value of the MSS option. We also found that two VPs always change the TCP Sequence number.

3.2 RFC1812-compliant routers

`tracebox` keeps track of each original packet sent and makes a comparison with the quoted IP packet when the ICMP `time-exceeded` message is received. Further, `tracebox` can potentially detect more middleboxes when routers return a *Full ICMP* packet. `tracebox`'s utility clearly increases with the number of RFC1812-compliant routers. Fig. 2 provides an insight of the proportion of RFC1812-compliant routers and their locations.

In particular, Fig. 2(a) gives the proportion of RFC1812-compliant routers (the horizontal axis) as a CDF. A value of 0, on the horizontal axis, corresponds to paths that contained no RFC1812-compliant router. On the other hand, a value of 1 corresponds to paths made only of RFC1812-compliant routers. Looking at Fig. 2(a), we observe that, in 80% of the cases, a path contains at least one router that replies with a *Full ICMP*. In other words, `tracebox` has the potential to reveal more middleboxes in 80% of the cases.

Fig. 2(b) estimates the position of the RFC1812-compliant routers in the probed paths. It provides the distance between the VP and the RFC1812-compliant routers on a given path. Note that, on Fig. 2(b), the X-Axis (i.e., the distance from the VPs) has been normalized between 1 and 10. Distances between 1 and 3 refer to routers close to the VP, 4 and 6 refer to the Internet core while, finally, distances between 7 and 10 refer to routers closer to the `tracebox` targets. The widespread deployment of RFC1812-compliant routers in the Internet core is of the highest importance since `tracebox` will be able to use these routers as "mirrors" to observe the middlebox interferences occurring in the access network [3].

Fig. 2(b) shows that for 22% of the paths, the RFC1812-compliant routers are close to the VP. This is approximatively the same proportion for routers close to `tracebox` targets. However, the majority of routers sending back a *Full ICMP* are located in the network core.

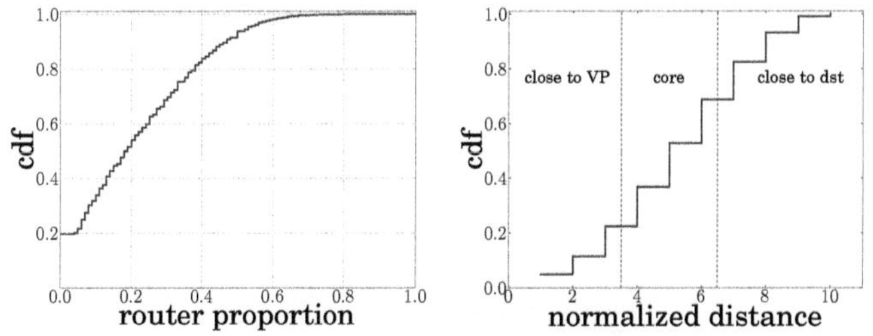

(a) Proportion of RFC1812-compliant routers on a path

(b) Normalized distance from VP to RFC1812-compliant router

Figure 2: RFC1812-compliant routers

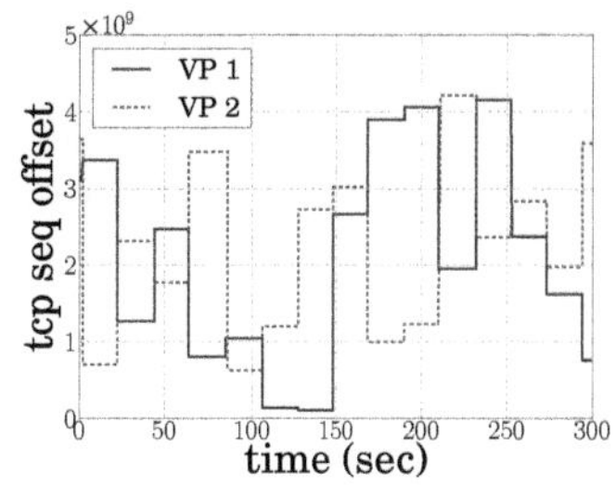

Figure 3: Time evolution of the TCP sequence number offset introduced by middleboxes

3.3 TCP Sequence Number Interference

The TCP sequence number is not supposed to be modified by intermediate routers. Still, previous measurements [4] showed that some middleboxes change sequence and acknowledgement numbers in the processed TCP segments. As the sequence number is within the first 64 bits of the TCP header, `tracebox` can detect its interference even though there are none RFC1812-compliant routers.

We analyze the output of `tracebox` from the 72 VPs. Our measurements reveal that two VPs always modify the TCP sequence numbers. The position of the responsible middlebox is close to the VP, respectively the first and third hop. We suspect that the middlebox randomizes the TCP sequence number to fix a bug in old TCP/IP stacks where the *Initial Sequence Number* (ISN) was predictable [17].

When used on a path that includes such a middlebox, `tracebox` can provide additional information about the sequence number randomization. Depending on the type of middlebox and the state it maintains, the randomization function can differ. To analyze it, we performed two experiments. First, we generated SYN probes with the same destination (IP address and port), the same sequence number, and different source ports. `tracebox` revealed that the middlebox modified all TCP sequence numbers as expected. A closer look at the modified sequence numbers revealed that the difference between the ISN of the probe and the randomized sequence number can be as small as 14510 and as large as 4294858380 (which corresponds to a negative difference of 108916 when the 32 bits sequence number space wrap). Our measurements show that these differences appear to be uniformly distributed for the different source ports.

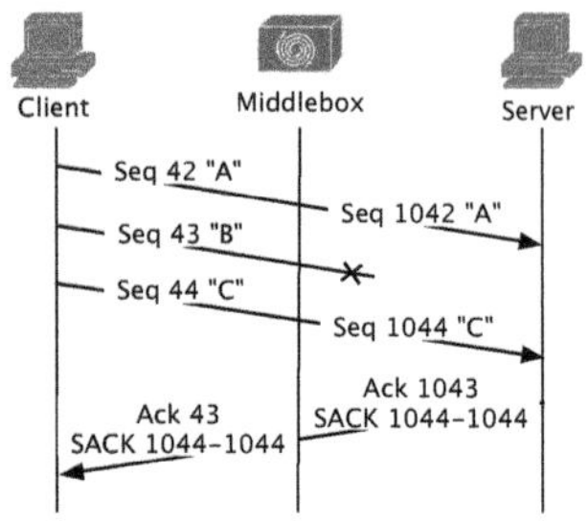

Figure 4: Example of invalid SACK blocks generated due to a middlebox.

For our second experiment, we used `tracebox` to verify how the randomization evolves over time. For this, we sent SYN probes using the same 5-tuple and different ISN during five minutes and evaluated the evolution of the TCP sequence number modifications. Fig. 3 shows the offset between the sent ISN and the randomized one for two different 5-tuples. `tracebox` reveals that the two middleboxes seem to change their randomization approximatively every 20 seconds. This suggests stateful middleboxes.

As explained by Honda et al. [4], changing the TCP sequence numbers has an impact on the TCP protocol evolvability. Unfortunately, it has also an impact on the utilization of widely deployed TCP extensions. Consider the TCP *Selective Acknowledgement* (SACK) option [18]. This TCP option improves the ability of TCP to recover from losses. One would expect that a middlebox changing the TCP sequence number would also update the sequence numbers reported inside TCP options. This is unfortunately not true, almost 18 years after the publication of the RFC [18]. We used `tracebox` to open a TCP connection with the SACK extension and immediately send SACK blocks. `tracebox` reveals that the middlebox changes the sequence number but does not modify the sequence number contained in the SACK block.

Fig. 4 shows the behavior of such a middlebox on the TCP sequence number and SACK blocks. In this scenario, the middlebox increases the TCP sequence number by 1,000 bytes causing the client to receive a SACK block that corresponds to a sequence number that it has not yet transmitted. This SACK block is invalid, but the acknowledgement is valid and correct. For the receiver, it may not be easy to always detect that the SACK information is invalid. The receiver may detect that the SACK blocks are out of the window, but the initial change may be small enough to carry SACK blocks that are inside the window.

If we know that a SACK block is invalid, algorithms that use SACK should understand that the SACK option does not give more information than a simple acknowledgment. In this view, such algorithms should have at least the same performance as they would have if SACK was not used at all. Unfortunately, this is not the case as the Linux TCP stack does not consider duplicate acknowledgment when SACK is enabled. When the offset is small the SACK blocks are potentially in-window. In this case the Linux TCP stack reacts correctly. However, when the SACK blocks are out-of-window then the TCP stack has to wait for a complete RTO instead of doing fast-retransmit. We performed a small measurement in a controlled environment and observed up to a 50% drop in performance with a large offset [19].

3.4 TCP MSS Option Interference

Our third use case for `tracebox` concerns middleboxes that modify the TCP MSS option. This TCP option is used in the SYN and SYN+ACK segments to specify the largest TCP segment that a host sending the option can process. In an Internet that respects the end-to-end principle, this option should never be modified. In the current Internet, this is unfortunately not the case. The main motivation for changing the TCP MSS option on middleboxes is probably to fix some issues caused by other middleboxes with Path MTU Discovery [20]. On top of changing the MSS option, we also discovered middleboxes, in a couple of ISPs, that add the option if it is missing.

Path MTU Discovery is a technique that allows a host to dynamically discover the largest segment it can send without causing IP fragmentation on each TCP connection. For that, each host sends large segments inside packets with the `Don't Fragment` bit set. If a router needs to fragment the packet, it returns an ICMP `destination-unreachable` (with code "Packet fragmentation is required but the 'don't fragment' flag is on") back to the source and the source updates its segment size. Unfortunately, some routers do not return such ICMP messages [21] and some middleboxes (e.g., NAT boxes and firewalls) do not correctly forward the received ICMP message to the correct source. MSS clamping mitigates this problem by configuring middleboxes to decrease the size reported in the MSS option to a smaller MSS that should not cause fragmentation.

We use our dataset to identify middleboxes that modify the MSS option in SYN segments. Fig. 5(a) provides, for each VP (the horizontal axis), the proportion of paths (the vertical axis, in log-scale) where the MSS option has been changed. We see that a few VPs encountered at least one MSS modification on nearly all paths while, for the vast majority of VPs, the modification is observed in only a couple of paths. We decided to remove those VPs from our data set for further analyses, meaning that only 65 VPs were finally considered for the use case.

Similarly to Fig. 5(a), Fig. 5(d) provides, for each target, the proportion of paths affected by an MSS modification. We see about ten targets that have a middlebox, probably their firewall or load balancer, always changing the MSS option. In the same fashion as the VPs that changed the MSS option, they also removed the Multipath TCP, MD5 and Window Scale options.

Fig. 5(b) indicates where, in the network, the MSS option is modified. In the fashion of Fig. 2(b), the distance from VP has been normalized between 1 and 10, leading to the rise of three network regions (i.e., close to VP, core, and close to targets). As shown by Fig. 5(b), `tracebox` can detect the MSS modification very close to the source (2.7% of the cases) while this detection mostly occurs in the network core (52% of the cases).

Remind that this distance does not indicate precisely where is actually located the middlebox responsible for the MSS modification. Rather, it gives the position of the router that has returned a *Full ICMP* and, in this ICMP packet, the quoted TCP segment revealed a modification of the MSS field. Actually, the middlebox should be somewhere between this position and the previous router (on that path) that has also returned a *Full ICMP* (or the VP if it was the very first *Full ICMP* on that path).

Fig. 5(c) refines our location of MSS modification by tak-

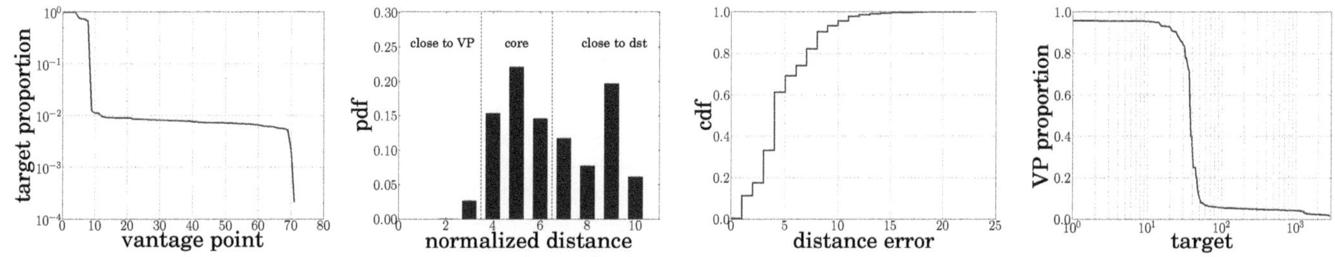

(a) VPs proportion modifying MSS

(b) Location

(c) Location error

(d) Targets proportion observing an MSS modification

Figure 5: MSS option modification

ing this aspect (i.e., the middlebox is somewhere on the path between the modification detection and the previous RFC1812-compliant router) into account. It gives thus an estimation of middlebox location error. This error is simply obtained by subtracting the distance at which tracebox reveals the modification and the distance at which the previous RFC1812-compliant router was detected by tracebox on that path. Obviously, lower the error, more accurate the location given in Fig. 5(b). On Fig. 5(c), we see that in 61% of the cases, the location estimation error is below (or equal to) four hops. All errors above 13 hops, that represents the length of around 60% of the paths, are uncommon (less than 1% each).

4. DISCUSSION

In Sec. 3, we showed that tracebox can provide a useful insight on known middleboxes interference. We believe that tracebox will also be very useful for network operators who have to debug strange networking problems involving middleboxes. While analyzing the data collected during our measurement campaign (see Sec. 3.1), we identified several strange middlebox behaviors we briefly explain in this section. We also discuss how tracebox can be used to reveal the presence of proxies and network address translators (NATs).

4.1 Unexpected Interference

We performed some tests with tracebox to verify whether the recently proposed Multipath TCP [6] option could be safely used over the Internet. This is similar to the unknown option test performed by Honda et al. [4]. However, on the contrary to Honda et al., tracebox allows one to probe a large number of destinations. To our surprise, when running the tests, tracebox identified about ten Multipath TCP servers based on the TCP option they returned. One of those server, www.baidu.com, belongs to the top 5 Alexa. All these servers where located inside China. A closer look at these options revealed that these servers (or their load balancers) simply echo a received unknown TCP option in the SYN+ACK. This is clearly an incorrect TCP implementation.

4.2 Proxy Detection

tracebox can also be used to detect TCP proxies. To be able to detect a TCP proxy, tracebox must be able to send TCP segments that are intercepted by the proxy and other packets that are forwarded beyond it. HTTP proxies are frequently used in cellular and enterprise networks [3]. Some of them are configured to transparently proxy all TCP connections on port 80. To test the ability of detecting proxies with tracebox, we used a script that sends a SYN probe to port 80 and, then, to port 21. If there is an HTTP proxy on the path, it should intercept the SYN probe on port 80 while ignoring the SYN on port 21. We next analyze the ICMP messages returned.

From our simple PlanetLab deployment, we identified two oddities. First, we found an HTTP proxy or more probably an IDS within a National Research Network (SUNET) as it only operated for a few destinations and that the path for port 80 was shorter than for port 21. Second, and more disturbing, tracebox identified that several destinations where behind a proxy whose configuration, inferred from the returned ICMP messages, resulted in a forwarding loop for probes that are not HTTP. We observed that the SYN probe on port 21, after reaching the supposed proxy, bounced from one router to the other in a loop as tracebox received ICMP replies from one router then another alternatively.

4.3 NAT Detection

NATs are probably the most widely deployed middleboxes. Detecting them by using tracebox would likely be useful for network operators. However, in addition to changing addresses and port numbers of the packets that they forward, NATs often also change back the returned ICMP message and the quoted packet. This implies that, when inspecting the received ICMP message, tracebox would not be able to detect the modification.

This does not prevent tracebox from detecting many NATs. Indeed, most NATs implement *Application-level Gateways* (ALGs) [22] for protocols such as FTP. Such an ALG modifies the payload of forwarded packets that contain the PORT command on the ftp-control connection. tracebox can detect these ALGs by noting that they do not translate the quoted packet in the returned ICMP messages. This detection is written as a simple script (shown in Fig 6) that interacts with tracebox. It builds and sends a SYN for the FTP port number and, then, waits for the SYN+ACK. The script makes sure that the SYN+ACK is not handled by the TCP stack of the host by configuring the local firewall (using the filter functionality, shown at line 7, of tracebox that configures iptables on Linux and ipfw on Mac OS X). It then sends a valid segment with the PORT command and the encoded IP address and port number as payload. tracebox then compares the transmitted packet with the quoted packet returned inside an ICMP message by an RFC1812-compliant router and stores the modification applied to the packet. If a change occurs and a callback function has been passed as argument, tracebox triggers the callback function. In Fig 6, the callback cb checks whether

```
1   -- NAT FTP detection
2   -- To run with: tracebox -s <script> <ftp_server>
3   -- Build the initial SYN (dest is passed to tracebox)
4   syn = IP / tcp{dst=21}
5   -- Avoid the host's stack to reply with a reset
6   fp = filter(syn)
7   synack = tracebox(syn)
8   if not synack then
9           print("Server did not reply...")
10          fp:close()
11          return
12  end
13  -- Check if SYN+ACK flags are present
14  if synack:tcp():getflags() ~= 18 then
15          print("Server does not seems to be a FTP server")
16          fp:close()
17          return
18  end
19  -- Build the PORT probe
20  ip_port = syn:source():gsub("%.", ",")
21  data = IP / tcp{src=syn:tcp():getsource(), dst=21,
22          seq=syn:tcp():getseq()+1,
23          ack=synack:tcp():getseq()+1, flags=16} /
24          raw('PORT '.. ip_port .. ',189,68\r\n')
25  -- Send probe and allow cb to be called for each reply
26  function cb(ttl, rip, pkt, reply, mods)
27          if mods and mods:__tostring():find("Raw") then
28                  print("There is a NAT before " .. rip)
29                  return 1
30          end
31  end
32  tracebox(data, {callback = "cb"})
33  fp:close()
```

Figure 6: Sample script to detect a NAT FTP.

there has been a payload modification. If it is the case a message showing the approximate position of the ALG on the path is printed (see line 29).

5. RELATED WORK

Since the end of the nineties, the Internet topology discovery has been extensively studied [23, 24]. In particular, `traceroute` [7] has been used for revealing IP interfaces along the path between a source and a destination. Since then, `traceroute` has been extended in order to mitigate its intrinsic limitations. From simple extensions (i.e., the types of probes sent [25, 26]) to much more developed modifications. For instance, `traceroute` has been improved to face load balancing [27] or the reverse path [28]. Its probing speed and efficiency has also been investigated [29, 30, 31].

To the best of our knowledge, none of the available `traceroute` extensions allows one to reveal middlebox interference along real Internet paths as `tracebox` does.

Medina et al. [21] report one of the first detailed analysis of the interactions between transport protocols and middleboxes. They rely on active probing with `tbit` and contact various web servers to detect whether Explicit Congestion Notification (ECN) [32], IP options, and TCP options can be safely used. The `TCPExposure` software developed by Honda et al. [4] is closest to `tracebox`. It also uses specially crafted packets to test for middlebox interference.

Wang et al. [3] analyzed the impact of middleboxes in hundreds of cellular networks. This study revealed various types of packet modifications. These three tools provide great results, but they are limited to specific paths as both ends of the path must be under control. This is a limitation since some middleboxes are configured to only process the packets sent to specific destination or ports. On the contrary, `tracebox` does not require any cooperation with the service. It allows one to detect middleboxes on any path, i.e., between a source and any destination. Our measurements reveal middleboxes that are close to the clients but also close to the server.

Sherry et al. [1] have relied on network configuration files to show the widespread deployment of middleboxes. Still, their study does not reveal the impact of these middleboxes on actual packets.

6. CONCLUSION

Middleboxes are becoming more and more popular in various types of networks (enterprise, cellular network, etc.). Those middleboxes are supposed to be transparent to users. It has been shown that they frequently modify packets traversing them, sometimes making protocols useless. Further, due to the lack of efficient and easy-to-use debugging tools, middleboxes are difficult to manage.

This is exactly what we tackled in this paper by proposing, discussing, and evaluating `tracebox`. `tracebox` is a new extension to `traceroute` that allows one to reveal the presence of middleboxes along a path. It detects various types of packet modifications and can be used to locate where those modifications occur. We deployed it on the PlanetLab testbed and demonstrated its capabilities by discussing several use cases. `tracebox` is open-source and publicly available [12].

`tracebox` opens new directions to allow researchers to better understand the deployment of middleboxes in the global Internet. In the coming months, we plan to perform large-scale measurement campaigns to analyze in more details middlebox interferences in IPv4 and IPv6 networks. `tracebox` could also be extended to fingerprint specific middleboxes.

Acknowledgments

We are grateful to the anonymous reviewers for their feedback. We would also like to thank Randy Bush, Matsuzaki Yoshinobu, Marc Neuckens, Pierre Reinbold, Bruno Delcourt and Claire Delcourt for assistance in understanding the middleboxes present in their networks.

This work is partially funded by the European Commission funded mPlane (ICT-318627) and CHANGE (INFSO-ICT-257422) projects and the BESTCOM IAP.

7. REFERENCES

[1] J. Sherry, S. Hasan, C. Scott, A. Krishnamurthy, S. Ratnasamy, and V. Sekar, "Making middleboxes someone else's problem: Network processing as a cloud service," in *Proc. ACM SIGCOMM*, August 2012.

[2] B. Carpenter and S. Brim, "Middleboxes: Taxonomy and issues," Internet Engineering Task Force, RFC 3234, February 2002.

[3] Z. Wang, Z. Qian, Q. Xu, Z. Mao, and M. Zhang, "An untold story of middleboxes in cellular networks," in *Proc. ACM SIGCOMM*, August 2011.

[4] M. Honda, Y. Nishida, C. Raiciu, A. Greenhalgh, M. Handley, and H. Tokuda, "Is it still possible to extend TCP," in *Proc. ACM/USENIX Internet Measurement Conference (IMC)*, November 2011.

[5] R. Stewart, Q. Xie, K. Morneault, C. Sharp, H. Schwarzbauer, T. Taylor, I. Rytina, M. Kalla,

L. Zhang, and V. Paxson, "Stream control transmission protocol," Internet Engineering Task Force, RFC 2960, October 2000.

[6] A. Ford, C. Raiciu, M. Handley, and O. Bonaventure, "TCP extensions for multipath operation with multiple addresses," Internet Engineering Task Force, RFC 6824, January 2013.

[7] V. Jacobson et al., "traceroute," UNIX, man page, 1989, see source code: ftp://ftp.ee.lbl.gov/traceroute.tar.gz.

[8] J. Postel, "Internet control message protocol," Internet Engineering Task Force, RFC 792, September 1981.

[9] F. Baker, "Requirements for IP version 4 routers," Internet Engineering Task Force, RFC 1812, June 1995.

[10] R. Ierusalimschy, L. H. de Figueiredo, and W. Celes, "LUA, an extensible extension language," *Software: Pactice & Experience*, vol. 26, no. 6, pp. 635–652, June 1996.

[11] P. Biondi, "Scapy," see http://www.secdev.org/projects/scapy/.

[12] G. Detal, "`tracebox`," July 2013, see http://www.tracebox.org.

[13] E. Kohler, R. Morris, B. Chen, J. Jannotti, and F. Kaashoek, "The click modular router," *ACM Transactions on Computer Systems*, vol. 18, no. 3, pp. 263–297, August 2000.

[14] B. Hesmans, "Mbclick," July 2013, see https://bitbucket.org/bhesmans/mbclick.

[15] A. Heffernan, "Protection of BGP sessions via the TCP MD5 signature option," Internet Engineering Task Force, RFC 2385, August 1998.

[16] V. Jacobson, R. Braden, and D. Borman, "TCP extensions for high performance," Internet Engineering Task Force, RFC 1323, May 1992.

[17] Microsoft, "Patch available to improve TCP initial sequence number randomness," Microsoft, Microsoft Security Bulletin MS99-066, October 1999, see http://technet.microsoft.com/en-us/security/bulletin/ms99-046.

[18] M. Mathis, J. Mahdavi, S. Floyd, and A. Romanow, "TCP selective acknowledgement options," Internet Engineering Task Force, RFC 2018, October 1996.

[19] C. Paasch, "Presentation ietf 87," July 2013, see http://tools.ietf.org/agenda/87/slides/slides-87-tcpm-11.pdf.

[20] J. Mogul and S. Deering, "Path MTU discovery," Internet Engineering Task Force, RFC 1191, November 1990.

[21] A. Medina, M. Allman, and S. Floyd, "Measuring interactions between transport protocols and middleboxes," in *Proc. ACM SIGCOMM Internet Measurement Conference (IMC)*, October 2004.

[22] P. Srisuresh and M. Holdrege, "IP network address translator (NAT) terminology and considerations," Internet Engineering Task Force, RFC 2663, August 1999.

[23] B. Donnet and T. Friedman, "Internet topology discovery: a survey," *IEEE Communications Surveys and Tutorials*, vol. 9, no. 4, December 2007.

[24] H. Haddadi, G. Iannaccone, A. Moore, R. Mortier, and M. Rio, "Network topologies: Inference, modeling and generation," *IEEE Communications Surveys and Tutorials*, vol. 10, no. 2, pp. 48–69, April 2008.

[25] M. Torren, "tcptraceroute - a traceroute implementation using TCP packets," UNIX, man page, 2001, see source code: http://michael.toren.net/code/tcptraceroute/.

[26] M. Luckie, Y. Hyun, and B. Huffaker, "Traceroute probe methode and forward IP path inference," in *ACM SIGCOMM Internet Measurement Conference (IMC)*, October 2008.

[27] B. Augustin, X. Cuvellier, B. Orgogozo, F. Viger, T. Friedman, M. Latapy, C. Magnien, and R. Teixeira, "Avoiding traceroute anomalies with Paris traceroute," in *Proc. ACM/USENIX Internet Measurement Conference (IMC)*, October 2006.

[28] E. Katz-Bassett, H. Madhyastha, V. Adhikari, C. Scott, J. Sherry, P. van Wesep, A. Krishnamurthy, and T. Anderson, "Reverse traceroute," in *Proc. USENIX Symposium on Networked Systems Design and Implementations (NSDI)*, June 2010.

[29] B. Donnet, P. Raoult, T. Friedman, and M. Crovella, "Efficient algorithms for large-scale topology discovery," in *Proc. ACM SIGMETRICS*, June 2005.

[30] R. Beverly, A. Berger, and G. Xie, "Primitives for active Internet topology mapping: Toward high-frequency characterization," in *Proc. ACM/USENIX Internet Measurement Conference (IMC)*, November 2010.

[31] T. Bourgeau and T. Friedman, "Efficient IP-level network topology capture," in *Proc. Passive and Active Measurement Conference (PAM)*, March 2013.

[32] K. Ramakrishnan, S. Floyd, and D. Black, "The addition of explicit congestion notification (ECN) to IP," Internet Engineering Task Force, RFC 3168, September 2001.

Demystifying the Dark Side of the Middle: A Field Study of Middlebox Failures in Datacenters

Rahul Potharaju
Purdue University
rpothara@purdue.edu

Navendu Jain
Microsoft Research
navendu@microsoft.com

ABSTRACT

Network appliances or *middleboxes* such as firewalls, intrusion detection and prevention systems (IDPS), load balancers, and VPNs form an integral part of datacenters and enterprise networks. Realizing their importance and shortcomings, the research community has proposed software implementations, policy-aware switching, consolidation appliances, moving middlebox processing to VMs, end hosts, and even offloading it to the cloud. While such efforts can use middlebox failure characteristics to improve their reliability, management, and cost-effectiveness, little has been reported on these failures in the field.

In this paper, we make one of the first attempts to perform a large-scale empirical study of middlebox failures over two years in a service provider network comprising thousands of middleboxes across tens of datacenters. We find that middlebox failures are prevalent and they can significantly impact hosted services. Several of our findings differ in key aspects from commonly held views: (1) Most failures are grey dominated by connectivity errors and link flaps that exhibit intermittent connectivity, (2) Hardware faults and overload problems are present but they are not in majority, (3) Middleboxes experience a variety of misconfigurations such as incorrect rules, VLAN misallocation and mismatched keys, and (4) Middlebox failover is ineffective in about 33% of the cases for load balancers and firewalls due to configuration bugs, faulty failovers and software version mismatch. Finally, we analyze current middlebox proposals based on our study and discuss directions for future research.

Categories and Subject Descriptors

C.2.3 [**Computer-Communication Network**]: Network Operations—*network management*

General Terms

Network management; Reliability

Keywords

Datacenters; Network reliability; Middleboxes

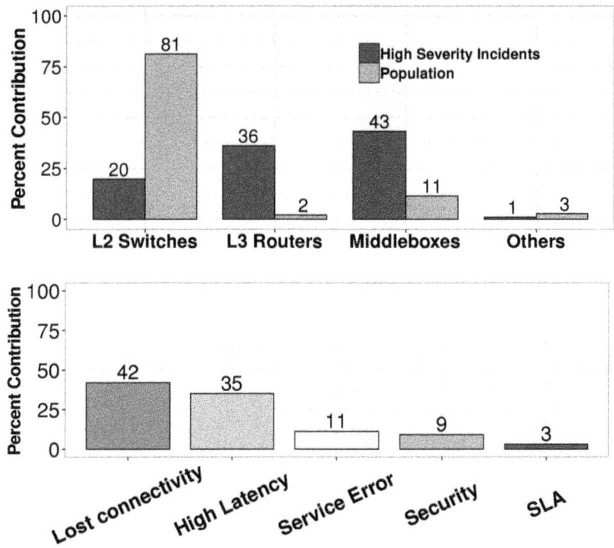

Figure 1: Middleboxes contribute to 43% of high-severity incidents despite being 11% of the population (top). The top-5 categories of service impact in these incidents caused by middleboxes (bottom).

1. INTRODUCTION

Today's datacenters and enterprises deploy a variety of intermediary network devices or *middleboxes* to distribute load (e.g., load balancers), enable remote connectivity (e.g., VPNs), improve performance (e.g., proxies) and security (e.g., firewalls, IDPS), as well as to support new traffic classes and applications [1–4]. Given these valuable benefits, the market for middleboxes is estimated to exceed $10B by 2016 [5], and their number is becoming comparable to that of routers in enterprise networks [1, 6].

These benefits, however, come at a high cost: middleboxes constitute a significant fraction of the network capital and operational expenses [1]; they are complex to manage and expensive to troubleshoot [6]; and their outages can greatly impact service performance and availability [7]. For instance, in December 2012, a load balancing misconfiguration affected multiple Google services including Chrome and Gmail [8]. In a 2011 survey of 1,000 organizations [9], 36% and 42% of the respondents indicated failure of a firewall due to DDoS attacks at the application layer and network layer, respectively; the very attack firewalls are deployed to protect against.

Table 1: The major findings of our study of middlebox failures and their implications.

Major findings	Implications
(1) Middlebox failures are prominent and can greatly degrade service performance and availability.	(1) The problem of middlebox failures is significant and worth special attention from the research community.
(2) Most failures are grey dominated by connectivity errors and link flaps that exhibit intermittent connectivity; fail-stop device failures occur, but they are not as often.	(2) Connectivity errors degrade service performance and availability e.g., due to timeouts, delayed protocol convergence, packet retransmissions, and parity errors. Robust network protocols (e.g., MP-TCP [10]) need to be developed to route traffic around interfaces exhibiting intermittent connectivity.
(3) Hardware faults, misconfigurations and overload problems are present, but they are not in majority in contrast to common perception [6].	(3) Hardware repairs risk long periods during which the network is operating at reduced or no redundancy. Load testing of middleboxes is needed to measure the maximum operating capacity under peak traffic.
(4) There are a variety of misconfigurations such as incorrect rules, VLAN misallocation and mismatched keys.	(4) Software-defined networks (SDNs) based configuration and management tools need to be developed to handle a wide range of middlebox misconfigurations.
(5) Middlebox redundancy is ineffective in about 33% cases for load balancers and firewalls due to configuration bugs, faulty failovers and software version mismatch.	(5) Middlebox failovers need rigorous testing and ensuring software version compatibility in redundant units. Explore commoditizing middleboxes to dynamically scale-out/in and to avoid single points of failure.
(6) A family of middleboxes having faulty PSUs and another exhibiting the few bad apples effect, could have been detected as early problem indicators.	(6) Trend analysis can be a useful tool in identifying failure trends in network datasets e.g., compare device categories/models to find the ones less reliable than others.

Our analysis, Figure 1 (top) of *high-severity* incidents (signifying high customer or business impact), over four years in the network we studied indicates that middleboxes contributed to about 43% of the incidents despite being 11% of the population. Figure 1 (bottom) shows the top-5 categories of service impact caused by middleboxes in this dataset. Operators tagged each incident to a problem category based on the primary issue experienced by impacted customers. We observe that loss of connectivity and high latency issues dominate, with a long tail of other issues such as service errors, security problems and SLA violations. Thus, understanding the characteristics and the impact of middlebox failures is important to improve performance and availability of hosted services.

Recent research proposals on middleboxes [2, 3, 6, 11–13] aim to alleviate many of their shortcomings, but they do not address how to improve middlebox reliability in existing deployments. These efforts, in turn, would benefit from a field study on middlebox failures as understanding their failures, causes and impact may help guide researchers to improve their reliability, cost-effectiveness and management, in spirit of recent efforts [14, 15].

Unfortunately, very few empirical studies have been conducted on middlebox failures and even they have a limited focus. For example, Allman et al. [16] perform active measurements of TCP traffic across two firewalls and load balancers to quantify their impact on end-to-end performance [16]. Sekar et al. [1, 11] presented anecdotal data on middleboxes from a large enterprise network. Sherry et al. [6] provide a useful survey of 57 network administrators to study enterprise middlebox deployments. They, however, do not report any empirical failure data, but rather the fraction of administrators who *estimated* one of three pre-defined issues to be the most common root cause. Our prior work on datacenter network failures observed that load balancers exhibit many short-term, transient faults [17]. However, it did not analyze their root causes, service impact, effectiveness of middlebox redundancy or study other types of middleboxes; we provide a detailed comparison to related work in Section 8.

1.1 Our contributions

In this paper, we present a large-scale empirical study of middleboxes in datacenters to (a) understand their failure characteristics, (b) analyze current middlebox proposals through the lens of reliability, and (c) derive implications for research on middleboxes. Specifically, our study focuses on answering the following key questions:

1. What are the failure characteristics of middleboxes?
2. What are the root causes and what actions are taken for resolution? How prevalent are misconfigurations and what are their different types?
3. Does reliability improve with new generations? Can we find *early problem symptoms* to enable proactive repair?
4. Is middlebox redundancy effective in masking failures?

To answer these questions, we collect network event logs over two years (July 24, 2010-12) across 10+ datacenters hosting 100k+ servers and 2k+ middleboxes; absolute counts omitted due to confidentiality reasons. Our measurement data covers a wide range of network event sources, including syslog and SNMP alerts, configuration files, a maintenance tracking system, trouble tickets, and traffic data. The details of our datasets and methodology are described in Section 2. Our major findings are summarized in Table 1.

To identify failure trends in network datasets, we propose using a simple technique of trend analysis which can uncover global problem trends rather than analyzing incidents in isolation. For instance, we observed that only a few devices contributed to a significant number of failures in one device family exhibiting the *few bad apples* effect, and a family of load balancers having faulty PSUs could have been detected as early problem indicators by aggregating failure root causes across that type, but they kept being repaired in isolation as observed in our failure dataset.

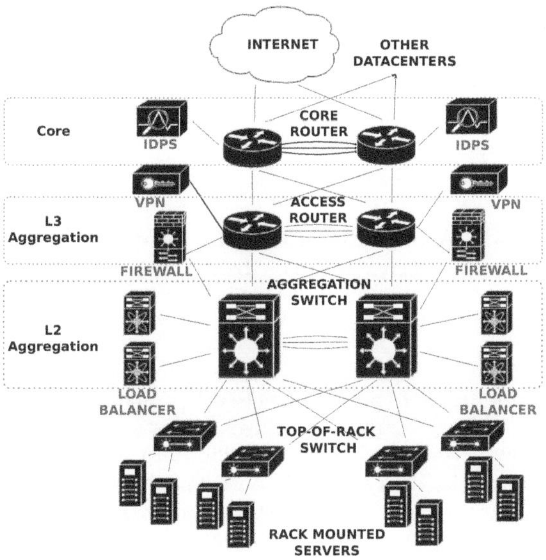

Figure 2: Example of a conventional datacenter network comprising middleboxes, switches and routers.

While we studied only our dataset, we believe it is fairly representative of a larger class of datacenters based on the scale (2k+ middleboxes across 10+ datacenters), diversity (multiple middlebox types and platforms), measurement duration (over two years), and validation with operators having high experience with middleboxes and some having previously worked at other sites. Further, the middleboxes we studied are from multiple leading network vendors having a significant share of the middlebox market.

2. BACKGROUND AND METHODOLOGY

In this section we provide a brief overview of the datacenter network architecture, and then describe the challenges and methodology for analyzing middlebox failures.

2.1 Datacenter network architecture

Figure 2 illustrates a topology[1] of a conventional datacenter network [18] comprising a variety of L2 switches, L3 routers and middleboxes such as firewalls, IDPS, load balancers, and VPNs.

Firewalls (FW) protect applications from unwanted traffic (e.g., DoS attacks) by examining packet fields at IP, transport and application layers against a specified set of rules. Network-based IDPS devices analyze traffic to safeguard against attacks such as malware and intrusions. Typically, hardware FWs and IDPSes are deployed to handle high traffic rates [19]. Load Balancers (LB) distribute application requests across hosted servers. Redundant pairs of LBs typically connect to each aggregation switch (AGG) and perform mapping between static (exposed to clients through DNS) and dynamic IP addresses of the servers. Recent hardware LBs also provide other features such as NAT, SSL acceleration, and data caching. VPNs are typically used to facilitate secure remote access for web and client/server applications. Some commercial offerings such as Cisco Catalyst 6509-E provide VPN functionality through IPSec and SSL. Due to the low population of other middleboxes such as NATs and media converters, our study did not include them.

[1]Other configurations are possible e.g., firewalls at the network edge.

2.2 Network Datasets

We examined multiple sources of network failure data for middleboxes over two years logged in the monitoring servers of a large service provider comprising 100k+ servers and 2k+ middleboxes across 10+ datacenters. The service provider uses middleboxes to deliver a variety of applications e.g., load balancers for web services, search, email, cloud computing and video streaming; firewalls and IDPS to protect confidential data (e.g., high business impact applications), and VPNs to enable remote access (e.g., to office network).

- **Event Logs**: Operators typically detect network failures from monitoring alarms such as syslog and SNMP traps, and track device/link status via ping and SNMP polling. These logs contain information about what type of network element experienced the event, event type, the other end-point of the interface, and a short machine-generated description.
- **Configuration data**: A configuration database stores and tracks changes to device configurations using a revision control system. It also provides a 'diff'-like functionality.
- **Maintenance Tracking System**: This system tracks network changes such as device provisioning, repairs, and code updates. Network engineers use this system to check for on-going and planned maintenance during failure triage.
- **Link-level traffic**: Traffic carried on each network interface is logged using SNMP [20] polling which averages packet and byte counts observed every five minutes. Most traffic monitoring systems use the MIB [21] format to store the data that includes fields such as the interface type (e.g., token ring, ethernet), the other endpoint, interface status (up/down), and the number of bytes sent/received. We correlate this data with network events to extract failures impacting network traffic, and to reverse-engineer the topology.
- **Trouble Tickets**: Network tickets record the activities of engineers while troubleshooting a problem [22]. Each ticket is assigned a unique identifier (TicketID) and contains multiple fields such as when and how a failure was discovered, and a diary of free-form text written by engineers describing the steps taken to mitigate the problem.

Note that since the datacenters we studied are managed by a central operations team, their failure characteristics are similar and thus we do not compare between datacenters.

2.3 Methodology

Failure definition. Intuitively, a failure can be defined as an event that causes a network device or link to be *unavailable* to carry traffic. However, precisely defining a middlebox failure is complicated because its impact is dependent on the device type. For instance, a faulty load balancer may cause a loss of throughput while a misconfigured firewall may incorrectly forward or drop legitimate traffic. Therefore, we consider all logged events as failures which cause a traffic impact (in terms of loss in traffic volume) or cause a device to function incorrectly in routing or processing traffic (based on problems observed in trouble tickets).

Challenges in analyzing data. There are several challenges in utilizing the network event logs to derive an accurate set of failure events and to characterize their impact:

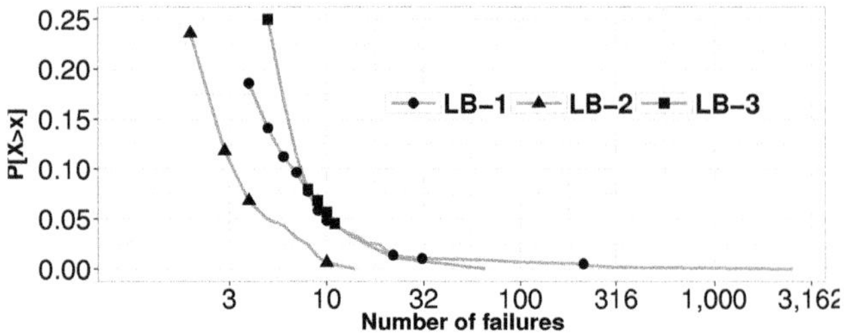

Figure 3: CCDF plot showing that a small fraction of devices log $\gg$ 100 failure events.

1. How can we differentiate noisy events from *meaningful* failures? For instance, syslog messages can be spurious where a device may log multiple 'down' events (even when it is operational) or when neighbors may send redundant notifications for the same device. Similarly, how to handle link flaps generating multiple and possibly overlapping down/up messages which get logged as separate events?

2. Is it accurate to consider all failures to characterize reliability? In particular, some down events are expected due to routine and scheduled maintenance e.g., code update. Operators aim to limit the planned downtime, and at the same time, prioritize detection and mitigation of unexpected failures. While prior efforts [16, 17] did not differentiate them, "lumping" all events together risks inflating failure rates.

3. How to handle *redundant failures* from devices that keep logging errors while undergoing repairs or being scheduled for replacement? Figure 3 shows the CCDF for different types of LBs in our dataset with some devices logging more than 1000 down messages over a few hours as the monitoring system did not suppress them during triage. Such events may bias measurement of device failures.

Event Filters: To address these challenges, we apply a pipeline of four event filters (Figure 4): (1) timing filter, (2) maintenance filter, (3) redundant failures filter, and (4) impact filter.

1. **Timing Filter**: This filter fixes various timing inconsistencies. First, it groups all events with the same start and end time originating on the same interface to remove duplicate events. Second, to avoid any problems due to clock drifts (typically small) and log buffering, multiple events within a 60 second window on the same interface are grouped into a single event by picking the earliest start and end times. If two events on the same interface have the same start time but different end times, we group them into a single event and assign the earliest end time as events may not always be quickly cleared after being fixed.

2. **Maintenance Filter**: We use the maintenance tracking system to filter failure events due to planned maintenance. As operators likely have a good understanding of scheduled repairs, this filtering enables computing device reliability only due to unexpected or unplanned problems.

3. **Redundant Failures Filter**: To filter redundant failures, we group events based on their unique trouble ticket identifiers as events within the same ticket are typically part of the common problem. We validated these events with operators assigned to trouble tickets for these failures.

4. **Impact Filter**: We measure the impact of a failure in two ways based on our definition of a middlebox failure: (a) traffic loss and (b) device malfunctioning.

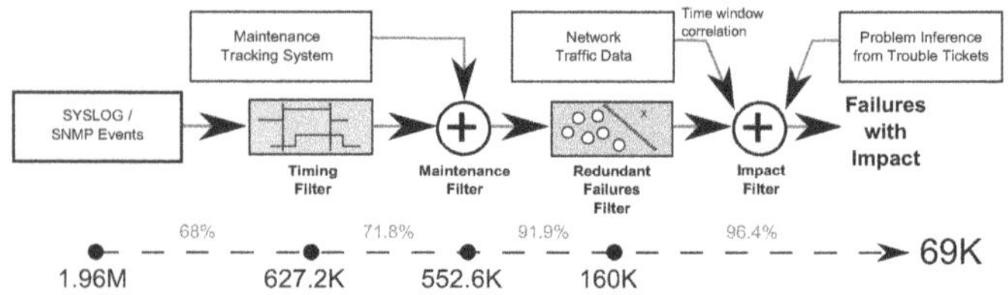

Figure 4: A pipeline of event filters applied to extract meaningful failures from the network data sources. The cumulative noise reduction at each step is shown below.

A. Traffic Impact: Since the network is shared and we did not have access to application logs, we estimate the failure impact by leveraging network traffic data and computing the ratio of the median traffic on a failed device/link during a failure and its value in the recent past (preceding a two hour window): a failure has traffic impact if this ratio is less than one [17]. Note that this filter is applied *after* a network alarm has been logged and a ticket opened to resolve the issue. Hence, it will not misclassify failures due to the inherent time-varying nature of traffic e.g., time of day effects. We perform hypothesis testing to validate this approach. Specifically, we use the Mann-Whitney-Wilcoxon (MWW) [23] test for validation, which is a non-parametric significance test to compare two populations. The *null hypothesis* to test is that the traffic values observed before a failure and during a failure have identical distribution functions. We randomly sampled 7k middlebox failure events and 7k time points from periods during which no known failures occurred. For the former, we obtained traffic values up to eight hours before the failure and during the failure, and up to eight hours before the event and up to two hours afterwards for the latter.

Figure 5 plots the distribution of the p-value to quantify the fraction of cases where we can reject the null hypothesis at a significance level of 0.05. The top figure shows that in 99.3% of the failures, p-value is less than 0.05; the remaining cases had insufficient traffic data points (e.g., due to best-effort logging). Hence the null hypothesis can be rejected in 99.3% of the cases. Similarly, the bottom figure shows that the distributions are identical during periods when no failures occurred. Further, a time window size of two hours and eight hours of traffic before the event yields the highest and lowest accuracy, respectively. Indeed, under more strict assumptions, a significant MWW test can be interpreted as showing a difference in medians [24]. Our prior work [17] also correlated failures with traffic deviations, but it did not evaluate its accuracy or specify the time window size before a failure to compute the traffic ratio with highest accuracy. As Figure 5 (top) shows, the accuracy is clearly dependent on the time window size.

B. Device Malfunction Impact: To measure impact due to incorrect device function, we leverage the information logged by operators in trouble tickets to determine the problem root causes when middleboxes fail. Specifically, we apply NetSieve [25], an automated problem inference system that analyzes the free-form text in a trouble ticket to generate its synopsis: (1) the problems observed e.g., link down, misconfigured rule, (2) troubleshooting performed e.g., check configuration, verify routes, and (3) actions taken for resolution e.g., replaced line card, cleaned fiber.

Table 2: Annual number of failures per middlebox and annualized failure rate (AFR) for devices that were present for at least a month in production.

Type	Mean	Stddev	25P	50P	75P	95P	COV	AFR% (July 2010-11)	AFR% (July 2011-12)
FW	2.1	2	1	2	3	5	0.9	19	13
IDPS	3.5	2.9	1	1	6	8.3	0.8	23	18
LB	1.5	0.9	1	1	2	3	0.6	31	19
VPN	3.4	2.2	2	3	5	7	0.7	7	12

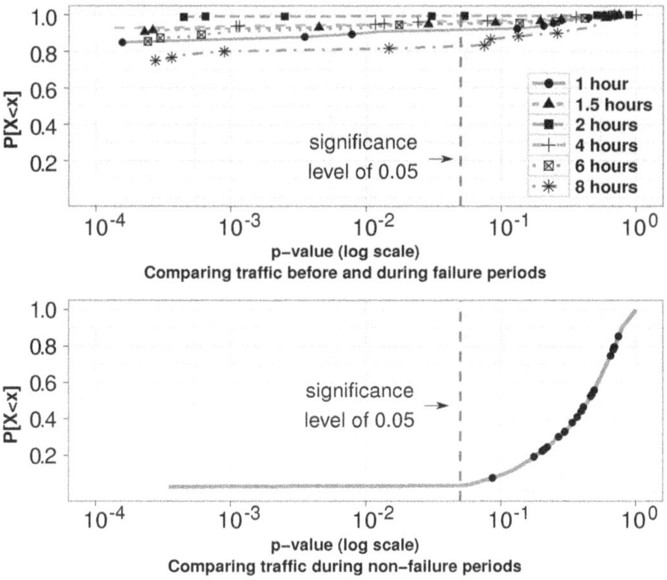

Figure 5: MWW test: p-value < 0.05 in 99.3% of the failures (top), and p-value > 0.05 in 99.2% of the events during no failure periods (bottom). Hence the null hypothesis can be rejected.

Our dataset comprised 1.96M raw events collected over two years for FWs, IDPSes, LBs and VPNs. Note that the high-severity incidents described in Figure 1 is a very small fraction compared to this dataset; we use the latter for analysis throughout the rest of this paper. Applying the pipeline of filters on this data resulted in about 17k events from the traffic filter and about 52k events from the device malfunction filter. To ensure 100% coverage of impactful failure events, we verified that our filtered dataset includes all the events recorded in tickets deemed 'actionable' by operators. Since typically multiple events logged close in time for a device attribute to a common problem and hence are likely to be merged in the same ticket, the number of tickets is significantly smaller than the number of events.

3. FAILURE CHARACTERIZATION

In this section we characterize reliability of the four types of middleboxes in our dataset: firewalls, IDPS, VPNs each spanning two generations (FW[1-2], IDPS[1-2], and VPN[1-2], respectively), and load balancers spanning three of them (LB[1-3]). For a middlebox type, its different generations are from the same network vendor, and they are ordered by their release date (1 is oldest). Where applicable, we first provide an inter-type comparison and then compare devices across different generations within a type.

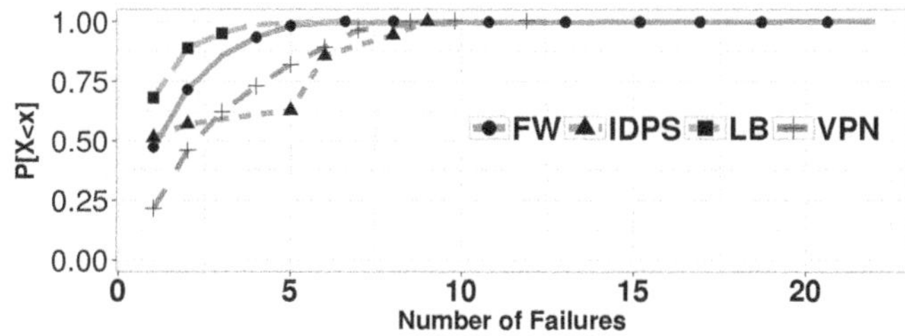

Figure 6: Failures per device per year for middleboxes.

3.1 How reliable are middleboxes?

Figure 6 shows the CDF of the number of failures per device per year for devices with at least a month in operation. Most devices experience few failures per year with a median value of at most three (Table 2), and they occur with low variability (COV < 1: COV [26] is defined as the ratio of standard deviation to the sample mean where a COV >> 1 indicates high variability) as expected in a service provider network carrying customer traffic. Across middlebox types, IDPS devices show relatively highest annual failures per device with a 95th percentile value of 8.3 while LBs exhibit lowest with a 95th percentile value of 3. The distribution for firewalls have a relatively long tail of up to 24 annual failures per device compared to other types.

We next compute the annualized failure rate (AFR) by dividing the number of devices of a given type that observe at least one failure by the population of that type.

Inter-type: Table 2 shows the AFR for different device types during July 2010-11 and July 2011-12. We observe that LBs are the least reliable with about a 1 in 3 chance of failure during July 2010-11 which improved to about a 1 in 5 chance in the next year. The reason for this improvement is due to on-boarding of the more reliable LB-3 platform in the deployment and the end-of-life retirement of some of the older LB-1 devices. FWs and IDPSes also exhibit improvement in AFR over the two years. VPNs show relatively the lowest AFR amongst all middleboxes.

Intra-type: Figure 7 shows the AFR and Figure 8 shows the fraction of failures and downtime, respectively, across different generations of each middlebox type. We find that during the first year, FW-2 exhibits relatively low failure rate of 14% whereas FW-1 exhibits 2x higher failure rate at 32%. Through trouble tickets, we found that the reliability of FW-2 started improving when the vendor released an end-of-life notice for FW-1 and provided faster bug fixes and better technical support to handle FW-2 failures. Figure 8 shows that FW-2 contributed majority to the total failures due to its dominant population while FW-1 devices decreased due to being decommissioned. This observation

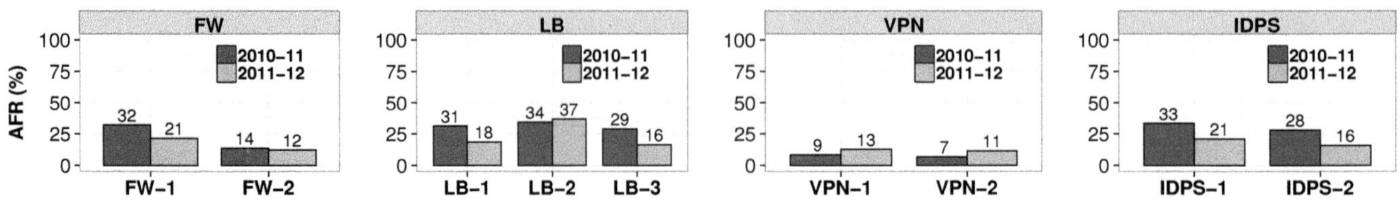

Figure 7: Comparing annualized failure rate across middleboxes over the two years measurement period.

combined with the relatively low AFR of FW-2 (Figure 7) indicates that a few devices contributed the most, due to limited device familiarity of operators with the new platform and unexpected hardware problems. Further, the number of failures contributed by FW-2 is roughly proportional to its downtime while they are relatively higher for FW-1. This indicates that most FW-1 failures seem to be relatively short-lived and resolved through reboot or rule reconfiguration.

In the case of load balancers, LB-1 exhibits a large AFR and contributes significantly (Figure 8) toward the total number of failures and downtime. However, note that in comparison to other LBs, the fraction of failures contributed is higher than the downtime indicating that most problems are short-lived. We validate this observation by using the time-to-repair (TTR) plots (Figure 9(c)) where a short TTR indicates transient problems. We find that a majority of these problems were due to link flapping i.e., interface continually goes up and down due to a bad cable, faulty line card, etc. In most cases, the network engineer adjusts/reseats the cable/network card or the problem gets self-corrected. LB-2, on the other hand, exhibited an increased AFR indicating that this generation experienced new types of problems such as unexpected reboots. However, these problems seem to have been resolved in its successor, LB-3, which exhibits relatively the highest reliability. Similar to the case of firewalls, note that the significant improvement in LB-3 reliability occurred due to the vendor releasing an end-of-life notice for older generations, as we observed through tickets.

Across the four middlebox types, VPN devices exhibit relatively higher reliability with failure rates between 7%-9% which increased slightly year over year to 11%-13%. The increase in AFR over time is due to (a) the older generation VPN-1 which was being decommissioned exhibiting an increasing number of connectivity errors, and (b) the newer generation VPN-2 exhibiting the infant mortality effect e.g., memory errors. Further, the failures contributed is roughly proportional to the downtime caused by both VPN-1 and VPN-2 suggesting that each failure roughly causes the same downtime on average. We find a common root cause of VPN failures to be VLAN misconfigurations. Similar to other middleboxes, we also observed an end-of-life announcement for VPN-1 recently.

Findings (1): (1) Firewalls and IDPS devices exhibit annualized failure rate of 19% and 23%, respectively, which improved to about 13% and 18% year over year due to timely bug fixes and decommissioning of older generation of devices. (2) About 1 in 3 load balancers experience a failure and exhibit the highest annualized failure rate during July 2010-11, which improved next year to about a 1 in 5 chance of failure due to new generations exhibiting relatively higher reliability. (3) VPN devices exhibit the relatively lowest annualized failure rate across middleboxes. (4) When vendors release an end-of-life notice for an old device generation, it often results in improved reliability of newer generations because of faster bug fixes and better technical support.

3.2 How often do middleboxes fail?

We define the time to failure (TTF) of a device as the time elapsed between two consecutive failures. As this metric requires that a device fail at least twice, we exclude devices having a single failure during our measurement period.

Inter-type: Figure 9(a) shows the TTF across middleboxes. We observe that the lines of FWs and LBs nearly overlap exhibiting a high similarity with a median TTF of 7.5 hours and 5.2 hours, respectively. Many FW failures are caused due to connectivity errors, hardware faults and overload conditions (Figure 11). Similarly, LB failures are mostly due to short-term transient faults, hardware and parity errors e.g., due to incompatible protocol versions between devices. For IDPS, the median is about 20 minutes while the 95th percentile is around 40 days. This indicates that even amongst devices that fail multiple times, there are two types: (a) robust ones that fail at most once in one or two months and (b) failure prone ones that experience numerous failures (the few bad apples effect), mostly within a few hours. In comparison, VPN devices show relatively the smallest median TTF of about 10 minutes due to connectivity errors (Figure 11) and 95th percentile of about three days.

In terms of availability, Figure 9(b) shows that FWs exhibit a median of four 9's and a 95th percentile of two 9's. VPNs perform slightly better with their 95th percentile above two 9's. While the median value for LBs is above four 9's, their 95th percentile is two 9's due to all three LB[1-3] generations exhibiting high AFR over the two year measurement period as observed in Figure 7.

3.3 How long do repairs take?

We define the time to repair (TTR) for a device as the time between a down notification for a device and when it is next reported as being back online. There are two main types of failures: *short-lived transient faults* where an engineer may not always intervene to resolve them and *long-term failures* where the device or its component is usually replaced or decommissioned. Note that for long-term failures, the failure durations may be skewed (up to days) by when the trouble ticket got closed e.g., till a spare is on-site. Figure 9(c) shows the TTR results. The 95th percentile values show that the distribution has a long tail for both LBs and FWs. Using problems inferred from trouble tickets, we found several incidents for device replacements and ambiguous customer complaints which resulted in an increased TTR. For instance, in several cases, after receiving vague complaints from many customers about occasional slow file-transfer rates between two datacenters, determining the rootcause was challenging as the problem could not be easily reproduced. The root-

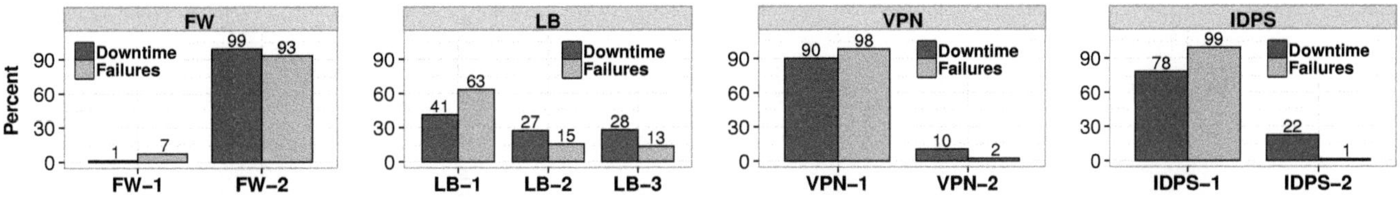

Figure 8: Comparing fraction of failures and downtime across middleboxes.

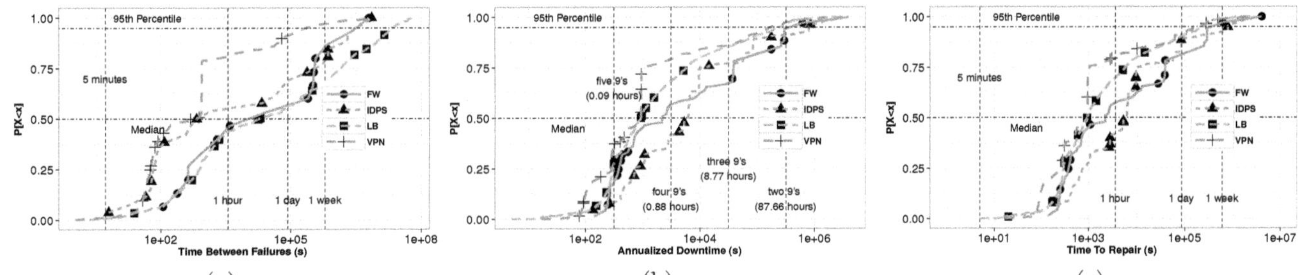

(a) (b) (c)

Figure 9: Comparing (a) Time to Failure, (b) Annualized downtime, and (c) Time to Repair across middleboxes.

cause, determined after three weeks, was a software bug that prevented some FWs from recognizing large flows.

Across device types, middleboxes exhibit typically a low median TTR, indicating short-lived failures that get resolved within a few minutes to at most a few hours in most cases. The short-lived failures for LBs are due to interface flaps and software problems (e.g, OS watchdog timer triggering a reboot) and the long-lived failures to delays in equipment replacement (due to spare unavailability), faulty spares and problem misdiagnosis. VPNs exhibited mostly link flapping and connectivity errors which get resolved quickly (e.g., protocol convergence, port disabled) resulting in a small TTR.

Findings (2): Middleboxes exhibit a low median TTR, suggesting most failures are short-lived due to connectivity errors and link flaps that get resolved within a few minutes to a few hours.

3.4 How to model failures and repairs?

Building statistical models of middlebox failures is important as researchers can use them to understand their failure modes, analyze a large number of network design solutions [14, 16, 27], and derive implications to improve fault detection and troubleshooting operations. Although this section discusses the specific case of LBs, note that our analysis can be extended to other types of middleboxes.

Before modeling the failure distribution, we need to first characterize their statistical properties. As Figures 9(a) and 9(c) show, the range of TTF and TTR durations can be several orders of magnitude across devices. To reduce this high variance, we use the Box-Cox transformation [28], a family of parametric power transformation techniques that transform data such that it approximately follows the normal distribution. Using this technique, we found that the logarithmic power transform yielded the best normal fit for our failure data which we verified using a Q-Q plot (not shown).

Figures 10(a) and 10(d) show the kernel density plot of the log-transformed TTF and TTR respectively. We observe that the distributions are right skewed and are clearly not unimodal (observe the peaks). To find these peaks automatically, we use a local peak finding algorithm where a peak is defined as the locally highest value in a time series, before a change in signal direction has occurred. Observe that the main peaks occur at 15 minutes for TTF (Figure 10(a)) and 5.6 minutes for TTR (Figure 10(d)). Further, there are secondary peaks, which are relatively small, at 14 days for TTF and 24 hours and 2.5 days for TTR.

These findings indicate that there are two or three qualitatively different *types* of failures and repairs in effect, respectively. For TTF, the peak at 15 minutes indicates that connection errors and interface flaps dominate middlebox failures, and the secondary peak at 14 days indicates problems due to both hardware faults (e.g., line card, memory errors) and software bugs. For TTR, most repairs take a short time ($<$ 6 minutes), but once the repair window exceeds a day (the 24 hours peak), it will likely take longer e.g., hardware replacement.

Failure Modeling: Based on prior work [14, 29], we first tried to fit existing heavy-tailed distributions to our failure data. However, they did not capture the multi-mode properties of our dataset. For instance, in the case of lognormal distribution, the Q-Q plots in Figures 10(b) and 10(e) show that the data does not follow the absolute line.

Intuitively, the presence of multiple peaks indicates that a two or three-component mixture of right-skewed distributions might be able to provide a good approximation of the process generating the data. We next present the mixture model framework [30] we used. Suppose the real-valued variables $\mathbf{X}_1, ..., \mathbf{X}_n$ are a random sample of time periods from a finite mixture of $m(> 1)$ arbitrary distributions, called *components*. The density of each $\mathbf{X}_i$ may then be written as:

$$h_{\theta}(\mathbf{x}_i) = \sum_{j=1}^{m} \lambda_j \phi_j(\mathbf{x}_i), \mathbf{x}_i \in \mathbf{R}^r \quad (1)$$

where $\boldsymbol{\theta} = (\boldsymbol{\lambda}, \boldsymbol{\phi}) = (\lambda_1, ...\lambda_m, \phi_1, ..., \phi_m)$ denotes the model parameter and $\sum_{j=1}^{m} \lambda_m = 1$. We further assume that ϕ_j

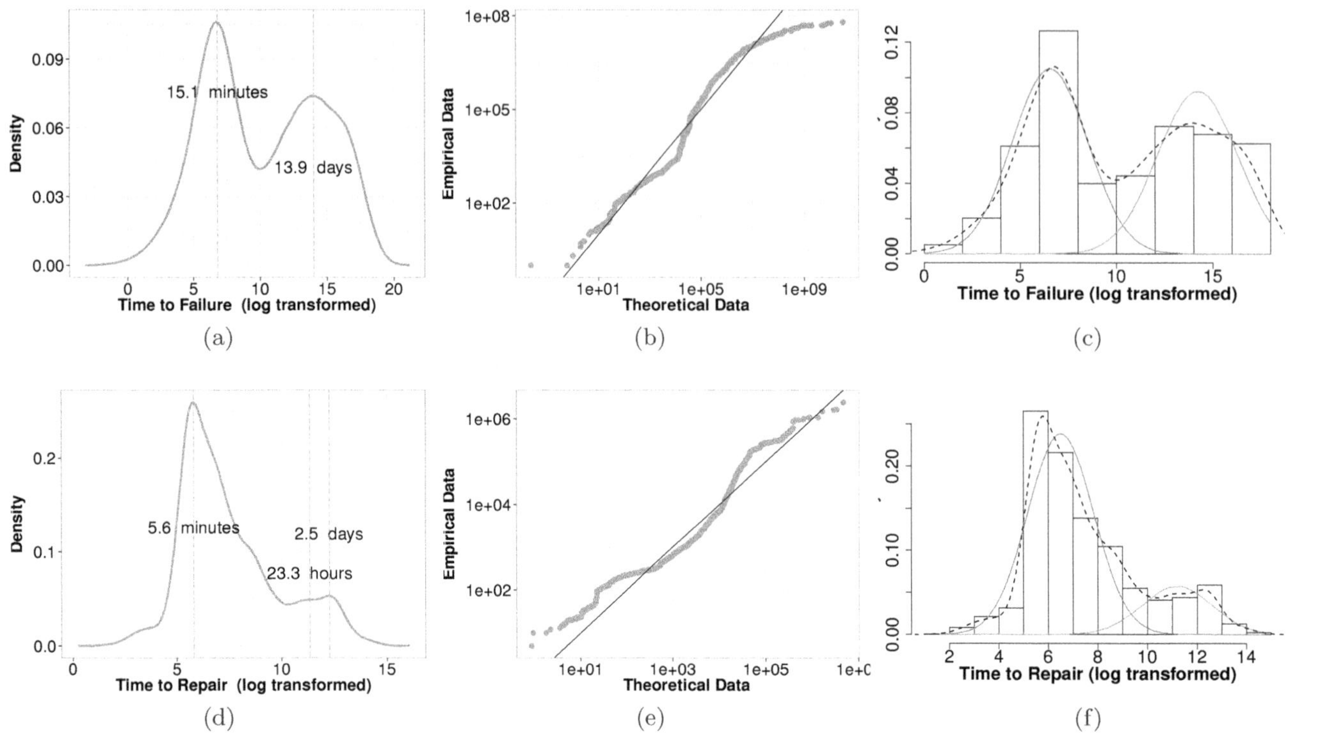

Figure 10: Modeling Time to Failure [a-c] and Time to Repair [d-f] for load balancers. Figures (a, d) show the kernel density plot of the log transformed TTF and TTR. Figures (b, e) show fit of a single log-normal distribution. Figures (c, f) show fit of a mixture of log-normal distributions.

are drawn from some family $\mathcal{F}$ of univariate density functions on $\mathbf{R}$. We consider a univariate lognormal family $\mathcal{F} = \{\phi(\cdot|\mu_{ln}, \sigma^2_{ln}\}$, in which μ_{ln} and σ_{ln} denote the mean and standard deviation in log scale. Thus, the model parameter reduces to $\boldsymbol{\theta} = (\boldsymbol{\lambda}, (\mu_{ln_1}, \sigma^2_{ln_1}), ..., (\mu_{ln_m}, \sigma^2_{ln_m}))$. By substituting these parameters, Equation (1) can be written as:

$$h_\theta(\mathbf{x}_i) = \sum_{j=1}^{m} \lambda_j \frac{1}{\sigma_{ln_j} \mathbf{x}_i \sqrt{2\pi}} e^{-\frac{(ln(\mathbf{x}_i) - \mu_{ln_j})^2}{2\sigma^2_{ln_j}}}, \mathbf{x}_i \in \mathbf{R}^r \quad (2)$$

We obtained a reasonable fit by choosing a two-component ($m = 2$) lognormal mixture, where our model from Equation (1) becomes: $\lambda f(\mu_{ln_1}, \sigma_{ln_1}) + (1 - \lambda) f(\mu_{ln_2}, \sigma_{ln_2})$. To obtain the model parameter λ, we use the well-known Expectation Maximization(EM) [31] algorithm. Table 3 gives the values of the parameters for the two-component lognormal mixture distribution. We use the two-sample Kolmogorov-Smirnov (KS) test [32] as a goodness-of-fit test to compare data generated from the two-component lognormal mixture distribution with our failure data. We obtain a p-value of 0.111 indicating that we cannot reject the *null hypothesis* that the samples are drawn from the same distribution.

Figures 10(c) and 10(f) show how this model fits our data; the dotted-line is the kernel density curve of our data and the solid lines are the individual mixture components. We observe that our model closely approximates the real-world data of load balancer failures in our study.

4. ROOT CAUSE ANALYSIS

In this section, we analyze the root causes of middlebox problems and the actions taken to mitigate them.

Table 3: Parameters for the two-component lognormal mixture distribution

Type	λ	μ_{ln_1}	σ_{ln_1}	μ_{ln_2}	σ_{ln_2}
TTF	0.516284	6.557005	1.963986	14.210978	2.090600
TTR	0.428609	6.045474	0.690533	8.524983	2.541691

4.1 What are the dominant problems?

As described in Section 2.3, we apply NetSieve to do automated problem inference on network trouble tickets [25] for determining the problem root causes when middleboxes fail. Table 4 shows the classification of the problems into five categories based on the ticket data and their example causes. Note that there are two potential issues to be considered in interpreting these categories. First, a problem observed in one category can be due to issues in another one. For instance, parity errors in VPNs indicate failed sanity checks which may be caused due to misconfigured pre-shared keys. Another example is that a malformed message could be due to incompatible protocol versions between devices. Second, in some cases, there may be multiple problems pertaining to the same failure. In these cases, we take a conservative approach and attribute each observed problem to its respective category.

Inter-type: Figure 11 shows the breakdown of problems observed across the four types of middleboxes. We find that connectivity errors dominate failures across all middleboxes as also validated from the results in Section 3. Connectivity errors are mainly interface/link flaps which can be due to many factors such as protocol convergence, line card errors, cpu overload, bit corruption and cable problems. As a

Table 4: Classification and examples of problem types observed across middleboxes.

Problem Classification	Example causes or explanation
Connectivity errors	Device/neighbor unreachable, link flaps, ARP conflicts, address not found, message/frame parity errors, checksum failed, malformed message, port errors
Hardware	faulty PSU/ASIC, memory error, defective chassis/disk/fan, failed SUP engine/line card
Misconfiguration	bad rule, VLAN misallocation, configuration conflict/out-of-sync/corrupted/missing, mismatched crypto keys, expired security association, incorrect clock causing certificate expiry, incorrect root password
Software	reboot/reload, firmware bug, OS errors
Overload	High utilization exceeding a specified load threshold

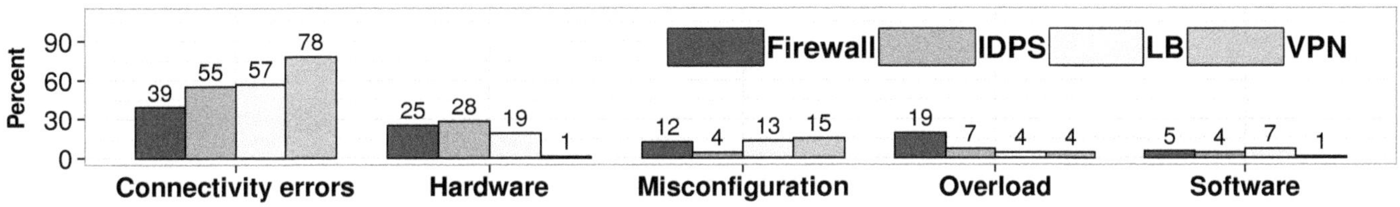

Figure 11: Problem types observed across middleboxes.

result, these errors can significantly degrade service performance and availability due to TCP timeouts, convergence delays, and retransmissions e.g., due to malformed packets or parity errors. The second main root cause is hardware problems except for VPNs where it accounts for only 1% of the problems. One implication of high percentage of hardware problems is long repair times as the faulty component or the device gets replaced. Another one is that this observation is in direct contrast to the industry view of equating hardware boxes with high reliability.

VPN problems are dominated by parity errors which may be attributed to faulty cables (e.g., copper, SFP fiber optics) and their common root causes are power surge, bad connectors, or a short circuit. For these problems, we observed mainly two repair actions of either cleaning the fiber or replacing them. In comparison, misconfigurations and overload problems are relatively in minority, contrary to the common view of being a dominant contributor [6].

Table 4 (row 3) gives the common categories of misconfigurations across device types. While bad rules as a common root cause ($\approx$70% cases) are expected, there are a wide variety of other problems such as VLAN misallocation, corrupted or missing configuration files, mismatched cryptographic keys, and expired certificates.

Across middleboxes, misconfigurations contribute lowest to IDPS problems due to the fact that centralized management in a datacenter continuously monitors and immediately enforces policy changes (e.g., security access) upon violation. Software problems contribute the minimum percentage to problems indicating that the software running on these devices exhibits reasonable stability. Finally, software problems are fixed relatively quickly e.g., via code update or power cycling the device.

Intra-type: Figure 12 shows the problems observed split by different generations for each of the four types of middleboxes. For Firewalls, FW-1 exhibits lower hardware and software problems compared to FW-2. However, the fraction of misconfigurations and connectivity errors is higher, due to better configuration tools and more reliable port connectors and cables for the new platform FW-2. Surprisingly, even though FW-2 has a higher capacity compared to FW-1, it experiences a high fraction of overload induced failures which are not observed in FW-1. Unlike firewalls, for IDPS devices, the port errors increased with the newer device IDPS-2, while contribution of the other problem types reduced. For load balancers, LB-3 exhibits fewer problems due to hardware and software improvements compared to its predecessors, LB-1 and LB-2. In sharp contrast to trends observed across FWs, IDPSes and LBs, VPN-2 exhibits a higher percentage of hardware faults and overload problems compared to VPN-1 due to the instability of the newer platform.

Overall, these trends provide a fine-grained analysis of what aspects of a new platform are improving over its predecessor and vice versa, to guide researchers and vendors in developing better designs and tools to improve middleboxes.

Findings (3): (1) Connection errors and interface problems dominate causes of middlebox failures, and (2) Hardware, misconfigurations and overload problems are present, but they are not in majority.

4.2 What are the main resolution actions?

Figure 13 shows the breakdown of actions taken to mitigate middlebox failures. The nine categories show the resolutions applied to faulty components at a fine granularity. For instance, the cable category implies that the cable was either cleaned or replaced. The software category denotes that either a patch was applied or the code was upgraded to the latest stable version. Similarly, the categories of different hardware components such as chassis, disk, fan, and PSU denote that they were replaced using on-site spare or sent back to the vendor for repairs, or warranty purposes.

We observe that across middleboxes, the most prevalent actions taken are replacing the cable and disks, and reboot to fix software-related issues. The former can be attributed to the relatively low-cost and high failure rates of these commodity components as operators tend to replace them quickly after observing a problem. In comparison, the decisions to replace specialized components such as chassis, supervisor engines, or even the device, requires a detailed

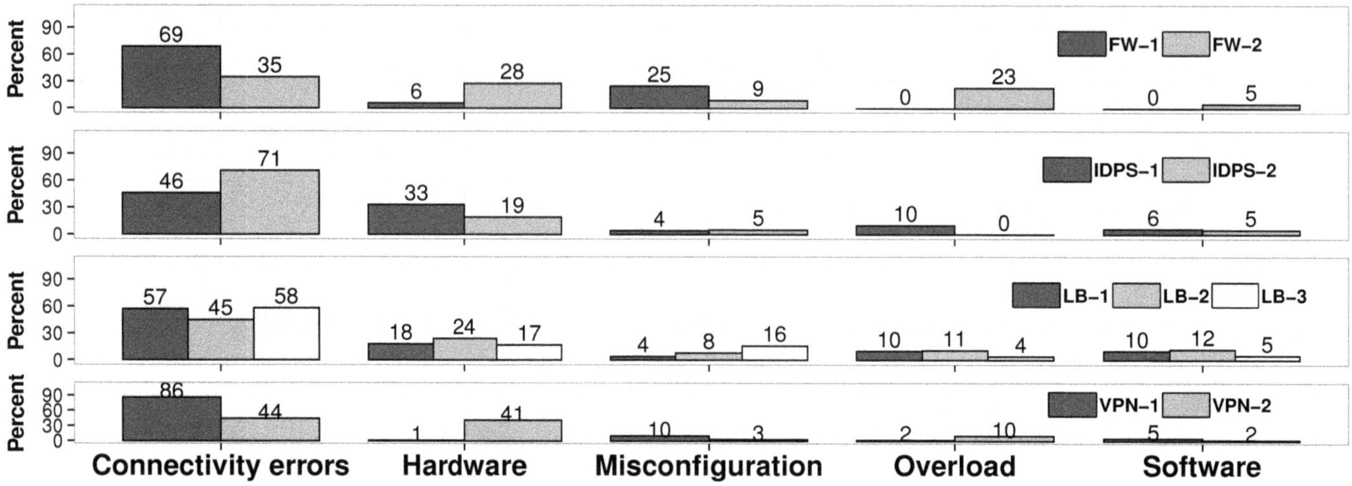

Figure 12: Comparison of problem types across different generations of middleboxes.

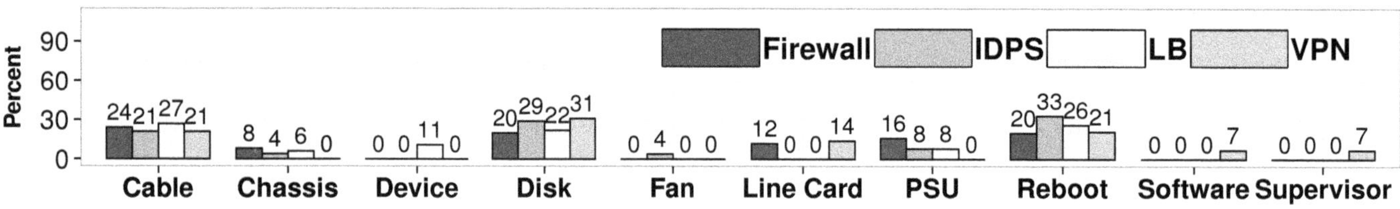

Figure 13: Resolution actions observed across middleboxes.

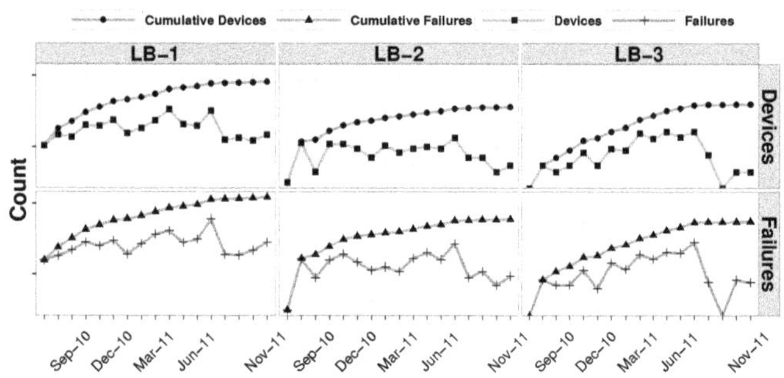

Figure 14: Failure trends across different generations of load balancers. The y-axes are unlabeled for confidentiality.

investigation due to their high cost and long turnaround time from their vendor. The reason for a high percentage of reboots is that it is a quick-fix solution in many cases and hence run as a popular first attempt to mitigate a problem to reduce downtime.

Findings (4): (1) Cables and disks are the most failing components, and (2) Device reboot is a popular quick-fix solution to mitigate middlebox problems.

5. FAILURE TREND ANALYSIS

In this section we analyze failure trends across different device generations of middleboxes. We use trend analysis as it is a useful tool to uncover outliers i.e., set of devices which

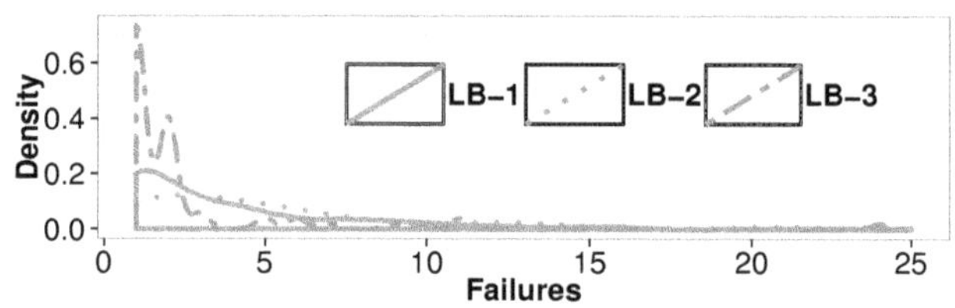

Figure 15: Distribution of load balancer failures.

are more failure-prone than the rest of the population. We present detailed case studies on LB[1-3].

Figure 14 shows the timeline for the number of failure events and the number of devices that failed; the Y-axis is on log scale. Each subplot shows two curves: a cumulative curve that sums up the number of failures (or devices that failed) across time and the other showing the actual number of failures (or devices that failed). For LB-1, the number of failure events far exceeds the number of devices that failed indicating that a few bad devices are responsible for a majority of their failures.

Validation. We validate this inference by computing two statistical metrics from the failure distribution (Figure 15). (1) skewness [33], an indicator used in distribution analysis as a sign of asymmetry where positive values indicate a right-skewed distribution and vice versa, and (2) COV. The observed skewness values are 2.2 (LB-1), 1.5 (LB-2) and 3.9 (LB-3), indicating that the distributions for LB-1 and LB-3 are right-skewed (tail on the right). Though the COV across all LBs is 0.6 (Table 2), the COV for LB-1 is 5.8 whereas it is 1.3 for LB-3 indicating that even though both have a right-skewed distribution, the "few bad devices" effect is higher in LB-1. Further, in Figure 14, the slope of the cumulative curve indicates the rate of increase of the observed value. Sudden increase in the slope indicates major problems during that period of observation. A key root cause of this behavior is connectivity problems as observed in Figure 12.

Combining failure rates with trouble tickets, trend analysis revealed two key issues:

1. **Early problem symptoms:** Inference on the problems observed in trouble tickets for LB-1 devices revealed a recurring PSU problem. Aggregating problem statistics across LB-1 tickets indicated that 46% of the tickets called for a device replacement due to a narrow focus of operators in mitigating a problem (compared to its diagnosis) and limited tools at their disposal in checking vendor-specific problems. In retrospect, a simple approach of aggregating root causes across a device generation can identify the problem patterns. In this case, failing PSUs could have been used as early indicators of problems with the product line. A *Cost of Ownership* analysis (§7) can then help decide whether to continue using LB-1 or gracefully upgrade it to a newer, more stable generation.
2. **The few bad apples affect:** LB-1 suffers from the *few bad apples* effect i.e., the rate of increase of the slope of the cumulative count of failures curve is higher than the rate of increase of the slope of the cumulative count of devices curve. This indicates that only a few devices are contributing to a majority of failures and is validated by high COV value for LB-1 of 5.8. There were several reasons why this happened. First, we observed a re-occurring fault using LB-1 trouble tickets with the regulated PSU, despite being redundant, that frequently caused power fluctuations leading to damaged parts. Even if the damaged parts are replaced, unless the fault is localized to the power supply unit, the problem likely will repeat itself. Second, a memory bit corruption (e.g., SDRAM ECC error) kept being masked temporarily by the quick-fix solution of reboots as observed in Figure 13.

These observations can be leveraged to (a) prioritize replacement of frequently failing devices and scheduling of repair actions based on the top-k observed problems, and (b) aid repair vs. replace analysis by combining early problem symptoms with a cost of ownership metric. Finally, frequently occurring hardware problems can aid in detecting faults at the vendor.

> **Findings (5)**: (1) A significant number of failures in one *generation* of load balancers exhibited the few bad apples effect, and (2) A family of load balancers having faulty PSUs could have been detected as early problem indicators using trend analysis.

6. REDUNDANCY ANALYSIS

In this section we first analyze the loss of traffic due to middlebox failures and then evaluate the effectiveness of redundancy in masking them.

6.1 How much traffic loss do failures cause?

Quantifying the impact of a failure is difficult as it requires attributing discrete outage levels to annotations used by network operators such as *severe, mild,* or *some impact.* As described in Section 2.3, we estimate the failure impact in terms of lost network traffic that would have been routed on a failed device in the absence of failure. Specifically, we first compute the median traffic (bytes/sec) on the device two hours before the failure and during the failure. The traffic loss is estimated as product of the failure duration and the difference between the two median traffic values.

Figure 16(a) shows the estimated traffic loss across the three LB generations. We observe the estimated median number of bytes lost during failures is about 1 GB for LB-1 (exhibiting a relatively high failure rate as seen in §3.1 and §5) while it is close to 5 MB for newer LB-3 generation devices, which have a low failure rate. Notice that LB-2, which also exhibited high failure rates compared to LB-3, shows a median traffic loss close to LB-1.

6.2 How effective is middlebox redundancy?

We next analyze how effective is middlebox redundancy, a *de-facto* technique for fault tolerance, in masking failures. Typically, middleboxes are deployed in 1:1 redundant groups, where one device is designated the primary and the other as backup. Based on the failure definition in Section 2.3, we evaluate redundancy effectiveness for LBs based on the traffic impact, and based on device malfunctioning for the other middlebox types.

Evaluating LB redundancy. To estimate the effectiveness of LB redundancy, we first compute the ratio of median traffic on a device during a failure and its median traffic before the failure, and then compute this ratio across all devices in the redundancy group where the failure occurred. Network redundancy is considered 100% effective if this ratio is close to one across a redundancy group. We refer to this ratio as *normalized traffic* [17].

Figures 16(b) and 16(c) show the distribution of normalized traffic for individual LBs and their redundancy groups. We observe that the redundancy groups are effective at moving the ratio close to one with 40% of the events experiencing no failure impact at the redundancy group level. The median traffic carried at the redundancy group level is 92% compared with 55% at the individual level, a relative improvement of 67.2% in median traffic as a result of middlebox redundancy.

Evaluating redundancy for other middleboxes. To analyze redundancy effectiveness for FWs, IDPSes, and VPNs, we measure the fraction of overlapping failure events where both the redundant pairs were down simultaneously. In particular, after one of the pair fails, we check if the other device also undergoes a failure before the former becomes operational. Our analysis of redundancy effectiveness across FWs, IDPSes and VPNs revealed that both the redundant pairs failed in 33% and 1% of the failure events for FWs and IDPS, respectively. In comparison, VPN redundancy exhibits 100% effectiveness in mitigating failures.

Analyzing unsuccessful redundancy failover. Based on applying NetSieve [25] on trouble tickets, we observed two main reasons why the redundancy failover was not successful for LBs and FWs in masking the failure impact:

- **Faulty Failovers**: The primary device failed when the backup was experiencing an unrelated problem and hence led to a *failed failover.* In other cases, protocol bugs, bad cables, and software issues such as version incompatibility caused an unsuccessful failover, often sending devices into a deadlock state.

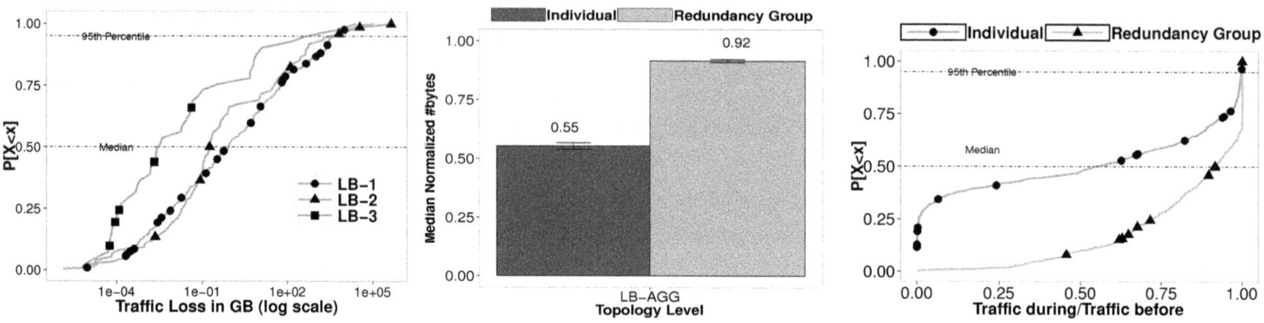

(a) (b) (c)

Figure 16: (a) Estimated traffic loss during failure events for LBs, (b) Normalized traffic (bytes) during failure events for a device as well as within a redundancy group and (c) Normalized bytes (quartiles) during failure events per device and across redundancy group compared across LBs.

- **Misconfigurations**: The same configuration error was made on both primary and backup devices. Primary reasons were due to copy-paste of the configuration files, mismatched cryptographic keys, and expired certificates.

Findings (6): (1) Middlebox redundancy is ineffective in 33% of the cases for load balancers and firewalls, and (2) Unsuccessful redundancy failover is mainly due to misconfigurations, faulty failovers and software version mismatch.

7. DISCUSSION

In this section, we discuss the research implications based on our middlebox reliability study.

Commoditize middleboxes: §1 and §3 indicated that hardware middleboxes contribute significantly to network failures, and that their failovers are not 100% effective (§6.2). Therefore, a natural alternative is to commoditize them [11–13] as they can enable a *scale-out* design and provide n:1 redundancy. While there has been promising work on software routers [34], achieving high performance, scalability and fault tolerance simultaneously poses several challenges. First, achieving high performance and programmability are often competing goals. For instance, the communication overhead introduced by software LBs may impact performance of latency-sensitive applications. Second, well-known software issues such as code bugs, frequent updates, and misconfigurations, may cause a commodity middlebox to be less reliable than hardware boxes. Finally, running a large number of commodity servers or VMs as middleboxes risks high operational costs such as power and cooling. Efforts such as [35,36] to reduce network energy footprint can be explored to address them. In some cases, strict application requirements for hardware accelerators such as hardware-based deep packet inspection (DPI) for IDPS and deep-packet modification for WAN optimizers, may become a limiting factor.

Middlebox verification: §4 indicated that connection errors and interface problems dominate middlebox failures, and that there is a wide range of misconfigurations observed on middleboxes. As a result, a key requirement for network operations is to automate management and debugging of network problems e.g., using SDN [37,38]. To improve network debugging, one approach is to do static and runtime verification of desired properties e.g., to check configurations, verify reachability, detect routing loops, guarantee isolation [37,39,40]. However, there are several challenges that need to be addressed. First, current tools lack support for common middlebox features such as tunneling and load balancing. Second, the task of parsing policy specifications and configurations is non-trivial and error-prone, as vendors use varying semantics which in-turn may change with device generations. Third, checking for correctness of policies involves designing a set of constraints that can be tested against the device configuration. However, defining a complete constraint set is difficult and evaluating it, computationally expensive [41]. Finally, the large-scale of data center networks makes it challenging to apply formal verification techniques due to the well-known state space explosion problem.

Detect early faulty product-line: In §5, we uncovered using trend analysis that an LB generation had lower reliability compared to other generations. This raises a serious dilemma: keep replacing faulty devices in existing deployment or upgrade to a new product line? While capital and operating costs dominate the cost vs. benefit analysis, answering this question is challenging for two additional reasons:

- Device familiarity: Upgrading devices with their high-speed, feature-rich counterparts will require additional training for network engineers (and has the undesirable consequence of increasing TTR due to unfamiliarity).
- Active/Standby Compatibility: Where 1:1 redundancy is dominant, both devices should be simultaneously upgraded to avoid unsuccessful redundancy failovers.

By computing a Cost of Ownership (COO) [42] metric, decisions such as whether to buy more spares for a faulty product line or to gracefully replace a product line can be made. The primary cost elements of the COO model are: (i) initial investment in purchasing the product, (ii) depreciation, (iii) cost of operation that includes space, personnel, and power expenses, (iv) cost of maintenance operations including downtime, repair cost, failure rates, and cost of spares, and (v) enhancement costs that include hardware/software upgrades and personnel training. Our reliability analysis attempts to provide some of these metrics as described in §3.1 and §3.3.

Feasibility of making middlebox processing as a cloud service: A recent proposal is to offload middlebox processing to the cloud [6]. Similar to CDNs, the idea is to use DNS-based redirection to route requests across multiple cloud PoPs and deploy middlebox instances in the cloud to process them based on defined policies. While this approach shifts the burden of owning and managing middleboxes from enterprises to the cloud, our study indicates that it risks making the problem worse as middlebox failures are prevalent in datacenters (§3.1) and redundancy is not 100% effective (§6.2) . Several other challenges also need to addressed before pushing middleboxes as a cloud hosted service: (a) how to guarantee correct middlebox traversal and coordinate state during churn? (b) how to manage the state and complexity for multiple tenants sharing the same set of middlebox instances? (c) how to address grey failures (§4.1) that can degrade service performance and availability? and (d) how to elastically scale-out and scale-in the processing capabilities (e.g., for stateful services) as demand changes? For instance, the stateful session nature of many middleboxes (e.g., load balancers) can limit how quickly instances can be (de)instantiated or risk a traffic spike as disconnected customers attempt to simultaneously rejoin when an instance is shutdown. To deliver traffic reliably in the presence of grey failures, multi-path protocols such as MP-TCP [10] can be explored.

Make the cost-metric of middlebox hardware reliability aware: To compare network hardware costs across platforms and vendors, the conventional metric is to use \$/Gb/s as the unit-cost basis e.g., \$ per 10 Gbps port. For instance, using this metric, we find that hardware LBs are about an order of magnitude more expensive than commodity Layer 3 switches. As §3 shows, middleboxes experience a significant fraction of failures, and incur substantial operating costs for repair and upgrade [6]. Thus, to balance the trade-off between improving service availability while cutting costs down, the cost metric should comprise both capital and operational expenses, e.g., \$/Gbps/99.9% availability, so that administrators can compute the total cost of ownership (TCO) and determine the network costs to provide a target SLA (e.g., 99.9%), to hosted services. Note that the accuracy of this metric needs to be continuously validated and improved by leveraging data from middlebox deployments in production.

8. RELATED WORK

Broadly, the research community has pursued two key directions to build better middleboxes:

1. **Middlebox Architectures**: Research in this direction proposes techniques for explicit control of the middleboxes e.g., middlebox communication (MIDCOM) [4, 43–45] and IETF Next Steps in Signaling (NSIS) [46]. The motivation behind these efforts draws from the fact that while operators increasingly require support for new applications (e.g., teleconferencing, cloud and mobile applications), they are unable to use third-party software/hardware specific to the application and are tied to their middlebox vendor to make the necessary upgrade [4, 6]. There has been some recent work [47, 48] in separating policy from reachability and centralized management of networks. Joseph et al. [2] proposed a policy-aware switching layer for data centers comprising inter-connected policy-aware switches that enable forwarding of different types of traffic through a specified sequence of middleboxes. dFence proposes adding DoS mitigation middleboxes on-demand on the data path to servers under attack [27].

2. **Middlebox Processing Analysis**: Research in this direction largely focused on either characterizing NAT properties such as mapping type and filtering rules [49, 50] or quantifying the end-to-end performance degradation induced by middleboxes [16]. Our work falls into the latter category of middlebox reliability analysis. We do not argue the benefits or shortcomings of current middlebox architectures but instead focus on analyzing their performance.

Failures in datacenters have received significant attention in the recent years [51–56]. Wang et al. measure the impact of middlebox policies on performance, energy and security in cellular networks [15]. However, they did not study middlebox failures. Our work is complementary to these efforts in that we focus on characterizing the device reliability across middleboxes and understanding the causes and impact of their failures.

Markopoulou *et al.* [54] studied failure in the Sprint backbone using passive optical taps and high-speed packet capture hardware. Their results indicated that 20% of all failures is due to planned maintenance and that maintenance is usually scheduled during periods of low network usage to minimize the impact on performance. As operators likely have a good understanding of problems under scheduled maintenance, we apply a planned maintenance filter on network events to analyze device-level reliability due to unexpected outages.

Our work draws some similarity with the analysis carried out by Turner et al. [56] and Gill et al. [17]. Turner et al. [56] used router configurations, syslog and email records to analyze network failures in the CENIC network that serves educational and research institutions in California. Gill et al. [17] study network failures in datacenters. Similar to us, they observe that LBs exhibit high annualized failure rates.

While we share the broader goal of studying network failures with these efforts, this work differs in three important ways driven by our goal of understanding the causes and impact of middlebox failures. First, we focus on several new questions to characterize middlebox reliability e.g., What are the key problems observed and their resolution actions? How prevalent are misconfigurations and what are their different types? Does reliability improve with new generations? and How effective is middlebox redundancy? that have not been addressed in the past. Second, our methodology filters maintenance events to identify "unexpected/unplanned" outages, filters events for devices with redundant failures, and performs hypothesis testing to validate traffic based impact filtering. Finally, our results provide useful guidelines to improve middlebox reliability.

9. CONCLUSION

Middleboxes form a critical component of the network infrastructure in datacenters and enterprises, yet, there have been few real-world studies on understanding the characteristics of middlebox failures. In this paper, we make one of the first attempts to do a large-scale characteristic study of real-world middleboxes to understand the causes and impact of their failures in datacenters. Our study reveals several surprising findings that differ from some commonly held views. We hope that this study motivates further research to improve middlebox reliability. In future work, we aim to leverage the middlebox failure models to predict their failures, develop techniques to improve middlebox redundancy, and build better tools for configuration management.

10. ACKNOWLEDGEMENTS

We thank our shepherd Z. Morley Mao and the anonymous reviewers for their feedback. Moises Goldszmidt and Nachiappan Nagappan provided invaluable help in verifying the failure analysis methodology. We are grateful to David St. Pierre for helping us understand the network data sets.

11. REFERENCES

[1] V. Sekar, S. Ratnasamy, M. Reiter, N. Egi, and G. Shi, "The Middlebox Manifesto: Enabling Innovation in Middlebox Deployment," in *HotNets*, 2011.

[2] D. Joseph, A. Tavakoli, and I. Stoica, "A Policy-Aware Switching Layer for Data Centers," in *SIGCOMM CCR*, 2008.

[3] M. Walfish, J. Stribling, M. Krohn, H. Balakrishnan, R. Morris, and S. Shenker, "Middleboxes No Longer Considered Harmful," in *OSDI*, 2004.

[4] P. Srisuresh, J. Kuthan, J. Rosenberg, A. Molitor, and A. Rayhan, "Middlebox Communication Architecture and Framework," *RFC 3303*, 2002.

[5] ABI, "Enterprise Network and Data Security Spending Shows Remarkable Resilience," http://goo.gl/t43ax, January 2011.

[6] J. Sherry, S. Hasan, C. Scott, A. Krishnamurthy, S. Ratnasamy, and V. Sekar, "Making Middleboxes Someone Else's Problem: Network Processing As a Cloud Service," in *SIGCOMM*, 2012.

[7] I. Week, "Data Center Outages Generate Big Losses," http://goo.gl/zBOfv, May 2011.

[8] "Why Gmail went down: Google misconfigured load balancing servers," http://goo.gl/NXTeW.

[9] "2011 ADC Security Survey Global Findings," http://goo.gl/A3b2Q.

[10] M. Scharf and A. Ford, "MP-TCP Application Interface Considerations," *draft-ietf-mptcp-api-00*, 2010.

[11] V. Sekar, N. Egi, S. Ratnasamy, M. Reiter, and G. Shi, "Design and Implementation of a Consolidated Middlebox Architecture," in *NSDI*, 2012.

[12] H. Uppal, V. Brajkovic, D. Brandon, T. Anderson, and A. Krishnamurthy, "ETTM: A Scalable Fault Tolerant Network Manager," in *NSDI*, 2011.

[13] A. Greenhalgh, F. Huici, M. Hoerdt, P. Papadimitriou, M. Handley, and L. Mathy, "Flow Processing and the Rise of Commodity Network Hardware," *SIGCOMM CCR*, 2009.

[14] V. Liu, A. Krishnamurthy, and T. Anderson, "F10: Fault-Tolerant Engineered Networks," in *NSDI*, 2013.

[15] Z. Wang, Z. Qian, Q. Xu, Z. Mao, and M. Zhang, "An Untold Story of Middleboxes in Cellular Networks," *SIGCOMM CCR*, 2011.

[16] M. Allman, "On Performance of Middleboxes," in *IMC*, 2003.

[17] P. Gill, N. Jain, and N. Nagappan, "Understanding Network Failures in Data Centers: Measurement, Analysis, and Implications," in *SIGCOMM*, 2011.

[18] "Cisco Data Center Network Architecture," http://goo.gl/kP28P.

[19] J. Lockwood, "Open Platform for Development of Network Processing Modules in Reprogrammable Hardware," in *DesignCon*, 2001.

[20] J. Case, M. Fedor, M. Schoffstall, and J. Davin, "Simple Network Management Protocol," SRI International Network Information Center, May 1990.

[21] M. McCloghrie, K. ad Rose, "Management Information Base for Network Management of TCP/IP-based internets," RFC 1213.

[22] D. Johnson, "NOC Internal Integrated Trouble Ticket System," RFC 1297, 1992.

[23] H. Mann and D. Whitney, "On a Test of Whether One of Two Random Variables is Stochastically Larger than the Other," in *The Annals of Mathematical Statistics*, 1947.

[24] A. Hart, "Mann-Whitney test is not just a test of medians: differences in spread can be important," 2001.

[25] R. Potharaju, N. Jain, and C. Nita-Rotaru, "Juggling the Jigsaw: Towards Automated Problem Inference from Network Trouble Tickets," in *NSDI*, 2013.

[26] C. E. Brown, "Coefficient of Variation," in *AMSGRS*, 1998.

[27] A. Mahimkar, J. Dange, V. Shmatikov, H. Vin, and Y. Zhang, "dFence: Transparent network-based denial of service mitigation," in *NSDI*, 2007.

[28] R. Sakia, "The Box-Cox Transformation Technique: A Review," in *JSTOR Statistician*, 1992.

[29] W. E. Leland, M. S. Taqqu, W. Willinger, and D. V. Wilson, "On the Self-Similar Nature of Ethernet Traffic (extended version)," in *IEEE ToN*, 1994.

[30] T. L. Bailey and C. Elkan, "Fitting a Mixture Model by Expectation Maximization to Discover Motifs in Bipolymers," in *ISMB*, 1994.

[31] T. K. Moon, "The Expectation-Maximization Algorithm," 1996.

[32] H. W. Lilliefors, "On the Kolmogorov-Smirnov Test for Normality with Mean and Variance Unknown," *JASA*, 1967.

[33] R. Bendel, S. Higgins, J. Teberg, and D. Pyke, "Comparison of Skewness Coefficient, Coefficient of Variation, and Gini Coefficient as Inequality Measures within Populations," in *Oecologia*, 1989.

[34] K. Argyraki, S. Baset, B. Chun, K. Fall, G. Iannaccone, A. Knies, E. Kohler, M. Manesh, S. Nedevschi, and S. Ratnasamy, "Can Software Routers Scale?" in *PRESTO*, 2008.

[35] S. Nedevschi, L. Popa, G. Iannaccone, S. Ratnasamy, and D. Wetherall, "Reducing Network Energy Consumption via Sleeping and Rate-adaptation," in *NSDI*, 2008.

[36] A. Greenberg, P. Lahiri, D. Maltz, P. Patel, and S. Sengupta, "Towards a Next Generation Data Center Architecture: Scalability and Commoditization," in *PRESTO*. ACM, 2008.

[37] P. Kazemian, G. Varghese, and N. McKeown, "Header space analysis: Static checking for networks," in *NSDI*, 2012.

[38] N. Handigol, B. Heller, V. Jeyakumar, D. Mazières, and N. McKeown, "Where is the debugger for my software-defined network?" in *Proceedings of the first workshop on Hot topics in software defined networks*. ACM, 2012, pp. 55–60.

[39] H. Mai, A. Khurshid, R. Agarwal, M. Caesar, P. Godfrey, and S. King, "Debugging the Data Plane with Anteater," *SIGCOMM CCR*, 2011.

[40] N. Feamster and H. Balakrishnan, "Detecting BGP configuration Faults with Static Analysis," in *NSDI*, 2005.

[41] A. Feldmann and J. Rexford, "IP network Configuration for Intra-domain Traffic Engineering," *Network, IEEE*, 2001.

[42] L. Ellram, "Total Cost of Ownership: An Analysis Approach for Purchasing," in *Journal of PDLM*, 1995.

[43] R. Swale, P. Mart, P. Sijben, S. Brim, and M. Shore, "Middlebox Communications Protocol Requirements," *RFC 3304*, 2002.

[44] B. Carpenter and S. Brim, "Middleboxes: Taxonomy and Issues," *RFC 3234*, 2002.

[45] M. Stiemerling and J. Quittek, "Middlebox communication (MIDCOM) protocol semantics," *RFC 4097*, 2008.

[46] R. Hancock, S. Bosch, G. Karagiannis, and J. Loughney, "Next steps in signaling (NSIS): Framework," in *IETF RFC 4080*, 2005.

[47] A. Greenberg, G. Hjalmtysson, D. Maltz, A. Myers, J. Rexford, G. Xie, H. Yan, J. Zhan, and H. Zhang, "Clean slate 4D approach to Network Control and Management," in *SIGCOMM*, 2005.

[48] M. Casado, M. Freedman, J. Pettit, J. Luo, N. McKeown, and S. Shenker, "Ethane: Taking Control of the Enterprise," in *SIGCOMM CCR*, 2007.

[49] J. Eppinger, "TCP connections for P2P Apps: Software Approach to Solving the NAT Problem," in *ISR*, 2005.

[50] A. Biggadike, D. Ferullo, G. Wilson, and A. Perrig, "NATBLASTER: Establishing TCP Connections Between Hosts Behind NATs," in *ACM SIGCOMM Workshop*, 2005.

[51] S. Kandula, R. Mahajan, P. Verkaik, S. Agarwal, J. Padhye, and P. Bahl, "Detailed Diagnosis in Enterprise Networks," in *SIGCOMM*, 2009.

[52] V. Padmanabhan, S. Ramabhadran, S. Agarwal, and J. Padhye, "A Study of End-to-End Web Access Failures," in *CoNext*, 2006.

[53] C. Labovitz, A. Ahuja, and F. Jahanian, "Experimental Study of Internet Stability and Backbone Failures," in *FTC*, 1999.

[54] A. Markopoulou, G. Iannaccone, S. Bhattacharyya, C. Chuah, Y. Ganjali, and C. Diot, "Characterization of Failures in an Operational IP Backbone Network," in *IEEE/ACM TON*, 2008.

[55] A. Shaikh, C. Isett, A. Greenberg, M. Roughan, and J. Gottlieb, "A Case Study of OSPF Behavior in a Large Enterprise Network," in *ACM SIGCOMM WIM*, 2002.

[56] D. Turner, K. Levchenko, A. Snoeren, and S. Savage, "California Fault Lines: Understanding the Causes and Impact of Network Failures," in *ACM SIGCOMM CCR*, 2010.

A Method for Identifying and Confirming the Use of URL Filtering Products for Censorship*

Jakub Dalek⋆, Bennett Haselton⋆, Helmi Noman⋆, Adam Senft⋆, Masashi Crete-Nishihata⋆, Phillipa Gill†⋆, Ronald J. Deibert⋆
⋆ The Citizen Lab, University of Toronto
† Dept. of Computer Science, Stony Brook University

Abstract

Products used for managing network traffic and restricting access to Web content represent a dual-use technology. While they were designed to improve performance and protect users from inappropriate content, these products are also used to censor the Web by authoritarian regimes around the globe. This dual use has not gone unnoticed, with Western governments placing restrictions on their export.

Our contribution is to present methods for identifying installations of URL filtering products and confirming their use for censorship. We first present a methodology for identifying externally visible installations of URL filtering products in ISPs around the globe. Further, we leverage the fact that many of these products accept user-submitted sites for blocking to confirm that a specific URL filtering product is being used for censorship. Using this method, we are able to confirm the use of McAfee SmartFilter in Saudi Arabia and the United Arab Emirates (UAE) and Netsweeper in Qatar, the UAE, and Yemen. Our results show that these products are being used to block a range of content, including oppositional political speech, religious discussion and gay and lesbian material, speech generally protected by international human rights norms.

Categories and Subject Descriptors: C.2.2 [Computer-Communication Networks]: Network Protocols

General Terms: Measurement **Keywords:** Censorship; Network Measurement; URL filtering

1. INTRODUCTION

URL filtering products, used for managing Web traffic and restricting access to content, are extremely common in corporate, educational and ISP networks around the globe. However, these technologies, which were designed to improve performance and filter inappropriate content in the enterprise setting, represent a dual-use technology. Indeed, there have been numerous reports of URL filtering products produced by Western companies being sold in countries with poor human rights records, where they are used for censorship and surveillance [2–5, 28, 30]. The use of technology developed in North America and Europe against citizens by authoritarian regimes presents many legal and ethical issues. In the past two years, the United States [26], Europe [29], and Israel [7] have all taken steps to limit the export of these technologies to countries under sanctions such as Syria and Iran. Further, as part of the OpenNet Initiative (ONI), we have documented numerous cases of products developed by Western companies being used to limit freedom of speech online via censorship and potentially surveillance [11, 13, 14, 21, 32] over the past ten years.

With the stakes so high, it is important that we have techniques for monitoring the use of specific technologies for censorship. These tools can help inform policymakers and even vendors, who may be unaware that their technology is being used for censorship. In 2009, Websense actually withdrew software update support once the ONI informed them that their technology was being used for censorship by the government of Yemen [35]. While our methodologies have sufficed thus far, recent legal implications of our observations beg for repeatable methodologies that produce high confidence results.

Challenges of measuring URL filtering deployments. Measuring URL filtering products is complicated by the fact that censorship is difficult to observe without vantage points located within the country of interest. Through our involvement in ONI, we have managed to gain access to measurements from within many countries with restrictive filtering regimes. However, performing client-based measurements in some countries is considered too risky (e.g., Cuba, North Korea), thus we cannot claim global coverage. Further, identifying installations of specific URL filtering products requires an understanding of distinct properties of the product under consideration (e.g., relevant HTTP headers) and careful validation to avoid false positives. Finally, even if a given product is installed in a country, it does not necessarily mean it is being used for censorship/surveillance purposes.

Our contribution. With these challenges in mind, we sought to design a simple, repeatable, methodology for *identifying* installations of URL filtering products and *confirming* their use for censorship. Our method for identifying URL filter installations (§3) serves to identify installations of filtering products where we can apply our confirmation methodology (§4); however, the confirmation methodology alone is enough to verify that a specific product is used for censorship in a given network. Our identification method-

*Data available at: `http://goo.gl/Cc1vO`

IMC'13, October 23–25, 2013, Barcelona, Spain.

http://dx.doi.org/10.1145/2504730.2504763 .

Table 1: Summary of products we consider.

Company	Headquarters	Product description	Previously observed
Blue Coat [1]	Sunnyvale, CA, USA	Web proxy (ProxySG) and URL Filter (Web Filter)	Burma, Egypt, Kuwait, Qatar, Saudi Arabia, Syria, UAE [14,32]
McAfee SmartFilter [16]	Santa Clara, CA, USA	Filtering of Web content for enterprises	Bahrain, Iran, Kuwait, Oman, Saudi Arabia, Tunisia, UAE [11,21,22]
Netsweeper [18]	Guelph, ON, Canada	Netsweeper Content Filtering	Qatar, UAE, Yemen [21]
Websense [34]	San Diego, CA, USA	Web proxy gateways including features to monitor for corporate data leakage.	Yemen (prior to 2009) [21]

ology hinges on the observation that some URL filter installations are visible on the global Internet (likely due to inexperienced network administrators). We came to this observation during initial study of Syria where external facing IP addresses were used to host Blue Coat products [32]. We develop methodologies to locate a set of these externally visible IPs and verify that (1) they are hosting the suspected product and (2) confirm the product is indeed used for censorship (when we have access to in-country measurements). Our study highlights the human rights implications of these products and can provide ground truth for Web proxy fingerprinting (as is done by Netalyzr [12,17]).

Key insights. Our study highlights many properties of URL filters that underscore the importance of studying their use. Specifically, we observe the use of these products in multiple North American ISPs which raises issues about monitoring how these products are being used on a global scale, and not just in jurisdictions commonly considered in censorship studies (§3). We further highlight complications in terms of how URL filters are implemented (e.g., inconsistent blocking and use of multiple products) that make characterizing their use challenging (§4). Finally, we demonstrate our proposed method by confirming the use of Netsweeper and McAfee SmartFilter for censorship of content protected by human rights norms in Qatar, Saudi Arabia, the UAE and Yemen (§5).

Limitations. We note that our methodology for identifying installations of URL filtering products requires that these installations be visible on the global Internet, thus the identification method is likely identifying installations that are not maintained by a technically sophisticated administrator. Further, we are not robust to products that attempt to evade our profiling. Thus, our results should be viewed as presenting a high confidence subset of URL filter deployments. We discuss these limitations in more detail in Section 6.

2. BACKGROUND

2.1 URL filtering products

There are multiple methods that may be used for implementing URL filtering systems. These products usually include a database of pre-categorized URLs, that allow the network operator to configure which categories to block within their network, and the ability to create custom categories for blocking. The products may also include a subscription/update component to push newly categorized URLs to the product's database. Depending on the functionality provided by the product (*e.g.,* whether it proxies all Web traffic), the product may be sold as software to be installed by the administrator or as a stand-alone middlebox in the case of proxies. Table 1 summarizes the products we consider.

2.2 Prior work by the OpenNet Initiative

The OpenNet Initiative has studied Internet censorship for the past decade [11,13,14,21,32]. Over the course of the project, we began to observe products developed by Western companies used for censorship by repressive regimes, starting with SmartFilter products in Tunisia in 2005. By 2010, we had documented extensive use of Western technologies for censorship in the Middle East and North Africa (MENA) region [21]. Table 1 highlights the products we have discovered, as well as the countries where we have located them. Initially, our methods for identifying these products consisted of manual analysis of block pages for company logos/branding and product names in HTTP headers. Over time, however, we observed Western vendors obscure the use of their products (*e.g.,* by omitting logos on block pages [21]). In response, we have been developing novel techniques to confirm use of URL filtering products. This paper expands upon these efforts by describing how we identify networks containing URL filter installations (§3) and how we confirm that these installations are in fact being used for censorship (§4).

The policy impacts of our efforts thus far, have been mixed. In 2009, our identification of Websense in Yemen led to the vendor discontinuing support of their product for the Yemen government [35]. In contrast, Netsweeper stated that is not against their company policies to aid foreign governments in implementing Internet censorship. Finally, we have observed Blue Coat withdraw update support from Syria [32], as a result of legal sanctions against the country [26]. However, the company still plays a role in Internet censorship in many countries around the world, and has even been named an "enemy of the Internet" by Reporters Without Borders [6]. Part of our goal in this study is to present a repeatable methodology for identifying and confirming the use of these products for censorship to inform future discussions with vendors and policy makers.

3. IDENTIFYING URL FILTERS

We begin by presenting our methodology to identify installations of URL filtering products. As described in Section 2.2, we previously leveraged user reports to identify URL filtering products. However, as vendors remove branding from block pages, it becomes more difficult for non-technical users to identify these products. Further, the individuals we engage with tend to be biased towards certain regions of interest (*e.g.,* the MENA region). In this section, we present an identification method that does not depend

Table 2: Summary of our methodology for identifying URL filtering products.

Product	Shodan keywords	WhatWeb signature
Blue Coat	"proxysg","cfru="	Built in detection or `Location` header contains hostname "www.cfauth.com"
McAfee SmartFilter	"mcafee web gateway", "url blocked"	`Via-Proxy` header or HTML title contains "McAfee Web Gateway"
Netsweeper	"netsweeper", "webadmin", "webadmin/","webadmin/deny", "8080/webadmin/"	Built in detection
Websense	"blockpage.cgi", "gateway websense"	`Location` header redirects to a host on port 15871 with parameter "ws-session"

on user reports and is more scalable than manual inspection, by examining HTTP headers and Web directory structure for evidence of filtering installations.

3.1 Methodology

Our methodology leverages the observation that URL filtering products are sometimes configured such that they are visible on the global Internet. Since they are visible on the global Internet, these products can be located via external scans of IP address space. Indeed, our group has previously leveraged network scans to identify Blue Coat installations in Syria [14, 32]. As a proof of concept, we demonstrate our techniques using the Shodan search engine [27] to locate IP addresses, but are working towards applying it on a larger scale with the Internet Census [10] data in ongoing work.

Locating potential installations. The Shodan search engine [27] indexes the IP addresses of externally visible devices on the Internet. Entries in Shodan consist of an IP address, along with meta-data and HTTP headers observed when the IP address was accessed by the search engine. By manually analyzing results from the ONI tests, we were able to identify commonly appearing keywords and headers for the products we consider (summarized in Table 2). These keywords include HTTP headers (e.g., "ProxySG" for Blue Coat) and paths known to be associated with the management console (e.g., "8080/webadmin" for Netsweeper). We search for these keywords, in combination with each of the two letter country-code top-level domains, to maximize the set of results we obtain from Shodan.

Validating URL filter installations. When locating IP addresses of the URL filters, we are not conservative, and rely on the following step to confirm that a given product is indeed installed on the identified host. We use the WhatWeb profiling tool [9] to confirm the product that is installed on a given host. For some products (e.g., Netsweeper) WhatWeb contains a pre-existing signature that we leverage in our validation, whereas in other cases we create signatures based on HTTP headers observed when running the WhatWeb tool on an IP address. Table 2 also summarizes how we identify the various products using WhatWeb.

Finally, we use geolocation data from MaxMind [15] and whois data from TeamCymru [31] to map the IP addresses matching WhatWeb signatures to country-level location and autonomous system (AS) number.

3.2 Networks with URL filtering installations

Figure 1 summarizes the countries where each product was observed. While ONI tends to focus on installations by national ISPs, our new methodology allows us to uncover URL filtering installations in a wider set of countries and networks. Indeed, we observe Blue Coat in many new countries and regions: South America (Argentina and Chile), Europe (Finland, Sweden), Asia (Philippines, Thailand and Taiwan) and the Middle East (Israel, Lebanon). Further, for the remaining three products all the installations we discover (with the exception of McAfee SmartFilter in Pakistan) were previously unknown.

Figure 1: Locations of URL filter installations

As expected, we observe installations on a diverse range of networks in the US, such as Websense in two Texas utilities' networks and Netsweeper installations in educational networks in West Virginia, Oklahoma and Missouri. However, we also observe Netsweeper installations in large ISP networks such as Global Crossing, AT&T, Verizon, and Bell South; and Blue Coat installations in Comcast and Sprint. Interestingly, we also observe an installation of Blue Coat on an IP address registered to the United States Information Systems Command (USAISC). The dual-use of these products for network management and censorship, requires confirming *how* they are used before drawing conclusions.

4. CONFIRMING USE OF URL FILTERS

Many of the products we identify play a legitimate role in network management. Thus, when evaluating the human rights implications of these technologies, it is important to validate that they are actually being used for censorship. Further, vendors may obscure the identities of their products by removing the headers we identified in Table 2. The confirmation method we present, is robust to a lack of signatures and does not require the IP address of the URL filter be externally visible. However, we use networks identified via the techniques in Section 3 as a case study of our technique.

4.1 In-network testing

To confirm that a URL filter is being used for censorship, we perform experiments from within the network under consideration, using our global network of testers. Tests of Web page accessibility are performed using a measurement client that accesses a specified list of URLs in the "field" i.e., the location where censorship is suspected. This client software also triggers the same set of URLs to be accessed from a server in our lab at the University of Toronto (which does not censor the type of content tested). The results of the Web page accesses in the field and lab are compared to determine if the page was blocked in the field location. For our measurements of URL filtering, we test short lists of URLs that are amenable to manual analysis of results. Further, the products we test tend to use block pages that explicitly state that content has been censored. Thus, we avoid ambiguities such as censorship via dropped packets or TCP resets.

4.2 Methodology

Our methodology seeks to answer the question: is the given URL filtering product used for censorship in the measured ISP? Since many URL filters provide a mechanism for users to submit sites that should be blocked, we wondered if we could use this mechanism to confirm the use of a specific URL filter. The basic idea is to test sites (under our control) that are not blocked within the ISP, and then submit a subset of these sites to the appropriate URL filter vendor. After 3-5 days, we retest the sites and observe whether or not the submitted sites are blocked. If they are blocked, it is highly likely that the URL filter under consideration is being used for censorship, and our submission of the sites triggered the blocking. We present case studies that explore the effectiveness of this idea to confirm the use of a variety of products in networks where we have in-country testers. Table 3 summarizes these case studies.

4.3 Case study: McAfee SmartFilter in UAE and Saudi Arabia

In 2009, the ONI identified McAfee SmartFilter being used in UAE's national ISP, Etisalat, and in a centralized blocking implementation in Saudi Arabia (effectively used for all ISPs) [23,24]. We use our proposed methodology to confirm whether these technologies are still deployed in these networks in 2012 and 2013.

ONI had previously observed Etisalat using SmartFilter to block content related to anonymizing proxies [24]. Thus, we created a set of 10 domains providing proxy services to test whether SmartFilter was still being used. These domains had the form of two random (non-profane) words registered with the ".info" top-level domain (e.g., `starwasher.info`) and contained the Glype proxy script [8] as their index page. We first ran measurements in the country to verify that these 10 domains were accessible. We then submitted five of these domains to SmartFilter for blocking. Within a few days we observed that the five submitted sites were blocked on Etisalat, thus confirming that the product was still in use within the country (Table 3).

Challenge 1: Access to sites that will be blocked. Our methodology requires access to Web sites that are blocked by the studied ISP. Unlike UAE, we found Web sites classified as proxies by SmartFilter were accessible in Saudi Arabia. Thus it appears that Saudi Arabia is not using the proxy category provided by SmartFilter in their deployment. However, Web sites classified as pornography by SmartFilter are blocked in Saudi Arabia. Thus, we perform a similar experiment as we did for UAE, except that the 10 created domains hosted an adult image found via a Google image search. (The image was only used for the duration of our experiment and then removed.) Using the ISP Bayanat Al-Oula, we verified that the 10 domains were accessible in Saudi Arabia. We then submitted five of the domains to SmartFilter for blocking. After four days, we observed that these five domains were blocked (Table 3). We repeated this methodology on Nournet, also in Saudi Arabia, and Etisalat to confirm SmartFilter is still used within these ISPs in 2013.

4.4 Case study: Netsweeper in Qatar, UAE and Yemen

Implementation details of censorship platforms can impact the ability of our method to confirm censorship. For example, we have observed Netsweeper queuing Web sites for categorization once they have been accessed within the country (to expand the set of categorized sites [19]). As a result, once we have validated that our set of URLs is accessible, they may be queued for categorization by Netsweeper, and eventually may be blocked. Thus, it is not possible for us to validate that our sites are accessible prior to submitting a subset of them to be blocked. As a result, we operate on the assumption that none of our sites will be blocked prior to submission.

Prior study by the ONI identified the use of Netsweeper in YemenNet in Yemen [25], Du, in UAE [24] and Ooredoo, in Qatar [21] to block content related to anonymizing proxies. Thus, we use these ISPs to test our proposed methodology. We created a list of 12 domains providing proxy services and submitted six of them to Netsweeper's "test-a-site" service for classification [20]. We then accessed these 12 domains in YemenNet, Du and Ooredoo, and observed whether the six submitted sites were blocked. In all three ISPs, the methodology was successful with 5 of the 6 sites blocked in Du and all six blocked in YemenNet and Ooredoo. (Table 3).

Challenge 2: Inconsistent blocking. Validating censorship in Yemen was complicated by inconsistent blocking. We observed cases where the blocking technology appeared to be temporarily "offline" within the country. For example, some proxy URLs are accessible on runs where other proxy URLs are blocked, while in later runs the reverse is true for the same set of URLs. Indeed, prior work by the ONI observed a Yemeni ISP using Websense with a limited number of concurrent user licenses. When the number of users exceeded the number of licenses no content would be filtered [25].

Inconsistent blocking means that we need to repeat the tests numerous times and require a larger set of domains for testing (as we cannot be sure that previously-accessed sites are not queued for classification). This inconsistency limits the scalability of our approach for validating Netsweeper installations in Yemen.

However, we identified another way to validate that Netsweeper is being used for censorship. To help with configuration of the middlebox, Netsweeper provides a Web site for operators to validate that censorship is working within their network by querying a set of 66 category-specific URLs (e.g., `denypagetests.netsweeper.com/category/catno/23` for pornography). While this method is only viable in networks where the tool has not been disabled, a manual test of this tool in YemenNet, in January 2013, indicated that five categories were blocked: adult images, phishing, pornography, proxy anonymizers, and search keywords.

Table 3: Summary of URL filter case studies.

Product	Country	ISP	Date	Sites submitted	Category	Sites blocked	Confirmed?
Blue Coat	UAE	Etisalat (AS 5384)	4/2013	3/6	Proxy Avoidance	0/3	N
Blue Coat	Qatar	Ooredoo (AS 42298)	4/2013	3/6	Proxy Avoidance	0/3	N
McAfee SmartFilter	Qatar	Ooredoo (AS 42298)	4/2013	5/10	Pornography	0/5	N
McAfee SmartFilter	Saudi Arabia	Bayanat Al-Oula (AS 48237)	9/2012	5/10	Pornography	5/5	Y
McAfee SmartFilter	Saudi Arabia	Nournet (AS 29684)	5/2013	5/10	Pornography	5/5	Y
McAfee SmartFilter	UAE	Etisalat (AS 5384)	9/2012	5/10	Anonymizers	5/5	Y
McAfee SmartFilter	UAE	Etisalat (AS 5384)	4/2013	5/10	Pornography	5/5	Y
Netsweeper	Qatar	Ooredoo (AS 42298)	8/2013	6/12	Proxy anonymizer	6/6	Y
Netsweeper	UAE	Du (AS 15802)	3/2013	6/12	Proxy anonymizer	5/6	Y
Netsweeper	Yemen	YemenNet (AS 12486)	3/2013	6/12	Proxy anonymizer	6/6	Y

Table 4: Summary of Web content blocked by URL filtering products.

Category		Media Freedom	Human Rights	Political Reform	LGBT	Religious Criticism	Minority Groups and Religions
Product	Where						
McAfee SmartFilter	UAE (AS 5384)	X	X	X	X	X	X
Netsweeper	Yemen (AS 12486)	X			X		X
Netsweeper	UAE (AS 15802)	X	X	X	X	X	X
Netsweeper	Qatar (AS 42298)	X	X	X	X	X	X

4.5 Case study: Blue Coat in UAE

Challenge 3: URL filtering and network management tools used in combination. Some of the products we consider in this study can be used in tandem to achieve the goals of an ISP. For example, software products such as SmartFilter can be configured to run on proxy appliances, such as Blue Coat's ProxySG. We observe this situation in Etisalat in the UAE, where we confirm that the ISP is using SmartFilter for URL filtering (§4.3). However, we also identified installations of Blue Coat products in Etisalat using our methodology in Section 3. We created a set of test URLs and submitted them to the "Proxy avoidance" category for filtering by Blue Coat (since we had previously observed proxies blocked using SmartFilter). Upon testing these URLs in Etisalat, we found that none of them were blocked. While it may be the case that the network is using the two vendors to block different types of content, the more likely cause of this discrepancy is Etisalat using SmartFilter for URL filtering atop a Blue Coat proxy which can provide further traffic management capabilities (e.g., policy enforcement, traffic shaping).

4.6 Ethical considerations

The case studies in the prior sections raise ethical issues concerning use of the interfaces provided by the vendors to submit Web sites. We emphasize that our approach does not harm the intended performance of the URL filter as we do not impact the classification of legitimate Web sites. Further, since the Web sites we submit are under our control, there is no collateral damage to existing sites. Finally, in the use of a pornographic image in Saudi Arabia we took care to remove the image promptly after our tests were done. To limit the testers' exposure to the pornographic content, we had them access a benign image file located on the host, rather than the page containing the offensive content. Since our tests indicate that even the benign content on the host was blocked, we conclude that blocking was at the granularity of hostname, thus this method of mitigating user risk does not impact the results.

5. CHARACTERIZING CENSORED CONTENT

Now that we have designed a methodology to identify and confirm the usage of URL filters, we consider the type of content these products are blocking. The types of content found blocked by URL filters was determined by querying lists of URLs through the measurement client (§4.1). Two lists of URLs were tested in each country; a "global list" of internationally relevant content which is constant for all countries, and a "local list" of locally relevant content which is designed for each country by regional experts and is unique for each country tested. Each of the URLs on these lists was assigned to one of 40 content categories (e.g. "human rights" or "gambling") under four general themes: political, social, Internet tools and conflict/security content.

Tests using the measurement client to characterize the type of content censored by URL filtering products were performed within 30 days of the confirmations in Section 4. Manual analysis identified regular expressions corresponding to the vendors' block pages and automated analysis identified all URLs which matched a given block page regular expression.

Results of these tests, presented in Table 4, show that all products are used to block a wide variety of content, including oppositional and critical political content, non-pornographic gay and lesbian content, human rights content, independent media, as well as content relating to minority groups and religious discussion. The blocking of such content contradicts internationally recognized human rights frameworks protecting freedom of expression, such as Article 19 of the Universal Declaration of Human Rights [33].

Table 5: Summary of methods presented in this paper, their limitations, and potential techniques vendors may use to evade them.

Step	Technique	Limitations	Evasionary tactics
Identify installations (§3.1)	Port scans (*e.g.,* Shodan [27], Internet Census [10])	Can only identify externally visible installations.	Do not allow device to be accessed externally
Validate installations (§3.1)	WhatWeb [9]	Requires distinctive use of protocol headers	Can remove evidence of product from headers.
Confirm censorship (§4)	In-country testing and URL submission	Requires in-country testers, knowledge of what categories are blocked, and a set of domains for submission.	Vendors may identify and disregard our submissions (non-trivial)

6. DISCUSSION

In this paper, we present an initial methodology for identifying and confirming the use of URL filtering products around the world and highlight challenges faced when applying this methodology. We now elaborate on how our techniques would fare in the face of vendors that attempt to mask the use of their products. Table 5 summarizes these limitations. We emphasize that the identification of products and confirmation that they are used for censorship are independent; thus the confirmation (§4) is robust even if the techniques presented in Section 3 are evaded.

6.1 Identifying and validating installations.

While our identification method serves as a useful filter when determining where to apply the techniques of Section 4, we observe that URL filter vendors can take simple steps to evade discovery. To prevent identification of their products, vendors could provide ISPs with scripts and configuration instructions that prevent the product from being visible on the global Internet, however they are still reliant on the ISP to implement this correctly. URL vendors may also take steps to remove evidence of their products from protocol headers which is fairly simple to do, but would require having all ISPs running the product perform a software update before the change would take effect.

If both of these tactics are implemented, we would become more reliant on local contacts to provide reports of products being used (*e.g.,* because of access to internal IP address space) in their region. Alternatively, we could apply the techniques of Section 4 more widely, but scalability issues would make this time consuming.

6.2 Confirming censorship

URL filtering products view their database of URLs as a key differentiator to their business, and many even advertise the number of URLs they have classified and the rate at which they add to their databases [19]. By allowing individuals/administrators to submit sites to be blocked in different categories, they effectively crowdsource the database maintenance process. As a result of this, vendors are unlikely to reject all submissions based on our approach.

However, they may attempt to identify our submissions and disregard them. The can be accomplished by identifying either (1) our IP or e-mail address when we submit URLs, or (2) hosting services we use to host the domains under our control (§4). The first is easy for us to evade using proxy services or Tor and many e-mail addresses from free Webmail providers. The second can be evaded by using a popular cloud or hosting provider for our URLs, thus making blocking URLs from the given provider too damaging to the vendor's database.

Even though we may be able to counter evasion tactics by vendors, such a cat-and-mouse game is undesirable. Thus, the design of more scalable techniques, that can use our methodology to provide ground truth, is critical for continued study of URL filtering technologies.

7. CONCLUSIONS

We have presented a methodology for identifying installations of specific URL filtering products and confirmed their use for censorship in networks with in-country testers. Through our case studies, we have confirmed the use of North American products to block content protected by human rights norms in Qatar, Saudi Arabia, UAE, and Yemen.

Future work. While our methodology moves us beyond manual analysis of these products, it still poses many challenges in terms of scalability. Specifically, the methods in Section 4 require that we identify which categories are blocked in each ISP before creating test sites. Further, these methods also require vantage points in the network being considered. We hope this paper spurs dialog in the network measurement community about how to characterize URL filtering products in a high confidence, yet scalable, way. Indeed, our methodology can provide a useful ground truth for more general identification of transparent proxies (*e.g.,* [12, 17]) to yield a more complete picture of URL filtering deployments.

8. REFERENCES

[1] Blue Coat. `http://www.bluecoat.com/`.

[2] B. Elgin. Israel didn't know high-tech gear was sent to Iran, 2011. `http://www.bloomberg.com/news/2012-02-15/syria-blocks-texts-with-dublin-made-gear.html`.

[3] B. Elgin and V. Silver. Syria crackdown gets Italy firm's aid with U.S.-Europe spy gear, 2011. `http://www.bloomberg.com/news/2011-11-03/syria-crackdown-gets-italy-firm-s-aid-with-u-s-europe-spy-gear.html`.

[4] B. Elgin and V. Silver. Syria disrupts text messaging of protesters with made-in-Dublin equipment, 2012. `http://www.bloomberg.com/news/2012-02-15/syria-blocks-texts-with-dublin-made-gear.html`.

[5] B. Elgin, V. Silver, and A. Katz. Iranian police seizing dissidents get aid of Western companies, 2011. `http://www.bloomberg.com/news/2011-10-`

31/iranian-police-seizing-dissidents-get-aid-of-western-companies.html.

[6] Era of the digital merceneries. *Reporters Without Borders*, 2013. http://surveillance.rsf.org/en/.

[7] J. Ferziger. Israeli lawmaker calls for investigation of Iran equipment sales, 2011. http://www.bloomberg.com/news/2011-12-23/israeli-lawmaker-calls-for-investigation-of-iran-equipment-sales.html.

[8] Glype proxy script. http://www.glype.com/.

[9] A. Horton. WhatWeb, 2011. http://www.morningstarsecurity.com/research/whatweb.

[10] Internet census 2012: Port scanning /0 using insecure embedded devices, 2012. http://internetcensus2012.bitbucket.org/paper.html.

[11] ONI research profile: Tunisia. http://opennet.net/studies/tunisia, 2005.

[12] C. Kreibich, N. Weaver, B. Nechaev, and V. Paxson. Netalyzr: Illuminating the edge network. In *The Internet Measurement Conference*, 2010.

[13] M. Marquis-Boire. From Bahrain with love: FinFisher's spy kit exposed? *The Citizen Lab*, 2011. https://citizenlab.org/wp-content/uploads/2012/08/09-2012-frombahrainwithlove.pdf.

[14] M. Marquis-Boire, J. Dalek, S. McKune, M. Carrieri, M. Crete-Nishihata, R. Deibert, S. Khan, H. Noman, J. Scott-Railton, and G. Wiseman. Planet Blue Coat: Mapping global censorship and surveillance tools. *The Citizen Lab*, 2013. https://citizenlab.org/wp-content/uploads/2013/01/Planet-Blue-Coat.pdf.

[15] Maxmind. http://www.maxmind.com/.

[16] McAfee Web protection. http://www.mcafee.com/us/products/web-protection.aspx.

[17] The ICSI Netalyzr. http://netalyzr.icsi.berkeley.edu/.

[18] Netsweeper content filtering. http://www.netsweeper.com/.

[19] Netsweeper by the numbers. http://www.netsweeper.com/what-we-do/netsweeper-by-the-numbers.

[20] Netsweeper Test-a-site. http://www.netsweeper.com/support/test-a-site.

[21] H. Noman and J. York. West censoring East: The use of Western technologies by Middle East censors 2010-2011. *The OpenNet Initiative Bulletin*, 2011. https://opennet.net/sites/opennet.net/files/ONI_WestCensoringEast.pdf.

[22] ONI research profile: Iran. http://opennet.net/research/profiles/iran, 2009.

[23] ONI research profile: Saudi arabia. http://opennet.net/research/profiles/saudi-arabia, 2009.

[24] ONI research profile: United arab emirates. http://opennet.net/research/profiles/united-arab-emirates, 2009.

[25] ONI research profile: Yemen. http://opennet.net/research/profiles/yemen, 2009.

[26] R. Runningen. Obama moves to block technology used by regimes on rebels, 2012. http://www.bloomberg.com/news/2012-04-23/obama-moves-to-block-technology-used-by-regimes-against-protests.html.

[27] Shodan - Computer Search Engine. http://www.shodanhq.com/.

[28] V. Silver. HP Computers underpin Syria surveillance, 2011. http://www.bloomberg.com/news/2011-11-18/hewlett-packard-computers-underpin-syria-electonic-surveillance-project.html.

[29] V. Silver. European Union bans exports to Syria of systems for monitoring web, phones, 2013. http://www.bloomberg.com/news/2011-12-01/european-union-bans-exports-to-syria-of-systems-for-monitoring-web-phones.html.

[30] V. Silver and B. Elgin. Torture in Bahrain becomes routine with help from Nokia Siemens, 2011. http://www.bloomberg.com/news/2011-08-22/torture-in-bahrain-becomes-routine-with-help-from-nokia-siemens-networking.html.

[31] IP to ASN Mapping, 2013. http://www.team-cymru.org/Services/ip-to-asn.html.

[32] Behind Blue Coat: Investigations of commercial filtering in Syria and Burma. *The Citizen Lab*, 2011. https://citizenlab.org/wp-content/uploads/2012/07/01-2011-behindbluecoat.pdf.

[33] Universal declaration of human rights: Article 19, 2013. http://www.un.org/en/documents/udhr/index.shtml#a19.

[34] Websense. http://www.websense.com/.

[35] J. York. Websense bars Yemen's government from further software updates, 2009. https://opennet.net/blog/2009/08/websense-bars-yemens-government-further-software-updates.

Peer-Assisted Content Distribution in Akamai NetSession

Mingchen Zhao[†] Paarijaat Aditya[‡] Ang Chen[†] Yin Lin[⋆◇]
Andreas Haeberlen[†] Peter Druschel[‡] Bruce Maggs[⋆◇] Bill Wishon[◇] Miroslav Ponec[◇]
[†]University of Pennsylvania [‡]MPI-SWS [⋆]Duke University [◇]Akamai Technologies

ABSTRACT

Content distribution systems have traditionally adopted one of two architectures: infrastructure-based content delivery networks (CDNs), in which clients download content from dedicated, centrally managed servers, and peer-to-peer CDNs, in which clients download content from each other. The advantages and disadvantages of each architecture have been studied in great detail. Recently, hybrid, or "peer-assisted", CDNs have emerged, which combine elements from both architectures. The properties of such systems, however, are not as well understood.

In this paper, we discuss the potential risks and benefits of peer-assisted CDNs, and we study one specific instance, Akamai's NetSession system, to examine the impact of these risks and benefits in practice. NetSession is a mature system that has been operating commercially since 2010 and currently has more than 25 million users in 239 countries and territories. Our results show that NetSession can deliver several of the key benefits of both infrastructure-based and peer-to-peer CDNs—for instance, it can offload 70–80% of the traffic to the peers without a corresponding loss of performance or reliability—and that the risks can be managed well. This suggests that hybrid designs may be an attractive option for future CDNs.

Categories and Subject Descriptors

C.2.4 [**Computer Systems Organization**]: Computer-Communication Networks—*Distributed Systems*; C.4 [**Computer Systems Organization**]: Performance of Systems

Keywords

Content distribution networks, peer-to-peer systems

1. INTRODUCTION

This paper presents a study of a hybrid CDN called NetSession in which most content is delivered by a set of peers whose operation is coordinated (and backstopped) by a dedicated infrastructure. Our study is motivated by the observation that hybrid CDNs seem to have reconciled two architectures with very different tradeoffs: On the one hand, peer-to-peer systems are inexpensive and easy to scale but seem to be plagued by security issues and low quality of service (QoS); on the other hand, infrastructure-based systems are expensive to set up and scale but can provide predictable QoS and reliable accounting, and ensure content integrity. We felt that the time was ripe to investigate what advantages a hybrid of these approaches might convey.

We find, perhaps surprisingly, that NetSession is able to achieve the "best of both worlds": it can offer most of the benefits of both architectures while avoiding most of the drawbacks. This is because the strengths of the infrastructure and the peers complement each other: The infrastructure provides a central point of coordination that can quickly match up peers and can add resources when peers cannot provide adequate QoS; the peers provide resources and scalability, and they extend the "reach" of the infrastructure to underserved areas.

Prior work has identified several potential concerns about hybrid CDNs; in particular, it has been suggested that hybrid CDNs might become a burden to Internet Service Providers (ISPs) by increasing inter-AS traffic [17, 24, 35]. We show that, at least in the case of NetSession, this concern appears to be unfounded. Finally, we report some observations from the day-to-day operation of the NetSession system. Among other things, we discover a surprising degree of user mobility in the system, and we describe what appear to be the effects of cloning and re-imaging client installations. In summary, this paper makes the following five contributions:

- an overview of the hybrid CDN design space, including a discussion of potential risks and benefits (Section 2);
- a description of NetSession's design goals and implementation (Section 3);
- a measurement study that provides an overview of the scale at which NetSession operates and the types of content it is used to deliver (Section 4);
- an analysis of whether NetSession meets its design goals and realizes the potential benefits of hybrid systems (Section 5); and
- an investigation into whether the risks associated with hybrid systems, such as undue burdens on ISPs or problems with untrusted end-user machines, are evidenced by NetSession in practice (Section 6).

We discuss related work in Section 7, and present our conclusions in Section 8.

IMC'13, October 23–25, 2013, Barcelona, Spain.
ACM 978-1-4503-1953-9/13/10. http://dx.doi.org/10.1145/2504730.2504752.

2. THE CDN DESIGN SPACE

We begin by sketching the design space for content distribution systems, and discuss the potential risks and benefits of hybrid designs.

2.1 To Peer or Not To Peer?

Traditionally, CDNs have fallen into two categories: some relied exclusively on a centrally managed infrastructure, while others operated entirely without one. Akamai's CDN [10] is an example of an *infrastructure-based* CDN: it uses an infrastructure of more than 137,000 servers in 87 countries within over 1,150 Internet networks, all owned and operated by Akamai. BitTorrent [8] is an example of a *peer-to-peer (p2p)* CDN: other than the tracker (which serves as an initial point of contact) and perhaps an initial seeder, it requires no infrastructure at all; all data is exchanged directly between the peers. Recent BitTorrent clients have even replaced the tracker with a distributed hashtable [9], removing the last remaining infrastructure element.

Infrastructure-based CDNs typically have the benefit of professional administrators and amply provisioned resources—they can control and authenticate the content they distribute, and they can achieve high performance and reliability, but they are also expensive to scale. Peer-to-peer CDNs must rely on resources contributed by their peers, which means that their properties are often the exact opposite: they require little up-front investment and scale organically, but can be plagued by spam and low-quality content, and their quality of service tends to be unpredictable. Thus, it is natural to ask whether it might not be possible to achieve the "best of both worlds" in a single system.

2.2 Why decide?

In this paper, we focus on hybrid CDNs that combine elements from both architectures: like peer-to-peer CDNs, they achieve scalability by leveraging resources from the client machines, but, like infrastructure-based CDNs, they also rely on dedicated, centrally managed elements, such as a central directory of file locations and dedicated servers that provide a backstop of delivery capacity. We refer to such CDNs as *peer-assisted CDNs*.

One way to characterize peer-assisted CDN designs is to look at the role they assign to the infrastructure. For instance, the infrastructure can provide *resources*, such as bandwidth, computation, or storage, which might be used to improve the quality of service or to keep rarely requested content available; it can provide *coordination* by building a global view of the system, e.g., to recognize attacks, to allocate resources, or to pair up peers with matching NATs; and it can provide *control*, e.g., by deciding which content may be distributed. Thus, there is an entire spectrum of possible designs, ranging from systems that rely mostly on the peers and have a very small infrastructure (such as tracker-based BitTorrent) to systems that rely primarily on the infrastructure and use the peers only as an optimization.

2.3 Potential benefits

Peer-assisted CDNs have substantial flexibility in dividing tasks between the peers and the infrastructure. Thus, they can potentially use each element where it is strongest. The potential benefits relative to a pure peer-to-peer CDN include:

Better quality of service: The infrastructure can be used as a "backstop" for the peers, i.e., it can help out with requests where the peers do not have much bandwidth, or where there is a lot of churn.
Reduced reliance on peer contributions: The infrastructure can absorb the cost of a certain degree of freeloading. Thus, it is not as important to force peers to reciprocate, or to "fairly" distribute the workload.
More reliable delivery: The infrastructure can authenticate content; there is no need to rely on heuristics or reputations to recognize content that has been corrupted or tampered with.
Less legal exposure: The infrastructure can ensure that all content is properly licensed; thus, peers can safely participate in swarming and upload content to others, without being at risk for accidental violations of the DMCA (and similar laws).
Better security: The infrastructure can use its global view to recognize and fight attacks, and it can provide professionally managed servers that can perform trusted functions.
Higher efficiency: The infrastructure can maintain a global view and perform global optimizations, e.g., by quickly locating copies of a file, or by matching up peers.

The potential benefits over a pure infrastructure-based system include:
Lower cost: Content providers can potentially deliver their data at lower cost (and can pass some of the resulting savings on to end users). Also, the CDN operator may be able to offer services to content providers who otherwise may not be able to afford a CDN.
Global coverage: Finally, in geographic areas with sparse infrastructure deployment, serving content from peers may increase the quality of service. Also, ISPs that are not hosting CDN servers should see less inter-ISP traffic for popular downloads.

2.4 Potential risks

Peer-assisted CDNs face some of the risks that affect pure infrastructure based and peer-to-peer architectures, and a few risks that are unique to them:
Need for revenue: Unlike peer-to-peer CDNs, peer-assisted CDNs must generate some revenue to defray the costs of the infrastructure.
Less transparency: Unlike infrastructure CDNs, peer-assisted CDNs are usually not transparent to users; they require the installation of software on each client.
Heterogeneity: Unlike most infrastructure CDNs, peer-assisted CDNs include a heterogeneous population of machines that are managed by users, with varying capabilities and complex failure modes.
Multiple administrative domains: Unlike infrastructure CDNs, peer-assisted CDNs inherently contain machines that are controlled by different parties, many of whom the CDN operator does not trust.
NATs and firewalls: Unlike infrastructure CDNs, peer-assisted CDNs rely on their clients' upstream links, which requires traversing a variety of middleboxes that may exist on the path.
Impact on ISPs: Peers in peer-assisted CDNs send *and* receive traffic; thus, these systems are creating a different traffic pattern, which can affect ISPs' networks and businesses.

3. THE NETSESSION SYSTEM

To examine how many of the potential benefits peer-assisted CDNs can deliver in practice, and how many of their potential risks they can avoid, we have studied the NetSession system, a peer-assisted CDN that was originally developed by RedSwoosh and has been commercially operated by Akamai since 2010. As of October 2012, NetSession has been in production use for five years and has almost 26 million users in 239 countries and territories.

3.1 Design goals

NetSession was designed with the following three high-level goals in mind:

1. A substantial fraction of the content should be delivered by the peers.
2. Peer-assisted delivery QoS should be comparable to that of infrastructure-based delivery; in particular,
   (a) downloads should be no less reliable; and
   (b) downloads should not be much slower.
3. The system should offer reliable accounting for services provided.

In other words, the system was meant to combine the key benefits of peer-to-peer CDNs (scalability) and infrastructure CDNs (quality of service). The third goal was an operational requirement: Content providers, who pay for the CDN's services, expect detailed logs that show the amount and the quality of the services provided. There were also two explicit non-goals:

1. The system need not be *more* reliable than an infrastructure-based CDN; and
2. Peers need not contribute equally.

The first point sets realistic expectations about security; the second point reflects the fact that the system has a large infrastructure to fall back on, so some proportion of peers who opt out of serving content to peers would not be a concern. Serving content reliably and with good QoS is more important than minimizing load on the infrastructure.

3.2 Architecture

NetSession distributes content via an infrastructure of *edge servers* that are operated by Akamai, and a number of user-operated peers that have special software, the *NetSession Interface* (Section 3.4), installed on them. In addition to the edge servers, the infrastructure also contains a group of NetSession-specific servers called the *NetSession control plane* (Section 3.6), which serve as coordinators and perform accounting, but do not directly serve any content. Figure 1 illustrates the high-level interaction between these components.

To avoid confusion, we use the term *content providers* to refer to the organizations and individuals who provide content for NetSession to distribute, and the term *users* to refer to those who download the content.

3.3 Example: Download Manager

We begin by briefly describing an example application, the Download Manager (DLM). The DLM is one of several applications that use the NetSession system; a typical use case is to distribute large objects that are several GBs in size, such as software installation images.

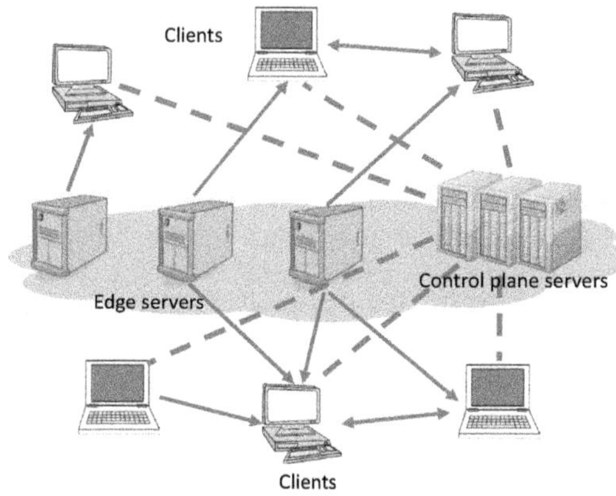

Figure 1: Overview of the NetSession system.

When a user attempts to download an object that is distributed using the DLM, she is first asked to install the NetSession Interface on her computer (unless it is already available from previous usage). Once installed, the NetSession Interface starts downloading the content from the edge servers; in parallel, it queries the control plane for a list of nearby peers that already have a copy of the object. If suitable peers are found, the local peer and the selected peers attempt to contact each other and exchange as much data as possible; however, the download from the edge servers continues in parallel. Thus, if a peer is "unlucky" and picks peers that are slow or unreliable, the infrastructure can cover the difference, so that user experience does not suffer as a result.

Users can pause and resume downloads, and they can continue downloads that were aborted earlier, e.g., because the peer lost network connectivity or the peer's hard drive was full. Once the download completes, the NetSession Interface software remains on the peer and can be reused for future downloads, or by other NetSession-enabled applications, and it can upload the downloaded content to other peers.

3.4 The NetSession Interface

The NetSession Interface is available for Windows and Mac OS. It is implemented as a background application that runs whenever the user is logged into their system. This design choice is different from many p2p clients, which must be launched explicitly by the user. The short session times that have been observed in p2p systems [4, 14, 27] suggest that users launch the client only when they intend to download something, so the time window in which objects can be uploaded to other peers tends to be very short. As a persistent background application, NetSession does not have this problem, but in return, it must take great care not to inconvenience the user. We discuss some of its best practices in Section 3.9.

Whenever the NetSession Interface is active and the peer is online, it maintains a TCP connection to the control plane. When a download is started, the peer uses this control connection to query the control plane for other peers. The connection is also useful for opening peer-to-peer connections through NATs, which in most cases requires coordination between the peers; the control plane can facilitate this by informing both endpoints using their control connection. Finally, peers use the connection to learn about configuration updates, and they report usage statistics, which are used for billing, performance monitoring, and to generate reports for content providers. Each peer has a unique GUID, which is chosen at random during installation.

NetSession uses the standard HTTP (or HTTPS) protocol to download content from edge servers; for downloads from peers, it uses a swarming protocol not unlike BitTorrent's. As in BitTorrent, objects are broken into fixed-size pieces that can be downloaded and their content hashes verified separately, and peers exchange information about which pieces of the file they have locally available.

A key difference to BitTorrent is the absence of an incentive mechanism: in NetSession, peers can always obtain the content from the infrastructure, so it is not as important to discourage "freeloading"—the infrastructure can easily absorb the cost of a few users who decide not to upload. Hence, a conscious decision was made not to include incentives, and to serve content to each peer at the best possible speed, regardless of how much bandwidth it is contributing to the system. There is no tit-for-tat strategy that would "choke" slow uploaders as in BitTorrent, only a globally configurable limit on the total number of upload connections a peer allows. In fact, NetSession Interface users have the option to turn off peer content uploads permanently or temporarily in the NetSession application preferences, without adverse effects on their download performance.

NetSession is predominantly used by content providers who distribute large objects and already require their clients to install software (e.g., games). NetSession also supports video streaming, but it currently does not serve much video traffic because of the requirement to install client software.

3.5 Interaction with edge servers

NetSession's HTTP(S) connections to the edge servers are used not only for downloading files, they also support many other critical functions.

One important function is to ensure content integrity. File pieces can be corrupted in transit or on the peers; additionally, content can change over time, so it is important that different versions are not mixed up in the same download. Edge servers generate and maintain secure IDs of content, which are unique to each version, as well as secure hashes of the pieces of each file. The IDs and the hashes are provided to the peers, so they can validate the content they have downloaded. If a peer cannot validate a file piece, it discards the piece and does not upload it to other peers.

Another key function is authorization. Before a peer can receive content from other peers, it must authenticate to an edge server over the HTTP(S) connection; this yields an encrypted token that can be used to search for peers. This is done to prevent users from downloading files from peers that they are not authorized to obtain from the infrastructure.

Finally, the HTTP(S) connections are used for configuration and reporting. A policy defined by the content provider is used to decide whether a particular file may be downloaded and uploaded; in addition, various configurable options apply to each download and upload. These policies and options are securely communicated to the peers through the trusted edge-server infrastructure. NetSession also uses information from the trusted edge servers to prevent accounting attacks [1], where compromised or faulty peers incorrectly report downloads and uploads.

3.6 The NetSession control plane

The NetSession control plane consists of a number of globally-distributed servers that are operated by Akamai. Its main function is to coordinate between the peers. Each control plane server runs some of the following components:

Connection node (CN): The CNs are the endpoints of the persistent TCP connections that the peers open to the control plane when they are active. The CNs receive and collect the usage statistics that are uploaded by the peers, and they handle queries for objects the peers wish to download. These persistent TCP connections are also used to tell peers to connect to each other in order to facilitate sharing of content. Such coordination is necessary for both security reasons and to overcome NATs and firewalls.

Database node (DN): The DNs maintain a database of which objects are currently available on which peers, as well as details about the connectivity of these peers. Peers appear in the database only when a) uploads are explicitly enabled on the peer, and b) the peer currently has objects to share.

STUN: Peers periodically communicate with STUN components over UDP and TCP to determine the details of their connectivity (which are then stored in the DN databases) and to enable NAT traversal. This involves a protocol with goals similar to [25], but NetSession uses a custom implementation.

Monitoring node: Peers upload information about their operation and about problems, such as application crash reports, to these nodes. Processing their logs helps to monitor the network in real-time, to identify problems, and to troubleshoot specific user issues during support procedures.

3.7 Peer selection

When a CN receives a query for an object with peer-to-peer delivery enabled, the CN asks the DNs to identify suitable peers that currently have a copy of the requested object. The CN then returns information about these peers to the querying peer, and it instructs both the querying peer and the chosen peers to initiate connections to each other. By default, up to 40 peers are returned, and if connections to some of these peers cannot be established, additional queries are issued until a sufficient number of peer connections succeed. Peers control the number and utilization of their connections based on current resource availability.

The DN chooses peers using a locality-aware strategy at two different levels. First, when a peer establishes its persistent TCP connection to the control plane, it is mapped to the closest available CN by Akamai's DNS system [10]. When a CN queries the DN for peers for a specific object, it prefers to contact only local DNs, i.e., DNs running on machines in the same network region as the CN that performs the query. (Network regions are defined by proximity to particular groups of servers.) Since the same process is used when a peer registers a local copy of a file, DNs tend to have information about their *local* peers. The CN/DN system is interconnected across regions, so it is possible in principle to search for peers from any region; however, long-term experimentation has shown that using only local DNs in searches does not negatively impact performance.

Since the current deployment has less than 20 network regions, the first, region-based selection strategy is not sufficiently fine-grained for popular content that is available on many peers. Hence, the DNs use another level of locality-based peer selection that is based on the geolocation of each peer. Each peer belongs to multiple sets, based on its public IP address and the Autonomous System (AS) it is located in. For example, a peer can simultaneously be in a universal *World* set, a subset for a large geographical region, a subset for a smaller region, and a subset for its specific AS.

DN selection begins with peers from the most specific set that the querying peer belongs to, and proceeds to less specific sets until enough suitable peers are found. An additional mechanism adds diversity: Occasionally, peers are selected from a less specific set, with probability proportional to the specificity of the set. Also, when a peer is selected, it is placed at the end of a peer selection list for fairness. The selection process can be modified with a set of configurable policies.

In addition to locality and file availability, the DN also takes the connectivity of the peers into account: it selects only peers that are likely to be able to establish a connection with each other, e.g., based on the type of their NAT or firewall. Due to the vast diversity in NAT implementations today, NAT hole punching is a complex issue, and the necessary code takes up a large fraction of the NetSession codebase.

3.8 Robustness

The design of NetSession employs the notions of soft state and fate sharing to provide robustness against failures. At first glance, it might seem that the loss of CN or DN components could be catastrophic to NetSession. Indeed, many peers rely on each CN: over 150,000 might be connected to one simultaneously. But ultimately, all of the data about the peers that matters is held by the peers themselves. If a CN goes down, the peers that are connected to that CN simply reconnect to another one. If a DN goes down, the CNs connected to that DN send a RE-ADD message to their peers, asking them to list the files that they are storing. The CN passes these lists on to the available DNs in order to repopulate their databases. In practice, failures of CN and DN nodes occur routinely, e.g., during server maintenance or during software updates. In fact, when a new CN/DN software version is released, all CNs and DNs are restarted in a short timeframe, and this does not negatively affect the service. (In the event of an unexpectedly large-scale failure, reconnections are rate-limited to ensure a smooth recovery.) Finally, if a peer is not able to connect to any CN at all, it retrieves the content directly from the edge servers; hence, even if the entire CN and DN infrastructure were to fail, the peers would simply fall to back to retrieving content from the CDN infrastructure.

The client software version is centrally controlled by the CDN infrastructure, and peers can perform automated upgrades in the background on demand. Most of the peer population can be upgraded to a new version within one hour. The ability to perform fast software upgrades without user interaction can help to respond quickly to security or performance incidents. Download and upload performance is constantly monitored, and automated alerts are in place to notify network engineers in case of large-scale problems.

3.9 Best practices

Since NetSession uses resources that are provided by the peers, it must carefully consider the users' interests. NetSession obtains consent from users through its EULA, and Akamai provides users with information about what the NetSession Interface is, and what it does. The software includes both a control panel user interface and a command line utility that enable users to determine what the software is doing, which files it is currently storing, which applications are using it, etc. These tools also allow users to turn uploading on or off, and it comes with an uninstaller.

Control plane logs:	
Time period covered	10/01 – 10/31, 2012
Log entries	4,150,989,257
Number of GUIDs	25,941,122
Control plane servers	197
Distinct URLs	4,038,894
Distinct IPs	133,690,372
Downloads initiated	12,508,764
Geolocation data:	
Distinct IPs	133,690,372
Distinct locations	34,383
Distinct autonomous systems	31,190
Distinct country codes	239

Table 1: Overall statistics for our data sets.

NetSession is designed to protect the privacy of its users; it does not capture personal information [3]. The data it keeps is similar to that of a normal web server. When peers download content from each other, they learn that other peers with certain GUIDs and IP addresses already have the requested file. However, this information is not displayed to users and is deleted from the peer once a download completes and the logs have been uploaded to the CNs for billing and monitoring.

To avoid inconveniencing users, the NetSession Interface is designed to stay in the background as much as possible. For example, a peer does not proactively download content; it only shares objects that the corresponding user has previously downloaded. Uploads are rate-limited, and peers upload each object at most a limited number of times. Finally, peers monitor the utilization of the local network connections and throttle or pause uploads when the connections are used by other applications. While it is important for users to experience good download performance, the performance of uploads is intentionally limited using custom protocols.

Users do not benefit directly from the bandwidth they donate, but NetSession offers a number of indirect benefits; for instance, the DLM enables users to resume aborted downloads and to download from multiple sources simultaneously. Also, peer-assisted downloads require fewer resources from the infrastructure and can thus be offered at a lower price. Content providers can pass on these savings to the users.

4. MEASUREMENT STUDY

We now turn to the question how well NetSession, as one instance of a peer-assisted CDN, is able to deliver the potential benefits of a hybrid architecture, and how well it is able to avoid the corresponding risks. To answer this question, we have performed a measurement study that is based on a set of logs from the production system.

4.1 Data set

Our logs cover the month of October 2012. At a high level, they contain information about *downloads* and information about *logins*. When a peer downloads a file from NetSession,

	Americas			Asia			Europe	Africa	Oceania
	US East	US West	Other	India	China	Other			
Customer A	–	–	12%	6%	6%	18%	51%	4%	3%
Customer B	2%	1%	1%	11%	–	61%	6%	17%	1%
Customer C	13%	6%	15%	1%	–	8%	55%	1%	2%
Customer D	22%	21%	6%	–	–	3%	45%	–	3%
Customer E	5%	3%	8%	2%	1%	29%	48%	2%	3%
Customer F	–	–	–	–	–	–	100%	–	–
Customer G	8%	3%	12%	2%	8%	20%	45%	2%	2%
Customer H	6%	4%	7%	4%	2%	20%	53%	2%	2%
Customer I	5%	2%	18%	–	–	15%	57%	1%	1%
Customer J	42%	24%	14%	–	–	5%	11%	1%	3%
All customers	7%	4%	11%	3%	2%	20%	46%	4%	2%

Table 2: Global distribution of downloads for the ten largest content providers.

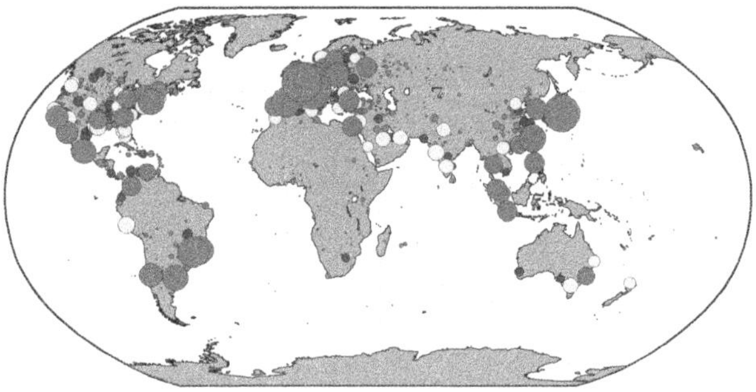

Figure 2: Global distribution of peers.

the CN records information about the download, including the GUID of the peer, the name and size of the file, the CP code (a number identifying a specific account of a content provider that is offering the file), the time the download started and ended, and the number of bytes downloaded from the infrastructure and from peers. This information is used for accounting and billing. Additionally, when a peer opens a connection to the control plane, the CN records the peer's current IP address, its software version, and whether or not uploads are enabled on that peer.

To localize the peers geographically and in the network, we also obtained geolocation data from Akamai's EdgeScape [2] service about each IP address that appears in the trace. This data includes an ISO 3166 country code, the name of a city and state, a latitude/longitude pair, a timezone, and a network provider name. (Note that territories and areas of geographical interest, such as Antarctica, can also have country codes.) The granularity of the location information varies by region; in the United States, locations are typically at the city/suburb granularity. For instance, the data set contains 218 unique locations in the state of Pennsylvania.

To protect the privacy of users and content providers, the data in our logs have been anonymized by hashing the file names, IP addresses, and GUIDs. Table 1 shows some overall statistics for our data set.

4.2 Number and location of the peers

We begin by giving an overview of the NetSession deployment as of October 2012, to illustrate the number and geographic distribution of the peers, as well as the type of content being served. The one-month trace contains about 26 million distinct GUIDs. (Recall that the NetSession software chooses a GUID when it is first installed, so the number of GUIDs should correspond roughly to the number of peers.) On a typical day, between 8.75 and 10.90 million of the GUIDs connect to the control plane at least once. The system has been growing steadily over time; for comparison, a trace from October 2010 contained 14.19 million distinct GUIDs, or slightly more than half the number in our trace.

Figure 2 shows the global distribution of the peers as a "bubble plot": the size of each bubble corresponds to the number of peers whose first connection to the system was from that particular location. Most of the peers are located in North America (27%) and Europe (35%), but there are also sizable groups of peers in South America and Asia. Overall, we observed connections from 239 different countries and territories across all continents, so NetSession is a truly global system.

4.3 Content providers

Each file that is available through NetSession is offered by a specific content provider—usually a large corporate customer. To illustrate how these customers are using the system, we selected the downloads served by the ten largest customers (here identified as Customers A through J), we associated each download with one of ten regions, and we counted the number of downloads per customer per region.

Table 2 show the results. Generally, we find that roughly half of the downloads occur in Europe. However, the downloads distribution depends on customer. Customer B's content, for example, is far more popular in Asia except China and Africa. Customer J's content is mostly requested from within the United States.

4.4 Available content

At the time our data was collected, a typical use case for NetSession was the distribution of software installers; data files and other content, such as music and video, made up a small portion. Overall, we observed downloads for 4,038,894 distinct objects in our trace. Figure 3(a) shows the distribution of requests for objects of a given size, for peer-assisted, infrastructure only, and all requests in NetSession. Peer-assisted downloads are strongly biased towards large files; 82% of peer-assisted requests are for objects larger than 500 MB. Because the benefits of peer assist are most pronounced for such large objects, content providers tend to enable it on such objects.

The object popularity distribution and temporal request pattern in NetSession's workload are shown in Figure 3(b) and (c). As expected, the former shows the nearly ubiquitous power law, while the latter shows the usual diurnal patterns.

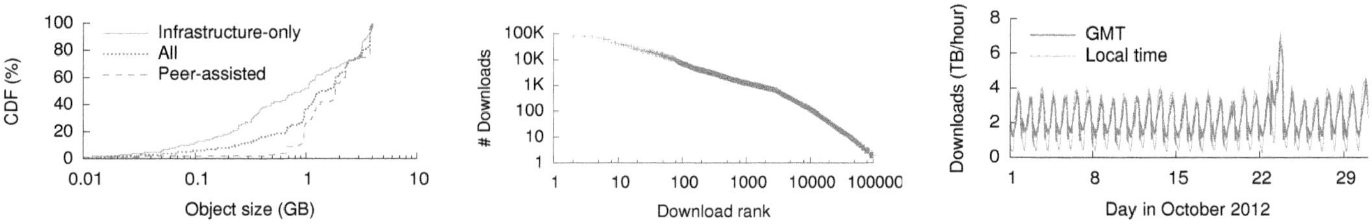

(a) Request distrib. by object size (b) Content popularity (c) Bytes served over time

Figure 3: Overall workload characteristics.

Uploads initially...	Nodes	Number of changes		
		0	1	≥ 2
Disabled	15,913,255	99.96%	0.03%	0.01%
Enabled	7,395,867	98.11%	1.80%	0.09%

Table 3: Observed changes to the setting that enables content uploads.

5. BENEFITS

Next, we focus on three questions that can be answered quantitatively based on our data, namely: 1) How well does peer assist work? 2) Does peer assist affect performance and reliability? And, 3) does peer assist help improve the CDN's global coverage?

5.1 How well does peer assist work?

Recall that NetSession peers are not required to contribute bandwidth: users are free to disable uploads to peers by changing their preferences in the NetSession GUI. This is a major difference from pure peer-to-peer systems like BitTorrent, which include incentive mechanisms like tit-for-tat to encourage uploading. In the literature, it is often assumed that users are "rational" and will avoid uploading if they don't benefit from it [8, 23]; it is therefore natural to ask whether NetSession peers are willing to contribute any bandwidth at all.

Do the peers contribute resources? To answer this question, we used the login records in our data set to determine the fraction of peers that have uploads enabled. However, the NetSession binary is available in two versions, one with uploads initially enabled and one with uploads initially disabled. This is chosen by the content provider who bundles the binary; some content providers use the software merely as a download manager, without the peer assist. For this reason, we additionally check whether users changed this setting between logins, and if so, how often.

Tables 3 and 4 show our results. About 31% of the peers have uploading enabled, but the setting is rarely changed—more than 99% of the peers keep their initial setting throughout our trace. As Table 4 shows, the initial setting depends on the content provider from who the user first downloaded the binary. Most users simply stick with whatever the default is. This tendency is well known in UI design [21, 31], but it also suggests that users either don't care enough about the uploads to change the setting or are not aware of the choice, despite its mention in the NetSession user agreement.

Uploading in peer-to-peer CDNs carries the risk of legal exposure and/or degraded network performance [29]. As a peer-assisted CDN, NetSession can avoid the first problem

Customer	A	B	C	D	E	F	G	H	I	J
p2p (%)	<1	20	2	94	2	45	47	<1	91	<1

Table 4: Fraction of peers that have content uploads enabled.

because its content is centrally controlled and vetted, and its back-off mechanism (Section 3.9) can avoid the second problem by consuming bandwidth only when the connection is idle. We speculate that this is part of the reason why most users don't seem to turn off peer uploads when they are enabled initially.

How much can be offloaded to the peers? As a peer-assisted CDN, NetSession can offload some of the bandwidth needed to satisfy the download requests to the peers. Content providers can control on a per-file basis whether or not peer-to-peer downloads are allowed. In our trace, we found that peer-to-peer downloads were enabled for only 1.7% of the files, but these downloads accounted for 57.4% of the downloaded bytes overall.

The key quantity of interest is the *peer efficiency* of the system, i.e., the fraction of bytes in peer-assisted downloads that are actually downloaded from the peers. (The peer efficiency for infrastructure-only downloads is zero.) In our trace, the average peer efficiency for peer-assisted downloads was 71.4%. This is a very good result, given that, even in a peer-assisted download, NetSession never *exclusively* downloads from the peers; there is always at least one connection to the infrastructure, to guarantee progress independent of the peers.

5.2 Does peer assist reduce performance?

Are peer-assisted downloads slower? NetSession relies on peer downloads, which are limited by peer reliability and the upstream bandwidth of broadband access networks, to which many of NetSession's peers are connected. This bandwidth is typically much smaller than the downstream bandwidth [11]. Hence, it is natural to ask how the performance of peer-assisted downloads compares to those that are served by the infrastructure.

Figure 4 makes this comparison for downloads from the two networks with the most downloads, AS X and AS Y. We identified all downloads from these networks where either a) all the bytes came from the edge servers, or b) at least 50% of the bytes came from peers. We then averaged the speed of each download across its entire length; the figure shows the results as a CDF.

We find that, although the peer-assisted downloads are somewhat slower, the speed is still quite high, with most downloads occurring at rates of multiple Mbps. When comparing the performance across networks, we find that the

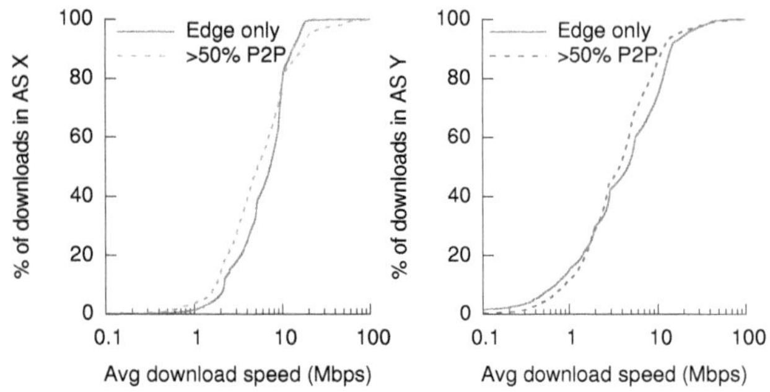

Figure 4: Edge-only vs peer-assisted download speed in two large ASes.

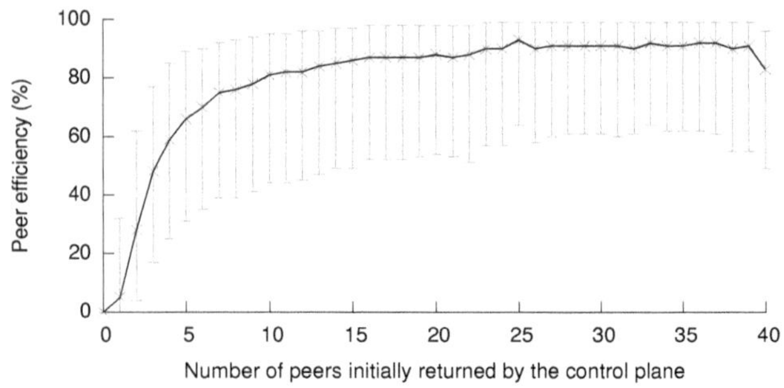

Figure 6: Impact of the number of peers on peer efficiency.

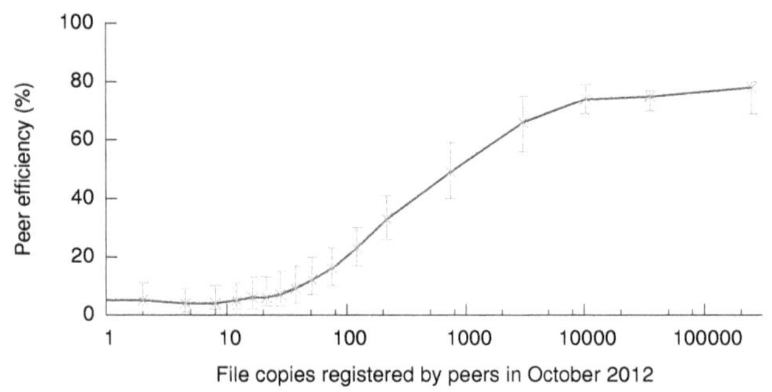

Figure 5: Number of registered file copies vs. peer efficiency

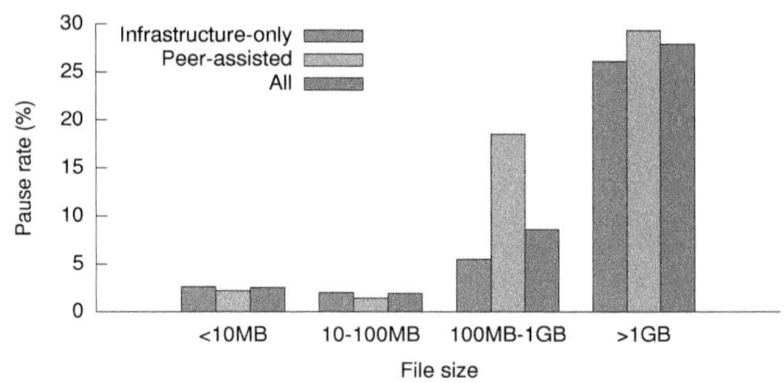

Figure 7: Downloads of larger files are terminated more often.

biggest differences between peer-assisted and infrastructure download speeds occur in the networks with the highest link bandwidths. One possible explanation is the high asymmetry of most high-speed broadband links (fast downstream and slow upstream), which would limit the available bandwidth from nearby peers.

How many peers are needed for good performance? Achieving good peer efficiency in a peer-assisted download requires a sufficient number of peers who have a copy of the requested file. We now ask how many copies are needed to achieve a good peer efficiency.

NetSession does not use predictive caching—i.e., a peer only downloads a file when it is requested by the local user. Once a file has been downloaded, the peer keeps it in a local cache for a certain amount of time and informs the control plane that it is willing to upload this file to other peers (if uploading is enabled). This creates entries in the DN log, and we counted these entries for each file to estimate how many copies of that file were available. We also calculated the average peer efficiency for each file.

Figure 5 shows the average peer efficiency as a function of the number of copies registered during the trace (the error bars show the 20th and 80th percentile). We found that, with less than 50 registered copies, peer efficiency was below 10%, but rose rapidly after that, and reached 80% for approximately 10,000 copies.

Another way to look at this question is to ask how many *peers* need to assist in a given download to achieve the highest efficiency. This question is difficult to answer precisely because peer efficiency depends on a variety of other factors, including the size of the object and the network connections of the peers, so we can only hope for a rough trend (with large error bars). To look for this trend, we grouped the downloads by the number of peers that the DN initially suggested to the downloading peer, and we computed the average peer efficiency for each group. Figure 6 shows our results. We find that 80% peer efficiency is generally reached with about 25–30 peers. This is consistent with earlier results for BitTorrent [5,14], which also requires a few tens of peers to achieve good performance.

Are peer-assisted downloads less reliable? To answer this question, we examined the eventual outcome of the downloads initiated in our trace. The logs can show three kinds of outcomes: a download can complete, it can fail, or it can be aborted/paused by the user and never resumed. When a download fails, the log also shows a specific cause; we divided these into system-related causes (e.g., too many corrupted content blocks) and other causes (e.g., the user's disk is full).

We find that 94% of the infrastructure-only downloads eventually complete, but only 92% of the peer-assisted downloads. At first glance, this discrepancy suggests that peer-assisted downloads are slightly less reliable. However, the rate of system-related failures is very small (0.1% for infrastructure-only versus 0.2% for peer-assisted), but infrastructure-only downloads are paused or terminated less often than peer-assisted ones (3% versus 8%).

A closer look reveals that the termination rate increases with the length of the download. While the download *speed* for infrastructure-only and peer-assisted downloads is approximately the same, the latter are typically used for larger files (see Figure 3(a) earlier), which naturally take longer to download. As Figure 7 shows, larger downloads are terminated more often—hence the discrepancy.

5.3 Do peers improve global coverage?

In theory, a hybrid CDN has another advantage over its infrastructure-based counterparts: it may be easier to obtain a globally distributed population of peers than to establish a truly global infrastructure. Thus, it should be possible for a hybrid system to provide better service for customers in under-served regions, where the closest infrastructure nodes are far away, but peers may be nearby.

To test whether this is the case for NetSession, we aggregated the completed downloads on a per-country basis, and we counted the number of bytes served by the infrastructure and by the peers. We then classified each country into one of three groups, which are shown as colored dots in Figure 8: countries where the infrastructure serves bytes more than the peers (circle), between 50% and 100% of the peers (plus), or less than 50% of the peers (square). Since not all content providers use peer-assisted downloads, and the popularity of the providers varies between regions, we show results for one typical, p2p-enabled provider here.

We find that, for NetSession, the picture is mixed: although the peers tend to contribute more in some regions, such as Africa and South America, the contributions do not vary much overall. We suspect that this is because NetSession relies on edge servers from Akamai's main CDN, which already has very good coverage around the globe.

Another potential benefit of a large peer population is that downloading peers might find a copy of the requested content within their local network, e.g., in a corporate LAN. In October 2012 this case appears to have been rare, but this could change, e.g., when NetSession is used to distribute large software updates.

5.4 Summary

NetSession demonstrates that peer-assisted CDNs can indeed deliver the key benefits of both peer-to-peer and infrastructure-based CDNs: they can offload a considerable fraction of the traffic to the peers, without a significant loss of speed or reliability. NetSession's 80% peer efficiency depends on many factors that may be different in other systems, but it provides a lower bound on what peer-assisted CDNs can achieve in a large-scale commercial deployment.

6. RISKS

We now turn to the question of how well NetSession, as an instance of a peer-assisted CDN, can avoid the risks inherent in this architecture. We again focus on two aspects we can examine quantitatively using our trace: 1) whether NetSession affects the traffic balance of ISPs, and 2) whether the presence of user-managed machines is causing problems.

6.1 Do ISPs suffer from NetSession?

The impact of peer-assisted CDNs on ISPs, and the potential conflict of interest between the two, has been a cause of some concern [17, 24, 35]. To determine how this conflict affects NetSession, we used detailed traffic statistics in our trace, which included, for each peer-assisted download, the GUID of each peer that has sent any content bytes to the downloading client. We first used the login data to map each GUID to the IP address it was using at the time, and then we used the EdgeScape data to map the IP address to the number of the Autonomous System (AS) to which it belongs. The result is a set of (N, AS_1, AS_2) tuples, which describe a flow of N bytes from AS_1 to AS_2. We aggregated the flows per AS, and we report our results at the granularity of ASes. We include only the content bytes, but not the packet headers or the protocol overhead; including the latter would add a small constant factor. We also neglect bytes sent by the infrastructure, since these would be sent by an infrastructure-based CDN as well, and since most of them would normally be sent from an edge server within the same AS anyway.

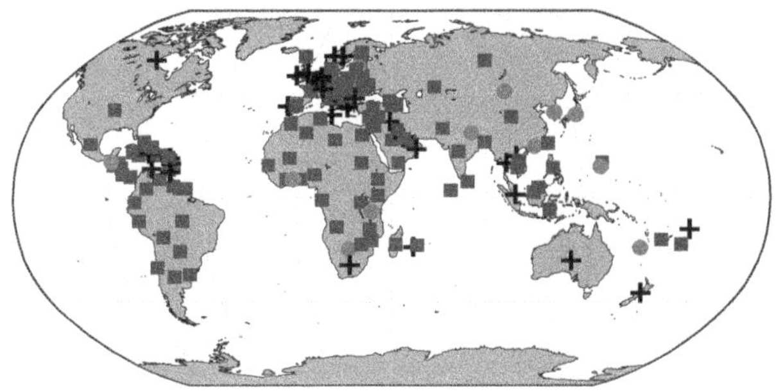

Figure 8: Peer contributions in different regions (for one exemplary content provider).

Which ASes are sending the most? Overall, our trace shows that 895 TB of content bytes were sent peer-to-peer, and that the peers involved in these transmissions were located in roughly 22,000 different ASes. (The number is different from that in Table 1 because not all GUIDs participated in a p2p transaction.) 18% of this traffic was sent between peers in the same AS; we do not further consider such intra-AS traffic here because it does not affect the inter-AS bandwidth cost.

To determine how the inter-AS traffic was distributed across the ASes, we sorted the ASes by the number of bytes they sent to peers in other ASes. Figure 9(a) shows the result as a CDF. Roughly half of the ASes did not send any inter-AS bytes at all, and 98% sent less than 163 GB over the entire month. However, there is a "heavy tail" of ASes that sent substantially more; the top contributor sent approximately 34.2 TB.

Figure 9(b) shows a different perspective on this result: a point (x, y) on this plot indicates that the cumulative contribution of ASes contributing less than x bytes amounted to y% of the total inter-AS p2p traffic. This plot shows that 98% of the ASes contributed just 10% of the bytes; the remaining 2% (394 ASes) were responsible for 90% of the p2p traffic. We refer to the former as "light" and "heavy" uploaders, respectively. Figure 9(c) shows that this uneven distribution has a natural explanation; the heavy uploaders simply contain a lot more peers.

How balanced is the traffic? Sending a large number of bytes to its neighbors is not necessarily expensive for an AS, as long as it receives an equally large number of bytes from them; balanced connections with peering ASes may be considered "settlement free". To examine whether NetSession's p2p traffic affects this balance, we separately counted the inter-AS bytes each AS sent and received. Figure 10 shows the result as a scatterplot. Note that the scales are logarithmic; since zero does not appear on a logarithmic scale, the points for ASes that have not uploaded and/or downloaded anything appear near the axes.

Figure 10 shows that ASes often have a substantial *relative* imbalance; many receive several Gigabytes but send

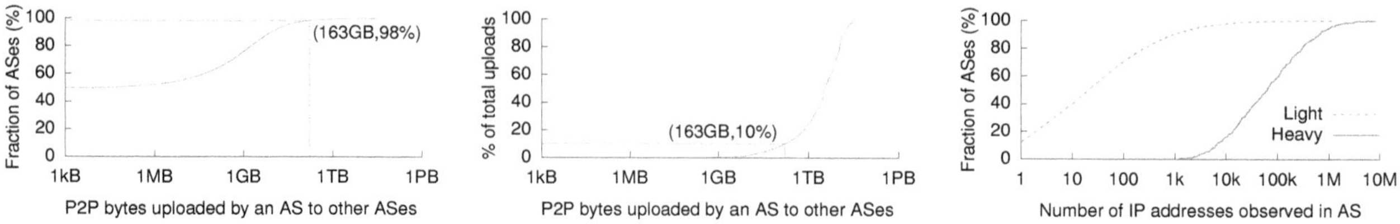

(a) Inter-AS traffic (b) Contributions of different ASes (c) Distinct IP addresses per AS

Figure 9: Traffic balance results.

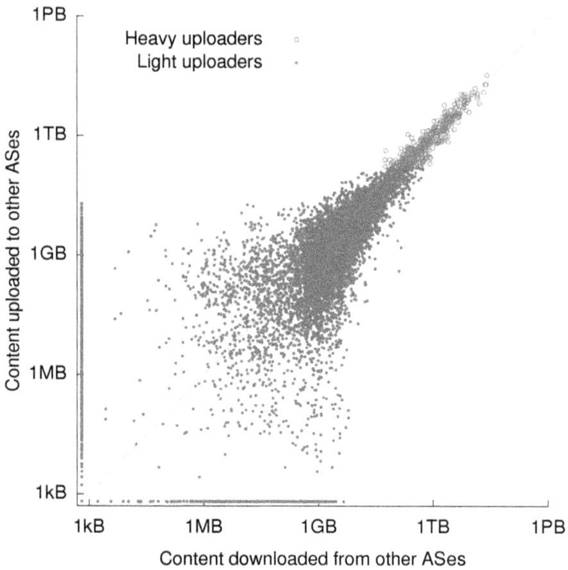

Figure 10: p2p bytes uploaded vs. downloaded for an AS. Only the bytes which cross AS boundaries are considered here.

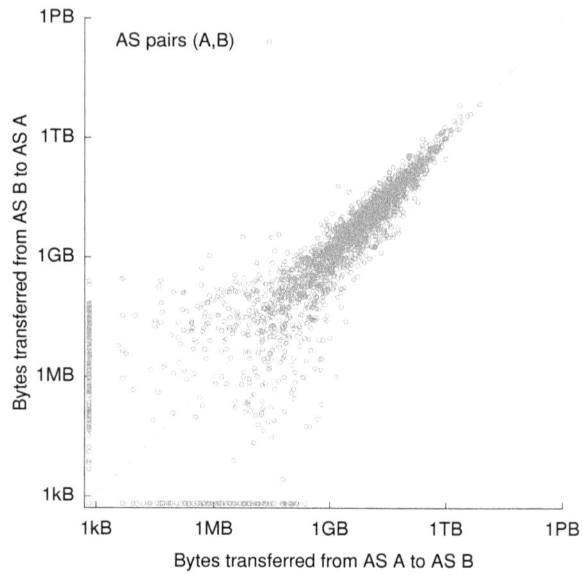

Figure 11: Traffic balance on AS-to-AS links.

hardly anything, or vice versa. However, this imbalance mostly affects ASes that are not carrying very much NetSession p2p traffic anyway. The traffic of the "heavy" uploaders (which appear in red towards the upper right end of the plot) tends to be well-balanced, i.e., they usually receive as much as they send. At a high level, this is not unexpected: if uploaders and downloaders are distributed roughly uniformly, the resulting traffic is naturally balanced. However, there are many effects that *could* bias this pattern—for instance, clients in certain ASes might have a higher upstream bandwidth and might therefore be chosen to upload more often. NetSession avoids such biases in part by limiting the number of times a peer will upload a file it has locally cached.

Note that we have only considered the origin and the destination of the traffic here. We cannot reliably estimate the effect of transit traffic because our data set does not contain traceroutes. Based on CAIDA's AS topology data [6], we estimate that out of the total inter-AS p2p bytes exchanged between the "heavy" uploaders, approximately 35% were exchanged between those that had a direct connection with each other.

So far, we have seen that the overall incoming traffic of an AS is largely balanced by its overall outgoing traffic. However, a *pairwise* imbalance could still exist between pairs of ASes. Figure 11 shows that this is not the case: analogous to above, the figure contains the distribution of p2p bytes exchanged between pairs of "heavy" uploaders that had a direct connection (though not necessarily a peering relationship) with each other. The trend is similar to Figure 10: heavy contributors tend to have a traffic balance that is roughly even.

We emphasize that our results should *not* be interpreted as saying that NetSession's traffic has no impact on ISPs. Our data only describes the traffic, and not the cost that ISPs may or may not charge each other for carrying that traffic. This cost depends on a variety of other factors as well, including the business relationships between the ISPs. Nevertheless, it is likely that a large traffic imbalance would eventually affect the business relationship and/or the cost, and our results do show that this particular problem does not seem to be occurring.

6.2 Impact of user-managed machines

How strong is the mobility-related churn? Unlike the servers in an infrastructure-based CDN, the NetSession peers can move; for instance, users can install NetSession on a laptop that they take to work in the morning and back home in the evening. Overall, we observed connections from 133.7 million different IP addresses in 31,190 different autonomous systems (ASes); 80.6% of the GUIDs connected from a single AS, 13.4% from two different ASes, and 6% from more than two ASes. The DNs must update their directories to keep track of this mobility, but the corresponding workload is moderate: on average, the control plane receives 20,922 new connections per minute.

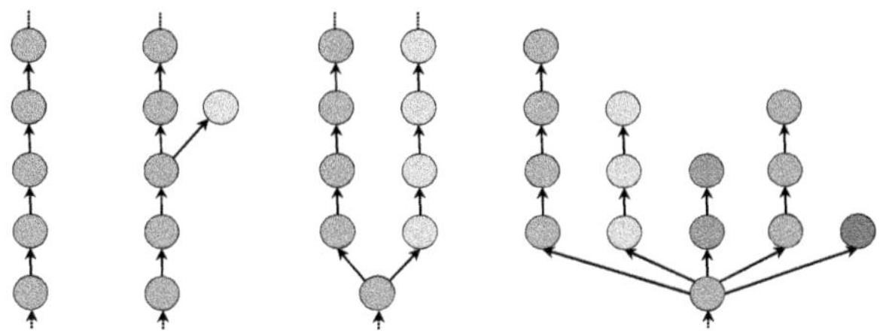

Figure 12: Expected sequence of secondary GUIDs (left) and common nonlinear patterns.

As an aside, to get a rough sense of the corresponding physical mobility, we computed for each GUID the two geolocations that were farthest apart. We found that 77% remained within 10 km, and that 23% were more than 10 km apart. We note that the actual mobility may be somewhat lower; for instance, if a user occasionally opens a VPN connection to her corporate headquarters, the geolocation of the latter may be far away.

Can malicious peers do damage? Unlike a centrally managed infrastructure, which mostly needs to be protected against external attackers, a peer-assisted CDN also needs protection against attacks from *within*—each user physically controls his or her machine and can change the software on it at will. Previous work has shown that this can lead to new vulnerabilities that are unique to hybrid architectures, such as accounting attacks [1], in which compromised peers misreport the amount of service they have provided, in an attempt to distort the reports the CDN provides to its customers. As mentioned in Section 3.5, NetSession relies on data from the (trusted) edge servers to detect such attacks and to filter out incorrect reports. Measures are in place to make modification of the client-side executable difficult, but we have seen users experiment with manually modifying data in configuration files.

GUID cloning and re-imaging: Even in the absence of attacks, the designer of a hybrid CDN must consider more failure modes than in an infrastructure-based system. Here, we cannot provide an exhaustive discussion due to lack of space, but we discuss an illustrative example. While analyzing an earlier set of traces, we noticed that certain GUIDs showed unusual behavior: they were logging in very frequently, sometimes from IP addresses in different countries and even on different continents. We initially suspected international travel, but some users appeared to be traveling at implausible speeds. We eventually suspected that some installations had to be sharing the same GUID.

To investigate further, we modified the NetSession software to support a random 160-bit "secondary GUID", which is chosen freshly every time the software *starts* (unlike the primary GUID, which is chosen when the software is first installed), and to report the last five secondary GUIDs to the control plane upon login. A normal NetSession installation would report overlapping sequences of secondary GUIDs, such as `5 4 3 2 1`, `6 5 4 3 2`, and so on. We then collected and analyzed the secondary GUIDs on a sample of 8 control plane servers, grouped them by primary GUID, and constructed graphs in which vertices represent secondary GUIDs and edges connect GUIDs that follow each other in a login entry. In total, we obtained 17.7 million connected graphs with at least three vertices.

99.4% of the graphs were linear chains (as in our example: $1 \rightarrow 2 \rightarrow 3 \rightarrow \ldots$), which would be expected for a normal NetSession installation. But the remaining 0.6% were trees, indicating that the corresponding installation had at some point been rolled back to an earlier state! Figure 12 shows the most common nonlinear patterns: one long branch with a single, one-vertex short branch (46.2%), two long branches (6.2%), and several short or medium branches (23.5%). We suspect that the first pattern corresponds to a failed software update and the second pattern to a restored backup; the third pattern might be due to re-imaging, e.g., in an Internet café that restores its machines every night, or due to cloning, e.g., in a large IT department that initializes new workstations from a master image. We also observed several highly irregular patterns for which we currently have no explanation.

Recall that this example was merely meant to illustrate that hybrid systems must deal with user actions that would not normally occur in a centrally managed infrastructure. However, this specific example was of some practical importance, since the number of distinct GUIDs plays a role in NetSession's internal accounting.

7. RELATED WORK

CDN measurement studies: There are several prior studies of content-distribution systems, including both peer-to-peer [13,26] and infrastructure [32] systems. The systems studied include p2p streaming systems [15,28,34] and one commercial hybrid CDN, LiveSky [36]. LiveSky delivers live-streaming video, so its architecture is necessarily different from NetSession's. To the best of our knowledge, the present paper is the first measurement study of a commercial hybrid CDN for static content.

Hybrid CDNs: The idea of combining a CDN infrastructure with peer-to-peer elements has been explored both in research [12,22] and in industry [33,34,36]; see [20] for a survey. The Antfarm system [22], in particular, has some similarities to NetSession. Antfarm combines peer-to-peer swarms with a coordinator, which carefully directs bandwidth provided by the infrastructure servers to maximize the aggregate bandwidth of the swarms. NetSession's control plane plays a similar role but, unlike Antfarm's coordinator, it does not implement an explicit incentive mechanism. Work on the potential benefits, specifically [16,17], has already been discussed in Section 5; likewise, work on the inherent risks, such as [1], has been discussed in Section 6.

Impact on ISPs: Several papers [7,17,24,35] have noted a potential conflict of interest between hybrid CDNs and ISPs because the former potentially increase the upstream traffic, and thus the cost, of the latter. The work in [7] demonstrated that a peer selection algorithm using CDN-based DNS "hints" can significantly reduce cross-ISP traffic. However, the general conclusion in this work is that the CDN can avoid a large impact on ISPs by using a simple locality-aware peer selection strategy.

Incentives: Swarming protocols like BitTorrent [8] typically include explicit incentives because they assume that users will not contribute bandwidth unless they can benefit from it. There is a large body of work on understanding specific incentive systems, e.g., [18,23], and on building systems that can deliver them more robustly, e.g., [19]; Dandelion [30] even introduces an infrastructure component similar to NetSession's control plane, although its main purpose is to implement a fair-exchange mechanism. The existence and efficient operation of NetSession does not contradict the basic assumptions on which these systems are based, but it does suggest that the users' actual motivations are more complex, and that avoiding bandwidth contributions may not be among their primary concerns.

8. CONCLUSION

In this paper, we have examined the risks and benefits of "hybrid" CDN architectures, which rely on a managed infrastructure but also include a peer-to-peer element to leverage resources contributed by clients. To determine how well a practical system can deliver the benefits (and avoid the risks), we have presented a measurement study of NetSession, a large commercial CDN that uses this architecture.

Our results show that NetSession is able to deliver the key benefits of a hybrid architecture: it can offload a high fraction (70–80%) of the traffic to peers, but it can *also* offer good performance and high reliability. NetSession appears to avoid a key risk—tilting the traffic balance of ISPs—but it does face other challenges that are inherent in its hybrid architecture, e.g., with respect to security or manageability.

Overall, our findings suggest that a hybrid architecture is an attractive design point for a CDN. The infrastructure and the peers can deliver many of their key benefits, and they can complement one another to avoid many of their key weaknesses. NetSession's performance shows what is possible in this space.

Acknowledgments

We thank our shepherd Craig Partridge and the anonymous reviewers for their comments and suggestions. This work was supported in part by NSF grants CNS-1040672, CNS-1054229, and CNS-1065130, by AFRL grants FA8750-11-1-0262 and FA8750-10-2-0193, and by the Max Planck Society.

9. REFERENCES

[1] P. Aditya, M. Zhao, Y. Lin, A. Haeberlen, P. Druschel, B. Maggs, and B. Wishon. Reliable client accounting for hybrid content-distribution networks. In *Proc. NSDI*, Apr. 2012.

[2] Akamai. EdgeScape brochure. `http://www.akamai.com/dl/brochures/edgescape.pdf`.

[3] Akamai Technologies. NetSession design principles. `http://www.akamai.com/html/solutions/client_design_principles.html`.

[4] R. Bhagwan, S. Savage, and G. M. Voelker. Understanding availability. In *Proc. IPTPS*, 2003.

[5] A. R. Bharambe, C. Herley, and V. N. Padmanabhan. Analyzing and improving a BitTorrent network's performance mechanisms. In *Proc. INFOCOM*, 2006.

[6] CAIDA. Archipelago measurement infrastructure. `http://www.caida.org/projects/ark/`.

[7] D. R. Choffnes and F. E. Bustamante. Taming the Torrent. In *Proc. SIGCOMM*, 2008.

[8] B. Cohen. Incentives build robustness in BitTorrent. In *Proc. P2PEcon*, June 2003.

[9] S. A. Crosby and D. S. Wallach. An analysis of BitTorrent's two Kademlia-based DHTs. Technical Report TR-07-04, Department of Computer Science, Rice University, May 2007.

[10] J. Dilley, B. Maggs, J. Parikh, H. Prokop, R. Sitaraman, and B. Weihl. Globally distributed content delivery. *IEEE Internet Computing*, 6(5):50–58, Sept. 2002.

[11] M. Dischinger, A. Haeberlen, K. P. Gummadi, and S. Saroiu. Characterizing residential broadband networks. In *Proc. IMC*, Oct. 2007.

[12] M. J. Freedman. Experiences with CoralCDN: A five-year operational view. In *Proc. NSDI*, 2010.

[13] K. P. Gummadi, R. Dunn, S. Saroiu, S. Gribble, H. Levy, and J. Zahorjan. Measurement, modeling and analysis of a peer-to-peer file-sharing workload. In *Proc. SOSP*, Oct. 2003.

[14] L. Guo, S. Chen, Z. Xiao, E. Tan, X. Ding, and X. Zhang. Measurements, analysis, and modeling of BitTorrent-like systems. In *Proc. IMC*, 2005.

[15] X. Hei, C. Liang, J. Liang, Y. Liu, and K. Ross. A measurement study of a large-scale P2P IPTV system. *Multimedia, IEEE Trans.*, 9(8):1672–1687, Dec. 2007.

[16] C. Huang, A. Wang, J. Li, and K. W. Ross. Understanding hybrid CDN-P2P: Why Limelight needs its own Red Swoosh. In *NOSSDAV*, 2008.

[17] T. Karagiannis, P. Rodriguez, and K. Papagiannaki. Should Internet service providers fear peer-assisted content distribution? In *Proc. IMC*, 2005.

[18] D. Levin, K. LaCurts, N. Spring, and B. Bhattacharjee. BitTorrent is an auction: Analyzing and improving BitTorrent's incentives. In *Proc. SIGCOMM*, 2008.

[19] H. C. Li, A. Clement, M. Marchetti, M. Kapritsos, L. Robison, L. Alvisi, and M. Dahlin. FlightPath: Obedience vs. choice in cooperative services. In *Proc. OSDI*, 2008.

[20] Z. Lu, Y. Wang, and Y. R. Yang. An analysis and comparison of CDN-P2P-hybrid content delivery system and model. *JCM*, 7(3):232–245, 2012.

[21] W. E. Mackay. Triggers and barriers to customizing software. In *Proc. CHI*, Apr. 1991.

[22] R. S. Peterson and E. G. Sirer. Antfarm: efficient content distribution with managed swarms. In *Proc. NSDI*, 2009.

[23] M. Piatek, T. Isdal, T. Anderson, and A. Krishnamurthy. Do incentives build robustness in BitTorrent? In *Proc. NSDI*, 2007.

[24] M. Piatek, H. V. Madhyastha, J. P. John, A. Krishnamurthy, and T. Anderson. Pitfalls for ISP-friendly P2P design. In *Proc. HotNets*, 2009.

[25] J. Rosenberg, R. Mahy, P. Matthews, and D. Wing. Session Traversal Utilities for NAT (STUN). RFC 5389, Oct. 2008.

[26] S. Saroiu, K. P. Gummadi, R. J. Dunn, S. D. Gribble, and H. M. Levy. An analysis of Internet content delivery systems. In *Proc. OSDI*, 2002.

[27] S. Saroiu, K. P. Gummadi, and S. Gribble. A measurement study of peer-to-peer file sharing systems. In *Proc. MMCN*, Jan. 2002.

[28] T. Silverston and O. Fourmaux. Measuring P2P IPTV systems. In *Proc. NOSSDAV*, 2007.

[29] M. Sirivianos, J. H. Park, R. Chen, and X. Yang. Free-riding in BitTorrent networks with the Large View exploit. In *Proc. IPTPS*, Feb. 2007.

[30] M. Sirivianos, J. H. Park, X. Yang, and S. Jarecki. Dandelion: Cooperative content distribution with robust incentives. In *Proc. USENIX ATC*, 2007.

[31] J. Spool. Do users change their settings? `http://www.uie.com/brainsparks/2011/09/14/do-users-change-their-settings/`.

[32] K. Sripanidkulchai, B. Maggs, and H. Zhang. An analysis of live streaming workloads on the Internet. In *Proc. IMC*, 2004.

[33] Velocix. Network architecture. `http://www.velocix.com/network_architecture.php`.

[34] L. Vu, I. Gupta, K. Nahrstedt, and J. Liang. Understanding overlay characteristics of a large-scale peer-to-peer IPTV system. *ACM Tr. Multim. Comp. Comm. Appl.*, 6:31:1–31:24, 2010.

[35] H. Xie, R. Yang, A. Krishnamurthy, Y. Liu, and A. Silberschatz. P4P: Provider portal for applications. In *Proc. SIGCOMM*, 2008.

[36] H. Yin, X. Liu, T. Zhan, V. Sekar, F. Qiu, C. Lin, H. Zhang, and B. Li. Design and deployment of a hybrid CDN-P2P system for live video streaming: experiences with LiveSky. In *Proc. MM*, 2009.

Analyzing the Potential Benefits of CDN Augmentation Strategies for Internet Video Workloads

Athula Balachandran
Carnegie Mellon University
abalacha@cs.cmu.edu

Vyas Sekar
Stony Brook University
vyas@cs.stonybrook.edu

Aditya Akella
University of Wisconsin Madison
akella@cs.wisc.edu

Srinivasan Seshan
Carnegie Mellon University
srini@cs.cmu.edu

ABSTRACT

Video viewership over the Internet is rising rapidly, and market predictions suggest that video will comprise over 90% of Internet traffic in the next few years. At the same time, there have been signs that the Content Delivery Network (CDN) infrastructure is being stressed by ever-increasing amounts of video traffic. To meet these growing demands, the CDN infrastructure must be designed, provisioned and managed appropriately. Federated telco-CDNs and hybrid P2P-CDNs are two content delivery infrastructure designs that have gained significant industry attention recently. We observed several user access patterns that have important implications to these two designs in our unique dataset consisting of 30 million video sessions spanning around two months of video viewership from two large Internet video providers. These include partial interest in content, regional interests, temporal shift in peak load and patterns in evolution of interest. We analyze the impact of our findings on these two designs by performing a large scale measurement study. Surprisingly, we find significant amount of synchronous viewing behavior for Video On Demand (VOD) content, which makes hybrid P2P-CDN approach feasible for VOD and suggest new strategies for CDNs to reduce their infrastructure costs. We also find that federation can significantly reduce telco-CDN provisioning costs by as much as 95%.

Categories and Subject Descriptors

C.4 [**Performance of Systems**]: performance attributes; C.2.4 [**Computer-Communication Networks**]: Distributed Systems—Client/server

General Terms

Experimentation, Measurement, Performance

Keywords

Internet video, Measurement, User behavior

IMC'13, October 23–25, 2013, Barcelona, Spain.

http://dx.doi.org/10.1145/2504730.2504743.

1. INTRODUCTION

Internet video has been consistently growing for the last few years, with some reports showing that around 51% of Internet traffic in 2011 was video [3]. Market predictions suggest that video will comprise over 90% of the traffic on the Internet in the next few years. The increasing video workload is placing the onus on content providers for efficient distribution of the content.

Today, content providers rely on CDNs to leverage their presence across different geographical locations to serve video content. With the ever-increasing amounts of video traffic, however, there are signs that the CDN infrastructure is being stressed [31, 32]. In this context, hybrid P2P-CDN and telco-CDN federation are two emerging strategies to augment the existing infrastructure that have received significant industry attention recently:

- Telco-CDN federation is based on the recent development amongst various CDNs operated by telecommunication companies to federate by interconnecting their networks and compete directly with the traditional CDNs [35, 10, 19, 4]. This would enable users to reach CDN caches that are closer. Interconnecting resources across telco-CDNs would also ensure better availability and will benefit the participating ISPs in terms of provisioning costs [4].
- A hybrid strategy of serving content from dedicated CDN servers using P2P technology (e.g., [16, 17]) has been around for a while in the research literature but has only recently seen traction in the industry [1, 37]. A hybrid P2P-CDN approach would provide the scalability advantage of P2P along with the reliability and manageability of CDNs.

Given that several industry efforts and working groups are underway on both fronts [35, 10, 19, 1, 37], it is crucial to analyze the potential benefits that these CDN augmentation strategies can offer for Internet video workloads. Our main contribution in this paper is in identifying video access patterns that have significant implications to these two strategies and analyzing the potential benefits of these two strategies. To the best of our knowledge, there has not been any previous large-scale study on the benefits of federated telco-CDN infrastructures. While there is prior work on analyzing the benefits of P2P augmentation, these were done long before Internet video became mainstream [16, 17], and hence were ahead of their times. Thus, it is also timely to revisit the benefits of P2P augmentation.

Using a dataset of around 30 million VOD and live sessions collected over two months from viewers across the United States, we characterize several video viewing patterns that have implications to these two designs including:

- **Regional interest:** Typically, we observe significant population induced difference in load across different regions (e.g., US East coast, US West coast, Mid-West). But, for live events with regional biases like a local team playing a match, we observe significantly skewed access rates from regions that exhibit low load in the typical case.
- **Temporal shift in peak load:** We observe strong diurnal effects in access patterns and also confirm temporal shifts between regions in the demand for VOD objects using cross-correlation analysis. The temporal shift in access pattern is caused by time zone differences. The video access load peaks at around 8pm local time for each region.
- **Evolution of interest:** We observe that peak demand for VOD objects occur on the day of release and the decay in demand in the subsequent days can be modeled using an exponential decay process. Interestingly, overall user viewing patterns are very different across genres (e.g., TV series, reality shows, news shows). For example, decay rates of news shows are much higher than TV series episodes. Also, TV series episodes have highly predictable and stable demand from week to week (i.e., across successive episodes).
- **Synchronized viewing patterns:** While we expect synchronous viewing behavior for live video, we unexpectedly observe synchrony in the viewership of VOD objects. This is especially true for popular shows during the peak demand period (e.g., evening of the day of release of the show).
- **Partial interest in content:** We reconfirm prior observations that users watch only part of the video during a session [11, 24]. For instance, in the case of VOD, a significant fraction of the viewers typically watch only the first 10 minutes of the video before quitting. We observe that around 4.5% of the users are "serial" early-quitters (analogous to channel surfing) while 16.6% of the users consistently watch videos to completion.

We develop simple models to capture the deployment of federated telco-CDNs and analyze the potential benefit of federation to increase availability and reduce provisioning required to serve video workloads. We also revisit the potential benefits that P2P-assisted architectures provide in the light of these video access patterns. Our key findings are:

- Telco-CDN federation can reduce the provisioning cost by as much as 95%. VOD workloads benefit from federation by offloading daily peak loads and live workloads benefit by offloading unexpected high traffic triggered by regional events.
- Using P2P can lead up to 87% bandwidth savings for the CDNs during peak access hours. Employing a strategy to filter out users who quit early by serving them using P2P can alone lead to 30% bandwidth savings for VOD traffic and 60% savings for live traffic.

In the rest of the paper, we discuss related work in Section 2 and provide an overview of our dataset in Section 3. We analyze the implications and potential benefits for federation across telco-CDNs and for hybrid P2P-CDNs in Section 4 and Section 5 respectively before concluding in Section 6.

2. RELATED WORK

In this section, we discuss the key similarities and differences with respect to past work in measuring different aspects of Internet video.

Video performance: Previous work confirms that video quality impacts user engagement across different content genres [20, 28]. Past work also identifies that many of the quality problems observed today are a result of spatial and temporal differences in CDN performance and suggest potential workarounds via cross-CDN optimization [31, 32]. The quality problems these studies uncover suggest that CDNs are stressed to deliver high-quality video and this motivates the need to explore strategies for augmenting CDNs.

Content popularity: There have been studies to understand content popularity in user-generated content systems (e.g., [18, 25]), IPTV systems (e.g., [13, 34, 12]), and other VOD systems (e.g., [27, 30, 21]). The focus of these studies was on understanding content popularity to enable efficient content caching and prefetching. Other studies analyze the impact of recommendation systems on program popularity (e.g., [38]) or the impact of flash-crowd like events (e.g. [22]). In contrast, our work focuses on analyzing the benefit of CDN augmentation techniques and extends these studies along two key dimensions. First, we model the longitudinal evolution in interest for different genres of video content and analyze its implications for designing a hybrid P2P-CDN infrastructure. Second, we analyze regional variations and biases in content popularity and its implications for provisioning a federated telco-CDN infrastructure.

P2P: Several pure P2P VOD systems aim to provide performance comparable to a server-side infrastructure at significantly lower cost (e.g., [14, 26, 27, 36]). There are already recent commercial efforts by CDNs to augment their infrastructures with P2P based solutions [1, 37]. Early work in the P2P space presented measurement-driven analysis on the feasibility and cost savings that hybrid-P2P technologies can bring [16, 17]. In some sense, these studies were ahead of their time—given that Internet video has really taken off only in the last 3-4 years, we believe it is critical to revisit these findings in light of new video viewing patterns. Specifically, our observations on synchronized viewing behavior for VOD and user join-leave patterns lead us to question the conventional wisdom in this space and we explore and evaluate new strategies for designing hybrid-P2P CDNs.

User behavior: Previous studies show that many users leave after a very short duration possibly due to low interest in the content (e.g., [11, 24]). While we reconfirm these observations, we also provide a systematic model for the fraction of video viewed by users using mixture model and gamma distributions, and highlight key differences between live and VOD viewing behavior. Furthermore, we analyze the implications of such partial user interest in the context of hybrid-P2P CDN deployments and explore new strategies for CDNs to reduce their bandwidth costs.

3. DATASET

The data used for this analysis was collected by `conviva.com` in real time using a client-side instrumentation library in the video player that collects information pertaining to a session. This library gets loaded when the user watches video on `conviva.com`'s affiliate content providers' websites. The library also listens to events from the player (e.g., seek, pause). The data is then aggregated and processed using Hadoop [5].

We focus on two of the most popular content providers (based in the US). These two providers appear consistently in the Top 500 sites in overall popularity ranking. Our analysis is based on data queried over two months—January 2012 and March 2012—and consists of over 30 million video viewing sessions during this period. We classify the video content into two categories:

- *VOD:* The first provider serves VOD objects that are between 35 minutes and 60 minutes long. These comprise TV series episodes, news shows, and reality show episodes.

- *Live:* The second provider serves sports events that are broadcast while the event is happening, and hence the viewing behavior is synchronized.

The VOD dataset consists of approximately 4 million users and 14 million viewing sessions and covers 1,000 video shows. The live dataset consists of around 4.5 million users and 16 million video viewing sessions covering around 10,000 different events. As in several prior studies on content popularity [30, 12], we also observe a heavy tailed Zipf distribution for overall popularity of objects for both VOD and live. Whereas most objects have few accesses over the two months, some extremely popular objects had significant viewership. On average, users viewed 4 VOD objects and 2 live events during the course of a month, which amounts to 85 minutes of VOD objects and 65 minutes of live events per month. We also observed a few heavy-hitters who watched upwards of 500 videos per month on these websites.

Session characteristics: In order to understand user behavior, we look at several characteristics of individual video sessions. Specifically, for each session we collected the following information:

- *ClientID:* The first time a client watches a video on the player, a unique identifier is assigned to the player and stored in a Flash cookie to be used by subsequent views.
- *Geographical location:* Country, state and city of the user.
- *Provider:* Information on the AS/ISP from which the request originated.
- *Session events:* Start time and duration of the session along with details on other user interaction events like pausing and stopping.
- *Session Performance:* Average bitrate, estimated bandwidth etc. during the playback.
- *Content:* Information on the content being watched, in particular, the name of the video (which we use for classifying videos into genres) and the actual duration of the content (e.g., 45 minute show).

Region	States
1	MA, NH, TV, ME, RI, CT
2	NY, PA, NJ
3	WI, MI, IL, IN, OH
4	MO, ND, SD, NE, KS, MN, IA
5	DE, MD, DC, VA, WV, NC, SC, GA, FL
6	KY, TN, MS, AL
7	OK, TX, AR, LA
8	ID, MT, WY, NV, UT, CO, AZ, NM
9	AK, WA, OR, CA, HI

Table 1: *List of Regions*

Geographical regions: We limit our study to clients within the United States. We classified the country into 9 regions using the censor bureau designated areas [2] as shown in Table 1. Not surprisingly, we observe that the average load in terms of number of accesses is significantly different across different regions, and they are largely correlated with the total population of the region. We observe that this pattern holds for both live and VOD traffic except in the case of some events that have regional bias. We explore this aspect further in Section 4.

4. ANALYZING TELCO-CDN FEDERATION

The tremendous increase in video traffic on the Internet over the past few years has caused great challenges for ISPs. The increasing traffic has strained the ISP networks leading to higher costs and maintenance issues. However, this trend has not significantly contributed to much increase in revenue for ISPs since most of the

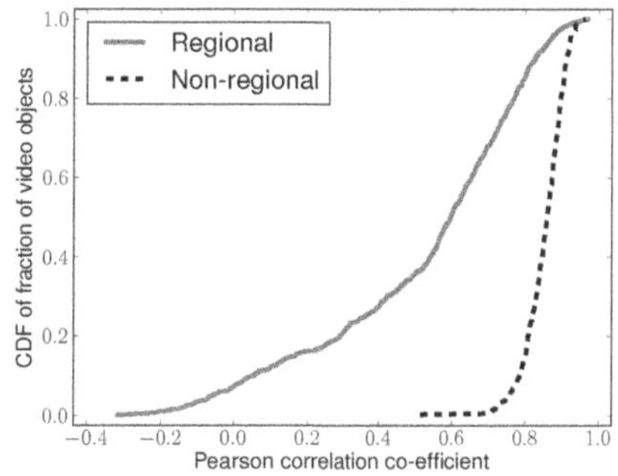

Figure 1: *The result shows the CDF of the correlation coefficient between the #views and the population of the region for the live dataset. Non-regional content is strongly correlated with population whereas regional content is uncorrelated or negatively correlated.*

video content is served by content providers using CDNs. As a result, several ISPs have started deploying proprietary CDNs inside their own network, providing services to content providers to serve content from caches closer to customers. This could result in increased revenue for the ISPs along with traffic reduction caused by content caching [4].

There has also been recent developments that point to interest among ISPs to deploy *telco CDN federations* by consolidating their CDN capacity and offering services to users in other ISPs [35, 10, 19]. By interconnecting telco-CDNs, consumers can reach CDN caches that are closer and are also ensured of better availability and service in case of local network congestion. Pooling resources across ISPs could potentially benefit the participating ISPs in terms of provisioning costs. It also enables ISPs to provide a global "virtual CDN" service to the content providers [4].

Although there have been pilot deployment efforts and initiatives for standardization of a federated-CDN architecture in the industry [4, 10], we are not aware of any study quantifying the benefits of telco-CDN federation, specifically in the context of Internet video. We first present video access patterns that we observed in our dataset that have significant implications for CDN federation in Section 4.1. We further quantify the potential benefits that telco-CDN federation can provide and put them in context with our findings on the user access patterns. To this end, we develop simple models to capture the deployment of telco-CDN federations that help us determine the potential benefits that such federation offers in Sections 4.2 and 4.3. We use this to evaluate the benefits of telco-CDN federation using our dataset for live and VOD content separately in Section 4.4. To the best of our knowledge this is the first large scale study to quantify the benefits of telco-CDN federation.

4.1 User Access Patterns

We observed video access patterns for live and VOD content that have implications to telco-CDN federation. For instance, in our live dataset, we observed unexpected surges in demand for certain objects from regions which can potentially be served using spare capacity in servers in other regions if CDNs federate. Similarly, we observed strong temporal shifts in when specific regions hit peak load in the VOD dataset opening up new possibilities for handling peak loads using federation. We finally also present statistics on ISP coverage and their relative performance which also have important implications when ISPs decide to federate.

4.1.1 Regional Interests

Typically, the number of accesses to a particular content from a geographical region is strongly correlated with the total population of the region. However, in our live dataset, we observed anomalies in the case of content with region-specific interest (e.g., when a local team is playing a game). Such unexpected surges in demands triggered by regional interests can potentially be served from servers in other regions if CDNs federate.

Our data consists of only clients within the United States and it does not contain tags with event region details. Hence, we manually classified the content as regional or non-regional based on whether it appeals to a particular region within the US. Sports matches between local teams within the US (e.g., NCAA) were classified as regional as opposed to events that are non-regional to the US viewers (e.g., Eurocup soccer).

We computed the Pearson correlation coefficient [33] between the number of accesses from each region to the population of the region (obtained from census data [2]). Figure 1 shows the CDF of the correlation coefficient across video objects for all the live objects. We observe that access rates of non-regional content show strong correlation to the population, whereas for regional matches it is uncorrelated or negatively correlated. This is because of skewed access rates from normally not so active regions because of a sporting event that has a local team. However, some regional matches show high correlation. These are highly popular events (e.g., final rounds of NCAA are of interest to everyone in the US).

Implications: The skeweness in access rates caused by regional interest is an important factor to be considered while provisioning the delivery infrastructure to handle unexpected high loads. Federation can potentially help offload such unexpected surges triggered by regional interests by using spare capacity in CDNs in other regions.

4.1.2 Temporal shift in peak loads

Figure 2a provides an overview of the VOD dataset by plotting the time series of the normalized number of videos accessed across all regions at per minute granularity for a week. As expected, we clearly observe strong time-of-day effects. To identify regional variations in peak load, we zoom into a day and plot the time series of the normalized number of accesses separately for each region in Figure 2b. Due to lack of space, we only show the results for the top 3 regions. The number of accesses peaks around 8 pm local time with a lull in the night. We observe that there is a difference between the time when the load peaks at different regions (caused by time zone difference). Also, we see that the peak loads are different across regions—they are largely correlated with the total population of the region.

We perform cross-correlation analysis to confirm the temporal shift in access patterns over the entire two months of data. Cross-correlation measures the degree of similarity between two time series as a function of a time lag applied to one of them. Let $X =< X_0, X_1, ..., X_i, ... >$ denote the time series of the number of accesses as a vector where X_i is the number of accesses at time index i and $E(X_i)$ and σ_{X_i} represents the expected value and standard deviation respectively. For a given time lag k, the cross-correlation co-efficient between two time series vectors $X =< X_0, X_1, ..., X_i, ... >$ and $Y =< Y_0, Y_1, ..., Y_j, ... >$ is defined as:

$$\tau(k) = \frac{E(X_iY_{i+k}) - E(X_i)E(Y_{i+k})}{\sigma_{X_i}\sigma_{Y_{i+k}}} \tag{1}$$

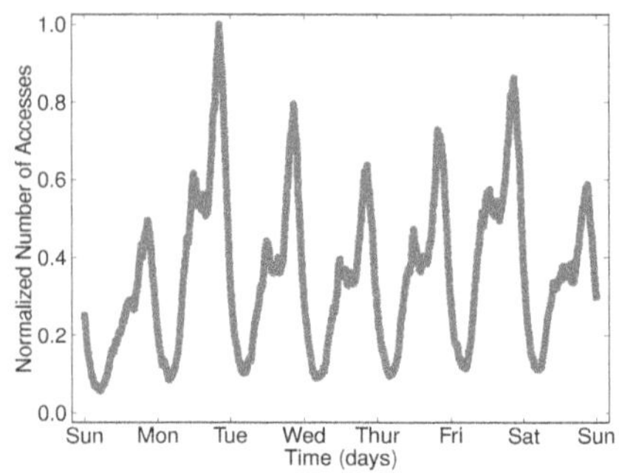

(a) Aggregate access pattern

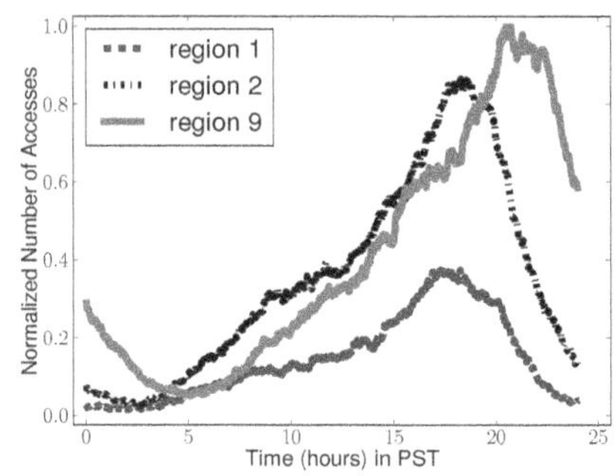

(b) Region-wise access pattern

Figure 2: *Diurnal characteristics of access pattern*

The cross-correlation coefficient lies in the range of [-1,1] where $\tau(k) = 1$ implies perfect correlation at lag k and $\tau(k) = 0$ implies no correlation at lag k. We use cross-correlation to analyze the time shift in the access pattern across regions. We performed analysis across all region pairs at lags of one hour each. Due to space constraint, we present the co-coefficients plotted at different lags for the top 3 region pairs in Figure 3. Regions 1 and 2 fall in the same time zone and hence the $\tau(k)$ is highest at $k = 0$. Region 9 is 3 hours behind regions 1 and 2 and hence $\tau(k)$ is highest at $k = 3$. We observe this pattern holds for all the region pairs.

Implications:
The temporal shift in peak access times across different regions opens up new opportunities to handle peak loads—e.g., spare capacity at servers in regions 1 and 2 can be used to serve content in region 9 when access rates peak at region 9.

4.1.3 ISP performance

We study the relative performance of the ISPs over the month in terms of video quality using two key metrics identified in [20]: (1) buffering ratio defined as the percentage of session time spent in buffering, and (2) the average bitrate for each session. We summarize the relative performance of top ISPs using box-and-whiskers plots (Figure 4) showing the minimum, 25%ile, median, 75%ile, and 90%ile values observed across sessions. Our results corroborate a similar report released by Netflix in May 2011 [6]. The mean performance of the ISPs are very similar, with cable ISPs like Comcast and Cox providing marginally better bitrates in the median case. We also see that wireless providers like Clearwire and Verizon Wireless provide lower bitrates compared to their wired counterparts. As observed in [20], majority of the sessions have very low buffering ratio. The median buffering ratio is zero for all

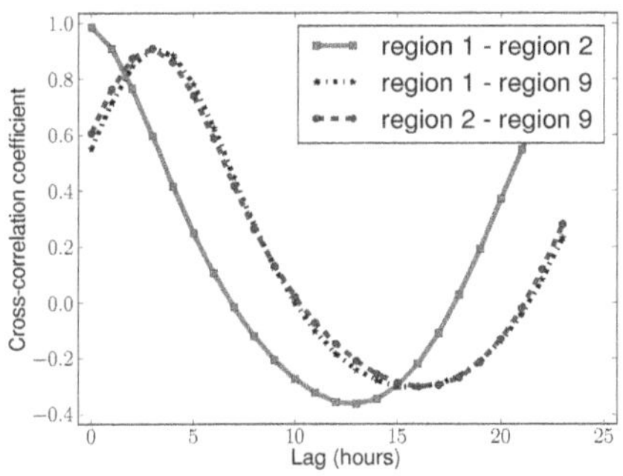

Figure 3: *Cross correlation analysis confirms the temporal shift in access pattern over two months of data*

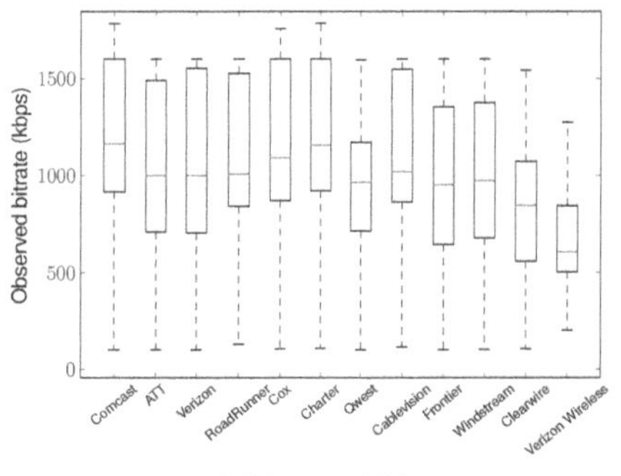

(a) Observed bitrate

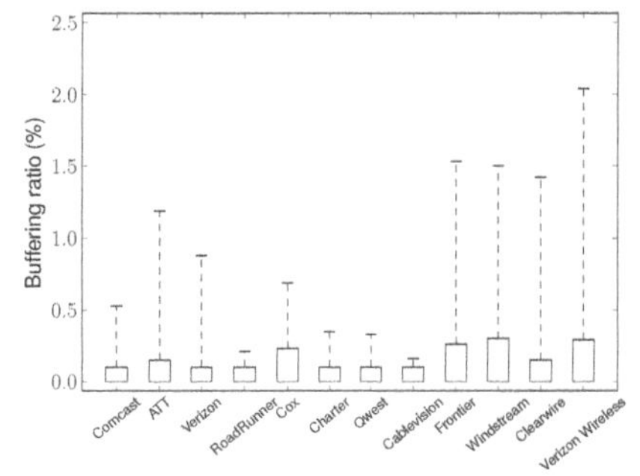

(b) Buffering ratio

Figure 4: *Performance of top ISPs*

the ISPs. Verizon Wireless and Windstream have marginally higher buffering ratio in the 75%ile and 90%ile case.[1]

Implications: Since the overall performance of most ISPs are very similar, they can potentially collaboratively use their resources without worrying that their customers may see poor performance from their federating "peers" due to network effects.

4.1.4 ISP Regional presence

ISP	NY (%)	LA (%)
Comcast	1.4	1.7
AT&T	6.1	24.7
Verizon	41.7	56.3
RoadRunner	34.1	2.0
Cox	-	-
Charter	-	1.2
Qwest	-	-
Cablevision	2.9	-
Frontier	-	-
Windstream	-	-
Others	13.8	14.1

Table 2: *Fraction of clients observed from individual ISPs for top-2 cities*

Table 2 shows a different split across ISPs for two large cities. We observe that ISPs have significant regional biases in their coverage. For instance, while Verizon and RoadRunner have a large fraction of clients in New York city, AT&T and Verizon have a more dominant presence in LA. We also observe that some ISPs have a small fraction of their clients in cities where they are not dominant. For example, RoadRunner appears to contribute 2% of the total users in LA and AT&T has 6% in NY.

Implications: An ISP may not want to roll out new video delivery infrastructure in regions where it does not already have a significant coverage and in this case might want to direct its customers to servers located in cooperating ISPs.

4.2 System Model

In order to analyze the potential benefits of federation, we use a simplified system model for federated telco-CDNs. Figure 5 provides a high-level overview of our system model. As we have discussed earlier, there are several geographical regions, represented by $Region_r$. We currently use the regions described in Table 1, but this could also be more fine-grained (e.g., city or metro-area). Each region may have several ISPs, each denoted by ISP_i and each such ISP has some provisioned CDN capacity (number of users that can be served) in each region denoted by $Cap_{r,i}$.

Similar to today's ISP peering for connectivity, we envision pre-established "peering" relationships between ISPs across different regions to share their spare capacity. Let $P(r, i)$ be the set of all region-ISP tuples with whom ISP_i in $Region_r$ has peering relationships. We use $r'i' \in P(r, i)$ to specify that $ISP_{i'}$ in $Region_{r'}$ has such a peering relationship with ISP_i in $Region_r$. This means that $ISP_{i'}$ in $Region_{r'}$ can offer its services or spare capacity to serve users from ISP_i in $Region_r$. This allows us to flexibly capture different kinds of telco CDN peering relationships.[2] For example, in the trivial case, without any cross-ISP federation or cross-region resource sharing $P(r, i)$ relationship only contains the current ISP-region combination. In the most general case, all ISPs can share capacity with each other.

Let $Demand_{ri}(t)$ be the number of video users in region $Region_r$ from ISP_i at a given epoch t. As a first step, we only focus on the number of users and not on the specific bitrates they choose. Let $N_{r',i'\to r,i}(t)$ denote the number of users served using servers located in $ISP_{i'}$ in $Region_{r'}$ to clients from ISP_i in $Region_r$. at epoch t. We use $L_{r'i';r,i}$ to denote the latency cost incurred in this process. For clarity of discussion, we use a simple latency function at the level of "region-hops" between neighboring regions; we can extend this to incorporate more fine-grained inter-ISP latency within and across regions.

[1]Even though these wireless providers have worse performance, we did not observe any significant difference in user behavior. This is somewhat surprising given recent studies on how quality affects behavior [28]. It probably points to how users get "trained" for lower expectations, thereby increasing their tolerance.

[2]ISPs can also employ other relationships and policies. For example, ISPs with higher server capacity can potentially employ "provider-customer" relationships. Our current model does not capture such fine-grained policies and cost models.

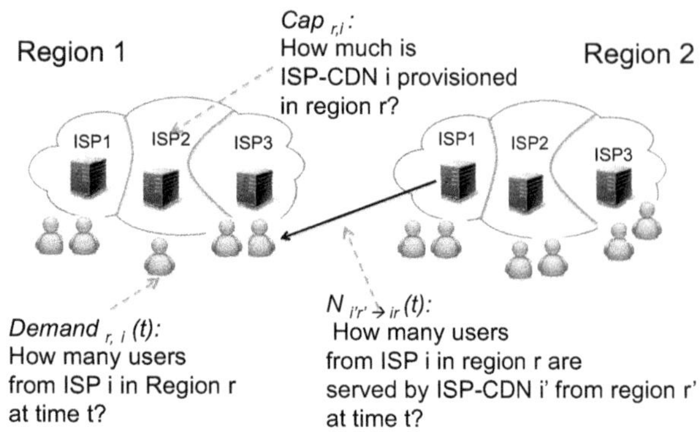

Figure 5: *System model for telco CDN federation*

$$\text{Minimize: } Latency(t) + \alpha \times Dropped(t)$$

$$\forall r, i : Dropped_{r,i}(t) = Demand_{r,i}(t) - \sum_{r',i':r',i' \in P(r,i)} N_{r',i' \to r,i}(t) \quad (2)$$

$$\forall r, i : Dropped_{r,i}(t) \geq 0 \quad (3)$$

$$Dropped(t) = \sum_{r,i} Dropped_{r,i}(t) \quad (4)$$

$$Latency(t) = \sum_{r,i:r'i' \in P(r,i)} L_{r'i';r,i} \times N_{r',i' \to ri}(t) \quad (5)$$

$$\forall r', i' : \sum_{ri:r'i' \in P(r,i)} N_{r'i' \to ri}(t) \leq Cap_{r'i'} \quad (6)$$

Figure 6: *Linear program for finding the optimal allocation in each logical epoch*

4.3 Global provisioning problem

Given this setup, we can now formulate the telco CDN federation problem as a *resource allocation* problem with the resources being the servers in different ISP/region combinations and the demands being the users in ISP/region combination. The linear program in Figure 6 formally describes the high-level optimization problem.

There are two high-level goals here. First, we want to accommodate as many users as possible given the current capacity provisioned at the different ISPs in various regions. Second, we want to minimize the network footprint of these assignments and ensure that requests are served as locally as possible. However, given a specific provisioning regime, it may not always be possible to fully meet the demands and some requests have to be invariably dropped. We trade off the relative importance of these objectives (i.e., latency vs. coverage) using the cost factor α in the objective function that captures the penalty for dropping users. By setting α to be very high, we can ensure that the demand is maximally met even if it requires fetching content from remote servers.

We capture the number of requests that are *dropped* in each ISP-region tuple Eq (2) and the total number of drops in Eq (4). (Of course, the number of requests dropped cannot be negative so we have the sanity check in Eq (3).) We model the overall latency footprint in Eq (5) using a simple weighted sum. Finally, we have a natural capacity constraint that in each region no ISP exceeds its provisioned capacity and this is captured in Eq (6).

4.4 Evaluation

We use the above formal model to evaluate the potential benefits of telco CDN federation for live and VOD content using our dataset.

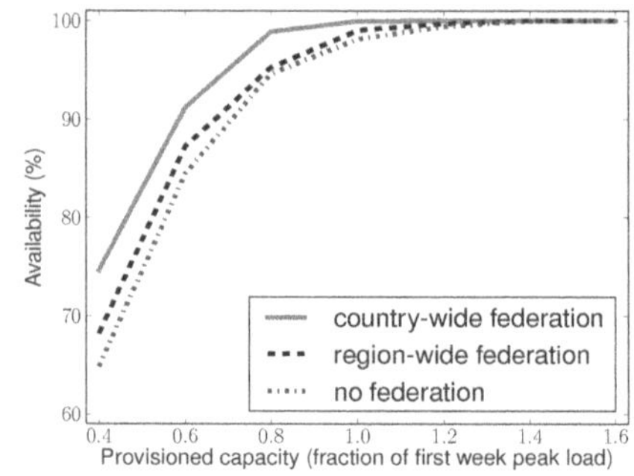

(a) Over multiple weeks

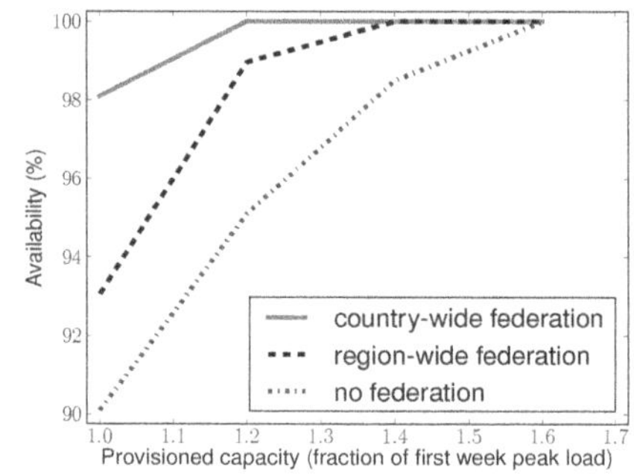

(b) 5 hour peak access time

Figure 7: *Benefits from federation for VOD*

Methodology: We use the user access behavior during the first week and find the peak load at each ISP_i in each $Region_r$ to determine a baseline for provisioning $Cap_{r,i}$ at each ISP-region combination. Specifically, we consider a provisioning exercise where each ISP-region combination is provisioned to handle a fraction of this peak load. Then, we use the remaining three weeks of user arrival patterns to analyze the effectiveness of such provisioning with and without federation. We set the value of α to be extremely high to minimize drops. The particular measure of interest in this exercise is the *availability* which we define as the fraction of requests that are served by the overall distribution infrastructure. Formally, this can be expressed as:

$$Availability = \frac{\sum_{r,i,t} \sum_{ri:r'i' \in P(r,i)} N_{r'i' \to ri}(t)}{\sum_{r,i,t} Demand_{ri}(t)} \quad (7)$$

In the following evaluation, we consider three scenarios:

- *No federation:* Here, $P(r, i)$ consists of just itself.
- *Region-wide federation:* $P(r, i)$ consists of all ISPs within the same region
- *Country-wide federation:* $P(r, i)$ consists of all ISPs in all regions.

Benefits for VOD content: Figure 7a shows the overall benefits of federation using the VOD dataset. As mentioned before, each telco-CDN provisions for a fraction of the observed peak load from the first week. For instance, as shown in Figure 7a, when each telco-CDN provisions for 40% of the observed peak load in the first week (this roughly corresponds to the average observed load), we see that there is almost a 5% increase in availability with just region-wide federation when evaluated over the workload from the next 3 weeks. Country-wide federation results in about 10% increase in availability of the system.

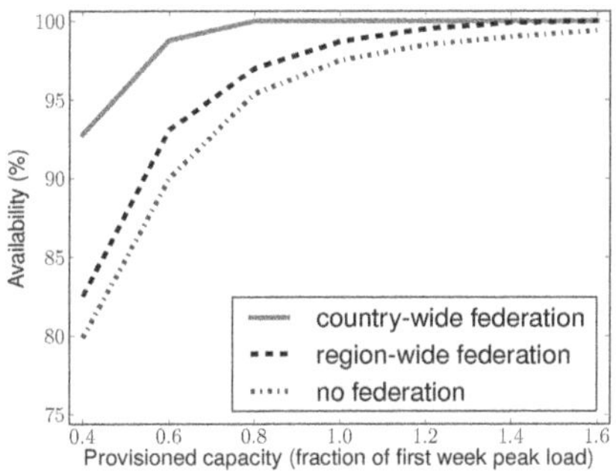

(a) Over multiple weeks

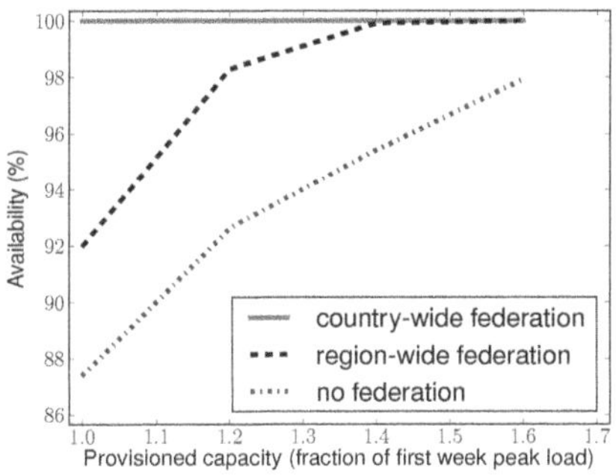

(b) During a popular regional event

Figure 8: *Benefits from federation for live*

Although peak loads are roughly predictable for VOD content, in order to achieve 100% availability without federation, each ISP-region needs to over-provision with 1.6 times the observed first week peak load. Whereas, provisioning with 1.4 times the peak load would be enough with region-wide cooperation and provisioning with 1.2 times the observed first week peak load is sufficient to sustain the workload over the next 3 weeks with country-wide federation. This points to the fact that despite the synchrony in viewing behavior, peak loads are slightly offset across different ISPs within a region enabling using spare resources from other ISPs within the same region to improve availability. Similarly, the temporal shift in peak loads across regions due to time zone effect enables even more sharing of resources, reducing the provisioning cost to meet unexpected demands.

This result focuses on the average availability across the entire three week period. The benefits of federation are the most pronounced during peak access times. In order to highlight this further, we evaluate the availability of the system during a five-hour peak access period in Figure 7b. This result shows that without federation, roughly 10% of users will need to be dropped if each ISP-region was simply provisioned for the peak load observed in the first week, whereas we get only 2% dropped users with country-wide federation.

Benefits for live content: Live events have more unpredictable workloads due to interest-induced regional effects leading to unexpected higher load from typically low-load regions (e.g., when the local team plays a match). Consequently, we expect that pooling in resources from other ISPs and regions via federation will be even more beneficial.

We use the live dataset and show the overall benefits from federation in Figure 8a. For instance, as seen in Figure 8a, when provisioned for 40% of the peak load from first week, region-wide federation would increase the availability by around 3% (lower than the VOD case) while country-wide federation would increase the availability by 13% (higher than VOD) when evaluated on the next 3 week workload.

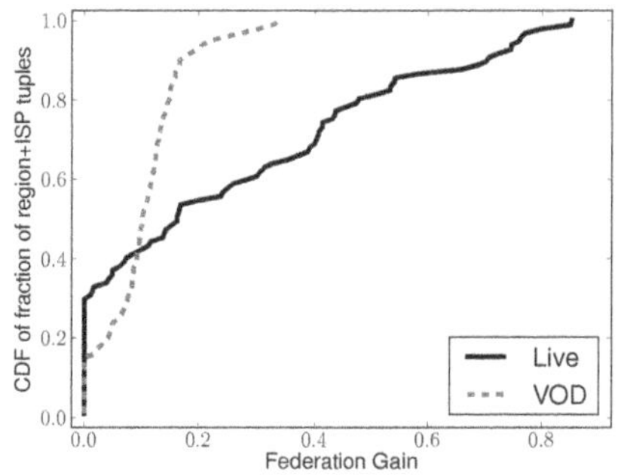

Figure 9: *CDF of federation gain*

We zoom into a peak access time of 3 hours when a regional match was being broadcasted and repeat the study to show the benefits of federation in Figure 8b. We observe that employing country-wide federation, the system can achieve 100% availability by just provisioning for the observed peak load from the first week. Region-wide federation would require provisioning the system with 1.4 times the peak load. Without any federation, we observed that provisioning for 20 times the peak load is required to meet 100% availability—i.e., federation decreases the required provisioning by around 95%. This clearly shows that live events can benefit a lot from federation because unpredictable local peaks in access rates are much more common.

Which ISPs benefit the most: The immediate question that arises when we consider peering and federation is fairness. We analyze if specific categories of ISPs and/or regions are more likely to gain from federation compared to others. To this end, we define a *federation gain* metric for each ISP-region combination as the ratio between the total volume of requests served by other ISP/regions to the total capacity of this ISP-region $\frac{TotalServedbyOthers}{Capacity}$. Figure 9 shows the CDF of federation gain over all ISP-region combinations using country-wide federation. We observe that federation gains are lower and more uniform for VOD (highest gain is 0.4) while they are more skewed and higher in value in the case of live (highest gain is 0.8). Looking at the ISP-region combinations that benefit the most, we observe that ISPs in typically low-load regions have higher benefits in the case of live. This is because of unpredictable local peaks caused by events of regional interest. In the case of VOD, the ISPs in high-load regions have larger benefits. The benefits were mostly from offloading unexpected daily peak loads.

Performance Costs: Employing telco-CDN federation might lead to the selection of CDN servers far from a user, which would increase latency. Our approach to limit these performance issues is to use a very simple hop-based latency model, but a more systematic scheme would take into consideration the impact of CDN server selection on users' quality-of-experience [32, 15]. Design and analysis of a system taking these into consideration is outside the scope of this paper.

4.5 Main observations

To summarize, the key observations are:

- Federation increases the overall availability of the system with lower provisioning overhead (as much as 95% reduction in the case of live). The benefits are higher with higher level of cooperation (the upper bound being pooling in all resources within the country).

- VOD workload benefits from federation by offloading daily peak loads. We notice that ISPs from typically high load regions benefit the most.
- Live workload benefits from federation by offloading unexpected high traffic triggered by regional events. Here, the benefits are higher for ISPs in typically low-load regions.

5. ANALYZING HYBRID P2P-CDN

The two predominant technologies for delivering videos to end users are CDNs based on the client-server model of delivery, and server-less P2P mechanisms. Whereas CDNs provide reliable delivery using a geographically distributed delivery infrastructure, P2P enables scalability by leveraging on the bandwidth resources of individual users. There has been renewed interest in the CDN industry to augment traditional CDN based video delivery with P2P technologies. This trend is driven by the need for higher quality (e.g., [7]), and is further enabled by new technologies that allow P2P modules to run within browsers and video players without requiring separate applications [9, 1, 8].

Conventional wisdom in the use of P2P-assisted hybrid CDNs suggests that:

- P2P is only likely to be useful for live content because VOD may have low synchrony with very few users viewing the same part of the video at the same time.
- It is better to use the CDN for the early bootstrap process as clients arrive and use P2P only for the steady-state once the "swarm" dynamics stabilize.

However, we observed several user access patterns and behaviors in our dataset that give us reason to revisit and question these traditional assumptions in hybrid CDN-P2P designs. We present these observations in Section 5.1. Based on these observations, we propose new strategies for CDNs to reduce their infrastructure costs by using a hybrid-P2P approach and evaluate these proposals in Section 5.2.

5.1 User Access Patterns

We observed several user access patterns that have very important implications to the design of hybrid P2P-CDN architecture. For example, we observed that several users watch only the first few minutes of a video in the case of both VOD and live content. This could imply that some parts of the video objects are more amenable to P2P than the rest. We also explore the evolution of interest for both VOD and live content to understand when it would be more beneficial to employ P2P strategies.

5.1.1 Partial Interest in content

We observed that several users had partial interest in the content that they are viewing and they quit the session without watching the content fully in the case of both VOD and live. If most users watch only the first few minutes of the video before quitting, P2P might be more amenable for the first few chunks since there will be more copies of them compared to the rest of the video. Hence, we further investigated the temporal characteristics of user behavior within a given video session and analyzed what fraction of a video object users typically view before quitting.

For VOD content, Figure 10a shows that based on the fraction of video that a user viewed within a session, users can be classified into three categories:

- **Early-quitter:** A large fraction of the users watch less than 10% of the video before quitting the sessions. These users might be "sampling" the video.
- **Drop-out:** We observe that further on, users steadily drop out of the video session possibly due to quality issues or lack of interest in the content.
- **Steady viewer:** A significant fraction of the users watch the video to completion.

We can model this using a mixture model with three separate components [33]. As shown in Figures 10b and 10c, we try to find the best fitting probability distribution for the early-quitter and steady viewer components. Inspecting visually and using mean squared error test, we choose the gamma distribution to represent both the early-quitter and the steady viewer components. We model the drop-out component using a uniform distribution. We then use expectation maximization [33] to estimate the mixture model parameters and obtain the model as shown in Figure 10a. These models can be used for simulating video viewing behaviors in the future.

The previous result considers the behavior of users in aggregate. A natural question then is whether specific users behave in a consistent way across multiple video sessions. To this end, we profile users' viewing history across multiple sessions by grouping sessions by the user as identified using their unique *ClientID*. We find that 4.5% of the users quit the session early for more than 75% of the sessions; i.e., these users are "serial" early quitters. Similarly, 16.6% of the users consistently viewed the video to completion; i.e., these are consistently steady viewers.

Similar to the analysis that we did for VOD content, we also analyze what fraction of the live content users typically view before quitting and plot the distribution in Figure 11a. We observe that based on the fraction of video viewed within a session, users watching live content can be classified into two categories:

- **Early-quitter:** A very large fraction of users watch less than 20% of the video before quitting the session.
- **Drop-out:** The remaining fraction of users steadily drop out of the video session.

Figure 11b zooms into the early-quitter part of the plot and shows how well different distributions fit the data. Inspecting visually and using mean squared error test, we find that the gamma distribution is the best fit and model it in Figure 11a. A large fraction of users quitting the session early for live content might imply that the first part of the event is the most popular part. However, as we see in Figure 11c users arrive randomly within the event and stay for short periods of time before quitting. Hence the first part of the event is not necessarily the most popular part.

We also profile users' viewing history (based on the unique *Client ID*) and notice that around 20.7% of the clients are "serial" early quitters—i.e., they quit the session early for more than 75% of the sessions for live content. We also observe several users joining and quitting multiple times during the same event. Since our dataset consists of sporting events, one possibility is that they might be checking for the current score of the match.

Contrasting the observations of live and VOD, we observe the following key differences:

- The early-quitters watch higher fractions of video in the case of live (up to 20% of the video) when compared to VOD (up to 10% of the video). Drop-out percentage is less pronounced in the case of live and we also do not observe a significant fraction of users viewing the entire event.
- In the case of VOD, users typically view the video from the start as opposed to live where people join at random times.

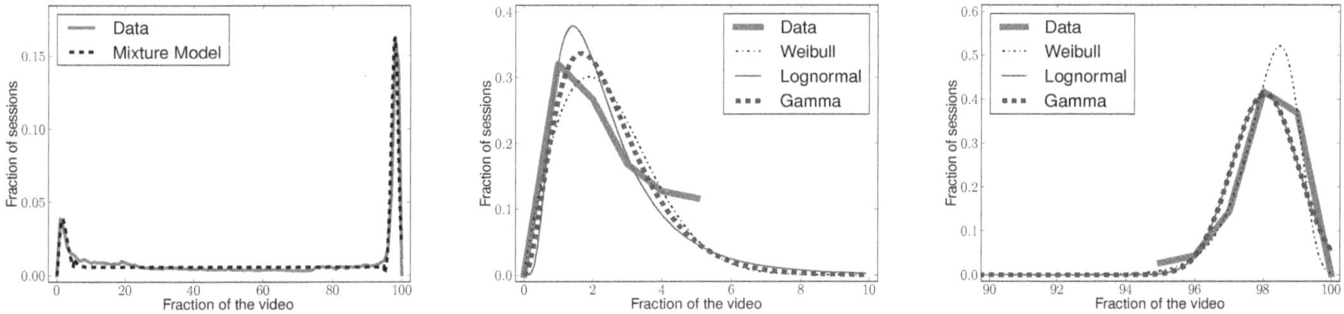

(a) PDF of fraction of video viewed before quitting

(b) Component 1: Early quitters

(c) Component 3: Steady viewers

Figure 10: *Distribution of the fraction of video viewed for VOD*

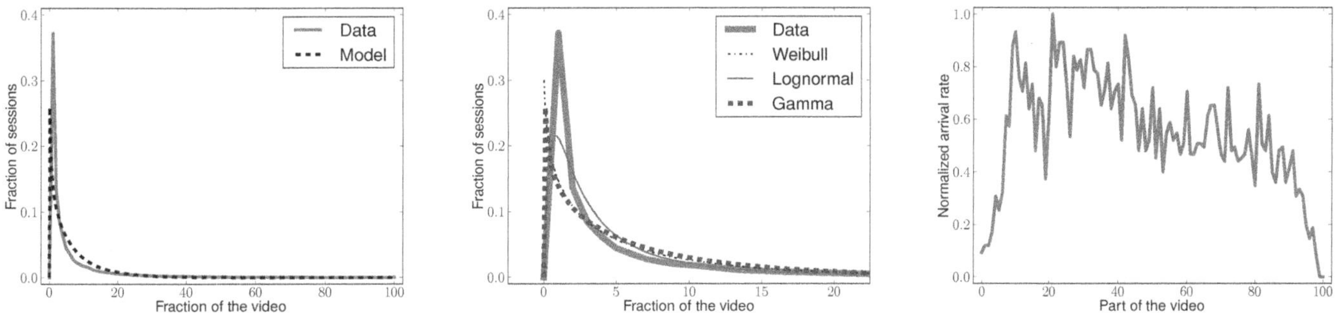

(a) PDF of fraction of video viewed

(b) Modeling fraction of video viewed

(c) Arrival rate

Figure 11: *Fraction of video viewed and arrival rate for live objects*

- We observe a higher fraction of "serial" early-quitters in the case of live.

Implications:
(1) This analysis is particularly relevant in the context of augmenting CDNs with P2P based delivery. For example, if most users are likely to only watch a small fraction of video, then P2P will be less effective at offloading some of the server load as there may not be sufficient number of cached copies of the content.
(2) Content providers and content delivery infrastructures can identify the early quitters and steady viewers and customize the allocation of resources (e.g., use P2P to serve the content to early quitters who are "sampling" the video).
(3) Although user behavior like early-quitting are similar for live and VOD, we need to consider the differences in access patterns. For example, since early-quitters watch the video for longer in the case of live, employing P2P to serve early-quitters might imply serving more content using P2P in the case of live than VOD.
(4) Similarly, the fact that users typically view VOD objects from the start and quit early might imply higher availability for the first few chunks of the video. For live, even though users quit quickly, they arrive randomly in between the event and hence the first part of the event may not necessarily be the most popular part.
(5) Beyond hybrid P2P designs, this analysis is very interesting because understanding such patterns is especially useful for content providers and content delivery infrastructures in order to maximize some higher-level objective (e.g., where to place ad impressions to maximize revenue).

5.1.2 Evolution of interest

It is crucial to investigate how popularity of content evolves over time since it could point to certain times when P2P strategies might be more beneficial. For example, if more users watch VOD videos on the day of release, there would be higher synchrony in viewership that could lead to higher benefits from employing P2P.

We classify VOD objects into three categories: TV series, news show or reality show and model the evolution in interest along two key dimensions: (1) temporal decay in popularity for a given object (i.e., a fixed episode for a fixed show) over days, and (2) demand predictability across multiple episodes for a given show. We develop models for these parameters that can be used for simulating video workloads in the future. Live objects are viewed while the event is happening and are not available afterwards. Hence, we explore how the interest in the content evolves during the event by analyzing hotspot points in events.

Figure 12 shows the temporal variation in popularity and how demand for the content decays for sample objects from the three categories of VOD objects. First, for TV series episodes, the demand for episodes appears relatively stable and predictable week to week, and it decays gradually over time. Second, for news shows, we see the demand hits a peak on the release date and decreases quite dramatically. Finally, for reality shows, while we see a decay in demand from the time of release, there is less predictable viewership across different episodes. We further characterize the temporal decay and demand predictability for VOD objects.

Temporal decay in popularity for VOD objects: We observe that the highest number of accesses occurs on the day of release for

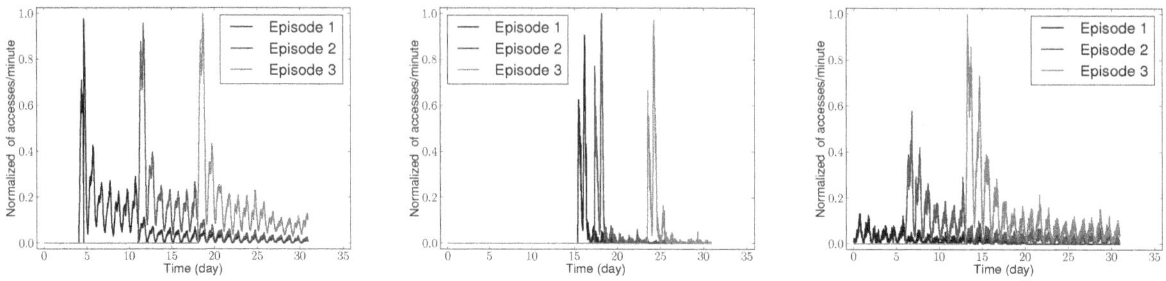

(a) TV series (b) News shows (c) Reality shows

Figure 12: *Temporal change in popularity of VOD objects*

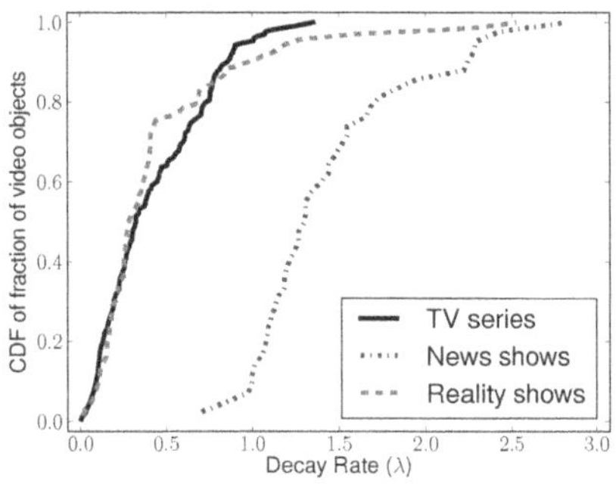

Figure 13: *CDF of decay rate for different genres*

all the VOD objects, and the daily peak number of access for each object decreases with time. Exponential decay appears to be the best fit for modeling the decay (compared to linear decay process) based on aggregate mean-squared error test across multiple objects. The decay in peak number of accesses can hence be characterized using an exponential decay function as follows:

$$P(t) = P_0 e^{-\lambda t} \tag{8}$$

where P_0 is the peak number of access on the day of release, $P(t)$ is the peak number of access on the day t since release and λ is the decay constant. Figure 13 shows the CDF of the estimated decay rate (λ) for all the VOD objects categorized by their genres. News shows have high decay rates which implies that these objects turn stale quicker and their demand decreases dramatically within a day of release. In contrast, TV shows have lower decay rates. The decay rate of reality shows have more variability.

Demand predictability for VOD objects: We analyze how predictable the demand for shows are based on their viewership history. For this, we use the viewership pattern of the latest episode as an estimate for the next episode.[3] We characterize (1) how close were the peak number of accesses on the day of release? (2) how similar were the decay patterns?

(1) *Estimation Error:* Using the most recent episode as a predictor for the peak demand for the next episode, we calculate:

$$Estimation\ error = \frac{|P_{actual} - P_{estimated}|}{P_{\texttt{actual}}} \tag{9}$$

where P_{actual} is the peak number of accesses on the day of release of the show and $P_{estimated}$ is the estimated peak number of accesses (i.e., the peak number of accesses observed for the previous show in the series). Figure 14a shows the CDF of relative error for different genres. We observe that TV series have lower relative error values, implying that their peak access rates across episodes are more steady and predictable. News shows and reality shows tend to have more variable peak accesses.

[3]Our dataset is limited to 2 to 4 episodes per show. Modeling viewership history over a larger span is an interesting direction for future work.

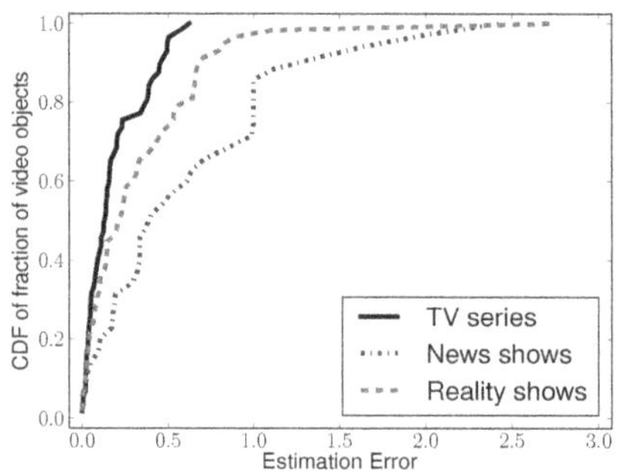

(a) Estimation Error

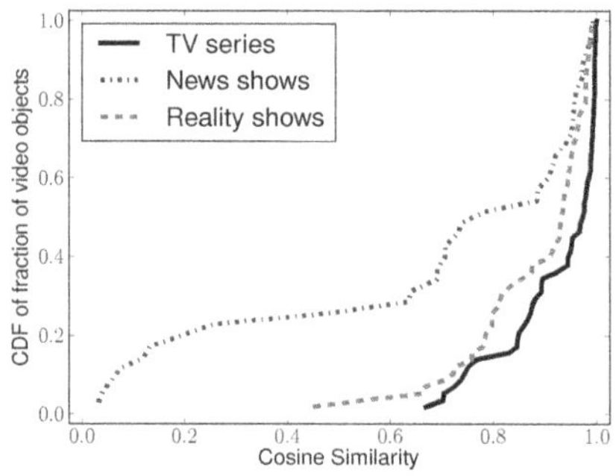

(b) Cosine Similarity

Figure 14: *Characterizing demand predictability*

(2) *Cosine similarity:* Apart from categorizing the predictability of the peak number of accesses, we also want to estimate how similar the decay patterns are across episodes within a series. If $X =< x_0, x_1, ..., x_i, ... >$ denotes the vector of the number of accesses for the object starting from the hour of release and $Y =< y_0, y_1, ..., y_j, ... >$ denote the vector of number of accesses for the previous episode of the series, we compute the similarity between the episodes as:

$$Cosine\ similarity = \frac{\sum_{i=0}^{n} x_i \times y_i}{\sqrt{\sum_{i=0}^{n}(x_i)^2} \times \sqrt{\sum_{i=0}^{n}(y_i)^2}} \tag{10}$$

Cosine similarity takes values in the range [0,1] where 1 implies high similarity and 0 indicates independence.[4] Figure 14b shows the CDF of cosine similarity for different VOD objects. We observe that TV series have the highest similarity. The access patterns of news shows tend to be very different from the previous episodes. The cosine similarity of reality shows falls in between the TV series and news shows.

Hotspots in live events: From a provisioning perspective, it is important to understand how the interest in the content evolves during the live event. Figure 15 gives two extreme examples of how overall interest in the content changes within a session. Figure 15a shows an example of an event where the number of viewers watching the event was steady throughout the event whereas Figure 15b is an example of an event where there was a particular point in the event where interest peaked and then it died down. We refer to the location with the peak number of simultaneous viewers as the *hotspot point* within the event.

Given these extremes, a natural question is what does a typical live event look like? To this end, we systematically analyze the live events on two dimensions: (1) where do hotspots occur in a video? (2) how pronounced is the hotspot? Figure 16a shows the CDF of the hotspot point location for all the live events. We see that there is no particular location where hotspots typically occur. To capture how pronounced a hotspot is, we compute the *peak-to-average* ratio of the number of simultaneous viewers at a given point of time during the session. Looking at the distribution of the peak-to-average ratio (Figure 16b), we observe that majority of the events have flat access rates (similar to Figure 15a). However, events with pronounced hotspots tend to have the hotspot point towards the beginning of the event.

Implications:
(1) The strong diurnal patterns observed from the time series plots again point to high synchrony of viewing even at a per-object basis. This bodes favorably in using P2P augmentation strategies for delivering VOD content.
(2) The decay rates indicate higher synchronous viewing behavior on the day of release of the show. This is also when we see higher demand in objects and when the CDNs might benefit more from using P2P strategies.
(3) Comparing genres, news shows have very high decay rates and are least predictable. This could potentially lead to sudden unexpected surges in demands and hence CDNs may need to invoke P2P-based strategies dynamically to handle these loads. However, TV series have more stable demands that are predictable and with lower decay. This means that the delivery infrastructure can be provisioned accordingly. Reality shows have much more variability in terms of decay and predictability.
(4) Since we do not observe any typical pattern for hotspot locations across live objects, CDNs may need to dynamically invoke strategies to handle the peak loads by using P2P depending on how interest evolves for the particular content.

5.2 Revisiting P2P-CDN benefits

Contrary to the conventional wisdom in this space, first, we posit that P2P might be more useful for VOD than previously assumed and that these benefits can be achieved even without assuming that each peer is caching the whole content as in [27]. Second, the presence of early quitters suggest CDNs may want to rethink how they allocate constrained server resources. Specifically, we leverage the higher interest in the early chunks coupled with the tendency of users to sample videos to consider a (possibly counter-intuitive) option where we can use P2P to bootstrap serving the content and later use the CDN servers. This allows the CDN to invest resources more usefully for viewers who are more likely to yield increased revenue from ad-impressions.

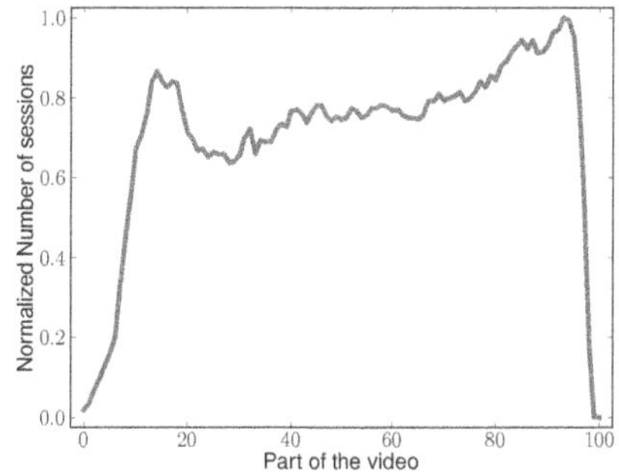

(a) Flat

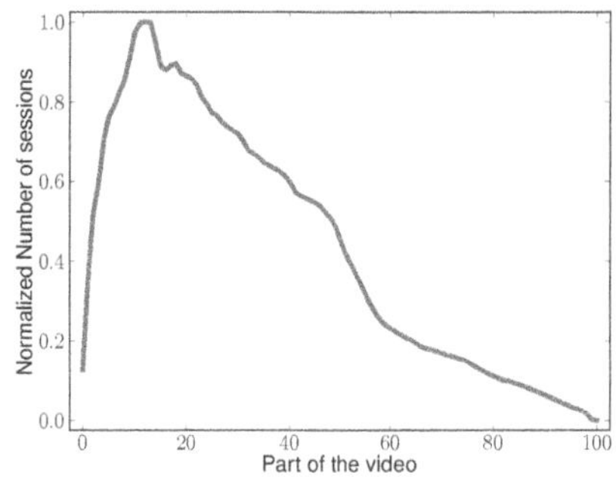

(b) Non-flat

Figure 15: *Two extreme examples of temporal change in interest in live content during the duration of the event*

Methodology: The metric of interest here is the reduced number of accesses at the CDN server as a result of using P2P. Our goal in this exercise is to evaluate the *potential benefit* of P2P-assisted CDNs. To this end, we consider a very simplistic P2P-assisted model where peers are organized in a swarm with a specific *scope* and *size*. For each swarm, we assume that only one request needs to go to CDN server and the remaining nodes receive the content through P2P. The scope represents a trade off between network-friendliness and the availability of peers who are in synchronized viewing:

- Nodes form peers only with nodes within the *same city+ISP*.
- Based on the region classification in Table 1, nodes form peers only with other nodes within the *same region+ISP*.
- Nodes form peers within the *same region*

Because our goal is to estimate the potential benefit, we do not model swarm dynamics or evaluate the choice of chunk selection policies [23]. We consider a simple sequential chunk selection policy where peers are organized in swarms corresponding to the location in the video. For live content we do not consider the impact of cache size since all viewers are in sync. However, for VOD we cache a limited number of previous chunks (e.g., several services like Netflix do not allow caching more than a few minutes of the content) and nodes typically peer with other nodes that have the required content cached. We set the chunk size to 5 minutes of the video consistent with what is predominant in the industry. We limit the maximum swarm size to 100.

[4]Because X and Y are both positive vectors, the cosine similarity can't be negative.

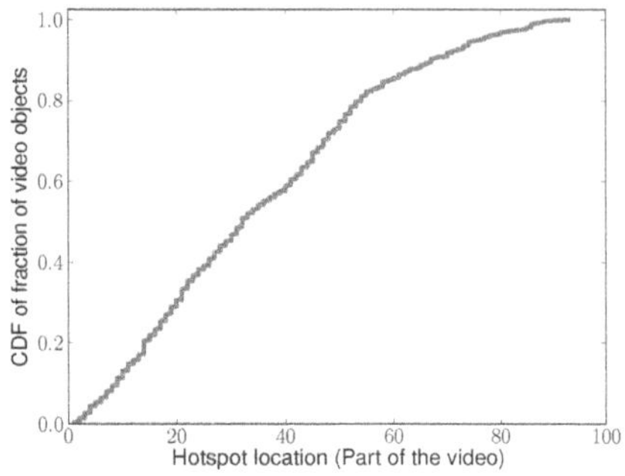

(a) Where do hotspots occur?

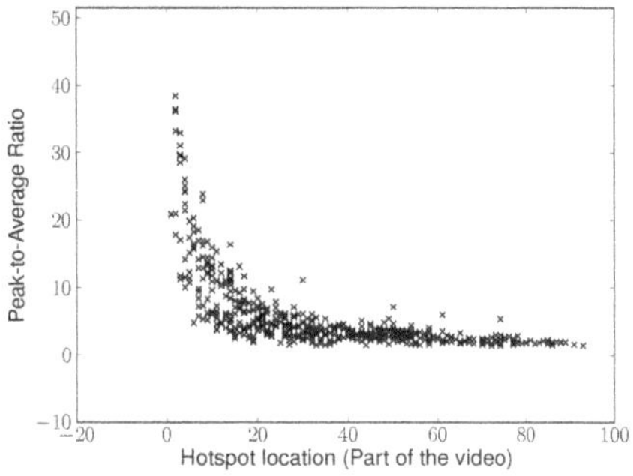

(b) How pronounced are the hotspots?

Figure 16: *Investigating hotspots in live content*

Scope	Live (%)	VOD (%)
Same region	98.94	87.09
Same region+ISP	96.91	40.90
Same city+ISP	92.65	13.79

Table 3: *Overall benefit for using P2P for different scopes*

Impact of varying scope: Table 3 summarizes the overall benefit from using a P2P-augmented CDN system for live and VOD content. Not surprisingly, live content has higher savings than VOD. For live, the potential savings are as high as 92% even with same city+ISP scope. While the benefits are higher as we increase the scope, the resulting increase in savings shows diminishing returns. This suggests that realizing simple and network-friendly P2P solutions to augment today's CDN infrastructure is a promising path. In the case of VOD, we limit the cache size to 1 chunk. We observe that savings can be as high as 87% when nodes are allowed to peer with other nodes within the same region. Unlike live content, however, the savings are not as large when the scope of peering is limited (e.g. same city + ISP).

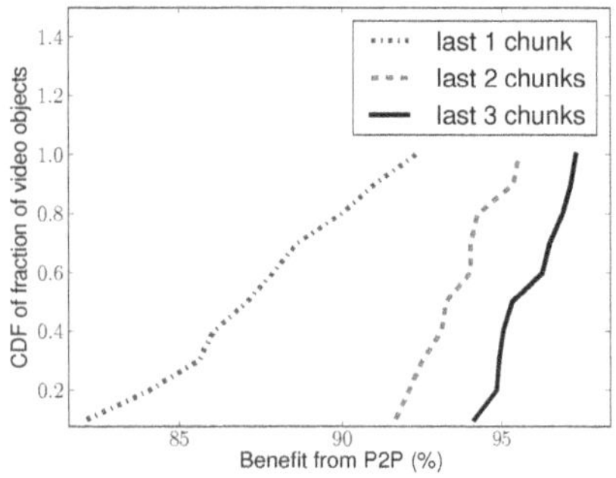

Figure 17: *Impact of cache size on the benefit of P2P for VOD*

Effect of varying cache size for VOD: In the case of VOD, it is interesting to investigate how increasing cache size affects the performance of the system. Figure 17 shows the CDF of the benefits from P2P for different VOD objects with same region scope. Although increasing cache size leads to greater savings, we observe diminishing returns for increased cache size.

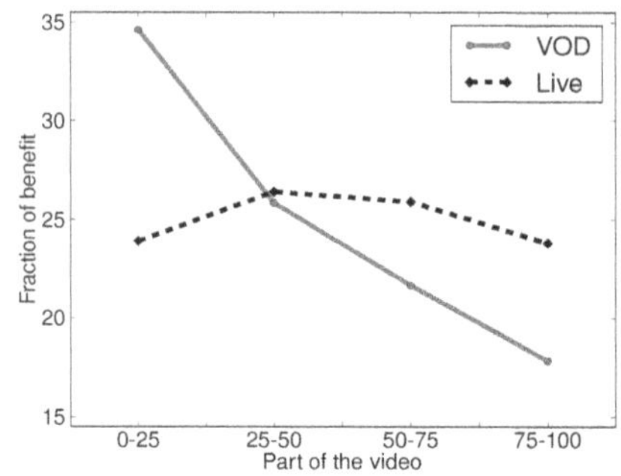

Figure 18: *Chunks that are more likely to benefit from P2P; for VOD we see that the early chunks are the ones that benefit the most*

Which part of the video gives most benefit? In Figure 18, we look at the percentage of savings that chunks in different parts of the video provide. We observe that most of the benefits for VOD is due to the earlier chunks. This is because users typically watch VOD videos from the start and the large number of early-quitters cause the earlier chunks to be more available than the later ones. However, in the case of live, the benefits appear to be more uniform. This is because of the pattern that we observed earlier—although users quit early, they also join the event at random times.

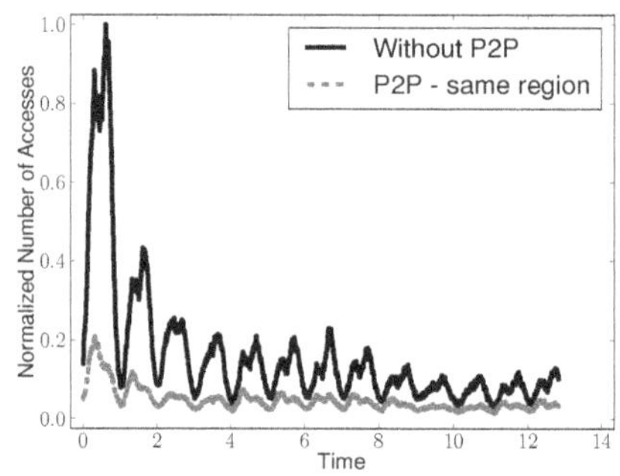

Figure 19: *Evolution of the benefit of P2P assistance over time*

How does the benefit of P2P vary over time: Unlike live events, VOD objects have demands that last several weeks. In this context, it is interesting to observe how the savings vary with time. Figure 19 shows the temporal variation in access demands at the server with and without P2P. We observe that the savings are as high as 80% during the peak access hour on the day of release because of larger number of users synchronously viewing content. This is also the time when the CDN would benefit the most from savings.

Using P2P earlier: Last, we explore the benefits via an alternative strategy of using P2P for the early chunks and later serving the content directly from the CDN. This can be a viewed as a mechanism to filter out the early quitters and serve them without wasting precious server resources. We analyze the benefits of serving only the first few chunks using P2P for both live and VOD in Figure 20. We observe that with about 2 chunks (which covers most of the early-quitter scenarios for VOD), we can get savings of around 30%. In

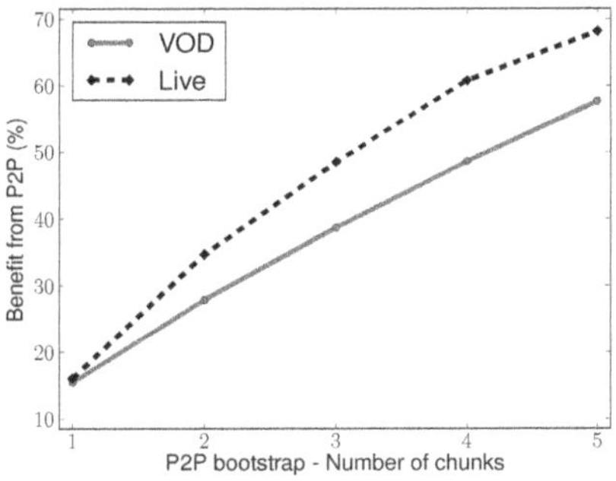

Figure 20: *Using P2P in the early stages of user arrival*

the case of VOD, this is almost equivalent to the savings obtained from the first 2 chunks of the video (as in Figure 18) since users typically watch the video from start. In the case of live, serving the first four chunks since the user starts the session (which covers all of the early-quitters) results in around 60% savings. However, note that this is not the same as the savings from the first 4 chunks of the video since users join at random times during the event and start viewing from random parts of the event.

Performance Costs: Using P2P to bootstrap video delivery might have an impact on the time it takes for the video to start playback (*start up delay*) [29]. Also, higher node churns in the P2P swarm can potentially result in disruptions in the video playback. System designs to circumvent such performance issues have been studied in previous work [37] and is not the focus of this paper.

5.3 Main observations

To summarize, the key observations are:

- VOD has more synchrony in viewership than expected, especially during the peak access hours on the day of release. This is also when we observe the highest demand for the object. Hence, P2P can be used to offload some of the load from the server during peak hours. We observed around 87% savings for P2P-assisted VOD.
- We explore the option of bootstrapping using P2P as a means of "filtering out" early-quitters for both VOD and live and see that this alone could lead to 30% savings in the case of VOD and 60% savings in the case of live.

6. CONCLUSIONS

As Internet-based video consumption becomes mainstream, the video delivery infrastructure needs to be designed and provisioned to deliver high-quality content to larger user populations. But current trends indicate that the CDN infrastructure is being stressed by the increasing video traffic. Telco-CDN federation and hybrid P2P-CDNs are two oft-discussed strategies to augment existing infrastructure, but there are no recent studies on the benefits of these two strategies. Given the ongoing industry efforts and discussions to deploy federated and P2P-based solutions, we believe our work is timely: we provide a quantitative basis to justify, motivate, and inform these initiatives.

Our analysis of over 30 million live and VOD sessions reveals several interesting access patterns that have important implications to these two strategies including regional and time of day effects, synchronous viewing behavior, demand predictability, and partial interest in content. Building on these observations, we analyzed the potential benefits of hybrid P2P-CDN approaches and telco-CDN federation. We found that federation can signiïňAçantly reduce telco-CDN provisioning costs and equivalently increase the effective capacity of the system by exploiting regional and cross-ISP skews in access popularity. Surprisingly, we found that P2P approaches can work for VOD content as well, especially at peak loads when we see highly synchronous viewing patterns, and proposed and evaluated new strategies for hybrid-P2P systems based on prevalent user behavior.

Acknowledgments

We thank our shepherd Kuai Xu and the anonymous reviewers for their feedback that helped improve the paper. We thank Conviva Inc. for making the video viewing data available for our study. We also thank the staff at Conviva for answering several questions about the dataset and the data collection infrastructure. This work is partially supported by the National Science Foundation under grants CNS-1050170, CNS-1017545, CNS-0905134 and CNS-0746531

7. REFERENCES

[1] Akamai NetSession. http://www.akamai.com/client/.
[2] Census Bureau Divisioning. http://www.census.gov/geo/www/us_regdiv.pdf.
[3] Cisco forecast. http://blogs.cisco.com/sp/comments/cisco_visual_networking_index_forecast_annual_update/.
[4] Cisco Report on CDN Federation - Solutions for SPs and Content Providers To Scale a Great Customer Experience.
[5] Hadoop. http://hadoop.apache.org/.
[6] Mail service costs Netflix 20 times more than streaming. http://www.techspot.com/news/42036-mail-service-costs-netflix-20-times-more-than-streaming.html.
[7] NFL What are HQ videos? http://www.nfl.com/help/faq.
[8] Use RTMFP for developing real-time collaboration applications. http://labs.adobe.com/technologies/cirrus/.
[9] WebRTC 1.0: Real-time Communication Between Browsers. http://www.w3.org/TR/webrtc/.
[10] B. Niven-Jenkins, F. L. Faucheur, and N. Bitar. Content distribution network interconnection (CDNI) problem statement. http://datatracker.ietf.org/doc/draft-ietf-cdni-problem-statement/, Jan. 2012.
[11] L. Plissonneau and E. Biersack. A Longitudinal View of HTTP Video Streaming Performance. In *Proc. MMSys*, 2012.
[12] H. Abrahamsson and M. Nordmark. Program popularity and viewer behavior in a large TV-on-Demand system. In *IMC*, 2012.
[13] D. Applegate, A. Archer, V. Gopalakrishnan, S. Lee, and K. K. Ramakrishnan. Optimal Content Placement for a Large-Scale VoD System. In *Proc. CoNext*, 2010.
[14] B. Cheng, L. Stein, H. Jin, and Z. Zheng. Towards Cinematic Internet Video-On-Demand. In *Proc. Eurosys*, 2008.
[15] A. Balachandran, V. Sekar, A. Akella, S. Seshan, I. Stoica, and H. Zhang. Developing a Predictive Model of Quality of Experience for Internet Video. In *SIGCOMM*, 2013.
[16] C. Huang, A. Wang, J. Li, and K. W. Ross. Understanding Hybrid CDN-P2P: Why Limelight Needs its Own Red Swoosh. In *Proc. NOSSDAV*, 2008.

[17] C. Huang, J. Li, and K. W. Ross. Can Internet Video-on-Demand be Profitable? In *Proc. SIGCOMM*, 2007.

[18] M. Cha, H. Kwak, P. Rodriguez, Y.-Y. Ahn, and S. Moon. I Tube, You Tube, Everybody Tubes: Analyzing the World's Largest User Generated Content Video System. In *Proc. IMC*, 2007.

[19] D. Rayburn. Telcos and carriers forming new federated cdn group called ocx (operator carrier exchange). http://goo.gl/wUhXr.

[20] F. Dobrian, V. Sekar, A. Awan, I. Stoica, D. A. Joseph, A. Ganjam, J. Zhan, and H. Zhang. Understanding the impact of video quality on user engagement. In *Proc. SIGCOMM*, 2011.

[21] J. Erman, A. Gerber, K. Ramakrishnan, S. Sen, and O. Spatscheck. Over the top video: The gorilla in cellular networks. In *IMC*, 2011.

[22] H. Y. et al. Inside the Bird's Nest: Measurements of Large-Scale Live VoD from the 2008 Olympics. In *Proc. IMC*, 2009.

[23] B. Fan, D. Andersen, M. Kaminsky, and K. Papagiannaki. Balancing Throughput, Robustness, and In-Order Delivery in P2P VoD. In *Proc. ACM CoNEXT*, 2010.

[24] A. Finamore, M. Mellia, M. Munafo, R. Torres, and S. G. Rao. Youtube everywhere: Impact of device and infrastructure synergies on user experience. In *Proc. IMC*, 2011.

[25] H. Yu, D. Zheng, B. Y. Zhao, and W. Zheng. Understanding User Behavior in Large-Scale Video-on-Demand Systems. In *Proc. Eurosys*, 2006.

[26] X. Hei, C. Liang, J. Liang, Y. Liu, and K. W. Ross. A measurement study of a large-scale P2P IPTV system. *IEEE Transactions on Multimedia*, 2007.

[27] Y. Huang, D.-M. C. Tom Z. J. Fu, J. C. S. Lui, and C. Huang. Challenges, Design and Analysis of a Large-scale P2P-VoD System. In *Proc. SIGCOMM*, 2008.

[28] S. Krishnan and R. Sitaraman. Video Stream Quality Impacts Viewer Behavior: Infering Causality Using Quasi-Experimental Designs. In *IMC*, 2012.

[29] B. Li, S. Xie, Y. Qu, and K. G.Y. Inside the New Coolstreaming: Principles, Measurement and Performance Implications. In *INFOCOMM*, 2008.

[30] Z. Li, J. Lin, M.-I. Akodjenou-Jeannin, G. Xie, M. A. Kaafar, Y. Jin, and G. Peng. Watching video from everywhere: a study of the pptv mobile vod system. In *IMC*, 2012.

[31] H. Liu, Y. Wang, Y. R. Yang, A. Tian, and H. Wang. Optimizing Cost and Performance for Content Multihoming. In *SIGCOMM*, 2012.

[32] X. Liu, F. Dobrian, H. Milner, J. Jiang, V. Sekar, I. Stoica, and H. Zhang. A Case for a Coordinated Internet-Scale Video Control Plane. In *Proc. SIGCOMM*, 2012.

[33] T. Mitchell. *Machine Learning*. McGraw-Hill.

[34] T. Qiu, Z. Ge, S. Lee, J. Wang, Q. Zhao, and J. Xu. Modeling channel popularity dynamics in a large IPTV system. In *Proc. SIGMETRICS*, 2009.

[35] R. Powell. The federated cdn cometh. May 2011. TelecomRamblings.com.

[36] S. Guha, S. Annapureddy, C. Gkantsidis, D. Gunawardena, and P. Rodriguez. Is High-Quality VoD Feasible using P2P Swarming? In *Proc. WWW*, 2007.

[37] H. Yin, X. Liu, T. Zhan, V. Sekar, F. Qiu, C. Lin, H. Zhang, and B. Li. Design and Deployment of a Hybrid CDN-P2P System for Live Video Streaming: Experiences with LiveSky. In *Proc. ACM Multimedia*, 2008.

[38] R. Zhou, S. Khemmarat, and L. Gao. The impact of YouTube recommendation system on video views. In *Proc. IMC*, 2010.

D-mystifying the D-root Address Change

Matthew Lentz mlentz@cs.umd.edu
Dave Levin dml@cs.umd.edu
Jason Castonguay castongj@umd.edu
Neil Spring nspring@cs.umd.edu
Bobby Bhattacharjee bobby@cs.umd.edu

University of Maryland

ABSTRACT

On January 3, 2013, the D-root DNS server hosted at the University of Maryland changed IP address. To avoid service disruption, the old address continues to answer queries. In this paper, we perform an initial investigation of the traffic at both the new and old addresses before, during, and since the flag day. The data we collected show non-obvious behavior: the overall query volume to the D-roots increases by roughly 50%, the old address continues to receive a high volume of queries months after the changeover, and far more queries to the old address succeed than those to the new one. Our analysis provides a window into how compliant resolvers change over and how non-standard and seemingly malicious resolvers react (or not) to the IP address change. We provide evidence that a relatively small number of implementation errors account for nearly all discrepancies that are not misconfigurations or attacks.

Categories and Subject Descriptors

C.2.3 [**Computer-Communication Networks**]: Network Operations; C.2.5 [**Computer-Communication Networks**]: Local and Wide-Area Networks—*Internet*

Keywords

Domain Name Service; Measurement; Root Server

1. INTRODUCTION

DNS is a foundational protocol of the Internet, and fundamental to DNS are its 13 root name servers, responsible for last-resort queries for top level domains (TLDs). To bootstrap DNS, root servers' IP addresses are widely disseminated, both out-of-band (via hints files) and in-band (via so-called priming queries, where one root server provides the others' IP addresses).

The University of Maryland hosts the D-root name server, originally referred to as terp.umd.edu (TERP). TERP has always been a root nameserver. 128.8.10.90 was an early IP address for TERP (D) appearing in BIND 4.2.1 in 1989. In order to support a robust anycasted service for "critical infrastructure," ICANN and ARIN have allocated several /24 IPv4 (and /30 IPv6) address blocks to different organizations. Root name server operators receive a new /24 IPv4 micro-allocation that is used to host anycasted root servers [8, 11]. Under this policy, the 199.7.91/24 block was allocated to the University of Maryland, and the D-root server address was changed from 128.8.10.90 to 199.7.91.13. The new /24 IPv4 block will be anycasted globally.

Though root servers very rarely change their IP addresses (historically, at most once each, to permit anycast addressing), there are some generally well-known phenomena that occur when they do. In particular, overall query volume increases, and queries persist at the old IP address, seemingly indefinitely (we review these prior observations in §2). Yet, surprisingly, there remains no explanation as to *why* these occur. This is almost our last chance to find out; D-root is the penultimate root server to change its IP address.

This paper presents and analyzes data we collected before, during, and for several months after D-root's address change. With these data, we observe the same phenomena of prior measurements at other root servers, and we identify a new one: widely differing query success rates between the old and new addresses (§3). We identify potential root causes to increases in query volume: we believe it to be largely due to a particular resolver, PowerDNS (§4). To explain persistent queries to the old address, we present a classification of name servers—those that only visit the new address after an extended period of time, those that only visit the old, and, surprisingly, those that rapidly swap between the two. We show that these different classes exhibit very different behavior, and can be used to help identify root causes (§5). We conclude that, while it can have wide-reaching effects on hosts throughout the Internet, changing a root name server's IP address can be helpful in identifying bugs, misconfigurations, and attacks, and that perhaps changing root servers' IP addresses should not be a historical event but rather a periodic, crude means of garbage collection (§6).

2. BACKGROUND AND RELATED WORK

In DNS, root name servers serve the "root zone," which lies at the top of the namespace hierarchy. Each root name server provides authoritative answers to queries regarding root zone records. For all other queries, they provide pointers to the authoritative name servers for the top level domain (TLD) (e.g., `com` or `edu`) as specified in the query.

As per its original design constraint that limited UDP responses to 512 bytes, the DNS protocol supports a maximum of 13 root name server addresses. Due to the expansive growth of the Internet, these servers quickly became under-provisioned to handle the large number of queries. In order to fix this limitation without patching the existing protocol, anycasting [8, 11] was suggested as a means

IMC'13, October 23–25, 2013, Barcelona, Spain.

http://dx.doi.org/10.1145/2504730.2504772.

Queries ($\times 10^3$)	01/02 00:00 - 01/03 09:53 Old	New	01/03 09:53 - 01/09 17:11 Old	New
Total	1,690,311	897	5,229,920	6,547,199
Invalid TLD	655,732	199	1,613,107	4,918,226
Malformed	3,934	0.6	6,802	9,104
Underscore	2,529	1.0	9,107	1,755
RFC1918 PTR	272	0.2	985	168
Non-Print Char	117	0	94	28
A-for-A	6	0	39	143
Invalid Class	4	0	19	29

Table 1: Scaled overall query volume (in thousands) broken down into reasons for invalidity for both the old and new server. The time interval is divided according to before and after the old server started advertising the new IP address (on Jan 3rd at 09:53).

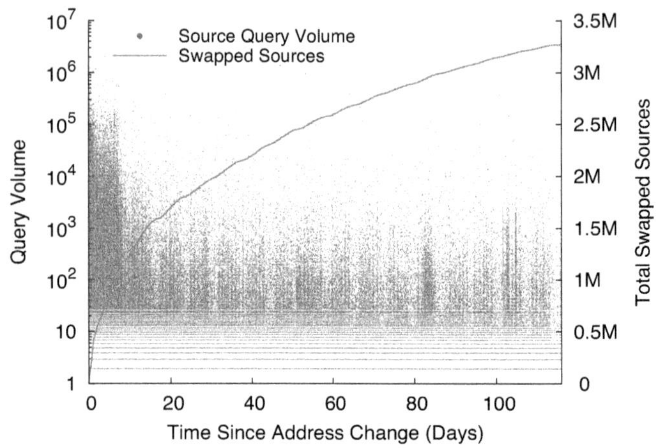

Figure 1: In the first two weeks, approximately 100,000 sources switched to the new address every day. In the following three months, this rate decreased to approximately 20,000 sources per day.

to distribute the root name server instances across a large number of global replicas.

DNS Root Server Traffic Analysis.

Prior analyses of traffic at DNS root name servers identified significant levels of malformed or invalid queries [3, 4, 7, 13]. A 2008 study by Castro et al. [4] found that only 1.8% of the traffic that arrives at 8 of the 13 root name servers was valid. Based on the traffic breakdown, the following four categories comprise 94.9% of the total: identical and repeated queries, failure to cache referrals, and invalid TLDs (e.g., `local`). These results validate and expand upon a 2003 study by Wessels and Fomenkov [13], which discovered only 2.15% legitimate traffic at F-root. These prior studies focus on behavior at steady state, whereas we study a rare event; however, if DNS resolvers transition to the new address as intended, we expect the steady state behavior at the new address to mimic the old.

D-root is not the first root server to be measured during an IP address change. Barber et al. measured the J-root address change [2], and Manning presented an overview of B-root's [10].

Both initiatives reported significant, prolonged levels of traffic at the old IP address—even two years after the change, despite the fact that root name server records have limited TTLs (currently 41 days for `A` records and 6 days for `NS` records). To determine the various software versions for the resolvers that appeared to be acting incorrectly, both the B- and J-root studies used the `fpdns` [1] fingerprinting tool. Newer resolver software versions (e.g., BIND9 [9]) appeared incorrect despite having implemented the mechanisms to (ostensibly) handle these IP address changes.

Nonetheless, the root cause behind this behavior has remained undetermined. While generally well-known that an increase of volume is imminent, there is surprisingly little insight into why. In this paper, we initiate a thorough analysis of D-root's address change and identify what we believe to be the major root causes behind this and other anomalies.

3. DATA COLLECTION AND OVERVIEW

In this section, we describe the data we collected, and identify three anomalies that drive our initial measurement analysis.

3.1 Data collection

The new address is hosted on a new interface on the same physical host as the old address. We port mirrored both interfaces, and collected two datasets. The first consists of full-payload packet captures using `tcpdump` on the aggregate traffic to both the new and old IP addresses. Unfortunately, the traffic volume ($\sim$20,000 queries per second on average) is too high to allow us to capture all packets for an extended period. Instead, once a minute, we capture 200,000 packets, which, after the changeover, results in approximately five seconds of packet capture every minute (i.e., we collect slightly more than 8.3% of all aggregate traffic).

We sampled complete packets for the week of the trace (one day prior and approximately six days after). In order to quantify steady state behavior, we sampled complete packets at irregular intervals (200,000 packets every 5–30 minutes, rather than once a minute) a few weeks prior to the address switch. We verified that our more complete data from the day before is representative of these earlier data. Finally, we sampled complete packets a few months after the address switch (April 29th to May 2nd) to measure traffic at both addresses.

Infrequent `tcpdump` packet captures may miss precisely when any given host first switched over. To measure this, we wrote a tool `switch` that captures (1) the precise time the source first contacts the new IP address, as well as (2) approximately how many queries it had issued to the old IP address since the changeover before switching over. This second dataset sacrifices full payloads in order to get more complete information regarding changeover times and behavior.

3.2 Overview of D-root's changeover

Table 1 summarizes the traffic at both addresses the week of the address change. Recall that our trace captures only the first 200,000 packets every minute; the query volumes in Table 1 are scaled up assuming the rate at which the first 200,000 packets are received is maintained for the entire minute. The new address was announced on DNS and operator mailing lists prior to the changeover and received a negligible amount of probe/test traffic the day before.

The line in Figure 1 plots the delay in resolvers discovering the new address. The dots represent their corresponding query volume; the highest volume resolvers find the new address relatively quickly. Figure 2 shows the query volume to the old and new addresses during the week of the changeover. Query volume to both the old and new addresses show the expected time-of-day variation. Further, the thin spikes are (usually DNSSEC amplification) attacks on the root servers, which have been previously documented [6].

The adoption of the new address is rapid, and the total traffic volume to the new address exceeds that to the old within 24 hours.

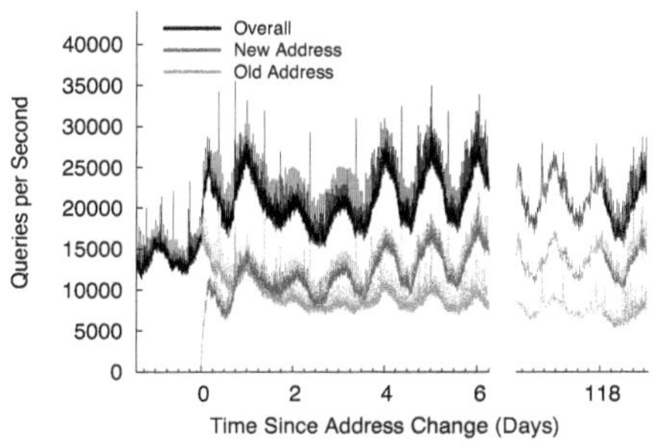

Figure 2: Number of queries per second sent to both the old and new address.

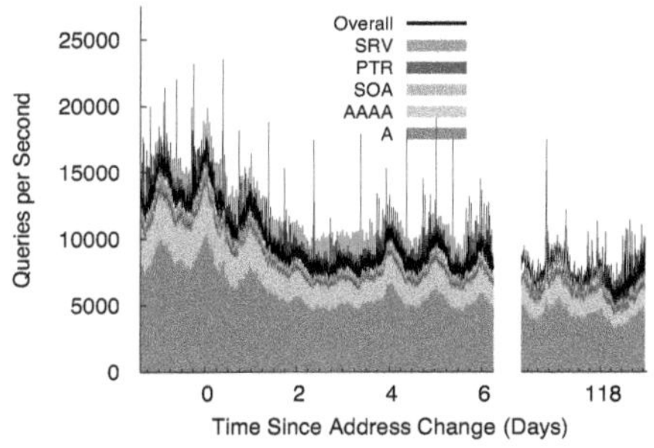

Figure 3: Query types at the *old address*, around the changeover time and several months later.

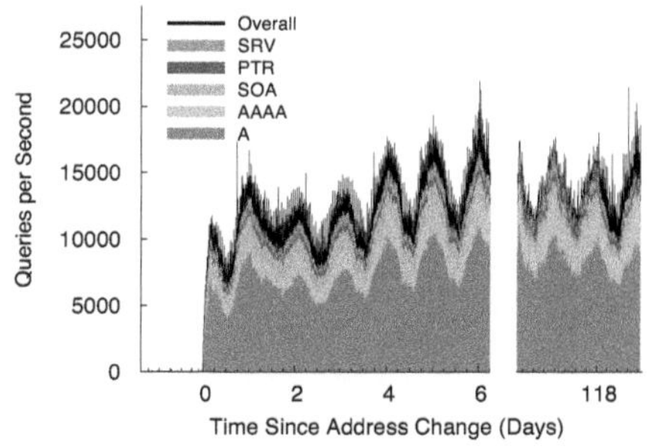

Figure 4: Query types at the *new address*, around the changeover time and several months later.

In contrast, it took nearly five days before the query volume to the new J-root address exceeded the old [2]. Note also that the new address is not initially attacked (the sharpest load spikes correspond only to queries at the old address).

Figure 2 shows that there is an immediate surge in traffic to the new address, and the rate at which it receives traffic far exceeds expected (and previously documented [2]) behavior. Further, the *total* query volume to the D-root increases dramatically, and that increase is sustained through the end of April (three months later). The old address continues to receive queries months after the changeover.

Figures 3 and 4 show the query volume to the old- and new server broken down by query type. The new address initially receives more `SOA` and `SRV` queries, but those queries are not sufficient to account for the increase in overall query volume. From Table 1, we also note that the new address receives far more invalid queries than the old address did. In contrast, the fraction of invalid queries to the old address decreases after the changeover.

These observations raise several questions that drive the analysis in the remainder of this paper:

(Q1) What causes the increase in overall traffic volume after the changeover day? Extra traffic after a root server changeover is to be expected, as resolvers will issue priming queries. But, with compliant name servers, these should constitute a small fraction of increased traffic and should dissipate once resolvers discover the root's new address and update their hints files. However, prior work has shown that there can be a prolonged increase in queries over time [2, 10]. Our data reflect this anomaly, as well (as seen in Figure 2). There are roughly 50% more queries shortly after the changeover than there were the day before, and this discrepancy continues for at least three months. While prior studies have observed this phenomenon, we are unaware of any investigation into the root cause, which is central to Q2.

(Q2) Why do servers continue to query the old address? It is not surprising that name servers continue to query the old address even months after the changeover date. Some very old BIND hints files contained exorbitantly long TTLs for root servers (99,999,999, or slightly more than three years), and given that root address changes are so uncommon, it is reasonable to assume that otherwise stable name server implementations may have faulty changeover logic. However, it is surprising that the overall volume to the old address has stabilized shortly—to approximately 50% of its original query volume—after the changeover.

(Q3) Why are queries to the old IP address on average more successful than those to the new address? Table 1 shows that the queries to the old address result in fewer `NXDOMAIN` responses than the queries to the new. To the best of our knowledge, we are the first to observe this phenomenon. Seemingly straightforward explanations for why a name server would remain at the old address—a misconfiguration or a faulty implementation—do not appear to explain these increased success rates.

4. WHY DOES QUERY VOLUME INCREASE?

Intuitively, there are two (not necessarily mutually exclusive) causes to an overall increase in volume: new resolvers could begin to query the D-root who did not before, or queries from some (possibly strict) subset of resolvers could increase. The number of servers contacting D-root did not change significantly in the 24 hours before and after the IP address change; in fact, they dropped slightly (1,336,167 sources before, 1,187,801 after).

4.1 Excitables issue many more queries

Overall query volume increases because a (relatively) small number of sources issue many more queries (100× or more) to the new address than they did to the old. We refer to these sources as *excitables*.

For each host querying the D-root, Figure 5 plots the ratio of queries per second one day before and one day after the address change. Along with the expected symmetric clustering around $y = x$ (the 1× line), Figure 5 clearly identifies the excitables: high volume hosts that increase their ratio by two or more orders of magnitude. By themselves, the top-1000 or so excitables account for ~58% of the increase in overall query volume. The top-1000 hosts that increase their query rate by at least 2× account for the entire increase in volume. Note that if high volume servers simply added the new address to their set of 13 root addresses (and if they queried each of the root servers uniformly) then their query volume would increase by $\frac{2/14}{1/13}$, less than 86%. Therefore, a different process is responsible for the increase in query volume.

4.2 Likely cause: Non-uniform server selection algorithms

Yu et al. [14] found that various versions of DNS resolvers (notably BIND and PowerDNS) adjust the rate at which they query different root servers based on RTTs, sometimes in nonintuitive ways. BIND 9.7, for instance, preferentially queries root servers with *greater* RTTs. In general, different versions of BIND do not distribute their query loads uniformly over all addresses that can

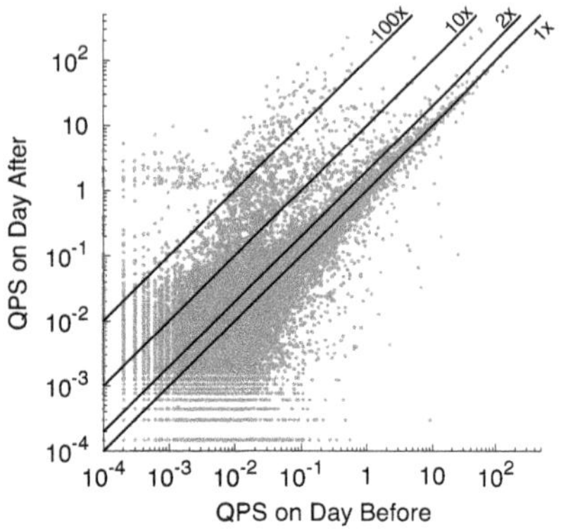

Figure 5: Comparison of queries per second (QPS) for each source in the 24 hours before and after the address change.

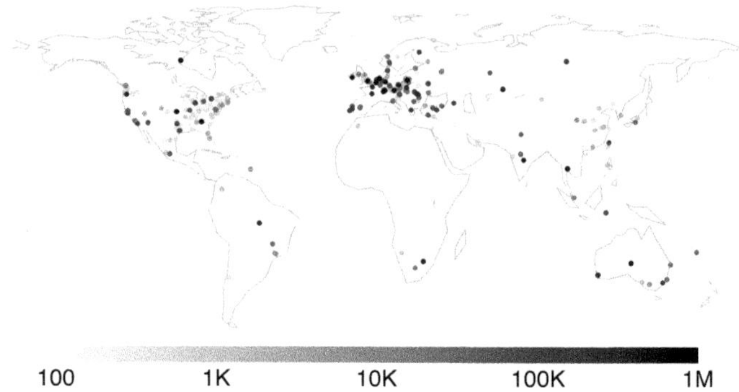

Figure 6: Locations and query volume of all excitables (resolvers whose query volume increased by at least 100× after the changeover). Most of the excitables' queries come from Europe.

serve a zone. Further, in our experiments, we see that relatively new versions of BIND (9.2, 9.5) do not implement priming correctly, and query both addresses, accounting for some of the increase in query volume, particularly in the 2×–10× range.

BIND implementations do not explain the sudden increase by 10×, 100× or more. PowerDNS, which is popular in Europe, on the other hand, exhibits a "spike distribution," causing it to almost exclusively contact the single lowest-RTT server [14]. Figure 6 shows the geographic distribution of servers whose query volumes increased by at least 100×; 62% of these servers are located in Europe, 20% in North America, 10% in Asia, 7% in Oceania, and the rest in South America and Africa. D-root, however, is not the lowest-RTT root server for European hosts; our measurements from both academic and residential hosts in Germany indicated that D-root (both old and new addresses) had an RTT one order of magnitude larger than the hosts' closest root server.

However, we have observed from an analysis of PowerDNS version 3.1 (the latest version on the D-root changeover date) that it will provide a greater weight to a *new* server, even though it does not have the lowest RTT. This can arise as certain corner cases may cause PowerDNS to stop updating the RTT-based server selection mechanism, causing PowerDNS to "stick" to a single server. It appears that the only way to exit this state is to restart the software. This bug, coupled with the fact that PowerDNS sends *all* its queries to the chosen server, could explain the increase in query volume. Further, PowerDNS has increased in popularity relatively recently, which would explain why prior address changes did not witness such extreme change in query volume. Finally, Figure 6 shows that most of the highest volume excitables are hosted in Europe, where PowerDNS is used extensively; PowerDNS reported in 2012 that they power around 30% of all domains in Europe [12]. **These observations point to resolvers using PowerDNS as being the primary source of increased traffic volume to D-root.**

Unfortunately, PowerDNS is not responsive to the latest version of the `fpdns` fingerprinting tool, and we have not yet developed a robust method for fingerprinting PowerDNS resolvers. (Reassuringly, the `fpdns` tool fails to identify the high volume hosts as BIND.) We are in the process of trying to both identify PowerDNS resolvers in the wild, and to reproduce the bug in older versions of PowerDNS which would enable definitive attribution of the increase in volume to PowerDNS.

5. WHO'S STILL USING THE OLD ADDRESS?

Technically, a DNS root IP address change does not require maintaining connectivity on the old IP address if all resolvers handle an individual failure by contacting any of the other 12 root servers. However, older resolvers that do not perform priming queries (and use outdated hints files) may completely break. A fundamental question facing a DNS root address change is: At what point can one responsibly shut down the old IP address? When all hosts switch over? When some fraction of traffic switches over? Or perhaps when it appears that the only hosts still contacting the old address are faulty?

The original expectations for D-root's changeover were that (1) the vast majority of traffic would migrate over to the new address relatively quickly, (2) the only remaining traffic would be due to faulty servers or botnets, and thus (3) a few months of running the old address would suffice.[1] However, the changeover has not been as rapid in practice: 63% of sources do not switch over after four months (by May 2, 2013), and they generate 4,721 queries per second on average.

In this section, we investigate why, after several months, the old address continues to see such a high volume of queries. We do not believe there to be a single reason for this. Instead, we seek to classify name servers among several groups, and to identify the likely causes among these groups.

5.1 Classifying resolvers

We begin by investigating the types of access behaviors resolvers exhibit towards the two addresses. So as not to confuse hosts who *never* change to the new address from those who have not *yet* changed, we focus on data collected in April and May 2013, three to four months after turning on the new IP address (and well beyond the 41 day TTL). Our hypothesis was that, after this much time, there would be very few hosts on the old address, most on the new address, and few to none who regularly contact both, as that would be incorrect behavior.

The results in Figure 7 tell another story. In this figure, we plot for each source viewed in our April/May data the difference between the fraction of queries it issued at the old address and the fraction it issued at the new. A resolver who contacted only the old address has a value of 1; a resolver who contacted only the new has value -1; a value of 0 corresponds to an equal amount of queries

[1] L-root had similar expectations, and in fact relinquished the old IP address after six months, which was "hijacked" soon after [5].

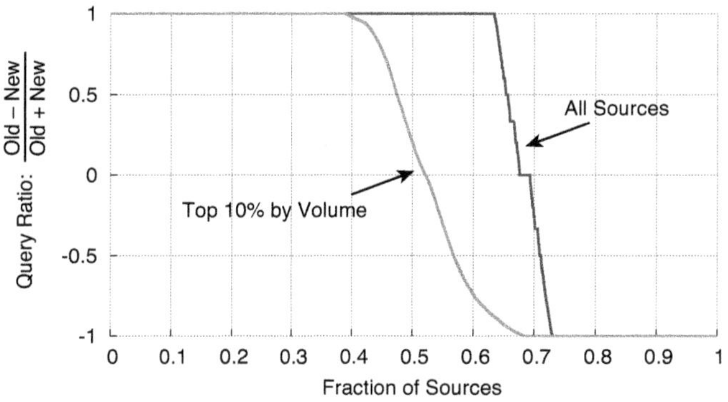

Figure 7: Fraction of sources with various query patterns to the old and new IP addresses. A query ratio of 1 or -1 corresponds to sources who only send to the old or new IP address, respectively.

to old and new, and so on. From this we see that of the top 10% of the hosts by volume (who constitute roughly 80% of the overall volume), a mere 32% contact the new address only. Approximately 40% of the resolvers we saw in April/May contact the old only. We refer to these hosts who latch onto the old address as *barnacles*.

This leaves a remainder of about 28% who swap between both old and new at varying rates—we refer to these as *swappers*. We investigated the rate at which these hosts swap (data not plotted). The majority do so infrequently (roughly once every 20 queries), though some (about 2%) swap at least as fast as every two queries they issue.

The rest of this section analyzes those who continue to query the old address after several months: the barnacles and the swappers. As a point of comparison, we also include a baseline of hosts which we refer to as *normals*: sources we expect to act in a reasonably correct manner. Specifically, a set of large ISP nameservers constitutes our "normals": Verizon DSL, Verizon HS, QWEST, COX, and Speakeasy/Megapath (business only).

5.2 Classifying root causes

For each host from each of the three classes of resolvers (barnacles, swappers, and normals), we measure it along two features. The first is the fraction of failed queries the host issues (including those that issue `NXDOMAIN` responses as well as malformed queries). The rationale behind this feature comes from a manual investigation of the data; we identified that some hosts never failed (because they issue the same small set of queries constantly), and some always failed (because they issued seemingly random strings, or incorrectly configured their internal root DNS servers and issued many queries for a TLD of `local` or `internal`). With a correctly implemented cache, one would expect high failure rates at the root (as the root knows of relatively few, long-TTL TLDs).

The second feature we measure a host against is its *query diversity*: the number of unique queries (in terms of domain name) it issues divided by the total number of queries it issues. Query diversity takes a value in (0,1], and with correctly implemented negative and positive caches, one would expect diversity to be high.

We present plots for all three types in Figure 8. We use the April–May dataset for classifying hosts as barnacles and swappers, and the more detailed January dataset for calculating their failure rates, query diversities, and query volumes.

Normals. As expected, the normals exhibit high failure rates and high diversity, forming a large cluster in the upper right corner of Figure 8(c). It is important to note, however, that a high failure rate and high query diversity does not necessarily imply correct behavior. For instance, 47% of the queries from a subset of the Google public DNS resolvers contain random strings (thus have high diversity) and include a TLD of `internal` (and thus have a high failure rate). This is likely caused by a misconfiguration of some of Google's name servers meant to serve a private namespace.

Barnacles. The vast majority of barnacles (Fig. 8(a)) exhibit low failure rates, suggesting that these are resolvers that are misconfigured, used for measurement, or used for attack. *Disproportionately low failure rates from hosts who never query the new address are a viable explanation for the anomaly wherein the old address experiences a lower failure rate than the new (Q3).*

Among the barnacles, we see resolvers that continually query for: (1) lists of known name servers (likely measurements), (2) DNSBLs (spambots or attacks), or (3) very small sets of names (embedded devices that implement their own resolver looking for updates and patches). We believe *all* of the barnacles with low error rates (<10%) are pieces of software issuing mechanized queries using incorrect DNS implementations. Moreover, we believe that barnacles with very low query diversity (wherein the resolver asks for the same name repeatedly) can be specifically attributed to misconfigurations or hard-coded attack software that does not have the facility for handling address changes.

There are a few very high volume barnacles that have approximately 30% query diversity and 50% failures. These are OpenDNS resolvers. Because OpenDNS resolvers are publicly available, we

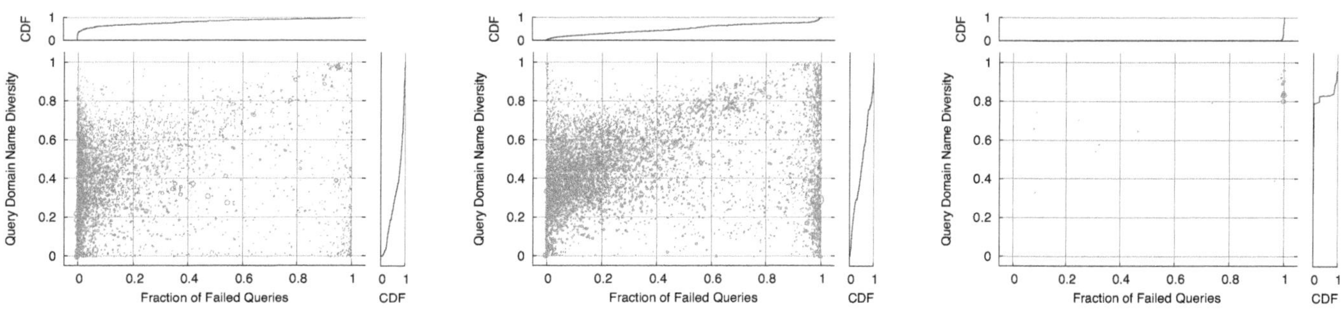

Figure 8: Diversity of domain names in queries versus the fraction of failed queries for the three types of resolvers. Each circle represents a source /24, where the area is a function of the query volume.

conjecture that their behavior is a composite of normal queries, attacks, and misconfigurations.

Swappers. Finally, swappers (Fig. 8(b)) exhibit a nearly uniform distribution of failures (note the linear CDF at the top of the plot). We believe that the very low error rate queries in this set also represent mechanized bots, as do the very low diversity queries. Moreover, there is a positive correlation between failure rates and diversity. We believe the bulk of these (relatively low volume) resolvers simply use both addresses interchangeably. We are in the process of fingerprinting each of these resolvers and with the hope of mapping the ones that respond to known implementations that prime incorrectly and use all known addresses.

6. DISCUSSION AND OPEN QUESTIONS

Many signs of excitables point to PowerDNS: it is most popular in Europe (where the majority of excitables come from), we have identified that some versions include both of D-root's IP addresses in its list of root name servers, and its root selection algorithm can send all queries to a single name server. However, our runs of `fpdns` have turned up only a single PowerDNS resolver running an old version of the software. `fpdns` is known to be unable to identify PowerDNS; further, the vast majority of the European resolvers are configured to not answer external queries. Validating our hypothesis—either by improving `fpdns` or by simply running a PowerDNS resolver from multiple vantage points (with different RTTs to the new and old addresses)—is an area of ongoing work.

Our analysis of why name servers continue to visit the old address identifies many examples of what appear to be misconfigurations, buggy code, or scanners. For example, many queries from these barnacles are redundant yet they infrequently fail; among these, we have identified resolvers that scan DNSBLs. One question is: do these bugs and behaviors occur at smaller scales for the less-concentrated TLD servers or even others, perhaps creating similarly inexplicable fluctuations in traffic volume? Answering this question may provide greater confidence that barnacle's redundant queries account for the large difference in query success rates between the old and new IP addresses.

Answering these questions may require old-fashioned footwork: getting in touch with operators. One promising, potential outcome of this is that a DNS root server IP address change may be able to assist in identifying and raising awareness about bugs, common misconfiguration errors, and possibly attacks.

Indeed, perhaps changing root DNS IP addresses should be done every so often as a matter of regular practice! So doing would possibly encourage operators to run serviceably recent versions of BIND or PowerDNS and discourage hard-coding. In the long run—and if our hypothesis is correct that many of the barnacles are buggy or forgotten code—then the occasional address change could serve as a crude form of garbage collection.

Acknowledgments

We thank Xiehua Li from Hunan University, the anonymous reviewers, and our shepherd, Mark Allman, for their helpful comments on the paper. We also thank James Litton for his help in analyzing the PowerDNS code. This work was supported in part by NSF Awards CNS-0917098, IIS-0964541, and CNS-1255314.

7. REFERENCES

[1] R. Arends and J. Schlyter. `fpdns`. `https://github.com/kirei/fpdns`.

[2] P. Barber, M. Larson, M. Kosters, and P. Toscano. Life and Times of J-Root. In *NANOG32*, Oct 2004.

[3] N. Brownlee, K. Claffy, and E. Nemeth. DNS Measurements at a Root Server. In *IEEE Global Communications Conference (GLOBECOM)*, 2001.

[4] S. Castro, D. Wessels, M. Fomenkov, and K. Claffy. A Day at the Root of the Internet. *ACM SIGCOMM Computer Communication Review (CCR)*, 38(5):41–46, 2008.

[5] D. Conrad. Ghosts of Root Servers Past. `http://blog.icann.org/2008/05/ghosts-of-root-servers-past/`.

[6] A. Cowperthwaite and A. Somayaji. The Futility of DNSSec. In *Annual Symposium Information Assurance (ASIA)*, 2010.

[7] P. Danzig, K. Obraczka, and A. Kumar. An Analysis of Wide-Area Name Server Traffic: A Study of the Internet Domain Name System. In *SIGCOMM Conference on Data Communication*, 1992.

[8] T. Hardie. Distributing Authoritative Nameservers via Shared Unicast Addresses. *RFC 3258*, Apr 2002.

[9] Internet Systems Consortium. BIND. `https://www.isc.org/software/bind`.

[10] B. Manning. Persistent Queries and Phantom Nameservers. In *CAIDA-WIDE Workshop*, 2006.

[11] C. Partridge, T. Mendez, and W. Milliken. Host Anycasting Service. *RFC 1546*, Nov 1993.

[12] PowerDNS Technologies. `https://www.powerdns.com/resources/PowerDNSTechnologies.pdf`.

[13] D. Wessels and M. Fomenkov. Wow, That's a Lot of Packets. In *Passive and Active Network Measurement Workshop (PAM)*, 2003.

[14] Y. Yu, D. Wessels, M. Larson, and L. Zhang. Authority Server Selection in DNS Caching Resolvers. *ACM SIGCOMM Computer Communication Review (CCR)*, 42(2):80–86, 2012.

Understanding the Domain Registration Behavior of Spammers

Shuang Hao
Georgia Tech
shao@cc.gatech.edu

Matthew Thomas
Verisign, Inc.
mthomas@verisign.com

Vern Paxson
ICSI & UC Berkeley
vern@cs.berkeley.edu

Nick Feamster
Georgia Tech
feamster@cc.gatech.edu

Christian Kreibich
ICSI & Lastline, Inc.
christian@icir.org

Chris Grier
ICSI & UC Berkeley
grier@cs.berkeley.edu

Scott Hollenbeck
Verisign, Inc.
shollenbeck@verisign.com

ABSTRACT

Spammers register a tremendous number of domains to evade blacklisting and takedown efforts. Current techniques to detect such domains rely on crawling spam URLs or monitoring lookup traffic. Such detection techniques are only effective after the spammers have already launched their campaigns, and thus these countermeasures may only come into play after the spammer has already reaped significant benefits from the dissemination of large volumes of spam. In this paper we examine the registration process of such domains, with a particular eye towards features that might indicate that a given domain likely has a malicious purpose at registration time, before it is ever used for an attack. Our assessment includes exploring the characteristics of registrars, domain life cycles, registration bursts, and naming patterns. By investigating zone changes from the `.com` TLD over a 5-month period, we discover that spammers employ bulk registration, that they often re-use domains previously registered by others, and that they tend to register and host their domains over a small set of registrars. Our findings suggest steps that registries or registrars could use to frustrate the efforts of miscreants to acquire domains in bulk, ultimately reducing their agility for mounting large-scale attacks.

Categories and Subject Descriptors

C.2.3 [**Computer-Communication Networks**]: Network Operations—*Network monitoring*; K.6.5 [**Security and Protection**]; K.4.1 [**Computers and Society**]: Public Policy Issues—*Abuse and crime involving computers*

General Terms

Measurement, Security

IMC'13, October 23–25, 2013, Barcelona, Spain.

http://dx.doi.org/10.1145/2504730.2504753.

Keywords

DNS; Domain Registration; Spam; Blacklist

1. INTRODUCTION

Spammers and other miscreants often make heavy use of domains registered in the DNS to direct victims to Web sites that host scams, malware, and other malicious content. To mitigate these threats, network operators employ blacklisting of domains, but the rate at which new domains appear makes developing decisions sufficiently quickly to blacklist domains particularly challenging. Ideally, such decisions could be made at *registration time* rather than at *usage time*, enabling "proactive blocking". However, developing registration-time decisions about which new domains will likely see subsequent malicious employment appears quite daunting given the very large rate at which new domains appear (tens of thousands per day for `.com`). Instead, existing DNS reputation systems use either evidence of malicious use (*e.g.*, appearance of names in a spam trap) or the characteristics of DNS lookup traffic [1, 4]. Such systems generally must observe a significant volume of DNS lookups before determining the reputation to associate with a domain.

In this work we seek to understand the nature of spammer domain registrations with an ultimate goal of hampering the ease with which attackers currently acquire large volumes of registered domains. We do so by analyzing a range of registration-time features as manifest in changes seen every 5 minutes to `.com` over a 5-month period. For partial ground truth in assessing which of these registrations reflected spammer activity, we draw upon domains identified by several large blacklist feeds associated with email spam campaigns.

Our study develops the following findings:

- We confirm the earlier finding that *only a handful of registrars account for the majority of spammer domains* [18]. 70% of spammer domains came from 10 registrars, though these registrars accounted for only about 20% of all new domains added to the zone. Thus, miscreants appear to prefer those specific registrars, and positive actions from these registrars could have significant impact in impeding the use of large volumes of newly registered domains for spam activity.
- *Groups of domains registered by a given registrar at a single time exhibit two statistically distinct patterns.* We show

that groups of registrations very often follow a distribution well-described by a compound Poisson process, but many registrars also exhibit registration "spikes" that this process would produce only with exceedingly low probability.

- *Spammer domains occur in such "spikes" with much more prevalence than in general (non-spike) registration activity.* This finding suggests that spammers find economic and/or management benefit to registering domains in large batches, and thus detection procedures that leverage the presence of such spikes could force spammers to adopt less efficient approaches for their registrations.
- *Spammers frequently re-register expired domains that originally had a clean history.* Presumably using such names alleviates spammers of the burden of generating plausible-looking names (though we also observe algorithmically generated names), providing textual diversity as well as a benign past reputation that may aid in initially avoiding detection.

We hope these findings will ultimately lead to the development of a detection procedure that can accurately identify names intended for malicious use at *time-of-registration* rather than only later at *time-of-use*.

The remainder of this paper is organized as follows. §2 introduces the taxonomy and §3 surveys the related work. §4 describes the datasets that we collected and used in our analysis. In §5 we use the datasets to illuminate the benefits of identifying spammer domains at registration time. We then proceed with investigating the prospects for doing so, starting in §6, which analyzes the distribution of spammer and non-spammer domains across registrars and DNS servers. §7 presents our findings regarding bulk registration and our approach to identify registration spikes. §8 associates the domain life cycle with registration to dissect spammers' strategies to acquire domains.

2. BACKGROUND: DNS REGISTRATION PROCESS AND LIFE CYCLE

To set the context for our work, here we sketch the process by which malicious parties (and others) register domains and the subsequent life cycle regarding use of the domains.

Figure 1 shows the domain registration process. There are three roles in the figure: registrants (domain registration applicants), registrars (*e.g.*, `GoDaddy`), registries (*e.g.*, Verisign). Registries are responsible for managing the registration of domain names within the top-level domains (TLDs) and generating the zone files that list domain names and their authoritative nameservers. For example, Verisign serves as the registrar for `.com`, CNNIC for `.cn`, and DENIC for `.de` [32]. In this work we focus on `.com`, the largest TLD [30], which has long reflected a major target abused by miscreants for spamming activities [27].

ICANN accredits registrars, which contract with TLD registries to provide registration service to the public. Presently around 900 registrars exist across all TLDs, the bulk of which serve `.com` (and often other TLDs) [25]. A registrant selects a *designated registrar* to register a domain. The designated registrar in turn connects to the registry's SRS (Shared Registration System) via EPP (Extensible Provisioning Protocol, RFC5730 [14]) or RRP (Registry Registrar Protocol, RFC3632 [13]) to manage the zones. The registry updates the corresponding DNS zone information in the database and uses RZU (Rapid Zone Update) to add the DNS information in the top-level domain nameservers. Domain registration operates in a real-time fashion, resulting in only a short interval between registration requests and domains becoming active in the zone.

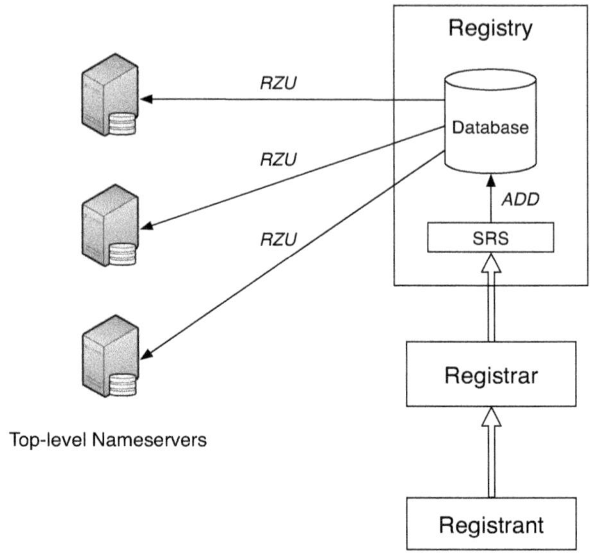

Figure 1: *Process of second-level domain registration.*

Figure 2 indicates the life cycle of a second-level domain in the `.com` zone. We show only a simplified cycle; see ICANN's registry agreements [15] for a full description of the possible states of a domain. In order to obtain a domain, registrants need to select available domain names that are not registered and in use. The registration term usually ranges from 1 year to 10 years. If the registrant chooses to renew a domain, the expiration date will be extended and the domain remains in the zone files. The renewal could occur at any time during the registration period, the *Auto-Renew Grace Period* (for domains the registrar has already marked for renewal) and the *Redemption Grace Period* (for domains marked for deletion). If the registrant chooses not to renew, the domain expires, gets removed from the zone and becomes available for others to register. Two special periods mark the beginning and end of a domain's life cycle. The 5-day *Add Grace Period* begins immediately after domain registration, allowing the registrant to change their mind, undo the registration, and receive full credit for the registration fee [16]. To limit *domain tasting* abuse, *i.e.*, taking advantage of no-cost trial periods for domains, registrars limit the number of registrations a registrant may revert per month. The domain enters a 5-day *Pending Delete Period* that prevents further alterations to the domain's status before it gets unregistered and becomes available for re-registration [29, 22]. We explore how this life cycle relates to the registration of spammer domains in §8.

3. RELATED WORK

DNS Resolution. Most previous DNS-based detection studies have focused on analyzing lookup traffic. These studies date back many years to work performed by Danzig *et al.* [6] and Jung *et al.* [17], both of which examined lookup behavior from the vantage point of lookups produced by individual sites. Notos [1] and EXPOSURE [4] leverage DNS lookup behavior within a local network to formulate reputations associated with domains. Kopis monitors the traffic to authoritative nameservers and top-level domain servers to achieve global visibility to detect abnormal activities [2]. Our previous work actively probed the DNS records and studied the lookup traffic of second-level domains after their registration to characterize those associated with Internet attacks [12]. In contrast, our

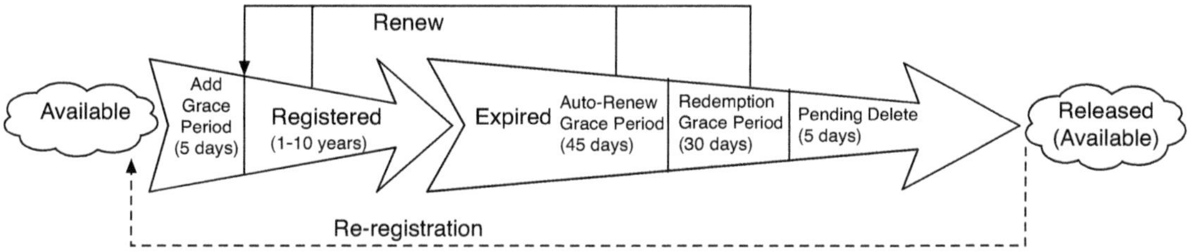

Figure 2: *Life cycle of a second-level domain.*

work here analyzes the *registration patterns* of spammer domains to illuminate potential opportunities for early detection of spammer domains.

Registrars and Registration. Several lines of recent work have examined the roles of registrars and registries. Coull *et al.* studied the registration abuse phenomenon, including domain-name speculation, tasting, and front-running (where registrars abuse insider information to obtain a domain, thus locking out other registrars) [5]. Liu *et al.* investigated the effect of registry policy changes and registrar actions taken to terminate domains used by illicit on-line pharmacies [19], finding domain pricing and domain takedowns to have at least temporary deterring effect. Felegyhazi *et al.* inferred groups of malicious domains based on the DNS servers and daily registration concurrency associated with known-bad *seed* domains [10]. While closest to the theme of our work, their approach's need to identify such seeds complicates its application at registration time. In addition, we provide a significantly more granular analysis (5-minute zone changes, modeling the registration process of individual registrars, statistical identification of "spikes"), and data broader in scope (non-spam registrations vs. spam registrations, domain life cycle, naming patterns).

Domain Generation Algorithms. In an effort to resist takedown of centralized command and control (C&C) servers, recent botnets such as Conficker, Kraken and Bobax have used domain generation algorithms (DGAs) to query a set of domains. The botmaster needs to only register one domain of the set to enable bots to access the C&C server. Yadav *et al.*studied different metrics to identify botnets by finding randomly generated domain names [31]. Antonakakis *et al.* developed clustering techniques to discover new DGA variants and compromised hosts [3]. Unlike these works, we examine the domain names as actually registered in the `.com` TLD in an attempt to identify lexical patterns distinguishing spammer domains.

4. DATA COLLECTION

In this section we describe the datasets used in our analysis, which we summarize in Table 1. Our primary dataset consists of changes made to the `.com` zone every five minutes for a 5-month period, March–July 2012. In addition, we interpret the significance (*i.e.*, spammer or otherwise) of new registrations in `.com` based on any subsequent appearance of a given domain in either a "spam trap" we operate or a well-known blacklist. We term a newly registered domain that appears in either the spam trap or on one of the blacklists as a *spammer domain*, and a domain that does not as a *non-spammer domain*.

Domain Registration. Verisign operates the `.com` zone under contract to ICANN. Changes to the zone appear in *Domain Name Zone Alert (DNZA)* files, which indicate (1) the addition of new

Data	*Collection period*	*Update granularity*	`.com` *domains*
DNZA	March–July 2012	5 minutes	12,824,401
Spam trap	March–October 2012	real time	65,298
URIBL	March–October 2012	hourly	149,555
SURBL	August–October 2012	hourly	490,439

Table 1: *Summary of data feeds.*

domains, (2) the removal of existing domains, and (3) changes to existing domains in terms of revisions to their associated nameservers. Our data includes captures of the DNZA files as recorded every five minutes, time periods we refer to as *epochs*.

Registrars and History. Domain registrations must be executed by an ICANN-accredited registrar chosen by the user registering the domain (the "registrant"). The registrant pays the registrar a fee for this service. In general, we have no visibility into the registrants associated with particular domains (sometimes `WHOIS` information provides their identities, but numerous registrars provide a "private registration" service that masks this information). One can however obtain information about a given domain's registrar based on `WHOIS` information, or using third-party services such as DomainTools [8]. Thus, we can only attempt to tease out the registration behavior of individual users as inferable from the registration activities of individual registrars.

A given domain added to the zone might reflect either a first-time registration or a re-registration of a previously registered domain. We can distinguish these two based on historical `WHOIS` information; for re-registered domains, we can obtain when the domain was previously deleted from the zone [28].

Identifying Spammer Domains. In general we would like to associate with domains a label indicating whether an attacker registered the domain for spamming purposes. Since we lack comprehensive ground truth regarding the ultimate use of domains, to this end we use two proxies: subsequent appearance of a newly registered domain in: (1) an email spam campaign, or (2) a domain blacklist.

For the first of these, we operated a spam trap, *i.e.*, our own domain with an associated mail server that has no legitimate email addresses. We can confidently consider all emails sent to the spam trap as spam. Although the spam contains non-spam related domains (*e.g.*, `youtube.com`), by restricting our focus to domains recently registered (March–July 2012) we can filter down the domains appearing in the spam trap to those very likely used for spamming.

For the second, we subscribed to three major DNS blacklists, URIBL, SURBL, and Spamhaus DBL. During our subsequent analysis we found strong indications that the Spamhaus DBL very

	New domains	Subset of new domains appearing in spam trap	Subset of new domains appearing in URIBL	Subset of new domains appearing in SURBL	Subset of new domains appearing in spam messages **or** blacklists
March 2012	2,832,867	6,072	12,572	18,875	24,458
April 2012	2,596,192	3,970	12,111	21,824	27,300
May 2012	2,641,466	4,091	10,726	21,616	25,936
June 2012	2,383,010	2,861	8,651	21,872	24,763
July 2012	2,389,636	2,958	8,875	29,525	32,394
Registrations over 5 months	12,824,401	19,930	52,857	113,358	134,455

Table 2: *Monthly data statistics.*

likely uses registration-time features to establish the reputation of a domain (see the discussion in §5.3). Given that, then since part of our focus is to assess to what degree registration-time features correlate with a domain's subsequent employment in an abusive context, for our purposes we cannot soundly use a domain's presence on the Spamhaus DBL as such an indicator. Consequently, we omit this source from our analysis other than to demonstrate the indicators that it uses such features for blacklisting.

Summary of Data. Table 2 shows the number of second-level `.com` domains registered in each month, and the subset of those registrations that later appeared in either our spam trap or on one of the two blacklists. Of the 12,824,401 second-level domains registered in the `.com` zone over five months, 134,455 reflect spammer domains.

5. LONGEVITY OF SPAMMER DOMAINS

In this section we look at several facets of the time periods over which spammers employ their domains: the age of domains (time since registration) when they appear on blacklists or in spam campaigns; the amount of time during which domains continue to see use once spammers begin to employ them; and the amount of time between a *recent* registration of a spammer domain and its subsequent appearance. Our examination shows that detecting spammer domains at the time of their registration can offer significant advantages.

5.1 Age of Domains Used for Spamming

We first consider the degree to which spammers employ relatively "fresh" (recently registered) domains in their spam campaigns. If spammers primarily rely upon long-lived domains, then we cannot hope to gain much benefit from disrupting the registration of new spammer domains.

Figure 3 shows the distribution of the amount of time elapsed between the registration of a given `.com` spammer domain and its appearance in either the URIBL blacklist or our spam trap. (We omit results for SURBL because we lack sufficiently long data from it to compute a comparable distribution.) In particular, for all `.com` domains that appeared in either URIBL or our spam trap from March–July 2012, we determine the domain's date of registration, and plot the difference between that time and the first such appearance. Overall, 35–40% of the domains were registered within the past 30 days, and 40–50% within 60 days. (In addition, since listings in URIBL will likely lag behind actual use, and the spam trap will include some long-lived benign domains such as `google.com`, the age of actual spammer domains at time of first use will skew somewhat lower than these figures.)

Because domain registrations represent a direct cost for spammers, the fact that spammers frequently employ domains registered quite recently (within a few months) indicates that they have an ongoing need to acquire new domains. Thus, if we impair their reg-

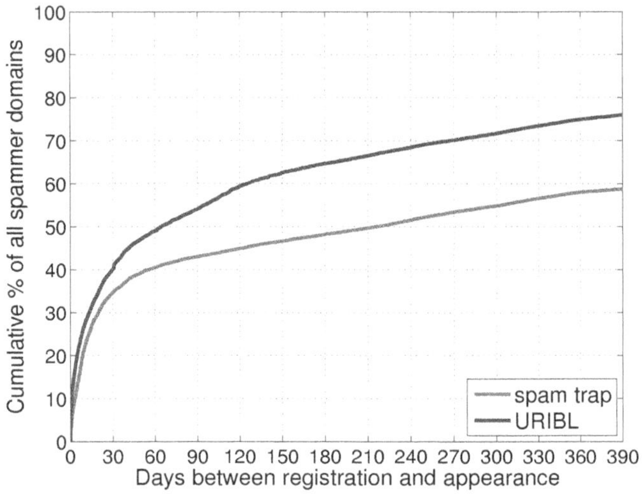

Figure 3: *Distribution of days between domain registration and appearance of a* `.com` *domain in either our spam trap (red) or URIBL (blue).*

istration activities, we can add friction to their general enterprise. In addition, given the quantity of domains that spammers use, we would expect that their need to continually acquire new domains will incline them towards registering new domains in batches, a feature that we analyze in §7.1.

5.2 Duration-of-Use in Spam Campaigns

Another facet of spammer domain longevity concerns for how long a spammer uses a given domain. If domains see only brief periods of use, then activity-based blacklisting will fail to effectively block the spammer's fruitful employment of a domain unless the blacklisting occurs very soon after the onset of use. If so, then the benefits of identifying spammer domains prior to use, such as at-time-of-registration, rise.

We can assess duration-of-use from our spam trap data, and indeed we find that more than 60% of the `.com` domains observed in the spam trap appear during only a single day (75% for $\leq$ 10 days, and only 5% for $\geq$ 60 days). This "single-shot" nature of most of the spammer domains complicates blacklisting efforts—though it also may reflect the efficacy of such efforts at narrowing the window during which spammers can profitably use their domains—and highlights the benefit of at-time-of-registration detection.

5.3 Lifetime of Recently Registered Domains

Finally, we examine the use by spammers of newly registered domains *given* that we flagged it as a spammer domain (and thus it necessarily appeared in our spam trap, or in one of our black-

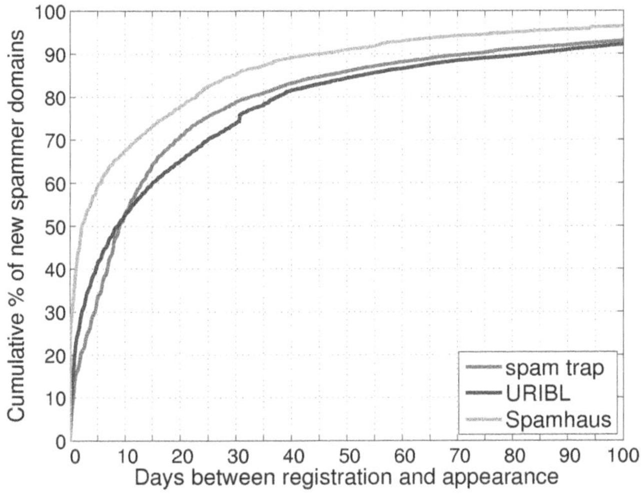

Figure 4: *Distribution of days between domain registration and appearance of a newly registered* `.com` *domain in either our spam trap, URIBL, or the Spamhaus blacklist.*

lists, during the coming months). Figure 4 shows the distribution of the time between the registration of such spammer domains and their appearance in our spam trap or in a blacklist.[1] We see that a number of days may pass after registration prior to the domain's appearance. This delay again indicates we might gain significant benefit from identifying spammer domains at the time of registration, before any activity takes place.

The figure also shows the delay between registration and blacklisting for the Spamhaus DBL. We observed that Spamhaus blacklists domains much earlier than URIBL—or even than the appearance of the domain in our spam trap. We confirmed with Spamhaus that they base their DBL entries in part on information gathered at registration time to facilitate more proactive blacklisting. Because Spamhaus uses registration-time features to construct their blacklist, the presence of a Spamhaus domain in a blacklist does not provide *independent* evidence that features we consider for at-registration-time detection indeed will have power for identifying spammer domains. Given this lack of independence, we refrain from further analysis treating the appearance of a domain on the Spamhaus blacklist as separate confirmation of the domain as one employed by spammers.

Finally, we examine the extent to which any particular blacklist covers the full set of spammer domains, and the extent to which these blacklists overlap with one another. Figure 5 shows the intersection of spammer domains registered from March–July 2012, based on the information from our spam trap, and from URIBL and SURBL. We observe that each data source identified many spammer domains that did not appear in the other information sources. This lack of overlap presumably indicates that different blacklist sources use different criteria to determine whether to include a domain in its blacklist.

[1]It is important to keep in mind the distinction between Figure 3 and Figure 4. The former is conditioned on any domain appearing in either the spam trap or the blacklist during the five-month period; the latter is conditioned on the appearance of any domain *registered* during the five-month period.

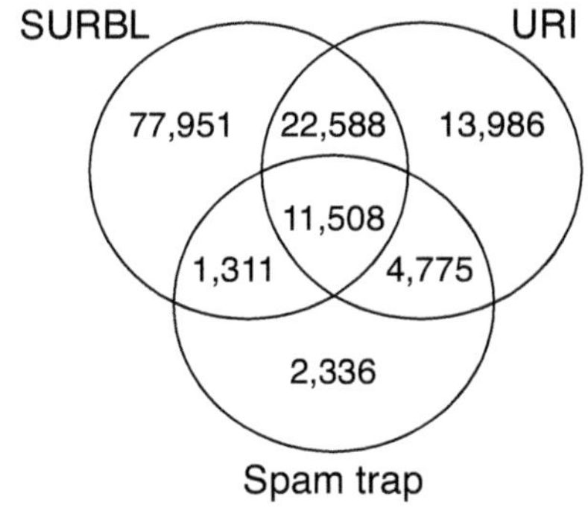

Figure 5: *Venn diagram of spammer domains for different identification methods.*

6. SPAM DOMAIN INFRASTRUCTURE

In this section we briefly look at the infrastructure supporting individual spammer domain registrations: the registrars used to register these domains, the DNS servers initially selected to resolve the domains, and how this infrastructure compares with that used for non-spammer domains. Our analysis supports the following:

- Nearly 70% of spammer domains originated from 10 registrars, while those registrars accounted for only 20% of all newly registered domains over the 5 months of our data.
- Spammer domains primarily use the regular authoritative DNS servers operated by the registrar, at least initially. This finding suggests that efforts to proactively blacklist spammer domains should focus on registrar-level analysis rather than DNS-server analysis.

We now develop these findings in more detail.

6.1 Registrars Used for Spammer Domains

We first examine the proportion of registrations at each registrar that correspond to spammer domains and how this proportion varies by registrar. Table 3 shows the registrars, ranked by the number of spammer domains that they registered over the five-month period of our study (shown in the second column); the third column shows the percentage of known spammer domains registered by that registrar. The fourth column indicates the cumulative percentage of spammer domains for the top registrars. Interestingly, 46% of the spammer domains correspond to just two registrars. This statistic implies that the positive actions from a small set of registrars might significantly frustrate the use of newly registered spammer domains. We treated `GoDaddy` separately because it manages significantly more domains than other registrars; hence, even though it registers a significant number of spammer domains, the number of spammer domains that it registers remains a small fraction of the total number of domains that it registers.

Our findings agree with a similar study by Levchenko *et al.* [18], and also with an independent study that ranks the registrars serving rogue Internet pharmacies [24]. Indeed, three registrars—`Moniker`, `Tucows` and `Bizcn.com, Inc.`—appeared in both studies as top-ten registrars for spammer domains.

Next, we explore how the registrars compare, in terms of the number of spammer and non-spammer domains that they register. Figure 6 shows the number of spammer and non-spammer domains that each registrar registered over the course of our study; each dot represents a registrar. Dots above the diagonal show registrars that registered more non-spammer domains than spammer

	Spammer domains			All registered domains	
Registrar	*Number*	*Percentage*	*Cumulative pct.*	*Percentage*	*Cumulative pct.*
eNom, Inc.	36,245	27.03	**27.03**	7.62	**7.62**
Moniker Online Services, Inc.	25,488	19.01	**46.05**	0.67	**8.30**
Tucows.com Co.	5,996	4.47	**50.52**	6.28	**14.57**
INTERNET.bs Corp.	5,786	4.32	**54.83**	0.70	**15.27**
Bizcn.com, Inc.	5,638	4.21	**59.04**	0.70	**15.97**
Trunkoz Technologies Pvt Ltd. d/b/a OwnRegistrar.com	4,577	3.41	**62.45**	0.05	**16.02**
PDR Ltd. d/b/a PublicDomainRegistry.com	3,595	2.68	**65.13**	3.08	**19.10**
OnlineNIC, Inc.	2,857	2.13	**67.26**	0.70	**19.80**
Center of Ukrainian Internet Names	2,781	2.07	**69.33**	0.06	**19.86**
Register.com, Inc.	2,540	1.89	**71.22**	2.18	**22.04**
GoDaddy.com, LLC	5,532	4.13	75.35	30.75	53.79

Table 3: *The 10 registrars that registered the greatest number of spammer domains.*

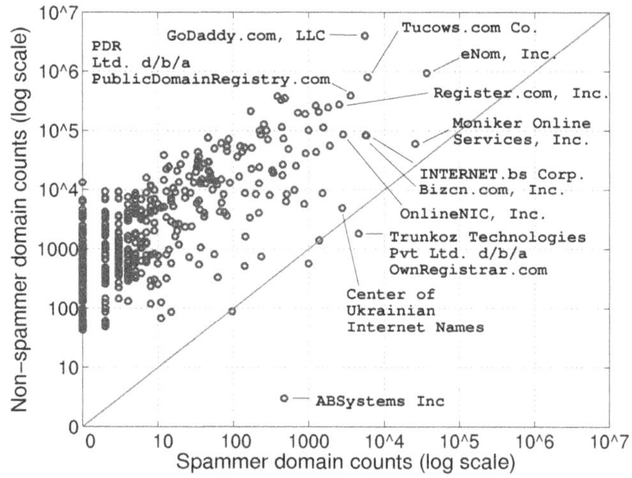

Figure 6: *Counts of spammer versus non-spammer domains on the registrars.*

ones, and dots below the diagonal line reflect a ratio towards higher spammer domain registrations than non-spammer. The figure labels the top registrars for spammer domains, and shows that 19 of the 919 registrars in our study registered more than 1,000 spammer domains. We see that spammers often use popular registrars to register spammer domains, perhaps because doing so may make it more difficult to identify spammer domains solely based on the registrar. On the other hand, for some registrars that do not register many domains, their fraction of spammer domains can be strikingly high (`ABSystems`, in particular [2]).

We speculate that the decisions by spammers regarding domain registrations are driven by both economic concerns (price of registration) as well as the ease of managing multiple domain registrations. Regarding the first of these, we note that registrars charge a range of fees. For example, `eNom` sets special prices for resellers, `GoDaddy` offers cheaper prices for bulk registration, and `INTERNET.bs` provides free private `WHOIS` protection. The management features that each registrar provides determine how easily a customer can manage a domain; for example, `eNom` provides APIs that allow users to manipulate the domain zone entries, and `Moniker` allows up to 500 domain registrations at a time.

6.2 Authoritative Nameservers

The zone updates we use for our study include NS records associated with each new domain. During March–July 2012, we observed 12,824,401 newly registered `.com` domains, but only 242,790 authoritative DNS servers assigned to those domains. We thought that we might find that spammer domains are disproportionately hosted on certain sets of authoritative DNS servers, which we assessed using three metrics:

- *Toxicity:* The percentage of domains that a nameserver hosts that are spammer domains. This metric represents the extent to which an authoritative nameserver sees use mainly in support of spamming activity. A toxicity of 100% indicates that the nameservers appear to operate solely under miscreant control; the presence of such nameservers in a new domain registration could effectively identify new spammer domains.
- *Duplication:* Owners of a given domain typically use multiple DNS servers to host the same domain to achieve redundancy in case of failure [20]. Intuitively, a group of domains hosted by the same set of authoritative nameservers likely have some relationship. We compute the Jaccard index to measure the similarity of the authoritative nameservers in terms of the domains they host. Suppose there exist N nameservers, each of which hosts a set of domains D_i. We compute $|\cap_{i=1}^{N} D_i| / |\cup_{i=1}^{N} D_i|$. A higher Jaccard index for a pair of nameservers indicates a high overlap in terms of the set of domains that those nameservers resolve. This association may ultimately help with identifying groups of nameservers commonly used to host spammer domains.
- *Association:* The percentage of domains hosted on a nameserver that belong to a particular registrar. We define the registrar with the highest association score for a nameserver as the *primary registrar* for that nameserver.

Figure 7 shows the cumulative distribution of spammer domains over the DNS servers. The X-axis shows the indexes of DNS servers ordered by their toxicity; 8,543 of 242,790 DNS servers hosted spammer domains. The figure has two Y axes. The blue dashed curve shows the toxicity of each DNS server and corresponds to the Y-axis on the left side. The red solid curve shows the cumulative percentage of spammer domains for the set of nameservers ranked by their toxicity, and maps to the Y-axis values on the right side of the plot. The nameservers hosting only spammer

[2] The badness of `ABSystems` comes as no surprise. This registrar effectively acts as the DNS infrastructure division of a large spamming operation known as "Quick Cart Pro."

DNS server	*Common spammer domains*	*Toxicity*	*Jaccard index*	*Primary registrar*	*Assoc. %*
ns[1,2].monikerdns.net	21,256	38.46	1.00	Moniker Online Services, Inc.	99.77
ns[3,4].monikerdns.net	17,012	33.74	1.00	Moniker Online Services, Inc.	99.75
dns[1-5].name-services.com	16,955	6.75	0.97	eNom, Inc.	99.88
dns[1-5].registrar-servers.com	11,016	4.58	0.99	eNom, Inc.	99.86
ns[1,2].google.com†	5,957	93.99	0.99	Trunkoz Technologies Pvt Ltd. d/b/a Own-Registrar.com	19.90
ns[1,2].directionfindfree.com	5,302	5.55	1.00	Tucows.com Co.	82.00
ns[1,2].speee.jp	2,400	37.94	1.00	OnlineNIC, Inc.	98.70
ns[1-4].name.com	1,345	1.52	0.96	Name.com LLC	99.76
ns0[7,8].domaincontrol.com	1,089	0.17	1.00	GoDaddy.com, LLC	95.35
ns[3,4].cnmsn.com	1,047	24.89	0.99	Bizcn.com, Inc.	99.38

Table 4: *Top nameservers hosting spammer domains.* †Note: *the domains registered on ns1.google.com and ns2.google.com migrated to other DNS servers immediately after registration.*

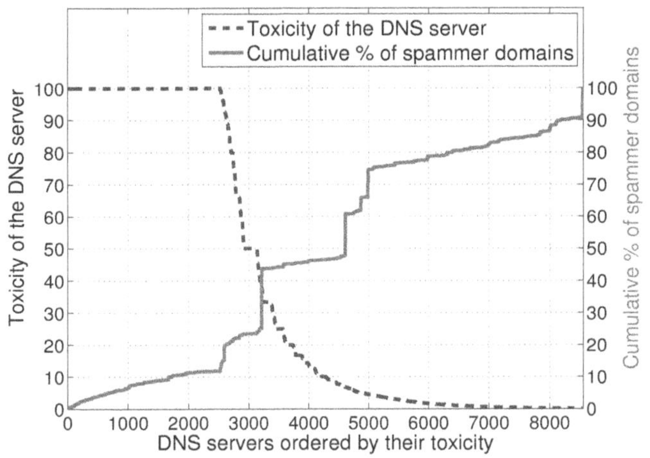

Figure 7: *Cumulative distribution of spammer domains on DNS servers (ordered by toxicity).*

domains (*i.e.*, with toxicity 100%) only account for about 10% of all spammer domains.

Table 4 lists the top nameservers associated with spammer domains, in terms of the total number of spammer domains that they host. We group servers together if their Jaccard index exceeds 0.95, to ensure grouping similarity; we use a regular expression to represent groups of similar domains. For nameservers in common groups, we calculate the metrics based on common domains. The second column shows the number of common spammer domains for each DNS server group; we rank the groups in descending order of the number of common spammer domains for that group. The third and fourth columns indicate the server toxicity and the Jaccard index of duplication, respectively. When spammer domains are sheltered in large registrars (like `Moniker` or `eNom`), these registrars provide and operate their authoritative DNS servers, also hosting a large number of legitimate domains.

It becomes clear from these results that although spammers prefer certain nameservers in some cases, no clear-cut separation exists between nameservers used for spamming and those used for benign purposes. Hence, our earlier hope fails to pan out: we do not see how to fruitfully leverage the nameservers associated with domain registrations to identify spammer domains. In the next section, we turn to exploring to what degree the patterns that spammer registrations exhibit can help distinguish spammer domain registrations from benign ones.

7. DETECTING REGISTRATION SPIKES

In this section we examine the extent to which spammers register domains in abnormally large batches ("spikes"). We first present evidence that suggests that domains associated with spamming are registered in groups. We then show that the number of domains that a given registrar registers in a given five-minute interval usually follows a distribution well-modeled by a compound Poisson process—but that many registrars also exhibit registration spikes that this process would produce only with exceedingly low probability. From this we conclude that these spikes represent a different underlying process than that corresponding to routine activity.

After deriving a model to explain both normal and anomalous registration activity, we show that spammers tend to register batches of domains in such spikes more often than do non-spammers. Our results suggest that methods to reliably identify registration spikes can serve as a useful feature for proactively detecting names that are subsequently used in spam campaigns.

7.1 Bulk Registrations by Spammers

Spammers acquire large volumes of domains to remain agile when conducting their operations [18]. We frequently observe spammer domains registered in spikes as large as hundreds of domains within a single five-minute `.com` update. We speculate that such registration behavior occurs due to: (1) convenience; (2) bulk pricing from registrars [11, 21]; or (3) the use of stolen credit cards to purchase a large number of domains in a short period of time, since the fraudulent purchases will trigger detection and result in voiding of the stolen credit card.

We use the term *bulk registration* to refer to the behavior of registering a batch of domains during a period of a few minutes. Since the registrants' information and behavior are not directly observable in the zone updates, we can only infer that a group of domains may represent a bulk registration by observing updates with multiple domains within the same ⟨registrar, 5-minute-epoch⟩ tuple. The granularity of data that we have provides only an approximation of the behavior of each registrant because different registrants may register simultaneously from the same registrar, and the same registrant could spread their registrations across multiple registrars. Still, we observe the general tendency for spammers to perform registrations in batches, as we develop below.

Figure 8 shows the distribution of the number of spammer domains registered in the same epoch. The X-axis shows the number of spammer domains observed for a given registrar within a single epoch, and the Y-axis shows the cumulative percentage of spammer domains within such epochs. The inlay shows that 50% of the spammer domains were registered in groups of ten or more. We find that only 20% of the spammer domains got registered in

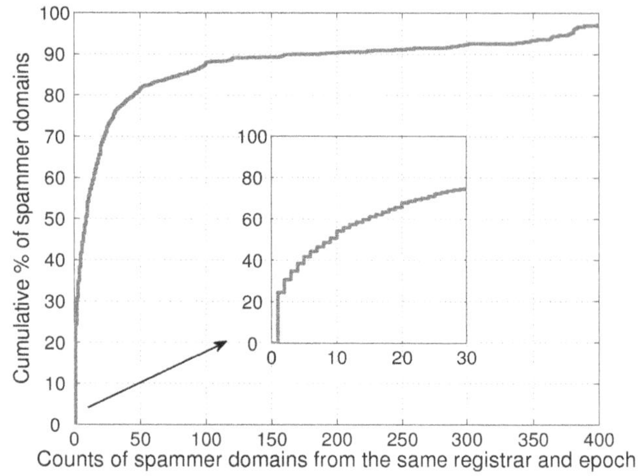

Figure 8: *Distribution of bulk spammer domain registration from the same registrar and epoch.*

isolation (with no other spammer domains), but more than 10% in batches exceeding 200 spammer domains.

We confirmed that the prevalence of multiple spammer domains registered together is not simply a reflection of general "overcrowding". In particular, when we examined the registration patterns for the ten registrars (other than `GoDaddy`) responsible for about 70% of all spammer domains (per Table 3), we observe that only 8% of all registration epochs contained any activity involving spammer domains. Indeed, only `Trunkoz` has more than 20% of its epochs including such domains; for this particular registrar, about 60% of the epochs involve registrations of spammer domains, indicating that this registrar clearly represents an outlier in terms of reflecting consistently bad behavior.

Thus, we see a general trend reflecting behavior where many (but not all) spammer domains are registered in bulk. In the next section, we attempt to capture this notion in more principled terms by fitting the bulk of temporal registration patterns to a compound Poisson process and identifying registration spikes as epochs that deviate significantly from this distribution.

7.2 Detecting Abnormal Registration Batches

The evidence from the previous section suggests that spammers often register multiple domains at the same time. This phenomenon motivates us to identify a way to determine whether a registrar's set of registrations during a given epoch is "abnormally large". If so, then we posit that those registrations are more likely to reflect domain registration activity by spammers. We aim to identify registration activity behavior that *qualitatively* differs from routine (and thus, we presume, likely benign) activity. As noted above, we refer to such a set of registrations as a "spike".

Developing a model for registration batch size. Our challenge is to determine that a given set of registrations crosses the line into "abnormally large", thus constituting a spike. The difficulty we face is that simple approaches for spike detection can lack soundness. For example, simply setting a single threshold (registrations per epoch) may cause us to miss numerous spikes that appear in the registrations for some of the smaller registrars, since for those registrars, an abnormally large set of registrations might not be all that large in terms of absolute volume. If, on the other hand, we instead pick a fixed quantile, such as "treat as spikes all registrations larger than the 99th percentile of a given registrar's registration sizes", then we will necessarily define a subset of each registrar's activity as "abnormally large"—failing to capture the notion of a *qualitative* difference.

Instead, we strive to develop a principled approach to identify qualitatively different (abnormally large) registration epochs, as follows. We hypothesize that a single model can capture the bulk of a registrar's registration activity (*i.e.*, the distribution of how many names the registrar registers during each of its epochs). We then look for epochs during which, according to that model, the volume of names registered was exceedingly unlikely (in a probabilistic sense). We deem such epochs as qualitatively different, and classify the corresponding set of registrations as a spike.

The first question we face concerns what sort of model to use to capture regular registrar activity. If registrars receive a steady stream of customers who act independently of one another, and each registers a single name, then a Poisson process should capture the corresponding activity well: during each epoch, the registrar registers a number of names corresponding to the number of customers who arrived since the last epoch. For this model, all we need to identify is the rate at which the customers arrive at the registrar with their requests. However, we would expect that diurnal patterns would cause the arrival rate at each registrar to vary over the course of each day, and indeed from inspection we find that this is the case. We adjust for this consideration by separately computing for each registrar the mean number of names they registered for each hour of the day, analogous to the nonhomogeneous Poisson processes used previously in characterizing network traffic [23]. For example, we determine a registrar's registration rate per epoch as the average over all epochs between 10 a.m. and 11 a.m., and then use that rate to parameterize a Poisson process to capture the number of registrations that we expect to occur in each such epoch.

We explored this simple Poisson model and found that while it works well for some registrars, for many registrars it often fails to produce convincing fits to the body of the distribution of names registered per epoch. This provides evidence that customers do not arrive at a registrar independently from one another, the rates at which they do vary significantly more rapidly than on a per-hour basis, and/or customers sometimes register more than a single name at a time in normal activity.

The first two of these possibilities appear somewhat at odds with how we expect users to function under normal circumstances, which leads us to consider instead the third option. By employing a *compound Poisson* process, we can capture customers who arrive independently at a fixed rate, but each of whom makes a number of registrations drawn from a given distribution. The general compound Poisson formalism does not require a particular family for this second distribution. However, we achieved quite good results by using a second Poisson distribution; we later discovered that previous work has also modeled consumer purchase behaviors using a compound Poisson process that employs a second Poisson distribution [26].

In summary, for normal registrar activity we capture the number of domain registrations per epoch as $Y = \sum_{i=1}^{N} X_i$, where N represents the number of registrants during the epoch, and follows one Poisson distribution, and X_i $(1 \leq i \leq N)$ are *i.i.d.* Poisson distributions capturing the number of domains each registrant registers. For this model, we have:

$$\begin{aligned} E(Y) &= E(N)E(X_i) \\ Var(Y) &= E(N)[Var(X_i) + E(X_i)^2] \end{aligned}$$

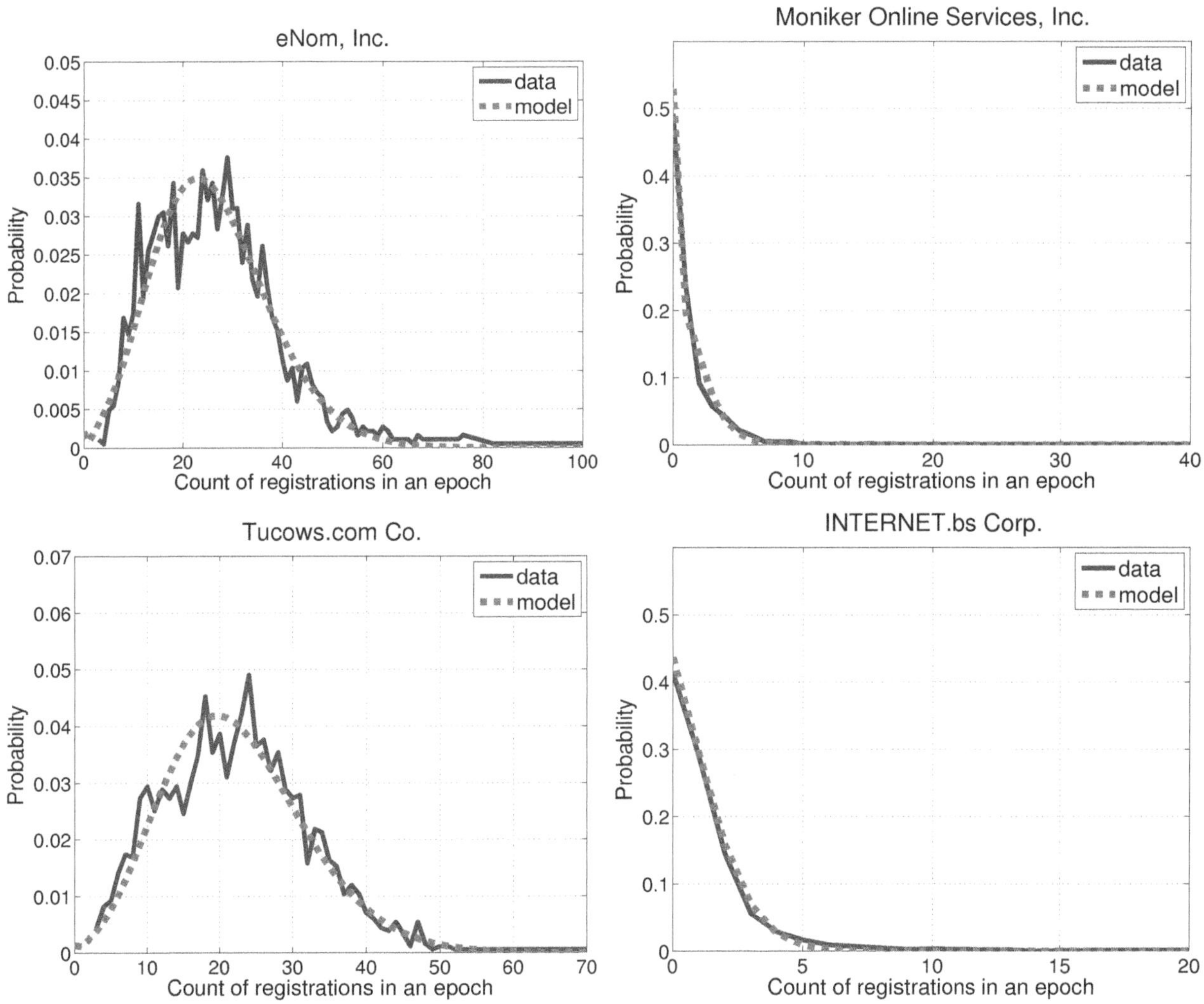

Figure 9: *Compound Poisson processes fitted to the count of registrations per epoch for 4 registrars (hourly window, 10AM–11AM ET).*

Fitting the distribution. Given this model, we now turn to how to fit it to a given registrar's activity. (A reminder, we do this for each hour of the day separately, to accommodate diurnal patterns.) We need to estimate N's parameter, λ_N, and that for the X_i, λ_X. Given they are Poisson distributions, we have: $E(N) = \lambda_N$, $E(X_i) = \lambda_X$, and $Var(X_i) = \lambda_X$, and therefore:

$$\lambda_X = \frac{Var(Y)}{E(Y)} - 1, \quad \lambda_N = \frac{E(Y)}{\lambda_X}.$$

Of course, we cannot simply compute these estimates from each registrar's registration process because our goal is precisely to try to identify registration events that do *not* conform to the registrar's usual activity. For any given registrar, we do not know whether any of these qualitatively different events even exist, but we have strong confidence that they do exist for at least some registrars.

We thus refine the process of fitting the distribution based on the following intuition. Because the events we seek to detect reflect abnormally large registration batches, they will occur in the upper tail of the distribution of all of a registrar's registrations. Therefore, for each registrar we progressively apply different *truncation thresholds* (proportion of the upper tail to discard) to see whether omitting extreme tail values provides us with a better fit of the remaining data to the compound Poisson process. Note that if all of the registration events indeed conform to the same compound Poisson process, then we would expect to do no better—and possibly a bit worse—as we discard upper tail events, since these in fact simply reflect the natural extremes of the process.

We use KL divergence to assess how well the model fits a truncated portion of a registrar's activity: given two probability distributions P and Q, the KL divergence of Q from P is $D_{KL}(P||Q) = \sum_i log_2(\frac{P(i)}{Q(i)})P(i)$, which captures the information lost when we use Q to approximate P. The smaller the KL divergence, the better a model fits the data. For each registrar, we compute the KL divergence for all of its data versus that for a compound Poisson processes fitted to that data; the same but using the data with the upper 99.5% tail discarded; again, but discarding the upper 99.0% tail; etc., through the 90% tail (*i.e.*, we discard the top 10% of largest registration events). We then take as the best fit the tail truncation (if any) that provides the lowest KL divergence. To demonstrate the fitting results, Figure 9 shows the models and epoch distributions of the first 4 registrars listed in Table 3 regarding to the hourly window between 10 AM and 11 AM US Eastern Time.

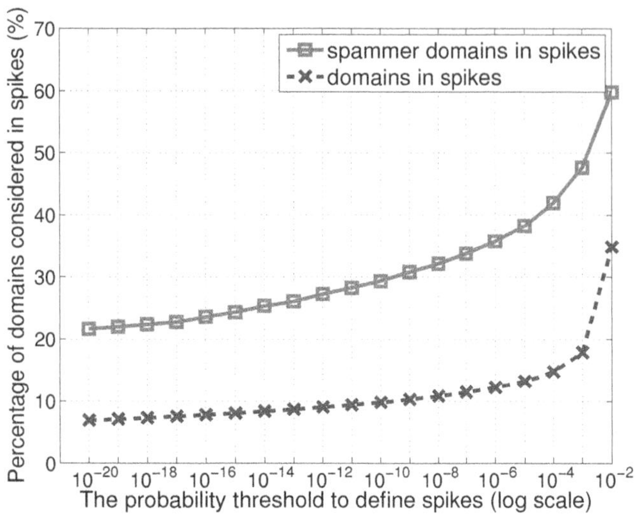

Figure 10: *Percentages of domains deemed as registered in spikes according to different thresholds.*

If we find that this fit worked best with some of the upper tail truncated, then this provides evidence that the most extreme registration epochs behave qualitatively differently from the bulk of the epochs. We can in addition then compute the probability of observing those extreme events given the model fitted to the truncated data. If the extreme events are not in fact all that unlikely, then they may simply reflect stochastic fluctuations of a single underlying (compound Poisson) model. For example, if when truncating the upper 1% tail, we find that truncated model predicts probabilities for the points in the tail as 0.5%, then in fact those points are not so extreme, given the model, and we should not consider them as reflecting qualitatively different behavior. On the other hand, if those points have predicted probabilities of 0.005%, then they are quite unlikely, bolstering evidence that they represent a fundamentally different process.

In the next section, we refine the model by assessing each of these probabilities and explain how we make a final determination of whether a given registration epoch reflects a truly abnormal "spike".

7.3 Refining Threshold Probabilities

The compound Poisson model that we have derived enables us to assess the probability of observing a given number of domains registered by a registrar in a five-minute epoch. A low probability indicates a rare event; if the probability is sufficiently low, we can then conclude the presence of an "abnormal" spike. Figure 10 shows the number of domains that were registered in spikes depending on how low we set this probability; the X-axis is log-scaled. The blue dashed curve shows the proportion for all newly registered `.com` domains, and the red solid curve shows the same statistic for spammer domains. Spammer domains appear in spikes with a much higher likelihood.

We also observe that the slope of the curves increases significantly at a probability of 10^{-3}, suggesting a modal change at that point. For this range of probabilities, the model incorporates spikes that arise simply due to stochastic fluctuations of the normal model, rather than reflecting qualitatively different registration behavior. To avoid mis-classifying registration events for this range of probabilities, we propose defining a spike as a registration size with probability $\leq 10^{-4}$. With that definition, we find about 15% of all domains were registered in spikes; in contrast, 42% of spammer domains were registered in such spikes.

8. DOMAIN REGISTRATION PATTERNS

Spammers can potentially use different strategies to decide on which names to register for use in their campaigns. In this section we analyze the history of domains registered by spammers to assess the different approaches they use. We first define different types of registrations in terms of the domain life cycle discussed in §2. We then show that some types are significantly more likely than others to correlate with spammer domains. We finish with a look at the nature of the names spammers choose when creating new domains.

8.1 Domain Categories

The most basic property of a domain registration concerns whether the domain is **brand-new**, *i.e.*, has never appeared in the zone before, and thus now gets registered for the first time. Such domains have no registration history.

On the other hand, a **re-registration** reflects a name that previously appeared in the zone that the registrant now registers once more after its expiry from the previous owners. For re-registration domains we possess registration history, such as previous registrar(s), registration time(s) and deletion time(s).

We further characterize re-registered domains as either *drop-catch* or *retread*. The former refers to a domain re-registered immediately after its expiry, a phenomenon that occurs quite frequently [7]. Conversely, if some time elapses between a domain's prior deletion and its re-registration, then we term it as a "retread". Thus, the "drop-catch" and "retread" categories are mutually exclusive, and together comprise all members of the "re-registration" category.

8.2 Prevalence of Registration Patterns

How common is each registration pattern? We define a domain registration as drop-catch if the domain was deleted and re-registered in the same 5-minute epoch. If more time elapses for a re-registered domain, then we consider it a retread. Among the spammer `.com` domains that were registered over the 5 months, 68% were brand-new, 30% were retread, and 2% were drop-catch.

Which registrations are more likely to reflect spammer domains? To better understand the role of each type of registration in spamming activity, we investigate the conditional probability that a registration reflects a spammer domain, given a specific category of registration. For example, to calculate the conditional probability of observing a spammer domain given that the registration is a retread, we divide the count of domains that are both retread and spammer by the count of retread domains.

This procedure then gives us the conditional probabilities of being a spammer domain given that the registration is retread, drop-catch, or brand-new as 1.34%, 0.33%, and 1.01%, respectively. Retread and brand-new have higher conditional probabilities of reflecting spammer domains compared to drop-catch registrations. One possible explanation for this could be that spammers simply use drop-catch domains less often in their spam campaigns. Usually registrars charge higher prices to purchase drop-catch domains; for example, three major drop catching services—Namejet.com, Pool.com, and Snapnames.com—charge $59, $60, and $69, respectively, for drop-catch registrations, significantly higher than typical domain registration rates of around $8–12 per registration [9].

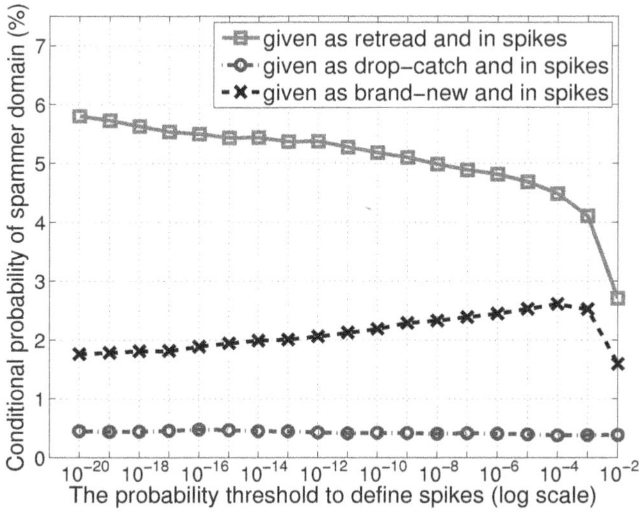

Figure 11: *Conditional probabilities of registrations reflecting spammer domains given that the registration appeared in a spike, for retread, drop-catch, and brand-new registrations.*

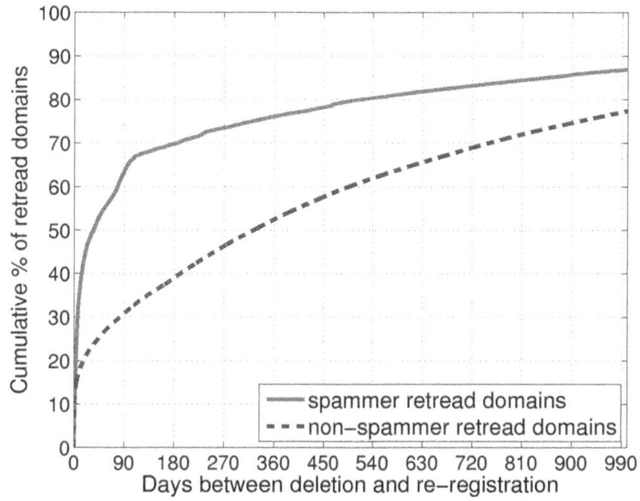

Figure 12: *Distribution of days between domain deletion and re-registration.*

Thus, drop-catch registrations appear significantly less economical for spammers.

Interestingly, if we *also* condition on the registration event occurring in a spike, certain types of registrations become much more likely to reflect spammer domains. Figure 11 shows the conditional probability of observing a spammer domain given a specific category *and* registration occurring in a spike (as defined in §7). The X-axis indicates the probability thresholds in log scale. Each curve shows the conditional probability of a spammer domain for different spike detection threshold values. The red solid curve shows that the conditional probability of a spammer domain given that the registration is a retread and appears in a spike reaches as high as 6%, significantly higher than the conditional probability of a given spammer domain being a retread alone (1.34%). This observation indicates spammers are adept at finding previously used but expired domains and re-registering them in bulk. The black dashed curve shows the same statistic for brand-new domains; for this category, the conditional probability of spammer domains roughly doubles when observing a spike. The highest conditional probability for spammer domains occurs around a threshold of 10^{-4}, which indicates that when spammers register new domains in bulk, the spikes may not be as large as they are for registration spikes for other categories of domains. This difference may arise from the difficulty of finding large numbers of brand-new domain names that are suitable for use in spam campaigns. Finally, the conditional probabilities for spammer domains occurring in drop-catch registrations are small and do not vary significantly depending on the detection threshold.

8.3 Retread Registration Patterns

We have seen that spammers commonly re-register expired domains, especially when performing bulk registrations. Information about domain expiration is publicly released via various channels [22, 29]; spammers, of course, have access to this information and appear to exploit it when selecting the domains to register for subsequent spam campaigns. The majority of the retread registrations that reflect spammer domains were deleted from the zone within 90 days, which indicates that spammers tend to select domains that have expired recently (although not so recently as to qualify as drop-catch domains). We now examine the registration patterns of retread domain registrations in more detail.

Do spammers perform reconnaissance to determine whether a re-registered domain has been previously blacklisted? We study whether the retread registrations that reflect spammer domains have typically appeared in spammer activity in the time period before the spammer decided to re-register the domain. This analysis allows us to better understand whether spammers specifically aim to re-register expired domains with clean histories. We use both the blacklist reports and spam trap observations from the preceding five months—from October 2011 to February 2012—as our source of historical information about spammer domains. (The SURBL blacklist data was only available for October and November 2011, but we also use it for historical information about spammer domains.) Only 6.8% of the retread registrations during March–July 2012 that reflected spammer domains had ever previously appeared in a blacklist, which suggests that spammers indeed deliberately re-register expired domains with clean histories.

How long are retread domains dormant between periods of registration? Next, we investigate the amount of time that typically elapses between domain expiration and a retread registration. The distribution of the dormancy periods for retread registrations that do not reflect spammer domains is much more uniform than the distribution for spammer domains, which tend to be reused more quickly after they expire. Figure 12 shows a cumulative distribution of the dormancy period for retread registrations; more than 65% of spammer domains were dormant for less than 90 days. If we condition on retread domains dormant for less than three months, and registered in moderately sized spikes (according to a threshold probability of 10^{-4}), the conditional probability of a retread domain being a spammer domain is 7.7%, again significantly higher than the conditional probability of being a spammer domain based on being a retread registration alone (1.34%).

8.4 Naming Patterns for Brand-New Domains

We now study the naming conventions that spammers use when registering brand-new domains, focusing in particular on such do-

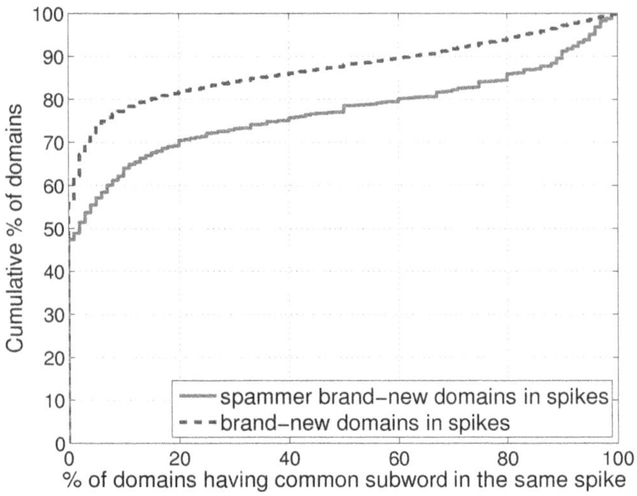

Figure 13: *Cumulative percentage of (brand-new) domains that appear in the same registration spike and have at least one English subword in common with another domain in the spike.*

mains registered in spikes (once again using 10^{-4} as the threshold probability for defining a spike). We first compare the proportion of spammer and non-spammer domains that are registered in spikes that contain English words. To do so, we compare the domain names against a dictionary, looking for matches against words of at least four letters. We find that about 84% of the brand-new spammer domain registrations occurring in spikes contain an English word, versus about 82% of such non-spammer registrations. Thus, it appears that spammers create names that for the most part will appear plausible, as opposed to employing simple algorithms to crank out gobbledygook. Perhaps spammers seek to avoid detection by domain reputation algorithms that use entropy as a feature (*e.g.*, [3]), or aim to diminish user suspicions and increase the likelihood that users will visit the corresponding website.

We hypothesized that when spammers register new domains in bulk, that they may register domains that represent various combinations of English words that relate to the campaign itself, perhaps with slight variations (*e.g.*, one might expect a spam campaign involving watches to involve the registration of many domains containing the word "watch"). To test this hypothesis, we counted the number of brand-new domains in the same registration spike that share a common word, again considering only English words that are at least four characters long. Figure 13 shows the results of this analysis; many domains in the same spike share no common English words, yet the spammer domains show a slightly higher tendency to have common words in spikes. For example, about 40% of brand-new domains that appear in the same spike contain a common subword overall, yet slightly more than 50% of brand-new spammer domains contain a common subword when they appear in the same registration spike.

9. SUMMARY

In this work we have analyzed the domain registration behavior of spammers, including both the infrastructure that they use to register their domains and the patterns that they exhibit when registering them. Our motivation in exploring these behaviors is ultimately to facilitate *time-of-registration* detection of such domains, enabling proactive blocking. We found that nearly half of spammer domains are less than 3 months old; spammer domains are often only used for short periods of time; and current blacklists (with the exception of Spamhaus DBL) identify spammer domains at time-of-use rather than time-of-registration.

We based our study on a large, fine-grained dataset that reflected all changes to the `.com` zone over a five-month period, as seen during five-minute intervals. We then analyzed this data in conjunction with several spam trap and blacklist feeds as *post facto* indicators of spammer domains. After confirming the previous finding that just a handful of registrars account for the bulk of spammer domain registrations, we examined the *registration process* of each registrar, finding two distinct types of registration activity. In the first, predominant mode, the number of domains registrars register is well-described by a compound Poisson process. By fitting such a process to the bulk of a registrar's registration epochs, we can associate probabilities with "outlier" epochs that register large numbers of domains, allowing us to identify registration spikes that *qualitatively differ* from the registrar's usual registration practices. We then showed that spammers often register their domains in such spikes, whereas non-spammers do so much less frequently.

Spammers also often prefer to re-register domains that previously existed in the zone but subsequently expired. While spammers do not engage in "drop-catching" (immediately re-registering domains that have just expired), they prefer domains that have recently expired (within the past few months) and that in their previous life did not appear to be associated with spamming.

We also analyzed two other time-of-registration features: (1) the degree to which spammers tend to use distinctive nameservers to host their domains, and (2) whether newly registered spammer domains contain common English words. We did not find much discriminatory power for either of these features.

Other than a couple of particularly abuse-prone registrars—which by themselves do not account for a significant portion of spam domains—none of the time-of-registration features that we examined by themselves serve as a "smoking gun". Nevertheless, many features exhibit different behavior for spammer domains versus non-spammer domains, suggesting that an apt application of machine learning may enable the development of an accurate time-of-registration detector that can enable us to nip spammer domain registrations in the bud.

Acknowledgments

This work was supported in part by the U.S. Army Research Office under MURI grant W911NF-09-1-0553, by the Office of Naval Research under MURI grant number N000140911042, and by the National Science Foundation under grants 0831535, 1111723, and 1237265. Any opinions, findings, and conclusions or recommendations expressed in this material are those of the authors and do not necessarily reflect the views of the sponsors.

REFERENCES

[1] M. Antonakakis, R. Perdisci, D. Dagon, W. Lee, and N. Feamster. Building a Dynamic Reputation System for DNS. In *Proc. 19th USENIX Security Symposium*, Washington, DC, Aug. 2010.

[2] M. Antonakakis, R. Perdisci, W. Lee, N. Vasiloglou, and D. Dagon. Detecting Malware Domains at the Upper DNS Hierarchy. In *Proc. 20th USENIX Security Symposium*, San Francisco, CA, Aug. 2011.

[3] M. Antonakakis, R. Perdisci, Y. Nadji, N. Vasiloglou, S. Abu-Nimeh, W. Lee, and D. Dagon. From Throw-Away Traffic to Bots: Detecting the Rise of DGA-Based Malware. In *Proc. 20th USENIX Security Symposium*, San Francisco, CA, Aug. 2011.

[4] L. Bilge, E. Kirda, C. Kruegel, and M. Balduzzi. EXPOSURE: Finding Malicious Domains Using Passive DNS Analysis. In *18th*

Annual Network & Distributed System Security Symposium, San Diego, CA, Feb. 2011.
[5] S. E. Coull, A. M. White, T.-F. Yen, F. Monrose, and M. K. Reiter. Understanding Domain Registration Abuses. In *Proc. 25th International Information Security Conference*, Brisbane, Australia, Sept. 2010.
[6] P. Danzig, K. Obraczka, and A. Kumar. An Analysis of Wide-Area Name Server Traffic: A Study of the Internet Domain Name System. *ACM SIGCOMM Computer Communication Review*, 22(4):292, 1992.
[7] How to Snatch an Expiring Domain. `http://www.mikeindustries.com/blog/archive/2005/03/how-to-snatch-an-expiring-domain`, 2005.
[8] DomainTools. `http://www.domaintools.com`, 2012.
[9] Backorder Price Wars: NameJet.com Lowers Minimum Bid On Pending Delete Domains to $59. `http://tinyurl.com/4mb2tgo`, 2011.
[10] M. Felegyhazi, C. Kreibich, and V. Paxson. On the potential of proactive domain blacklisting. In *3rd USENIX Workshop on Large-Scale Exploits and Emergent Threats*, San Jose, CA, Apr. 2010.
[11] Godaddy Bulk Registration. `http://www.godaddy.com/domains/searchbulk.aspx`, 2012.
[12] S. Hao, N. Feamster, and R. Pandrangi. Monitoring the Initial DNS Behavior of Malicious Domains. In *Proc. ACM SIGCOMM Internet Measurement Conference*, Berlin, Germany, Nov. 2011.
[13] S. Hollenbeck. *VeriSign Registry Registrar Protocol Version 2.0.0*. Internet Engineering Task Force, Nov. 2003. RFC 3632.
[14] S. Hollenbeck. *Extensible Provisioning Protocol*. Internet Engineering Task Force, Aug. 2009. RFC 5730.
[15] .COM Agreement Appendix 7, Functional and Performance Specifications. `http://www.icann.org/en/about/agreements/registries/verisign/appendix-07-01mar06-en.htm`, 2006.
[16] Add Grace Period Limits Policy. `http://www.icann.org/en/resources/registries/agp/agp-policy-17dec08-en.htm`, 2008.
[17] J. Jung, E. Sit, H. Balakrishnan, and R. Morris. DNS Performance and the Effectiveness of Caching. In *Proc. ACM SIGCOMM Internet Measurement Workshop*, San Fransisco, CA, Nov. 2001.
[18] K. Levchenko, N. Chachra, B. Enright, M. Felegyhazi, C. Grier, T. Halvorson, C. Kanich, C. Kreibich, H. Liu, D. McCoy, A. Pitsillidis, N. Weaver, V. Paxson, G. M. Voelker, and S. Savage. Click Trajectories: End-to-End Analysis of the Spam Value Chain. In *Proc. IEEE Symposium on Security and Privacy*, Oakland, CA, May 2011.
[19] H. Liu, K. Levchenko, M. Felegyhazi, C. Kreibich, G. Maier, G. M. Voelker, and S. Savage. On the effects of registrar-level intervention. In *4th USENIX Workshop on Large-Scale Exploits and Emergent Threats*, Boston, MA, Mar. 2011.
[20] P. V. Mockapetris. *Domain names - concepts and facilities*. Internet Engineering Task Force, Nov. 1987. RFC 1034.
[21] Moniker Bulk Registration. `https://www.moniker.com/bulkdomainname.jsp`, 2012.
[22] NameJet Domain Name Aftermarket. `http://www.namejet.com/pages/downloads.aspx`, 2012.
[23] V. Paxson and S. Floyd. Wide-area traffic: The failure of poisson modeling. *IEEE/ACM Transactions on Networking*, 3(3):226–244, 2005.
[24] Rogues and Registrars: Top 10 List. `http://blog.legitscript.com/2012/10/rogues-registrars-top-10-list-october-2012`, 2012.
[25] List of ICANN Accredited Registrars. `http://www.icann.org/registrar-reports/accredited-list.html`, 2013.
[26] J. Springael and I. V. Nieuwenhuyse. A Lost Sales Inventory Model with A Compound Poisson Demand Pattern. *Working paper*, July 2005.
[27] Symantec Intelligence Report. `http://www.symantec.com/theme.jsp?themeid=state_of_spam`, 2012.
[28] Verisign Who was Service. `http://www.icann.org/en/registries/rsep/verisign-whowas-01jul09-en.pdf`, 2009.
[29] Verisign Domain Countdown. `http://domaincountdown.verisignlabs.com`, 2011.
[30] The Domain Name Industry Brief. `http://www.verisigninc.com/en_US/why-verisign/research-trends/domain-name-industry-brief/index.xhtml`, 2012.
[31] S. Yadav, A. K. K. Reddy, A. Reddy, and S. Ranjan. Detecting Algorithmically Generated Malicious Domain Names. In *Proc. ACM SIGCOMM Internet Measurement Conference*, Melbourne, Australia, Nov. 2010.
[32] Root Zone Database. `http://www.iana.org/domains/root/db`, 2012.

On Measuring the Client-Side DNS Infrastructure

Kyle Schomp[†], Tom Callahan[†], Michael Rabinovich[†], Mark Allman[‡]
[†]Case Western Reserve University, Cleveland, OH, USA
{kyle.schomp,tom.callahan,michael.rabinovich}@case.edu
[‡]International Computer Science Institute, Berkeley, CA, USA
mallman@icir.org

ABSTRACT

The Domain Name System (DNS) is a critical component of the Internet infrastructure. It allows users to interact with Web sites using human-readable names and provides a foundation for transparent client request distribution among servers in Web platforms, such as content delivery networks. In this paper, we present methodologies for efficiently discovering the complex client-side DNS infrastructure. We further develop measurement techniques for isolating the behavior of the distinct actors in the infrastructure. Using these strategies, we study various aspects of the client-side DNS infrastructure and its behavior with respect to caching, both in aggregate and separately for different actors.

Categories and Subject Descriptors

C.2 [**Computer-Communication Networks**]: Miscellaneous; C.4 [**Performance of Systems**]: Measurement Techniques

Keywords

Internet Measurement; Domain Name System (DNS)

1. INTRODUCTION

DNS plays a foundational role in today's Internet. From its initial function of providing the mapping between human-readable names (e.g., "amazon.com") and obtuse network-level addresses, it evolved to form a basis for building scalable and agile Web platforms. In particular, by changing name-to-address bindings dynamically and providing different bindings to different clients, Web sites can transparently distribute client load among replicated Web servers or redirect client requests from their own servers to content delivery networks (CDNs), while CDNs and similar platforms can direct incoming requests to specific nodes in the platform.

With the crucial role DNS plays, the complexity of the DNS infrastructure—especially the client-side query-resolving aspect—has increased dramatically. No longer are address lookups a simple matter of end devices querying a local DNS resolver, which in turn queries authoritative nameservers on clients' behalf. Rather, facilitated by the simplicity of the stateless and connectionless protocol, DNS has developed into a complex ecosystem often involving several layers of shared resolvers which can, in turn, peer with additional resolvers. The path a DNS query takes through this infrastructure is often complex and hidden. This complexity makes it difficult to understand the behavior of the resolving infrastructure and to attribute responsibility for distinct behaviors to the individual actors.

This study targets the above challenge and makes the following contributions. First, we develop a set of methodologies for discovering the client-side DNS infrastructure efficiently. Given the vastness of this infrastructure and a short lifetime of some of its actors [8,13], probing strategies that improve the rate of discovery can facilitate subsequent measurements. Second, we develop measurement techniques for teasing apart the behavior of the actors within the system, some of whom cannot be accessed directly. Third, we apply our methodologies and strategies to assess some aspects of the client-side DNS infrastructure and its behavior with respect to caching, both in aggregate and separately for different actors. Our key observations from this assessment include the following:

- We double, from 15 to 32 million, previous estimates of the number of open resolvers on the Internet.
- We find evidence of wide adoption of complex resolution topologies including large shared pools of resolvers at certain layers in the infrastructure.
- We observe that DNS queries frequently travel large distances *within* the resolving infrastructure—both in terms of geography and network delay. We find 20% of open resolvers experiencing at least 100 msec of delay before their queries leave the resolution infrastructure.
- To the best of our knowledge, we contribute the first assessment of how various actors treat the time-to-live (TTL) settings given by authoritative nameservers to set the behavior of DNS caches. Despite being a simple notion, we find that different actors handle the TTL differently. The overall effect is that in many cases the TTL is distorted before reaching the original requesting client. We find that only 19% of all open resolvers consistently return correct TTL values to all our probes. A 2004 study [17] reports a wide violation of TTLs by end-clients while a 2012 study from a client site with "honest" resolvers shows a much lower violation rate by clients [6]. We expand upon these studies by demonstrating not only which actors cause violation but also how they behave regarding the TTL setting and, thus, cause other actors to violate TTL.
- We assess the time an unused record stays in the cache of various actors within the resolving infrastructure, which in particular determines whether the TTL or cache capacity is

IMC'13, October 23–25, 2013, Barcelona, Spain.

http://dx.doi.org/10.1145/2504730.2504734 .

the cause of eviction. We find scant evidence of a general capacity limitation problem .

2. RELATED WORK

The over-arching methodology we use to study the DNS ecosystem—as developed in the next three sections—involves actively discovering and characterizing DNS resolvers that will answer queries from arbitrary hosts throughout the Internet. In this manner, we can determine how the client-side DNS infrastructure behaves with regard to a wide range of test queries. The closest related work to ours is [8], which scans open resolvers in order to assess answer rewriting occurring on DNS paths. That work further contributes the idea of building a mapping between resolvers found by probing Internet hosts and the resolvers that ultimately contact an authoritative DNS server. We build upon that technique to attribute DNS behavior to specific actors. Our work extends the probing methodology presented in [8] to effectively discover resolver pools and examines many resolver characteristics not discussed in that paper.

Efficiently scanning the IPv4 address space for service discovery (including DNS) while avoiding complaints is discussed in [13]. While [13] explores reducing the burden of probing, we focus on reducing the number of probes required without losing insight. Our additional methodological contributions are in probing strategies that (*i*) increase the discovery rate, (*ii*) identify pools of recursive resolvers, and (*iii*) soundly assess specific behavior of the various actors in the system.

We also consider this work related to [2], which performs DNS lookups from several vantage points in order to compare performance among various local resolvers and public DNS services. [2] finds that ISP-provided resolvers often outperform public DNS services in query latency. Another performance-centric study is [14], which characterizes the difference in observed DNS performance for common DNS names from a variety of vantage points. Additionally, [14] reports on the behavior of the DNS time-to-live, which we also explore in more depth in this paper. Finally, [22] reports on several facets of DNS servers, including security configuration and support for DNS protocol components such as DNSSEC [5].

Several studies [10, 18, 23] show that information gleaned from DNS resolvers may be used to measure various aspects of the Internet such as popularity of Web sites and inter-host delays. Our work supports these efforts by developing effective discovery strategies and showing the diversity of behavior in differing implementations.

Several prior studies consider the number of open resolvers on the Internet [13, 22], the distance between clients and their resolvers [4, 11, 15, 20] and TTL violations [6, 17, 21]. We contrast our findings with these studies throughout this paper.

3. CLIENT-SIDE DNS INFRASTRUCTURE

The architecture of the client-side DNS infrastructure varies across providers. The actors can be loosely grouped into three roles: (*i*) "ingress" servers that receive DNS queries directly from user devices, (*ii*) "egress" servers that directly communicate with authoritative DNS servers (ADNS), which maintain hostname to IP address mappings for their respective domains, and (*iii*) hidden servers that act as intermediaries between the ingress and egress but are not exposed to either clients requesting mappings or authoritative servers providing mappings. To avoid confusion, in the rest of the paper we use the following terminology to describe the various components of the client-side DNS infrastructure that is charged with obtaining a hostname to IP address binding from an ADNS. The actors are also illustrated in Figure 1.

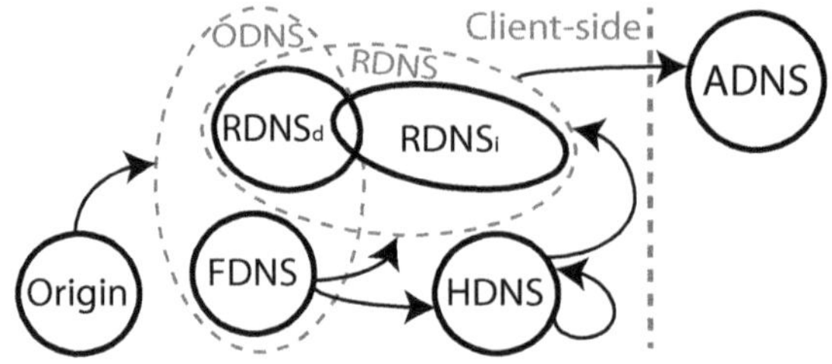

Figure 1: Structure of the client-side DNS infrastructure.

- Origin devices are either user devices or the sources of our DNS requests sent to probe the client-side DNS infrastructure.
- ODNSes ("open DNS") are ingress servers that accept requests from any host.
- RDNSes ("recursive DNS resolvers") are egress resolvers that communicate directly with authoritative DNS servers.
- FDNSes ("forwarding ODNS") refers to an ODNS that does not itself resolve a query, but rather forwards the request along to another resolver. The FDNS servers are a subset of the ODNS servers, or the ingress points that origin devices query.
- $RDNS_d$es ("direct RDNS") are RDNSes that are also ODNSes. In other words, an $RDNS_d$ is both an ingress and egress server.
- $RDNS_i$es ("indirect RDNS") are RDNSes observed at the authoritative DNS server resolving queries on behalf of an FDNS. Note: The $RDNS_i$ and $RDNS_d$ sets overlap. That is, we find some RDNS servers that both (*i*) accept and resolve queries from arbitrary origin devices and (*ii*) act on behalf of a set of FDNS servers we detect in our survey.
- HDNSes ("hidden DNS") are servers which operate between FDNSes and RDNSes. Since these servers are neither ingress nor egress servers, they are invisible externally. While we cannot directly detect these servers, their existence is confirmed by DNS operators [9] and therefore we must keep them in mind as their actions may impact our results.

A typical example path through the maze of DNS-related devices has a client computer (Origin) starting the process by sending a DNS request to a home routing device (FDNS), which in turn forwards the request through a chain of zero or more HDNSes and ultimately to an $RDNS_i$. The $RDNS_i$ sends the request to the appropriate ADNS. Note that the $RDNS_i$ may cooperate with other $RDNS_i$es and subsequent requests from the same FDNS may be handled by a different $RDNS_i$. We call such structures "RDNS pools". We discuss RDNS pools in more detail in §6. This typical example accounts for nearly all of our experimental observations.

4. METHODOLOGY OVERVIEW

In this section we sketch our general methodology and datasets. The specific methodology for each of our experiments is described in subsequent sections. Our measurements cover only a fraction of the Internet and therefore we must consider bias, namely, the degree to which the DNS infrastructure we discover and assess is representative of the broader Internet. We defer this question to §8—after we have further developed experiments that can be brought to bear on the question.

Scan	Format	Start	Dur. (days)	ODNSes	RDNSes
S_1	Random IP	2/29/12	17	1.09M	69.5K
S_2	Random IP	7/3/12	32	1.98M	72.6K
S_3	Random /24	8/5/12	17	841K	43.9K
S_4	Scan on First Hit	10/4/12	25	17.6M	72.1K
S_5	Rescan of S_3	11/16/12	9	892K	29.9K
S_6	Scan on First Hit	2/26/13	31	11M	65.8K

Table 1: Dataset characteristics

Non-Interference With Normal Operation: While we are investigating the various components of the DNS ecosystem, we use our registered domain. Our probing rates are limited to insure we do not interfere with normal operation of any of the components of the system, and, although some of our techniques involve cache injection, all DNS requests are for subdomains of our own domain and we dot not interfere with any actual name-to-address bindings in use.

Discovering DNS Infrastructure: To examine the client-side DNS infrastructure, we must have an efficient method for finding both ODNSes and RDNSes. Discovering DNS infrastructure is a challenge because many of the components have policy restrictions preventing the acceptance of DNS requests from arbitrary hosts. Our basic discovery technique is an extension of the process described in [8]. We registered a domain name[1] and deployed an ADNS for this domain. We then leverage approximately 100 PlanetLab [7] nodes as our origins and randomly probe the IP address space with DNS requests for various hostnames within our domain. By embedding the probed IP address in the hostname request and observing the queries arrive at our ADNS, we collect the IP addresses that are willing to handle our probes—thus discovering ODNSes. The IP addresses from which the queries ultimately arrive at our ADNS illuminate the set of RDNSes. Finally, since the ADNS has the addresses of both the RDNS and ODNS, we can associate FDNSes with the RDNSes they use for DNS resolution. Thus, we can elicit a response from an RDNS that will not respond to direct probes by indirectly probing via the FDNS.

Attribution of Behavior: When measuring DNS behavior, it is often necessary to identify the actor responsible for the behavior, e.g., when a violation of the DNS protocol is detected. A key contribution of this paper is measurement techniques to isolate FDNS behavior from RDNS and HDNS behavior. Through cache injection[2] on FDNSes, to which we found a sizable fraction of FDNSes are susceptible, we short-circuit HDNS and RDNS from processing a measurement probe. Therefore, any artifacts are the sole result of the FDNS. Similarly, we develop a technique of coordinated probing through two or more FDNSes to determine the behavior of a shared RDNS in near isolation from FDNS behavior. We validate the latter technique using the RDNS$_{di}$es —which we can probe both through an FDNS and directly—as ground truth of RDNS behavior. Estimating from our experiments, over 77% of RDNS$_i$es will not respond to direct DNS requests from external hosts and are assumed hidden from an outside observer; despite that, our technique provides the ability to assess their behavior.

ODNS Lifetimes: We note that during our measurements we find that ODNSes are often short-lived—with around 40% becoming unreachable within one day (see §5.1.1). Since the duration of our experiments is typically longer than one day, we rediscover the resolvers anew for each new experiment we discuss below. Hence, techniques for quick rediscovery are important. We describe these techniques below and use them to collect different datasets for different experiments, as summarized in Table 1. We describe the details of each scan as needed throughout the remainder of the paper. Our datasets are publicly available [19].

[1]dnsresearch.us

[2]A technique for inserting records into a DNS cache against the spirit of the protocol.

Criterion	No. ODNSes	% ODNSes
RomPager	258K	24%
Basic auth realm	265K	24%
PBL Listed by SpamHaus	566K	51%
PBL Listed by ISP	180K	17%
Wrong port	529K	48%
Total	849K	78%

Table 2: Home network device criteria

5. METHODOLOGY DETAILS

We first turn our attention to discovering various components of the client-side DNS infrastructure. To facilitate our exploration of discovery methodologies, we use two datasets. The first dataset is from the S_2 scan in Table 1 and represents the probing of 255M unique random IP addresses using 267M DNS requests from 7/3/2012 to 8/3/2012. Our S_2 scan discovered 1.9M ODNSes and 73K RDNSes. The second dataset is from the S_3 scan in Table 1 and was collected between 8/5/2012 and 8/21/2012 using a methodology based on completely scanning random /24 IP address blocks. This scan represents a probing of 465K random /24 address blocks—11.9M IP addresses—via 121M DNS requests. The S_3 dataset includes 841K ODNSes and 44K RDNSes. The number of probes exceeds the number of IP addresses because some ODNSes use RDNS pools, which we attempt to discover through repeated probes to ODNSes (see §5.2 for details).

ODNSes appear to be mostly home network devices. During the S_1 scan of random IP addresses we gather detailed information about roughly 1.09M ODNSes. We find that 78% are likely residential networking devices as they meet at least one of the following criteria as shown in Table 2: (*i*) HTTP probes to the device show that the Web server reports itself as RomPager, which is a well-known software package for creating Web interfaces in embedded devices, (*ii*) HTTP probes to the device show the use of basic authentication with a realm indicating a likely home device (e.g., "3068 DSL-2641R"), (*iii*) the IP address is listed in the Spamhaus PBL, or (*iv*) the device replies to a DNS probe from a port other than the port to which the probe was directed. We speculate that the final criteria is caused by a low-end NAT device that is performing translation on its own packets. Together, these indicators provide supporting evidence that the ODNSes we discover are overwhelmingly low-end network devices residing in residential settings.

5.1 ODNS Discovery

The fundamental aspect of discovery is finding ODNSes since, as we will show, these are the windows into the client-side DNS infrastructure. Several projects leverage full scans of the Internet address space [1, 13] to understand the prevalence of open resolvers. However, we are interested not only with discovering the existence of ODNSes, but also with understanding their characteristics and behavior, which entails sending far more requests than discovery would dictate (as detailed in subsequent sections). Additionally, we find—as previously developed in the literature [8, 13]—the window of accessibility for ODNSes to be in general fairly short (see below). Therefore, we must do in-depth probing in conjunction

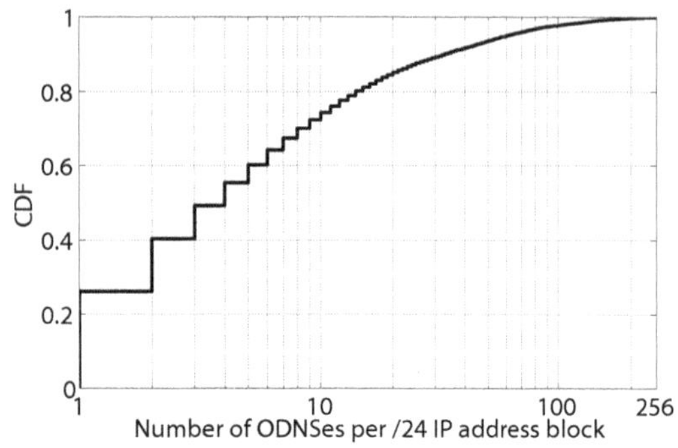

Figure 2: Distribution of ODNSes per /24 IP address block, excluding empty blocks.

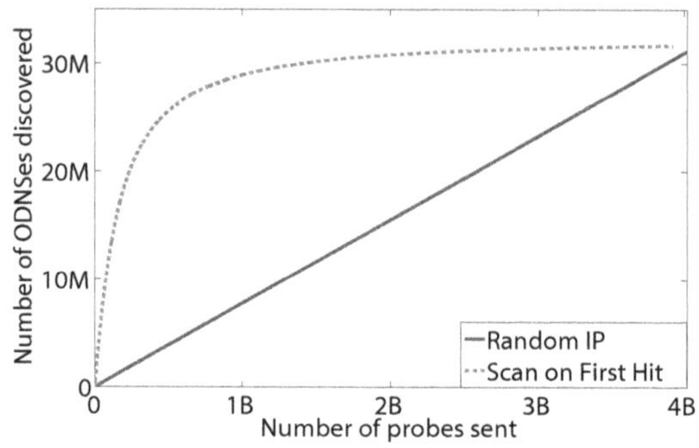

Figure 3: ODNS discovery rate versus DNS requests sent (extrapolation from the S_3 scan to the Internet scale).

with ODNS discovery as returning to the given address later may well be fruitless. Finally, our probing rate has to result in a manageable load on the ADNS—both the server itself and the hosting network—where ultimately the measurement traffic converges. For our ADNS, the resource constraints and desire to finish experiments in a reasonable time frame necessitates a partial scan. The key questions that arise from this choice involve (i) understanding the effectiveness of randomly probing arbitrary IP addresses with DNS requests in the hope of stumbling upon ODNSes, and (ii) whether there are probing strategies to improve the efficiency of this process.

Our first observation is that ODNSes are unevenly distributed throughout IP space. As sketched above, in S_3 we choose and probe random /24 address blocks. We find that only 14% of these blocks contain ODNSes. Further, as Figure 2 shows, the distribution of ODNSes among the blocks that have some ODNSes is uneven. We find a small number of "dense" blocks with many ODNSes. For instance, the top 10% of the address blocks each contain over 30 ODNSes while 40% of the blocks have no more than two ODNSes. The average across all blocks with at least one ODNS is approximately 13 ODNSes per /24 block.

Discovery within such a sparse address space requires extensive scanning. For collecting a sample of ODNSes with a partial scan, we examine two methods of ODNS discovery. The first method is a random scanning of IP addresses labeled "Random IP". The second method, "Scan on First Hit", acts like "Random IP" but, once an ODNS is discovered, proceeds to scan the entire /24 block in which the ODNS resides. This latter method utilizes the above observation of uneven ODNS distribution among /24 blocks to increase the ODNS discovery rate.

To compare the two methods fairly, we simulate both of them based on the same dataset from the S_3 scan using the following methodology. We consider the Internet's 2^{32} IP addresses divided into 2^{24} /24 blocks. We mark a random 14% of /24 blocks as "productive" —which as previously discussed is the fraction of /24 blocks found to contain at least one ODNS server—and in each productive block we mark a number of IP addresses as ODNS according to the distribution from Figure 2. "Random IP" is then simulated by selecting randomly without replacement from the full 2^{32} address range and counting the rate of discovering ODNS. For "Scan on First Hit", we again select an address randomly without replacement. If the selected address is an ODNS, we count not only this address, but also all addresses marked as ODNS in the encompassing /24 block and remove the block from the address pool for further selection.

Figure 3 shows the discovery rate for both methods. We find a drastically higher initial discovery rate using the "Scan on First Hit" strategy, which maintains its advantage for all scan sizes until the techniques converge to discover the entire set of ODNSes with a complete scan. The discovery rate of "Scan on First Hit" decreases over time. The reason is that the more dense a /24 address block is the higher the probability of finding an ODNS; therefore, dense /24 address blocks have a greater chance of being discovered early. The purely random scan shows steady progress across the entire scan but is overall less productive for limited scans. As noted above, only 14% of the /24 blocks contain ODNSes. So, the random scan misses opportunities to learn about the "neighborhood" when finding an ODNS and chances are that neighborhood is populated with additional ODNSes.

While the "Scan on First Hit" strategy discovers more ODNSes with fewer probes, it has a downside in that it introduces a bias in the set of discovered ODNSes. Blocks with higher concentrations of ODNSes have a greater chance of being discovered, thus biasing the resulting dataset towards ODNS in well-populated address blocks. Thus, when using this efficient discovery method, one must consider implications of its bias. We consider effects of this bias on our results in §8.

5.1.1 Rediscovery and Whitelisting

ODNSes have previously been found to be short lived [8,13] and we confirm these results. In our S_6 scan conducted from 2/26/2013 through 3/28/2013 we repeatedly probe discovered ODNSes for a period of 1M seconds after discovery. Details of the S_6 scan and the intervals at which the ODNSes were probed are discussed in §7. As shown in Figure 4, 40% of the discovered ODNSes answer queries for no more than one day and 80% of the ODNSes cease answering queries within one week. As noted above, there is evidence that the ODNSes we find are predominantly home network devices. Therefore, we suspect that short ODNS lifetimes are due to DHCP lease expirations. Thus, we conclude that our lists of ODNSes become stale and biased quickly and for this reason we discover ODNSes anew for each phase of our study.

Rescanning can be an expensive and time consuming process. Fortunately, we find that ODNSes demonstrate a tight IP spatial cohesion: while an individual ODNS can be short lived, productive /24 blocks tend to remain productive. We rescanned the same /24 address blocks from the S_3 scan between 11/16/2012 and 11/24/2012, nearly three months after the S_3 scan ended; this scan is labeled S_5 in Table 1. We also find that 76% of the 67K produc-

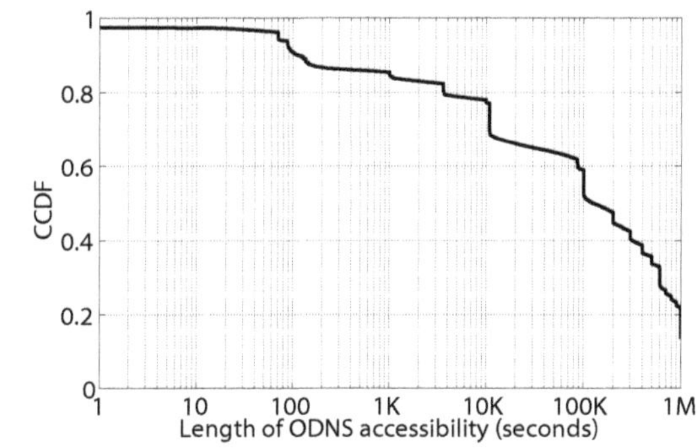

Figure 4: Distribution of the duration of ODNS accessibility.

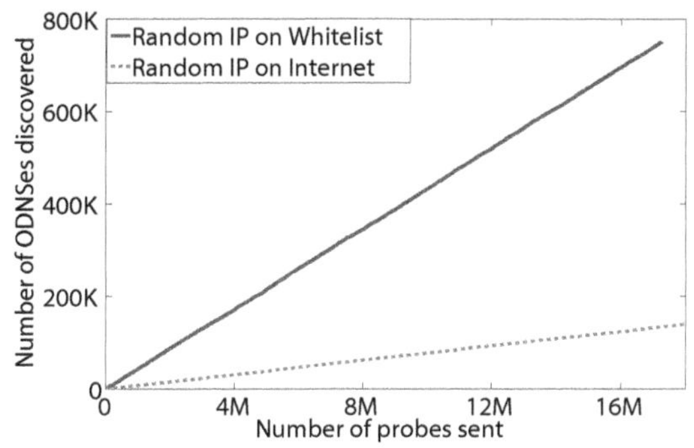

Figure 5: ODNS discovery rate using whitelisting in the S_5 scan compared to the discovery rate of the S_2 scan.

tive /24 address blocks during the former scan remain productive during the repeat scan. This spatial cohesion over time enables the use of "whitelisting" to rescan just those /24 address blocks which were previously productive. Using the same simulation methodology we employ to explore Random IP vs. Scan on First Hit above (Figure 3) we study re-scanning previously productive /24 blocks. Figure 5 shows the discovery rate for rescanning the 67K productive /24 address blocks from the S_5 scan using Random IP—i.e., scanning random IP addresses from the whitelisted /24 address blocks—in contrast to random IP selection from the entire Internet address space based on the S_2 scan. Clearly, rescanning using whitelisting is more efficient than random scanning. We also note that whitelisting may be used in conjunction with the "Scan on First Hit" strategy to generate a whitelist containing dense /24 address blocks. Rescanning using such a whitelist would likely have a much higher discovery rate than Figure 5 suggests.

5.2 RDNS Discovery

RDNS discovery provides more of a challenge than ODNS discovery for two reasons. First, unlike ODNS discovery, RDNS discovery is an indirect process whereby the characteristics and behaviors of the ODNSes may impact the process. Second, the RDNS resolver topologies are complex, unlike the ODNS population, which is by definition just a set of simple servers. In particular, an ODNS may forward DNS queries to a *pool* of resolvers, which may optionally utilize another layer of resolvers before the queries egress the infrastructure and are visible at our ADNS. For example, Google's public DNS utilizes a two-level topology that hashes the requested hostnames to particular egress resolvers to improve their cache effectiveness [9]. Unfortunately, we can only discover the egress RDNSes and do not have a technique for discovering HDNSes in the middle of the infrastructure.

We use a two-pronged approach for RDNS discovery. First, for a given ODNS we send multiple DNS requests for hostnames within our domain in an attempt to spread those requests throughout the RDNS pool—if such exists. For this we use unique hostnames such that each request must move through the entire infrastructure and end up at our ADNS. Second, our ADNS returns a variable-length chain of CNAME records to queries from RDNSes[3]. We know from experience that the RDNS that sends a DNS request is often *not* the same RDNS that resolves the CNAME redirections. We use both these mechanisms until we stop discovering new members of the observed RDNS pool. Specifically, our strategy is as follows.

- When a first probe to a newly discovered ODNS arrives at our ADNS through a previously discovered RDNS, the ADNS responds with a special A record indicating that no new RDNS discovery has occurred.
- However, when this first query arrives from a previously unknown RDNS, the ADNS responds to a query with a CNAME record of a new subdomain. After receiving the subsequent query for this new subdomain we repeat the process four additional times. When this batch of five CNAME queries leads to the discovery of at least one new RDNS then the entire process is repeated with five additional CNAMEs. This process continues until no new RDNS is found, at which point a special A record is returned to the client indicating that new RDNSes were discovered.
- When the A record returned—through the ODNS—indicates new RDNS were discovered, the client sends five more probes for distinct subdomains to this ODNS. Note that these subsequent probes may trigger a series of CNAME responses by our ADNS as described above. As long as the A record from the ADNS indicates new RDNS discovery, probing extends with another batch of five probes.
- When the A record returned to the client indicates that no new RDNSes were found, the discovery process terminates.

Our S_2 scan uses the above procedure. Furthermore, to enable exploration of alternate scanning strategies—as well as to discover RDNS pools in §6—our S_3 scan uses a modified version of the above procedure that triggers a new CNAME batch as long as new RDNSes are discovered *for the current ODNS* rather than consulting the full set of RDNSes from all probing.

We test this basic RDNS discovery mechanism with four ODNS probing strategies: "Random IP", "Scan On First Hit", and "Random /24 Block" described earlier, plus "Aborted Random Block", which is a scan of random /24 address blocks that terminates after the first ODNS in that block is found. The idea behind the last strategy is that the ODNSes in a /24 block will all share the same RDNS infrastructure and so the first ODNS will trigger the discovery of the lion's share of the RDNSes. The results for all four strategies reflect simulations driven by the dataset collected by the S_3 scan.

Figure 6 shows the discovery rates of our four methods. The "Scan on First Hit" method has a higher rate than the alternate strategies for two reasons. First, we find that ODNSes within the same /24 address block do not all use the same RDNS or RDNS pool—contrary to our intuition. Therefore, learning about the "neighborhood" is beneficial not only for ODNS discovery but also for RDNS discovery. This accounts for "Scan on First Hit"

[3]A CNAME record indicates a "canonical" name for the hostname queried. On receiving this record, the resolver will issue a new query for the name contained in the CNAME record.

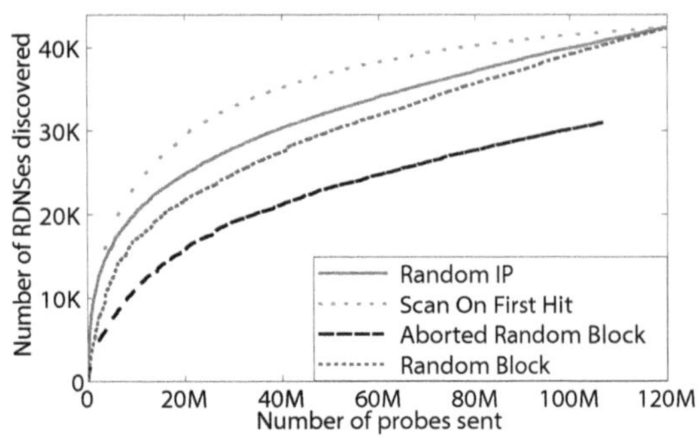

Figure 6: RDNS discovery rate versus DNS requests sent, simulated from the S_3 scan.

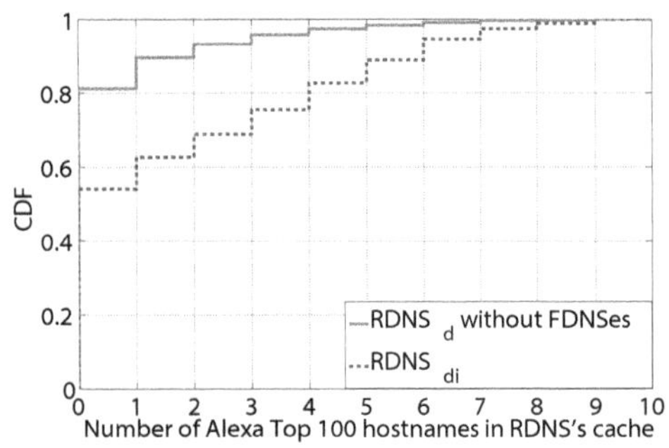

Figure 7: Number of the Alexa top 100 Web sites in the caches of RDNSes.

achieving a higher RDNS discovery rate than Random IP. Second, because the vast majority of /24 blocks do not contain any ODNSes, much of the scanning in Aborted Random Block and Random Block is wasted. We note that Aborted Random Block was unable to discover 13K of the 43.9K RDNSes within the S_3 dataset. The undiscovered RDNSes were not reachable through the first ODNS found within each /24 block. The "Scan on First Hit" technique provides the best ODNS and RDNS discovery rate in terms of scanning infrastructure cost and time.

5.2.1 $RDNS_d$ Evaluation

The RDNS_des deserve special attention here. These servers have been counted during both ODNS and RDNS discovery. Yet, it is unclear if all RDNS_des serve clients. They could, for instance, be misconfigured authoritative DNS servers that happen to be willing to accept external queries for external domains as discussed in [10]. We find that 51% of the RDNS_des in the S_2 scan are used by at least one FDNS, i.e., are in fact RDNS_{di}es. The remaining 49% could be resolvers which might be accessed by origins directly, or whose client FDNSes are hidden from our scans' view or have been missed by our scans.

To determine if the 49% (17K) of RDNS_des which are *not* used by any FDNSes in our dataset from the S_2 scan are actually acting as resolvers for some client population we query them for the top 100 Web sites as listed by Alexa [3]. If the RDNS_des are resolvers, then they are likely handling DNS requests from their clients for some of these Web sites. Therefore, some of these popular hostnames should be in the RDNS_des' caches. We detect if a record is in the cache by sending a DNS request for the hostname to the RDNS_d and comparing the returned time-to-live (TTL) value with the TTL we expect to be set by the Web site's ADNS—which we established separately. A TTL value in a DNS response that is less than the ADNS assigned TTL indicates that the Web site's record is in the RDNS_d's cache, suggesting that some real client previously requested the record. Figure 7 shows the distribution of the number of popular Web site records that appear to be in the caches of RDNS_des *without* FDNSes and in the caches of RDNS_{di}es. Although we later show that RDNSes are prone to inaccurate reporting of TTLs, the difference between the two curves indicates a difference in the behavior of the two sets of RDNSes. We opt to remove RDNS_des without FDNSes from our analysis since their purpose is unclear. Instead, we focus the remainder of our study upon RDNS_ies which have a clear purpose within the client-side DNS infrastructure.

5.3 Techniques for Untangling Behavior

We now discuss techniques we developed to tease apart the behavior of FDNS from RDNS.

5.3.1 Measuring FDNS

As we previously note, the vast majority of ODNSes we discover are in fact FDNSes (over 95% across all datasets). Gaining an understanding of FDNSes in isolation from the remainder of the client-side DNS infrastructure is a challenge. Fortunately, we find that a fraction of FDNSes allow a primitive form of cache injection which we leverage to gain insight into the behavior of this FDNS subset. Specifically, these FDNSes do not perform any of the following security checks on DNS responses which could prevent cache injection: (i) change and/or verify the transaction ID, (ii) verify the source IP address, and (iii) verify the destination port number. The absence of such checks makes it straightforward to follow a request to an FDNS with an acceptable response which only involves the FDNS and not the rest of the infrastructure.

Hence, we can study these FDNSes in isolation from HDNSes and RDNSes using the following procedure. We begin by sending a DNS request for a hostname within our domain to the FDNS under study and then immediately issue a DNS response for the same hostname to the FDNS that binds the requested name to IP address X. On the other hand, when the request arrives to our ADNS in a normal way, the latter answers with a response containing IP address Y. Then, any subsequent requests made by our probing host that are responded to with IP address X must have come from the FDNS's cache and the FDNS is effectively isolated from the rest of the client-side infrastructure, which never touched record X. We stress that the FDNSes we study may be a biased set since the set only includes FDNSes that exhibit the cache injection vulnerability.

5.3.2 Measuring RDNS

Since typically we cannot query RDNS_ies directly, we utilize FDNSes as our window into RDNS_i behavior. This, however, poses a problem as FDNSes may alter DNS requests, responses and caching phenomena, hence obscuring RDNS behavior. A second response for a domain name through a single FDNS may be returned from either the FDNS's cache or the RDNS_i's cache, ambiguously. Fortunately, it is common to find multiple FDNSes which use the same RDNS_i. We leverage a general experimental strategy which requires at least two FDNSes per RDNS_i to succeed—F_1 and F_2. While the exact details of the technique vary with different experiments and will be detailed separately, the general framework is as follows. We begin by requesting a unique subdomain of our domain from F_1. Our ADNS responds to this query with a randomly generated record, which should be cached

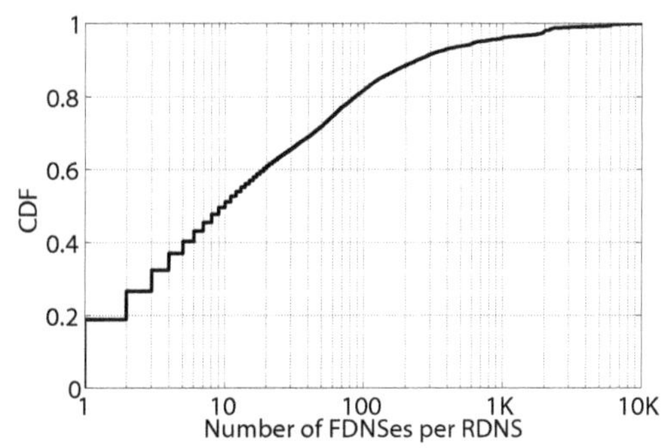

Figure 8: Number of FDNSes per RDNS$_i$ in the S_3 scan.

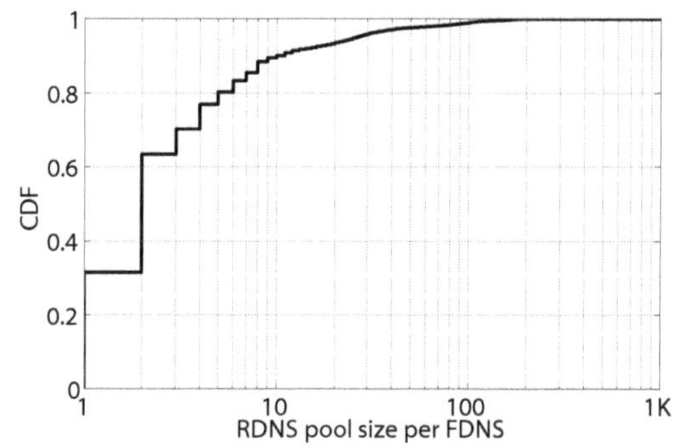

Figure 9: Distribution of the RDNS pool size for each FDNS.

at the RDNS$_i$ on the return path to F_1. Then, after a predetermined amount of time, we query for the same subdomain through F_2. If the RDNS$_i$ still has the record in its cache, the response from F_2 will match the response from F_1. In this case, we further know that the record is from the RDNS$_i$'s cache and not from F_2 because the request was previously unseen by F_2. If the record is no longer in the RDNS$_i$'s cache, the request will arrive at our ADNS, which will respond with a different record. In this way, we eliminate FDNS caching behavior when studying RDNS$_i$ caching behavior.

This technique relies upon discovering two FDNSes which use the same RDNS$_i$ at roughly the same time. Figure 8 shows the number of FDNSes per RDNS$_i$ in the S_3 dataset. Over 80% of the RDNS$_i$es are used by more than one FDNS and the coordinated probing technique has a chance of succeeding. Further, 50% of RDNS$_i$es appear with at least 10 FDNSes in the dataset, vastly increasing the chances of successful measurement.

FDNS behavior may still distort the measurement by altering records. We discuss ways to mitigate this problem—such as using all available FDNSes— in §7.

6. TOPOLOGY

In this section, we address the size and structure of the client-side DNS infrastructure.

6.1 Estimating Global ODNS Population

Extrapolating from our limited scans of IP space, we estimate that there are approximately 32M ODNSes on the Internet today. We arrive at this result from two independent scans. First, we find almost 2M ODNS within a set of 254.7M probed IPs in the "Random IP" scan S_2 where addresses are chosen randomly from the complete 2^{32} address space. Therefore, we estimate the population size as $2M/254.7M \times 2^{32} = 33M$ ODNSes across the Internet. Second, from the "Random /24" scan S_3, the fraction of productive /24 address blocks (those with at least one ODNS) is 0.141 and a productive block contains on average 13 ODNSes. Therefore, the ODNS population across the entire Internet is $0.141 \times 13 \times 2^{24} = 31M$ (a similar number is also obtained from simulations in Figure 3).

These estimates significantly exceed previous results of complete Internet scans [13] and estimates [22], which show around 15M responding DNS resolvers. One of our *partial* scans using the "Scan on First Hit" strategy directly identifies 17.6M ODNSes—more than found in previous full scans. Additionally, [1], a complete Internet scan, reports 33M open resolvers as of May 2013 which agrees with our estimate. The results show the population of ODNSes on the Internet has increased since previous studies.

6.2 RDNS Pool Sizes

The ODNSes we find in both our S_2 scan and S_3 scan utilize RDNSes in roughly 99% of the cases—i.e., they are in fact FDNSes. Moreover, approximately 70% of FDNSes use an RDNS pool in both scans. Per §5.2, we use repeated DNS requests and CNAME chaining triggered by per-ODNS discovery of a new RDNS to identify RDNS pools used by an FDNS. Figure 9 shows the size distribution of the discovered RDNS pools in the S_3 scan. The plot shows that 10% of FDNSes use RDNS pools consisting of more than 10 servers. Also, note that these pools can encompass multiple providers, e.g., an ISP's own DNS infrastructure and OpenDNS, which could occur when either the FDNS is configured to use both, e.g., one as the primary DNS server and the other as the secondary DNS server, or the ISP is utilizing some alternate DNS infrastructure for some queries.

6.3 Distance between FDNSes and RDNSes

As discussed in §5.1.1, ODNSes—and consequently FDNSes—are predominantly in residential settings. Many Internet platforms—notably content delivery networks—rely on the assumption that client machines are close to their RDNS in that the platforms direct the client to a nearby node within the platform based on the location of the client's RDNS. To test this assumption, we use a geolocation database [16] to calculate the distance between FDNSes and the RDNSes they employ for resolution. We perform this on the S_6 dataset. Figure 10 presents the distribution of these distances[4]. Since an FDNS may use several RDNSes, we plot the minimum, maximum, and mean distance between an FDNS and all of the RDNSes it utilizes. We find that FDNSes are often quite close to their RDNSes with the median being approximately 100 miles. However, one in ten FDNSes appear to be over 8K miles from at least one of their RDNSes; these FDNSes experience a high cache miss cost and potentially incorrect redirections by content delivery networks to nodes that are not nearby. Prior studies [4, 11] also consider the geographical distance between the client hosts and their DNS resolvers and report different results. In particular, [11] observes shorter distances between FDNSes and RDNSes, with 60% of clients to be within 17 miles from their resolvers, while [4] reports fewer client-resolver pairs at the low distance range, with only 25% of pairs being within 500 miles from each other, and also fewer extremely distant pairs, with just 5% of pairs more than 2000 miles apart. The differences with our experiment could be due to different vantage points. Both [11] and [4]

[4]The accuracy of our results rests upon the accuracy of the MaxMind geolocation database which varies by country. For example, MaxMind claims 81% accuracy within 25 miles for IP addresses inside the USA. See [16] for accuracy in other countries.

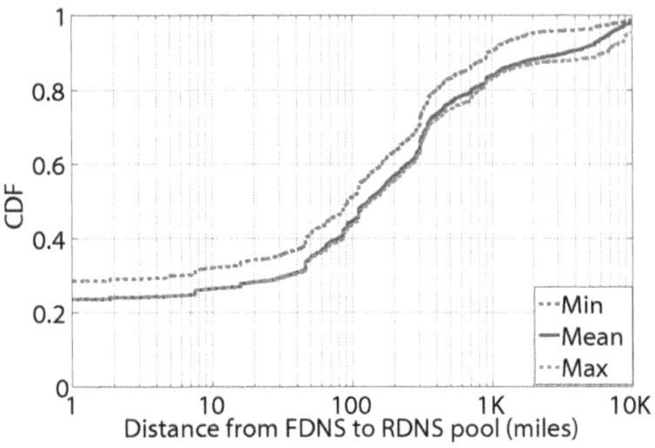

Figure 10: Distribution of the geographic distance from FDNS to RDNS.

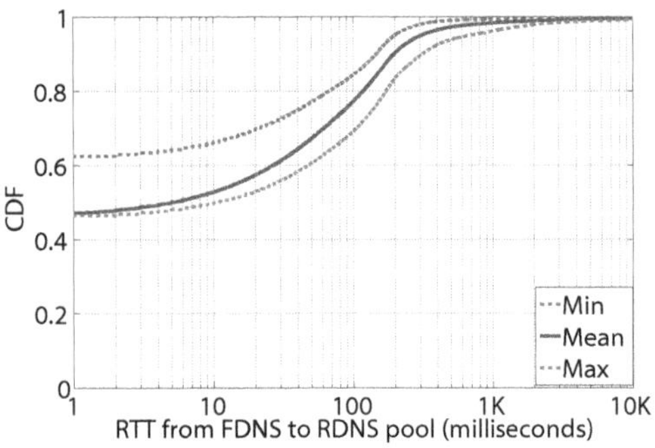

Figure 11: Distribution of round trip time between FDNS and RDNS.

instrumented a Web page and passively observed FDNS/RDNS pairs via DNS requests and subsequent HTTP connections, where as our study is an active scan which exhaustively explores all FDNS/RDNS pairs. Therefore, we discover FDNS/RDNS pairs that may not appear in prior studies.

Additionally, we found that some FDNSes respond to ICMP pings. In the S_6 scan, we obtained (1) the round trip time from our measurement point to the 22% of the FDNSes that were responsive to a ping and also (2) the round trip time between our measurement point and the respective RDNS through the FDNS for 6.3M FDNS/RDNS pairs. The later leverages our coordinated probing technique. We add a record to the RDNS' cache via a probe from the first FDNS. We then obtain the distance from our measurement point to the RDNS through the second FDNS by querying for the same record through the second FDNS. The difference between (2) and (1) is the round trip time in milliseconds between the second FDNS and the RDNS. We also repeat the process by swapping the roles of the two FDNS servers. We perform this measurement for each FDNS pair we discover using the same RDNS during discovery. Using this technique, we are able to obtain the round trip time from FDNS to RDNS for 5.6M FDNS/RDNS pairs across 1.3M unique FDNSes. In the case of multiple measurements per FDNS/RDNS pair, we choose the minimum delay value as it most accurately reflects the actual network delay between the FDNS and RDNS. We plot the results in Figure 11. The median round trip time is about 10 ms, however nearly 20% of the FDNSes experience delays in excess of 200 ms to at least one of their RDNSes.

7. CACHING BEHAVIOR

Caching aids the scalability of the DNS system and hides delay for hostname resolution. Additionally, DNS caching has important performance and security implications.

In terms of performance, DNS caching complicates Internet sites' traffic engineering ability because a single hostname-to-address binding may pin all clients behind a given resolver to the selected server for an extended period of time. Not only does this handicap sites' control over client request distribution but it also complicates the removal of unneeded infrastructure without risking failed interactions from clients using old bindings. DNS nominally provides sites with the capability to bound these effects by specifying a time-to-live (TTL) value within DNS responses to limit the amount of time recipients can reuse the response. However, recipients are known to disobey TTL [6, 17, 21]. With regard to security, caching determines the lingering effect of a successful record injection (e.g., using the Kaminsky attack [12]).

The extent of these phenomena depends on two inter-related aspects: how long a resolver keeps a record in its cache and how the resolver treats the TTL. We first explore the aggregate behavior of all components of the client-side DNS infrastructure, as this will be the view of the clients leveraging the infrastructure. We then use the measurement techniques described above to tease apart the behavior of the components in isolation to gain insight into which components are responsible for various behavior.

The results in this section come from the S_6 scan (see Table 1). The scan covers 79M IP addresses with 1.3B DNS requests from 2/26/2013 through 3/28/2013. The S_6 scan encompasses 11M ODNSes and 65.8K RDNSes—46K of which are RDNS$_i$es. The S_6 dataset uses the "Scan on First Hit" methodology to increase the ODNS discovery rate and thus the probability of finding multiple FDNSes which use the same RDNS$_i$ at roughly the same time. This assists with the coordinated probing strategy sketched in §5.3.2.

7.1 Aggregate Behavior

To investigate aggregate behavior of the DNS resolution infrastructure, we perform in-depth probing of 2.4M FDNSes during the S_6 scan. We did not test all of the FDNSes because of limitations in the amount of traffic our ADNS can handle. Therefore, we limit the number of FDNSes which can be concurrently assessed to 25K per measurement origin (PlanetLab node). When a measurement origin finds a new FDNS we skip in-depth measurement if 25K FDNSes are presently being assessed.

We examine how FDNSes and RDNS$_i$es behave when presented with DNS records with different TTL values: 1, 10, 30, 60, 100, 120, 1,000, 3,600, 10,000, 10,800, 86,400, 100,000, 604,800 and 1,000,000 seconds. For each TTL value, we re-probe at various intervals to determine whether the records are still available. We use intervals slightly below the TTL values (by two seconds), to check if the record is retained for the full TTL. We also use intervals slightly above the TTL values (by two seconds), to check if the record is retained *longer* than the TTL. For this experiment, our ADNS returns a random IP address. Thus, if subsequent DNS requests for the same hostname return the same IP address we know—with high likelihood—the request was satisfied by a cache somewhere within the resolving infrastructure, either at the FDNS, HDNSes, or RDNS$_i$.

Our first observation is that some of the responses arrive at the client with incorrect TTL values, i.e., different from those set by our ADNS. Furthermore, even when the client receives the correct TTL for the *initial* request for a hostname, we find *subsequent* requests result in responses with incorrect TTL values. We interpret the latter as due to the DNS actor distorting TTL not when con-

Behavior	Percentage of Measurements
Honest	19%
Lie on Initial	38%
Lie on Subsequent	9%
Constant TTL	7%
Increment TTL	1%

Table 3: Aggregate TTL Behavior

Expected (sec)	% <	% >	Mode Lie	
			Value	% of All Lies
1	0%	11%	10000	35%
10-120	$\leq$ 1%	$\leq$ 8%	10000	$\geq$ 37%
1000	1%	3%	10000	62%
3600	2%	2%	10000	51%
10000	5%	0%	3600	40%
10800	8%	0%	3600	27%
86400	16%	0%	21600	36%
100000	22%	0%	21600	27%
604800	22%	0%	21600	26%
1000000	64%	0%	604800	67%

Table 4: Aggregate TTL Deviations

veying the record back to the requester but when storing the record in its cache. Table 3 summarizes our results for aggregate behavior. In total, 19% of the FDNSes and their underlying infrastructure always report the correct TTL value. Meanwhile, 38% of the FDNSes respond with an incorrect TTL value to an initial request and 9% of FDNSes respond with an incorrect TTL value to the subsequent requests. The fact that at least 62% of FDNSes honestly report the TTL on the first DNS request will be important in studying RDNS$_i$es below.

Beyond changing the TTL of DNS records, we find some FDNSes fail to correctly decrement the TTL over time[5]. We find that 7% of the FDNSes return a constant TTL value, never decrementing. An additional 1% of the FDNSes actually begin to *increment* the TTL after it counts down to zero! Both these behaviors eventually result in a TTL which disagrees with the initial setting by the ADNS. Downstream devices—regardless of how they treat the TTL—may unwittingly use such records in violation of the intent of the ADNS.

Table 4 shows the TTL deviations we observe including those in response to both the initial and subsequent requests. The table shows the percentage of cases when TTL is less than ("< %") and greater than ("> %") the ADNS-assigned value. In addition, we show the most common TTL violation (mode lie) and the percentage of the lies the mode represents. For example, we find 11% of FDNSes deviate from a 1 second authoritative TTL. Further, 35% of the lies are for a TTL of 10,000 seconds. The prevalence of lies increases for both small and large TTL values. For instance, most resolvers appear to cap the TTL at one week (604,800 seconds).

We next consider how long a record remains cached and accessible in the client-side DNS infrastructure. Using repeated probes at the intervals mentioned above, we record the latest time at which a record is returned to our probing host. While it is possible that the record was still in some cache at this point and resolution merely took a different path through the infrastructure, our experiment reflects the behavior a user of the system would experience. Figure 12 shows the length of time records remain in some cache within the resolving infrastructure. We present results for records with TTLs

[5]A resolver is supposed to decrement the TTL to account for time spent in the resolver's cache.

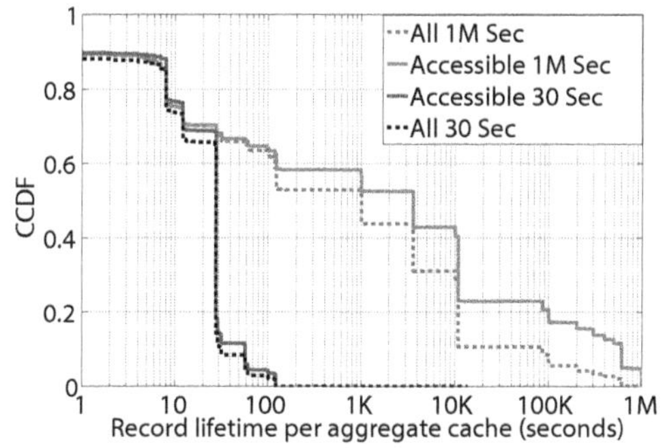

Figure 12: Aggregate cached record lifetimes.

of 30 seconds, a short TTL value similar to those used by content delivery networks (e.g., Akamai uses 20 seconds and Limelight uses 350 seconds). Additionally we use records with TTLs of 1 million seconds, a value chosen to determine how long the infrastructure will retain rarely used records. The "All" lines reflect the longest record lifetime we observe from a given FDNS. However, a number of FDNSes become unreachable in the course of the experiment. When this happens due to IP address reassignments as discussed in §5.1.1, the records may still be in the cache. Thus, the "All" line may be an underestimate of the length of time the infrastructure retains DNS records. Consequently, we report results separately for the 189K FDNSes that remain accessible throughout the experiment (the "Accessible" line). The true cache duration lies somewhere between these two lines.

Our results show that 90% of FDNSes and their supporting infrastructure retain records with a TTL of 30 seconds for no longer than the TTL—with 60% of the FDNSes retaining the record for the full 30 seconds. We find that 10% of FDNSes retain the record for longer than the TTL—with 4% retaining the record for over 100 seconds. This indicates that in general short TTLs are relatively effective in controlling DNS caching behavior. These results deviate from the findings from a 2004 passive study that shows TTL violations on the order of hours were not uncommon [17]. Furthermore, the records assigned a TTL of 1 million seconds show much longer retention, with 40% active for more than 1 hour. This indicates that short cache retention of the records with TTLs of 30 seconds is due to the TTL setting rather than cache capacity constraints.

7.2 FDNS Behavior

We now study the behavior of FDNSes in isolation by using the record injection technique described in §5.3.1. We find 683K FDNSes in the S_6 dataset (6%) accept our injected response records and were thus amenable to our measurement.

We utilize the same experimental technique as in §7.1 with the exception that we follow up the initial DNS request for a hostname with a DNS response that binds the hostname to IP address X. The same binding is never returned by our ADNS, so whenever X appears in a DNS response we know the request was satisfied from the FDNS' cache. If the DNS response contains an address other than X we know X is no longer in the FDNS' cache. We perform the experiment for the same TTL values and re-probe intervals as in §7.1.

Table 5 summarizes our general findings on FDNS' TTL behavior. First, 60% of the FDNSes never lie with respect to the TTL. However, we find that 12% of FDNSes lie in response to the initial request and 30% lie in response to the subsequent requests. As we

Behavior	Percentage of Measurements
Honest	60%
Lie on Initial	12%
Lie on Subsequent	30%
Constant TTL	26%
Incrementing TTL	10%

Table 5: FDNS TTL Behavior

Expected (sec)	% <	% >	Mode Lie	
			Value	% of All Lies
1	0%	31%	10000	88%
10-3600	≤ 1%	19%	10000	≥ 95%
10000	1%	0%	60	92%
10800	19%	0%	10000	97%
86400	19%	0%	10000	97%
100000	19%	0%	10000	97%
604800	19%	0%	10000	97%
1000000	25%	0%	10000	75%

Table 6: FDNS TTL Deviations

note above, we interpret this latter behavior as due to the FDNS distorting TTL not when conveying the record back to the origin but when storing the record in its cache. We also determine that 26% of FDNSes report a constant TTL value without ever decrementing it. Finally, 10% of the FDNSes began to increment the TTL value upon decrementing it to zero.

Table 6 shows the TTL deviations we observe for FDNSes, including both initial and subsequent deviations. The table shows the same general trend as aggregate behavior but with more deviations at the low end of TTL spectrum and less prevalence of capping the TTL at 1 week. The number of cases where the authoritative short TTL is replaced by a 10,000 second value jumps by roughly 50% for the authoritative TTL of 1 second as compared to 10 seconds. Thus, the ADNS often will retain better control over FDNS caching by assigning a TTL larger than 1 second.

We now consider how long a record remains accessible in the cache of FDNSes. Using repeated probes at the intervals mentioned above, we record the latest time at which the injected record is returned to our probing host. Again, we present results for records supplied by our ADNS with the TTLs set to 30 seconds and 1 million seconds. Figure 13 shows how long the records are retained in the caches. See §7.1 for an explanation of the "All" and "Accessible" lines. For this experiment, the "Accessible" line contains the results for 22.5K (3.3%) of the 683K tested FDNSes.

The results show that roughly 40% of the FDNSes retain the record with a TTL of 30 seconds for longer than the TTL. Additionally, 28% of FDNSes hold the record for over 100 seconds, more than twice the TTL. This deviates from the aggregate results in Figure 12 indicating that FDNSes which allow cache injection are more likely to retain records past the TTL value than the general FDNS population. We find records with a TTL of 1 million seconds are retained for at least 10,000 seconds in 50% of the FDNSes.

7.3 RDNS$_i$ Behavior

We now turn to the behavior of RDNS$_i$es in near isolation from FDNSes. RDNS$_{di}$es are particularly convenient in that we can examine their behavior in perfect isolation since there is no other actor to interfere with our results. We have results for 4.9K RDNS$_{di}$es. We use the same experimental technique as in §7.1 with the same TTL values and re-probe intervals. Table 7 shows our general results while Table 8 shows the TTL deviations we observe. RDNS$_{di}$es do not exhibit either the constant TTL nor the pathological TTL incrementing behavior we observe in FDNSes and the aggregate data. However, there is more TTL distortion with virtually no consistently honest RDNS$_{di}$es.

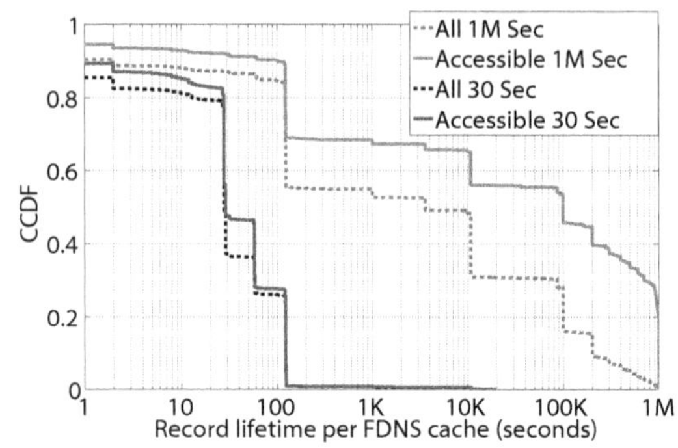

Figure 13: Distribution of record availability in FDNS caches for records with TTLs of 30 and 1 million seconds.

Behavior	Percentage of Measurements
Honest	2%
Lie on Initial	80%
Lie on Subsequent	18%
Constant TTL	0%
Incrementing TTL	0%

Table 7: RDNS$_{di}$ TTL Behavior

For RDNS$_i$es that do not respond to direct probes, we leverage the coordinated probing strategy to assess their violations. As described in §5.3.2, we begin by requesting a unique hostname via FDNS F_1. Our ADNS responds to this query with two IP addresses, one random and the second uniquely bound to the RDNS$_i$ from which the DNS request arrives. We assign the same set of TTL values as in §7.1. Both records pass through RDNS$_i$ on the return path to F_1 and may be cached for subsequent requests. Next, our experiment requests the same hostname via F_2. If the RDNS$_i$ still has the records in its cache and is leveraged by both F_1 and F_2, the random IP address from the response to F_1 will be re-used and hence the response to F_2 will show the same address.

However, at this point, any TTL deviations cannot be attributed to the RDNS$_i$, the FDNSes or even some HDNS in the path. To gain confidence in our attribution of TTL deviations to RDNS$_i$, we leverage two pieces of information. First, as noted in the previous two sections, a significant number of FDNSes are honest on the initial DNS response. We find 62% of FDNSes are honest on the

Expected (sec)	% <	% >	Mode Lie	
			Value	% of All Lies
1-120	0%	22%	3600	≥ 52%
1000	3%	19%	3600	53%
3600	3%	7%	86400	69%
10000	16%	7%	3600	53%
10800	16%	7%	3600	52%
86400	16%	0%	3600	72%
100000	40%	0%	86400	59%
604800	40%	0%	86400	59%
1000000	88%	0%	604800	54%

Table 8: RDNS$_{di}$ TTL Deviations

Behavior	Percentage of Measurements
Honest	36%
Lie on Initial	55%
Lie on Subsequent	5%
Constant TTL	5%
Incrementing TTL	0%

Table 9: RDNS$_i$ TTL Behavior

initial response in §7.1 and 88% of FDNSes are honest on the initial response in §7.2. Second, we can utilize more than two FDNSes in coordinated probing to mitigate the effect of FDNS lies. Instead of F_1 and F_2 representing single FDNSes in the above description of the experiment, we utilize up to 10 FDNSes that we divide into two sets. We send the same request through each FDNS at roughly the same time.

If any FDNS responds with the correct TTL value, then we conclude the RDNS$_i$ must be truthful since every component was truthful in this case. On the other hand, if no FDNS responds with the correct TTL, then it is probable that the RDNS$_i$ is responsible for the lie. In this situation, there are three scenarios. First, some of the FDNSes are in the set of FDNSes that were honest in initial responses *and* the TTL values from these FDNSes all agree. In this ideal case, their responses collectively identify the actual TTL the RDNS$_i$ provides. In the second scenario, the TTL values arriving at honest FDNSes do not agree. One potential cause of this case is HDNSes interposing between some of the FDNSes and the RDNS$_i$. In this case, we assume that the RDNS$_i$ returns the most common TTL value among the honest FDNSes. In the final scenario, none of the FDNSes are honest. In this case, we assume that the RDNS$_i$ returns the most common TTL value among all the FDNSes.

If the majority of FDNSes access an RDNS$_i$ through the same HDNS, then our experiment will conflate the behavior of the RDNS$_i$ and the HDNS. However, we note that if an RDNS$_i$ is *only* accessible through a single HDNS, then learning the RDNS$_i$'s behavior in isolation is moot because only the aggregate behavior of both components will ever impact client devices in the real system.

We validate our technique for determining RDNS$_i$ TTL behavior using RDNS$_{di}$es, which allow us to obtain ground truth by direct probing. The results using our coordinated probing technique agree with the ground truth in 98% of the cases, and not only in detecting whether an RDNS$_i$ is honest but also in determining the quantitative TTL violations (as we will show, most lies are from a small fixed set of TTLs).

In our dataset, there are 46K RDNS$_i$es and we conduct in-depth probing for 22K of them (due to logistical issues, as sketched above). Table 9 shows our findings. We determine that 36% of RDNS$_i$es are honest. Further, 55% of RDNS$_i$ lie on the initial response to F_1, but only 5% of RDNS$_i$es lie in response to subsequent requests from F_2 indicating that the behavior of caching a different TTL than initially returned is less prevalent in RDNS$_i$es than FDNSes. This supports our conjecture that FDNSes, being mostly home-based devices, represent more primitive implementations of DNS. In addition to incorrect TTLs, we find 8% of RDNS$_i$es return constant TTL values without decrementing. The TTL deviations from RDNS$_i$es, merged with the results for RDNS$_{di}$es are shown in Table 10.

We now consider how long a record remains cached and accessible at RDNS$_i$es. Again, we use the experimental setup described earlier in this section with one exception. Instead of querying from F_2 immediately after receiving the response from F_1, we wait before repeating the query (using the same intervals as in §7.1 up to

Expected (sec)	% <	% >	Mode Lie	
			Value	% of All Lies
1-120	$\leq$ 1%	$\leq$ 1%	300	$\geq$ 34%
1000	1%	0%	900	29%
3600	1%	0%	80	19%
10000	2%	0%	3600	35%
10800	2%	0%	7200	20%
86400	5%	0%	21600	32%
100000	11%	0%	86400	55%
604800	11%	0%	86400	53%
1000000	49%	0%	604800	71%

Table 10: RDNS$_i$ TTL Deviations

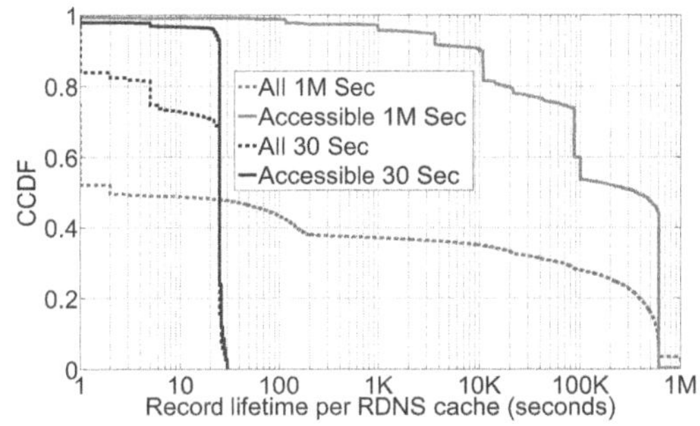

Figure 14: Distribution of record availability in RDNS$_i$ caches for records with TTLs of 30 and 1 million seconds.

the TTL value[6]). For each RDNS$_i$, we track the latest time at which the record is available.

Again, when FDNSes become unavailable in the course of the experiment we cannot detect how much longer a record stays in the RDNS's cache. Thus, Figure 14 shows the duration of record retention separately for all measured RDNSes (the "All" lines, representing 22K tested RDNS$_i$es and underestimating the result) and for those RDNSes that remained accessible throughout the experiment (the "Accessible" lines, representing 8.8K and 2.4K RDNS$_i$es for the 30 second TTL and the 1 million second TTL, respectively).

Concentrating on the "Accessible" lines as more reliable, we show that DNS records with a TTL of 1 million seconds stay in the cache for a long time, with the records still present 10K seconds (2.8 hours) after being inserted in 90% of the cases. Furthermore, step-wise drops indicate record evictions at fixed values of time in cache, indicating some configuration parameters rather than capacity eviction, and a more gradually descending line in the aggregate behavior (Figure 12) is likely due to FDNS affects. The record with a TTL of 30 seconds remains in the cache for the full TTL in 94% of the tested RDNS$_i$es.

8. DATASET REPRESENTATIVENESS

Finally, we return to the issue of bias in our datasets first mentioned in §4. Since our scans do not encompass the entire Internet, it is possible that our results are not demonstrative of the entire population of FDNSes and RDNS$_i$es due to biases in our scanning methodology. In particular, our results on FDNS behavior encompass a subset of FDNSes, i.e., those which allow cache injection. Similarly, our results for RDNS$_i$es include only those RDNS$_i$es

[6]Unfortunately, we neglected to measure intervals beyond TTL and hence do not check if RDNSes cache records beyond the authoritative TTL as we did for FDNSes.

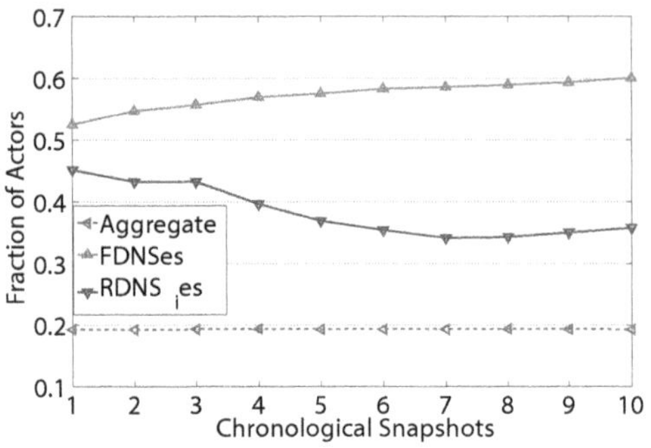

Figure 15: Fraction of honest actors over the discovery process.

for which we discover at least two FDNSes. For these two, we demonstrate here that our dataset is representative of the respective subsets of the whole population. On the other hand, we can validate the aggregate behavior against the whole population.

We assess representativeness of our datasets by calculating the fraction of actors which honestly report the TTL value for all TTL values we utilize. We divide our datasets into ten slices ordered by the time of discovery. For the aggregate behavior and FDNS behavior, the 10 slices each include an identical number of measured FDNSes while for the RDNS$_i$ behavior, the 10 slices each include an identical number of measured RDNS$_i$es. We then calculate a cumulative snapshot of the fraction of honest actors found in the first n slices for 1–10 slices. The cumulative rate should flatten out if the dataset is typical of the broader population.

Figure 15 shows the results. The fraction of honest actors in the aggregate data remains constant throughout the 10 snapshots, indicating that we quickly discover a representative sample in this study. In particular, these results indicate that the "Scan on First Hit" method of discovery used in this study and which has a bias potential, does not bias this particular metric. The fraction of honest RDNS$_i$es decreases over time but appears to converge to a constant value by the 7th snapshot. This shows that (1) honest RDNS$_i$es are discovered at a higher rate towards the beginning of the scan and (2) we discover a sufficient number of RDNS$_i$es to be representative of the general population. Finally, the fraction of honest FDNSes increases throughout the 10 snapshots though the growth is flattening. This result indicates that our dataset is not sufficient to capture a representative set of FDNSes that allow cache injection. The fraction of honest FDNSes in the true population is likely higher than what we report in this paper.

A larger question of representativeness is whether open DNS resolvers are representative of the overall population of DNS resolvers users employ. In other words, do the behaviors we find in ODNSes more broadly apply to first hop resolvers in general? Our methodology does not afford any way to directly assess this question given that we would have to do so from inside many edge networks to gain an understanding of resolver behavior for first hop resolvers that are not arbitrarily accessible. This problem does not apply to our RDNS results because given the window that the myriad ODNSes provide we are readily able to get "inside" the RDNSes' networks and assess their behavior.

9. CONCLUSION

In this paper, we present a set of methodologies for efficiently discovering the client-side DNS infrastructure and, once discovered, teasing apart the behavior of the actors within the system including components that cannot be directly probed. Using these methodologies, we assess various aspects of the client-side DNS infrastructure and its behavior with respect to caching, both in aggregate and separately for different actors. In terms of the infrastructure, we double previous estimates of the number of open resolvers on the Internet, find evidence of wide use of shared resolver pools, and observe significant distances DNS messages travel within the infrastructure. In terms of caching behavior, we show how long various actors retain records and how they report TTL values. In general, we observe that the authoritative TTL value is frequently modified by the client-side DNS infrastructure. We show that large TTLs are reduced in 64% of the cases, and small TTLs are increased in 11% of our measurements. We tease apart these behaviors and attribute the former behavior predominantly to RDNS$_i$es and the latter behavior predominantly to FDNSes. Additionally, we find that cache evictions due to capacity limits occur infrequently in RDNS$_i$es even for rarely accessed records. At the same time, while the TTL is frequently mis-reported to clients, resolvers themselves do not retain records much past authoritative TTL. We observe that records are returned past TTL in only 10% of the cases, even for records with a relatively short TTL of 30 seconds.

Acknowledgments

This work was supported in part by NSF through grants CNS-0831821, CNS-1213157 and CNS-0831535. The authors would like to thank the anonymous reviewers – and in particular our shepherd, Meeyoung Cha – for their assistance in improving the paper.

10. REFERENCES

[1] Open Resolver Project. http://openresolverproject.org/.

[2] B. Ager, W. Mühlbauer, G. Smaragdakis, and S. Uhlig. Comparing DNS Resolvers in the Wild. In *10th ACM SIGCOMM IMC*, pages 15–21, 2010.

[3] Alexa. http://www.alexa.com/topsites.

[4] H. A. Alzoubi, M. Rabinovich, and O. Spatscheck. The Anatomy of LDNS Clusters: Findings and Implications for Web Content Delivery. In *22d Int. WWW Conf.*, 2013.

[5] R. Arends. DNS Security Introduction and Requirements, 2005. RFC 4033.

[6] T. Callahan, M. Allman, and M. Rabinovich. On Modern DNS Behavior and Properties. *ACM SIGCOMM CCR*, 43(3):7–15, 2013.

[7] B. Chun, D. Culler, T. Roscoe, A. Bavier, L. Peterson, M. Wawrzoniak, and M. Bowman. PlanetLab: An Overlay Testbed for Broad-Coverage Services. *ACM SIGCOMM CCR*, 33(3):3–12, 2003.

[8] D. Dagon, N. Provos, C. Lee, and W. Lee. Corrupted DNS Resolution Paths: The Rise of a Malicious Resolution Authority. In *NDSS*, 2008.

[9] I. Google. https://developers.google.com/speed/public-dns/docs/performance#loadbalance.

[10] K. Gummadi, S. Saroiu, and S. Gribble. King: Estimating Latency Between Arbitrary Internet End Hosts. In *2nd ACM SIGCOMM Workshop on Internet Measurment*, pages 5–18. ACM, 2002.

[11] C. Huang, D. Maltz, J. Li, and A. Greenberg. Public DNS System and Global Traffic Management. In *IEEE INFOCOM*, pages 2615 –2623, 2011.

[12] D. Kaminsky. Black Ops 2008: It's the End of the Cache As We Know It. *Black Hat USA*, 2008.

[13] D. Leonard and D. Loguinov. Demystifying Service Discovery: Implementing an Internet-wide Scanner. In *10th ACM IMC*, pages 109–122, 2010.

[14] R. Liston, S. Srinivasan, and E. Zegura. Diversity in DNS Performance Measures. In *2nd ACM SIGCOMM Workshop on Internet Measurment*, pages 19–31. ACM, 2002.

[15] Z. M. Mao, C. D. Cranor, F. Douglis, M. Rabinovich, O. Spatscheck, and J. Wang. A Precise and Efficient Evaluation of the Proximity Between Web Clients and Their Local DNS Servers. In *USENIX ATC*, pages 229–242, 2002.

[16] Geoip. maxmind llc, 2012.

[17] J. Pang, A. Akella, A. Shaikh, B. Krishnamurthy, and S. Seshan. On the Responsiveness of DNS-based Network Control. In *4th ACM SIGCOMM IMC*, pages 21–26, 2004.

[18] M. Rajab, F. Monrose, A. Terzis, and N. Provos. Peeking Through the Cloud: DNS-based Estimation and its Applications. In *Applied Cryptography and Network Security*, pages 21–38. Springer, 2008.

[19] K. Schomp, T. Callahan, M. Rabinovich, and M. Allman. Client-Side DNS Infrastructure Dataset, Oct. 2013. `http://dns-scans.eecs.cwru.edu/`.

[20] A. Shaikh, R. Tewari, and M. Agrawal. On the Effectiveness of DNS-based Server Selection. In *INFOCOM*, pages 1801–1810, 2001.

[21] C. Shue, A. Kalafut, M. Allman, and C. Taylor. On Building Inexpensive Network Capabilities. *ACM SIGCOMM CCR*, 42(2), Apr. 2012.

[22] G. Sisson. DNS Survey: October 2010. `http://dns.measurement-factory.com/surveys/201010/`, 2010.

[23] C. E. Wills, M. Mikhailov, and H. Shang. Inferring Relative Popularity of Internet Applications by Actively Querying DNS Caches. In *3rd ACM SIGCOMM IMC*, pages 78–90, 2003.

Internet Nameserver IPv4 and IPv6 Address Relationships

Arthur Berger
MIT CSAIL / Akamai
awberger@csail.mit.edu

Nicholas Weaver
ICSI / UCSD
nweaver@icsi.berkeley.edu

Robert Beverly
Naval Postgraduate School
rbeverly@nps.edu

Larry Campbell
Akamai
lcampbel@akamai.com

ABSTRACT

The modern Domain Name System (DNS) provides not only resolution, but also enables intelligent client routing, e.g. for Content Distribution Networks (CDNs). The adoption of IPv6 presents CDNs the opportunity to utilize different paths when optimizing traffic, and the challenge of appropriately mapping IPv6 DNS queries. This work seeks to discover the associations between Internet DNS client resolver IPv6 address(es) and IPv4 address(es). We design and implement two new techniques, one passive and one active, to gather resolver pairings. The passive technique, deployed in Akamai's production DNS infrastructure, opportunistically discovered 674k (IPv4, IPv6) associated address pairs within a six-month period. We find that 34% of addresses are one-to-one, i.e. appear in no other pair, a fraction that increases to $\approx$ 50% when aggregating IPv6 addresses into /64 prefixes. The one-to-one associations are suggestive, but not a sufficient condition, of dual-stack DNS recursive resolvers. We further substantiate our inferences via PTR records and software versions, and manual verification of sample pairings by three major Network Operators. Complex associations, where e.g. distributed DNS resolution leads to inferred address groupings that span continents and many autonomous systems exist, a subset of which we explore in more depth using the active probing technique. Among potential uses, Akamai is currently utilizing screened output from the passive technique, in conjunction with prior knowledge of IPv4, to inform IPv6 geolocation within its CDN.

Categories and Subject Descriptors

C.2.3 [**Computer Communication Networks**]: Network Operations—*network monitoring*

General Terms

Measurement, Experimentation

IMC'13, October 23–25, 2013, Barcelona, Spain.
Copyright 2013 ACM 978-1-4503-1953-9/13/10 ...$15.00.
http://dx.doi.org/10.1145/2504730.2504745.

Keywords

DNS; Nameservers; Resolvers; IPv6

1. INTRODUCTION

After languishing for decades, IPv6 [13] is experiencing renewed interest [17], in large part due to economics and politics [10, 23]. However, IPv4 and IPv6 are expected to co-exist for the foreseeable future. Transition strategies, practical constraints, and inertia imply that portions of the IPv6 infrastructure will depend on IPv4, where hosts and infrastructure are "dual-stacked."

Previous measurement research has explored IPv6 penetration of the broader client population, for instance via web instrumentation [11, 32, 27]. Several initiatives [18, 19] and anecdotal evidence [28] suggest that IPv6 infrastructure deployment is proceeding in advance of client adoption. For instance, many large residential networks [12] and content providers [1] fully support IPv6. An important component of any provider's transition plans is enabling IPv6 on their Domain Name System (DNS) servers, including local recursive client resolvers.

Our motivation is interest in associating Internet DNS resolver IPv6 address(es) with IPv4 address(es). Operationally, such association is especially important to Content Distribution Networks (CDNs), where information of a client's recursive resolver is used to perform intelligent client routing and load balancing. We are particularly interested the simple case of one-to-one associations as such pairs are candidates for being on the same machine, or even interface, and thus collocated, which can be used as an input to IPv6 geolocation.

Our work is concerned with developing techniques for associating IPv4 and IPv6 DNS resolver addresses, and performing large-scale measurements to collect such associations. While out of scope for the present paper, obtaining DNS resolver associations between the two protocols has several potential future applications:

1. ***Internet Evolution:*** As IPv6 deployment continues, the infrastructure supporting each protocol will evolve. The techniques herein can be used in the future for a longitudinal study of tracking the inter-relationship of IPv4 and IPv6 nameservers.

2. ***IPv6 Geolocation:*** There is potential to leverage prior knowledge of geolocation of IPv4 addresses [5] to inform IPv6 geolocation when the addresses are correlated. One-to-one DNS resolver associations are con-

sistent with, but not proof of, the corresponding IPv4 and IPv6 addresses being assigned to the same machine, and thus being at the same physical location. Further screening of such pairs, discussed in §5.1, can pick out those that are more likely to be collocated. However, as with other inputs to geolocation, our associations are likely to be noisy and thus must be appropriately weighted. Akamai Technologies is currently using screened output from the opportunistic passive technique, §2.1, in conjunction with prior knowledge of IPv4, as one of the inputs for IPv6 geolocation within its CDN.

3. ***Security:*** IPv4, IPv6 nameserver pairs that are likely on the same machine are of interest from a security viewpoint. Not only are many old IPv4 attacks feasible in IPv6 [7], IPv6 introduces new attack vectors [16]. An attack directed against the IPv6 address of a DNS server may also impact an organization's corresponding IPv4 service.

Our hope is that our techniques and data from this research can be used as a first step toward future work on these important applications.

To this end, we develop two novel techniques for discovering associated IPv4 and IPv6 resolver addresses: i) a passive, opportunistic technique that uses a two-level DNS hierarchy that encodes IPv4 addresses within IPv6 nameserver records; and ii) an active technique whereby we probe resolvers to induce various lookup behaviors. Our techniques provide new methods to characterize a small, but critical, portion of the Internet infrastructure.

The passive technique has been implemented in the Akamai CDN, and for 674k (IPv4, IPv6) address pairs observed over a six month period, we find that 34% of the collected resolver addresses have a one-to-one association, i.e. appear in no other address pair. This percentage increases to almost 50% when the IPv6's are aggregated to /64 prefixes, (creating pairs of an IPv4 address with an IPv6 /64 prefix). We also discover complex, connected sets of address pairs that, at the extreme, span continents and hundreds of Autonomous Systems, where large cluster resolvers and public DNS providers play a major role. Additionally, we find evidence of abnormal use of 6to4 tunnels.

To help substantiate our results, we analyze the PTR records and software versions of the association inferences. For more precise validation of a subset of the associations, we employ our active measurement technique to perform a data collection over 13 hours to minimize temporal address assignment changes and corroborate the extant complexity discovered passively. Last, for samples sent to personal contacts at six major networks, three responded and manually confirmed that all of our inferred one-to-one associations that they checked were correct and indeed assigned to the same machine.

In total, this paper makes four primary contributions:

1. A new passive technique for *opportunistically* pairing IPv4 and IPv6 addresses of DNS resolvers.

2. A novel approach for *active*, targeted, DNS resolver probing to discover associated address pairs.

3. Real-world deployment of the passive technique on a commercial CDN to gather a large cross section of Internet resolvers.

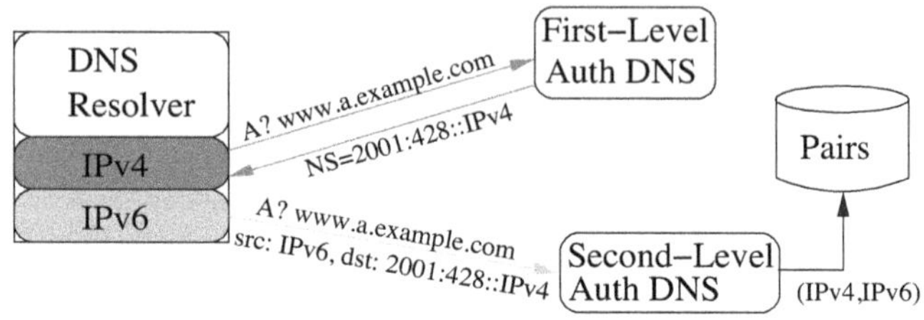

Figure 1: DNS Resolver IPv4/IPv6 Address Inference: A multi-level authority returns second-level nameserver AAAA records encoding a query's IPv4 source in the lower-order bits. The second-level nameserver associates IPv6 sources with the IPv4 encoded in the destination IPv6.

4. Analysis of observed DNS resolver address pairs that finds a significant proportion, 34%, have a one-to-one association (almost 50% when the IPv6's are aggregated to /64 prefixes) and also finds complex, connected sets of address pairs.

The remainder of this paper is organized as follows. Section 2 details the two measurement techniques comprising our system as well as our deployment. We summarize the collected data in §3, present its analysis in §4, and discuss findings in §5. Finally, we conclude in §6 with a summary of implications and suggestions for future work.

2. METHODOLOGY

Our system includes two novel measurement techniques. First, we develop a *passive*, opportunistic method to discover candidate IPv4 and IPv6 addresses of DNS resolvers. Second, we create a custom DNS server that permits *active* measurement of DNS resolvers. In this section, we detail these techniques.

2.1 Opportunistic DNS Technique

Clients rely on local recursive resolvers to perform DNS resolution. We seek to ascertain the IPv4, IPv6 addresses of dual-stacked DNS resolvers by inducing them to reveal their addresses as part of their natural lookup process.

Our technique exploits: 1) a two-level authoritative DNS resolution, and 2) the ability to encode an IPv4 address in the lower order bits of an IPv6 address. For the purpose of exposition, assume we control, and deploy our technique on, the DNS authority of `example.com`.

Consider a recursive DNS resolver servicing a local client requesting resolution of `www.a.example.com`. As depicted in Figure 1, the resolver requests resolution (typically an `A` record) for this host from the first-level authoritative nameserver via an IPv4 DNS query. The first-level nameserver responds with the second-level `NS`, and corresponding "additional" `A` and `AAAA`, records [22]. Crucially, the `AAAA` records of the second-level `NS`, as returned by our first-level nameserver, are formed dynamically. The first-level DNS *encodes a query's IPv4 source address in the lower-order bits of the response's additional* `AAAA` *record.*

For example, Figure 1 shows the first-level DNS responding to a DNS resolver's query with the authoritative `NS` record of the second-level DNS, including an additional `AAAA` record for the second-level nameserver that includes the querying resolver's IPv4 source address in the low-order bits. The recursive DNS resolver may use either the `A` or `AAAA` address for the second-level resolution. When the latter is used, the second-level DNS can pair the IPv6 source address of the query it receives with the IPv4 address encoded in the IPv6 destination of the query. Note that the dynamically generated `AAAA` nameserver record is valid as the second-level DNS accepts queries from an entire prefix; we use a /80 prefix.

Akamai Technologies has deployed this passive technique within its production infrastructure [26], making use of its pre-existing multi-level DNS hierarchy (whose primary purpose is to resolve names to CDN addresses that can best serve the client), and has activated it for a selection of domains. Akamai has used the resulting data collection during the revision of its request-routing software to support IPv6, and continues to use it as one of the inputs into Akamai's geolocation product [5] where the extensive prior knowledge of IPv4 can be used to aid in the location of IPv6 when the IPv4 and IPv6 addresses are inferred to be correlated.

As a practical issue, the first-level authoritative DNS in Figure 1 does not know whether the client's nameserver is IPv6 capable, as the incoming DNS query arrives over IPv4. Thus, in Akamai's implementation, of eight `NS` records returned, only one or two of the associated glue records are `AAAA`. Also, even when the client's nameserver is dual stacked, it may not select the `AAAA`; selection order typically depends on historical load and performance characteristics.

Note that this technique is opportunistic: a client resolver must first contact our authoritative DNS for resolution of an object within our portion of the DNS namespace. No additional packets are sent when one deploys the technique for domain names that are being used anyway. Because the technique is passive, where the collection of address pairs is simply a by-product of the client's resolver requesting a domain under our authority, there are no restrictions on the population of resolvers we can measure. In particular, we are not limited to open resolvers as the entity collecting the data is not initiating the DNS query.

Also note that the passive technique only checks whether the client's resolver can send IPv6, but does not check whether it can receive IPv6. If it can not receive responses over IPv6, the query will timeout, and the resolver can fallback to retry using an IPv4 glue record. In such a scenario, we still record an (IPv4, IPv6) pair. This ambiguity does not occur with the active technique of §2.2.

The passive technique can be implemented on any authoritative nameservers under common control along a DNS namespace hierarchy. It can be implemented even on a single machine, with multiple addresses, where the IPv4 glue address for the NS record for `example.com` is distinct from the IPv4 and IPv6 glue addresses for the NS record that causes the lookup to the second level. However, our deployment using separate first and second-level authorities is most compatible with the existing Akamai infrastructure, where deployment on Akamai affords us a rich and diverse dataset.

2.1.1 Advantageous Complications

Figure 1 illustrates the simple case where the DNS queries come from a single, dual-stacked machine. However, the reality of Internet DNS resolution can be much more complex. Recall that the (IPv4, IPv6) addresses that are logged are addresses seen by the authoritative nameservers. They need not be associated with the same machine. It is well-known that DNS servers and resolvers experience significant load, and that many approaches exist for balancing DNS query load [25, 3, 15, 4]. A relatively common case, especially among large providers, is that a provider maintains a set of servers at a location that share the load, and also may share a cache or may distribute obtained resolutions. Further, DNS resolver implementations may perform record pre-fetching [4] in an effort to improve performance.

In Akamai's implementation, the `NS` records returned by the first-level authoritative DNS have a TTL of 12 hours. Thus, if there is shared cache or if the results are distributed, then another nameserver may subsequently use cached results and send a query over IPv6, in which case the second-level nameserver will discover multiple IPv6 addresses associated with a single IPv4 address. A short TTL on the final `A` or `AAAA` record (20 seconds in the Akamai implementation) increases reuse of the cached `NS` record. Furthermore, after the `NS` TTL expires, if some other nameserver in the cluster does the lookup at the first-level, then another IPv4 address could be seen by the authoritative nameserver. In which case the data set will contain multiple pairs which have IPv4 or IPv6 addresses in common, all of which are associated with a given cluster of DNS servers at a given location. This complexity is an advantageous complication from a number viewpoints. For geolocation, one has discovered additional addresses that are likely collocated. For CDN's that wish to associate clients to nameservers, one might generalize an observed set of (client address, nameserver address) pairs to any of these clients potentially being associated with any of these nameservers. Further, from the viewpoint of survivability, or robustness, one has gained some insight into how the ISP has chosen to architect its DNS.

However, clusters of DNS servers complicate the discovery of pairs of (IPv4, IPv6) addresses that can be inferred to exist on the same interface or machine. However, in [8], we describe preliminary work on an active fingerprinting technique that seeks to determine whether or not candidate address pairs are indeed on the same machine.

Another complication is when sometimes there is an intermediary machine between the client's nameserver and the authoritative first and second-level nameservers, as for example when a Network Operator has deployed a DNS cache hierarchy. Another case is when a public DNS, e.g. [2], is used for the IPv6 but not the IPv4, or vice versa. The presence of intermediary machines is a negative complication from the viewpoint of wishing to associate addresses to a common machine or set of machines at a given location. Though, it is interesting from the viewpoint of discovery of DNS architecture and how the DNS is being used, as discussed in §4.1.3.

Note that when using the discovered (IPv4, IPv6) pairs for geolocation one needs to take into account that the data set will likely contain misleading information, as some of the pairs will have addresses that are in distinct locations. However, noisy inferences are not a new problem, but rather a well-known attribute of many of the inputs used for geolocation; and one must sort, weigh, and filter conflicting information from multiple sources.

2.1.2 Example Nameserver Pairs

To illustrate the potential complexity of the associations we gather passively, we present several example resolver pairs in this subsection. Often (to be quantified in §4.1.1) a given IPv4 address and a given IPv6 appear in only one pair.

For example, the two addresses in the pair:

```
(119.63.216.69,  2402:7400:0:c::5)
```

are only observed in this pair. However, just as common are more complex relationships. For example the IPv6 address `2001:380:515:1::201` is observed in two pairs:

```
(210.227.79.198,  2001:380:515:1::201)
(210.227.79.230,  2001:380:515:1::201)
```

and these two IPv4 addresses are only seen for this IPv6. Similarly, the IPv4 address `120.119.28.2` is observed in four pairs:

```
(120.119.28.2, 2001:e10:c41:49:c5e5:281b:44f8:80bd)
(120.119.28.2, 2001:e10:c41:51:226:b0ff:fedc:f970)
(120.119.28.2, 2001:e10:c41:1::2)
(120.119.28.2, 2001:e10:c41:59:cabc:c8ff:fe92:e8d6)
```

and these four IPv6 addresses are only seen in these pairs. The associations can become more involved, for example the following six pairs:

```
(193.137.16.65,  2001:690:2280:1::65)
(193.137.16.65,  2001:690:2280:801::135)
(193.137.16.75,  2001:690:2280:801::135)
(193.137.16.75,  2001:690:2280:1::75)
(193.137.16.145, 2001:690:2280:801::135)
(193.137.16.145, 2001:690:2280:801::145)
```

form a connected set of associations, in that starting at any address and following the associations, one would eventually touch each of the addresses in this set.

Such sets of address pairs can be complex. In the 6-month data set, Section 3, there is one particularly large group consisting of about a third of the 674,000 address pairs, and spanning hundreds of autonomous systems (ASes) and multiple continents. This large group occurs, at least in part, due to open, public nameservers such as GoogleDNS, and is of interest from the viewpoint of how DNS is being used, and is discussed in Section 4.1.3.

2.1.3 *Bipartite Graph and Equivalence Classes*

We abstract the observed resolver pairs as a bipartite graph between a set of IPv4 addresses and a disjoint set of IPv6 addresses. Each of the observed address pairs is an edge of the graph connecting a vertex in the IPv4 set to a vertex in the IPv6 set. The graph is not fully connected, but rather consists of many subsets of connected edges.

We call a set of connected edges (and the address pairs they represent) an "equivalence class," abbreviated "eq. class." Figure 2 illustrates an example bipartite graph consisting of five IPv4 addresses, seven IPv6 addresses, and eight address pairs (edges). Let m-n denote an equivalence class containing m IPv4 and n IPv6 addresses. In Figure 2 the address pairs partition into four equivalence classes, two of which are *1-1*, one is *2-1* and one is *1-4*.

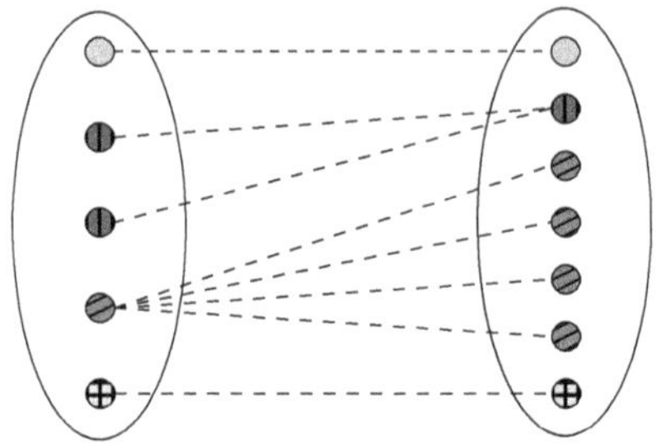

Figure 2: Equivalence Classes: The associations (edges) between IPv4 and IPv6 addresses form a bipartite graph. The connected components form equivalence classes of various sizes. In this hypothetical example, the nodes in each equivalence class are shaded uniquely. Two of the four equivalence classes are 1-1 (one IPv4, one IPv6 node), one is 2-1, and one is 1-4.

2.2 Active DNS Measurements

In addition to the opportunistic, passive DNS data collection, we develop an active DNS measurement to both validate and better understand our passive results.

We use this active technique to probe the subset of passively gathered resolvers that respond to external requests, e.g. the subset containing open and forwarding resolvers [6]. More generally, this technique can be used on any resolver that will respond to probes from one's vantage point, such as those of one's own network, or the numerous open DNS forwarders on the public Internet.

One actively probes the resolvers issuing specially crafted queries for DNS records for which we are authoritative. In this way, we control both the DNS probes and the authority of the DNS records being probed, thereby permitting testing of open DNS recursive resolvers in our dataset. Figure 3 depicts the high-level active DNS probing methodology.

Our authoritative domains are served by a custom DNS server that is standards compliant [14]. Our authoritative server listens on both IPv4 and IPv6, but returns different results depending upon the incoming request. The server handles multiple domains that support either IPv4 or IPv6 requests, where the choice of domain impacts the IP protocol used by a recursive resolver.

We initiate queries to the open and forwarding resolvers. The results from our DNS server for the queried object induce the resolver under test to issue a series of queries that alternate between IPv4 and IPv6 for network transport. We maintain state between requests by specially encoding the returned results such that the final response to the recursive query is a "chain" of IPv4 and IPv6 addresses used by the resolver under test. Mao et al. [21] also encode an Internet address in a domain name, though in the different context of associating IPv4 clients with the client's recursive resolver address, and where a web bug is inserted in volunteer web pages. Figure 4 provides an example timing diagram of the interaction of our prober and an authoritative DNS server with an open resolver whose addresses we wish to infer. In this example, the resolver has IPv6 addresses=$A1, A3$ and IPv4 addresses=$A2, A4$.

The prober queries the open resolver or forwarder for a single `TXT` record. The resolver can only fetch this name using IPv6, but instead of returning the record's value, our server returns a canonical name (`CNAME`) alias. This `CNAME` encodes the IPv6 address which contacted our server; for example an IPv6 address `2001:f8b0::91` is encoded into the `CNAME`:

```
2001yf8b0yy91.v4.dnstest.icsi.berkeley.edu
```

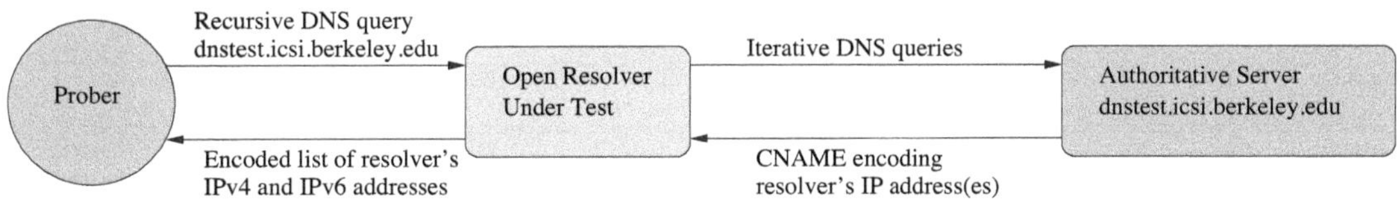

Figure 3: Active DNS Probing: We send queries for DNS records whose authority is under our control (shaded blue), thereby permitting testing of open resolvers in our dataset. Our authoritative server is specially designed to: 1) force the recursive resolver to alternate between IPv4 and IPv6 transport; and 2) encode the resolver's source IP addresses. The result of our DNS probes is an encoded list of the resolver's IPv4 and IPv6 addresses.

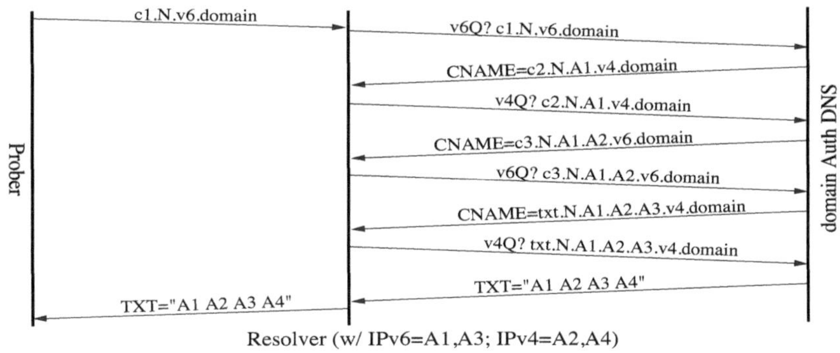

Figure 4: Active DNS Probing: Our authoritative DNS server returns a series of `CNAME` results with alternating IPv6 and IPv4 glue. We probe a resolver under test for our special domain, including a nonce N. State is maintained on addresses the resolver uses by encoding the IPs along the chain. The final result is the sequence of IPv4, IPv6 addresses used by the resolver (here $A1, A2, A3, A4$).

This returned `CNAME` exists within the IPv4-only domain. The next `CNAME` redirects back to IPv6, encoding both IPs. After following another `CNAME` back to the IPv4 domain, our server finally returns a `TXT` record reporting the sequence of four IP addresses which contacted our server. Note that while DNS authority servers may typically include multiple records in a single returned result, our server only returns one result at a time in order to force multiple lookups and infer the chain. Our `CNAME` encoding scheme, combined with DNS message compression [22], ensure that, even in the worst case ASCII IPv4 and IPv6 encoding expansion, our chains of length 4 are less than 512 bytes. As 512B is the limit for DNS over UDP, we ensure that our chains rely on neither truncation nor EDNS0 [30].

Note that our methodology includes several techniques to ensure accuracy. First, each query includes a nonce that prevents effects due to DNS caching. Second, all state is maintained in the queries themselves, thereby removing the potential for miscorrelation of IPv4 and IPv6 addresses. For example, to infer a set of IPv4 and IPv6 addresses used by the Google public DNS resolvers, we query:

```
dig +short TXT @8.8.8.8 \
 cname1e6464.n123.v6.dnstest.icsi.berkeley.edu
```

where the Google DNS resolver, after stepping through the CNAME's, finally sends a query for the `TXT` record:

```
txt.n123.2607yf8b0y4004yc00yy153.64x233x168x86. \
2607yf8b0y4004yc00yy156.v4.dnstest.icsi.berkeley.edu.
```

The authoritative DNS, notes the three addresses contained in the requested domain, and notes the source address of the incoming query. The authoritative DNS then returns the TXT record that includes the nonce and the sequence of addresses that contacted our server to resolve the request; in this example:

```
"n123" \
"2607:f8b0:4004:c00::153" "64.233.168.86" \
"2607:f8b0:4004:c00::156" "64.233.168.85"
```

As we will show in §4, many large-scale resolvers are actually clusters, not individual systems. A cluster might be behind a single publicly facing IP address with load distributed among multiple backend machines, or might encompass multiple publicly visible IP addresses. Thus, one can repeat the active DNS probes multiple times in order to gain a more complete picture of cluster structure when present. Since the DNS specification [14] requires that the recursive resolver process the entire `CNAME` chain, these four IP addresses should represent the same "system" responsible for completing the DNS resolution.[1] The replies themselves have a 0 second TTL and the request contains a counter, thus a resolver should never cache the result.

[1]We initially noticed a complication where a NAT forwarder could send an initial lookup to our server but, after receiving our `CNAME` reply, it queries instead a configured recursive resolver for the `CNAME`, as the initial IPv4 address was only used in the first of the two IPv4 queries and did not otherwise cluster well with the rest of the resolution change. We speculate that most such systems are not IPv6 capable, so we changed our query's order from V4/V6/V4/V6 to V6/V4/V6/V4 to prevent a NAT from initiating the request directly, forcing it to contact the configured recursive resolver first to complete the resolution process.

Table 1: Data sets

Set	Method	Collection Period	Num. IPv4	Num. IPv6	Num. Pairs	Notes
6-month data set	Passive	Mar. 17 to Sep. 13, 2012	270,000	282,000	674,000	From Akamai's production deployment. Includes first and last time the address pair was recorded.
12-day data set	Passive	Apr. 18 to 30, 2012	47,000	46,000	119,000	From Akamai's production deployment. Includes the number of times an address pair was recorded.
1-day data set	Active	Apr. 19 to 20, 2013	5,000	8,000	41,000	200 repeated tests to 7,000 open resolvers of the 6-month data set.

Although limited to probing IPv6-capable open resolvers and forwarders (thus excluding most corporate networks), the active measurement has several advantages over the passive measurements. This technique forces the resolver to use IPv6 (instead of relying on a resolver's preference for IPv6 over IPv4). Since the measurements all occur within a short time window, this measurement is not affected by network changes. It also produces a set of up to four associations, allowing it to more effectively and precisely map the structure of a cluster resolver.

3. DATA SETS

We examine three data sets, summarized in Table 1. The 6-month data set is from Akamai's production deployment. The address pairs are obtained by the passive, opportunistic DNS technique, described in §2.1. Akamai observes a significant cross-section of global DNS traffic in its role as a large CDN; the dataset includes resolvers from over 213 countries [5] and contains: 674,000 unique (IPv4, IPv6) pairs with 271,000 unique IPv4 and 282,000 unique IPv6 addresses.

The 12-day data set is also from Akamai's deployment and the passive DNS technique, though the logs were collected and aggregated via a script that records the number of observations of each address pair. A measure of the popularity of an address pair is useful as an additional criteria when screening for collocated addresses, and it is being incorporated into a revised collection and aggregation of the Akamai logs.

The 1-day data set is obtained by the active technique of §2.2. We test the addresses in the 6-month data set to determine whether they return a response from our prober, i.e. whether they are open[2], and we receive responses from 5,308 IPv4 and 1,677 IPv6 resolver addresses. While this is only a subset of the full data, it permits validation against a meaningful pool of systems. These addresses are then repeatedly probed, at least 200 times over the next hours.[3] We use this active data set to investigate the additional complexity in the DNS infrastructure that is revealed by repeated probes to a given set of resolvers.

[2]We again emphasize that while our active technique requires an open resolver, the passive technique does not.

[3]The returned v6/v4/v6/v4 4-tuple often contains addresses distinct from the addresses probed, thus, from ≈7,000 open resolvers probed, ≈13,000 addresses occur in the 4-tuples, Table 1. The number of systems probed is significantly lower than the number of open "recursive resolvers" because this only included systems supporting IPv6 and only included true open resolvers, rather than the bulk of misconfigured home NATs and other DNS forwarders.

4. RESULTS

This section analyzes results from deploying the aforementioned techniques on the IPv4 and IPv6 Internet. We first examine the six-month passive data set, focusing on the *1-1* eq. classes, and the ability to limit the prevalence of complex associations via various forms of aggregation. To better understand the remaining complexity, which is a small fraction of the eq. classes, but a large number of addresses, we examine one of the largest eq. classes. Using our active technique, we exploit the subset of open resolvers in the six-month passive data set to show similarly complex eq. classes. We then consider the additional attribute of the frequency that an address pair is observed. Last, we perform three forms of validation to increase the confidence in our results: probing for consistent software version and PTR records, and manual verification by network operators.

4.1 Passive Technique Address Discovery (Six-Month Data Set)

We examine the address pairs of the 6-month data set. Recall that we define an "Equivalence Class" to be a set of connected edges (address pairs) in a bipartite graph (§2.1.3). A *m-n* eq. class consists of m IPv4 and n IPv6 addresses, and a *1-1* eq. class is the simple case of an address pair where neither address has been observed in any other pair, and is consistent with (but not a guarantee of) the two addresses being assigned to a common resolver.

Figure 5 is a scatter plot of all eq. classes, using their relative frequency as the color key. We observe that the small eq. classes, *1-1* and *1-2*, are the most common, and that there exists a broad range of sizes, with larger eq. classesoften representing a singular occurrence. We focus first on the *1-1* eq. classes, and then examine the larger ones.

4.1.1 Focus on 1-1 Equivalence Classes

The canonical case of a simple dual-stack server with a single routable IPv4 and IPv6 address would be observed as a *1-1* eq. class, though the converse need not hold as a *1-1* relationship may also be the public facing portion of a more complicated architecture. From the perspective of finding candidate dual-stack servers more *1-1* eq. classes is better.

As shown in the first row of Table 2, 34% of the addresses (IPv4 plus IPv6) of the 6-month data set are in *1-1* eq. classes. Although, not a majority, it is still a substantial portion, and increases to almost 50% when we consider aggregation to prefixes.

Aggregation to Prefixes.

Frequently, multiple addresses of a non-*1-1* equivalence class reside in a given network prefix. Therefore, for each equivalence class, we examine aggregating addresses by pre-

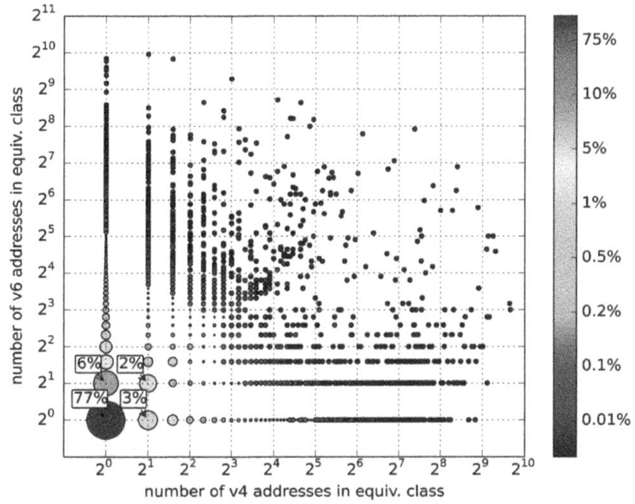

Figure 5: Scatter plot of number of IPv4 and IPv6 addresses in the equivalence classes. Only the *1-1*, *1-2*, *2-1*, and *2-2* eq. classescomprise more than 1% of the total population, however there are a small number of large eq. classesof varied sizes.

Table 2: Prevalence of 1-1 equivalence classes in the 6-month data set

Data Set	Entity	% of IPv4+IPv6 addresses in 1-1 eq class
6-month data set	addresses	34%
6-month data set	prefixes - , /64	47.6%
6-month data set	prefixes /30, /64	47.9%
6-month data set	prefixes /27, /64	48.2%
6-month data set	prefixes /24, /64	48.6%
6-month data set	prefixes /24, /48	49.7%
6-month data set	prefixes /16, /32	62.4%
6-month data set	AS's	80%
Restrict to final week	addresses	71%
Random subset; same num of pairs as in last week	addresses	51%±0.5%
Example in Fig 2	addresses	33%

fix, thereby forming network-specific eq. classes. There is a trade-off regarding the chosen size of the prefix, where larger prefixes lead to more *1-1* eq. classes, but also increase the chance of pooling together unrelated equipment. For example, aggregating to prefixes as advertised by BGP would produce eq. classes with a natural association to the networks. However, the Network Operator that advertises a given prefix is not claiming that the addresses therein are located in a given Point of Presence, and are unlikely to be so for larger prefixes.

Here, we concern ourselves with *1-1* eq. classes whose addresses are likely candidates to be collocated. Therefore, we consider smaller prefixes to increase the chance of collocation. For IPv6, a natural choice is to aggregate across the interface ID in the lower 64 bits. Established practice is for IPv6 addresses in a given /64 to be on a common subnet, or may even be associated with a single interface where the interface ID is varied for anonymity, [24]. For IPv4 there is no natural choice for aggregation. Commonly, not always, operators assign to servers in a given rack (or subnet, or building) addresses that are close to one another in address space. A reasonable assumption (but for which there would be exceptions) is that addresses of servers in the same /30 would be in the same building. Assuming a /29 is a somewhat more aggressive, and so on. Fortuitously, given the arbitrariness in choice of prefix, we find that for the *1-1* eq. classes there is an insensitivity, at least up to /24's and /48's.

As an example of aggregation, the following five pairs:

```
(122.1.94.240, 2001:380:150::1053)
(122.1.94.240, 2001:380:11c::1053)
(122.1.94.240, 2001:380:11c::2053)
(122.1.94.242, 2001:380:11c::1053)
(122.1.94.243, 2001:380:11c::2053)
```

form a *3-3* eq. class of addresses. When aggregated to prefixes /30, and /64 they become:

```
(122.1.94.240/30, 2001:380:150::/64)
(122.1.94.240/30, 2001:380:11c::/64)
```

a *1-2* eq. class of prefixes /30, /64.

For a more dramatic example, paired with `88.191.68.83` are 101 IPv6 addresses. All of the IPv6 addresses are in the single prefix `2a01:e0b:1:68/64`. The 6-month data set includes timestamps of when a given pair is first and last seen, and these IPv6's were almost always observed in disjoint 24-hour periods. This is likely an example where there is a single interface and the interface identification (the 64 lowest order bits) varies. Thus, whereas the addresses form a *1-101* equivalence class, after aggregating the IPv6's to /64 prefixes, we obtain *1-1* eq. class of prefixes.

The second through seventh rows of Table 2 report the aggregation to prefixes for different masks, where the equivalence classes are now of prefixes. When aggregating just the IPv6's and to /64's, the second row, the percent of addresses that are in the *1-1* eq. class jumps from 34% to 47.6%. When we also aggregate the IPv4's to prefixes, there is only a minor increase in the percentage even for aggregation to /24 and /48 respectively, which is rather aggressive from the viewpoint of addresses that are likely to be on the same subnet or location. (Aside: the choice of prefix has a more noticeable impact for eq. classes greater than *1-1*; see §4.1.2.) Out of curiosity, when we do an extreme aggregation to /16 and /32 prefixes, we get that 62%.

In summary, from the viewpoint of finding (IPv4, IPv6) address pairs that are candidates for being collocated, we observe that aggregating the IPv6's to /64's yields almost 50% of the addresses to be in the *1-1* equiv. class, and that there is little need for the somewhat more dubious step of also aggregating the IPv4's. See §5.1 for further comments.

Aggregation to AS's.

Shifting the focus from addresses that are candidates for being collocated, and to consider their distribution across networks, we consider aggregation to AS's. We exclude pairs where the IPv6 address is 6to4, as such addresses have ambiguous AS assignments. With 6to4 excluded, 80% of the addresses are in the *1-1* eq. class of AS's, Table 2. However, this includes the circumstance when the two AS's are not equal to each other. (This issue does not arise for prefixes, as the IPv4 is always distinct from the IPv6.) When the two AS's are different, by far the most common case is where the IPv6 AS is 6939, the tunnel broker Hurricane Electric. If we remove the address pairs of Hurricane Electric, then 51% of the remaining addresses are in the *1-1* of AS's where we impose the additional condition that the two AS's are equal to each other. Of the remaining *1-1* eq. classes of AS's where the two AS's are different, often the two AS's belong to the same organization. For example, of these AS pairs with distinct elements, the most popular AS is 7018, ATT. And of the AS's that are paired with 7018, 82% are AS 7132, SBIS-AS ATT Internet Services, and another 9% are AS 6389, BellSouth.net Inc. As an example of different organizations, when AS 3320, Deutsche Telekom, is in a *1-1* eq. class with a different AS, the most popular other AS is 8422 NetCologne, which suggest business relations besides what can be inferred from interconnection.

Restriction to a Shorter Observation Interval.

As the data set is a collection over a six month period, some address assignments and configurations likely changed during this period. These changes are reflected as larger eq. classes, as additional complexity, when in actuality, these large eq. classes may not have ever existed at a given moment in time. In this section, we examine this effect by considering a shorter observation interval.

However, when we restrict to a shorter time interval, we actually introduce *two* effects that reduce the larger eq. classes, and increase the proportion of addresses in the *1-1* eq. class: 1) less opportunity for changes in address assignments; and 2) a smaller data set. With a smaller data set, there is less opportunity for extant complexity to be revealed. (Imagine the extreme case of just a few observations, in which case large eq. classes are not possible.)

In order to separate these two effects, we also take random subsets of the full data set, where the subsets have the same number of pairs as present in the shorter observation interval. As the random subsets have address pairs from the full, 6-month observation interval, they exhibit just the first effect of a smaller data set.

The 6-month data set includes the time epoch the given pair was last observed. Thus, we can pick a time period, and then examine the subset of the pairs that are last observed during that period. We pick the length to be a week, which is short enough that the opportunity for address reassignments is much less as compared with 6 months, and long enough that we get an appreciable number of pairs, to somewhat mitigate the impact of the smaller data set. Also, we pick the week to be final week of the 6-month period, as these are the pairs that are most active, and there are two to eight times as many pairs, 83,000, as compared with any other week on the six months.

Table 2 shows the results for the restriction to the final week, as well as for the random subsets, where for the latter, 10 subsets were taken and the table reports the mean values and the range. Table 2 shows that the fraction of addresses in the *1-1* eq. classes increases from 34% to 51% when we take the random subsets, which is the effect of a smaller data set. And the percentage increases further to 71% when we restrict to the final week, where the increment from 51% is the effect of reduced opportunity for changes in configuration.

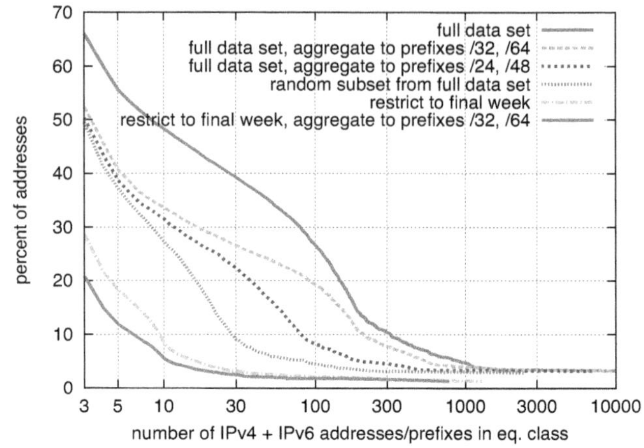

Figure 6: Percent of IPv4 + IPv6 addresses in equivalence classes of at least a given size

4.1.2 *All Equivalence Classes*

In this and the next three sub-sections, we shift the focus from the *1-1* eq. classes, and candidate address pairs that likely are on the same machine or subnet, to the non-*1-1* eq. classes.

Figure 6 shows the percent of addresses that are in eq. classes of at least a given size, where "size" is the sum of IPv4 plus IPv6 addresses (prefixes) in the eq. class. One can view Figure 6 as the complementary distribution of an address being in an equivalence class of a given size. For example, looking at the full data set, the red line, 40% of the addresses are in equivalence classes of size at least 27. While, when aggregating IPv6 to /64 prefixes, the green line, 40% of the addresses are in equivalence classes (of prefixes) of size at least 5. Note that with the x-axis beginning at 3, one can infer the percent of addresses in *1-1* eq. classes, e.g. the y-intercept of 66% means that 34% of the addresses are in an eq. class of size 2, as reported in Table 2. The curves that are higher up in the Figure indicate that, overall, the equivalence classes are larger and more complex – the distribution has a heavier tail.

Figure 6 shows that although the aggregation of IPv6 to /64 noticeably reduces the tail of the distribution, still 20% of the addresses are in eq. classes of size 90 or more. As expected, with greater aggregation, to /24 and /48 prefixes, the tail of the distribution is further reduced. A more substantial reduction occurs when we take a random subset from the full data set, where the number of pairs in the subset equals the number of pairs observed in the final week, §4.1.1.[4] This reduction is due to the smaller sample size as compared to the full data set. That is, the additional observations in the full data set reveals substantial more complexity. We use the active technique of §2.2, to perform a more controlled data collection, over a short time period, and examine the additional complexity discovered with additional probing in §4.2. When we restrict the data to the final

[4]The plots for the different random subsets are very similar to one another.

week, there is a significant reduction as compared with the random subset. Although the random subset has the same number of address pairs, it covers a period of six months, and thus there is a greater opportunity for changes in address assignments and configurations. Lastly, as expected, there is somewhat further reduction when the IPv6's are aggregated to /64's for the eq. classes of the final-week data set.

In all of the cases of Figure 6, there is a long tail. This is due to the tendency for there to be one eq. class that is much larger than the others, as discussed next.

4.1.3 "Mammoth" equivalence class

Here, we examine the largest equivalence class. As mentioned in §2.1.2, one of the equivalence classes is huge, 8037 IPv4 addresses and 9582 IPv6's, *8037-9582*, which we call the "mammoth" eq. class – it contains 3% of the addresses and 37% of the address pairs. (The next largest eq. class contains 0.3% of the addresses and 0.2% of the pairs.) This huge eq. class, whose addresses span multiple continents and are in over 750 AS's, is of interest from the viewpoint of how DNS is being used and architected, and how such a diverse set addresses could be associated with one another (and clearly does not represent a set of load balanced nameservers at a single location).

The much larger percent of pairs, 37%, as compared with percent of addresses, 3%, occurs because a minority of the addresses are in many pairs. In terms of the bipartite graph, some of the vertices have many edges.

Figure 7 shows the complementary degree distribution of the vertices in the mammoth eq. class. That is, the percent of addresses (vertices) in the mammoth eq. class that are in at least a given number of pairs (edges). Figure 7 shows that the degree distribution for the IPv4 vertices is roughly the same as for the IPv6, though with a somewhat heavier tail. Although 54% of the addresses are in just one address pair, i.e. have degree one,[5] as seen from the y-intercept, 8% of the addresses are in at least 100 pairs, 4% in at least 300 pairs, and 1% in at least 500 pairs. As a comparison, for the full 6-month data set 89% of the addresses have degree one, and only 1% have degree at least 15.

AS 15169, Google, plays a major role in this mammoth eq. class.[6] Although just 9% of the addresses in the mammoth eq. class are in AS 15169, 90% of the address pairs have one or both address(es) in that AS. 97% of the addresses that appear in at least 100 pairs are in AS 15169.

Whenever the IPv6 address is in AS 15169, then so is the paired IPv4. However, whenever the IPv4 address is in 15169, the paired IPv6 is not quite always in 15169 - 1% of the IPv6's are 6to4 and another 1% are scattered across a hundred different AS's. This is how addresses outside AS 15169 become a part of this eq. class. Some of these non-15169 IPv6 addresses may still be a part of Google's DNS architecture, assuming that Google has deployed servers in local ISP's with that ISP's addresses. And also, some may be separate from GoogleDNS - if the client's nameserver, using the public GoogleDNS for IPv4, obtained and cached the NS records returned by the first-level authoritative nameserver; and then for subsequent resolutions, sent a DNS query over IPv6 to the low-level authoritative nameserver.

[5]A degree one vertex in the bipartite graph does not imply that the vertex is in a a *1-1* eq. class. as the paired vertex can have degree greater than one.

[6]Other third-party DNS providers, such as OpenDNS and DynDNS, are present in the data set, but to a much lesser extent compared with GoogleDNS.

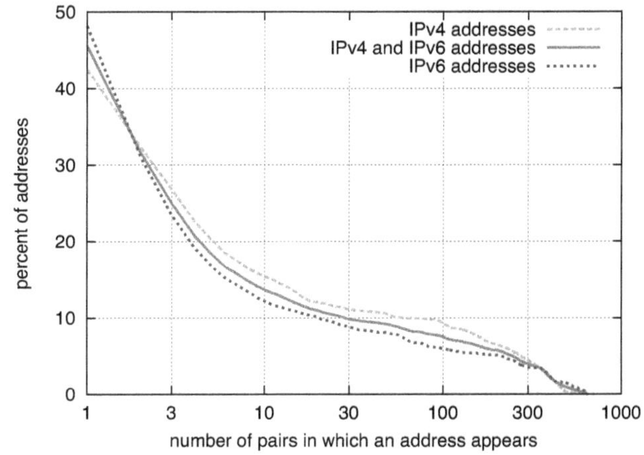

Figure 7: Percent of addresses in the "mammoth" eq. class that are in at least a given number of pairs. (Complementary distribution of node degree in bipartite graph of "mammoth" eq. class.)

Table 3: Impact on the largest equivalence class of the 6-month data set when selected address pairs are removed

Action	After action, recompute eq. classes. Resulting largest eq. class contains: Num of IPv4 addr.	Num of IPv6 addr.	Num of addr. pairs
no change to data set	8,000	9,600	247,000
omit 6to4	4,000	5,100	230,000
omit AS 15169	5,600	4,900	18,000
omit 6to4 and AS 15169	900	2,000	3,400
random subset from full data set; same number of pairs as prior line	2,623 ± 214	2,626 ± 335	78,778 ± 603

6to4 addresses also play a significant role in the mammoth eq. class. Although 6to4 addresses are in only 6% of the pairs, they are 42% of the IPv6 addresses in this eq. class (an imbalance that is the opposite of AS 15169). Interestingly, for many of the 6to4 addresses, the embedded IPv4 address does not equal the observed paired IPv4. See §4.1.4 which discusses 6to4 in the full data set, not just the mammoth eq. class.

It is of interest to see what becomes the largest eq. class when, say, AS 15169 addresses are removed. Note that if one removes a set of addresses from the mammoth eq. class, the mammoth eq. class can partition into multiple smaller eq. classes - the remainder need not be a connected set of edges in the bipartite graph. Thus, we start with the full data set, and remove pairs that contain the addresses in question, and then with the reduced set of pairs, we recompute the equiv. classes and then note which is the largest one. Table 3 shows the results for selected removals.

As discussed in Section 4.1.1, some of the reduction is simply due to a smaller number of address pairs. Thus, ten random subsets from the full 6-month data set are taken, where the number of pairs in the subset is the same as in the fourth line of the Table, 225,000 pairs, down from 674,000. Given that the cases of the fourth and fifth line have the same number of pairs, their differences are due the selective removal of particular pairs, the fourth line, versus random removal. The mean value and range is reported in fifth line, and shows that the major cause for the lower complexity reported in line four is not due the smaller sample, but rather the selected pairs that are omitted.

Even with the omission of 6to4 and AS 15169, the resulting largest eq. class still has thousands of address pairs. In §4.3 we continue the examination of largest eq. classes where we consider the 12-day data set, which has the additional information of the popularity of an address pair, and we show that significant further simplification is obtained when we omit infrequently observed pairs.

4.1.4 *Abnormal behavior with 6to4*

Auto-tunneled [9] addresses raise a natural question whether the embedded IPv4 address (i.e. the 32 bits that come after the "`2002:`") matches the paired IPv4 address from the discovery technique. Somewhat surprisingly, in 63% of the pairs where the IPv6 address is 6to4, the embedded IPv4 address is different from the paired address. Overall, any 6to4 traffic is probably a bug: Given a choice between an IPv4 address and a 6to4 address, a host should always prefer IPv4 unless executing a "happy eyeballs" strategy. Since the resolver also receives an IPv4 glue record, the resolver should prefer the IPv4 glue record, never attempting to connect to the DNS authority using 6to4.

Sometimes the 6to4 address is paired with hundreds of IPv4's. For example, `2002:aca8:101::aca8:101` appears with 270 IPv4's. The embedded address is `172.168.1.1`, on AOL, and located in the USA. The paired IPv4's are mostly in Brazil, but also Germany, Saudi Arabia, and Turkey.

A likely explanation is some sort of buggy resolver software with a hardcoded 6to4 address. That we receive such 6to4 traffic also suggests that the 6to4 gateway processing this traffic isn't validating that the embedded IPv6 address corresponds to the IPv4 address. It is not likely to be an attack as, if an attacker took advantage of this, the query the attacker would employ would cause significantly more amplification than the name lookups present in an Akamai-ed domain.

Also, there are stranger cases where the 6to4 is again paired with many IPv4's but the embedded IPv4 is not routable. For example 2002:6464:64cd::6464:64cd is paired with over 250 IPv4's and the embedded address is 100.100.100.205, or 2002:10::1:219:dbff:fef9:aa4f with embedded address 0.16.0.0. Again, this suggests buggy software misusing 6to4.

Although further investigation would be needed for a definitive explanation, it is clear that the collection of nameserver associations has turned out to have the additional feature of revealing abnormal activity.

Note: in calculating the percent of addresses that are in one-to-one associations, §4.1.1, we kept all of the complexities in the data set, including the abnormal associations. To the extent we remove any, the percentages would just get better.

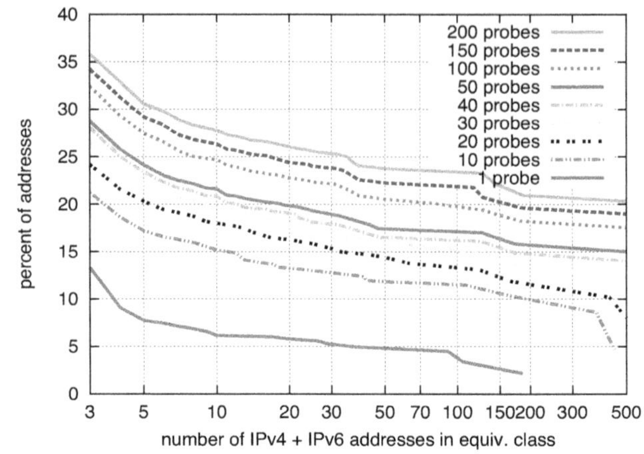

Figure 8: Percent of IPv4 + IPv6 addresses in equivalence classes of at least a given size, for open resolvers probed at least 200 times on April 19-20, 2013

4.1.5 *IPv4 address within IPv6 address (non-6to4)*

We mention briefly that of the few, 92, pairs with Teredo IPv6 addresses, (`2001:0000::/32`) only one has an embedded IPv4 equal to the paired IPv4. Of the pairs where the IPv6 address is neither 6to4 nor Teredo, just 0.6% have an embedded IPv4 equal to the paired IPv4. Of these, 57% embed the IPv4 address in the lowest 32 bits.

We also confirm an interesting human-centric convention in at least one major ISP's DNS infrastructure that has been previously observed [16]. The operator assigns the lower 64 bits of the IPv6 address, using 16 bits to encode each octet of the IPv4 address, so that the hexadecimal values render as the decimal equivalent of the IPv4 address, such as `2001:558:1014:f:68:87:76:181`. which is paired with the IPv4 address `68.87.76.181`.

4.2 Discovery of Complexity in Resolver Associations Using Active DNS Measurements

Here, we corroborate the passively discovered complexity using the Active DNS Measurement technique of §2.2 to perform a controlled data collection over a short time period. We first determine the open resolvers in the 6-month data set, for which we find about 7,000: 5,308 IPv4's and 1,677 IPv6's[7]. We probe each of these open resolvers via our active technique at least 200 times on April 19-20, 2013, requesting resolution for our special domain which induces chains of lookups across IPv6 and IPv4 glue. Thus, we obtain a data set over a short period of time, about 13 hours, and for which the same set of nameservers is probed repeatedly. Each 4-tuple of IPv6/IPv4/IPv6/IPv4 yields either 1, 2, or 4 (IPv4, IPv6) address pairs, depending on whether the two IPv4's and two v6's are the same.

We are interested in the marginal benefit of *repeated* active probing of the open resolvers, from the perspective of discovering the complexity in the IPv4, IPv6 nameserver associations using a different methodology than the passive

[7]While there exists a much larger population of open DNS resolvers in the Internet, we focus only on the subset of open resolvers that support IPv6 and appear within our passively collected six-month data set.

technique. We examine those resolvers for which the 4-tuple is obtained at least 200 times, and then compute equivalence classes conditioned on different amounts of probing.

Figure 8 shows the percent of addresses that are in equivalence classes of at least a given size, as a function of the number of probes. The curves that are higher up in the Figure indicate that, overall, the equivalence classes are larger and more complex – the distribution has a heavier tail. The lowest curve in the plot is of equivalence classes of addresses from those 4-tuples discovered as a result of just the *first* probe to each of the resolvers. That is, even though at least 200 probes were made, the lowest curve considers just the first one. The next curve above that one is from those 4-tuples discovered from the first ten probes, and so on. The Figure shows that with increased sampling, additional nameserver addresses are discovered, and the equivalence classes overall become larger. Note that the curves are stacked on top of each other, and where the spacing varies. There is a relatively large jump between the curve for 1 probe to that of 10 probes. Then, as progressively ten more probes are incorporated, up to 50 probes, the spacing tends to get smaller. And likewise, there is a relatively large jump between the curve for 1 probe to that of 50 probes, as compared with the incremental spacing from 50 to 100, which in turn is larger than from 100 to 150 probes, and which is about the same from 150 to 200 probes. Thus, with the additional probing, additional existing complexity is discovered, though often the marginal increase is decreasing. Moreover (and particularly given the impact of going from 150 to 200 probes being about the same as from 100 to 150), even after 200 probes, in all likelihood we have not discovered all of the existing complexity associated with this given set resolvers. As with the six-month data set, the largest eq. classes have addresses that span multiple continents and many AS's.

We obtain analogous results to Figure 8 when in each eq. class, we aggregate the IPv6's to /64 prefixes. In summary, the active DNS measurement technique also finds complex associations, even when the probing is done over a short period of time. Repeated probing reveals additional complexity, though the marginal increase will decrease.

4.3 Worthwhile to Record the Frequency Address Pairs are Observed

Akamai's initial code that aggregated the logs of the Passive DNS Measurement technique did not compute a measure of the frequency that an address pair was observed. Jointly with the present study, Akamai is revising the code to include this measure.

In the present section we present one application of this measure: detecting the additional complexity in nameserver associations due to address pairs that are less frequently observed.

The 12-day data set is a one-time collection from Akamai's production deployment, and in contrast to the 6-month data set, includes the number of times an address pair was observed during this period. This data set is a precursor to the production deployment. The counts range from 1 to over 17 million, with a median value of 12. The pairs with highest counts belong to Comcast and ATT.

We are interested in the impact of restricting the set of address pairs to those that were observed at least 12 times in the 12 days, as well as further restrictions. We start with the full data set, and remove pairs that contain the addresses in question, and then with the reduced set of pairs, we recompute the eq. classes. The results are shown in Table 4. The Table is comparable to Table 3 for the 6-month data set, and also contains aspects of Table 2.

Table 4: The *1-1* and the largest equivalence class in the 12-day dataset, and subsets there of

Case	% of IPv4+IPv6 in 1-1 eq cls	within the largest eq cl: Num of IPv4	Num of IPv6	Num of pairs
12-day data set	66%	683	624	62,000
at least 12 occurrences	78%	447	455	30,000
omit AS 15169 & 6to4	72%	346	47	764
at least 12 occurrences; and omit AS 15169 & 6to4	82%	1	34	34
random subsets from full data set; same num of pairs as prior line	76% ± 0.7%	468 ± 5.7	508 ± 12.5	11,112 ± 75.3

As a sanity check, Table 4 includes info on the *1-1* eq. class. As shown in the first row, 66% of the addresses are in the *1-1* eq. class. This is in between the 34% for the 6-month data set, and the 71% when that data set is restricted to the final week, where the latter is more comparable in duration to present case of 12 days.

The largest eq. class contains 52% of the address pairs, which is even a greater share than the 37% of the "mammoth" eq. class of the 6-month dataset (§4.1.3). When we omit the pairs whose addresses are in AS 15169 and whose IPv6 is 6to4, the third row, the number of pairs in the largest eq. classes is just 764, which is about 1% of what it is for the full 12-day data set, the first row. This is the same percentage reduction as occurred with the 6-month data set, Table 3. Now, when in addition we omit pairs with fewer that 12 occurrences, the number of pairs in the largest eq. class is just 34, a further 20 fold reduction.

To distinguish from reduction due simply to a smaller number of pairs, we take ten random subsets of the full 12-day data set, where here the subsets have the same number of pairs as the fourth row of the Table 4, 21,000 pairs. The fifth row reports the mean value and range. The number of pairs in the largest eq. class is back up at 11,000, thus showing that the major cause for the relatively low complexity reported in line four is not due the smaller sample, but rather the selected pairs that were omitted.

4.4 Validation

To assess the IPv4 to IPv6 associations inferred via the passive DNS technique, we examine two sources of external information about the resolvers: PTR records and software version. Also, we were able to get feedback from three ISP's regarding sample data.

4.4.1 PTR *Records*

DNS PTR records map an IPv4 or IPv6 address to a human readable name. We perform a DNS PTR query for every address in the 6-month dataset. For 14.5% of the pairs, both addresses have a PTR record. For these 97,821 pairs, Table 5 shows the percent of PTR record matches for the full data set, and then partitioned by those address pairs

Table 5: Agreement between associated IPv4 and IPv6 equivalence classes and their corresponding DNS PTR records.

Set	# Pairs with PTR	Exact Match	Second-Level Match
All	97,821	4821 (4.9%)	47,752 (48.8%)
1-to-1	8461	3500 (41.4%)	5679 (67.1%)
Non 1-to-1	89,360	1321 (1.5%)	42,073 (47.1%)

Table 6: Agreement between associated IPv4 and IPv6 equivalence classes and their corresponding bind.version.

Set	Num of Pairs with bind.version	Exact Match
All	8475	6951 (82.0%)
One-to-One	4650	4619 (99.3%)
Non One-to-One	3825	2332 (61.0%)

that are a *1-1* eq. class, and those in a larger eq. class. Of the addresses in *1-1* eq. classes, we see that 41% have `PTR` records that match exactly, as compared to only 1.5% of the non *1-1* eq. classes. Identical `PTR` records is supporting, though not definitive, evidence that the two addresses are either on the same server, or are the public-facing interfaces to a DNS server cluster.

Next, we examine the agreement between the IPv4 and IPv6 `PTR` records for just the second-level domain portion of the name, e.g. `foo.bar.com` and `faz.bar.com` match at the second-level. Whereas an exact `PTR` record match might suggest that the IPv4 and IPv6 address correspond to a common host, a load-balanced or distributed resolver might assign different hostnames to different machines, albeit with the same second-level domain. Supporting this conjecture is that while only 1.5% of the non *1-1* eq. class pairs have exactly matching `PTR` records, 47.1% have a second-level `PTR` match. Whereas the difference is not as pronounced with pairs in *1-1* eq. classes, with 41.4% matching exactly and 67.1% matching at the second-level. While DNS `PTR` records are frequently incorrect or misleading, these findings increase our confidence that our passive technique is discovering meaningful structure.

4.4.2 Software Version

We examine the version of software reported by the DNS resolvers discovered in the eq. classes of the 6-month dataset. To ascertain the software version, we perform a DNS Chaosnet class (`CHAOS`) `TXT` type query for the object `version.bind`. 35,921 of the addresses respond. An example response is:

"`9.7.0-P2-RedHat-9.7.0-10.P2.el5_8.1`"

For a baseline of what is the chance that two unrelated addresses have the same `version.bind`, we repeatedly randomly pick a IPv4 and a IPv6 address from this set (ignoring whether or not they are observed as a pair), which yields a 3% match rate.

For 8,475 of the address pairs, both addresses return a value for `version.bind`. As shown in Table 6, the version matches for 82% of these pairs, a value significantly higher than the 3% random baseline. Moreover, 99.3% of the *1-1* eq. classes have resolvers that report exactly the same version.

Together, these `PTR` and `version.bind` results help support the validity of our associations and equivalence classes. While we can not definitively ascertain whether the two addresses of a pair are on the same machine, our in-progress work [8] considers other means to make a more definitive determination.

4.4.3 Feedback from Network Operators

We sent sample address associations to personal contacts at six major networks and got responses from three. All three confirmed that the IPv4 and IPv6 addresses of all of the one-to-one associations that they checked are assigned to the same physical machine. One respondent, a cable operator, further explained that some of the addresses were of clients. Therefore, some of the associations we observe correspond to resolvers that are run on machines of customers of said cable operator.

5. DISCUSSION

This Section discusses additional details and implications of our methodology and results. In particular, we discuss the need to filter when making collocation inferences, and potential root causes for the non 1-1 eq. classes we observe.

5.1 Screening for collocated addresses

An interest in this paper is the discovery of IPv4, IPv6 address of resolvers that likely are on the same machine, or, from the viewpoint of geolocation, exist at a common location, e.g. data center. With this aim, we first wish to discover the complexity that exists in the Internet of IPv4, IPv6 resolver associations, so as to avoid the false conclusion of a simple association when reality is more complicated. Our findings demonstrate that, given the complexity of address associations, the observed pairs must be filtered in order to be most valuable to higher-level objectives, e.g. geolocation.

Natural candidates of value are address pairs that are in the *1-1* eq. class and have remained so over a period of time, such as six-months, or remained so after repeated, active probing, or repeated, passive observations. However, eq. classes larger than *1-1* also provide value, for instance eq. classes where the IPv6's differ only in the lower 64 bits, given the common practice that such addresses reside on a common subnet, or may be associated with a single interface where the interface ID is varied for anonymity.

Excluding non-native IPv6 addresses is natural as these only associate the IPv4 address with the infrastructure of a particular transition strategy. If we exclude address pairs whose IPv6 is 6to4, and then compute eq. classes, and aggregate IPv6's in the eq. classes to /64 prefixes, then for the six-month data set, we find that 50% of the addresses are associated with the *1-1* eq. classes of prefixes, which again is an appreciable proportion.

Having discovered address pairs that may be on the same server, we would like a technique that could make a definitive determination. In on-going work, we are developing an active, fingerprinting technique with that goal – see [8] for an initial description.

5.2 Large Equivalence Classes

There are several potential causes of equivalence classes larger than *1-1*; for DNS resolvers specifically:

- DNS queries that subvert our multi-level hierarchy, e.g. manual or automated probes from different locations directed to specific nameservers.

- Shared distributed caches, such as those commonly employed by large public DNS resolvers [15]. If NS records returned from the first-level are saved in a shared cache (with TTL of 12 hours for the present data set) and subsequently used by another resolver that sends a query over IPv6, then the second-level will discover multiple IPv6's associated with a single IPv4. A short TTL on the final A or AAAA record (20 seconds in the data set) increases reuse of the cached NS record. Furthermore, after the NS TTL expires and some other resolver using the shared cache does the lookup at the first-level, then another IPv4 address could be added to the equivalence class.

However, our results offer a more general caution in efforts that attempt to pair IPv4 and IPv6 addresses. Complicating factors that contribute to the complexity observed in our data, but are not specific to DNS and may affect other measurement efforts, include:

- Hosts and interfaces with multiple IPv4 and/or IPv6 addresses.
- Network Address Translation (NAT) [29] of either IPv4 or IPv6, where we observe multiple addresses of the non-translated protocol that correspond to a smaller set of addresses from the other. Such translation may occur at the edge, or within the carrier [20].
- Other forms of middleboxes, including load balancers, e.g. [3].
- Auto-tunneling, including 6to4, Teredo, etc [9].
- Address changes over time, including ephemeral addresses [31] and IPv6 privacy extensions [24].

6. CONCLUSIONS

This paper seeks to characterize the inter-relation of IPv4 and IPv6 among Internet DNS resolvers. We deploy both active and passive measurement techniques to discover and analyze sets of associated pairs of IPv4, IPv6 addresses.

While prior work has examined IPv4, IPv6 associations for clients, to our knowledge this paper is the first to begin to examine such associations for equipment within operators' networks, which can be a leading indicator of IPv6 adoption [12, 1].

We develop and deploy two novel measurement systems: i) a passive, opportunistic technique using a two-level DNS hierarchy that encodes IPv4 addresses within IPv6 nameserver records; and ii) an active DNS probing system that induces a combination of IPv4 and IPv6 DNS resolver lookups in a single resolution operation.

For a six-month passive data collection, we find that 34% of the addresses have a one-to-one association, i.e. appear in no other address pair. This percentage increases to almost 50% when the IPv6's are aggregated to /64's. We consider this a positive result for finding candidate address pairs that likely are on the same server or subnet, and are collocated. Supporting evidence is provided via matching PTR records and software versions, and confirmation from three major Network Operators of sample pairings. Companion, in-progress work seeks to develop a fingerprinting technique that would confirm whether an address pair is on the same server, [8].

In contrast to such simple associations, we also find complex, connected sets of address pairs that, at the extreme, span continents and hundreds of ASes, where third-party resolvers with distributed shared caches [15] play a major role. We also observe multiple instances of abnormal use of 6to4 tunnels, where a 6to4 address is paired with hundreds of different IPv4's that again span multiple continents, and where the IPv4 embedded in the 6to4 does not equal any of the paired IPv4's.

The active technique, which was designed, implemented, and deployed completely separately from the passive one, also discovers significant complexity on the address-pair associations. It did so in the context of a controlled experiment of repeated probing of a given set of open resolvers over a short period of time, 13 hours.

The passive technique has been implemented in Akamai Technologies' DNS infrastructure, where the collected pairs, after appropriate filtering, are being used to bootstrap geolocation of IPv6 addresses, and were helpful for revisions to request-routing software to handle IPv6.

Acknowledgments

Matthew Levine had the original idea for the opportunistic nameserver technique, while Steve Hill, James Kretchmar, and Brian Sniffen contributed to its design and implementation at Akamai Technologies. Patrick Gilmore provided insights into common practice of network operators, and via his contacts obtained feedback on sample address pairs. Our shepherd, John Heidemann, helped to review and properly frame the work. Thanks to the anonymous reviewers, Mark Allman, Billy Brinkmeyer, Aaron Hughes, and Geoffrey Xie for invaluable feedback on initial drafts of this work. This work supported in part by NSF grants CNS-1111445, CNS-1111672, and CNS-1213157. This material represents the position of the authors and not necessarily that of the NSF, Akamai Technologies, or the U.S. Government.

7. REFERENCES

[1] IPv6 Implementors Conference, 2010. https://sites.google.com/site/ipv6implementors/2010/agenda.

[2] Public DNS: Performance Benefits, 2013. https://developers.google.com/speed/public-dns/docs/performance.

[3] J. Abley. A software approach to distributing requests for DNS service, 2004. http://ftp.isc.org/isc/pubs/tn/isc-tn-2004-1.html.

[4] B. Ager, W. Mühlbauer, G. Smaragdakis, and S. Uhlig. Comparing DNS resolvers in the wild. In *Proceedings of the 10th ACM IMC*, pages 15–21, 2010.

[5] Akamai. Edgescape geolocation, 2012. http://www.akamai.com/html/technology/products/edgescape.html.

[6] R. Arends, R. Austein, M. Larson, D. Massey, and S. Rose. DNS Security Introduction and Requirements. RFC 4033, Mar. 2005.

[7] R. Beverly, A. Berger, Y. Hyun, and k. claffy. Understanding the efficacy of deployed internet source address validation filtering. In *Proceedings of the 9th ACM IMC*, pages 356–369, 2009.

[8] R. Beverly, A. Berger, N. Weaver, and L. Campbell. Inferring Internet Server IPv4 and IPv6 Address Relationships. Technical Report NPS-CS-13-002, Naval Postgraduate School, 2013. http://calhoun.nps.edu/public/handle/10945/34089.

[9] B. Carpenter and K. Moore. Connection of IPv6 Domains via IPv4 Clouds. RFC 3056, Feb. 2001.

[10] k. claffy. Tracking IPv6 evolution: data we have and data we need. *SIGCOMM Comput. Commun. Rev.*, 41(3):43–48, July 2011.

[11] L. Colitti, S. H. Gunderson, E. Kline, and T. Refice. Evaluating IPv6 adoption in the internet. In *Proceedings of the 11th international conference on Passive and active measurement*, PAM'10, pages 141–150, 2010.

[12] Comcast. IPv6 Information Center, 2012. http://www.comcast6.net/.

[13] S. Deering and R. Hinden. Internet Protocol, Version 6 (IPv6) Specification. RFC 2460, Dec. 1998.

[14] R. Elz and R. Bush. Clarifications to the DNS Specification. RFC 2181, July 1997.

[15] Google. Public DNS, 2012. https://developers.google.com/speed/public-dns/.

[16] M. Heuse. Recent advances in IPv6 insecurities. In *Chaos Communications Congress*, 2010.

[17] G. Huston. IPv6 BGP Statistics, 2013. http://bgp.potaroo.net/v6/as2.0/.

[18] ISOC. World IPv6 Day, 2011. http://www.internetsociety.org/ipv6/archive-2011-world-ipv6-day.

[19] ISOC. World IPv6 Launch, 2012. http://www.worldipv6launch.org.

[20] S. Jiang, D. Guo, and B. Carpenter. An Incremental Carrier-Grade NAT (CGN) for IPv6 Transition. RFC 6264 (Informational), June 2011.

[21] Z. M. Mao, C. D. Cranor, F. Douglis, M. Rabinovich, O. Spatscheck, and J. Wang. A Precise and Efficient Evaluation of the Proximity Between Web Clients and Their Local DNS Servers. In *Proceedings of the General Track of the annual conference on USENIX Annual Technical Conference*, ATEC '02, pages 229–242, 2002.

[22] P. Mockapetris. Domain names - implementation and specification. RFC 1035 (Standard), Nov. 1987.

[23] R. Mohan. Will U.S. Government Directives Spur IPv6 Adoption?, Sept. 2010. http://www.circleid.com/.

[24] T. Narten, R. Draves, and S. Krishnan. Privacy Extensions for Stateless Address Autoconfiguration in IPv6. RFC 4941 (Draft Standard), Sept. 2007.

[25] Nominum. Intelligent DNS, 2012. http://www.nominum.com/.

[26] E. Nygren, R. K. Sitaraman, and J. Sun. The Akamai network: a platform for high-performance internet applications. *SIGOPS Oper. Syst. Rev.*, 44(3):2–19, Aug. 2010.

[27] RIPE NCC. World IPv6 Day Measurements, 2011. http://v6day.ripe.net.

[28] N. Sarrar, G. Maier, B. Ager, R. Sommer, and S. Uhlig. Investigating IPv6 traffic: what happened at the world IPv6 day? In *Proceedings of PAM*, 2012.

[29] P. Srisuresh and K. Egevang. Traditional IP Network Address Translator (Traditional NAT). RFC 3022 (Informational), Jan. 2001.

[30] P. Vixie. Extension Mechanisms for DNS (EDNS0). RFC 2671 (Proposed Standard), Aug. 1999.

[31] Y. Xie, F. Yu, K. Achan, E. Gillum, M. Goldszmidt, and T. Wobber. How dynamic are IP addresses? In *Proceedings of SIGCOMM*, pages 301–312, 2007.

[32] S. Zander, L. L. H. Andrew, G. Armitage, G. Huston, and G. Michaelson. Mitigating Sampling Error with Measuring Internet Client IPv6 Capabilities. In *Proceedings of the SIGCOMM IMC*, 2012.

Understanding IPv6 Internet Background Radiation

Jakub Czyz, Kyle Lady, Sam G. Miller, Michael Bailey
University of Michigan
Ann Arbor, MI
{jczyz, kylelady, sgmiller, mibailey}@umich.edu

Michael Kallitsis
Merit Network, Inc.
Ann Arbor, MI
mgkallit@merit.edu

Manish Karir
Department of Homeland Security
Sci. and Tech. Directorate
Cyber Security Division
Washington, DC
manish.karir@hq.dhs.gov

ABSTRACT

We report the results of a study to collect and analyze IPv6 Internet background radiation. This study, the largest of its kind, collects unclaimed traffic on the IPv6 Internet by announcing five large /12 covering prefixes; these cover the majority of allocated IPv6 space on today's Internet. Our analysis characterizes the nature of this traffic across regions, over time, and by the allocation and routing status of the intended destinations, which we show help to identify the causes of this traffic. We compare results to unclaimed traffic in IPv4, and highlight case studies that explain a large fraction of the data or highlight notable properties. We describe how announced covering prefixes differ from traditional network telescopes, and show how this technique can help both network operators and the research community identify additional potential issues and misconfigurations in this critical Internet transition period.

Categories and Subject Descriptors

C.2.3 [**Computer-Communication Networks**]: Network Operations—*Network management, Network monitoring*

Keywords

IPv6; Darknet; Routing; Network Pollution; Internet Background Radiation; Measurement

1. INTRODUCTION

We have reached a turning point in IPv6 adoption. The entire IPv4 address space has now been allocated from the Internet Assigned Numbers Authority (IANA) to the Regional Internet Registries (RIRs). Two of these already have run out of their pool of addresses and are reduced to a final /8, from which only very small assignments are given to customers. As a result, IPv4 network growth has slowed to an almost linear rate over time from its historically exponential rate, while IPv6 networks have gone from a linear growth rate in the past to an exponential one [40]. Since World IPv6 Day in June 2011, native IPv6 traffic has doubled [34], and IPv6 traffic constitutes approximately 0.2% of peak bits per second in large cross-provider samples [21].

IMC '13 Barcelona, Spain
Copyright 2013 ACM 978-1-4503-1953-9/13/10$15.00.
http://dx.doi.org/10.1145/2504730.2504732.

Historically, network telescopes that capture traffic to "dark" (i.e., unreachable) destinations have frequently been used in IPv4 as sensors to observe phenomena that result as side effects of various applications and events on the Internet (e.g., [31], [38]). For instance, network telescopes can be used to detect worm scanning behavior, backscatter from Denial of Service (DoS) attacks, malicious vulnerability scanning, misconfiguration, and even Internet censorship. Observations of such Internet background radiation serve two purposes: to understand the original phenomenon and to aid in raising awareness regarding issues (e.g., bugs, bad practices, or misconfigurations) that potentially could be fixed. As an example of the latter, one of the results of the work of Wustrow *et al.* was the adoption of a policy to quarantine a particularly polluted block of IPv4 address space from being allocated to the public [38].

As networks attempt to enable an increasing number of IPv6 applications and services, it is highly likely that inexperience, system configuration differences, or even software or hardware bugs will result in errors that can lead to Internet background radiation. Observing such undesired traffic can provide valuable insight to help navigate the rocky start of the new technology. Identifying these issues early in the adoption process minimizes the cost of fixing them and can provide a best-practice template for future IPv6 network operators. In addition, by observing this traffic, we can be alerted to the emergence of malicious activity, such as scanning and worms, via the new protocol.

The primary contribution we make is to report on a large sample of IPv6 background radiation. We conduct the broadest IPv6 network-telescope-based longitudinal study ever preformed by concurrently announcing *BGP prefixes that cover the majority of allocated IPv6 space* used for allocations by each of the five (RIRs)—86% of allocated /64 networks outside of 6to4. We announced the prefixes: 2400::/12, 2600::/12, 2800::/12, 2c00::/12, 2a08::/13, and 2a04::/14 for over a three-month period. For a few days, we also announced RIPE's 2a00::/12. This perspective and scale allows us to capture both spatial and temporal features of the network telescope data. We also compare our results to a week of IPv4 network telescope traffic from unallocated portions of a large ≈/8 prefix captured at the same time as one of our IPv6 collection periods.

Second, we show that a *covering prefix* methodology for network telescopes in IPv6 leads to a much larger sample of data—and of qualitatively different data—than that afforded by a traditional network telescope based on only unallocated address space. We find that 95% of the packets we captured were from allocated space, and we show that captured traffic is clustered close to used prefixes. As the IPv6 address space is particularly sparse (e.g., each IPv6 subnetwork is, by default, 64 bits—an entire IPv4 Internet address space, squared), this methodology is critical to network telescope studies.

Our contributions include:

- A characterization of IPv6 background radiation, including:
  - We observe a mere 1Mbps of traffic in our study.
  - We find significant, qualitative differences between IPv4 background radiation and our observations.
  - We uncover little or no evidence of large-scale malicious scanning, and find that most traffic we see is due to misconfiguration.
- An exploration of the type of traffic observable via a covering prefix methodology, which reveals
  - 95% of the traffic we observed would not have been visible using a traditional network telescopes.
  - This traffic consists of packets misdirected due to IPv6 routing instability (36%) and apparent leakage of address space meant for internal use (59%).

2. RELATED WORK

Related work in this area can be divided into the following broad categories: early IPv6 network telescope measurements; IPv4 background radiation analysis; and Internet background radiation collection considerations. In the following sections we discuss the key prior research under each of these three umbrellas.

Early IPv6 Network Telescope Measurements. The earliest known study to collect IPv6 background radiation advertised an extremely small /48 prefix for a month in 2006 and only collected 12 packets over that time period [14]. More recent studies have announced a single covering /12 prefix [12,20]. Both of these works served as an initial inspiration for our own experiment. In the shorter term study, Deccio *et al.* collected two weeks of data and reported an average of 74 packets/second of pollution traffic [12]. In the longer term study, Huston *et al.* collected data for 115 days and presented analysis of observed traffic [20]. They reported minimal-to-no increase in average pollution traffic rate during that period. That study also presented a detailed analysis of traffic address destinations. Our results confirm a major finding of that work, which was that the vast majority (≈95%) of captured traffic was for *allocated* networks.

The results we report complement these earlier efforts by scaling up the basic approach in order to better understand global and regional trends. In addition, we also adopt a more rigorous approach by quantifying not only the BGP-control-plane reachability of our prefix announcements, but also data-plane-traffic reachability. Further, we attempted to verify that our global-scale experiment did not negatively impact actual IPv6 traffic on the Internet. Lastly, we present a more thorough analysis of the collected data, providing greater confidence about the generalizability of our results to overall IPv6 pollution.

IPv4 Background Radiation Analysis. Wustrow *et al.* analyzed a five-year sample of data collected passively from an unallocated IPv4 /8 block in addition to several newly-allocated-but-unused /8 network telescope prefixes [38]. Their temporal and spatial analysis revealed that background pollution traffic increased four-fold over the course of their sample and that pollution traffic was increasingly dominated by traffic resulting from misconfiguration and other errors.

In work by Pang *et al.*, Yegneswaran *et al.*, and Cooke *et al.*, the authors utilize active responders in order to gain additional insight into the sources of pollution traffic [9, 31, 39]. Bailey *et al.* discuss the advantages of an active-responder-based network telescope monitor [4]. We did not use active responders in our study in an effort to ensure that we did not directly affect valid IPv6 traffic during this critical transition period; given that we were advertising a *covering prefix* such active response could have interfered with legitimate host traffic.

Glatz *et al.* and Brownlee *et al.* examine sources of Internet pollution and attempt to create classification schemes for this traffic based on various parameters, such as source address, protocol, and inter-arrival times. They present data that quantifies the amount of such traffic on a given network, as well as its properties [7, 15].

Internet pollution traffic has also been analyzed to provide insight into large-scale scanning activities [10], Internet censorship [25], and even large-scale physical events such as outages from earthquakes and hurricanes [1, 11]. Barford *et al.* use similar data to find the location of malicious hosts [6].

Background Radiation Collection Considerations. Similar techniques to the ones used in our study have previously been discussed in the work of Bailey *et al.*, which describes the use of honeypots with network telescope monitoring [5]. They analyzed a distributed network telescope with over 60 smaller network telescopes and 17 million routable addresses to determine the difficulties in implementing such a hybrid monitoring system.

The size and spatial location of a network telescope are also an important factor in determining the amount of pollution traffic it receives. Moore *et al.* describe the effect the size of a network telescope has on the types of security events witnessed, such as worm spreading, scanning, and distributed denial of service (DDoS) attacks. Similarly, Cooke *et al.* examine Internet background radiation data over ten distributed monitors and study how location effects the collected data [8,30]. These various studies all conclude that location, visibility, route announcement propagation, and filtering all have the potential to effect the observed traffic. Based on these conclusions, we paid particular attention to these data-collection details when designing our study.

3. METHODOLOGY

In this section, we describe the design of our experiment and our data collection methodology, as well as the mitigating steps and proactive measurements we conducted to ensure a minimal impact of our covering routes. A long-running study by Huston *et al.* demonstrates that it is possible to conduct a safe IPv6 covering prefix experiment [20]. We sought both to replicate and to greatly expand the scope of that experiment with our work.

3.1 The BGP Announcements

In early October 2012, we contacted each of the five RIRs to request permission to announce the entire /12 IPv6 address block that had been allocated to them by IANA. After deliberation, each RIR granted us a Letter of Authority (LOA) temporarily allowing us to announce these prefixes via BGP for the duration of our four-month experiment.

Next, we coordinated with AT&T and Hurricane Electric, the upstream IPv6 providers to Merit Network, Inc., our ISP and research partner. This was necessary to ensure that they would accept our announcements of these unusually large blocks. As anticipated, they both needed to execute special configuration changes (i.e. removing sanity filters) to allow us to make such short covering prefix announcements.

After a series of test announcements, on November 8, 2012 we began announcing all five of the covering /12 prefixes for our experiment. We set up a collection server at Merit Network and advertised it as the final destination for each route. All IPv6 traffic on the Internet that was destined for RIR address space—*but not explicitly claimed by another network via a more specific route*—was routed to our collector and archived. The only large, in-use blocks of IPv6 addresses that fall outside the covering prefixes we advertised were 2001::/12 (used by all RIRs in older allocations), 2002::/16 (used for 6to4 transition), and 2003::/18.

On November 13, RIPE NCC asked us to limit our announcements by withdrawing the /12 route and replacing it with a /13 and a /14, the portion of their address space that hasn't been allocated to customers yet. As explored more fully in the following sections, this change gave us a unique control that helped us discern the nature of Internet background radiation in IPv6. During the course of our experiment, we received four inquiries regarding our BGP announcements from the Internet operations community, which were addressed by providing pointers to a detailed study description. With the exception of the RIPE region's change, we did not need to modify our experiment in throughout the four-month experiment.

3.2 Routing Visibility

Since our own providers needed policy changes to accept our routes, we believed that policy could play a role in how broadly visible these routes were. To determine the extent to which the BGP announcements were being accepted and propagated across the broader Internet, we analyzed data from both the Route Views [35] and RIPE NCC Routing Information Service [33] BGP archives.

As seen in Table 1, our announcements were visible from 8 of the 9 IPv6-capable monitors from the Route Views project, including Australia, Brazil, California, Georgia (USA), Japan, South Africa, Virginia, and the UK. The only Route Views monitor that did not see our routes was KIXP in Kenya. In addition, 9 of the 12 IPv6-capable monitors maintained by RIPE NCC saw our announcement, including Austria, California, Italy, Japan, the Netherlands, New York, Sweden, Switzerland, and the UK. We were partially visible by DE-CIX (Germany), which saw two of the six routes (2600::/12 and 2400::/12). Our routes were not visible from MSK-IX in Russia or PTTMetro-SIP in Brazil.

Examining the Route Views peer perspectives more closely, we found that, on average, of the 93 peers at all sites during period A, 74 peers saw our /12 announcements. Likewise, during period B, 75 of the 98 peers saw our /12 announcements. This compares favorably with the number of peers that saw the average IPv6 prefix known to Route Views (66 and 68, respectively). The smaller /13 and /14 RIPE prefixes during period B were just as highly visible for the first half of the period (through mid-January), but only visible to 5 (of 98) Route Views peers in the second half.

Based on our analysis, we conclude that these announcements were visible at the vast majority of IPv6-capable route monitors.

3.3 Validating Data Plane Effects

In general, Internet traffic is routed to the most specific prefix in the BGP routing table; therefore, as our experiment consists of announcing shorter (i.e., less specific) prefixes, we would expect to only capture unclaimed IPv6 traffic. However, due to the immature nature of the IPv6 Internet, we were concerned that the longest-match rule, a core routing principle, might not be implemented correctly at every IPv6 node. To identify any potential negative effects, we performed a series of short test announcements (as detailed above) before announcing all of the prefixes. We also closely monitored data plane connectivity during these periods and into the first month of the long-term announcement, as discussed next.

Table 1: Visibility in Route Views and RIPE Monitors

Route Server	LACNIC 2800/12	ARIN 2600/12	APNIC 2400/12	RIPE 2a04/14+ 2a08/13	AFRINIC 2c00/12
Route Views					
r-v.eqix	✓	✓	✓	✓✓	✓
r-v.isc	✓	✓	✓	✓✓	✓
r-v.jinx	✓	✓	✓	✓✓	✓
r-v.linx	✓	✓	✓	✓✓	✓
r-v.kixp					
r-v.saopaulo	✓	✓	✓	✓✓	✓
r-v.sydney	✓	✓	✓	✓✓	✓
r-v.telxatl	✓	✓	✓	✓✓	✓
r-v.wide	✓	✓	✓	✓✓	✓
RIPE RIS					
rrc00	✓	✓	✓	✓✓	✓
rrc01	✓	✓	✓	✓✓	✓
rrc03	✓	✓	✓	✓✓	✓
rrc04	✓	✓	✓	✓✓	✓
rrc05	✓	✓	✓	✓✓	✓
rrc06					
rrc07	✓	✓	✓	✓✓	✓
rrc10	✓	✓	✓	✓✓	✓
rrc11					
rrc12		✓	✓		
rrc13					
rrc14	✓	✓	✓	✓✓	✓
rrc15					

Table 2: Distribution of the 12,418 IPs used to assess impact of route announcements during testing.

RIR Region	No. of IPs	No. of Unique ASNs
APNIC	1622	603
ARIN	1219	530
LACNIC	159	62
RIPE	9,409	3,654
AFRINIC	9	8
Total	12,418	4,857

In order to validate minimal impact on data plane connectivity, we performed the following: We collected a set of public IPv6 addresses by querying the Alexa top 1M domains [2] for AAAA records. We then categorized these by AS number and covering prefix (i.e., RIR region). We conducted ping tests to the resulting set of twelve thousand hosts, which were spread among diverse ASes and regions, summarized in Table 2. *The response rates we saw before and after our announcements were comparable.*

Port Filtering. In another approach to validating the representativeness of the captured data, we attempted to detect port blocking between our collection system and sample Internet locations. To this end, we obtained access to a small set of globally-distributed native IPv6 hosts. These hosts were located in Atlanta (AS3595), Japan (AS2516), South Africa (AS33764), Tanzania (AS37084), and the United Kingdom (AS15830). From these hosts, we were able to actively probe our network telescope and examine the data coming into the collection infrastructure. It should be noted that the server in the United Kingdom was unable to have packets routed to the our blocks. However, this appears to be a filtering policy of only the upstream ISP (TelecityGroup Limited), as all of our routes were observed at the London Internet Exchange (LINX, RIS server `rrc01` in Table 1), and AS15830 is a member of LINX.

We began a series of probes of the network telescope prefixes from the remaining four servers. We scanned arbitrarily chosen addresses within the otherwise-unrouted portions of our announcements, such that the scanning packets would be routed to us. We then separated these synthetic packets from organic traffic received by the collector, and discard the scan packets we generated for the rest of the analyses presented here. Upon aggregating the probes, we found *no port-based packet filtering in TCP or UDP* between our four hosts and our collector at Merit Network (AS237). This lies in stark contrast to the experiments conducted by Kreibich, *et al.*, which illustrated widespread port blocking by ISPs for IPv4, as high as 50% for the most commonly blocked ports in IPv4: NetBIOS (TCP/139), SMB (TCP/445), and RPC (TCP/135) [26].

3.4 Complications of a Covering Prefix

One interesting difference that emerges in the study of network telescopes that are based on a covering prefix versus traditional ones that are based on unused address space is the impact of routing instability. In a network telescope based on completely *unused* address space, routing instability has no impact, as there are no prefix allocations within the telescope. In the case of a covering prefix, however, the network telescope is effectively the union of all address space (under that prefix) not being otherwise advertised by BGP at any given point in time—whether it is allocated to networks or not. This results in a much more complete telescope but also in complications when the allocated address blocks exhibit instability. In such scenarios, address space can rapidly shift between the network telescope and an allocated and announced address block. As a result, traffic captured due to such instability is much more likely to be composed of otherwise *normal network packets* that happen to be caught by the network telescope due to a (perhaps brief) drop of the more specific route. As such, care must be taken in interpreting and comparing results from network telescopes that do versus ones that do not use a covering prefix announcement. We discuss how we categorized our data with this in mind in Section 3.5.

Benefits of a Covering Prefix. During the current transition towards greater adoption of IPv6-enabled networks and services, it is critical to understand any routing instability, as it can help to identify and address the misconfigurations, bad practices, or bugs in software or hardware that are the root cause.

In addition to the ability to observe instability, the main advantage of a covering-prefix-based network telescope study is *much better visibility* due to the known clustering of Internet background radiation near active network prefixes. For instance, Bailey, *et al.* and Cooke, *et al.* have shown that, with an IPv4 network telescope, much more data is gathered when it is located near live hosts [4,8]. Likewise, Harrop *et al.* discuss, in the context of enterprise IPv4 networks, the advantages of *greynets*, which have unused addresses interspersed with live addresses to produce visibility similar to that of a large, contiguous network telescope [17]. Since the IPv6 address space is vast, compared to IPv4, (and, consequently, sparse) this locality advantage is even more necessary to capture a network telescope sample of any meaningful size. Our results bear this out.

As mentioned above, we initially announced each of the five /12 prefixes that have been assigned by IANA to the RIRs. However, after several days RIPE requested that we reduce our 2a00::/12 announcement to 2a04::/14 and 2a08::/13. Although our reduced RIPE announcement still covered 75% of the initial RIPE address space under the /12, the volume of traffic decreased disproportionately from around 300–900 kilobits per second to 0–80 bits per second for RIPE. On most days, no packets arrived for these RIPE prefixes and we collected an aggregate of only 2,635 RIPE packets over the entire course of the three-month period they were announced[1]. These results agree with previous work in IPv4 [8] and in IPv6 [14,20], showing more packets near used space.

[1] While the traffic dropped by three orders of magnitude right away, as mentioned in section 3.2, the two smaller prefixes did have reduced global visibility during the second half of the three-month period as well, which further reduced collected data.

3.5 Data Categorization

We sought to segregate the packets we captured according to whether they would be seen by a traditional network telescope methodology or only by a covering prefix, as we suspected differences. This way, we could characterize traditional Internet background radiation traffic separately from what is otherwise potentially valid traffic to instantaneously unreachable destinations that are normally routed. Likewise, focusing on the traditionally collected traffic would allow an apples-to-apples comparison of this IPv6 data with other IPv4 background radiation studies.

We started by aggregating all of the routed BGP prefixes seen by all Route Views monitors. We combined initial RIBs on the first hour of each experiment period with every subsequent update file (a digest of BGP packets) from all Route Views monitors for each dataset. Since we aimed for a *conservative filtering to produce what we considered traditional background radiation data*, we recorded all prefixes ever announced in any BGP message throughout the entire data collection period, no matter how briefly or sparsely. We excluded from consideration prefixes *shorter* than our own announcements (e.g., a sparse announcement of 2000::/3), as those would not affect our packets.

Next, we aggregated the five RIRs' allocation data and built a list of all prefixes which were allocated by the RIRs prior to the end of each of our two data collection periods. The resulting list in each period, along with the routed prefix list discussed above, constituted our *"allocated"* and *"routed"* filters for that period, respectively. The Cartesian product of these two binary filters gives us four categories of packets.

The type of packets that network telescopes have traditionally captured are the "unallocated and unrouted" category. These are packets destined to prefixes that have not been assigned to any organization by an RIR and which are not normally advertised in the global BGP table—not until the operators of the network telescope announce them. Packets in this category are what have typically been studied when examining background radiation in IPv4 (e.g., the work of Wustrow, *et al.* [38]). Thus, these packets serve as the core data that we use in our characterization of background radiation in IPv6, as discussed in section 4. For succinctness, we term this traffic "dark" in the sections that follow, but we use this term interchangeably with "background radiation". We discuss the other three categories of packets in detail in section 5.

Table 5: Breakdown of address space under our covering prefixes at the end of February 2013, showing percentage allocated and routed. Also shown is size (in /24 subnets) of non-covering IPv4 network telescope prefix we compare some results to. Note that the size of the entire IPv4 address space is 2^{32}, which the square root of the size of a single IPv6 /64 subnet.

RIR	Prefix	Size of Space in /64 Subnets	Alloc.	Routed
APNIC	2400::/12	$2^{52} = 4,503,599,627,370,496$	3.29%	1.31%
ARIN	2600::/12	$2^{52} = 4,503,599,627,370,496$	1.85%	0.20%
LACNIC	2800::/12	$2^{52} = 4,503,599,627,370,496$	6.75%	0.46%
RIPE NCC	2a00::/12	$2^{52} = 4,503,599,627,370,496$	2.66%	2.15%
RIPE NCC	2a08::/13	$2^{51} = 2,251,799,813,685,248$	0.00%	0.00%
RIPE NCC	2a04::/14	$2^{50} = 1,125,899,906,842,624$	0.25%	0.04%
AFRINIC	2c00::/12	$2^{52} = 4,503,599,627,370,496$	0.43%	0.41%
IPv4	35≈/8	A total of 54,784 /24 subnets	None	None

3.6 Dataset Description

Table 3 summarizes the complete datasets that we captured. We present data from two periods: dataset A (a 24-hour-long capture

Table 3: Packet counts, rates, and protocol breakdown in the complete datasets, by RIR.

RIR	Dataset A.Complete (24 hr.; with RIPE /12) 2012-11-12T17:00:00 to 2012-11-13T16:59:59							Dataset B.Complete (3 mon.; with RIPE /13 & /14 only) 2012-12-01T00:00:00 to 2013-02-28T23:59:59						
	kPackets	Average (peak)		% Protocol Type				kPackets	Average (peak)		% Protocol Type			
		pkts/sec	kbits/sec	UDP	TCP	ICMP	Other		pkts/sec	kbits/sec	UDP	TCP	ICMP	Other
APNIC	11,826	85 (149)	310 (552)	48.5	4.8	46.1	0.6	1,345,425	172 (811)	523 (1868)	45.5	20.9	33.2	0.4
ARIN	12,146	88 (517)	299 (1169)	72.7	3.9	23.0	0.4	2,481,476	318 (21185)	418 (28685)	23.3	67.1	9.1	0.5
LACNIC	8,936	69 (130)	210 (370)	50.4	2.1	46.4	1.1	504,848	65 (875)	238 (768)	28.8	4.6	65.6	1.0
RIPE	25,490	175 (8750)	235 (6211)	20.6	41.0	38.4	< 0.1	3	< 0.1	< 0.1	8.3	27.4	64.2	0.1
AFRINIC	298	2 (9)	4 (16)	56.7	7.9	35.2	0.2	20,290	3 (88)	4 (114)	54.4	6.5	38.8	0.3
Overall	58,696	419 pps	1.06 Mbps	41.7	19.9	38.0	0.4	4,352,040	558 pps	1.18 Mbps	30.9	45.4	23.3	0.4

Table 4: Categorization of packets by destination in each dataset. "Allocated" are packets with destinations matching a prefix that was allocated by an RIR; "routed" match a BGP prefix known to Route Views any time during collection. Unique number of destinations as well as total TCP payload in each category is also shown.

Category	Dataset A				Dataset B			
	Packets	%	Unique Dest.	TCP Bytes	Packets	%	Unique Dest.	TCP Bytes
Unallocated, Unrouted ("dark")	2,997,540	5.11	36,855	21,880,029	208,988,570	4.80	1,274,798	2,901,567,271
Unallocated, Routed (UR)	456	0.001	28	0	13,948	< 0.01	848	39,216
Allocated, Unrouted (AU)	35,426,005	60.36	4,784	239,960	2,576,456,636	59.20	85,956	18,857,335
Allocated, Routed (AR)	20,271,633	34.54	22,335	36,435,501	1,566,581,006	36.00	1,580,052	424,971,873
Total (Complete)	58,695,634		64,002	58,555,490	4,352,040,160		2,941,654	3,345,435,695

starting on 12 November 2012), and dataset B (a three-month-long capture starting on 1 December 2012). An outage caused by undetected power failure occurred between 5-9 January 2013; we have no packets from that period.

The covering prefixes we announced for each RIR subsumed varying amounts of address space. Table 5 shows the percentage of space under each announced covering prefix that was allocated at any time prior to the last day of the three-month (B) period and that was routed, even briefly, at any time during the period.

Packet and Dataset Categories. Table 4 shows the breakdown of the two datasets according to the categories explained in section 3.5. For each category, we also include the number of unique destinations, which gives a sense of the spatial nature of each target address set, as well as TCP payload bytes. The "unallocated and unrouted" subset is the background radiation data that traditional (non-covering prefix) network telescopes have captured.

As Table 4 also shows, due to the covering prefix nature of our route advertisements, we were able to capture a broader spectrum of invalid traffic than would be possible via the traditional network telescope approach. In fact, 95% of the packets we captured were due to our use of a covering prefix. That traffic falls into three categories: unallocated/routed, allocated/unrouted, and allocated/routed. As this traffic is distinct from Internet background radiation as previously studied, we treat it separately and aim to explain and characterize each category in section 5.

Basic Statistics. Before we move to a deep analysis of the "dark" subset of our data, we first provide basic high-level statistics about the overall (unfiltered) captured packets. Table 3 shows the volume of all packets per RIR collected during the longer (three-month-long) dataset B time frame (i.e., B.Complete).

An analysis of packet TTL values reveals that the vast majority of received packets (90% captured during time period A and 97% during B) appear to be sent by Windows operating systems (TTL between 64 and 128).

During the 24-hour period selected to be dataset A we received 18.7 GiB in 59M packets. The APNIC, ARIN, LACNIC, and RIPE NCC blocks all received a similar order of magnitude of data, while AFRINIC received two orders less. A similar distribution was observed over the three months that constitute dataset B, except for the loss of nearly all data from RIPE due to withdrawal of 2a00::/12 in favor of two smaller RIPE prefixes. We collected 1,141 GiB via 4.4Bn packets in dataset B. As shown in Table 3, we received an aggregate rate of nearly 1.1 Mbps of traffic during period A and nearly 1.2 Mbps during period B. Since RIPE data in B was nearly zero, we refrain from separately analyzing RIPE in dataset B in the sections that follow, except where noted.

Protocols. As Table 3 also shows, the protocol distribution in the overall data is dominated by no single protocol but is made up of between 20 and 50 percent of each of TCP, UDP, and ICMP, though TCP (with 45% of packets) ranks higher than the other protocols in the complete three-month dataset while UDP is the most common protocol in in the unfiltered 24-hour dataset (42%).

Transition Addresses. One question of importance when studying the state of IPv6 deployment is the relative proportion of native IPv6 hosts versus those using IPv6 transition technologies. We took advantage of the large and global nature of our collection to explore the distribution of source addresses that were used for 6to4 and Teredo, two of the most prevalent IPv6 transition technologies. We found that, of the 12.5M unique sources observed in dataset B, 12.4% were using 6to4 prefixes. Teredo was used by another 21.7%. Thus, over 34% of sources seen were transition addresses. Note that, since 53% of sources fell under a single native /36 prefix, removing that outlier would yield 72% transition sources. This is approaching the higher 96% seen in an ad-based experiment conducted by Karir *et al.* [23]. We caution, however, that since our sample is largely based on traffic intended for networks that are misconfigured or unstable, it may not accurately reflect the overall IPv6 client population.

4. BACKGROUND RADIATION RESULTS

4.1 Background Radiation Data Description

As our first aim is to characterize IPv6 background radiation traffic and compare it to IPv4 background radiation, the core statistics we report in this section focus on the unallocated/unrouted ("dark") category of data. We leave explorations of the other three categories of collected packets to the sections that follow.

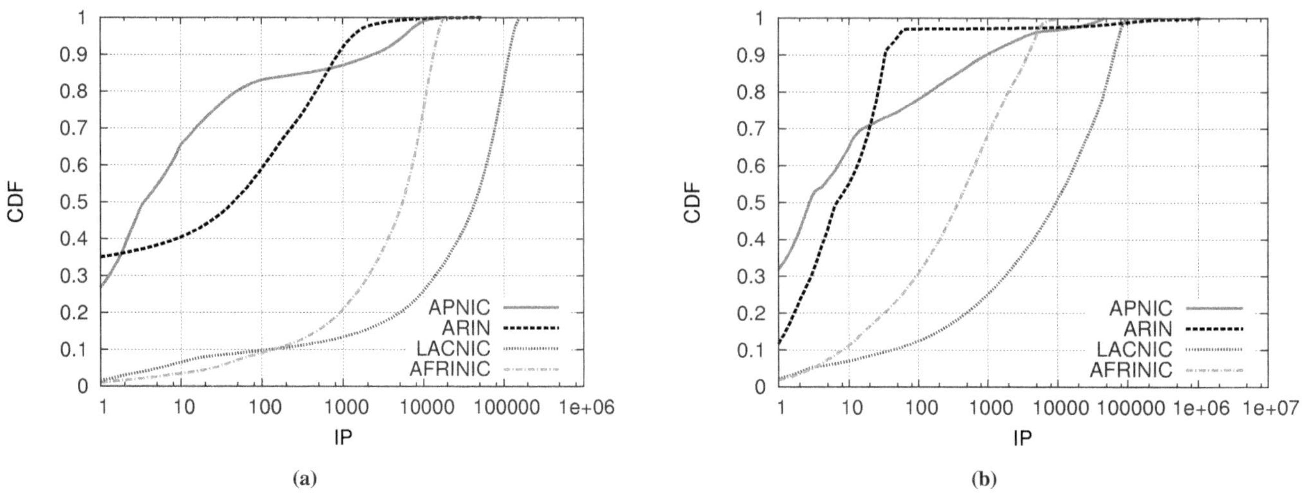

Figure 1: Cumulative distribution of source (1a) and destination (1b) IP addresses in B.Dark, sorted by number of collected packets

4.2 Spatial Analysis

In this section, we provide a comparative analysis of spatial features of the dark traffic we observed.

Traffic Volumes and Patterns. For the three-month-long background radiation dataset, B.Dark, we observed a total of just 209m packets across all five prefixes. ARIN's traffic dominated the packet count with about 205m packets. We collected about 1m packets in the APNIC dataset. The LACNIC dataset contains 3m packets, and both the AFRINIC and RIPE dataset contain a relatively low number of packets (325k and 2.5k respectively). We refrain from including RIPE in several of the following analyses, due to the negligible number of packets captured after reducing the announcement, as discussed in Section 3.4.

Source Distributions. Figure 1a shows the cumulative distribution of source addresses sorted by packet contribution in B.Dark. In both the ARIN and APNIC datasets, we see a few source addresses account for a significant portion of the traffic. In particular, one source address contributes around 30% of the packets, and 90% of these two regions' traffic is accounted for by 1–2k IPs. The other two regions (AFRINIC and LACNIC) both have higher source address diversity, and it takes more than 10k and 100k unique sources to account for 90% of the packets, respectively.

Destination Distributions. Figure 1b shows the distribution of destination addresses in B.Dark. Here, we see a slightly greater concentration of destinations and most prominently so for ARIN, where fewer than 30 destination IPs account for 90% of the traffic. In the other three RIRs' datasets, fewer than 10k destinations make up 95% of the packets seen. LACNIC has the most diversity again, with more than 30k unique destinations needed to account for 90% of packets.

4.3 Protocol and Port Analysis

Protocols. Figure 2a shows the protocol breakdown in the darknet datasets. Just as observed in the discussion of the overall data in Section 3.6, the protocol volumes in the three-month dataset (B.Dark) are heavily biased toward ICMP. However, in the APNIC dataset, we find that TCP dominates the traffic, at 72%, with another 22% of observed packets being ICMP.

In the one-day dataset with RIPE's network blocks, we see 62% UDP traffic, with TCP and ICMP both contributing about 20%. A surprising 95% of all observed packets in the ARIN dataset were ICMP. We investigate this further in section 4.6.1.

These numbers lie in contrast to typical IPv4 network telescope measurements (e.g., [38]), where TCP dominates, UDP contributes about half as much as TCP, and ICMP is present with only single digits of percentage points of volume. Our own comparison IPv4 analysis, described in Section 4.5, also bears this out, as we see TCP constituting 82% of packets.

TCP/UDP Ports. Table 6 presents the top 5 TCP source and destination ports observed in Dataset B.Dark. Source ports 80 and 443 appear in the top 10 or top 20 ports for all datasets. Source port 53 is also the second-most-common port in the ARIN dataset. These suggest that much of the collected traffic is likely to be misdirected responses from DNS and web services. A high number of TCP port 7 packets, used by the Echo protocol to measure round trip times, suggests possible network testing traffic.

Similarly, Table 7 shows the top 5 UDP ports observed in our our different datasets. Port 53, in both source and destination fields, clearly dominates the UDP traffic. While only 6% of UDP packets have source port 53, 28% of the bytes received in UDP packets were in packets sent on port 53. Additionally, nearly 85% of received UDP packets were destined for port 53. These constitute DNS responses and queries, respectively. Another notable pattern in UDP is the significant prevalence of traffic both to and from port 123, which is primarily used for Network Time Protocol packets [29]. Further analysis of some of these features is explored as separate case studies in section 4.6.

TCP Flags. The most interesting flag combinations for network telescope research are SYN and SYN+ACK. The former indicates packets where a connection is being attempted (ultimately unsuccessfully to an unreachable address) such as when a host is scanning ports or IPs to connect to. SYN+ACK indicates the response to a previous connection attempt, such as might be seen when an attempt to make a connection is made using a source address that is within the network telescope, and the contacted host replies. When this is done for malicious reasons, it is called backscatter and is often observed during certain classes of DDoS attacks, but this can also be observed in cases of misconfiguration.

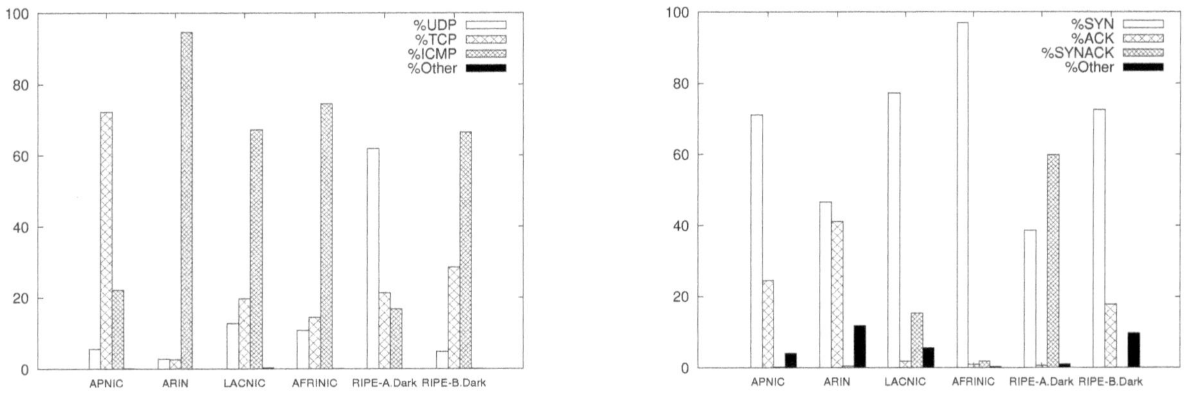

(a) (b)

Figure 2: Breakdown of Protocols (2a) and TCP Flags (2b) by RIR (from B.Dark unless otherwise noted)

Table 6: Top 5 TCP Ports by Packets for Each RIR and Overall in Dataset B.Dark and for RIPE in A.Dark

APNIC		ARIN		LACNIC		AFRINIC		B.Dark Overall, %of TCP Pkts.			
src	dest	src	dest	src	dest	src	dest	src	%	dst	%
56583	80	22	7	445	80	993	39236	22	30.32	7	32.40
49561	443	53	22	135	45682	443	45682	56583	1.59	80	14.44
49559	2001	51211	80	12829	56024	143	24739	445	1.22	22	10.13
49558	445	51208	34521	80	61638	80	26823	49561	0.59	443	1.11
49560	5222	51207	443	49155	29671	5222	52232	53	0.49	34571	0.85

RIPE (A.Dark)			
src	%	dst	%
80	35.62	179	31.10
443	20.45	25	2.18
993	2.73	53	1.03
49166	0.85	80	0.92
5228	0.80	40000	0.91

Figure 2b illustrates the regional differences in the TCP flag combinations in the data we collected. The relatively low volume of SYNACK packets (1.7% in B.Dark) indicates that spoofed-random-source DDoS attacks do not appear to be prevalent in IPv6. However, while low as a percentage of all dark traffic, SYNACKs do constitute a large percentage of the single-day RIPE dataset (59.8%). Our collected TCP packets are overwhelmingly SYN packets; this is most apparent in the AFRINIC dataset, 97% of which are SYN packets. As SYN packets form a plurality, if not the majority, of the TCP packets we see (40.5% in A.Dark and 52.6% in B.Dark), we can infer that a majority of dark TCP traffic coming to the network telescope is connection attempts to unreachable networks.

4.4 Temporal Analysis

Overall, we see no clear trend in the volume of IPv6 background radiation over the three-month period of our study. As Figure 3 shows, however, there is a slight decrease in total traffic volume observed by the network telescope in the last two weeks of the B dataset. This is primarily due to a drop in traffic volume to the ARIN region from approximately 30 packets per second to 10. The decreased traffic is related to a reduction in ICMP probing of a small set of ARIN destinations that are heavy recipients of ICMP traffic. We discuss this traffic in section 4.6.1.

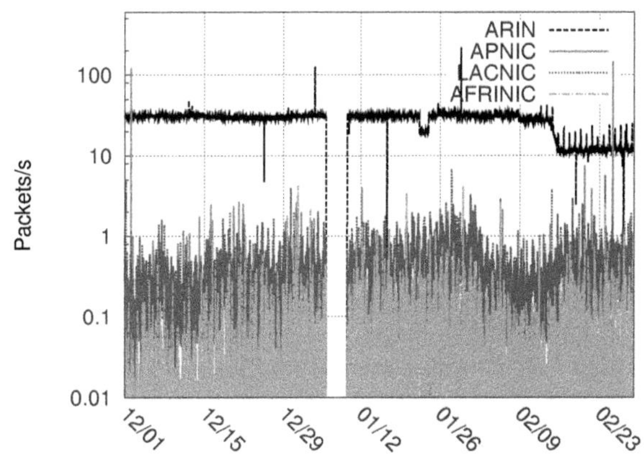

Figure 3: Background radiation (i.e., dark) packet rate for the four /12s prefixes we announced over three months (dataset B.Dark). The ARIN prefix received about 30 packets per second, whereas the other regions all saw only between 0.1 and 1.0 pps. The hole in January was caused by a power outage.

4.5 Comparison to IPv4

Our work follows a series of seminal IPv4 network telescope experiments that characterized the background radiation of unallocated address space in IPv4, as well as its evolution over time (e.g., [31, 38]). Our IPv6 network telescope results suggest several important differences (and some similarities) compared to that body of work. To produce a more recent and valid comparison, we analyzed a single week of IPv4 background radiation captured during the course of our ongoing IPv6 packet capture.

The methodology used to capture this data is identical to that described in Section 3.1, with the main differences, aside from the protocol, being that (a) the IPv4 space we monitor is completely *unallocated and unrouted* (by our definition) and thus not a covering prefix; and (b) the size of the address space is considerably smaller: our IPv4 network telescope is composed of address blocks encompassing 13,915,136 total host addresses (≈55k typical subnets). This is equivalent to about 84% of an IPv4 /8, far smaller than our announced IPv6 address space (see Table 5). We subset the three-month background radiation IPv6 data (B.Dark), focusing on the same week (beginning 4 February 2013) for both it and the IPv4 data. We next highlight important differences between the two protocols' background radiation.

Table 7: Top 5 UDP Ports by Packets for Each RIR and Overall in Dataset B.Dark and for RIPE in A.Dark

APNIC		ARIN		LACNIC		AFRINIC		B.Dark Overall, %of UDP Pkts.				RIPE (A.Dark)			
src	dest	src	dest	src	dest	src	dest	src	%	dst	%	src	%	dst	%
53	53	53	53	12929	53	53	39236	53	5.96	53	84.81	53	10.50	53	88.60
16703	16703	123	123	53	45682	45682	45682	123	1.20	123	1.19	32833	0.07	389	0.50
45682	39045	33336	30718	45682	3702	12829	24739	12829	0.61	30718	0.71	12589	0.05	40000	0.18
12407	37385	54709	33336	123	123	48359	26823	33336	0.31	33336	0.31	500	0.04	16881	0.04
54593	45682	500	500	18600	29671	20904	37648	45682	0.14	45682	0.12	123	0.03	500	0.04

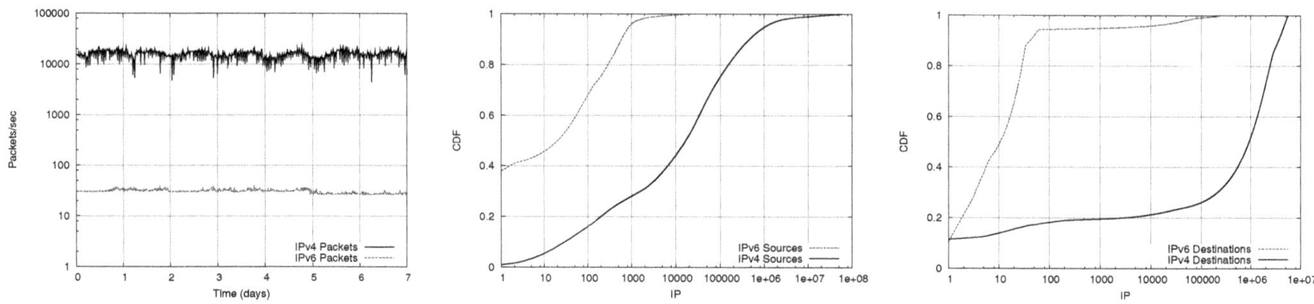

(a) Overall packet volume over the week (b) CDF of source IPs sorted by packets (c) CDF of destination IPs sorted by packets

Figure 4: Comparison of IPv4 and IPv6 background radiation during the week starting on 4 February 2013.

Table 8: IPv4 and IPv6 protocol breakdown for traffic during the week of February 4, 2013 in the aggregate B.Dark IPv6 dataset and in the IPv4 35.x.y.z network telescope.

Darknet Packets	% TCP	% UDP	% ICMP	% Other
IPv4 (35.x.y.z)	81.7	15.8	2.3	0.2
IPv6 (All /12)	3.3	2.9	93.8	< 0.1

Traffic Volume. The first striking difference between the two background radiation samples is the relative volume of traffic collected. The IPv6 telescope, as Figure 4a shows, collected an aggregate packet rate of approximately 30 packets per second. In stark contrast, the IPv4 telescope sustained a rate of around 15,000 pps, a 500-fold difference. The bitrate difference (not shown) is similarly unmistakeable. This disparity is expected, due to the still-low adoption of IPv6 and the dearth of malicious traffic over the new protocol. Even the rate of total traffic we received (i.e., with all categories of packets counted), is only about 20-fold higher, at 558 pps. This is in spite of the vastly larger address space covered by our IPv6 announcements as compared to the /8 in IPv4 (as discussed in the previous section).

Spatial Analysis. Examining the spatial distributions of the sources and destinations in the two samples, shown in Figures 4b and 4c, respectively, reveals several differences. In the source distributions, we see the IPv4 source contribution ramp-up is slow, taking more than 100 top sources to account for 20% of packets. In the IPv6 data (top line), however, a single source contributes nearly 40% of the packets; we elaborate on that source in Section 4.6.2. The two distributions have similar shape except that the IPv6 line is shifted to the left, as we would expect based on the lower volume of IPv6 traffic, and up, due to the single outlier.

The distributions of the destination IPs, however, suggest a qualitative difference between the two protocols. Namely, the IPv6 sample has many more heavily-hit IPs relative to the total set of destinations, while IPv4 has a small number of heavy hitters. The vast majority of IPv4 destinations only see a relatively low number of packets—e.g., 16.3% of destinations account for just 50% of the IPv4 packets. On the other hand, less than 0.01% (10) of the IPv6 destinations account for 50% of the traffic. We recall that the size of the entire destination address space monitored by the IPv4 network telescope is on the order of 2^{24} (nearly 14M unique destinations), whereas the address space of the IPv6 telescope—detailed in Table 5—is on the order of 2^{118} hosts, and only a very small percent of routed space generally outside of our visibility. Thus, the fact that so few hosts contacted the IPv6 space we monitored (and that so few IPs are contacted within the space) is itself a significant difference from IPv4.

Table 9: Top 10 TCP Ports with Percentages in the IPv4 Sample and Comparative Ranking in IPv6 Dark Dataset (if Present) for the Week of 2013-02-04.

Source Port	%	v6 Rank	Dest. Port	%	v6 Rank
80	10.07	#47	445	47.75	#4,268
6000	2.83	#27,826	12350	7.14	
30800	0.73		23	4.97	
0	0.70	#5,914	80	4.15	#710
22	0.67	#1	443	4.03	#685
38121	0.54	#20,825	3389	3.91	
4935	0.51		22	2.44	#442
7777	0.49	#25,981	1433	1.68	
6005	0.38		3072	1.03	
21	0.36		1024	1.03	

Protocol Differences. In Table 8 we see the protocol breakdown of the IPv4 background radiation compared to that of the aggregated IPv6 B.Dark data for the comparison week. As can be seen, while TCP is the most prevalent protocol in the IPv4 sample (82%), in the IPv6 sample the dominating protocol is, by far, ICMPv6, making up 94% of the packets in the B.dark dataset. This suggests that *there is relatively less pollution traffic in the IPv6 dark space from scanning and backscatter and more from probing, diagnostic, and management traffic.* However, as discussed more in Section 4.6.1, a small block of heavily-hit destinations is responsible for the vast majority of ICMP packets in the dark IPv6 dataset; these inevitably skew these results. That said, as IPv6 is at an early stage of deployment, we certainly expect the properties of its traffic to differ from IPv4.

Table 10: Top 10 UDP Ports with Percentages in the IPv4 Sample and Comparative Ranking in IPv6 Dark Dataset (if Present) for the Week of 2013-02-04.

Source Port	%	v6 Rank	Dest. Port	%	v6 Rank
19288	1.60	#51,473	10320	35.88	#31,731
39776	1.55	#18,816	5060	4.85	#61,409
17148	1.55	#39,266	47458	2.99	#46,486
58843	1.54	#12,809	53	1.99	#1
17190	1.54	#43,881	137	1.39	
10688	1.52	#48,799	3544	1.24	#37,930
18864	1.51	#1,315	39455	1.17	#2,117
24048	1.48	#25,676	65535	0.58	#62,982
8090	1.48	#60,075	1900	0.44	#58,668
10042	1.42	#59,877	161	0.35	

Port Distribution. Tables 9 and 10 show the top ten source and destination ports for each of TCP and UDP, respectively, in IPv4. Next to each port is that port's placement in the corresponding rankings from the IPv6 data during the same week. We do not separately show all the top ports for this week of IPv6 data, as they closely match the top ports seen in the overall dark data (shown in Tables 6 and 7). Looking at the top IPv4 ports, we first observe that, unlike in the IPv6 data where UDP port 53 dominates both directions (78% of destination and 13% of source ports during this comparison week), it is not among the top IPv4 source ports (though it is the fourth destination port). In fact, it ranks as only the 192nd most common source port, accounting for just 0.02% of IPv4 UDP packets. This suggests that relatively little stray DNS traffic is entering the IPv4 network telescope, while this type of traffic is common in our IPv6 data. Indeed, both the prevalence of DNS and ICMP traffic in IPv6 background radiation are congruent with previous findings (e.g., [24]) for overall IPv6 usage, which reported high fractions of these two types of traffic via the new protocol. Other than port 53, we find no coexistent ports in the top 10 lists for UDP in the two samples. For TCP, we also see little similarity, with just port 22 in both protocols' top source port lists and 22 and 80 in both top destination port lists.

Significant absences are TCP/23 (Telnet) and UDP/137 (NetBIOS) from the IPv6 dataset from that week. Despite our earlier discussion of the lack of any port filtering in IPv6 in Section 3.3 and the prevalence of these both in IPv4, we saw zero Telnet packets and only a single NetBIOS packet in that week's IPv6 data. In general, there is a markedly different overall distribution of ports between the two datasets, supporting the hypothesis that *there is a qualitative difference in the nature of traffic in IPv4 and IPv6 background radiation—it is not just a matter of volume.*

TCP Flags. Lastly, we compare the proportions of TCP flags in the IPv4 dataset to that in IPv6. As discussed earlier in section 4.3, the most interesting flag combinations for Internet background radiation research are SYN and SYN+ACK. We tabulated SYN and SYN+ACK packets in the IPv4 dataset and found the two categories to make up 83% and 14%, respectively. The IPv6 percentages in this dataset for these two flag combinations are 25% SYN, and 1% SYN+ACK. These differences suggest that *scanning (which manifests itself as SYN packets to dark space) and backscatter (which manifests as SYN+ACK packets to dark space) are both less prevalent in IPv6 background radiation than in IPv4.*

4.6 Darknet Case Studies

4.6.1 ICMPv6 Probing/Scanning

As described earlier, we see a significant amount of ICMPv6 traffic in our background radiation dataset. Of particular interest to us was whether we would observe signs of large-scale scanning. We see clear evidence of sequential scanning in a handful of cases, though it was generally limited to smaller subnets rather than randomized scans of the entire address space.

Focusing on just the background radiation subset of the data, we find 16 APNIC, 1,646 ARIN, 9 LACNIC, and 3 AFRINIC addresses sourcing over 1,000 ICMP packets in B.Dark. Of these, we find 249 addresses in ARIN with over 100k ICMP packets and five with over a million. Of those five, one begins with fe80:: (discussed in Section 4.6.2), while two are in Akamai Technologies address space.

An interesting specific example is the single ARIN Region IP address 2600:140f:b::b81a:a21f, which is also from address space belonging to Akamai. It generated 2.5M total ICMPv6 packets to 141 unique destinations. Other IP addresses from the Akamai address space sent similarly large amounts of ICMPv6 traffic that was received by our network telescope. In total, we observed over 17M ICMPv6 packets originated by Akamai in B.Dark. We speculate that Akamai probes hosts that provide IPv6 content when making redirection or other content-update decisions.

In one extreme case, we saw fe80::224:38ff:fe7e:af00, a single, link-local ([18]) IP address, send over 71M ICMPv6 packets to only 27 unique destinations, all within the same /120 prefix (i.e., with only the last 8 destination bits varying) under 2607:fc86::/32. A similar number of packets (around 2.6M) were sent to each address, suggesting a repeated automated scan of this small set of destinations. While we do not know the source of these particular packets, it is possible that the misconfigured host was attempting to monitor the availability of a small group of devices, except that the address range of those devices is in neither publicly advertised space nor allocated space. Interestingly, this is not the only source address probing those same destination addresses.

Upon deeper inspection, we find that hosts within the same /120 subnet along with a closely-addressed second /120, both under the same 2607:fc86::/32 block, were probed by an additional 100M packets. This addition brings the total amount of traffic destined for this unallocated block to 192M packets. Thus, *a staggering 92% of our total background radiation packets was ICMPv6 traffic to or from these hosts.* There are over 3,500 unique source IPs that sent traffic to these two /120 groups, which totaled just 66 destination addresses. The sources originate from a wide swath of 378 different /32s, mostly in ARIN space but with some in each region.

We found that the size of these ICMPv6 payloads was either 10 (about 40% of the packets), 1,000 (30%), or 64 (30%) bytes. Sixty-three percent of the packets are echo requests, and the rest are echo replies. This suggests that traffic from hosts addressed in this block is being sent and with solicitation of replies, which we end up capturing. Indeed, an examination of the other datasets reveals some packets sourced from hosts in this block, which we end up capturing because they themselves happen to contact, for example, allocated-but-unrouted addresses. For example, this is the case for four hosts in this range sending around 5k packets in the B.AU dataset and one host sending ten packets in the B.AR dataset.

While we are unable to track down the location of the hosts using this invalid address block, the case study highlights how a single misconfigured network prefix can cause a large volume of pollution—92% of our background radiation packets.

4.6.2 Link-local Leakage

We mentioned above that we saw a very large fraction of packets from the IPv6 address fe80::224:38ff:fe7e:af00. This address's packets were the largest single contributor to our background radiation data, accounting for 34% of all received packets.

As addresses beginning with $fe80$ are "link-local" and meant to only be valid on local networks, their presence in our collection indicates a misconfiguration [18]. This address appears to use the EUI-64 encoded MAC address format for the host portion of the address (indicated by the FF:FE in the middle of the last 64 bits). Using this information, we determined that it corresponds to a MAC address whose vendor ID is assigned to Brocade (formerly Foundry Networks), a maker of SAN and network equipment. Assuming the MAC is not spoofed, this may indicate a faulty router. Even though it contributes a large volume of packets to background radiation, as the address is link-local and not allocated, we have no way to determine the operator to contact about possible remediation or root cause determination.

In total, we observe 205 link-local addresses in our background radiation data and over 605 in our overall three-month data, indicating that this is not a single occurrence. Likewise, we found 63 sources in our dark data and 1,678 overall sourcing packets from "unique-local" address space, which is analogous to RFC 1918 private address space and should not be globally routed [19].

These results suggests that current configurations on at least some Internet backbone and edge routers are allowing local IPv6 addresses to be globally visible, which is potentially dangerous, since it can allow a remote host to appear local to another host on the opposite end of the Internet.

4.6.3 Worm Activity

One of the traffic artifacts we were interested in was worm activity in IPv6. In particular, even randomly scanning worms should be visible to some degree in our data, if they exist, due to the sheer size and duration of our study. We would expect that even with a single scanning host using a slow scanning rate, such as 10 packets per second, we could expect to observe at least one packet within our four /12 blocks with 99.999% probability in 19.6 minutes [30]. Even though there had been no reports of any IPv6-capable variants of the major worms in IPv4, we decided to look for early signs of worm activity on two ports used by popular worms in IPv4.

We focused on UDP/1434 and TCP/445. These ports are used by Microsoft SQL Server and the Direct Hosted SMB protocol, respectively, and, in IPv4, they are exploited by worms such as SQL Slammer via UDP/1434, and, for example, Conficker and Sasser via TCP/445. The Slammer worm continues to be quite active in IPv4 despite the passage of a decade since the first outbreak [22]. Conficker scanning is also still highly prevalent, ranking it as the second most detected worm in the second half of 2012 [28, 37]. Validating some of this in our own work, the background radiation from the IPv4 network telescope we report on in Section 4.5 revealed over 99k UDP 1434 packets over the course of a week. We were able to positively confirm these as Slammer activity by its payload signature [36].

In our analysis of the IPv6 dark data, we noticed some small amounts of traffic on these two ports. However, upon closer inspection the data showed no signs of worm activity on either port. Our dark data contained just 18 packets to UDP port 1434, and it did not appear to be Slammer. The larger complete collected dataset also revealed nothing implicating worm activity on this port. Similarly, though we also observed some activity on port 445 (88k packets, involving a total of 92 unique IPs in the dark data), closer observations revealed that this traffic consisted of conversations between a single pair or a handful of IP address—not a typical scanning pattern. Likewise, expanding the search to the complete set of collected packets showed no indications of any scanning on these ports.

Overall, *we found no evidence of broad scanning nor prevalent malicious traffic in our data, a sharp departure from IPv4.*

4.6.4 NTP/BGP Services

Interestingly, we are able to find data destined to critical services such as NTP and BGP in our datasets. We find NTP traffic from over 62k unique IP addresses in the background radiation data. There are just 28 unique source IPs to 62,395 unique destinations among the packets we captured. Of the 28 sources, six are in 6to4 space (2002::/16), while the remaining are from 12 unique prefixes originated by 12 ASes—one Brazilian, one Canadian, one Mexican, and nine U.S., including two large ISPs. In B.Dark, the port used by NTP is the second most common source and destination UDP port, suggesting possible prevalent disruption of NTP activity by IPv6 misconfiguration we observe (although we note that clients often configure several NTP servers for resiliency, possibly prolonging the time to detection of the misconfiguration).

We also find a significant amount of BGP traffic in the background radiation data. In B.Dark, we see BGP packets between 338 unique IPv6 addresses. Examining the IPs of the 150 unique packet sources, we found that ten were clearly invalid, with addresses beginning with 6001::/16, a001::/16, or 1::/16, none of which fall under the global unicast address space (2000::/3); 26 of the sources were out of unrouted space, and the remaining 114 sources were originated from eight unique prefixes advertised by seven unique origin ASes: four US, two German, and one from the Philippines. These included four telecom operators and one very large global Internet search provider. In the one-day dataset, BGP traffic is the top contributor to RIPE's TCP traffic, comprising over 31% of the RIPE TCP packets, and involving eight IPs in six unique /32 blocks. The significance of BGP traffic among background radiation is that it indicates brokenness on the Internet's control plane itself, and 346 routers (if we assume no aliasing) with sources in several ASes shows that the problem is not isolated.

5. BEYOND BACKGROUND RADIATION

Although we used a covering prefix methodology in order to maximize our visibility, the data that we ended up collecting greatly exceeded the traditional background radiation (dark) data that we initially set out to study. We focused on deeply characterizing the dark data in section 4 because it constitutes the first large and long-term glimpse into global background radiation in IPv6, but we now turn to an analysis of this new non-traditional background radiation data, which constitutes the majority ($\approx$95%) of the packets we captured. In the subsections that follow, we examine each of the other three types of packets: allocated/routed (AR), allocated/unrouted (AU), and unallocated/routed (UR); these comprise 35%, 60%, and <0.01% of the packets we captured, respectively.

5.1 Allocated/Routed (AR) Packets

As previously shown in table 4, 34.5% of the packets collected in dataset A and 36.0% of those collected in dataset B were destined to *allocated* and *routed* prefixes. Recall that, because we ended up receiving these packets, it is necessarily the case that a more-specific route to that prefix must not have been globally available at the time of the packet—at least not available between the packet's source and Merit's upstreams (AT&T and Hurricane Electric). Indeed, for several sample days we performed finer-grained analysis comparing the precise time stamp of each packet and the state of the global and local (Merit's) routing tables in order to validate that this was the case—i.e., the longest-matching-prefix routing rule was being followed. Packets only came to us when, at that instant, there was no known more-specific route, not to Merit's upstreams or not globally. In this section we first present a general examination of this allocated/routed (AR) traffic, followed by a description of a routing analysis we conducted to identify characteristics of this subset of IPv6 prefixes.

5.1.1 Traffic Characterization

Table 4 provides some high-level statistics for our AR data subset, which includes the number of packets, unique destinations, and TCP payload volume of the data in this category. Overall, we observe 4.32B packets in the three-month dataset. Of these, we categorized 1.56B packets as allocated/routed and these were directed to over 1.5M unique destination IP addresses. Below we highlight two of the key features that differentiate this data subset from the traditional background radiation. Recall that, since routes to prefixes in this category are temporarily or regionally available, *this category is more likely to be "normal" IPv6 traffic that is briefly disrupted, rather than traffic that permanently fails, as in the other categories.*

In terms of TCP flags, we find that, overall, SYNACK (76%) dominates SYN (22%) packets in the three-month dataset, B.AR. In the 24-hour collection, A.AR, it is SYN with 76%, and SYNACK at 5%. However, we note that in the A dataset, as shown earlier in Table 3, TCP packets are dominated by RIPE, which has a high percentage of SYN (78%) and very low SYNACK (just 2%). Recall that in the dark data, shown in Figure 2b, SYN packets generally dominated, i.e., connection attempts were more common. The general dominance here of SYNACK, instead suggests replies to SYN packets from these networks—replies that are unable to find a path back to the source of the antecedent packet due to the lack of a valid route.

TCP source ports are dominated by 443 and 80, at 22% and 14%, with port 5528 at 2% and all others (the next 6 being 25, 993, 995, 587, 110, and 22) below 1% of traffic. This indicates a large number of responses from web servers in the AR traffic. Notable also is the absence of port 53 in the top ten, which was the most common in the dark data. In the opposite direction, TCP destination ports are dominated by port 80 (10%) with other ports in the top 10 all under 1%. In descending order, they are: 113, 179, 22, 25, 51413, 53, 8008, 443, and 11171. This suggests some web traffic, along with client connections to services in AR nets. The presence of BGP (TCP/179 is a destination of 0.2% of packets), just as in the dark data, shows some control plane misconfiguration. In the RIPE data in dataset A.AR, the lists are similar, with 80 and 443 topping the port list in both directions. Overall, the port and protocol AR data, along with the high presence of SYNACK packets, fits the profile of client networks being prominent among AR networks.

5.1.2 AR Network Prefix Properties

To better explain this large fraction of our traffic, we sought to more closely characterize the networks in the AR set of destinations. Through our analysis (as described in 3.5) we were able to identify 311 AR networks in the dataset A and 1,669 in dataset B. Figure 5 shows the cumulative distribution function of these prefixes according to their contribution of packets to the AR data. We note that just one prefix is responsible for over 46% of the packets in A and just one (different) prefix for 21% of the packets in B, and that the top 10 prefixes account for 90% and 71% of the packets, respectively.

We hypothesized that these networks may differ systematically from the overall pool of IPv6 networks. To study this, we examined several properties of these prefixes and their origin autonomous systems (AS). For each prefix seen in the data, we tabulated the number of Route Views peers that had routes to that prefix. This is a measure of *prefix propagation*. We also counted the number of withdrawal events (which we define as the number of withdrawal messages divided by the number of peers) for each prefix seen. This is a measure of *stability*.

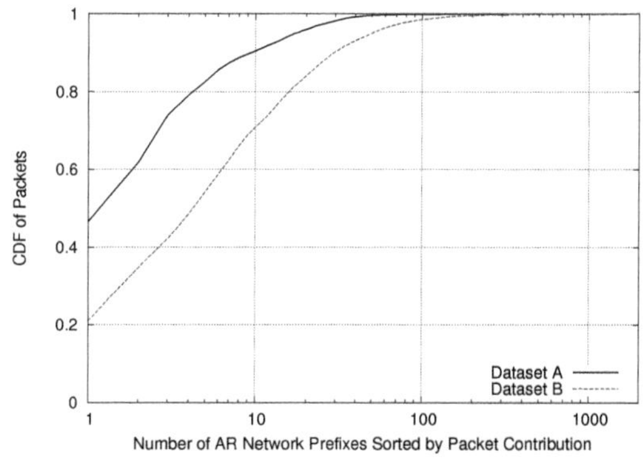

Figure 5: Cumulative distribution of contribution of packets by 311 AR nets in dataset A and 1,669 AR nets in dataset B.

Table 11: Three properties of AR destination prefixes and their origin ASes as well as averages for the Internet at large (IPv6 and IPv4). All numbers are averages over the dataset, except for withdrawal events, which are averages per 24 hours.

	Dataset A			Dataset B		
	IPv4	IPv6	A.AR	IPv4	IPv6	B.AR
Route Analysis (over entire dataset)						
Networks	485,233	12,841	311	502,483	13,462	1,669
R.V. Peers	95.22	65.67	28.68	102.75	68.34	65.48
Withdrawals	0.12	0.65	8.22	0.09	0.33	0.55
K-Core Decomposition Analysis (First Day of Dataset)						
Origin ASes	36,559	6,511	247	36,651	6,586	1,018
AS Coreness	2.23	9.87	8.94	2.21	9.23	6.62

Lastly, for each sample day, we examined the *coreness* [3,16] of all origin ASes. In graph theory, a k-core is a maximal subgraph in which every vertex has at least degree k. The coreness of a vertex v indicates the maximum value of N for which v is in the N-core. As used in studying routing topology, coreness is a measure of AS *connectivity*. The coreness values for each origin AS were obtained via an analysis of BGP table snapshots collected from Route Views and from RIPE RIS on the first day of each dataset period.

For each of the three measures, we tabulated the overall averages for all Internet IPv4 and IPv6 prefixes, separately, as well as the values for just our list of seen AR prefixes in each sample. Table 11 summarizes our results.

Propagation. As can be seen, there appear to be differences between the pool of AR prefixes and the overall pool of IPv6 prefixes according to our measures. The average count of Route Views collector BGP peers advertising paths to the seen AR prefixes is about half the count of the average IPv6 prefix in the one-day sample (A), though much closer (65.48 versus 68.34) in the three-month sample (B). As with the stability measure discussed next, the difference between the three-month dataset and the one-day dataset likely has to do with the larger aggregated pool of AR prefixes over the three month period. Even a single captured packet destined to a mostly stable prefix due to a brief withdrawal would land it in our AR list. Thus, the longer time period is likely to include more stable routes than period A. We have confidence in these numbers as we also conducted these types of analyses for three single-day subsamples of the B time period and obtained very similar results to the single-day numbers for A presented here. The difference between AR prefix and overall IPv6 prefix peer counts suggests that these *AR prefixes have weaker propagation* in the global BGP routing table.

Stability. Next, examining the withdrawal events, we see that the overall pool of IPv6 prefixes sees an average of 0.65 withdrawal events per prefix per day for the single-day dataset, A, and 0.33 for the three-month, B. Here, we see a stark difference, as the AR prefixes exhibit 8.22 withdrawals per day in A and 0.55 withdrawal events in B. Even the latter difference is meaningful, since it indicates that the average AR prefix has 66% more withdrawals per day than the average IPv6 prefix (at 0.33 withdrawals). This suggests that AR prefixes are *much less stable* than average networks.

Through a fine-grained analysis of timestamps, mentioned above, we initially observed that some AR networks ought to have received packets that, instead, we received. We say "ought to" as routes to these networks were available in some part of global BGP, based on Route Views data. The stability and connectivity measures here explain why we received these packets in spite of their intended routes being seen by at least some Route Views peers: the routes must have been unavailable to Merit's providers. Our deeper analysis of Merit's BGP perspective confirmed that Merit's upstreams did *not* have more specific routes for the given weakly-routed prefixes at the instant each packet arrived. *Operators can mitigate lost traffic in this category via route monitoring, such as by consulting Route Views or an alert service.*

Connectivity. Coreness is utilized to assess the connectivity and centrality of a network. Intuitively, high coreness indicates a better-connected AS, such as a large ISP. Typical values for all IPv6-enabled ASes range from 0 (stub networks) to 70 (the best-connected ISPs). The measured coreness of 8.94 in dataset A (versus 9.87 for all IPv6 prefixes) and 6.62 for the three-month sample suggest that *the origin of these unstable and weakly-advertised prefixes is more likely to be a small network.* This is to be expected, since smaller networks might be less likely to be managed as rigorously as large Internet service providers, whose main business is the network.

5.1.3 IPv6 Prefix Comparison to IPv4

Compared to the overall pool of advertised IPv6 prefixes, we found that AR prefixes had poorer propagation, were less stable, and were originated by less well-connected autonomous systems. As IPv6 is still at an early deployment phase, we expect IPv6 prefixes, as a whole, to have poor routing. To perform a systematic juxtaposition of IPv4 against IPv6, we repeated the analyses described above to obtain the corresponding IPv4 metrics.

Table 11 also depicts these measures applied to the entire pool of IPv4 prefixes. We first observe that the IPv4 networks are, in general, better-connected to Route Views monitors, with average peer counts of 95.22 and 102.75 for the A and B samples, respectively. Examining the average withdrawals, we see that IPv4 prefixes are much more stable, exhibiting just 0.12 (A) and 0.09 (B) withdrawal events per prefix per day. Finally, we see that the average coreness of IPv4 prefixes is much lower than that of IPv6. This means that the average IPv4 prefix is originated by a smaller network than the average IPv6 prefix. This is not surprising, since it has been shown that IPv6 deployment is more prevalent at the core of the Internet than at the edges [13], and, both by definition and by necessity, the core is highly connected.

These findings suggest that, indeed, IPv6 routing is not as mature as IPv4, and that the AR networks are an even less mature subset of the IPv6 pool. This result is intuitive, given the early stage of IPv6 deployment, the fact that it only carries a small fraction ($\approx$0.2%) of Internet traffic [21], that operators generally have much less experience with the new protocol, and that both hardware and software support for the new protocol is still not on par with IPv4 support.

5.2 Allocated/Unrouted (AU) Packets

As table 4 shows, 60.4% of dataset A and 59.2% of B packets are destined for addresses that match *allocated but unrouted* prefixes. This is interesting, as it suggests traffic to networks that were assigned and configured but which were not intended to be globally reachable—perhaps because they were intended for internal (i.e. "private") organizational use, in spite of existence of the *unique local* prefix, fc00::/7, analogous to IPv4 RFC 1918 space, for this purpose [19, 32]. Indeed, traffic patterns of the two largest contributors we found in this category, were confirmed examples of this.

Together with the Allocated/Routed (AR) packets, this category of traffic constitutes nearly 95% of packets we saw. This high-level finding, that a majority of collected traffic via a covering prefix network telescope belongs to allocated networks, is consistent with an earlier experiment with just APNIC's /12 reported by Geoff Huston [20]. Here, we highlight some of the largest contributors we discovered in this subset of the data.

We observed periodic spikes in the overall volume of traffic in the ARIN dataset. These large jumps, resulting in a one or two order of magnitude spike in ARIN traffic, occurred daily at around noon UTC. Upon investigation, we found that they were largely composed of DNS replies. All of these packets had their destinations set to the same value, which we omit here to preserve organizational privacy. In total, we received over 444M packets (over 423M of which were DNS responses) destined to this one IP. It is the top contributor and accounts for over 17% of all packets in the AU dataset. The address is in a network block that has been allocated to a managed hosting company but is not seen in any routing tables visible to any Route Views monitors.

We contacted operators at this organization to inform them of the traffic and learn the cause. It was quickly determined that the source of the traffic was a misconfigured DNS server. The server was assigned a (globally unique) address meant by the organization for internal use, but it was using this address as the source of external packets it sent. Since this address was from a prefix that was not globally advertised in BGP, the replies to that DNS server all ended up being routed, via our covering prefix, to our collector. This misconfigured server was not previously noticed by its operators because it was part of a cluster of several resolvers, which *were* correctly configured. After the company began advertising the network block in which this server was addressed in mid-August 2013, we stopped receiving these packets, and our total ARIN traffic, in bytes, fell by about half.

Another large contributor to the AU dataset is traffic destined to a network block allocated to the R&D unit of a large U.S. wireless phone provider. We received 1.1Bn packets destined to 216 destinations in one prefix allocated to this organization. This constitutes nearly 44% of the packets in the AU dataset. There were over 6M unique IPs sending traffic to these 216 destinations, and nearly 6M were from the same /32 block as the destinations. Most of the sources were from sub-blocks of the /32 that were publicly routed. This strongly suggested that the prefix in question was being used internally but that some routing misconfiguration was causing traffic from other prefixes within that organization to be misdirected out to the Internet instead of toward that internal network. We established contact with the company and they confirmed that this address space is used internally and not meant to be globally reachable. At publication deadline, they were still investigating why these internal hosts were sending their traffic to our collector instead of to the local private network. In general, operators can avoid leaking such internal traffic by either using unique local addressing internally or by placing access lists on edge routers to either block or log such unintended address use.

5.3 Unallocated/Routed (UR) Packets

The third and final category, accounting for less than 0.01% of packets in both the A and B time periods, is those whose destination address matching prefixes that were not allocated by an RIR but which did have routes in the BGP routing table at least temporarily during our data collection period. Again, recall that, these prefixes were not globally reachable during the instant we captured a given packet, otherwise it would not be routed to us. We suspected that these unallocated but either partially- or temporarily-routed prefixes may be either the result of RIRs withdrawing allocations while operators continued to use the address space, the result of experimentally-advertised prefixes, or the result of misconfiguration.

In dataset period A, there were two prefixes in this category, 2a02:510::/32 and 2606:8900::/32, and there were also two during period B: 2607:fd20::/32 and 2406:7a00::/31. Each of these four prefixes was unallocated at the end of our data collection windows. However, the first of the four was in allocation for several years prior to our collection, the second was allocated a few days after the collection period, the third was allocated for part of our B collection period then returned, and the last was never allocated (but a prefix one bit longer was).

In each case, these prefixes were known to Route Views by only a single peer router (versus $\approx$75 for the overall average IPv6 prefix, as discussed in section 3.2), suggesting very limited announcements, likely for testing or due to misconfiguration. Because of this, the traffic in this category most closely resembles the unallocated and unrouted (i.e. background radiation) traffic.

Focusing on the packets, we find that ICMPv6 comprised 94.5 and 98.1% of the traffic in this category in datasets A.UR and B.UR, respectively. Upon further examination, we discovered that the vast majority of packets were due to traffic from hosts associated with researchers. In dataset B, for example, 83.5% of packets came from what we confirmed with CAIDA to be their experimental hosts. Another 8.8% of the packets were confirmed by BBN Technologies as hosts that are part of their experiments. A third source, with 2.8% of these packets was confirmed as belonging to another research organization we contacted, in Canada. *In total, at least 95.1% of the packets in the B.UR (and 97.5% in the A.UR) dataset were the result of confirmed researcher activity.*

5.4 Near Misses

When we modified our initial RIPE NCC /12 announcement into a /13 and a /14, eliminating the 25% of the address space from which RIPE was making customer allocations, the volume of RIPE traffic we saw dropped disproportionately—by three orders of magnitude. We considered whether this was representative of a general case, i.e., if the majority of network telescope traffic we received was clustered near allocated address space. We discussed most of the answer to this above by showing that, after our allocation and routing analysis, around 95% of the captured traffic was, indeed, destined for allocated prefixes (the AU and AR data subsets). However, what about traffic to unallocated-and-unrouted space?

We hypothesized that if misconfiguration was a large source of the traffic to unallocated networks, then the target destinations might be addresses that are lexically close to existing, active prefixes (i.e., "fat finger" errors). To examine this systematically, we conducted a Levenshtein distance [27] analysis of each packet's destination in fully-expanded ASCII format, comparing it to all known routed networks (up to the prefix length). An analysis of three day-long samples of destination IPs of packets we captured (all of dataset A, as well as all packets on the first day of each month of dataset B) yielded the somewhat unexpected result that *every destination address had some minimal edit distance of at most 2*. Between 39% and 81% of packets, depending on the sample, were within one hex character change away from an existing routed prefix, and the rest were within two. Since our other analyses showed that such a large percentage of traffic is for allocated networks, this should not be too surprising, as routed prefixes are often part of or near other allocated addresses. However, that this held even for the pure "dark" traffic to unrouted-and-unallocated space was unexpected. While we can't confirm this, it suggests that one explanation for the dark traffic could simply be typos, as a single character change would bring each packet we saw under a legitimate routed prefix.

6. CONCLUSION

In this paper, we presented results from our broad observation of Internet pollution on the IPv6-enabled Internet. To the best of our knowledge, this study, which relies on five large covering prefixes, is the first of its kind in terms of visibility.

Our results show that misconfiguration is prevalent in the IPv6 network, although concurrent measurements we made in IPv4 indicate that the shear volume of background radiation is minuscule (500-fold less) in IPv6 despite a vastly larger covered address space. In fact, in the IPv6 traditional background radiation data, a single block with just 66 unique addresses was responsible for 92% of the packets—nearly all were ICMPv6 echo requests or replies. Happily, we found no evidence of prevalent malicious traffic in the captured IPv6 data due to worms, scanning, or backscatter, which are all common in IPv4 background radiation. We continue our collection, in an effort to understand the long-term trends as well as to identify particular configuration and stability findings that can be shared with the broader Internet operations community.

We found that only about five percent of the packets we captured were destined for unallocated and unrouted address space, the type of addresses that network telescopes traditionally monitor. Thus, our use of a covering prefix is a departure from most network telescope studies in the past. It provided unique visibility into routing and configuration errors previously hidden from this type of study—i.e., those affecting allocated prefixes. Nearly 60% of packets we captured were destined to allocated but unrouted destinations, likely due to traffic sourced by networks meant for internal use being "leaked" into the Internet; this was the case for the two largest contributors to this category, which we contacted, accounting for 61% of packets. Another 36% of packets were destined to allocated space that had, at least briefly or sparsely, advertised routes. We examined updates for these prefixes and found them to be less stable and advertised than the average IPv6 prefix, which is itself less stable and less well-advertised than the average IPv4 prefix. We received these packets due to unavailable routes. The final category of data was mostly explained by researcher traffic, which we confirmed by contacting several organizations. In aggregate, we identified the cause of a majority of all captured packets. We aim to continue covering-prefix-based network telescope studies, including in IPv4 space, due to the increased insight they provide.

Acknowledgments

This work was supported in part by the Department of Homeland Security Science and Technology Directorate under contract numbers D08PC75388, FA8750-12-2-0314, and FA8750-12-2-0235; the National Science Foundation (NSF) under contract numbers CNS

1111699, CNS 091639, CNS 08311174, CNS 0751116, CNS 1330142, and CNS 1255153; and the Department of the Navy under contract N000.14-09-1-1042. We are also grateful for help from Rick Reinecke at Merit, from our shepherd, and from the anonymous IMC reviewers who provided valuable manuscript feedback.

7. REFERENCES

[1] E. Aben, A. King, K. Benson, Y. Hyun, A. Dainotti, and K. Claffy. Lessons learned by "measuring" the Internet during/after the Sandy storm. In *In Proceedings of FCC Workshop on Network Resiliency 2013*, Feb. 2013.

[2] Alexa Internet, Incorporated. Top 1,000,000 Sites. `http://s3.amazonaws.com/alexa-static/top-1m.csv.zip`.

[3] J. I. Alvarez-Hamelin, L. Dall'Asta, A. Barrat, and A. Vespignani. k-core decomposition: a tool for the visualization of large scale networks. *CoRR*, abs/cs/0504107, 2005.

[4] M. Bailey, E. Cooke, F. Jahanian, A. Myrick, and S. Sinha. Practical Darknet Measurement. In *Proceedings of the 40th Annual Conference on Information Sciences and Systems (CISS '06)*, pages 1496–1501, Princeton, New Jersey, USA, Mar. 2006.

[5] M. Bailey, E. Cooke, F. Jahanian, N. Provos, K. Rosaen, and D. Watson. Data Reduction for the Scalable Automated Analysis of Distributed Darknet Traffic. *Proceedings of the USENIX/ACM Internet Measurement Conference*, Oct. 2005.

[6] P. Barford, R. Nowak, R. Willett, and V. Yegneswaran. Toward a Model for Source Address of Internet Background Radiation. In *Passive and Active Measurement Conference (PAM)*, 2006.

[7] N. Brownlee. One-Way Traffic Monitoring with iatmon. In N. Taft and F. Ricciato, editors, *PAM*, volume 7192 of *Lecture Notes in Computer Science*, pages 179–188. Springer, 2012.

[8] E. Cooke, M. Bailey, Z. M. Mao, D. Watson, and F. Jahanian. Toward understanding distributed blackhole placement. In *Proceedings of the 2004 ACM Workshop on Rapid Malcode (WORM-04)*, New York, Oct 2004. ACM Press.

[9] E. Cooke, M. Bailey, D. Watson, F. Jahanian, and J. Nazario. The Internet motion sensor: A distributed global scoped Internet threat monitoring system. Technical Report CSE-TR-491-04, University of Michigan, Electrical Engineering and Computer Science, July 2004.

[10] A. Dainotti, A. King, K. Claffy, F. Papale, and A. Pescapè. Analysis of a "/0" Stealth Scan from a Botnet. In *Internet Measurement Conference (IMC)*, Nov 2012.

[11] A. Dainotti, C. Squarcella, E. Aben, K. C. Claffy, M. Chiesa, M. Russo, and A. Pescapé. Analysis of country-wide internet outages caused by censorship. In *Proceedings of the 2011 ACM SIGCOMM conference on Internet measurement conference*, IMC '11, pages 1–18, New York, NY, USA, 2011. ACM.

[12] C. Deccio. Turning Down the Lights: Darknet Deployment Lessons Learned. Technical report, Sandia National Laboratories, 2012.

[13] A. Dhamdhere, M. Luckie, B. Huffaker, K. Claffy, A. Elmokashfi, and E. Aben. Measuring the Deployment of IPv6: Topology, Routing and Performance. In *Proceedings of the 12th ACM SIGCOMM Conference on Internet Measurement (IMC 2012)*.

[14] M. Ford, J. Stevens, and J. Ronan. Initial Results from an IPv6 Darknet. In *International Conference on Internet Surveillance and Protection*, 2006.

[15] E. Glatz and X. Dimitropoulos. Classifying internet one-way traffic. pages 417–418, 2012.

[16] G. Gürsun, N. Ruchansky, E. Terzi, and M. Crovella. Inferring visibility: who's (not) talking to whom? *SIGCOMM Comput. Commun. Rev.*, 2012.

[17] W. Harrop and G. Armitage. Defining and evaluating greynets (sparse darknets). In *Proceedings of the The IEEE Conference on Local Computer Networks 30th Anniversary*, LCN '05, pages 344–350, Washington, DC, USA, 2005. IEEE Computer Society.

[18] R. Hinden and S. Deering. RFC 4291: IP Version 6 Addressing Architecture, 2006.

[19] R. Hinden and B. Haberman. RFC 4193: Unique Local IPv6 Unicast Addresses, 2005.

[20] G. Huston. IPv6 Background Radiation. Technical report, 2012. Slides of a talk given at DUST 2012 – The 1st International Workshop on Darkspace and UnSolicited Traffic Analysis, May 14–15, San Diego, California.

[21] J. Czyz, M. Allman, J. Zhang, S. Iekel-Johnson, E. Osterweil, and M. Bailey. Measuring IPv6 Adoption. ICSI Technical Report TR-13-004, August 2013.

[22] J. Jarmoc. SQL Slammer âĂŞ 10 years later. `http://www.secureworks.com/resources/blog/research/general-sql-slammer-10-years-later/`, Mar. 2013.

[23] M. Karir, G. Huston, G. Michaelson, and M. Bailey. Understanding ipv6 populations in the wild. In *Passive and Active Measurement (PAM '13)*. 2013.

[24] E. Karpilovsky, A. Gerber, D. Pei, J. Rexford, and A. Shaikh. Quantifying the Extent of IPv6 Deployment. In *Proceedings of the 10th International Conference on Passive and Active Network Measurement*, 2009.

[25] A. King. Syria disappears from the Internet. `http://blog.caida.org/best_available_data/2012/12/05/syria-disappears-from-the-internet/`, 2012.

[26] C. Kreibich, N. Weaver, B. Nechaev, and V. Paxson. Netalyzr: illuminating the edge network. In *Proceedings of the 10th ACM SIGCOMM conference on Internet measurement*, IMC '10, pages 246–259, New York, NY, USA, 2010. ACM.

[27] V. I. Levenshtein. Binary codes capable of correcting deletions, insertions and reversals. *Sov. Phys. Dokl.*, 6:707–710, 1966.

[28] Microsoft. Microsoft Security Intelligence Report - July–December 2012. `http://download.microsoft.com/download/E/0/F/E0F59BE7-E553-4888-9220-1C79CBD14B4F/Microsoft_Security_Intelligence_Report_Volume_14_English.pdf`, 2013.

[29] D. Mills, J. Martin, J. Burbank, and W. Kasch. Network Time Protocol Version 4: Protocol and Algorithms Specification. RFC 5905 (Proposed Standard), June 2010.

[30] D. Moore, C. Shannon, G. M. Voelker, and S. Savage. Network telescopes. Technical Report CS2004-0795, UC San Diego, July 2004.

[31] R. Pang, V. Yegneswaran, P. Barford, V. Paxson, and L. Peterson. Characteristics of Internet background radiation. In *Proceedings of the 4th ACM SIGCOMM conference on Internet measurement*, pages 27–40. ACM Press, 2004.

[32] Y. Rekhter, B. Moskowitz, D. Karrenberg, G. J. de Groot, and E. Lear. Address Allocation for Private Internets, 1996.

[33] RIPE NCC. Routing Information Service (RIS). `http://www.ripe.net/ris/`.

[34] N. Sarrar, G. Maier, B. Ager, R. Sommer, and S. Uhlig. Investigating IPv6 Traffic - What Happened at the World IPv6 Day? In *Proceedings of the 13th International Conference on Passive and Active Network Measurement*, 2012.

[35] University of Oregon. Route Views project. `http://www.routeviews.org/`.

[36] VigilantMinds. MS-SQL Slammer Signature. `http://seclists.org/snort/2003/q1/871`, Jan. 2003.

[37] S. Walls and M. Karir. Internet pollution - part 2. Presented at the 51st North American Network Operators Grooup (NANOG51) Meeting in Miami, Florida, Feb. 2011.

[38] E. Wustrow, M. Karir, M. Bailey, F. Jahanian, and G. Houston. Internet Background Radiation Revisited. In *Proceedings of the 10th ACM SIGCOMM Conference on Internet Measurement (IMC '10)*, Melbourne, Australia, November 2010.

[39] V. Yegneswaran, P. Barford, and D. Plonka. On the design and use of Internet sinks for network abuse monitoring. In *Recent Advances in Intrusion Detection—Proceedings of the 7th International Symposium (RAID)*, Sophia Antipolis, French Riviera, France, 2004.

[40] G. Zhang, B. Quoitin, and S. Zhou. Phase changes in the evolution of the IPv4 and IPv6 AS-Level Internet topologies. *Computer Communications*, 34(5), Apr. 2011.

Speedtrap: Internet-Scale IPv6 Alias Resolution

Matthew Luckie
CAIDA / UC San Diego
mjl@caida.org

Robert Beverly
Naval Postgraduate School
rbeverly@nps.edu

William Brinkmeyer
Naval Postgraduate School
wdbrinkm@nps.edu

kc claffy
CAIDA / UC San Diego
kc@caida.org

ABSTRACT

Impediments to resolving IPv6 router aliases have precluded understanding the emerging router-level IPv6 Internet topology. In this work, we design, implement, and validate the first *Internet-scale alias resolution technique* for IPv6. Our technique, *speedtrap*, leverages the ability to induce fragmented IPv6 responses from router interfaces in a particular temporal pattern that produces distinguishing per-router fingerprints. Our algorithm surmounts three fundamental challenges to Internet-scale IPv6 alias resolution using fragment identifier values: (1) unlike for IPv4, the identifier counters on IPv6 routers have no natural velocity, (2) the values of these counters are similar across routers, and (3) the packet size required to collect inferences is 46 times larger than required in IPv4. We demonstrate the efficacy of the technique by producing router-level Internet IPv6 topologies using measurements from CAIDA's distributed infrastructure. Our preliminary work represents a step toward understanding the Internet's IPv6 router-level topology, an important objective with respect to IPv6 network resilience, security, policy, and longitudinal evolution.

Categories and Subject Descriptors

C.2.5 [**Local and Wide-Area Networks**]: Internet; C.2.1 [**Network Architecture and Design**]: Network topology; C.2.3 [**Computer Communication Networks**]: Network Operations—*network monitoring*

Keywords

Internet topology; alias resolution; IPv6

1. INTRODUCTION

The Internet operations and engineering community is putting significant effort into deploying IPv6 [10, 8, 6]. As IPv6 gains importance, the research community is in a position to study the deployment of this new Internet protocol using lessons learned studying the IPv4 Internet [5]. In this paper, we introduce *speedtrap*, our Internet-scale IPv6 alias resolution technique. IPv6 alias resolution is the process of determining if two IP addresses are assigned to different interfaces of the same physical router [15]. *speedtrap* is an active measurement technique that reduces an interface-level graph inferred from traceroute measurements to a router-level graph, facilitating better understanding of the resilience and robustness properties of the network [30].

Several IPv4 router alias inference techniques exist, each empirically providing varying degrees of success such that a combination of methods yields the best results: Ally [27], RadarGun [2], and MIDAR [16] use the Identifier (ID) field built into the IPv4 header; DisCarte [25] uses the record route IP option and graph analysis; Mercator [11] uses common source addresses in reply packets; Sherry et al. [24] use the pre-specified timestamp IP option. However, these methods rely on characteristics of IPv4 that are not present in IPv6. The IPv6 header does not include an ID field, there is no record route or pre-specified timestamp options, and the source address of ICMP6 responses must match the destination probed if it exists on the host [7].

Because of the protocol-level differences between IPv4 and IPv6, prior work on IPv6 alias resolution has sought protocol features in IPv6 that could be exploited to resolve aliases, in particular the IPv6 source routing feature (e.g. [29, 23, 22]). However, the IPv6 source routing has been deprecated [1] and the number of probes required scale $O(N^2)$ with the number of interfaces to compare. More recently, we showed that it is possible to obtain ID values in IPv6 useful for alias resolution by inducing routers to send fragments [4]. However, that method scales $O(N^2)$, limiting its application.

This paper describes an Internet-scale application of the technique, dubbed *speedtrap* as it induces velocity in normally stationary ID counters; other than responses to our probes, routers do not send fragments. We show its efficacy by running it on the IPv6 Internet where we obtain ≈ 11k routers from ≈ 53k interfaces. Validation against ground truth from network operators yields 451 of 453 correct inferences, comprising 2% of the 11,181 routers we infer. While not exhaustive, our technique represents a step toward understanding the IPv6 topology. *speedtrap* is implemented in the freely available scamper [19] tool, and the IPv6 router-level graphs are available from CAIDA. The remainder of the paper reviews related work (§2), details the *speedtrap* algorithm (§3), and presents results (§4). We then provide preliminary properties of the IPv6 topology (§5) and suggest avenues for further exploration.

IMC'13, October 23–25, 2013, Barcelona, Spain.
Copyright 2013 ACM 978-1-4503-1953-9/13/10 ...$15.00.
http://dx.doi.org/10.1145/2504730.2504759.

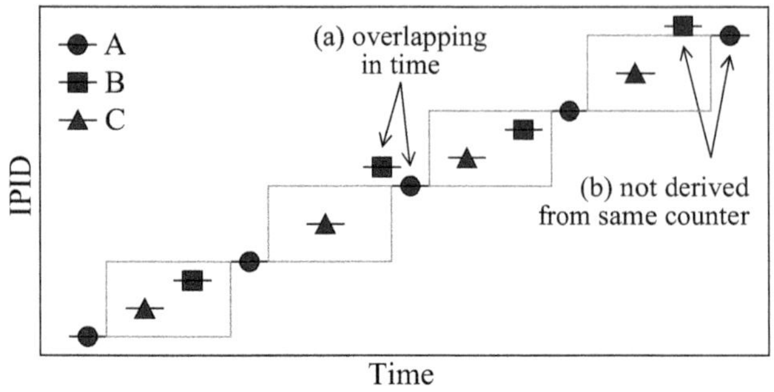

Figure 1: The Monotonic Bounds Test (MBT) used by MIDAR. For two interfaces to share a counter, non-overlapping IPID samples must strictly increase. The horizontal lines with each sample indicate the length of time each probe was outstanding in the network. The boxes between IPID samples from A show the bounds within which samples from aliases must be observed. The MBT suggests that A and C share a counter, but that A and B do not. The samples annotated with (a) are not used to determine shared counter status because it is not possible to determine packet arrival order.

2. RELATED WORK

Three alias resolution techniques for IPv4 use the ID field: Ally [27], RadarGun [2] and MIDAR [16], with RadarGun addressing scaling issues of Ally, and MIDAR addressing accuracy issues of RadarGun. A fundamental property these techniques exploit is that many router implementations use a single, shared ID counter across all of their interfaces. This section summarizes this prior work, with particular focus on the Monotonic Bounds Test (MBT) used by MIDAR, a modified version of which is utilized by *speedtrap*; [16] contains a thorough discussion of MIDAR's MBT and the accuracy of Ally, RadarGun, and MIDAR.

Ally's main limitation is that the number of probe packets required to resolve a graph for aliases scales $O(N^2)$ with the number of interfaces in the graph. RadarGun [2] surmounts Ally's scaling limitation by sending probes to all interfaces in multiple rounds to build a time series: two interfaces are then aliases if they both produce a linear time series and the time series are within a threshold. Unfortunately, the time series of two different routers can be within the threshold, producing a false router. MIDAR [16] provides better accuracy than RadarGun by using a Monotonic Bounds Test (MBT). The MBT is illustrated in figure 1: for two interfaces to be aliases, the ID values returned from a sequence of non-overlapping probes must strictly increase over time. If they do not, as with the points annotated with (b) in figure 1, then the interfaces cannot be using a shared counter.

In this paper, we use the MBT of MIDAR for *speedtrap*. We tailor our probing algorithm to features and challenges unique to IPv6, specifically: (1) no ID field in the IPv6 header, thus requiring us to induce the interface to send an IPv6 fragment header [4], (2) a 32-bit ID counter, as opposed to 16-bit in IPv4, (3) lack of ID velocity (see §3), and (4) the absence of entropy in ID values from unrelated routers. Further, to elicit an IPv6 fragment ID as in [4], we must manage the load induced by the large probe packets we require.

3. TECHNIQUE AND DATA

In this section, we describe the primitive we used to infer aliases, issues in applying existing alias resolution techniques to IPv6, and the Internet-scale alias resolution technique we use to infer aliases. We also describe our application of the technique to the IPv6 interface-level graph captured by CAIDA's Archipelago (Ark) infrastructure [14] for March 2013. The graph consists of *all* the 52,986 IPv6 interfaces numbered within the 2000::/3 unicast prefix captured from all 27 Ark vantage points (VPs) with IPv6 connectivity.

3.1 Obtaining and using the IPv6 ID f eld

The IPv6 header differs from the IPv4 header in many ways; one important difference is the absence of the ID field used for fragmentation and reassembly. The IPv6 protocol shifts the burden of fragmentation to the sender; no in-network packet fragmentation is done by routers. If a sender must fragment a packet, it includes an IPv6 extension header on the fragments which includes a 32-bit ID field necessary for reassembly.

Building on our technique in [4], *speedtrap* obtains an ID field by sending a router an ICMP packet too big message (PTB) with an MTU field smaller than the size of the packets solicited from it. In this work, we send 1300-byte ICMP echo request packets; when we receive 1300-byte echo replies, we send the router a PTB message with an MTU of 1280 bytes. If the router follows the IPv6 protocol [9], it will subsequently send (induced) fragmented echo replies to our hosts. In our dataset, 32.1% of interfaces we probed sent fragmented echo replies with incrementing ID field values; 17.9% sent responses with a random value in the ID field, and 50.0% did not send fragments because they either did not respond to the echo request (30.2%), or appeared to ignore PTB messages (19.8%). Section 4.4 reports on the marginal gains possible by probing interfaces from multiple VPs; a different VP may receive fragmented responses from a router where another VP received no response. To better understand IPv6 fragmentation behavior implemented in various hardware, we obtained hardware ground truth from several commercial service providers via email communication. In our testing, routers manufactured by Cisco, Huawei, Vyatta, HP, and Mikrotik all return sequential fragment identifiers; only Juniper routers, originally based on BSD, return random identifiers. Inevitably an IPv6 router-level map will be composed using multiple complementary inference techniques, as with IPv4.

Soliciting fragments requires us to send large (>1280 byte) probe packets, compared with IPv4 where 28-byte probe packets are sufficient. The requirement to send packets 46 times larger than sent in IPv4 restricts the rate at which packets can be sent. However, we have found it rare for routers to fragment traffic in their normal operation. When we began our work, 28% of probed interfaces replied with an initial fragment ID value of zero or one [4], suggesting they had not sent any fragmented traffic since booting. Figure 2 shows the distribution of IPID values derived from a counter: 80% of the samples occupy 0.00002% of the sample space (i.e. have an ID $<$ 1000 where the ID is a 2^{32} bit value).

Except for responses to our alias resolution probes, routers do not currently source fragmented traffic and so there is no background velocity. It seems unlikely that there will be background velocity in the future. ICMP error messages are limited to 1280 bytes in size so they do not require fragmen-

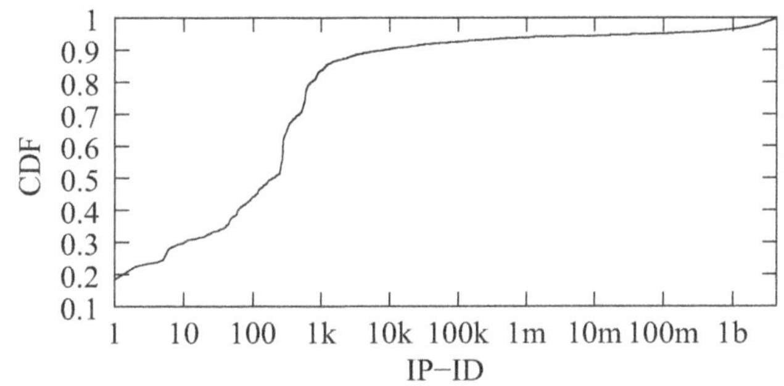

Figure 2: The first IPID value observed from April 2013 interfaces where a counter was inferred. Because there is no natural velocity to the ID counter in IPv6, 80% of the IPID values are less than 1000.

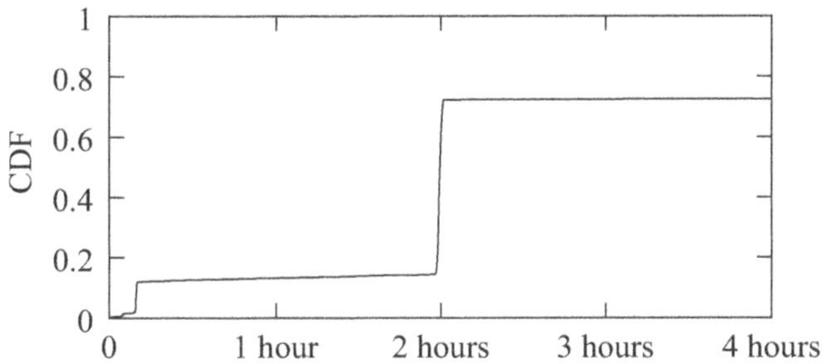

Figure 3: Length of time between sending a PTB and the final fragmented packet received from interfaces that assign IDs from a counter. 78% of interfaces send fragments for at least two hours; 8.7% send fragments for 10 minutes, and 0.8% send fragments for 5 minutes.

tation [7], and it is unlikely that routing protocol traffic will be fragmented in the future if it is not currently.

The minimum MTU in IPv6 is 1280 bytes; it is possible to send 5TB before the 32-bit field contains a duplicate value. Therefore, we can conduct Internet-scale alias resolution with a moderate probing rate without impairing our ability to accurately infer aliases. Routers are required to cache the Path-MTU when they receive a PTB. How long a router caches the Path-MTU depends on the implementation; RFC1981 [20] requires a system to cache for at least five minutes and recommends at least ten minutes. Figure 3 shows that a small fraction of routers cache for the recommended length of time; 78% of interfaces send our host fragments for at least two hours after we sent it a PTB message. This caching helps because it reduces the number of PTB messages sent to routers during the alias resolution process.

3.2 Speedtrap algorithm

We use the same MBT test as is used by MIDAR: for two interfaces to be aliases, the IPID sequence received from non-overlapping probes must strictly increase. Our probing strategy is tailored to determine aliases using the minimum number of probe packets necessary given that the ID field has no velocity except that caused by our probing. Briefly, we (1) determine the set of interfaces in our set that send responses with an IPID derived from a counter, (2) determine which interfaces appear to share a counter, (3) try to cause the counters of distinct routers to diverge, and (4) confirm aliases with pairwise probing. Given the absence of velocity in ID counters and the large probes required for the technique to work, we probe at a low rate of 20pps from a single VP, producing 26Kbps of traffic. We evaluate the performance of our technique in section 4.

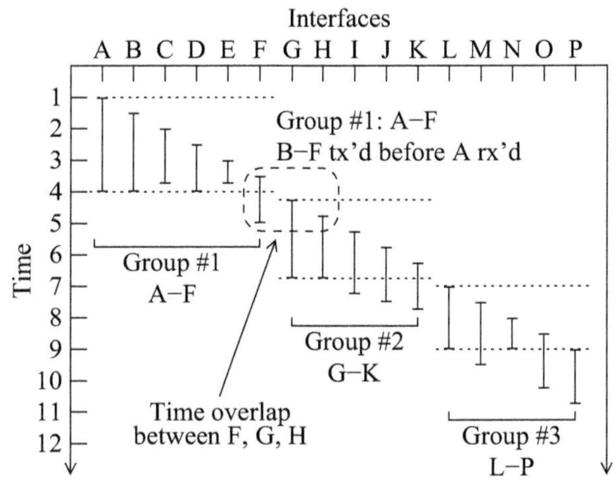

Figure 4: Grouping interfaces during step 2. The vertical bars represent the time a probe is outstanding in the network: between when we transmit and then receive a reply. Each group includes only probes transmitted before a response to the first was received. These groups can then be probed in parallel if there is no overlap between members of the groups in time: #1 and #3 can be probed simultaneously, but #2 cannot be probed at the same time as #1 because G and H (in #2) were transmitted before F (in #1) was received.

Step 1: determine IPID behavior of interfaces. We send each interface six echo requests one second apart. We probe interfaces in a sliding window: probing at 20pps means we test 20 different interfaces at a time. We infer the interface is deriving fragment ID values from a counter provided we receive at least three responses and the difference in ID values for adjacent responses is less than 65,535. In practice, 99.8% of interfaces return perfectly sequential IPID values during this step if they use a counter. This step prevents the following stages from sending probes that will not help resolve router aliases.

Step 2: solicit a sequence of non-overlapping fragments from all interface-pairs. To test if interfaces A and B are aliases, we obtain a sequence of ID values A-B-A or B-A-B where the probes soliciting the ID values were not overlapping. We break this step into three rounds. In each round, we solicit a single ID value from every interface that we inferred to be deriving ID values from a counter; if we do not receive a fragment (and thus no ID value), we probe the interface up to two further times after waiting at least one second.

In the first round, we solicit a single fragmented response from all interfaces, probing in parallel to obtain samples quickly. Because this first round of probing is conducted in parallel, many ID samples are taken while multiple probes were in flight concurrently. To obtain the non-overlapping sequence necessary to infer if two interfaces might share a counter, we assemble groups of interfaces where the previous samples were overlapping in the network. In the second round, we solicit a single fragmented response from each interface in the group one at a time. Figure 4 illustrates the grouping process: we visit samples in order of their transmission time and assemble a group by including all probes subsequently transmitted before the response to the first probe in the group was was received. To achieve time efficiency, we probe interface groups in parallel provided no members overlap between the groups in time. In Figure 4, group #2 cannot be probed at the same time as #1 because of overlap between samples from F, G, and H; however, we can probe group #3 at the same time we probe group #1 because no samples were taken concurrently. In the third round, we solicit a single fragmented response from all interfaces in parallel as we did in round one. On completion, we have obtained packet triplets (A-B-A or B-A-B) with non-overlapping probes for all pairs of interfaces (A, B), which allows us to test whether the interfaces might share a counter.

Step 3: distill candidate routers. We use the data acquired in step 2 to produce sets using a transitive closure (TC) of all interface-pairs that individually passed the MBT using the samples obtained in step 2. Because each closure can contain multiple distinct routers, we probe the interfaces in each closure that holds more than three interfaces, to try to force counters on different routers to diverge. Given a closure (A, B, C, D, E) we try to cause a divergence by sampling an interface between every other interface in the set, e.g. A, B, A, C, A. While the algorithm scales $O(N!)$ worst case, only the subset of interface-pairs that passed the MBT in step 2 will require testing. In addition, in this step we only have to interleave A where the previous sample was monotonically increasing; if a sample for B did not monotonically increase, then we can probe C without interleaving A because B could not have shared a counter with A and caused A's counter to increment. Because the closures represent distinct routers, we can probe separate closures in parallel without inducing rate limiting. After probing each set, we process the interfaces to form smaller closures where the MBT has ruled out shared counters between interfaces.

Step 4: pair-wise testing of candidate routers. The final step is to test each candidate pair of interfaces in each closure that remains after step 3. This step is necessary because there can be large time gaps between previous samples. For a pair of interfaces (A, B) we probe (A, B, A, B, A) and declare aliases if the MBT suggests a shared counter. Because the closures represent distinct routers, we again probe separate closures in parallel. The output from this process is a set of routers and their associated interface addresses.

4. RESULTS

This section provides our results. We first detail our real-world alias success rate, and properties of the aliases we infer. Second, we report our validation results, which relied on a combination of methods and out-of-band interaction with four providers. Of the inferred alias we could validate, > 99% of them were correctly assigned. Third, we evaluate the scalability of *speedtrap* and suggest future avenues of improvement to the algorithm. Fourth, we quantify the marginal benefit of performing *speedtrap* from multiple VPs to mitigate ICMP6 filtering and identify those networks likely to be filtering.

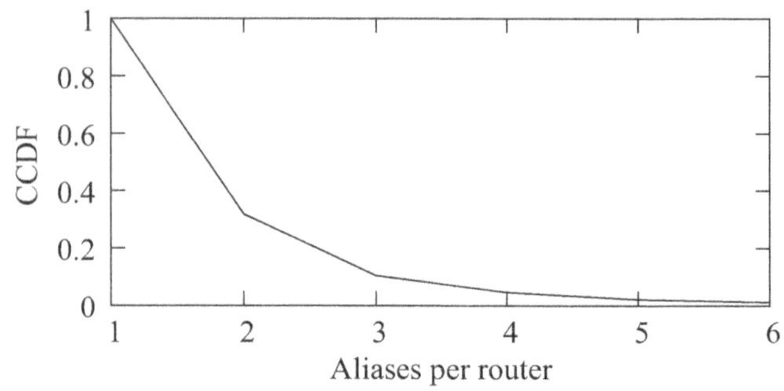

Figure 5: CCDF of number of interfaces observed per router, inclusive of interfaces that assign ID values from a counter. Our dataset contains a single interface for most routers.

Step		Packets	Time
1	IPID behavior	317,814	5:35:44
2	Non-overlapping sequence	80,017	1:15:31
3	Distill candidate routers	34,659	1:15:43
4	Pair-wise testing	63,765	1:01:12
Total:		496,255	9:08:10

Table 1: Packets and time required to complete each step evaluating 52,969 interfaces at 20pps. More than half of the time is spent determining the IPID behavior of interfaces in the set.

4.1 Inferred IPv6 Aliases

Overall, 17,002 interfaces (32.1%) sent echo replies with an incrementing IPID value. Speedtrap inferred 11,181 routers involving these interfaces; figure 5 shows the number of aliases inferred for each router. We observed a single interface on 68% of routers in our set, and two interfaces on 21%. Our validation in section 4.2 suggests that we only observed a single interface on those routers with traceroute, and not that interfaces belonging to the same router use independent counters. The largest router we observed contained 25 aliases. We are confident all aliases we inferred are true aliases because of the cleanness of the data collected in pair-wise testing: 11,083 of 11,086 pairs tested had perfectly sequential ID values in step 4. Table 1 shows the number of packets sent and the time taken to complete. Most time is used and packets sent in step 1; in section 4.3 we show increasing the probe rate and using multiple VPs reduces the time required.

4.2 Validation

We obtained validation data from four networks: a large access provider (AP), two small transit providers (STP-1, STP-2), and a Tier-1 network. Three of the four sets of validation data were obtained by deriving and then confirming an IP address naming convention used in DNS entries with operators of the networks. Additional networks were contacted but their naming conventions were not sufficiently clean to be used as validation data. The fourth set of validation data was obtained by extracting interfaces from a RANCID database [26]. Stale information was found in three of the four sources of validation data, including the RANCID database, which required in-depth discussion with the network operators involved. Table 2 shows the outcome of our

Validation name	STP-1	STP-2	AP	Tier1
Data source	RANCID	DNS	DNS	DNS
Routers				
Incr. IPID	43	40	86	50
Random IPID		43	85	98
No Fragments		11	84	77
No Echo replies			8	11
Mixed			4	3
Total Routers	70	94	267	239
Interfaces	151/750	85/279	138/1008	79/625
Correct	150/151	85/85	137/138	79/79

Table 2: Validation of IP to router assignments. Overall, 451 of 453 (99.6%) of assignments were correct. There exists surprising heterogeneity in router behavior in these networks.

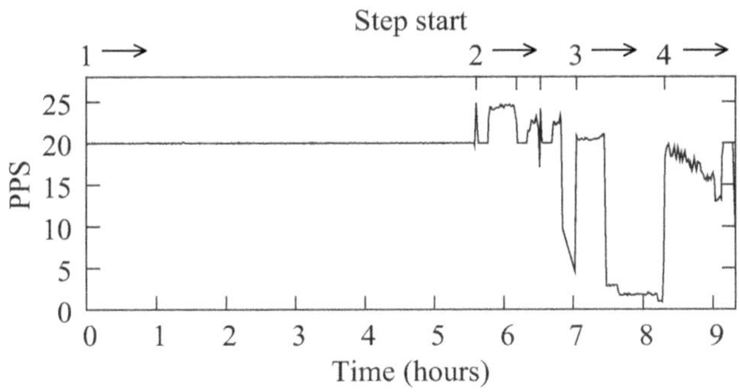

Figure 6: Data collection rate measured by packets-per-second (PPS) over time. Steps 1 (IPID behavior classification) and 2 (non-overlapping sequence) are limited by the configured PPS rate. Steps 3 (distill candidate routers) and 4 (pair-wise testing) are algorithmically limited). The reduction in PPS rate immediately before step 3 is due to $O(N^2)$ (pair-wise) IP-ID comparisons that distill the candidate routers.

validation exercise. Overall, 451 of 453 (99.8%) assignments were made correctly, and we validated 219 of 11,181 routers (2%). The two incorrect assignments were where a single interface was not correctly matched with its aliases, implying that we observed no aliases for the two interfaces. Both cases were due to our not receiving a response to probes sent in round 2 of step 2.

4.3 Scalability

Figure 6 evaluates the scalability of *speedtrap*, focusing on the PPS rate as data collection progressed. We configured scamper's probing rate at 20pps; for nearly the first seven of nine hours the experiment is limited by the configured probing rate; increasing the probing rate or using a distributed set of vantage points linearly reduces the time taken to complete these steps. Steps 3 and 4 are algorithmically limited; because we only probe one address in each candidate router at a time, the time these steps take to complete is limited by the size of the largest candidate router. At present, steps 3 and 4 probe all pairs of addresses in a candidate router. These steps can be improved by building a transitive closure as addresses are evaluated; if an incrementing sequence of IP-ID values is observed probing addresses A and B, then both A and B do not need to be tested against C. With a separate experiment, we confirmed that increasing the probing rate results in a linear reduction of the time to complete steps 1 and 2, and that steps 3 and 4 are currently algorithmically limited. As with MIDAR [16] and RadarGun [2], the number of packets required scales linearly with the number of interfaces to test.

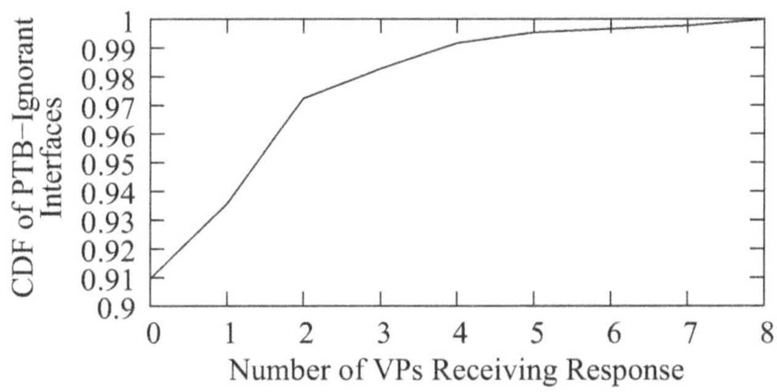

Figure 7: Dependence on vantage point (VP). We observed ≈9% of interfaces that were unresponsive from the first VP responding from at least one of eight different VPs. We observed diminishing marginal success with more vantage points.

4.4 Dependence on Vantage Point

We examined the impact of ICMP6 and fragment filtering by focusing on the set of 10,497 interfaces (19.8%) that do not send fragmented packets after we respond to their echo reply with a PTB, a set we term *PTB-ignorant*. Since we cannot know whether the PTB message arrived at the destination, we instead study their responsiveness using eight Ark VPs distributed around the world (2 in North America, 4 in Europe, 1 in Asia, 1 in Australia). Figure 7 shows the cumulative fraction of the PTB-ignorant interfaces versus the number of VPs that received a fragmented response. Overall, 9,548 (≈ 91%) of these still did not receive fragments from any of the eight VPs, implying that filtering is close to the interfaces. 949 interfaces that were seemingly PTB-ignorant replied with fragments when probed from a different VP. Of the 949 interfaces, only 7.2% returned sequential IDs; we leave understanding why the behavior of these interfaces differs from the whole set to future work.

We then mapped interfaces to autonomous systems (ASes) using the longest matching prefix observed in BGP. For 3% of ASes, all of their PTB-ignorant interfaces were reachable from at least one of the eight VPs. However, for 87% of the ASes, none of their interfaces returned fragments when probed from any of our eight VPs. These findings suggest that various forms of ICMP6 filtering exist in the production IPv6 Internet, perhaps due to security concerns [18].

We therefore performed tomography to infer which ASes might filter PTBs. We performed a traceroute from each of our 8 VPs to infer the forward paths to the interfaces, and then used the global IPv6 BGP table as available from Routeviews [21] to infer the forward AS path. Thus, from each VP to each candidate interface, we have both the AS path, and an understanding of whether that path returned fragments. For all $(VP, interface)$ paths where we received fragments, we infer that no ICMP6 filtering is in place for the ASes along that path, and assemble a set of ASes that do not filter. Then, for all paths where we received unfragmented ICMP6 echo responses, we find the first AS along the

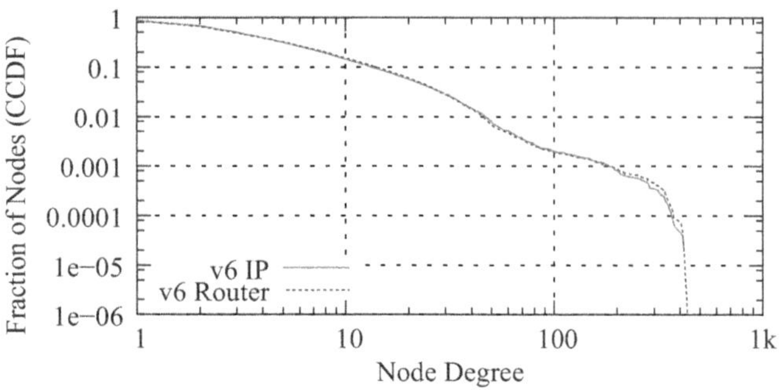

Figure 8: CCDF of IPv6 interface and router degree, inferred from 4.9M Ark traces (Apr, 2013).

path that is not in the unfiltered set. This first "closed" AS is likely the root of the filtering, since it appears in none of the AS paths where fragments are returned. We gathered the most prevalent ASes that likely filter ICMP6, which include: 5511 (France Telecom), 3265 (XS4ALL), 6327 (Shaw), 7843 (Time Warner), 10026 (Pacnet), and 3209 (Vodafone). Thus, performing *speedtrap* from multiple VPs can decrease the fraction of interfaces that do not return fragments, and increase the number of inferred aliases.

5. TOWARD AN IPV6 ROUTER MAP

We used *speedtrap* to resolve the IPv6 interface topology obtained from Ark during April 2013 into a router-level topology. The April 2013 data includes 4.9M IPv6 traces. Our analysis considered only the portion of the trace containing hops that sent ICMP6 time-exceeded messages. Using the *speedtrap*-inferred aliases, we reduced the graph from 49,542 distinct IPv6 interfaces connected by 165,832 edges (average degree of 6.69) to 42,929 nodes connected by 144,377 edges. 39,049 of the 49,542 interfaces (79%) have no known alias, which is similar to the corresponding ratio in a recent study of IPv4 aliases [12]. Figure 8 is a complementary CDF of the node degree distribution for the Ark IPv6 interface and *speedtrap* router-level topologies.

We manually investigated the 81 nodes with degree 100 or greater. 25 of 81 belong to the Tiscali group, including Tinet/Intelliquent, while 11 nodes belong to Level 3. Ten of these large degree nodes correspond to Hurricane Electric (HE) tunnel broker [13] servers, with `ams1.he.net` and `fra1.he.net` having 405 and 303 interfaces respectively. Within the IP-level topology and without alias resolution, `ams1.he.net` was inferred to be *different* nodes of degree 218, 194, 178, 189, 136, where some of the IPv6 interfaces corresponded to address space other than that owned by HE. This example illuminates the danger in using interface-level topologies, and the value in alias resolution for IPv6, where individual nodes may be disproportionately important at this stage of IPv6 evolution, or in the future. This finding is consistent with other recent measurements of BGP paths where HE, Level 3, and Tinet also appear as important parts of the IPv6 topology [10].

A limitation of our approach is that 17.9% of interfaces return random fragment identifiers, a function of the underlying router implementation. Unfortunately, MBT cannot make alias inferences over interfaces that return random identifiers. One potential enhancement to our technique is to use the PTB MTU as a nonce such that an alias of the interface to which the PTB is sent would return fragments of a distinguishing size. The ability to leverage MTU size for IPv6 alias resolution depends on the PMTU destination cache being shared across interfaces. In our testing, we find that Huawei, Vyatta, HP, and Mikrotik use a shared per-destination PMTU cache. However, we can already resolve aliases of these devices using *speedtrap*. Unfortunately, Juniper routers use a per-interface, per-destination PMTU cache. Thus, resolving the aliases of Juniper routers remains an open problem.

6. CONCLUSION

While researchers continue to make progress toward understanding the Internet's IPv4 topology, little is known about the IPv6 router-level topology. Relying on interface topologies such as those revealed by traceroute yields incorrect inferences and conclusions about the structure and resilience of the network [17, 30]. Alias resolution is crucial to producing a topology that represents actual equipment (routers and links). In IPv6, tunnels and virtual interfaces are common, and one cannot assume that nodes in the network core have low degree as might be dictated by physical router density constraints. Similarly, tunnels can directly connect distant IPv6 routers over many IPv4 hops. Understanding the IPv6 router-level topology is thus important both from security and Internet evolution perspectives [5].

We do not claim that our inferred IPv6 router-level topology is representative of the IPv6 Internet. In particular, our current research explores how to more efficiently and effectively perform active probes in IPv6 amid large amounts of topological sparsity encountered in random probes [3]. Further, combining graph analysis techniques such as those detailed in [15] will likely uncover additional router-level structure. However, our work represents an important step forward in more completely understanding the true IPv6 topology, and the first IPv6 router-level topologies.

In February 2013 the IETF updated the specification of the ID field in IPv4 so that the ID field is only set when a packet is fragmented [28]. If this RFC is followed, *speedtrap* will soon be required for IPv4 router alias resolution as well as IPv6. A related question is what fraction of IPv4 routers that set a constant (zero) ID field would set an incrementing IPID field if they were required to fragment responses.

Acknowledgments

We thank Owen DeLong, Aaron Hughes, and Brandon Ross for operational insight and ground truth, and the four anonymous operators of the networks (STP-1, STP-2, AP, Tier1) who confirmed our interpretation of their router naming convention which we used to validate our inferred router-level map. Bradley Huffaker supplied IPv4 degree distribution data for comparison purposes. Our shepherd, Lachlan Andrew, and the anonymous reviewers provided invaluable feedback. The work was supported by the NSF under grants CNS-1111445 and CNS-1111449, and by the U.S. Department of Homeland Security (DHS) Science and Technology (S&T) Directorate Cyber Security Division (DHS S&T/CSD) BAA 11-02 and SPAWAR Systems Center Pacific via contract number N66001-12-C-0130. This material represents the position of the author(s) and not necessarily that of NSF or DHS.

7. REFERENCES

[1] J. Abley, P. Savola, and G. Neville-Neil. Deprecation of type 0 routing headers in IPv6, Dec. 2007. RFC 5095.

[2] A. Bender, R. Sherwood, and N. Spring. Fixing Ally's growing pains with velocity modeling. In *ACM SIGCOMM IMC*, pages 337–342, Vouliagmeni, Greece, Oct. 2008.

[3] R. Beverly, A. Berger, and G. G. Xie. Primitives for active internet topology mapping: toward high-frequency characterization. In *ACM SIGCOMM IMC*, pages 165–171, 2010.

[4] R. Beverly, W. Brinkmeyer, M. Luckie, and J. P. Rohrer. IPv6 alias resolution via induced fragmentation. In *PAM*, Mar. 2013.

[5] k. claffy. Tracking IPv6 evolution: data we have and data we need. *CCR*, 41(3):43–48, July 2011.

[6] Comcast. Comcast Launches IPv6 for Business Customers, 2013. `http://corporate.comcast.com/comcast-voices/comcast-launches-ipv6-for-business-customers`.

[7] A. Contra, S. Deering, and M. Gupta. Internet control message protocol (ICMPv6) for the Internet protocol version 6 (IPv6) specification, Mar. 2006. RFC 4443.

[8] J. Czyz, M. Allman, J. Zhang, S. Iekel-Johnson, E. Osterweil, and M. Bailey. Measuring IPv6 adoption. Technical Report TR-13-004, ICSI, Aug. 2013.

[9] S. Deering and R. Hinden. Internet protocol, version 6 (IPv6) specification, Dec. 1998. RFC 2460.

[10] A. Dhamdhere, M. Luckie, B. Huffaker, K. Claffy, A. Elmokashfi, and E. Aben. Measuring the deployment of IPv6: Topology, routing, and performance. In *ACM SIGCOMM IMC*, pages 537–550, Boston, MA, USA, Nov. 2012.

[11] R. Govindan and H. Tangmunarunkit. Heuristics for Internet map discovery. In *IEEE INFOCOM*, pages 1371–1380, Tel-Aviv, Israel, Mar 2000.

[12] B. Huffaker, M. Fomenkov, and k. claffy. Internet Topology Data Comparison. Technical report, Cooperative Association for Internet Data Analysis (CAIDA), May 2012.

[13] Hurricane Electric. IPv6 tunnel broker service, 2013. `http://tunnelbroker.net/`.

[14] Y. Hyun and k. claffy. Archipelago measurement infrastructure, 2013. `http://www.caida.org/projects/ark/`.

[15] K. Keys. Internet-scale IP alias resolution. *ACM SIGCOMM CCR*, 40(1):50–55, Jan. 2010.

[16] K. Keys, Y. Hyun, M. Luckie, and k claffy. Internet-scale IPv4 alias resolution with MIDAR. *IEEE/ACM Transactions on Networking*, pages 383–399, Apr. 2013.

[17] B. Krishnamurthy and W. Willinger. What are our standards for validation of measurement-based networking research? *SIGMETRICS Perform. Eval. Rev.*, 36(2):64–69, Aug. 2008.

[18] S. Krishnan. Handling of Overlapping IPv6 Fragments. RFC 5722 (Proposed Standard), Dec. 2009.

[19] M. Luckie. Scamper: a scalable and extensible packet prober for active measurement of the internet. In *ACM SIGCOMM IMC*, pages 239–245, 2010.

[20] J. McCann, S. Deering, and J. Mogul. Path MTU discovery for IP version 6, Aug. 1996. RFC 1981.

[21] D. Meyer. University of Oregon RouteViews, 2013. `http://www.routeviews.org`.

[22] S. Qian, Y. Wang, and K. Xu. Utilizing destination options header to resolve IPv6 alias resolution. In *IEEE Globecom*, Miami, FL, USA, Dec. 2010.

[23] S. Qian, M. Xu, Z. Qiao, and K. Xu. Route positional method for IPv6 alias resolution. In *ICCCN*, 2010.

[24] J. Sherry, E. Katz-Bassett, M. Pimenova, H. V. Madhyastha, T. Anderson, and A. Krishnamurthy. Resolving IP aliases with prespecified timestamps. In *ACM SIGCOMM IMC*, pages 172–178, Melbourne, Australia, Nov. 2010.

[25] R. Sherwood, A. Bender, and N. Spring. DisCarte: a disjunctive Internet cartographer. In *ACM SIGCOMM*, pages 303–314, Seattle, WA, USA, Aug. 2008.

[26] Shrubbery Networks, Inc. RANCID - Really Awesome New Cisco conflg Differ. `http://www.shrubbery.net/rancid/`.

[27] N. Spring, R. Mahajan, and D. Wetherall. Measuring ISP topologies with Rocketfuel. In *ACM SIGCOMM*, pages 133–145, Pittsburgh, PA, USA, Aug. 2002.

[28] J. Touch. Updated specification of the IPv4 ID field, Feb. 2013. RFC 6864.

[29] D. G. Waddington, F. Chang, R. Viswanathan, and B. Yao. Topology discovery for public IPv6 networks. *ACM SIGCOMM CCR*, 33(3):59–68, July 2003.

[30] W. Willinger, D. Alderson, and J. C. Doyle. Mathematics and the Internet: A source of enormous confusion and great potential. *Notices of the AMS*, 56(5), 2009.

A Fistful of Bitcoins: Characterizing Payments Among Men with No Names

Sarah Meiklejohn Marjori Pomarole Grant Jordan
Kirill Levchenko Damon McCoy[†] Geoffrey M. Voelker Stefan Savage

University of California, San Diego George Mason University[†]

ABSTRACT

Bitcoin is a purely online virtual currency, unbacked by either physical commodities or sovereign obligation; instead, it relies on a combination of cryptographic protection and a peer-to-peer protocol for witnessing settlements. Consequently, Bitcoin has the unintuitive property that while the ownership of money is implicitly anonymous, its flow is globally visible. In this paper we explore this unique characteristic further, using heuristic clustering to group Bitcoin wallets based on evidence of shared authority, and then using re-identification attacks (i.e., empirical purchasing of goods and services) to classify the operators of those clusters. From this analysis, we characterize longitudinal changes in the Bitcoin market, the stresses these changes are placing on the system, and the challenges for those seeking to use Bitcoin for criminal or fraudulent purposes at scale.

Categories and Subject Descriptors

K.4.4 [**Electronic Commerce**]: Payment schemes

Keywords

Bitcoin; Measurement; Anonymity

1. INTRODUCTION

Demand for low friction e-commerce of various kinds has driven a proliferation in online payment systems over the last decade. Thus, in addition to established payment card networks (e.g., Visa and Mastercard) a broad range of so-called "alternative payments" has emerged including eWallets (e.g., Paypal, Google Checkout, and WebMoney), direct debit systems (typically via ACH, such as eBillMe), money transfer systems (e.g., Moneygram) and so on. However, virtually all of these systems have the property that they are denominated in existing fiat currencies (e.g., dollars), explicitly identify the payer in transactions, and are centrally or quasi-centrally administered.[1]

[1]In particular, there is a central controlling authority who has the technical and legal capacity to tie a transaction back to a pair of individuals.

IMC'13, October 23–25, 2013, Barcelona, Spain.

http://dx.doi.org/10.1145/2504730.2504747.

By far the most intriguing exception to this rule is Bitcoin. First deployed in 2009, Bitcoin is an independent online monetary system that combines some of the features of cash and existing online payment methods. Like cash, Bitcoin transactions do not explicitly identify the payer or the payee: a transaction is a cryptographically-signed transfer of funds from one public key to another. Moreover, like cash, Bitcoin transactions are irreversible (in particular, there is no *chargeback* risk as with credit cards). However, unlike cash, Bitcoin requires third party mediation: a global peer-to-peer network of participants validates and certifies all transactions; such decentralized accounting requires each network participant to maintain the entire transaction history of the system, currently amounting to over 3GB of compressed data. Bitcoin identities are thus *pseudo-anonymous*: while not explicitly tied to real-world individuals or organizations, all transactions are completely transparent.[2]

This unusual combination of features has given rise to considerable confusion about the nature and consequences of the anonymity that Bitcoin provides. In particular, there is concern that the combination of scalable, irrevocable, anonymous payments would prove highly attractive for criminals engaged in fraud or money laundering. In a widely leaked 2012 Intelligence Assessment, FBI analysts make just this case and conclude that a key "advantage" of Bitcoin for criminals is that "law enforcement faces difficulties detecting suspicious activity, identifying users and obtaining transaction records" [7]. Similarly, in a late 2012 report on Virtual Currency Schemes, the European Central Bank opines that the lack of regulation and due diligence might enable "criminals, terrorists, fraudsters and money laundering" and that "the extent to which any money flows can be traced back to a particular user is unknown" [6]. Indeed, there is at least some anecdotal evidence that this statement is true, with the widely publicized "Silk Road" service using Bitcoin to trade in a range of illegal goods (e.g., restricted drugs and firearms). Finally, adding to this urgency is Bitcoin's considerable growth, both quantitatively — a merchant servicer, Bitpay, announced that it had signed up over 1,000 merchants in 2012 to accept the currency, and in April 2013 the exchange rate soared to 235 USD per bitcoin before settling to a more modest 100 USD per bitcoin — and qualitatively via integration with existing payment mechanisms (e.g., Bitinstant offering to tie users' Bitcoin wallets to Mastercard accounts [5] and Bitcoin Central's recent partnership with the French bank Crédit Mutuel Arkéa to gateway Bitcoin into the banking system [16]) and the increasing attention of world financial institutions (e.g., Canada's recent decision to tax Bitcoin transactions [3] and FinCEN's recent regulations

[2]Note that this statement is not strictly true since private exchanges of Bitcoin between customers of a single third party exchange, such as Mt. Gox, need not (and do not) engage the global Bitcoin protocol and are therefore not transparent.

on virtual currencies [8]). In spite of this background of intense interest, Bitcoin's pseudo-anonymity has limited how much is known about how the currency is used and how Bitcoin's use has evolved over time.

In this context, our work seeks to better understand the traceability of Bitcoin flows and, through this understanding, explore the evolution in how Bitcoin has been used over time. Importantly, our goal is not to generally de-anonymize all Bitcoin users — as the abstract protocol design itself dictates that this should be impossible — but rather to identify certain *idioms of use* present in concrete Bitcoin network implementations that erode the anonymity of the users who engage in them. Our approach is based on the availability of the Bitcoin *block chain*: a replicated graph data structure that encodes all Bitcoin activity, past and present, in terms of the public digital signing keys party to each transaction. However, since each of these keys carries no explicit information about ownership, our analysis depends on imposing additional structure on the transaction graph.

Our methodology has two phases. First, in Section 3, we describe a re-identification attack wherein we open accounts and make purchases from a broad range of known Bitcoin merchants and service providers (e.g., Mt. Gox and Silk Road). Since one endpoint of the transaction is known (i.e., we know which public key we used), we are able to positively label the public key on the other end as belonging to the service; we augment this attack by crawling Bitcoin forums for "self-labeled" public keys (e.g., where an individual or organization explicitly advertises a key as their own). Next, in Section 4, we build on past efforts [2, 17, 18, 21] to cluster public keys based on evidence of shared spending authority. This clustering allows us to amplify the results of our re-identification attack: if we labeled one public key as belonging to Mt. Gox, we can now transitively taint the entire cluster containing this public key as belonging to Mt. Gox as well. The result is a condensed graph, in which nodes represent entire users and services rather than individual public keys.

From this data we characterize Bitcoin use longitudinally, focusing in particular on the evolution of services and their role in the Bitcoin network. Finally, in Section 5, we combine what we have learned to examine the suitability of Bitcoin for hiding large-scale illicit transactions. Using the dissolution of a large Silk Road wallet and notable Bitcoin thefts as case studies, we demonstrate that an agency with subpoena power would be well placed to identify who is paying money to whom. Indeed, we argue that the increasing dominance of a small number of Bitcoin institutions (most notably services that perform currency exchange), coupled with the public nature of transactions and our ability to label monetary flows to major institutions, ultimately makes Bitcoin unattractive today for high-volume illicit use such as money laundering.

2. BITCOIN BACKGROUND

Our heuristics that we use to cluster addresses depend on the structure of the Bitcoin protocol, so we first describe it here, and briefly mention the anonymity that it is intended to provide. Additionally, much of our analysis discusses the "major players" and different categories of bitcoin-based services, so we also present a more high-level overview of Bitcoin participation, as well as some general statistics about the Bitcoin network.

2.1 Bitcoin protocol description

Bitcoin is a decentralized electronic currency, introduced by (the pseudonymous) Satoshi Nakamoto in 2008 [15] and deployed on January 3 2009. Briefly, a bitcoin[3] can be thought of as a chain of *transactions* from one owner to the next, where owners are identified by a *public key* (in practice, a public key for the ECDSA signature scheme) that serves as a pseudonym; i.e., users can use any number of public keys and their activity using one set of public keys is not inherently tied to their activity using another set, or to their real-world identity (so that, e.g., a user can use a different public key to deposit bitcoins into his Silk Road account than to withdraw bitcoins from his Mt. Gox account, and expect that these activities cannot be linked to either his real identity or to each other). In each transaction, the previous owner signs — using the secret signing key corresponding to his public key — a hash of the transaction in which he received the bitcoins (in practice, a SHA-256 hash) and the public key of the next owner. This signature (i.e., transaction) can then be added to the set of transactions that constitutes the bitcoin; because each of these transactions references the previous transaction (i.e., in sending bitcoins, the current owner must specify where they came from), the transactions form a chain. To verify the validity of a bitcoin, a user can check the validity of each of the signatures in this chain.

To prevent double spending, it is necessary for each user in the system to be aware of all such transactions. Double spending can then be identified when a user attempts to transfer a bitcoin after he has already done so. To determine which transaction came first, transactions are grouped into *blocks*, which serve to timestamp the transactions they contain and vouch for their validity. Blocks are themselves formed into a chain, with each block referencing the previous one (and thus further reinforcing the validity of all previous transactions). This process yields a *block chain*, which is then publicly available to every user within the system.

This process describes how to transfer bitcoins and broadcast transactions to all users of the system. Because Bitcoin is decentralized and there is thus no central authority minting bitcoins, we must also consider how bitcoins are generated in the first place. In fact, this happens in the process of forming a block: each accepted block (i.e., each block incorporated into the block chain) is required to be such that, when all the data inside the block is hashed, the hash begins with a certain number of zeroes. To allow users to find this particular collection of data, blocks contain, in addition to a list of transactions, a *nonce*. (We simplify the description slightly to ease presentation.) Once someone finds a nonce that allows the block to have the correctly formatted hash, the block is then broadcast in the same peer-to-peer manner as transactions. The system is designed to generate only 21 million bitcoins in total. Finding a block currently comes with an attached reward of 25 BTC; this rate was 50 BTC until November 28 2012 (block height 210,000), and is expected to halve again in 2016, and eventually drop to 0 in 2140.

In summary, the dissemination of information within the Bitcoin network is as follows (and as depicted in Figure 1): first, users generate at least one signing keypair, and publicize the public key, or *address* — in the rest of the paper we use these terms interchangeably — to receive bitcoins (and again, users can choose to use a single public key or arbitrarily many). If a user has bitcoins that she wishes to transfer, she broadcasts a *transaction*, proving that she has the bitcoins and indicating the address of the recipient to her peers, who in turn broadcast it to their peers. Eventually, this transaction reaches a miner, who collects the transactions he hears about into a *block*, and works on finding the right data/nonce bal-

[3]Following established convention, we use the capitalized term *Bitcoin* when referring to the payment system and peer-to-peer network and the lowercase term *bitcoin* (abbreviated *BTC*), when referring to the unit of currency.

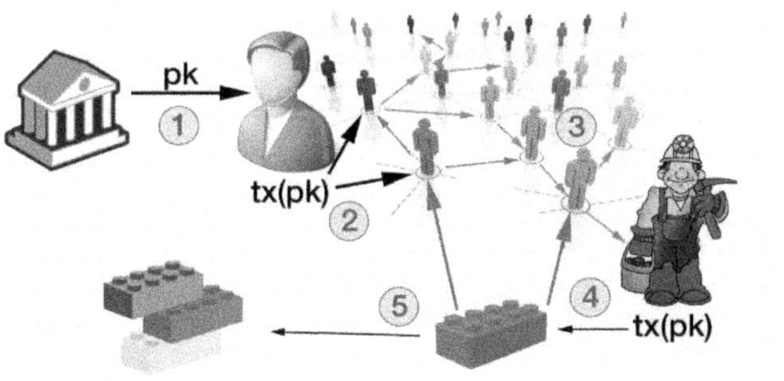

Figure 1: The main players in the Bitcoin landscape. In (1), a user wishing to deposit bitcoins into a bank receives a *public key*, or *address*, belonging to the bank. In (2), the user incorporates both his own public key and the one sent to him by the bank into a *transaction*, which he then broadcasts to his peers. In (3), the transaction floods the network. In (4), the transaction is eventually received by a *miner*, who works to incorporate the transaction into a *block*. In (5), this block is then flooded through the network, and in this way is incorporated into the global *block chain*. The bitcoins now belong to the public key of the bank, and thus have been successfully deposited.

ance to hit the target hash. He also includes in the block a special *coin generation* transaction that specifies his address for receiving the block reward. Finally, when the miner does find such a block, he broadcasts it to his peers, who again broadcast it to their peers. As his reward, the block reward and all the fees for the included transactions are credited to his specified address. When another block has been formed, referencing his block as the previous block, his block can now be considered part of the *block chain*.

2.2 Participants in the Bitcoin network

In practice, the way in which Bitcoin can be used is much simpler than the above description might indicate. First, generating a block is so computationally difficult that very few individual users attempt it on their own. Instead, users may join a *mining pool* such as Deepbit, in which they contribute "shares" to narrow down the search space, and earn a small amount of bitcoins in exchange for each share.

Users may also avoid coin generation entirely, and simply purchase bitcoins through one of the many *exchanges*, such as Mt. Gox. They may then keep the bitcoins in a wallet stored on their computer or, to make matters even easier, use one of the many *wallet services* (i.e., banks) that exist online (although the two most popular of these, MyBitcoin and Instawallet, have both shut down due to thefts).

Finally, to actually spend their bitcoins, users could gamble with one of the popular dice games such as Satoshi Dice. They could also buy items from various online vendors, such as Bitmit ("the eBay of Bitcoin"), the notorious Tor-based service Silk Road, or with vendors, such as Wordpress, that might ordinarily accept only US dollars but accept bitcoins through BitPay, a payment gateway that takes bitcoins from the buyer but offers the option of payment in USD to the seller (thus eliminating all Bitcoin-based risk for the vendor). Finally, users wishing to go beyond basic currency speculation can invest their bitcoins with firms such as Bitcoinica (shut down after a series of thefts) or Bitcoin Savings & Trust (later revealed as a major Ponzi scheme). In Section 3, we more fully describe the role and impact of these and other services within the Bitcoin network.

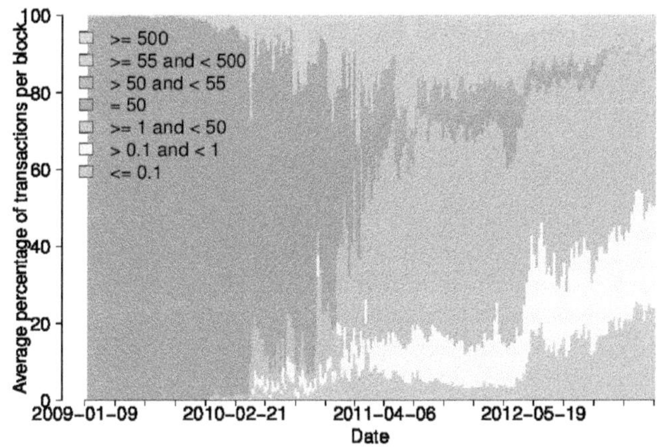

Figure 2: The distribution, over time and averaged weekly, of transaction values. The plot and legend both run, bottom to top, from the smallest-valued transactions to the highest.

2.3 Bitcoin network statistics

We used the `bitcoind` client to download the block chain, and parsed it into a PostgreSQL database using a modified version of the `bitcointools` library developed by Gavin Andresen [1]. We last parsed the block chain on April 13 2013, when there were 231,207 blocks, containing 16,086,073 transactions and 12,056,684 distinct public keys.

To begin, we looked at the size of transactions; i.e., the number of bitcoins sent in a transaction. Figure 2 depicts the changing percentage of various transaction sizes over time. Not surprisingly, until approximately April 2010 — the first 15 months that Bitcoin was deployed — almost all transactions involved exactly 50 bitcoins (the initial reward for mining a block), and indeed these transactions became a minority of all transactions only in January 2011. This activity reflects the adoption phase of Bitcoin, in which most blocks contained the coin generation transaction and nothing more. (In later phases, the mining reward is likely a little more than 50 because it includes miner fees, which is why we created a separate bin for values between 50 and 55.) We also see a second turning point in early 2012, in which the percentage of transactions carrying less than a single bitcoin in total value doubled abruptly (from 20% to 40%), while the percentage of transactions carrying less than 0.1 BTC tripled.

We also observed how quickly bitcoins were spent; i.e., once they were received, how long did it take the recipient to spend them? Figure 3 shows breakdowns both in terms of public keys (how many recipient public keys spent their contents in a certain time window) and in terms of value (how many of the bitcoins that were received were spent in a certain time window).

Looking at this figure, we again see two clear turning points. The first, in early 2011, represents a point at which users began meaningfully spending bitcoins, rather than just "hoarding" them; in fact, from this point on a negligible fraction of bitcoins are hoarded. Nevertheless, these early hoarders in fact took most of the bitcoins out of circulation; as observed by Ron and Shamir [18], a significant majority of all bitcoins are in these "sink" addresses that have to date never spent their contents (at the time they parsed the block chain it was 75%, whereas we observed it to be 64%), meaning only 4 million bitcoins are currently in circulation. Nevertheless, these remaining coins are circulating quite actively, as seen in the second turning point in Figure 3: in April 2012, the percentage of bitcoins being spent *immediately* (i.e., in the same block in which

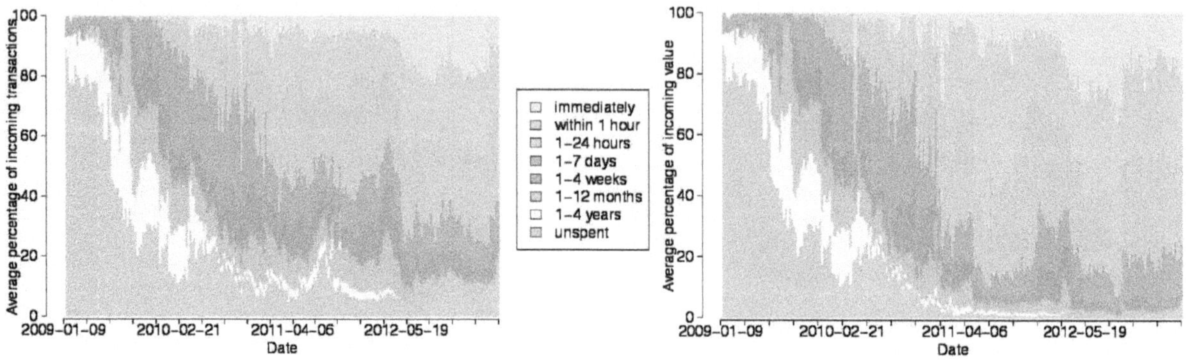

Figure 3: The trend, over time and averaged weekly, of how long public keys hold on to the bitcoins received. The plot on the left shows the percentage over all public keys, and the plot on the right shows the percentage over all value transacted. The values run bottom to top, from longest to spend (unspent as of now) to shortest to spend (spent within the same block).

they were received) doubled, and more generally half of all bitcoins are now spent within an hour of being received and 80% of bitcoins are spent within a day.

As it turns out, and as we see in Section 5.1, both these recent trends of smaller transactions and faster spending can be largely attributed to a single service: the gambling site Satoshi Dice. Thus, even a longitudinal study of the Bitcoin network already makes clear the effect that services have on current Bitcoin usage.

3. DATA COLLECTION

To identify public keys belonging to the types of services mentioned in Section 2.2, we sought to "tag" as many addresses as possible; i.e., label an address as being definitively controlled by some known real-world user (e.g., Mt. Gox or Instawallet). As we will see in Section 4.3, by clustering addresses based on evidence of shared control, we can bootstrap off the minimal ground truth data this provides to tag entire clusters of addresses as also belonging to that user.

Our predominant method for tagging users was simply transacting with them (e.g., depositing into and withdrawing bitcoins from Mt. Gox) and then observing the addresses they used; additionally, we collected known (or assumed) addresses that we found in various forums and other Web sites, although we regarded this latter kind of tagging as less reliable than our own observed data.

3.1 From our own transactions

We engaged in 344 transactions with a wide variety of services, listed in Table 1, including mining pools, wallet services, bank exchanges, non-bank exchanges, vendors, gambling sites, and miscellaneous services.

Mining pools. We attempted to mine with each of the major mining pools (a pie chart depicting the relative productivity of mining pools can be found at `blockorigin.pfoe.be/chart.php`). To do this, we used an AMD Radeon HD 7970, capable of approximately 530 million SHA-256 computations per second; this effort allowed us to trigger a payout of at least 0.1 BTC (often the minimum payout for pools) with 11 different pools, anywhere from 1 to 25 times. For each payout transaction, we then labeled the input public keys as belonging to the pool. One of these pools, Eligius, split the coin among the miners immediately upon being mined, and we were thus unable to tag any of their public keys using this method.

Wallets. We kept money with most of the major wallet services (10 in total), and made multiple deposit and withdrawal transactions for each. Three of these services — My Wallet, Easycoin, and Strongcoin — kept the funds of their users separate, which meant we were unable to link many addresses together for them.

Bank exchanges. Most of the real-time trading exchanges (i.e., in which the exchange rate is not fixed) also function as banks. As such, we tagged these services just as we did the wallets: by depositing into and withdrawing from our accounts (but rarely participating in any actual currency exchange). We kept accounts with 18 such exchanges in total.

Non-bank exchanges. In contrast, most of the fixed-rate exchanges did not function as banks, and are instead intended for one-time conversions. We therefore were able to participate in fewer transactions with these exchanges, although we again tried to transact with most of the major ones at least once (8 in total).

Vendors. We purchased goods, both physical and digital, from a wide variety of vendors. Some of the vendors, such as Bitmit and CoinDL, function more as marketplaces (the "eBay" and "iTunes" of the Bitcoin economy, respectively), while others were individual merchants. Although we purchased from Etsy, they do not provide a Bitcoin payment interface and we instead negotiated individually with the merchant. Many of the vendors we interacted with did not use an independent method for accepting bitcoins, but relied instead on the BitPay payment gateway (and one used WalletBit as a payment gateway). We also kept a wallet with Silk Road, which allowed us to tag their public keys without making any purchases. Figure 4 depicts all of our physical purchases.

Gambling. We kept accounts with five poker sites, and transacted with eight sites offering mini-games and/or lotteries. Many of the dice games (Satoshi Dice, BTC Dice, etc.) advertised their public keys, so we did fewer transactions with these services.

Miscellaneous. Four of the additional services we interacted with were *mix* or *laundry* services: when provided with an output address, they promised to send to that address coins that had no association with the ones sent to them; the more sophisticated ones offered to spread the coins out over various transactions and over time. One of these, BitMix, simply stole our money, while Bitcoin Laundry twice sent us our own coins back, indicating we were possibly their only customer at that time. We also interacted with Bit Visitor, a site that paid users to visit certain sites; Bitcoin Advertisers, which provided online advertising; CoinAd, which gave out free bitcoins; Coinapult, which forwarded bitcoins to an email address, where they could then be redeemed; and finally, Wikileaks, with whom we donated to both their public donation address and two one-time addresses generated for us via their IRC channel.

Mining		
50 BTC	BTC Guild	Itzod
ABC Pool	Deepbit	Ozcoin
Bitclockers	EclipseMC	Slush
Bitminter	Eligius	
Wallets		
Bitcoin Faucet	Easywallet	Strongcoin
My Wallet	Flexcoin	WalletBit
Coinbase	Instawallet	
Easycoin	Paytunia	
Exchanges		
Bitcoin 24	BTC-e	Aurum Xchange
Bitcoin Central	CampBX	BitInstant
Bitcoin.de	CA VirtEx	Bitcoin Nordic
Bitcurex	ICBit	BTC Quick
Bitfloor	Mercado Bitcoin	FastCash4Bitcoins
Bitmarket	Mt Gox	Lilion Transfer
Bitme	The Rock	Nanaimo Gold
Bitstamp	Vircurex	OKPay
BTC China	Virwox	
Vendors		
ABU Games	BTC Buy	HealthRX
Bitbrew	BTC Gadgets	JJ Games
Bitdomain	Casascius	NZBs R Us
Bitmit	Coinabul	Silk Road
Bitpay	CoinDL	WalletBit
Bit Usenet	Etsy	Yoku
Gambling		
Bit Elfin	BitZino	Gold Game Land
Bitcoin 24/7	BTC Griffin	Satoshi Dice
Bitcoin Darts	BTC Lucky	Seals with Clubs
Bitcoin Kamikaze	BTC on Tilt	
Bitcoin Minefield	Clone Dice	
Miscellaneous		
Bit Visitor	Bitfog	CoinAd
Bitcoin Advertisers	Bitlaundry	Coinapult
Bitcoin Laundry	BitMix	Wikileaks

Table 1: The various services we interacted with, grouped by (approximate) type.

3.2 From other sources

In addition to our own transactions, many users publicly claim their own addresses; e.g., charities providing donation addresses, or LulzSec claiming their address on Twitter. While we did not attempt to collect all such instances, many of these tags are conveniently collected at `blockchain.info/tags`, including both addresses provided in users' signatures for Bitcoin forums, as well as self-submitted tags. We collected all of these tags — over 5,000 in total — keeping in mind that the ones that were not self-submitted (and even the ones that were) could be regarded as less reliable than the ones we collected ourselves.

Finally, we searched through the Bitcoin forums (in particular, `bitcointalk.org`) looking for addresses associated with major thefts, or now-defunct services such as Tradehill and GLBSE. Again, these sources are less reliable, so we consequently labeled users only for addresses for which we could gain some confidence through manual due diligence.

4. ACCOUNT CLUSTERING HEURISTICS

In this section, we present two heuristics for linking addresses controlled by the same user, with the goal of collapsing the many public keys seen in the block chain into larger entities. The first

Figure 4: The physical items we purchased with bitcoins, including silver quarters from Coinabul, coffee from Bitcoin Coffee, and a used Boston CD from Bitmit. The items in green were purchased from CoinDL; in blue from Bitmit; and in red using the payment gateway BitPay.

heuristic, in which we treat different public keys used as inputs to a transaction as being controlled by the same user, has already been used and explored in previous work, and exploits an inherent property of the Bitcoin protocol. The second is new and based on so-called *change addresses*; in contrast to the first, it exploits a current *idiom of use* in the Bitcoin network rather than an inherent property. As such, it is less robust in the face of changing patterns within the network, but — as we especially see in Section 5.2 — it provides insight into the current Bitcoin network that the first heuristic does not.

4.1 Defining account control

Before we present our heuristics, we clarify what the results of our clustering algorithms imply; in particular, we must define what we mean by address *control*. Put simply, we say that the controller of an address is the entity (or in exceptional cases multiple entities) that is expected to participate in transactions involving that address. While this requirement implies a priori that the controller of an address knows the corresponding private key (recall that transactions are signatures, and thus knowledge of the signing key is necessary to form a valid transaction), knowledge of the private key is not a sufficient requirement for control. Consider, for example, buying physical bitcoins from a vendor such as Casascius. To form the physical bitcoin to send to you, Casascius must know the private key. Then, once you receive the bitcoin, you also learn the private key. Finally, if you redeem this private key with a service such as Mt. Gox, that service also learns the private key. In such a case, control defined solely by knowledge of the secret key is therefore not well defined.

In the above case, however, the controller of the address is in fact quite clear: as you redeemed the private key with Mt. Gox and thus stored any bitcoins inside with them, the expected entity responsible for forming transactions on behalf of that address is Mt. Gox (otherwise, if you plan to form your own transactions, why store your money with them?).

Finally, we emphasize that our definition of address control is quite different from account *ownership*; for example, we consider a wallet service such as Instawallet to be the controller of each of the addresses it generates, even though the funds in these addresses are owned by a wide variety of distinct users.

4.2 Graph structure and definitions

To define our heuristics formally, we consider two important directed graph structures for the Bitcoin network: a transaction graph and a public key graph. In the former, vertices represent transactions, and a directed edge from a transaction t_1 to a transaction t_2 indicates that an output of t_1 was used as an input in t_2. Using this graph, we define in degrees and out degrees for transactions, which correspond exactly to the in and out degrees in the graph (i.e., the number of edges incident to and from the node, respectively).

DEFINITION 4.1. *The* in degree *for a transaction t, denoted by* $d^+_{\mathsf{tx}}(t)$*, is the number of inputs for the transaction. The* out degree *for a transaction t, denoted by* $d^-_{\mathsf{tx}}(t)$*, is the number of outputs for the transaction.*

We can also construct a graph using public keys, in which vertices are public keys and directed edges again represent the flow of money from one public key to another; here, however, the in degree of a public key reflects the number of inputs to the transaction in which it received bitcoins, so a public key that received bitcoins only once could have an in degree of (for example) five. For our purposes, we would instead like the in degree of the output public keys to be independent of how many public keys are provided as input to the transaction. We therefore define, rather than in/out degree, the *in/out count* for a public key.

DEFINITION 4.2. *The* in count *for a public key* pk*, denoted* $d^+_{\mathsf{addr}}(\mathsf{pk})$*, is the number of times* pk *has been an output in a transaction. The* out count *for a public key* pk*, denoted* $d^-_{\mathsf{addr}}(\mathsf{pk})$*, is the number of times* pk *has been an input in a transaction.*

One of the defining features of the Bitcoin protocol is the way that bitcoins must be spent. When the bitcoins redeemed as the output of a transaction are spent, they must be spent all at once: the only way to divide them is through the use of a *change address*, in which the excess from the input address is sent back to the sender. A public key can therefore spend money only as many times as it has received money (again, because each time it spends money it must spend all of it at once).

4.3 Our heuristics

Heuristic 1.

The first heuristic we use, in which we link input addresses together, has already been used many times in previous work [2, 17, 18, 21]; for completeness, we nevertheless present it here. Briefly, if two (or more) public keys are used as inputs to the same transaction, then we say that they are controlled by the same user.

HEURISTIC 1. *If two (or more) addresses are inputs to the same transaction, they are controlled by the same user; i.e., for any transaction t, all* $\mathsf{pk} \in \mathsf{inputs}(t)$ *are controlled by the same user.*

The effects of this heuristic are transitive and extend well beyond the inputs to a single transaction; e.g., if we observed one transaction with addresses A and B as inputs, and another with addresses B and C as inputs, then we conclude that A, B, and C all belonged to the same user. It is also quite safe: the sender in the transaction must know the private signing key belonging to each public key used as an input, so it is unlikely that the collection of public keys are controlled by multiple entities (as these entities would need to reveal their private keys to each other).

Using this heuristic, we partitioned the network into 5,579,176 clusters of users. By naming these clusters — using the data collection described in Section 3 — we observed that some of them corresponded to the same user; e.g., there were 20 clusters that we tagged as being controlled by Mt. Gox. (This is not surprising, as many big services appear to spread their funds across a number of distinct accounts to minimize the risk in case any one gets compromised.) This cross-cluster naming was nevertheless not too common, and we thus ended up with 5,577,481 distinct clusters (recall we started with 12,056,684 public keys). Factoring in "sink" addresses that have to date never sent any bitcoins (and thus did not get clustered using this heuristic) yields at most 6,595,564 distinct users, although we consider this number a quite large upper bound.

Heuristic 2.

Although Heuristic 1 already yields a useful clustering of users, restricting ourselves to only this heuristic does not tell the whole story. To further collapse users, our second heuristic focuses on the role of change addresses within the Bitcoin system. A similar heuristic was explored by Androulaki et al. [2] (who called them "shadow" addresses), although there are a number of important differences. In particular, their definition of shadow addresses relied upon assumptions that may have held at the time of their work, but no longer hold at present. For example, they assumed that users rarely issue transactions to two different users, which is a frequent occurrence today (e.g., payouts from mining pools, or bets on gambling sites).

As discussed above, change addresses are the mechanism used to give money back to the input user in a transaction, as bitcoins can be divided only by being spent. In one idiom of use, the change address is created internally by the Bitcoin client and never re-used; as such, a user is unlikely to give out this change address to other users (e.g., for accepting payments), and in fact might not even know the address unless he inspects the block chain. If we can identify change addresses, we can therefore potentially cluster not only the input addresses for a transaction (according to Heuristic 1) but also the change address and the input user.

Because our heuristic takes advantage of this idiom of use, rather than an inherent property of the Bitcoin protocol (as Heuristic 1 does), it does lack robustness in the face of changing (or adversarial) patterns in the network. Furthermore, it has one very negative potential consequence: falsely linking even a small number of change addresses might collapse the entire graph into large "superclusters" that are not actually controlled by a single user (in fact, we see this exact problem occur in Section 4.5). We therefore focused on designing the safest heuristic possible, even at the expense of losing some utility by having a high false negative rate, and acknowledge that such a heuristic might have to be redesigned or ultimately discarded if habitual uses of the Bitcoin protocol change significantly.

Working off the assumption that a change address has only one input (again, as it is potentially unknown to its owner and is not re-used by the client), we first looked at the outputs of every transaction. If only one of the outputs met this pattern, then we identified that output as the change address. If, however, multiple outputs had only one input and thus the change address was ambiguous, we did not label any change address for that transaction. We also avoided certain transactions; e.g., in a coin generation, none of the outputs are change addresses.

In addition, in custom usages of the Bitcoin protocol it is possible to specify the change address for a given transaction. Thus far, one common usage of this setting that we have observed has been to provide a change address that is in fact the same as the input address.[4] We thus avoid such "self-change" transactions as well.

DEFINITION 4.3. *A public key* pk *is a* one-time change address *for a transaction t if the following conditions are met:*

1. $d^+_{\mathsf{addr}}(\mathsf{pk}) = 1$*; i.e., this is the first appearance of* pk.
2. *The transaction t is not a coin generation.*
3. *There is no* $\mathsf{pk}' \in \mathsf{outputs}(t)$ *such that* $\mathsf{pk}' \in \mathsf{inputs}(t)$*; i.e., there is no self-change address.*
4. *There is no* $\mathsf{pk}' \in \mathsf{outputs}(t)$ *such that* $\mathsf{pk}' \neq \mathsf{pk}$ *but* $d^+_{\mathsf{addr}}(\mathsf{pk}') = 1$*; i.e., for all the outputs in the transaction, condition* 1 *is met for only* pk.

HEURISTIC 2. *The one-time change address is controlled by the same user as the input addresses; i.e., for any transaction t, the controller of* $\mathsf{inputs}(t)$ *also controls the one-time change address* $\mathsf{pk} \in \mathsf{outputs}(t)$ *(if such an address exists).*

4.4 The impact of change addresses

To see the impact of change addresses on user clustering, consider the following illustrative example: suppose we want to measure the *incoming value* of the major services with whom we interacted; i.e., we want to know how many bitcoins they received over time. If we consider the incoming value of services across seven different categories — exchanges that function as banks, mining pools, wallet services, gambling sites, vendors, fixed-rated exchanges that do not function as banks, and investment schemes — then, using Heuristic 1, we obtain the results shown in Figure 5a.

Looking at Figure 5a cumulatively, we might first notice that, for the past year and a half, the major users we tagged account for anywhere from 20% to 40% of the total incoming value. Comparing across categories, we see that exchanges account for a considerable fraction of the total value of these users. More surprisingly, given the payout-based nature of mining pools, Figure 5a also seems to indicate that mining pools are receiving a large portion of incoming value. This percentage is artificially inflated, however, by certain artifacts of how mining pools, and Deepbit in particular, pay their miners. In fact, as we see in Figure 5b, over 80% of the value Deepbit receives is as change from itself.

While the particular mechanism that Deepbit uses allows us to eliminate this "self-churn" even using Heuristic 1 (as they always use a self-change address), more generally we cannot eliminate the self-churn of all users with just Heuristic 1. We are able to identify self-churn only if we know that the change address is controlled by the same user as the input address(es).

Eliminating this self-churn is therefore where Heuristic 2 becomes crucial. To see the effect it has, we compare the self-churn of Mt. Gox as determined using the two heuristics. Figure 5c shows that finding additional change addresses for Mt. Gox using Heuristic 2 essentially doubles the estimate of churn activity of Mt. Gox compared to using Heuristic 1 (and we observed a similar doubling when considering the churn in bitcoin value rather than activity).

4.5 Refining Heuristic 2

Although effective, Heuristic 2 is more challenging and significantly less safe than Heuristic 1. In our first attempt, when we used it as defined above, we identified over 4 million change addresses. Due to our concern over its safety, we sought to approximate the false positive rate. To do this even in the absence of significant ground truth data, we used the fact that we could observe the behavior of addresses over time: if an address and transaction met the conditions of Definition 4.3 at one point in time (where time was measured by block height), and then at a later time the address was used again, we considered this a false positive. Stepping through time in this manner allowed us to identify 555,348 false positives, or 13% of all labeled change accounts.

We then considered ways of making the heuristic more conservative. First, however, a manual inspection of some of these false positives revealed an interesting pattern: many of them were associated with transactions to and from Satoshi Dice and other dice games. By looking further into the payout structure of these games, it became clear that these were not truly false positives, as when coins are sent to Satoshi Dice, the payout is sent back to the same address. If a user therefore spent the contents of a one-time change address with Satoshi Dice, the address would receive another input back from Satoshi Dice, which would appear to invalidate the "one-timeness" of the address. We therefore chose to ignore this case, believing that addresses that received later inputs solely from Satoshi Dice could still be one-time change addresses. By doing so the false positive rate reduces to only 1%. We next considered waiting to label an address as a change address; i.e., waiting to see if it received another input. Waiting a day drove the false positive rate down to 0.28%; waiting a week drove it down to 0.17%, or only 7,382 false positives total.

Despite all these precautions, when we clustered users using this modified heuristic, we still ended up with a giant super-cluster containing the public keys of Mt. Gox, Instawallet, BitPay, and Silk Road, among others; in total, this super-cluster contained 1.6 million public keys. After a manual inspection of some of the links that led to this super-cluster, we discovered two problematic patterns. First, especially within a short window of time, the same change address was sometimes used twice. If this change address were then used the second time with a new address, the new address would appear to be the change address and be falsely labeled as such. Second, certain addresses would occasionally be used as "self-change" addresses (recall the second requirement in Definition 4.3), and then later used as separate change addresses; again, if the time they were used separately was with a new address, the new address would be falsely labeled as the change address. This behavior is likely due to the advanced features in some wallets, such as My Wallet and the desktop client Armory, that allow users to explicitly specify the change address for a transaction.

We thus further refined our heuristic by ignoring transactions involved with either of these types of behavior. For transactions in which an output had already received only one input, or for transactions in which an output had been previously used in a self-change transaction, we chose to not tag anything as the change address. Doing so, and manually removing a handful of other false positives (with no discernible pattern), we identified 3,540,831 change addresses.

Using this refined Heuristic 2 produces 3,384,179 clusters, which we were able to again collapse slightly (using our tags) to 3,383,904 distinct clusters. Of these clusters, we were able to name 2,197 of them (accounting for over 1.8 million addresses); although this might seem like a small fraction, recall that by participating in 344 transactions we hand-tagged only 1,070 addresses, and thus Heuristic 2 allowed us to name 1,600 times more addresses than our own

[4]This usage is quite common: 23% of all transactions in the past six months are self-change transactions. For example, it is the standard option for the popular wallet service My Wallet, hosted by `blockchain.info`, as well as the way the Deepbit mining pool does its payouts.

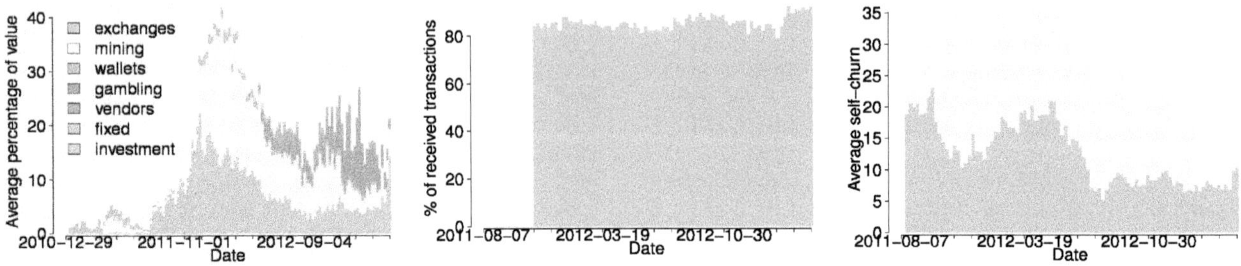

(a) The incoming value over time, as a percentage of total weekly incoming value, for each of the major categories. The teal and yellow categories are exchanges and mining pools respectively.

(b) Of transactions sent to Deepbit, the percentage that were sent by Deepbit itself (i.e., the percentage that was self-churn). The transactions from Deepbit account for over 80% of its incoming transactions.

(c) The percentage of all transactions received by Mt Gox that were sent by Mt Gox. The teal shows self-churn identified by Heuristic 1; the yellow shows *additional* churn identified by Heuristic 2.

Figure 5: Figures illustrating the effect of self-churn on measurements, and the different ways Heuristics 1 and 2 deal with self-churn.

manual observation provided. Furthermore, as we see in the visualization of the user graph depicted in Figure 6, and will argue in Section 5, the users we were able to name capture an important and active slice of the Bitcoin network.

Having finally convinced ourselves of both the safety of Heuristic 2, by refining it substantially, and its effectiveness, as illustrated in Figure 5c, we use Heuristic 2 exclusively for the results in the next section.

5. SERVICE CENTRALITY

In this section, we focus on two notable parts of the user graph seen in Figure 6: the component consisting of Satoshi Dice and the individuals who interact with it, and the heavily connected component consisting of most of the services we tagged. For both of these components, we argue that the demonstrated centrality of these services makes it difficult for even highly motivated individuals — e.g., thieves or others attracted to the anonymity properties of Bitcoin — to stay completely anonymous, provided they are interested in cashing out by converting to fiat money (or even other virtual currencies).

5.1 The effect of popular services

One of the largest stresses on the Bitcoin system to date has been the introduction of so-called dice games, and in particular Satoshi Dice, a betting game introduced in late April 2012. Briefly, users may place bets with various addresses, each of which is associated with a probability of winning (ranging from a 0.0015% chance of winning to a 97% chance). After determining if the user has won (using an algorithm involving the bet transaction and a random number), Satoshi Dice then sends some multiplier of the user's bet back to him if he won (e.g., 1.004 times his bet if he sent to the address with 97% winning odds), and 1 satoshi (0.00000001 BTC) if he lost.

Within weeks of being introduced, Satoshi Dice became wildly popular. Figure 7a shows its activity as compared to the activity of the Deepbit mining pool, which was arguably the most active user prior to the introduction of dice games. Satoshi Dice engages in tens of thousands of transactions per day, or about 60% of the overall activity in the Bitcoin network. It has also spawned a number of clones, such as BTC Dice, BTCLucky, Clone Dice, and DiceOnCrack (which, although less popular, are nevertheless quite well connected, as seen in Figure 6).

A number of factors help explain the popularity of Satoshi Dice. First, it allows users to place very small bets: the minimum bet for each category is 0.01 BTC, and over 21% of all bets (896,864 out of 4,127,979) are exactly this minimum value. Figure 7b shows that Satoshi Dice — just in terms of its outgoing transactions — accounts for anywhere between 30% and 40% of such micro-valued transactions (we found very similar results looking instead at the incoming transactions for Satoshi Dice). Referring back to Figure 2 and the rise of micro-valued transactions, we conclude that a large fraction of this rise can be attributed just to Satoshi Dice. In addition to allowing small bets, Satoshi Dice also acts extremely quickly. Once a bet is placed, the outcome is decided immediately and the payout is returned within seconds, as shown in Figure 7c. As with micro-valued transactions, referring back to Figure 3 indicates that Satoshi Dice also accounts for much of the rise of immediate spending (as a weekly average, nearly 50% of immediate transactions are due to Satoshi Dice).

Because of its immense popularity, and the extent to which it has inflated the size of the block chain (an extra 30,000 transactions translates into an extra 14MB added to the overall block chain daily), the opinion of Satoshi Dice in the Bitcoin community is somewhat mixed: some decry it as a DoS attack,[5] while others appreciate that it has stress-tested the Bitcoin network.

It might be tempting to additionally think that, given the large amounts of bitcoins flowing through it, Satoshi Dice could act as a mix service:[6] if "dirty" bitcoins were gambled using 97% winning odds, and the resulting bitcoins were paid out to a different address, these bitcoins might at first glance appear to have no association with the gambled money (especially if they came from a different address than the gambled money was sent to, as is sometimes the case). Because the addresses that Satoshi Dice uses are public, however, it is trivial to observe when users are gambling; furthermore, in sending a bet to Satoshi Dice, a user must explicitly identify where the payout should be sent. Thus, without using services such as Satoshi Dice as a co-conspirator (which they seem to have no incentive to do, as they made over $500,000 in their first eight months alone [11]), the bitcoins paid out are indelibly linked to the ones that were placed as a bet.

5.2 Traffic analysis of illicit activity

We next turn our attention to another dominant category of service: exchanges. Although not nearly as active as Satoshi Dice, exchanges have essentially become chokepoints in the Bitcoin economy: to buy into or cash out of Bitcoin at scale, we argue that using

[5] `http://en.bitcoin.it/wiki/SatoshiDice`

[6] See, for example, early concerns at `bitcointalk.org/index.php?topic=79079.0` and related discussions.

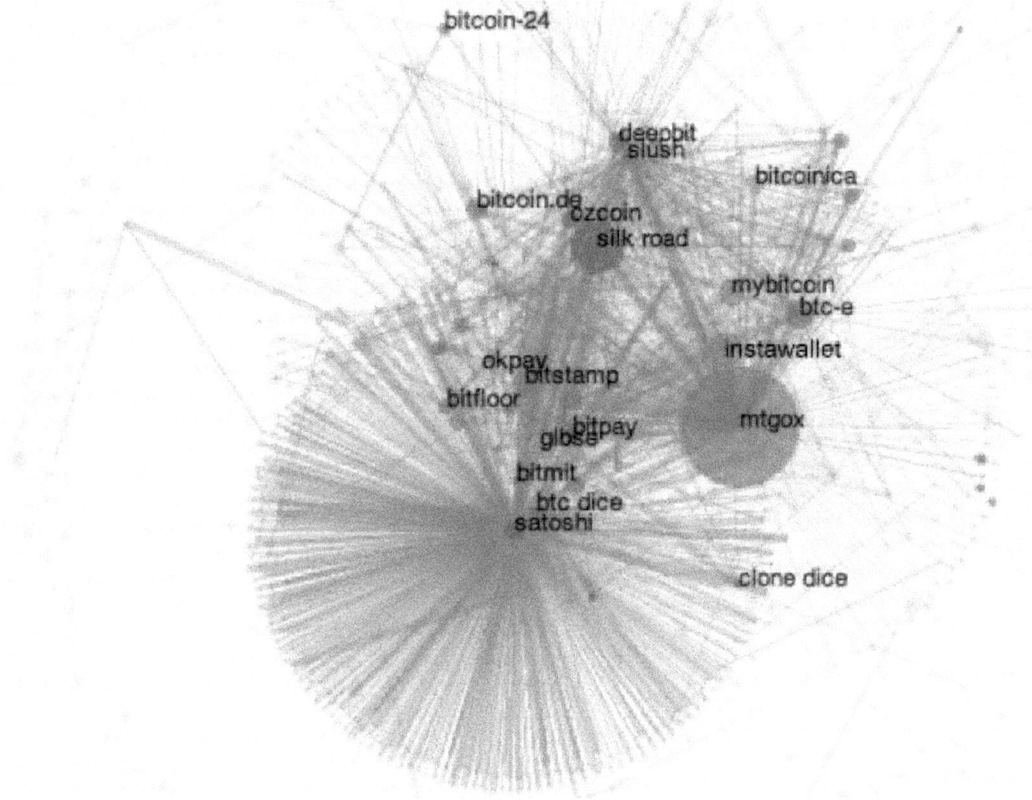

Figure 6: A visualization of the user network. The area of the cluster represents the external incoming value; i.e., the bitcoins received from other clusters but not itself, and for an edge to appear between two nodes there must have been at least 200 transactions between them. The nodes are colored by category: blue nodes are mining pools; orange are fixed-rate exchanges; green are wallets; red are vendors; purple are (bank) exchanges; brown are gambling; pink are investment schemes; and grey are uncategorized.

an exchange is unavoidable. While sites like `localbitcoins.com` and `bitcoinary.com` do allow you to avoid exchanges (for the former, by matching up buyers directly with sellers in their geographic area), the current and historical volume on these sites does not seem to be high enough to support cashing out *at scale*.

For criminals, this centrality presents a unique problem: if a thief steals thousands of bitcoins, this theft is unavoidably visible within the Bitcoin network, and thus the initial address of the thief is known and (as most exchanges try to maintain some air of reputability) he cannot simply transfer the bitcoins directly from the theft to a known exchange.[7] While he might attempt to use a mix service to hide the source of the money, we again argue that these services do not currently have the volume to launder thousands of bitcoins. As such, thieves have developed various strategies for hiding the source of the bitcoins that we explore in this section. In particular, we focus on the effectiveness of Heuristic 2 in de-anonymizing these flows, and thus in tracking illicitly-obtained bitcoins to exchanges (and thus, e.g., providing an agency with subpoena power the opportunity to learn whose account was deposited into, and in turn potentially the identity of the thief). For this approach to work, we do not need to (and cannot) account for each and every stolen bitcoin, but rather need to demonstrate only some flow of bitcoins directly from the theft to an exchange or other known institution.

To demonstrate the effectiveness of Heuristic 2 in this endeavor, we focus on an idiom of use that we call a "peeling chain." The usage of this pattern extends well beyond criminal activity, and is seen (for example) in the withdrawals for many banks and exchanges, as well as in the payouts for some of the larger mining pools. In a peeling chain, a single address begins with a relatively large amount of bitcoins (e.g., for mining pools it starts with the 25 BTC reward). A smaller amount is then "peeled" off this larger amount, creating a transaction in which a small amount is transferred to one address (e.g., 0.1 BTC for a miner payout), and the remainder is transferred to a one-time change address. This process is repeated — potentially for hundreds or thousands of hops — until the larger amount is pared down, at which point (in one usage) the amount remaining in the address might be aggregated with other such addresses to again yield a large amount in a single address, and the peeling process begins again. By using Heuristic 2, we are able to track flows of money by following these change links systematically: at each hop, we look at the two output addresses in the transaction. If one of these outputs is a change address, we can follow the chain to the next hop by following the change address (i.e., the next hop is the transaction in which this change address spends its bitcoins), and can identify the meaningful recipient in the transaction as the other output address (the "peel").

Silk Road and Bitcoin Savings & Trust.

[7]Indeed, the Bitcoin community has recently demonstrated both the inherent traceability of thefts and the unwillingness to accept stolen money (see `bitcointalk.org/index.php?topic=14085.msg1910231`). After 923 BTC was stolen from the mining pool Ozcoin and transferred to a Strongcoin wallet, Strongcoin intercepted the bitcoins when the thief attempted to withdraw them and returned them to Ozcoin.

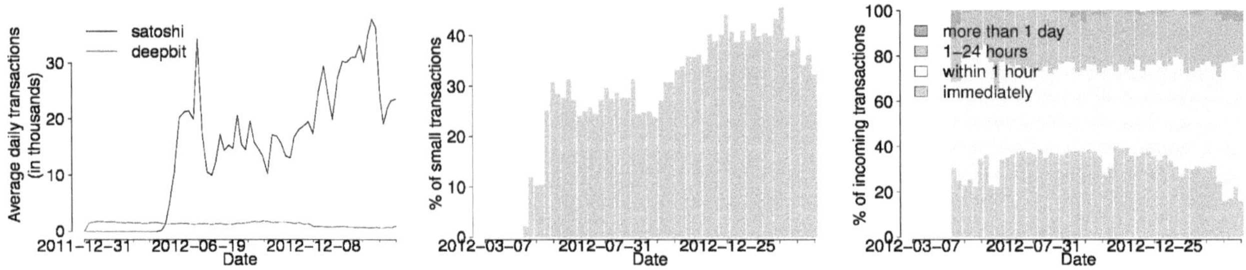

(a) The overall daily activity, in terms of number of both incoming and outgoing transactions, for Satoshi Dice, as compared to the overall activity for the mining pool Deepbit.

(b) The percentage of transactions with less than 0.1 BTC in total value in which Satoshi Dice participated as the sender, shown as an average weekly percentage.

(c) A breakdown of how quickly Satoshi Dice spends the money it receives: teal is immediately, yellow is within an hour, purple is within a day, and red is more than a day.

Figure 7: The effect Satoshi Dice has had on the Bitcoin network, in terms of both activity and its influence on trends.

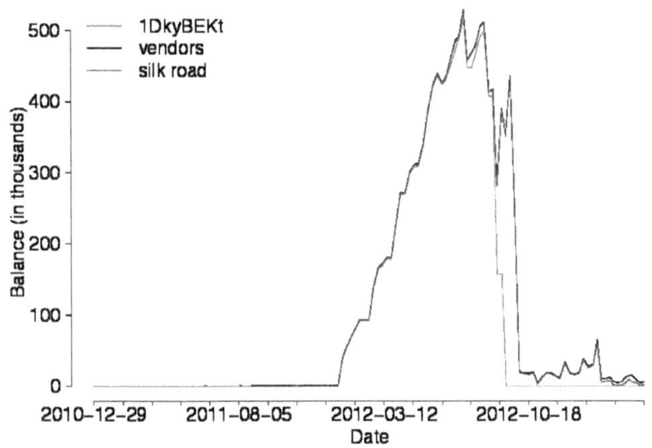

Figure 8: The balance of the vendors category (in black, although barely visible because it is dominated by Silk Road), Silk Road (in blue), and the 1DkyBEKt address (in red).

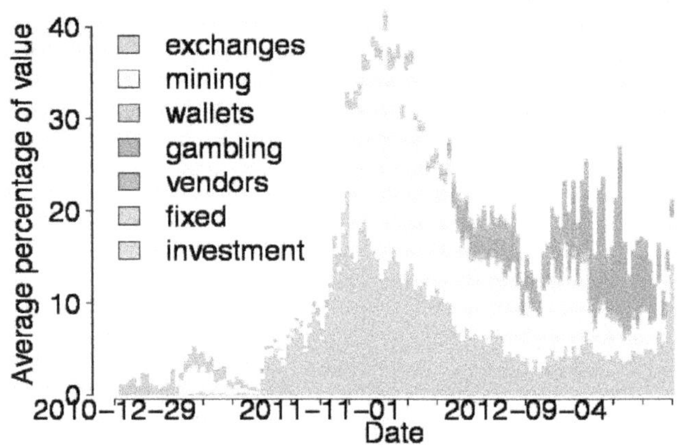

Figure 9: The balance of each major category, represented as a percentage of total active bitcoins; i.e., the bitcoins that are not held in sink addresses.

One of the most well-known and heavily scrutinized addresses in Bitcoin's history is 1DkyBEKt,[8] which is believed to be associated with Silk Road and was active between January and September 2012. Starting in January, the address began to receive large aggregate sums of bitcoins; in the first of these, the funds of 128 addresses were combined to deposit 10,000 BTC into the 1DkyBEKt address, and many transactions of this type followed (including one transaction in which the funds of 589 addresses were combined to deposit 8,000 BTC). All together, the address received 613,326 BTC in a period of eight months, receiving its last aggregate deposit on August 16 2012.

Then, starting in August 2012, bitcoins were aggregated and withdrawn from 1DkyBEKt: first, amounts of 20,000, 19,000, and 60,000 BTC were aggregated and sent to separate addresses; later, 100,000 BTC each was sent to two distinct addresses, 150,000 BTC to a third, and 158,336 BTC to a fourth, effectively emptying the 1DkyBEKt address of all of its funds. The balance of this address over time, as well as the balance of Silk Road and of vendors as a whole (as we consider Silk Road a vendor), is shown in Figure 8.

Due to its large balance (at its height, it contained 5% of all generated bitcoins), as well as the curious nature of its rapidly accumulated wealth and later dissolution, this address has naturally been the subject of heavy scrutiny by the Bitcoin community. While it is largely agreed that the address is associated with Silk Road (and indeed our clustering heuristic did tag this address as being controlled by Silk Road), some have theorized that it was the "hot" (i.e., active) wallet for Silk Road, and that its dissipation represents a changing storage structure for the service. Others, meanwhile, have argued that it was the address belonging to the user pirate@40, who was responsible for carrying out the largest Ponzi scheme in Bitcoin history (the investment scheme Bitcoin Savings & Trust, which is now the subject of a lawsuit brought by the SEC [20]).

To see where the funds from this address went, and if they ended up with any known services, we first plotted the balance of each of the major categories of services, as seen in Figure 9. Looking at this figure, it is clear that when the address was dissipated, the resulting funds were not sent en masse to any major services, as the balances of the other categories do not change significantly. To nevertheless attempt to find out where the funds did go, we turn to the traffic analysis described above.

In particular, we focus on the last activity of the 1DkyBEKt address, when it deposited 158,336 BTC into a single address. This address then peeled off 50,000 BTC each to two separate addresses, leaving 58,336 BTC for a third address; each of these addresses then began a peeling chain, which we followed using the methodology described above (i.e., at each hop we continued along the chain by following the change address, and considered the other output address to be a meaningful recipient of the money). After follow-

[8]Full address: 1DkyBEKt5S2GDtv7aQw6rQepAvnsRyHoYM.

	First		Second		Third	
Service	Peels	BTC	Peels	BTC	Peels	BTC
Bitcoin-24			1	2	3	124
Bitcoin Central					2	2
Bitcoin.de					1	4
Bitmarket					1	1
Bitstamp			5	97	1	1
BTC-e					1	250
CA VirtEx	1	3	1	10	3	22
Mercado Bitcoin					1	9
Mt. Gox	11	492	14	70	5	35
OKPay	2	151			1	125
Instawallet	7	39	5	135	2	43
WalletBit	1	1				
Bitzino					2	1
Seals with Clubs	1	8				
Coinabul			1	29		
Medsforbitcoin	3	10				
Silk Road	4	28			5	102

Table 2: Tracking bitcoins from `1DkyBEKt`. Along the first 100 hops of the first, second, and third peeling chains resulting from the withdrawal of 158,336 BTC, we consider the number of peels seen to each service, as well as the total number of bitcoins (rounded to the nearest integer value) sent in these peels. The services are separated into the categories of exchanges, wallets, gambling, and vendors.

ing 100 hops along each chain, we observed peels to the services listed in Table 2.

Looking at this table, we see that, although a longitudinal look at the balances of major services did not reveal where the money went, following these chains revealed that bitcoins were in fact sent to a variety of services. The overall balance was not highly affected, however, as the amounts sent were relatively small and spread out over a handful of transactions. Furthermore, while our analysis does not itself reveal the owner of `1DkyBEKt`, the flow of bitcoins from this address to known services demonstrates the prevalence of these services (54 out of 300 peels went to exchanges alone) and provides the potential for further de-anonymization: the evidence that the deposited bitcoins were the direct result of either a Ponzi scheme or the sale of drugs might motivate Mt. Gox or any exchange (e.g., in response to a subpoena) to reveal the account owner corresponding to the deposit address in the peel, and thus provide information to link the address to a real-world user.

Tracking thefts.

To ensure that our analysis could be applied more generally, we turned finally to a broader class of criminal activity in the Bitcoin network: thefts. Thefts are in fact quite common within Bitcoin: almost every major service has been hacked and had bitcoins (or, in the case of exchanges, other currencies) stolen, and some have shut down as a result.

To begin, we used a list of major Bitcoin thefts;[9] some of the thefts did not have public transactions (i.e., ones we could identify and study in the block chain), so we limited our attention to the ones that did. For each theft, we first found the specific set of transactions that represented the theft; i.e., the set of transactions in which the sender was the service being stolen from, and the recipient was the thief. Starting with these transactions, we did a preliminary manual inspection of the transactions that followed to determine their approximate type: we considered aggregations, in which bitcoins were moved from several addresses into a single one; folding, in which some of the addresses involved in the aggregation were not clearly associated with the theft, and thus were potentially there to "clean" the stolen money; splits, in which a large amount of bitcoins was split among two or more addresses; and finally peeling chains, in which relatively small amounts were peeled off from a succession of one-time change addresses holding a large amount of bitcoins. Our results are summarized in Table 3.

Theft	BTC	Date	Movement	Exchanges?
MyBitcoin	4019	Jun 2011	A/P/S	Yes
Linode	46,648	Mar 2012	A/P/F	Yes
Betcoin	3171	Mar 2012	F/A/P	Yes
Bitcoinica	18,547	May 2012	P/A	Yes
Bitcoinica	40,000	Jul 2012	P/A/S	Yes
Bitfloor	24,078	Sep 2012	P/A/P	Yes
Trojan	3257	Oct 2012	F/A	No

Table 3: Tracking thefts. For each theft, we list (approximately) how many bitcoins were stolen, when the theft occurred, how the money moved after it was stolen, and whether we saw any bitcoins sent to known exchanges. For the movement, we use A to mean aggregation, P to mean a peeling chain, S to mean a split, and F to mean folding, and list the various movements in the order they occurred.

Briefly, the movement of the stolen money ranged from quite sophisticated layering and mixing to simple and easy to follow. Examining thefts therefore provides another demonstration of the potential for anonymity provided by Bitcoin, and the ways in which current usage falls short of this potential: for the thieves who used the more complex strategies, we saw little opportunity to track the flow of bitcoins (or at least do so with any confidence that ownership was staying the same), but for the thieves that did not there seemed to be ample opportunity to track the stolen money directly to an exchange.

One of the easiest thefts to track was from Betcoin, an early gambling site that was shut down after its server was hacked on April 11 2012 and 3,171 BTC were stolen in four installments of 2,902, 165, 17, and 87 BTC each. The stolen bitcoins then sat in the thief's address until March 15 2013 (when the bitcoin exchange rate began soaring), when they were aggregated with other small addresses into one large address that then began a peeling chain. After 10 hops, we saw a peel go to Bitcoin-24, and in another 10 hops we saw a peel go to Mt. Gox; in total, we saw 374.49 BTC go to known exchanges, all directly off the main peeling chain, which originated directly from the addresses known to belong to the thief. For some of the other thefts, de-anonymizing the flow of bitcoins was similarly straightforward: for the May 2012 Bitcoinica theft, for example, we observed one peeling chain, occurring directly after an aggregation of addresses belonging to the thieves, in which large amounts (i.e., hundreds of bitcoins) were peeled off directly to known exchanges; in total, we saw 4,588 BTC peeled off to three different exchanges (BTC-e, CampBX, and Bitstamp). Again, although we do not account for every stolen bitcoin, watching even a portion of them flow to exchanges provides the opportunity we need to potentially compromise the anonymity of the thieves.

[9] `https://bitcointalk.org/index.php?topic=83794.0`

In contrast, some of the other thieves used more sophisticated strategies to attempt to hide the flow of money; e.g., for the Bitfloor theft, we observed that large peels off several initial peeling chains were then aggregated, and the peeling process was repeated. Nevertheless, by manually following this peel-and-aggregate process to the point that the later peeling chains began, we systematically followed these later chains and again observed peels to multiple known exchanges: the third peel off one such chain was 191.09 BTC to Mt. Gox, and in total we saw 661.12 BTC sent to three popular exchanges (Mt. Gox, BTC-e, and Bitstamp).

Even the thief we had the most difficulty tracking, who stole bitcoins by installing a trojan on the computers of individual users, seemed to realize the difficulty of cashing out at scale. Although we were unable to confidently track the flow of the stolen money that moved, most of the stolen money did not in fact move at all: of the 3,257 BTC stolen to date, 2,857 BTC was still sitting in the thief's address, and has been since November 2012.

With these thefts, our ability to track the stolen money provides evidence that even the most motivated Bitcoin users (i.e., criminals) are engaging in idioms of use that allow us to erode their anonymity. While one might argue that thieves could easily thwart our analysis, as Heuristic 2 is admittedly not robust in the face of adversarial behavior, our observation is that — at least at present — none of the criminals we studied seem to have taken such precautions. We further argue that the fairly direct flow of bitcoins from the point of theft to the deposit with an exchange provides some evidence that using exchanges to cash out at scale is inevitable, and thus that — again, at present — Bitcoin does not provide a particularly easy or effective way to transact large volumes of illicitly-obtained money.

6. RELATED WORK

Since its inception, questions regarding the security — and in particular the anonymity — of Bitcoin have received considerable interest. On the first front, much work has concerned the strength of Bitcoin's settlement mechanism and the difficulty of an adversary in subverting it. The two best known explorations concerning Bitcoin "double spending" are from Karame et al. [9] and Meni Rosenfeld [19]. At their core, both focus on the tradeoffs between latency (the number of confirmations made through the Bitcoin network) and the computational requirements of an attacker — a tradeoff that implicitly explains the different risk regimes operational in the Bitcoin ecosystem today.

The second thrust of Bitcoin security research, closer to our own interest, has focused on the anonymity of its transactions. In 2011, fueled by the high-profile MyBitcoin theft, Reid and Harrigan [17] provided one of the first written analyses. Using a clustering algorithm similar to our Heuristic 1, they obtained a condensed "user" graph, and used it to describe the flow of stolen money from the aforementioned theft. In a more recent paper, Ron and Shamir [18] performed a similar analysis over the user graph (again using an heuristic similar to our Heuristic 1), and provided an in-depth examination of the largest transactions in Bitcoin history. From this data they conclude that there is massive hoarding in the Bitcoin system and that the vast majority of capital does not circulate. Concurrently with the work of Ron and Shamir, Androulaki et al. [2] applied a similar analysis, but focused more squarely on privacy concerns. Unlike Ron and Shamir, their analysis attempts to account for the complexity of "change" accounts which are central to how Bitcoin is used in practice. Applying this analysis to a *simulated* Bitcoin graph (in which ground truth data was known), 40% of user identities were correctly classified through such clustering. As we mention briefly in Section 4.3, their approach is insufficient for an empirical characterization of Bitcoin traffic since the assumptions it makes (particularly around the use of multi-output transactions) are routinely violated today. On the constructive side, Miers et al. [12] presented Zerocoin, a system designed to cryptographically amplify the anonymity guarantees in Bitcoin, precisely motivated by potential of the analysis techniques described in this paper.[10] Most recently, Möser [14] examined the anonymity of three Bitcoin mix services, and found that some were more successful than others, although all had a distinct transaction graph pattern due to their centralized nature.

Finally, we are aware of three analyses of key parts of the Bitcoin economy: Kroll et al.'s economic analysis of Bitcoin mining [10], Christin's study of the Silk Road marketplace [4] and Moore and Christin's analysis of Bitcoin exchange failures [13]. The first paper applies a game-theoretic analysis to the mining mechanism of Bitcoin, and in particular creates a formal model for a 51% (or "Goldfinger") attack, in which a cartel of miners are responsible for over half of the blocks being mined. They then discuss the circumstances under which such an attack could take place, and conclude that Bitcoin governance is not only inevitable but also necessary for the future of the currency. The second effort uses regular Web crawling of the Silk Road marketplace to characterize the popularity of illicit goods (typically controlled substances) and to estimate the total market value of such transactions. While this work does not examine the Bitcoin block chain at all, it could be used in tandem with our analysis to estimate the spread of such "dirty money" in the Bitcoin graph. Finally, the third paper is driven by the central role of Bitcoin exchanges, which are commonly used to deposit user funds. However, by escrowing funds with a third party outside the protections of the Bitcoin protocol, users can, and are, exposed to the risk of these exchanges failing. Moore and Christin provide a meta-analysis showing that almost half of all such exchanges have failed, and that failure is positively correlated to transaction volume (which they hypothesize is because the risk of a data breach is related to the value a criminal may obtain through such an action). While the authors do not focus on anonymity, we note that such breaches also provide large amounts of labeling data by which the broader Bitcoin graph can be de-anonymized.

7. CONCLUSIONS

In this study, we presented a longitudinal characterization of the Bitcoin network, focusing on the rise of services and the growing gap — due to certain idioms of use — between the potential anonymity available in the Bitcoin protocol design and the actual anonymity that is currently achieved by users. To accomplish this task, we developed a new clustering heuristic based on change addresses, allowing us to cluster addresses belonging to the same user. Then, using a small number of transactions labeled through our own empirical interactions with various services, we identify major institutions and the interactions between them. Even our relatively small experiment demonstrates that this approach can shed considerable light on the structure of the Bitcoin economy, how it is used, and those organizations who are party to it.

Although our work examines the current gap between actual and potential anonymity, one might naturally wonder — given that our new clustering heuristic is not fully robust in the face of changing behavior — how this gap will evolve over time, and what users can do to achieve stronger anonymity guarantees. We argue that to

[10]The authors write, "There is reason to believe that sophisticated results from other domains (e.g., efforts to deanonymize social network data using network topology) will soon be applied to the Bitcoin transaction graph."

completely thwart our heuristics would require a significant effort on the part of the user, and that this loss of usability is unlikely to appeal to all but the most motivated users (such as criminals). Nevertheless, we leave a quantitative analysis of this hypothesis as an interesting open problem.

Acknowledgments

We would like to thank Brian Kantor and Cindy Moore for managing our systems and storage needs, and for helping to set up and maintain our mining rig. We are also grateful to Andreas Pitsillidis for his advice in creating figures and overall useful discussions. Finally, we thank our anonymous reviewers and our shepherd, Katerina Argyraki, for their helpful feedback and guidance.

This work was supported by National Science Foundation grants NSF-1237264 and NSF-1237076, by the Office of Naval Research MURI grant N00014-09-1-1081, and by generous research, operational and/or in-kind support from Google, Microsoft, Yahoo, and the UCSD Center for Networked Systems (CNS).

8. REFERENCES

[1] G. Andresen. bitcointools. github.com/gavinandresen/bitcointools.

[2] E. Androulaki, G. Karame, M. Roeschlin, T. Scherer, and S. Capkun. Evaluating User Privacy in Bitcoin. In *Proceedings of Financial Cryptography 2013*, 2013.

[3] CBC News. Revenue Canada says BitCoins aren't tax exempt, Apr. 2013. www.cbc.ca/news/canada/story/2013/04/26/business-bitcoin-tax.html.

[4] N. Christin. Traveling the Silk Road: A Measurement Analysis of a Large Anonymous Online Marketplace. In *Proceedings of WWW 2013*, 2013.

[5] B. P. Eha. Get ready for a Bitcoin debit card. CNNMoney, Apr. 2012. money.cnn.com/2012/08/22/technology/startups/bitcoin-debit-card/index.html.

[6] European Central Bank. Virtual Currency Schemes. ECB Report, Oct. 2012. www.ecb.europa.eu/pub/pdf/other/virtualcurrencyschemes201210en.pdf.

[7] Federal Bureau of Investigation. (U) Bitcoin Virtual Currency Unique Features Present Distinct Challenges for Deterring Illicit Activity. Intelligence Assessment, Cyber Intelligence and Criminal Intelligence Section, Apr. 2012. cryptome.org/2012/05/fbi-bitcoin.pdf.

[8] FinCEN. Application of FinCEN's Regulations to Persons Administering, Exchanging, or Using Virtual Currencies, Mar. 2013. www.fincen.gov/statutes_regs/guidance/pdf/FIN-2013-G001.pdf.

[9] G. Karame, E. Androulaki, and S. Capkun. Double-Spending Fast Payments in Bitcoin. In *Proceedings of ACM CCS 2012*, 2012.

[10] J. A. Kroll, I. C. Davey, and E. W. Felten. The Economics of Bitcoin Mining, or Bitcoin in the Presence of Adversaries. In *Proceedings of WEIS 2013*, 2013.

[11] J. Matonis. Bitcoin Casinos Release 2012 Earnings. Forbes, Jan. 2013. www.forbes.com/sites/jonmatonis/2013/01/22/bitcoin-casinos-release-2012-earnings/.

[12] I. Miers, C. Garman, M. Green, and A. D. Rubin. Zerocoin: Anonymous Distributed E-Cash from Bitcoin. In *Proceedings of the IEEE Symposium on Security and Privacy*, 2013.

[13] T. Moore and N. Christin. Beware the Middleman: Empirical Analysis of Bitcoin-Exchange Risk. In *Proceedings of Financial Cryptography 2013*, 2013.

[14] M. Möser. Anonymity of Bitcoin Transactions: An Analysis of Mixing Services. In *Proceedings of Münster Bitcoin Conference*, 2013.

[15] S. Nakamoto. Bitcoin: A Peer-to-Peer Electronic Cash System, 2008. bitcoin.org/bitcoin.pdf.

[16] M. Peck. Bitcoin-Central is Now The World's First Bitcoin Bank...Kind Of. IEEE Spectrum: Tech Talk, Dec. 2012. spectrum.ieee.org/tech-talk/telecom/internet/bitcoincentral-is-now-the-worlds-first-bitcoin-bankkind-of.

[17] F. Reid and M. Harrigan. An Analysis of Anonymity in the Bitcoin System. In *Security and Privacy in Social Networks*, pages 197–223. Springer New York, 2013.

[18] D. Ron and A. Shamir. Quantitative Analysis of the Full Bitcoin Transaction Graph. In *Proceedings of Financial Cryptography 2013*, 2013.

[19] M. Rosenfeld. Analysis of hashrate-based double-spending, Dec. 2012. bitcoil.co.il/Doublespend.pdf.

[20] Securities and Exchange Commission. SEC Charges Texas Man With Running Bitcoin-Denominated Ponzi Scheme, July 2013. www.sec.gov/News/PressRelease/Detail/PressRelease/1370539730583.

[21] znort987. blockparser. github.com/znort987/blockparser.

Follow the Money

Understanding Economics of Online Aggregation and Advertising

Phillipa Gill
Stony Brook University
phillipa@cs.stonybrook.edy

Vijay Erramilli
Telefonica Research
vijay@tid.es

Augustin Chaintreau
Columbia University
augustin@cs.columbia.edu

Bala Krishnamurthy
AT&T Labs – Research
bala@research.att.com

Dina Papagiannaki,
Pablo Rodriguez
Telefonica Research
dina@tid.es,
pablorr@tid.es

ABSTRACT

The large-scale collection and exploitation of personal information to drive targeted online advertisements has raised privacy concerns. As a step towards understanding these concerns, we study the relationship between *how much* information is collected and *how valuable* it is for advertising. We use HTTP traces consisting of millions of users to aid our study and also present the first comparative study *between* aggregators. We develop a simple model that captures the various parameters of today's advertising revenues, whose values are estimated via the traces. Our results show that per aggregator revenue is skewed (5% accounting for 90% of revenues), while the contribution of users to advertising revenue is much less skewed (20% accounting for 80% of revenue). Google is dominant in terms of revenue and reach (presence on 80% of publishers). We also show that if all 5% of the top users in terms of revenue were to install privacy protection, with no corresponding reaction from the publishers, then the revenue can drop by 30%.

Categories and Subject Descriptors

H.1.0 [**Models and Principles**]: General

General Terms

Economics, Measurement

Keywords

Advertising, Privacy, CPM, Do-not-track, Publishers, Aggregators

IMC'13, October 23–25, 2013, Barcelona, Spain.
Copyright 2013 ACM 978-1-4503-1953-9/13/10 ...$15.00.
http://dx.doi.org/10.1145/2504730.2504768.

1. INTRODUCTION

Online advertising plays a critical role in the Web ecosystem today. Most Web services[1] are offered for free to end users and these Web services operate by relying on revenues generated by online advertising. A lot of work has been done on different facets of online advertising: whether it be understanding the mechanisms used for advertising [25], privacy concerns [13] or combating click spam [10]. However, little is known about the *economics* of online advertising, chiefly the economics of collecting and using personal information of users for facilitating targeted advertising.

Understanding the relationship between personal information and its economic value sheds light on debates around privacy and network economics. Economics of online advertising can highlight information vectors that can lead to higher revenues, the users who supply these vectors and its impact on online privacy. Network economics literature has not considered revenues generated for Web services by the users via ads and a fine-grained characterization can lead to better models and accurate understanding of the flow of money [19].

Our key contribution is characterizing advertising revenue as a function of users' information that is used to drive online advertising, specifically how much information do different parties collect, and the value of this information to them. We begin by developing a model of online advertising revenue based on discussions with advertising professionals and literature [16, 6] (Sec. 2). Our model includes content-hosting publishers, users browsing content and aggregators tracking these users across publishers. We then perform a data-driven analysis using our model to study today's advertising ecosystem, using multiple large Web traces (Sec. 3- 4). The unique nature of our traces also lets us compare different aggregators – impossible to do by studying the click-stream of a single aggregator. To highlight the utility of understanding revenues as a function of information, we investigate what would happen to revenues if users were to adopt a privacy solution such as do-not-track (DNT), and show why such unilateral actions will not be supported by Web services (Sec. 5). Our main findings include:

Today's advertising ecosystem. In Sec. 4.2, we observe that: (a) Google is a dominant player in the online ad in-

[1]By services, we refer to online search, social networks, email as well as providing content

dustry, with presence on 80% of publishers in our datasets, with highest revenues as an aggregator but is not the top publisher in terms of revenue, and Facebook is increasing its presence around the Web with their 'Like' button, reaching 23% of publishers, (b) a few aggregators account for most of the revenue (5% accounting for 90% of revenues), however, users' contribution to advertising revenue is much less skewed (20% accounting for 80% of revenue) and (c) popular publishers account for highest revenues, while less popular ones have low revenues.

DNT/Blocking can decrease overall revenue by 75%. We learn that there can be up to 75% drop in ad revenues if blocking is near-total, without any repercussions from aggregators (Sec. 5), and just the top 5% of users (in terms of revenue contribution) blocking is enough to decrease the advertising revenue by 30%.

2. ONLINE ADVERTISING MODEL

The reason stated by online aggregators for collecting information is to increase advertising effectiveness. Hence, we focus on online advertising.

2.1 Online advertising entities

The online advertising ecosystem consists of three main entities[2]:

Users ($\mathcal{U}$) access Web content and services. We focus on content and services the user accesses for free.

Publishers ($\mathcal{P}$) host content and services that are provided free-of-charge to users. Publishers gain revenue by selling space on their Web pages to advertisers. Examples include `nytimes.com` and `slate.com`.

Aggregators ($\mathcal{A}$) map advertisers to the most effective Web page placements based on content of the Web site and any information they have about users viewing the page. To facilitate this process, aggregators track user behavior using a combination of Web-bugs, cookies, analytics *etc.*(see [18] and references therein).

Examples include DoubleClick (owned by Google) and more recently Facebook that tracks users (for social purposes) via the ubiquitous "Like" button [26]. Some large aggregators like Google also host content (*e.g.,* Youtube), hence can be publishers as well.

2.2 The role of users

In an implicit exchange for free services, users contribute to advertising revenue by viewing advertisements when they visit a publisher. We denote the number of visits a user u makes to publisher p as $\mu_u(p)$. Each visit a user makes to a Web page produces impressions that may be sold to advertisers.

2.3 Revenue for publishers and aggregators

Aggregators and publishers share advertising revenue generated by displaying ads on Web sites. We assume the aggregator retains a constant fraction of the advertising revenue (α) and passes the remaining amount on to the publisher. Google AdSense, for instance, keeps $\alpha \sim 0.32$ [21]. (We use this value in the paper.)

We consider ad revenue on a "cost-per-mille" (CPM) (*i.e.,* price for 1,000 ad impressions) basis as this is the *primary* method of purchasing targeted display ads [16]. Our model can be extended to handle cost-per-click (CPC) but this is left for future work. The amount an advertiser will pay for impressions depends on user u, ad network a and publisher p.

$$CPM(u, p, a) = RON_a \times TQM_p \times \mathcal{I}_a(u) \tag{1}$$

Run-of-network (RON_a). RON_a is the base price for an impression in ad network a. A RON ad is a generic ad that is shown to users about whom little is known and may be shown on *any* publisher that a is affiliated with [6]. It has been observed that CPM for a *targeted* ad can go anywhere between 2-10X the price of a normal RON ad [16].

Traffic quality multiplier (TQM_p). TQM_p is a multiplier of the impression price that captures the quality of the publisher, ad location and hence the value of the impression.

User Intent $\mathcal{I}_a(u)$. The value of an impression increases as a function of the estimated purchasing intent of the user. Currently, aggregators segment users based on their interests [5], as inferred through online tracking. Certain segments are determined to have higher purchasing intent (*e.g.,* cell phone shoppers) and these users' impressions are worth more. This relative value, in turn, is reflected in the price that ad-networks charge for reaching these users via keywords and/or bid values.

We use implicit intent $II_a(u)$ to represent the intent value an aggregator can *infer* about a user. It naturally depends on the presence of an aggregator on the sites the user visits. We distinguish this from explicit intent $EI(u)$ that is computed with knowledge of *all* sites the user visits. Consider the example: user Bob visits (`espn.com, swimming.com, pets.com`). Aggregator A is present on the first two publishers, while aggregator B is present on the third one. Implicit intent for aggregator A about Bob would be limited to Bob being interested in sports, while for aggregator B, it is that Bob is interested in pets. The explicit intent $EI(u)$ is that Bob is interested in sports *and* pets. We assume that $II_a(u) \leq EI(u)$; implicit intent is capped by explicit intent. We note that while having longitudinal data helps in getting more accurate estimates of user intent, an aggregator would need to be present on *all* publishers to accurately estimate explicit intent $EI(u)$.

The total revenue[3] then of the online advertising ecosystem is the following:

$$\mathcal{R} = \sum_{u \in \mathcal{U}} \sum_{p \in \mathcal{P}} \left[\left(\sum_{a \in \mathcal{A}} \frac{\mu_u(p)}{1000} CPM(u, p, a) \right) \right] \tag{2}$$

3. DATA ANALYSIS METHODOLOGY

We use traces[4] of HTTP traffic in multiple networks to study advertising in relation to information gathered from the users. While having access to an aggregator or a publisher's clickstream would aid our study, it would provide

[2]The actual online ad ecosystem is staggeringly complex with multiple entities (*e.g.,* data management and demand-side platforms) `http://www.liesdamnedlies.com/online_advertising_business_101.html`. We want to understand relation between information and monetization at a first order approximation and so ignore the full chain.

[3]Note that this an estimate of revenue; we use 'revenue' to refer to this estimate

[4]No personally identifiable information was gathered or used. To the extent, any data was used, it was anonymous and aggregated data.

Table 1: **Summary of data sets.**

Trace	Setting	Country	Users	Sessions
HTTP	Neighborhood	A (4/2011)	$\sim$ 5K	40M
mHTTP	Country	B (8/2011)	$\sim$ 3M	1.5B
Univ	Campus	C (9/2010)	$\sim$ 8K	30M

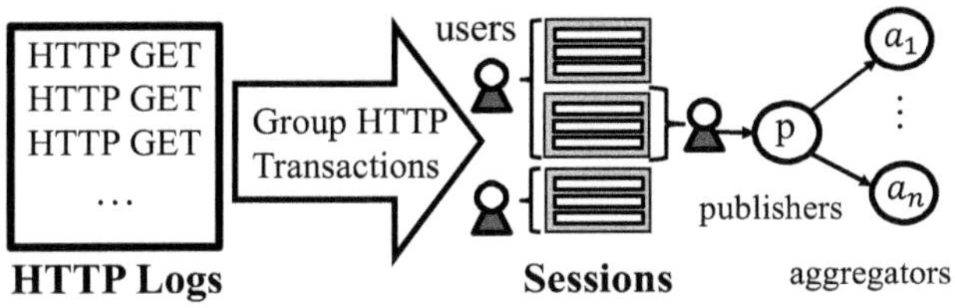

Figure 1: Data analysis pipeline to extract users, publishers and aggregators.

only a single point-of-view. In contrast, HTTP traces give us near complete visibility into the set of publishers and aggregators that the user population interacts with when they are present in the network. We also describe how we assign values to the parameters described in Sec. 2 from the data.

3.1 Data analysis overview

We use three data sets, summarized in Table 1. Both Univ and HTTP deal with traffic over a wired network, while mHTTP is traffic over a mobile network.

We first group each (anonymized) user's HTTP transactions in the HTTP traces into sessions and then identify publishers and aggregators within each session yielding a set of publishers and aggregators per user. We use the set of publishers to compute user intent ($II_a(u)$ and $EI(u)$ from Sec. 2). With intent values and values for RON_a and TQM_p, we compute $CPM(u,p,a)$ for each user-publisher-aggregator triple (Eqn. 1), and thus the overall revenue (Eqn. 2). The first two steps (Fig. 1) are described next.

3.2 Extracting HTTP sessions

We initially group HTTP transactions into sessions representing Web site visits using these heuristics.

1. StreamStructure [17]. For Univ we use the `Referer` header to group HTTP requests into sessions using the StreamStructure method proposed in [17]. This method has been shown to have precision and recall values between 0.8 and 0.9 using Alexa data [17].

2. Content-type and time. HTTP and mHTTP traces did not contain the `Referer` header so we group requests using the `Content-Type` header. We group requests between `TEXT/HTML` requests into sessions. We require that requests be more than 1s apart to avoid separating Web site frames into separate sessions. This method has been shown to be robust to thresholds between $0.5-2s$ with precision and recall values of between 0.7 and 0.8 using Alexa data [17]. We note here that while we may mis-identify a third party as a first party, the opposite would be much less likely as we use the `Content-Type`.

3. User-Agent. For mHTTP , we exploit the fact that mobile applications use HTTP for their communications and set the `User-Agent` field to indicate which application is making the request. When the `User-Agent` is not a mobile browser we group requests for the same application based on `User-Agent`.

For the three methods above we also exclude known third party domains (*e.g.,* those identified in [18]) from consideration as a publisher. We also require that sessions contain more than one request as most Web pages today contain more than one object (*e.g.,* images).

Identifying publishers and aggregators. After sessionizing HTTP transactions, we assign the first domain in the session to be the publisher. We consider any domain hosted on a different AS than the publisher to be a third party. We use RIPE's `whois` to perform the IP to AS mapping.

Using AS numbers to distinguish publisher and aggregator organizations has limitations. For example, CDNs hosting embedded content are classified as aggregators. Indeed, we observed CDNs as some of the most common aggregators. That emphasizes their potential to enter the aggregation business [4]. To mitigate the impact of CDNs on our results we exclude well known CDNs from consideration as aggregators (*e.g.,* Amazon (AS16509/14618), Akamai (AS16625/20940), and Limelight(AS22822)). Secondly, publishers and aggregators that are owned by one entity (*e.g.,* Gmail and Doubleclick) cannot be disambiguated. This is not a problem as we assume they share information (Google has a unified privacy policy [23]). We attempted using an alternate technique, combining ADNS entries and AS numbers. However, it divided some popular organizations (*e.g.,* Microsoft uses both msecd and nsatc as ADNS domains). For cases where multiple publishers are hosted on the same AS (*e.g.,* a CDN) we identify publishers using their host domain.

3.3 Computing intent $\mathcal{I}_a(u)$

The ability to profile users based on their purchasing intent is what drives advertisers to pay more for targeted advertisements. Advertisements targeted to specific audience segments can command 2-10X the base RON_a price (depending on the predicted purchasing intent of the segment) with an average increase of 3.3X [16]. Reverse engineering the data mining algorithms used to determine purchasing intent is beyond the scope of this paper. However, to lend realism to our calculations, we rely on values assigned by ad-networks themselves to key-words in combination with categories that can be assigned to publishers. So we use the following process.

1. Categorize user-visited publishers Users' interests and intent can be inferred based on publishers visited (*e.g.,* `espn.com`: sports) in the same way as aggregators do it [12]. Using Alexa's standard site categorization of our datasets mimics advertisers planning campaigns. When publishers appear in multiple categories in Alexa (*e.g.,* `bbc.co.uk`, bbc.co.uk: arts and news) we pick the highest ranking category. Note that this is conservative as publishers who map to different categories can lead to higher revenue.

2. Determine intent values for categories. Once we know the Web sites categories a user visits, we need to convert these categories into a multiplier value between 2 and 10 (as this is the increase in value of an impression due to targeting). We use *suggested* bid amounts for the categories provided by the Google AdWords Contextual Advertising Tool[5], to estimate the *relative value* of different categories.

[5]Can be found at `adwords.google.com`.

Once we have the bid amount for each category, we normalize by the highest category value and rescale into the range 2-10. Hence, every publisher gets mapped to a category and using the category, an intent value is assigned.

3. Compute intent. We use the set of publishers a user visits to calculate two different intent values for the user: *implicit* $II_a(u)$ for an aggregator a, computed by taking the *average* of intent value of publishers that u visits where a is present as a third party (results in an average $II_a(u)$ of 3.1 in the Univ and HTTP datasets and 3.8 in mHTTP) and *explicit* $EI(u)$ to be max of the average intent value across *all* publishers u visits or $II_a(u)$. The difference between the intents approximates the added value of having visibility into the full set of sites visited. Relative frequency of visits to different publishers can also be part of our calculations.

3.4 Additional parameters

Traffic quality multiplier (TQM_p). TQM_p captures additional factors (ad placement, quality of publisher) impacting the value of impressions. Capturing all of these factor is beyond the scope of this work. We instead, focus on TQM_p as based on the quality of the publisher. Reasonable values of TQM_p are 2 for popular publishers (*e.g.,* New York Times) or 0.1 for disreputable sites (*e.g.,* illegal file hosting). Thus, we assign publishers appearing in the top 500 sites on Alexa $TQM_p = 2$. We assign publishers with IPs on a DNS blacklist[6] $TQM_p = 0.1$. We assign the remaining publishers $TQM_p = 1$. We note that a publisher may be outside the Alexa top 500 but can still be a prime/reputable site, but the penalty for mis-classifying such sites is a factor of two. However, we want to ensure we never assign disreputable sites (as given by the blacklist) a high score, hence we assign a number that differs by an order of magnitude (0.1)

Run-of-network (RON_a). We use a value of \$1.98 for RON_a as this is the average run-of-network price found in advertising literature [6].

Limitations: We used published numbers for our parameters but they may vary in practice; our results are *not* meant to predict absolute values. Hence, we focus on distributions and trends in ad revenues that are not impacted by scalar values such as TQM_p or RON_a. There may be issues with relying on a certain method to classify publishers/aggregators or on certain resources (Alexa, Adwords) but methodology remains the same.

4. TODAY'S ADVERTISING REVENUE

We now combine the advertising model (Sec. 2) with the datasets (Sec 3) to see: (1) how much do aggregators know about users through tracking? (2) which users, publishers and aggregators generate the most ad revenue? We mostly present results from mHTTP due to space constraints.

4.1 How much do aggregators know?

Aggregators are able to estimate intent accurately for 50% of users. Fig. 2 shows the ratio of explicit to implicit intent for user-aggregator pairs. Recall, that for each user, the aggregator infers intent based on the subset of sites where the aggregator is present as a third party. We find that more than half of aggregators in all datasets inferring the correct value of $EI(u)$ for those users. This accuracy stems from many users visiting sites in a small number of categories (median: 2.2 categories, mHTTP).

[6]`http://dnsbl.inps.de`

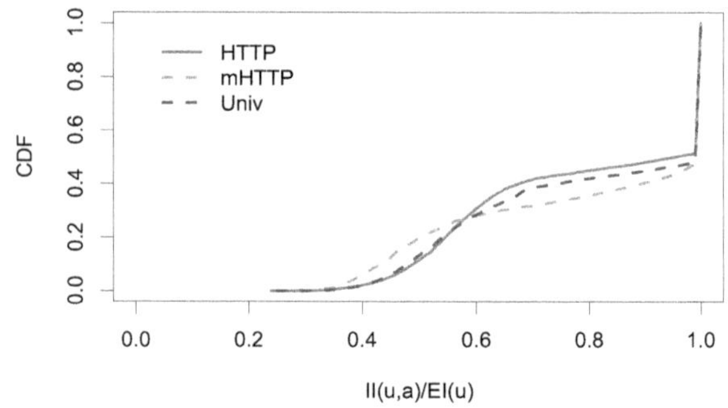

Figure 2: CDF of inferred intent ($II_a(u)$) normalized by explicit intent ($EI(u)$).

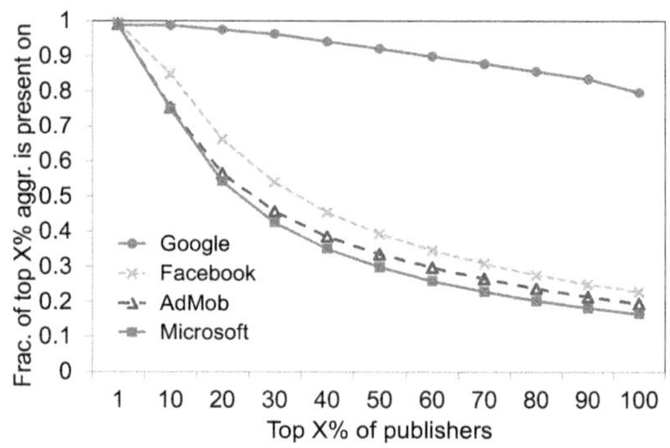

Figure 3: Presence of the top four aggregators on publishers with the most revenue, mHTTP.

Aggregators know most about popular sites. In Table 2, we show the reach of top (in terms of revenue) aggregators across all publishers in our datasets. Maintaining presence on many publishers requires aggregators to build and maintain business relationships. Fig. 3 shows the fraction of publishers the top four aggregators are present on for varying numbers of top (in terms of popularity) publishers. Top aggregators are focusing on popular publishers with the top aggregators present on more than 70% of the top 10% of sites. As we consider less popular sites presence by top aggregators correspondingly decreases with Facebook dropping from presence on 85% of the top 10% of publishers to presence on only 23% of all publishers. This suggests that studies considering third party tracking on popular publishers (*e.g.,* [18]) are seeing an upper bound on tracking. In terms of implications to privacy, we find most aggregators are present on a low number of publishers (Google being an exception, Table 2).

4.2 How valuable is this information?

Ad revenue is generated by many users. Ad revenue generated by users is only slightly skewed, with 90% of revenue derived from 55% of HTTP and 35% of mHTTP and Univ users, respectively (Fig. 4). We find strong correlation between user revenue and the number of sessions per user with a correlation (r-value) of 0.64 for mHTTP. Unsurprisingly, users who browse more are more valuable in the impression-based revenue model.

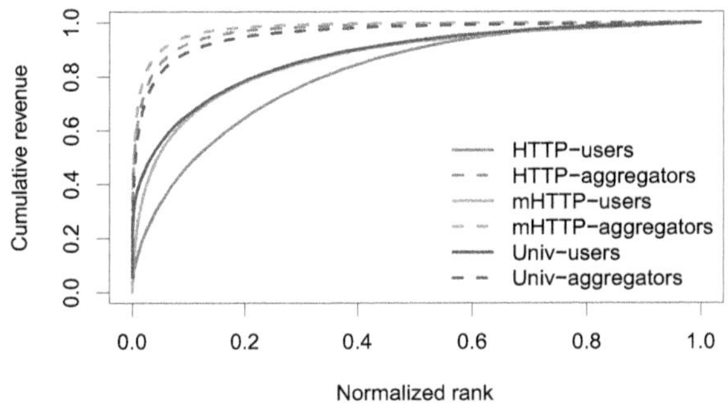

Figure 4: Cumulative fraction of revenue attributed to each aggregator and user.

Table 2: High revenue aggregators(mHTTP).

Aggregator	Frac. Rev.	Frac. Users	Frac. Pubs.
Google	0.18	0.17	0.80
Facebook	0.06	0.09	0.23
GlobalCrossing (AdMob)	0.04	0.11	0.19
AOL	0.03	0.04	0.07
Microsoft	0.03	0.04	0.17
Omniture	0.03	0.05	0.07
Yahoo! (AS42173)	0.03	0.04	0.07

Which information vectors are most lucrative? As mentioned earlier, number of sessions play a more central role in determining revenue. However, we find that some categories are more lucrative than others ('Recreation' for mHTTP), but this is reflected in the bid prices for different categories (Sec. 3.3). In addition, the bid prices also reflect the relative popularity of the categories (publishers classified as 'Recreation' are the most visited in mHTTP). Simultaneously, we find that publishers that are least visited belong to categories that have the lowest bid prices. From a privacy perspective, if we consider k-anonymity, then the most popular publishers (and most lucrative) would be the most private while the least lucrative/popular would be less private.

Most popular publishers do not necessarily generate most revenue. Table 3 shows the top publishers in the mHTTP dataset. We find that while Google (`google.com`) is the most visited publisher with 18% of users visiting Google as a publisher[7], Facebook (`facebook.com`) actually generates the most revenue: 9%. We see Facebook's CDN `fbcdn.net` also generating significant revenue since it also serves Facebook Web pages. Revenue is correlated with the number of aggregators present on each publisher, in the mHTTP dataset, we find a correlation of 0.61 (r-value) between number of aggregators and revenue per publisher.

Google is the top aggregator Table 2 shows the top aggregators in the mHTTP dataset. As in previous work [18], we observe Google playing an active role as an aggregator. Google is present on significantly more publishers than the other aggregators, with presence on 80% of publishers in the mHTTP dataset. Fig. 4 shows that advertising revenue is concentrated by a few aggregators with the top 5-10% of aggregators getting 90% of the ad revenue. Facebook also

Table 3: High revenue publishers (mHTTP).

Publisher	Frac. Rev.	Frac. Users	Category
facebook.com	0.09	0.15	society
google.co.uk	0.04	0.11	computers
bbc.co.uk	0.03	0.07	arts
fbcdn.net	0.03	0.13	society
twitter.com	0.03	0.04	computers
yahoo.com	0.03	0.04	computers
google.com	0.02	0.18	computers

ranks highly as an aggregator reaching 9% of users with presence on 23% of first parties in the mHTTP dataset.

5. REVENUE WITH PRIVACY

We study how unilateral privacy preserving actions by users affect advertising revenues. We consider blocking technologies, that disrupt tracking by third parties, downloading of online ads [3], deny cookies, limit Javascript execution to selective sites [22] as well as obfuscation methods where the key idea is to either inject noise in services that profile users, like search [15] or mobile apps [14] or to impersonate users [1]. The users' privacy is protected as their 'behavior' is obfuscated/attributed to someone else. The aggregators clearly lose out as the data they obtain is corrupted.

We note that these methods may not be effective and few might use them [11, 9]. Likewise, measures like the Do Not Track initiative [2] relies on aggregators honoring the intent. In addition, publishers and aggregators may retaliate by refusing service when they detect blocking, decreasing the utility for the user. Whatever the outcome might be in such a cat-and-mouse game, the intention from the users' is clear – to opt-out of tracking. Hence blocking prevents aggregators from tracking users and reduces revenue generated by targeted advertisements. We quantify this loss.

5.1 Quantifying revenue loss

The amount of information available to aggregators may differ based on privacy protection measures used and can be captured in the model from Sec. 2.

The cost of blocking When users deploy privacy preserving measures they may experience decreased functionality. Modeling the utility decrease due to blocking is beyond the scope of this paper.

User Intent $\mathcal{I}_a(u)$. Recall that user intent captures the interests of the user (Sec. 2). Privacy preservation techniques hinder aggregators from being able to infer the intent of users through tracking. This gives two potential values for $\mathcal{I}_a(u)$ in our model:

$$\mathcal{I}_a(u) = \begin{cases} II_a(u) & u \text{ and } p \text{ do nothing} \\ 1 & \text{otherwise} \end{cases} \quad (3)$$

Implicit intent ($II_a(u)$) is as described in Sec. 3.3. Recall that implicit intent ($II_a(u)$) is what aggregators can infer, while explicit intent ($EI(u)$) can consist of all the information the user possesses. And when the user or publisher block tracking there is no increase in CPM as a result of intent, hence it is set to 1.

Quantifying the cost of blocking Fig. 5 shows how much value is currently derived from implicit intent which stands to be lost if users block. The average value of $II_a(u)$ is 4.2

[7]Domain is used to identify publishers (google.co.uk/google.com are different) and given possible overlap among users we cannot sum the fraction.

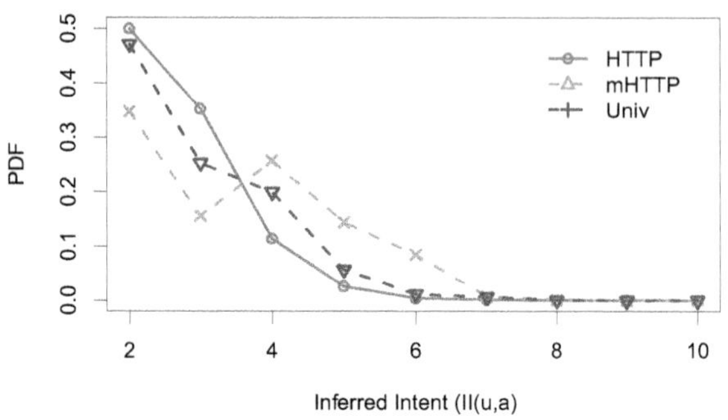

Figure 5: Distribution of implicit intent, $II_a(u)$.

in the HTTP, 3.8 in mHTTP and 3.1 in the Univ traces, respectively. Indeed, when we compute revenue with all users blocking (*i.e.*, $\mathcal{I}_a(u) = 1$) revenue decreases by a factor of 4.2 in the HTTP, 3.8 in mHTTP, and 3.2 in the Univ traces, respectively. A large population of users blocking – in the worst case, if the Do Not Track (DNT) header [2] became default – would represent a significant threat to advertising revenue. If proposals like DNT are honored by aggregators this may lead to lowered quality of service as the publisher will lose out on additional revenues. Blocking also poses the potential to decrease functionality of Web sites for users (*e.g.*, blocking Javascript via NoScript [22]). Hence, for these reasons, it can be argued that most users will not take the extreme step of blocking entirely. However, we find that even if 5% of the top users (Fig. 4) block, the revenue drop is between 35%-60%. Regarding obfuscation, assuming that incorrect targeting is worse than no targeting, the drop in revenues due to blocking will be a lower bound on *revenue loss* due to obfuscation.

6. RELATED WORK

Much work has been done on understanding the effectiveness of behavioral targeting [6, 29], users' attitudes towards targeting [20], and designing systems for mining interests of users for targeting [8]. The actual behavioral targeting mechanisms are not known as they tend to be proprietary. Likewise, recent work has focused on the problem of combating clickspam [10] and characterizing mobile advertising [28]. In addition, past work has also focused on understanding the role online ads play in decision making [24, 27] or how to properly set CPM values [7]. Our paper tries to shed light on part of the advertising landscape using real data from an economics perspective – understanding advertising revenue as a function of user's information.

7. CONCLUSIONS

Using HTTP traces, we looked into the relationship between how much information is collected by aggregators and quantified how valuable this information can be. We developed a simple revenue model for targeted advertising to aid us. Our results indicate that revenue is highly skewed towards few aggregators, while it is not that skewed from a user perspective. We also studied possible revenue drop if users were to adopt unilateral privacy protection.

Acknowledgments

We would like to thank the reviewers and our shepherd, Craig Partridge for helpful comments. We would like to thank Martin Arlitt for providing us with the university Web traces and infrastructure for analysis. We also thank Glenn Ellison, Jonathan Smith, John Byers and Georgios Siganos for comments on a draft of this work. Phillipa Gill was supported by the AT&T VURI program.

8. REFERENCES

[1] Bug me not. bugmenot.com.

[2] Do not track. donottrack.us.

[3] Adblock plus. http://adblockplus.org/.

[4] Akamai (Press Release). Akamai introduces advertising decision solutions; Announces agreement to acquire Acerno, 2012. http://www.akamai.com/html/about/press/releases/2008/press_102108.html.

[5] AudienceScience. The audiencescience targeting segments, 2012. www.audiencetargeting.com.

[6] H. Beales. The value of behavioral targeting. *National Advertising Initiative*, 2010.

[7] H. Cannon. Addressing new media with conventional media planning. *Journal of Interactive Advertising*, Vol 1, No 2, 2001.

[8] Y. Chen, D. Pavlov, and J. F. Canny. Large-scale behavioral targeting. In *In Proc. of ACM SIGKDD*, KDD '09, 2009.

[9] Cybernet News. Less than 3% of Firefox users block Ads, 2008. http://cybernetnews.com/less-than-3-of-firefox-users-block-ads/.

[10] V. Dave, S. Guha, and Y. Zhang. Measuring and Fingerprinting Click-Spam in Ad Networks. In *Proceedings of the Special Interest Group on Data Communication (SIGCOMM)*, Helsinki, Finland, Aug 2012.

[11] P. G. Leon et al. Why johhny can't opt out? a usability evaluation of tools to limit online behavioral advertising. Technical report, CMU, 2011.

[12] Google. Your data on Google: Advertising, 2012. http://www.google.com/goodtoknow/data-on-google/advertising/.

[13] S. Guha, B. Cheng, and P. Francis. Privad: Practical Privacy in Online Advertising. *Proc. of NSDI*, 2011.

[14] P. Hornyack et al. "These Aren't the Droids You're Looking For": Retrofitting Android to Protect Data from Imperious Applications. In *Proc. of ACM CCS*, 2011.

[15] D. Howe and H. Nissenbaum. Trackmenot: Resisting surveillance in web search. In I. Kerr, C. Lucock, and V. Steeves, editors, *On the Identity Trail: Privacy, Anonymity and Identity in a Networked Society*. 2008.

[16] A. Hunter, M. Jacobsen, R. Talens, and T. Winders. When money moves to digital, where should it go? identifying the right media-placement strategies for digital display. Technical report, Comscore and ValueClick Media, 2010.

[17] S. Ihm and V. S. Pai. Towards understanding modern web traffic. In *In Proc. of the ACM SIGCOMM IMC*, 2011.

[18] B. Krishnamurthy and C. Wills. Privacy Diffusion on the Web: A Longitudinal Perspective. In *Proc. ACM WWW*, page 541. ACM Press, 2009.

[19] R. T. B. Ma, D. M. Chiu, J. C. S. Lui, V. Misra, and D. Rubenstein. On cooperative settlement between content, transit, and eyeball internet service providers. *IEEE/ACM Trans. Netw.*, 19(3):802–815, June 2011.

[20] A. M. McDonald and L. F. Cranor. Americans' attitudes about internet behavioral advertising practices. In *WPES*, 2010.

[21] N. Mohan. The AdSense revenue share, 2010. http://adsense.blogspot.com/2010/05/adsense-revenue-share.html.

[22] No script. http://noscript.net/.

[23] NYTimes. Europe presses google to change privacy policy, 2013. http://www.nytimes.com/2012/10/17/business/global/17iht-google17.html?pagewanted=all&_r=1&.

[24] P. Patwardhan and J. Ramaprasad. Rational integrative model of online consumer decision making. *Journal of Interactive Advertising*, Vol 6, No 1, 2005.

[25] A. Reznichenko et al. Auctions in Do-Not-Track Compliant Internet Advertising. *ACM CCS*, 2011.

[26] R. Richmond. As ŚlikeŠ buttons spread, so do facebookŠs tentacles, 2011. http://bits.blogs.nytimes.com/2011/09/27/as-like-buttons-spread-so-do-facebooks-tentacles/.

[27] S. Rodgers and E. Thorson. The interactive advertising model: How users perceive and process online ads. *Journal of Interactive Advertising*, Vol 1, No 1, 2000.

[28] N. Vallina-Rodriguez, J. Shah, A. Finamore, Y. Grunenberger, K. Papagiannaki, H. Haddadi, and J. Crowcroft. Breaking for commercials: characterizing mobile advertising. In *Proceedings of the 2012 ACM conference on Internet measurement conference*, IMC '12.

[29] Y. Yan et al. How much can behavioral targeting help online advertising? In *In Proc. of WWW*, 2009.

Understanding the Effectiveness of Video Ads: A Measurement Study

S. Shunmuga Krishnan
Akamai Technologies
sarumuga@akamai.com

Ramesh K. Sitaraman
University of Massachusetts, Amherst
& Akamai Technologies
ramesh@cs.umass.edu

ABSTRACT

Online video is the killer application of the Internet. Videos are expected to constitute more than 85% of the traffic on the consumer Internet within the next few years. However, a vexing problem for video providers is how to monetize their online videos. A popular monetization model pursued by many major video providers is inserting ads that play in-stream with the video that is being watched. Our work represents the first rigorous scientific study of the key factors that determine the effectiveness of video ads as measured by their completion and abandonment rates. We collect and analyze a large set of anonymized traces from Akamai's video delivery network consisting of about 65 million unique viewers watching 362 million videos and 257 million ads from 33 video providers around the world. Using novel quasi-experimental techniques, we show that an ad is 18.1% more likely to complete when placed as a mid-roll than as a pre-roll, and 14.3% more likely to complete when placed as pre-roll than as a post-roll. Next, we show that completion rate of an ad decreases with increasing ad length. A 15-second ad is 2.9% more likely to complete than a 20-second ad, which in turn is 3.9% more likely to complete than a 30-second ad. Further, we show the ad completion rate is influenced by the video in which the ad is placed. An ad placed in long-form videos such as movies and TV episodes is 4.2% more likely to complete than the same ad placed in short-form video such as news clips. Finally, we show that about one-third of the viewers who abandon leave in the first quarter of the ad, while about two-thirds leave at the half-way point in the ad.Our work represents a first step towards scientifically understanding video ads and viewer behavior. Such understanding is crucial for the long-term viability of online videos and the future evolution of the Internet.

Categories and Subject Descriptors

C.4 [**Performance of Systems**]: Performance attributes, Measurement techniques; C.2.4 [**Computer-Communication Networks**]: Distributed Systems—*Client/server*

IMC'13, October 23–25, 2013, Barcelona, Spain.

ACM 978-1-4503-1953-9/13/10 ...$15.00.
http://dx.doi.org/10.1145/2504730.2504748.

General Terms

Economics, Human Factors, Measurement

Keywords

Online videos; Advertisements; Monetization; User behavior; Internet content delivery; Multimedia.

1. INTRODUCTION

Online video is the killer application of the Internet. According to a recent Cisco study more than half of the consumer traffic on the Internet today is related to videos and that fraction is expected to exceed 85% in 2016 [9]. As all forms of traditional media such as news, entertainment and sports migrate to the Internet, video on-demand traffic is expected to triple by 2016 from the levels seen in 2011. Video providers who offer online videos include news channels (such as CNN and Fox News), sports channels (such as ESPN and MLB), movie outlets (such as Hulu and NetFlix), and entertainment providers (such as NBC, ABC, and CBS). Video providers bear the costs of acquiring and delivering the videos to their audience of viewers. Acquisition costs may include production costs for original content or licensing costs and/or revenue sharing for third-party content. The delivery costs often involve contracting with a content delivery service (such as Akamai [18]), who in turn incur the costs for the servers, software, bandwidth, colocation, and power. The runaway success of online videos leaves video providers and the media industry with perhaps their single most vexing problem. How can online videos be monetized? How can they be made viable and profitable?

While successful models for video monetization are still evolving, there are broadly three monetization models that are gaining popularity in the industry. The *subscription-based* model requires users to pay a fee on a periodic basis (usually monthly) to watch videos. The *pay-per-view* model requires users to pay a fee usually on a per-event basis. Finally, a popular model more relevant to our work is the *ad-based* model where viewers do not pay a fee but are shown ads that are placed *in-stream* in the video content.[1]

Driven by both the rapid increase in online video consumption and the intense need to monetize that consumption, it is perhaps not surprising that video ads were the

[1]We use the term "video" to describe the video being watched, such as a news clip, sports event, or movie. We use the term "ad" to indicate the ad that is played in-stream with the video that is being watched.

fastest growing category of online ads with spending increasing by about 50% in 2012 [8]. But, how effective are video ads? Are there general causal rules of viewer behavior that govern their effectiveness? What key factors of the ad, of the video, and of the viewer influence an ad's effectiveness? These questions are of great importance to the long-term viability of online videos that are a key part of the Internet ecosystem. However, to our knowledge, they have not been studied in a rigorous scientific fashion, and hence our focus.

1.1 Understanding Ad Effectiveness

The question of how to measure the effectiveness of a video ad is complex. Ads convey a message to the viewer and the key metric for ad effectiveness that is widely used in the media industry is *ad completion rates*. Ad completion rate is the percentage of ads that the viewer watched *completely* without abandoning in the middle. Completion rates are perhaps the most tracked metric in an ad campaign since a viewer watching an ad to completion is more likely to be influenced by it. A related metric is *ad abandonment rate* that measures what fraction of viewers watched what fraction of the ad. The goal in any advertising campaign is to maximize completion rates and minimize abandonment.

In addition to ad completion, there are a few other metrics that are tracked that attempt to measure the response of the viewer after watching the ad. Primary among those is the click-through rate (CTR) that measures the percentage of users who click on a link associated with the ad during or after watching the ad. CTR has the advantage over ad completion rates of capturing an active user response. Though many have argued that CTRs capture only a immediate response but not the long-term impact of the ad that advertiser is hoping to achieve [12].

Another class of metrics for ad effectiveness take the more direct approach of surveying a sample of users who have viewed the ad to determine how much the ad may have increased brand awareness, brand loyalty, and the viewer's intent to buy. While the directness of the approach is an advantage, such surveys are difficult to do at scale and suffer from biases that relate to how the questions are framed and who opts to participate in the survey.

While the video ad industry is yet to evolve a consensus on how to integrate the different ways of measuring ad effectiveness, there is consensus that a basic and important measure is ad completion rate. Thus, we focus on ad completion rate and the associated metric of ad abandonment rate as indicators of ad effectiveness in our study. Our current data set does not currently allow us to measure CTRs or survey responses. But, comparing the different metrics of ad effectiveness is an interesting avenue for future work.

1.2 Our contributions

To our knowledge, our work is the first in-depth scientific study of video ads and their effectiveness. We explore how ad effectiveness as measured by completion rate is impacted by key properties of the ad, of the video, and of the viewer. A key contribution of our work is that we go beyond simple characterization to derive causal rules of viewer behavior that are predictive and more generally applicable. To derive such rules we develop and use a novel technique based on quasi-experimental designs (QEDs).

Our data set is one of the most extensive cross-sections of enterprise videos used in a scientific study of this kind. The data used in our analysis was collected from 33 video providers over a period of 15 days consisting of 362 million videos and 257 million ad impressions that were watched by 65 million unique viewers located across the world.

The metrics that we study such as completion and abandonment rates are critical in the media industry and are widely tracked and reported by ad networks and analytics providers. We expect that the deeper scientific understanding that our work provides for these metrics will have a significant impact on the evolution of monetization models for video. We now list our specific key contributions below.

(1) "Mid-roll" ads placed in the middle of a video had the highest completion rate of 97% while "pre-roll" ads placed in the beginning and "post-roll" ads placed in end yielded drastically smaller completion rates of 74% and 45% respectively. The intuitive reason is that viewers are more engaged with the video during a mid-roll ad causing them to be more patient, while viewers are less engaged in the beginning and at the end of the video. By designing a quasi-experiment, we verify the above intuition by showing that the position of an ad can causally impact its completion rate. We show that an ad is 18.1% more likely to complete when placed as mid-roll than as a pre-roll, and 14.3% more likely to complete when placed as pre-roll than as a post-roll.

(2) 20-second ads had the least completion rate of 60% in our data set, with 15-second and 30-second ads completing at higher rates of 84% and 90% respectively. However, using a quasi-experiment, we show that longer ads are in fact *less* likely to complete. Our causal analysis bolsters our intuition that viewers have less patience to wait for longer ads and would complete fewer of them, provided the other confounding factors are kept similar.

(3) Ads played within long-form video such as TV episodes and movies completed at a higher rate of 87%. While ads played within short-form video such as news clips completed at a lower rate of 67%. A plausible reason is that viewers are more willing to complete an ad that they view as a "cost" if they perceive a greater "benefit" in return from watching the associated video. And, on average, viewers tend to perceive greater benefit from a long-form video than a short-form one. Using a quasi-experiment, we confirm this intuition by showing that an ad is 4.2% more likely to complete if placed in a long-form video than if it is placed in a short-form video, provided all other factors are similar. Note that the magnitude of impact of video length on ad completion rates is smaller when confounding factors are accounted for than what a simple correlation suggests (4.2% versus 20%).

(4) Using information gain ratios, we show that the contents of the video and the ad have high relevance for completion rates, while the connectivity of the viewer had the lowest relevance.

(5) Industry folklore suggests that viewers are less likely to abandon ads when watching them in the evenings or weekends when they tend to be more relaxed and have more spare time. However, we did not find any supporting evidence in our data as we did not observe a significant influence of either time-of-day or day-of-week on ad completion rates.

(6) In our study of ad abandonment rates, we show that a significant set of viewers abandon soon after the ad starts. The abandonment rate is initially higher but tapers off over time as the ad plays. About one-third of the viewers who eventually abandon leave in the first quarter of the ad, while about two-thirds leave at the half-way point in the ad.

2. BACKGROUND

2.1 The Video Ads Ecosystem

The video ad ecosystem consists of four types of entities. *Video providers* own and manage video content, e.g., NBC, CBS, CNN, Hulu, Fox News, etc. Advertisers offer ads that can be played in-stream with the video. Ad insertion is managed by an ad delivery network such as Freewheel [5], Adobe Auditude [1], or Video Plaza [7]. The ad network brings together the video providers (i.e., publishers) who offer videos and the advertisers who offer ads. An ad network has an ad decision component that decides what ads to play with which videos and where to position those ads. Both the ads from the advertisers and the videos from the video providers need to be streamed to the viewer with high performance. For that reason, both the ads and videos are typically delivered to the viewers using content delivery networks (CDNs) such as Akamai [10, 18]. Thus, CDNs are cognizant of both the video content and ads embedded within them. The mechanism for inserting the ad is commonly performed by the user's media player when it is playing the video. When it is time to play an ad, the media player redirects to the ad network that choses the ad and plays it within an ad player.When the ad completes the control returns to the user's media player that continues to play the video content.

2.2 Views, viewers, and visits

We describe a user watching a video with ads, defining terms along the way that we will use in this paper.

Viewer. A viewer is a user who watches one or more videos using a specific media player installed on the user's device. A viewer is uniquely identified and distinguished from other viewers by using a GUID (Globally Unique Identifier) value that is set as a cookie when the media player is accessed. To identify the viewer uniquely, the GUID[2] value is generated to be distinct from other prior values in use.

Views. A view represents an attempt by a viewer to watch a specific video. A typical view would start with the viewer initiating the video playback, for instance, by clicking the play button of the media player[3] (see Figure 1). During a view, the media player might first play an ad called a *pre-roll* before the actual video content begins. (We use the term *video* to denote the actual video that the viewer wants to watch to distinguish it from the *ad* that the viewer is also shown.) Further, the video may be interrupted in the middle with one or more ads called *mid-rolls*. Finally, an ad might be shown when the video ends called a *post-roll*. Each showing of an ad, whether or not it is watched completely, is called an *ad impression*. *Ad completion rate* is the percent of ad impressions that were played to completion[4].

Typically, viewers do not have the ability to "skip" ads and must either watch the ad in order to watch the video content that follows, or just abandon the ad and the view all together. Our data sets have such non-skippable ads that is the standard for enterprise video. Recently YouTube that has a large fraction of user-generated videos has been experimenting with pre-roll ads that have a mandatory non-skippable part that must be viewed but can be skipped beyond that point. But, it is not yet common within enterprise videos and is not represented in our data set.

[2]In most implementations, the GUID is tied to the device or the desktop of the viewer. Thus, we cannot always detect cases where one user watches video on another user's device.

[3]In other cases, a view may be initiated automatically using a play list or by other means.

[4]If an ad is played completely it is *likely* that it was watched completely by the viewer. However, we are not able to measure whether or not a viewer is actually watching the ad or if he/she has shifted focus elsewhere when the ad is playing.

Type	Factor	Description
Ad	Content	defined by unique name
	Position	Pre-, mid-, post-roll
	Length	15-, 20-, and 30-second
Video	Content	defined by unique url
	Length	Short-form, Long-form
	Provider	News, Movie, Sports, Entertainment
Viewer	Identity	defined by unique GUID
	Geography	Country and Continent
	Connection Type	Mobile, DSL, Cable, Fiber
	Temporal	Time of day, Day of week

Table 1: Potential factors that influence viewer behavior and ad completion.

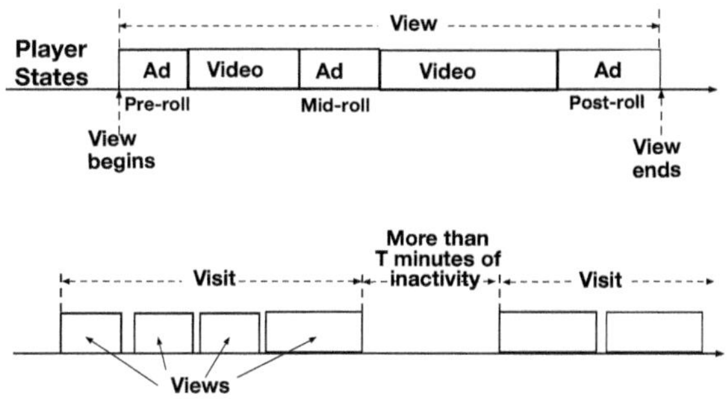

Figure 1: Views and Visits

Visits. A visit is intended to capture a single session of a viewer visiting a content provider's site to view videos. A visit is a maximal set of contiguous views from a viewer at a specific video provider site such that each visit is separated from the next visit by at least T minutes of inactivity, where we choose $T = 30$ minutes[5](see Figure 1).

2.3 Potential factors that impact ad completion

We study three sets of key factors that potentially influence ad completion that we list in Table 1 and discuss below.

Ad-related factors. The actual ad and its contents as identified by its unique name is a first factor. Ad position relates where it was inserted in a video view and can either be pre-roll, mid-roll, or post-roll. The most common ad lengths in our study are 15-second, 20-second, and 30-second ads.

[5]Our definition is similar to the standard notion of a visit (also called a session) in web analytics where each visit is a set of page views separated by a period of idleness of at least 30 minutes (say) from the next visit.

Video-related factors. The first factor is the video content itself as identified uniquely by its url[6]. Besides the actual content of the video itself, we isolate two important factors. The *video length* can be used to differentiate short-form from long-form videos. The IAB (Interactive Advertising Bureau) which is a major industry body for online video advertising defines long-form video as videos lasting over 10 minutes and short-form as those under 10 minutes [6]. We adopt this standard definition in our work. Typically, short-form and long-form videos are qualitatively different. Short-form video are usually smaller clips for news, weather, etc. Long-form videos are typically TV episodes, movies, sports events, etc. Most long-form videos possess a "content arc" with a beginning, middle and end.

Viewer-related factors. A viewer can be uniquely and anonymously identified by their GUID. Besides their identity, we consider three important attributes of the viewer. The geographical location of the viewer at the country level encapsulates several social, economic, religious, and cultural aspects that could influence his/her viewing behavior. In addition, the manner in which a viewer connects to the Internet, both the device used and typical connectivity characteristics can influence viewer behavior. The primary connection types are mobile, DSL, cable, and fiber (such as AT&T's Uverse and Verizon's FiOS). Finally, it is plausible that the time-of-day and the day-of-week[7] when the ad was watched could potentially influence its completion rate. For instance, folklore holds that people have more time in the weekend and evenings, leading them to be more relaxed and more patient with video ads. However, as we show in Section 5.3.3, we did not observe a significant influence of either time-of-day or the day-of-week on ad completion rates.

It is worth noting that many of the video and viewer related factors considered here are known to significantly impact viewer behavior in the context of viewer tolerance to performance degradation from our prior work [14]. So, it is natural to consider these in the different behavioral context of viewer tolerance to ads. The ad-related factors considered here, besides being natural to consider, are widely tracked in industry benchmarks.

3. DATA SETS

The data sets that we use for our analysis are collected from a large cross section of actual users around the world who play videos using media players that incorporate the widely-deployed Akamai's client-side media analytics plug-in [2]. When video providers build their media player, they can choose to incorporate the plugin that provides an accurate means for measuring a variety of video and ad metrics. When the viewer uses the media player to play a video, the plugin is loaded at the client-side and it "listens" and records a variety of events that can then be used to stitch together an accurate picture of exactly what the viewer experienced and what the viewer did.

When a view is initiated, say with the user clicking the play button, metrics such as the time when the view was initiated, the video url that uniquely identifies the content, video length, whether it is live or on-demand, the video provider, the amount of video watched, the bitrate(s) at which it was streamed, and several other detailed characteristics pertaining to the video are recorded. Likewise, when an ad is inserted, ad-related metrics such at what point in the video the ad was inserted, the ad name that uniquely identifies the content of the ad, the ad length, the amount of the ad that was actually played, and whether the ad completed or not are recorded. Further, detailed information about the viewer is recorded including the GUID that uniquely identifies the viewer, current ip address, network, geography, and connection type. Once the metrics are captured by the plugin, the information is "beaconed" to an analytics backend that we use to process the huge volumes of data. From every media player at the beginning and end of every view, the relevant measurements are sent to the analytics backend. Further, incremental updates are sent at a configurable periodicity as the video is playing, typically once every 300 seconds. All relevant fields in the data set used in our study are measured and stored in an *anonymized* fashion so as to not include any PII or sensitive information.

3.1 Data Characteristics

The Akamai CDN serves a significant fraction of world's online videos and ads. We selected a large, characteristic cross-section of 33 video providers including news sites, sports sites, movie providers, and entertainment channels who have an ad-based monetization model. We tracked all videos and ads for these providers over a period of 15 days in April 2013. About 94% of the video views were for on-demand content and the rest were live events. We only consider on-demand videos that currently form the bulk of the videos for our study.

Our data is among the most extensive ever studied for video ads and consisted of 257 million ad impressions that were watched by over 65 million unique viewers located in all major continents of the world. On average, viewers spent 8.8% of their time watching ads as opposed videos. Table 2 summarizes some basic statistics of our data. The geography

	Total	Per View	Per Visit	Per Viewer
Views	362 mil	N/A	1.3	5.6
Ad Impressions	257 mill	0.71	0.92	3.95
Video Play (in minutes)	777 mil	2.15	2.79	11.96
Ad Play (in minutes)	75 mil	0.21	0.27	1.15

Table 2: Key statistics of our data set.

of the viewer was mostly concentrated in North America, and Europe that together originate the bulk of video traffic. One continent where we could not obtain proportional representation is Asia that accounts for significant video traffic but where many video providers do not yet have the software changes required in their media player to track ads. The connection types were dominated by cable, though the other categories have a solid representation as well (cf. Table 3).

[6]Note that if two different providers are showing the same movie with different urls, we consider them different videos. Detecting them to be the same content is intrinsically very difficult as there is no universally accepted naming system across video providers.

[7]Time-of-day and day-of-week is computed using the *local* time for the viewer based on his/her geographical location.

Viewer Geography	Percent Views	Connection Type	Percent Views
North America	65.56%	Fiber	17.14%
Europe	29.72%	Cable	56.95%
Asia	1.95%	DSL	19.78%
Other	2.77%	Mobile	6.05%

Table 3: Geography and connection type.

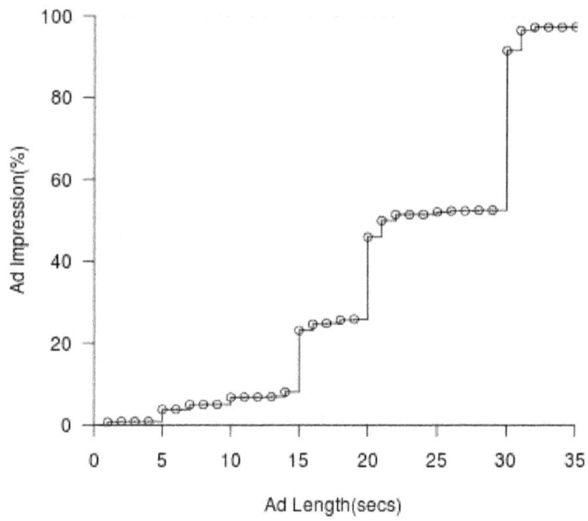

Figure 2: CDF of ad length showing the three major clusters at 15-, 20- and 30-seconds.

The ad length distribution is shown in Figure 2. The ad lengths clustered around 15-, 20- and 30-second marks and were clustered into those categories respectively.

The distribution of the video lengths for short-form and long-form videos are shown in Figure 3. The mean length of a short-form video is 2.9 minutes and that of long-form video is 30.7 minutes. The most popular duration for long-form video was 30 minutes that is typical for a TV episode.

4. ANALYSIS TECHNIQUES

We seek to understand how a set of key factors such as those in Table 1 impact viewer behavior metrics such as ad completion and abandonment rates. We use *correlational tools* such as Kendall correlation and information gain described in Section 4.1 to characterize the observed data. While correlational analysis is important as a description of *what is*, they don't necessarily have the ability to predict *what will be*. The ability to predict often requires a deeper inference of a *causal* rule between the key factor and the viewer behavior metric. To provide an example, a correlational analysis of the observed data will be able to say that mid-roll ads have a higher completion rate than pre-roll ads in the observed data. However, this fact does necessarily imply a causal rule that states that placing an ad as mid-roll will likely cause higher completions than placing the same

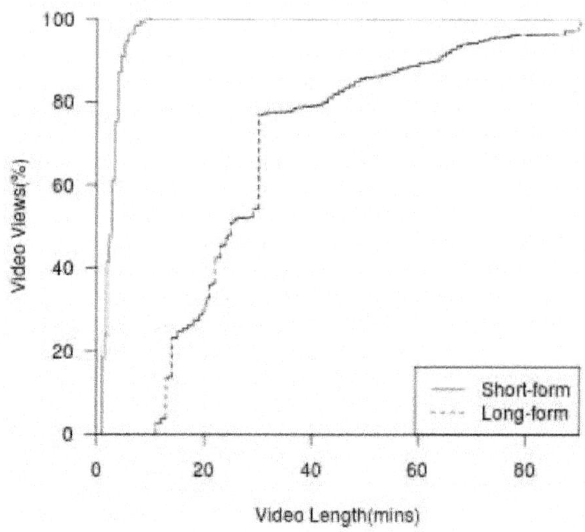

Figure 3: CDF of video length for long-form and short-form videos.

ad as a pre-roll. The value of causal inference over a purely correlational one is that it extracts general rules of viewer behavior from the data that can be applied to a more general or even different context. In our prior work [14], we introduced an innovative tool called Quasi Experimental Design (QED) that we adapted from the social and medical sciences for use in network measurement research. In this work, we take the next step and further evolve this technique to extract causal rules pertaining to video ads. We describe our technique in Section 4.2.

4.1 Correlational Analysis

To study the impact of a key factor X (say, ad length) with a viewer behavioral metric Y (say, completion rate), we start by visually plotting factor X versus metric Y in the observed data. Then, when relevant, we compute Kendall's correlation coefficient τ that takes values in the interval $[-1, 1]$ where τ near 1 means that larger values of X are associated with larger values for Y, τ near -1 means that larger values of X are associated with smaller values of Y, and τ near 0 means that X and Y are independent.

A key technique that we use to quantify the influence of factor X on metric Y is the *information gain ratio* [13]. Information gain ratio measures the extent to which the variability of Y is reduced by knowing X. That is, information gain is the entropy of Y (denoted by $H(Y)$) minus the entropy of Y given X (denoted by $H(Y|X)$). Normalizing the information gain, we obtain the information gain ratio denoted by

$$IGR(Y,X) = \frac{H(Y) - H(Y|X)}{H(Y)} \times 100.$$

It is instructive to view the two extreme cases. Suppose knowing X perfectly predicts Y, then $H(Y|X)$ is zero since there is no variability left in Y and $IGR(X,Y)$ is 100%. In the other extreme, suppose that X and Y are statistically independent. In that case, $H(Y|X)$ simply equals $H(Y)$

since knowing X says nothing about Y and $IGR(Y,X)$ is 0%. In all our results, IGR is somewhere in between and is a quantitative indicator of the extent of a factor's influence on a viewer behavioral outcome.

4.2 Causal Analysis using QEDs

A correlational analysis of factor X (say, ad length) and a viewer behavior metric Y (say, completion rate) could show that X and Y are associated with each other. A primary threat to a causal conclusion that an *independent variable* X causes the *dependent variable* Y is the existence of *confounding variables* that can impact both X and Y. To take an example that we describe in greater detail in Section 5.1.3, suppose we want to infer a causal rule that a longer ad causes viewers to complete the ad less often. Simply correlating completion rate and ad length is not sufficient. In fact, 20-second ads complete less often than 30-second ads in the observed data, apparently violating the rule. To derive a causal conclusion, one would need to account for the confounding factor of ad position, since 30-second ads are often placed as mid-rolls and as we show mid-rolls have a higher completion rate independent of length.

A primary technique for showing that an independent variable X (also called the treatment variable) has a causal impact on a dependent variable Y (called the outcome variable) is to design a *quasi-experiment*. Quasi-experiments were developed by social and medical scientists and has more than 150 years of history in those domains [20]. In particular, we use a specific type of QED called the matched design [19] where a treated individual (in our case, a view or viewer) is randomly matched with an untreated individual, where both individuals have similar values for the confounding variables. Consequently, any difference in the outcome for this pair can be attributed to the treatment. By creating a large collection of matched pairs and assessing the differential outcome of the paired individuals, one can isolate the causal impact of X on Y.

Adapting QEDs to our situation, our population typically consists of views. The independent variable is one of the factors in Table 1 (say, ad position). The treated and untreated sets have two different values of the independent variable that we want to compare (say, mid-roll versus pre-roll). Our outcome is a function of the behavioral metric under study, such as ad completion. The confounding factors that need to be matched so that they have similar values are typically other key factors in Table 1 except the independent variable that is varied, since the other factors could confound the outcome. We form comparison sets by randomly matching each treated view with an untreated view such that they have similar values for the confounding variables and differ only in the independent variable. For instance, to study the impact of ad position, we match views that belong to similar viewers watching the same ad within the same video, neutralizing the impact of the confounding variables. By forming a large number of such pairs and by studying the behavioral outcomes of matched pairs one can deduce whether or not the treatment variable X has a causal effect on variable Y, with the influence of the confounding variables neutralized.

Statistical Significance of the QED Analysis.

As with any statistical analysis, it is important to evaluate whether the results are *statistically significant* or if they could have occurred by random chance. As is customary in hypothesis testing [16], we compute the p-value which evaluates the probability that the observed outcome from a QED happened by chance, assuming that the null hypothesis holds. The null hypothesis states that there is no impact of the treatment on the outcome. To evaluate the p-value we use the sign test that is a non-parametric test that makes no distributional assumptions and is particularly well-suited for evaluating matched pairs in a QED setting [21]. A low p-value means that our results are statistically significant. The choice of the threshold is somewhat arbitrary and in medical sciences a treatment is considered effective if the p-value is at most 0.05. We can achieve much higher levels of significance owing to the large numbers of treated-untreated pairs in our QEDs (order of 100,000) in relation to what is typical in the medical sciences (in the 100's). However, our results are unambiguously significant and not very sensitive to the choice of significance level. We refer to our prior work [14] for a more detailed treatment of QEDs.

Type	Factor	IGR
Ad	Content	32.29%
	Position	15.1%
	Length	12.79%
Video	Content	23.92%
	Length	18.24%
	Provider	15.24%
Viewer	Identity	59.2%
	Geography	9.57%
	Connection Type	1.82%

Table 4: Information gain ratio (IGR) for ad completion rate.

Some Caveats.

It is important to understand the limitations of our QED tools, or for that matter *any* experimental technique of inference. Care should be taken in designing the quasi-experiment to ensure that the major confounding variables are explicitly or implicitly captured in the analysis. If there exists confounding variables that are not easily measurable (example, the gender of the viewer) and/or are not identified and controlled, these unaccounted dimensions could pose a risk to a causal conclusion, but only if they turn out to be significant. *Our work on deriving a causal relationship by systematically accounting for the confounding variables must not be viewed as a definitive proof of causality, as indeed there can be no definitive proof of causality. But, rather, our work increases the confidence in a causal conclusion by accounting for potential major sources of confounding.* This is of course a general caveat that holds for all domains across the sciences that attempt to infer causality from observational data.

5. AD COMPLETION RATE

We study the ad completion rate metric that is a key measure of ad effectiveness. The completion rate can be influenced by the characteristics of three entities that we examine in turn: the ads themselves, the videos that the ads are embedded in, and the viewer who is watching the videos and ads. We evaluate the relevance of each of these factors to the completion rate by computing their information gain ratio shown in Table 4. Enormous effort goes into creating the

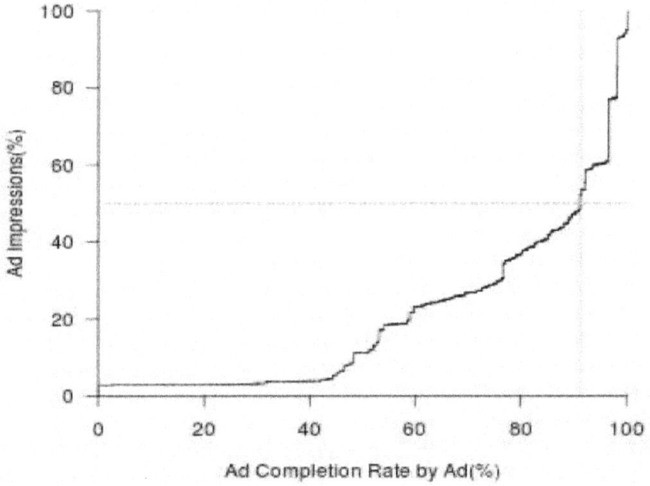

Figure 4: The percent of ad impressions y attributed to ads with ad completion rate smaller than x. 50% of the ad impressions are from ads with completion rate at most 91%.

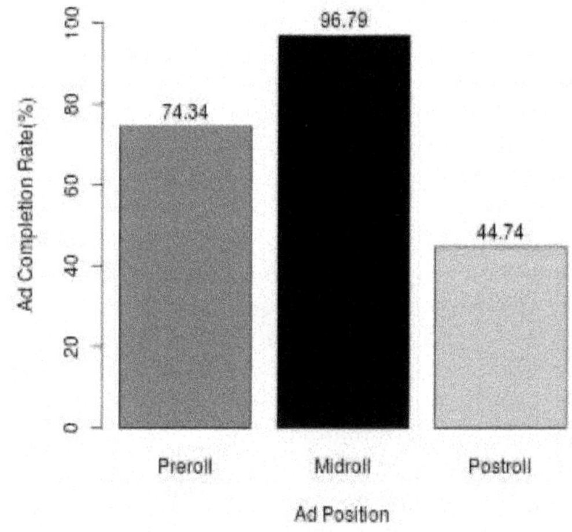

Figure 5: Mid-roll ads complete most often as the viewer is already engaged by the video and wants to watch more.

ad and video content to make it as captivating as possible. It is interesting that both show high information gain, perhaps indicating that content does matter.The information gain ratio of the viewer is very high. This is at least in part due to the fact that 51% of the viewers watched only one ad resulting in either a 0% or 100% completion rate. In those cases, knowing the viewer perfectly predicts the completion rate. Information gain is known to be counter-intuitive for factors like viewer that can take millions of values each with small individual weights. The information gain from connection type was the least, as viewers showed lesser variations in their patience for completing ads across the different connection types. This is in contrast with our earlier work on viewer patience in the context of video performance [14] where viewers with worse connectivity had more patience for a video to start up.

5.1 Impact of Ad-related Factors

We examine three factors that relate to the ad itself: the ad's content as identified by its unique name, the position in which the ad was played, and the length of the ad.

5.1.1 Ad Content

For each unique ad, we can define its completion rate as simply the fraction of ad impressions where the ad was watched to completion by the viewer. We plot the percent of ad impressions (y-axis) attributed to ads with completion rate smaller than some x-value (cf. Figure 4). We can see from the figure that ads complete at varying rates with some having low completion rates with others completing 90+% of the time. Further, 25% the ad impressions come from ads with completion rate under 66%, and 50% come from ads with completion rate under 91%.

5.1.2 Ad Position

We analyze the impact of ad position on the likelihood that a viewer watches the ad to completion. We first take a simple correlational approach of categorizing the position in which the ad was played and computing the completion rates for each category. Our analysis shows that mid-roll ads completed most often, followed by pre-roll and post-roll ads (cf. Figure 5).

Assessing Causal Impact.

Our observational results support the intuition that ads placed in the middle of the content has the most likelihood of being watched, since the viewer is engaged with the content when the ad is shown, wants to watch the rest of the video, and is thus more willing to tolerate the ad. Whereas ads placed as pre-roll run a greater risk of viewers abandoning and going elsewhere, since they have not yet started watching their content and hence are not yet engaged with it. Further, an ad placed at the end of the content as a post-roll runs an even greater risk of viewers leaving since the content that they wanted to watch has completed, and so they are less motivated to sit through an ad. Based on our observational results, we assert the following causal rule.

RULE 5.1. *On average, a viewer is more likely to complete watching an ad that is placed as a mid-roll than when the same ad is placed as a pre-roll. In turn, a viewer is more likely to complete watching an ad that is placed as a pre-roll than when the same ad is placed as a post-roll.*

Note that the correlational analysis in Figure 5 is not sufficient to show that the rule holds, as there are potential confounding factors such as the ad length, video length, content provider, viewer geography, and viewer connectivity that can negate such an assertion. For instance, the following plausible scenario could be threat to our asserted rule. It *could* be possible that mid-roll ads appear largely in longer content such as TV episodes and movies, and perhaps ads placed in longer content have higher completion rates than ads placed in shorter content *irrespective* of their position. Thus, mid-roll ads could have a higher completion, not by virtue of

Matching Algorithm

Matched: similar viewer, same ad, same video.
Independent: ad position.

1. *Match step.* Let the treated set T be the set of all views that had a mid-roll ad and let the untreated set C be the set of all views that had a pre-roll ad. For each $u \in T$ that had some ad α as mid-roll, we pick uniformly and randomly from the set of candidate views $v \in C$ such that u and v belong to similar viewers with the same geography and connection type who are watching the same video and the same ad α, except that the ad α was played as mid-roll in u but played as pre-roll in v[a]. The matched set of pairs $M \subseteq T \times C$ have the same or similar attributes for the confounding variables that are matched and differ only on the independent variable.

2. *Score step.* For each pair $(u, v) \in M$, we compute an $outcome(u, v)$ to be $+1$ if the matched ad was completed in u but not completed in v, - 1 if the matched ad was completed in v but not in u, and 0 otherwise. Now,

$$Net\ Outcome = \frac{\sum_{(u,v)\in M} outcome(u, v)}{|M|} \times 100.$$

[a]If no match v exists for a u, then no pair is formed.

Figure 6: The matching algorithm that compares ads placed as mid-roll (treated) versus pre-roll (untreated) while accounting for the other confounding variables such as the ad, video, and viewer characteristics.

them being placed in the middle of the content, but simply by being more likely to be placed in longer content.

QED. To carefully assess the impact of ad position in isolation by accounting for other potential confounding factors, we design a quasi-experiment as described by the matching algorithm in Figure 6. To compare the effect of placing an ad as mid-roll versus placing as pre-roll, the algorithm finds matched views (u, v) from two similar viewers who have the same connection type and geography. Further, the two matched views are for exactly the same video and the same ad. The primary difference between the matched views is that the ad was played in different positions, i.e., one view u has the ad as a mid-roll while the other view v has the same ad as a pre-roll. Note that a positive value for net outcome provides positive (supporting) evidence for the rule that an ad in mid-roll completes more often than the same ad as pre-roll, while a negative value provides negative evidence for the asserted rule. The algorithm in Figure 6 can be used to compare any pair of ad positions with minor modifications. For instance, to compare pre-roll with post-roll, we can apply the same algorithm with pre-roll as the treated set T and post-roll as the untreated set C.

QED Results. The results for the quasi-experiment are shown in Table 5. These results show that on average ads run in the mid-roll position are 18.1% percent more likely to complete than the same ad run in the pre-roll position for the same video content for a similar viewer. Further, ads

Treated/Untreated	Net Outcome
mid-roll/pre-roll	18.1%
pre-roll/post-roll	14.3%

Table 5: Net QED outcomes support the rule that placing an ad as a mid-roll can cause greater completions than as a pre-roll or as a post-roll.

run in the pre-roll position are 14.3% percent more likely to complete than the same ad run in the post-roll position for the same video content for a similar viewer. The results confirm the causal impact of ad position on completion rates and establish Rule 5.1 in a causal and quantitative manner. Further, using the sign test, the p-value for each quasi-experiment was at most 1.98×10^{-323}, confirming the statistical significance of the results.

Discussion.
(1) Note that the impact of ad position on ad completion rates turns out to be smaller (but still significant) when the confounding factors are accounted for than in the simpler correlational analysis of Figure 5.
(2) If mid-rolls are so effective, why not place only mid-roll ads? While our results show that positioning an ad as mid-roll increases its likelihood of completion, it is not a recommendation for advertisers to place only mid-roll ads. If an ad network wants to achieve a certain number of completed ad impressions one needs to worry about both the audience size and the ad completion rate. Audience size for pre-roll ads are larger than mid-roll ads simply because viewers drop off before the video progresses to a point where a mid-roll ad can be played. Likewise, the audience size of a mid-roll ad is typically larger than that of a post-roll ad. Thus, an ad positioning algorithm would have to carefully consider this tradeoff when deciding where to place ads. Our work provides an important input to such an algorithm, though designing optimal ad placement algorithms is beyond the scope of our work. However, our results do show that post-roll ads are generally inferior to mid-roll and pre-roll ads, since post roll ads have both smaller audience sizes and lesser ad completion rates.

5.1.3 Ad Length

We classify each ad into the three common categories, 15-second, 20-second, and 30-second ads, and compute the completion rate for each category (cf. Figure 7). Ads of length 30 seconds had the highest completion rate and 20-second ads have the least. A fundamental question is how the ad length causally influences its completion rate. With a purely correlational analysis such as that shown in Figure 7, one is liable to incorrectly conclude that 20-second ads are detrimental to ad completion and the sweet spots are 15-second and 30-second ads. Further, the results appear to contradict the intuition that longer ads are more likely to be abandoned, since viewers are more likely to loose patience.

To dig deeper, we analyzed the ad positions of the different ad lengths (cf. Figure 8). We noticed that 30-second ads are placed most often as mid-rolls since advertisers intuitively realize what we quantified in Section 5.1.2 that the viewer is more engaged in the middle of video and tend to place their longest ads there. Thus, the observed high completion rate for 30-second ads could be an influence of its ad position

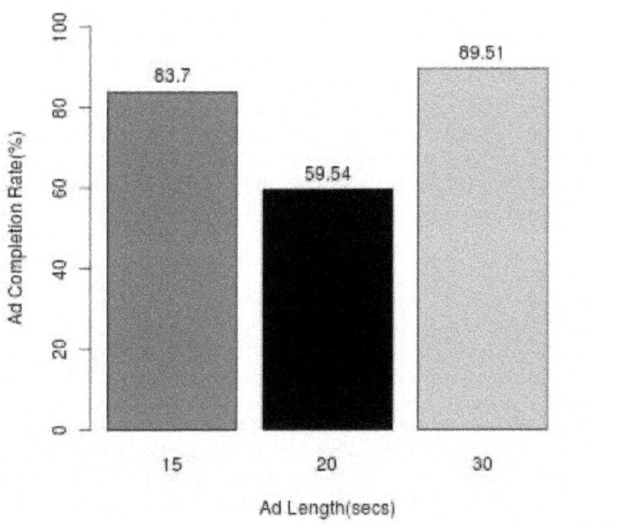

Figure 7: The measured ad completion rates in our data set did not decrease with ad length as expected. The 30-second ad, while longer, had the highest completion rate in part due to being placed more frequently in the mid-roll position.

that counteracts its larger length. Further, 15-second ads are placed most often as pre-roll and 20-second ads have a greater chance of being a post-roll than other ad lengths. We have to compensate for the confounding effect of variables such as ad position to isolate the true impact of ad length on ad completion rates. To that end, we design the quasi-experiment described below.

Assessing Causal Impact.

QED. We design a quasi-experiment where the independent variable is the ad length (15-second, 20-second, or 30-second) and the other potential confounding variables are matched. For a given pair of ad-lengths $x \neq y$ and $x, y \in \{15, 20, 30\}$ seconds, we design a quasi-experiment with the treated set consisting of videos that contained an ad of length x and the untreated set consisting of videos that contained an ad of length y. The matching algorithm that we use is similar to that in Figure 6 with the following differences. When forming the matched pair of views $(u, v) \in M$, we ensure that view u played an ad of length x and view v played an ad of length y. To account for the influence of ad position, we ensure that the ads were played in the same position. Further, we ensure that the viewers of u and v are similar with the same geography and connection type and are watching exactly same video. The scoring step is identical to the matching algorithm of Figure 6.

QED Results. The results of the quasi-experiments are shown in Table 6. Our results show that 15-second ads completed 2.86% more often than the 20-second ones in a head-to-head comparison that accounts for the confounding factors. Likewise, 20-second ads completed 3.89% more often than the 30-second ones in the head-to-head comparison. Further, using the sign test, the p-value for the quasi-experiment is at most 8.52×10^{-30}, confirming the statistical significance of the results. Thus we state the following rule.

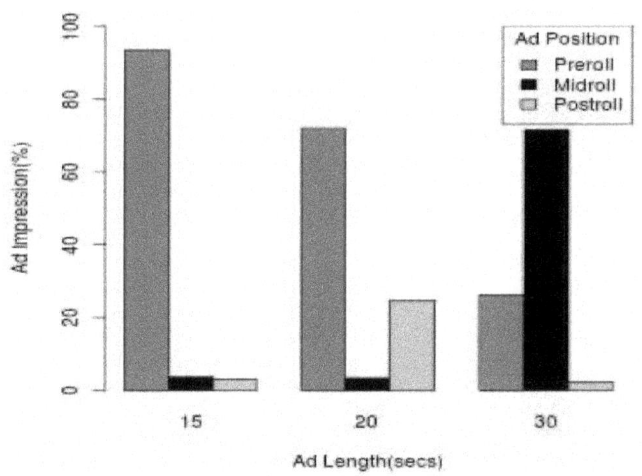

Figure 8: 30-second ads are most commonly mid-rolls, and 15-second ads most commonly pre-rolls. 20-second ads are more often post-rolls than other lengths.

Treated/Untreated	Net Outcome
15 sec/20 sec	2.86%
20 sec/30 sec	3.89%

Table 6: Net QED outcomes support the assertion that longer ads result in fewer completions.

RULE 5.2. *On average, a shorter ad is more likely to complete than a longer ad, when the other confounding factors are neutralized.*

5.2 Impact of Video-related Factors

We examine two factors that relate to the video: its content as identified by its unique url, and its length.

5.2.1 Video Content

People typically watch ads so that they are allowed to watch the video. Therefore, it is reasonable to ask what influence the video itself has on the completion rate of the ads embedded within it. Videos in our traces are uniquely identified by their urls. A video could have been viewed multiple times, and multiple ads could have been shown as part of each view. The ad completion rate of a video is simply the percentage of all ad impressions shown with that video that completed. *Ad completion rate of a video is not to be confused with the unrelated metric of video completion rate that relates to whether the video itself completed or not.* One could imagine that the ad completion rates vary from video to video, with videos with compelling content having high ad completion rates and videos with boring content having lower ad completion rates. In Figure 9, we do indeed see a large variation in ad completion rate across different videos with half the ad impressions coming from videos that have an ad completion rates of 90% or smaller.

5.2.2 Video Length

We narrow our focus to the length of video to assess how it relates to the ad completion rate. We bucket the video

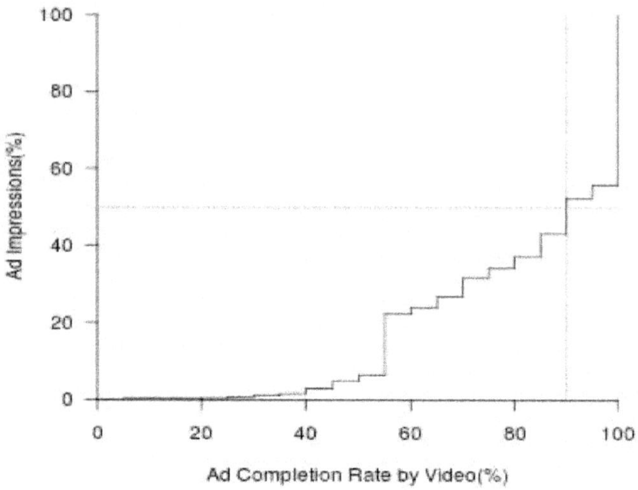

Figure 9: The percentage of ad impressions $y\%$ from videos with ad completion rate at most $x\%$, plotted in 5% buckets of ad completion rate. Half the ad impressions belonged to videos with completion rate 90% or smaller.

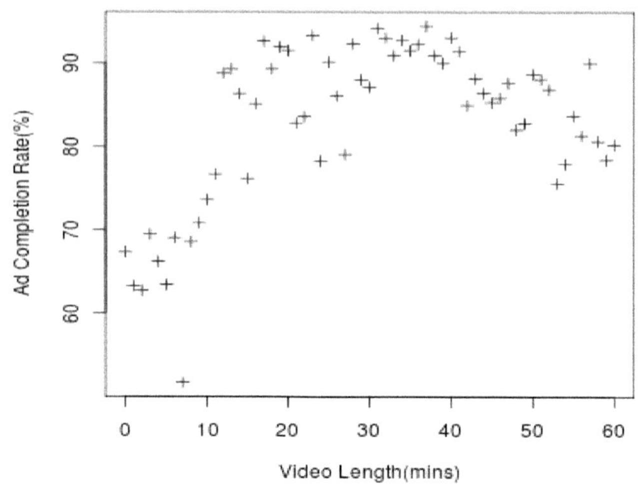

Figure 10: Ad completion rate and video length have a positive correlation with a Kendall coefficient of 0.23.

length into one minute buckets and compute the average ad completion rate of the videos in each bucket. (Each video is weighted by the number of ad impression shown with that video for computing the average.) We plot ad completion rate as a function of the video length in Figure 10. The ad completion rate shows a positive correlation with video length with Kendall correlation of 0.23. One can further bucket the videos according to whether they are short-form or long-form and one can see that short-form video has a smaller ad completion rate than the long-form (cf. Figure 11).

Our initial correlational results support the intuition that a viewer exhibits more patience for an ad to complete if they are watching long-form content such as a TV episode or a movie that are often perceived to be of greater value than short-form content. Such a phenomena is known to hold in the physical world where researchers who study the psychology of queuing [15] have shown that people have more patience for waiting in longer queues if the perceived value of the service that they are waiting for is greater. Duration of the service often influences its perceived value with longer durations often perceived as having greater value. In [14], we showed that viewers are more likely to wait without abandoning for a longer video to startup than a shorter one. Our current work implies that a similar phenomenon holds for viewer patience for ads to complete.

Assessing Causal Impact.

Based on our correlational evidence above, we would like to establish the following causal rule by a carefully designed quasi-experiment.

RULE 5.3. *On average, placing an ad in long-form video can cause a greater completion rate in comparison to placing the same ad in a short-form video.*

QED. We conduct a quasi-experiment where the independent variable is the video length (long-form versus short-form) and other potential confounding variables are matched. The matching algorithm that we use is similar to that in Figure 6 with the following differences. Since the independent variable is video length, the treated set consists of long-form videos with ads, while the untreated set consists of short-form videos with ads. When forming the matched pair of views $(u, v) \in M$, we ensure that the paired views played the same ad in the same position, i.e., the ad was pre-roll, mid-roll, or post-roll in both views. Further, the viewers of u and v are similar in that they are from the same geography and have the same connection type. Finally, even though u and v are watching different videos, one long-form and the other short-form, we ensure that they are watching videos from the same video provider. The scoring step is identical to the matching algorithm of Figure 6.

QED Results. The results of the quasi-experiment produced a net outcome of 4.2%. The positive net outcome supports Rule 5.3 by showing that on average an ad that is placed in long-form video is 4.2% more likely to complete than the same ad placed in short-form video. Further, using the sign test, the p-value for the quasi-experiment was at most 9.9×10^{-324}, confirming the statistical significance of the results.

Discussion.

The impact of video length on ad completion rate is confounded by factors such as ad position. For instance, mid-roll ads that tend to have higher completion rates are more commonly embedded in long-form video than in short-form video. Thus, the influence of ad position must be neutralized to get a clearer picture of the impact of video length in isolation. Accounting for such confounding factors in the QED analysis shows a smaller (but still significant) impact of video length, though that impact is smaller than what is implied by the simpler analysis of Figure 11.

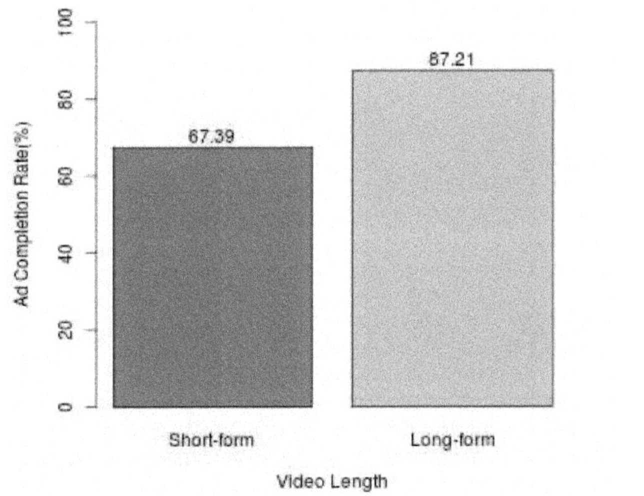

Figure 11: Ads embedded in long-form video such as a TV episode or a movie complete more often than ads embedded in short-form video such as a news clip.

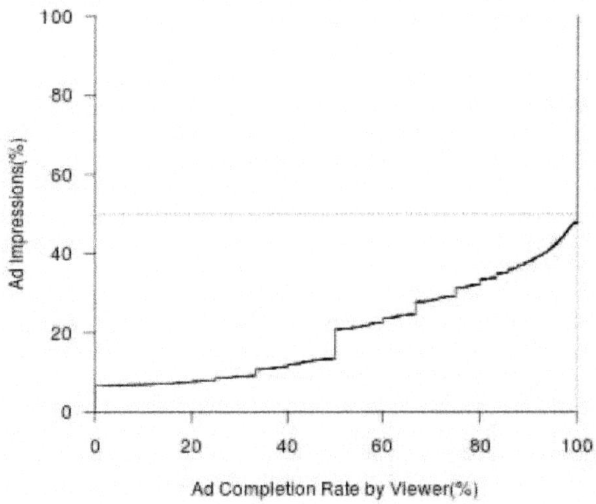

Figure 12: The percentage of ad impressions $y\%$ from viewers with completion rate at most $x\%$.

5.3 Impact of Viewer-related Factors

We examine three factors that relate to the viewer in more depth: the viewer as identified by his/her unique GUID, the viewer's geographical location, and the temporal factors when the ad was played.

5.3.1 *Viewer's identity*

We compute the ad completion rate of each viewer as simply the percentage of ad impressions that the viewer watched to completion. In Figure 12, we plot the percent of ad impressions $y\%$ that were watched by viewers with completion rate less than or equal to $x\%$. One can notice the concentrations of viewers around completion rates of 0%, 50%, and 100%. These concentrations are an artifact of the fact that a large fraction of viewers see a small number of ads. For instance, 51.2% see one ad contributing to concentrations around 0% and 100%. And, 20.9% see only two ads, contributing to concentrations around integer multiples of $1/2$. More generally, one can observe concentrations around integer multiples of $1/i$, where i is a small integer.

5.3.2 *Geography*

In Figure 13, we show the ad completion rates across different continents in the world. Perhaps the most striking contrast are between the two most trafficked continents with Europe having the lowest completion rate and North America having the highest.

5.3.3 *Temporal factors*

A plausible hypothesis that exists as a folklore is that viewers are more likely to watch ads (and complete them) in the weekend or in the evenings where they tend to be more relaxed, more patient, and have more spare time. Indeed, both video and ad viewership peaks in the late evening as shown in Figures 14 and 15 respectively. However, as shown in Figure 16, ad completion rates did not show much time-of-day variation and were nearly identical between weekday and weekend.

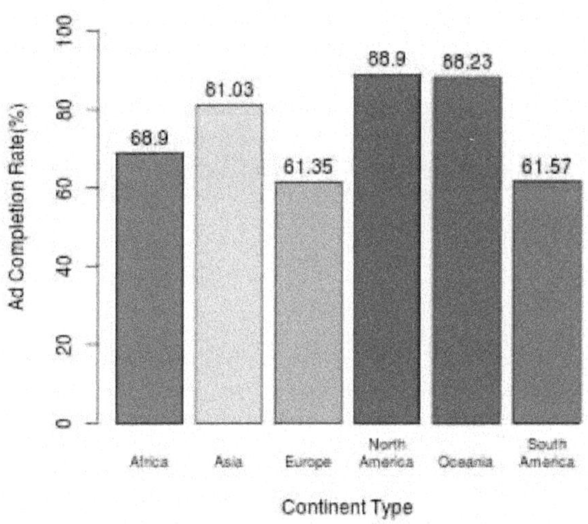

Figure 13: Europe has the smallest completion rate while North America has the greatest.

6. AD ABANDONMENT RATE

While ad completion rates measure whether viewers complete watching an ad or not, ad abandonment rates measure what portion of the ad was played before the viewer abandoned. Thus, abandonment rates provide more granular information than completion rates. We define metrics we use to study abandonment. Suppose we have an ad of length L time units. *Ad play time* x, $0 \le x \le L$, refers to the amount of time that the ad was played by the viewer

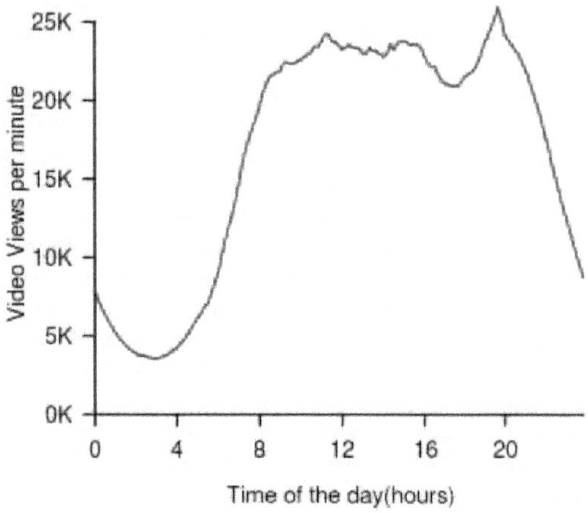

Figure 14: Video viewership is high during the day, dips slightly in the evening, and peaks in the late evening.

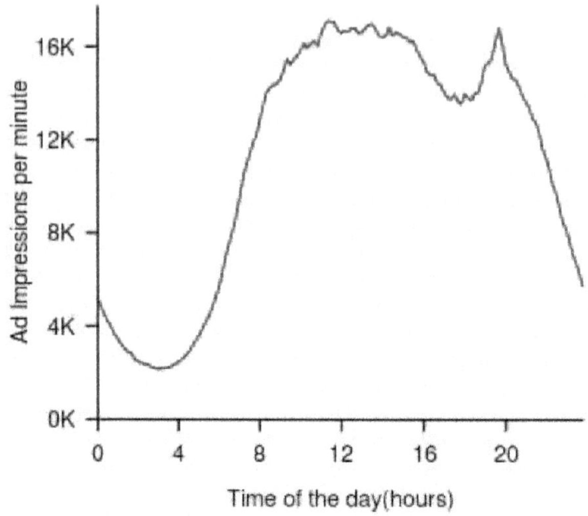

Figure 15: Ad viewership roughly follows the same trend as video viewership.

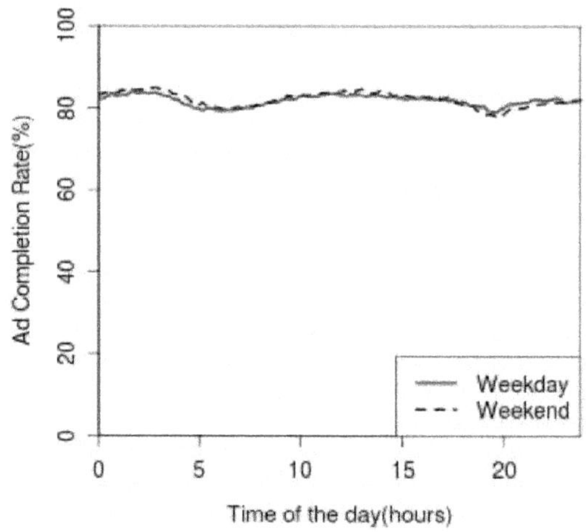

Figure 16: However, ad completion rates do not show major weekday/weekend or time-of-day variations.

during an ad impression. The abandonment rate at time x, $0 \leq x \leq L$, is the percentage of ad impressions that have ad play time less than x, i.e., the percentage of ad impressions where the ad was watched for fewer than x time units. By definition, the abandonment rate of the ad at time $x = L$ is 100 minus that ad's completion rate, since viewers who did not abandon and watched all L time units completed the ad. When aggregating abandonment rates across ads with different lengths, we plot ad abandonment rate as a function of a normalized value called *ad play percentage* which is (ad play time/ad length) $\times$ 100. Further, we define *normalized abandonment rate* to be

$$(\text{ad abandonment rate}/(100 - \text{ad completion rate})) \times 100.$$

Aggregated over all ad impressions in our study, the abandonment rate when ad play percentage equals 100% is 17.9%, which equals 100 minus the system-wide completion rate of 82.1%. In Figure 17, we plot the *normalized* abandonment rate as a function of the ad play percentage. Normalized ad abandonment rate is a concave function with viewers abandoning at a greater rate initially that subsequently tapers off. One can observe from the figure that when 25% of the ad is played, the normalized abandonment rate is already 33.3%, i.e., one-third of the viewers who eventually abandon have abandoned on or before the quarter-way mark in the ad. Likewise, at 50%, the normalized abandonment rate is 67%, i.e., two-thirds of the viewers who eventually abandon have abandoned on or before the half-way mark in the ad.

Next, in Figure 18, we plot the normalized abandonment rate as a function of ad play time to examine how viewers abandon for each of the three ad lengths. By definition, the three abandonment curves reach the normalized abandonment rate of 100% at 15, 20, and 30 seconds respectively. However, the normalized abandonment rates are nearly identical for the first few seconds and diverge beyond that point. This suggests that perhaps a significant fraction of viewers abandon as soon as the ad starts independent of its length.

Finally, in Figure 19, we show the normalized abandonment rate for the different connection types. Our results do not show major differences between the four major connection types for when viewers who eventually abandon stop watching the ad. One *plausible* explanation could be that viewers have a similar expectations on how long they would have to wait for an ad to complete, independent of their connectivity. This could be contrasted with the situation where viewers are waiting for a video to start up after a play is initiated. In this situation, viewers with high-speed connectivity (say, fiber) rightfully expect the video to start up sooner than viewers on a mobile connection. Indeed, in this situation we showed in our prior work [14] that viewers with faster connectivity abandoned the video sooner than

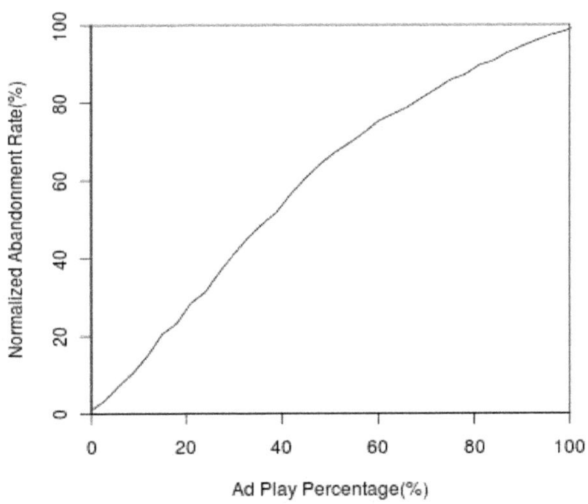

Figure 17: Normalized abandonment rate as a function of ad play percentage has a concave form. Of the viewers who eventually abandon the ad, about a third of the them have abandoned before the quarter-way mark and two-thirds of them have abandoned before the half-way mark.

those with slower connectivity, presumably because the former had greater expectations for a quicker startup and hence showed less patience for the video to start up.

7. RELATED WORK

We are not aware of large-scale scientific studies of video ads and their impact akin to our work. However, given its importance, the metrics that we study such as ad completion rate, abandonment rate are widely reported on a quarterly or yearly basis by ad networks such as FreeWheel [5], Adobe[1], and Bright Roll [3] and analytics providers such as comScore [4]. Since the business of online video relies on ad completion rates, audience size and other such metrics, the major industry standards body IAB [6] provides guidelines on how such video monetization metrics ought to be measured. Our work on systematically understanding the impact of various factors on ad viewing behavior and extracting general rules via quasi-experiments is unique and significantly contributes to our scientific understanding of ad efficacy and video monetization.

There has recently been research on understanding the impact of video performance on viewer behavior [11, 14], and in the use of client-side measurements for better video delivery [17]. These work share a commonality with our current work in the sense of using large amounts of data collected from media players, but are targeted towards very different research goals.

In terms of the techniques, our prior work [14] used quasi-experiments in a network measurement setting. In this paper, we develop the QED technique further and use it in a different context for the study of video ads. While seldom used in measurement studies of networked systems prior to our work in [14], quasi-experiments have a long and distinguished history of use in the social and medical sciences that is well documented in [20].

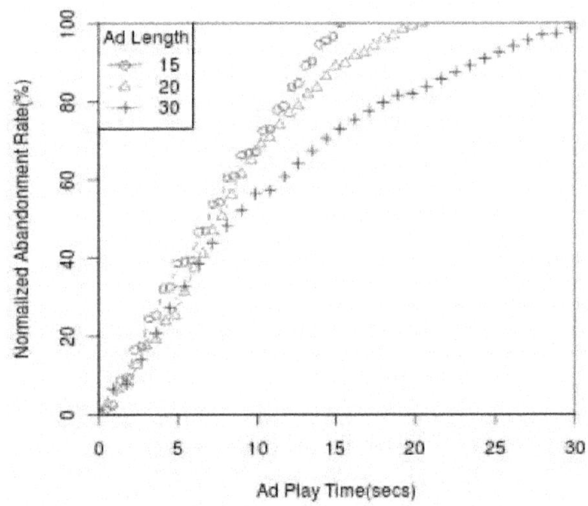

Figure 18: Normalized abandonment rate for different ad lengths.

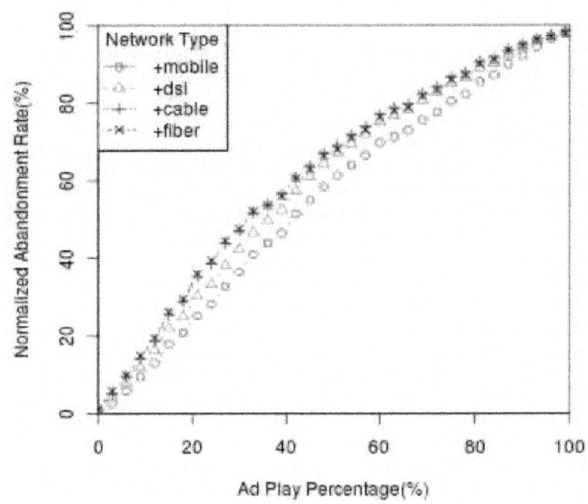

Figure 19: Normalized abandonment rates are roughly similar for the different connection types.

8. CONCLUSIONS

To our knowledge, our work is the first in-depth scientific study of video ads and their effectiveness. We explored how ad effectiveness as measured by ad completion rate is impacted by key properties of the ad, of the video, and of the viewer. A key contribution of our work is that we go beyond simple characterization to derive causal rules of viewer behavior using quasi-experimental designs (QEDs). We show that an ad is 18.1% more likely to complete when placed as a mid-roll than as a pre-roll, and 14.3% more likely to complete when placed as pre-roll than as a post-roll. Next, we show that completion rate of an ad decreases with increasing ad length. A 15-second ad is 2.9% more likely to complete than a 20-second ad, which in turn is 3.9% more likely to complete than a 30-second ad. Further, we show that the ad completion rate is influenced by the video in which the ad is placed. An ad placed in long-form videos such as movies and TV episodes is 4.2% more likely to complete than the same ad placed in short-form video such as news clips. We also studied the abandonment rate metric and showed that viewers abandon more quickly in the beginning of the ad and abandon at slower rates as the ad progresses. Our work represents a first step towards scientifically understanding video ads and viewer behavior. Such understanding is crucial for the long-term viability of online videos and the future evolution of the Internet ecosystem.

9. ACKNOWLEDGEMENTS

We thank Girish Bettadpur for his deep insights into the video ecosystem, Rick Weber for providing computing resources, and Harish Kammanahalli for his support. Any opinions expressed in this work are solely those of the authors and not necessarily those of Akamai Technologies.

10. REFERENCES

[1] Adobe Auditude. http://goo.gl/iI7Mc.
[2] *Akamai Media Analytics.* http://goo.gl/lnFwF.
[3] Bright roll. http://www.brightroll.com.
[4] comscore. http://www.comscore.com.
[5] Freewheel. http://www.freewheel.tv.
[6] Interactive Advertising Bureau (IAB). http://www.iab.net.
[7] Video Plaza. http://www.videoplaza.com.
[8] Cynthia Boris. What is the fastest growing online ad format? Video! http://goo.gl/ylnX8.
[9] Cisco. Visual Networking Index. http://bit.ly/KXDUaX.
[10] John Dilley, Bruce M. Maggs, Jay Parikh, Harald Prokop, Ramesh K. Sitaraman, and William E. Weihl. Globally distributed content delivery. *IEEE Internet Computing*, 6(5):50–58, 2002.
[11] Florin Dobrian, Vyas Sekar, Asad Awan, Ion Stoica, Dilip Joseph, Aditya Ganjam, Jibin Zhan, and Hui Zhang. Understanding the impact of video quality on user engagement. In *Proceedings of the ACM SIGCOMM Conference on Applications, Technologies, Architectures, and Protocols for Computer Communication*, pages 362–373, 2011.
[12] eMarketer. Click rates complicate online video ad metrics. http://goo.gl/vPGzs.
[13] John T Kent. Information gain and a general measure of correlation. *Biometrika*, 70(1):163–173, 1983.
[14] S Shunmuga Krishnan and Ramesh K Sitaraman. Video stream quality impacts viewer behavior: inferring causality using quasi-experimental designs. In *Proceedings of the ACM conference on Internet measurement conference*, pages 211–224. ACM, 2012.
[15] R.C. Larson. Perspectives on queues: Social justice and the psychology of queueing. *Operations Research*, pages 895–905, 1987.
[16] E.L. Lehmann and J.P. Romano. *Testing statistical hypotheses.* Springer Verlag, 2005.
[17] X. Liu, F. Dobrian, H. Milner, J. Jiang, V. Sekar, I. Stoica, and H. Zhang. A case for a coordinated internet video control plane. In *Proceedings of the ACM SIGCOMM Conference on Applications, Technologies, Architectures, and Protocols for Computer Communication*, pages 359–370, 2012.
[18] E. Nygren, R.K. Sitaraman, and J. Sun. The Akamai Network: A platform for high-performance Internet applications. *ACM SIGOPS Operating Systems Review*, 44(3):2–19, 2010.
[19] H. Oktay, B.J. Taylor, and D.D. Jensen. Causal discovery in social media using quasi-experimental designs. In *Proceedings of the First Workshop on Social Media Analytics*, pages 1–9. ACM, 2010.
[20] W.R. Shadish, T.D. Cook, and D.T. Campbell. *Experimental and quasi-experimental designs for generalized causal inference.* Houghton, Mifflin and Company, 2002.
[21] D.A. Wolfe and M. Hollander. Nonparametric statistical methods. *Nonparametric statistical methods*, 1973.

Follow the Green: Growth and Dynamics in Twitter Follower Markets

Gianluca Stringhini, Gang Wang, Manuel Egele†, Christopher Kruegel, Giovanni Vigna, Haitao Zheng, Ben Y. Zhao
Department of Computer Science, UC Santa Barbara
†Carnegie Mellon University
{gianluca, gangw, chris, vigna, htzheng, ravenben}@cs.ucsb.edu, megele@cmu.edu

ABSTRACT

The users of microblogging services, such as Twitter, use the count of followers of an account as a measure of its reputation or influence. For those unwilling or unable to attract followers naturally, a growing industry of "Twitter follower markets" provides followers for sale. Some markets use fake accounts to boost the follower count of their customers, while others rely on a pyramid scheme to turn non-paying customers into followers for each other, and into followers for paying customers. In this paper, we present a detailed study of Twitter follower markets, report in detail on both the static and dynamic properties of customers of these markets, and develop and evaluate multiple techniques for detecting these activities. We show that our detection system is robust and reliable, and can detect a significant number of customers in the wild.

Categories and Subject Descriptors

J.4 [**Computer Applications**]: Social and Behavioral Sciences; K.6 [**Management of Computing and Information Systems**]: Security and Protection

General Terms

Measurement, Security

Keywords

Twitter, Follower Markets, Sybils, Online Social Networks

1. INTRODUCTION

Microblogging services such as Twitter have become important tools for personal communication as well as spreading news. Twitter users can "follow" accounts that they find interesting, and start receiving status updates that these accounts share in real-time. As Twitter use grows, the influence and reputation of a person or business entity are increasingly associated with their number of Twitter followers [8, 18]. Third party services, such as Klout, estimate the influence of accounts ranging from normal users to celebrities and politicians [19] based on a series of features such as the number of followers and the frequency with which content is re-shared.

IMC'13, October 23–25, 2013, Barcelona, Spain.
Copyright 2013 ACM 978-1-4503-1953-9/13/10 ...$15.00.
http://dx.doi.org/10.1145/2504730.2504731.

For many users hoping to achieve fame and "influence" on Twitter, growing a significant follower population is a difficult and time consuming process. Some follow random users in the hope that these users might follow back. Others join groups where each member agrees to follow all the others in the group. Unfortunately, none of these techniques are efficient enough for users who need large numbers of followers fast [16].

The demand of quick Twitter followers has led to the growth of an industry that caters to users who want to quickly grow their population of followers, even if it means paying for them. Some of these "customers," such as politicians or celebrities, might want to give the appearance of a large fan base [4, 9, 10]. Other, more malicious entities seek followers so they can quickly spread malware and spam [12, 14, 29, 30]. We refer to such enterprises as *Twitter follower markets* and to the operators as *follower merchants*.

There are two ways for follower merchants to deliver followers to their customers. One way is to create fake accounts that imitate real users [10, 31, 33, 34]. However, these accounts have less "value," as quantified by popular metrics that establish reputation based on quantities such as a user's follower to followee ratio and tweets per follower. Fake accounts, or *Sybils*, provide lower additive value in this system, given their small follower counts and low volume of tweets. On the other hand, legitimate accounts are more attractive as followers to cybercriminals, because these accounts have real followers, share content, and add real value to customers seeking a higher reputation. Unfortunately for these markets, legitimate users are unlikely to voluntarily follow their customers, unless they were first compromised or controlled without their knowledge[1].

In our work, we perform a detailed measurement study of Twitter follower markets. Note that unlike prior work that studied black markets for social network accounts [25, 31], these merchants only provide "followers," not access to compromised or fake accounts. In our work, we observe two types of behavior in Twitter follower merchants. First, some merchants provide their customers with fake accounts (*i.e.*, Sybils). Second, we also observe the rise of a new type of follower merchants centered on pyramid schemes. In this case, follower merchants lure in unsuspecting users with promises of free followers, compromise their accounts, and then add them as new followers to each other and (more importantly) to other paying customers; Since these accounts are compromised by the market operators, we call them *victims*. We call the operators of pyramid markets *pyramid merchants*.

In this paper, we perform a comprehensive study of Twitter follower markets. First, we study in detail both the static properties

[1]We consider an account as compromised if a third party obtained access to it, and is using it in a way that violates Twitter's terms of service [3].

and the dynamic behavior of market customers. Then, we develop and evaluate multiple techniques for detecting these activities. We first introduced the notion of Twitter follower markets and some ad hoc observations of pyramid merchants in our preliminary work [28]. Compared to our preliminary work, we make the following contributions:

- We explored methods to detect follower markets and proactively obtained ground-truth composed of 69,222 victim accounts, and 2,909 market customers.
- We analyzed the characteristics of victim accounts and market customers, with particular focus on the dynamics of their followers. Intuitively, we expect customers of follower markets to experience dramatic increases in the number of followers followed by a steady decrease as compromised accounts unfollow. This happens because victim accounts did not willingly follow the customers, and often times they find the content that the customer posts uninteresting.
- We developed a detection system that uses follower dynamics to detect the customers of follower markets. We show that our system is robust and reliable, and that it is able to detect a large number of customers in the wild.

2. METHODOLOGY AND BACKGROUND

According to anonymous follower merchants, follower markets have already become a multimillion-dollar business [26]. Driven by their increasing popularity and effects on Twitter's ecosystem, we want to understand via empirical measurements the key characteristics of these markets, particularly the newly-emerged *pyramid merchants*, and develop effective countermeasures against them. Our study is motivated by two observations.

First, there is no concrete understanding on the characteristics of these markets as well as the key factors leading to their success and impact. To the best of our knowledge, the only known prior work is our preliminary study which detected a follower market [11].

Second, there are no effective countermeasures against these markets and follower merchants. Existing detection techniques can spot fake accounts or spammers [5, 14, 29], but are not effective against pyramid merchants as the purchased followers are real users. Instead, we believe that a fundamentally different method can effectively address this challenge. Specifically, if one can identify customers who bought Twitter followers from these markets, then once Twitter starts to systematically and heavily penalize or even suspend their customers, the markets will soon lose their revenue stream and eventually go out of business.

In the remainder of the paper, we describe our efforts to empirically characterize the accounts involved in follower markets and build detection algorithms. In Section 2.1 we briefly introduce the operations of Pyramid merchants to provide background for our study. We then discuss our data collection process (Section 3), followed by analysis on the market characteristics (Section 4) and its key players (Section 5). We then use insights from our analysis to develop a comprehensive detection system for identifying the market customers and to experiment on real Twitter data (Section 6).

2.1 Background: Pyramid Merchants

Unlike typical Twitter follower markets that trade fake accounts, pyramid markets sell real accounts as followers. They usually offer two kinds of subscriptions: *premium* and *free*. Premium users pay to get the services from the market, and are mostly companies or

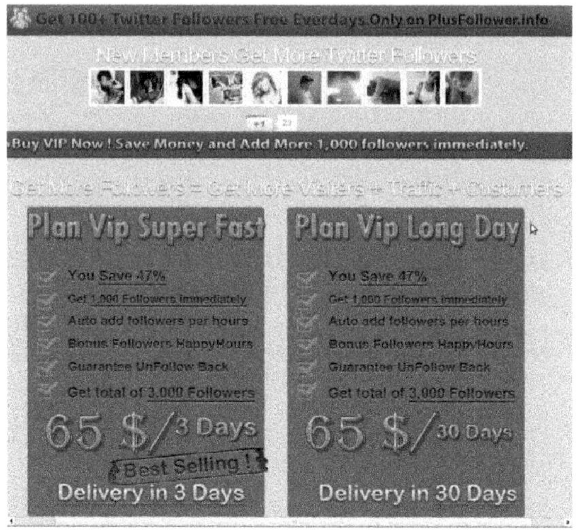

Figure 1: A Twitter follower market website. The market provides two options, depending on how fast the customer wants to obtain his followers.

Figure 2: A tweet advertising a Twitter follower market. The link in the tweet points to the homepage of the Twitter follower market being advertised.

individuals who are interested in increasing their follower count and reaching a broader audience (we refer to them as *customers*).

Free users, on the other hand, are typically offered a small number of followers for free. In exchange for this service, free users are requested to give control of their account to the pyramid merchant. The merchant gains control of a user account by asking the user to authorize an OAuth application [2], or by having the user give away her profile name and password. Because these "free" subscribers give control of their account to a third party, we consider them as compromised, and refer to them as *victims*. The pyramid merchants leverage their victims to carry out many tasks, from following other accounts to periodically tweeting advertisements for the markets (see Figure 2 for an example). Although certain pyramid markets announce to their victims that their accounts might be used to follow other people or to send tweets, this practice violates Twitter's term of service [3].

In their attempt to shut down market operations, Twitter blocks the OAuth applications that are used by such schemes. However, pyramid merchants overcome this problem by periodically creating new OAuth applications and using the victims' credentials to authorize such applications [11]. Furthermore, to hide their involvement in any follower market, customers who purchased followers typically add these followers slowly. In fact, some follower markets advertise that it can take up to one month for a customer to add 3,000 followers.

3. DATA COLLECTION

In this section, we present our efforts to collect a large set of Twitter accounts that actively interact with follower markets, essentially building the ground-truth data on customers who bought followers from the markets and victims who were compromised by the markets and traded as followers. Our data collection includes two steps. First, we locate popular follower markets. Second, we collect accounts of customers and victims as well as legitimate Twitter users for further analysis. In this section, we describe these two steps in detail.

3.1 Locating Follower Markets

In general, a Twitter follower market offers services through a website where customers can directly make purchases. An example is shown in Figure 1. To locate as many markets as possible, we explored three different approaches, including *locating suspicious clusters of Twitter accounts*, *searching for advertisement tweets*, and *querying a search engine*. We found that the search engine-based approach is the most effective and thus used this technique for our subsequent data collection. Next, we discuss each method in detail.

Clustering Twitter Accounts. We first encountered evidence of Twitter follower markets from our previous study [11], in which we detected a viral Twitter campaign advertising a follower market (`Bigfollow.net`). To attract customers, follower markets often send advertising tweets (with a link to the follower market's website) using compromised Twitter accounts under their control (*i.e.*, victims). Therefore, one way of detecting these markets is by grouping Twitter accounts that demonstrate similar suspicious behaviors (*e.g.*, sending similar tweets) [11]. This method, however, has two key limitations. First, not all Twitter follower markets use Twitter to promote themselves (in particular, the non-pyramid markets typically do not); therefore this method cannot provide full coverage of popular markets. Second, this method also requires significant manual effort to examine suspicious clusters and exclude benign ones and those representing non-Twitter-market campaigns.

Searching Advertisement Tweets. The second approach is to directly search for tweets advertising the follower markets using the Twitter API. These tweets usually contain links pointing to the markets and keywords like "buy Twitter followers" or "get more followers" (Figure 2). Therefore, by searching for specific keywords in the tweet stream, we could identify various markets. After performing the above keyword search from the 1.4 billion tweets that we collected from Twitter's stream, we identified eleven Twitter follower markets that send advertisement tweets in bulk. The limitation of this approach is that it requires access to a large volume of tweets and it is also prone to false positives. Since our tweet dataset was collected between May 13, 2011 and August 12, 2011, we can only identify markets that actively advertised during this time frame.

Querying Search Engine. As it is difficult to gain a comprehensive picture of the follower markets directly from Twitter, we decided to leverage search engines. To attract customers, these markets should be able to make their sites indexed by Google. We confirmed this hypothesis by sending the query "more Twitter followers" to Google and analyzing the returned results. Other than links to the actual Twitter follower markets, we also found links pointing to news or blog articles talking about Twitter follower markets. For this reason, we cannot solely rely on the results returned by Google to detect follower markets.

To distinguish between real Twitter follower markets and benign websites, we developed a Support Vector Machine (SVM) classifier. We extracted 30 features from the URL, domain, and HTML content of the market website. The detailed features are listed in Table 1. The keywords were chosen by mining the web pages of known Twitter follower markets. This effectively exclude news article pages talking about markets, since the index page of news portals usually has no Twitter follower markets features.

Feature Category	Feature Description
URL (3)	Level of URL depth Length of URL Length of domain
HTML (7)	Number of $ sign Number of hyper links Number of outgoing links Number of image tags Number of Javascript tags Number of buttons Word count
Keywords (20)	twitter, followers, buy, social, service, facebook, services, youtube, views, likes, contact, order, within, fans, real, marketing, 100, privacy, account, website

Table 1: Features to locate Twitter follower markets by querying search engines.

Market	$ for 10K Followers	$ for 1K (Re)Tweets	Twitter Only?	Pyramid?
newfollow.info	$216	N/A	YES	YES
bigfolo.com	$91.99	N/A	YES	YES
bigfollow.net	$70	$500	YES	YES
intertwitter.com	$65	$550	NO	NO
justfollowers.in	$95	N/A	NO	YES
twiends.com	$169	N/A	YES	YES
socialwombat.com	$49	$79	YES	NO
devumi.com	$64	$97	NO	NO
hitfollow.info	$214	N/A	YES	YES
plusfollower.info	$214	N/A	YES	YES
buyactivefans.com	$40	N/A	NO	NO
getmorefollows.com	$127	N/A	YES	NO
followmania.co	$48	N/A	YES	YES

Table 2: Popular Twitter follower markets. Different markets have different prices, and some of them are not Twitter-specific. The follower markets that do not use a pyramid scheme are likely selling fake accounts as followers.

To evaluate the effectiveness of this method, we manually verified the first 100 websites returned by Google, and constructed a ground-truth set with 56 Twitter follower markets and 44 benign websites. A ten-fold cross-validation leads to a 97% accuracy. On February 2013, the query "more Twitter followers" offered 7,210,000 results in Google, while Google only returned the first 680 sites. We ran the classifier on all the returned 680 websites and located 303 Twitter markets. In Table 2 we list the 13 highest-ranked markets by Google. We believe this approach provides a reasonable coverage of current popular Twitter follower markets.

3.2 Locating Customers and Victims

Our next step is to locate a large set of accounts corresponding to customers and victims of the follower markets, as well as legitimate Twitter users. We use these sets of accounts as ground-truth for our further experiments.

Market	Victims	Customers
BigFollow	16,185	2,781
Bigfolo	1,404	37
JustFollowers	20,897	91
NewFollow	10,307	N/A
InterTwitter	20,429	N/A
Total	69,222	2,909

Table 3: Identified market victims and customers among the six Twitter follower markets that we monitored.

Collecting Market Victims. To identify a large number of ground-truth victim accounts, we purchased followers from the most popular follower markets in Table 2: *NewFollow*, *Bigfolo*, *InterTwitter* and *JustFollowers*. Here *InterTwitter* is the only non-pyramid market as it does not offer free-subscriptions.

Specifically, we registered one account as premium user for *Bigfolo* and *NewFollow*, and two accounts each at *InterTwitter* and *JustFollowers*. Since our accounts were newly-created with no followers, we consider any account that started following them a market victim. We made our purchases on March 27, 2013. Within two weeks we identified 53,037 victims (1,404 on *Bigfolo*, 20,429 on *InterTwitter*, 20,897 on *JustFollowers*, and 10,307 on *NewFollow*). However, at the end of the first week, Twitter banned two of our premium accounts, one at *JustFollowers* and another one at *Bigfolo*.

Unfortunately, we were not able to buy followers from the market *BigFollow*, the third highest ranked market, because their website did not accept payments from our credit card. Fortunately, the victims in this market are very recognizable, because they post very specific tweets (i.e., the tweets contain the hashtag *#BigFollow*). Therefore, we searched Twitter for tweets advertising this market, and considered any account posting such tweets as a victim. In total, we identified 16,185 victims for this market.

Overall, we were able to identify 69,222 victims. We refer to them as $\mathbf{A}_v$. A detailed breakdown of victims per market can be found in Table 3.

Collecting Market Customers. The core part of a Twitter follower market business is to sell followers. Therefore, to understand the phenomenon we need to monitor and study the characteristics of a set of customers in the wild. The problem with selecting a set of customers is that it is hard to determine which accounts purchased followers on Twitter. To overcome this problem, we registered 180 newly-created Twitter accounts as victims to the target follower markets (*BigFollow*, *NewFollow*, *Bigfolo*, and *JustFollowers*). We call this set of accounts $\mathbf{A}_g$. Since the accounts in $\mathbf{A}_g$ were newly-created, and had no followers or friends [2], we can assume that any account that established a friend or follower relation with them is somehow involved in the follower market (as either a victim or a customer). We did not subscribe to *InterTwitter*, because their website does not offer a free subscription service. This in fact raises an interesting question: where do the victims of this market come from? One possibility is that *InterTwitter* does not use free-subscribers as victims but uses massively-created fake accounts to follow their customers. We will further explore this intuition in the data analysis section (Section 5).

As previously explained, after signing up to the follower market, victims will start following customers, as well as other victims. For this reason, we cannot build a set of known customers just by looking at the friends of the accounts in $\mathbf{A}_g$. Instead, we leverage the following observation: market victims periodically post tweets that advertise the market. Such tweets are likely to be similar across the victims of the same market. To detect customers among the friends of the accounts in $\mathbf{A}_g$, we apply the following algorithm. This process returns a set $\mathbf{A}_c$ of identified customers.

1. At the beginning, the set of known customers $\mathbf{A}_c$ is empty.

2. For each account a in $\mathbf{A}_g$, we retrieve the tweets posted by a. We call this set $\mathbf{T}_a$. We also retrieve the set of friends that a has, and call it $\mathbf{F}_a$.

3. For each account b in $\mathbf{F}_a$, we extract the set of tweets posted by b. We call this set $\mathbf{T}_b$.

4. For each tuple $< t_1, t_2 >$ composed of one tweet from $\mathbf{T}_a$ and one tweet from $\mathbf{T}_b$, we compare t_1 and t_2. If t_1 and t_2 are similar, we consider b as a victim, and move to the next account in $\mathbf{F}_a$. More precisely, we consider t_1 and t_2 to be similar if they share four or more consecutive words (4-grams). This similarity metric has already been used in previous work, and has proven to be robust [11]. Note that the accounts in $\mathbf{A}_g$ never posted any legitimate tweet, therefore our approach will only match tweets that advertise follower markets and not, for example, popular tweets that both accounts happen to have shared.

5. If no pair $< t_1, t_2 >$ resulted similar, it means that b has never advertised the follower market. Therefore, we assume that the owner of b paid to get her followers, and add b to the set of known customers $\mathbf{A}_c$.

In total, we identified 2,909 market customers by using the described algorithm, 2,781 from *BigFollow*, 37 from *Bigfolo* and 91 from *JustFollowers*. We did not manage to identify any customer for the market *NewFollow*, because Twitter suspended our victim accounts shortly after we subscribed them, probably because the tweets advertising the market that these accounts sent were considered spam. A summary of identified customer and victim accounts is shown in Table 3. We noticed a disparity in the number of customers identified from these markets. The reason might be that some markets are more successful than others in attracting customers; alternatively, it might be that some markets have more victims, and therefore each victim follows a smaller number of customers. We will investigate these possibilities in Section 5.4. In the rest of the paper, we refer to the entire set of 2,909 customers as $\mathbf{A}_c$.

Selecting Legitimate Users. Finally, we wanted to gather a large number of regular Twitter users to draw comparison with market customers. At a high level, we selected two sets of legitimate users for different purposes. First, we picked one set of 2 million randomly-sampled users $\mathbf{A}_{lr}$ from the general Twitter population, which serves as baseline for our profile analysis. The second set, that we call $\mathbf{A}_l$, is our key legitimate user dataset, which focused on legitimate users who are comparable with market customers. For $\mathbf{A}_l$, we excluded users that are obviously non-customers (*i.e.* users with a relatively low follower count). To this end, we constructed $\mathbf{A}_l$ by extracting another two million unique accounts whose number of followers exceeded 100. In our later analysis (Section 5), we will show that choosing 100 as a threshold is reasonable. Both legitimate user sets were sampled from our dataset of a stream of 10% of all public Twitter messages [11]. Note that we cannot be sure that the accounts in $\mathbf{A}_l$ and $\mathbf{A}_{lr}$ did not purchase followers on Twitter. However, since the accounts were collected at random, we are confident that they are representative enough of the Twitter

[2]In Twitter's jargon, a friend is a profile that the account follows.

Market	Tweets	Victims
BigFollow	662,858	90,083
Bigfolo	4,732,016	611,825
JustFollowers	302	257
NewFollow	77,865	38,341
InterTwitter	0	0
Total	5,473,041	740,506

Table 4: Tweets advertising markets and victims identified in the wild. These results show that some markets are significantly larger than others.

population, and that they will show different characteristics than the set $\mathbf{A}_c$, that is solely composed of customers. In fact, the results reported in the rest of the paper confirm this assumption.

Summary. In total, we identified 4 million legitimate users ($\mathbf{A}_{lr}$ and $\mathbf{A}_l$), 69,220 market victims ($\mathbf{A}_v$) and 2,909 market customers ($\mathbf{A}_c$) for analysis. Using this dataset as our ground-truth, we analyze the behavior patterns of different parties that interact with Twitter follower markets. Then, we leverage potential behavior features to build systems to detect customers on Twitter. We will illustrate the details of the performed analysis and of the proposed detection in the following sections.

4. ANALYZING FOLLOWER MARKETS

In this section we analyze the Twitter follower markets that we discovered. In particular, we study the size of these markets and the price distribution for their offered services.

4.1 Market Prices

All the markets that we found offer Twitter followers for sale. Some of them offer additional services related to Twitter, such as having a tweet chosen by the customer retweeted a number of times. In addition, some of the markets do not only provide Twitter-related services but also target other social networks such as Facebook and Youtube.

The price for buying Twitter followers varies depending on the market, and ranges from \$40 to \$216 for 10,000 followers. Some markets go further, offering followers of a certain guaranteed "quality" (for example, each of the purchased followers will have 100 or more followers of their own). Intuitively, having "high quality" followers makes it possible to reach a broader audience, in case some of them retweet messages posted by the customer. The price for promotional tweets and retweets on the markets that we identified varies between \$79 and \$550 for 1,000 tweets (or retweets). In general, pyramid markets charge higher than non-pyramid markets as they can deliver real, compromised users as followers.

4.2 Market Sizes

We want to understand how prominent the Twitter follower markets are within the Twitter ecosystem, and in particular how many victims they are able to recruit. To answer this question, we searched for tweets advertising these markets in the Twitter stream. In particular, we had access to a random 10% sample of all public tweets for the period between January 16, 2013 and May 7, 2013. This accounted for 3.3 billion total tweets. To detect tweets advertising the markets in this stream, we proceeded as follows:

1. We group victim accounts in $\mathbf{A}_v$ based on the market that they belong to. For each market, we extract the set of victims of that particular market, which we call $\mathbf{A}_m$.
2. We group the tweets sent by the accounts in $\mathbf{A}_m$, based on text similarity. In particular, we group together those tweets that share four or more identical words.
3. For each group of tweets of size greater than one, we extract the URLs and hashtags contained in those tweets. We add these keywords to the set $\mathbf{K}_m$ of keywords indicative of the market m.
4. For each keyword in $\mathbf{K}_m$, we search the Twitter stream for tweets containing that word. We consider every hit as a tweet advertising the market m, and the account that posted the tweet as a victim of m.

The results are shown in Table 4. Although these results were derived from only 10% of the total tweets, the sheer volume of the victims is significant, confirming the impact of the follower markets on Twitter. Moreover, Twitter has a particularly hard time in dealing with this problem: since victims are usually legitimate accounts that got compromised, Twitter cannot just suspend them, but has to try alternative mitigation techniques, such as blocking the OAuth applications that are used by these markets.

Across the five identified markets, *Bigfolo* appears to be larger than the others, followed by *BigFollow* and *NewFollow*. *JustFollowers* appears to be considerably smaller. Our analysis on *InterTwitter* terminated at step 2 where we did not find similar tweets across victims advertising the market. Since *InterTwitter* does not offer a free subscription, it is likely that the victims are fake accounts with no real followers. Thus there is no point for victims to post advertisement tweets to attract more victims.

We then looked at the number of victims who advertise more than one market. These are users who, to get more "free" followers, handed out their credentials to multiple markets. In total, we found that only 22,702 out of 740K (or 3%) victims advertise more than one market.

We suspect that the size difference across these markets is the key reason of why the number of identified customers varies significantly across the markets. In particular, the fact that *Bigfolo* has so many more victims might mean that each victim follows a smaller number of customers, and therefore makes it harder for us to identify these customers. In Section 5.4, we will discuss more on how each follower merchant "distributes" their victims to service their customers.

5. ANALYZING CUSTOMERS AND VICTIMS

In this section, we analyze the characteristics of the key players of Twitter follower markets: market customers and victims, and we compare them to the characteristics of regular Twitter accounts. The goal is to identify behavioral features that can effectively distinguish between the follower purchasing phenomenon and an organic follower growth, typical of legitimate users.

5.1 Customer Account Characteristics

We first characterize the differences between market customers and legitimate accounts. We start by analyzing static characteristics of Twitter accounts, such as the current number of followers or friends that an account has. Figure 3 shows the cumulative distribution function (CDF) of the number of followers of market customers in $\mathbf{A}_c$ and 2 million randomly-sampled legitimate users $\mathbf{A}_{lr}$. Compared with regular Twitter users, market customers typically have more followers. The figure also indicates that customers typically have more than 100 followers.

Another interesting aspect is that, as Figure 4 shows, legitimate Twitter accounts typically have a more balanced follower-to-friend

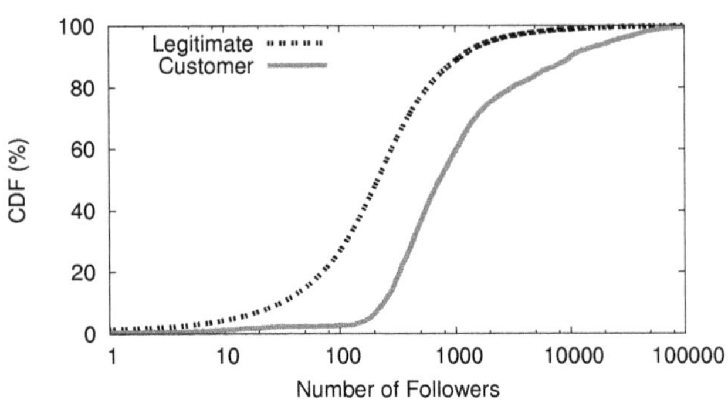

Figure 3: Cumulative distribution function of the number of followers of market customers, compared to legitimate users. Customers typically have one hundred followers or more.

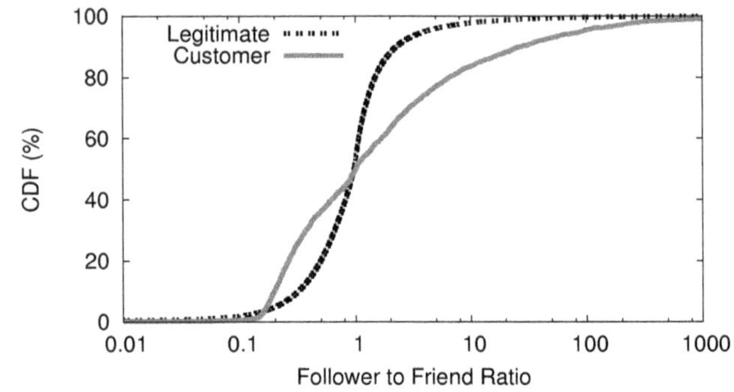

Figure 4: Cumulative distribution function of the follower to friend ratio of market customers, compared to legitimate users. 20% of market customers have at least ten times more followers than friends.

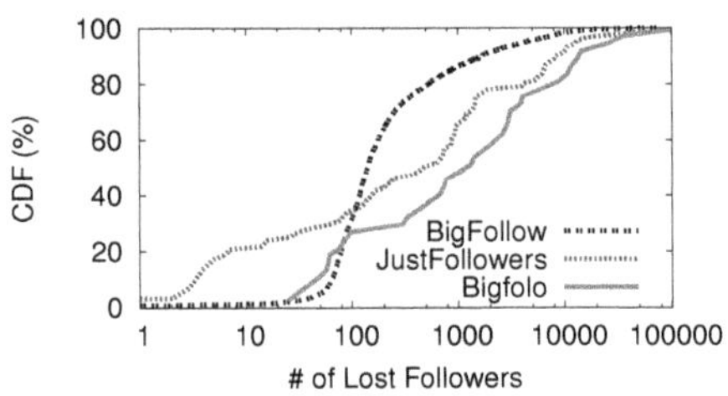

Figure 5: Cumulative distribution function of the number of followers that ever unfollowed the customer.

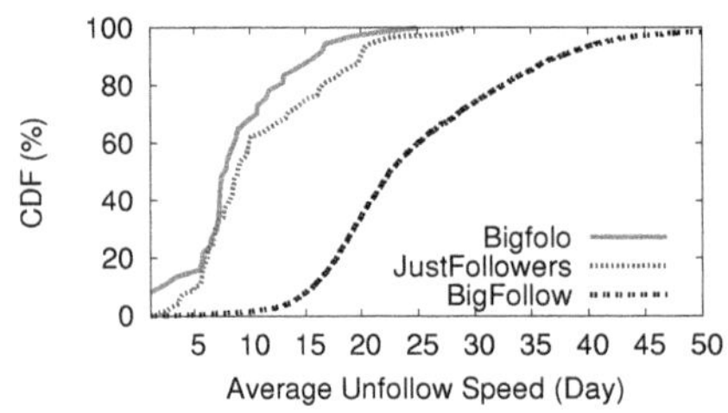

Figure 6: Cumulative distribution function of the average time it takes before followers unfollow the customer.

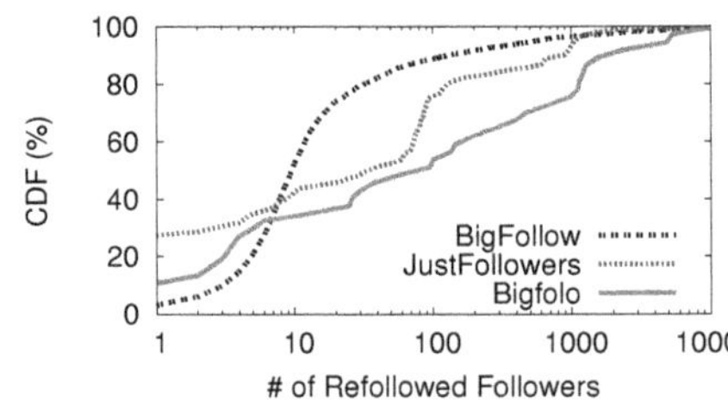

Figure 7: Cumulative distribution function of the number of followers that ever unfollow-then-refollow the customer.

ratio (*i.e.*, the number of followers an account has, divided by its number of friends) compared to accounts that purchased followers. In particular, 20% of the customers in $\mathbf{A}_c$ have at least ten times more followers than friends, while 98% of legitimate users in $\mathbf{A}_{lr}$ cannot achieve this. In addition, about 50% of the customers have more friends than followers. It turns out that despite buying followers, these customers also use other techniques to increase their number of followers, such as massively following random users with the expectation that some of them will follow back.

To analyze the people who followed the customers in $\mathbf{A}_c$, we crawled the follower list of the accounts in $\mathbf{A}_c$ on an hourly basis, from January 23, 2013 to May 7, 2013. We call the sequence of the followers for an account, crawled over multiple hours, *follower dynamics* for that account.

One of our hypothesis is that some market victims, who unwillingly followed a customer, would eventually unfollow the customer. So here, we try to verify whether customers in $\mathbf{A}_c$ lose followers over time. Figure 5 plots the distribution of the number of followers that ever unfollowed the accounts in $\mathbf{A}_c$. It shows that almost all the customers from the three markets have lost followers during our observation time. About 70% of customers have lost more than 100 followers. Figure 6 shows how long the "following" relationship will last before followers unfollow the accounts in $\mathbf{A}_c$. It shows that the *BigFollow* market provides followers with better loyalty, as 80% of the average "following" relationship can last at least 2 weeks. Victims of the other two markets usually unfollow the customer within 2 weeks.

We also observe that some followers who unfollowed customers would follow them again. Figure 7 shows the number of followers that ever unfollow-then-refollow the customer. This might indicate that some customers have bought the service more than once, and that the markets use the same set of victims for the same customer.

5.2 Follower Dynamics

We then wanted to understand whether there are differences in the way in which legitimate users and market customers acquire their followers over time. The datasets used to analyze follower dynamics are $\mathbf{A}_l$ and $\mathbf{A}_c$. Similarly to what we did for $\mathbf{A}_c$, the follower dynamics for the accounts in $\mathbf{A}_l$ were also collected by crawling their followers on an hourly basis, from January 23, 2013 to May 7, 2013. To this end, we first need to define a model for the dynamics of Twitter followers.

We define the current fluctuation in followers for an account a as

$$\Delta_a[f_h] = f_h - f_{h-1},$$

where h is the current observation period (of an hour). In a nutshell, $\Delta_a[f_h]$ represents the number of followers that account a gained (or lost) during hour h. Given this basic definition, we define four characteristics in the follower dynamics of an account: *increases in followers*, *steady decreases in followers*, *intervals of stationary followers*, and *follower fluctuations*.

Increases in Followers. Twitter accounts tend to increase the number of their followers over time. Generally, users experience a regular increase in followers, and sudden spikes in the number of followers are rare for legitimate users. On the other hand, those accounts that purchase followers might have many of these followers added in a short period of time. Given an account a, we say that the account experienced a follower increase of height t if, during

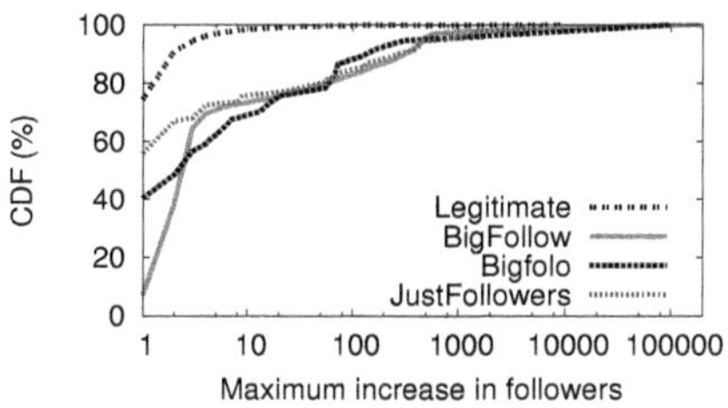

Figure 8: Cumulative distribution function of the sudden increase of followers experienced by customers, compared to legitimate profiles.

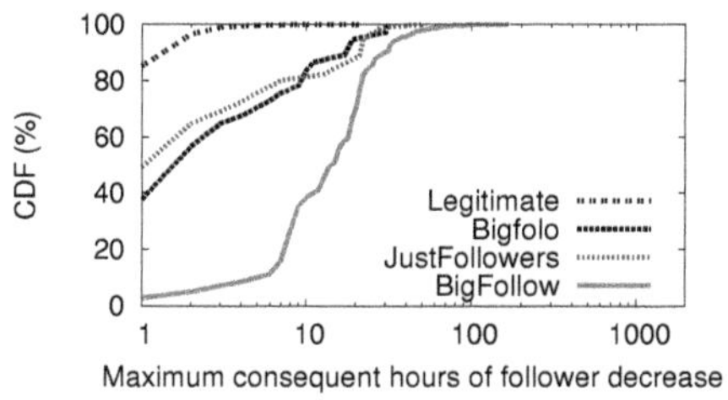

Figure 9: Cumulative distribution function of the maximum period of follower decrease experienced by customers, compared to legitimate profiles.

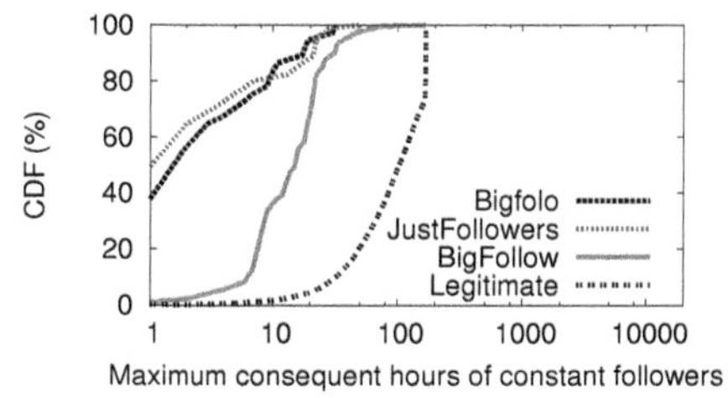

Figure 10: Cumulative distribution function of the maximum period of constant followers experienced by customers, compared to legitimate profiles.

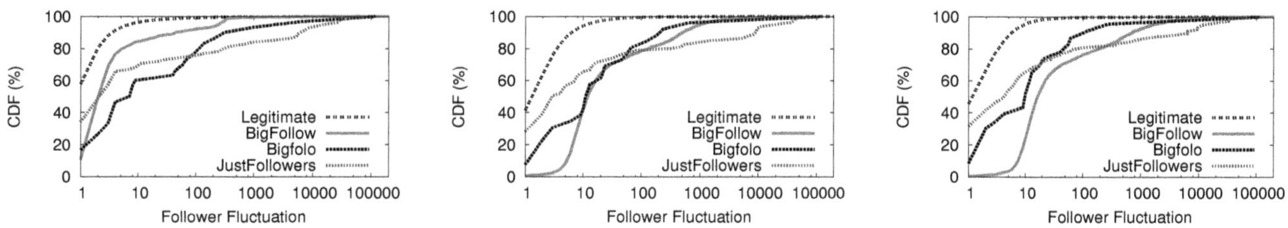

(a) 1-hour Interval

(b) 12-hour Interval

(c) 24-hour Interval

Figure 11: Cumulative distribution function of the follower fluctuation with different interval lengths for market customers and legitimate users. Increasing the observation period, market customers show higher fluctuations than legitimate users.

the hour of observation, $\Delta_a[f_h]$ for the account is greater or equal than t.

To investigate these differences, we analyzed the dynamic characteristics of the users in $\mathbf{A}_l$ and $\mathbf{A}_c$. What we observed is that it is more common for market customers to experience a large increase in followers over a one-hour period than it is for legitimate users. Figure 8 shows this phenomenon. In particular, it is quite common for market customers (20%) to experience increases of 50 or more followers during a period of an hour, while only a small fraction (0.4%) of legitimate accounts experience the same.

Steady Decreases in Followers. Legitimate users get followed because they share interesting content, and engage their audience. Market customers, however, are usually trying to promote themselves or a brand, and the content that they share is not considered useful by many users. For this reason, many of the followers that a customer bought are likely to unfollow him after a certain time. We already verified this hypothesis in Section 5.1. Given an account a, we say that a experiences a steady decrease in followers of length d hours if, for a number d of consecutive hours, $\Delta_a[f_h]$ has been negative (*i.e.*, the account lost followers).

Figure 9 shows the CDF of the longest sequence of consecutive hours in which customers and legitimate users lost followers, over an observation period of one week. As it can be seen, the accounts in $\mathbf{A}_c$ show long periods in which they lose followers. In particular, 60% of the customers of *BigFollow* experienced periods of 10 or more consecutive hours in which their followers steadily decreased.

Intervals of Stationary Followers. Although Twitter accounts experience variations in their number of followers, we expect this number of followers to change slowly over time. In fact, most Twitter accounts will keep the same number of followers over periods of multiple hours, while market customers tend to constantly experience increases in followers or decreases in the number of their followers. For this reason, we expect legitimate Twitter accounts to show intervals of multiple hours in which their followers do not change more often than market customers. Given an account a, we say that a experienced an interval of constant followers of length d hours if, for a number d of consecutive hours, $\Delta_a[f_h]$ has been equal to zero.

Figure 10 shows the CDF of the longest sequence of consecutive hours in which market customers and legitimate users kept their followers unchanged, over an observation period of one week. As it can be seen, 30% of legitimate users did not experience changes in their followers at all. On the other hand, market customers rarely have their followers remain constant for longer than ten consecutive hours.

Follower Fluctuations. An important aspect in follower dynamics is the fluctuation of followers. Twitter accounts gain and lose followers, depending on how interesting the content that they share is, as well as other factors. In general, we expect the follower fluctuations of legitimate Twitter accounts to be rather small. On the other hand, accounts that bought followers are likely to show fluctuations that are more pronounced.

To investigate this phenomenon, we define the change in the number of followers over a period of n hours as

$$\Delta_a[f_{nh}] = f_h - f_{h-n}.$$

We then look for consecutive intervals of length n hours in which this variation had the same sign (positive or negative). For each interval in which the follower variation had the same sign, we calculate the total number of followers that the account gained (or lost) during that interval. By doing this, two consecutive intervals will have opposite signs, indicating, for example, an interval in which the followers of an account increased steadily, followed by an interval in which its followers decreased. Given two consecutive inter-

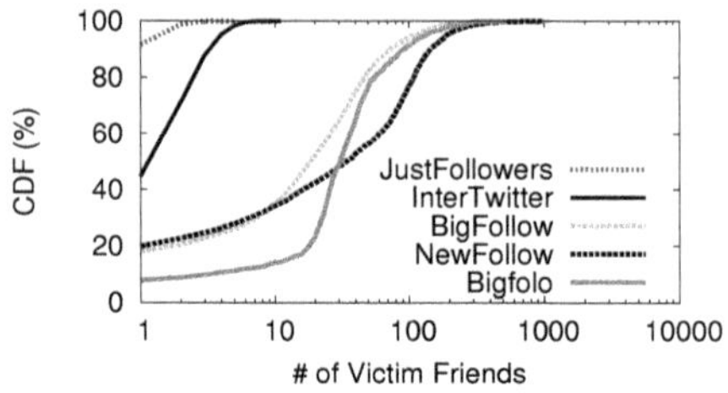

Figure 12: Cumulative distribution function of the number of other victims that market victims followed.

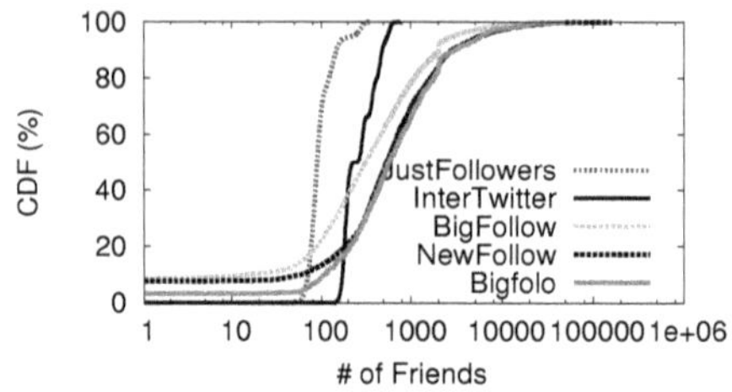

Figure 13: Cumulative distribution function of the total number of unique friends of victim accounts.

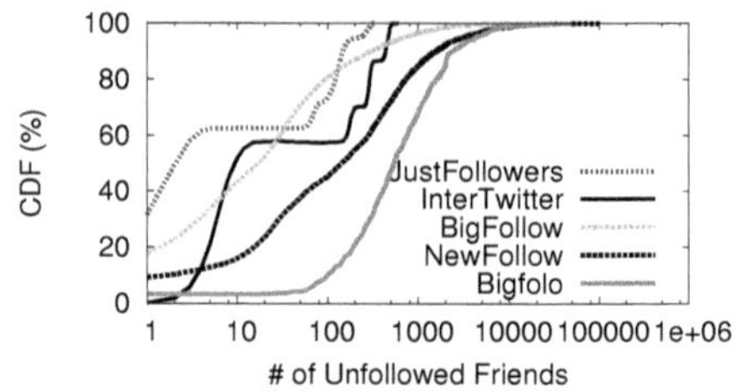

Figure 14: Cumulative distribution function of the number of friends that a victims unfollowed.

vals, we define the follower fluctuation Fl_n for periods of length n between those two intervals as the absolute value of the difference between the change of followers in the two intervals.

Intuitively, we expect accounts that have bought followers to show higher fluctuations than legitimate accounts. To verify this assumption, we calculated the fluctuation of followers for the accounts in $\mathbf{A}_l$ and $\mathbf{A}_c$ over a period length n of one hour, twelve hours, and 24 hours. For each account, we calculated the maximum value of Fl_n observed during the measurement period. Figure 11 shows the CDFs for these fluctuations. As it can be seen, legitimate accounts experience relatively low fluctuations, while customers tend to experience larger ones. Also, using longer time intervals (12 and 24 hours) leads to better distinction between the two groups of users. This indicates that both legitimate users and customers would experience short-terms fluctuations, while in the long term the fluctuations experienced by customers are more evident.

5.3 Victim Account Characteristics

In this section, we analyze the characteristics of victims in $\mathbf{A}_v$. We want to understand whether victims tend to follow other victims of the same market. Also, we want to verify whether victims would consistently follow and then unfollow other users.

In order to check the following behavior of users in $\mathbf{A}_v$, we crawled their friend list (*i.e.*, users they follow) every two hours from April 3, 2013 to April 30, 2013. During the data collection period, we observed that some of the victims got banned by Twitter. The victims of *InterTwitter* were suspended more frequently (31%) than the victims from other markets (*BigFollow* 8%, *Bigfolo* 11%, *JustFollowers* 17%, and *NewFollow* 23%). Note that *InterTwitter* is the only market among these five that does not offer a free-subscription service. It is likely that *InterTwitter* recruits victims by massively creating fake accounts, and existing countermeasures already detect such accounts. On the other hand, the remaining markets sell real accounts as followers. For Twitter, dealing with these accounts is more challenging, because blocking them might generate complaints by the accounts' owners.

To study the characteristics of victim accounts, we first want to see whether victims would follow each other. Figure 12 shows the distribution of the number of other victims that a victim followed. As shown, most victims of the markets *Bigfolo*, *BigFollow* and *NewFollow* would follow other victims. This way, victims can increase each other's follower count. However, the vast majority (more than 95% of them) of victims of *JustFollowers* followed at most one other victim from the same market. Victims of *InterTwitter* also show a low interconnection between victims: more than 90% of the victims have followed less than 3 other victims. Since *InterTwitter* does not offer free-subscriptions, victims do not have to follow each other. For *JustFollowers*, one possible explanation is that this market is considerably smaller compared to the others.

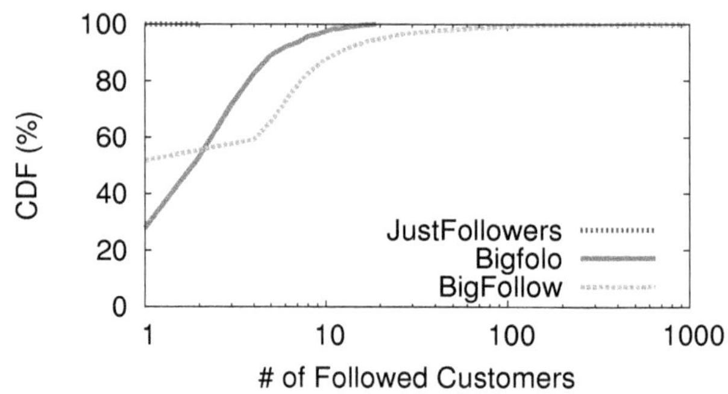

Figure 15: Number of customers that victims followed. Some markets have their victims follow many customers, while others have each victim follow a small number of customers.

This is confirmed by the number of victims for this market that we identified in the wild (see Table 4).

Figure 13 shows the total number of friends of the victim accounts in $\mathbf{A}_v$. This number is a cumulative count of all friends that we observed during the data collection period. We can see that victims of *InterTwitter* and *JustFollowers* strictly limit their number of friends below 500, while victims of the other three markets would follow more people. Normally, the friend count of a Twitter account cannot exceed 2,000, which is the hard limit set by Twitter. A small portion (about 10%) of victims of the markets *Bigfolo*, *BigFollow* and *NewFollow* have followed more than 2,000 people during one month. The possible explanation is that victims would unfollow some of their friends in order to follow new ones. This can be confirmed in Figure 14, which shows the number of friends that the victims in $\mathbf{A}_v$ unfollowed during the data collection period. As we can see, market victims typically unfollow many of their friends. For example, 90% of the victims of *Bigfolo* have unfollowed more than 100 people during the period that we observed, while 30% of victims have unfollowed more than 1,000 people. Previous research showed that it is not uncommon for legitimate Twitter users to unfollow other profiles, but at rates a lot lower than this [22].

5.4 Different Strategies for Operating Markets

As we have observed, the Twitter follower markets that we have analyzed share common traits, but also feature distinguished characteristics. In this section, we study the different strategies that follower merchants use to operate their markets, and analyze advantages and disadvantages of these strategies.

The most evident difference is that the followers offered by *InterTwitter* seem to be fake accounts, unlike those of all other markets, which are real accounts. The first consequence of this choice is that such followers will not provide an increase in popularity to their customers, but just an increase in their follower count. Fake accounts will not purchase the products advertised by the customer, for instance. In addition, as we have shown, it is easier for Twitter to deal with fake accounts, because the social network can just suspend them, without anybody complaining. The follower merchants can create new fake accounts, but this is not effortless.

The main difference between the other three markets (*BigFollow*, *Bigfolo*, and *JustFollowers*) is in the way they manage their victims. First of all, as we showed in Section 4.2, some markets can count on more victims than others. Intuitively, the victims of the larger markets will have less connections to the customers of the market, meaning that each victim will follow a smaller number of customers. Figure 15 shows the CDF of how many accounts in $\mathbf{A}_c$ are followed by the victims in $\mathbf{A}_v$. As it can be seen, the victims of *JustFollowers* follow a very small number of customers, while the ones of *Bigfolo* and *BigFollow* follow a larger number of them. Another way in which follower merchants can control the way in which they deliver followers is how fast they add them: as we have shown in Figure 8, *BigFollow* provides customers in a more abrupt way than *Bigfolo* and *JustFollowers*. Another interesting aspect is whether follower merchants provide the same followers twice, in case the customer purchased their service more than once. As we show in Figure 7, *JustFollowers* and *Bigfolo* tend to give the same followers to their users more than once more often than *BigFollow*. Given the number of tweets advertising these two markets that we observed in the wild, and that are summarized in Table 4, the reason for this is probably that *Bigfollow* can count on a larger number of victims, while *JustFollowers* is a lot smaller.

6. DETECTING MARKET CUSTOMERS

Previously we analyzed the characteristics of market victims and customers. Some of these characteristics can be leveraged to detect accounts that purchased followers on Twitter (i.e., market customers). Detecting customers is very important to fight against the phenomenon of Twitter follower markets: while crooks can compromise more accounts and sell them as followers, it is much harder for them to attract new customers, especially if Twitter starts to systematically suspend customer accounts. In principle, Twitter could start suspending customer accounts, because they are violating the terms of service that specifically prohibit to take part in Twitter follower market activity [3]. However, to date we are not aware of any countermeasures taken by Twitter against market customers.

We propose a method that leverages the dynamics of the followers of an account, and raises an anomaly if they show the patterns that we described in Section 5.2. We also explore different filters that can help in discarding many accounts that are unlikely to be customers, and a classifier that can tell if an account is likely a market customer just by looking at its static characteristics. Eventually, we discuss how these techniques can be used in combination, and leverage them to detect customers in the wild.

6.1 Follower Dynamics Detection

As explained in Section 5.2, Twitter follower market customers tend to experience sudden increases in their followers, and steady decreases of the number of their followers for long periods of time. We are interested in leveraging these observations to detect accounts whose owners bought followers on Twitter (i.e., customers). To this end, we observe the follower dynamics of Twitter accounts for a number d of observation periods (hours), and we leverage the follower dynamics that are typical of accounts that bought followers to detect customers in the wild. Based on our observations, we developed three types of features to perform this task: *increase* features, *decrease* features, and *stationary followers* features. We describe them in detail in the following.

Increase Features. These features count the number of times during the observation period in which an account experienced an increase in followers higher or equal than t during one hour. We define 1,000 features of this type, with t ranging from 1 to 1,000.

Decrease Features. These features count the number of periods of length l hours in which the followers of a user steadily decreased. We define d features of this type, where the length of the steady decrease ranges from 1 hour to d hours.

Stationary Features. These features are similar to the steady decrease features, but look for consecutive hour intervals in which the user's number of followers did not change. Again, we define d features, from 1 hour to d hours.

In Section 5.2 we defined another characteristic of the follower dynamics of an account, the *follower fluctuation*. However, this characteristic embodies the same information provided by the *increase* and *decrease* features. In particular, if we look for accounts that ever experienced a sudden increase of followers of height greater or equal than 15, or that experienced a steady decrease in followers that lasted for at least ten hours, we already cover 97.6% of the accounts in $\mathbf{A}_c$. On the other hand, only 1% of the accounts in $\mathbf{A}_l$ show the same characteristics. Since the follower fluctuation is more resource-intensive to compute than the increase and decrease features, we decided not to use this type of features for our classification.

When analyzing follower dynamics, we have to observe Twitter accounts for a certain period of time. One of the challenges is to determine the optimum length of the observation period. If we picked an observation period that is too short, our system would probably not be able to observe the dynamics typical of market customers during that period. Also, the dynamics that are typical of a purchase of followers do not last forever, but instead tend to stabilize after a certain point. For this reason, to successfully detect a customer, we need the purchase to happen during our observation period, or shortly before it. We experimented with different observation periods, and found that having an observation period of one week (d =168 hours) is a good choice. In the next section, we perform an analysis of the classifier built from these features.

6.1.1 Dynamics-based Classifier Evaluation

We built a classifier based on the follower dynamics features, and analyzed its efficiency. To this end, leveraged Support Vector Machines trained with Sequential Minimal Optimization (SMO) for classification [27] as provided by the WEKA machine learning toolkit [15].

For our training set, we leveraged the set $\mathbf{A}_c$ as examples of accounts that bought followers, and a random set of 10,000 accounts from $\mathbf{A}_l$ as examples of legitimate accounts. We call this set $\mathbf{A}_{lt}$. We then extracted the follower dynamics for the accounts in our training set, for the period between April 16, 2013 and April 23, 2013. A ten-fold cross validation on this dataset shows that the classifier works well. We obtained a true positive rate of 98.4% among the market customers, and a false positive rate close to zero: only two of the profiles in $\mathbf{A}_{lt}$ were flagged as customers. The reason for this is that both accounts experienced several high increases in followers during the observation period. By manually analyzing these accounts, one was a foreign news site, and is probably a false positive, while the other one is belongs to a local DJ. We cannot tell if this particular account is a false positive or not.

The features that are most representative of a market customer are high increases in followers. However, it is very rare for a customer to experience an increase of more than 200 followers during an hour. Long intervals of steady decreases in followers (longer than ten consecutive hours) are also indicative of customers. Surprisingly however, shorter intervals (one or two hours) of steady decreases in followers are more common in legitimate accounts. The stationary features have less influence on the model.

Although this classifier is very strong, a market might try to avoid detection, by adding followers slowly. We argue that while customers of such a market might not look suspicious with regard to the features that deal with increases in followers, they will still show anomalous steady decreases in followers, because this is not an element that the follower merchants have control over.

6.2 Static Detection of Customers

We showed that it is possible to reliably detect accounts that bought followers on Twitter by looking at their follower dynamics. However, this method requires to observe an account for a long period of time. In our case in particular, it is unfeasible to monitor the whole population of Twitter, because Twitter limits us in the number of API calls that we can perform per hour. To be able to run our customer detection system at Twitter scale, we would need a lightweight system that discards as many benign users as possible before we start tracking the possible customers, to analyze their dynamics. To this end, we analyzed three possible strategies: using a *follower filter*, a *static filter*, or a *static classifier*. In the following, we analyze the three methods in detail.

Follower Filter. As Figure 3 illustrates, almost all market customers have more than 100 followers. Conversely, 26% of legitimate Twitter users are below that threshold. This shows that a quick way of getting rid of profiles that are unlikely to be customers is considering only accounts that have more than a hundred followers. In practice, this is what we already did by using the dataset $\mathbf{A}_l$ as our test dataset.

Static Filter. A more advanced way of filtering out accounts that are unlikely to be market customers is looking at static characteristics of a profile, such as the number of followers and the number of friends. The idea is to leverage the observations that we discussed in Section 5.1 to identify possible customer candidates. In the following, we describe the features used by this static filter in detail.

- **Number of Friends.** This is the number of friends of the Twitter account.
- **Number of Followers.** As we previously explained, market customers have, on average, more followers than normal Twitter users.
- **More Followers than Friends.** As we show in Figure 4, it is slightly more likely for market customers to have more followers than friends than it is for legitimate users. This feature is Boolean, and it is set to one if the number of followers is higher than the number of friends.
- **Followers to Friends Ratio.** As we show in Figure 4, customer accounts tend to have a higher follower-to-friend ratio than legitimate users.

This filter has the advantage of being fast, and being able to quickly discard accounts that are most probably not market customers. However, since it only takes into account the number of friends and followers of an account, it might generate many false positives. Since we use this filter to discard accounts that are not likely to be market customers, before starting to monitor account dynamics, this is not a big problem.

Dynamic Classifier	TP rate	FP rate
SVM (SMO)	98.4%	0.02%
Static Filter	TP rate	FP rate
Random Forest (cost-sensitive)	93.7%	63%
Static Classifier	TP rate	FP rate
Decision Tree	90%	3.7%
Random Forest	91%	3.3%

Table 5: Performance of the different classifiers. The dynamic classifier has both high recall and low false positives. The static methods are useful as prefilters to discard as many accounts that are unlikely to be market customers as possible.

Static Classifier. To be more precise in assessing whether an account is likely a market customer or not, we can add two additional features to the static filter.

- **Influence.** For a legitimate account, having a high number of followers means that people find this account interesting, and re-share the content that the account posts often. This indicates that such an account has high influence. Accounts that bought their followers, typically do not have very engaged audiences. We used the *Klout* service to measure an account influence [19]. This service analyzes the activity of Twitter accounts, and returns an influence score that is function of how many followers, mentions, and retweets an account has. This score performs well in our case. However, any service that provided a similar information would work for our purposes.
- **Number of Victim Followers.** Since Twitter follower markets use compromised accounts as followers for their customers, we expect market customers to be followed by many victims. To calculate this feature, for each follower b, of an account a, we look for tweets advertising an account market, similar to what we did in Section 3.2. We set this feature to the number of followers that follow a and have advertised a Twitter follower market.

The static classifier is more robust than the static filter, because it takes into account information about the activity of the account, as well as its social network. However, as we will see, it is not as lightweight.

In the following, we analyze the performance of the static filter and the static classifier, and describe their advantages and disadvantages.

6.2.1 Evaluation of the Static Methods

We performed an analysis of the two methods listed in the previous section: the static filter and the static classifier. Similarly to what we did for the follower dynamics classifier, we used the accounts in $\mathbf{A}_c$ as examples of market customers, and the accounts in $\mathbf{A}_{lt}$ as examples of legitimate users.

Our goal with the static filter is to discard as many benign accounts as possible, and analyze the remaining ones with the dynamic classifier. To perform this task, we require recall to be high, but allow false positives. First, we performed a 10-fold cross validation on the training dataset for the static filter. To this end, we used random forests, and we penalized a false negative 100 times more than a false positive. The 10-fold cross validation returned a true positive rate of 93.7%, and a false positive rate of 63%. As we can see, the static filter is able to detect most customer accounts, and is able to cut the number of candidates for the dynamic classifier by almost a half. Therefore, it is a useful pre-filter.

We then wanted to understand how much the features added to the static classifier improve over the simple filter, and whether performing this type of classification could be useful. To this end, we first performed a 10-fold cross validation, using decision trees. The 10-fold cross validation returned a true positive rate of 90%, and a false positive rate of 3.7%. The most important features in the decision tree were, in order, the number of followers, whether the account has more friends than followers, and the influence score. A random forest algorithm gave slightly better results [24], with a true positive rate of 91%, and a false positive rate of 3.3%. The results that we obtained for different approaches are summarized in Table 5.

The 10-fold cross validation on the static classifier shows that the features that we developed are effective in discriminating between users who acquired followers in a legitimate fashion and those who purchased followers. In principle, we could use this approach to detect market customers in the wild. Unfortunately, from our perspective, Twitter limits the number of API calls that we can make in an hour. Some of the features that we described, in particular the "Number of Victim Followers" and the "Influence" ones, require many API calls to compute, since they require us to download the timeline for every single follower that an account has, as well as the past tweets of the user. For these reasons, although we acknowledge that the static classifier might help in detecting customers in the wild, we did not use it to this end.

A market customer might evade detection by the static classifier by using other means of getting followers in conjunction with purchasing them. For example, a customer who constantly follows random users, and gets followed by a fraction of them, would have a more balanced number of friends and followers than average market customers, and might avoid detection. However, Twitter is already monitoring and blocking accounts that show this behavior [32].

6.3 Possible Uses of the Two Methods

We presented a method to monitor the follower dynamics of Twitter accounts, and determine if they increased their followers organically, or they purchased followers. This method works very well, but is not instantaneous, since it requires a long observation period before making a decision (in our setup, a week). Also, monitoring the follower dynamics of Twitter accounts is resource intensive. To mitigate these problems, we developed two methods to discard those accounts that are unlikely to be market customers (*follower filter* and *static filter*), and a method to tell if a profile is likely a market customer by only looking at it (*static classifier*). There are different ways in which these techniques can be combined effectively.

The most reasonable deployment would be applying the follower filter, followed by the static classifier first. Both methods are fast, and work well in discarding unlikely customers. Then, we can apply the dynamics classifier to the remaining set of accounts. We investigate this possible setup in the next section. Another possible deployment is to use the dynamic and the static classifier in parallel. As we have mentioned in the previous sections, both classifiers might be actively evaded by follower merchants and customers, and having two detection mechanisms in place might help in detecting these evasive accounts.

6.4 Detecting Customers in the Wild

We ran our detection algorithms on $\mathbf{A}_l$. In particular, we extracted the follower dynamics for the 2 million accounts for a period of two weeks, from April 19, 2013 to May 3, 2013.

First, we ran our dynamic classifier over the two-week data, on each week separately. Our system flagged 684 accounts as market customers. As we explained previously, this means that these accounts purchased followers during our observation period, or right before that, and that they showed follower dynamics that are typical of market customers. By manually looking at those accounts, they mostly belonged to wanna-be celebrities or small businesses, which is the type of accounts that we would expect to purchase Twitter followers to bootstrap their popularity. Although it is not possible to establish precise ground truth for our results, none of the detected customers looked like a false positive (for example, no account belonged to an established celebrity or a popular business).

We then looked at how applying the filter methods that we discussed in Section 6.3 would have affected our results. As we have shown in Figure 3, applying the follower filter would discard between 20 and 30% legitimate Twitter accounts, while keeping the vast majority of customers in the candidate set. For our purposes, we do not need to apply this filter, since the accounts in $\mathbf{A}_l$ have been selected to have more than 100 followers. We then applied the static filter to the accounts in $\mathbf{A}_l$. In total, the filter discarded 983,810 accounts, almost cutting the candidate set in half. After applying this filter, we ran the dynamics classifier on the remaining accounts. Our system flagged 631 accounts as market customers. This means that the static filter is fairly successful in keeping most customers in the candidate set – 92.3% of the total detected customers were still in it – and shows that having a static filter is a good option if the number of accounts that one can monitor is limited (like in our case).

6.5 Analysis of the Identified Customers

In this section, we analyze the characteristics of the 684 market customers that we identified. These customers are detected by the dynamic classifier, so not surprisingly, their dynamic characteristics are very similar to the ones of the customers in the training dataset $\mathbf{A}_c$. We found that their static characteristics show strong customer-like signals too: Figure 16 shows the distribution of the number of followers of the identified customers, compared to legitimate users. The identified customers typically have more than 1,000 followers, which is more than the number of followers for 80% of the regular Twitter user population. In addition, Figure 17 shows that the follower-to-friend ratio of identified customers is typically higher than one.

As we said, by manually looking at the identified customers we found that those accounts mostly belong to small businesses or wannabe celebrities, who try to boost their popularity. We then wanted to assess whether the purchase of followers actually helps in this process. To this end, we analyzed the influence score of these customers, according to Klout [19]. The CDF of the influence of the identified customers is shown in Figure 18, indicating that about half the customers have a Klout score lower than 45. However, the median Klout score of Twitter accounts is precisely 45 [1] (on a scale 1-100). This shows that, although purchasing followers can boost an account's social network, it does not really help in making the account popular. Since the followers did not willingly follow the profile, it is unlikely that they will engage the user, and share her content.

As a last element, we wanted to understand whether Twitter is detecting and blocking these customer accounts. After one week from detecting them, only two accounts had been suspended by

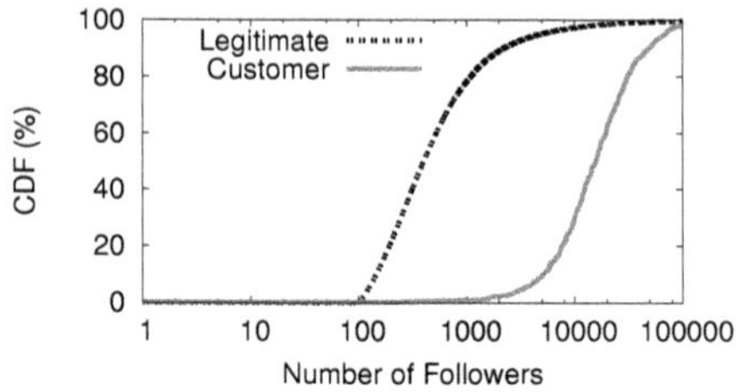

Figure 16: Followers of identified customers and legitimate users.

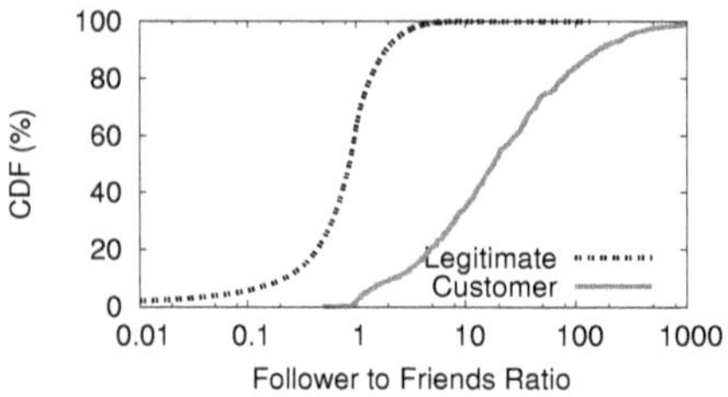

Figure 17: Follower-friend ratio of identified customers and legitimate users.

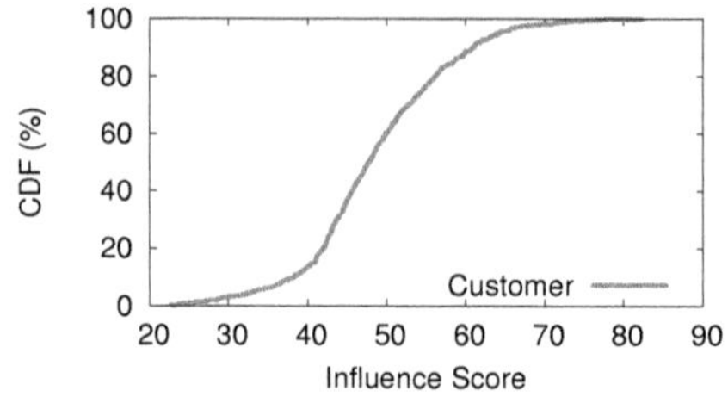

Figure 18: Influence (Klout) score of identified customers.

Twitter. This shows that it is hard for Twitter to detect which accounts purchased followers, and that the type of techniques proposed in this paper could actively help Twitter in fighting this phenomenon.

7. DISCUSSION

Follower markets enable dishonest users on social networks and microblogging sites to inflate their perceived credibility. Due to the lack of alternative means to gauge a user's influence, social network users often take the number of connections of an account as face-value for the account's influence. The techniques proposed in this work can help the social network operator to automatically detect the participants in these follower markets. More importantly, our system distinguishes between customers and victims of these schemes. This distinction allows the social network operator to focus mitigation approaches on market customers and potentially disrupt the economic foundations of follower market services. Furthermore, unsuspecting victims need not be punished and their participation in the social network can continue. As a consequence, the intuition that accounts with many followers are influential is restored.

Additionally, our techniques can also be leveraged by users that strive to keep their online social networking relations confined to trustworthy peers. To this end, a user can employ our techniques to identify market customers among the users in her social graph. Due to the high precision of our detection system, the user can remove the identified market customers from her social graph without fear that she would break connections to legitimate users in the social network.

Of course, once our detection mechanism impacts the bottom line of follower markets, follower merchants might try to adapt their operations to evade our techniques. However, our detection techniques leverage a key observation about the victims of these services – the fact that many victims unfollow the customers the merchants connect them to. Therefore, as long as follower markets exploit real victims for their operations we expect that these characteristics will persist. Follower merchants can still slow down the rate at which victims are added to customers to evade detection. While this would be a viable long term strategy for the follower merchants, it dramatically impacts one of the markets' key promises – to gain followers fast. These considerations do not apply to those follower markets that use fake accounts instead of real ones. However, this modus operandi has higher operational costs and overhead for the follower merchants, because they have to create and manage a substantial number of fake accounts. Such an operation by itself is non-trivial at best and would expose these fake accounts to existing detection techniques already employed by today's online social networks.

8. RELATED WORK

Over the last few years, many researchers focused their studies on Twitter, and online social networks [8, 20–22, 35, 36]. In particular, several works showed the security threats linked to the use of social networks [12–14]. Previous research showed that one of the main advantages of spreading malicious content through social networks is that users are more likely to click on content posted on these media than they are of doing so for more traditional media (*e.g.*, email) [6, 17].

Researchers developed several systems to detect malicious activity on social networks such as Twitter. Early systems focused on spammers and fake accounts (*Sybils*), and developed feature-based detection systems [5, 23, 29]. Others rely on the social network structure and detect clustered malicious accounts in the social graph [7, 37]. These techniques give a good first-level defense against social network threats.

More recently, miscreants started to send malicious content from legitimate accounts that had been compromised [12, 14]. Detecting compromised accounts is a very different problem compared to detecting fake ones, because such accounts can have a long history of legitimate activity, and typically do not show similar characteristics. Existing systems either look at the URLs that the malicious messages point to [30], at accounts that send the same malicious content in large-scale campaigns [12], or look for accounts that suddenly change their typical behavior [11].

Most existing detection techniques focus on the actual accounts sending out offending content. Once detected, social network administrators can suspend these malicious accounts. However, this modus operandi does not fundamentally remove the threats, as more malicious accounts could be created, or other legitimate profiles could get compromised. In this paper, we propose to detect and disrupt Twitter follower market operations by identifying and possibly suspending the accounts that fund these malicious enterprises – the markets' customers. By doing this, we hope to cause a major economical hit to the Twitter follower market schemes, up to a point in which they will not be profitable anymore.

Thomas et al. studied marketplaces where miscreants can buy fake accounts, and use them to spread malicious content [31]. Instead, we focus on markets that sell followers to their customers. The concept of Twitter follower markets was first introduced in our previous work [28]. In this paper, we studied the phenomenon more broadly, and focused on characterizing the behavioral patterns of key players of account markets. In particular, we leveraged the follow/unfollow dynamics to detect market customers, which the previous approach did not explore. Kwak et al. studied the unfollow dynamics on Twitter with a focus on normal users [21], while our study leveraged unfollow dynamics for anomaly detection from a security angle.

9. CONCLUSIONS

Our work studies Twitter follower markets, where followers are sold to customers for a fee. We use ground-truth to reveal interesting patterns in the dynamics of the users involved in these markets, and in particular, the follower populations of their customers. We use our insights to build a system for detecting these behaviors in the wild, and use real experiments to show that it is both scalable and robust.

10. ACKNOWLEDGMENTS

This work was supported by the Office of Naval Research (ONR) under Grant N000140911042, the Army Research Office (ARO) under grant W911NF0910553, the National Science Foundation (NSF) under grant CNS-0845559 and grant CNS-0905537, and Secure Business Austria. Gang Wang, Haitao Zheng, and Ben Y. Zhao were partially supported by NSF grants IIS-0916307, CNS-1224100, IIS-1321083, and DARPA grant BAA-12-01. Any opinions, findings, and conclusions or recommendations expressed in this material are those of the author(s) and do not necessarily reflect the views of the National Science Foundation.

We would like to thank our shepherd Cecilia Mascolo for her support, and the anonymous reviewers for their insightful comments and observations.

11. REFERENCES

[1] Klout blog. http://corp.klout.com/blog/2011/11/do-you-have-google-klout/?goback=%2Egmp_4159546%2Egde_4159546_member_212786154.

[2] Oauth community site. http://oauth.net.

[3] Twitter terms of service. http://support.twitter.com/articles/18311-the-twitter-rules.

[4] Justin Bieber Twitter followers 50% fake says report, 2013.

[5] BENVENUTO, F., MAGNO, G., RODRIGUES, T., AND ALMEIDA, V. Detecting Spammers on Twitter. In *Conference on Email and Anti-Spam (CEAS)* (2010).

[6] BILGE, L., STRUFE, T., BALZAROTTI, D., AND KIRDA, E. All Your Contacts Are Belong to Us: Automated Identity Theft Attacks on Social Networks. In *World Wide Web Conference (WWW)* (2009).

[7] CAI, Z., AND JERMAINE, C. The latent community model for detecting sybils in social networks. In *Symposium on Network and Distributed System Security (NDSS)* (2012).

[8] CHA, M., HADDADI, H., BENVENUTO, F., AND GUMMADI, K. Measuring User Influence in Twitter: The Million Follower Fallacy. In *International AAAI Conference on Weblogs and Social Media* (2010).

[9] COLDEWEY, D. Romney twitter account gets upsurge in fake followers, but from where? *NBC News* (2012).

[10] CONSIDINE, A. Buying their way to twitter fame. *The New York Times* (2012).

[11] EGELE, M., STRINGHINI, G., KRUEGEL, C., AND VIGNA, G. COMPA: Detecting Compromised Accounts on Social Networks. In *Symposium on Network and Distributed System Security (NDSS)* (2013).

[12] GAO, H., HU, J., WILSON, C., LI, Z., CHEN, Y., AND ZHAO, B. Detecting and Characterizing Social Spam Campaigns. In *ACM SIGCOMM Internet Measurement Conference* (2010).

[13] GHOSH, S., VISWANATH, B., KOOTI, F., SHARMA, N. K., KORLAM, G., BENEVENUTO, F., GANGULY, N., AND GUMMADI, K. P. Understanding and combating link farming in the twitter social network. In *World Wide Web Conference (WWW)* (2012).

[14] GRIER, C., THOMAS, K., PAXSON, V., AND ZHANG, M. @spam: the underground on 140 characters or less. In *ACM Conference on Computer and Communications Security (CCS)* (2010).

[15] HALL, M., FRANK, E., HOLMES, G., PFAHRINGER, B., REUTEMANN, P., AND WITTEN, I. H. The weka data mining software: an update. *SIGKDD Explor. Newsl. 11*, 1 (Nov. 2009), 10–18.

[16] HUTTO, C. J., YARDI, S., AND GILBERT, E. A longitudinal study of follow predictors on twitter. In *SIGCHI Conference on Human Factors in Computing Systems (CHI)* (2013).

[17] JAGATIC, T., JOHNSON, N., JAKOBSSON, M., AND JAGATIF, T. Social phishing. *CACM 50*, 10 (2007), 94–100.

[18] KING, R. How companies use Twitter to bolster their brands. In *BusinessWeek Online* (2008).

[19] klout. http://klout.com.

[20] KRISHNAMURTHY, B., GILL, P., , AND ARITT, M. A few chirps about twitter. In *USENIX Workshop on Online Social Networks* (2008).

[21] KWAK, H., CHUN, H., AND MOON, S. Fragile online relationship: a first look at unfollow dynamics in twitter. In *SIGCHI Conference on Human Factors in Computing Systems (CHI)* (2011).

[22] KWAK, H., LEE, C., PARK, H., AND MOON, S. What is Twitter, a social network or a news media? In *World Wide Web Conference (WWW)* (2010).

[23] LEE, K., CAVERLEE, J., AND WEBB, S. Uncovering social spammers: social honeypots + machine learning. In *International ACM SIGIR Conference on Research and Development in Information Retrieval* (2010).

[24] LIAW, A., AND WIENER, M. Classification and regression by randomforest. *R news* (2002).

[25] MOTOYAMA, M., MCCOY, D., LEVCHENKO, K., SAVAGE, S., AND VOELKER, G. An analysis of underground forums. In *ACM SIGCOMM Internet Measurement Conference* (2011).

[26] PERLROTH, N. Fake twitter followers become multimillion-dollar business. *The New York Times* (2013).

[27] PLATT, J. C. Fast training of support vector machines using sequential minimal optimization. In *Advances in Kernel Methods - Support Vector Learning* (1998).

[28] STRINGHINI, G., EGELE, M., KRUEGEL, C., AND VIGNA, G. Poultry Markets: On the Underground Economy of Twitter Followers. In *SIGCOMM Workshop on Online Social Networks* (2012).

[29] STRINGHINI, G., KRUEGEL, C., AND VIGNA, G. Detecting Spammers on Social Networks. In *Annual Computer Security Applications Conference (ACSAC)* (2010).

[30] THOMAS, K., GRIER, C., MA, J., PAXSON, V., AND SONG, D. Design and Evaluation of a Real-Time URL Spam Filtering Service. In *IEEE Symposium on Security and Privacy* (2011).

[31] THOMAS, K. AND MCCOY, D. AND GRIER, C. AND KOLCZ, A. AND PAXSON, V. Trafficking Fraudulent Accounts: The Role of the Underground Market in Twitter Spam and Abuse. In *USENIX Security Symposium* (2013).

[32] TWITTER. The twitter rules. http://support.twitter.com/entries/18311-the-twitter-rules, 2010.

[33] WANG, G., KONOLIGE, T., WILSON, C., WANG, X., ZHENG, H., AND ZHAO, B. Y. You are how you click: Clickstream analysis for sybil detection. In *USENIX Security Symposium* (Washington, DC, 2013).

[34] WANG, G., MOHANLAL, M., WILSON, C., WANG, X., METZGER, M., ZHENG, H., AND ZHAO, B. Y. Social Turing tests: Crowdsourcing sybil detection. In *Symposium on Network and Distributed System Security (NDSS)* (2013).

[35] WILSON, C., BOE, B., SALA, A., PUTTASWAMY, K., AND ZHAO, B. User Interactions in Social Networks and Their Implications. In *ACM European conference on Computer systems (EuroSys)* (2009).

[36] YANG, C., HARKREADER, R., AND GU, G. Die Free or Live Hard? Empirical Evaluation and New Design for Fighting Evolving Twitter Spammers. In *Symposium on Recent Advances in Intrusion Detection (RAID)* (2011).

[37] YU, H., KAMINSKY, M., GIBBONS, P., AND FLAXMAN, A. Sybilguard: defending against sybil attacks via social networks. *ACM SIGCOMM Computer Communication Review* (2006).

Next Stop, the Cloud: Understanding Modern Web Service Deployment in EC2 and Azure

Keqiang He, Alexis Fisher, Liang Wang, Aaron Gember, Aditya Akella, Thomas Ristenpart
University of Wisconsin – Madison
{keqhe,afisher,liangw,agember,akella,rist}@cs.wisc.edu

ABSTRACT

An increasingly large fraction of Internet services are hosted on a cloud computing system such as Amazon EC2 or Windows Azure. But to date, no in-depth studies about cloud usage by Internet services has been performed. We provide a detailed measurement study to shed light on how modern web service deployments use the cloud and to identify ways in which cloud-using services might improve these deployments. Our results show that: 4% of the Alexa top million use EC2/Azure; there exist several common deployment patterns for cloud-using web service front ends; and services can significantly improve their wide-area performance and failure tolerance by making better use of existing regional diversity in EC2. Driving these analyses are several new datasets, including one with over 34 million DNS records for Alexa websites and a packet capture from a large university network.

Categories and Subject Descriptors

C.2.0 [**Computer-Communication Network**]: General; C.4 [**Performance of Systems**]: Metrics—*performance measures*

General Terms

Measurement

Keywords

Web Service, Cloud Computing, EC2, Azure, DNS, trace analysis

1. INTRODUCTION

Up until a few years ago, web services were hosted in heterogeneous server clusters or co-location centers that were widely distributed across different network providers and geographic regions. Today, web services are increasingly being deployed in infrastructure-as-a-service (IaaS) clouds such as Amazon EC2, Windows Azure, and Rackspace. Industry and the media claim that over 1% of Internet traffic goes to EC2 [31] and that outages in EC2 are reputed to hamper a huge variety of services [4, 6, 24, 35].

IMC'13, October 23–25, 2013, Barcelona, Spain.
Copyright 2013 ACM 978-1-4503-1953-9/13/10 ...$15.00.
http://dx.doi.org/10.1145/2504730.2504740.

Despite the popularity of public IaaS clouds, we are unaware of any in-depth measurement study exploring the current usage patterns of these environments. Prior measurement studies have quantified the compute, storage, and network performance these clouds deliver [29, 30], evaluated the performance and usage patterns of specific services that are hosted in these clouds, e.g., Dropbox [23], or examined cloud usage solely in terms of traffic volume [28].

We present the first in-depth empirical study of modern IaaS clouds that examines *IaaS cloud usage patterns* and identifies *ways in which cloud tenants could better leverage IaaS clouds*. We focus specifically on web services hosted within IaaS clouds, which our study (unsurprisingly) indicates is a large and important use case for IaaS.

We first examine *who is using public IaaS clouds*. We generate a dataset of cloud-using domains using extensive DNS probing in order to compare the IPs associated with websites on Alexa's top 1 million list [1] against published lists of cloud IP ranges. This identifies that ≈40K popular domains (4% of the Alexa top million) have a subdomain running atop Amazon EC2 or Windows Azure, two of the largest public clouds. We extract an additional ≈13K cloud-using domains from a one week packet capture from a large university network, and we use this capture to characterize the network traffic patterns of cloud-hosted web services. These results indicate that a large fraction of important web services are already hosted within public IaaS clouds.

We proceed to dissect *how these services are using the cloud*. EC2 and Azure both have a veritable potpourri of features, including virtual machines, load balancers, platform-as-a-service (PaaS) environments, content-distribution networks (CDNs), and domain name services. They also give tenants the choice of deploying their services in several different regions (i.e., geographically distinct data centers), and EC2 provides several different "availability zones" within each region. We couple analysis of DNS records with two different cloud cartography techniques [34] to identify which features, regions and zones web services use. We identify several common front end deployment patterns and report estimates of the percentages of Alexa subdomains using each of the patterns. In particular, we find that about 4% of EC2-using web services use load balancers and 8% of them leverage PaaS. Only 5% of the DNS servers used by cloud-using subdomains run on VMs inside EC2 or Azure. We also show that 97% of the subdomains hosted on EC2 and 92% of the subdomains hosted on Azure are deployed in only a single region. Counted among these are the subdomains of most of the top 10 (by Alexa rank) cloud-using domains. Services deployed in EC2 also appear to make limited use of different availability zones: our measurements estimate that only 66% of subdomains use more than one zone and only 22% use more than two. This lack of redundancy means that many (even highly ranked

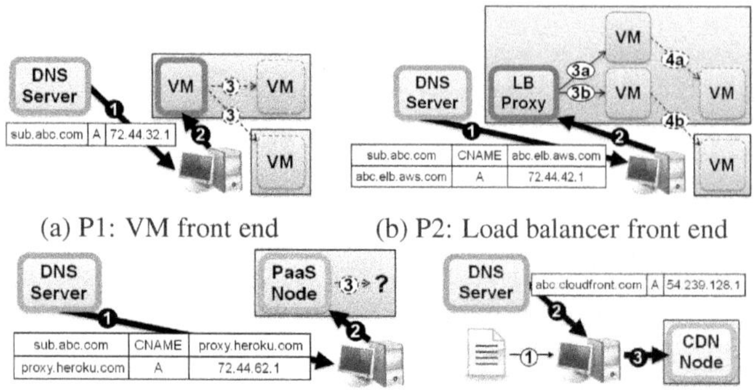

(a) P1: VM front end (b) P2: Load balancer front end

(c) P3: PaaS front end (d) P4: Leverage CDN

Figure 1: Deployment patterns for web services.

Alexa) services will not tolerate single-region or even single-zone failures.

Finally, we use a series of PlanetLab-based [17] active measurements and simulations to *estimate the impact of wide-area route outages and the potential for wide-area performance improvement.* We find that expanding a deployment from one region to three could yield 33% lower average latency for globally distributed clients, while also substantially reducing the risk of service downtime due to downstream Internet routing failures.

The remainder of our paper is organized as follows. We first provide background on Amazon EC2 and Windows Azure and discuss the primary datasets we use in our study (§2). We then examine who is using the cloud (§3), and which cloud features, regions, and zones are used by the cloud-using web services we identified (§4). Based on these observations, we proceed to estimate the wide-area-failure tolerance of current web service deployments and the potential for performance improvement (§5). Finally, we discuss related work (§6) before concluding (§7).

2. MEASUREMENT SCOPE & DATASETS

Public IaaS clouds, such as Amazon EC2, Windows Azure, and Rackspace, allow tenants to dynamically rent virtual machine (VM) instances with varying CPU, network, and storage capacity. Cloud tenants have the option of renting VMs in one or more geographically distinct data centers, or *regions*. Some clouds, such as EC2, further divide these regions into multiple distinct availability *zones*. Each zone has separate compute and power infrastructure to make certain failure modes zone-specific and to allow cloud tenants to replicate their deployments across multiple zones for smooth failover.

Beyond simple VMs, IaaS providers, as well as third parties, offer a wide-range of value-added features: load balancers (e.g., Amazon Elastic Load Balancer and Azure Traffic Manager), platform-as-a-service environments (e.g., Amazon Elastic Beanstalk, Heroku, and Azure Cloud Services), content-distribution networks (e.g., Amazon CloudFront and Azure Media Services), DNS hosting (e.g., Amazon route53), etc. The result is a complex ecosystem of interdependent systems operating at multiple layers of abstraction, and, in turn, a large variety of possible deployment patterns for cloud tenants. In this paper, we study four popular deployment patterns. We describe these using a series of examples.

In Figure 1, we show the steps involved in a client accessing an EC2-hosted web service that is using one or more of the aforementioned features. When a client wants to access a web service, it first performs a DNS lookup of the service's domain name. The response may contain an IP address associated with a VM (deployment pattern *P1*), a load balancer (*P2*), or a platform-as-a-service (PaaS) node (*P3*). With *P2*, the client request is subsequently directed to a VM[1]. Tenants using *P1–P3* may also rely on additional VMs or systems (dashed lines) to handle a client's request; these additional components may or may not be in the same region or availability zone (indicated by the gray boxes). An object returned to a client (e.g., a web page) may sometimes require the client to obtain additional objects (e.g., a video) from a content-distribution network (*P4*).

We focus on studying the front end portions of web service deployments within the above four deployment patterns (indicated by the thicker lines in Figure 1). These portions are encountered within the initial few steps of a client making a request. We leave an exploration of deployment/usage patterns covering the later steps (e.g. back-end processing) for future work.

2.1 Datasets

We use two primary datasets: (*i*) a list of cloud-using subdomains derived from Alexa's list of the top 1 million websites, and (*ii*) packet traces captured at the border of the UW-Madison campus network. Both datasets leverage the fact that EC2 [12] and Azure [8] publish a list of the public IPv4 address ranges associated with their IaaS cloud offerings. Below, we provide details on our Alexa subdomains and packet capture datasets. We augment these data sets with additional traces and active measurements to aid specific analyses; we describe these at the appropriate places in subsequent sections.

Top Cloud-Using Subdomains Dataset. Our first dataset is a list of subdomains which use EC2 or Azure and are associated with domains on Alexa's list of the top 1 million websites [1]. We consider a subdomain to use EC2 or Azure if a DNS record for that subdomain contains an IP address that falls within EC2 or Azure's public IP address ranges.

To construct this dataset, we first identified the subdomains associated with each domain on Alexa's list of the top 1 million websites. We started with Alexa's top 1 million list from Feburary 6, 2013 and attempted to issue a DNS zone transfer (i.e., a DNS query of type AXFR) for each domain on the list. The query was successful for only about 80K of the domains. For the remaining domains, we used dnsmap [16] to identify subdomains by brute-force. Dnsmap uses a pre-defined word list, which we augmented with the word list from knock [15], to construct potential subdomain names. Dnsmap then runs DNS queries to check if the potential subdomains actually exist. This brute-force approach misses some subdomains, but it allows us to provide a lower bound on the number of subdomains which use public IaaS clouds and explore the deployment patterns of these known cloud-using subdomains. We distributed this task to 150 globally-distributed PlanetLab nodes, producing a list of 34 million valid subdomains.

To limit the list of subdomains to cloud-using subdomains, we performed a series of DNS lookups using the UNIX dig utility. We first performed a single DNS lookup from one PlanetLab node (chosen from our set of 150 nodes) for each subdomain. If the DNS record contained an IP address within EC2 or Azure's public IP ranges[2], we included it on our list of the top cloud-using subdomains. This resulted in a list of 713K cloud-using subdomains. We then performed a DNS lookup for each of the cloud-using subdomains on every node in a set of 200 globally-distributed PlanetLab nodes. Figure 2 shows the geographic location of these PlanetLab

[1]Or PaaS nodes, as is done by Amazon Elastic Beanstalk and Azure Traffic Manager.

[2]We assume the IP address ranges published by EC2 and Azure are relatively complete.

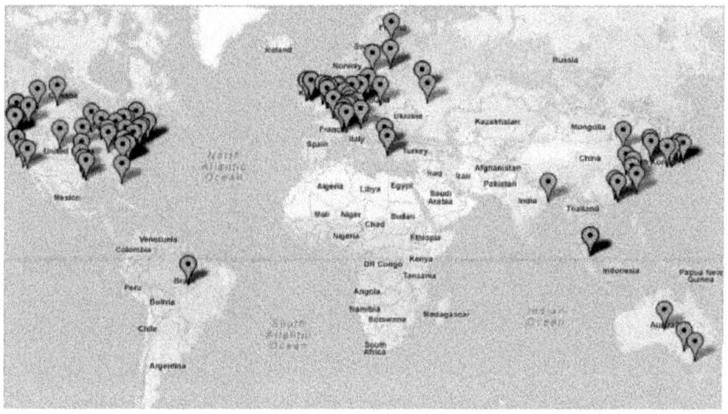

Figure 2: PlanetLab nodes used for DNS lookups

nodes, which are spread across North America, South America, Europe, Asia, and Australia. The queries were performed March 27-29, 2013. These distributed DNS queries help ensure that we gather a comprehensive set of DNS records for each cloud-using subdomain and capture any geo-location-specific cloud usage.

We refer to the list of cloud-using subdomains, and their associated DNS records, as the Alexa subdomains dataset.

Packet Capture Dataset. Our second primary dataset is a series of packet traces captured at the border of the University of Wisconsin-Madison campus network[3]. We captured full IP packets whose source or destination IP address fell within the public address ranges published by EC2 and Azure. The capture was performed from Tuesday, June 26 to Monday, July 2, 2012 giving us a full week of traffic and a total of 1.4TB of data. The total Internet traffic averaged approximately 7Gbps during the capture, with about 1% of the traffic going to/coming from EC2 or Azure. Due to the relatively low rate of traffic being captured, no loss occurred during the capture process (according to tcpdump and counters reported by the border router). To protect user privacy, we anonymized the IP addresses of clients within the university network, and we only report aggregate statistics.

Since our traces contain full packets, we were able to perform an in-depth analysis of network and transport layer information (e.g., IP addresses, protocols, ports), application layer information (e.g., HTTP hostnames, HTTP content-type, HTTPS certificates), and packet payloads. We extracted relevant information from the traces using Bro [33], a network monitoring and traffic analysis tool. We refer to these traces as the packet capture dataset.

We recognize that a packet trace from a single campus vantage point may not reflect the "typically" usage patterns of services deployed in IaaS clouds. Correspondingly, we only leverage the packet capture for analysis which cannot be conducted using our Alexa subdomains dataset—namely, protocol usage (§3.1), popularity estimates based on traffic volume and flow counts (§3.2), and flow characteristics (§3.3).

3. WEB-FACING CLOUD TENANTS

In this section, we explore what applications are being hosted on public IaaS clouds. We start by analyzing the packet capture to identify the types of applications being hosted. This analysis suggests (unsurprisingly) that web applications represent a large, important set of cloud tenants. We then turn to examining which of the most popular websites are using clouds. We view popularity both globally, via the Alexa top website rankings, and locally, via the volume of traffic associated with each domain in the packet capture. We also analyze the traffic patterns of cloud-using services, including flow characteristics and content types served.

[3]The university has seven /24 IP blocks and one /16 IP block

Cloud	Bytes	Flows
EC2	81.73	80.70
Azure	18.27	19.30
Total	100	100

Table 1: Percent of traffic volume and percent of flows associated with each cloud in the packet capture.

	EC2		Azure		Overall	
Protocol	Bytes	Flows	Bytes	Flows	Bytes	Flows
ICMP	0.01	0.03	0.01	0.18	0.01	0.06
HTTP (TCP)	16.26	70.45	59.97	65.41	24.24	69.48
HTTPS (TCP)	80.90	6.52	37.20	6.92	72.94	6.60
DNS (UDP)	0.11	10.33	0.10	11.59	0.11	10.58
Other (TCP)	2.40	0.40	2.41	1.10	2.40	0.60
Other (UDP)	0.28	0.19	0.31	14.77	0.28	3.00
Total	100	100	100	100	100	100

Table 2: Percent of traffic volume and percent of flows associated with each protocol in the packet capture.

3.1 Protocols and Services

We first examine the fraction of bytes and flows in the packet capture that are associated with each cloud (Table 1). We only consider flows that were initiated within the university and destined for EC2 or Azure. We observe that the majority of cloud traffic, both as measured by volume and number of flows, is EC2-related: 81.73% of bytes (80.70% of flows) are associated with EC2, while Azure accounts for 18.27% of bytes (19.30% of flows).

Next, we use the packet capture to study the application-layer protocols used by cloud tenants. Table 2 shows the percentage of bytes (and flows) using a specific protocol relative to the total number of bytes (and flows) for EC2, Azure, and the capture as a whole.

We observe that more than 99% of bytes in the packet capture are sent and received using TCP, with less than 1% of bytes associated with UDP or ICMP. The vast majority of this TCP traffic is HTTP and HTTPS. The proportion of HTTPS traffic is far higher than that seen for general web services in the past (roughly 6% [18]); as we will show later, HTTPS traffic is dominated by cloud storage services. Interestingly, the majority of Azure's TCP traffic is HTTP (59.97%) while the majority of EC2's TCP traffic is HTTPS (80.90%)

The breakdown by flow count is less skewed towards TCP, with UDP flows accounting for 14% of flows in the packet capture. This is largely due to DNS queries, which account for 11% of flows but carry few bytes.

As one would expect, public IaaS clouds are also used for non-web-based services. In the packet capture, we find a small fraction of non-HTTP(S) TCP traffic and non-DNS UDP traffic going to both EC2 and Azure. This traffic includes SMTP, FTP, IPv6-in-IPv4, SSH, IRC, and other traffic that Bro could not classify.

Summary and implications. While we analyze a single vantage point, our measurements suggest that web services using HTTP(S) represent an important set of WAN-intensive cloud tenants. The extent to which compute-intensive workloads (that may not result in a large impact on network traffic) are prevalent as cloud tenants remains an interesting open question. In the following sections we dig into what tenants are hosting web services on public clouds as well as diving deeper into their traffic patterns.

3.2 Popular Cloud-Using (Sub)Domains

Cloud-using Alexa domains. We now consider what subset of the Alexa top 1 million websites use the cloud to (partly) host their services. Recall that Alexa provides an estimate of the most pop-

Provider	# Domains (%)	# Subdomains (%)
EC2 only	3,277 (8.1%)	685,725 (96.1%)
EC2 + Other	34,721 (86.1%)	21,628 (3.0%)
Azure only	184 (0.5%)	6,328 (0.9%)
Azure + Other	1,858 (4.6%)	225 (<0.01%)
EC2 + Azure	293 (0.7%)	4 (<0.01%)
Total	40,333 (100.0%)	713,910 (100.0%)
EC2 total	38,291 (94.9%)	707,357 (99.1%)
Azure total	2,335 (5.8%)	6,557 (0.9%)

Table 3: Breakdown of domains and subdomains based on their use of EC2, Azure, and/or other hosting services.

ular domains worldwide. Their ranking is based on the number of unique visitors and the number of page views over the last 3 months, aggregated at the domain level[4] [1]. Using our Alexa subdomains dataset, we can determine which Alexa sites are hosted in EC2/Azure.

We find that 40,333 (>4%) of the domains on Alexa's top 1 million list have a subdomain that uses EC2 and/or Azure. Under these domains, there are a total of 713,910 cloud-using subdomains. Note that these are lower bounds on cloud use, since our analysis approach (see §2.1) means we do not flag as cloud-using any domains that use a layer of indirection (e.g., via services like CloudFlare [11]) before requests are sent to EC2 or Azure.

Table 3 provides a breakdown of the domains and subdomains in terms of whether they use EC2, Azure, or other hosting services (the last indicating IP addresses not associated with EC2 or Azure). Note that "other" could in fact be public clouds besides EC2 and Azure. A subdomain is marked as *EC2 only* if it always resolves only to IP addresses within EC2; similarly for Azure. We mark a subdomain as *EC2+Azure*, *EC2+Other*, or *Azure+Other* if it resolves to IP addresses associated with the appropriate subset of EC2, Azure, and other. Domains are counted as *EC2 only* if all of their subdomains only use EC2; similarly for Azure. Domains are marked as *EC2+Azure*, *EC2+Other*, or *Azure+Other* if they have subdomains associated with the indicated subset of EC2, Azure, and other.

The vast majority of cloud-using domains (94.9%) use EC2, and the majority of these domains use other hosting for some of their subdomains (i.e., EC2 + Other). Only 5.8% of domains use Azure. Additionally, a small fraction (0.7%) of cloud-using domains use both EC2 and Azure; hence the *EC2 total* and *Azure total* rows in Table 3 sum to more than 100%. A list of the top 10 (by Alexa rank) EC2-using domains appears in Table 4. This list will be used in several later sections with results specific to EC2, which is why we excluded the four top Azure domains that would otherwise have been in the top 10: live.com, msn.com, bing.com, and microsoft.com.

The distribution of Alexa ranks for cloud-using domains is skewed: higher ranked domains are more likely to be cloud-using than lower ranked domains. Notably, 42.3% of cloud-using domains have ranks in the first 250,000 sites versus only 16.2% of the bottom 250K domains.

The most frequent prefix used by cloud-using subdomains in our Alexa subdomains dataset is www (3.3% of all cloud-using subdomains). The other top 10 prefixes (each <1%) are, in order: m, ftp, cdn, mail, staging, blog, support, test, and dev. The majority of subdomains are hosted either only in the cloud or only elsewhere, although a small fraction (3%) appear to be hosted both on EC2 and other providers, what we might call a hybrid-cloud deployment.

[4]Except for domains hosting personal sites, e.g., wordpress.com, where subdomains are ranked individually.

Rank	Domain	Total # Subdom	# EC2 Subdom
9	amazon.com	68	2
13	linkedin.com	142	3
29	163.com	181	4
35	pinterest.com	24	18
36	fc2.com	89	14
38	conduit.com	40	1
42	ask.com	97	1
47	apple.com	73	1
48	imdb.com	26	2
51	hao123.com	45	1

Table 4: Top 10 (by Alexa rank) EC2-using domains, their total number of subdomains, and the number of EC2-using subdomains.

High traffic volume domains. We complement the above with an analysis of the top domains seen in the packet capture, as measured by traffic volume. We use Bro to extract hostnames within HTTP requests and common names within the server certificates embedded in HTTPS flows[5]. Aggregating the hostnames and common names by domain, we find 13,604 unique cloud-using domains: 12,720 use EC2 and 885 use Azure. Of these 13,604 domains, 6902 were also identified as cloud-using via the Alexa dataset; the remainder were not in the Alexa top 1 million. Table 5 lists the highest 15 such domains in terms of traffic volume. A few tenants are responsible for a large fraction of the traffic. Most notably, dropbox.com accounts for almost 70% of the combined HTTP(S) traffic volume. This also explains why HTTPS (used by dropbox.com) dominates HTTP in terms of volume (though not number of flows, refer to Table 2).

It is informative to compare our analysis of top EC2-using domains by traffic volume to the analysis by DeepField networks [28], which was conducted three months before we collected the packet capture. They used data from customers of their network analysis products. Seven of the domains on our top 15 list also appear within the top 15 on DeepField's list (indicated with a (d) in Table 5).

Summary and implications. A substantial fraction of the world's most popular websites rely in whole or in part on public IaaS clouds, especially EC2. Most cloud-using domains have some subdomains hosted on a cloud service while other subdomains are hosted elsewhere. Perhaps surprisingly a small, but noticeable fraction of subdomains use both a cloud and other hosting solutions. Finally, traffic volume appears to be dominated by a few cloud tenants (we discuss traffic patterns more next). Depending on how tenants' deploy their services (e.g., how many and which regions they use), these observations have implications for availability of web-based cloud-resident services. We explore the underlying deployments in more detail in §4.

3.3 Traffic Patterns

Our packet capture enables us to analyze not only who is running on the cloud, but also the traffic patterns between clients in our university and cloud-resident web services.

Flow-level properties. We first study the number of flows observed for various cloud-using domains in the packet capture. Figures 3a and 3b show CDFs of the number of HTTP and HTTPS flows, respectively, per-domain across our entire packet capture. We observe that ≈50% of domains have fewer than 1,000 HTTP flows, and more than 80% of domains have fewer than 1,000 HTTPS flows. Upon further analysis, we found that the top 100 cloud-using domains are responsible for about 80% of the HTTP flows

[5]TLS encryption hides the hostname associated with the underlying HTTP requests, so we use the common names found in TLS server certificates as a proxy.

EC2			Azure		
Domain	**Rank**	**Traffic (%)**	**Domain**	**Rank**	**Traffic (%)**
dropbox.com (d)	119	595.0 (68.21)	atdmt.com	11,128	27.0 (3.10)
netflix.com (d)	92	14.8 (1.70)	msn.com	18	20.9 (2.39)
truste.com (d)	15,458	9.2 (1.06)	microsoft.com	31	19.7 (2.26)
channel3000.com	29,394	6.4 (0.74)	msecnd.net	4,747	13.5 (1.55)
pinterest.com (d)	35	5.1 (0.59)	s-msn.com	25,363	12.5 (1.43)
adsafeprotected.com (d)	371,837	4.7 (0.53)	live.com	7	11.8 (1.35)
zynga.com	799	3.9 (0.44)	virtualearth.net	147,025	9.2 (1.06)
sharefile.com	20,533	3.6 (0.42)	dreamspark.com	35,223	7.1 (0.81)
zoolz.com	272,006	3.2 (0.36)	hotmail.com	2,346	6.3 (0.72)
echoenabled.com (d)	-	2.7 (0.31)	mesh.com	-	4.5 (0.52)
vimeo.com	137	2.3 (0.26)	wonderwall.com	-	3.2 (0.36)
foursquare.com	615	2.2 (0.25)	msads.net	-	2.5 (0.29)
sourcefire.com	359,387	1.9 (0.22)	aspnetcdn.com	111,859	2.3 (0.26)
instagram.com (d)	75	1.5 (0.17)	windowsphone.com	1,597	2.0 (0.23)
copperegg.com	122,779	1.5 (0.17)	windowsphone-int.com	-	2.0 (0.23)

Table 5: Domains with highest HTTP(S) traffic volumes (in GB) in the packet capture. Percentages are relative to the total HTTP(S) traffic across both clouds in the capture. Domains marked with (d) appeared on DeepField's Top 15 [28].

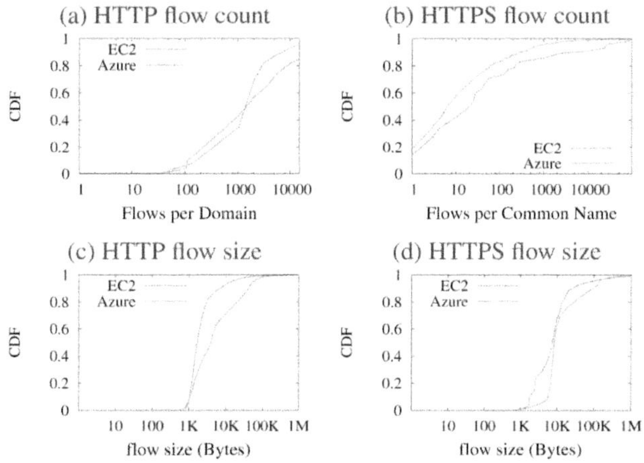

Figure 3: CDFs for HTTP/HTTPS flow counts and sizes.

Content	Bytes (GB)	%	mean (KB)	max (MB)
text/html	57.9	24.10	16	3.7
text/plain	56.2	23.37	5	24.4
image/jpeg	25.6	10.64	20	18.7
application/x-shockwave-flash	20.8	8.66	36	22.9
application/octet-stream	18.9	7.85	29	2,147
application/pdf	7.6	3.15	656	25.7
text/xml	7.5	3.10	5	4.9
image/png	7.1	2.94	6	24.9
application/zip	6.8	2.81	1,664	5,010
video/mp4	5.3	2.21	6,578	143

Table 6: HTTP content types by byte counts (in GB), as well as mean (in KB) and max (in MB) object sizes.

in EC2, and nearly 100% of the HTTP flows in Azure; a long tail follows for both clouds (CDF excluded for brevity).

Flow sizes and durations generally appear to fit heavy-tailed distributions (we omit durations in Figure 3 for brevity); similar properties have been observed for flows in other networking contexts (e.g., in data centers [21]). We note interesting differences between HTTP and HTTPS: in particular, HTTPS flows are larger and last longer than HTTP flows across both EC2 and Azure (e.g., median sizes for EC2 are 10K and 2K, respectively). This is expected given our observation that a large percentage of HTTPS traffic is from file storage services. In both cases, we see large flows that are more than a few MB in size and long flows that last for a few hours.

Content types. We next look at the types of content served by web-facing cloud tenants. We use Bro to extract the Content-Type and Content-Length fields from replies in HTTP flows. Unfortunately, we cannot extract these details for HTTPS flows because the HTTP headers are encrypted. The top content types, by byte count, for HTTP flows are shown in Table 6, along with the mean and max content sizes. About half of all content is html or plain text, and these type of objects are generally smaller in size. The majority of the remaining content is a mixture of images, Flash, generic binary data (i.e., octet-stream), PDFs, and XML; these objects are generally much larger. This suggests that EC2 and Azure HTTP traffic is primarily conveying web sites, and not (say) for file transfer. We see that some objects can be very large in size; e.g., we see binaries that are 5GB in size, and even some plain text files that are as large as 24MB.

Summary and Implications. We find that most flows arise from the top few domains. A majority of the flows are short, and HTTPS flows are generally larger in size and last longer than their HTTP counterparts. Most web services appear to be using the cloud to serve html or plain text content. These observations have implications for content delivery systems targeted toward cloud-resident services. For instance, the predominance of plain text and HTML traffic (as opposed to compressed images, binaries, videos, etc.) points to the fact that compression could be employed to save WAN bandwidth and improve content delivery latency [18].

4. TENANTS' DEPLOYMENT POSTURE

In this section, we attempt to understand *how* tenants use the cloud for deploying their front ends. We start by analyzing the deployment patterns employed by cloud-using (sub)domains. We first focus on the four patterns identified in Figure 1. We then quantify how many, and which, regions and availability zones are leveraged by cloud-using (sub)domains' front ends.

4.1 Deployment Patterns

In this section, we use the DNS records from our Alexa subdomains dataset and a variety of heuristics to detect and quantify usage of the deployment patterns outlined in Figure 1. Specifically, we estimate the use of virtual machines (VMs), platform-as-a-service (PaaS) environments, load balancers, content-distribution networks (CDNs), and domain name servers within the front ends of web services hosted in both EC2 and Azure. In general, we discuss EC2 and Azure separately because of differences in the cloud architectures.

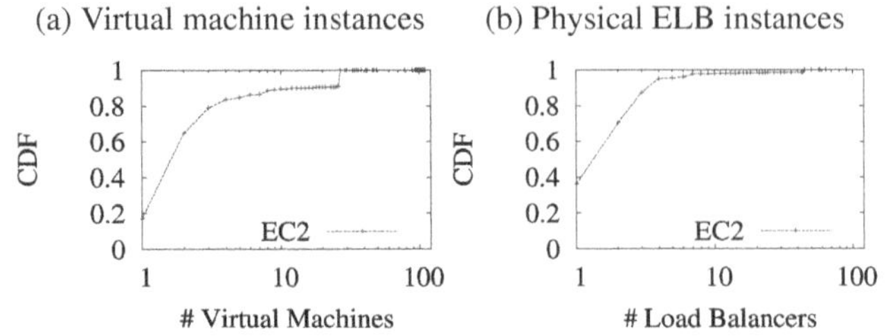

Figure 4: CDFs for the # of feature instances per subdomain (only includes subdomains which use the feature).

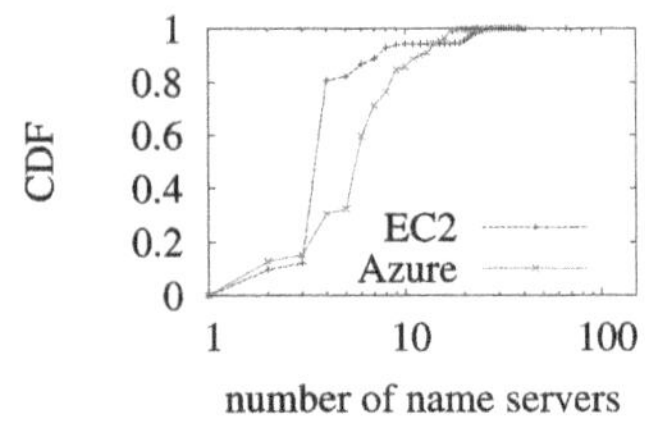

Figure 5: CDF of the # of DNS servers used per subdomain.

VM front end in EC2. Each VM instance in an IaaS cloud combines a set of virtual resources (CPU core(s), memory, local storage, and network bandwidth) whose capacity depends on the instance type. In EC2 each instance is assigned an internal IP address within a region-specific private network; EC2 tenants may optionally assign a public (i.e., Internet-routable) IP address to a VM.

We identify usage of VMs as directly-reachable web service front ends—i.e., deployment pattern *P1* (Figure 1a)—by examining if the DNS query for an EC2-using subdomain directly returns an IP address (instead of a CNAME), which we then associate with a VM instance. We find that 505,578 (72%) EC2-using subdomains leverage front end VMs. Figure 4a shows a CDF of the number of front end VM instances used by each EC2-using subdomain; this CDF only includes subdomains which use front end VMs. We observe that about half of such subdomains use 2 front end VMs and 15% use 3 or more front end VMs.

Aggregating by domain, we find that 52% of EC2-using domains have at least one subdomain which uses at least one front end VM. If we sum the number of front end VMs used across all subdomains of a given domain, we find that 10% of domains which use front end VMs in EC2 use 3 or more front end VMs in total.

PaaS front end in EC2. PaaS systems offer a hosted environment for deploying web applications, avoiding the need for tenants to manage low-level system details. PaaS systems are frequently built atop existing IaaS infrastructure: e.g., Amazon's Elastic Beanstalk [5] and Heroku [14] both run atop EC2. A Beanstalk environment always includes an Amazon Elastic Load Balancer (ELB) instance (discussed in more detail below), reflecting deployment pattern *P2* (Figure 1b, replace VMs with PaaS nodes). A Heroku environment may or may not include an ELB, reflecting usage of deployment patterns *P2* or *P3* (Figure 1), respectively.

We say that a subdomain uses Beanstalk or Heroku if the subdomain's DNS record has a CNAME that (*i*) includes 'elasticbeanstalk' or any of 'heroku.com', 'herokuapp', 'herokucom', and 'herokussl' and (*ii*) resolves to an IP in EC2's public IP address range. In the case of Heroku without ELB, the IPs to which the CNAME resolves represent PaaS nodes; we associate these IPs with the subdomain whose DNS record contains the corresponding CNAME.

A total of 201,666 (28%) EC2-using subdomains in our Alexa subdomains dataset contain a CNAME in their DNS record. Applying the above filters for PaaS, we find that 60,273 (8%) EC2-using subdomains use a front end PaaS environment in EC2. Of these, over 97% (59,991) are using Heroku; only 3% use Elastic Beanstalk. Amazon always includes an ELB in a Beanstalk environment, but Heroku only sometimes leverages ELBs—only 3% of subdomains (1,850) which use Heroku also use ELB. We therefore conclude that, in the case of EC2, PaaS systems are predominantly used according to deployment pattern *P3* (Figure 1c).

We now focus on the 58,141 (59,991 - 1,850) subdomains that use Heroku without ELB. We find that these are associated with just 94 unique IPs. Although we have no insight into the number of worker instances used by Heroku, this shows that Heroku is multiplexing PaaS functionality among a relatively large number of subdomains: in particular, we find that about one-third of subdomains using Heroku share the CNAME 'proxy.heroku.com'.

Load balancer front end in EC2. Load balancers divide traffic among a set of "worker" VMs or PaaS nodes, as reflected in deployment pattern *P2* (Figure 1b). Amazon Elastic Load Balancers (ELBs) [13] are Amazon-managed HTTP proxies. An EC2 tenant requests an ELB in a specific region and subsequently associates VM instances, in one or more zones, with this ELB. The ELB automatically round-robins requests among zones and among the VMs in each zone. In fact, traffic is routed to zone-specific ELB proxies by rotating the order of ELB proxy IPs in DNS replies. ELB can also be used with PaaS, as discussed above.

When a subdomain uses an ELB, the subdomain's DNS record contains a CNAME ending in 'elb.amazonaws.com'; the CNAMEs resolve to IP addresses for one or more ELB proxies. We identify ELB-using subdomains in our Alexa subdomains dataset based on the presence of such CNAMEs; we refer to each distinct CNAME as a "logical ELB instance". We also associate with the subdomain the IPs of the specific ELB proxies to which the CNAME resolves; we refer to these as "physical ELB instances".

We find that 27,154 (4%) EC2-using subdomains use ELB as their front end. Of the subdomains that use ELB, 280 (1%) use it in the context of Elastic Beanstalk and 1,850 (6.8%) use it with Heroku. Aggregating by domain, we find that 9,851 (26%) EC2-using domains use front end ELB(s).

Across all ELB-using subdomains, we observe 15,703 physical ELB instances (i.e., distinct IPs associated with ELB CNAMEs). Hence, while each subdomain has its own logical ELB(s), the physical ELB proxies that perform the actual load balancing appear to be shared across multiple, even unrelated, subdomains. In particular, we analyzed the number of subdomains per physical ELB and found that ≈4% of the physical ELB instances are shared by 10 or more subdomains.

Figure 4b shows a CDF of the number of physical ELB instances associated with each subdomain; this CDF only includes subdomains which use ELB. We observe that about 95% of ELB-using subdomains are associated with 5 or fewer physical ELB instances. A few ELB-using subdomains (e.g., dl.outbrain.com and m.netflix.com) use many physical ELB instances: 58 and 90, respectively.

Front ends in Azure. Azure's architecture differs from EC2 insofar as clients cannot distinguish whether a web service uses a VM, PaaS, or load balancer front end. In Azure, VMs and PaaS environments are both encompassed within logical "Cloud Services" (CS). An individual CS may contain (*i*) a single VM, (*ii*) a collection of related VMs, or (*iii*) a PaaS environment. Each CS is assigned a unique DNS name ending with 'cloudapp.net' and a corresponding public IP address. Traffic sent to this public IP goes through a transparent proxy—which performs NAT and, optionally, load balancing—before directing traffic to a VM or PaaS node. Thus, a CS may reflect deployment patterns *P1*, *P2* (with VMs or PaaS nodes), or *P3* (Figure 1), all of which appear the same from a client perspective.

We examine the DNS records for Azure-using subdomains in the Alexa subdomains dataset to identify subdomains which use a CS (i.e., VM, PaaS, or load balancer) front end. If the DNS query for an Azure-using subdomain either directly returns an IP address or returns a CNAME ending in 'cloudapp.net', then we say the subdomain uses a CS front end. We associate the directly returned IP or the CNAME, and its corresponding IP, with a CS instance.

A total of 1,153 (17%) Azure-using subdomains directly resolve to an IP address and 5,404 (82%) Azure-using subdomains contain a CNAME in their DNS record. Applying the above filters for CS, we find that 4,581 (70%) Azure-using subdomains use a CS front end. Aggregating by domain, we find that 57% of Azure-using domains have at least one subdomain which uses a CS front end.

Azure also offers a unique feature (which has no parallel in EC2) for load balancing across front ends: Azure Traffic Manager (TM) [9] uses DNS to direct traffic to different CSs, which may be spread across multiple regions. TM can, based on a tenant's preference, do performance-based load balancing (finding the CS closest to the client), failover load balancing (picking the next active CS), or simple round-robin load balancing. When a subdomain uses TM, its DNS record contains a CNAME ending in 'trafficmanager.net', similar to ELB. However, TM performs all load balancing using DNS—unlike ELB which uses a combination of DNS and physical proxies—so TM CNAMEs resolve directly to a CNAME for a specific CS (e.g., 'abc.cloudapp.net'). We find that only 100 (2%) Azure-using subdomains (corresponding to 52 domains) use TM.

The aforementioned CNAME-based filters for ELB, Beanstalk, Heroku, CS, and TM were not applicable to 116,323 (16%) EC2-using subdomains, and 1,938 (30%) Azure-using subdomains. We are investigating techniques to understand the deployment patterns underlying these subdomains.

Content distribution networks. We now focus on the use of CDNs, which we illustrated in deployment pattern *P4* (Figure 1d). Note that CDNs can be employed alongside any of the other three deployment patterns.

Both Microsoft and Amazon run their own CDNs, which we focus on studying. Amazon's CloudFront CDN [3] uses a different public IP address range than the rest of EC2. Hence, we determine if a subdomain uses CloudFront by observing if its DNS records contain one or more IPs in CloudFront's IP range. Azure's CDN [7] uses the same IP address ranges as other parts of Azure, so we detect whether a subdomain uses the Azure CDN based on whether a subdomain's DNS records contain CNAMEs with 'msecnd.net'.

We find 7,622 subdomains (corresponding to 5,988 domains) use CloudFront and 68 subdomains (corresponding to 54 domains) use Azure's CDN. Despite the much smaller number of domains using Azure's CDN, there is still a significant volume of traffic associated with msecnd.net in our packet capture dataset (Table 5). Azure's CDN is clearly being used within some Microsoft properties, perhaps to host embedded content or cookies.

Domain name servers. The first step in accessing a cloud-resident service is to resolve its name (Figure 1). In what follows, we examine cloud-resident subdomain's use of DNS, focusing on the extent to which they rely on cloud providers for DNS services as well.

We identifed the "location" of a cloud-using subdomain's authoritative name server(s) as follows: For each DNS record associated with a given subdomain in our Alexa subdomains dataset, we extract all the domains specified in the NS records. We then performed a DNS lookup on each of these domains from 50 globally-distributed PlanetLab nodes. We flushed and reset the cache of the local resolver between each DNS lookup, and we added the 'norecurse' flag to each DNS query to minimize the influence of caching. We compare the resulting IP addresses to the public IP address ranges for EC2, CloudFront, and Azure.

Cloud	Feature	# Domains	# Subdomains	# Inst.
EC2	VM	19.9K (52.5%)	505.6K (71.5%)	28.3K
	ELB	9.9K (25.9%)	27.1K (3.8%)	15.7K
	BeanStalk (w/ ELB)	188 (0.5%)	280 (< 0.01%)	455
	Heroku (w/ ELB	622 (1.6%)	1.9K (0.3%)	2.4K
	Heroku (no ELB)	1.3K (3.5%)	58.1K (8.2%)	94
Azure	CS	863 (37.0%)	4.5K (68.3%)	790
	TM	52 (2.2%)	100 (1.5%)	78

Table 7: Summary of cloud feature usage.

Rank	Domain	# Cloud Subdom	Front-end VM	Front-end PaaS	Front-end ELB	ELB IPs	Use CDN
9	amazon.com	2	0	1	2	27	0
13	linkedin.com	3	0	1	1	1	0
29	163.com	4	0	0	0	0	4*
35	pinterest.com	18	4	0	0	0	0
36	fc2.com	14	10	0	4	68	0
38	conduit.com	1	0	1	1	3	0
42	ask.com	1	1	0	0	0	0
47	apple.com	1	1	0	0	0	0
48	imdb.com	2	0	0	0	0	1
51	hao123.com	1	0	0	0	0	1*

Table 8: Cloud feature usage for the highest ranked EC2-using domains (* indicates use of a CDN other than CloudFront).

We observe a total of 23,111 name servers supporting the 713K cloud-using subdomains in our Alexa subdomains dataset. Many subdomains use the same name servers, leading to a smaller set of name servers than subdomains. Figure 5 shows a CDF for the number of name servers used by each cloud-using subdomain; we observe that nearly 80% of subdomains use 3 to 10 name servers. We categorize the name servers as follows: 2,062 were hosted in CloudFront, which appears to host Amazon's route53 DNS service as many of these name servers had 'route53' in their domain name; 1,239 were running inside EC2 VM instances; 22 were hosted inside Azure VM instances or Azure CS; and 19,788 were hosted outside any of EC2, CloudFront, or Azure;

The above analyses are summarized in Table 7 which shows how many (sub)domains in our Alexa subdomains dataset use each cloud feature. We also show the number of instances (identified by IP address) of that feature.

Analysis of top domains. As notable exemplars, Table 8 gives a detailed breakdown of the cloud feature usage of the most popular (according to Alexa rankings) EC2-using domains. We observe that the majority of subdomains associated with the top domains have VM or ELB front ends. Of those using ELB front ends, amazon.com and fc2.com use ELB the most (i.e., there are more physical ELB IPs associated with these domains). Three of the top domains have subdomains which use a CDN, but only one of these domains uses the CloudFront CDN.

Summary and implications. In summary, we find that the majority (71.5%) of EC2-using subdomains use a VM front end (deployment pattern *P1*); hence most EC2 tenants are using EC2 as a true IaaS cloud. Only a small fraction use an ELB front end (3.8%) or PaaS front end (8.5%). Due to limited use, failures of value-added features are unlikely to have a major impact on EC2-using subdomains. In Azure, we are able to identify the usage of VM, PaaS, or load balancing front ends (we cannot distinguish which) for 70% of subdomains. A small fraction (1.5%) of Azure-using domains

Region	Location	# Dom	# Subdom
ec2.us-east-1	Virginia, USA	25,722	521,681
ec2.eu-west-1	Ireland	6,834	116,366
ec2.us-west-1	N. California, USA	3,950	40,548
ec2.us-west-2	Oregon, USA	1,548	15,635
ec2.ap-southeast-1	Singapore	1,800	20,871
ec2.ap-northeast-1	Tokyo, Japan	2,223	16,965
ec2.sa-east-1	São Paulo, Brazil	625	14,866
ec2.ap-southeast-2	Sydney, Australia	313	554
az.us-east	Virginia, USA	268	862
az.us-west	California, USA	161	558
az.us-north	Illinois, USA	590	2,071
az.us-south	Texas, USA	1,072	1,395
az.eu-west	Ireland	564	1,035
az.eu-north	Netherlands	573	1,205
az.ap-southeast	Singapore	379	632
az.ap-east	Hong Kong	333	502

Table 9: EC2 and Azure region usage Alexa subdomains

leverage TM to balance traffic across different front ends. The majority of DNS servers used by cloud-using subdomains reside outside of EC2 or Azure, giving subdomains the option of routing traffic to different resources (in another cloud or a private data center) in the event of cloud failure.

4.2 Region Usage

EC2 and Azure give tenants the choice of using one or more geographically distinct regions (i.e., data centers). Regions provide a mechanism for robustness in the case of catastrophic failures, e.g., regional power or service outages [4, 6, 24, 35]. In this section, we examine how many, and which, of the eight regions offered by each cloud provider are leveraged by the front ends of cloud-using (sub)domains.

We ascertain the region(s) used by each subdomain in the Alexa subdomains dataset by comparing the IP addresses associated with that subdomain against the per-region IP address ranges published by EC2 [12] and Azure [8]. We only consider IPs associated with VM, PaaS, and ELB/TM.

Figure 6a shows a CDF (note the Y-axis starts at 90%) of the number of regions used by each subdomain in the Alexa subdomains. Over 97% of EC2-using and 92% of Azure-using subdomains exclusively use one region. Across all domains (Figure 6b), the trend of low region usage is largely the same, although, the fraction of Azure-using domains that only use one region (83%) is smaller than the fraction of subdomains that only use one region (92%).

The number of (sub)domains (from the Alexa subdomains) in each region are shown in Table 9. We observe that the usage of EC2 regions is heavily skewed towards a few regions: 74% of EC2-using subdomains use *US East* and 16% use *Europe West*. Azure, relatively speaking, has a more even distribution of subdomains across regions, but each region has significantly fewer subdomains. The most used Azure regions are *US South* and *US North*.

Analysis of top domains. We now focus on region usage of subdomains corresponding to the most popular (according to Alexa rankings) domains. Our analysis is summarized in Table 10. As with the rest of our results above, we see that in all but two cases, subdomains appear to use a single region. The exceptions are msn.com and microsoft.com, where 11 of the 89 subdomains and 4 of 11 subdomains, respectively, use two regions each. No popular subdomain uses three or more regions. We also note that in some cases, a domain may deploy different subdomains across different regions: e.g., live.com's 18 subdomains are spread across 3 regions. Contrarily, there are domains whose subdomains are all deployed in one region (e.g., pinterest.com).

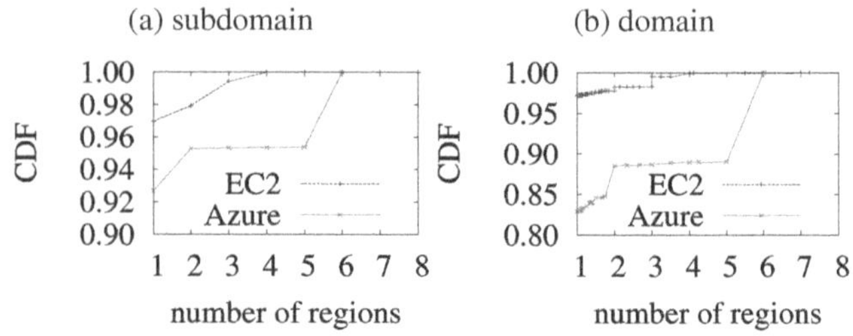

Figure 6: (a) CDF of the number of regions used by each subdomain (b) CDF of the average number of regions used by the subdomains of each domain.

Rank	Domain	# Cloud Subdom	Total # Regions	*k*=1	*k*=2
7	live.com	18	3	18	0
9	amazon.com	2	1	2	0
13	linkedin.com	3	2	3	0
18	msn.com	89	5	78	11
20	bing.com	1	1	1	0
29	163.com	4	1	4	0
31	microsoft.com	11	5	7	4
35	pinterest.com	18	1	18	0
36	fc2.com	14	2	14	0
42	ask.com	1	1	1	0
47	apple.com	1	1	1	0
48	imdb.com	2	1	2	0
51	hao123.com	1	1	1	0
59	go.com	4	1	4	0

Table 10: Region usage for the top cloud-using domains. The third column is the number of cloud-using subdomains; fourth is the total number of regions used by a domain; and the $k = 1$ and $k = 2$ columns are the number of subdomains which use one or two regions, respectively.

Analysis of subdomain deployment vs. customer location. An interesting question about cloud service deployment is whether subdomains are deployed near their customers? The answer to this question reveals whether current cloud services are deployed in an "optimal" manner, because deploying a service near customers usually leads to better client network performance (lower latency and higher throughput).

To answer this question, we leverage the client geo-location information provided by the Alexa web information service [2]. For example, at the time of writing, Alexa reported that 47% of clients accessing pinterest.com are from the United States, 10.4% from India, 3.2% from the United Kingdom, 3.1% from Canada, and 2.1% from Brazil. For each domain, we define the "customer country" as the country where the largest fraction of clients are located. We assume the customer country is the same for all of a website's subdomains, as Alexa does not track subdomains separately. For instance, the United States is the customer country for pinterest.com (and its subdomains) based on our definition.

We performed the analysis for all of the cloud-using subdomains (about 713K) in our dataset. Our measurement methodology was able to successfully identify approximately 538K (75% of the total) subdomains' customer country. We find that 252K (47%) subdomains' customer country is not the same as the country where this subdomain is hosted. Moreover, 174K (32%) subdomains are not even hosted on the same continent as the subdomains' customer country. This implies that a large fraction of web services are prob-

Instance type	Zone of probe destination ec2.us-east-1a	ec2.us-east-1c	ec2.us-east-1d
t1.micro	0.6 / 0.6	1.4 / 1.5	1.9 / 2.0
m1.medium	0.5 / 0.6	1.5 / 1.6	2.0 / 2.1
m1.xlarge	0.4 / 0.5	1.4 / 1.5	1.8 / 1.9
m3.2xlarge	0.4 / 0.5	1.5 / 1.7	1.9 / 2.0

Table 11: RTTs (least / median) in milliseconds over 10 probes from a micro instance in ec2.us-east-1a to an instance with a certain type (rows) and zone (columns).

ably not deployed in an optimal manner in terms of network performance. We suspect that the current deployment posture is affected by computing, storage, and network costs and/or how long the cloud region has existed. In §5, we explore how much opportunity exists for improving wide-area performance through changes in region usage.

Summary and implications. Our key finding in this section is that most popular domains and subdomains appear to be using a single region. This has significant implications on both the robustness and performance of cloud-using web services. From an availability perspective, an outage of EC2's *US East* region would take down critical components of at least 2.3% of the domains (61% of EC2-using domains) on Alexa's list of the top 1 million websites. This is a lower bound, as our results do not include dependencies between domains. From a performance perspective, our analysis of web service deployment and customer locations reveals that a considerable fraction of client traffic may travel farther than necessary due to suboptimal provisioning.

4.3 Availability Zone Usage

Within each region of EC2, cloud tenants have the choice of deploying across multiple zones. EC2 zones offer a means for improving service robustness as they are claimed to use separate compute, network, and power infrastructure so that a failure in any of these will not affect more than one zone. There seems to be no equivalent of zones in Azure.

We now focus on determining the zone deployment for EC2-using services' front ends. Unlike the regions, which are easily distinguished based on the IP address of a subdomain and the advertised ranges [8, 12], there is no direct way to associate an IP address to a zone. We therefore turn to cloud cartography techniques [34]. We use two methods to identify zones: network latency and proximity in the internal addresses to instances with a known zone (i.e., VMs we launched).

Latency-based identification. The first technique (originally used in [34]) aims to estimate whether a target physical instance (e.g., VM instance, physical ELB instance, etc.) is in the same zone as an instance under our control by measuring the RTT to the target. The RTT will be significantly smaller when both instances are in the same zone, compared to when they are in different zones, presumably reflecting a longer path in the latter case. We performed a simple experiment to confirm that RTTs follow this trend. We setup an m1.micro instance in the ec2.us-east-1a zone and measured the RTT (over 10 trials) to one instance of each type in each of the three zones ec2.us-east-1a, ec2.us-east-1c, and ec2.us-east-1d. Table 11 shows both the minimum and median RTTs. It is clear that the instances in the same availability zone have the smallest RTTs (about 0.5ms) regardless of the instance type. We repeated this experiment in each of the EC2 regions with similar results.

Our experiment corroborates similar previous ones [34] regarding the efficacy of latency-based zone estimates. However, there are several complicating factors when attempting to deploy this

Region	# tgt IPs	# resp.	1st zn	2nd zn	3rd zn	% unk
ec2.us-east-1	34,194	25,085	11,592	2,835	10,658	16.6
ec2.us-west-1	3,663	2,471	1,050	1,367	N/A	32.5
ec2.us-west-2	1,869	1,679	600	755	324	10.1
ec2.eu-west-1	8,581	7,023	1,935	2,095	2,993	18.2
ec2.ap-northeast-1	2,558	1,260	1,129	N/A	131	50.7
ec2.ap-southeast-1	2,296	1,987	968	1,019	N/A	13.5
ec2.ap-southeast-2	333	298	146	152	N/A	10.5
ec2.sa-east-1	701	616	376	240	N/A	12.1

Table 12: Estimated distribution of instance IPs across zones using latency method ($T = 1.1$). Second column is total number of IPs derived from subdomains, followed by the number that responded to probes, and the estimates of how many were in each of the zones. The final column is the percentage of the responding IPs for which no zone could be estimated.

methodology for zone measurement in practice. First, our and prior experiments used a limited number of otherwise idle EC2 instances—RTT times may be significantly more noisy across a broader set of instances and for more heavily loaded instances. Second, in some regions (ec2.us-east-1) we are unable to run an instance in each zone. Nevertheless, we perform, to the best of our knowledge, the first use of latency-based zone measurement at scale.

For each region, we launch three m1.medium instances in each zone from which to perform probes; we refer to these as probe instances. In ec2.us-east-1, we use ten additional m1.small instances in each zone because a large fraction of IPs are in this region. This region proved more challenging, due to a higher density of instances, a lack of full coverage of zones by probe instances, and more network noise. For each target physical instance in a region, we first map the public IP address to an internal IP address via an appropriate DNS query from a probe instance in that region. We then use hping3 to perform 10 TCP pings from a probe instance in each zone in the region to both the internal IP address and the public IP. While probes are very lightweight, we nevertheless limited the frequency of our probing, and the probing process was repeated 5 times on each probe instance. The experiment was performed over the course of five days (April 4th to April 8th, 2013). The minimal RTT is taken as the probe time. For a region with k zones (for ec2.us-east-1 we have $k = 3$, even though it has five zones), we end up with k probe times $t_1, \ldots, t_k$ and we let i be such that $t_i < t_j$ for all $i \neq j \in [1..k]$. If there exists no such i (due to a tie), then we mark the target IP (physical instance) as having unknown zone. If t_i is less than a threshold T then we conclude that the target physical instance is in zone i. Otherwise, we mark the target as having an unknown zone.

Setting $T = 1.1$, we end up with a zone estimate for physical instance IPs from our Alexa subdomains dataset in most regions. The results are shown in Table 12. The technique worked well for all regions except for ec2.ap-northeast-1. The unknown rate is affected by two factors: (*i*) Whether we can set up instances in all zones; for example, we can not set up instances in ec2.ap-northeast-1's zone #2 after January, 2013, but, according to our observation in January, the number of IPs in zone #1 and zone #2 is quite similar. (*ii*) How many times we repeat the probes to reduce network noise; with more probe data, the unknown rate can be further reduced.

Address-proximity-based identification. We supplement the latency measurements with sampling using our own accounts and an estimation mechanism based on proximity of a target internal IP address to a sampled IP address. As shown in prior work [34], it is very likely that two instances running in the same /16 subnet are

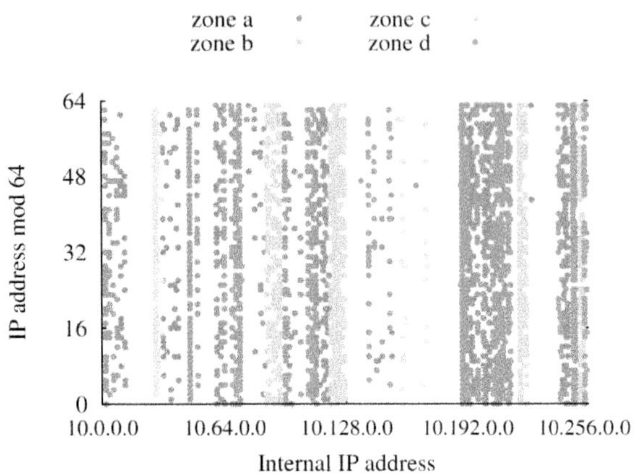

Figure 7: Sampling data for address proximity measurement.

co-located in the same zone (and are potentially even of the same instance type). We launched 5096 instances (in aggregate over the course of several years) under a number of our AWS accounts. The result is a set of account, zone label, internal IP triples (a_i, z_i, ip_i) for $i \in [1 .. X]$. A complicating factor is that, for $a_i \neq a_j$ (different accounts), it may be that the EC2-provided zone labels are not the same. Meaning, for account a_i it may be that the ec2.us-east-1a is not the same actual zone as ec2.us-east-1a for account a_j. Let Z be the set of zone labels.

We thus take the following straightforward approach to merge data across multiple different accounts. Consider a pair of accounts a, b. Find the permutation $\pi_{b \to a}$: $Z \to Z$ that maximizes the number of pairs of /16 IPs $ip_i/16 = ip_j/16$ such that $a_i = a$, $a_j = b$ and $\pi_{b \to a}(z_j) = z_i$. This can be done efficiently by ordering all triples of the accounts a and b by IP address, and inspecting the zone labels associated to each account for nearby IP addresses. One can repeat this for all pairs of accounts and solve the integer programming problem associated with finding an optimal set of permutations π, but it proved effective to take the simpler approach of finding $\pi_{b \to a}$ for one pair, merging the pair's triples by applying $\pi_{b \to a}$ appropriately, and then repeating with the next account c, etc. The outcome of applying this process to samples from ec2.us-east-1 is shown in Figure 7. Each binned IP address is a point, with the distinct colors representing distinct availability zones.

We now apply the sampling data to the physical instances from the Alexa subdomains dataset. If we have at least one sample IP in the same /16 subnet as the IP associated with a target physical instance, we conclude that the target instance is in the same zone as the sample instance. Otherwise, we mark the target instance as having an unknown zone. With this approach, we are able to identify the zone for 79.1% of the EC2 physical instances in the Alexa subdomains dataset.

Treating these zone identifications as ground truth, we check the accuracy of the latency-based zone identifications. Table 13 shows for each EC2 region the total number of physical instances in the Alexa subdomains dataset, the number of instances for which the two zone identification approaches agree, the number of instances whose zone cannot be identified using one or both methods, the number of instances where the two methods disagree, and the error rate of the latency-based method. The error rate is defined as the number of mismatched instances / (the total number of instances - the number of unknown instances). We observe that latency based method's overall error rate is 5.7%. Its error rate is less than 3.9%

Region	count	match	unknown	mismat.	error rate
all	37876	28640	7494	1742	5.7%
ec2.ap-northeast-1	1260	965	295	0	0.0%
ec2.ap-southeast-1	1987	1558	428	1	<0.1%
ec2.ap-southeast-2	298	201	97	0	0.0%
ec2.eu-west-1	6102	3359	1597	1146	25.0%
ec2.sa-east-1	616	0	616	0	N/A
ec2.us-east-1	23518	19228	3748	542	2.7%
ec2.us-west-1	2417	2032	385	0	0.0%
ec2.us-west-2	1678	1297	328	53	3.9%

Table 13: Veracity of latency-based zone identification.

Region	1st zone		2nd zone		3rd zone	
	#Dom	#Sub	#Dom	#Sub	#Dom	#Sub
ec2.us-east-1	16.1	419.0	6.2	155.4	9.5	292.9
ec2.us-west-1	1.6	33.2	3.0	37.4	N/A	N/A
ec2.us-west-2	0.9	13.4	1.0	9.6	0.8	7.3
ec2.eu-west-1	2.3	77.0	2.9	63.9	4.5	98.7
ec2.ap-northeast-1	0.4	3.7	1.3	11.3	1.5	12.9
ec2.ap-southeast-1	0.9	11.3	1.2	19.1	N/A	N/A
ec2.ap-southeast-2	0.2	0.3	0.2	0.3	N/A	N/A
ec2.sa-east-1	0.5	14.4	0.2	8.9	N/A	N/A

Table 14: Estimated number of domains and subdomains using various EC2 zones. Some regions only have 2 zones.

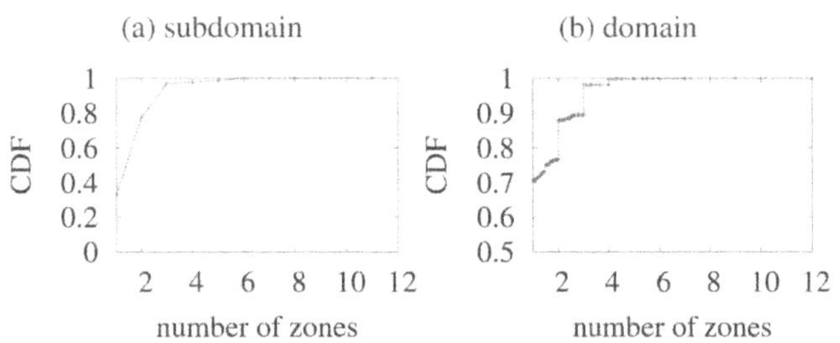

Figure 8: (a) CDF of the number of zones used by each subdomain (b) CDF of the average number of zones used by the subdomains of each domain.

for all regions except Europe West[6]. In particular, the error rate in the US East region (where the majority of the instances reside) is quite low (2.7%).

Combined identification. We combine the two zone identification methods to maximize the fraction of physical instances whose zone we can identify. We give preference to our address-proximity-based zone identifications, and use our latency-based identifications only for instances whose zone cannot be identified using the former method. Combining the two methods allows us to identify the EC2 availability zone for 87.0% of all physical EC2 instances in the Alexa subdomains dataset.

Table 14 summarizes the number of (sub)domains using each region and zone. In all but one region (Asia Pacific Southeast 2), we observe a skew in the number of subdomains using each zone in a region. Asia Pacific Northeast and US East regions have the highest skew across their three zones: 71% and 63% fewer subdomains, respectively, use the least popular zone in those regions compared to the most popular zone.

We also look at the number of zones used by each (sub)do-main. Figure 8a shows a CDF of the number of zones used by each subdomain. We observe that 33.2% of subdomains use only one zone, 44.5% of subdomains use two zones, and 22.3% of subdomains use

[6]We were unable to decrease the error rate for Europe West even after gathering additional latency measurements.

Rank	domain	# subdom	# zone	k=1	k=2	k=3
9	amazon.com	2	4	0	0	2
13	linkedin.com	3	5	1	1	1
29	163.com	4	1	4	0	0
35	pinterest.com	18	3	10	0	8
36	fc2.com	14	5	1	11	2
38	conduit.com	1	2	0	1	0
42	ask.com	1	1	1	0	0
47	apple.com	1	1	1	0	0
48	imdb.com	2	1	2	0	0
51	hao123.com	1	1	1	0	0

Table 15: Zone usage estimates for top using zones. Column 4 is estimated total number of zones used by all subdomains. Columns 4–6 indicate the estimated number of subdomains that use k different zones.

three or more zones. Of the subdomains that use two or more zones, only 3.1% use zones in more than one region. Figure 8b shows the average number of zones used by the subdomains of each domain. We observe that most domains (70%) only use one zone for all subdomains; only 12% of domains use two or more zones per subdomain on average.

Even for the top EC2-using domains, a large fraction of their subdomains only use a single zone (Table 15). For example, 56% of pinterest.com's EC2-using subdomains and 33% of linkedin.com's are only deployed in one zone.

Summary and implications. Our two key findings in this section are that *(i)* the majority of EC2-using subdomains only use one (33.2%) or two (44.5%) zones, and *(ii)* the subdomains using a given EC2 region are not evenly spread across the availability zones in that region. The former implies that many EC2-using subdomains would be completely unavailable if a single zone failed, and many others would be severely crippled: e.g., a failure of ec2.us-east-1a would cause 16.1% of subdomains to be completely unavailable. Our later key finding implies that an outage of a particular zone in a region may have a greater negative impact than an outage of a different zone in the same region: e.g., a failure of ec2.us-east-1a would impact ≈419K subdomains, while a failure of ec2.us-east-1b would only impact ≈155K.

5. WIDE-AREA PERFORMANCE AND FAULT TOLERANCE

Our results in the last section revealed that several services, even highly ranked Alexa domains, appear to use only a single region or even just a single availability zone. In this section, we explore the impact of these choices on web services' wide-area performance and tolerance to failures. We focus on EC2-using web services.

5.1 Wide-area Performance

The choice of region(s) by a cloud service may impact performance in at least two ways. First, clients' geo-distribution may be poorly matched to particular regions; such clients may experience poor latency and throughput compared to a more judicious deployment. Second, there could be temporary changes in which region performs best for a client due to congestion [19] or routing problems [36].

While the impact of diverse deployment of services (e.g., via CDNs) has been previously studied in other settings [27], we are unaware of any studies that assess its impact for the available diversity of modern public IaaS clouds. We therefore perform measurements to help us answer the following two questions: *(i)* To what extent does the choice of region impact performance experienced by clients of a web service? *(ii)* To what extent does the use

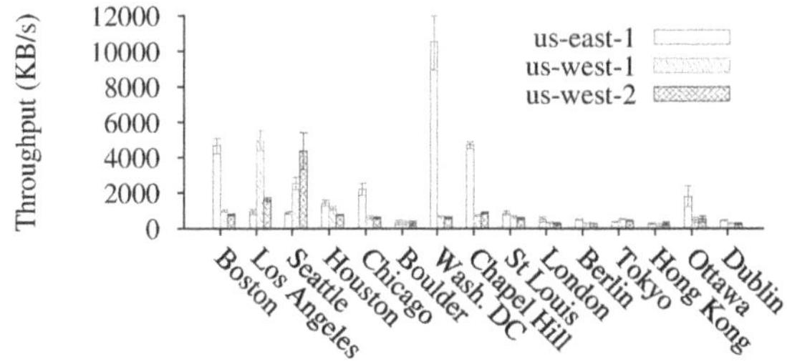

Figure 9: Average throughput between representative clients and EC2 regions in the US.

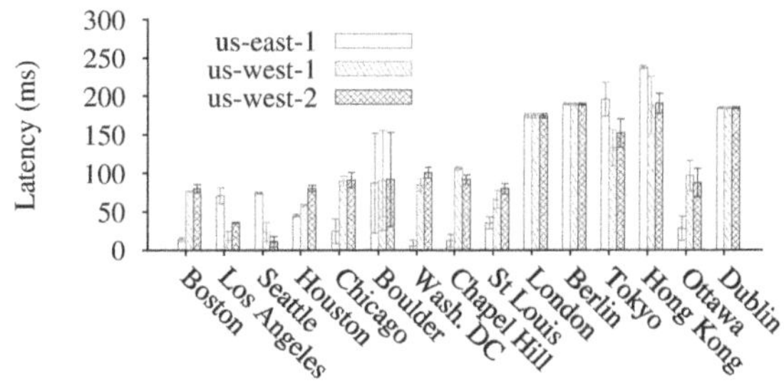

Figure 10: Average latency between representative clients and EC2 regions in the US.

of multiple regions (or zones) improve the client-perceived performance?

Latency measurements. To study per-region latency performance, we set up 40 m1.medium instances, 2 in each of the 20 availability zones available to us on EC2. We selected 80 geographically distributed PlanetLab [17] nodes as stand-ins for real clients and we used the hping3 utility to conduct 5 TCP pings to each of the 40 instances, from which we derive the average RTT. Pings that timed out were excluded from the calculations of the average. Probing was performed once every 15 minutes for three consecutive days.

Throughput measurements. We used the same set of 40 m1.medium EC2 instances and 80 PlanetLab nodes to measure throughput. We divided the PlanetLab nodes into two groups of 40. Each node in each group performed an HTTP get of a 2 MB file to one of the 40 EC2 instances (which were running Apache web server). At any given time, only one HTTP connection was established with each EC2 instance to avoid contention across throughput measurements. In particular, the clients in each group performed an HTTP get operation every 11.25 seconds; the download was canceled if it took more than 10 seconds. Each client accessed all 40 servers in each round, which means it took 450 seconds for one group to finish a round of downloading the file from each of the servers. So, in total, it took 15 minutes for 80 clients to perform one round of throughput measurements. The final throughput is measured as file_size / download_time. We ran the measurements for three consecutive days, for a total of 288 data points per client. The throughput measurements were intermingled with the latency measurements.

Performance across different regions. Figures 9 and 10 show the latency and throughput measurements for 15 representative PlanetLab locations and for the three US EC2 regions. The PlanetLab nodes are spread across the US and other parts of the world. We make a few key observations: *(i)* Single-region deployments must carefully choose a region. For example, the two US west regions do not offer equivalent "across-the-board" performance, with ec2.us-west-1 offering better average latency and throughput (130 ms and 1143 KB/s) than ec2.us-west-2 (145 ms and 895 KB/s) (averaged across all client locations). *(ii)* The charts show that the region

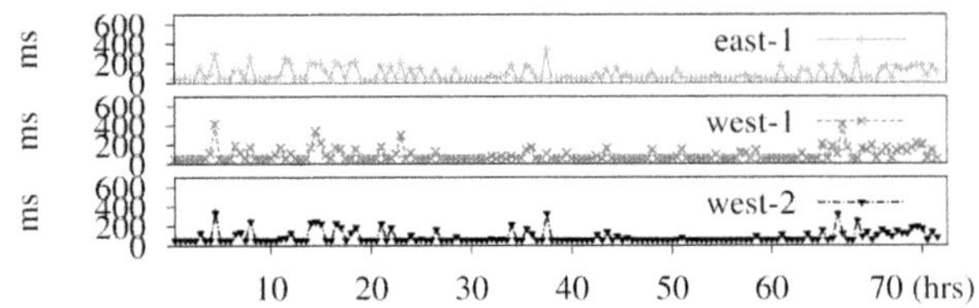

Figure 11: Latencies between Boulder site and three EC2 US regions. The best performing region changes over time.

chosen to serve content to a given client can have a significant performance impact. For example, for the client in Seattle, using the ec2.us-west-2 region can reduce latency by close to a factor of 6 and improve throughput by close to a factor of 5 compared to using ec2.us-east-1. (*iii*) We also note that the way a region is chosen may depend on the client's location: always choosing ec2.us-west-1 for the Seattle client is a good idea, but for the client in Boulder, the best choice of region may change dynamically (see Figure 11).

We now examine the relative benefits of, and choices underlying, multi-region deployments in more detail. We start by deriving an upper bound on the performance from a k-region deployment of a service. To do this, we determine the best k regions out of the 8, for $1 \leq k \leq 8$. Using our measurement data we determine the overall performance that the clients would have achieved given a routing algorithm that picked the optimal region from the k for each client and at each point in time. More specifically, for each value of k we: (*i*) enumerate all size-k subsets of regions; (*ii*) for each size-k subset compute the average performance across all clients assuming each client uses the lowest latency or highest throughput region of the k at each time round (15 min); and (*iii*) choose from these the size-k subset with lowest latency or highest throughput. Figure 12 shows the results. We find that while average performance can be increased a significant amount by adding more regions to one's deployment, there is evidence of diminishing returns after $k = 3$. In particular, latency decreases by 33% when $k = 3$ compared to $k = 1$, but only decreases by 39% when $k = 4$.

We now examine what constitutes the best k regions to use. The choice of best regions, by throughput, is as follows: ec2.us-east-1 ($k = 1$); ec2.us-east-1,ec2.eu-west-1 ($k = 2$); ec2.us-east-1, ec2.eu-west-1, ec2.us-west-1 ($k = 3$); and ec2.us-east-1, ec2.eu-west-1, ec2.us-west-1, ec2.ap-southeast-1 ($k = 4$). The choice of best regions, by latency, is: ec2.us-east-1 ($k = 1$); ec2.us-east-1,ec2.ap-northeast-1 ($k = 2$); ec2.us-east-1, ec2.ap-northeast-1, ec2.us-west-1 ($k = 3$); and ec2.us-east-1, ec2.ap-northeast-1, ec2.us-west-1, ec2.ap-southeast-1 ($k = 4$).

Performance across different zones. We also investigated the difference in performance should one use different zones in the same region. We found that the zone has little impact on latency, with almost equivalent average RTTs for all clients across the two days (results omitted for brevity). For throughput, the variation appears to be somewhat higher, but not as significant as that seen across regions. We believe such variation is due to local effects, such as contention on shared instances or network switches. This is suggested as well by other recent measurements of EC2 performance variability [25]. Moreover, in the next section we show that the Internet path variability between zones is low as well.

Summary and Implications. We find that using multiple regions can improve latency and throughput significantly. However, leveraging multiple regions may not be easy: while a given region always offers best performance for some clients, the choice of region for other clients will have to adapt in an online dynamic fashion.

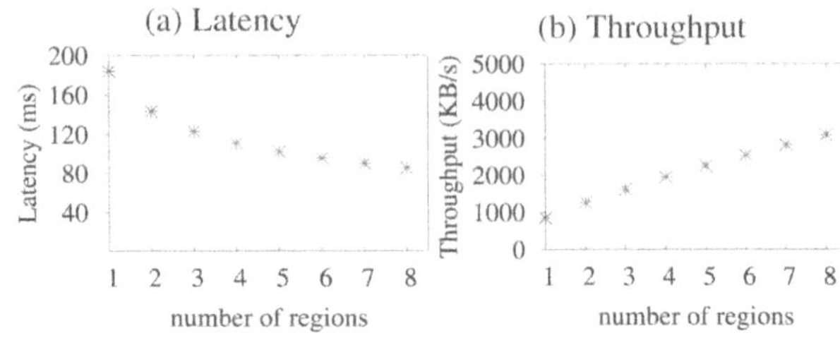

Figure 12: Average latency/throughput across all clients using an optimal k-region deployment.

Region	AZ1	AZ2	AZ3
ec2.us-east-1	36	36	34
ec2.us-west-1	18	19	n/a
ec2.us-west-2	19	19	19
ec2.eu-west-1	10	11	13
ec2.ap-northeast-1	9	n/a	9
ec2.ap-southeast-1	11	12	n/a
ec2.ap-southeast-2	4	4	n/a
ec2.sa-east-1	4	4	n/a

Table 16: Number of downstream ISPs for each EC2 region and zone.

This could be achieved via global request scheduling (effective, but complex) or requesting from multiple regions in parallel (simple, but increases server load).

While a multiple region deployment helps improve web service performance and protects against major cloud failures, cloud tenants must also consider other factors in making their decision of how many and which regions to use. First, cloud providers charge for inter-region network traffic, potentially causing tenants to incur additional charges when switching to a multi-region deployment. Second, the design of particular cloud features may restrict how a tenant's data can be shared across regions: e.g., objects stored in Amazon's Simple Storage Service (S3) can only be stored in one region at a time and Amazon Machine Images (AMIs) cannot be shared between regions. Lastly, deployments that rely on fewer features may be less susceptible to failures—e.g., deployments which only use VMs, and not other services like Amazon Elastic Block Storage or Amazon ELB, have not been affected by some major outages [4, 6]—reducing the need for resiliency through the use of multiple regions.

5.2 ISP Diversity

We now investigate tolerance to wide-area faults. Having in previous sections already established the reliance of many cloud-using services on one zone or region, we now focus on diversity in the immediate downstream ISPs at each EC2 zone. Greater diversity, and an even spread of routes across downstream ISPs, generally indicates greater tolerance to failures in Internet routing.

To do this study, we set up three m1.medium instances in each of the available EC2 availability zones. Then we ran *traceroute* 50 times from each of these instances to each of 200 geographically diverse PlanetLab nodes (Figure 2). Finally, we used the UNIX 'whois' utility to determine the autonomous system (AS) number associated with the first non-EC2 hop, and we count that AS as an immediate downstream ISP for the zone hosting the instance. The discovered ASs constitute a lower bound for the true number of ASs. Table 16 gives the number of distinct ASs seen for each zone and region. We note that: (*i*) different zones in a region have (almost) the same number of downstream ISPs; and (*ii*) the extent of diversity varies across regions, with some connected to more than 30 downstream ISPs and others connected to just 4. Except for South America and Asia Pacific Sydney, other regions are well-multihomed.

We also studied the spread of routes across downstream ISPs (not shown). We found it to be rather uneven: even when using well-connected regions – e.g., ec2.us-west-1 and ec2.eu-west-1– we found that up to 31% (ec2.us-west-1) and 33% (ec2.eu-west-1) of routes use the same downstream ISP.

Summary and Implications. Although individual regions are multihomed, the uneven spread of routes implies that local failures in downstream ISPs can cause availability problems for large fractions of clients of cloud-using web services. This could be overcome by using multiple regions at once, or by leveraging dynamic route control solutions [20].

6. RELATED WORK

There have been several studies of the network characteristics of data centers (DCs). For example, Kandula et al. [26] focus on measuring the flow level characteristics. Benson et. al [21] studied three types of DCs: universities, private enterprise and public cloud. They characterize the internal network traffic, and infer the applications deployed in the DCs as well. Similarly, Mishra et al. [32] characterize cloud backend workloads inside Google compute clusters. Li et al. [29] benchmark and compare the computing and storage service's performance across different public cloud providers. They also measure the network bandwidth between DCs. In roughly the same vein, Chen et al. [22] study the wide-area traffic patterns between Yahoo! DCs. Our work, in contrast, is more "user-facing" than the above, in that we focus on characterizing deployment patterns of the front ends of cloud-using web services, the wide-area traffic they impose, and the implications of these properties on client perceived performance and availability. Our work therefore extends prior works on DC and cloud workload characterization along important new axes.

7. CONCLUSION

In this work we performed the first extensive measurement study of usage of modern infrastructure-as-a-service (IaaS) clouds, in particular Amazon EC2 and Windows Azure. This measurement study, which combined data from a university packet capture, interrogation of DNS records for websites listed on the Alexa top 1 million list, and lightweight probing, confirms the oft-reported anecdotes about the extent to which modern web services use these cloud systems. We profile the deployment patterns observed for popular web services. We uncover that, in many ways, these deployments are somewhat precarious, as the vast majority of (even very popular) websites use only one cloud region. In addition to resiliency benefits, we show that multi-region deployments could significantly increase latency and throughput performance in EC2. Beyond providing a snapshot on the state of cloud usage, we believe our work will spark further research on tracking cloud usage, as well as developing cloud-region-aware routing and deployment mechanisms. Finally, we make all data sets used in this paper publicly available [10], with the exception of the packet capture.

8. ACKNOWLEDGMENTS

We would like to thank Dale Carder, Michael Hare and Mark Tinberg from the Department of Information Technology at the of University of Wisconsin-Madison for helping capture packet traces. We would also like to thank our shepherd and the anonymous reviewers for their insightful feedback. This work is supported by NSF awards 1040757 and 1065134.

9. REFERENCES

[1] Alexa. http://alexa.com/topsites.

[2] Alexa Web Information Service. http://aws.amazon.com/awis/.

[3] Amazon CloudFront. http://aws.amazon.com/cloudfront.

[4] Amazon ELB Service Event in the US-East Region. http://aws.amazon.com/message/680587/.

[5] AWS Elastic Beanstalk. http://aws.amazon.com/elasticbeanstalk.

[6] AWS Service Event in the US-East Region. https://aws.amazon.com/message/680342/.

[7] Azure CDN. http://msdn.microsoft.com/en-us/library/windowsazure/ee795176.aspx.

[8] Azure Datacenter IP Ranges. http://microsoft.com/en-us/download/details.aspx?id=29840.

[9] Azure TM. http://msdn.microsoft.com/en-us/library/windowsazure/hh744833.aspx.

[10] Cloud Measurement Data. http://pages.cs.wisc.edu/~keqhe/cloudmeasure_datasets.html.

[11] Cloudflare CDN. http://cloudflare.com.

[12] EC2 public IP ranges. https://forums.aws.amazon.com/ann.jspa?annID=1528.

[13] ELB. http://aws.amazon.com/elasticloadbalancing.

[14] Heroku. http://heroku.com.

[15] Knock. http://code.google.com/p/knock.

[16] Passive DNS Network Mapper. http://code.google.com/p/dnsmap/.

[17] PlanetLab. http://planet-lab.org/.

[18] B. Agarwal, A. Akella, A. Anand, A. Balachandran, P. Chitnis, C. Muthukrishnan, R. Ramjee, and G. Varghese. EndRE: An End-System Redundancy Elimination Service for Enterprises. In *NSDI*, pages 419–432, 2010.

[19] A. Akella, S. Seshan, and A. Shaikh. An Empirical Evaluation of Wide-area Internet Bottlenecks. In *Proceedings of the 3rd ACM SIGCOMM conference on Internet measurement*, pages 101–114. ACM, 2003.

[20] A. Akella, S. Seshan, and A. Shaikh. Multihoming Performance Benefits: An Experimental Evaluation of Practical Enterprise Strategies. In *USENIX Annual Technical Conference, General Track*, pages 113–126, 2004.

[21] T. Benson, A. Akella, and D. A. Maltz. Network Traffic Characteristics of Data Centers in the Wild. In *Proceedings of the 10th ACM SIGCOMM conference on Internet measurement*, pages 267–280. ACM, 2010.

[22] Y. Chen, S. Jain, V. K. Adhikari, Z.-L. Zhang, and K. Xu. A First Look at Inter-Data Center Traffic Characteristics via Yahoo! Datasets. In *INFOCOM, 2011 Proceedings IEEE*, pages 1620–1628. IEEE, 2011.

[23] I. Drago, M. Mellia, M. M Munafo, A. Sperotto, R. Sadre, and A. Pras. Inside Dropbox: Understanding Personal Cloud Storage Services. In *Proceedings of the 2012 ACM conference on Internet measurement conference*, pages 481–494. ACM, 2012.

[24] J. Edberg. Post-Mortem of October 22, 2012 AWS Degradation. http://techblog.netflix.com/2012/10/post-mortem-of-october-222012-aws.html.

[25] B. Farley, A. Juels, V. Varadarajan, T. Ristenpart, K. D. Bowers, and M. M. Swift. More for Your Money: Exploiting Performance Heterogeneity in Public Clouds. In *Proceedings of the Third ACM Symposium on Cloud Computing*, page 20. ACM, 2012.

[26] S. Kandula, S. Sengupta, A. Greenberg, P. Patel, and R. Chaiken. The Nature of Data Center Traffic: Measurements & Analysis. In *Proceedings of the 9th ACM SIGCOMM conference on Internet measurement conference*, pages 202–208. ACM, 2009.

[27] R. Krishnan, H. V. Madhyastha, S. Srinivasan, S. Jain, A. Krishnamurthy, T. Anderson, and J. Gao. Moving beyond End-to-End Path Information to Optimize CDN Performance. In *Proceedings of the 9th ACM SIGCOMM conference on Internet measurement conference*, pages 190–201. ACM, 2009.

[28] C. Labovitz. How Big is Amazon's Cloud? `http://deepfield.net/blog`, April 2012.

[29] A. Li, X. Yang, S. Kandula, and M. Zhang. CloudCmp: Comparing Public Cloud Providers. In *Proceedings of the 10th ACM SIGCOMM conference on Internet measurement*, pages 1–14. ACM, 2010.

[30] A. Li, X. Zong, S. Kandula, X. Yang, and M. Zhang. CloudProphet: Towards Application Performance Prediction in Cloud. In *ACM SIGCOMM Computer Communication Review*, volume 41, pages 426–427. ACM, 2011.

[31] R. McMillan. Amazon's Secretive Cloud Carries 1 Percent of the Internet. `http://www.wired.com/wiredenterprise/2012/04/amazon-cloud/`, 2012.

[32] A. K. Mishra, J. L. Hellerstein, W. Cirne, and C. R. Das. Towards Characterizing Cloud Backend Workloads: Insights from Google Compute Clusters. *ACM SIGMETRICS Performance Evaluation Review*, 37(4):34–41, 2010.

[33] V. Paxson. Bro: A System for Detecting Network Intruders in Real-Time. In *USENIX Security Symposium (SSYM)*, 1998.

[34] T. Ristenpart, E. Tromer, H. Shacham, and S. Savage. Hey, You, Get Off of My Cloud: Exploring Information Leakage in Third-party Compute Clouds. In *Proceedings of the 16th ACM conference on Computer and communications security*, pages 199–212. ACM, 2009.

[35] J. Schectman. Netflix Amazon Outage Shows Any Company Can Fail. `http://blogs.wsj.com/cio/2012/12/27/netflix-amazon-outage-shows-any-company-can-fail/`, 2012.

[36] R. Teixeira, A. Shaikh, T. Griffin, and J. Rexford. Dynamics of Hot-potato Routing in IP Networks. In *ACM SIGMETRICS Performance Evaluation Review*, volume 32, pages 307–319. ACM, 2004.

Choreo: Network-Aware Task Placement for Cloud Applications

Katrina LaCurts, Shuo Deng, Ameesh Goyal, Hari Balakrishnan
MIT Computer Science and Artificial Intelligence Lab
Cambridge, Massachusetts, U.S.A.
{katrina, shuodeng, ameesh, hari}@csail.mit.edu

ABSTRACT

Cloud computing infrastructures are increasingly being used by network-intensive applications that transfer significant amounts of data between the nodes on which they run. This paper shows that tenants can do a better job placing applications by understanding the underlying cloud network as well as the demands of the applications. To do so, tenants must be able to quickly and accurately measure the cloud network and profile their applications, and then use a network-aware placement method to place applications. This paper describes Choreo, a system that solves these problems. Our experiments measure Amazon's EC2 and Rackspace networks and use three weeks of network data from applications running on the HP Cloud network [15]. We find that Choreo reduces application completion time by an average of 8%–14% (max improvement: 61%) when applications are placed all at once, and 22%–43% (max improvement: 79%) when they arrive in real-time, compared to alternative placement schemes.

CATEGORIES AND SUBJECT DESCRIPTORS

C.4 [**Performance of Systems**]: Measurement Techniques

KEYWORDS

Application Placement; Bottlenecks; Cloud Computing; Cross Traffic; Datacenters; Measurement; Throughput

1. INTRODUCTION

A significant number of applications that run on cloud computing infrastructures are *network-intensive*, transferring large amounts of data between machines. Examples include Hadoop jobs [12], analytic database workloads, storage/backup services, and scientific or numerical computations (see `http://aws.amazon.com/hpc-applications`). Such applications operate across dozens of machines [31], and are deployed on both public cloud providers such as Amazon EC2 and Rackspace, as well as enterprise datacenters ("private clouds").

The performance of such applications depends not just on computational and disk resources, but also on the network throughput between the machines on which they are deployed. Previous research [4, 11] has shown that the datacenter network is the limiting factor for many applications. For example, the VL2 paper reports that "the demand for bandwidth between servers inside a datacenter is growing faster than the demand for bandwidth to external hosts," and that "the network is a bottleneck to computation" with top-of-rack (ToR) switches frequently experiencing link utilizations above 80% [11].

Much previous work has focused on better ways to design datacenter networks to avoid hot spots and bottlenecks. In this paper, we take a different approach and ask the converse question: given a network architecture, what is the impact of a network-aware task placement method on end-to-end performance (e.g., application completion time)? Our hypothesis is that by measuring the inter-node rates and bottlenecks in a datacenter network, and by profiling applications to understand their data transfer characteristics, it is possible to improve the performance of a mix of applications.

A concrete context for our work is a tenant (an organization paying for computing resources) of a cloud computing provider with a set of network-intensive cloud applications. To run these applications, the tenant requests a set of virtual machine (VM) instances from the cloud provider; to contain costs, the tenant is thrifty about how many VMs or instances it requests. When it gets access to the VMs, the tenant now has a decision to make: how should the different applications be placed on these VMs to maximize application performance? A common tenant goal is to minimize the run-time of the application.

For network-intensive applications, an ideal solution is to map an application's tasks to the VMs taking the inter-task network demands as well as the inter-VM network rates into consideration. We use "tasks" as an intuitive term: a task may map to a collection of processes in an application, for instance a map or reduce task during a MapReduce job. As a simple example, suppose an application has three tasks, S, A, and B, where A and B communicate often with S, but not much with each other. If we are given three VMs (in general on different physical machines) and measure the network rates between them to be different—say, two of them were higher than the third—then the best solution would be to place S on the VM with the highest network rates to the other two VMs. By not taking the performance of the underlying network into account, applications can end up sending large amounts of data across slow paths, while faster, more reliable paths remain under-utilized. Our goal is to build on this insight and develop a scalable system that works well on current cloud providers.

This paper makes two contributions. The first is a network-aware placement system, called **Choreo**, which tenants can use to place a mix of applications on a cloud infrastructure. Choreo has three sub-systems: a low-overhead measurement component to obtain inter-VM network rates, a component to profile the data transfer characteristics of a distributed application, and an algorithm to

IMC'13, October 23–25, 2013, Barcelona, Spain.

http://dx.doi.org/10.1145/2504730.2504744.

map application tasks to VMs so that tasks that communicate often are placed on VMs with higher rates between them. These sub-systems must overcome four challenges: first, inter-VM network rates are not constant [6]; second, cloud providers often use a "hose model" to control the maximum output rate from any VM; third, any practical measurement or profiling method must not introduce much extra traffic; and fourth, placing a subset of tasks changes the network rates available for subsequent tasks. Moreover, an optimal placement method given the network rates and application profile is computationally intractable, so any practical approach can only be approximate. To the best of our knowledge, the problem of matching compute tasks to nodes while taking inter-VM network properties into account has not received much prior attention.

The second contribution is an evaluation of how well Choreo performs compared to other placement methods that do not consider network rates or inter-task communication patterns. We collect network performance data from Amazon's EC2 and Rackspace, as well as application profiles from the HP Cloud [15], to evaluate Choreo. We find that it is possible to use packet trains to estimate TCP throughput within a few minutes for 90 VM pairs. We find that Choreo can reduce the average running time of applications by 8%–14% (max improvement: 61%) when applications are placed all at once, and 22%–43% (max improvement: 79%) when applications arrive in real-time, compared to alternative placement methods on a variety of workloads. These results validate our hypothesis that task mapping using network measurements and application communication profiles are worthwhile in practice.

2. CHOREO

Choreo has three sub-systems, which perform three distinct jobs: (1) profile the tenant's application tasks, (2) measure the performance of the network between the VMs allotted by the cloud provider, and (3) place and monitor application tasks.

2.1 Profiling Applications

Choreo uses a network monitoring tool such as sFlow or `tcpdump` to gather application communication patterns. Choreo assumes that by profiling an application offline (during a testing phase or in production for long-running services), it will have reasonably accurate knowledge of the application's communication pattern online. For batch computations, this assumption may be reasonable because the relative amounts of data sent between different application tasks might not change dramatically between testing and production; on an encouraging note, some previous work suggests that application traffic patterns are predictable [4]. The dataset we use for our evaluation (see Section 6.1) justifies this assumption; in this dataset, we found that data from the previous hour and the time-of-day are good predictors of the number of bytes transferred in the next hour.

Choreo models the inter-task network needs of an application by profiling the *number of bytes sent*, rather than the rate observed. The reason is that the network rate achieved depends on what else is going on in the network, whereas the number of bytes is usually independent of cross-traffic in cloud applications.

The output of the application profiling step is a matrix whose rows and columns are the application's tasks, where each entry A_{ij} is a value proportional to the number of bytes sent from task i to task j.

2.2 Measuring the Network

Choreo measures the network path between each pair of VMs to infer the TCP throughput between them. When we started this project over a year ago, we found that the TCP throughput between the VMs obtained on Amazon's EC2 was highly variable, as shown in Figure 1. Over the past few months, however, we have observed a significant change in how EC2 (and Rackspace) manage their internal bandwidth.

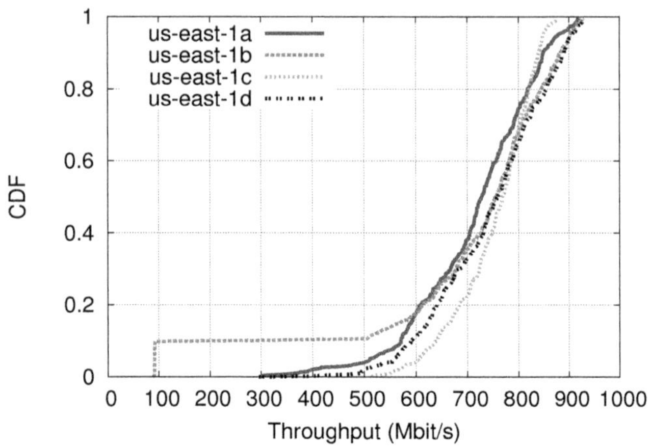

Figure 1: TCP throughput measurements on Amazon EC2 taken roughly one year ago, in May, 2012. Each line represents data from a different availability zone in the US East datacenter. Path throughputs vary from as low as 100 Mbit/s to almost 1 Gbit/s.

To measure spatial stability, we used 19 10-instance topologies made up of medium Amazon EC2 instances, and 4 10-instance topologies made up of 8-GByte Rackspace instances. For each of the paths in a given topology, we measured the TCP throughput on the path by running `netperf` for 10 seconds. This method gives us 1710 data points in total across the 19 topologies for EC2, and 360 data points for Rackspace. Figure 2 shows a CDF of the throughputs we observed on the instances in both networks. In EC2 (Figure 2(a)), although the CDF shows a large range of spatial variability, with throughputs ranging from 296 Mbit/s to 4405 Mbit/s, most paths (roughly 80%) have throughputs between 900 Mbit/s and 1100 Mbit/s (the mean throughput is 957 Mbit/s and the median is 929 Mbit/s). Not shown on the CDF are 18 paths that had extremely high throughput (near 4 Gbit/s). We believe that most of these paths were on the same physical server (see Section 4.2). Because all of these measurements were taken at roughly the same time, we can conclude that the variability in 20% of the paths is not strictly a function of the time of day.

Another interesting feature of Figure 2(a) is the distinct knees around 950 Mbit/s and 1100 Mbit/s. We suspect that this is partly due to a correlation between path throughput and path length; see Section 4.2.

In Rackspace (Figure2(b), there is very little spatial variation. In fact, every path has a throughput of almost exactly 300 Mbit/s, which is the advertised internal network rate for the 8 GByte Rackspace instances.[1] This implies that if a tenant were placing a single application on the Rackspace network, there would be virtually no variation for Choreo to exploit. However, Choreo is still effective in this type of network when a tenant is placing multiple applications in sequence, as traffic from existing applications causes variations in available throughput (Section 6.3).

In all our experiments, we have found that both of these networks are rate-limited and implement a *hose model* [10] to set a maximum outgoing rate for each VM. Figures 2(a) and 2(b) give evidence for such rate-limiting, as the typical throughput for a path remains close

[1] `http://rackspace.com/cloud/servers/pricing`

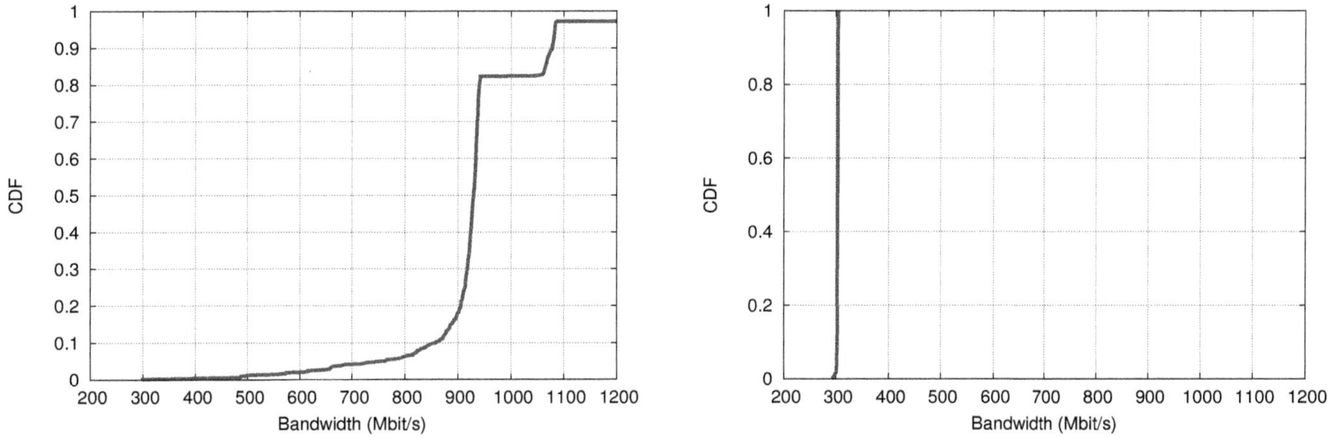

(a) EC2 (b) Rackspace

Figure 2: TCP throughput measured in May, 2013 on 1710 paths for EC2 and 360 paths for Rackspace. We see some variation on EC2, but less than in Figure 1. Rackspace exhibits almost no spatial variation in throughput.

to a particular value for each network (1 Gbit/s for EC2, 300 Mbit/s for Rackspace). We develop techniques to confirm both of these hypotheses in Section 3, and verify them on EC2 and Rackspace in Section 4.3.

Our approach to estimating TCP throughput in these figures was to use `netperf`, but this approach induces significant overhead for online use. Choreo must also measure the network quickly, so that applications can be placed in a timely manner. Moreover, if Choreo's measurement phase takes too long, there is a chance the network could change between measurement time and placement (we discuss the temporal stability of public cloud networks in Section 4.1).

To overcome this issue, Choreo uses packet trains to measure available throughput. We discuss this method, as well as Choreo's methods for assessing rate limits and bottlenecks, in Section 3. Briefly, packet trains allow Choreo to get a snapshot of the network within just a few minutes for a ten-node topology, including the overhead of retrieving throughput measurements from each machine back to a centralized server.

2.3 Placing Applications

Once the network has been measured and the application profiled, Choreo must place each application's tasks on the network. In the Appendix, we show how to formulate the problem of task placement as an integer linear program (ILP). Because solving ILPs can be slow in practice, we develop a greedy placement algorithm that takes far less time to run, and in practice gives near-optimal results (see Section 5).

2.4 Handling Multiple Applications

A tenant may not know all of the applications it needs to run ahead of time, or may want to start some applications after others have begun. To run a new application while existing ones are running, Choreo re-measures the network, and places its tasks as it would normally (presumably there is more variation in the network in this case, because existing applications create cross traffic). It is possible, however, that placing applications in sequence in this manner will result in a sub-optimal placement compared to knowing their demands all at once. For that reason, every T minutes, Choreo re-evaluates its placement of the existing applications, and migrates tasks if necessary. T can be chosen to reflect the cost of migration; if migration is cheap, T should be smaller. This re-evaluation also allows Choreo to react to major changes in the network.

3. MEASUREMENT TECHNIQUES

Choreo's primary function is placing application tasks on a set of VMs. To do this, it needs to know three things. First, the available throughput on each path, which tells Choreo what the throughput of a single connection on that path is. Second, the amount of cross traffic in the network, which tells Choreo how multiple connections on the same path will be affected by each other. For instance, if one connection gets a throughput of 600 Mbit/s on a path, it is possible that two connections on that path will each see 300 Mbit/s—if they are the only connections on a path with link speed of 600 Mbit/s—or that they will each see 400 Mbit/s—if there is one background TCP connection on a path with a link speed of 1200 Mbit/s. Third, which paths share bottlenecks, which tells Choreo how connections between different pairs of VMs will be affected by each other. For instance, knowing that $A \rightsquigarrow B$ shares a bottlenecks with $C \rightsquigarrow D$ informs Choreo's estimated rate of a new connection on $A \rightsquigarrow B$ when connections exist on $C \rightsquigarrow D$.

3.1 Measuring Pair-Wise Throughput

The first measurement that Choreo does is to estimate the pairwise TCP throughput between the cloud VMs, to understand what the throughput of a single connection will be. Estimating the pairwise TCP throughput between N VMs by running bulk TCP transfers takes a long time for even modest values of N. Packet trains, originally proposed in [18] and also used in [7], have been adapted in various ways, but with only varying success over Internet paths [27, 28]. The question is whether more homogeneous and higher-rate cloud infrastructures permit the method to be more successful.[2]

Choreo's measurement module sends K bursts of P-byte UDP packets, each burst made up of a sequence of B back-to-back packets. Bursts are separated by δ milliseconds to avoid causing persistent congestion. This collection of K bursts is one packet train; to estimate throughput on a path, we send only one packet train on that path.

At the receiver, the measurement module observes the kernel-level timestamps at which the first and last packet of each burst b_i was received using the `SO_TIMESTAMPNS` socket option, and records this time difference, t_i. If either the first or last packet of a burst is

[2]In our experiments, "packet pairs", in which only two packets are sent, were not very accurate on any cloud environment, and so Choreo does not use that method.

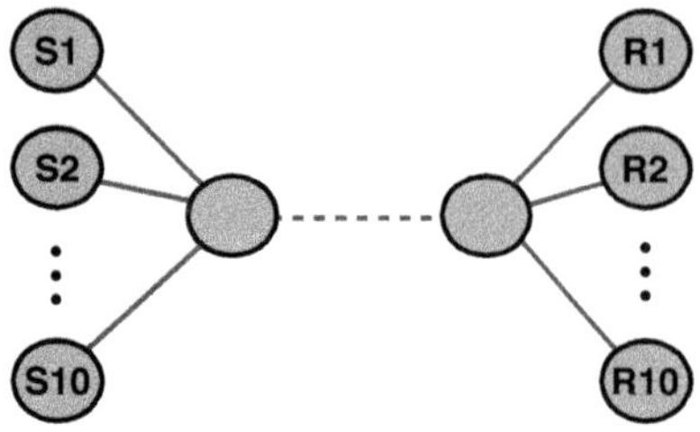

(a) Simple topology. All links are 1 Gbit/s.

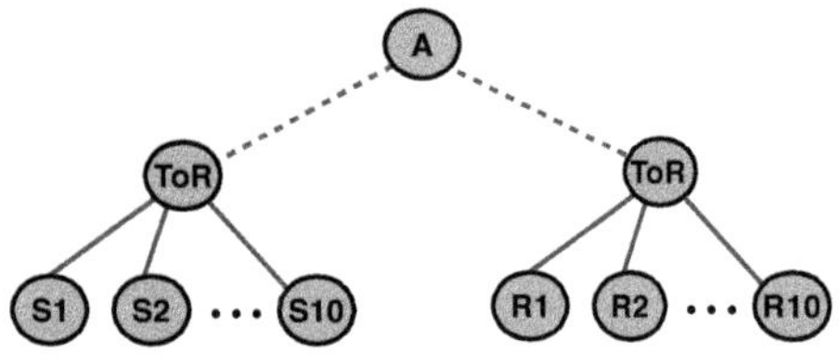

(b) Cloud topology. Links between sender/receiver nodes and ToR switches are 1 Gbit/s, and links between ToR switches and the aggregate switch (labeled "A") are 10 Gbit/s.

Figure 3: ns-2 simulation topologies for our cross traffic method. The dashed lines are bottlenecks where cross traffic will interfere.

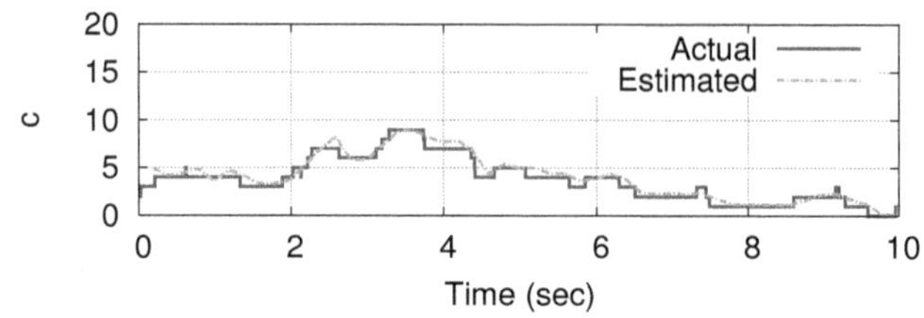

(a) Simulation results for $c < 10$ on a simple topology.

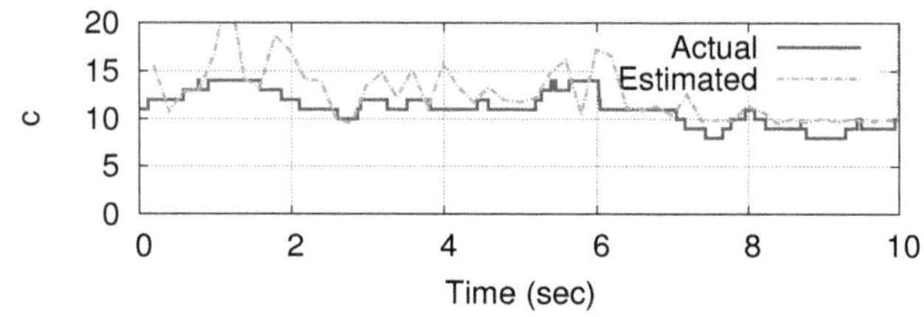

(b) Simulation results for $c \geq 10$ on a more realistic cloud topology.

Figure 4: ns-2 simulation results for our cross traffic method. We are able to quickly and accurately determine the number of background connections, particularly for small values of c, even when the number of background connections changes rapidly.

lost (which we can determine via the sequence numbers we inserted into the UDP payload), we adjust t_i to take into account what the time difference should have been, by calculating the average time it took to transfer one packet and adjusting for the number of packets missing from the beginning or end of the burst. We also record the number of packets received in each burst, $n_i \leq B$.

Using this data, we estimate the bulk TCP throughput as

$$\frac{P \cdot \sum_{i=1}^{K} n_i}{\sum_{i=1}^{K} t_i}.$$

This throughput estimate is equivalent to estimating the throughput as $\frac{P(N-1)(1-\ell)}{T}$, where N is the number of packets sent, ℓ is the packet loss rate, and T is the time between the receipt of the first packet and the last packet. An alternative method for estimating TCP throughput is to use the formula $\frac{MSS \cdot C}{RTT \cdot \sqrt{\ell}}$, where C is the constant of proportionality, roughly $\sqrt{3/2}$ [23]. This formula, however, is an upper-bound on the actual throughput, and departs from the true value when ℓ is small, and is not always useful in datacenter networks with low packet loss rates. Our estimator combines these two expressions and estimates the throughput as:

$$\min\left\{P(N-1)(1-\ell)/T, MSS \cdot C/RTT \cdot \sqrt{\ell}\right\}.$$

Section 4.1 evaluates this method on EC2 and Rackspace.

3.2 Estimating Cross Traffic

The second measurement that Choreo makes is to estimate cross traffic on the network, to understand how multiple connections on the same path will be affected. As part of this task, Choreo also needs to understand how the cross traffic on a path varies over time; e.g., does the number of other connections on a path remain stable, or does it vary significantly with time?

To estimate the "equivalent" number of concurrent bulk TCP connections along a path between two VMs, we send one bulk TCP connection between two instances (e.g., using `netperf`), run it for ten seconds, and log the timestamp of each receiving packet at the receiver. This method allows us to measure the throughput of the connection every 10 milliseconds. Given the maximum path rate, the throughput of our connection should indicate how many other connections there are. For instance, if the path rate is 1 Gbit/s, and our connection sees 250 Mbit/s of throughput, then there is the equivalent of three other bulk TCP connections on the path. In general, if the path rate is c_1, and our connection gets a throughput of $c_2 \leq c_1$, then there are $c = c_1/c_2 - 1$ other bulk connections on the path. We measure the throughput frequently to account for the fact that background connections may come and go.

In this method, we have made a few assumptions: first, that we know the maximum rate of the path; second, that TCP divides the bottleneck rate equally between bulk connections in cloud networks; and third, that the background connections are backlogged, sending as fast as possible. In public clouds, it is not hard to obtain a maximum link rate (e.g.., it is usually 1 Gbit/s today on EC2) using simple measurements or because the provider advertises it (e.g., Rackspace). If the maximum rate is unknown, however, then we can solve this problem by sending one connection on the path, and then two connections; the change in the throughputs will allow us to estimate c.

For the second assumption, we ran `netperf` on the EC2 network and observed that when one connection could obtain 1 Gbit/s of bandwidth (the maximum rate), the rate did decrease by roughly 50% when we added a second connection. This result is unsurprising, given the homogeneity of cloud networks, and the fact that both connections were capable of sending at the maximum rate.

As for the third assumption, our method of estimating c also gives us a reasonable estimate of how throughput will be affected in many cases even when the other connections are not backlogged. For instance, if there is one background connection on a 1Gbit/s link that has an offered load of only 100 Mbit/s, our measured throughput will be 900 Mbit/s, and our estimated throughput of two connections on that link will be 450 Mbit/s. Although Choreo will incorrectly assume that there is no background traffic, it will not be a problem in terms of throughput estimates until Choreo tries to place a significant number of connections on the path (10, in this example—enough to decrease the rate of the initial 100 Mbit/s connection).

The quantity c is an estimate of the cross traffic on the bottleneck link, measured in terms of the equivalent number of concurrent bulk transport connections. We should interpret the quantity c as a measure of load, not a measure of how many discrete connections exist. A value of c that corresponds to there being one other connection on the network simply means that there is load on the network equivalent to one TCP connection with a continuously backlogged sender; the load itself could be the result of multiple smaller connections.

To test this method, we used ns-2 simulations. First, we simulated a simple topology where 10 sender-receiver pairs share one 1 Gbit/s link, as shown in Figure 3(a). In this simulation, the pair S1 $\rightsquigarrow$ R1 serves as the foreground connection, which transmits for 10 seconds, and the rest (S2 $\rightsquigarrow$ R2,..., S10 $\rightsquigarrow$ R10) serve as the background connections, and follow an ON-OFF model [2] whose transition time follows an exponential distribution with $\mu = 5$s. Figure 4(a) shows the actual number of current flows and the estimated value using c. Here, $c_1 = 1$ Gbit/s. Second, we simulated a more realistic cloud topology, shown in Figure 3(b). Figure 4(b) shows the actual and estimated number of cross traffic flows. In this cloud topology, the links shared by cross traffic are links between ToR switches and an aggregate switch, A. Because these links have a rate of 10 Gbit/s each, compared to the 1 Gbit/s links between sender/receiver nodes and their ToR switches, the cross traffic throughput will decrease only when more than 10 flows transfer at the same time. Thus, in Figure 4(b), the smallest estimated value is 10.

The difference in accuracy between Figure 4(a) and Figure 4(b) comes from the possible throughputs when c is large. For instance, given a 1 Gbit/s link, if we see a connection of 450 Mbit/s, we can be relatively certain that there is one existing background connection; the expected throughput was 500 Mbit/s, and 450 Mbit/s is not far off. However, if we see a connection of 90 Mbit/s, multiple values of c (e.g., $c = 10, c = 11$) are plausible.

Section 4.2 describes the results of this method running on EC2 and Rackspace.

3.3 Locating Bottlenecks

Choreo's final measurement is to determine what paths share bottlenecks, which it can use to determine how connections on one path will be affected by connections on a different path. There is a long-standing body of work on measuring Internet topologies [19, 33, 35]. Typically, these works use traceroute to gain some knowledge of the topology, and then use various clever techniques to overcome the limitations of traceroute. Datacenter topologies, however, are more manageable than the Internet topology; typically they have a structured, hierarchical form. In this section, we explore how traceroute measurements combined with topological assumptions can allow us to discover features of datacenter networks that we typically cannot discover in the Internet at-large.

3.3.1 Typical Datacenter Topologies

Datacenter topologies are often multi-rooted trees, as shown in Figure 5 and described in [9]. In these topologies, virtual machines lie on physical machines, which connect to top-of-rack (ToR) switches. These switches connect to aggregate switches above them, and core switches above those. To route between virtual machines on the same physical machine, traffic need travel only one hop. To route between two physical machines on the same rack, two hops are needed: up to the ToR switch and back down. To route to a different rack in Figure 5, either four or six hops are needed, depending on whether traffic needs to go all the way to the core. In general, all paths in this type of topology should use an even number of hops (or one hop). If we assume that a datacenter topology conforms to

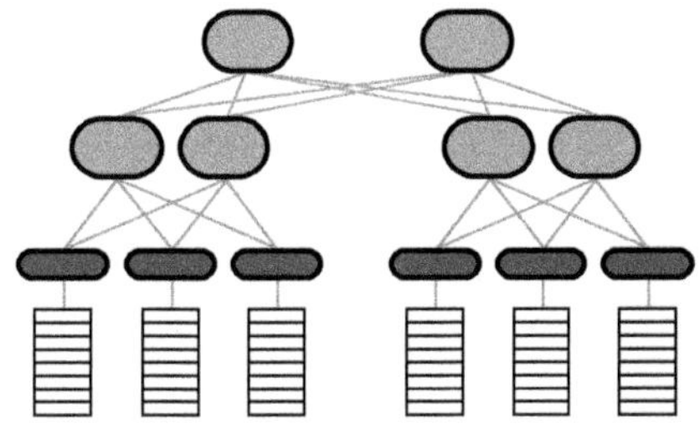

Figure 5: Typical multi-tier datacenter topology.

this structure, inferring where machines are placed in the topology is easier; in some sense, we can make the same measurements as traditional techniques, and "fit" a multi-rooted tree onto it.

3.3.2 Locating Bottlenecks

With this knowledge of the topology, we turn our attention to determining whether two paths share a bottleneck link, and where that bottleneck link occurs: at the link to the ToR switch, the link from the ToR switch to the aggregate layer, or the link to the core layer. One way to determine whether two paths share a bottleneck is by sending traffic on both paths concurrently. To determine whether path $A \rightsquigarrow B$ shares a bottleneck with $C \rightsquigarrow D$, we send `netperf` traffic on both paths concurrently. If the throughput on $A \rightsquigarrow B$ decreases significantly compared to its original value, we say that $A \rightsquigarrow B$ shares a bottleneck with $C \rightsquigarrow D$.

We are interested in whether a connection from $A \rightsquigarrow B$ will interfere with one from $C \rightsquigarrow D$. We note the following rules:

1. If the bottleneck is on the link out of the ToR switch, the two connections will interfere if either of the following occur:
   (a) they come from the same source, i.e., $A = C$.
   (b) A and C are on the same rack, and neither B nor D is on that rack.
2. If the bottleneck is on the link out of the aggregate layer and into the core, the two connections will potentially interfere if they both originate from the same subtree and must leave it, i.e., if A and C are on the same subtree, and neither B nor D is also located on that subtree. Note that even in this case, the connections may not interfere; $A \rightsquigarrow B$ may not get routed through the same aggregate switch as $C \rightsquigarrow D$.

These rules allow Choreo to estimate bottlenecks more efficiently than a brute force method that measures all pairs of paths. Because we can cluster VMs by rack, in many cases, Choreo can generalize one measurement to the entire rack of machines. For instance, if there is a bottleneck link on the ToR switch out of rack R, then any two connections out of that rack will share a bottleneck; Choreo does not need to measure each of those connections separately.

Choreo's bottleneck-finding technique can also determine what type of rate-limiting a cloud provider may be imposing. For instance, if the datacenter uses a hose model, and rate-limits the hose out of each source, our algorithm will discover bottlenecks at the end-points—indicating rate-limiting—and that the sum of the connections out of a particular source remains constant—indicating a hose model.

Section 4.3 evaluates this method on EC2 and Rackspace.

4. MEASUREMENT RESULTS

We evaluated the techniques described in Section 3 on EC2 and Rackspace to validate the techniques and measure how these two cloud networks perform.

4.1 Packet Train Accuracy and Temporal Stability

The packet train method from Section 3.1 is parameterized by the packet size, P, the number of bursts, K, and the length of each burst, B. To tune these parameters, we compared the accuracy of various packet sizes, burst lengths, and number of bursts, against the throughputs estimated by `netperf` on 90 paths in EC2 and Rackspace (we use the `netperf` throughputs as the "ground truth" for this experiment). Each path gives us one datapoint (one `netperf` measurement and one packet train estimate). Figure 6 displays the accuracy of estimating throughputs via packet trains averaged over all paths, for a packet size of 1472 bytes and a time δ of 1 millisecond.

In general, we see from Figure 6 that the accuracy improves with the burst length and number of bursts, as expected. Beyond a point, however, the accuracy does not improve (diminishing returns). We found that 10 bursts of 200 packets works well on EC2, with only 9% error, and sending 10 bursts of 2000 packets worked well on Rackspace, with only 4% error (this configuration also works well on EC2). In our measurements, an individual train takes less than one second to send, compared to the ten seconds used by `netperf` (in our experiments, we found that using `netperf` for a shorter amount of time did not produce a stable throughput estimate). To measure a network of ten VMs (i.e., 90 VM pairs) takes less than three minutes in our implementation, including the overhead of setting up and tearing down tenants/servers for measurement, and transferring throughput data to a centralized server outside the cloud.

Because the best packet train parameters for EC2 and Rackspace differ, before using a cloud network, a tenant should calibrate their packet train parameters using an approach similar to the one proposed above. This phase takes longer than running only packet trains, but only needs to be done once.

Although Choreo can get an accurate snapshot of the network quickly using packet trains, such a snapshot will not be useful if the network changes rapidly, i.e., has low temporal stability. In this case, Choreo will have trouble choosing the "best" VMs on which to place tasks. To measure temporal stability, we used 258 distinct paths in Amazon EC2, and 90 in Rackspace. On each of these paths, we continuously measured the throughput using 10-second `netperf` transfers for a period of 30 minutes, giving us one throughput sample every ten seconds for each path.

We analyze temporal throughput stability by determining how well a TCP throughput measurement from τ minutes ago predicts the current throughput. Given the current throughput measurement, λ_c, and the throughput τ minutes ago, $\lambda_{c-\tau}$, Figure 7 plots a CDF of the magnitude of the relative error, i.e., $|\lambda_c - \lambda_{c-\tau}|/\lambda_c$, for various values of τ (1, 5, 10, and 30 minutes). In EC2, for every value of τ, at least 95% of the paths have 6% error or less; the median error varies between .4% and .5%, while the mean varies between 1.4% and 3%. As suspected from Figure 2(b), the error in Rackspace is even lower: at least 95% of the paths have 0.62% error or less; the median varies between 0.18% and 0.27%, while the mean varies between 0.27% and 0.39%.

Thus, we find that although some path throughputs vary spatially, they exhibit good temporal stability. Hence, Choreo can measure path throughputs infrequently to gather useful results for making decisions about application placement. The temporal stability result is somewhat surprising because EC2 and Rackspace are popular cloud infrastructures, and one would expect significant amounts of cross traffic. In the next section, we measure the amount of cross traffic on these networks, finding that it is small. We then explore the locations of the bottlenecks, finding that the hose model provides a good explanation of the currently observed network performance on EC2 and Rackspace.

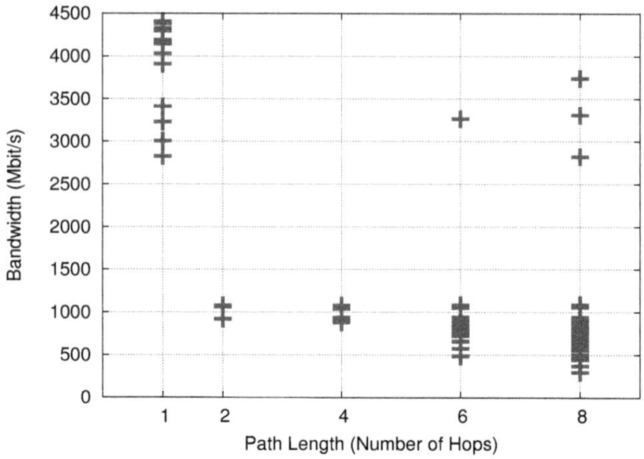

Figure 8: Comparison of path length with bandwidth. Path length is not entirely correlated with throughput, as evidenced by the eight-hop paths with throughput over 2500Mbit/s.

4.2 Cross Traffic

We first return to a result from Section 2.2, shown in Figure 2(a). Initially, we expected that path throughput would be correlated with path length, in part because it should correlate with physical topology: the longer the paths, the more likely they are traversing the middle of the network, and thus cross traffic there would be to interfere and lower the throughput.

Figure 8 plots the various path lengths observed over a collection of 1710 paths in EC2; these are the same paths that we used in Section 2.2. The first thing to note from this figure is that the path lengths are only in the set $\{1,2,4,6,8\}$. These lengths are consistent with a multi-rooted tree topology. Second, many of the paths are more than one or two hops, indicating that a significant number of VMs are not located on the same rack. In the Rackspace network (not shown in the picture), we saw paths of only 1 or 4 hops. Because the throughputs in the Rackspace network are all approximately 300 Mbits/s, there is no correlation with path length. It is also curious that we do not see paths of any other lengths (e.g., 2); we suspect that Rackspace's traceroute results may hide certain aspects of their topology, although we cannot confirm that.

From Figure 8, we see that there is little correlation between path length and throughput. In general, we find that the highest throughput pairs are one hop apart, an unsurprising result as we would expect the highest-throughput pairs to be on the same physical machine. However, there are four high-throughput paths that are six or eight hops away. Moreover, although we see that the lower throughputs tend to be on longer paths, we also see that a "typical" throughput close to 1 Gbit/s appears on all path lengths. This result leads us to believe that there is very little cross traffic that affects connections on the EC2 network, so we did not run our cross traffic algorithm from Section 3.2 on it; instead, we turned our attention towards locating bottlenecks, speculating that the bottlenecks may be at the source. This result would imply that Choreo can determine how multiple connections on one path are affected by each other simply by knowing the throughput of that path.

4.3 Bottleneck Locations and Cross Traffic

From Figure 8, we hypothesized that Amazon rate-limits at the source, and that cross traffic in the middle of the network has very little effect on connections (and thus the bottleneck link is the first hop). To test this hypothesis, we ran Choreo's bottleneck-finding algorithm from Section 3.3. We ran an experiment on twenty pairs of

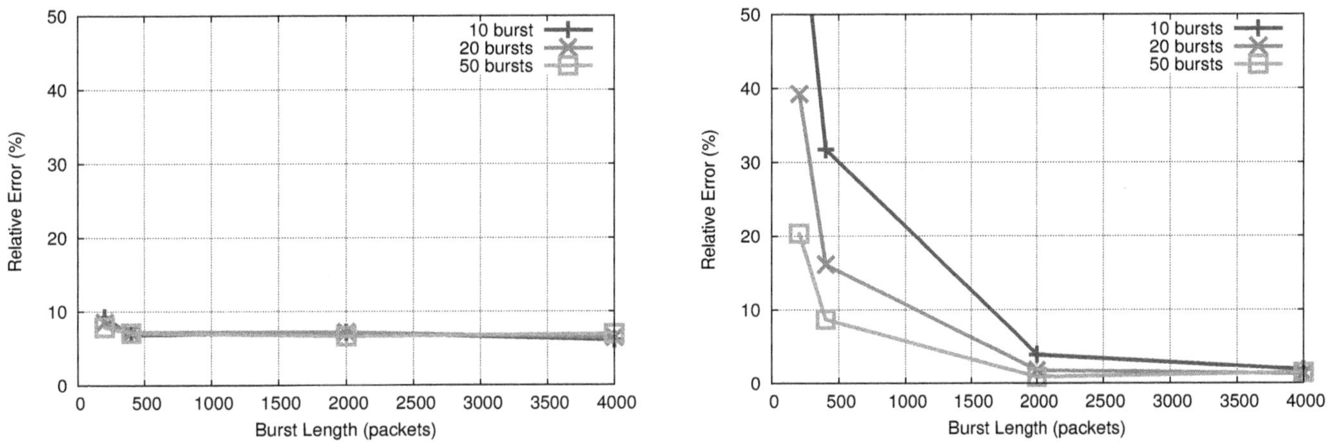

(a) EC2

(b) Rackspace

Figure 6: Percent error for packet train measurements using different burst lengths and sizes. EC2 displays a consistently low error rate over all configurations, while Rackspace's error rate improves dramatically once the burst length is at least 2000.

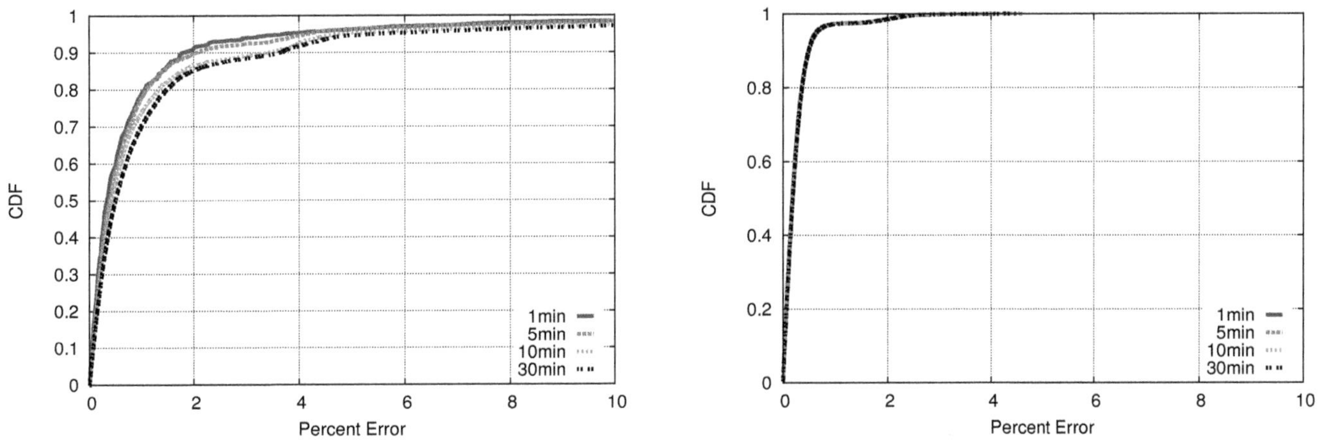

(a) EC2. More recent measurements are more accurate, but even with values of $\tau = 30$min, over 90% of paths see 4% error or less.

(b) Rackspace. The results for Rackspace are virtually the same for all values of τ, hence the appearance of only one line on the graph.

Figure 7: Percent error when a measurement from τ minutes ago is used to predict the current path bandwidth.

connections between four distinct VMs, and twenty pairs of connections from the same source. We found that concurrent connections among four unique endpoints never interfered with each other, while concurrent connections from the same source always did. This result indicates that EC2 bottlenecks occur on the first hops of the paths. Figure 7 also supports this conclusion, as paths with little cross traffic tend to be relatively stable over time.

We also hypothesized that rate-limiting at the source was prevalent on Rackspace, since most path throughputs are so close to 300Mbit/s. Additionally, we verified that connections out of the same source always interfered. These results imply that connections placed on a particular path are affected by other connections out of the source, not just other connections on the path. However, they are not affected by connections emanating from a different source.

4.4 Discussion

In summary, these results suggest that the EC2 and Rackspace networks are both rate-limited and use the hose model. Rackspace has very little spatial variability in throughput; EC2 has some, but the overwhelming majority of paths see similar throughputs near 1Gbit/s.

Despite this lack of a lot of natural variation in the two public cloud networks, Choreo is still able to exploit variation that comes with a tenant running multiple applications at once (see Section 6.3), and to avoid the few paths in EC2 that do see low throughput. Moreover, paths on these networks are temporally stable, indicating that Choreo does not need to update its measurements very frequently to take into account high-variance paths.

We also note that cloud networks can change over time. In fact, our results from Figure 1 indicated a larger range of spatial variation. For that reason, we believe that Choreo's measurement techniques are worthwhile beyond simply measuring a tenant's own applications, because higher network variation could appear in other cloud networks, or in EC2 and Rackspace in the future.

5. CHOREO'S PLACEMENT METHOD

Here, we discuss the placement of one application's tasks; the placement of a sequence of applications follows naturally. Our goal is to minimize application completion time. This goal can be formulated as an integer linear program (ILP), which we detail in the

Appendix. In practice, we found that this ILP occasionally took a very long time to solve, hampering our ability to place applications quickly. Moreover, the larger the number of machines in the network and the number of tasks in the application, the longer the mathematical optimization will take.

As a result, Choreo uses an alternate network-aware placement algorithm, shown in Algorithm 1 below. This algorithm works by trying to place the pairs of tasks that transfer the most data on the fastest paths. Because intra-machine links are modeled as paths with (essentially) infinite rate, the algorithm captures the heuristic of placing pairs of transferring tasks on the same machines. Though not guaranteed to result in a globally optimal placement (see Figure 9), this method scales better to larger topologies. We compared our greedy algorithm to the optimal algorithm on 111 different applications, and found that the median completion time with the greedy algorithm was only 13% more than the completion time with the optimal algorithm.

It is possible that an application may have other goals, such as minimizing latency or increasing fault tolerance, or even goals unrelated to the network, such as minimizing the monetary cost to the user. Users may also want to impose more constraints on CPU or storage systems. The basic principles of Choreo can be extended to all of these types of goals; we refer readers to our technical report on the subject [20]. In general, Choreo can support any goal that can be expressed as an ILP (all of the previous examples can be); it is not clear, though, whether every goal has a corresponding greedy heuristic, as minimizing completion time does. We have also not evaluated Choreo's performance improvements for these additional goals; we leave this to future work.

Algorithm 1 Greedy Network-aware Placement

transfers = a list of $\langle i,j,b\rangle$ tuples, ordered in descending order of rates, b. $\langle i,j,b\rangle$ means Task i transfers b bytes to Task j.
for $\langle i,j,b\rangle$ in *transfers* **do**
    if i has already been placed on machine k **then**
        P = set of paths $k \rightsquigarrow N\ \forall$ nodes N
    if j has already been placed on machine ℓ **then**
        P = set of paths $M \rightsquigarrow \ell\ \forall$ nodes M
    if neither i nor j have been placed **then**
        P = set of paths $M \rightsquigarrow N\ \forall$ nodes M and $\forall$ nodes N
    for path $m \rightsquigarrow n$ in P **do**
        if placing i on m or j on n would exceed the CPU constraints of m or n **then**
            Remove $m \rightsquigarrow n$ from P
    for path $m \rightsquigarrow n$ in P **do**
        $rate(m,n)$ = the rate that the transfer from i to j would see if placed on $m \rightsquigarrow n$. This rate takes into account all other task pairs already placed on $m \rightsquigarrow n$ for a "pipe" model, or all other connections out of m for a "hose" model.
    Place i and j on path $m \rightsquigarrow n \in P$ such that $rate(m,n)$ is maximized.

6. EVALUATION

We evaluate two different scenarios with Choreo. First, a case where a tenant wants to run multiple applications all at once, and second, a case where a tenant wants to run multiple applications, the entire sequence of which is not known up front. In each case, we compare Choreo's placement to three alternate existing placement algorithms: Random, Round-robin, and Minimum Machines.

Random: Tasks are assigned to random VMs. This assignment makes sure that CPU constraints are satisfied, but does not take the network into account. This type of placement acts as a baseline for comparison.

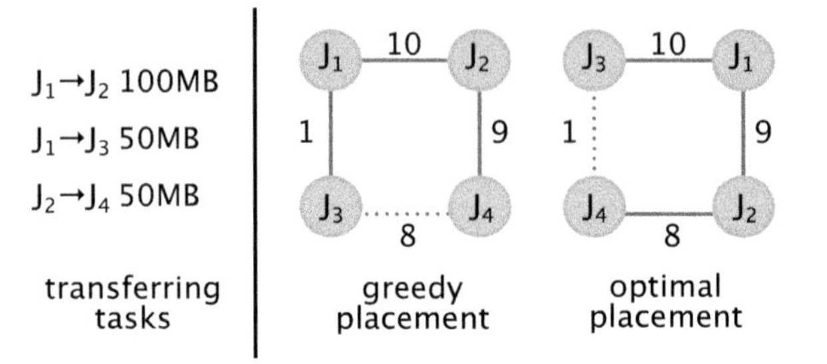

Figure 9: An example topology where the greedy network-aware placement is sub-optimal. Because the greedy placement algorithm first places tasks J_1 and J_2 on the path with rate 10, it must also use the path with rate 1 to place J_1 and J_3. The optimal placement avoids this path by placing J_1 and J_2 on the path with rate 9.

Round-robin: This algorithm assigns tasks in a round-robin order to VMs; a particular task is assigned to the next machine in the list that has enough available CPU. As before, CPU constraints are satisfied, but the network is not taken into account. This placement is similar to one that tries to load balance, and minimize the amount of CPU used on any particular VM.

Minimum Machines: This algorithm attempts to minimize the number of machines used. If possible (given CPU constraints), a task will be placed onto a VM that is already used by another task; a new VM will be used only when no existing machine has enough available CPU. This algorithm may be of interest to cloud customers who aim to save money; the fewer machines they use, the lower the cost (at, perhaps, the expense of longer-running applications).

6.1 Dataset and Experimental Set-up

To evaluate Choreo, we ran experiments on EC2. In each experiment, we measure an EC2 topology, and then place an application or sequence of applications on that topology. The applications are composed from the real traffic matrices gathered using sFlow at the ToR and aggregation switches in the HP Cloud network [15]. For each application, we know the observed start time on the cloud as well as its traffic matrix. From this data, we can accurately model sequences of applications. We model each component of an application as using between 0.5 and four CPU cores, and each cloud machine as having four available cores (the actual CPU data was not available in our dataset).

Once the applications are placed, we transfer data as specified by the placement algorithm and the traffic matrix. Note that these experiments transfer *real traffic* on EC2; we do not merely calculate what the application completion time would have been based on the measured network, placement, and traffic matrix. Thus, these experiments are susceptible to any changes in the network, as well as the effects of any cross traffic.

6.2 All Applications at Once

For our first set of experiments, we modeled a tenant with multiple applications, whose network demands (amount of data transferred between tasks) are known a priori. We randomly chose between one and three applications and made one combined application out of them, combining each application's traffic demand matrix and CPU vector in the obvious way. Then, we placed this combined application and ran it, using each of the four placement algorithms in turn. Our CDFs do not explicitly account for measurement time, because it is the same (approximately three minutes for a ten-node

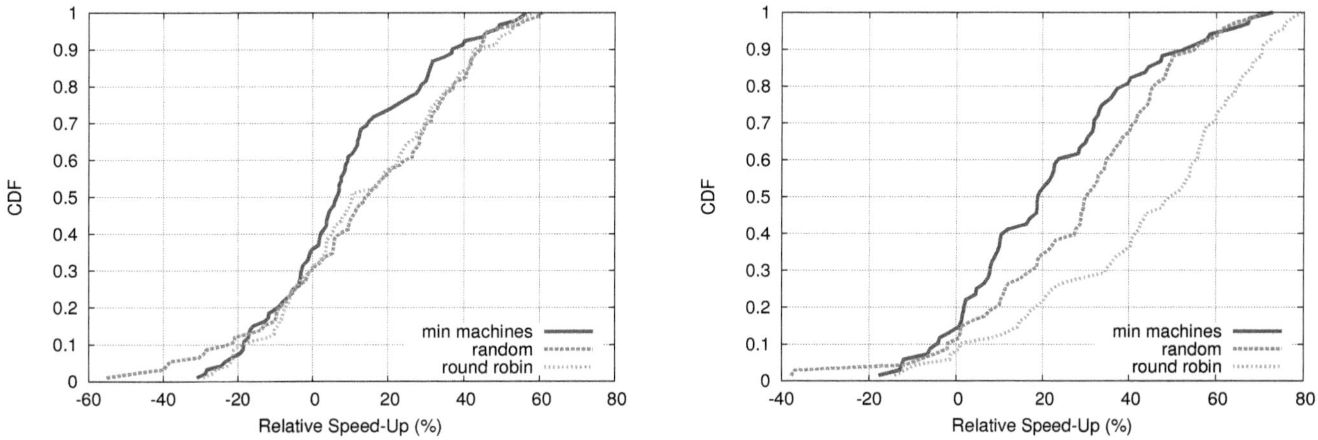

(a) All applications at once

(b) Sequences of applications

Figure 10: Relative speed-up for applications using Choreo vs. alternate placement algorithms.

topology) regardless of the length of an application's run. We note that Choreo is not meant for short-lived applications where the three-minute time-to-measure will exceed any reductions in the completion time from Choreo.

Figure 10(a) shows the results from this experiment. Each line in the CDF compares Choreo to one of the alternate placement algorithms. The x-axis plots the relative speed-up, defined as the amount of time that Choreo saved (or added) to the completion time of an application. For instance, if an application took five hours with the random placement algorithm, and four hours using Choreo, the relative speed-up would be $(5-4)/5 = 20\%$.

From Figure 10(a), we can see that in roughly 70% of the applications, Choreo improves performance, with improvements as large as 60%. The mean improvement over other approaches in *all* cases is between 8% and 14%, while the median improvement is between 7% and 15%; restricted to the 70% of applications that show improvement, these values rise to 20%–27% (mean) and 13%–28% (median). In the other 30% of applications, Choreo reduces performance; in these cases, the median slow-down is (only) between 8% and 13%.

These numbers imply that, if we could predict the types of applications where Choreo typically provides improvement, it would improve performance by roughly 13%–28%. We leave this type of prediction to future work.

6.3 Applications in Sequence

For our second set of experiments, we modeled a tenant wishing to run multiple applications whose demands are not all known a priori. Instead, the applications arrive one-by-one, and are placed as they arrive. We randomly chose between two and four applications and ordered them by their observed start times. We placed the applications in sequence according to these start times. Applications may overlap in time in this scenario.

Because multiple applications arrive in sequence, it does not make sense to measure the entire sequence's completion time. Instead, we determine the total running time of each application, and compare the sum of these running times for each placement algorithm.

Figure 10(b) shows the results from this experiment. As in Figure 10(a), each line in the CDF compares Choreo to one of our alternate placement algorithms. We see similar results as in Figure 10(a), in that for most applications, Choreo provides an improvement over all other placement schemes. With sequences of applications, we see an improvement in 85%–90% of all applications, with a maximum observed improvement of 79%. Over all applications, the mean improvement ranges from 22%–43%; the median from 19%–51% across different alternative algorithms. Restricted to the applications that show improvement, the mean rises slightly to 26%–47% and the median to 23%–53%. For the applications whose performance degraded, the median slow-down was only 10%.

In general, Choreo performs better when applications arrive in sequence than when all demands are known up front and applications can be placed at once. This result is likely due to the fact that applications arriving in sequence allows us to spread their network demands out more; placing multiple applications at once will use more network resources than placing the applications as they arrive, in general.

In cases where an in-sequence placement seems to be going poorly, however, Choreo can re-evaluate its placement during a run, and migrate applications if the tenant deems that worthwhile (as mentioned in Section 2.4). However, we can see from Figure 10(b) that even without this behavior, Choreo's relative performance improvement over the other schemes when constrained to no re-evaluations is significant.

7. DISCUSSION

Although Choreo can improve the completion time of many cloud applications, it is not appropriate for every application nor for every cloud environment. Here, we discuss some use-cases that are not particularly well-served by Choreo, as well as how we expect Choreo to fare as cloud networks evolve.

7.1 Limitations of Choreo

Choreo was designed with network-intensive applications in mind. Though it is a general framework, there are certain applications for which it likely will not provide any improvement. For example, for applications that only need a few minutes to run, the cost of Choreo's measurement phase would cancel out any improvement. Applications that have relatively uniform bandwidth-usage also would not see much improvement from Choreo, because there is not a lot of room for improvement. Here, because every pair of VMs uses roughly the same amount of bandwidth, it does not help to put the "largest" pair on the fastest link. We observed this traffic pattern in some map-reduce applications.

Finally, interactive applications would probably not see much improvement from Choreo, in part because the current version of Choreo does not model how applications change over time. Even if it did, the interactive phases would likely be difficult to model, although Choreo could potentially re-evaluate its placement after every interactive phase for some applications.

Choreo is also only appropriate for certain cloud environments. For instance, Choreo will not offer a great deal of improvement in cloud environments with an abundance of network bandwidth. After all, if the cloud provider can afford to give every pair of tasks a dedicated path, for instance, there is not much need to optimize task placement. Choreo will offer more improvement as cloud networks become more utilized. Although we do not believe that today's cloud networks are blessed with an excess of network bandwidth, they also may not be as heavily utilized as they could be; thus, Choreo may offer more more substantial improvements as cloud networks evolve and become more heavily utilized.

7.2 Future Work

Currently, Choreo models an application with one traffic matrix that captures the total number of bytes transferred between each task. Notably, Choreo loses information about how an application changes over time. Choreo could capture that information by modeling applications as a time series of traffic matrices; this method will naturally lead to a more complicated task placement algorithm. A straw-man approach is to determine the "major" phases of an application's bandwidth usage, and use Choreo as-is at the beginning of each phase. We leave an evaluation of this method, as well as a more involved approach as future work.

We also leave a study of how Choreo performs with multiple users as future work. In general, we believe that Choreo would succeed in this case, because each user would measure the network individually (and so would be able to place their application with the knowledge of how the network was being affected by the other Choreo users). How this approach compares to using a centralized Choreo controller to orchestrate all users remains to be seen.

The final piece of future work is studying how the accuracy of Choreo's measurements trades off with its improvement. Though Choreo's measurement phase does not require much overhead (taking only three minutes to measure 90 VM-pairs), it is possible that the system would still be able to improve performance with even less accurate measurements. For instance, if Choreo's measurements were only 75% accurate, as opposed to approximately 90% accurate (as in Section 4.1), would the performance improvement also fall by 15%, or only by a few percent?

7.3 Longevity of Choreo

Cloud networks are an evolving environment. The way providers manage their network, including enforcing rate-limits, or migrating VMs, could change, and it is difficult to predict how Choreo will be affected by these changes. However, because Choreo starts by measuring the cloud network, we believe that it could provide improvement—or, at the very least, not be detrimental—in the face of some of these changes. For example, if rate limits are enforced, Choreo should be able to pick up on that when it explicitly measures the links. If VMs are migrated during an application's run, Choreo will account for that, as it measures periodically. Determining the correct frequency for these measurements would likely require some fine-tuning.

Today's cloud providers offer little in the way of network QoS or SLAs to their customers. In the future, these types of guarantees may become commonplace; a customer may be able to pay for a particular level of bandwidth in their network. We believe that Choreo could be complementary in this scenario, determining the best placement for an application within the guaranteed network. However, for some customers, Choreo may provide diminishing returns; the provider's SLA may be "good enough" on its own.

Today's version of Choreo may not be appropriate for cloud networks years from now. But we believe that the general approach of measuring the network and adapting to it will remain useful, and that future versions of Choreo could be built under the same principles to adapt to future cloud networks.

8. RELATED WORK

We break related work into two sections: work related to improving various aspects of cloud performance, and work related to the measurement of public cloud networks and datacenters.

8.1 Improving Cloud Performance

Previous papers on network virtualization and optimization for cloud computing systems and datacenters address one of two problems: how to choose paths between fixed machines or how to choose machines given a fixed network. Choreo falls into the second category, as work in the first generally assumes a level of control over the network that public cloud tenants do not have.

How to choose paths: Given a fixed network, there are many ways to choose paths in the network to route from one machine to another. Many datacenters choose paths with load balancing in mind. A popular method is Equal-Cost Multi-Path forwarding [9], where a flow's path is selected based on a hash of various header fields. VL2 [11] uses Valiant Load Balancing on a Clos network as a means for selecting routes. Hedera [3] designed a dynamic flow scheduling system, which can move flows in a network to efficiently utilize all network resources. Other approaches to load balancing in datacenters include software-defined networking, as in [13].

Other schemes, such as Seawall [34] and NetShare [21], focus on choosing routes for performance isolation, ensuring that network bandwidth is shared among tenants based on some weight function. All of these systems differ from Choreo in that they have control, at a minimum, of the routing protocol in the network. Tenants of public cloud infrastructures do not have this type of control.

How to choose machines: Now we turn our attention to the following problem: Given a large network of machines, how do we pick which machines to run a particular workload on? Here we assume that the routes between machines are fixed. Oktopus [4] uses a virtual topology to place tenant VMs such that they meet bandwidth and oversubscription requirements. This system must be deployed by cloud providers rather than tenants, but offers more stable workload completion times (the goal of Oktopus is to improve the accuracy of predicted completion times, rather than to focus on finding an optimal placement). Researchers have also designed an algorithm to place VMs on physical machines with the goal of minimizing the number of physical machines used while also meeting the VMs' requirements for CPU, memory, and bandwidth [24]. Unlike our work, they model network requirements as the percentage of network I/O required, rather than amount of data to be transferred between tasks, which limits the speed of a particular transfer even if the network capacity is available. It is not clear whether virtual machines are allowed to transfer data to multiple machines, nor is it clear how this system would operate in general; the only simulation is done on an extremely small topology with a highly structured workload. Purlieus [26] reduces MapReduce job execution times by placing Map/Reduce nodes in a locality-aware manner. This method requires information about the network topology, which is usually not provided by public cloud providers.

The largest difference between Choreo and these works is that we present network-aware placement schemes that run with *no changes to the network*; imposing no virtual topologies, assuming no knowledge of the topology is assumed, and not introducing a new routing protocol. Although there are features of Choreo that cloud providers can take advantage of (such as incorporating network topology knowledge), Choreo can be run entirely by tenants.

Our idea of network-aware placement is in contrast to workload placement systems that only take CPU constraints into account [1, 29]. These systems generally attempt to load balance across machines or minimize the number of physical machines used.

8.2 Measurement

In accordance with the popularity of datacenters, there have been many recent measurement studies in this environment [5, 6, 22]. These studies corroborate the assumptions in this paper, for example the typical datacenter topology used in Section 3.3.1. However, these studies are not focused on the performance of the network and how it varies, which can affect the performance of network-intensive applications. There have been a few efforts to understand the network performance of Amazon EC2 [25], though only at a very small scale.

In [8], Butler conducts measurement for network performances for five major cloud providers, focusing on the throughputs when cloud users upload/download files from outside the cloud, while Choreo focuses on measuring the throughputs between VMs inside the cloud. CloudTalk [30] measures EC2 topology to help optimize latency sensitive applications such as web search. As we show in Section 4.2, the topology information, i.e, hop-count from traceroute, has no strong correlation with throughput. Thus, compared to CloudTalk, Choreo's throughput measurement techniques are more helpful to big data applications whose performance depends more on throughput instead of latency. Schad, et al [32] measured network throughput between Amazon EC2 instances using `iperf`. They observed similar throughput variation results as ours in both US and European zones. Wang, et al [36] measured TCP/UDP throughput between VMs in EC2. Similarly, they observed spatial variation in both Small and Medium instances, and they observed temporal variation over a 150-hour period, which is a much larger time scale than we discussed in this paper.

We borrow the basis of many of our measurement techniques from existing techniques, such as the early work by Bolot [7] and Jain [18] on packet trains. Further related work in this area [27, 28] has indicated that packet trains are not always an accurate measure of path throughput due to their susceptibility to cross traffic. Packet trains are also similar to the "history-based" methods in He, et al [14], but requires significantly less data (He's method requires 10-20 TCP transfers to make a throughput prediction on a path). We did not consider methods that estimate the available bandwidth of a path [16, 17], as that is not equivalent to the TCP throughput.

9. CONCLUSION

In this paper, we motivated the need for network-aware application placement on cloud computing infrastructures. As applications become more network-intensive, they can become bottlenecked by the network, even in well-provisioned clouds. Without a network-aware system for placing workloads, poor paths can be chosen while faster, more reliable paths go unused. By placing applications with the goal of minimizing the total completion time, Choreo is able to improve application-level performance. Choreo's placement also tends to place tasks that transfer large amount of data on the same machines if possible, avoiding any network transmission time, as well as avoiding slow paths in the network.

Our experiments on Amazon EC2 showed that Choreo improves application completion time by an average of 8%–14% (max improvement: 61%) when applications are placed all at once, and 22%–43% (max improvement: 79%) when they arrive in real-time, compared to alternative placement schemes studied on realistic workloads.

We also note that tenants may be interested in adding other requirements to their workload; some of the tasks could be specified as "latency-constrained", or certain tasks could be specified as being placed "far apart" for fault tolerance purposes. We believe that all of these types of constraints are reasonable and would be beneficial to tenants. Moreover, they can be formulated as part of our optimization problem, as shown in [20].

In addition to our results from Choreo, we also developed and tested techniques for measuring public cloud networks quickly and accurately. We found that packet trains could be used to measure public cloud networks, with a mean error of only 9% on EC2, and a mean error of 4% on Rackspace. Choreo uses these measurements to quickly place applications, and they are accurate enough that applications see improvement over existing placement methods.

ACKNOWLEDGMENTS

We are indebted to Jeff Mogul for help with data collection and for discussions on this work, and to Gavin Pratt and Sujata Banerjee for permitting us to analyze Choreo with data collected from HP. We thank our shepherd, Morley Mao, and the IMC reviewers for their insightful comments. This work was supported in part by the National Science Foundation under grants 0645960, 1065219, and 1040072.

10. REFERENCES

[1] A. Aboulnaga, K. Salem, A. A. Soror, U. F. Minhas, P. Kokosielis, and S. Kamath. Deploying Database Appliances in the Cloud. In *Bulletin of the IEEE Computer Society Technical Committee on Data Engineering*, 2009.

[2] A. Adas. Traffic Models in Broadband Networks. *Communications Magazine, IEEE*, 35(7):82–89, 1997.

[3] M. Al-Fares, S. Radhakrishnan, B. Raghavan, N. Huang, and A. Vahdat. Hedera: Dynamic Flow Scheduling for Data Center Networks. In *NSDI*, 2010.

[4] H. Ballani, P. Costa, T. Karagiannis, and A. Rowstron. Towards Predictable Datacenter Networks. In *SIGCOMM*, 2011.

[5] T. Benson, A. Akella, and D. A. Maltz. Network Traffic Characteristics of Data Centers in the Wild. In *IMC*, 2010.

[6] T. Benson, A. Anand, A. Akella, and M. Zhang. Understanding Data Center Traffic Characteristics. In *WREN*, 2009.

[7] J.-C. Bolot. Characterizing End-to-End Packet Delay and Loss in the Internet. *Journal of High Speed Networks*, 2(3):289–298, 1993.

[8] B. Butler. Microsoft Azure Overtakes Amazon's Cloud in Performance Test. `http://www.networkworld.com/news/2013/021913-azure-aws-266831.html`.

[9] Cisco Data Center Infrastructure 2.5 Design Guide. `http://www.cisco.com/univercd/cc/td/doc/solution/dcidg21.pdf`.

[10] N. Duffield, P. Goyal, A. Greenberg, P. Mishra, K. Ramakrishnan, and J. E. van der Merwe. A Flexible Model for Resource Management in Virtual Private Networks. In *SIGCOMM*, 1999.

[11] A. Greenberg, J. R. Hamilton, N. Jain, S. Kandula, C. Kim, P. Lahiri, D. A. Maltz, P. Patel, and S. Sengupta. VL2: A Scalable and Flexible Data Center Network. In *SIGCOMM*, 2009.

[12] Apache Hadoop. `http://hadoop.apache.org`.

[13] N. Handigol, M. Flagslik, S. Seetharaman, R. Johari, and N. McKeown. Aster*x: Load-Balancing as a Network Primitive. In *ACLD (Poster)*, 2010.

[14] Q. He, C. Dovrolis, and M. Ammar. On the Predictability of Large Transfer TCP Throughput. In *SIGCOMM*, 2005.
[15] HP Cloud Services. `http://hpcloud.com/`.
[16] M. Jain and C. Dovrolis. Ten Fallacies and Pitfalls on End-to-End Available Bandwidth Estimation. In *IMC*, 2004.
[17] M. Jain and C. Dovrolis. End-to-end Estimation of the Available Bandwidth Variation Range. In *Sigmetrics*, 2005.
[18] R. Jain and S. A. Routhier. Packet Trains: Measurements and a New Model for Computer Network Traffic. *IEEE Journal on Selected Areas in Communications*, 4:986–995, 1986.
[19] E. Katz-Bassett, H. V. Madhyastha, V. K. Adhikari, C. Scott, J. Sherry, P. van Wesep, T. Anderson, and A. Krishnamurthy. Reverse Traceroute. In *NSDI*, 2010.
[20] K. LaCurts, S. Deng, and H. Balakrishnan. A Plan for Optimizing Network-Intensive Cloud Applications. Technical Report MIT-CSAIL-TR-2013-003, MIT CSAIL, 2013.
[21] T. Lam, S. Radhakrishnan, A. Vahdat, and G. Varghese. NetShare: Virtualizing Data Center Networks Across Services. In *Technical Report CSS2010-0957, University of California, San Diego*, 2010.
[22] A. Li, X. Yang, S. Kandula, and M. Zhang. CloudCmp: Comparing Public Cloud Providers. In *IMC*, 2010.
[23] M. Mathis, J. Semke, J. Mahdavi, and T. Ott. The Macroscopic Behavior of the TCP Congestion Avoidance Algorithm. *SIGCOMM CCR*, 27(3), 1997.
[24] E. Mohammadi, M. Karimi, and S. R. Heikalabad. A Novel Virtual Machine Placement in Cloud Computing. *Australian Journal of Basic and Applied Sciences*, 2011.
[25] Network Performance Within Amazon EC2 and to Amazon S3. `http://blog.rightscale.com/2007/10/28/network-performance-within-amazon-ec2-and-to-amazon-s3`.
[26] B. Palanisamy, A. Singh, L. Liu, and B. Jain. Purlieus: Locality-aware Resource Allocation for MapReduce in a Cloud. In *International Conference for High Performance Computing, Networking, Storage and Analysis*, 2011.
[27] V. Paxson. End-to-End Internet Packet Dynamics. In *SIGCOMM*, 1997.
[28] R. S. Prasad, M. Murray, C. Dovrolis, and K. Claffy. Bandwidth Estimation: Metrics, Measurement Techniques, and Tools. *IEEE Network*, 17:27–35, 2003.
[29] A. Quiroz, H. Kim, M. Parashar, N. Gnanasambandam, and N. Sharma. Towards Automatic Workload Provisioning for Enterprise Grids and Clouds. In *IEEE/ACM International Conference on Grid Computing*, 2009.
[30] C. Raiciu, M. Ionescu, and D. Niculescu. Opening Up Black Box Networks with CloudTalk. In *Hotcloud*, 2012.
[31] Scaling Hadoop to 4000 Nodes at Yahoo! `http://developer.yahoo.net/blogs/hadoop/2008/09/scaling_hadoop_to_4000_nodes_a.html`.
[32] J. Schad, J. Dittrich, and J.-A. Quiané-Ruiz. Runtime Measurements in the Cloud: Observing, Analyzing, and Reducing Variance. *Proceedings of the VLDB Endowment*, 3(1-2):460–471, 2010.
[33] R. Sherwood, A. Bender, and N. Spring. DisCarte: A Disjunctive Internet Cartographer. In *SIGCOMM*, 2008.
[34] A. Shieh, S. Kandula, A. Greenberg, C. Kim, and B. Saha. Sharing the Data Center Network. In *NSDI*, 2011.
[35] N. Spring, R. Mahajan, and D. Wetherall. Measuring ISP Topologies with Rocketfuel. In *SIGCOMM*, 2002.
[36] G. Wang and T. E. Ng. The Impact of Virtualization on Network Performance of Amazon EC2 Data Center. In *INFOCOM*, 2010.

APPENDIX

The problem of minimizing application completion time can be modeled as a quadratic optimization problem. In our formulation, we assume that there is no unknown cross-traffic in the network. We show in Section 4.2 that this assumption generally holds in the Amazon EC2 and Rackspace networks, and also discuss how we could change our formulation if the assumption were not true.

To describe the existing network of M machines, we require two matrices:

- $C_{M\times 1}$, the CPU constraint vector. C_m is the CPU resource available on machine m, i.e., the number of cores on the machine.
- $R_{M\times M}$, the network constraint matrix. R_{mn} is the bulk TCP throughput of the path from Machine m to n, assuming no one else is sending traffic on the path.

To describe the J tasks:

- CR_J, the CPU demand vector. CR_j is the CPU demand for Task j, i.e., the number of cores required for Task j.
- $B_{J\times J}$, the network demand matrix. B_{ij} is the amount of data Task i needs to transfer to Task j.
- $X_{J\times M}$, the task assignment matrix. $X_{jm} = 1$ if Task j is placed on Machine m, and 0 otherwise.

A placement of the J tasks onto the M machines is an X such that:

$$\sum_{m=1}^{M} X_{jm} = 1, \forall j \in [1,J]$$

That is, each task must be placed on exactly one machine. In addition, the placement of tasks on each machine must obey CPU constraints, i.e.,

$$\sum_{j=1}^{J} CR_j \cdot X_{jm} \le C_m, \forall m \in [1,M]$$

Given a particular placement of tasks, we need to calculate how long an application running with this placement will take to complete. By definition, this completion time is equal to the time taken to complete the longest-running flow.

Let $f_1,\ldots,f_k$ be a set of flows that share a bottleneck link ℓ with rate R. The flows transmit $b_1 \le,\ldots,\le b_k$ bytes of data, respectively. The amount of data traversing link ℓ is then $\sum_{i=1}^{i=k} b_i$. Since there is no cross traffic (by our assumption), the total amount of time these flows take is $\sum_{i=1}^{i=k} b_i/R$. The total completion time for the workload placement, then, is $max \sum_{i=1}^{i=k} b_i/R$ over all sets of flows that share a bottleneck link. Choreo's goal is to minimize that time over all possible placements.

To formulate this objective so that it can be solved by quadratic program solvers, we need to express it using matrices. In particular, we need a way to define whether two flows will share a bottleneck link. Let S be an $M^2 \times M^2$ matrix such that $S_{mn,ab} = 1$ if the path $m \rightsquigarrow n$ shares a bottleneck link with path $a \rightsquigarrow b$. Let D_{mn} be the $M \times M$ matrix expressing the amount of data to be transferred between machines m and n ($D = X^T BX$). Let $E_{mn} = \sum_{m'=1,n'=1}^{m'=M,n'=M} D_{m'n'} \times S_{mn,m'n'}$.

E_{mn} expresses the amount of data traveling on $m \rightsquigarrow n$'s bottleneck link. Note that the rate of that path is, by definition, R_{mn}. Our objective, then, is min $\max_{m,n} E_{mn}/R_{mn}$, such that all CPU constraints are still satisfied. In Section 4.4, we show that VMs in both EC2 and Rackspace cloud follow a hose model: the outgoing bandwidth for each VM is limited by a certain threshold. We can model this type of rate-limiting with the following: $S_{mi,mj} = 1$ $(m \neq i, m \neq j)$.

What happens if a tenant does not know the physical topology of the network, i.e., does not know the correct values for S? In this case, Choreo assumes that every entry in S is zero, i.e., there are *no* shared bottlenecks in the network (effectively, this S models a network with unique paths between every pair of machines). If this value is incorrect, i.e., there are certain paths that share bottlenecks, our formulation will likely calculate the workload completion time incorrectly. However, we show in Section 6 that in practice, significant performance gains can still be seen without knowledge of S.

It turns out that our problem can be converted into a linear programming problem. For each quadratic term in above constraints, $X_{im} \cdot X_{jn}, i < j$, we define a new variable, z_{imjn} ($i < j$ forces $X_{im} \cdot X_{jn}$ and $X_{jn} \cdot X_{im}$ to be equal). Now the problem is as follows:

minimize: z
subject to:

$$z - \sum_{i=1}^{J} \sum_{j=1}^{J} \frac{B_{ij} \cdot z_{imjn}}{R_{mn}} \geq 0 \; \forall \; m,n \in [1,M]$$

$$C_m - \sum_{i=1}^{J} CR_i \cdot X_{im} \geq 0 \; \forall \; m \in [1,M]$$

$$\sum_{m=1}^{M} X_{im} = 1 \; \forall \; i \in [1,J]$$

$$z_{imjn} - X_{im} \leq 0, \text{ and } z_{imjn} - X_{jn} \leq 0 \; \forall \; i,j \in [1,J]$$

$$\sum_{n,m} \sum_{j=i+1}^{J} z_{imjn} + \sum_{n,m} \sum_{j=1}^{i-1} z_{jnim} = J-1 \; \forall \; i \in [1,J]$$

$$z \geq 0$$

binaries:

$$X_{im}, z_{imjn} \; (i < j, \; i,j \in [1,J], \; m,n \in [1,M])$$

The constraints serve the following purposes, in order: To force z to represent the maximum amount of data transferred between two machines, to make sure the computation capability of any machine is not exceeded, to make sure each task is placed on exactly one machine, to force $z_{imjn} \leq X_{im} \cdot X_{jn}$, and to force $z_{imjn} \leq X_{im} \cdot X_{jn}$.

Benchmarking Personal Cloud Storage

Idilio Drago
University of Twente
i.drago@utwente.nl

Enrico Bocchi
Politecnico di Torino
enrico.bocchi@studenti.polito.it

Marco Mellia
Politecnico di Torino
mellia@tlc.polito.it

Herman Slatman
University of Twente
h.slatman@utwente.nl

Aiko Pras
University of Twente
a.pras@utwente.nl

ABSTRACT

Personal cloud storage services are data-intensive applications already producing a significant share of Internet traffic. Several solutions offered by different companies attract more and more people. However, little is known about each service capabilities, architecture and – most of all – performance implications of design choices. This paper presents a methodology to study cloud storage services. We apply our methodology to compare 5 popular offers, revealing different system architectures and capabilities. The implications on performance of different designs are assessed executing a series of benchmarks. Our results show no clear winner, with all services suffering from some limitations or having potential for improvement. In some scenarios, the upload of the same file set can take seven times more, wasting twice as much capacity. Our methodology and results are useful thus as both benchmark and guideline for system design.[1]

Categories and Subject Descriptors

C.2 [**Computer-Communication Networks**]: Miscellaneous; C.4 [**Performance of Systems**]: Measurement Techniques

Keywords

Measurements; Performance; Comparison; Dropbox

1. INTRODUCTION

Personal cloud storage services allow to synchronize local folders with servers in the cloud. They have gained popularity, with companies offering significant amounts of remote storage for free or reduced prices. More and more people are being attracted by these offers, saving personal files, synchronizing devices and sharing content with great simplicity. This high public interest pushed various providers to enter the cloud storage market. Services like Dropbox, SkyDrive and Google Drive are becoming pervasive in people's routine. Such applications are data-intensive and their increasing usage already produces a significant share of Internet traffic [3].

Previous results about Dropbox [3] indicate that design and architectural choices strongly influence service performance and network usage. However, very little is known about how other providers implement their services and the implications of different designs. This understanding is valuable as a guideline for building well-performing services that wisely use network resources.

The goal of this paper is twofold. Firstly, we investigate how different providers tackle the problem of synchronizing people's files. For answering this question, we develop a methodology that helps to understand both system architecture and client capabilities. We apply our methodology to compare 5 services, revealing differences on client software, synchronization protocols and data center placement. Secondly, we investigate the consequences of such designs on performance. We answer this question by defining a series of benchmarks. Taking the perspective of users connected from a single location in Europe, we benchmark each selected service under the same conditions, highlighting differences manifested in various usage scenarios and emphasizing the relevance of design choices for both users and the Internet.

Our results extend [3], where Dropbox usage is analyzed from passive measurements. In contrast to the previous work and [12, 16] that focus on a specific service, this paper compares several solutions using active measurements. The results in [3] are used to guide our benchmarking definition. The authors of [11] benchmark cloud providers, but focusing only on server infrastructure. Similarly to our goal, [9] evaluates Dropbox, Mozy, Carbonite and CrashPlan. Motivated by the extensive list of providers, we first propose a methodology to automate the benchmarking. Then, we analyze several synchronization scenarios and providers, shedding light on the impact of design choices on performance.

Our results reveal interesting insights, such as unexpected drops in performance in common scenarios because of both the lack of client capabilities and architectural differences in the services. Overall, the lessons learned are useful as guidelines to improve personal cloud storage services.

[1]Our benchmarking tool and the measurements used in our analyses are available at the SimpleWeb trace repository: `http://www.simpleweb.org/wiki/cloud_benchmarks`

IMC'13, October 23–25, 2013, Barcelona, Spain.

ACM 978-1-4503-1953-9/13/10 ...$15.00.
http://dx.doi.org/10.1145/2504730.2504762.

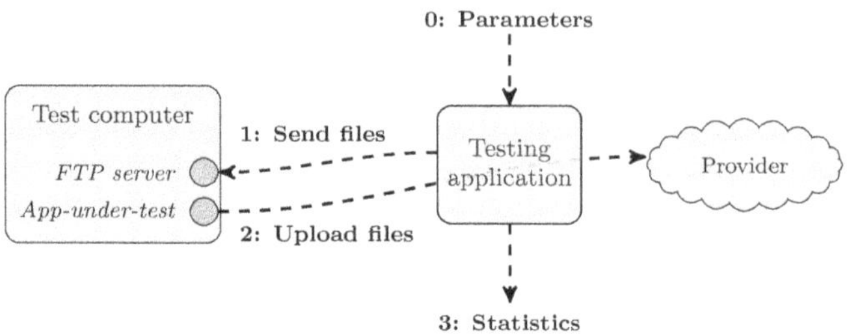

Figure 1: Testbed to study personal storage services.

2. METHODOLOGY AND SERVICES

This section describes the methodology we follow to design benchmarks to check capabilities and performance of personal storage services. We use active measurements relying on a testbed (Fig. 1) composed of two parts: (i) a *test computer* that runs the application-under-test in the desired operating system; and (ii) our *testing application*. The complete environment can run either in a single machine, or in separate machines provided that the testing application can intercept traffic from the test computer.

We build the testbed in a single Linux server for our experiments. The Linux server both controls the experiments and hosts a virtual machine that runs the test computer (Windows 7 Enterprise).[2] Our testbed is connected to a 1 GB/s Ethernet network at the University of Twente, in which Internet connectivity is not a bottleneck.

Our testing application receives as input benchmarking parameters (step 0 in Fig. 1) describing the sequence of operations to be performed. The testing application acts remotely on the test computer, generating specific workloads in the form of file batches, which are manipulated using a FTP client (step 1). Files of different types are created or modified at run-time, e.g., text files composed of random words from a dictionary, images with random pixels, or random binary files. Generated files are synchronized to the cloud by the application-under-test (step 2) and the exchanged traffic is monitored to compute performance metrics (step 3). These include the amount of traffic seen during the experiments, the time before actual synchronization starts and the time to complete synchronization.

2.1 Architecture and Data Centers

The used architecture, data center locations and data center owner are important aspects of personal cloud storage, having both legal and performance implications. To identify how the analyzed services operate, we observe the DNS name of contacted servers when (i) starting the application; (ii) immediately after files are manipulated; and (iii) when the application is in idle state. For each service, a list of contacted DNS names is compiled.

To reveal all IP addresses of the front-end nodes used by a service, DNS names are resolved to IP addresses by contacting more than 2,000 open DNS resolvers spread around the world.[3] In fact, cloud services rely on the DNS to distribute workload, returning different IP addresses according to the originating DNS resolver [2].

The owners of the IP addresses are identified using the `whois` service. For each IP address, we look for the geographic location of the server. Since popular geolocation databases are known to have serious limitations regarding cloud providers [14], we rely on a hybrid methodology that makes use of: (i) informative strings (i.e., International Airport Codes) revealed by reverse DNS lookup; (ii) the shortest Round Trip Time (RTT) to PlanetLab nodes [15]; and (iii) active `traceroute` to spot the closest well-known location of a router. Previous works [2, 5] indicate that these methodologies provide an estimation with about a hundred of kilometers of precision, which is sufficient for our goals.

Table 1: Benchmarks to assess client performance.

Random bytes			Plain text		
Set	Files	Size	Set	Files	Size
1	1	100 kB	5	1	100 kB
2	1	1 MB	6	1	1 MB
3	10	100 kB	7	10	100 kB
4	100	10 kB	8	100	10 kB

2.2 Checking Capabilities

Previous work [3] shows that personal storage applications can implement several capabilities to optimize storage usage and to speed up transfers. These capabilities include the adoption of *chunking* (i.e., splitting content into a maximum size data unit), *bundling* (i.e., the transmission of multiple small files as a single object), *deduplication* (i.e., avoiding re-transmitting content already available on servers), *delta encoding* (i.e., transmission of only modified portions of a file) and *compression*.

For each case, a specific test has been designed to observe if the given capability is implemented. We describe each test directly in Sect. 4. In summary, our testing application produces specific batches of files that would benefit from a capability. The exchanged traffic is analyzed to determine how the service operates.

2.3 Benchmarking Performance

After knowing how the services are designed in terms of both data center locations and system capabilities, we check how such choices influence synchronization performance and the amount of overhead traffic.

Results in [3] show that up to 90 % of Dropbox users' uploads carry less than 1 MB. While 50 % of the batches carry only a single file, a significant portion (around 10 %) involves at least 100 files. Based on these results, we design 8 benchmarks varying (i) number of files; (ii) file sizes and (iii) file types, therefore covering a variety of synchronization scenarios. Tab. 1 lists our benchmark sets. All files in the sets are created at run-time by our testing application. Other types of files, used in Sect. 4 for checking capabilities, are not included in the benchmarks for the sake of space.

Each experiment is repeated 24 times per service, allowing at least 5 min between experiments to avoid creating abnormal workloads to servers. The benchmark of a single storage service lasts for about 1 day. Synchronization startup, upload time and protocol overhead are discussed in Sect. 5. It is important to reinforce that all measurements

[2]OS X and Linux clients have also been checked whether available and show no differences.

[3]The list has been manually compiled from various sources and covers more than 100 countries and 500 ISPs.

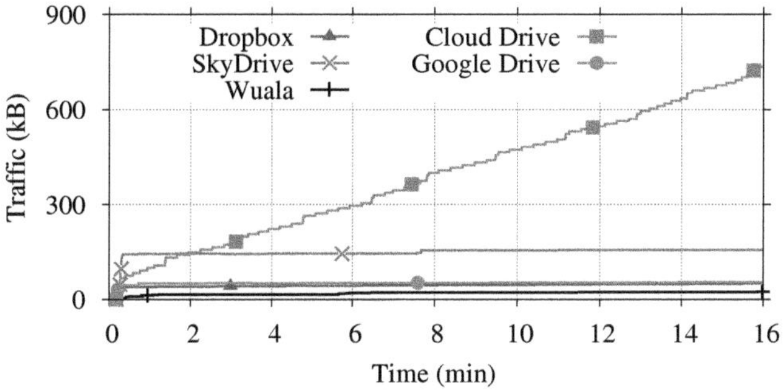

Figure 2: Background traffic while idle.

Figure 3: Google Drive's edge nodes.

have been taken from a single location, in the same controlled environment. While results for each service may vary when measuring from other locations or longer intervals, our conclusions in the following are independent of that. Repeating the experiments from different locations is planned to future works.

2.4 Tested Storage Services

We focus on 5 services for the sake of space, although our methodology is generic and can be applied to any other service. We restrict our analysis to native clients, since previous results [3] show that this is the largely preferred means to use personal cloud storage services.

Tab. 2 lists the analyzed services. Dropbox [4], Google Drive [6] and SkyDrive [13] are selected because they are among the most popular offers, according to the volume of search queries containing names of cloud storage services on Google Trends [8]. Wuala [10] is considered because it is a system that offers encryption at the client-side. We want to verify the impact of such privacy layer on synchronization performance. Finally, we include Cloud Drive [1] to compare its performance to Dropbox, since both services rely on Amazon Web Services (AWS) data centers.

Table 2: Analyzed personal cloud storage services.

Name	Version
Dropbox	2.0.8
Microsoft SkyDrive	1.8.4357.4863
Google Drive	17.0.2006.0314
LaCie Wuala	*Strasbourg*
Amazon Cloud Drive	2.0.2013.841

3. SYSTEM ARCHITECTURE

3.1 Protocols

All clients exchange traffic using HTTPS, with the exception of Dropbox notification protocol, which relies on plain HTTP. Interestingly, some Wuala storage operations also use HTTP, since users' privacy has already been secured by local encryption.

All services but Wuala use separate servers for control and storage. Their identification is trivial by monitoring the traffic exchanged when the client (i) starts; (ii) is idle; and (iii) synchronizes files. Both server names and IP addresses can be used to identify different operations during our tests. For Wuala, we use flow sizes and connection sequences to identify storage flows.

We notice some relevant differences among applications during login and idle phases. Fig. 2 reports the cumulative number of bytes exchanged with control servers considering an initial 16 min in idle state. Two considerations hold. Firstly, the applications authenticate the user and check if any content has to be updated. Note how SkyDrive requires about 150 kB in total, 4 times more than others. This happens because the application contacts many Microsoft Live servers during login (13 in this example). Secondly, once login is completed, the applications keep exchanging data with the cloud. Wuala is the most silent, polling servers every 5 min on average – i.e., equivalent background traffic of about 60 b/s. Google Drive follows close, with a lightweight 40 s polling interval (42 b/s). Dropbox and SkyDrive use intervals close to 1 min (82 b/s and 32 b/s, respectively).

Amazon Cloud Drive is completely different: polling is done every 15 s, each time opening a new HTTPS connection. This notification strategy consumes 6 kb/s – i.e., about 65 MB per day. This information is relevant to users with bandwidth constraints (e.g., in 3G/4G networks) and to the system: 1 million users would generate approximately 6 Gb/s of signaling traffic alone! As the results for other providers demonstrate, such design is not optimal and seems indeed possible to be improved.

3.2 Data Centers

Next, we analyze data center locations. Dropbox uses own servers (in the San Jose area) for client management, while storage servers are committed to Amazon in Northern Virginia. Cloud Drive uses three AWS data centers: two are used for both storage and control (in Ireland and Northern Virginia); a third one is used for storage only (in Oregon). SkyDrive relies on Microsoft's data centers in the Seattle area (for storage) and Southern Virginia (for storage and control). We also identified a destination in Singapore (for control only). Not surprisingly, most data centers are located in the U.S. Wuala data centers instead are located in Europe: two in the Nuremberg area, one in Zurich and a fourth in Northern France. None is owned by Wuala. All these services follow a centralized design where clients contact the servers using the public Internet, as expected.

Google Drive follows a different approach: TCP connections are terminated at the closest Google's *edge node*, from where the traffic is routed to the actual storage/control data center using the private Google's network. Fig. 3 shows the

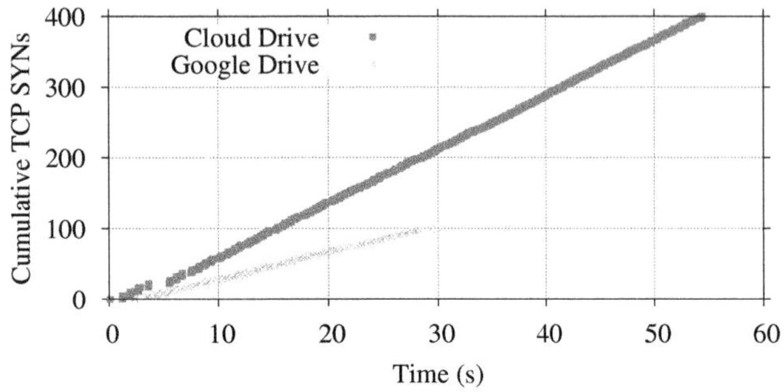

Figure 4: Uploading 100 files of 10 kB.

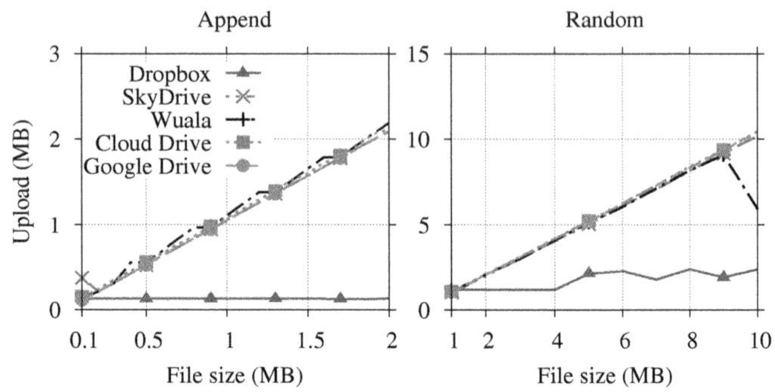

Figure 5: Delta encoding tests. Note the x-axes.

locations identified in our experiments.[4] Overall, more than 100 different entry points have been located. Such architecture allows to reduce client-server RTT and to offload storage traffic from the public Internet. Performance implications are discussed in Sect. 5.

4. CLOUD SERVICE CAPABILITIES

4.1 Chunking

Our first test aims at understanding how the services process large files. By monitoring throughput during the upload of files differing in size, we determine whether files are exchanged as single objects (no pause during the upload), or split into *chunks*, each delimited by a pause. Our experiments show that only Cloud Drive does not perform chunking. In fact, Google Drive uses 8 MB chunks while Dropbox uses 4 MB chunks. SkyDrive and Wuala apparently use variable chunk sizes.

Chunking seems advantageous because it simplifies upload recovery in case of failures: partial submission becomes easier to be implemented, benefiting users connected to slow networks, for example.

4.2 Bundling

When a batch of files needs to be transferred, files could be bundled and pipelined so that both transmission latency and control overhead impact are reduced. Our tests to check how services handle batches of files consist of 4 upload sets, each containing exactly the same number of bytes (1 MB), which are split into 1, 10, 100 or 1000 files, respectively.

These experiments reveal a variety of synchronization strategies. Google Drive and Cloud Drive open one separate TCP (and SSL) connection for each file. Considering management, Cloud Drive opens 3 TCP/SSL control connections per file operation. Fig. 4 shows the number of TCP `SYN` packets observed when Google Drive and Cloud Drive have to store 100 files of 10 kB each: 100 and 400 connections are opened respectively, requiring 30 s and 55 s to complete the upload. Sect. 5 will confirm that such design strongly limits the client performance when several files have to be exchanged, owing to TCP and SSL negotiations.

Other services reuse TCP connections. However, SkyDrive and Wuala submit files sequentially, waiting for application layer acknowledgments between each upload. This can be determined by counting packet bursts, which are proportional to the number of files in our experiments. We conclude that only Dropbox implements a file-bundling strategy.

[4]Our results match with Google's points of presence [7]. Understanding how Google manages traffic inside its network is outside the scope of this paper.

4.3 Client-Side Deduplication

Server data deduplication eliminates replicas on the storage server. In case the same content is already present on the storage, replicas in the client folder can be identified to save upload capacity too.

To check whether this feature is implemented, we design the following test: (i) a random file is inserted in an arbitrary folder; (ii) the same random payload is used to create a replica with a different name in a second folder; (iii) the original file is copied to a third folder; and (iv) after all copies are deleted, the original file is placed back. The last step determines whether deduplication fails after files are deleted from the local folder.

Results allow to conclude that only Dropbox and Wuala implement deduplication. All other services have to upload the same data even if it is readily available at the storage server. Interestingly, Dropbox and Wuala can identify copies of users' files even after they are deleted and later restored. In the case of Wuala, deduplication is compatible with local encryption, i.e., two identical files generate two identical encrypted versions.

4.4 Delta Encoding

Delta encoding is a specialized compression technique that calculates file differences among two copies, allowing the transmission of only the modifications between revisions. To verify which services implement delta encoding, a sequence of changes are generated on a file so that a portion of content is added/changed at each iteration. Three cases are considered: new data added/changed at the end, at the beginning, or at a random position within the file. This allows us to check whether rolling hash mechanisms are implemented. In all cases, the modified file replaces its old copy.

Fig. 5 shows that only Dropbox fully implements delta encoding, i.e., the volume of uploaded data corresponds to the actual part that has been modified. Results in which bytes are inserted at the end and at random positions are shown on the left and right plots, respectively. In the former case, file sizes have been chosen up to 2 MB. Larger files are instead considered in the latter case to highlight the combined effects with chunking and deduplication. Focusing on Dropbox, observe that the amount of sent traffic increases when files are bigger than Dropbox 4 MB-long chunk. This happens because the original content may be shifted, chang-

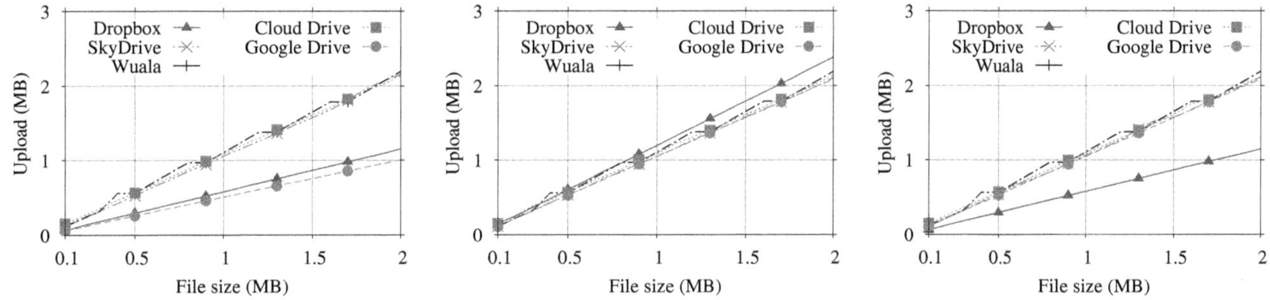

(a) Random readable text (b) Random bytes (c) Fake JPEGs

Figure 6: Bytes uploaded during the compression test.

ing two or more chunks at once. As such, the volume of data to be transmitted is larger than the added data.

Wuala does not implement delta encoding. However, deduplication prevents the client from uploading those chunks not affected by the change. This can be seen in Fig. 5, when data is added at a random offset, forming a 10 MB file. In this case, only two chunks (among 3) are modified, and thus uploaded.

4.5 Data Compression

We next verify whether data is compressed before a transfer. Compression could, in general, reduce traffic and storage requirements at the expense of processing time. The compression capability is checked with two distinct file sets. The first set (Fig. 6(a)) is made of highly compressible text files (sizes from 100 kB to 2 MB). Files in the second set (Fig. 6(b)) contain pure random bytes so that no compression is possible. Fig. 6(a) reveals that Dropbox and Google Drive compress data before transmission, with the latter implementing a more efficient scheme. Fig. 6(b) confirms that Dropbox has the highest overhead in this scenario.

Naturally, compression is advantageous only for some file types. Compression has a negligible or negative impact when already compressed files are going to be transmitted. A possible approach would be to verify the file format before trying to compress it (e.g., using *magic numbers*). We check whether Google Drive and Dropbox implement smart policies by creating fake JPEGs – i.e., files with JPEG extension and JPEG headers, but actually filled with text. Fig. 6(c) shows that Google Drive identifies JPEG content and avoids compression. Dropbox instead compresses all files independently of their content.

4.6 Summary

Tab. 3 summarizes the capabilities of each service. It shows that Dropbox has the most sophisticated client from the point of view of features to enhance synchronization speed. Wuala, Google Drive and SkyDrive come next, implementing some capabilities. Finally, Cloud Drive is the simplest client, as none of the capabilities are implemented.

5. CLIENT PERFORMANCE

5.1 Synchronization Startup

We first evaluate how much time each service needs before synchronization starts. This metric could reveal, for instance, whether implementing advanced capabilities increases initial synchronization delay. The metric is computed from the moment when files start being modified in the test computer until the first storage flow is observed.[5]

Fig. 7(a) shows average delays over 24 repetitions. Only 4 scenarios using binary files are shown, since similar conclusions are obtained with plain text files. Dropbox is the fastest service to start synchronizing single files. Its bundling strategy, however, slightly delays start up with multiple files. As we will show next, such strategy pays back in total upload time. SkyDrive is by far the slowest, waiting at least 9 s before starting submitting files. The root cause of this delay is unclear, since SkyDrive client does not report any activity during this period. Moreover, SkyDrive gets slower as batches increase, taking more than 20 s to start sending 100 files of 10 kB. Wuala also increases its startup time when multiple files are submitted.

5.2 Completion Time

Next, we test how long each service takes to complete upload tasks. This is measured as the difference between the first and the last packet with payload seen in any storage flow. We ignore TCP tear-down delays, and control messages sent after the upload is complete.

Fig. 7(b) summarizes our results (note the logarithmic scale on the y-axis). A mixed figure emerges. When synchronizing single files of 100 kB or 1 MB, the distance between our testbed and the data centers dominates the metric. Google Drive (26,49 Mb/s) and Wuala (33,34 Mb/s) are the fastest, since each TCP connection is terminated at data centers nearby our testbed. Dropbox and SkyDrive, on the other hand, are the most impacted services. SkyDrive (160 ms of RTT) needs almost 4 s to upload a 1 MB file, whereas Google Drive requires only 300 ms (15 ms of RTT).

When multiple files are stored, the client capabilities become central. The rightmost bars on Fig. 7(b) show a striking difference on completion time when 100 files of 10 kB are used. Dropbox wins by a factor of 2 because of bundling, topping to 0,8 Mb/s of upload rate. Interestingly, Google Drive's advantage due to its distributed topology is canceled by the usage of separate TCP/SSL connections per file. It takes 42 s on average – i.e., 189 kb/s. Other services are also penalized by their lack of bundling, with Cloud Drive taking about 60 s (132 kb/s) to complete some tests.

[5] This includes delays of our testing application to send files to the test computer. The artifact, however, does not affect our conclusions, since all experiments are equally affected.

Table 3: Summary of the capabilities implemented in each service.

	Dropbox	SkyDrive	Wuala	Google Drive	Cloud Drive
Chunking	4 MB	var.	var.	8 MB	no
Bundling	**yes**	no	no	no	no
Compression	always	no	no	**smart**	no
Deduplication	**yes**	no	**yes**	no	no
Delta-encoding	**yes**	no	no	no	no

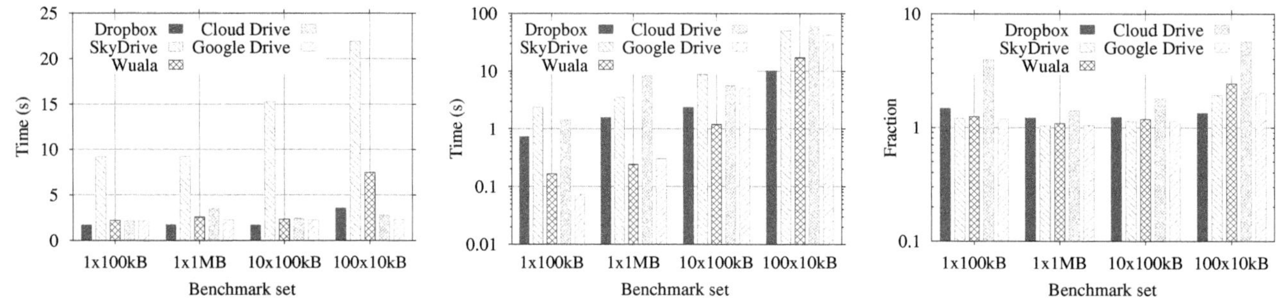

(a) Synchronization start up time (b) Duration (note log y-axis) (c) Overhead (note log y-axis)

Figure 7: Average benchmarking results when uploading binary files.

Results with plain text files are not shown for the sake of space, but similar conclusions can be drawn. Dropbox has a small improvement in its upload time because of compression, although network latency still dominates the metric. Google Drive profits from its smart compression when sending single plain text files of moderate sizes. However, the service is again among the slowest when multiple small text files are synchronized, showing that its smart compression advantage is also canceled by the lack of bundling.

5.3 Protocol Overhead

Finally, we evaluate protocol overhead as the total storage and control traffic over the benchmark size. Fig. 7(c) shows that all services have a moderate to high overhead when small binary files are synchronized. Cloud Drive presents a very high overhead because of its high number of control flows opened for every file transfer (see Fig. 2). Dropbox exhibits the highest overhead among the remaining services (47 % for 100 kB files and 22 % for 1 MB files), possibly owing to the signaling cost of implementing its advanced capabilities.

The lack of bundling dramatically increases overhead when multiple small files are sent. Google Drive, for instance, exchanges twice as much traffic as the actual data size when sending 100 binary files of 10 kB. Cloud Drive shows even more overhead – i.e., more than 5 MB of data are exchanged to commit 1 MB of content. A similar pattern is generally seen in the experiments with plain text files. Dropbox and Google Drive are the exceptions, owing to their compression strategies, which naturally reduce network overhead.

6. CONCLUSIONS

In this paper we presented a methodology to check both capabilities and system design of personal cloud storage services. We then evaluated the implications of design choices on performance by analyzing 5 services.

Our analysis shows the relevance of *client capabilities* and *protocol design* to personal cloud storage services. Dropbox implements most of the checked capabilities, and its sophisticated client clearly boosts performance, although some protocol tweaks seem possible to reduce network overhead. On the other extreme, Cloud Drive bandwidth wastage is an order of magnitude higher than other offerings, and its lack of client capabilities results in performance bottlenecks. SkyDrive shows some performance limitations, while Wuala generally performs well. More importantly, Wuala deploys client side encryption, and this feature does not seem to affect Wuala synchronization performance.

These 4 examples confirm the role played by *data center placement* in a centralized approach: taking the perspective of European users only, network latency is still an important limitation for U.S. centric services, such as Dropbox and SkyDrive. Services deploying data centers nearby our test location, such as Wuala, have therefore an advantage.

Google Drive follows a different approach resulting in a mixed picture: it enjoys the benefits of using Google's capillary infrastructure and private backbone, which reduce network latency and speed up the system. However, protocols and client features limit performance, especially when multiple files are considered.

As future work, we intend to extend our analysis with measurements from other locations and longer time intervals. This will allow us to quantify long-term effects of design choices for users connected in different geographic areas. Moreover, we plan to define new benchmarks by collecting data from volunteers, thus creating realistic benchmarks that mix files of different types in a single set.

7. ACKNOWLEDGMENTS

This work was partly funded by the Network of Excellence project *Flamingo* (ICT-318488) and the EU-IP project *mPlane* (n-318627). Both projects are supported by the European Commission under its Seventh Framework Programme.

8. REFERENCES

[1] Amazon. Cloud Drive v. 2.0.2013.841. http://www.amazon.com/gp/feature.html?docId=1000828861.

[2] I. N. Bermudez, S. Traverso, M. Mellia, and M. M. Munafò. Exploring the Cloud from Passive Measurements: the Amazon AWS case. In *The 32nd Annual IEEE International Conference on Computer Communications*, INFOCOM'13, 2013.

[3] I. Drago, M. Mellia, M. M. Munafò, A. Sperotto, R. Sadre, and A. Pras. Inside Dropbox: Understanding Personal Cloud Storage Services. In *Proceedings of the 12th ACM Internet Measurement Conference*, IMC'12, pages 481–494, 2012.

[4] Dropbox. v. 2.0.8. https://www.dropbox.com/release_notes.

[5] B. Eriksson and M. Crovella. Understanding Geolocation Accuracy using Network Geometry. In *The 32nd Annual IEEE International Conference on Computer Communications*, INFOCOM'13, 2013.

[6] Google. Drive v. 1.9.4536.8202. https://tools.google.com/dlpage/drive.

[7] Google. Network Introduction. https://peering.google.com/about/delivery_ecosystem.html.

[8] Google. Trends. http://www.google.com/trends/.

[9] W. Hu, T. Yang, and J. N. Matthews. The Good, the Bad and the Ugly of Consumer Cloud Storage. *ACM SIGOPS Operating Systems Review*, 44(3):110–115, 2010.

[10] LaCie. Wuala v. *Strasbourg*. http://www.wuala.com/.

[11] A. Li, X. Yang, S. Kandula, and M. Zhang. CloudCmp: Comparing Public Cloud Providers. In *Proceedings of the 10th ACM SIGCOMM Conference on Internet Measurement*, IMC'10, pages 1–14, 2010.

[12] T. Mager, E. Biersack, and P. Michiardi. A Measurement Study of the Wuala On-line Storage Service. In *Proceedings of the IEEE 12th International Conference on Peer-to-Peer Computing*, P2P'12, pages 237–248, 2012.

[13] Microsoft. SkyDrive v. 17.0.2006.0314. https://skydrive.live.com/.

[14] I. Poese, S. Uhlig, M. A. Kaafar, B. Donnet, and B. Gueye. IP Geolocation Databases: Unreliable? *SIGCOMM Comput. Commun. Rev.*, 41(2):53–56, 2011.

[15] R. Torres, A. Finamore, J. R. Kim, M. Mellia, M. M. Munafò, and S. Rao. Dissecting Video Server Selection Strategies in the YouTube CDN. In *Proceedings of the 31st International Conference on Distributed Computing Systems*, ICDCS'11, pages 248–257, 2011.

[16] H. Wang, R. Shea, F. Wang, and J. Liu. On the Impact of Virtualization on Dropbox-like Cloud File Storage/Synchronization Services. In *Proceedings of the IEEE 20th International Workshop on Quality of Service*, IWQoS '12, pages 11:1–11:9, 2012.

Measuring and Mitigating Web Performance Bottlenecks in Broadband Access Networks

Srikanth Sundaresan
Georgia Tech
srikanth@gatech.edu

Nick Feamster
Georgia Tech
feamster@cc.gatech.edu

Renata Teixeira
CNRS & UPMC
renata.teixeira@lip6.fr

Nazanin Magharei
Cisco Systems
n.magharei@gmail.com

ABSTRACT

We measure Web performance bottlenecks in home broadband access networks and evaluate ways to mitigate these bottlenecks with caching within home networks. We first measure Web performance bottlenecks to nine popular Web sites from more than 5,000 broadband access networks and demonstrate that when the downstream throughput of the access link exceeds about 16 Mbits/s, latency is the main bottleneck for Web page load time. Next, we use a router-based Web measurement tool, Mirage, to deconstruct Web page load time into its constituent components (DNS lookup, TCP connection setup, object download) and show that simple latency optimizations can yield significant improvements in overall page load times. We then present a case for placing a cache in the home network and deploy three common optimizations: DNS caching, TCP connection caching, and content caching. We show that caching only DNS and TCP connections yields significant improvements in page load time, even when the user's browser is already performing similar independent optimizations. Finally, we use traces from real homes to demonstrate how prefetching DNS and TCP connections for popular sites in a home-router cache can achieve faster page load times.

Categories and Subject Descriptors

C.2.3 [**Computer-Communication Networks**]: Network Operations—*Network Management*; C.2.3 [**Computer-Communication Networks**]: Network Operations—*Network Monitoring*

Keywords

Broadband Networks; Web performance; Bottlenecks; Popularity-based prefetching; Connection caching; DNS prefetching

1. INTRODUCTION

Home broadband Internet access is getting faster: the OECD reports that broadband speeds are increasing by about 15–20% every year. Average advertised broadband speeds are now about 16 Mbits/s in the U.S. and 37.5 Mbits/s across OECD areas [43].

IMC'13, October 23–25, 2013, Barcelona, Spain.
Copyright 2013 ACM 978-1-4503-1953-9/13/10 ...$15.00.
http://dx.doi.org/10.1145/2504730.2504741 .

As downstream throughput continues to increase, one might expect the Web to get faster at home, as well. Meanwhile, Internet service providers and application providers are increasingly cognizant of the importance of reducing Web page load times; even seemingly small differences in latency can introduce significant effects on usability (and revenue). The Bing search engine experiences reduced revenue of 1.2% with just a 500-millisecond delay [53], and a 400-millisecond delay resulted in a 0.74% decrease in searches on the Google search engine [14]. Forrester research found that most users expected online shopping sites to load in two seconds or fewer [40]. Content providers struggle to mitigate any network performance bottleneck that can slow down Web page loads in access networks by even tens of milliseconds. Thus, it is crucial to understand both how network properties of access networks such as latency can introduce bottlenecks in Web page load times and the extent to which various optimizations can help further mitigate these bottlenecks.

Towards this goal, in this paper, we use measurements from a router-based Web performance measurement tool, Mirage, to analyze Web page load times to nine popular Web sites. This tool has been deployed in over 5,000 home networks as part of the FCC/SamKnows deployment in the US. We also deploy the tool in our own smaller deployment, BISmark. We examine how access network latency and throughput can introduce performance bottlenecks and evaluate how to mitigate these bottlenecks by deploying various caching optimizations on the router in the home network. Next, we demonstrate that caching on a home router can improve page load time, even if the router does not cache any content (*i.e.*, even if it only caches DNS records and TCP connections), and even if the end host or Web browser is already independently performing similar optimizations. Finally, we show how prefetching DNS records and TCP connections from the home router can improve cache hit rates; we use a trace-based emulation to show that prefetching can help achieve these performance improvements in real home networks. We now describe each of these contributions in more detail.

First, we measure Web performance from 5,556 broadband access networks to nine popular Web sites and identify bottlenecks that contribute to Web page load time in these networks (Section 5). Our results suggest that latency is the main bottleneck for Web page load times for access links whose downstream throughput exceeds about 16 Mbits/s. Last-mile latency is an important contributor to the end-to-end latency, and an increase in last-mile latency of just 10 milliseconds can sometimes induce delays of hundreds of milliseconds for page load times of popular sites. In the case of small objects, we find that TCP latency overhead exceeds the actual download time of the object. Our results corroborate and quantify anecdotal evidence from users, Internet service providers, and content providers who are increasingly finding that latency is becoming a critical performance bottleneck [28,40].

Second, we use Mirage to deconstruct page load time into its constituent components (*i.e.*, DNS lookup, TCP connection setup, content download) and show that even small improvements in latency can yield significant improvements in overall page load times (Section 6). To our knowledge, this paper presents the first study to compare the relative benefits of content caching, DNS caching, and TCP connection caching from within home networks. As part of this analysis, we explore how the page load time that Mirage measures relates to Web page load time measured by other tools (*e.g.*, Phantomjs, Web browsers). We find that latency is a significant contributor to all factors that affect page load time. These results—in conjunction with previous studies that have observed that characteristics of the access network can introduce significant latency [55]—present the case for *home caching*, the process of caching DNS lookups, TCP connections, and content from the home router.

Third, we deploy an OpenWrt module that performs various caching optimizations in home routers on the BISmark testbed and show that such a cache can yield improvements in page load time, even if it does not cache content, and *even if the browser is already performing similar optimizations* (Section 7). As expected, content caching offers the most significant reductions in page load time and can reduce page load times by up to 53% in some cases. Yet, simply caching TCP connections and DNS records at the home router can reduce mean page load times by 20% and 7%, respectively, even if the ISP and browser are also independently performing their own caching optimizations.

Finally, to improve cache hit rates in real home networks, we introduce *popularity-based prefetching*, which prefetches DNS records and TCP connections for Web sites that are commonly accessed from a home network. Using Web traces from twelve home networks, we find that prefetching DNS records and TCP connections for only the twenty most popular sites significantly increases DNS and connection cache hit rates and therefore could offer significant improvements in page load times.

The Web performance measurements from the SamKnows deployment are available on the FCC Web site [52]. We have published both the Web performance measurements from the BISmark experiments [13] and the OpenWrt module that performs popularity-based prefetching [48].

2. BACKGROUND

Factors that affect page load time. Web downloads begin by downloading the home page of the requested Web page. The home page object typically contains references to other objects that the browser must subsequently retrieve. Each of these objects is referenced with another URL, which the browser retrieves with additional HTTP requests. These objects are either static, in which case the URL is in the home page itself; or dynamic, in which case the URL is determined by running active scripts (*e.g.*, Javascript) that determine which objects to download. Modern Web sites typically contain a mix of static and dynamic objects. Browsers minimize the download time of the individual objects using many optimizations such as parallel fetches, DNS caching, TCP connection reuse, and optimizations for processing scripts and rendering. Different browsers implement different sets of optimizations.

Because the time for the browser to render a page depends on the choice of browser and machine configuration, we instead define *page load time* as the time from the initial request to the time when all objects for the page have been retrieved. The retrieval time for each object has the following components: (1) the *DNS lookup time* for the domain referenced in the object URL; (2) the *TCP connection time*, which is the time to complete the TCP three-way handshake to the server; (3) the *server response time*, which is the time it takes for the server to start sending the object once it has been requested; and (4) the *object download time*, which is the time to download the object itself over TCP. Some of these factors, such as the DNS lookup and TCP connection times, are bound by latency; others, such as the object download time, are bound by both latency and throughput.

Optimizations to improve page load time. A number of optimizations have been proposed and implemented in the quest to minimize page load time. Server-side optimizations include HTTP replacements [50, 54] and TCP modifications [11, 12, 19, 20, 26]. Recent proposals suggest using a larger initial congestion window sizes on servers for TCP connection, so that small objects can be transferred with significantly fewer round trips [26]. Al-Fares *et al.* studied the effects of server-side optimizations, such as increasing TCP's initial congestion window (ICW) and enabling HTTP pipelining on Web page load times [7]. They found that increasing the ICW can reduce page load times by several hundred milliseconds in many cases. Although these server-side optimizations can improve page load times, they do not reduce certain components that contribute to page load time, including DNS lookup and the TCP connection setup time.

Many client-side optimizations from the browser have also been developed. HTTP/1.1 introduced persistent connections and pipelining. Persistent connections allow the client to retrieve multiple objects over the same TCP connection (thereby amortizing the three-way handshake and TCP congestion window ramp up cost over multiple objects). Pipelining allows the client to initiate a request for the next object as soon as it sees a reference to that object in another object (rather than waiting for the object download to complete). Nielsen *et al.* showed the superior performance of HTTP/1.1 over HTTP/1.0 [42]. However, most browsers do not enable pipelining by default, and some servers do not enable persistent connections. Zhou *et al.* propose a new protocol that minimizes connection time by having DNS resolvers set up TCP connection on the client's behalf [61]. Browsers also download multiple objects in parallel and have highly optimized engines for parsing and rendering objects.

Content caching is also a common optimization. Content Distribution Networks (CDNs) are large distributed caches that are typically deployed at the edge of ISPs to reduce the latency between the end-host and the content. Ihm *et al.* characterized five years of Web traffic traces from a globally distributed proxy service; they observe that Web caches typically have a 15–25% hit rate, and these rates could almost double if caches operated on 128-byte blocks [31]. Previous studies have reported object cache hit rates in the range of 35–50%, although these cache hit rates have continued to drop over time [2, 16, 30, 41, 60]. Some browsers also support content prefetching [39]; Padmanabhan *et al.* proposed predictive content prefetching using server hints [45].

To improve cache hit ratios, Web browsers prefetch DNS records anticipating client requests; the browser parses certain downloaded pages (*e.g.*, a search result page) for domains and resolves them before the user clicks on them [24]. To reduce the time associated with DNS lookups, browsers and intermediate DNS servers employ caching and prefetching [21, 22]. Jung *et al.* studied DNS performance and the effectiveness of DNS caching [34], and saw that DNS cache hit rates can be as high as 80%, even with only a few clients [33]. Feldmann *et al.* observed in Web traces from AT&T home users that 47% of objects retrieved incur more than half of the total download time from TCP connection setup [29]. Based on this observation, the study proposes a *connection cache* in the ISP network to reduce connection setup time, which reduces download times by up to 40%.

3. RELATED WORK

There is much previous work on measuring and modeling Web performance, ranging from protocol modeling to empirical analysis to designing techniques to improve performance. Many of these previous studies were performed before the growth of broadband access networks, content distribution networks, and modern browsers. This evolution suggests that it is time for a reappraisal of some past studies in the context of broadband access networks, although it is important to put our study in the context of previous work. Below, we compare past work in measuring and modeling Web performance to the study in this paper. This study is a more complete version of our own previously published work, which explored the contribution of latency to Web page load time [57] and the positive performance benefits of proactive caching and prefetching [56].

Measuring Web performance. Barford *et al.* analyzed the contribution of server, client, and network delays to HTTP 1.0 transaction times [10]; the authors used virtual clients on several campus networks to request files from a virtual Web server. They found that for small files, server load is the dominant factor for performance, while for large files, the network properties dominate. Krishnamurthy and Wills analyzed the impact of variants of TCP (*i.e.*, Tahoe, Reno) and HTTP (*i.e.*, persistent, parallel, or pipelined) on Web performance; they also studied the effects of network latency and server load on observed performance [36]. These studies were performed more than ten years ago. During this time period, the Web has changed dramatically, in terms of the type of content is served, how content is hosted, and how browsers operate. Additionally, broadband Internet access has proliferated since the late 1990s. It is also much faster than it was when these original studies were conducted and is now a predominant mode of Internet access. To our knowledge, this study is the first to explore Web page load times from broadband access links, and the first to quantify the extent to which latency becomes a bottleneck on high-throughput access links.

More recent work has studied the performance of CDNs [32] and caching [27]. Akella *et al.* [3–6] studied the effects of the performance of 68 CDN sites across 17 cities, focusing on how server multihoming can improve CDN performance for clients. "Why-High?" identifies cases where a certain set of clients experience higher Web page load times [37]. Butkiewicz *et al.* recently studied how the complexity of modern Web sites may contribute to slower page load times and found that more than 60% of the Web sites they profiled retrieve content from five non-origin sources that contribute to more than 35% of the bytes downloaded [15]. Our work complements existing literature by exposing how access networks introduce bottlenecks and assessing how well existing Web performance optimizations work when they are deployed in homes.

The online service `webpagetest.org` [59] analyzes the contribution of different network components to overall page load time via a "waterfall"; the analysis is similar to the decomposition that we perform in this paper, although the software we develop can run directly on home routers, unlike `webpagetest.org`, which runs from data centers. Keynote [35] and Compuware [23] perform end-to-end Web performance measurements from a variety of vantage points, but they do not study how individual network factors such as latency, loss, or throughput ultimately contribute to page load time.

Metric	Type	Description
Page load time	Total	The time to look up DNS, set up TCP connections and retrieve all objects.
DNS lookup time	Per Domain	The DNS lookout time for the main domain of the site.
Time to first byte	Per Object	The time from the initiation of the TCP connection to the arrival of the first byte of the requested object (including server processing time).
Object download time	Per Object	The time to download an object, excluding the DNS lookup time and time to first byte.

Table 1: *Performance metrics. For each per-object metric, Mirage measures the maximum, minimum, and average times for each object in the transaction.*

Modeling Web performance. Previous work developed models for TCP and HTTP performance based on various network properties such as latency and packet loss [8, 9, 17, 18, 44]. We present an empirical study of Web performance from thousands of access networks. This empirical approach provides new insights into how access network characteristics affect each component of page load time. WebProphet [38] and WProf [58] analyze dependencies between Web page objects to predict browser-level response time and study bottlenecks in the critical path of page load times. These tools are valuable in the quest to improve page load times by exposing inefficiencies in Web site design, but they are difficult to deploy at scale.

4. MEASURING PAGE LOAD TIME

The notion of page load time depends on many factors, including the underlying network, the design of the Web site, and the endhost, including the browser. Every browser downloads pages using different methods (and different optimizations), and the pages themselves may be optimized for different browsers and devices. In this paper, we explore how the characteristics of broadband networks affect Web page load times. Page load time will necessarily vary depending on the above characteristics. Thus, to conduct controlled experiments of the effects of network characteristics on page load time, we use a single tool on a common platform to measure page load times as various network conditions change. We now explain the design of the active measurement tool that we use, and how the numbers it yields compares to that of a browser.

4.1 Mirage: Home Router-Based Web Testing

We use measurements from the FCC/SamKnows deployment of routers across the US [55]. The deployment uses a custom tool, which we call *Mirage*, to measure page load time. Mirage is a headless Web client designed by SamKnows for deployment on home router devices; the initial deployment of Mirage was sponsored by the Federal Communications Commission (FCC) on more than 5,000 homes across the US. We also use it in the BISmark deployment.

4.1.1 How Mirage Works

Mirage downloads the home page of a Web site and parses it to determine the static objects that are needed to render the page. It then performs all the DNS lookups at once before downloading the rest of the objects. The tool is based on `libcurl`, which can de-

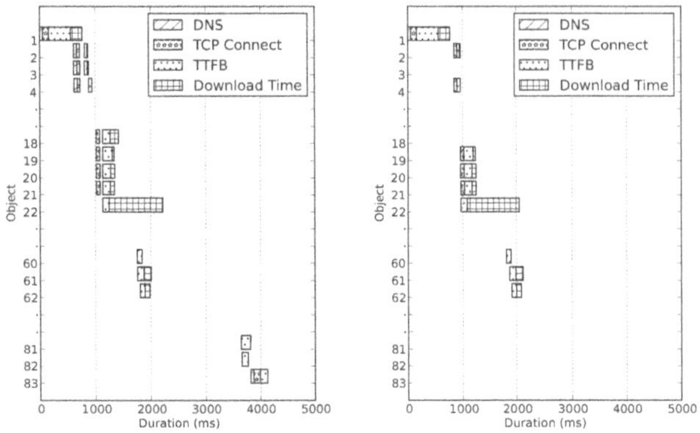

(a) *Real Browser* **(b)** *Mirage*

Figure 1: *Comparison of a real browser (from* `webpagetest.org`*) with Mirage for* `www.ebay.com`*; some objects are omitted. The browser optimizes object retrieval differently, and also retrieves more objects. Still, the performance bottlenecks are similar for both.*

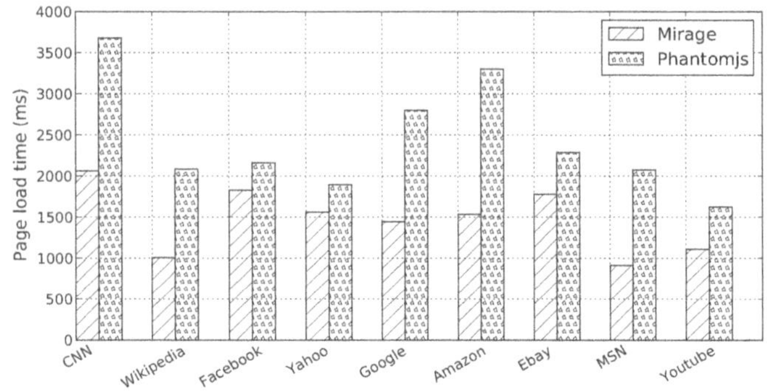

Figure 2: *Comparison of Mirage to Phantomjs. We see that Mirage underestimates the page load times: real load times are higher than what we measure.*

compose the overall page load time into the download times for individual objects. Mirage separates the page load time into the time to perform DNS lookups, the time to first byte (which combines the TCP connection time and the server processing time), and the actual load time for each object. It uses persistent TCP connections if the server supports them and up to eight parallel TCP connections to download objects. Because Mirage uses many of the basic network optimizations that a browser uses including persistent TCP connections and parallel TCP connections, it approximates the that a real browser might see, even though it does not emulate any particular browser. Table 1 shows the performance metrics for each download and how the performance measurements from Mirage compare to those from `webpagetest.org`.

Mirage is ideal for our goal of studying the effect of the characteristics of broadband access networks on Web performance for a number of reasons. First, because Mirage can be deployed directly on home routers, it provides measurements from a single platform that is directly connected to the access link, thereby normalizing some of the effects that might otherwise affect page load times (*e.g.*, the use of different browsers, home network effects). Second, Mirage is already in use in the large FCC/SamKnows deployment, which provides longitudinal measurements of the same set of diverse access links. Because Mirage breaks down each object into its constituent parts, it exposes important performance bottlenecks in access networks. Finally, Mirage is freely available and portable; we have used Mirage in our own BISmark deployment.

4.1.2 Validation

Comparing Mirage to real browser behavior. Mirage's behavior differs from a browser in several ways. We explain these differences using the example download in Figure 1. This figure shows the partial breakdown of the page load time for Ebay both using a real browser through `webpagetest.org` and Mirage. First, Mirage waits to download the home page before processing it and downloading subsequent objects; in contrast, many modern browsers start downloading objects as they process the home page. This difference is visible in objects 2–4 in Figure 1, where the real browser initiates the download before object 1 is complete. Mirage also performs DNS queries for all the unique domains after parsing the home page before downloading any of the remaining objects; it adds the maximum DNS time to the total time to download the objects. Although Mirage performs the DNS queries before downloading any objects, the effect on total page load time is not significant. The time to retrieve each individual object and the time spent on each component of the object retrieval is nearly identical for the case of the real browser and Mirage.

Mirage also downloads a slightly different, smaller set of objects than a real browser. Modern Web sites, especially content-heavy ones, employ active scripts. These scripts result in additional processing latency and also frequently result in the browser downloading more objects. Mirage only processes static objects, so it downloads a subset of the objects that are downloaded by a real browser, usually resulting in a smaller page load time than a normal browser would see. For example, in Figure 1, the browser downloads 83 objects, while Mirage downloads 62 objects.

Validation with Phantomjs. To understand how the differences between Mirage and a real browser affect overall page load time, we compare Mirage's measurements to those of a real browser environment. For this comparison, we use Phantomjs [46], a headless client that implements the Webkit browser engine and has a JavaScript API. Phantomjs is used extensively for Web benchmarking and testing [47].

Figure 2 shows the median page load time of Mirage and Phantomjs for an emulated 10 Mbits/s access link with a last-mile latency of 40 ms; the results also hold for lower latency (10 ms) links. Mirage always underestimates the actual page load time because it downloads fewer objects than a real browser would. Depending on the amount of dynamic content on the site, the difference may vary: in some cases, Mirage underestimates load times by up to 50%; in others, its measured page load time is close to the load time that Phantomjs sees.

The implementation differences between Mirage and real browsers imply that the page load times that Mirage sees may not reflect the times that any real browser would see. Yet, page load times will always differ across different browsers, and we do not aim to estimate page load time from any particular browser. Our goal is to illustrate how components of network latency (*e.g.*, DNS lookup time, TCP connect time) contribute to Web page load times. Mirage decomposes Web page load time into these components, which will be the same regardless of browser or any optimizations that a browser might perform. Mirage also allows us to evaluate how optimizations that a browser might perform can mitigate vari-

Target	Objects			Lookups			Connections			Size (KB)		
	Sam-Knows	BISmark US	BISmark non-US	Sam-Knows	BISmark US	BISmark non-US	Sam-Knows	BISmark US	BISmark non-US	Sam-Knows	BISmark US	BISmark non-US
`edition.cnn.com`	26	25	26	4	4	4	12	12	12	1199	1022	1023
`www.amazon.com`	24	31	32	4	4	4	21	24	23	589	840	851
`www.ebay.com`	29	33	32	12	14	14	16	17	19	595	613	615
`www.facebook.com`	8	8	7	2	2	2	7	8	7	437	389	289
`www.google.com/mobile`	32	20	20	1	1	1	8	8	8	1398	289	291
`www.msn.com`	24	24	54	8	8	8	14	14	16	377	348	641
`www.wikipedia.org`	16	15	16	1	1	1	16	15	15	56	56	56
`www.yahoo.com`	74	69	66	7	7	8	32	32	29	927	887	818
`www.youtube.com`	8	7	8	2	2	2	9	8	8	488	423	414

Table 2: *Properties of the Web sites in our data set. The values represent the average of the parameters over all transactions.* Objects *denotes the number of objects that must be downloaded;* lookups *are the number of DNS lookups required; and* connections *are the number of unique TCP connections the client set up to download all objects in the page. The number of connections depends on whether the server supports persistent connections, whether the objects are located on one or more domains, and the order in which objects are retrieved.* Size *denotes the number of bytes for all of the objects for a site.*

ISP	Number of homes	Avg. last-mile latency (ms)	Avg. downstream tput (Mbits/s)
AT&T	718	18	8.7
Cablevision	209	6	34.1
CenturyLink	248	23	5.8
Charter	579	7	27.4
Comcast	932	8	22.8
Cox	618	7	21.2
Mediacom	242	14	18.7
TimeWarner	952	8	16.0
Qwest	299	30	10.0
Verizon	608	5	38.0
Windstream	251	20	5.9

Table 3: *The SamKnows deployment in the US.*

Location	# of homes	Avg. last-mile latency (ms)	Avg. downstream tput (Mbits/s)
US	43	12	24.2
Europe	3	24	8.3
N. Amer. (non-U.S.)	3	15	5.5
E. Asia/Australia	4	3	46.5
Southeast Asia	8	12	5.7

Table 4: *The BISmark deployment across the world.*

Page load times for users outside the US are significantly higher for many sites; these higher times result mostly because of higher latencies to these sites.	§5.1, Fig. 3
Page load times stop improving beyond a downstream throughput of about 16 Mbits/s. For higher throughputs, latency is the performance bottleneck.	§5.2, Fig. 5a
The time to first byte can exceed the object load time in the cases of many small objects and for some pages can be as much as 21% of the page load time. The last-mile latency can be up to 23% of the time to first byte.	§5.3, Fig. 6b

Table 5: *Highlights of Section 5 results.*

ous network bottlenecks under different network conditions. When we evaluate the effects of different optimizations in Section 7, we again "close the loop" by showing that the benefits as predicted by Mirage are realized, even from a browser that is already performing its own optimizations.

4.2 Deployment

We use data from the FCC/SamKnows deployment, spanning 5,556 homes in the US; and the BISmark deployment, spanning 61 homes across the world. For both deployments, we use Mirage to characterize nine sites as chosen by SamKnows/FCC. Because it is difficult to measure a large number of Web sites from home routers and constrained access links, we focus on nine of the most popular sites around the world. Table 2 shows the sites that we measure and their properties. All of the measurements from both deployments are public. In some cases, the properties of the sites are different across deployments. Because both deployments use the same tool, these differences may result from either the vantage point or the time that the measurements were conducted. Because we do not compare measurements across the two deployments, however, these differences are not consequential.

- We analyze measurements from 5,556 participants in the FCC/SamKnows study across 11 ISPs in the US from October 2011, April 2012, and September 2012. We include only users who have reported more than 100 measurements during the duration of the study from ISPs with more than 100 users. Table 3 summarizes the deployment; our previous study describes it in more detail [55]. We report on results from September 2012; the results that we present are consistent with measurements from October 2011 and April 2012.
- We also analyze measurements from the BISmark deployment [49]. Table 4 characterizes the homes in the BISmark deployment by region. *BISmark-US* collects measurements from 44 routers across the US, and *BISmark-nonUS* collects measurements from 18 routers in other parts of the world, including Europe, North America (excluding the US), and Asia. The BISmark-US data is from May 17–June 7, 2012, and the BISmark-nonUS data is from May 24–June 7, 2012. The URLs are the same for both datasets, and we rely on DNS to locate the local version of a site, if one exists.

5. CHARACTERIZING BOTTLENECKS

We study page load times for popular sites and evaluate how downstream throughput and latency of an access link affects these times. Table 5 summarizes our results.

We find that *latency is a performance bottleneck for Web page load time in access networks whose downstream throughput ex-*

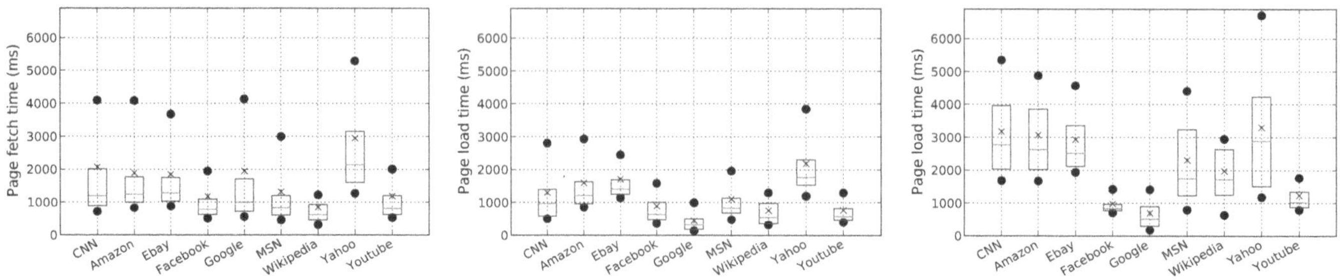

(a) *SamKnows* **(b)** *BISmark-US* **(c)** *BISmark-nonUS*

Figure 3: *Page load times for popular sites. The lower edge of each box indicates the 25th percentile of the distribution of page load times for each site, the upper edge is the 75th percentile, the middle line is the median, the cross represents the average, and the dots the 10th and 90th percentile page load times.*

ceeds about 16 Mbits/s. Last-mile latency (*i.e.*, the latency between the home network and the first hop in the access ISP) is a significant overall contributor to both DNS lookup times and the time to first byte. Therefore, *even when Web caches are deployed at the edge of access ISPs, optimizations in the home network that reduce the effects of last-mile latency can still offer significant performance improvements in page load time.*

5.1 Page Load Times of Popular Web Sites

We study the page load times to nine popular Web sites. Figure 3a shows the load times for access links in the SamKnows deployment while Figure 3b shows load times for links in the BISmark deployment (both in the US). Figure 3c shows page load times for links in the BISmark deployment outside of the US. As expected, page load time varies both by site and the location of the access network. Some variability results from differences in page size and design (see Table 2); the largest four sites (CNN, Yahoo, Amazon, and Ebay) also have the largest load times (*e.g.*, the median for CNN in the US is more than one second).

Figure 3c shows that access links outside of the US typically experience higher page load times for a given site than links in the US. The median and variance is higher for all sites we measure from outside the US, as well. A few sites have different sizes depending on the from which the page is requested, but most performance differences result from the fact that content is farther away from clients that are outside of the US. Figure 4 illustrates this phenomenon; the figure shows that the average time to first byte is in general higher in most regions outside the US. Our measurements also indicate that the global deployment of content distribution networks is somewhat spotty for certain sites. Sites with more expansive CDNs (*e.g.*, Google, YouTube) have low median and maximum page load times, whereas other sites have more variable performance, both in the US and abroad. Even Google has relatively poor performance from Southeast Asia; we discussed this phenomenon with network operators at Google, who confirmed that Google's CDN deployment is not extensive in that region.

5.2 Effects of Downstream Throughput

We study how page load time and its components vary with downstream throughput using measurements from the SamKnows deployment. We use the 95th percentile of the distribution of downstream throughput over the duration of the measurements for a given user to capture the capacity of each access link. We group access links according to downstream throughput into seven bins that reflect common ranges of Internet access plans in the dataset: 0–1 Mbits/s, 1–2 Mbits/s, 2–4 Mbits/s, 4–8 Mbits/s, 8–16 Mbits/s, 16–32 Mbits/s, and 32–64 Mbits/s. Figure 5a shows the median page load time for each category for five representative sites.

Median page load time decreases as downstream throughput increases, up to about 16 Mbits/s. As downstream throughput increases further, page load times decrease only modestly. For example, the median time for CNN is 8.4 seconds for links with throughput 0–1 Mbits/s and 1.3 seconds when throughput is 8–16 Mbits/s. Yet, when downstream throughput exceeds 32 Mbits/s, the page load time is 790 ms, only slightly better than for links with 8–16 Mbits/s.

We study how each component of page load time varies with access link throughput. Page load time is heavily influenced by the maximum DNS lookup time and the maximum time to download a single object (regardless of any caching, parallel lookups, or other optimizations), so we can interpret the maximum times for these values as a lower bound on page load time. Large objects also have a correspondingly lower TCP overhead. Figure 5b shows how these values decrease as throughput increases; each point shows the median value for the group of hosts with the corresponding range of downstream throughput. As downstream throughput increases to 32–64 Mbits/sec, object load time decreases from 3.2 seconds to 530 ms. In contrast, the time to first byte decreases as the throughput of the link increases from 0–1 to 1–2 Mbits/s, but does not improve further for higher values of throughput. DNS lookup time decreases from about 50 ms to about 15 ms. In summary, as downstream throughput increases beyond 8–16 Mbits/sec, time to first byte and DNS times become a larger component of page load time and depend more on latency than on throughput—even for large objects.

Page load times for clients outside of the US illustrate the effect of latency on page load time. For example, the average page load time for Facebook is 1.7 seconds in southeast Asia, 990 ms in east Asia and Australia, and 924 ms in Europe. Table 4 shows that clients in east Asia have higher average throughput than Europe, but do not necessarily see a corresponding improvement in page load times because latency bottlenecks negate the effects of higher throughput.

5.3 Effects of Last-Mile Latency

Our previous study of access links in the US observed that last-mile latency contributes significantly to end-to-end latencies [55]. To study the effect of last-mile latency on page load times, we group access links into 10 ms bins, according to the 10th percentile last-mile latency. Figure 6a shows the median page load time for

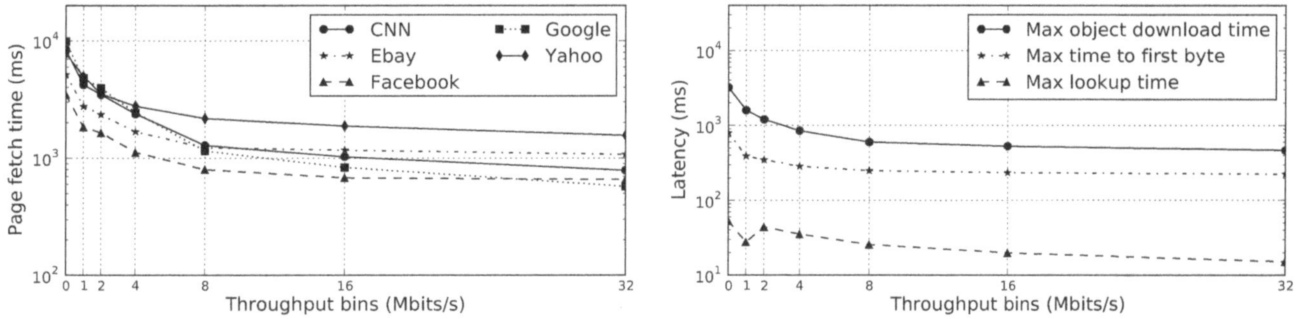

(a) *Page load times*

(b) *Components of page load time*

Figure 5: *Page load times decrease with downstream throughput, but only up to 8–16 Mbits/s. X-axis labels denote the start of each throughput bin* (e.g., *"0" is the set of users with downstream throughput up to 1 Mbits/s.) (SamKnows)*

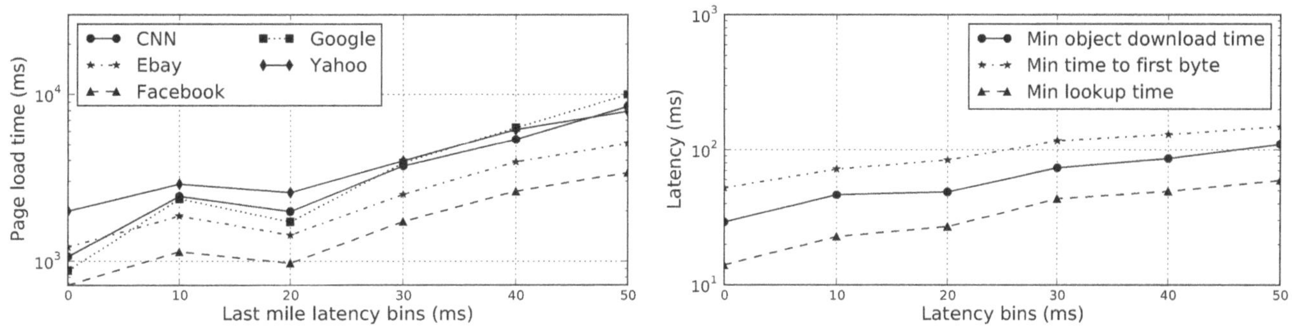

(a) *Page load times*

(b) *Components of page load time*

Figure 6: *Page load times increase with last-mile latency. X-axis labels denote the start of each latency bin. (SamKnows)*

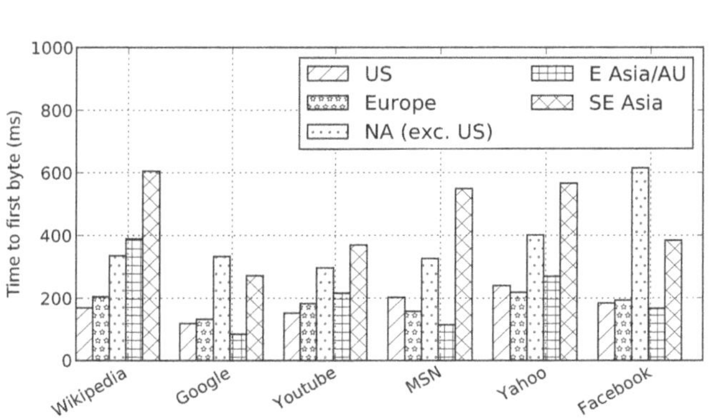

Figure 4: *Average time to first byte to six representative sites from BISmark clients broken down by location.*

each group for five representative sites. In general last-mile latency has a multiplicative effect on page load time, which is intuitive because it affects all packets in the transaction. The increase we see is not monotonic because other factors such as downstream throughput also affect page load time and some groups have more links than others: 75% of links have less than 10 ms last-mile latency. Even accounting for differences in throughput, an increase in last-mile latency of only 10 ms can result in a few hundred milliseconds increase in page load time. Increasing downstream throughput beyond 16 Mbits/s yields only marginal improvements, but decreasing last-mile latency can have a larger impact on page load time.

To understand the overhead of TCP on small objects, we look at the minimum object download time and compare it to the minimum time to first byte and DNS lookup time. Figure 6b shows the median of each of these values for each group of links. For smaller objects, the time to establish the TCP connection to the server is often greater than the time to actually transfer the object. Although the effect is magnified in smaller objects, we saw that it exists across all objects; in fact, we found that the average time to first byte ranges from 6.1% (for Yahoo) to 23% (for Wikipedia) of the total page load time. We also observed that last-mile latency can be as much as 23% of the time to first byte.

5.4 Conclusion: Optimize Latency

The results in this section suggest that for the increasing number of homes that have downstream throughput above 16 Mbits/s, the most effective way to reduce Web page load time is to focus on reducing latency as much as possible.

Improving Object Fetch Time. Because most pages have many objects, the time to download all of them can dominate other factors when downstream throughput is small. Links with less than 16 Mbits/s will thus benefit the most from content caching. For links with higher downstream throughput, however, reducing object download time is less important than reducing latency. Thus, intuition suggests that faster access links can realize significant improvements in Web page load time simply by caching DNS records and TCP connections, without even having to cache any content. Our evaluation in Section 6 confirms this intuition.

Improving DNS Lookup Time. Figure 6b shows that minimum lookup time increases as last-mile latency increases. Minimum lookup times are about 15 ms, and they increase as the last-mile latency increases. The only approach to eliminate the last-mile latency is to cache DNS records inside the home itself. Even when the resolver is well-placed in the access ISP network, DNS lookup latencies are bound by last-mile latency (previous work confirms this observation [1]).

Improving Time to First Byte. Optimizations in the home network cannot improve server processing time, but they can improve TCP connection setup time. The connection setup time depends on the round-trip latency to the server. Web service providers use content distribution networks to place servers as close to users as possible. Figure 4 shows that servers are in general closer to homes in the US, but even users in the US can experience slowdowns in TCP connection setup time due to the last-mile latency. Client-side optimizations such as connection caching [29] can reduce this latency by maintaining TCP connections to popular sites, thereby reducing overhead for new connections.

6. THE CASE FOR HOME CACHING

We use Mirage to evaluate the benefits of DNS caching, TCP connection caching, and content caching in a home network. Although the optimizations that we evaluate are well known, the placement of these optimizations in the home router is new. Our analysis in this section offers two important contributions: (1) It is the first study to quantify the benefits of deploying them in the home network, where many users now access Web content; (2) To our knowledge, it is also the first study to quantify both the relative benefits to DNS caching, TCP connection caching, and content caching across a large number of popular sites and the holistic benefits of performing all three optimizations together.

Table 6 summarizes the main results in this section. Perhaps the most important takeaway from this section is that *optimizations that reduce latency can significantly reduce page load time, even if content caching is not used*. This result offers good news, since so much Web page content is dynamic, and since caching a large amount of content on end-hosts or inside home networks may prove infeasible. This finding also emphasizes the importance of placing optimizations inside the home network, since even the last-mile access link can introduce additional latency on the order of tens of milliseconds [55]. Similar optimizations already exist in the browser; we explain how a home cache provides additional benefits beyond browser-based optimizations in Section 7.

Performing DNS caching inside the home can improve maximum lookup times by about 15–50 milliseconds, compared to simply relying on the ISP's DNS resolver.	§6.2, Fig. 7
Connection caching reduces median page load time by 100–750 milliseconds depending on the Web site.	§6.2, Fig. 8
Placing a content proxy inside the home versus in a nearby network improves median page load times between 150 and 600 milliseconds, depending on the site.	§6.3, Fig. 10
Applying all three optimizations together can reduce Web page load times by up to 60% at the router.	§6.4, Fig. 11

Table 6: *Highlights of Section 6 results.*

Measurement	Proxy Location	DNS	Conn.	Content
	Baseline Measurements			
No Proxy, ISP DNS	—			
Cold Home Proxy	—	•		
ISP Proxy	Network	•	•	•
	Optimizations			
Home DNS	Home	•		
Home Conn. Caching	Home	•	•	
Home Proxy	Home	•	•	•

Table 7: *The measurements we perform to evaluate the benefits of DNS, connection, and content caching in the home.*

6.1 Experiment Setup

We develop a controlled experiment to investigate how deploying three different caching optimizations in the home—DNS caching, TCP connection caching, and content caching—contribute to reducing page load time. We use the BISmark deployment described in Section 4 for our measurements. Mirage runs on the BISmark router; it uses a locally running DNS resolver and an HTTP proxy. `dnsmasq` is a lightweight caching DNS resolver [25] that caches up to 150 domains and honors the TTL values of the lookups. To evaluate TCP connection and content caching, we use `polipo`, a HTTP proxy that splits the TCP connection by opening a connection to the requested domain on behalf of the client and communicates with the client over a separate connection and reuses TCP connections where possible. We run `polipo` with a 4 MByte cache in RAM.

Measuring Baseline Performance. Table 7 illustrates how we measure baseline performance and compare it with performance for each optimization. To measure the three *baseline* performance measurements, the client first performs the following three sets of requests:

1. **ISP DNS Cache ("No Proxy, ISP DNS").** The client clears the local DNS cache and fetches the page directly from the server. This measures the baseline performance of fetching the Web page. The DNS lookups required for this measurement may reflect caching in the ISP's DNS resolver.
2. **Empty Caching Proxy in the Home ("Cold Home Proxy").** The client fetches the same page by directing the request through a fresh `polipo` instance running in the router. Because `polipo`'s cache is empty at this point, this measurement reflects the performance of a "cold" proxy. This step takes advantage of any DNS caching that `dnsmasq` performs in the previous step.
3. **Shared ISP Caching Proxy ("ISP Proxy").** We cannot control a Web cache in a real ISP's network, so we approximate the behavior of an ISP cache by deploying a caching proxy in our university network. To measure the benefits of performing DNS, connection, and content caching at a shared proxy (the most common setup for content caches), the client first fetches the page through a `polipo` proxy running on a university server to warm the cache. It then immediately repeats the step. We perform the measurements from eleven BISmark routers that are less than 35 ms away from the proxy, so that it emulates nearby ISP caches.

Quantifying the Benefits of Caching in Home Networks. After collecting the baseline measurements, the client then performs three additional requests to measure the relative benefit of performing different optimizations in the home.

4. **Home DNS caching only ("Home DNS").** The client fetches the same page directly from the servers. This measures the benefits of DNS caching in the home (since `dnsmasq` caches the DNS responses from earlier measurements).
5. **Home proxy with DNS caching, persistent connections, and content caching ("Home Proxy")** The client fetches the page through the local `polipo` again; this measurement takes advantage of DNS, content and connection caching, since the proxy would have cached any cacheable objects and reused TCP connections where possible from the requests in the "Cold Home Proxy" experiment.
6. **Home proxy with DNS caching and persistent connections only ("Home Connection Caching")** The client clears the `polipo` cache on the home router — this gets rid of the content in the cache, *but keeps the TCP connections from the previous step alive.* It then fetches the page through the proxy again. All content is retrieved again from the origin service, but the TCP connections from the previous step are reused.

These experiments allow us to isolate the effects of (1) the relative benefits of performing DNS, connection, and content caching inside the home network and (2) placing a cache inside the home versus elsewhere (*e.g.*, in the ISP).

6.2 Effects of Home Caching on Latency

Benefits of DNS caching in the home vs. in the ISP. To quantify the benefits of DNS caching in the home, we compare the maximum lookup time for the *Home DNS Cache* and *No Proxy, ISP DNS* cases. Figure 7 shows the CDF of the improvement in the maximum lookup time for the page load. In the median case, DNS caching in the home reduces the maximum lookup time by 15–50 ms, depending on the site. Certain clients outside the US can reduce their lookup time by several hundred milliseconds for certain sites like Ebay and CNN by caching DNS responses in the home. For a small fraction of cases, DNS caching in the home actually slightly impairs performance; in these cases, the detriment in small and may result from changes in network conditions between experiments (this effect occurs for some of our TCP connection caching and content caching experiments, too).

Benefits of TCP connection caching in the home. Figure 8 shows the additional improvement in page load time due to connection caching by measuring the difference between the load times for the *Home Connection Caching* and the *Home DNS Cache* measurements. The median improvement varies from 100–750 ms depending on the site. Ebay and Yahoo experience the most improvement in load times because both sites require many objects from many domains to render; connection caching can significantly reduce TCP overhead in such cases.

6.3 Effects of Home Caching on Throughput

Benefits of content caching vs. connection caching. Figure 9 shows the improvement in page load time due to content caching over connection caching. We compute the improvement by subtracting the page load time for the *Home Proxy* experiment from that for the *Home Connection Caching* experiment. Caching content inside the home can decrease median page load times in the US by 75–400 ms over connection caching, depending on the site. Obviously, sites with more cacheable content will benefit more. Our analysis shows that this benefit is even more significant for clients outside the US; at least 20% of clients experienced an improvement of 500 ms or more for all sites.

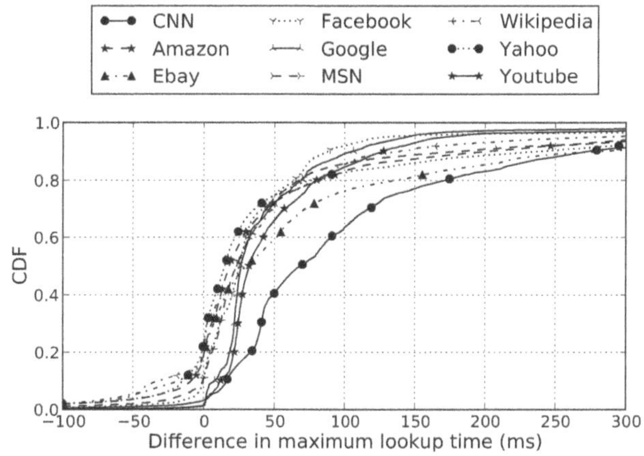

Figure 7: *Caching DNS in the home can reduce the maximum DNS lookup time by 15–50 ms.* (Home DNS *Measurement vs.* No Proxy, ISP DNS *Measurement)*

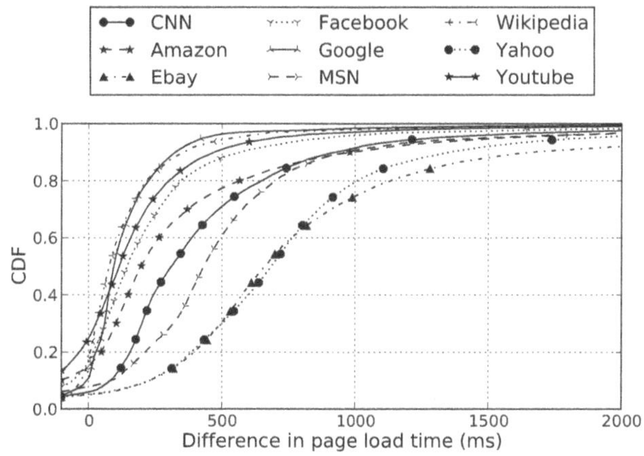

Figure 8: *Connection caching in the home can reduce median page load times by 100–750 ms.(*Home Connection Proxy *vs.* Home DNS *Measurements)*

Benefits of content caching in the home vs. in the ISP. We compare the Web page load time when using a remote HTTP proxy (the *ISP Proxy* measurement from Table 7) versus using a local HTTP proxy running on the router (the *Home Proxy* measurement). Figure 10 shows that a proxy in the home can offer a median improvement in page load time of 150–600 ms, depending on the site. Yahoo and CNN experience the most benefits, likely because these pages are larger and have many objects (Table 2). A cache in the upstream ISP is still constrained by the access link's throughput and last-mile latency, while a local cache is not. For some sites, the remote proxy performs better than the home proxy about 20% of the time, perhaps because of varying access link characteristics across tests (due to cross traffic) or because the proxy is in a university network that potentially has better connectivity to these sites.

6.4 Putting It Together

We now quantify the collective benefit from performing all three optimizations. We use Mirage's *No Proxy, ISP DNS* measurement

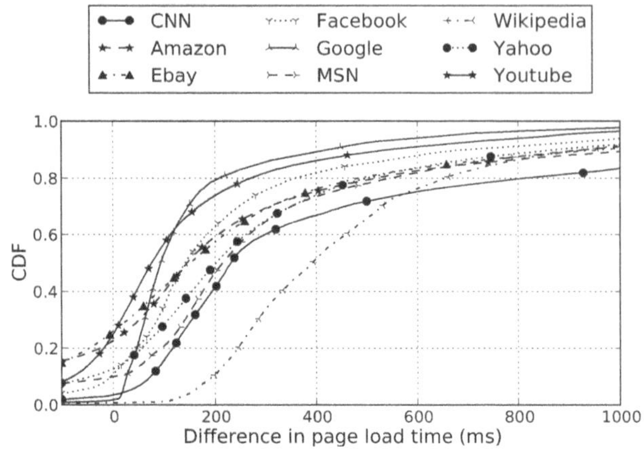

Figure 9: *Content caching reduces the median page load time by 75–400 ms over connection caching alone. For sites with more cacheable content, the benefit is greater (*Home Proxy *vs.* Home Connection Caching *Measurements)*

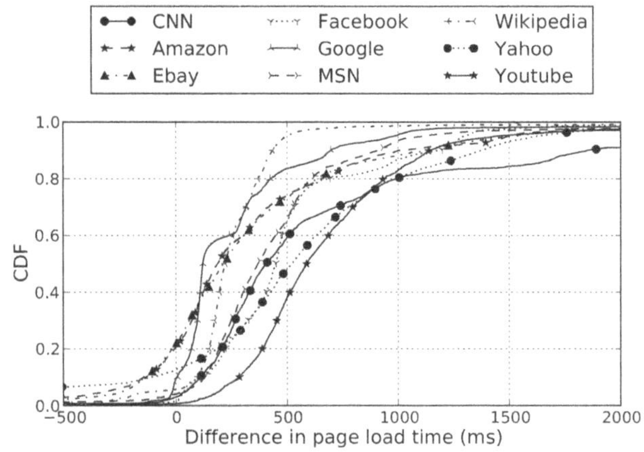

Figure 10: *Running a proxy in the home improves median page load times by 150–600 ms versus running a proxy in the ISP. (*Home Proxy *vs.* ISP Proxy *Measurement)*

as the baseline. We compute the *relative improvement* as $(b-v)/b$, where b is the baseline load time and v is the optimized load time.

Figure 11a shows the relative improvement of each optimization relative to the baseline of performing no optimizations in BISmark-US. Applying all three optimizations improves page load time by as much as 60%. *Even without content caching, connection caching can yield up to a 35% improvement in load time, and DNS caching alone can improve page load time by as much as 10%.* Figure 11b shows the relative improvement for clients outside the US. The improvement is slightly less than for the users within the US because the absolute page load times for users outside the US are already higher (Figure 3). The variance is also higher because of the wide range of operating conditions outside the US (Table 4 and Figure 4). The improvements we measure represent the best-case scenario because the quick succession of Web page retrievals will always induce a cache hit at the router. In the next section, we explore how to design a cache in the home that achieves high cache hit rates in practice.

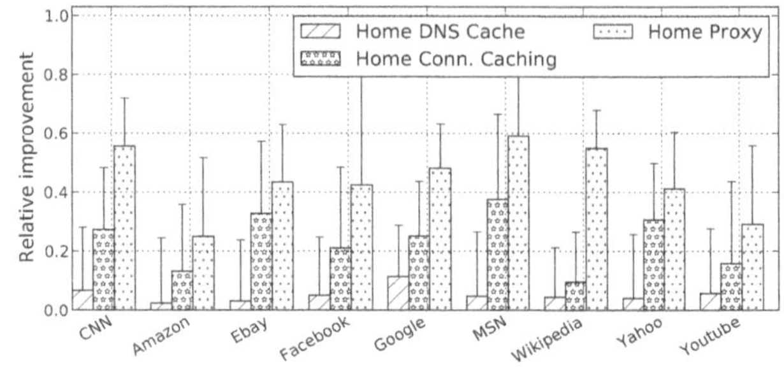

(a) *BISmark-US*

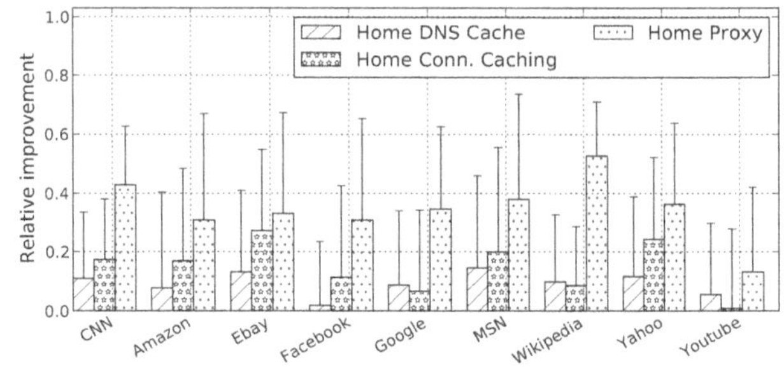

(b) *BISmark-nonUS*

Figure 11: *Average relative improvement in page load times for various optimizations, as observed from the* **router**. *Error bars denote standard deviation.*

7. HOME CACHING IN PRACTICE

The previous section demonstrated how home caching can improve page load times in the best-case scenario, but the results measured the benefits in isolation from other optimizations (*e.g.*, browser caching) and also assumed that these cache hits could be realized in practice. Thus, our experiments from Section 6 raise two questions:

1. *How can users inside a home network practically realize cache hits on a home cache?* Prefetching DNS queries and maintaining open TCP connections to all sites visited by a user is not practical. To intelligently determine which DNS records and TCP connections to cache, we implemented a lightweight router-based *popularity-based prefetching* system that prefetches and caches DNS records and maintains active TCP connections to popular domains to help improve cache hit rates. We analyzed cache hit ratios resulting from this system with a trace-driven simulation using passive traces collected from twelve homes. (Section 7.1)

2. *Are the performance benefits that home caching offers significant, in light of the fact that browsers already perform some amount of caching and prefetching?* To answer this question, we retrieve Web pages from a laptop in a home network using Phantomjs under a variety of emulated access link characteristics with various caching optimizations enabled on the home router. (Section 7.2)

Our results indicate that popularity-based prefetching can complement existing browser optimizations.

7.1 Popularity-based Prefetching

We design, implement, and evaluate a *popularity-based caching and prefetching* systemthat prefetches DNS records and keeps TCP connections to Web servers active based on the sites that users in the household visit most frequently. We develop a proof-of-concept OpenWrt module, which is publicly available [48]. The system consists of (`dnsmasq`) and (`polipo`), instrumented to track popular DNS lookups and HTTP domains respectively. The system tracks popularity and refreshes DNS lookups and maintains an active TCP connection to popular domains by using a simple caching mechanism. The system aims to maximize the hit rate of the DNS and TCP connection caches. The two parameters that affect the hit rate are (1) *the number of domains to be tracked*: the system actively prefetches DNS records and maintains active connections to these domains; the system maintains the two lists separately; and (2) *timeout thresholds*: the system tracks the time since a lookup or a TCP connection was requested to a domain and removes the domain from the popular list if this time exceeds a threshold. The system does not prefetch content but exploits any content caching that `polipo` performs by default.

Does popularity-based prefetching improve Web page load times in homes? To analyze whether popularity-based prefetching can improve performance, we perform a trace-based simulation using real browsing activity in home networks, with optimizations enabled and disabled. We capture Web browsing activity of users from routers deployed in twelve homes in the US for the period October 15–31, 2012 to evaluate the potential improvements from proactive DNS and connection caching in home networks. We capture DNS and HTTP traffic. We record the timestamp, hashed domain, and TTL of all resolved DNS responses. Each HTTP flow event has a timestamp of all connections, hashes of their corresponding IP addresses, flow duration, and TCP connection time. To preserve user privacy, we do not capture packet payloads, so we do not evaluate cache hit ratios for content.

Using these traces, we run a trace-driven simulation that maintains the DNS cache using the timestamp, hashed domain, and TTL of resolved DNS responses from the trace. When prefetching a domain, the simulation delays each incoming DNS response by a random interval between 50 and 200 ms; the TTL value is set according to the value in the trace. Requests for domains waiting for a DNS response are considered cache misses. To characterize the benefit of TCP connection caching, the simulation maintains the TCP connection cache based on the timestamp, five-tuple flow identifier, and duration of both the entire TCP connection and its connection establishment of all port 80 requests from the passive traces. For each new request, the simulation compares it with the entries in the connection cache. In the event of a cache miss, or when a connection to an IP address is in use by another request, we establish a new connection with the flow and TCP connection establishment durations that correspond to the TCP connection in the trace. Upon a cache hit, the simulation denotes the cache entry to be in use for the duration of TCP connection minus the connection establishment time to that IP.

Baseline DNS cache hit rates without popularity-based prefetching vary from 11–50%, depending on the home; the baseline cache hit ratio for TCP connection ranges from 1–8% across homes. Setting a cache size of 20 and a timeout threshold of 120 seconds for both DNS and connection prefetching causes DNS hit ratios improve to 19–93%, representing at least a 40% improvement over the baseline in every home. Connection cache hit ratios increase to 6–21% across homes. These results show that popularity-based prefetching for only a few sites and with a short timeout can significantly improve performance.

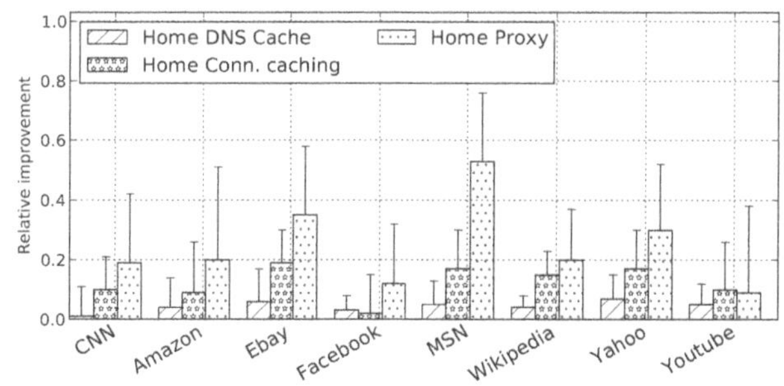

Figure 12: *Average relative improvement in page load times for various optimizations, as observed from the* **browser**. *Error bars denote standard deviation.*

7.2 Benefits of Home Caching from Browsers

We evaluate the benefit of home caching as seen from a browser by analyzing the improvement in page load times from Phantomjs with various caching optimizations enabled. We measure page load times from a Web browser using Phantomjs running on a Linux laptop that is connected through a wired link to a Netgear home router; the router shapes the uplink to represent different home network throughputs and latencies. We use two settings for the downstream throughput of the access link (10 Mbits/s and 20 Mbits/s) and three settings for the latency of the access link (0 ms, 20 ms, and 40 ms). We download each of the sites 25 times for each setting. These parameters approximate common access-link throughputs and last-mile latencies. The router also runs popularity-based prefetching, discussed in Section 7.1.

Home caching complements browser optimizations. Figure 12 shows the relative improvement in Web page load times as a result of deploying various caching optimizations from a home router, as observed from the laptop running Phantomjs. Because we had problems with Phantomjs using `polipo` for Google, we omit results for it. DNS caching improves page load times by as much as 7%; connection and DNS caching improve load times by about 20%; all three optimizations together reduce load times by as much as 60%, depending on the site. The benefits as measured using Phantomjs are lower, but they are comparable to what we observe at the router in Figure 11. Although the improvements in page load time that a browser realizes obviously depends on many factors, our results demonstrate that *home caching complements existing optimizations that browsers already perform.*

To further illustrate these benefits, we show the page load time for Ebay, for a single experiment. Figure 13 shows how DNS and TCP connection caching improves per-object downloads. It shows the time to download the first ten objects of the site using Phantomjs. We measure the total time for the first ten objects. The left plot shows the baseline case without optimization, and the second plot shows the benefits that the browser observes when the home router performs DNS and connection caching. We observe an 6.4% reduction in page load time for the home page alone when the home router performs both DNS and TCP caching. The improvements are relatively more significant for smaller objects. The numbers next to the objects show the percentage improvement in the baseline. All objects show some improvement; objects that are cacheable see more improvement.

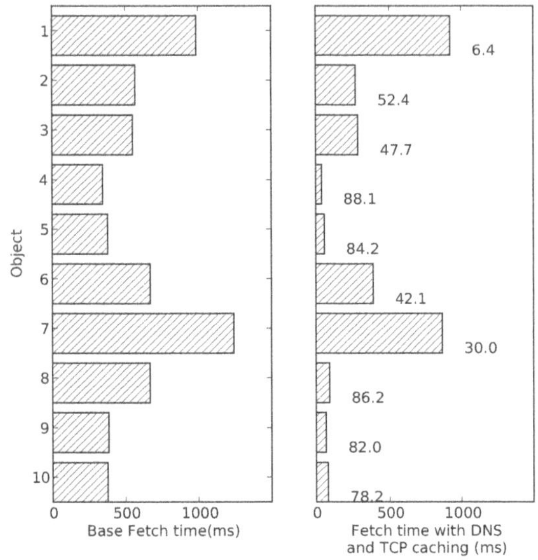

Figure 13: *The time to load the first ten objects for Ebay using Phantomjs. We plot the total download time for the first ten objects. The first plot shows the breakdown for the base case; the second when there is DNS and TCP connection caching. The numbers in the second plot denote the percentage improvement over the base case.*

8. CONCLUSION

We presented the first large-scale study of Web performance bottlenecks in broadband access networks. We first characterize performance to nine popular Web sites from 5,556 access networks using Mirage, a router-based Web measurement tool, and identify factors that create Web performance bottlenecks. Regardless of the optimizations that clients, servers, and browsers may perform, the access link is a fundamental limit to the efficacy of optimizations. As throughput increases, latency becomes more important, to the extent that even having caches on the edge of ISPs could prove to be insufficient. We show that Web page load times stop improving as throughput rates increase beyond 16 Mbits/s. We also show that last-mile latency contributes to the time required for performing DNS lookups, completing TCP connection setup, and downloading Web objects and can be up to 23% of the time to first byte.

Moreover, we evaluate techniques to mitigate latency bottlenecks by implementing *home caching*, which performs DNS and TCP connection caching and prefetching inside the home network. We demonstrate that home caching can improve Web performance, even if the ISP and browser are already independently performing similar optimizations. TCP connection caching alone can improve Web page load times by up to 20%, depending on the site. Performing all three optimizations together from the home router can reduce page load times by up to 53%.

Although the optimizations we describe can be implemented anywhere in the home network, we believe that the home router is a reasonable location for caching and prefetching DNS records and TCP connections. In addition to further reducing page load times, even in the presence of similar optimizations that browsers already implement, it is worth noting that there are many Web-based applications that do not run from a standard browser. Any device in the home network that retrieves Web content can benefit from home caching. Indeed, as Singhal and Paoli state, "apps—not just browsers—should get faster too" [51]. Our publicly available OpenWrt module for popularity-based prefetching may serve as yet another important component for reducing page load times in home networks.

Acknowledgments

This research was funded in part by NSF award CNS-1059350, a Google Focused Research Award, and the European Community's Seventh Framework Programme (FP7/2007-2013) no. 258378 (FIGARO). We would like to thank the Federal Communications Commission and SamKnows for access to the data. We would also like to acknowledge BISmark volunteers worldwide for supporting the platform.

REFERENCES

[1] B. Ager, W. Mühlbauer, G. Smaragdakis, and S. Uhlig. Comparing dns resolvers in the wild. In *Proceedings of the 10th annual conference on Internet measurement*, IMC '10, pages 15–21, New York, NY, USA, 2010. ACM.

[2] B. Ager, F. Schneider, J. Kim, and A. Feldmann. Revisiting cacheability in times of user generated content. In *INFOCOM IEEE Conference on Computer Communications Workshops, 2010*, pages 1–6. IEEE, 2010.

[3] A. Akella, B. Maggs, S. Seshan, and A. Shaikh. On the performance benefits of multihoming route control. *IEEE/ACM Transactions on Networking*, 16(1), Feb. 2008.

[4] A. Akella, B. Maggs, S. Seshan, A. Shaikh, and R. Sitaraman. A measurement-based analysis of multihoming. In *Proc. ACM SIGCOMM*, Karlsruhe, Germany, Aug. 2003.

[5] A. Akella, J. Pang, B. Maggs, S. Seshan, and A. Shaikh. A comparison of overlay routing and multihoming route control. In *Proc. ACM SIGCOMM*, Portland, OR, Aug. 2004.

[6] A. Akella, S. Seshan, and A. Shaikh. Multihoming performance benefits: An experimental evaluation of practical enterprise strategies. In *Proc. USENIX Annual Technical Conference*, Boston, MA, June 2004.

[7] M. Al-Fares, K. Elmeleegy, B. Reed, and I. Gashinsky. Overclocking the Yahoo! CDN for faster Web page loads. In *Proceedings of Internet Measurement Conference*, 2011.

[8] E. Altman, K. Avrachenkov, and C. Barakat. A stochastic model of tcp/ip with stationary random losses. In *ACM SIGCOMM*, 2000.

[9] M. Arlitt, B. Krishnamurthy, and J. Mogul. Predicting Short-transfer Latency from TCP arcana: a Trace-based Validation. In *Proc. ACM SIGCOMM Internet Measurement Conference*, New Orleans, LA, Oct. 2005.

[10] P. Barford and M. Crovella. Critical path analysis of tcp transactions. In *IEEE/ACM Transactions on Networking*, 2000.

[11] M. Belshe. A Client-Side Argument for Changing TCP Slow Start. `http://goo.gl/UDKXz`.

[12] M. Belshe. More Bandwidth Doesn't Matter (much). `http://goo.gl/OIv47`.

[13] BISmark Web Performance data. `http://data.gtnoise.net/bismark/imc2013/webperf/bismark_webperf_data.tgz`.

[14] J. Brutlag. Speed matters for Google Web search. `http://services.google.com/fh/files/blogs/google_delayexp.pdf`, June 2009.

[15] M. Butkiewicz, H. Madhyastha, and V. Sekar. Understanding website complexity: Measurements, metrics, and implications. In *Proc. Internet Measurement Conference*, Berlin, Germany, Nov. 2010.

[16] R. Caceres, F. Douglis, A. Feldmann, G. Glass, and M. Rabinovich. Web proxy caching: The devil is in the details. June 1998.

[17] J. Cao, W. S. Cleveland, Y. Gao, K. Jeffay, F. D. Smith, and M. Weigle. Stochastic models for generating synthetic http source traffic. In *IN PROCEEDINGS OF IEEE INFOCOM*, 2004.

[18] N. Cardwell, S. Savage, and T. Anderson. Modeling tcp latency. In *Proc. IEEE INFOCOM*, Tel-Aviv, Israel, Mar. 2000.

[19] Y. Cheng and Others. *TCP Fast Open*. IETF, Sept. 2011. http://www.ietf.org/id/draft-cheng-tcpm-fastopen-00.txt.

[20] J. Chu and Others. *Increasing TCP's Initial Window*. IETF, Oct. 2011. http://tools.ietf.org/html/draft-ietf-tcpm-initcwnd-01.

[21] E. Cohen and H. Kaplan. Prefetching the means for document transfer: A new approach for reducing Web latency. In *Proc. IEEE INFOCOM*, volume 2, pages 854–863, Tel-Aviv, Israel, Mar. 2000.

[22] E. Cohen and H. Kaplan. Proactive caching of DNS records: Addressing a performance bottleneck. In *Symposium on Applications and the Internet (SAINT)*, pages 85–94, 2001.

[23] Compuware. http://www.compuware.com/en_us/application-performance-management/products/application-aware-network-monitoring/web-services/overview.html.

[24] DNS Prefetching (or Pre-Resolving). http://blog.chromium.org/2008/09/dns-prefetching-or-pre-resolving.html.

[25] Dnsmasq. http://thekelleys.org.uk/dnsmasq/doc.html.

[26] N. Dukkipati, T. Refice, Y. Cheng, J. Chu, T. Herbert, A. Agarwal, A. Jain, and N. Sutin. An argument for increasing tcp's initial congestion window. *SIGCOMM Comput. Commun. Rev.*, 40:26–33, June 2010.

[27] J. Erman, A. Gerber, M. Hajiaghayi, D. Pei, and O. Spatscheck. Network-aware forward caching. In *Proceedings of the 18th international conference on World wide web*, 2009.

[28] FCC Measuring Broadband America Report. http://www.fcc.gov/measuring-broadband-america/2012/july, July 2012.

[29] A. Feldmann, R. Caceres, F. Douglis, G. Glass, and M. Rabinovich. Performance of web proxy caching in heterogeneous bandwidth environments. In *Proc. IEEE INFOCOM*, New York, NY, Mar. 1999.

[30] S. Gribble and E. Brewer. System Design Issues for Internet Middleware Services: Deductions from a Large Client Trace. In *Proc. 1st USENIX Symposium on Internet Technologies and Systems (USITS)*, Monterey, CA, Dec. 1997.

[31] S. Ihm and V. Pai. Towards understanding modern web traffic. In *Proc. Internet Measurement Conference*, Berlin, Germany, Nov. 2010.

[32] A. jan Su, D. R. Choffnes, A. Kuzmanovic, and F. E. Bustamante. Drafting behind akamai (travelocity-based detouring. In *Proc. ACM SIGCOMM*, Pisa, Italy, Aug. 2006.

[33] J. Jung, A. W. Berger, and H. Balakrishnan. Modeling TTL-based Internet Caches. In *IEEE Infocom 2003*, San Francisco, CA, April 2003.

[34] J. Jung, E. Sit, H. Balakrishnan, and R. Morris. DNS Performance and the Effectiveness of Caching. In *Proc. ACM SIGCOMM Internet Measurement Workshop*, San Fransisco, CA, Nov. 2001.

[35] Keynote. http://www.keynote.com/products/web_performance/web-performance-testing.html.

[36] B. Krishnamurthy and C. Wills. Analyzing factors that influence end-to-end Web performance. In *Proc. Twelfth International World Wide Web Conference*, Amsterdam, The Netherlands, May 2000.

[37] R. Krishnan, H. V. Madhyastha, S. Jain, S. Srinivasan, A. Krishnamurthy, T. Anderson, and J. Gao. Moving beyond end-to-end path information to optimize CDN performance. In *Proc. Internet Measurement Conference*, 2009.

[38] Z. Li, M. Zhang, Z. Zhu, Y. Chen, A. Greenberg, and Y.-M. Wang. Webprophet: Automating performance prediction for web services. In *Proc. 7th USENIX NSDI*, San Jose, CA, Apr. 2010.

[39] Link Prefetching FAQ. https://developer.mozilla.org/En/Link_prefetching_FAQ.

[40] S. Lohr. For Impatient Web Users, an Eye Blink Is Just Too Long to Wait. http://www.nytimes.com/2012/03/01/technology/impatient-web-users-flee-slow-loading-sites.html, Mar. 2012.

[41] J. C. Mogul, Y. M. Chan, and T. Kelly. Design, implementation, and evaluation of duplicate transfer detection in HTTP. In *Proc. First Symposium on Networked Systems Design and Implementation (NSDI)*, San Francisco, CA, Mar. 2004.

[42] H. Nielsen, J. Gettys, A. Baird-Smith, E. Prud'hommeaux, H. W. Lie, and C. Lilley. Network performance effects of http/1.1, css1, and png. In *Proc. ACM SIGCOMM*, Cannes, France, Sept. 1997.

[43] OECD. *OECD Communications Outlook*. OECD Publishing, July 2011.

[44] J. Padhye, V. Firoiu, D. Towsley, and J. Kurose. Modeling TCP Throughput: A Simple Model and its Empirical Validation. In *Proc. ACM SIGCOMM*, pages 303–323, Vancouver, British Columbia, Canada, Sept. 1998.

[45] V. Padmanabhan and J. Mogul. Using predictive prefetching to improve world wide web latency. *ACM SIGCOMM Computer Communication Review*, 26(3):22–36, 1996.

[46] Phantomjs. http://phantomjs.org/.

[47] Phantomjs Users. https://github.com/ariya/phantomjs/wiki/Users.

[48] OpenWRT Module for Popularity-based Prefetching. http://data.gtnoise.net/bismark/imc2013/webperf/popularity_prefetch.tgz.

[49] Project bismark. http://projectbismark.net.

[50] QUIC: Quick udp internet connections. http://goo.gl/O2r6rM.

[51] S. Singhal and J. Paoli. Speed and Mobility: An Approach for HTTP 2.0 to Make Mobile Apps and the Web Faster, Mar. 2012. http://goo.gl/1uWCl.

[52] April 2012 FCC/SamKnows data. http://www.fcc.gov/measuring-broadband-america/2012/validated-data-april-2012.

[53] S. Souders. Velocity and the bottom line. http://radar.oreilly.com/2009/07/velocity-making-your-site-fast.html, July 2009.

[54] SPDY: An experimental protocol for a faster web. http://www.chromium.org/spdy/spdy-whitepaper.

[55] S. Sundaresan, W. de Donato, N. Feamster, R. Teixeira, S. Crawford, and A. Pescapè. Broadband internet performance: A view from the gateway. In *Proc. ACM SIGCOMM*, Toronto, Ontario, Aug. 2011.

[56] S. Sundaresan, N. Magharei, N. Feamster, and R. Teixeira. Accelerating last-mile web performance with popularity-based prefetching. In *Proceedings of ACM SIGCOMM 2012 (Poster)*, SIGCOMM '12. ACM, 2012.

[57] S. Sundaresan, N. Magharei, N. Feamster, R. Teixeira, and S. Crawford. Web performance bottlenecks in broadband access networks. In *Proceedings of ACM SIGMETRICS 2013 (Poster Paper)*, SIGMETRICS '13. ACM, 2013.

[58] X. S. Wang, A. Balasubramanian, A. Krishnamurthy, and D. Wetherall. Demystifying page load performance with wprof. Apr. 2013.

[59] Web page test. http://webpagetest.org/.

[60] A. Wolman, G. M. Voelker, N. Sharma, N. Cardwell, A. Karlin, and H. M. Levy. On the scale and performance of cooperative web proxy caching. In *Proc. 17th ACM Symposium on Operating Systems Principles (SOSP)*, Kiawah Island, SC, Dec. 1999.

[61] W. Zhou, Q. Li, M. Caesar, and P. Godfrey. Asap: A low-latency transport layer. In *Proceedings of the Seventh COnference on emerging Networking EXperiments and Technologies*, page 20. ACM, 2011.

Studying Interdomain Routing over Long Timescales

Giovanni Comarela
Boston University
Boston, USA
gcom@bu.edu

Gonca Gürsun
Boston University
Boston, USA
goncag@bu.edu

Mark Crovella
Boston University
Boston, USA
crovella@bu.edu

ABSTRACT

The dynamics of interdomain routing have traditionally been studied through the analysis of BGP update traffic. However, such studies tend to focus on the volume of BGP updates rather than their effects, and tend to be local rather than global in scope. Studying the global state of the Internet routing system over time requires the development of new methods, which we do in this paper. We define a new metric, MRSD, that allows us to measure the similarity between two prefixes with respect to the state of the global routing system. Applying this metric over time yields a measure of how the set of total paths to each prefix varies at a given timescale. We implement this analysis method in a MapReduce framework and apply it to a dataset of more than 1TB, collected daily over 3 distinct years and monthly over 8 years. We show that this analysis method can uncover interesting aspects of how Internet routing has changed over time. We show that on any given day, approximately 1% of the next-hop decisions made in the Internet change, and this property has been remarkably constant over time; the corresponding amount of change in one month is 10% and in two years is 50%. Digging deeper, we can decompose next-hop decision changes into two classes: churn, and structural (persistent) change. We show that structural change shows a strong 7-day periodicity and that it represents approximately 2/3 of the total amount of changes.

Categories and Subject Descriptors

C.2.3 [**Network Operations**]: Network monitoring; C.2.5 [**Local and Wide-Area Networks**]: Internet – BGP

General Terms

Measurement

Keywords

BGP; Interdomain Routing

IMC'13, October 23–25, 2013, Barcelona, Spain.

http://dx.doi.org/10.1145/2504730.2504771.

1. INTRODUCTION

There are many aspects of the interdomain routing system that are important to understand, including its stability, scalability, and security. However, a particularly difficult problem is understanding the overall structure of interdomain routing and how it evolves over time. The immense size, complexity, and continuous growth of the system make it challenging to gain a useful understanding of the nature of routing changes over time.

This problem is important because currently there are no metrics able to provide useful information about the rate of routing changes of the interdomain routing system. Such metrics could contribute at the understand the impact of de-peering disputes, link failures, merging of autonomous systems and any other event that may affect globally the routing structure of the Internet.

To address this challenge, we focus in this paper on answering basic questions about how Internet routing has changed over time. As a first step, we are interested in characterizing the *rate of change* of the routing system and the dynamics of its change. We seek to answer these questions for the system as a whole (i.e., globally) and over long timescales. In this respect we differ from most prior work which has asked more specific questions about the evolution of Internet routing.

We believe that one reason that temporal change has not been extensively studied to date is that good methods and metrics to study it have not existed. Accordingly, the first contribution we make is to propose a metric that can be used to capture the dynamics of routing change, and show how to apply it to available BGP data. The key idea behind our approach is that the entire state of the global routing system at any time can be captured as a large set of tuples that express the next-hop decisions made by each AS with respect to each prefix. From this starting point, we define a natural measure of change for this set of next-hop decisions, and then show the utility of the measure.

This kind of approach to the study of interdomain routing moves away from studying the system in terms of an AS topology. Rather than focusing on an imperfectly understood topology, we focus on the fundamental decisions that are made by each AS, namely, its next-hop choices. Further, our approach also avoids the problems of studying routing in terms of BGP update messages, which are very difficult to interpret in a global fashion. Analyzing BGP updates is problematic, requiring special methods and heuristics, because BGP traffic represents a variety of effects (table dumps as well as route changes) and because many messages do not result in actual changes to the routing systems (e.g., updates that do not trigger new next-hop decisions in the recipient).

The new metric we develop is based on the general concept of *Routing State Distance* (RSD) [7]. However, we show that RSD as originally used is insufficient to study the dynamics of a system that changes over time. Hence, we develop a significant improvement to RSD, called *Multiple Next-hop Routing State Distance* (MRSD). MRSD has the advantage of being applicable in a much wider set of routing systems than the original RSD, while still capturing the same concept. Further, whereas the original concept of RSD was developed to compare different prefixes, in this study we apply MRSD to compare routing to the *same* prefix at *different times*. We refer to the application of MRSD over time as *Temporal MRSD* (TRSD).

We use TRSD to address our motivating questions by applying it to a large corpus of BGP data. Our raw data comes from BGP Routing Information Bases (RIBs) made available through the Route Views and RIPE measurement projects. We convert downloaded RIBs to a cleaned format for processing. The converted data is smaller than the raw RIBs but still comprises more than 1TB (uncompressed); we store it in *Hadoop Distributed File System* (HDFS) and process it using *Hadoop MapReduce*.[1]

Our study looks at routing change at two granularities: at a daily level, and at a monthly level. At the finer timescale, we study the daily evolution of the routing system during three distinct years: 2005, 2008 and 2011. At the coarser timescale, we study the monthly evolution of the routing system over 8 years, from the beginning of 2005 until the end of 2012.

Our results reveal some interesting aspects of Internet routing. We show that approximately 1% of all visible next-hop decisions change each day, and that this rate is about 10% at the timescale of one month and 50% at the timescale of 2 years. Surprisingly, we show that that these values are remarkably constant over the period investigated, despite the immense change and growth of the network during our period of study. We also show a decomposition of the daily TRSD time series in two components, intended to capture the difference between sustained (policy-driven) changes in routing versus churn (temporary changes, e.g., due to equipment failures). About 2/3 of changes on a daily basis fall into the sustained category, with the remaining 1/3 classified as churn. Interestingly, we show that sustained changes show a strong weekly periodicity, with the majority of sustained changes made in the workweek. On the other hand, routing churn is better described as noise without a strong periodic component. Finally, we also study the relative rate of routing changes across different ASes. We show that this rate is very long-tailed, i.e., that a small fraction of ASes are responsible for the vast majority of changes to next-hop decisions.

The remaining of this paper is organized as follows. Section 2 briefly summarizes some related work. Section 3 presents the notation and definitions while Section 4 presents our data collection methodology. Measurement results are presented in Section 5 and finally, discussions, conclusions and future work directions are stated in Section 6.

2. RELATED WORK

The goals and methods of our study differ from or build on prior work in a number of ways.

BGP instability measurement: Considerable prior work has looked at the stability (or instability) of the interdomain routing system, including [11, 8, 12, 9, 4]. On one hand, these studies are related to ours in also performing long timescale studies of the BGP system. However, these studies do not emphasize the global evolution of routing *decisions* but focus mainly on the dynamics of routing *traffic*. They focus on characterization and analysis of BGP messages: how to understand BGP traffic dynamics over time, and how to characterize stability of BGP routing for specific destinations. Our focus is on the changes to next-hop decisions made throughout the global routing system.

Longterm Internet evolution: Some other studies have looked at global properties of the AS-level Internet over multi-year timescales. In particular, [13] explores a dataset composed of AS paths collected from 2005 to 2009, in order to show that the Internet is flattening. Another study is [3], in which the authors analyzed the growth of the Internet over a period of 10 years, focusing on the economical roles played by each AS, the types of relationship between ASes, and differences across geographical regions. Our work complements those studies by looking at similarly long timescales, but focusing on more basic questions such as the rate of change in routing, the nature of routing churn, and the ASes responsible for the most routing changes.

Routing State Distance: Finally, we mention that Routing State Distance (RSD) was originally used in [7] and [6], but the definition of RSD differs in important ways from the more general MRSD metric we define here. Our definition of MRSD is a generalization of RSD; it extends RSD to additional routing configurations that RSD could not handle, while remaining equivalent to RSD for any cases in which RSD can be used.

3. NOTATION AND DEFINITIONS

In this section we define the metrics we use to analyze change in the global routing system.

3.1 Multiple next-hop RSD

Our starting point is the notion of Routing State Distance (RSD) as defined in [7]. Briefly, RSD is a metric that defines the 'distance' between two destinations (e.g., prefixes) as the *number of nodes* which choose different next-hops for the two destinations.

While this general concept is a good starting point for studying routing changes, it has drawbacks. The main problem with RSD as defined in [7] is that it assumes that each node in the network has a unique next-hop towards any destination. In interdomain routing, where nodes are ASes and destinations are prefixes, this property does not hold. In [7], the authors decided to proceed as [10], i.e., they partitioned Autonomous Systems in such a way that each of its parts (denoted "quasi-routers") did not have more than one routing option to reach any prefix. Although that was a natural choice, this solution has a number of drawbacks. First, it can not be easily generalized to other routing sytems with multiple next-hops, such as OSPF with Equal Cost Multi-Path (ECMP). Second, identifying quasi-routers optimally is a NP-hard problem [5]. Third, and most important for our study, there is no natural way to extend the quasi-router approach to routing systems that change over time, which introduces serious problems for longitudinal analyses.

Hence, we need to define a new metric that handles the case of multiple next-hops in a cleaner, more robust fashion: MRSD. MRSD avoids the problems of RSD by allowing next-hops decisions to be expressed as sets (instead of unique elements). MRSD then uses *Jaccard distance* to compare the next-hop sets.

Formally, let $G(V, E)$ be a directed graph where V is a set of vertices and E is the set of edges. For all source-destination pairs $(u, v) \in V \times V$ we define $N_{u,v}$ as the set of *next-hops* from u towards v. More formally, a vertex $w \in N_{u,v}$ if and only if, the edge (u, w) starts a path from u to v.

DEFINITION 1. *Let $G(V, E)$ be a graph and S ($\neq \emptyset$) and P subsets of V denoting sets of sources and destinations respectively. For each pair $(d, d') \in P \times P$ we define the* Multiple next-hop

[1] Our source code is available by email request to the authors.

Routing State Distance *(MRSD) over S by*

$$MRSD(d, d') = \frac{\sum_{s \in S} \delta_s(d, d')}{|S|}, \quad (1)$$

where $\delta_s(d, d') = 1 - J(N_{s,d}, N_{s,d'})$ *and* $J(A, B)$ *denotes the Jaccard Index of any pair of sets A and B.*

The intuition behind MRSD is that when $MRSD(d, d')$ is close to 0 then d and d' are very similar in terms of the next-hop choices made by all nodes in the set S. On the other hand, when $MRSD$ approaches 1 we have that those destinations are routed very differently through the network. Note that MRSD is always a value between 0 and 1, and it can be interpreted as the *fraction* of next-hop decisions that differ, across all nodes in the network. It is also important to remark that when all destinations always have unique next-hops ($|N_{s,d}| = 1$ for all s and d), this definition is equivalent to the one presented in [7], and so in that case MRSD reduces to (normalized) RSD.

3.2 Temporal MRSD

Next we show how to apply the definition of the last section in the context of interdomain routing on the Internet in order to conduct a longitudinal analysis.

Consider P and S being respectively a set of IP prefixes $\{p_1, \ldots, p_{|P|}\}$ and sources (autonomous systems) $\{s_1, \ldots, s_{|S|}\}$ on the Internet seen by a set of monitors at times $t_1, \ldots, t_T$ ($t_i - t_{i-1} > 0$ for $i = 2, \ldots, T$). We define $N_{s,p}(t)$ as the set of next-hops (autonomous systems) that source s may use at time t in order to reach prefix p, where $p \in P$, $s \in S$ and $t = t_i$ for some $i \in \{1, \ldots, T\}$.

DEFINITION 2. *For a prefix p we define the* Temporal multiple next-hop Routing State Distance *(TRSD) over a set of sources S between time* t_i *and* t_j ($1 \leq i < j \leq T$) *as:*

$$TRSD_p(t_i, t_j) = \frac{\sum_{s \in S} \delta_{s,p}(t_i, t_j)}{|D_p(t_i, t_j)|}, \quad (2)$$

where $\delta_{s,p}(t_i, t_j) = 1 - J(N_{s,p}(t_i), N_{s,p}(t_j))$ *if both* $N_{s,p}(t_i)$ *and* $N_{s,p}(t_j)$ *are non empty sets and zero otherwise,* $D_p(t_i, t_j) = \{s \in S : N_{s,p}(t_i) \neq \emptyset \text{ and } N_{s,p}(t_j) \neq \emptyset\}$ *and* $J(A, B)$ *denotes the Jaccard Index of any pair of sets A and B.*

This definition is similar to the one presented in the last section, but has some key differences. The differences are: first, TRSD is specialized to the specific case of interdomain routing. Second, TRSD compares the next-hops of the same prefix in two different times instead of two different prefixes at the same time. And third, TRSD normalizes in a slightly different way, namely, the set S of sources becomes $D_p(t_i, t_j)$ which may vary with time. This was done by design, to address the fact that networks may grow over time.

To illustrate the definition, Figure 1 presents graphs related to the routing decisions towards a prefix p (hosted on AS x_p) at times t_i and t_{i+n} ($n > 0$). Table 1 shows the intermediate computations for TRSD over the set $S = \{a, b, c, d, e, f\}$.

From Table 1 we have that $|D_p(t_i, t_{i+n})| = 5$ and as consequence $TRSD_p(t_i, t_{i+n}) = 0.283$. This can be interpreted as saying that from time t_i to t_{i+n}, the network's next-hop decisions changed 28.3% with regard to p. It is important to remark that, in this example, the last row (related to the source f) did not contribute anything to TRSD (because it was not considered in the composition of the set $D_p(t_i, t_{i+n})$ and $\delta_{f,p}(t_i, t_{i+n}) = 0$). This shows an important aspect of our definition, i.e., TRSD was designed with the intention of capturing routing *changes*, and hence does not increase simply due to the *growth* of the network.

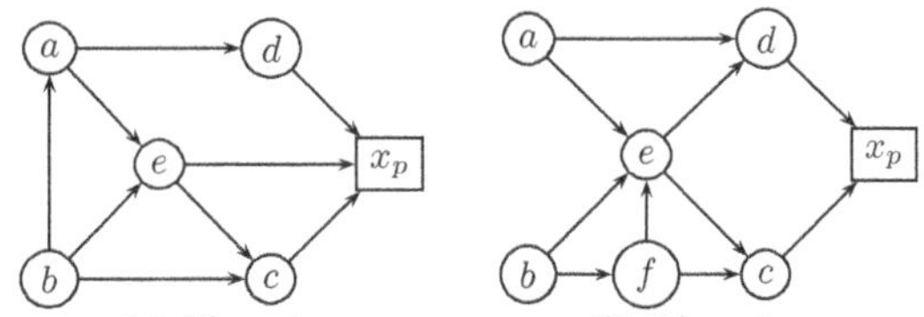

(a) Time t_i (b) Time t_{i+n}

Figure 1: Routing decisions towards p at t_i and t_{i+n}

Table 1: TRSD computation for Figure 1

s	$N_{s,p}(t_i)$	$N_{s,p}(t_{i+n})$	$\delta_{s,p}(t_i, t_{i+n})$
a	$\{d, e\}$	$\{d, e\}$	0
b	$\{a, c, e\}$	$\{e, f\}$	$\frac{3}{4}$
c	$\{x_p\}$	$\{x_p\}$	0
d	$\{x_p\}$	$\{x_p\}$	0
e	$\{c, x_p\}$	$\{c, d\}$	$\frac{2}{3}$
f	$\{\}$	$\{c, e\}$	0

4. DATASET DESCRIPTION

To explore the evolution of Internet routing over time, we collected four datasets comprising Routing Information Bases (RIBs) from RIPE [1] and Route Views [2]. Datasets 1, 2 and 3 consist of all RIBs on a daily basis for the entire years of 2005, 2008 and 2011 respectively. The fourth data set consists of all RIBSs for the first day of each month from 2005 to 2012. Since RIBs are made available at a coarser granularity than BGP updates (every 2 hours for Route Views and 8 hours for RIPE) we did not attempt to remove the effects of short term convergences, i.e., for each day, we kept all available distinct AS paths. It is important to remark that we collected data only for IPv4 prefixes.

Each RIB is a collection of records containing information about how to reach a prefix p from a specific autonomous system. From these records we extracted the following information: *route dumping date*, *autonomous system path* $a_0, a_1, \ldots, a_r$ ($r \geq 1$) and *destination prefix* p, hosted in the AS a_r. After that we decomposed each record into r 4-tuples of the form [*route dumping date*, a_i, a_{i+1}, p], for $i = 0, \ldots, r-1$. The semantics of each 4-tuple is: at the time of *route dumping date*, in order to reach the prefix p, AS a_i uses AS a_{i+1} as (one of its) next-hops. In the rest of the paper, AS a_i will be referred to as a *source*, prefix p will be referred to as a *destination*, and AS a_{i+1} will be referred to as a *next-hop*.

To apply the definitions presented in Section 3 to this data, S is the set of all sources (a_i) and P is the set of all prefixes (p) found in a dataset. Table 2 presents a summary of each dataset collected after transformation into a collection of 4-tuples as described above.

Table 2: Summary of the four datasets

	Dataset 1	Dataset 2	Dataset 3	Dataset 4
Granularity	daily	daily	daily	monthly
First	01/01/05	01/01/08	01/01/11	01/01/05
Last	12/31/05	12/31/08	12/31/11	12/01/12
Size (GB)	200	500	680	160
$\|S\|$	5,086	6,934	9,093	14,829
$\|P\|$	316,519	517,773	616,714	1,157,670

To see the need for using Jaccard Index in Definitions 1 and 2, we note that, in our dataset on each day, approximately 7% of the sources have more than one next-hop choice towards a specific prefix.

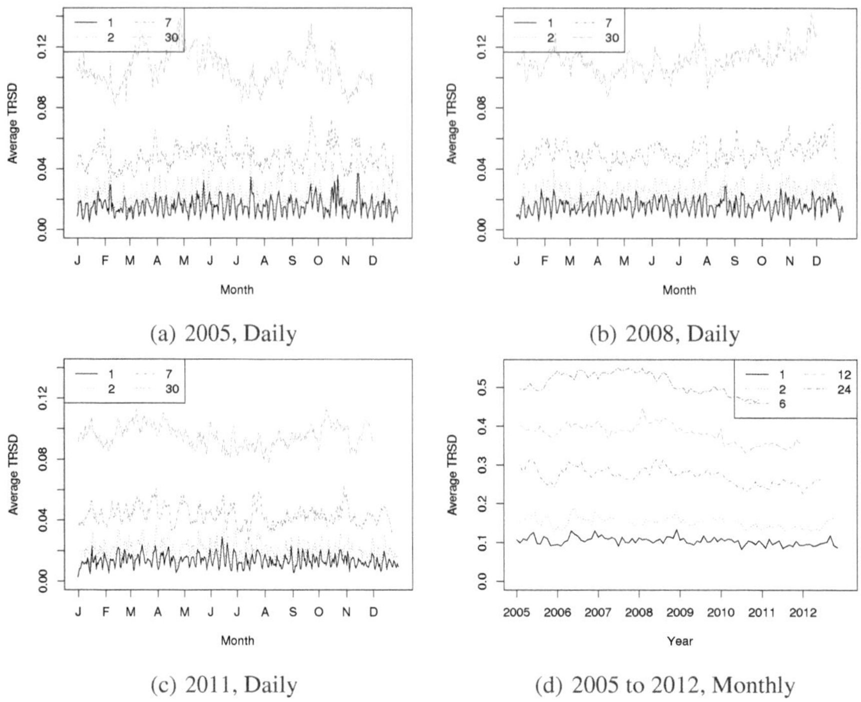

(a) 2005, Daily

(b) 2008, Daily

(c) 2011, Daily

(d) 2005 to 2012, Monthly

Figure 2: $r(i,n)$ versus i for different values of n

5. MEASUREMENTS

In this section we show how TRSD can be used to extract useful knowledge about interdomain routing dynamics.

5.1 Analyzing TRSD

To analyze routing dynamics in the four datasets we compute time series of TRSD, averaged over all prefixes. Specifically, let $r_p(i,n) = TRSD_p(t_i, t_{i+n})$ for $1 \leq i \leq T-n$ and some $1 \leq n \leq T-1$. We then define $r(i,n)$ as the average of all $r_p(i,n)$ that can be computed, i.e., for all prefixes that have routing information at times t_i and t_{i+n} in our datasets. We use average of $r_p(i,n)$ because it gives a measure of the total magnitude of change. Thus, $r(i,n)$ represents average proportion of change in next-hop decisions at timescale n.

Figure 2 presents the time series of $r(i,n)$ for our 4 datasets, where n is 1, 2, 7 and 30 days for datasets 1 to 3 (daily), and n is 1, 2, 6, 12 and 24 months for dataset 4 (monthly). From now on, to simplify discussion, we assume that time indices always represent days for datasets 1, 2 and 3, and represent months for dataset 4.

The first striking aspect of these time series is that they are all are approximately stationary. That is, they fluctuate around a mean value, but do not show any long-term trend. Furthermore, the mean values of TRSD do not show significant differences across years, from 2005 to 2012. This indicates that despite the considerable growth of the Internet in terms of ASes and Prefixes (which might suggest more next-hop options per AS) there is an approximately constant rate of routing decision changes over time. For example, for $n = 30$ days in the daily datasets we have that $r(i,n)$ is approximately 0.1, meaning that from month to month, on average, 10% of the Internet changes in terms of next-hop routing decisions. The same value can be seen in the monthly dataset for the curve $n = 1$ month.

The next observation is that as n grows so does $r(i,n)$. This implies that at least a portion of the routing changes that happen over time are persistent, i.e., are not undone quickly so as to return to a previous routing state. On the other hand, we cannot say that it is a system governed by system-wide changes. To see that we can refer to the curve $r(i,24)$ of the monthly dataset. From this curve we can see that in a time window of 2 years, approximately 50% of the next-hop choices persisted (because 50% changed). This fact indicates many routes are stable over a long period of time.

Yet another property that can be seen in the daily datasets is related to seasonality. One can note that for $n = 1$ day there is pattern of weekly variation in the data. This may be explainable as evidence of human input (network operators) in the system. We explore this conjecture in the following section.

5.2 Analyzing Routing Changes

After analyzing the results of the last section one question that arises is: of the total set of next-hop changes that happen over the time, what portion is related to *sustained* (changes that persist in the system for some time) and which fraction is related to *churn* (changes that change again in the near future)?

To answer this question we decompose the TRSD time series ($r(i,1)$) into two components: $s(i,k)$ and $c(i,k)$, standing for *sustained* TRSD and *churn* TRSD respectively. Sustained TRSD ($s(i,k)$) captures the portion of $r(i,1)$ that represents next-hop decisions that changed from t_i to t_{i+1} but did *not* subsequently change from t_{i+1} to t_{i+k}. In the same vein we define $c(i,k)$ as the portion of $r(i,1)$ that represents next-hop decisions that changed from t_i to t_{i+1} and then changed *again* from t_{i+1} to t_{i+k}.

Formally, we define $s(i,k)$ as the average over all $s_p(i,k)$, where $s_p(i,k)$ is a measure for sustained changes for a specific

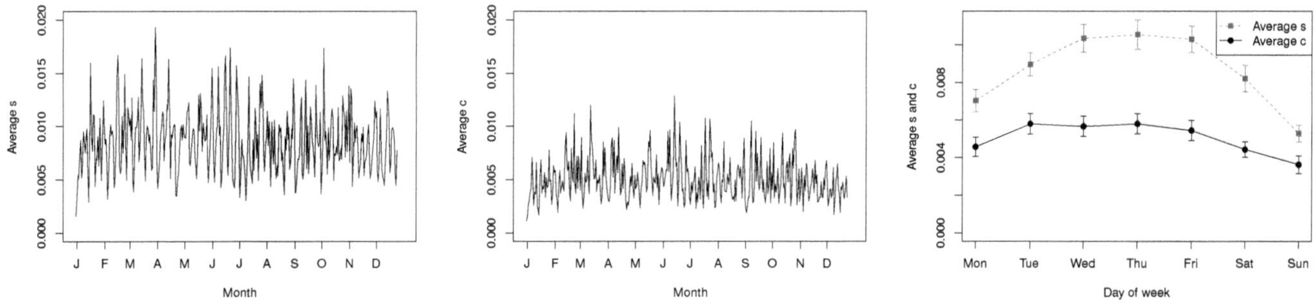

(a) $s(i,k)$, $k = 7$ days

(b) $c(i,k)$, $k = 7$ days

(c) weekly average of $s(i,7)$ and $c(i,7)$. Error bars are 95% Confidence Intervals

Figure 3: $s(i,k)$ and $c(i,k)$ for 2011, daily

prefix p given by:

$$s_p(i,k) = \frac{\sum_{s \in S} \delta'_{s,p}(i,k)}{|D'_p(i,k)|}, \quad (3)$$

where $D'_p(i,k)$ is the set of all sources for which the sets $N_{s,p}(t_i)$, $N_{s,p}(t_{i+1})$ and $N_{s,p}(t_{i+k})$ are not empty and $\delta'_{s,p}(i,k)$ is the fraction of elements, which belong to the set $N_{s,p}(t_i) \cup N_{s,p}(t_{i+1})$, that satisfy any of the two following conditions: *i)* the element is in $N_{s,p}(t_i)$ but it is not in $N_{s,p}(t_{i+1})$ nor in $N_{s,p}(t_{i+k})$; or *ii)* it is in $N_{p,s}(t_{i+1})$ and $N_{s,p}(t_{i+k})$ but it is not in $N_{s,p}(t_i)$.

Then proceeding analogously to Equation (3) we can compute $c(i,k)$. One important observation is that $s_p(i,k)$ and $c_p(i,k)$, by definition, form a partition of $r_p(i,1)$, i.e., $s_p(i,k) + c_p(i,k) = r_p(i,1)$, for all p and k that have available routing information at times t_i, t_{i+1} and t_{i+k}.

Figure 3 presents $s(i,7)$ and $c(i,7)$ for the daily dataset of 2011. (Results for 2005 and 2008 are similar). The choice of $k = 7$ means that routing changes that persist for a week are considered to be sustained. The first observation, obtained by comparing Figures 3(a) and 3(b), is that sustained routing changes ($s(i,7)$) have more impact on TRSD than $c(i,7)$. The average value of $s(i,7)$ is around 0.007 (0.7%), while $c(i,7)$ has an average value of approximately 0.004 (0.4%).

The next observation is that $s(i,k)$ inherits the weekly periodicity of $r(i,1)$ while $c(i,k)$ is more similar to noise. This weekly periodicity suggests that there is some sort of human interaction with the system. Our conjecture is that those changes are triggered by BGP policy management and resulting changes to BGP configurations. In order to dig deeper we computed the average of $c(i,k)$ and $s(i,k)$ over days of the week. Figure 3(c) presents the results, where we can see that both curves indicate more activity in the workweek and less on the weekends. However, the difference between week and weekend behavior is much more significant in the case of the sustained changes, i.e., $s(i,k)$. These results corroborate with the idea of human interaction with the system, since we can understand them as the ASes avoiding intentional routing changes on weekends (probably due to reduced number of network operators working full time).

The decomposition into sustained TRSD and churn TRSD is also informative on long timescales. Figure 4 presents $s(i,2)$ and $c(i,2)$ for dataset 4 (2005 to 2012, monthly). Here we adopt the assumption that routing changes that persist for one month are considered to be sustained. This Figure shows that on average, about 3% of all routing decisions churn on a monthly basis, while about 8% of all routing decisions show a sustained change. Comparing Figures 4 and 3, one can see that the sustained and churn TRSD on a monthly basis are greater than the corresponding values on a weekly basis, which is to be expected. However, the difference between sustained and churn TRSD is much greater on the monthly timescale, showing that sustained TRSD captures the accumulation of intentional changes to the routing system over time, while churn TRSD reflects the continuous background noise in the system.

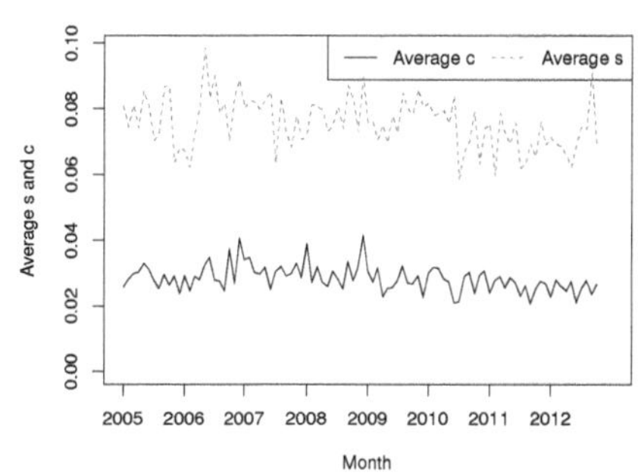

Figure 4: $s(i,k)$ and $c(i,k)$, monthly dataset with $k = 2$

The relative stability of $s(i,2)$ in Figure 4 shows that large-scale, system-wide changes to Internet routing are rare. There are only a couple of points in time where there are noticeable peaks in the amount of sustained change in Internet routing – one peak in mid 2006 and one in late 2012. Initial investigation of these events shows evidence that system-wide routing changes took place: a large fraction of all prefixes were affected by next-hop changes during these events. A deeper investigation of these events is ongoing.

5.3 Contribution of Sources

Our final set of results aims at answering the following question: *what is the contribution of each source AS to TRSD?* in other words, are the changes represented by TRSD uniformly spread over all ASes or are they concentrated in a small set? To start this analysis we sampled randomly chosen days in 2011 and computed the contribution of each AS over the total TRSD of that day. Figure 5(a) presents the Complementary Cumulative Distribution Function (CCDF) of this contribution for the first day of 2011 (results for other days are similar). The figure shows that the contribution of ASes is long-tailed, and that most ASes, approximately 90%, make little or no contribution to TRSD.

In order to inspect whether this is common behavior over time, for the entire year of 2011 we compute the fraction of ASes that

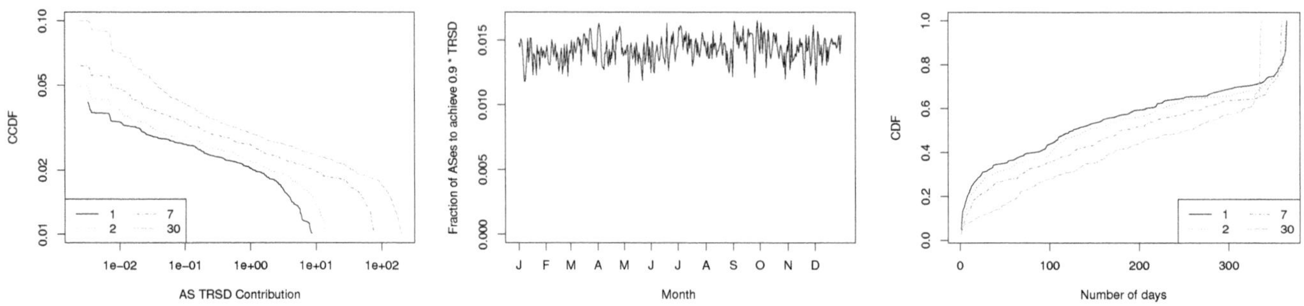

(a) 01/01/11, for $n = 1, 2, 7, 30$

(b) Fraction of top contributors for $n = 1$

(c) Number of days that each AS top contributor appears at Figure 5(b), for $n = 1, 2, 7, 30$

Figure 5: AS Contribution, 2011

are necessary to achieve 90% of TRSD. The result is presented in Figure 5(b), where we can see that less than 2% of all ASes are in fact necessary to capture 90% of TRSD. This result holds for the other datasets with a threshold of 2.5%.

A question that may naturally arise then is: *are these heavy-hitter ASes the same over the time?* In order to answer it we counted in how many days each AS appears during the computation of Figure 5(b), in other words, in how many days each AS was among the set of sources responsible for 90% of the daily TRSD over 2011. The Cumulative Distribution Function (CDF) of this quantity is presented in Figure 5(c). We can see that approximately 40% of ASes that appear on at least one day, appear in at least 300 days. Further, there is a group of approximately 20% of ASes that appear in all days. An initial investigation shows that many of them are in or are near to the network core.

6. CONCLUSIONS AND FUTURE WORK

In this work we proposed a new way to study the Internet at the AS level. We introduced a new measure, TRSD, allowing us to characterize rate of change in the interdomain routing system over long periods of time.

Using this measure we are able to uncover several interesting aspects of the global Internet routing system. First, we showed that the rate of change in routing decisions has been stable over time, despite the growth in the network overall. Second, we showed how to decompose TRSD into components that reflect sustained change versus churn. We showed that the rate of sustained changes shows a persistent weekly periodicity suggestive of a tendency of operators to make sustained (intentional) routing changes in the workweek. Finally, we showed that the locations of the routing changes in the Internet are generally concentrated among a small set of ASes, often those that are near or in the core. Throughout the entire study we consider various timescales and show how the magnitude of routing change (both sustained and churn) varies with timescales from days to months.

Although these are interesting results that characterize the Internet in a new way, it is important to note that this is a work in progress. In particular, there are several interesting observations that need further study in order to understand their implications. Moreover, the results presented here suggest several directions for future research: *i)* it may be valuable to group prefixes according to their TRSD similarity, as prefixes whose routing changes in similar ways may form important clusters; *ii)* TRSD may be usefully applied to individual prefixes, i.e., in a microscopic analysis as compared to the macroscopic view in this study; *iii)* it may be informative explore spatial and temporal dimensions at the same time; *iv)* TRSD may help understanding types of routing changes and how an AS's routing changes affect its neighbors; *v)* TRSD may be usufully applied in analyzing router-level topologies. Although a router-level study is a challenge due to the lack of publicly available data, an analysis at this granularity would be interesting because the same AS path may have traffic flowing through different physical paths. Finally, our long-term goal is to apply the methods of this paper to identify and understand major structural changes or reorganizations of the Internet. We hope to create a methodology that identify "interesting" events in the TRSD time series and find the responsible sources and prefixes associated with those events.

7. ACKNOWLEDGEMENTS

This material is based upon work supported by the National Science Foundation under Grant Numbers CNS-0905565, CNS-1018266, CNS-1012910, and CNS-1117039, and supported by the Army Research Office under grant W911NF-11-1-0227. We are also grateful to the anonymous reviewers and to our shepherd, John Heidemann, for their valuable comments.

8. REFERENCES

[1] Ripe's routing information service raw data project. `http://www.ripe.net/data-tools/stats/ris/ris-raw-data`.

[2] University of oregon route views project. `http://www.routeviews.org`.

[3] Amogh Dhamdhere and Constantine Dovrolis. Ten years in the evolution of the internet ecosystem. In *Proceedings of the 8th ACM SIGCOMM conference on Internet measurement*, IMC '08, pages 183–196, 2008.

[4] Ahmed Elmokashfi, Amund Kvalbein, and Constantine Dovrolis. Bgp churn evolution: A perspective from the core. *IEEE/ACM Trans. Netw.*, 20(2):571–584, April 2012.

[5] Gonca Gürsun. *Inferring Hidden Features in the Internet*. PhD thesis, Boston University, 2013.

[6] Gonca Gürsun, Natali Ruchansky, Evimaria Terzi, and Mark Crovella. Inferring visibility: who's (not) talking to whom? In *Proceedings of the ACM SIGCOMM 2012 conference on Applications, technologies, architectures, and protocols for computer communication*, SIGCOMM '12, pages 151–162, 2012.

[7] Gonca Gürsun, Natali Ruchansky, Evimaria Terzi, and Mark Crovella. Routing state distance: a path-based metric for

network analysis. In *Proceedings of the 2012 ACM conference on Internet measurement conference*, IMC '12, pages 239–252, 2012.

[8] Craig Labovitz, G. Robert Malan, and Farnam Jahanian. Internet routing instability. *IEEE/ACM Trans. Netw.*, 6(5):515–528, October 1998.

[9] Jun Li, Michael Guidero, Zhen Wu, Eric Purpus, and Toby Ehrenkranz. Bgp routing dynamics revisited. *SIGCOMM Comput. Commun. Rev.*, 37(2):5–16, March 2007.

[10] Wolfgang Mühlbauer, Steve Uhlig, Bingjie Fu, Mickael Meulle, and Olaf Maennel. In search for an appropriate granularity to model routing policies. In *Proceedings of the 2007 conference on Applications, technologies, architectures, and protocols for computer communications*, SIGCOMM '07, pages 145–156, 2007.

[11] Dimitri Papadimitriou, Florin Coras, and Albert Cabellos. Path-vector routing stability analysis. *SIGMETRICS Perform. Eval. Rev.*, 39(3):22–24, December 2011.

[12] Jennifer Rexford, Jia Wang, Zhen Xiao, and Yin Zhang. Bgp routing stability of popular destinations. In *Proceedings of the 2nd ACM SIGCOMM Workshop on Internet measurment*, IMW '02, pages 197–202, 2002.

[13] Yang Xiang, Xia Yin, Zhiliang Wang, and Jianping Wu. Internet flattening: Monitoring and analysis of inter-domain routing. In *ICC*, pages 1–6, 2011.

AS-level Topology Collection through Looking Glass Servers

Akmal Khan, Ted "Taekyoung" Kwon, *Hyun-chul Kim, Yanghee Choi
Seoul National University,*Sangmyung University
akmalshabaz,hyunchulk@gmail.com, tkkwon,yhchoi@snu.ac.kr

ABSTRACT

While accurate and complete modeling of the Internet topology at the Autonomous System (AS) level is critical for future protocol design, performance evaluation, simulation and analysis, still it remains a challenge to construct its accurate representation. In this paper, we collect BGP route announcements of ASes from Looking glass (LG) servers. By querying LG servers, we build an AS topology estimate of around 116 K AS links, from which we discover 11 K new AS links and 686 new ASes. We conclude that collecting BGP traces from LG servers can help enhance the current view of the AS topology from the BGP collector projects (e.g., RouteViews).

Categories and Subject Descriptors

C.2.2 [**Network Protocols: Routing Protocols**]:

Keywords

Inter-domain Routing, Border Gateway Protocol (BGP), Looking Glass servers

1. INTRODUCTION

The Internet consists of Autonomous Systems (ASes) that exchange inter-domain routing information using Border Gateway Protocol (BGP) [1]. The entire Internet can be viewed as an AS-level topology graph where each AS is a node, and a BGP connection between two ASes is a link. The importance of the AS topology has been highlighted through many studies, such as analyzing Internet topological properties [3,5,9], inferring AS relationships [12], building network topology generators for simulations [13], and evaluating the effectiveness of new protocols and improvements [11]. Considering the importance of the AS topology in many areas of networking research, significant efforts [2,7–10,14,19,20] have been made to discover and construct it. However, it still remains as a challenge to develop a complete and accurate view of the AS-level topology [4,7–9,22].

IMC'13, October 23–25, 2013, Barcelona, Spain.
Copyright 2013 ACM 978-1-4503-1953-9/13/10 ...$15.00.
http://dx.doi.org/10.1145/2504730.2504758.

There have been three main approaches to construct the AS topology, each of which has its own limitations: (i) passive measurements by collecting BGP routing tables and updates [18] suffer from routing policy filters and best path selection decisions made by the neighboring ASes of BGP collectors [22], (ii) active measurements using traceroute [14,19] are error-prone and generate potentially false AS links due to non-responsive hosts or errors in converting IP addresses to AS numbers (IP-to-AS mapping) [15,16], and (iii) Internet routing registry (IRR) [21] is known to have incomplete and/or outdated information and possibly biased towards RIPE region [6,17].

In this paper, we focus on the construction of the AS topology by using Looking glass (LG) servers, which are web-based portals run by Internet service providers (ISPs) or network operation centers (NOCs), that help understand network status like connectivity, path, and routing information. We collect around 116 K AS links from 245 LG servers across 110 countries. Then, we analyze the LG server-based AS topology against BGP (IRL [18]), traceroute (Ark [19] and iPlane [20]), and IRR based [21] AS topologies. The main findings of our study are as follows.

We observe 620 neighboring ASes of the LG servers that are not sharing their BGP traces with any of RouteViews [31], RIPE-RIS [32], and PCH [33]. We find 11 K new AS links in the AS topology from the LG servers. By comparing the AS topology from the LG servers against the BGP-based AS topology (i.e., IRL [18]), we observe the increase in the connectivity of some popular content providers, such as 22% more for Microsoft. We discover 686 new ASes in the AS topology from the LG servers that are hidden from other AS topologies. Moreover, 98% of the newly discovered ASes have only one provider AS. Overall, we conclude that collecting BGP traces from the LG servers help increase the narrow view of BGP observed from current BGP collectors [22].

2. LOOKING GLASS SERVERS

Looking glass (LG) servers are web based portals operated by network operators to provide a look into the BGP routing tables of the ASes in which the server resides. For example, from a response of a query to an LG server, a network problem can be traced back to its reasons like misconfigured BGP route advertisement, wrong route aggregation, or misconfigured AS path prepending. By an LG server, we mean a web site that allows running commands (e.g., traceroute) from one or more BGP routers that are under the control of the

Table 1: A sample result of the `show ip bgp summary` command.

Router: cr1-eqx3-pa3 Local AS Number: 29075					
Command: show ip bgp summary					
Neighbor	**AS#**	**State**	**Time**	**Received**	**Sent**
195.42.144.104	6939	ESTAB	61d	36,464	153

Table 2: A sample result of the `BGP neighbor ip advertised routes` command.

Router: cr1-eqx3-pa3 Local AS Number: 29075		
Command: BGP neighbor 195.42.144.104 advertised routes		
Prefix	**Next Hop**	**AS PATH**
149.154.80.0/21	195.42.144.71	29075 50618 57141
91.227.48.0/24	195.42.144.71	29075 50618 25091 56728

LG server[1]. For instance, the LG server of Hurricane Electric[2] provides facilities to run LG commands on its BGP routers that are distributed across 92 locations worldwide.

The importance of LG servers in constructing the Internet AS-level topology has been highlighted in many studies [2, 7, 9]. For instance, Augustin *et al.* [2] uses the `show ip bgp summary`[3] and `traceroute` commands to map IXPs, their members, and their peering matrices. While prior studies have shown the usefulness of LG servers, it is not clear what other information (apart from those available with the `show ip bgp summary` command) is available with LG servers for the purpose of collecting the AS topology. Thus, we conducted a comprehensive investigation to find out how many LG servers are operational and what functionalities are provided by individual LG servers. We first build a list of LG servers from the following sources: peeringDB [23], Traceroute.org [24], Traceroute.net.ru [25], BGP4.as [26], BGP4.net [27], and Virusnet [28]. After removing the overlapping LG servers from the above sources, we find 1.2 K LG servers, only 420 of which were in operation at the time of this study, in the month of March 2013. Our scripts can query 388 LG servers since the web sites of the other 20 LG servers are not parsable and 12 LG servers limit automated queries.

We queried 388 LG servers (running on 410 ASes) to learn their supported functionalities. We find that as many as two dozen commands[4] are supported by different LG servers, while a few of them are more widely supported than others. For example, all the 388 LG servers support `traceroute` and `ping` commands from 4.4 K (in total) locations in the Internet. Another widely supported command is `show ip bgp summary`, which is supported by 245 LG servers from 1.9 K locations. The regional Internet registries (RIR) wise distribution of 245 LG servers are as follows: RIPE (175), ARIN (40), APNIC (15), LACNIC (13), and AfriNIC (2).

Table 1 illustrates a sample result of querying a router (cr1-eqx3-pa3 operating at Paris Equinix) with the `show ip bgp summary` command through the LG server provided by Ielo (AS29075). It shows that Ielo has a BGP session with Hurricane Electric (AS6939) at Paris Equinix. It also shows other important information, such as (i) how long the BGP session has been alive (61 days), (ii) 36,464 routes received from the BGP neighbor, and (iii) 153 routes advertised to the BGP neighbor over this link.

[1]A BGP router under the control of an LG server is called an LG router.

[2]Hurricane Electric LG. http://lg.he.net

[3]`show ip bgp summary` lists the BGP sessions established with an LG router, and details the ASN and IP address of its peering BGP router, for each BGP session.

[4]The full list of LG commands along with all the datasets collected in this study can be found at http://mmlab.snu.ac.kr/traces/lg.

We also find that 59 LG servers (distributed over 250 locations) allow us to run the `BGP neighbor ip advertised routes` command, which helps observe IP prefix announcement(s) advertised by an LG router to its peering BGP routers. Table 2 shows a sample result of the `BGP neighbor ip advertised routes` command on the BGP router cr1-eqx3-pa3. Each row shows an IP prefix, its next hop address and AS path information.

3. AS-LEVEL TOPOLOGIES

We first describe our methodology to build an AS topology from LG servers. We also briefly describe AS topology snapshots derived from other data sources, such as BGP traces.

3.1 AS Topology derived from LG servers

We design a tool to automate a querying process to the 388 LG servers. Our tool issues 30 queries in parallel to the LG servers and waits for 15s between successive queries to the same LG server to avoid overloading them. Collecting data from an LG server is a multi-step process. First, for each LG server our tool learns, by parsing LG server websites, the supported LG commands and its LG routers to which our tool sends queries to collect the data. Second, to each LG router, our tool sends the `show ip bgp summary` command to the LG server. Third, from the returned response of `show ip bgp summary`, our tool extracts IP address(es) of the neighboring router(s) of the LG router. Fourth, by using the IP addresses of the neighboring routers, our tool sends a query of `BGP neighbor ip advertised routes` to collect the BGP routes advertised by the LG router to its neighboring routers. Finally, all the responses of the `show ip bgp summary` and `BGP neighbor ip advertised routes` commands from the LG server are stored in text files for constructing the AS topology.

We queried 245 LG servers that provide the option of running `show ip bgp summary` command from around 1.9 K locations (distributed across 110 countries), twice a week in the month of March 2013. Total 8 snapshots are combined to create an AS link dataset, which consists of around 70 K AS links. We find 77% of the AS links are intra-AS links, i.e., the source and destination ASes of a link are the same. As we are only interested in inter-AS links in this study, we filter out these intra-AS links and selected only 16 K inter-AS links. Throughout this paper, AS links refer to those inter-AS links.

We also queried 59 LG servers (out of the 245 ones) that provide the option of running `BGP neighbor ip advertised routes` command, once a week in the month of Mar. 2013. Their LG routers are located in 250 locations distributed across 40 countries. Moreover, these LG servers advertise routes to 5 K routers of their neighboring ASes. From the

BGP traces collected from the 59 LG servers, we extracted around 2 million AS paths and broke down these AS paths into around 103 K AS links.

Overall, by running the `show ip bgp summary` and `BGP neighbor ip advertised routes` commands on the LG servers, we have collected 116 K unique AS links (103 K+16 K=119 K-3 K overlapping AS links). To the best of our knowledge, this is the first study that investigates not only `show ip bgp summary` but also `BGP neighbor ip advertised routes` commands to construct the AS topology.

3.2 Other AS-level Topologies

In this section, we describe other AS topologies: BGP based (IRL [18]), traceroute based (Ark [19], iPlane [20]), and IRR [21] based, all of which are used in this paper. We have decided to use the recently (and regularly) published AS topology datasets only, not including ones such as Ono [10], which had been collected using BitTorrent P2P clients in 2007-2008. Since we cannot quantify how much of this AS topology dataset is outdated, we decided not to use it. Similarly, we exclude DIMES [14] as it has not been updated since Apr. 2012. Note that all the AS topologies are collected in March 2013.

IRL: UCLA IRL [18] regularly publishes the AS topology extracted from the BGP traces shared by RouteViews [31], RIPE-RIS [32], Packet Clearing House (PCH) [33], and Internet2 [34]. We find 179 K AS links in the AS topology published by IRL in March 2013.

Ark: CAIDA Archipelago (Ark) [19] provides the AS topology derived from the traceroute based measurements. As of March 2013, there are 71 Ark monitors distributed across the Internet. We used Ark's IPv4 Routed/24 AS link dataset, which includes direct and indirect AS links. A direct AS link means that a pair of connected ASes have a pair of adjacent hops in the traceroute path, while an indirect AS link means that two connected ASes are separated by one or more unmapped or non-responsive hops. We discarded indirect AS links and used direct AS links. We find 116 K direct AS links from the Ark dataset in March 2013.

iPlane: Madhyastha *et al.* proposed the iPlane [20] service that performs traceroute from around 300 PlanetLab locations daily to map the Internet topology. We find 81 K AS links from the iPlane AS topology in March 2013.

Internet Routing Registry (IRR): The Internet Routing Registry (IRR) [21] is a set of globally distributed databases with which ASes can register their routing and address related information. The IRR has been reported to contain stale records [6]. Nevertheless, the IRR contains AS links that are not observed in BGP and traceroute based AS topologies [9]. we downloaded the IRR data from the RIPE Routing Registry (RR) [29] and RADB [30] in March 2013. To derive AS link information from the IRR, we investigate *aut-num* objects' import, export and default attributes. We extract 206 K AS links from the IRR, most of which (75%) come from the RIPE RR.

To remove possibly outdated AS links from the IRR dataset, earlier studies like [7] have relied on `changed` attribute of an IRR record, which shows the last updated date of the IRR record. However, we find that RIPE no longer publishes `changed` attribute in the IRR records. To remove outdated AS links from the IRR, we collected the AS topology snapshots published by IRL [18] dating back till 2004. We want to check whether some of the AS links in the IRR were observed in the historical BGP based AS topologies. Such comparison confirms that some of the AS links found in the IRR were operational in BGP but are not currently visible from BGP. Using the above method, we find as many as 46 K (out of 206 K) outdated IRR AS links. We removed these AS links and have used around 160 K AS links from the IRR.

4. COMPARISON OF BGP FEEDERS

There are three popular BGP collector projects: RouteViews [31], RIPE-RIS [32], and PCH [33]. The ASes sharing their BGP traces to the BGP collector projects are known as BGP feeders [22]. In this section, we are interested in finding out whether, by querying LG servers, we can collect BGP traces from ASes that are not BGP feeders of RouteViews, RIPE-RIS, and PCH. Such analysis indicates whether BGP traces collected from the LG servers help discover new AS links that are not found in the other AS topology datasets (e.g., IRL [18]). Moreover, collecting BGP traces from new BGP feeders help widen our limited view of BGP observed from current BGP collectors [22].

We have collected information regarding the BGP feeders (i.e., ASNs and IP addresses of routers) of RouteViews [31], RIPE-RIS [32], and PCH [33] from their websites in the month of March 2013. The comparison between the BGP feeders of different projects are based on the ASN and IP address of BGP routers sharing the BGP traces. That is, if the ASN and/or IP address of a BGP router matches between the LG servers and RouteViews BGP feeders, then it is considered that the same BGP router (of an AS) is sharing its BGP traces with both RouteViews and the LG servers.

Table 3 shows the number of common BGP feeders (ASes and routers) sharing their BGP traces with the RouteViews, RIPE-RIS, PCH, or LG server datasets. The diagonal (in bold) is the number of BGP feeders available only in one dataset; either in RV, RIPE, PCH, or LG servers. We observe differences in the number of ASes and router IPs overlapping between different datasets. For example, 63 neighboring ASes of LG servers are sharing their traces with RV. However, only 36 router IPs are matched between LG servers and RV. Further investigation leads us to find the following two reasons for such mismatches: (i) An AS can be peering on an IPv4 connection with RV while on an IPv6 connection with LG servers. In that case, when two datasets are compared to check for the overlapping ASNs and router IPs, the observed router IPs can be different in both datasets though they are with the same ASN. (ii) An AS can be peering with RV at a different location in the Internet from where an LG server is located, thus the observed router IPs between the two datasets can be different as well, while they have the same ASNs.

Moreover, we find that 545 (out of 1.1 K) neighboring ASes of the LG servers overlap with RouteViews, RIPE-RIS, or PCH. More importantly, we observe that 620 neighboring ASes of the LG routers are not sharing their BGP traces with RouteViews, RIPE-RIS, nor PCH. We further inspect the number of routes announced by each neighboring ASes of LG servers to find that 70% (of the 1.1 K) neighboring ASes of the LG servers announce a small number (1 to 100) of BGP routes, since most of these ASes are stub ASes. The remaining (30%) neighbors of LG servers announce BGP routes in the range of 100 to 450 K. Overall, we were able

Table 3: The number of overlapping and unique (in bold) ASes and peering routers between various BGP feeders (RouteViews (RV), RIPE-RIS, PCH, and LG servers).

Collector (Total # of ASes and Routers)	RV ASes (Routers)	RIPE	PCH	LG servers
RV (179 and 368)	**72 (276)**	46 (27)	76 (44)	63 (36)
RIPE (343 and 599)	46 (27)	**51 (314)**	235 (215)	191 (133)
PCH (1.2 K and 2.7 K)	76 (44)	235 (215)	**719 (2 K)**	428 (615)
LG servers (1.1 K and 3.3 K)	63 (36)	191 (133)	428 (615)	**620 (2.6 K)**

Table 4: The number of overlapping and unique (in bold) AS links between various AS topology datasets.

Source (Links)	LGs	IRL	IRR	Ark	iPlane
LGs (116 K)	**11 K**	99 K	46 K	67 K	45 K
IRL (179 K)	99 K	**51 K**	62 K	75 K	48 K
IRR (160 K)	46 K	62 K	**93 K**	36 K	24 K
Ark (116 K)	67 K	75 K	36 K	**30 K**	51 K
iPlane (81 K)	45 K	48 K	24 K	51 K	**25 K**

to collect 128 BGP routing tables of around 450 K prefixes from the LG servers, which is approximately equal to the size of full BGP routing table in the current Internet [35].

The analysis presented so far in this section suggests that there are many ASes who are willing to publicly share their BGP traces by operating LG servers, which in turn begs the question that why such ASes have yet to offer feeds to route collectors. We suggest two possible reasons: (i) In the past, network operators were motivated to share their BGP feeds to the route collectors in order to advertise their rich connectivity and dominance (especially Tier-1's) in the Internet [22]. However, they may not need to do that any more as maintaining an LG server serves that purpose too. Besides, maintaining an LG server by an AS is helpful for operational reasons such as troubleshooting routing issues. (ii) BGP collector projects such as RouteViews have presence at a limited number of locations in the Internet (e.g., large IXPs) and mostly collect traces from ASes present at those locations (e.g., members of large IXPs). Thus, RouteViews can not collect traces from the ASes which are not located at these locations but are sharing their feeds to the LG servers.

5. ANALYSIS OF AS-LEVEL TOPOLOGIES

In this section, we present the analysis of the AS topology generated by the LG server datasets in comparison to the ones from the other datasets.

5.1 Overlapping/Unique AS Links

We compare AS topologies generated from different datasets, to find overlapping and unique AS links among them. Such analysis are important in quantifying how many AS links are newly discovered from the LG servers. Table 4 indicates the number of common AS links for each pair of datasets. The diagonal zone from upper-left to bottom-right (in bold) reports the count of AS links appearing in only one dataset, i.e., either in LGs, IRL, IRR, Ark or iPlane only. We observe 11 K unique AS links in the AS topology from the LG servers. We find 51 K unique AS links in IRL, which suggests that there are a significant number of AS links not observed

Table 5: Top 10 ASes in terms of the number of newly discovered AS links through LG servers. The number of AS links found in the IRL (2nd column), the number of newly discovered AS links from the LG servers (3rd column), and the corresponding increase in the AS connectivity in percentage (4th column).

AS Name (ASN)	In IRL	New in LGs	Percent Incr.
Level3 GBLX (AS3549)	3,290	112	3.40%
Abovenet(AS6461)	1,119	109	9.74%
Google (AS15169)	164	31	18.90%
Globalnet (AS31500)	115	29	25.22%
GlobalSol. (AS12713)	86	27	31.40%
Microsoft (AS8075)	122	27	22.13%
Yahoo (AS10310)	150	23	15.33%
Amazon (AS16509)	132	22	16.67%
EdgeCast (AS15133)	112	19	16.96%
Facebook (AS32934)	99	19	19.19%

from the BGP feeders of LG servers. The IRR contains 93 K unique AS links, some or many of which might have been outdated. However, as noted earlier in Section 3.2, there is no clear way of filtering out the outdated information from the IRR. Finally, Ark and iPlane have their contribution of unique AS links, while many of these AS links may not be accurate either, due to the traceroute measurement issues such as IP-to-AS mapping [15,16].

To better understand the geographic location of newly discovered AS links from the LG servers, we use the Team Cymru WHOIS service [37] to map the ASes in the newly discovered 11 K AS links to the regional Internet registries (RIRs). We find 6.5 K AS links whose source AS (in an AS link) is from RIPE, 3.4 K from ARIN, 0.8 K from APNIC, 295 from LACNIC, and 88 from AfriNIC. Considering that the IRR registration is popular in RIPE [6], it is surprising to observe that the largest portion (6.5 K out of 11 K) of newly discovered AS links are from RIPE. That is, there are still many ASes in the RIPE region who do not correctly maintain their routing policies in the IRR. Further inspection reveals that most of these 11 K AS links do not go beyond their RIR regions. For instance, 80% of the newly discovered AS links from the the RIPE region have both of the source and destination ASes in that region.

Finally, we analyze the differences in the AS connectivity of all the 4 K source ASes (i.e., every source AS of the 11 K newly discovered AS links) with respect to the AS connectivity of the ASes observed in IRL [18], which is known as the most complete BGP-based AS topology dataset [7]. Table 5 shows, for each of top 10 ASes in terms of the number of new AS links found from our LG dataset, the number of AS links found in the IRL (2nd column), the number of newly discovered AS links from the LG servers (3rd column), and the corresponding increase in AS connectivity in percentage (4th column). We found 112 and 109 new AS links for the Tier-1 ASes Level 3 and Abovenet, respectively, through the LG servers. We also observe the increase in the AS connectivity of some other large ASes, e.g., 18.9% increase in the AS connectivity of Google (AS15169).

Why do the LG servers miss AS links observed in other datasets? While the AS topology collected from LG servers reports new AS links (11 K), it is missing many AS links visible in other datasets, e.g., 51 K in the IRL. This can be due to the following reasons. First, BGP feeders may provide a full feed to the router collector projects such as RouteViews while they may share only partial feed to LG servers due to economic relationships (such as Peer-to-Peer) with ASes operating the LG servers. Second, LG servers also suffer from vantage point bias. More specifically, depending on the view of a BGP feeder and its location in the Internet, only a specific part of AS topology can be discovered by an LG server. Third, it is not clear whether all the AS links published by the traceroute and IRR datasets are correct.

Why do the other datasets not see AS links discovered using LG servers? The reasons are different depending on different AS topology datasets. First, the incompleteness of BGP-based datasets has been reported in a few studies [7, 22], which is due to the limited number of ASes sharing their BGP feeds to RouteViews and RIPE-RIS. Moreover, AS topology view from BGP-based datasets is also biased, as current route collector projects have better views of the core rather than the other parts of the Internet; Tier-1s more actively share their BGP traces than other ASes [22]. Second, traceroute-based datasets suffer from limited vantage points, selectively probing prefixes, IP-to-AS mapping issues [15, 16], and can not discover backup links [20]. Finally, many of the ASes, except in the RIPE region, do not actively use the IRR to register their routing policy related information [17, 36]. Thus, topology collection from LG servers result in discovering otherwise unobserved part of the Internet as LG servers provide new BGP feeders from geographically diverse locations in the Internet. Note that new AS links found in the AS topology from the LG servers can be hidden from other router collectors due to traffic engineering practices (such as route aggregation) of ASes in BGP [7, 10].

5.2 Overlapping/Unique ASes

Table 6 shows the number of common ASes for each pair of the datasets. The diagonal zone from upper-left to bottom-right (in bold) reports the count of ASes appearing in only one dataset. We observe 686 unique ASes from LG servers while IRL has only 181 unique ASes. There are around 6.2 K unique ASes in the IRR; mostly from RIPE and APNIC regions suggesting the popularity of the IRR usage in these regions [17]. We do not find any unique ASes in Ark, which suggests their accurate use of the BGP traces since Ark relies on BGP traces from RouteViews to convert IP-to-AS paths collected from traceroute measurements. Finally, iPlane shows 281 unique ASes. On further investigation, we find that these ASes were not operational in BGP in the month of March 2013. For example, (i) AS1448 (DPEC Partners) had been visible until February 18, 2013, (ii) AS40027 (Netflix) had been visible until February 23, 2012, and (iii) AS42411 (Vereya) had been visible until March 16, 2012, but not any more. The reason why we observed 281 unique ASes in iPlane is because it uses BGP traces that contain older data collected from July 2006 to March 2013 during the IP to AS mapping process, constructing its AS topology.

Table 6: The number of overlapping and unique (in bold) ASes found in various AS topology datasets.

Source (ASes)	LGs	IRL	IRR	Ark	iPlane
LGs (45.4 K)	**686**	44.1 K	28.7 K	36.9 K	25.4 K
IRL (44.9 K)	44.1 K	**181**	28.8 K	37.1 K	25.5 K
IRR (35.7 K)	28.7 K	28.8 K	**6.2 K**	24.5 K	17.4 K
Ark (37.1 K)	36.9 K	37.1 K	24.5 K	**-**	23.6 K
iPlane (26.1 K)	25.4 K	25.5 K	17.4 K	23.6 K	**281**

We check the RIR wise distribution of these 686 new ASes found from the LG servers, and find that 548 ASes are operational in ARIN, 71 in RIPE, 31 in APNIC, 28 in LACNIC, and 8 in AfriNIC. Most of the ASes are from the ARIN region, possibly due to the lower popularity of the IRR registration practice in that region, compared with the RIPE and APNIC ones [17]. We also check the length of IP prefixes announced by the new 686 ASes to find that 90% of the ASes announce IP prefixes of length between /19 and /24, which suggests that these IP prefixes are possibly aggregated by their provider ASes. Thus, the practice of IP prefix aggregation in BGP is one of the possible reasons that many of the new ASes observed from the LG servers are hidden from RouteViews, RIPE-RIS, and PCH BGP collectors. Yet, we observe that the practice of IP prefix aggregation in BGP may not be the only reason for these 686 hidden ASes since we also observe a few IP prefixes of length between /16 and /18, which needs further study.

Finally, we check the provider degree (i.e., the number of provider ASes of an AS) of each of the 686 ASes, and find that 98% of the ASes have only one provider AS. That is, an AS with a small provider degree is more likely to be hidden behind their provider ASes [7, 9]. Still, there are some ASes with their provider degrees ranging between 2 and 10. For instance, AS410 (754th Electronic Systems Group) has 10 provider ASes. To further investigate 686 hidden ASes, we queried two popular WHOIS services: Team Cymru and Hurricane Electric's WHOIS service [38]. These WHOIS services reportedly have access to the BGP feeds of ASes that are not the BGP feeders of RouteViews and RIPE-RIS [10]. Thus, they can provide some more insights related to the operation of these hidden ASes. While the WHOIS records confirm the operation of 150 (out of 686) ASes found from the LG servers, most of the ASes do not have their details in the WHOIS services either.

5.3 AS Degree Distribution

In this section, we investigate whether the different methods of collecting AS topologies result in different AS degree distributions. The **AS degree distribution** is the probability that a randomly selected AS is k-degree: $P(k) = n(k)/n$; where n is the number of ASes and $n(k)$ is the number of ASes with degree k. The degree distribution is the most frequently used topology characteristic [5].

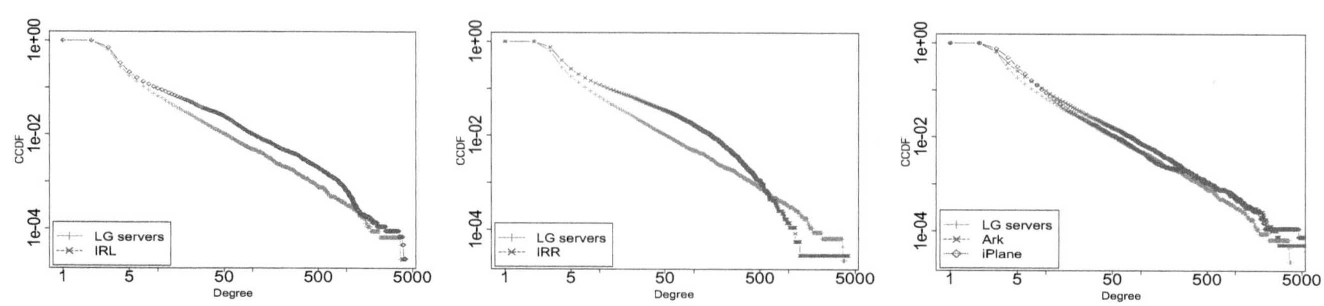

(a) LG and BGP-based (b) LG and IRR (c) LG and Traceroute-based

Figure 1: AS degree distribution (CCDF) of the AS topology obtained from the LG server dataset, as compared to those of other datasets.

Figure 1 shows the CCDFs of the AS topology datasets plotted along with that of the LG server-derived AS topology. Figure 1(a) shows that IRL provides more connectivity information related to moderate degree ASes than the LG servers.

Figure 1(b) shows that IRR has many more AS links for the moderate degree ASes which implies that the IRR is popular in the realm of smaller ISPs. Large ISPs have shown little interest in the IRR as it is difficult to manage complex routing policies in the IRR [36]. Figure 1(c) shows that LG servers and iPlane closely match for the low degree ASes. However, iPlane reports more AS links for higher degree ASes. To find out the reasons, we analyze the traceroute IP paths collected from the iPlane in March 2013. We observe that iPlane has a selective list of IP prefixes (120 K out of approximately 450 K IP prefixes that are currently operational in BGP [35]) to probe the Internet and this list seems to concentrate more on probing the core Internet [20]. Thus, iPlane discovers more connectivity of higher degree ASes. Finally, Ark reports more connectivity of the moderate degree ASes than the LG severs and iPlane. Overall, traceroute based projects such as Ark and iPlane suffer from limited vantage points, selectively probing IP prefixes, errors in the translation from IP to AS Path. Such factors impact the AS topology view observed from traceroute measurements, which can also be error prone [15,16].

6. RELATED WORK

There have been a number of measurement studies related to the AS topology discovery [2,7–9,14,18,19]. To quote the most recent efforts, He *et al.* [9] provide a large scale comprehensive synthesis of the available routing data sources such as BGP routing tables, IRR, and traceroute data. Augustin *et al.* [2] build on the work of He *et al.* [9], but the focus is on the IXP substrate, not on the AS topology as a whole. Active measurement platforms such as Ark [19], DIMES [14], and iPlane [20] are providing the AS topology views, but suffer from the small number of vantage points to run traceroute measurements. To overcome the limitation, Chen *et al.* [10] propose to send traceroute probes from a large number of (992,000 P2P user IPs in 3,700 ASes) P2P clients.

So far, LG servers have been considered as a secondary source of inter-domain routing data for discovering links in the Internet topology [2,7,9,18]. That is, LG servers have been used to augment some AS links to the AS topology extracted from BGP traces [7], or used to help verify the AS links found in the IRR [9]. To the best of our knowledge, this paper is the first to show that LG servers are yet another non-negligible source for building Internet AS topology. Moreover, collecting BGP traces from the LG servers can help widen the narrow view of BGP observed from the current BGP collector projects, such as RouteViews, RIPE-RIS, and PCH [22].

7. CONCLUSION

In this paper, we highlight the less-known capabilities of Looking glass (LG) servers to construct Internet AS topology. By collecting **show ip bgp summary** command responses from 245 LG servers (from 1.9 K locations in 110 countries) and **BGP neighbor ip advertised routes** command responses from 59 LG servers (from 250 locations in 40 countries) in March 2013, we build an AS topology estimate of around 116 K AS links. We newly discovered 11 K AS links and 686 ASes that are not found in BGP, traceroute, and IRR based AS topologies. Clearly, LG servers help in augmenting the current AS topology collection efforts reliably as BGP based methods are less error prone as compared to traceroute-based ones. However, the AS topology view from the LG servers suffers from limited vantage points of the LG servers and BGP export policies employed by the neighboring ASes of LG servers. Overall, we envision that more LG servers are deployed in the Internet in the future as they are important operational tools deployed by ASes. Thus, the research community needs to be aware of the facilities provided by them to discover Internet AS topology.

8. ACKNOWLEDGEMENTS

We are grateful to the anonymous IMC reviewers for their insightful comments. This research was supported in part by the KCC (Korea Communications Commission), Korea, under the R&D program supervised by the KCA (Korea Communications Agency) (KCA-2013-11-911-05-002) and by the MSIP (Ministry of Science, ICT & Future Planning), Korea in the ICT R&D Program 2013, and by Basic Science Research Program through the National Research Foundation of Korea (NRF) funded by the Ministry of Education (NRF-2013R1A1A2010474). The corresponding authors of this paper are Ted "Taekyoung" Kwon and Hyun-chul Kim.

9. REFERENCES

[1] Y. Rekhter, T. Li, and S. Hares. A Border Gateway Protocol. *RFC 4271*, January, 2006.

[2] B. Augustin, B. Krishnamurthy, and W. Willinger. IXPs: mapped?. *ACM IMC*, November, 2009.

[3] G. Gursun, N. Ruchansky, E. Terzi, and M. Crovella. Routing state distance: a path-based metric for network analysis. *ACM IMC*, November, 2012.

[4] B. Ager, N. Chatzis, A. Feldmann, N. Sarrar, S. Uhlig, and W. Willinger. Anatomy of a Large European IXP. *ACM SIGCOMM*, August, 2012.

[5] P. Mahadevan, D. Krioukov, M. Fomenkov, X. Dimitropoulos, K. Claffy, and A. Vahdat. The internet AS-level topology: three data sources and one definitive metric. *ACM SIGCOMM CCR*, vol. 36, no. 1, January, 2006.

[6] K. Butler, T. Farley, P. McDaniel, and J. Rexford. A Survey of BGP Security Issues and Solutions. *Proc. of the IEEE*, vol. 98, no. 1, January, 2010.

[7] R. Oliveira, D. Pei, W. Willinger, B. Zhang, and L. Zhang. The (In) Completeness of the Observed Internet AS-level Structure. *IEEE/ACM TON*, vol. 18, no. 1, February, 2010.

[8] H. Chang, R. Govindan, S. Jamin, S. Shenker, and W. Willinger. Towards Capturing Representative AS-Level Internet Topologies. *Computer Networks*, vol. 44, no. 6, April, 2004.

[9] Y. He, G. Siganos, and M. Faloutsos. Lord of the Links: A Framework for Discovering Missing Links in the Internet Topology. *IEEE/ACM TON*, vol. 17, no. 2, April, 2009.

[10] K. Chen, D. Choffnes, R. Potharaju, Y. Chen, F. Bustamante, D. Pei, and Y. Zhao. Where the Sidewalk Ends: Extending the Internet AS Graph Using Traceroutes From P2P. *ACM CoNEXT*, December, 2009.

[11] John S. Otto, M. Sanchez, D. Choffnes, F. Bustamante, and G. Siganos. On Blind Mice and the Elephant – Understanding the Network Impact of a Large Distributed System. *ACM SIGCOMM*, August, 2011.

[12] X. Dimitropoulos, D. Krioukov, M. Fomenkov, B. Huffaker, Y. Hyun, K. claffy, and G. Riley. AS relationships:Inference and validation. *ACM SIGCOMM CCR*, vol. 37, no. 1, January, 2007.

[13] P. Mahadevan, C. Hubble, D. Krioukov, B. Huffaker, and A. Vahdat. Orbis: rescaling degree correlations to generate annotated internet topologies. *ACM SIGCOMM*, August, 2007.

[14] Y. Shavitt, E. Shir. DIMES: Let the Internet measure itself. *ACM SIGCOMM CCR*, vol. 35, no. 5, October, 2005.

[15] Y. Zhang, R. Oliveira, Y. Wang, S. Su, B. Zhang, J. Bi, H. Zhang, and L. Zhang. A Framework to Quantify the Pitfalls of Using Traceroute in AS-Level Topology Measurement. *IEEE JSAC*, vol. 29, no. 9, October, 2011.

[16] P. Marchetta, W. Donato, A. Pescapé. Detecting Third-party Addresses in Traceroute Traces with IP Timestamp Option. *PAM*, March, 2013.

[17] A. Khan, H. Kim, T. Kwon, and Y. Choi. A comparative study on IP prefixes and their origin Ases in BGP and the IRR. *ACM SIGCOMM CCR*, vol. 43, no. 3, July, 2013.

[18] UCLA IRL, http://irl.cs.ucla.edu/topology.

[19] CAIDA ARK. http://www.caida.org/projects/ark.

[20] H. V. Madhyastha, T. Isdal, M. Piatek, C. Dixon, T. Anderson, A. Krishnamurthy, and A. Venkataramani. iPlane: An Information Plane for Distributed Services. *USENIX NSDI*, May, 2006.

[21] Internet Routing Registry. http://www.irr.net.

[22] E. Gregori, A. Improta, L. Lenzini, L. Rossi, and L. Sani. On the incompleteness of the AS-level graph: a novel methodology for BGP route collector placement. *ACM IMC*, November, 2012.

[23] PeeringDB, http://www.peeringdb.com.

[24] traceroute.org, http://www.traceroute.org.

[25] traceroute.net.ru, www.traceroute.net.ru.

[26] bgp4.as, http://www.bgp4.as/looking-glasses.

[27] bgp4.net, wiki, http://www.bgp4.net.

[28] virus-net.ru, http://www.virus-net.ru.

[29] RIPE DB, ftp://ftp.ripe.net/ripe/dbase.

[30] RADB, ftp://ftp.radb.net/radb/dbase.

[31] RouteViews, http://www.routeviews.org.

[32] RIPE-RIS, http://www.ripe.net/ris.

[33] Packet Clearing House, https://www.pch.net/resources/data.php.

[34] Internet2, http://ndb7.net.internet2.edu/bgp.

[35] BGP potaroo, http://bgp.potaroo.net.

[36] Route Filter Panel, Nanog43, June, 2008. http://www.nanog.org/meetings/nanog43.

[37] Team Cymru WHOIS service, http://asn.cymru.com.

[38] BGP Toolkit, http://bgp.he.net.

AS Relationships, Customer Cones, and Validation

Matthew Luckie
CAIDA / UC San Diego
mjl@caida.org

Bradley Huffaker
CAIDA / UC San Diego
bradley@caida.org

Amogh Dhamdhere
CAIDA / UC San Diego
amogh@caida.org

Vasileios Giotsas
University College London
V.Giotsas@cs.ucl.ac.uk

kc claffy
CAIDA / UC San Diego
kc@caida.org

ABSTRACT

Business relationships between ASes in the Internet are typically confidential, yet knowledge of them is essential to understand many aspects of Internet structure, performance, dynamics, and evolution. We present a new algorithm to infer these relationships using BGP paths. Unlike previous approaches, our algorithm does not assume the presence (or seek to maximize the number) of valley-free paths, instead relying on three assumptions about the Internet's inter-domain structure: (1) an AS enters into a provider relationship to become globally reachable; and (2) there exists a peering *clique* of ASes at the top of the hierarchy, and (3) there is no cycle of p2c links. We assemble the largest source of validation data for AS-relationship inferences to date, validating 34.6% of our 126,082 c2p and p2p inferences to be 99.6% and 98.7% accurate, respectively. Using these inferred relationships, we evaluate three algorithms for inferring each AS's *customer cone*, defined as the set of ASes an AS can reach using customer links. We demonstrate the utility of our algorithms for studying the rise and fall of large transit providers over the last fifteen years, including recent claims about the flattening of the AS-level topology and the decreasing influence of "tier-1" ASes on the global Internet.

Categories and Subject Descriptors

C.2.5 [**Local and Wide-Area Networks**]: Internet; C.2.1 [**Network Architecture and Design**]: Network topology

Keywords

AS relationships; routing policies; customer cones

1. INTRODUCTION

The Internet consists of thousands of independent interconnected organizations, each driven by their own business model and needs. The interplay of these needs influences, and sometimes determines, topology and traffic patterns, i.e., connectivity between networked organizations and routing across the resulting mesh. Understanding the underlying business relationships between networked organizations provides the strongest foundation for understanding many other aspects of Internet structure, dynamics, and evolution.

Business relationships between ASes, which are typically congruent with their routing relationships, can be broadly classified into two types: customer-to-provider (c2p) and peer-to-peer (p2p). In a c2p relationship, the customer pays the provider for traffic sent between the two ASes. In return, the customer gains access to the ASes the provider can reach, including those which the provider reaches through its own providers. In a p2p relationship, the peering ASes gain access to each others' customers, typically without either AS paying the other. Peering ASes have a financial incentive to engage in a *settlement-free* peering relationship if they would otherwise pay a provider to carry their traffic, and neither AS could convince the other to become a customer. Relationships are typically confidential so must be *inferred* from data that is available publicly. This paper presents a new approach to inferring relationships between ASes using publicly available BGP data.

Measurement and analysis of Internet AS topologies has been an active area of research for over a decade. While yielding insights into the structure and evolution of the topology, this line of research is constrained by systematic measurement and inference challenges [32], many of which our approach proactively addresses. First, the BGP-based collection infrastructure used to obtain AS-level topology data suffers from artifacts induced by misconfigurations, poisoned paths, and route leaks, all of which impede AS-relationship inference. Our algorithm incorporates steps to remove such artifacts. Second, AS topologies constructed from BGP data miss many peering links [6]. We show this lack of visibility does not hinder the accuracy of inferences on the links we do observe. Third, most AS-relationship algorithms rely on "valley-free" AS paths, an embedded assumption about the rationality of routing decisions that is not always valid [32], and which our algorithm does not make. Fourth, import and export filters can be complicated; some operators caveat their c2p links as being region or prefix specific. However, they still describe themselves as customers even if they do not receive full transit. Therefore, we make a c2p inference when any transit is observed between two ASes. We argue that relationship inferences can still be c2p or p2p with the caveat that the c2p relationship may be partial. We develop techniques to mitigate the effects of such *hybrid relationships* when computing an AS's customer cone, described later in

IMC'13, October 23–25, 2013, Barcelona, Spain.
Copyright 2013 ACM 978-1-4503-1953-9/13/10 ...$15.00.
http://dx.doi.org/10.1145/2504730.2504735.

this section. Finally, a single organization may own and operate multiple ASes; we leave the inference of *sibling relationships* as future work because it is difficult to distinguish them from route leaks. We make the following contributions:

We introduce a new algorithm for inferring c2p and p2p links using BGP data. Our algorithm builds on three generally accepted assumptions about industry structure: (1) there is a clique of large transit providers at the top of the hierarchy; (2) most customers enter into a transit agreement to be globally reachable; and (3) cycles of c2p links (e.g., where ASes A, B, and C are inferred to be customers of B, C, and A respectively) should not exist for routing to converge [19]. Our algorithm achieves *near-perfect accuracy* for both p2p and p2c links for the subset of relationships we were able to validate, using the largest set of externally gathered AS relationship validation data collected to date. Since even our three different sources of validation data disagree by 1%, our algorithm reaches the limit of accuracy achievable with available data.

We evaluate our algorithm's accuracy by validating 43,613 (34.6%) of our inferences – the largest validation of AS-relationships performed to date. First, we received nearly 2400 directly reported relationship assertions from operators through the interactive feedback functionality of our public repository of AS relationships [1]. Second, we use policy information encoded in the RIPE WHOIS database to extract more than 6,500 unique relationships; we extract only relationships between ASes where both ASes have policies recorded in the database and both policies are expressed consistently. Third, we extract more than 41,000 relationships using community strings encoded in BGP messages by ASes who publish how these strings map to AS relationships. Our validation data, 97% of which we can share (we cannot share directly reported relationships) will itself contribute to a research area that has long suffered from lack of validation.

We introduce a new algorithm for inferring the *customer cone* of an AS. The customer cone of AS X is defined as the set of ASes that X can reach using p2c links; for AS X the customer cone includes X's customers, as well as X's customers' customers, and so on. The customer cone is not a methodologically clean construct, since some ASes have hybrid relationships; for example, they peer in some regions (or some prefixes), but one AS will purchase from the other for other regions (or other prefixes). We compare the strengths and weaknesses of three distinct approaches for computing customer cones, and explain why we believe one approach is more accurate. We also show how this construct informs our understanding of evolutionary trends such as the flattening of the Internet topology and the financial consolidation of the Internet transit industry.

2. RELATED WORK

Gao [18] was the first to study the inference of AS relationships. Her solution relies on the assumption that BGP paths are hierarchical, or *valley-free*, i.e., each path consists of an uphill segment of zero or more c2p or sibling links, zero or one p2p links at the top of the path, followed by a downhill segment of zero or more p2c or sibling links. The valley-free assumption reflects the typical reality of commercial relationships in the Internet: if an AS were to announce routes learned from a peer or provider to a peer or provider (creating a valley in the path), it would then be offering transit for free. Gao's algorithm thus tries to derive the maximum number of valley-free paths, by selecting the largest-degree AS in a path as the top, and assuming that ASes with similar degrees are likely to be peers (p2p). Gao validated her results using information obtained from a single Tier-1 AS (AT&T). Xia and Gao [36] proposed an improvement to Gao's algorithm that uses a set of ground truth relationships to seed the inference process. Transit relationships are then inferred using the valley-free assumption. Gao's algorithm [18] is used for remaining unresolved links. They validated 2,254 (6.3%) of their inferences using 80% of their validation data and found their algorithm was accurate for 96.1% of p2c links and 89.33% of p2p links.

Subramanian *et al.* [34] formalized Gao's heuristic into the Type of Relationship (ToR) combinatorial optimization problem: given a graph derived from a set of BGP paths, assign the edge type (c2p or p2p, ignoring sibling relationships) to every edge such that the total number of valley-free paths is maximized. They conjectured that the ToR problem is NP-complete and developed a heuristic-based solution (SARK) that ranks each AS based on how close to the graph's core it appears from multiple vantage points. Broadly, as in Gao [18], ASes of similar rank are inferred to have a p2p relationship, and the rest are inferred to have a p2c relationship. Di Battista, Erlebach *et al.* [9] proved the ToR problem formulation was NP-complete in the general case and unable to infer p2p relationships. They reported that it was possible to find a solution provided the AS paths used are valley-free. They developed solutions to infer c2p relationships, leaving p2p and sibling inference as open problems. Neither Subramanian *et al.* or Di Battista, Erlebach *et al.* validated their inferences; rather, they determined the fraction of valley-free paths formed using their inferences.

Dimitropoulos *et al.* [16] created a solution based on solving MAX-2-SAT. They inferred sibling relationships using information encoded in WHOIS databases. Their algorithm attempted to maximize two values: (1) the number of valley-free paths, and (2) the number of c2p inferences where the node degree of the provider is larger than the customer. The algorithm uses a parameter α to weight these two objectives. They validated 3,724 AS relationships (86.2% were c2p, 16.1% p2p, and 1.2% sibling) and found their algorithm correctly inferred 96.5% of c2p links, 82.8% of p2p links, and 90.3% of sibling links. Their validation covered 9.7% of the public AS-level graph and has thus far been the most validated algorithm. However, MAX-2-SAT is NP-hard and their implementation does not complete in a practical length of time for recent AS graphs.

UCLA's Internet Research Laboratory produces AS-level graphs of the Internet annotated with relationships [3]. The method is described in papers by Zhang *et al.* [37] and Oliveira *et al.* [29]. Their algorithm begins with a set of ASes inferred to be in the Tier-1 clique, then infers links seen by these ASes to be p2c; all other links are p2p. Zhang [37] describes a method to infer the clique; Oliveira [29] assumes the Tier-1 ASes are externally available, such as a list published by Wikipedia. There are a growing number of region-specific c2p relationships visible only below the provider AS, causing this approach to assign many p2p relationships that are actually p2c. Gregori *et al.* [23] used a similar approach; for each AS path, their algorithm identifies the relationships possible and infers the actual relationship based on the lifetime of the paths. None of [23, 29, 37] describes validation.

The problematic lack of validation puts AS relationship inference research in a precarious scientific position. Nonetheless, research continues to build on the assumption that meaningful AS relationship inference can be achieved and applied to the study of the Internet, from deployment of security technologies [21], Internet topology mapping [6, 8, 12] and evolution [13, 14], to industry complexity [17] and market concentration [15]. Due to the diversity in inter-domain connectivity, relationship inferences do not (by themselves) consistently predict paths actually taken by packets; such predictive capabilities remain an open area of research [27].

Given its importance to the field of Internet research, we revisited the science of AS relationship inference, with particular attention to validation. Our algorithm does not seek to maximize the number of valley-free (hierarchical) paths, since at least 1% of paths are non-hierarchical (section 3.6). We make inferences using AS path triplets (adjacent pairs of links) which allow us to ignore invalid segments of paths that reduce the accuracy of valley-free path maximization approaches. We also rely on two key assumptions: (1) an AS enters into a c2p relationship to become globally reachable, i.e. their routes are advertised to their provider's providers, and (2) there exists a *clique* of ASes at the top of the hierarchy that obtain full connectivity through a full mesh of p2p relationships. We acquired external validation for 34.6% of the links in our AS graph, which was certainly a challenge but not one as insurmountable as has been suggested (e.g. [9, 18, 23, 33, 34]).

3. DATA

In this section we present the sources of data we use: public BGP data, a list of AS allocations to RIRs and organizations, and multiple sources of validation data.

3.1 BGP paths

We derive BGP paths from routing table snapshots collected by the Route Views (RV) project [5] and RIPE's Routing Information Service (RIS) [4]. Each BGP peer is a *vantage point* (VP) as it shows an AS-level view of the Internet from that peer's perspective. For each collector, we download one RIB file per day between the 1st and 5th of every month since January 1998, and extract the AS paths that announce reachability to IPv4 prefixes. When we extract the AS paths, we discard paths that contain AS-sets and compress path padding (i.e. convert an AS path from "A B B C" to "A B C"). We record all AS paths that are seen in any of the five snapshots and use the union to subsequently infer relationships. We use all paths and not just "stable" paths because backup c2p links are more likely to be included if we use all AS paths, and temporary peering disputes may prevent a normally stable path from appearing stable in our five-day window of data.

Figure 1 shows the number of ASes peering with RV or RIS between 1998 and 2013. We also show the number providing full views (routes to at least 95% of ASes). RV is the only source that provides BGP data collected between 1998 and 2000, and while more than two thirds of its peers provided a full view then, it had at most 20 views during these three years. For the last decade, approximately a third of contributing ASes provide a full view. Most (64%) contributing ASes provide routes to fewer than 2.5% of all ASes. The operators at these ASes likely configured the BGP session with the collector as p2p and therefore advertise only customer routes.

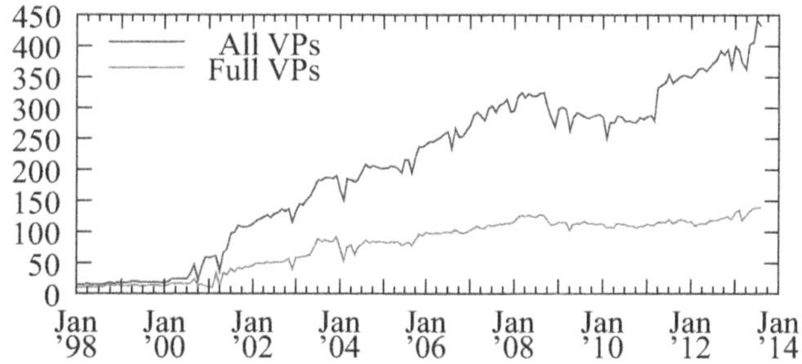

Figure 1: Number of ASes providing BGP data to Route Views and RIS over time. Currently, a third of all contributors provide a full view. The number of ASes providing a full view has not grown since 2008.

3.2 Allocated ASNs

We use IANA's list of AS assignments [2] to identify valid AS numbers assigned to organizations and RIRs. We filter out BGP paths that include unassigned ASes, since these ASes should not be routed on the Internet.

3.3 Validation data directly reported

Our website provides the ability to browse our relationship inferences and submit validation data. We use corrections to two separate inferred datasets, created in January 2010 and January 2011 using a previous relationship inference algorithm. This older algorithm did not produce a cycle of p2c links but assigned many more provider relationships than ASes actually had; 93% of the website feedback consists of p2p relationships, and 62% of that consists of correcting our inference of a c2p relationship to a p2p relationship. In total, we received 129 c2p and 1,350 p2p relationships from 142 ASes through our website. The disparity between our previous inferences and the submissions motivated the new algorithm that we present in this paper.

We separately followed up on unchanged inferences with operators, as well as submissions that seemed erroneous compared to observations in public BGP paths. We received responses from more than 50 network operators. 18 relationships submitted through our website were later acknowledged by the submitting operator to have been inaccurately classified (9 by one operator) or to have changed subsequent to the submission. Additionally, based on email exchanges with operators, we assembled a file containing 974 relationships – 285 c2p and 689 p2p (contained within the "directly reported" circle of figure 2, described further in section 3.6).

3.4 Validation data derived from RPSL

Routing policies are stored by network operators in public databases using the Routing Policy Specification Language (RPSL) [7]. The largest source of routing policies is the RIPE WHOIS database, partly because many European IXPs require operators to register routing policies with RIPE NCC. The routing policy of an AS is stored as part of the *aut-num* record [7]. The aut-num record lists import and export rules for each neighbor AS. An import rule specifies the route announcements that will be accepted from the

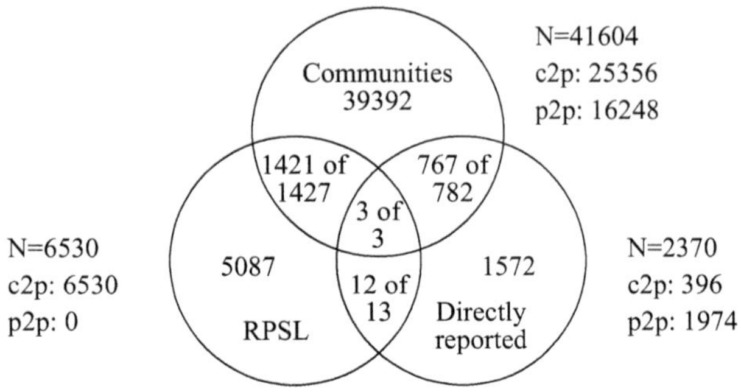

Figure 2: Summary of validation data sets collected and agreement among sets (first number inside intersections is number of overlapping relationships that agree). Overall, 2203 of 2225 relationships agree (99.0%) suggesting a limit on the accuracy of any source of validation data.

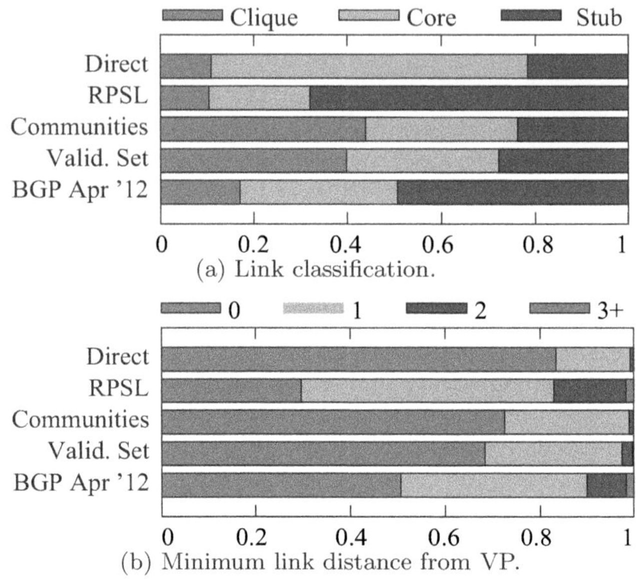

Figure 3: Characteristics of validation data. Relative to BGP data, *clique* links and links directly connected to VPs are over-represented and *stub* links are under-represented.

neighbor, while an export rule specifies what routes will be advertised to the neighbor. The special rule ANY is used by an AS to import/export all routes from/to the neighbor, and is indicative of a customer/provider relationship. Using the RIPE WHOIS database from April 2012, we extracted a set of c2p relationships using the following method: if X has a rule that imports ANY from Y, then we infer a c2p relationship if we also observe a rule in Y's aut-num that exports ANY to A. Limiting ourselves to records updated between April 2010 and April 2012 provided us with 6,530 c2p links between ASes with records in RIPE NCC's database.

3.5 Validation data derived from communities

AS relationships can be embedded in BGP community attributes included with each route announcement. Community attributes can be *tagged* to a route when it is received from a neighbor. Community attributes are optional transitive attributes; they can be carried through multiple ASes but could be removed from the route if that is the policy of an AS receiving the route [11]. The tagging AS can annotate the route with attributes of the neighbor and where the route was received, and the attributes can be used to control further announcements of the route. The commonly used convention is for the tagging AS to place its ASN, or that of its neighbor, in the first sixteen bits. The use of the remaining 16 bits is not standardized, and ASes are free to place whatever values they want in them. Many ASes publicly document the meaning of the values on network operations web sites and in IRR databases, making it possible to assemble a dictionary of community attributes and their policy meanings. We used a dictionary of 1286 community values from 224 different ASes assembled from [22] to construct a set of relationships from BGP data for April 2012; in total, there are 41,604 relationships in our set (16,248 p2p and 23,356 c2p).

3.6 Summary of validation data

Figure 2 uses a Venn diagram to show the size and overlap of our validation data sources. Overall, 2203 of 2225 relationships that overlap agree (99.0%), with multiple explanations for the discrepancies. For the directly reported source, some operators reported a few free transit relationships as peering relationships, i.e., they were reported in the traditional economic sense rather than in a routing sense. For the RPSL source, some providers mistakenly imported all routes from their customers and some customers mistakenly exported all routes to their providers. For the BGP communities source, some customers tagged routes exported to a Tier-1 AS as a customer. While there are limits to the accuracy of all our sources of validation, the 99.0% overlap in agreement gives us confidence in using them for validation.

We assembled our validation data set by combining our four data sources in the following order: (1) directly reported using the website, (2) RPSL, (3) BGP communities, and (4) directly reported in an email exchange. Where a subsequent source classified a link differently, we replaced the classification; we trust relationships acquired through email exchanges more than relationships submitted via the website. Our validation data set consists of 48,276 relationships: 30,770 c2p and 17,506 p2p.

To estimate possible biases in our validation data set, we compared its characteristics with those of the April 2012 BGP dataset in terms of the link types and the minimum distance from a VP at which those links were observed. The closer the link is to a vantage point, the more likely we are to see paths that cross it. We classify links as *clique* (one endpoint is in the clique), *core* (both endpoints are not in the clique and are not stubs), and *stub* (one endpoint is a stub and the other endpoint is not in the clique). Figure 3(a) shows *clique* links are over-represented in our validation data set as compared to BGP data, while *stub* links are under-represented. This disparity is due to the validation data from BGP communities, which mostly comes from large ASes. Figure 3(b) shows links directly connected to a VP (distance 0) are over-represented in our validation data relative to April 2012 BGP data, likely due to the communities dataset, many of which involve ASes that provide VPs.

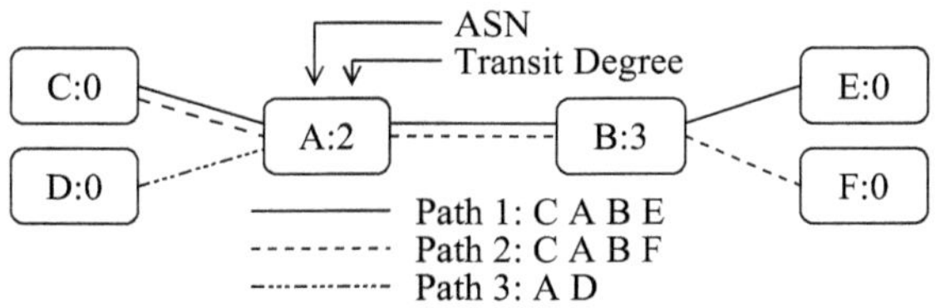

Figure 4: Computing the transit degree of ASes using paths. While the node degrees of ASes A and B are both three, A's transit degree is two because A it is not observed to announce D's prefixes to any neighbors. Nodes with a transit degree of zero (C, D, E, F) are stub ASes.

4. RELATIONSHIP INFERENCE

Our algorithm uses two metrics of AS connectivity: the *node degree* is the number of neighbors an AS has; and the *transit degree* is the number of unique neighbors that appear on either side of an AS in adjacent links. Figure 4 illustrates the transit degree metric; ASes with a transit degree of zero are stub ASes. We use transit degree to initially sort ASes into the order in which we infer their relationships, breaking ties using node degree and then AS number. ASes inferred to be in the clique are always placed at the top of this rank order. Sorting by transit degree reduces ordering errors caused by stub networks with a large peering visibility, i.e., stubs that provide a VP or peer with many VPs.

4.1 Assumptions

We make three assumptions based on discussions with operators and generally understood industry structure.

Clique: multiple large transit providers form a peering mesh so that customers (and indirect customers) of a transit provider can obtain global connectivity without multiple transit provider relationships.

A provider will announce customer routes to its providers. All ASes, except for those in the clique, require a transit provider in order to obtain global connectivity. We assume that when X becomes a customer of Y, that Y announces paths to X to its providers, or to its peers if Y is a clique AS. Exceptions to this rule include backup and region-specific transit relationships.

The AS topology can be represented in a directed acyclic graph. Gao *et al.* argue there should be no cycle of p2c links to enable routing convergence [19].

4.2 Overview

Algorithm 1 shows each high-level step in our AS relationship inference algorithm. First, we sanitize the input data by removing paths with artifacts, i.e., loops, reserved ASes, and IXPs (step 1). We use the resulting AS paths to compute the node and transit degrees of each AS, and produce an initial rank order (step 2). We then infer the clique of ASes at the top of the hierarchy (step 3). After filtering out poisoned paths (step 4), we apply heuristics to identify c2p links (steps 5-10). Finally, we classify all remaining unclassified links as p2p. Our algorithm contains many steps, a consequence of trying to capture the complexity of the real-world Internet and mitigate limitations of public BGP data [32]. The output from this process is a list of p2c and p2p relationships with no p2c cycles, by construction.

Algorithm 1 AS relationship inference algorithm.

Require: AS paths, Allocated ASNs, IXP ASes

1: Discard or sanitize paths with artifacts .(§4.3)
2: Sort ASes in decreasing order of computed transit degree, then node degree (§4)
3: Infer clique at top of AS topology (§4.4)
4: Discard poisoned paths (§4.3)
5: Infer c2p rels. top-down using above ranking (§4.5)
6: Infer c2p rels. from VPs inferred not to be announcing provider routes (§4.5)
7: Infer c2p rels. for ASes where the provider has a smaller transit degree than the customer (§4.5)
8: Infer customers for ASes with no providers (§4.5)
9: Infer c2p rels. between stubs and clique ASes (§4.5)
10: Infer c2p rels. where adjacent links have no relationship inferred (§4.5)
11: Infer remaining links represent p2p rels. (§4.5)

4.3 Filtering and Sanitizing AS Paths

We first sanitize the BGP paths used as input to our algorithm, especially to mitigate the effects of BGP path poisoning, where an AS inserts other ASes into a path to prevent its selection. A poisoned path implies a link (and thus relationship) between two ASes, where in reality neither may exist. We infer poisoning, or the potential for a poisoned path, in AS paths (1) with loops, or (2) where clique ASes are separated. We filter out paths with AS loops, i.e., where an ASN appears more than once and is separated by at least one other ASN. Such paths are an indication of poisoning, where an AS X prevents a path from being selected by a non-adjacent upstream AS Y by announcing the path "X Y X" to provider Z, so if the route is subsequently received by *Y* it will be discarded when the BGP process examines the path for loops [24]. For BGP paths recorded in April 2012, 0.11% match this rule. After we have inferred the clique in step 3, we also discard AS paths where any two ASes in the clique are separated by an AS that is not in the clique. This condition indicates poisoning, since a clique AS is by definition a transit-free network. For BGP paths recorded in April 2012, 0.03% match this rule.

We also filter out paths containing unassigned ASes; in BGP paths from April 2012, we observed 238 unassigned ASes in 0.10% of unique paths. 222 of these ASes are reserved for private use and should not be observed in paths received by route collectors. In particular AS23456, reserved to enable BGP compatibility between ASes that can process 32-bit ASNs and those that cannot [35], is prevalent in earlier public BGP data and can hinder relationship inferences.

We also remove ASes used to operate IXP route servers because the relationships are between the participants at the exchange. Unfortunately we know of no public database of IXP route server ASes, nor do we know of any algorithm that reliably identifies an IXP route server. To identify IXP route server ASes, we manually searched for IXP ASes using a combination of routing and WHOIS data: if the name of the AS in WHOIS contains RS or IX, we include the AS in our list if the AS announces less address space than a /23. This process yielded a list of 25 ASes known to operate route servers; we remove these ASes from paths so that the IX participants are adjacent in the BGP path.

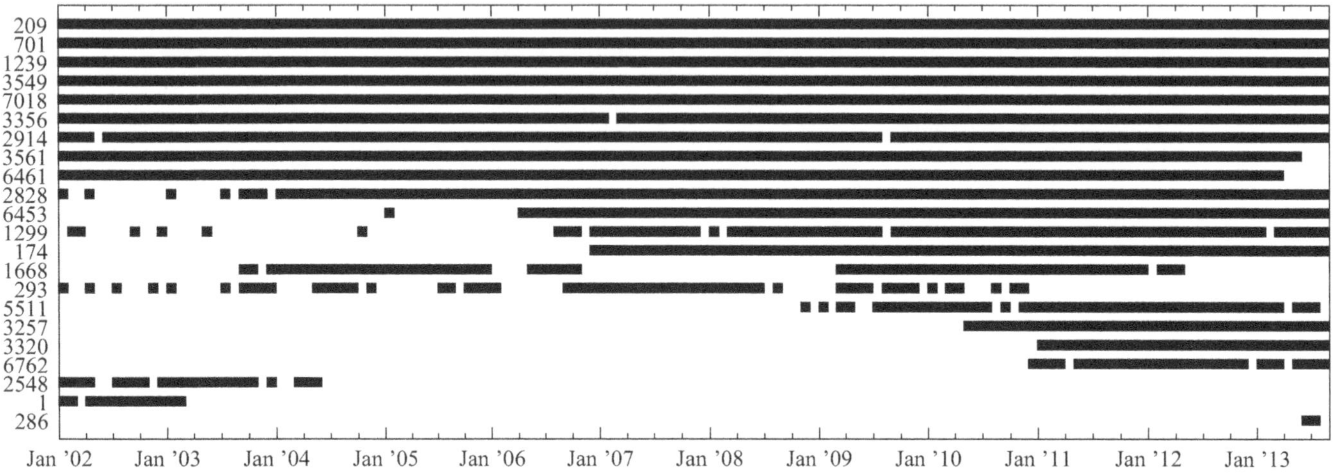

Figure 5: ASes inferred to be in the clique over time. We plot the 22 of the 26 ASes inferred to be in the clique at any time after January 2002. The clique's small size and consistent membership lend confidence in our inference methodology. AS names change over time so we do not label them. As an artifact of the AS3356/AS3549 merger process in 2013, clique member AS6461 was inferred not to be in the clique.

Finally, we discarded all paths from 167.142.3.6 for May and June 2003, and from 198.32.132.97 between March and November 2012; the former reported paths with ASes removed from the middle of the path, and the latter reported paths inferred from traceroute.

4.4 Inferring Clique

We attempt to infer the ASes present at the top of the hierarchy. Since Tier-1 status is a financial circumstance, reflecting lack of settlement payments, we focus on identifying transit-free rather than Tier-1 ASes. First, we use the Bron/Kerbosch algorithm [10] to find the maximal clique C_1 from the AS-links involving the largest ten ASes by transit degree.[1] Second, we test every other AS in order by transit degree to complete the clique. AS Z is added to C_1 if it has links with every other AS in C_1 and it does not appear to receive transit from another member of C_1; i.e. no AS path should have three consecutive clique ASes. Because AS path poisoning may induce three consecutive clique ASes in a false BGP path "X Y Z", we add AS Z to C_1 provided there are no more than five ASes downstream from "X Y Z". A nominal value of five ASes will still capture clique ASes even in paths poisoned multiple times, yet is unlikely to wrongly place a large transit customer in the clique since a clique AS is likely to announce (and we are likely to observe [28]) more than five customers of large transit customers. If an AS would be admitted to C_1 except for a single missing link, we add that AS to C_2. Finally, because an AS might be in C_1 but not in the clique, we re-use the Bron/Kerbosch algorithm to find the largest clique (by transit degree sum) from the AS-links involving ASes in C_1 and C_2. The product of this step is a clique of transit-free ASes.

Figure 5 shows ASes inferred to be in the clique since January 2002. Nine ASes have been in the clique nearly every month, and ASes that are inferred to be in the clique are almost continuously present. The consistency of the inferred clique and our discussions with operators give us confidence in our clique inference methodology. However, peering disputes and mergers of ASes can disrupt our inference of the clique. ASes may form alliances to prevent de-peering incidents from partitioning their customers from the Internet. If such a disconnection incident triggers activation of a backup transit relationship, a peer will disappear from the clique and instead be inferred as a customer of the allied peer. The process of merging ASes can can also result in peers being inferred as customers. For example, in 2013 Level3 (AS3356) gradually shut down BGP sessions established with Global Crossing (AS3549), shifting sessions to AS3356. In order to maintain global connectivity during this merger process, Level3 advertised customers connected to AS3549 to peers that were only connected to AS3356. As a result, ASes in the clique appeared to be customers of AS3356, when in reality they were peers. Specifically, in figure 5, AS6461 was not inferred to be a member of the clique because it had shifted all peering ports with Level3 to AS3356.

[1] Starting with ten ASes reveals most clique ASes and is small enough to prevent the incorrect inference of a clique below the top of the hierarchy. If there are multiple cliques, we select the clique with the largest transit degree sum.

4.5 Inferring Providers, Customers, and Peers

The remainder of the algorithm infers p2c and p2p relationships for all links in the graph. Step 3 infers p2p relationships for the full mesh of links between clique ASes. The rest of this section uses figure 6 as reference.

AS path triplets: We make inferences using only AS path triplets (adjacent pairs of links). Triplets provide the constraints necessary to infer c2p relationships while allowing us to ignore non-hierarchical segments of paths, and are more computationally efficient than paths. For example, in figure 6 we break path 1 into two triplets: "1239 3356 9002" and "3356 9002 6846".

Notation: We use the notation in table 1 to describe relationships between ASes. A p2c relationship between X and Y is presented as "X > Y". The notation reflects providers as typically greater (in degree or size or tier of a traditional hierarchical path) than their customers. A triplet with no inferred relationships is presented as "X ? Y ? Z".

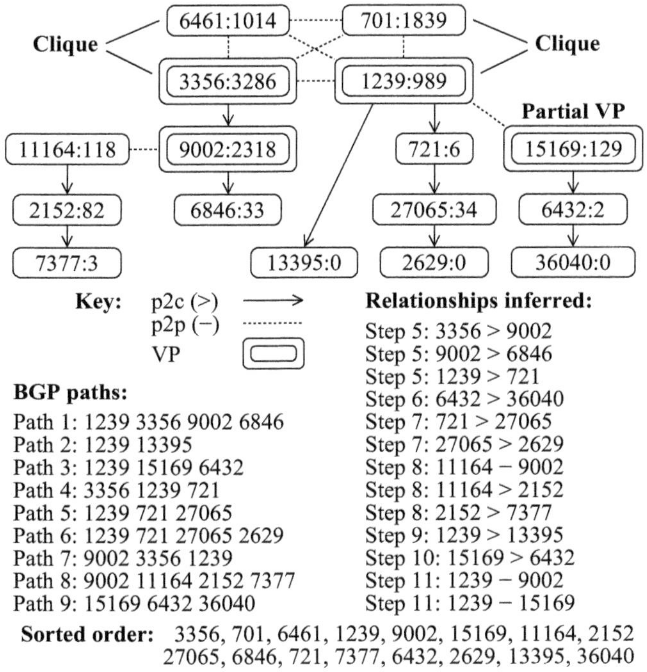

Figure 6: Inferring providers, customers, and peers. Each AS is labeled "AS Number:Transit Degree". VPs are in double squares, and (by definition) on the left side of all raw BGP paths. We use this set of paths to illustrate the inferences made at each step of our algorithm. Relationships listed use notation in Table 1.

Notation	Description
X < Y	X is a customer of Y
X – Y	X is a peer of Y
X ? Y	No inferred relationship

Table 1: Notation used to describe relationships.

Sorting of ASes: We sort ASes in the order we will estimate their c2p relationships. ASes in the clique are placed at the top, followed by all other ASes sorted by transit degree, then by node degree, and finally by AS number to break ties. We sort by transit degree rather than node degree to avoid mistaking high-degree nodes (but not high-transit degree, e.g., content providers) for transit providers. Figure 6 shows the sorted order of the ASes in that graph.

Preventing cycles of p2c links: When we infer a c2p relationship we record the customer AS in the provider's customer cone, and add the AS to the cones of all upstream providers. Any ASes in the customer's cone not in the cones of its upstream providers are also added to the cones of those providers. We do not infer a c2p relationship if the provider is already in the AS's cone, to prevent a cycle of p2c links.

Step 5: Infer c2p relationships top-down using ranking from Step 2. This step infers 90% of all the c2p relationships we infer, and is the simplest of all our steps. We visit ASes top-down, skipping clique ASes since they have no provider relationships. When we visit AS Z, we infer Y > Z if we observe "X – Y ? Z" or "X > Y ? Z". To have observed "X – Y", X and Y must be members of the clique (step 3). To have inferred "X > Y" by now, one must have visited Y in a previous iteration of this step. No cycle of c2p links can be formed because c2p relationships are assigned along the *degree gradient*, i.e. no c2p relationship is inferred between two ASes where the provider has a smaller transit degree, a necessary condition to create a cycle. For example, in figure 6, we first consider (after the four clique ASes) c2p relationships for 9002 (3356), then 15169 (none), etc.

The order of the ASes in the triplet is important, at this step and for most of the remaining steps. To minimize false c2p inferences due to misconfigurations in one direction of a p2p relationship (an AS leaks provider or peer routes to peers), we infer a c2p relationship when we observe the provider or peer closer than the customer to at least one VP in at least one triplet. This heuristic builds on the intuition that an AS enters a provider relationship to become globally reachable, i.e., at least one VP should observe the provider announcing the customer's routes. For example, when we infer 3356 > 9002 in figure 6, we use triplet "1239 3356 9002" from path 1 and not triplet "9002 3356 1239" from path 7 because 3356 appears before 9002 in path 1.

Step 6: Infer c2p relationships from VPs inferred to be announcing no provider routes. We assume that "partial VPs" providing routes to fewer than 2.5% of all ASes either (1) export only customer routes, i.e., the VP has configured the session with the collector as p2p; or (2) have configured the session as p2c, but have a default route to their provider, and export customer and peer routes to the collector. Given a path "X ? Y ? Z" where X is a partial VP and Z is a stub, the link XY can either be p2c or p2p, requiring Y > Z. In figure 6, we use path 9 and the inference of 15169 as a partial VP to infer 6432 > 36040.

Step 7: Infer c2p relationships for ASes where the customer has a larger transit degree. Given a triplet "W > X ? Y" where (1) Y has a larger transit degree than X, and (2) at least one path ended with "W X Y" (i.e. Y originates a prefix to X), then we assign X > Y. We assume c2p relationships against the degree gradient are rare, although they can arise from path poisoning. Condition (2) mitigates the risk of using poisoned paths because poisoned segments of a path do not announce address space. In figure 6 we infer 721 (X) > 27065 (Y) because path 5 shows 27065 announcing a prefix to 721. In the absence of path 5, we would infer that 2629 poisoned path 6 with 27065 and we would not assign a c2p relationship. When we assign X > Y, we also assign Y > Z where we observe triplets "X > Y ? Z"; in figure 6 we use path 6 to infer 27065 > 2629.

Step 8: Infer customers for provider-less ASes. We visit provider-less ASes top-down, skipping clique members because their customers were inferred in step 5. This step is necessary because steps 5 and 7 require an AS to have a provider in order to infer customers. Examples of provider-less ASes are some regional and research networks, e.g., TransitRail. For each provider-less AS X, we visit each of its neighbors W top-down. When we observe triplet "W X Y", we infer W – X because we never observed W announcing X to providers or peers in previous steps; therefore, X > Y. We remove the condition in step 5 that the peer AS must be closest to the VP, because provider-less ASes are mostly observed by downstream customers providing a public BGP view. In figure 6, 11164 (X) is a provider-less AS; we use path 8 to infer 9002 (W) – 11164 (X) and 11164 (X) > 2152 (Y). When we assign X > Y, we also assign Y > Z where we

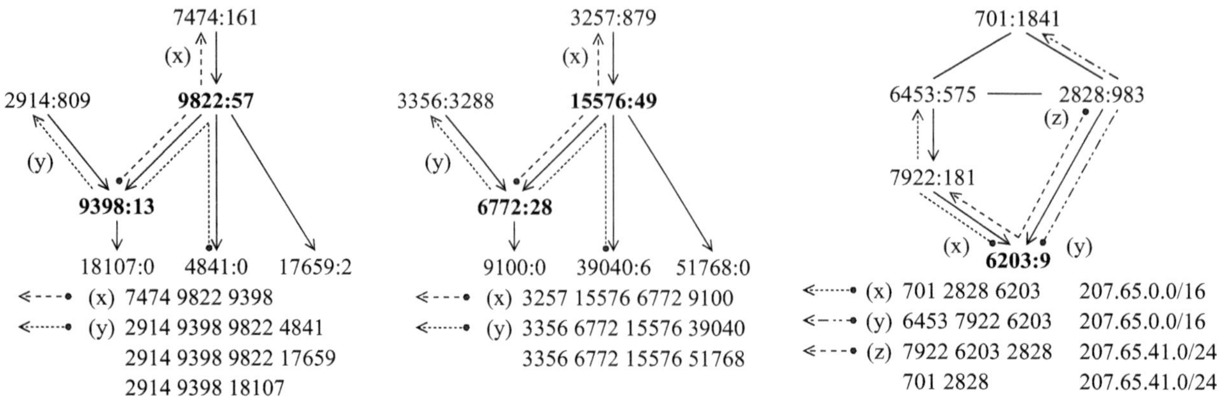

(a) Siblings (9398 and 9822) (b) Mutual Transit (6772 and 15576) (c) Leaking or Poisoning (6203)

Figure 7: p2c-c2p valleys caused by unconventional routing policies between (a) siblings, (b) mutual transit, and (c) leaking/poisoning. Each AS is labeled with its transit degree, which influences the order of p2c inferences. An AS-to-organization map would resolve (a) but not (b) because the ASes in (b) are independent ASes. Leaking as in (c) results in paths with spurious p2c-c2p valleys when an AS leaks a route from a provider to another provider. Note that in (c) AS6203 could instead be poisoning to prevent AS2828 from selecting the more specific route (traffic engineering); we believe (c) to be an example of a prefix-list leak because AS2828 is the only origin AS observed for that prefix. All examples are present in April 2012 BGP data.

observe triplets "X > Y ? Z"; in figure 6 we also use path 8 to infer 2152 (Y) > 7377 (Z).

Step 9: Infer that stub ASes are customers of clique ASes. If there is a link between a stub and a clique AS, we classify it as c2p. This step is necessary because step 5 requires a route between a stub and a clique AS to be observed by another clique AS before the stub is inferred to be a customer. Stub networks are extremely unlikely to meet the peering requirements of clique members, and are most likely customers. In figure 6, path 2 reveals a link between 1239 and 13395, but there is no triplet with that link in the set, perhaps because it is a backup transit relationship.

Step 10: Resolve triplets with adjacent unclassified links. We again traverse ASes top down to try to resolve one link as p2c from triplets with adjacent unclassified links. We do this step to avoid inferring adjacent p2p links in step 11, since adjacent p2p links imply anomalous behavior, e.g., free transit or route leakage. We loosen the requirement in step 5 that the first half of the triplet must be resolved. When we visit Y, we search for *unresolved triplets* of the form "X ? Y ? Z", and attempt to infer Y > Z. For each unresolved triplet "X ? Y ? Z", we look for another triplet "X ? Y < P" for some other P. If we find one, we infer X < Y (and Y will be inferred as a peer of Z in step 11). Otherwise we search for a triplet "Q ? Y ? X", which implies Y > X, and therefore we would resolve both sides of the original unresolved triplet to X < Y and Y > Z. Since we are only confident of resolving one side of the original triplet (embedding an assumption that most p2c links have already been resolved at earlier steps), we make no inferences in this case. Otherwise, we infer Y > Z in this step, and X – Y in step 11.

Step 11: Infer p2p links: We assign p2p relationships for all links that have no inferred relationships.

4.6 Complex Relationships

Sibling Relationships and Mutual Transit: Our algorithm does not infer sibling relationships, where the same organization owns multiple ASes, which can therefore have unconventional export policies involving each sibling's peers, providers, and customers. Similarly, we do not infer mutual transit relationships, where two independent organizations provide transit for each other in a reciprocal arrangement. Both of these arrangements can lead to paths (and triplets) that violate the valley-free property, and in particular produce p2c-c2p valleys in paths. Gao's algorithm [18] inferred that two ASes involved in a non-hierarchical path segment were siblings, which maximizes the number of valley-free paths. Dimitropoulos *et al.* used WHOIS database dumps to infer siblings from ASes with similar organization names, because policy diversity among siblings makes it difficult to infer siblings from BGP data [16]. Our algorithm does not attempt to resolve these unconventional routing policies because it is difficult to accurately classify them; as a result, our algorithm produces p2c-c2p valleys in paths.

Figure 7 provides three examples of non-hierarchical path segments caused by siblings (figure 7(a)), mutual transit (figure 7(b)), and route leaks or path poisoning (figure 7(c)). In figure 7(a), ASes 9398 and 9822 are ASes owned by the same organization, Amcom Telecommunications, which implements complex export policies with these ASes. Specifically, we observe customers of 9822 are exported to 9398's peers and providers, and routes originated by 9398 are exported to 9822's providers. These policies induce a p2c-c2p valley in a path, because we infer 9398 is a customer of both 9822 (path x) and 2914, and observe 9398 to announce customers of its inferred provider 9822 to its other inferred provider (path y). In figure 7(b), independently operated ASes 6772 and 15576 implement mutual transit, owing to complementary traffic profiles: AS6772 is an access provider with mostly inbound traffic, while AS15576 is a content provider, with mostly outbound traffic. A WHOIS-derived database of sibling relationships does not help infer mutual transit arrangements. Finally, route leaks and path poisoning can also result in a p2c-c2p valley in a path. Figure 7(c) provides an example of a route leak from 6203,

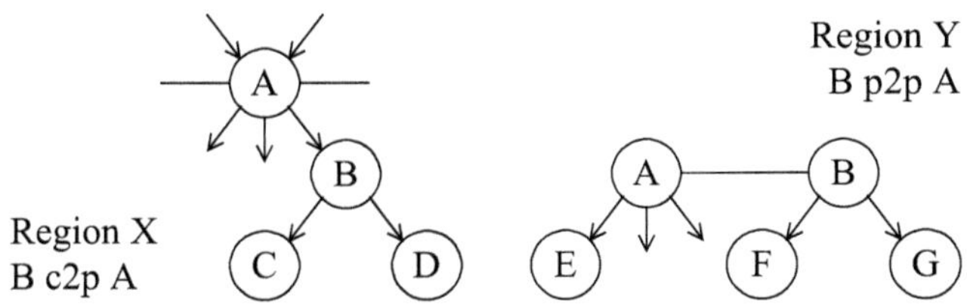

Figure 8: Two ASes may have hybrid relationships. In this example B is a customer of A in region X and B is a peer of A in region Y. However, our algorithm infers a single relationship between B and A: c2p. If A routes rationally, it will only advertise paths to F and G from B to customers.

where it provides transit to a /24 prefix announced by one of its providers (AS2828) to another provider (AS7922). The prefix AS2828 announces is a more specific prefix of a /16 prefix that AS6203 announces, and has likely leaked because of a prefix list configured in AS6203. An alternative explanation is that AS6203 is poisoning that path so that AS2828 cannot select the more specific prefix. We believe a route leak is the more plausible explanation because AS2828 is the only AS to originate the prefix. Without the use of prefixes, it is not possible to distinguish this valley from mutual transit or siblings. We do not currently use prefixes in our inference algorithm; detecting and validating route leaks and path poisoning remains an open problem.

We used sibling inferences derived from WHOIS database dumps [25] to evaluate how the sibling links in our topology were classified. We did not use these sibling inferences in our algorithm because (1) we did not have supporting WHOIS databases going back to 1998, (2) in validation the sibling inferences contained a significant number of false-positives (where two ASes were falsely inferred to belong to an organization), and (3) they do not help distinguish mutual transit between independent ASes from other anomalies such as path poisoning and route leaks. In total, there were 4537 links observed between inferred siblings for April 2012; we inferred 4238 (93%) of these to be p2c. Because we inferred most of the siblings to have p2c relationships (i.e. a transit hierarchy) we also used the sibling inferences to examine if the ordering of ASes in paths supported the classification. Of the 312 organizations for which we observe at least two siblings in a path, 275 (88%) had a strict ordering; i.e. AS x was always observed in a path before sibling AS y. For example, we observed 21 Comcast sibling ASes in BGP paths with at least two siblings present; all of these ASes were connected beneath AS7922. It is possible that Comcast's siblings exported routes received from their peers (if any) to other siblings. However, we did not see any peer links from beneath AS7922 (perhaps due to limited visibility), and it would make more engineering sense to share peer routes among siblings by connecting the peer to AS7922.

Partial Transit, Hybrid Relationships, and Traffic Engineering: Our algorithm infers either a p2p or c2p relationship for all links. A partial transit relationship typically restricts the propagation (and visibility) of routes beyond a provider to the provider's peers and customers. Similarly, complex import and export policies can produce hybrid relationships [27]. Figure 8 depicts an AS pair with a c2p relationship in one region, and a p2p relationship elsewhere. Because publicly available BGP data only includes the best paths announced from each AS, there is no way to distinguish hybrid relationships from traffic engineering practices such as load balancing across providers. Similarly, ASes A and B may enter into a p2p relationship, but B may not advertise all customers or prefixes to A, requiring A to reach those via a provider. We consider hybrid relationships and traffic engineering when computing the customer cone of each AS, which we describe in section 5. Modeling routing policies remains an open problem [27].

The presence of hybrid relationships can cause our algorithm to incorrectly infer a c2p link as a p2p link. In figure 8, if we observe no providers of A announcing routes to E via A then our algorithm infers the c2p link between A and E as p2p. This inference occurs because step 10 collapses triplets with no relationships inferred for either link; i.e., it does not adjust the triplet "E ? A > B". A separate step is necessary to distinguish partial transit relationships visible from a VP below the provider from peering relationships.

Paid Peering: An assumption behind c2p and p2p relationships is that the customer pays the provider and p2p relationships are settlement-free, as historically p2p relationships were viewed as mutually beneficial. Modern business relationships in the Internet are more complicated; ASes may enter into a paid-peering arrangement where an AS pays settlements for access to customer routes only. Multiple network operators confirmed several aspects of paid-peering: (1) approximately half of the ASes in the clique (figure 5) were paid-peers of at least one other AS in the clique as of June 2012; (2) paid-peering occurs between ASes at lower-levels of the AS topology; and (3) routes from paying and settlement-free peers have the same route preference. This last condition prevents us from distinguishing paid-peering from settlement-free peering using BGP data alone.

Backup Transit: A backup transit relationship occurs when a customer's export policies prevent their routes from being exported outside a provider's customer networks. The export policies used while the provider is in backup configuration are identical to peering; the difference between backup transit and paid peering is due to export filters instead of a contractual agreement. Our algorithm infers most backup transit relationships as peering.

4.7 Validation

In this section we evaluate the positive predictive value (PPV) and true positive rate (TPR, or *recall*) of our heuristics against our validation dataset (section 3.6). Our AS relationships dataset consists of 126,082 links; we validated 43,613 (34.6%) of these. Table 2 shows the PPV of inferences made at each step of our algorithm. Most relationship inferences are made in steps 5 (56.4%) and 11 (37.7%), and both of these stages have excellent PPV (99.8% and 98.7%).

Table 3 compares the PPV of our inferences and those made by four other popular inference algorithms for April 2012 BGP paths. Our algorithm correctly infers 99.6% of c2p relationships and 98.7% of p2p relationships. We asked the authors of SARK [34], CSP [27], and ND-ToR [33] for the source code for their algorithm, or for a set of relationships inferred from April 2012 BGP paths; we did not receive either. Gao's PPV for p2p relationships is the highest of the algorithms tested because it makes the fewest number of p2p inferences of all the algorithms, inferring many more c2p relationships than exist in the graph. The algorithm that per-

Step	Description	Validation (PPV)	Fraction
3	clique at top of AS topology	136 p2p @ 100%	153 (0.12%)
5	**c2p relationships top-down**	26664 c2p @ 99.8%	**71160 (56.4%)**
6	c2p relationships from VPs announcing no provider routes	116 c2p @ 99.1%	532 (0.42%)
7	c2p relationships to smaller degree providers	205 c2p @ 96.1%	2420 (1.92%)
8	relationships for ASes with no providers	120 c2p @ 93.3%	842 (0.67%)
		152 p2p @ 96.7%	333 (0.26%)
9	c2p relationships for stub-clique	422 c2p @ 95.0%	651 (0.52%)
10	collapse adjacent links with no relationships	524 c2p @ 94.7%	2474 (1.96%)
11	**p2p relationships for all other links**	15274 p2p @ 98.7%	**47517 (37.7%)**
		43613 @ 99.3%	126082 (100%)

Table 2: Validation of inferences (PPV) and number/fraction of inferences made at each step.

Algorithm	c2p PPV (%)	c2p TPR (%)	c2p Errs (1/)	p2p PPV (%)	p2p TPR (%)	p2p Errs (1/)
CAIDA	99.6	99.3	250	98.7	99.3	77
UCLA	99.0	94.7	100	91.7	98.8	12
Xia+Gao	91.3	98.6	11	96.6	81.1	29
Isolario	90.3	98.0	10	96.0	82.4	25
Gao	82.9	99.8	5.8	99.5	62.5	200

Table 3: Our AS relationship algorithm accurately classifies both c2p and p2p relationships, with high precision (PPV) and recall (TPR).

forms closest to ours is UCLA's; our improvements result in six times fewer false peering inferences. We assembled additional historical validation datasets by extracting relationships from archives of the RIPE WHOIS database (RPSL, section 3.4) and public BGP repositories (BGP communities, section 3.5) at six month intervals between February 2006 and April 2012. The validation performance of Gao, UCLA, and CAIDA algorithms are quantitatively similar as shown in table 3.

We investigated the types of errors that these four algorithms produce, focusing on the two cases with significant occurrence: where we correctly infer c2p (p2p), but another algorithm mistakenly infers p2p (c2p). We note that when the ground truth is p2p, Gao often infers the link as c2p, usually with the customer having a smaller degree than the provider. On the other hand, UCLA and Isolario produce errors where a p2p link is inferred to be c2p, often with the customer having a larger degree than the provider. The UCLA algorithm often infers c2p links to be p2p because it uses the visibility of a link from tier-1 VPs to draw inferences, and defaults to a p2p inference for links it cannot see (see section 2). We agree with the intuition behind this visibility heuristic and use a variant of it in our algorithm, but we use additional heuristics to accommodate for phenomena that inhibit visibility through tier-1 VPs, e.g., traffic engineering, selective announcements.

We compared our inferences with 82 partial transit relationships that were flagged by a community string. Our algorithm correctly inferred 69 (84%) of them as p2c; 66 p2c inferences where made in step 10. In comparison, UCLA's dataset identified only 13 (16%) of the partial transit relationships as p2c. We also compared our inferences against a small set of 27 backup p2c relationships, of which only 2 were correctly identified as p2c. Validation data for partial and backup transit relationships is scarce because of their rarity and their limited visibility.

It is well-known that the public view misses a large number of peering links [6]. While our algorithm can only make inferences for links we observe, an important question is whether its accuracy is affected by a lack of (or increasing) visibility. We performed the following experiment 10 times. We start with paths selected from a random set of 25% of VPs, and successively add VPs to obtain topologies seen from 50%, 75% and all VPs. We measure the PPV of our inferences on each topology subset. We found that the PPV of c2p inferences was consistently between 99.4% and 99.7% on all topology subsets. We found that the PPV of p2p links varied between 94.6% and 97.7% with 25% of VPs, and 97.2% and 98.4% with 50% of VPs, indicating that our algorithm performs better when it has more data (VPs) available. Consequently, if our visibility of the AS topology increases in the future (e.g., due to new VPs at IXPs), the accuracy of our algorithm at inferring the newly visible links should not be affected.

We agree that collecting validation data is difficult and time-consuming [9, 16, 18, 34] because the relationships are considered confidential and often covered by a non-disclosure agreements, but we gathered validation data from multiple sources that represent more than a third of the publicly available graph. The previous most validated work was Dimitropoulos *et al.* [16], which validated 9.7% of inferences.

5. CUSTOMER CONES

In this section, we use our AS relationship inferences to construct the *customer cone* of each AS. The customer cone is defined as the ASes that a given AS can reach using a customer (p2c) link, as well as customers of those customers (indirect customers). An AS is likely to select a path advertised by a customer (if available) over paths advertised by peers and providers because the AS is paid for forwarding the traffic. The most profitable traffic for an AS is traffic forwarded between customers, as the AS is paid by both.

The customer cone is a metric of influence, but not necessarily of market power. Market power requires the ability to restrict the mobility of customers; in general, an AS can enter into a provider relationship with whoever offers a suitable service. For large transit providers, particularly those in the clique where a full p2p mesh is required for global connectivity, the customer cone defines the set of ASes whose service might be disrupted if the AS were to have operational difficulty. We compare three algorithms to infer an AS's customer cone, and reason why one construction is the most realistic. We discuss the effect of topology flattening on the utility of the customer cone metric, and use our inferences to show how the Internet has flattened from an inter-domain routing perspective.

5.1 Algorithms to compute the customer cone

Due to ambiguities inherent in BGP data analysis, there are multiple methods to infer the customer cone of a given AS. We compare three methods: recursively inferred, BGP observed, and provider/peer observed. All three methods infer the set of ASes that can be reached from a given AS following only p2c links, and the three methods infer the same customer cone for nearly all but the largest ASes.

Recursive: the customer cone of an AS A is computed by recursively visiting each AS reachable from A by p2c links. For example, if B is a customer of A, and C is a customer of B, then A's customer cone includes B and C. Some prior work has defined and used the recursive customer cone (e.g. [15,16]), but this definition unrealistically assumes that a provider will receive all of its customers' routes, and thus be able to reach them following a customer link. This definition can thus distort the size of a customer cone.

BGP observed: given a set of relationships and corresponding BGP paths, C is included in A's customer cone if we observe a BGP path where C is reached following a sequence of p2c links from A. This method addresses two problems of the recursive method. First, A may provide transit for some prefixes belonging to B, but not for B's customers; the BGP observed method will not recursively include customers of B in A's cone that are never announced to A. Second, the error induced by hybrid relationships is reduced because an AS should not announce prefixes received from the peer segment of the hybrid relationship to providers; in figure 8, A's providers will not include E and F in their customer cone unless they receive routes to those ASes from another customer, though A's cone will include those ASes. The main limitations of the BGP observed cone method are: (1) the customer cones of ASes with hybrid relationships will still include customers of peers, and (2) the customer cones of ASes that provide a VP are more likely to be complete and therefore larger as an artifact of the collection apparatus.

Provider/Peer observed: given a set of relationships and corresponding BGP paths, we compute the customer cone of A using routes observed from providers and peers of A. This method addresses the two limitations of the BGP observed method: because A will not announce paths received from the peering portion of a hybrid relationship with AS B to providers and peers, we will not include customers of B observed from the peering portion in the customer cone of AS A. Similarly, because the customer cone of A is computed based on what neighbors of A announce, the presence of a VP at A will no longer inflate A's customer cone relative to ASes that do not provide a VP. The limitation of the provider/peer observed method is that we are only able to view best paths, rather than all paths, so we may underestimate the customer cones of some ASes.

5.2 Evaluation

Table 4 displays the customer cone sizes of the 15 largest ASes as a percentage of all ASes in the graph using the three methods, as well as their rank order. The rank order is largely independent of the method used to compute the customer cone; for example, the same seven ASes are the largest seven ASes computed with all algorithms. But the table also shows that the recursive cone is significantly larger than the BGP observed cone – for nine of the fifteen ASes shown in Table 4, the recursively defined customer cone is at least twice the size. We found significant incongruity between the customer cones constructed for ASes for which there is also a VP; for example, AS3356 only reaches 60-76% of the ASes in its recursively-defined customer cone over a p2c link. This incongruity makes the recursive method less realistic than the two alternatives we describe.

ASN	VP	PP Obs.	BGP Obs.	Recursive
3356	⋆	46.8 (1)	59.1 (1)	78.0 (1)
3549	⋆	45.2 (2)	54.2 (2)	72.3 (2)
3257	⋆	32.6 (3)	33.8 (5)	59.3 (5)
174		31.1 (4)	39.9 (4)	65.1 (3)
1299	⋆	29.3 (5)	40.0 (3)	64.6 (4)
2914	⋆	24.6 (6)	29.8 (6)	57.4 (6)
6453	⋆	18.9 (7)	28.1 (7)	55.8 (7)
6762	⋆	16.9 (8)	18.5 (9)	44.5 (11)
1239	⋆	15.2 (9)	21.0 (8)	51.0 (8)
3491		13.8 (10)	13.9 (12)	32.1 (13)
701	⋆	12.0 (11)	18.2 (10)	47.4 (9)
2828		11.3 (12)	11.4 (13)	45.7 (10)
7018	⋆	10.2 (13)	15.3 (11)	43.7 (12)
1273		8.4 (14)	8.4 (14)	26.7 (14)
6939	⋆	8.1 (15)	8.3 (15)	18.6 (15)

Table 4: For April 2012, the fifteen largest ASes by provider/peer observed customer cone size, their customer cone sizes inferred with recursive and BGP observed algorithms, and their rank by customer cone size. The size of each AS varies significantly, but their ranks are similar.

The BGP observed cone is often larger than the provider/peer observed customer cone for large ASes. There are three exceptions in table 4: ASes 1273, 2828 and 3491, none of which provide a VP. AS174's BGP observed cone is larger than its provider/peer observed cone despite not providing a VP, because one of its customers does. The provider/peer observed method avoids over-inflating ASes that provide a VP relative to ASes that do not, as an AS relies on peers and providers selecting their routes and those routes being observed by a VP to reveal the AS's entire customer cone.

Figure 9 shows the customer cone sizes of ASes that were in the top three (by customer cone size) at any point over the past eleven years, computed using BGP observed and provider/peer observed algorithms. BGP observed cones (figure 9(a)) have spikes that coincide with views of some peering routes received from neighbors with whom the AS has a hybrid relationship. In particular, AS1239's customer cone is consistently larger between October 2009 and May 2010 because a customer provided a view of the routes advertised by AS1239's peer. The provider/peer observed cones (figure 9(b)) have fewer such spikes because these peer routes were not advertised to other peers. A notable exception is AS1239's customer cone between June and December 2006, which corresponds incorrect inference of backup provider links as peer links due to an adjacent hybrid relationship (see section 4.6). In figure 8, if our algorithm incorrectly infers the c2p link between E and A as p2p, it will also infer that F and G are in A's customer cone. The provider/peer

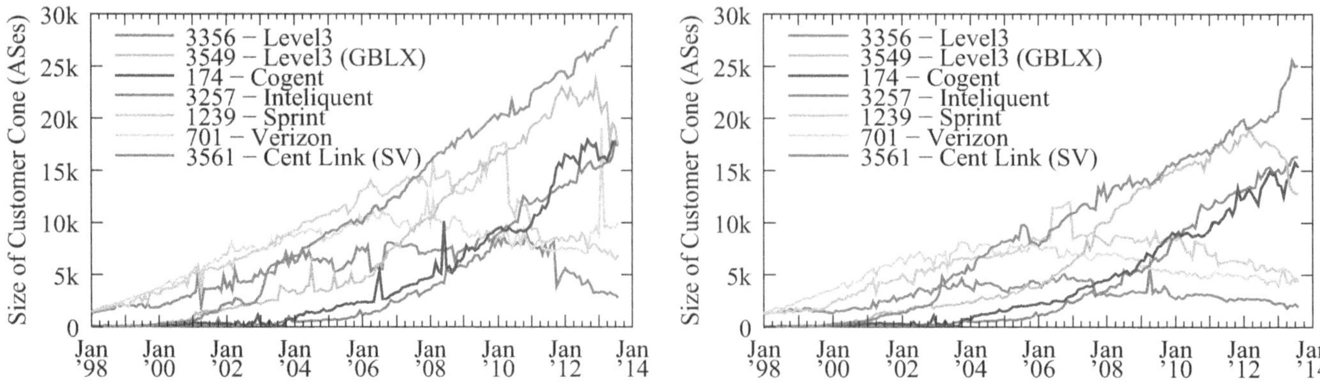

(a) BGP observed customer cone (b) Provider/peer observed customer cone

Figure 9: The size of the customer cones using BGP observed and provider/peer observed algorithms for the seven ASes that were among the three largest ASes between Jan. 1998 and Aug. 2013. The three largest ASes in Jan. 1998 (701, 1239, and 3561) are no longer in the top three. The BGP observed cone has several spikes, including a six-month spike for AS1239 between Oct. 2009 and May 2010 that is not present in the provider/peer observed cone. We believe the provider/peer observed customer cone is the more realistic customer cone method.

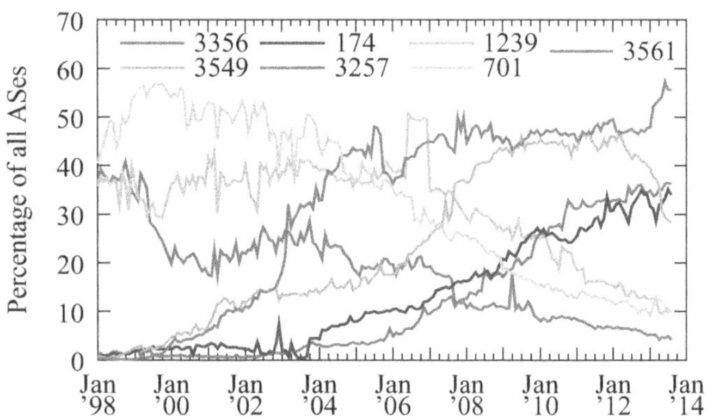

Figure 10: Relative size of provider/peer observed cone over time. 701 acquired part of 3561 in 1999 and moved customers across.

observed cone seems to be the most robust methodology available to infer AS customer cones provided a customer link is not mistakenly inferred as a peer link.

5.3 Customer cone over time

Figure 9(b) plots the seven ASes that ranked in the top three ASes by provider/peer observed customer cone size at any point from January 1998. We can observe several interesting trends with just these seven ASes. First, the three ASes ranked in the top three for January 1998 (ASes 701, 1239, and 3561) are no longer in the top three. In absolute terms, the customer cone of 701 decreased in size between January 2002 and October 2012. The customer cone of 3356 reflects two other interesting events: (1) in early 2003, AS1 (Genuity/BBN) merged with 3356 to create the third largest network at the time, and (2) in late 2010, 3549 (the second largest AS by customer cone) was purchased by Level3 (the largest AS by customer cone). 3549's customer cone has since shrunk as new customers connect to 3356 and some of 3549's customers moved across.

Figure 10 plots the customer cone sizes for the same seven ASes, but as a fraction of the topology size. We see: (1) ASes 701, 1239, and 3561 all had the same customer cone size in January 1998, (2) some customers of 3561 (MCI) shifted into 701 (Worldcom) due to the MCI-Worldcom merger in 1998, (3) 1239 held a third of the ASes in its customer cone for ten years until 2008, and (4) while 3356 had the largest customer cone in 2012, its relative cone size, i.e., as a fraction of the entire AS topology, was slightly smaller than AS701's was in January 2000. This last fact reflects massive growth in the Internet's AS topology since 2000, in addition to the consolidation undertaken by both ASes, yielding the largest customer cones of the two respective decades.

Since most companies providing Internet transit are by now also in other lines of business and do not report financial information specific to their transit business, we cannot correlate BGP consolidation with financial performance. But we know that of the three ASes whose relative customer cone sizes have plummeted in the last decade (701, 1239, 3561), two of them (Verizon and Sprint) have moved into more profitable cellular service.

Renesys produces market intelligence data using the customer cone notion [31]. They declined to share their data or method with us to enable a comparison because it is core to one of their commercial products. Comparing our rank order in table 4 with their "Bakers Dozen" from 2012 [30] shows minor differences in rank order.

5.4 Topology Flattening

The introduction of CDNs and richer peering has resulted in a flattening of the Internet topology [20, 26] where ASes avoid sending traffic via transit providers. An intriguing question is how valid is the customer cone in a flattened Internet topology? How many paths still travel to the top of a given cone to reach destinations?

We develop a new metric to track this potential shift in routing behavior as flattening occurs. While public BGP data contains a small fraction of all peering links [6] we can study shifts in routing behavior from the paths of individual

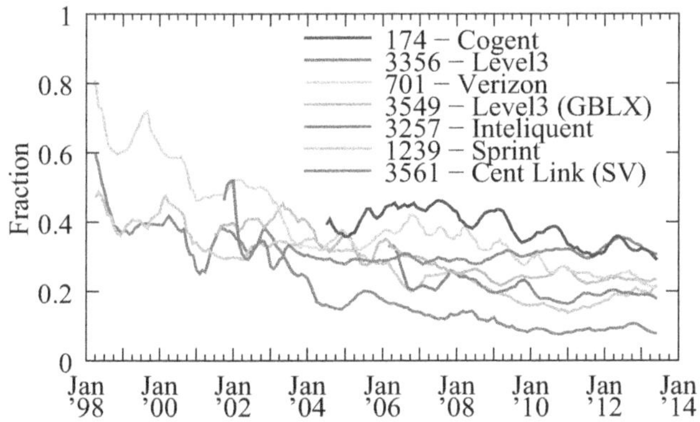

Figure 11: Fraction of ASes in X's customer cone that were reached via X from an AS in X's customer cone over time. Most ASes show a decline in the fraction of cone-internal paths.

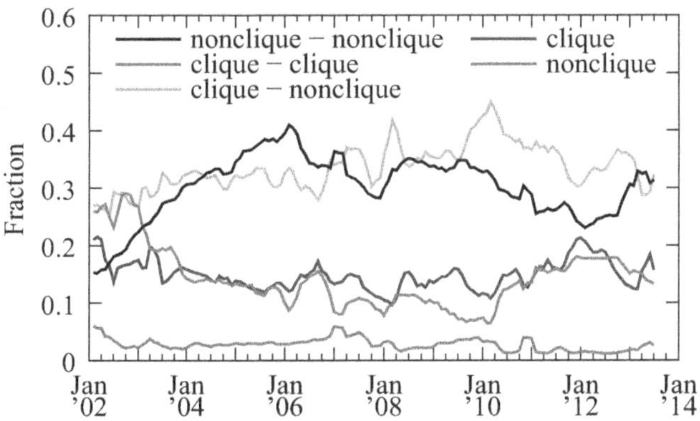

Figure 12: Characteristics of nodes or links at top of each path. The fraction of paths crossing a nonclique peering link peaked in January 2006.

VPs because they reveal the peering links they use. For each VP that provides a full view to RV or RIS and is also in X's customer cone, we compute the fraction of *cone-internal* paths, i.e., fraction of paths from that VP that transit X (the cone's top provider) when reaching another AS in X's cone which is not also in the customer cone of the VP. Figure 11 shows the five-month moving average of this fraction for the seven ASes once they have at least 1000 ASes in their cone. Five of these networks show a steady decline in the fraction of cone-internal paths.

To explore this decline in the use of these top (clique) providers to transit traffic, we evaluate the topological characteristics of top links of each path. Figure 12 plots the fraction of nodes or links in each topological category since 2002, for a set of seven VPs that consistently provided a public view.[2] Between 2002 and 2006 the fraction of paths where the top link was a peering link between two non-clique ASes rose from 15% to 40% of paths, while the fraction of paths where the top link was a peering link between two clique ASes fell from 30% to 10% of paths in 2009. Since 2006, the fraction of observed paths crossing a peering link between a clique AS and a lower-tier AS has increased, while the fraction of paths using a non-clique peering link has dropped. Considering all paths using clique ASes to reach destinations (clique-nonclique links, clique-clique links, or clique nodes at the top of paths), over 80% of paths used some clique AS back in 2002, bottoming out in 2006 (just above 60%), followed by a slow rise back to 77% today. This trend reversal is perhaps a result of Tier-1 ASes adjusting peering strategies as a reaction to ASes peering below the clique (so-called *donut peering*) to recover some transit revenue.

Our AS relationship inferences also shed light on the continually increasing richness of peering in the Internet. As the number of full VPs has increased an order of magnitude since 2000 (from 12 to 125 in October 2012), the number of p2p links observable from these VPs jumped by two orders of magnitude (from about 1K to 52K), and increased as a fraction of the entire graph from 10% (in 2000) to 38%. (even after the number of full VPs stabilized in 2008). This increase in peering (flattening) was not observed by individual VPs, most (75%) of which experienced almost no change in the *fraction* of links inferred as p2p. Instead, the increase in relative presence of p2p links in the graph is due to individual VPs seeing more unique p2p links.

6. SUMMARY AND FUTURE WORK

We have presented, and validated to an unprecedented level, a new algorithm for inferring AS relationships using publicly available BGP data. Our algorithm tolerates prevalent phenomena that previous algorithms did not handle. We validated 34.6% of our relationship inferences, finding our c2p and p2p inferences to be 99.6% and 98.7% accurate, respectively. Since even different sources of our validation data disagree by 1%, our algorithm reaches the limit of accuracy achievable with available data. We have published 97% of the validation data set, the relationship inference code, and inferred relationships publicly at `http://www.caida.org/publications/papers/2013/asrank/`

Analysis of the Internet at the AS granularity is inherently challenged by measurement and inference in a dynamic complex network. A known concern is that public views of the AS topology capture only a fraction of the p2p ecosystem, since so few ASes share their full view of the Internet with BGP data repositories. Another challenge is the variety of complex peering relationships that exist, which may be possible to infer by adapting our algorithm or incorporating additional data from either the control or data plane. Meanwhile, we have derived techniques to mitigate the effects of such relationships on application of relationship inferences.

Our inferences shed new light on the flattening Internet topology, revealing a decline in the fraction of observed paths traversing top-level (clique) ASes from 2002 (over 80%) bottoming out in 2006 (just above 60%), followed by a slow rise back to 77% today, perhaps as these clique ASes adjust their peering strategies to try to recover some transit revenue. Our customer cone metric reveals other interesting aspects of Internet evolution: the largest customer cone in the Internet has rarely had more than half of the routed ASes in it. In 2000, AS701 had a customer cone that contained half of the active ASes, and today AS3356's cone has half of the active ASes. An area of future research would be to explore the predictive capabilities of customer-cone-related metrics on Internet evolution and dynamics, such as characteristics that correlate with an impending switch from a c2p to a p2p relationship.

[2] ASes 513, 1103, 1221, 2497, 3333, 4608, and 4777.

Acknowledgments

We thank the numerous operators who contacted us with validation data and candidly discussed aspects of their network's operations. We thank Robert Beverly, David Clark, Xenofontas Dimitropoulos, Dimitri Krioukov, and Olaf Maennel for their feedback on an earlier version of this paper. We also thank the anonymous reviewers and Ethan Katz-Bassett for their feedback. The work was supported by the National Science Foundation under grants CNS-0958547 and CNS-1017064, and by the U.S. Department of Homeland Security (DHS) Science and Technology (S&T) Directorate Cyber Security Division (DHS S&T/CSD) BAA 11-02 and SPAWAR Systems Center Pacific via contract number N66001-12-C-0130. This material represents the position of the author(s) and not necessarily that of NSF or DHS.

7. REFERENCES

[1] AS Rank Website. `http://as-rank.caida.org/`.

[2] Autonomous System (AS) Numbers. `http://www.iana.org/assignments/as-numbers/as-numbers.xml`.

[3] Internet Topology Collection. `http://irl.cs.ucla.edu/topology/`.

[4] RIPE (RIS). `http://www.ripe.net/ris/`.

[5] U. Oregon Route Views Project. `http://www.routeviews.org/`.

[6] B. Ager, N. Chatzis, A. Feldmann, N. Sarrar, S. Uhlig, and W. Willinger. Anatomy of a Large European IXP. In *ACM SIGCOMM*, 2012.

[7] C. Alaettinoglu, C. Villamizar, E. Gerich, D. Kessens, D. Meyer, T. Bates, D. Karrenberg, and M. Terpstra. Routing policy specification language (RPSL), 1999.

[8] B. Augustin, B. Krishnamurthy, and W. Willinger. IXPs: Mapped? In *ACM SIGCOMM IMC*, 2009.

[9] G. D. Battista, T. Erlebach, A. Hall, M. Patrignani, M. Pizzonia, and T. Schank. Computing the Types of the Relationships Between Autonomous Systems. *IEEE/ACM Transactions on Networking*, 2007.

[10] C. Bron and J. Kerbosch. Algorithm 457: Finding All Cliques of an Undirected Graph. *CACM*, 1973.

[11] R. Chandra, P. Traina, and T. Li. BGP Communities Attribute, 1996.

[12] K. Chen, D. R. Choffnes, R. Potharaju, Y. Chen, F. E. Bustamante, D. Pei, and Y. Zhao. Where the Sidewalk Ends: Extending the Internet AS Graph Using Traceroutes from P2P Users. In *ACM CoNEXT*, 2009.

[13] A. Dhamdhere and C. Dovrolis. The Internet is Flat: Modeling the Transition from a Transit Hierarchy to a Peering Mesh. In *ACM CoNEXT*, Dec 2010.

[14] A. Dhamdhere and C. Dovrolis. Twelve Years in the Evolution of the Internet Ecosystem. *IEEE/ACM Transactions on Networking*, 2011.

[15] A. D'Ignazio and E. Giovannetti. Antitrust Analysis for the Internet Upstream Market: a Border Gateway Protocol Approach. *Journal Of Competition, Law and Economics*, 2006.

[16] X. Dimitropoulos, D. Krioukov, M. Fomenkov, B. Huffaker, Y. Hyun, and kc claffy. AS Relationships: Inference and Validation. *CCR*, 2007.

[17] P. Faratin, D. Clark, S. Bauer, W. Lehr, P. Gilmore, and A. Berger. The Growing Complexity of Internet Interconnection. *Communications and Strategies*, 2008.

[18] L. Gao. On Inferring Autonomous System Relationships in the Internet. *IEEE/ACM Transactions on Networking*, 2001.

[19] L. Gao and J. Rexford. Stable Internet Routing Without Global Coordination. *IEEE/ACM Transactions on Networking*, 2001.

[20] P. Gill, M. Arlitt, Z. Li, and A. Mahanti. The flattening Internet topology: Natural evolution, unsightly barnacles or contrived collapse? In *PAM*, 2008.

[21] P. Gill, M. Schapira, and S. Goldberg. Let the Market Drive Deployment: A Strategy for Transitioning to BGP Security. In *ACM SIGCOMM*, 2011.

[22] V. Giotsas and S. Zhou. Valley-free Violation in Internet Routing - Analysis Based on BGP Community Data. In *IEEE ICC*, 2012.

[23] E. Gregori, A. Improta, L. Lenzini, L. Rossi, and L. Sani. BGP and Inter-AS Economic Relationships. In *IFIP Networking*, 2011.

[24] G. Huston. Exploring Autonomous System Numbers. *The Internet Protocol Journal*, 2006.

[25] K. Keys and B. Huffaker. Mapping autonomous systems to organizations: CAIDA's inference methodology.

[26] C. Labovitz, S. Iekel-Johnson, D. McPherson, J. Oberheide, and F. Jahanian. Internet inter-domain traffic. In *ACM SIGCOMM*, 2010.

[27] W. Mühlbauer, S. Uhlig, B. Fu, M. Meulle, and O. Maennel. In Search for an Appropriate Granularity to Model Routing Policies. In *ACM SIGCOMM*, 2007.

[28] R. Oliveira, D. Pei, W. Willinger, B. Zhang, and L. Zhang. In search of the elusive ground truth: the Internet's AS-level connectivity structure. In *ACM SIGMETRICS*, June 2008.

[29] R. Oliveria, D. Pei, W. Willinger, B. Zhang, and L. Zhang. Quantifying the Completeness of the Observed Internet AS-level Structure. Technical Report TR-080026-2008, UCLA CS Dept., 2008.

[30] Renesys. A baker's dozen, 2012 edition. `http://www.renesys.com/blog/2013/01/a-bakers-dozen-2012-edition.shtml`.

[31] Renesys. Rankings, damned rankings, and statistics. `http://www.renesys.com/tech/presentations/pdf/menog2.pdf`.

[32] M. Roughan, W. Willinger, O. Maennel, D. Perouli, and R. Bush. 10 lessons from 10 years of measuring and modeling the Internet's autonomous systems. *JSAC*, 2011.

[33] Y. Shavitt, E. Shir, and U. Weinsberg. Near-Deterministic Inference of AS Relationships. In *ConTel*, 2009.

[34] L. Subramanian, S. Agarwal, J. Rexford, and R. H. Katz. Characterizing the Internet Hierarchy from Multiple Vantage Points. *IEEE INFOCOM*, 2002.

[35] Q. Vohra and E. Chen. BGP Support for Four-octet AS Number Space, 2007.

[36] J. Xia and L. Gao. On the evaluation of AS relationship inferences. In *IEEE Globecom*, 2004.

[37] B. Zhang, R. Liu, D. Massey, and L. Zhang. Collecting the Internet AS-level Topology. *CCR*, 2005.

RILAnalyzer: a Comprehensive 3G Monitor On Your Phone

Narseo Vallina-Rodriguez*
ICSI
narseo@icsi.berkeley.edu

Andrius Aucinas
Computer Laboratory
University of Cambridge
andrius.aucinas@cl.cam.ac.uk

Mario Almeida
Telefonica Research
4knahs@gmail.com

Yan Grunenberger
Telefonica Research
yan@tid.es

Konstantina Papagiannaki
Telefonica Research
dina@tid.es

Jon Crowcroft
Computer Laboratory
University of Cambridge
jon.crowcroft@cl.cam.ac.uk

ABSTRACT

The popularity of smartphones, cloud computing, and the app store model have led to cellular networks being used in a completely different way than what they were designed for. As a consequence, mobile applications impose new challenges in the design and efficient configuration of constrained networks to maximize application's performance. Such difficulties are largely caused by the lack of cross-layer understanding of interactions between different entities - applications, devices, the network and its management plane. In this paper, we describe RILAnalyzer, an open-source tool that provides mechanisms to perform network analysis from within a mobile device. RILAnalyzer is capable of recording low-level radio information and accurate cellular network control-plane data, as well as user-plane data. We demonstrate how such data can be used to identify previously overlooked issues. Through a small user study across four cellular network providers in two European countries we infer how different network configurations are in reality and explore how such configurations interact with application logic, causing network and energy overheads.

Categories and Subject Descriptors

C.2.3 [**Computer-communication networks**]: Network OperationsNetwork Monitoring

General Terms

Design, Measurement, Performance

Keywords

Energy, Mobile, Radio, Cellular, Networks, RNC

*This work was done while the author was a PhD student at the University of Cambridge.

IMC'13, October 23–25, 2013, Barcelona, Spain.
Copyright 2013 ACM 978-1-4503-1953-9/13/10 ...$15.00.
http://dx.doi.org/10.1145/2504730.2504764.

1. INTRODUCTION

The success of mobile apps has exposed new issues for end-users (battery life, erratic connectivity), and network providers (coverage and dynamic load management) that were not initially expected on its design. As opposed to wired and WiFi networks, cellular networks have clearly separated control-plane for signaling traffic and user-plane for user traffic respectively. Unfortunately, as previous research has revealed [1,2], the control plane directly impacts on user plane performance and vice-versa.

The way applications use the network affect its control-plane by increasing signaling traffic. The effects also depend on the network configuration. On one hand, the goal is to minimize the network load and improve spectrum efficiency. On the other hand, inappropriate network configurations can decrease the battery life of the handset and increase its communication latency. The two factors are not orthogonal and it is necessary to take into account both the way applications use the network (i.e. user plane) as well as the way network configuration affects applications (i.e. control plane) to alleviate network and energy inefficiencies.

In order to understand application-network dynamics and their inter-dependencies, it is important to follow a cross-layer approach that spans from applications and user events, to the behavior of the control-plane. A major challenge for such analysis is accessing the different layers: neither control-plane information is generally exposed by the radio driver to the mobile OS (only from within the operator), nor user and application events other than network packets are sent to the mobile operator. As a consequence, most of the previous research has been performed either thanks to privileged access to internal and proprietary data from mobile carriers [3–5], expensive test-beds [2] and diagnostic tools [6], or by emulating low-level control-plane events on the terminal [7]. In this paper, we present *RILAnalyzer*, a software and handset-oriented approach that enables gathering of accurate control-plane and user-plane data, including any layer on the protocol stack, *"in the wild"* with real users traffic load, and network configurations.

Firstly, we review the classical vantage points in cellular network research, including low-level diagnostic tools. We discuss their capability and openness in capturing the ground truth in terms of control plane events, user plane, as well as their scope in terms of scale and layers. Previous research is classified based on the type of data and vantage point they use in their analysis. Secondly, we present an

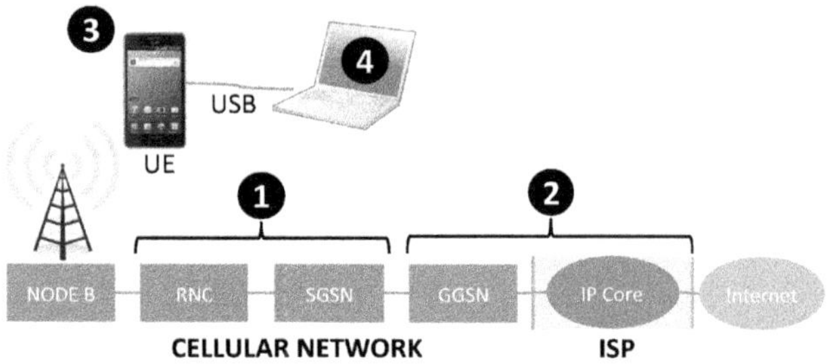

Figure 1: Basic UMTS cellular network deployment and possible probing points.

open source tool motivated by the limitations of these vantage points, we built *RILAnalyzer*, an accurate cross-layer open-source solution capable of reporting and correlating control and user plane events for Android handsets. We demonstrate the capabilities and limitations of our tool by looking at issues that would be difficult to analyze with current methodologies. In particular, we study *i)* the diversity of RNC state machines across different mobile carriers, and *ii)* the network cost associated to TCP operations to reach the back-end infrastructure in popular apps like Facebook, Skype, WhatsApp and Google's Push Notification Service.

2. CELLULAR NETWORK BACKGROUND

As opposed to wired networks, communication on cellular networks induces signaling overhead necessary to control limited spectrum resources and manage devices' power state. Figure 1 shows the basic components of a cellular network. Among all the elements present, the RNC plays a key role managing the spectrum and battery life of the handsets.

The UMTS standard defines three main client power modes known as RRC power states: `IDLE` that corresponds to no connection and low power; `CELL_DCH` (Dedicated Channel) the highest power state with highest throughput and lowest latency; and `CELL_FACH` (Forward Access Channel), a low capacity channel shared across all the mobile users. With the time and successive evolutions, an additional channel known as `CELL_PCH` (Cell Paging Channel) has been introduced between `IDLE` and `CELL_FACH` to enable paging the user equipment at a lower energy cost than `CELL_FACH`. For simplicity, they will be referred to as IDLE, DCH, FACH and PCH respectively. A similar state machine has been defined for LTE standards [8].

The promotions between RRC states are governed by the RNC based on traffic demand, whereas the demotions are defined by inactivity timeouts, unofficially referred to as $T1$ (DCH to FACH), $T2$ (FACH to PCH), and $T3$ (PCH to IDLE) [1]. Their configuration is highly vendor and operator dependent. High inactivity timers can lead to power waste on some devices, as these devices remain at high power states for longer. This has been called as the *tail-energy* [9, 10]. *Fast Dormancy* has been later introduced to minimize the effect of the tail-energy by allowing the handset to demote itself earlier if there is no more traffic [2].

Signaling happens during the promotion and demotion events, and throughout the entire DCH phase as the RRC protocol requires the handset to periodically report its state to the RNC. As signaling traffic is transmitted on a shared channel with limited capacity, its efficient use is critical for correct operation of the network. In fact, if signaling channels get congested, they can even cause network blackouts [2, 11]. Reducing RNC state changes is crucial for cellular operators to reduce spectrum overhead and signaling traffic, but also to extend battery life of mobile handsets. Consequently, understanding the way applications and cellular networks behave is essential to achieve optimal configurations that can satisfy the needs of applications, operating system, cellular networks, and ultimately, the mobile user.

3. ANALYSING CELLULAR NETWORKS

In order to analyze performance of cellular networks and behavior of mobile applications in the network, it is possible to obtain data traces from different vantage points as exemplified in Figure 1 for a 3G network: control-plane traces gathered at network components deployed in commercial networks or dedicated test-beds **(1)**, user-plane information collected from the GGSN or from proxies deployed in the IP core of the ISP **(2)**, user-plane data collected from mobile handsets **(3)**, and chipset-specific engineering/debugging tools running on an external monitoring station to collect *"in situ"* control-plane traces from mobile handsets**(4)**. Their scope and limitations are summarized in Table 1.

Network traces collected from a cellular network have been a convenient way of getting insight into network and application behavior [5]. Although they span across millions of mobile devices, their scope is limited to a single layer of the protocol stack (often HTTP) due to the large amount of signaling and user-plane traffic generated in cellular networks [2]. Gathering extensive control-plane information is only feasible for a limited period of time on a specific element of the cellular network chain like the RNC or a special network testbed **(1)** [5, 12]. Unfortunately, it covers a limited geographic area and logs are only accessible from the mobile operator or network equipment manufacturer.

Most of the previous cellular network studies rely on aggregated application layer data [3, 4, 13], such as web logs, collected and provided by an operator for its Network Operation Center (NOC) **(2)**. As these traces lack control-plane and OS events, researchers have used pre-built models of control-plane operations using advanced ways of modeling RNC state machine based on power measurements and binary search for commercial 3G [1] and LTE networks [8]. RNC models were frequently combined with reverse-DNS techniques to identify which applications generate traffic and to estimate their associated energy consumption and network signaling [3–5, 14]. Such approach can be proven inaccurate on actual mobile apps which combine several online services such as advertising modules, analytics, third-party APIs or even CDNs [3]. Network activity can therefore only be accurately attributed to applications by identifying the process owning a given network socket. We discuss these limitations in more detail in Section 5.

At the terminal level, it is possible to obtain accurate traces of mobile traffic at the user-plane (e.g. using **`tcpdump`** or **`iptables`**), user interaction patterns, application and OS events **(3)** [7, 14–16] due to the open-source nature of some OSes (such as Android). Control-plane information can also be extracted from terminals using vendor-specific tools, either licensed such as Qualcomm's XDM [6] **(4)** for Qualcomm, or open-source such as **`xgoldmon`** [17] for Intel XGold chipsets. Unfortunately, both tools run outside the mobile device using the USB port as a channel for collecting

Vantage point	Control plane	User plane	Scale	Process ID	OS/User events	Access
1. Cellular network components	Ground truth		Large			Operator/Vendor
2. GGSN and IP Core	Inferred	✓	Large	Reverse DNS		Operator/Vendor
3. Mobile OS	Inferred	✓	Medium	✓	✓	Open
4. Engineering tools	Ground truth		Small			Licensed/Open

Table 1: Comparison of the different vantage points used for characterizing cellular networks and mobile application performance along six different axis.

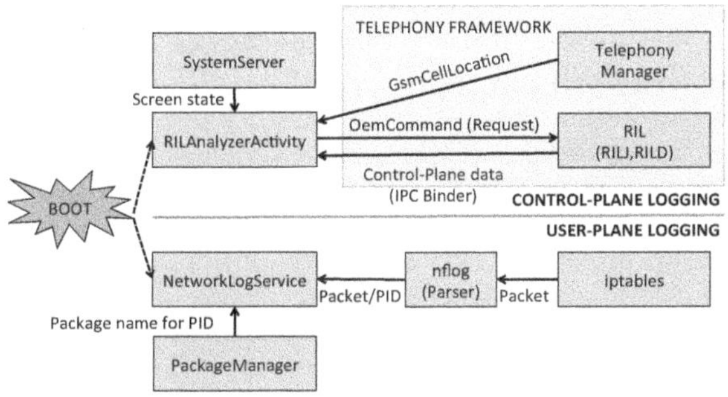

Figure 2: Data flow between the different components

Plane	Data
Control	Cellular technology (GPRS/UMTS/HSPA), RNC state, number of HSPA channels, SNR indicators (e.g. RSCP and EC/IO), Cell ID
Data	Screen state, transport/network layer header, IP header, process ID owning socket

Table 2: Data collected by RILAnalyzer.

data on an external terminal for processing. This makes it difficult to correlate between control-plane information and on-device logs, as well as perform *"in situ"* experiments.

Overall, some vantage points can offer privileged access to the network's ground truth at the expense of gathering limited data across the layers or geographical areas, different operators, number of events captured *etc.* By leveraging terminal capabilities, one could achieve open and decent accuracy across multiple levels (UI events, application, OS events), but even in that case, OS and network design, and current monitoring tools make performing experiments out of the research lab unrealistic. This leaves out an interesting possibility: *how can nearly complete, integrated ground truth knowledge be obtained at the terminal level in the wild?*

4. INTRODUCING RILANALYZER

To overcome the limitations described above, we implemented RilAnalyzer for rooted Android devices with Intel/Infineon XGold chipsets. The tool is publicly available at [18]. Some of the most popular Android devices (e.g. Samsung Galaxy SII/SIII) use this chipset. Figure 2 and Table 2 describe its software architecture and the information it collects. As opposed to other analysis based on data collected from the OS [15, 19], our implementation allows for gathering and correlation of user, application, and OS events with control and user-plane data in a single memory space **from** within the mobile handset.

Control-plane logging: Most mobile platforms are shipped with a dedicated modem chip which runs a real-time firmware in isolation. The main OS of the phone (e.g. Android) communicates with the baseband using the Radio Interface Layer (RIL). A typical Android's RIL spans across three different software sub-components: high-level RILJ (Java module that exposes RIL interface at the Android framework level), the low-level vendor RIL library (that implements vendor-specific messages communication with the modem serial interface), and a RIL Daemon (that runs in memory and translates packets and commands between RILJ and vendor RIL). Although developers can access events such as ongoing calls and the type of cellular network with the public APIs exposed by RILJ, the OS is not capable of accessing directly any control-plane information such as RNC states [1]. This information by default stays in the firmware.

The communication between RILJ and vendor RIL happens through special commands (similar to *AT commands* for PSTN modems) handled by the RILD. Some modems, including those in highly popular Android devices (e.g. Samsung Galaxy SII/SIII) also facilitate a way of sending special, and chipset-dependent commands to the vendor RIL for field-test and debugging measurements reserved to radio engineers. In the case of Samsung's XGold-based handsets, this information is displayed on a foreground application that is launched by entering `*##*197328640#*#*` on the dialer. Among many other low-level information, it provides access to RF status (e.g. RNC state, HSPA channels), signaling traffic, and control-plane information such as the band of radio access technology (RAT) by converting GUI events into special commands used to poll the radio modem for specific control-plane data.

Although multiple control-plane events can be obtained with such codes, they are not publicly documented. As a result, we had to identify the necessary requests triggering the information we were interested on by adding hooks on RILJ. In particular, we are interested in logging RNC states, which are obtained through the code `*##*0011#*#*`. Furthermore, any application that interacts with RIL has to use specific radio system permissions, and use non-public RILJ's methods to send `OemCommands` to RIL Daemon on a request/reply basis. To overcome these limitations, we implemented a system tool that runs in the background and polls the modem at the maximum frequency the device responds at, approximately every second (1291 $\pm$ 119 ms).

User-plane logging: To log user-plane information we chose to extend and improve `NetworkLog` [20], an open source tool that uses `iptables` with `Nflog` target to log packets in user space. A daemon called `Nflog` reads and parses `netlink` sockets to extract full network and transport layer headers (Figure 2). Once parsed, the information is sent to NetworkLogService (Java background service) to identify the process name for a given PID using the *PackageManager* public API. This solution provides a more accurate traffic to app mapping than other approaches that are based on information available on the `/proc` filesystem [7], especially for short-lived TCP connections and UDP traffic.

4.1 Validation

To verify accuracy of the tool we cross-checked the packets reported by RILAnalyzer against the ones captured by `tcpdump`. We ran 10 series of 100 ICMP packets, at 1 second and 10 ms intervals, DNS lookups to `google.com`, and HTTP requests (BBC's front-page), as well as a full over-night execution with real user-traffic. Exactly the same packets were logged by both RILAnalyzer and `tcpdump`.

Accurate packet timing is a hard problem to solve at the user space: `Nflog` only reports timestamps for outgoing packets as recorded by the Linux kernel. Consequently, they need to be added at the time of processing packets in user-space, which may be significantly later than the actual packet arrival time. This granularity is sufficient for analysing app traffic and control-plane interactions as baseband polling interval is currently limited to 1 second. To record more accurate timing information both modem firmware and Linux kernel require improvements.

Because of the difficulty of obtaining control plane information, we had to verify that RILAnalyzer correctly logs such events in two steps. First, we verified that the vendor-specific tool `xgoldmon` [17] logs control-plane information correctly by comparing its traces against control-plane traces obtained from a cellular network testbed. Given `xgoldmon`'s verbosity when compared against RILAnalyzer (e.g. it logs RRC messages which indicate RNC state changes while RILAnalyzer logs only RNC states), we only had to verify that the polling frequency is compatible with the frequency of occurrence of state changes for basic network operations in several locations under controlled conditions, and that the state reported by the tool is correct.

We used the following technique as both tools cannot run simultaneously on the same handset (due to exclusive use of the same modem interface). We observed that despite the different types of loads (ICMP pings and TCP packets of different size) and different events (3G activation/deactivation) the resulting RNC state events extracted from `xgoldmon` traces were all separated at least by 3-4 seconds, hence the polling frequency of 1 second is not a limiting factor.

4.2 Performance and limitations

Current RILAnalyzer version is limited to Intel Infineon XGold chipsets. Some of the most popular Android devices use the chipsets: Samsung Galaxy SII, SIII, Note 2 and Nexus. We tested our system with the SII and SIII versions. Although the same commands work for LTE networks, we could not test them given limited deployment in Europe. Focusing on single chipsets may induce particular behavior and interaction problems on its own due to Vendor RIL implementation differences, however we perform our case-study (Section 5) on devices shipped with the same radio baseband, hence we still discover network and application differences accurately. As licensed monitoring tools for Qualcomm chipsets are available, we expect finding similar features in other product vendors. Providing support for other chipsets is limited by the effort it takes to reverse-engineer the hidden commands. A more efficient solution would be for vendors to expose the information to the OS.

We observed CPU and memory consumption of RILAnalyzer both idle and under stress conditions on a Samsung Galaxy S2 (Dual-core 1.2 GHz Cortex-A9). The idle experiment was conducted over three hours with Google Services, Skype and Facebook apps active in the background but without any user interaction. Stress conditions were simulated using Speedtest application [21]. During the idle experiment, RILAnalyzer consumed an average of 0.16% of CPU and 22 MB of physical memory. In this period, applications generated periodic traffic that produced variations on the CPU consumption that remained below 10%. In the stress test, at the maximum observed download throughput (+5 Mbps) the maximum observed CPU consumption was 47% using close to 42 MB of physical memory. The high memory load is due to the number of different components logging all aspects of the running systems as well as polling the radio periodically for its state.

The increase is due to the way network packets are logged by our `iptables`-based approach: each packet is duplicated and forwarded to `Nflog`, annotated with the additional information as described above and recorded. Because of platform limitations, the current version of the tool is forced to rely on polling mechanisms to achieve association between applications, network traffic, and cellular state. This adds computational and energy overheads on embedded systems like Android, which have aggressive sleeping policies [22]. Although such overheads are not desirable, they would only be decreased if vendors open their APIs to efficiently gather control plane data within the system.

The current version relies on sufficient internal storage to log data for mid-term studies. The volume of logs generated is 62±2 bytes per RNC promotion, and 130±10 bytes per logged packet (including process name). In its current iteration, RILAnalyzer is meant to be used for limited duration studies as a measurement tool in a real environment, rather than a data collection app adopted by a large userbase. Nevertheless, we plan to extend the control-plane traces using other hidden codes, and build an online facility for collecting and processing anonymized data for users, researchers and developers interested in identifying network and apps inefficiencies.

5. CASE STUDIES

In order to demonstrate RILAnalyzer's capabilities, we instrumented eight Samsung Galaxy SII handsets owned by experienced Android users subscribed to different mobile operators. They were asked to run the tool for one complete week, with their normal set of apps. The logged data accounts for more than 1200 hours of mobile activity. During this period of time, 70 applications sent or received more than 2.6M packets, causing +138K RNC transitions (29K promotions to connected states such as FACH (shared) - and DCH (dedicated)). Using the data collected with RILAnalyzer, we characterize the diversity of RNC state machines across the different networks and their effects on resource consumption (Section 5.1). Finally, we evaluate the network costs associated to TCP operations to reach the back-end infrastructure in four popular applications (Section 5.2).

5.1 RNC state machine dynamics

In the past, RNC state machine has been modeled using probes and external power meters [1,9]. Although this identified one of the main energy sinks of mobile systems, they are static and inaccurate as they are obtained *"in situ"*. In contrast, we have used *RILAnalyzer* to record actual device RNC states and demonstrate that RNC state machines are much more diverse, necessitating more complex solutions for improving device performance and energy consumption.

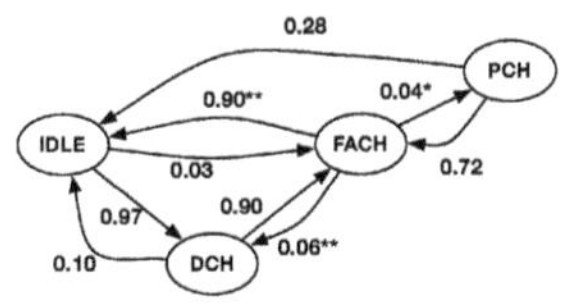

a Operator A

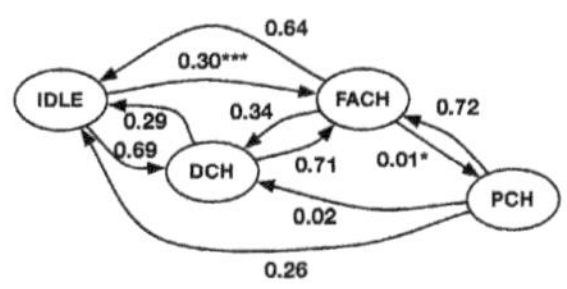

b Operator C

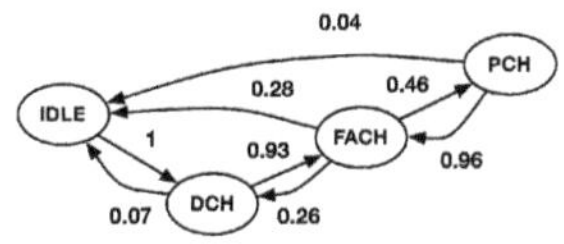

c Operator B

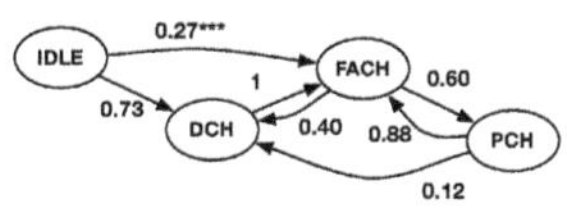

d Operator D

Figure 3: Observed RNC state transition likelihood

Figure 3 shows such differences. Although RNC promotions are triggered by user traffic, sequences of state transitions are very different.

Figure 3 shows observed transitions between RNC states for 4 different networks, *i.e.* if we look into RNC states in isolation, what is the likelihood of observing a particular transition from one state to another. A number of interesting observations can be made from this figure alone, not least that RNC state machines of these networks are quite different. *Firstly*, it is easy to see that transitions to PCH state in operators A and C are not common (labelled with (*) on figure). PCH is a RNC state introduced in HSPA standards to save battery power during periods of inactivity in the downlink while enabling an efficient paging in case of incoming data. This is likely caused by partial feature deployment in the network thus devices subscribed to these operators without complete PCH state support will experience different behaviors in terms of performance as well as signaling and energy costs.

Secondly, there are only 6% transitions from FACH to DCH vs 90% to IDLE in network A (** on figure). This is caused either by a very short FACH timeout, or by the users' set of applications not generating traffic within this timeout period. The former case would have adverse effects to both the network (largely increased signaling) and the user (control-plane latency due to connectivity reacquisition).

Finally, networks C and D contrast with network A and B in that they have a large proportion of transitions from IDLE to FACH compared to one from IDLE to DCH (*** on figure). This implies that these networks allow devices to use FACH for small messages as opposed to going to DCH for all communication.

We can explain some of these transitions better by also looking at RNC state demotion timeouts as described by Qian *et al.* [1]. The violin plots[1] in Figure 4 show the distribution of the RNC inactivity timeouts T1 (from DCH to FACH) and T2 (from FACH to IDLE or PCH) for the different networks as observed by participating users. We measured the timeouts as time difference between the last packet seen on the interface and the time RNC state is recorded as changed. As shown in Figure 3, a lower density of points indicates less frequent transitions.

Results show a large variability of RNC timeouts. T1 is mostly homogeneous around 5-6 seconds, often reported

[1]Similar to box plots, except that they show the probability density of the data at different values along y axis.

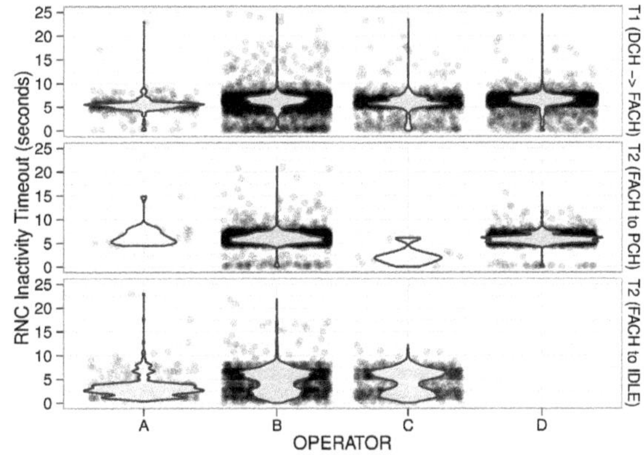

Figure 4: RNC inactivity timers (T1 and T2) in UMTS/HSPA for the different operators

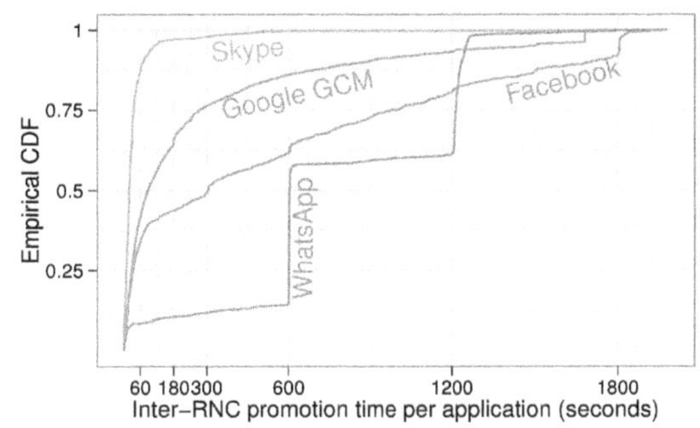

Figure 5: Empirical CDF of inter-RNC promotion time

in previous research work, however there are smaller values (1-2 seconds) that may be associated to Fast Dormancy support at some locations. In fact, inactivity timeouts are highly vendor and operator dependent and the duration can vary depending on traffic demand. It turns out, T1 can be set to different values depending on allocated throughput (8, 16, 32, 64, 128, 256, 384 kbit/s) and is recommended to be set to smaller values for higher throughput to save DCH capacity [23]. Both networks B and C, have two distinctly different values of T2: 6 and 2 seconds, showing fast dormancy behavior. T2 for network A, however, is the lowest one and as discussed above, it causes demotion to IDLE too soon for any promotions back up to DCH to happen. As a result, a lot of signaling and control-plane latency is added.

Both Figure 3 and 4 confirm the low number of transitions from FACH to PCH in networks A and C. This suggests that these transitions occur on rare locations for the users under study. Furthermore, there are no transitions from FACH to IDLE in network D, implying a good use of PCH, which reduces control-plane latency for devices in the network.

5.2 Unveiling cross-layer inefficiencies

To demonstrate the strengths of our approach, we chose to display the costs of basic TCP operations, such as heartbeats and FINs, in terms of RNC state changes on a per-application basis.

Figure 5 shows the empirical CDF of the time between promotion triggered by Facebook, WhatsApp, Skype and Google push notification service (a service shared across multiple applications such as Facebook, and WhatsApp). Here we aggregate inter-promotion times across all users and all networks in the study, therefore ignoring user-specific in-

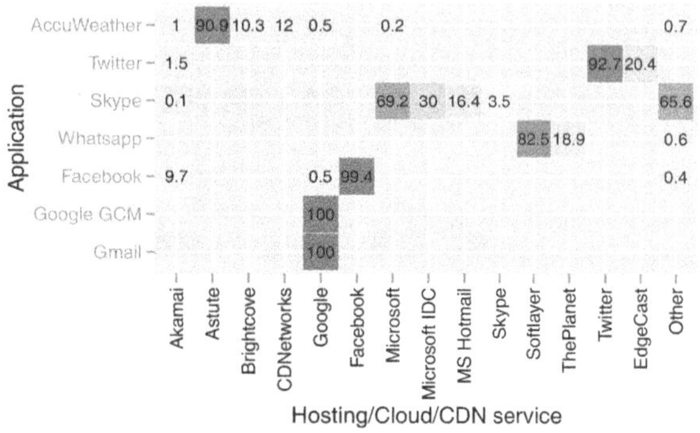

Figure 6: Percentage of observed RNC promotions per application to different backends

teraction patterns, but taking into account RNC behavior of each device as recorded by RILAnalyzer. We count promotions to both FACH and DCH states. As we can see, applications have different frequencies in terms of RNC promotion frequency and the steps on the lines (especially clear in the cases of WhatsApp and Facebook) represent periodic messages, such as TCP or HTTP/1.1 keepalives.

Apps have to rely heavily on backend infrastructure, such as CDNs, advertising networks [3], push mechanisms [24], and authentication APIs (e.g. OAuth), often managed by different organizations. An often overlooked fact is that a lot of overheads are exactly due to distributed backends' lack of coordination even in a single app, as indicated by Figure 6. Every long lived TCP connection is kept alive individually. Using reverse DNS to map network traffic to applications would incorrectly attribute it to the apps developed by the same company that owns the backend infrastructure.

Something that is only accurately feasible from within a device (e.g. using RILAnalyzer) is demonstrated in Figure 6: the proportion of RNC promotions in which there is traffic to a particular backend (a few more apps are included for comparison). Each network packet is assigned promotion ID during which it is transmitted and the percentage is obtained by combining organization name obtained from reverse DNS with the promotion ID. Naturally, there are promotions during which traffic goes to multiple backends. This happens when the sum of percentages for an app is more than 100%.

Skype here demonstrates a pathological case due to its P2P nature: RNC promotions are triggered every 30 seconds on average to maintain connections with other connected users. In addition, it relies on distributed services to monitor QoS, billing, and to guarantee reachability and resilience (managed by Microsoft or Skype). As much as 74% of connections are directly to other peers although surprisingly they only account for 57% of packets. Google's GCM, on the other hand, aggregates notifications for multiple applications (Google's own and ones that use it for push notifications) reducing the amortized cost for each application - only one open TCP connection is needed to a single entity serving multiple applications. We can not isolate per-application information from Google GCM protocol and have to analyze the entity as a whole.

Another problem with distributed backends is due to the fact that cellular networks are controlled by middleboxes for security and performance [25]. Such middleboxes impose restrictions on the way applications maintain their connections at the transport [26] and application layer [27]. We found us-

App	Hearbeats & FIN (%)	Server-side (%)
Facebook	3.2	12.6
Google GCM	6.1	69.6
Skype	15.9	40.2
WhatsApp	47.1	3.0
All apps	41.0	58.9

Table 3: Per-App promotions triggered by TCP operations and initiated by a server

ing RILAnalyzer that TCP heartbeats and FINs (messages that are driven by these restrictions) alone account for a significant proportion of RNC promotions (Table 3). In the case of WhatsApp, a large fraction of RNC promotions associated with these operations are due to TCP hearbeats maintaining connections, while the others often also include application-level information.

For network-intensive applications such as Skype and push notification mechanisms, a large portion of total promotions are triggered by packets sent from the server-side, indicating where connection maintenance logic is located. On the other hand, applications such as Facebook rely on Google's push notifications, thus reducing the need to maintain their own TCP connections. These observations suggest that to reduce the energy and network overheads of mobile traffic, it is essential to control downlink traffic (e.g. using middleboxes or enhancement proxies) in addition to the classic approach of controlling uplink on the mobile handset [1,3,4,9,28].

6. CONCLUSION

In this work we presented a tool which facilitates researchers to analyze cellular network issues in a new light without requiring access to the internal components of the cellular network. We prototyped the tool, RILAnalyzer, on the Android platform for popular smartphone devices. RILAnalyzer is meant to be used outside of laboratory environment and therefore allows open accurate mobile device measurement studies across many users, applications, networks and geographical regions. We evaluated performance of the tool and discussed its limitations - some of them inherent to running within a mobile device and not relying on external resources.

We have demonstrated the ability of RILAnalyzer to accurately perform cross-layer analysis on mobile systems. First, we demonstrated important RNC state machines differences across 4 mobile operators in two European countries. Second, to demonstrate the strengths of RILAnalyzer, we exposed inefficient connection maintenance logic for a few popular applications, caused by the large number of backend systems they rely on and sub-optimal use of TCP. We are releasing the tool publicly [18] for the mobile research community to use, extend and improve.

Acknowledgments

This material is based upon work supported by the EPRSC INTERNET Project, the Department Homeland Security under Contract N66001-12-C-0128, by the NSF under grant 1213157, and by the European Commission under grant agreement FP7-318627 (mPlane). The authors would also like to thank the volunteers, the anonymous reviewers and our shepherd Aditya Akella (University of Wisconsin-Madison) for constructive feedback on preparation of the final version of this paper.

7. REFERENCES

[1] F. Qian, Z. Wang, A. Gerber, Z. M. Mao, S. Sen, and O. Spatscheck. Characterizing radio resource allocation for 3G networks. In *Proceedings of ACM IMC*, 2010.

[2] Nokia Siemens Networks Smart Labs. Understanding smartphone behavior in the network. `http://www.nokiasiemensnetworks.com/sites/default/files/document/Smart_Lab_WhitePaper_27012011_low-res.pdf`, 2011.

[3] N. Vallina-Rodriguez, J. Shah, A. Finamore, Y. Grunenberger, K. Papagiannaki, H. Haddadi, and J. Crowcroft. Breaking for commercials: characterizing mobile advertising. In *Proceedings of ACM IMC*, 2012.

[4] J. Huang, F. Qian, Z. M. Mao, S. Sen, and O. Spatscheck. Screen-off traffic characterization and optimization in 3G/4G networks. In *Proceedings of ACM IMC*, 2012.

[5] F. Qian, Z. Wang, Y. Gao, J. Huang, A. Gerber, Z. M. Mao, S. Sen, and O. Spatscheck. Periodic transfers in mobile applications: network-wide origin, impact, and optimization. In *Proceedings of WWW Conference*, 2012.

[6] Qualcomm Extensible Diagnostic Monitor. `http://www.qualcomm.com/media/documents/qxdm-professional-qualcomm-extensible-diagnostic-monitor`.

[7] F. Qian, Z. Wang, A. Gerber, Z. M. Mao, S. Sen, and O. Spatscheck. Profiling resource usage for mobile applications: a cross-layer approach. In *Proceedings of ACM MobiSys*, 2011.

[8] J. Huang, F. Qian, A. Gerber, Z. M. Mao, S. Sen, and O. Spatscheck. A close examination of performance and power characteristics of 4G LTE networks. In *Proceedings of ACM MobiSys*, 2012.

[9] N. Balasubramanian, A. Balasubramanian, and A. Venkataramani. Energy consumption in mobile phones: a measurement study and implications for network applications. In *Proceedings of ACM IMC*, 2009.

[10] N. Vallina-Rodriguez and J. Crowcroft. Energy management techniques in modern mobile handsets. *Communications Surveys Tutorials, IEEE*, 2013.

[11] Z. Shafiq, L. Ji, A. Liu, J. Pang, S. Venkataraman, and J. Wang. A first look at cellular network performance during crowded events. In *Proceedings of ACM SIGMETRICS*, 2013.

[12] J. Erman, A. Gerber, K. K. Ramadrishnan, S. Sen, and O. Spatscheck. Over the top video: the gorilla in cellular networks. In *Proceedings of ACM IMC*, 2011.

[13] M. Z. Shafiq, L. Ji, A. X. Liu, J. Pang, and J. Wang. A first look at cellular machine-to-machine traffic: large scale measurement and characterization. In *Proceedings of ACM SIGMETRICS*, 2012.

[14] H. Falaki, R. Mahajan, S. Kandula, D. Lymberopoulos, R. Govindan, and D. Estrin. Diversity in smartphone usage. In *Proceedings of ACM MobiSys*, 2010.

[15] L. Zhang, B. Tiwana, Z. Qian, Z. Wang, R. P. Dick, Z. M. Mao, and L. Yang. Accurate online power estimation and automatic battery behavior based power model generation for smartphones. In *Proceedings of IEEE/ACM CODESS*, 2010.

[16] P. Abhinav, Y. C. Hu, and M. Zhang. Where is the energy spent inside my app?: fine grained energy accounting on smartphones with Eprof. In *Proceedings of ACM EuroSys*, 2012.

[17] Github. XGoldMon project. `https://github.com/2b-as/xgoldmon`.

[18] RILAnalyzer. `http://rilanalyzer.smart-e.org/`.

[19] X. Wei, L. Gomez, I. Neamtiu, and M. Faloutsos. ProfileDroid: multi-layer profiling of android applications. In *Proceedings of ACM Mobicom*, 2012.

[20] Github. Network Log. `https://github.com/pragma-/networklog`.

[21] Speedtest android application. `https://play.google.com/store/apps/details?id=org.zwanoo.android.speedtest&hl=en`.

[22] A. Jindal, A. Pathak, Y. C. Hu, and S. Midkiff. Hypnos: understanding and treating sleep conflicts in smartphones. In *Proceedings of ACM EuroSys*, 2013.

[23] Nokia. 3G radio optimisation parameter testing guide. `http://www.scribd.com/doc/103289214/Parameter-Testing-Reference-Quide`.

[24] Google Cloud Messaging. `http://developer.android.com/google/gcm/index.html`.

[25] Z. Wang, Z. Qian, Q. Xu, Z. M. Mao, and Ming Zhang. An untold story of middleboxes in cellular networks. In *Proceedings of the ACM SIGCOMM Conference*, 2011.

[26] F. Busatto. TCP Keepalive HOWTO. `http://tldp.org/HOWTO/TCP-Keepalive-HOWTO`.

[27] R. Fielding, J. Gettys, J. Mogul, H. Frystyk, L. Masinter, P. Leach, and T. Berners-Lee. Hypertext Transfer Protocol – HTTP/1.1, 1999.

[28] F. Qian, Z. Wang, A. Gerber, Z. M. Mao, S. Sen, and O. Spatscheck. TOP: Tail Optimization Protocol For Cellular Radio Resource Allocation. In *Proceedings of IEEE ICNP*, 2010.

Signals from the Crowd: Uncovering Social Relationships through Smartphone Probes

Marco V. Barbera, Alessandro Epasto, Alessandro Mei, Vasile C. Perta, and Julinda Stefa
Department of Computer Science, Sapienza University of Rome, Italy,
{barbera, epasto, mei, perta, stefa}@di.uniroma1.it.

ABSTRACT

The ever increasing ubiquitousness of WiFi access points, coupled with the diffusion of smartphones, suggest that Internet every time and everywhere will soon (if not already has) become a reality. Even in presence of 3G connectivity, our devices are built to switch automatically to WiFi networks so to improve user experience. Most of the times, this is achieved by recurrently broadcasting automatic connectivity requests (known as *Probe Requests*) to known access points (APs), like, e.g., "Home WiFi", "Campus WiFi", and so on. In a large gathering of people, the number of these probes can be very high. This scenario rises a natural question: "Can significant information on the social structure of a large crowd and on its socioeconomic status be inferred by looking at smartphone probes?".

In this work we give a positive answer to this question. We organized a 3-months long campaign, through which we collected around 11M probes sent by more than 160K different devices. During the campaign we targeted national and international events that attracted large crowds as well as other gatherings of people. Then, we present a simple and automatic methodology to build the underlying social graph of the smartphone users, starting from their probes. We do so for each of our target events, and find that they all feature social-network properties. In addition, we show that, by looking at the probes in an event, we can learn important sociological aspects of its participants—language, vendor adoption, and so on.

Categories and Subject Descriptors

C.2 [**Computer-communication networks**]: Network Architecture and Design—*Wireless communication*

Keywords

Smartphones; Wi-Fi probe requests; social networks.

1. MOTIVATION AND GOALS

WiFi access points (APs) are becoming increasingly ubiquitous in our homes, offices and public places. Initially, the APs were used to free our portable computers (laptops) from the ADSL/LAN cable. Nowadays, APs also represent a viable option for mobile devices to get fast and cheap connectivity. So, it is becoming more and more common for mobile devices to automatically switch to WiFi connectivity whenever possible. To facilitate this automatic process, current smartphone OSes store the list of the names (SSID) of the networks the user typically connects to. Periodically, many of our smartphones broadcast these SSIDs in the form of *Probe Request* to search for available networks [20, 11, 4]. This is done every few seconds, even when we are far from the WiFi access points we usually connect to. In a large crowd of people, a very high number of probe requests are sent every minute. In this paper we consider the following questions: "What information can we get on a large crowd from their probe requests?"; "Is it possible to infer important information on the crowd like its social structure or its socioeconomic status?"; and lastly: "If yes, can this analysis be done in a simple and automatic way?". To answer all these questions, we organized a campaign of probe collection: We targeted large gatherings of people at city-wide, national, and international events as well as a university campus. Our campaign lasted three months, and we managed to collect, using commodity hardware only, a total of 11,136,711 probes sent by 164,740 different devices.

Our main contribution and findings in this work are the following:

- We develop a simple and automated methodology that allows to extract, starting from our datasets, the existing social connections among the smartphone owners, and use it to uncover, for the first time, the underlying social network of the participants in each event;
- we analyze the properties of these social graphs and show that they all feature social-network attributes in many aspects such as diameter, clustering coefficient and degree distribution;
- we show that important information on the nature of large events can be learnt from the probes:
  - the distribution of the languages of SSIDs, as detected by our methodology, shows a clear relationship between the international nature of the event and the density of foreign participants;
  - the distribution of the smartphone vendors varies across the events and matches the expected socioecomomic characteristics of the participants.
- by using our datasets, we validate the well-known sociological theories of homophily and social influence in the context of smartphone vendor adoption;

IMC'13, October 23–25, 2013, Barcelona, Spain.
Copyright 2013 ACM 978-1-4503-1953-9/13/10 ...$15.00.
http://dx.doi.org/10.1145/2504730.2504742.

- we perform a temporal analysis of the data collected in our long-term university campus deployment that uncover strong correlation between the frequency of the co-occurrence of devices in the same time slot and the strength of the relationship inferred by our methodology;

An anonymized version of the dataset is available online [41]. The paper is organized as follows: Section 2 reviews the related work in this area. Section 3 introduces our data collection methodology and the events targeted by our analysis. Section 4 presents our main finding and contribution. Finally, Section 5 draws our conclusions and discusses possible future works.

2. RELATED WORKS

The use of probe requests as a way to discover nearby known WiFi networks has recently gained the attention of the community. In the last few years, the security community has focused on the potential perils of this technology. Zovi et al. [11], show how both Windows XP and OSX implementations of this feature exposes users to a man-in-the-middle attack, where a malicious access point (AP) pretends to be part of a trusted network (see also Klaus [20]). More recently, the same concern has been raised for mobile devices too [4]. In addition, probe requests have been shown to jeopardize users' privacy. Franklin et al. [15] show how the timings of passively collected probe requests can be exploited to fingerprint the wireless network interface driver. Loh et al. [12] expand on this idea by noting that not just the driver but also the network device and the OS can influence the timings between the probes. Finally, Pang et al. [28] show how, by combining information leaked by probe requests with other implicitly revealed identifiers, one can recognize users even when MAC addresses and names are replaced by pseudonyms.

Probe requests can also help WiFi monitoring and user tracking. Musa et al. [32] describe how to exploit probes to passively track smartphones and infer the trajectory of their users. Rose et al. [34] show how probes can be used to reveal past behavior of users. Cunche et al. [9] use probe requests to decide whether two devices potentially belong to socially linked users. They leverage the intersection between the SSIDs in the probe requests of the two devices and use a metric inspired by the Adamic-Adar [1] similarity to smooth out the influence of frequently used SSIDs. Later on, Cheng et al. [7] extended the previous analysis with spatial temporal information on probe requests on a small sample of users. These works focus on pairs of users, possibly recurrently observed over time, and aim at best characterizing their relationship.

In this work, we take a different approach: We focus on large scale events involving thousands of users. We capture the probe requests of the devices during the event, and, from that, we aim at building a snapshot of the society that the participants represent. A snapshot rich enough to reflect, as accurately as possible, the sociological features and peculiarities of the crowd in the event (e.g. language, wealth), and, simultaneously, the properties and features of the emerging social-network. Our datasets are collected at a large scale and target city-wide, campus-like, national, and international events.

Our methodology builds also on the work of [26, 25, 22, 40, 23], which analyze the social graphs induced by affiliation networks. To the best of our knowledge, we are the first to adapt and refine these techniques to large datasets of probes. This allows us to introduce an easily automated methodology through which it is possible to define and analyze large-scale social networks of mobile devices users. Finally, for the first time we perform language detection on the broadcast SSIDs, and exploit the vendor ID of the captured devices to validate the theory of homophily and social influence between smartphone users.

3. DATA COLLECTION METHODOLOGY

According to the 802.11 standard [37], a WiFi access point can announce its presence by broadcasting *Beacons*—frames containing network configuration parameters such as the service set identifier (SSID) and supported data rates. In particular, the SSID is a string that identifies the WiFi AP in a human readable format (e.g., "Home network", "Free WiFi"). Client devices—referred to as *Stations* by the standard—can use two methods to detect access points in range: *Passive* and *active* scanning. In the former, the client passively listens for beacons of nearby access points and uses them to decide which network to connect to. Conversely, with active scanning, it is the client that actively searches for available networks by sending *Probe Request* frames. The probe requests can be either *directed* to a specific network, by indicating its SSID, or *broadcast* to any network within range. An example of both types of probes is given in Table 1. Upon receiving a Probe Request, any AP belonging to the network the probe is directed to replies with a *Probe Response* enabling the client to initiate a connection.

Probe requests are an efficient way for energy-limited devices (like smartphones) to detect known and unknown WiFi networks within range. By sending active probes, a mobile device can keep the WiFi radio on for just a few milliseconds, the amount of time it takes for any response to be received. Directed probe requests are also useful for connecting to "hidden" networks whose APs do not broadcast its SSID. To further improve this mechanism, a *Preferred Network List* (from now on *PNL*) of networks a device has connected to in the past is maintained by the OS to transparently connect or switch between known networks whenever possible.

3.1 Probes collection: Technical details

Mobile devices periodically send probe requests with a frequency that is vendor specific but that we observed to be typically between 15 and 60 seconds, depending on the power state of the device. Since probe requests are used in the discovery phase that comes before the actual association to the access point, they are sent in the clear over all transmission channels in sequence. This makes intercepting (sniffing) probe requests an easy task, requiring just commodity hardware like the internal wireless card of a laptop set in monitor mode.

In our collection campaign we used the following hardware:

- 4 × MacbookPro equipped with a Broadcom BCM43xx card;
- 1 × ThinkPad X61 equipped with an Atheros network card;
- 1 × fixed external Ubiquity SuperRange Cardbus antenna[1].

Overall, we collected around 11M probes sent by around 160K unique devices. We collected data in more than eight different events and locations with large gatherings of people. After data collection we used the *tshark* network analyzer to filter out all corrupted probes with a bad checksum (field `FCS` in Table 1). Then, we built a database that associates each device, as identified by its MAC address (field `SA`), to the list of SSIDs (field `SSID`) derived from its probes.

3.1.1 Description of the datasets

As many metropolises, Rome hosts several important events with both national and international audience and is a recurrent venue of large political and religious gatherings. Some of these events became target of our study. In particular, in our data collection campaign we targeted the following scenarios: 1) Events of national

[1] `http://dl.ubnt.com/src_datasheet.pdf`

Frame Ctrl	Duration	DA	SA	BSSID	Seq Ctl	SSID	FCS
...	...	ff:ff:ff:ff:ff:ff	10:9a:42:42:42:42	ff:ff:ff:ff:ff:ff	...	null (Broadcast)	...
...	...	ff:ff:ff:ff:ff:ff	10:9a:42:42:42:42	ff:ff:ff:ff:ff:ff	...	"Free WiFi"	...
...	...	ff:ff:ff:ff:ff:ff	10:9a:42:42:42:42	ff:ff:ff:ff:ff:ff	...	"Home WiFi"	...

Table 1: Example of Probe Requests sent by device with MAC address 10:9a:42:42:42:42. One broadcast probe (on top), and two directed to the "Free WiFi" and the "Home WiFi" networks respectively.

audience; 2) events of international audience; 3) events with audience consisting of mostly local residents; 4) a train station; 5) a university campus; 6) other. The first four were one-shot events lasted from 40 minutes to 6 hours each. Data collection was physically carried out by a team of 5 researchers that joined the event equipped with their laptops. The fifth dataset was collected through a fixed hardware placed in a university campus over a continuous period of 6 weeks. The last dataset includes probes collected by the research group in other occasions (e.g. commuting from home to office). In the remaining of this section we describe in details each of the scenarios/events that we targeted. Details on the number of devices and number of probes of each datasets are given in Table 2.

3.1.2 *National Events*

In our collection campaign we targeted the political meetings of two very large parties in Italy: The Movimento Cinque Stelle (M5S), a recently-established progressive party that unexpectedly got 28% of the votes, and the conservative party Popolo della Libertà (PDL), one of the most important parties in the Italian political scene. The Movimento Cinque Stelle closed its electoral campaign in Rome, with a meeting held on February 22th 2013 in one of the largest square in Rome area ("Piazza San Giovanni"). This event is denoted in our dataset as *Politics 1*. The Popolo della Libertà called for a post-electoral meeting in Rome on March 23rd. The meeting was held in a famous square in the city center ("Piazza del Popolo"). This dataset is denoted as *Politics 2*. As the police reported, in both cases the event participants came from all over Italy.

3.1.3 *International Events*

On February 11th, 2013, Pope Benedict XVI announced his resignation, after 8 years of service as the Head of the Catholic Church. The day of his farewell Angelus[2], February 24th, Vatican City was literally invaded by pilgrims and tourists from all around the world, as police reported. The same happened on March 17th, when the newly elected Pope Francis delivered his first Angelus. The datasets relative to these two events are denoted as *Vatican 1* and *Vatican 2* respectively.

3.1.4 *City-wide probes: The Mall*

For this case study we aimed at collecting data from local residents of Rome. So, we targeted a location known for hosting many families and groups of friends all at once: One of the biggest malls in Rome (Porta di Roma). To make sure to get a relevant affluence of people, we chose to collect the data on a special afternoon, right before Easter (March 30th, 2013), when many Romans like to shop. The data collection lasted 3 hours and a half.

3.1.5 *Train Station*

In this case study we targeted Termini, the Rome central train station, and collected the probes for a total of 7 hours split in a time range of four days. The collection was carried out by positioning at vantage points in the station so as to maximize the area covered.

3.1.6 *University*

This dataset was collected by deploying an antenna in a fixed point located at one of the main entries of our university campus. Differently from the other datasets, in this case we collected probes continuously for a period of 6 weeks, collecting probes requests mostly transmitted by devices of students entering and leaving the campus.

3.1.7 *Others*

This dataset consists of probes collected individually by 3 members of our research group during several tours across the city performed in a time span of 4 weeks while, for example, commuting from home to work or shopping.

3.1.8 *All*

Our last dataset, denoted as *All*, is generated by merging all the previously described datasets together. We will refer to this dataset when giving global statistics on the aggregate data we collected.

4. DATA ANALYSIS

Our objective is to show how WiFi probe requests collected in big events or in a given area of a city reveal a number of insights on the sociological characteristics of the crowd in the event or on the target population. We do so by means of a methodology comprising social networks analysis techniques, sociological theories and natural language processing.

4.1 Vendors of the devices in the datasets

Today's market of mobile devices is very dynamic and lively. Periodically, the major vendors either launch newer versions of their flagship products or introduce a product line destined to a new segment of the market. We hereby investigate what type of influence this has on the data we collected. To do so, we grouped by vendor the over 160K devices we detected (see Table 2) and computed the percentage of devices of each vendor. The vendor of a device can be obtained by looking at the sequence of the first 3 bytes of the MAC address field of any of its WiFi probes and matching it against the IEEE Public OUI[3] list. This is the official database that lists the space of MAC addresses assigned to each vendor. The 6 most common vendors we found in our datasets are shown in Figure 1. The most common vendor in out datasets is Apple (57% of devices), followed by Samsung (17%), Nokia (6%), HTC (1%), Sony (1%) and RIM (1%). These results do not necessarily measure the market penetration of these brands—a number of factors may have influenced the distribution of the vendors like the range of the WiFi antennas, the probability that users leave the WiFi interface on, or the frequency with which devices scan for nearby networks. However, they are qualitatively similar to those obtained

[2]The Angelus is the Pope's speech and prayer delivered every Sunday at noon from his window overlooking Saint Peter's square.

[3]`http://standards.ieee.org/develop/regauth/oui/oui.txt`

Dataset	Devices	PNLs (%)		Total Probes	Directed Probes (%)		Broadcast Probes (%)		SSIDs
Politics 1 (P1)	16,695	4,677	(28.0%)	1,190,481	406,002	(34.1%)	784,479	(65.9%)	14,740
Politics 2 (P2)	12,619	4,144	(32.8%)	330,936	117,644	(35.5%)	213,292	(64.5%)	11,145
The Mall (M)	9,731	3,859	(39.6%)	820,806	394,184	(48.0%)	426,622	(52.0%)	10,451
Train Station (TS)	14,640	5,371	(36.6%)	393,143	218,234	(55.5%)	174,909	(44.5%)	17,295
University (U)	17,131	8,853	(51.6%)	5,349,894	2,803,104	(52.4%)	2,546,790	(47.6%)	14,751
Vatican 1 (V1)	23,430	7,631	(32.5%)	1,234,416	555,361	(45.0%)	679,055	(55.0%)	29,533
Vatican 2 (V2)	22,219	6,817	(30.6%)	507,945	208,028	(40.0%)	299,917	(60.0%)	23,345
Others	60,445	21,824	(36.1%)	1,309,090	642,526	(49.0%)	666,564	(51.0%)	42,105
All	164,740	59,684	(36.2%)	11,136,711	5,345,083	(48.0%)	5,791,628	(52.0%)	133,351

Table 2: Statistics on the probes captured in our target events. The column "PNLs" reports the number (and percentage) of devices that disclosed at least one entry of their Preferred Network List.

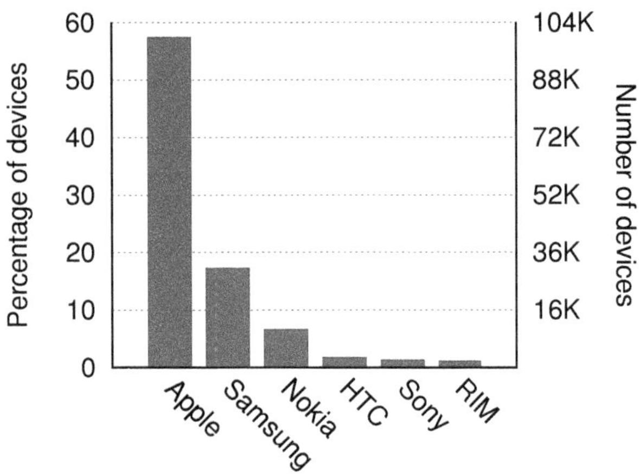

Figure 1: Vendors distribution (All datasets).

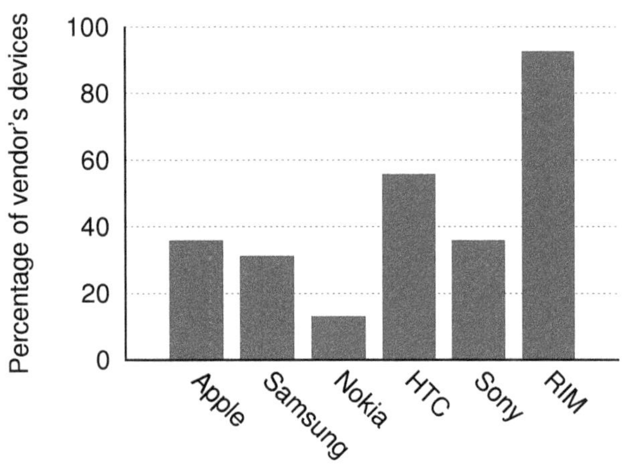

Figure 2: Vendor percentage of devices that exposed part or all the SSIDs in their Preferred Network List (dataset All).

by Musa et. al. in [32], and we can observe that all vendors in our list are amongst the market leaders of mobile devices, such as smartphones and tablets. This suggests that our datasets indeed capture a representative sample of the most commonly used mobile devices.

A question that we raise is how the choice of a particular vendor affects the probability that all or part of the PNL is exposed by means of directed probe requests. This is relevant for our analysis, and may also be an important information from a security and privacy point of view. An adversary, by using just commodity hardware, might collect the SSIDs in the PNL of a user's device and perform an Evil Twin man-in-the-middle attack [4] against the user. Also, the names of the networks may reveal sensible information on the user, such as the place where she lives or works, the communities she belongs to, and the places she likes or frequently visits. The percentage of devices of each of the most common vendors in the datasets is reported in Figure 2: 92% of RIM devices disclosed part of their PNL, followed by HTC (55%), Sony (35%), Apple (35%), Samsung (31%) and Nokia devices (13%).

4.2 SSIDs Analysis

Today it is becoming more and more common to find WiFi access points not only in homes and workplaces, but also in public environments such as restaurants, hotels, and pubs. As a result, the probability that users connect to the WiFi networks of the places they visit is increasing too. Intuitively, this should produce two side effects: First, SSIDs of WiFi networks of public places that are popular among the people that participated to an event should be found in many of their devices. Second, a significant fraction of the PNLs of these devices should store more than one SSID—e.g. home WiFi, office WiFi, and so on. We investigate whether the datasets we collected confirm these two intuitions. To do so, we reconstructed the PNLs of the devices in our datasets by collecting all the directed probe requests we logged. The total number of devices with a non-empty PNL is around 59K. The results of our analysis for Politics 1 (P1), Vatican 1 (V1), University (U) and the Mall, as well as for all the datasets together (All), are shown in Figure 3. The other datasets show similar trends.

The distributions of the popularity of the SSIDs are reported in Figure 3(a) for a selection of the datasets, one for each type of event we targeted. As the figure shows, in our datasets the distributions are heavy-tailed, with very few highly popular access points coexisting with hundred of thousands of SSIDs stored in a handful of PNLs. It is also interesting to notice that this result is consistent across different datasets independently on the data collection methodology. In fact, the datasets collected in local events (P1, Mall), those collected in international events (V1), and the long term dataset (U) show the same type of distribution. As expected, many popular SSIDs are relative to the WiFi network of public places, such as airports, tourist attractions, university campuses and so on. Among them, there are also SSIDs of a number of city-wide WiFi networks, such as "Provincia WiFi", serving around

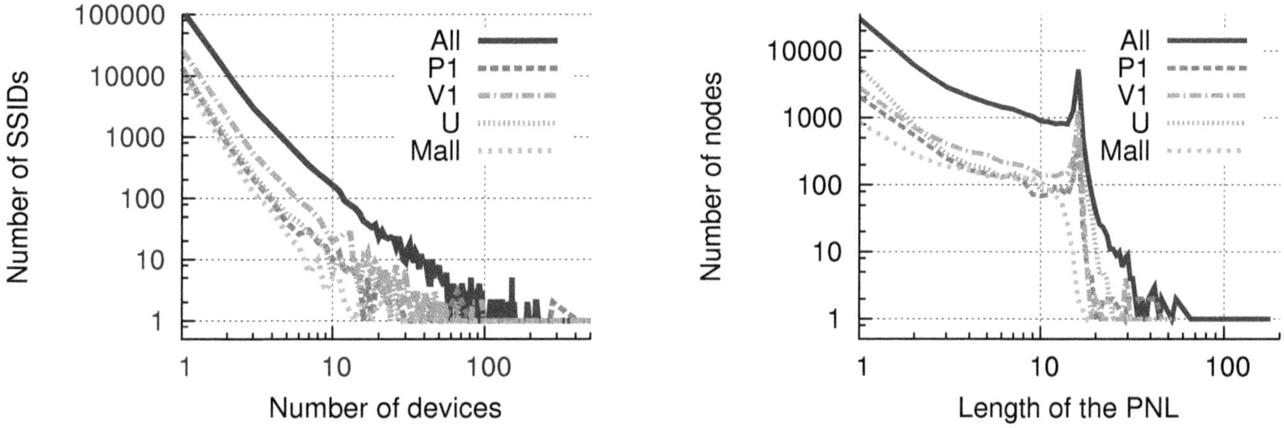

(a) SSIDs

(b) PNLs

Figure 3: Distribution of the popularity of the SSIDs (a) and of the sizes of the PNLs (b) relative to the All, Politics 1 (P1), Vatican 1 (V1), University (U), and The Mall (Mall) datasets.

300K users in Rome, and "Guglielmo", a WiFi network with more than 9K hotspots across Europe. Although we found SSIDs that are popular only because they have very generic names (e.g., "Hotspot" or "Dlink"), our results suggest that popular, public networks can indeed be detected by our data collection methodology.

The distributions of the lengths of the PNLs are shown in Figure 3(b). All the distributions present a peculiar shape: Up to about 16, the curves approximately follow a heavy-tailed distribution, then we observe a peak and a very steep drop. This behavior is easily explained by the fact that many vendors limit the number of different networks to which send directed probe requests to 16. For instance, we found that in the Android OS this limit is hard-coded as a constant with value 16 in the wireless driver source code[4]. These results, which are consistent across all the datasets, confirm the intuition that a significant fraction of users have more than just 1 SSID in the PNL of their device. More in detail, for the All dataset, 50% of the PNLs of all the devices store one SSID only, around 30% store between two and 10 SSIDs, and the remaining 20% store more than 10 SSIDs.

4.3 Uncovering the underlying social network

A contribution of our work is to show how WiFi probes can be used as a new lens to look at a crowd and uncover important information about it. One relevant information is the social structure of the set of people in the crowd.

We can regard the PNL of a device as a list of significant places visited by the user—significant enough that the user spent some time to connect to the access point. Therefore, the fact that two users share one or more SSIDs in the PNL of their devices should intuitively provide some information on the existence of a social relationship between the two. This intuition is supported by recent findings on the spatio-temporal properties of human behavior that have shown how social relationships can be correctly inferred between people sharing similar location trails [14, 10]. We investigate whether, by considering social links inferred from WiFI probes, we can uncover a *social network* that underlies the crowd that participated to the events we targeted. We do so by describing an automatic method for inferring social links between users starting from the PNLs of their mobile devices. We then apply this method to show how full-fledged social networks emerge from our datasets.

4.3.1 From affiliation networks to social networks

The SSIDs in the PNLs of a set of devices can be represented in the form of an *affiliation network* [23, 5]. An affiliation network, denoted as $G = (V_1, V_2, E)$, is a bipartite graph that connects a set V_1 of *actors* and a set V_2 of *groups* they belong to. In our case, V_1 is the set of devices that disclosed at least one entry of their PNL, V_2 is the set of the network SSIDs we collected, and an edge $(v_1, v_2) \in E$ represents v_1 having v_2 in its PNL. Statistics of the affiliation networks relative to each of our datasets are reported in Table 3.

Starting from an affiliation network of devices and SSIDs we can build a social network $\bar{G} = (V_1, \bar{E})$ between devices as follows: First, we define a *similarity measure* $f : V_1 \times V_1 \to \mathbb{R}$ that, given two devices u and v, yields the strength of the social relationship between their respective users. Then, we impose a minimum threshold τ and place an edge $\{u, v\} \in \bar{E}$ only if $f(u, v) > \tau$. A first possible choice of a similarity measure would be one based the size of the intersection between the PNLs of the two devices. In order for an edge to be placed, we would require at least $\tau = k$ common SSIDs. Although widely used in the literature [22, 23], this similarity measure would not work in our case as it gives the same importance to all SSIDs regardless of their popularity. In fact, in Section 4.2 we have seen how very popular SSIDs correspond to city-wide free networks, or to networks with very generic names (e.g., "Dlink") that, intuitively, should not produce strong social links. On the other hand, less popular SSIDs of home or small private networks clearly denote a potential strong relationship between users that connect to them. We therefore need a similarity measure that takes into account *both* the intersection of the PNLs *and* the popularity of the SSIDs. The similarity measure we found out to be the one best matching our needs is the Adamic-Adar [1] which penalizes SSIDs of popular networks in favour of those of networks shared by few people only (see Figure 4). More formally, the Adamic-Adar measure is defined as follows:

$$f_{ADA}(u, v) = \sum_{w \in N(u) \cap N(v)} \frac{1}{\log_2(|M(w)|)} \tag{1}$$

where $N(u)$ is the PNL of the device u, and $M(w)$ is the set of devices with the SSID w in their PNLs. In other words, the Adamic-

[4]`http://androidxref.com/4.1.1/xref/external/wpa_supplicant_8/src/drivers/driver.h`

Dataset	$\lvert V_1 \rvert$	$\lvert V_2 \rvert$	$\lvert E \rvert$	d_1	d_2
Politics 1 (P1)	4,677	14,740	24,494	5.24	1.66
Politics 2 (P2)	4,144	11,145	17,722	4.28	1.59
The Mall (M)	3,859	10,451	19,374	5.02	1.85
Train Station (TS)	5,371	17,295	27,515	5.12	1.59
University (U)	8,853	14,751	32,608	3.68	2.21
Vatican 1 (V1)	7,631	29,533	48,498	6.36	1.64
Vatican 2 (V2)	6,817	23,345	37,149	5.45	1.59
Others	21,824	42,105	80,502	3.69	1.91
All	59,684	133,351	277,214	4.64	2.08

Table 3: Statistics on the affiliation networks of the probes detected in the various experimental settings. The values $\lvert V_1 \rvert$ and $\lvert V_2 \rvert$ refer, respectively, to the number of devices and SSIDs extracted from the directed probe requests. The value $\lvert E \rvert$ is the number of links between the devices and SSIDs. The average number of SSIDs each smartphone is linked to, and the average number of smartphones announcing an SSID are given in the columns d_1 and d_2 respectively.

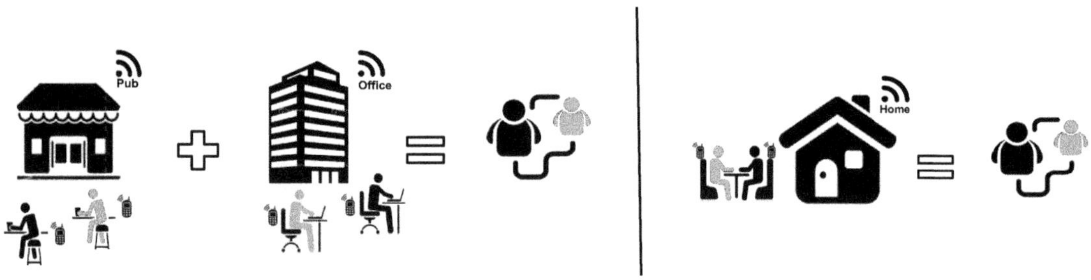

Figure 4: Adamic-Adar similarity: Several networks (e.g., pubs, workplaces) shared by a moderate or large amount of people are necessary for a relationship between two users to be correctly inferred. On the other hand, a single, private home network used by just a handful of persons may be enough.

Adar measure discounts the importance of an SSID by a factor that is logarithmic in the number of the devices that connected to it, which also well adapts to the heavy-tail distribution of the SSIDs popularities reported in Figure 3(a).

Among the other possible graph similarity measures found in the literature [21, 17, 1, 19, 27], those based on the Jaccard Coefficient [27] would not work because they do not reduce the importance of popular SSIDs. Measures based on random walks and nodes distance [27, 19] are instead not directly applicable in our case as affiliation networks are bipartite. Finally, measures based on textual similarity of SSIDs, determined by applying standard techniques in information retrieval [29], would not be suited in our context, as two nodes with exactly the same single (and very common) SSID would receive the maximum possible similarity score.

4.3.2 *Topological properties of the social networks*

We studied a number of structural properties of the social networks we extracted from our datasets and compared them with those of commonly studied online social networks [24]. We found that, consistently in all our datasets, Adamic-Adar with threshold values close to $\tau = 0.3$ generates social networks with structural properties that are similar to those of other well-known social networks. We therefore discuss the results obtained with this threshold. Note that in our discussion we ignore nodes without edges as they are irrelevant to our study.

Table 4 reports, for each of our social networks: The number $\lvert V \rvert$ and $\lvert E \rvert$ of nodes and edges in the network, the average node degree $\bar{d}$, the number of connected components NC, the size of the biggest connected component BCC, the diameter D, and the effective diameter D_{eff} of the BCC (the 90th percentile of the length of the shortest paths between nodes of the biggest connected component), the triadic closure t_c, and the clustering coefficient c_c. As we can observe, although our networks feature a large number of connected components (column NC), the biggest one (column BCC) always includes between 75.9% and 94.2% of all the nodes. The length of the longest shortest path (column D) and the 90th percentile of the shortest paths lengths (column D_{eff}) of the BCCs of our networks are close to those of popular online social networks. For comparison, those computed on a publicly available Facebook dataset are equal to 8 and 4.7 respectively [30]. We found structural similarities between our networks and popular online social networks also when we measured their density by means of the clustering coefficient (column c_c) and the triadic closure [39, 16] (column t_c). These are close to those computed in a publicly available Twitter dataset, which are 0.56 and 0.06 respectively [30]. Consistently with other social networks, in our networks too the distribution of the nodes degrees follows a power law [3]. These distributions are reported in Figure 5 for a group of datasets spanning the various types of events we targeted: Politics 1, Vatican 1, the Mall, and the long-term University dataset. Finally, for the same datasets, we report in Figure 6 the distributions of the connected components sizes. These show that most of the connected components, excluding the biggest component, contain between 1 and 10 nodes. The same property can be found in the other datasets too.

Overall, these results show that the Adamic-Adar metric allows to bring to light meaningful social structures from all our datasets. We show experimentally why the same cannot be said about a similarity measure based just on the size k of the intersection between

Dataset	$\|V\|$	$\|E\|$	$\bar{d}$	NC	BCC (%)		D	D_{eff}	t_c	c_c
Politics 1 (P1)	2,119	28,250	13.33	89	1,896	(89.4%)	9	3.88	0.144	0.491
Politics 2 (P2)	1,566	9,452	6.04	77	1,375	(87.8%)	10	4.57	0.154	0.505
The Mall (M)	1,742	33,835	19.42	74	1,533	(88.0%)	8	3.66	0.189	0.537
Train Station (TS)	2,397	16,045	6.69	90	2,164	(90.2%)	10	4.56	0.127	0.484
University (U)	2,448	96,498	39.42	59	2,307	(94.2%)	8	3.49	0.200	0.549
Vatican 1 (V1)	4,337	44,502	10.26	159	3,936	(90.7%)	9	4.47	0.145	0.453
Vatican 2 (V2)	3,423	32,239	9.42	172	3,003	(87.7%)	10	4.56	0.149	0.469
Others	8,770	134,188	15.30	798	6,662	(75.9%)	10	4.44	0.132	0.507
All	26,410	572,519	21.68	1,244	23,241	(88.0%)	11	4.70	0.132	0.460

Table 4: Structural properties of the social networks induced by using the Adamic-Adar measure with threshold $\tau = 0.3$.

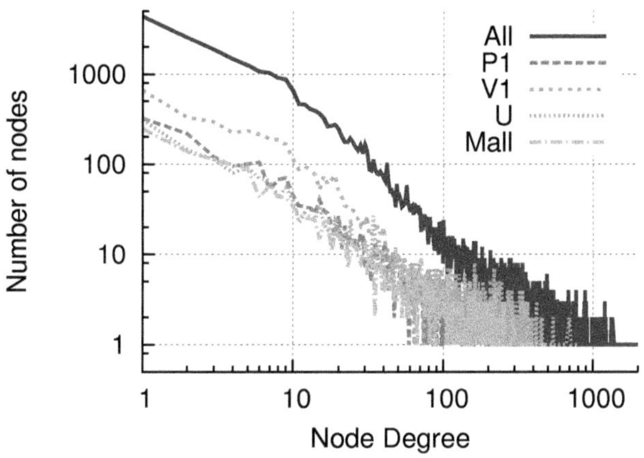

Figure 5: Degree distribution of the social networks induced by Adamic-Adar with threshold $\tau = 0.3$ from the All, Politics, Vatican 1, University and The Mall datasets.

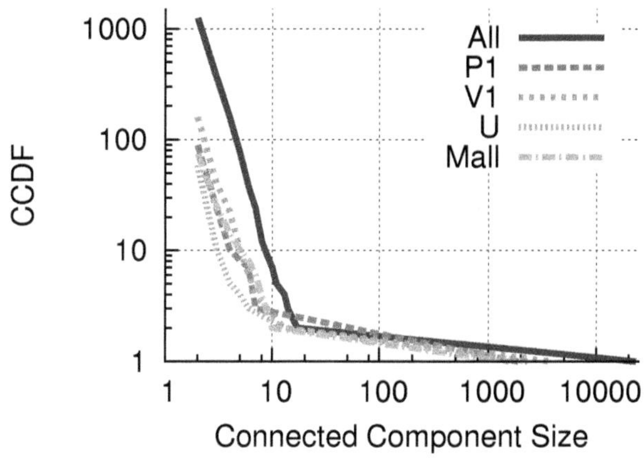

Figure 6: Distribution of the sizes of the connected components in the social networks induced by Adamic-Adar with threshold $\tau = 0.3$ from the All, Politics, Vatican 1, University and The Mall datasets.

two PNLs. To do so, we use a KNC-Plot, a tool for analysing the macroscopic properties of the graphs generated from our affiliation networks defined by Kumar et al. [22]. A KNC-Plot provides a visual indication on how the number of connected components and the size of the biggest connected component (BCC) change according to the minimum number k of common SSIDs required for an edge to be placed. Figure 7 shows a sample of the KNC-Plots of the Politics 1, Vatican 1, the Mall and University datasets. According to the figure, when the threshold k is equal to 1 almost all the nodes are connected. But increasing just slightly k produces a steep degradation in the connectivity structure of the graphs. For instance, with $k = 2$ the BCCs shrink to around 50% of the nodes, whereas with $k = 3$ they shrink to about the 25%. In other words, the similarity measure based on the size of the intersection of the PNLs generates an all-or-nothing effect that makes it hard to gain any insight on the social structure that underlies our datasets. A similar result was observed in a user-interest graph derived from Flickr [22].

4.4 Homophily and social influence in vendor adoption

Social networks based on WiFi probes may be a useful tool for studying the effects that physical proximity has on people in our society. Indeed, the way we derived our social networks leverages the intuition that users that connect to the same WiFi access point are likely to be socially connected to each other—the higher the Adamic-Adar measure that generates a link, the higher the chance that two users meet regularly or even live in the same place. According to a widely studied sociological theory known as *homophily* [31], physical proximity should cause interconnected users to be related in terms of, for instance, interests, social extraction, age, or gender. Starting from this observation, we evaluate whether our large scale data collection methodology may be used to experimentally confirm theories like that of homophily and social influence. We do so by measuring the homogeneity in device vendors adoption in groups of socially interconnected people. In fact, the choice a user makes of a particular vendor over another results from a number of factors, such as the user's wealth or age or social influence. We therefore expect people closely related to each other to tend to use devices of the same vendor.

As a measure of the homogeneity in device vendor adoption between socially connected users, we use the *assortativity* [33]. In our case, the assortativity quantifies the extent to which users of devices of a given vendor are likely to be connected to each other rather than with users of devices of different vendors. More formally, given a social network $G = (V, E)$ and a partition C of its nodes according to their respective vendors, the assortativity of G is defined as follows:

$$a(G) = \frac{\sum_{i \in C} e_{ii} - \sum_{i \in C} c_i^2}{1 - \sum_{i \in C} c_i^2}$$

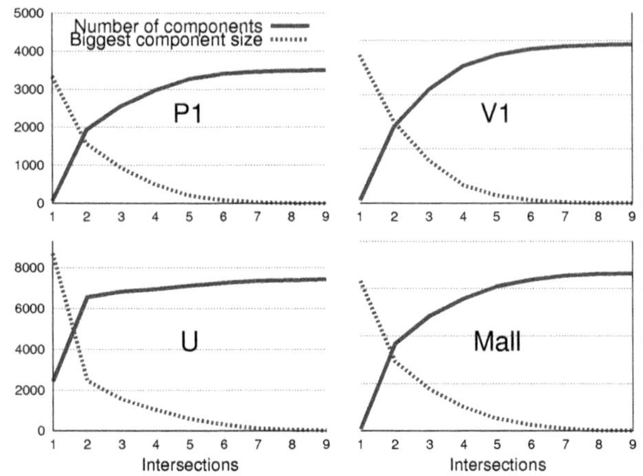

Figure 7: KNC-Plot for the Politics 1 (P1), Vatican 1 (V1), University (U), and The Mall datasets.

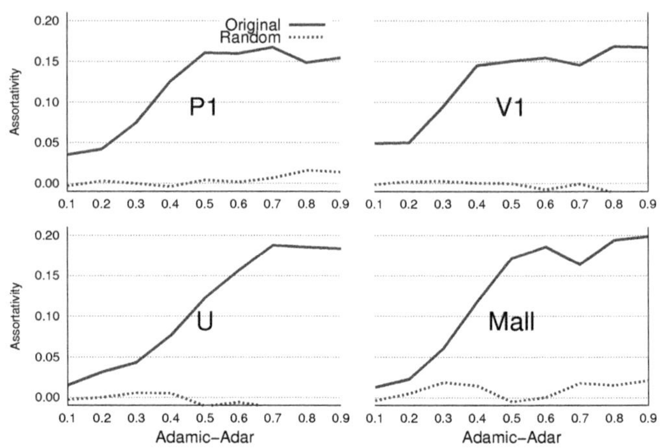

Figure 8: Vendor assortativity of the social network ("Original") vs. vendor assortativity of the randomized social network ("Random") for different Adamic Adar threshold τ values.

where c_i is the fraction of nodes that belong to vendor i and e_{ij} is the fraction of edges connecting nodes of vendor i to nodes of vendor j. The assortativity gets values in the $[-1,1]$ range. If most of the social relationships are between users who chose the same device vendor, then assortativity is positive, as $\sum_{i \in C} e_{ii}$ is close to 1. In the opposite case, that is, if most of the social relationships are between users who chose different device vendors, then assortativity is negative, as the values e_{ii} are close to 0. Finally, if social relationships are independent of the device vendor, then assortativity has values close to 0, as $e_{ii} \approx c_i c_i$.

For each dataset, we study how the assortativity of the corresponding social network varies according to Adamic-Adar threshold τ, so that we can verify whether mutual influence increases with the strength of the social links. We also perform a significance test to rule out the possibility that the assortativity of the graph depends only on the distribution of vendors popularity (shown in Figure 1). The test consists in generating, for each dataset, a randomized version of the corresponding affiliation network with the same in-degree and out-degree distribution as the original one. This is done by iteratively switching the endpoints of pairs of randomly selected edges until the affiliation network converges to a random bipartite graph. Then, we compare the assortativity of the social networks obtained from the original and randomized affiliation network with a given Adamic-Adar threshold.

The results of our measurements are reported in Figure 8 for a sample of our datasets. The other datasets present similar characteristics. As the figure shows, the vendor assortativity of our networks is not only always positive, but also significant, and the assortativity of the randomized network approximates zero. Second, as the Adamic-Adar threshold increases, the assortativity increases too, meaning that stronger social links are associated to stronger mutual influence.

4.5 Social Analysis

Collecting probe requests of a large number of mobile devices is an effective way to take a social snapshot of a crowd that participated to an event or that live in a certain area. So far, we have proved it by showing how it is possible to infer the social relationships between people in the crowd by leveraging the SSIDs in the PNLs of the devices. The social networks we extracted share the main properties of those emerging from other contexts, which confirms that our analysis methodology is sound. We now take a further step. We show that certain characteristics of the population that participated to the different events might be inferred from the probe requests sent by their devices. In particular, we focus on users' language and on vendors popularity.

4.5.1 Inferring user languages

We observed that a large fraction of the SSIDs stored in directed probe requests consist of natural language strings. In fact, as already discussed in Section 4.2, the SSIDs of many public WiFi networks reveal the name of touristic attractions (e.g., "Tour Eiffel"), hotels ("manhattan hotel"), bars ("Caffe Barberini"), and so on. On the other hand, we found that many broadband subscribers customized the SSID of their WiFi network in a number of different ways. For instance, some of them use their name. Some others use their SSID as a way to communicate something to their neighbors ("Please don't steal our WiFi"), or even to cheer for their favorite football club ("Forza Roma"). Intuitively, this should make it possible to get a hint on the language of the social context where a user lives by just looking at the SSIDs in the PNL of her device. The language would correspond either to the nationality of the user, if she lives in her country, or to the language of the country where she spends most of the time. Following this intuition, we defined an automatic and scalable user language identification procedure based on the name of the networks in the PNLs. When applied to one of our datasets, this technique helps deduce the national or international nature of the event, and the composition in terms of nationality of the crowd in the event.

Automatic language detection.

Inferring the language of an SSID is not always an easy task as SSIDs are very short (about 13 characters on average) and typically difficult to analyze due to the lack of white spaces or the use of special characters. This makes even the state-of-the-art methods for language identification of short texts [2, 6] unsuitable for our task. We therefore opted for a simple, ad-hoc methodology that turned out to be very effective. Given an SSID, we tokenize it after removing special characters and stop-words (including common words such as "WiFi" and "aDSL"). Each of the words is then

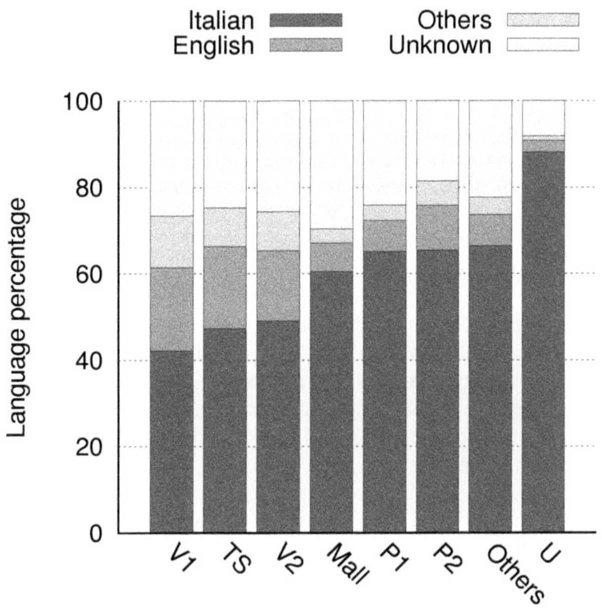

Figure 9: Distribution of languages in the different scenarios. Datasets are sorted by percentage of Italian devices.

searched in a large corpora[5] of texts in 5 languages (Italian, English, French and German) and assigned the language where it appears with highest frequency. The language of an SSID is then given by the language of the majority of its words. If no language is detected, or in case of ties, the language of the SSID is classified as unknown. Similarly, the language of a user is set to be that of the majority of the SSIDs in the PNL of her device, classifying it as unknown in case of ties. We also improved the accuracy of our automatic classification by complementing it in two ways. First, we manually annotated the language of the first 2K most popular SSIDs ($\sim$ 2% of the total) in our All dataset. Due to the skewed distribution of SSIDs popularity (see Figure 3), these SSIDs appear in a very large fraction of PNLs ($\sim$ 75%), thus greatly improving the detection accuracy with a manual task that requires just a few minutes to be completed. Second, we associated to SSIDs containing the name of popular broadband providers the language of the country where the provider operates. For instance, "FASTWEB" is assigned to Italian, "Orange" to French, "Verizon" to English and so on. This is particularly useful to classify the language of those broadband WiFi networks that were left with their default SSID.

We checked the accuracy of our classification method over a randomized sample of 1000 devices manually annotated by a panel of three independent judges. On average, the judges found the percentage of correctly classified devices to be 92%. To measure the level of agreement between the judges, we used a standard NLP approach known as Free-Marginal k agreement [38]. The resulting agreement value of $k = 82\%$ validates the reliability of our manual review process.

Results.

Figure 9 reports the distribution of the languages detected in our datasets. For clarity, in the figure we explicitly show the Italian and English languages only, aggregating all the remaining ones as "Others". Our results show a strong correlation between the percentage of Italian devices and the international nature of the events. More in detail, Vatican 1 (V1) and Vatican 2 (V2)—described as international events in Section 3.1.1—are amongst the datasets with the lowest percentage of Italian devices. The Train Station (TS) dataset too shows characteristics typical of an international event. This is a direct consequence of the fact that the central train station in Rome is located in one of the most international areas of the city. The train station also happens to be the main hub connecting the city to its airports, which makes it an almost forced stop of any tourist that visits Rome. The Mall, Politics 1 (P1), Politics 2 (P2), and Other datasets show, instead, a high (i.e., $> 50\%$) percentage of Italian devices, confirming the fact that these events mostly consisted of an Italian crowd. Nevertheless, the percentage of Italian devices that were detected in these datasets is still significantly lower than that of the University (U) dataset. This is because the surroundings of the university entrance where we positioned our fixed antenna (see Section 3.1.1) were almost exclusively frequented by students. As in our university there are very few courses that are taught in English, these students are either Italian, or foreigners speaking Italian and living in an Italian social context.

Assortativity of SSIDs' languages.

Our SSID language detection method can also be used to verify the intuition that people tend to connect to networks of the same nationality. To do it, we first build the graph G_{SSID} of WiFi networks that share common users. More specifically, we add an edge between two networks if there is at least one device that connected to both of them. Then, we compute the language assortativity of G_{SSID} with the same technique described in Section 4.4 but, this time, by partitioning the nodes of the graph according to their language. The result confirms our intuition as we found a positive and significant language assortativity of 0.20. By comparison, the language assortativity of the randomized graph of SSIDs is -0.01, showing that the result does not depend on the distribution of language popularity.

4.5.2 *Demographics of brand penetration*

We now focus on device vendors. Our objective is to understand what the distribution of vendors in a dataset reveals about the categories and the socioeconomic status of people that participated to the corresponding event. In Figure 10 we show the distributions of the device vendors of each of our datasets. Notice how the distribution of vendors varies in a less marked way from event to event with respect to that of users languages. This is expected, as language characterizes people in a much stronger way than the choice of a device vendor. However, note that the vendor distribution is computed over the total number of devices in each dataset, which can be up to 4 times higher than the number of devices we could infer the language of (compare column "Devices" with column "PNLs" on Table 2). Therefore, small variations in the distributions can be considered significant in this case. That said, there are two trends that emerge from our results. First, the Vatican 1, Vatican 2 and Train Station datasets all feature a very similar vendor distribution, which is characterized by a high ($\sim$ 62%) percentage of Apple devices and a low ($\sim$ 15%) percentage of Samsung devices with respect to most of the other datasets. Interestingly, these datasets correspond also to the events where we observed a significant presence of tourists. Based on the observation that Apple devices are typically more expensive that the others, these results can suggest that foreigners visiting Rome may represent a sample of people that are, on average, wealthier than those that participated to the local

[5]Available at `http://wacky.sslmit.unibo.it/doku.php?id=corpora`

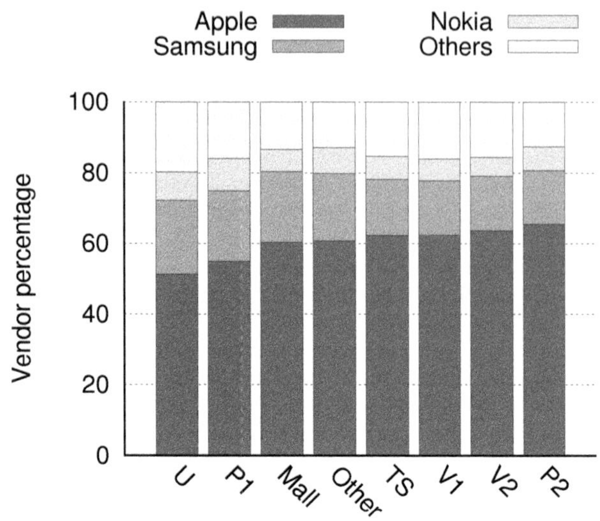

Figure 10: Distribution of vendors in the different scenarios. Datasets are sorted by percentage of Apple devices.

events. This is reasonable, since a trip to a foreign country, especially in a historical city like Rome, can be rather expensive. Local events, on the opposite, have the potential to attract an audience which is wider both in terms of social extraction and economic status. Second, we noticed that the differences in vendor popularity between local events is correlated with the difference we observed in the average age and social status of the people that participated. Again, this may be caused by Apple devices being more expensive. More in detail, we can notice a steep drop in the percentage of Apple devices when comparing the Politics 2 ($\sim$ 65%) to the Politics 1 ($\sim$ 54%) dataset, and the Mall ($\sim$ 60%) to the University ($\sim$ 51%) dataset. In fact, the people that participated to the Politics 2 event organized by the conservative party were, on average, older and wealthier than those that participated to the Politics 1 event. Also, the Mall is frequented by a wider range of people with respect to the University, which is mainly frequented by students who are typically on a budget. Finally, notice how the Others ($\sim$ 60% of Apple devices) dataset shows a distribution very similar to that of the Mall dataset. Both datasets, in fact, represent a rather uniform sample of population. Overall, these results suggest that difference in vendor distribution between two events might reveal a significant difference in the people that participated to them. The most compelling evidence of this fact is that the difference in age and socioeconomic status we observed between supporters of Politics 1 and Politics 2 parties is well represented by their difference in terms of popularity of Apple devices.

4.6 Temporal analysis on the University dataset

As opposite to the other datasets, which have been collected during one-shot events, the University dataset is the result of a 6 weeks long observation period performed from a fixed vantage point at the campus entrance. In this section we show how this long-term dataset allows to characterize the social dynamics of an observed area and to get further insights on its target population. Also, we study the correlation between co-occurrence of people and the strength of their social relationship as inferred by using the Adamic-Adar metric. Our studies are related to those regarding the characteristics of human social behavior [18, 35].

4.6.1 Recurrent patterns

Figure 11(a) reports the number of new (solid column) and known (dashed column) devices that were detected in each day of observation. Figure 11(b) reports, instead, the number of detected devices in a sample day. Our observations are consistent with the intuition that students' life is very predictable. Indeed, according to Figure 11(a), the number of detected devices abruptly decreases in correspondence of both week-ends and days when courses are suspended due to seasonal vacations (e.g., Week 1). Plus, consistently across all working days, the number of detected devices has a peak around lunch time (Figure 11(b)) and decreases in the evening. Also the repetitive schedule typical of students' life is captured in this dataset, as it takes only a few days for the number of newly detected devices to drop down to 30% of the total (Figure 11(b)). This suggests that the probability that a student does not visit the campus for more than a couple of working days in a row is small. In fact, most of them visit the campus with a very high frequency, which is confirmed by Figure 12 where we plot the distribution of the number of times the devices were detected in different time slots of 1 hour. According to the distribution, 40% of the devices were detected more than 100 times ($\sim$ 2 times per day on average).

Overall, these results show how a long-term collection of probes requests adds a further dimension to the characterisation of a target population. In our case, we found a number of properties that match the typical students' movements patterns. This complements the other insights we inferred on students' language and socioeconomic status.

4.6.2 Smartphone co-occurrences

As observed in other contexts [8, 13, 36], the simultaneous presence of pairs of people in a given place denotes the existence of a possible social relationship between them. At the same time, the Adamic-Adar similarity we defined in Section 4.3 is based on a similar intuition, as it assigns a higher strength to social links connecting people that are more likely to frequent the same places. Intuitively, there should be a correlation between these two ways of inferring social links. The long-term University dataset allows to confirm this by verifying whether increasing values of the Adamic-Adar similarity between two devices correspond to a higher probability of their simultaneous occurrence. To do so, we first divide the time in slots of 120 seconds, which are sufficiently large to allow most of the devices to transmit their probes. Then, we group pairs of devices together in buckets according to their Adamic-Adar similarity. Finally, we average the number of co-occurrences observed for the pairs in each bucket. The results, shown in Figure 13, confirm our hypothesis, as we can observe a positive correlation between the Adamic-Adar similarity and the average number of co-occurrences (Pearson coefficient 0.858. 1-tailed p-value < 0.005).

5. CONCLUSIONS AND FUTURE WORK

Probe requests, both broadcast and directed ones, are a useful tool that enables energy-limited mobile devices to efficiently and transparently discover available access points and switch between them. The goal of this work was to show that, besides from their basic utility, smartphone probes actually bring insightful and interesting information about a crowd at an event or about a target population. To fully investigate this idea, we organized a three months long campaign of probe collection. During our campaign we targeted scenarios differing in both terms of scale and characteristics of the population involved: From campus and city-wide, to national

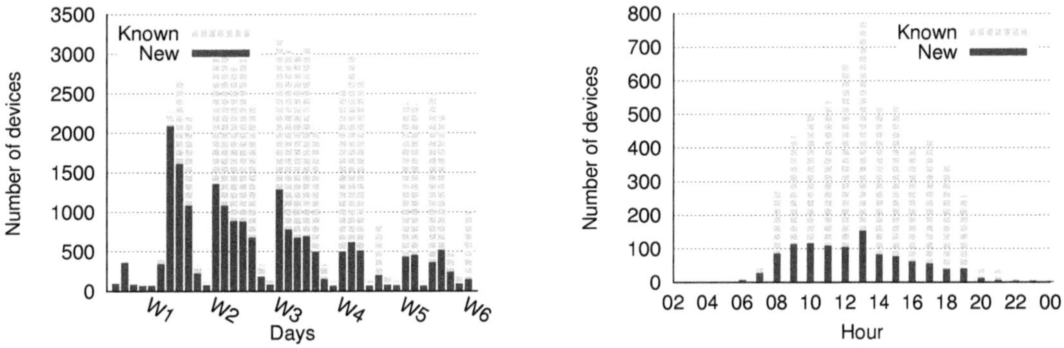

(a) Daily number of devices discovered. W1, W2, W3, W4, W5, and W6 mark the beginning of each week. Irregularities in W1, W4, and W5 correspond to classes breaks due to national holidays.

(b) Hourly number of devices discovered in a sample day.

Figure 11: Number of devices discovered in the University dataset for the whole collection period (a) and for a sample day (b). 'New' refers to the number of devices seen for the first time, 'Known' to the other ones.

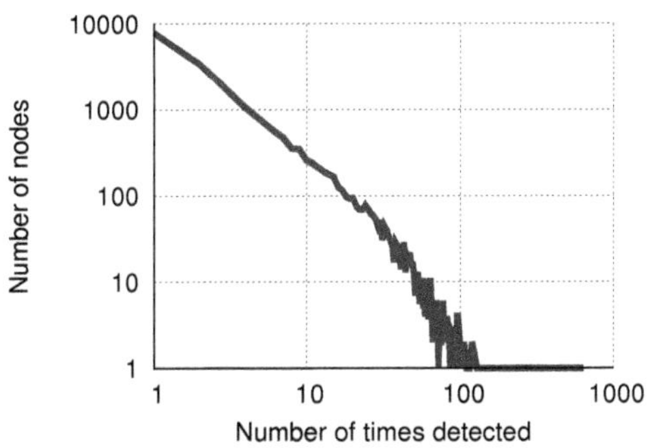

Figure 12: Distribution of the number of times the devices have been detected in the University dataset.

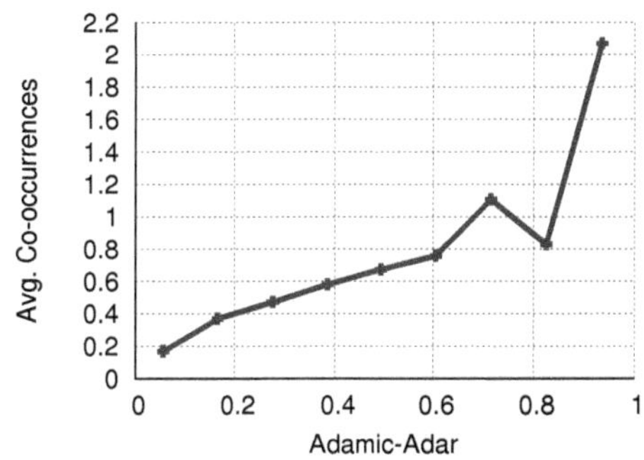

Figure 13: Expected number of co-occurrence per couple of nodes vs. their Adamic-Adar similarity in the University dataset.

and international scenarios. As a result we collected more than 11M probes sent by more than 160K different smartphone devices overall.

In this paper, we presented an in-depth study of these novel and large-scale datasets. The most important findings of our study are the following: First, we developed an automated methodology through which to derive the underlying relationship graphs between the users in each scenario, and showed how all these graphs feature properties that are typical of social networks—user and SSID degrees distributed as a power law, short diameter, high clustering coefficient and so on. Then, we studied how, in our social networks, groups of interconnected people tend to choose the same device vendor with a probability that increases with the strength of their social relationship. These results support the theory of homophily and social influence between people living in geographical proximity. We also performed, for the first time, language detection on the broadcast SSIDs, and exploited the vendor ID to show how the probes can directly reflect the sociological aspects of the people involved in each scenario like nationality, age, and socioeconomic status.

We believe this is just a first step towards a new, non invasive methodology for uncovering non-online social networks. As a future work, we plan to include information regarding the location of the networks referred to by the probes. This could be done, for instance, by using crowd sourced databases of 802.11 networks observed around the world, like Wigle[6]. This extra information will help us to achieve an even stronger characterization of the sample of the population contained in our datasets.

Acknowledgments

This work is partly supported by the Italian Government under the PRIN program (Progetti di rilevante interesse nazionale). We thank Sokol Kosta for his contribution to the data collection campaign.

6. REFERENCES

[1] L. A. Adamic and E. Adar. Friends and neighbors on the web. *Social networks*, 25(3):211–230, 2003.

[2] T. Baldwin and M. Lui. Language identification: The long and the short of the matter. In *Human Language Technologies*. Association for Computational Linguistics, 2010.

[3] A.-L. Barabási and R. Albert. Emergence of scaling in random networks. *Science*, 286(5439):509–512, 1999.

[4] J. Bhardwaj. Naked security blog: What is your phone saying behind your back?

[6] `https://wigle.net/`

[5] R. L. Breiger. The duality of persons and groups. *Social forces*, 53(2):181–190, 1974.
[6] S. Carter, W. Weerkamp, and M. Tsagkias. Microblog language identification: Overcoming the limitations of short, unedited and idiomatic text. *Language Resources and Evaluation*, pages 1–21, 2013.
[7] N. Cheng, P. Mohapatra, M. Cunche, M. A. Kaafar, R. Boreli, and S. Krishnamurthy. Inferring user relationship from hidden information in wlans. In *Military Communications Conference*. IEEE, 2012.
[8] D. J. Crandall, L. Backstrom, D. Cosley, S. Suri, D. Huttenlocher, and J. Kleinberg. Inferring social ties from geographic coincidences. *Proceedings of the National Academy of Sciences*, 107(52):22436–22441, 2010.
[9] M. Cunche, M. A. Kaafar, and R. Boreli. I know who you will meet this evening! linking wireless devices using wi-fi probe requests. In *Proceedings of the International Symposium on World of Wireless, Mobile and Multimedia Networks (WoWMoM)*. IEEE, 2012.
[10] J. Cranshaw, E. Toch, J. Hong, A. Kittur, and N. Sadeh. Bridging the gap between physical location and online social networks. In *Proceedings of the 12th International Conference on Ubiquitous Computing*. ACM, 2010.
[11] D. A. Dai Zovi and S. A. Macaulay. Attacking automatic wireless network selection. In *Proceedings from the Sixth Annual SMC*. IEEE, 2005.
[12] L. C. C. Desmond, C. C. Yuan, T. C. Pheng, and R. S. Lee. Identifying unique devices through wireless fingerprinting. In *Proceedings of the first conference on Wireless Network Security*. ACM, 2008.
[13] N. Eagle and A. Pentland. Reality mining: sensing complex social systems. *Personal and ubiquitous computing*, 10(4):255–268, 2006.
[14] N. Eagle and A. S. Pentland. Eigenbehaviors: Identifying structure in routine. *Behavioral Ecology and Sociobiology*, 63(7):1057–1066, 2009.
[15] J. Franklin, D. McCoy, P. Tabriz, V. Neagoe, J. V. Randwyk, and D. Sicker. Passive data link layer 802.11 wireless device driver fingerprinting. In *Proceedings of the 15th USENIX Security Symposium*, 2006.
[16] M. S. Granovetter. The strength of weak ties. *American journal of sociology*, pages 1360–1380, 1973.
[17] M. Heymans and A. K. Singh. Deriving phylogenetic trees from the similarity analysis of metabolic pathways. *Bioinformatics*, 19(suppl 1):i138–i146, 2003.
[18] T. Karagiannis, J.-Y. Le Boudec, and M. Vojnovic. Power law and exponential decay of intercontact times between mobile devices. *Transactions on Mobile Computing*, 9(10):1377–1390, 2010.
[19] L. Katz. A new status index derived from sociometric analysis. *Psychometrika*, 18(1):39–43, 1953.
[20] C. Klaus. Wireless 802.11b security faq. `https://lwn.net/2001/1011/a/wlan-security.php3`.
[21] J. M. Kleinberg. Authoritative sources in a hyperlinked environment. *Journal of the ACM (JACM)*, 46(5):604–632, 1999.
[22] R. Kumar, A. Tomkins, and E. Vee. Connectivity structure of bipartite graphs via the knc-plot. In *Proceedings of the international conference on Web search and web data mining*. ACM, 2008.
[23] S. Lattanzi and D. Sivakumar. Affiliation networks. In *Proceedings of the 41st annual symposium on Theory of computing*. ACM, 2009.
[24] J. Leskovec. Stanford large network dataset collection. `http://snap.stanford.edu/data/`.
[25] J. Leskovec, L. A. Adamic, and B. A. Huberman. The dynamics of viral marketing. *ACM Transactions on the Web (TWEB)*, 1(1):5, 2007.
[26] J. Leskovec, J. Kleinberg, and C. Faloutsos. Graph evolution: Densification and shrinking diameters. *ACM Transactions on Knowledge Discovery from Data (TKDD)*, 1(1):2, 2007.
[27] D. Liben-Nowell and J. Kleinberg. The link-prediction problem for social networks. *Journal of the American society for information science and technology*, 58(7):1019–1031, 2007.
[28] J. Pang, B. Greenstein, R. Gummadi, S. Seshan, and D. Wetherall. 802.11 user fingerprinting. In *Proceedings of the 13th annual international conference on Mobile computing and networking*. ACM, 2007.
[29] C. D. Manning, P. Raghavan, and H. Schütze. *Introduction to information retrieval*, volume 1. Cambridge University Press Cambridge, 2008.
[30] J. McAuley and J. Leskovec. Learning to discover social circles in ego networks. In *Advances in Neural Information Processing Systems 25*, pages 548–556, 2012.
[31] M. McPherson, L. Smith-Lovin, and J. M. Cook. Birds of a feather: Homophily in social networks. *Annual review of sociology*, pages 415–444, 2001.
[32] A. Musa and J. Eriksson. Tracking unmodified smartphones using wi-fi monitors. In *Proceedings of the 10th Conference on Embedded Network Sensor Systems*. ACM, 2012.
[33] M. E. Newman. Mixing patterns in networks. *Physical Review E*, 67(2):026126, 2003.
[34] I. Rose and M. Welsh. Mapping the urban wireless landscape with argos. In *Proceedings of the 8th Conference on Embedded Networked Sensor Systems*. ACM, 2010.
[35] M. Salathé, M. Kazandjieva, J. W. Lee, P. Levis, M. W. Feldman, and J. H. Jones. A high-resolution human contact network for infectious disease transmission. *Proceedings of the National Academy of Sciences*, 107(51):22020–22025, 2010.
[36] S. Scellato, A. Noulas, R. Lambiotte, and C. Mascolo. Socio-spatial properties of online location-based social networks. *ICWSM*, 11:329–336, 2011.
[37] I. C. Society. Ieee standardd 802.11, 2012.
[38] M. J. Warrens. Inequalities between multi-rater kappas. *Advances in data analysis and classification*, 4(4):271–286, 2010.
[39] D. J. Watts and S. H. Strogatz. Collective dynamics of 'small-world' networks. *nature*, 393(6684):440–442, 1998.
[40] E. Zheleva, H. Sharara, and L. Getoor. Co-evolution of social and affiliation networks. In *Proceedings of the 15th international conference on Knowledge discovery and data mining*. ACM, 2009.
[41] M. V. Barbera, A. Epasto, A. Mei, S. Kosta, V. C. Perta, and J. Stefa. CRAWDAD data set sapienza/probe-requests, 2013.

Rise of the Planet of the Apps: A Systematic Study of the Mobile App Ecosystem

Thanasis Petsas
FORTH-ICS, Greece
petsas@ics.forth.gr

Antonis Papadogiannakis
FORTH-ICS, Greece
papadog@ics.forth.gr

Michalis Polychronakis
Columbia University, USA
mikepo@cs.columbia.edu

Evangelos P. Markatos
FORTH-ICS, Greece
markatos@ics.forth.gr

Thomas Karagiannis
Microsoft Research, UK
thomkar@microsoft.com

ABSTRACT

Mobile applications (apps) have been gaining rising popularity due to the advances in mobile technologies and the large increase in the number of mobile users. Consequently, several app distribution platforms, which provide a new way for developing, downloading, and updating software applications in modern mobile devices, have recently emerged. To better understand the download patterns, popularity trends, and development strategies in this rapidly evolving mobile app ecosystem, we systematically monitored and analyzed four popular third-party Android app marketplaces. Our study focuses on measuring, analyzing, and modeling the app popularity distribution, and explores how pricing and revenue strategies affect app popularity and developers' income.

Our results indicate that unlike web and peer-to-peer file sharing workloads, the app popularity distribution deviates from commonly observed Zipf-like models. We verify that these deviations can be mainly attributed to a new download pattern, to which we refer as the *clustering effect*. We validate the existence of this effect by revealing a strong temporal affinity of user downloads to app categories. Based on these observations, we propose a new formal clustering model for the distribution of app downloads, and demonstrate that it closely fits measured data. Moreover, we observe that paid apps follow a different popularity distribution than free apps, and show how free apps with an ad-based revenue strategy may result in higher financial benefits than paid apps. We believe that this study can be useful to appstore designers for improving content delivery and recommendation systems, as well as to app developers for selecting proper pricing policies to increase their income.

Categories and Subject Descriptors

D.4.8 [**Operating Systems**]: Performance—*Measurements; Modeling and prediction; Simulation*

Keywords

Appstores; Mobile Apps; Workload Characterization; App Popularity; Clustering effect; App Pricing; Revenue

IMC'13, October 23–25, 2013, Barcelona, Spain.
Copyright 2013 ACM 978-1-4503-1953-9/13/10 ...$15.00.
http://dx.doi.org/10.1145/2504730.2504749.

1. INTRODUCTION

With more than 640 million active mobile devices as of July 2012 [9], the market of mobile devices is one of the fastest growing. Along with this growth, recent advances in mobile technologies facilitated a plethora of *mobile applications (apps)*; for example, the Android Market experienced a sevenfold increase in the number of offered apps from 100,000 to 700,000 within the last two years [8]. Typically, apps are hosted and distributed to end users through an increasing number of *mobile application stores (appstores)*. Appstores provide a new way of developing, downloading, and updating software applications for mobile devices, and create new business opportunities for application developers.

Despite this rapid evolution, there have been only a few large-scale studies of mobile appstores, mostly focusing on security and privacy aspects of mobile apps [32,33,44,45]. However, appstores provide essentially a public marketplace matching mobile users and developers, and hence can offer valuable insights across a diverse set of dimensions ranging from app download patterns and popularity trends, to developers' revenue strategies. To this end, through a study of four popular third-party Android appstores over several months, our work aims to better understand appstore properties by focusing on two main aspects:

- *Q1:* How can we characterize the popularity of different mobile applications?
- *Q2:* What are the pricing and revenue strategies followed by app developers?

To examine *Q1*, we first characterize the app popularity distribution. Our results highlight a typical "Pareto effect," with 10% of the apps accounting for 70–90% of the total downloads. While such phenomena have also been observed in the popularity of web objects [25] and video content [21], the app popularity distribution appears truncated at both head and tail, and this observation is consistent across all examined appstores. Our analysis shows that truncation at the head of the distribution is caused by the "fetch-at-most-once" property, also found in peer-to-peer file sharing systems [34]. Contrary, we attribute tail truncation to a phenomenon we refer to as the "clustering effect," which captures the tendency of users to show a strong temporal affinity to app categories, by selectively downloading apps from certain categories over time. These insights lead us to propose a new model to approximate the popularity distributions observed in appstores, and through simulation results we show that it closely captures the observed behaviors.

Typically, appstores offer two categories of mobile apps: paid and free. In *Q2*, we examine whether offering a paid or free ad-based app is a better revenue-making strategy for developers. To this end, we first study the differences between paid and free apps.

While as expected free apps are far more popular, interestingly, paid apps appear to follow a different popularity distribution, which more closely resembles a Zipf distribution. We conjecture that this is the result of users being more selective when paying for apps.

Looking at developers' income from paid apps, we find that the majority of them earn a very small income, and offering a large number of apps does not lead to larger income; quality is more important than quantity. In contrast, by inspecting application binaries, we find that 67.7% of the free apps include at least one library that belongs to the 20 most popular advertising networks. Our analysis suggests that, on average, a free app needs to make just $0.21 per download through ads to match the income offered by a paid app. For popular apps, this number drops to $0.033. Hence, opting for a free app appears to be a more lucrative strategy.

Overall, we believe that our study offers multiple insights to both appstore designers and app developers. By understanding app popularity patterns, appstore and mobile operators can improve performance (e.g., by caching the most popular applications as shown by the Pareto effect), usability (e.g., by pre-installing very popular applications to mobile devices), and the relevance of recommendation and search systems (e.g., by taking into account the clustering effect). Similarly, insights on app monetization can be crucial for developers. Indeed, our study further shows that choosing an appropriate app category significantly affects the expected income.

The main contributions of this work are:

- We study the popularity distribution of mobile apps and compare it to the popularity distributions seen in web, peer-to-peer file sharing, and user-generated content. We show that app downloads follow a power-law distribution with truncated edges and have a highly-skewed Pareto effect, with 10% of apps accounting for 70–90% of total downloads.
- We provide a model of app download distribution and validate it using data from four Android appstores. We show that our model fits the measured data much more closely than previously proposed models for web and peer-to-peer file sharing. We attribute this difference to the "clustering effect," which we validate with a study of user behavior patterns.
- We study the differences between paid and free apps and show that (i) they have different download distributions, and (ii) they lead to fundamentally different revenue patterns for developers. We show that, in most cases, free apps that follow an ad-based revenue strategy may result in higher financial benefits than paid apps.

2. DATA COLLECTION

In this section we describe the data sources we used, our data collection architecture, and summarize the collected data, which are analyzed in the rest of the paper.

2.1 Monitored Appstores

For our study we systematically collected information from four popular Android app marketplaces: SlideMe [16], 1Mobile [13], AppChina [15], and Anzhi [14]. SlideMe is one of the oldest Android marketplaces, founded in 2008, containing more than 20,000 apps. 1Mobile is one of the largest third-party appstores, with more than 150,000 apps. AppChina and Anzhi are very popular appstores located in China, with more than 50,000 apps each. All marketplaces provide a website through which users can browse, search, download, and buy apps. They also provide an application manager tool that allows users to manage, search, and download apps directly from their Android device, in a similar way as the official Google Play Store App. Anzhi is often found as the pre-configured appstore on HTC smartphones in China. Many tablet manufacturing companies like *Disgo*, as well as many telecommunication providers like *Vodafone*, offer their devices pre-installed with SlideMe [5, 17]. More than 120 OEM device models use SlideMe as their default appstore [35].

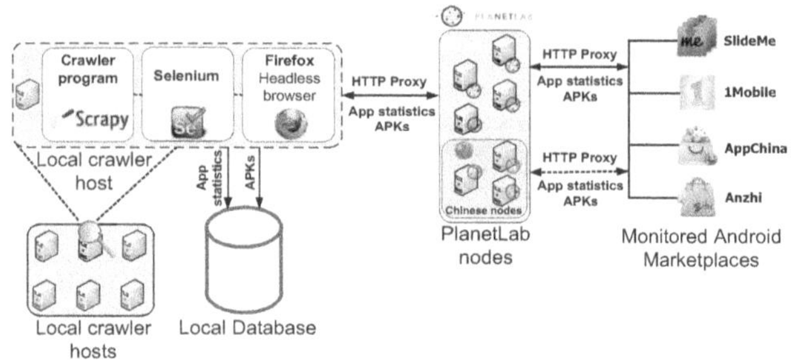

Figure 1: *Data collection architecture.* Local crawler hosts use Planetlab nodes as proxies to download per-app statistics and APKs, which are stored in a local database.

To explore similarities and differences among various appstores, we chose a representative and diverse sample of the available marketplaces. In terms of geographical distribution, Anzhi and AppChina target the quickly rising mobile app market of China, while 1Mobile and SlideMe are mostly used by developers and clients located in Europe and the United States. In terms of the number of available apps, 1Mobile is one of the largest appstores, Anzhi and AppChina are considered as medium-size appstores, while SlideMe is a smaller one. The appstores also differ in the degree of popularity in terms of daily downloads. SlideMe provides both free and paid apps, while the rest provide only free apps.

One of the main reasons for choosing these appstores is that all of them provide the accurate number of downloads for each app, an aspect that is of great interest for our study. On the other hand, the official Android market Google Play [6], as well as other third-party marketplaces [1, 3, 4], do not provide a precise number of downloads or installations per app. Instead, they give only range approximations, which make any kind of systematic analysis very difficult. Besides the coarse-grained available information, Google's terms of service do not allow access to Google Play through any type of automated means.

2.2 Data Collection Architecture

For each appstore, we collect information in two phases. Initially, we gather a snapshot of the available apps by crawling the appstore through its web interface, and store all data into a local database. Then, the crawling process is repeated on a daily basis. Each day, our crawling system re-visits the web pages for the already indexed apps to update their daily statistics. It also collects information for all the newly added apps, which are also stored into the database expanding the initial dataset. For each app, we collect statistics such as the number of downloads, user ratings and comments, current version, category, price, and information about the developer. We also download any updated APK files (i.e., the app itself), collecting this way all versions of every app in the marketplace. Note that we download each app version only once, so we do not affect the actual number of downloads.

Figure 1 shows our data collection architecture. The system consists of a set of local machines, each hosting several crawler instances. We also use a set of nodes (roughly around 100) from the PlanetLab infrastructure [23], which act as HTTP proxies. Before sending an HTTP request to an appstore, each crawler instance

Appstore	Crawling period	Total apps (first day / last day)	New apps per day (average)	Total downloads (first day / last day)	Daily downloads (average)
Anzhi	2012-06-04 – 2012-08-03	58,423 / 60,196	29.6	1,396 M / 2,816 M	23.7 M
AppChina	2012-03-30 – 2012-06-03	33,183 / 55,357	336.0	1,033 M / 2,623 M	24.1 M
1Mobile	2012-03-21 – 2012-08-01	128,455 / 156,221	210.4	367 M / 453 M	651.5 K
SlideMe (free)	2012-03-01 – 2012-08-01	12,296 / 16,578	28.0	63 M / 96 M	215.7 K
SlideMe (paid)	2012-03-01 – 2012-08-01	4,606 / 5,606	6.5	111 K / 914 K	5.2 K

Table 1: *Summary of collected data.* We collected data about more than 300,000 apps while monitoring four different appstores for 2–5 months. AppChina has the largest number of daily downloads and new apps per day.

randomly selects one of these proxies. This distributed crawling scheme was necessary to avoid any IP address blacklisting. The Chinese appstores apply rate limiting to hosts away from China, so we used only the PlanetLab nodes that are located in China for proxying their crawling connections.

We implemented a specific crawler for each appstore using the Scrapy framework [10]. We designed our crawlers to comply with the thresholds set by each appstore in terms of requests per time unit. To gather data from pages with dynamically generated content with JavaScript, we used the Selenium Remote Control (RC) [11], a browser automation tool, combined with a headless Firefox browser running on an X virtual framebuffer. For such pages, the crawler was altered to make the HTTP requests through Selenium with the controlled headless browser, so that Scrapy collects all the required information from the already rendered HTML page.

2.3 Data Set

Table 1 summarizes the collected data. For SlideMe, 74.7% of the apps we collected are free, while the rest 25.3% are paid. As of August 2013, the examined appstores had 316,143 apps and 7 billion downloads in total; this is roughly 52.7% of the 600,000 apps and 35% of the 20 billion downloads featured in Google Play at the same time [7]. This implies that our dataset comprises a significant part of the mobile app ecosystem.

We see that a small number of new apps are added to SlideMe and Anzhi by app developers every day. On the other hand, a higher number of new apps are added every day to AppChina and 1Mobile. This is probably due to the increasing popularity of the AppChina marketplace, while 1Mobile hosts the largest number of apps among these appstores. Indeed, we see that AppChina is the most popular appstore in terms of user downloads, with more than 24 million of downloads per day. It seems that this popularity attracts an increasing number of developers that choose this marketplace to distribute their applications. Although 1Mobile hosts the largest number of apps, it has a lower number of downloads than AppChina and Anzhi, which target smartphone users in China. We also observe that paid apps receive significantly less downloads than free apps, and fewer paid apps are added per day to SlideMe.

3. APP POPULARITY

First, we study app popularity based on the distribution of downloads of each app among the different appstores.

3.1 Is There a Pareto Effect?

Previous studies have shown that web content [25] and video downloads [21] usually follow the Pareto Principle: 20% of the objects are responsible for 80% of the downloads. Figure 2 shows the CDF of the percentage of app downloads as a function of the app ranking (ranked from the most popular to the least popular) for the different appstores. The results confirm that a small percentage of apps is responsible for a large percentage of downloads. For example, in AppChina and Anzhi, about 10% of the apps are responsible for close to 90% of all downloads. Similarly, 10% of the

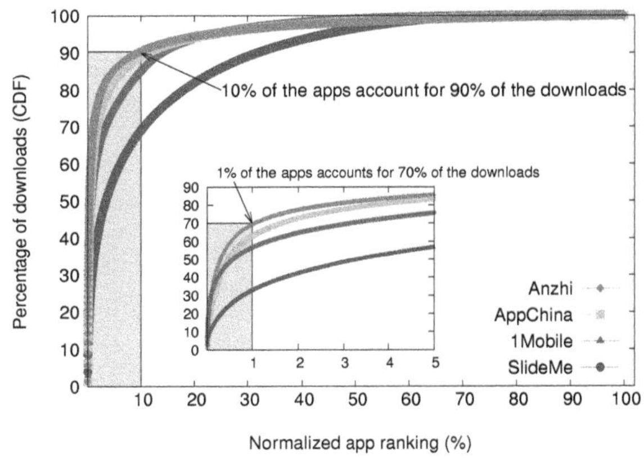

Figure 2: *A few apps account for most of the downloads.* The CDF of downloads per app shows that 10% of the apps account for 90% of the total downloads.

1Mobile apps are responsible for more than 85% of the downloads, and 10% of the SlideMe apps are responsible for more than 70% of all downloads in this appstore. We see that this uneven distribution of popularity goes all the way into the top 1% of the applications, which are responsible for more than 70% of downloads in Anzhi, more than 60% in AppChina, more than 55% in 1Mobile, and more than 30% in SlideMe. This evidence for the existence of the Pareto effect is significant for the design of efficient caching mechanisms for application delivery to end users. For example, a cache large enough to hold 1% of the apps will have a hit rate as high as 70%.

3.2 Is There a Power-law Behavior?

Although it is clear that app downloads follow a pareto principle, we would like to explore whether the app downloads follow a power law distribution much like web downloads do [20]. Figure 3 shows the number of downloads per app, when all apps are sorted in the x axis according to their rank based on their total downloads. We see that all distributions share a similar pattern: their main "trunk" has a linear slope indicating a Zipf distribution, which is truncated at both ends (i.e., for small and large x values).

The truncation for small x values (i.e., most popular apps) seems to follow similar patterns shown in the downloads of file sharing systems [34] and video downloads in YouTube [21]. This truncation on these systems was attributed to the *fetch-at-most-one* principle. That is, objects shared in a file sharing system, such as music, videos, movies, etc., tend to be downloaded at most once by each user. Therefore, the curve for very popular content (i.e., small values in the x axis) tends to flatten out and reach a value close to the number of users in the system. We see the same behavior in Figure 3: for very small x the number of downloads stays almost horizontal (especially in AppChina and Anzhi appstores), which is probably due to the fetch-at-most-one principle. It is reasonable to expect that smartphone users will also download each app at most once, apart from apps which are updated.

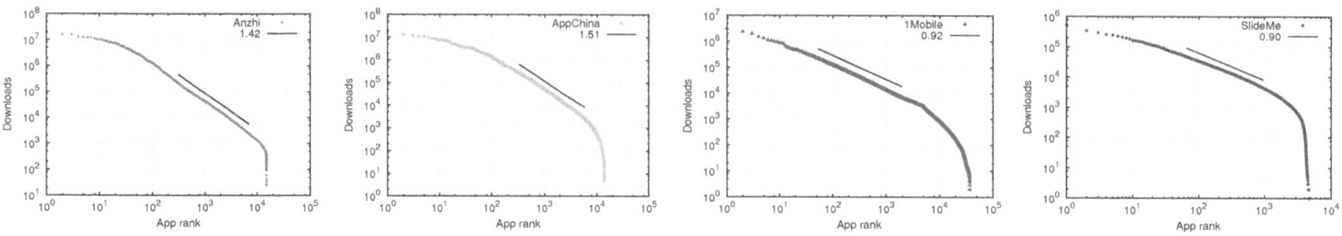

(a) Anzhi (b) AppChina (c) 1Mobile (d) SlideMe

Figure 3: ***App popularity distribution deviates from Zipf at both ends.*** **The distribution of total downloads per app as a function of app's rank shows a main trunk that follows a Zipf distribution with truncated ends. The truncation for small x values can be attributed to the *fetch-at-most-once* property observed in most popular apps. We explain the truncation for large x values with another phemomenon we call as *clustering effect*.**

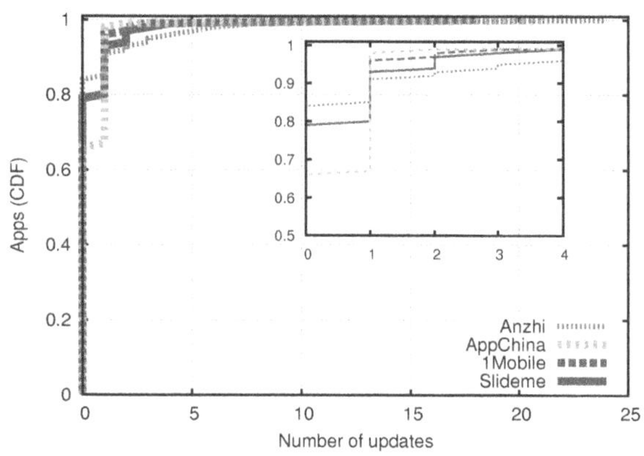

Figure 4: ***Apps are not updated often.*** **CDF of the number of updates per app within two months shows that a small percentage of apps was updated in this period. This implies that users download most apps just once, or very few times, verifying the fetch-at-most-once property.**

To validate that the fetch-at-most-once property exists in mobile appstores as well, and it is not affected by application updates, we plot in Figure 4 the CDF of the number of updates per app in the four appstores for a period of two months. We see that more than 80% of the apps are not updated at all within this period. Even the apps that are updated, they have a very small number of updates, e.g., the 99% of the apps have less than four updates. Since the fetch-at-most-once property affects only the most popular apps, limiting their downloads to the number of users in the market, we focused only on the top 10% most popular apps. We found that these apps are also rarely updated: 60%-75% of them have no updates in this period, while 99% of these apps have up to six updates. These results imply that the fetch-at-most-once property applies to mobile app market, as apps are not updated often.

Moreover, Figure 3 clearly shows that there is a significant curvature for large x values (less popular apps) as well. Observed in user-generated content downloads [21], but not in file sharing [34], this curvature has been thought to be attributed to search engines and recommendation systems. Previous works argue that these systems tend to favor the most popular content, due to information filtering, which results to the observed truncation of power law [22,37]. However, we feel that this curvature is an instance of a more general phenomenon, to which we refer as the *clustering effect*.

The clustering effect suggests that apps are grouped into (static or dynamic) sets. Apps within the same set (cluster) are correlated: if a user downloads one of them, then the same user will probably download another app of the same set rather than switching to another set, or to a totally unrelated app. These clusters can be formed, for example, by the semantic classification of apps to categories, by user communities as a result of positive comments, by the appstore as a result of the recommendation algorithm used, or by other grouping forces. To validate our clustering effect hypothesis, we define and measure the affinity of user downloads among the several app categories in Section 4. Then, we propose a model for user downloads based on clustering effect and we validate it with simulations comparing to the actual gathered data in Section 5.

4. THE CLUSTERING EFFECT

In our next set of measurements we explore whether the previously suggested "clustering effect" hypothesis can be validated. One way to validate the hypothesis would be to show that (A) apps are categorized into clusters, and (B) once users have downloaded an app from one cluster, it is more likely to download another app from the *same* cluster, rather than switching to another one.

Fortunately, point (A) above is easy to show. Most appstores already group apps into clusters that are usually thematically related to the app's content. For example, there exists a cluster for "games," a cluster for "e-books," a cluster for "business and finance," and so on. To validate point (B), we would like to study the download patterns of individual users and see if they tend to concentrate around a few clusters or not. Unfortunately, appstores tend not to reveal the download patterns of individual users, mostly due to privacy concerns, and thus it is not easy to study them. Instead, we use publicly available user comments to approximate their download patterns and interests. If a user posts a publicly available comment for a particular app, we assume that the user has download the app. Thus, publicly available comments provide us with access to a subset of the download patterns of individual users.

4.1 Users Focus on a Few Categories

In this set of measurements we focused only on data from the Anzhi appstore, because it provides user comments with precise timestamps. We considered only user comments that are accompanied by a rating of the app, which is a strong indication of actual downloads. During the crawling process of the Anzhi appstore, we recorded and stored into our database the comments of each user on each app. The crawling process of user comments from the Anzhi marketplace resulted in a dataset of 361,282 users to 60,196 apps in 34 categories. Figure 5(a) shows the distribution of the number of comments per user. We see that 99% of the users made up to 30 comments. In many categories, there were a few users with a very large number of comments. We found that these users were posting spam, possibly using an automated script.

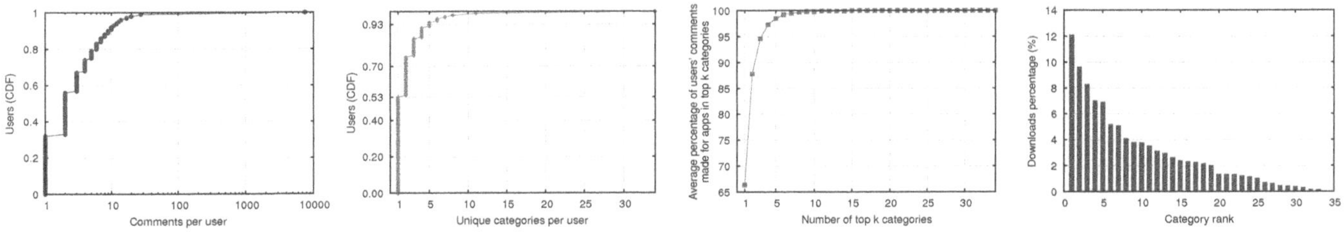

(a) Comments per user (b) Unique categories per user (c) Comments on top k categories (d) Downloads per app category

Figure 5: *Users focus on a few categories.* (a) shows that 92% of the users made up to 10 comments, while 2% of the users made more than 20 comments. (b) shows that 53% of the users leave feedback on apps from a single category, while 94% comment on up to five categories. (c) shows that 66% of the comments are for a single category, while 95% are made for up to three categories. (d) shows that there is no dominant category in terms of downloads, as the most popular app category has 12% of the total downloads.

Figure 5(b) shows the CDF of unique categories for which each user comments on, for users that posted at least one comment. We see that 53% of the users commented on apps from a single category, and 94% of the users commented on apps from up to just five categories. Thus, only 6% of the users made comments in more than five categories, which is significantly lower than the percentage of users that made more than 5 comments in general (20%), as shown in Figure 5(a). Similarly, in Figure 5(c) we present the average percentage of user comments made for the top k categories, as a function of k. We have excluded users that made comments on a single app in this figure. We observe that the 66% of the comments of an average user were made for a single category, while 95% of the user comments were made for no more than five categories.

These findings indicate that most users tend to download apps from a single or very few categories, which implies a clustering effect. One could argue that the popularity distribution of app categories can influence user downloads. For example, *games* are more likely to be downloaded than apps belonging to the *tools* category, as the *games* category has a higher number of total downloads than *tools*. Therefore, a few popular categories could attract most of the users downloads. Figure 5(d) shows the distribution of app downloads across the different app categories. We see that the most popular category has just 12% of the total downloads, while the majority of categories have less than 4% of the total downloads. This fact indicates that there are no dominant categories in terms of downloads, and the popularity of app categories does not seem to have a considerable influence on users downloads. Consequently, the main reason for the small number of categories observed in each user's comments appears to be the clustering effect.

4.2 Temporal Affinity to App Categories

To study the download patterns in more detail and validate the existence of the clustering effect, we will first define and then measure the *temporal affinity* metric of users to app categories. During the crawling process of the Anzhi appstore we have recorded the stream of comments for each user on each app. We suppressed successive comments of the same user on the same app. For example, if a user commented on apps $a_1a_2a_3a_3a_1a_4$ we kept the sequence $a_1a_2a_3a_4$, which we refer to as *app string*. In addition, we know that appstore has already categorized each app a_i into a category $c(a_i)$. Using this knowledge, for each app string $a_1a_2a_3a_3a_4$ we construct the *category string*: $c(a_1)c(a_2)c(a_3)c(a_4)$.

Given a category string S of n elements $c_1c_2c_3...c_n$ with the respective categories of a user's n comments in chronological order, we define the *temporal affinity* metric Aff as the number of elements that are in the same category with their previous element, divided by $n-1$, using the following formula:

$$\text{Aff} = \frac{\sum_{i=2}^{n} \text{Affinity}(c_i, c_{i-1})}{n-1} \quad (1)$$

where $\text{Affinity}(c_i, c_j)$ equals to one if c_i and c_j are the same, and zero otherwise. For example, a user with a category string $c_1c_1c_1c_1$ will have temporal affinity equal to $3/3$, a user with a category string $c_1c_1c_1c_2$ will have temporal affinity equal to $2/3$, and a user with a category string $c_1c_1c_2c_3$ will have affinity equal to $1/3$.

This affinity metric is an indication of whether users tend to comment on apps from the same category or on apps from different categories. Indeed, if affinity approaches the highest value (i.e., one), then users tend to repeatedly comment on apps from the same category, indicating that the users may tend to successively download apps from the same category. On the contrary, if the affinity is low, then users tend to switch from one category to another.

Note that if we have C categories of roughly equal volume, then if users randomly wander from one category to another, the affinity will be around $1/C$. However, in practice, the apps are not evenly distributed among the different categories. To calculate the accurate affinity probability of a random walk in the Anzhi marketplace we used the actual distribution of apps to the C different categories in this appstore from our dataset. Let A be the total number of apps in the appstore and $A(i)$ the number of apps that belong to category i. Given this distribution, the random walk affinity probability $\text{Aff}_{\text{random walk}}$, i.e., the probability that two random app choices belong to the same category, is equal to:

$$\text{Aff}_{\text{random walk}} = \frac{\sum_{i=1}^{C} A(i) \times (A(i)-1)}{A \times (A-1)} \quad (2)$$

since out of the $A \times (A-1)$ possible random app choices, the number of app choices for which the two apps belong to the same category are equal to the sum of $A(i) \times (A(i)-1)$ for all categories. We need the affinity probability of a random walk as a base case to compare with the actual affinity we measure from Anzhi.

So far we have defined the affinity metric as the percentage of consecutive app pairs that belong to the same category. In this way, however, we miss users that may oscillate between few categories. For instance, the category string $c_1c_2c_1c_2$ has affinity equal to zero according to our previous definition, but we can see a clear affinity of this user to c_1 and c_2 categories. To address this issue, we define the affinity metric using the *depth* notion. That is, the affinity Aff with depth d for a category string with n elements is defined as the number of elements in the category string for which at least

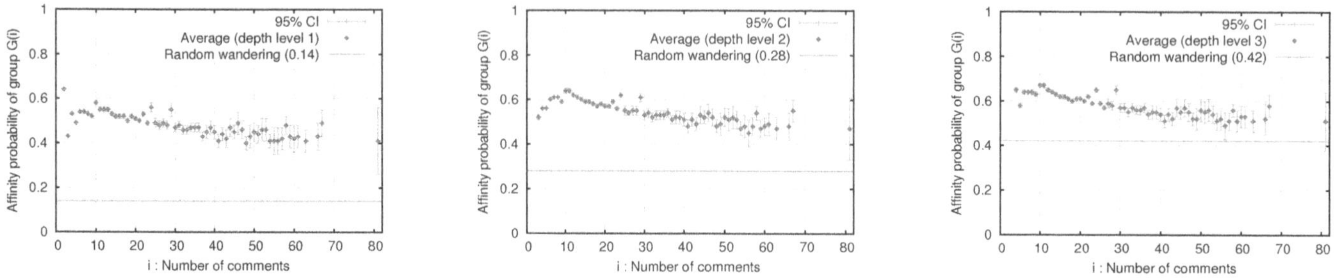

(a) Depth=1 (b) Depth=2 (c) Depth=3

Figure 6: *Successive user selections are from the same category with higher probability.* Temporal affinity for depth levels up to 3 for users grouped by their number of comments. We see that for depth=1, users select an app of the same category as the previous one with probability 0.55, which is 3.9 times higher than the base case of random walk. As expected, affinity increases with depth level.

one element among its previous d elements belongs to the same category, divided by $n - d$:

$$\text{Aff} = \frac{\sum_{i=d}^{n} \text{Affinity}(c_i, \{c_{i-1}, c_{i-2}, \ldots, c_{i-d}\})}{n - d} \tag{3}$$

where $\text{Affinity}(c_i, \{c_{i-1}, c_{i-2}, \ldots, c_{i-d}\})$ is equal to one if at least one of the $\{c_{i-1}, c_{i-2}, \ldots, c_{i-d}\}$ belongs to the same category with c_i, and zero otherwise. For example, the affinity of depth equal to two is defined as the percentage of app selections that belong to the same category with one of the previous two selections. To calculate the affinity metric for this depth, we first divide the n apps of the category string into $n - 2$ triplets. Then we check which of these triplets have affinity, i.e., if the third element belongs to the same category with the second or with the first one in the triplet. Finally, we sum the triplets that have affinity and divide them with the total number of triplets, as shown in Equation 3.

Using Equation 2 we find the affinity probability of a random walk for depth equal to one. To calculate the affinity for an arbitrary depth d we use the following equation:

$$\text{Aff}_{\text{random walk}} = \frac{\sum_{i=1}^{C} A(i) \times (A(i) - 1) \times d \times \prod_{k=2}^{d} (A - k)}{\prod_{k=0}^{d} (A - k)} \tag{4}$$

4.3 Users Exhibit a Strong Temporal Affinity to App Categories

We measure the temporal affinity metric as defined in Equation 3, based on the actual app distribution of the 34 categories of the Anzhi appstrore. Figure 6 shows the measured affinity for depth levels from 1 up to 3, as a function of the number of comments per user. We have grouped together all users that made the same number of comments, and we plot the average values and the 95th confidence intervals from each group. We plotted only the groups that had more than 10 samples, excluding, in this way, the spam users as well. In case of depth equal to one, we see that the average affinity for most groups is around 0.55. This implies that once a user comments on an app from one category, the same user will comment on another app of the same category with probability close to 0.55. To place these numbers in context, we also calculated the estimated affinity of the base case as well, i.e., the case where a user wanders from one app to another randomly. The random walk affinity probability in our dataset for depth one is 0.14, shown as a horizontal line in Figure 6(a). Thus, we see that Anzhi users are 3.9 times more likely to stay in the same category compared to the base case of random walk. This outcome indicates a strong temporal affinity between users and categories.

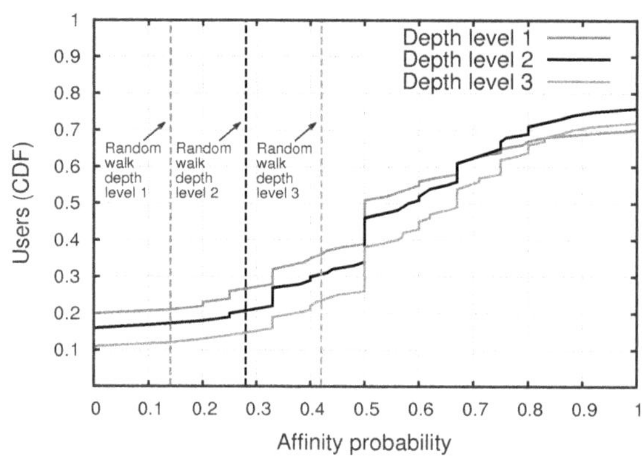

Figure 7: *Most users exhibit a strong temporal affinity to app categories.* The CDF of the affinity metric for each depth level shows that 50% of the users have significantly higher affinity than the base case of random walk.

To explore how the temporal affinity increases for higher depth levels, we plot in Figures 6(b) and 6(c) the affinity metric of the same user groups, as well as the random walk affinity probability, for depths equal to two and three respectively. We see that user affinity to app categories increases with depth, as it was expected, and remains higher than the respective random walk affinity probability. To explore how the affinity varies among users, we plot the CDF of temporal affinity among all Anzhi users for the three different levels in Figure 7. We observe that the median value for depth one is 0.5, while for depths two and three the median values are 0.58 and 0.67 respectively. Overall, our results show that there is a clear temporal affinity of users' comments to app categories, which is a strong indication that users tend to download successive apps from the same categories.These observations validate our hypothesis about the existence of clustering effect in user downloads.

5. A MODEL FOR APPSTORE WORKLOADS

We now define a model of appstore usage called APP-CLUSTERING, based on fetch-at-most-once and clustering effect properties. The model will enable us to further explore our hypothesis and validate the effect of app clustering on app popularity distribution.

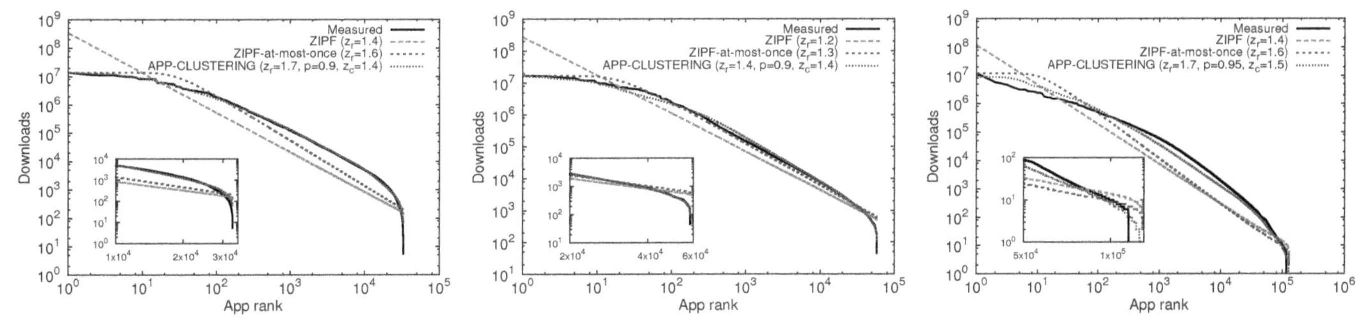

(a) AppChina (b) Anzhi (c) 1Mobile

Figure 8: *Predicted versus measured app popularity for each appstore.* We see that APP-CLUSTERING fits very closely the measured data. ZIPF-at-most-once fits the data better than a pure ZIPF distribution, but diverges for large x values.

Symbol	Parameter Description
A	Number of apps
U	Number of users
D	Total downloads
d	Downloads per user (average)
z_r	Zipf exponent for overall app ranking
Z_G	Overall Zipf distribution of all apps
C	Number of clusters
p	Percentage of downloads based on the clustering effect
z_c	Zipf exponent for cluster's app ranking
Z_c	Zipf distribution of apps in cluster c
$D(i,j)$	Predicted downloads for app with total rank i and rank j in its cluster

Table 2: APP-CLUSTERING model parameters.

5.1 Model Description and Analysis

Table 2 summarizes the key parameters used in our model. We assume that all apps are categorised in C clusters so that each app belongs to exactly one cluster. When a user downloads the first app, this download is drawn from a Zipf-like distribution Z_G. Once a user has downloaded at least one app, subsequent downloads will be from the same category of a previous download with probability p, and from a different category with probability $1-p$. Downloads from the same category of a previous download also follow a Zipf-like distribution Z_c. Therefore, each app has two rankings: its overall ranking i, taking values between 1 and A, and its ranking j within its category, taking values between 1 and the number of apps in that category. Thus, the APP-CLUSTERING model suggests that each user behaves as follows:

1. Download the first app according to the Z_G distribution.
2. Download another app:
   - **2.1.** with probability p the app will be downloaded from the same cluster c of a previously downloaded app. The cluster c is randomly chosen from previous downloads with a uniform probability. The app from cluster c is drawn from distribution Z_c. If the app has been downloaded go to 2.1.
   - **2.2.** with probability $1-p$ the app will be drawn from Z_G. If the app has been downloaded go to 2.2.
3. If user's downloads are less than d go to 2.

Analysis. We assume an appstore with U users, where each user downloads d apps. Out of the d downloads per user, $(1-p) \times d$ are app selections based on a pure Zipf distribution. That is, an app with rank i has a probability to be selected for downloading equal to $(1/i^{z_r})/(\sum_{k=1}^{A} 1/k^{z_r})$. Similarly, when apps are selected from a specific cluster C_a, an app with rank j in this cluster will be selected with probability equal to $(1/j^{z_c})/(\sum_{l=1}^{S_{C_a}} 1/l^{z_c})$, where S_{C_a} the size of cluster C_a. For simplicity we assume that all C clusters have the same size S_C. Overall, the expected downloads $D(i,j)$ for an app with overall rank i and rank j in its respective cluster with the APP-CLUSTERING model are:

$$D(i,j) = \sum_{u=1}^{U} 1 - \left(1 - \frac{1/i^{z_r}}{\sum\limits_{k=1}^{A} 1/k^{z_r}}\right)^{(1-p)\times d} \times \left(1 - \frac{1/j^{z_c}}{\sum\limits_{l=1}^{S_C} 1/l^{z_c}}\right)^{p \times d} \quad (5)$$

The expected downloads per app are estimated by adding the probability of all users to download this app. The probability of a single user to download this app is one minus the probability for not downloading this app with $(1-p) \times d$ Zipf-based selections and $p \times d$ clustering-based selections. We see that the number of downloads per app is limited by the number of users U.

5.2 Simulation-based Model Validation

To validate our model and understand the impact of clustering effect on the app downloads distribution, we developed three Monte Carlo simulators of an appstore, using ZIPF, ZIPF-at-most-once, and APP-CLUSTERING models. In the ZIPF simulator all downloads are drawn from Z_G. In the ZIPF-at-most-once simulator all downloads are drawn from Z_G, but each user can never download the same app more than once. Then we ran these simulators for all appstores in our dataset while varying their key parameters, in order to approximate the observed distribution of app downloads as close as possible. To measure how close each simulation approaches the actual downloads distribution of A apps we calculate the distance between the observed and simulated downloads of each app using the mean relative error:

$$distance = \frac{1}{A} \sum_{i=1}^{A} \frac{|D_o(i) - D_s(i)|}{D_o(i)} \quad (6)$$

where $D_o(i)$ and $D_s(i)$ are the observed and simulated downloads, respectively, for the app with overall rank i.

5.2.1 Comparing Modeled and Actual Downloads

Figure 8 compares the simulation results of the ZIPF, ZIPF-at-most-once, and APP-CLUSTERING models with the measured downloads in AppChina, Anzhi, and 1Mobile. We tuned the parameters of each model to produce the best data fit, by running simulations with all parameter combinations, and measuring the distance from actual data. We plot the results of each model using

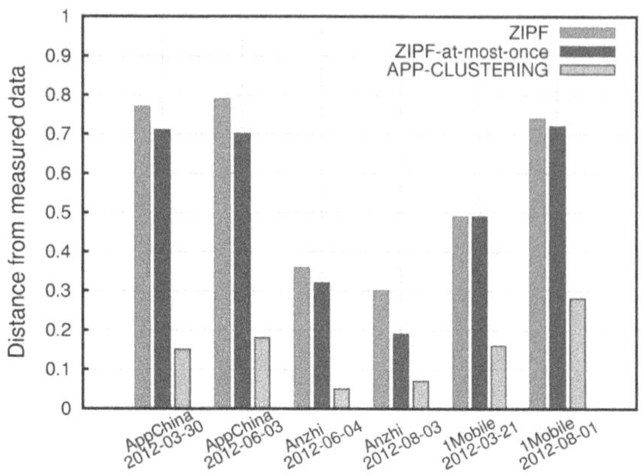

Figure 9: *APP-CLUSTERING has the smallest distance from measured data.* APP-CLUSTERING approximates the actual downloads up to 7.2 times closer than ZIPF and up to 6.4 times closer than ZIPF-at-most-once.

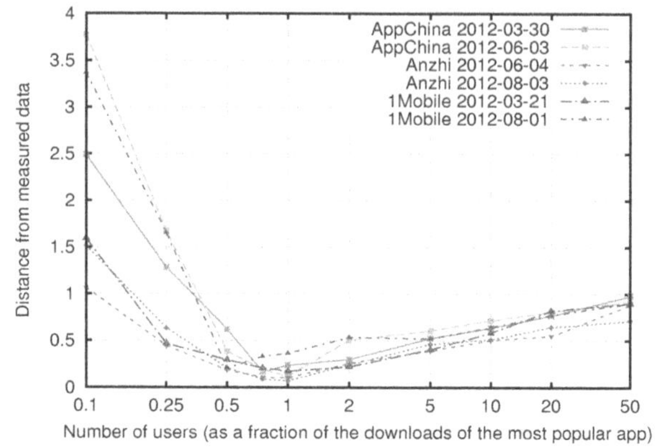

Figure 10: *Downloads of the most popular app are a good estimate of the number of users.* We see the minimum distance from the actual downloads when the number of users is close to the downloads of the most popular app.

the parameters that produced the minimum distance from actual downloads. We first see that in all figures the pure ZIPF distribution (dashed red line) clearly deviates from the measured data. The deviation is obvious: ZIPF is a straight line (in log-log scale) while the measured data follow a curved line at both ends of the x spectrum. Indeed, for small x (i.e., popular apps) ZIPF overshoots the measured data by more than an order of magnitude. ZIPF-at-most-once (dashed blue line) fits the data better than ZIPF, especially for small x (i.e., for popular apps), but deviates from the actual data mainly for large x values. On the other hand, APP-CLUSTERING matches the data very close, better than any other model, both for small x and especially for large x values (i.e., least popular apps).

As we increase p, i.e., the percentage of simulated downloads based on clustering, we see that the distance of APP-CLUSTERING from the actual data is reduced, and data fitting is improved. The best approximations of the actual data are achieved when the percentage p of clustering-based downloads is 90–95%. This outcome provides strong evidence that clustering affects app downloads distribution and is responsible for the observed tail behavior.

Figure 9 shows the distance of the three models from the measured data for the first and last day of our crawling period in AppChina, Anzhi, and 1Mobile. We see that APP-CLUSTERING has the smallest distance from measured data for all appstores. For instance, in the first day AppChina dataset, APP-CLUSTERING predictions result in 0.15 distance from the actual downloads, which is 4.7 times better than ZIPF-at-most-once and 5.1 times better than ZIPF. We see similar results from simulations of other appstores as well. Overall, we observe that APP-CLUSTERING model is able to approximate the actual downloads of all appstores very well from the first day up to the last day of our measurement period.

5.2.2 Choosing the Right Number of Users

Using the APP-CLUSTERING simulator we also explore how the number of users U influences the simulation results. Since we do not have access to the logs of the appstores, we do not know the actual number of users who have accessed each appstore. We know the total number of downloads, the total number of apps, but we do not know the total number of users. Nevertheless, we conduct simulations in order to explore whether there is a reasonable range for the number of users of the appstores studied that results to very close approximations of the actual downloads distribution per app. Given that different appstores have a different actual number of users, we express the number of users as a function of the total number of downloads of the most popular app.

Figure 10 shows our simulation results while varying the number of users U and setting the rest of the simulation parameters to the values that produce the minimum distance from the actual data. The x-axis is the number of the simulated users, as a ratio of the total number of downloads of the most popular app, and the y-axis reports the distance between the simulation results and the measured downloads. We plot the simulation results for the app downloads of the first and last day of the AppChina, Anzhi, and 1Mobile appstores. We see that in all cases the minimum distance from the measured data is achieved when the number of users is very close to the number of downloads of the most popular app.

6. APP PRICING AND INCOME

Among the four appstores we studied, AppChina, Anzhi, and 1Mobile offer solely free apps—only SlideMe provides both free and *paid* apps. One might wonder why developers choose third-party marketplaces to upload paid apps instead of Google Play, which could result in increased app visibility. There are several reasons to do so. First, many developers upload their apps in as many alternative markets as possible in order to gain more popularity, increase their income, and attract users with devices that have third-party appstores pre-installed, such as SlideMe, as explained in Section 2. Also, Google Play supports only specific locations for merchants [12]. Since developers living in countries not supported by Google cannot upload paid apps to Google Play, they usually choose an alternative market like SlideMe. Finally, third-party marketplaces may provide benefits to developers, e.g., SlideMe does not charge transaction fees besides a payment processing fee [35].

Paid apps usually have more advanced functionality and do not include advertisements. In this section, we focus on the SlideMe appstore to study how price affects app popularity, how revenue is distributed among developers and categories, and how different pricing strategies may affect developers' income. The main questions that drive our analysis regarding app pricing and developers' income are the following: (Q1) Which are the main differences between paid and free apps? (Q2) What is the developers' income range? (Q3) Which are the common strategies when offering an app, and how do these strategies affect revenue? In the rest of this section we explore these questions in more detail using the dataset of the SlideMe appstore.

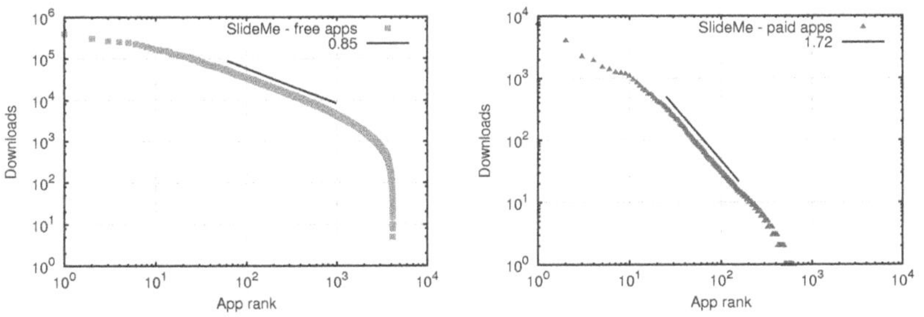

(a) SlideMe - free apps (b) SlideMe - paid apps

Figure 11: ***Paid apps follow a clear Zipf distribution.*** **The downloads distribution of free and paid apps shows that paid apps clearly follow a power-law distribution, while free apps follow the same distribution we observed in Section 3.2.**

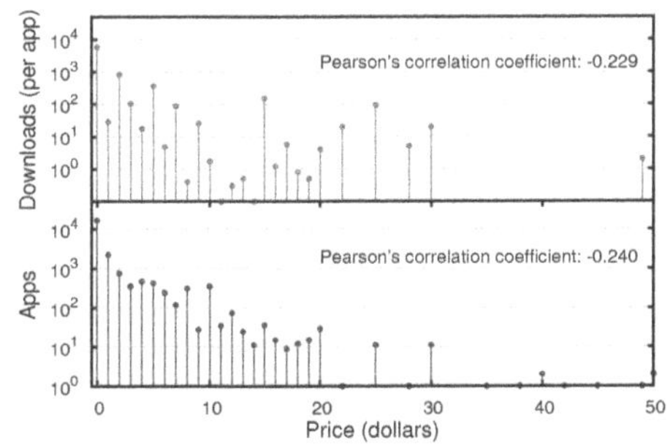

Figure 12: ***Expensive apps are less popular.*** **Number of downloads and apps as a function of price. We see that the number of downloads and number of apps are negatively correlated with price.**

6.1 The Influence of Cost on App Popularity

First, we explore how cost affects app popularity. To understand the different download patterns between paid and free apps (Q1), Figure 11 shows the distribution of downloads for free and paid apps separately. Free apps follow a similar distribution as the one observed in Section 3.2. Interestingly, we see that paid apps clearly follow a pure power-law distribution, with no significant deviations. This is probably due to the fact that users are more selective when downloading paid apps: they are less influenced by recommendation systems and more considerate about cost. Thus, less popular apps tend to stay that way and are deprived from any casual downloads. Contrary, free apps enjoy much more downloads and even less popular apps get a decent number of downloads.

Figure 12 shows the average number of downloads per app, as well as the number of apps as a function of price. Since the app price may change, we use the average price of each app we observed within our measurement period. We group together all apps that their price is within a range of one dollar, e.g., apps with price between two and three dollars belong to the same bin, and we plot the number of apps for each bin (in the lower part) and the average number of downloads among the apps of each bin (upper part). It is expected that apps with higher prices will get less downloads. Indeed, we observe a negative correlation between price and downloads, with Pearson's correlation coefficient equal to -0.229. This means that apps with higher prices are less likely to become popular. Similarly, the results indicate that there is a negative correlation between price and number of apps as well, i.e., we see more apps with lower prices, with a correlation coefficient equal to -0.240. This means that most developers offer their apps in lower prices, hoping for increased popularity.

6.2 Developers' Income

Next, we set out to explore how the app market's revenue from paid apps are distributed among the developers, and which parameters affect the developers' income (Q2). To estimate the income of each developer we rely on the total number of downloads (purchases) of each paid app offered by this developer, multiplied by the average price of this app during our measurement period. The average revenue of a single paid app is \$3.9. Appstores usually get a commission from purchases, typically around 20–30% of the app's price, and the remaining amount is the actual developer's income. However, SlideMe has one of the lowest commissions on app purchases: it gets 5% of the app's price for each download. From the total revenue, which is close to 4 million dollars in our dataset, SlideMe should get around 200 thousand dollars as commission. For simplicity in our measurements we assume that developers get the whole amount from each download of a paid app.

Figure 13 shows the CDF of total income per developer. We see that half of the developers made less than \$10, while 27% of them had no income from their paid apps. The 80% of the developers made less than \$100, and 95% of them less than \$1,500. However, we observe that there is a small percentage of developers, roughly around 1%, with income higher than 2 million dollars from very popular applications. Overall, it is clear that the majority of developers in the SlideMe appstore had a negligible income by selling paid apps, while only a very small percentage of them made a significant income.

An interesting question that comes up is whether the total income of a developer is correlated with the number of apps that this developer creates. In other words, can a developer earn more by creating more applications? To answer this question we plot in Figure 14 the number of paid apps per developer versus the average total income of the developers with this number of paid apps. We see that the developer's income does not increase with the number of apps, and there is no clear relation between them. The Pearson's correlation coefficient between income and number of apps per developer is equal to 0.008, which validates that these values are not correlated. Therefore, it seems that a developer will not necessarily reach a wider set of users by simply offering more apps. This is very interesting, because it shows that quality is more important than quantity for the developers' income.

We also measure how the revenue from paid app installations is distributed to app categories, and whether the percentage of apps and developers per category are related to the category's revenue fraction. Figure 15 shows the percentage of the total revenue per app category, along with the percentage of apps and developers for the same categories. We see that 67.7% of the revenue comes from paid apps of the music category, 19.7% from games, while 3.9% and 3.7% of the revenue comes from utilities and productivity categories respectively. Overall, 95% of the revenue comes from these four categories, while the rest 16 categories contribute only with 5% of the developers' income. These four categories include the 30.4% of the apps and 72% of the developers. Despite the fact that music produces 67.7% of the total revenue, we see that it contains just 1.6% of the paid apps, and only 4.3% of the developers have made at least one app in this category. We also observe that 33.2% of the apps are in the e-books category, created by only 1.6% of the developers, and they result to just 0.1% of the total revenue. On the other hand, 18.3% of the apps are games, offered by 36.2% of the developers, resulting to 19.7% of the total revenue, which is a reasonable ratio. Overall, we see that the fraction of revenue per

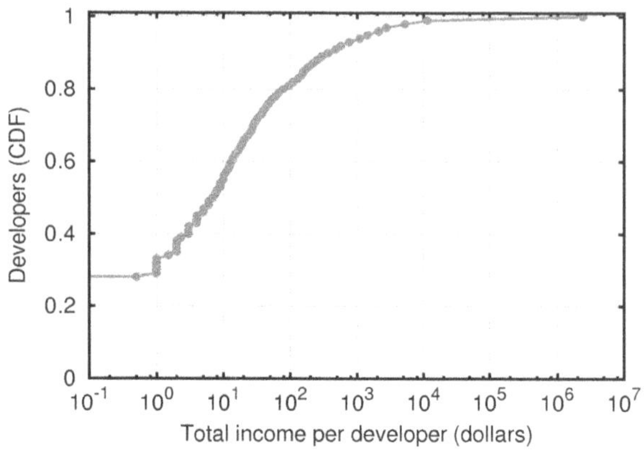

Figure 13: ***Most developers have negligible income from paid apps.* 80% of the developers made less than $100, while 1% of them gained more than 2 million dollars.**

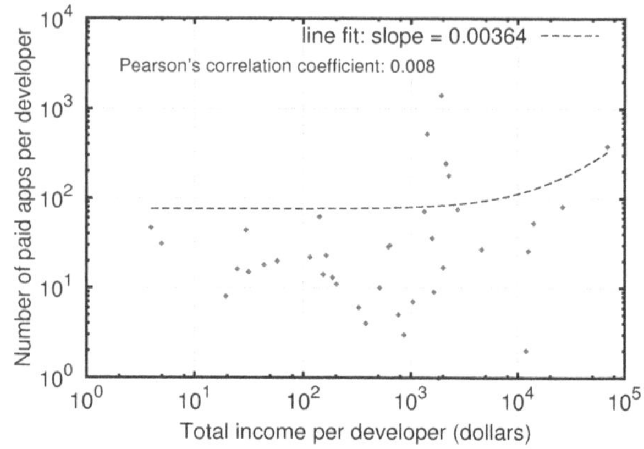

Figure 14: ***Quality is more important than quantity.* We see that developer's income is not correlated with the number of apps that this developer offers.**

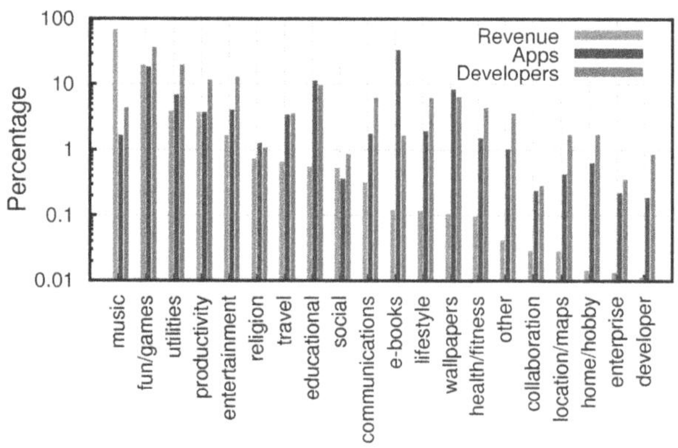

Figure 15: ***Revenue comes from few categories.* We see that 95% of the total revenue comes from the music, games, utilities, and productivity categories. The revenue per category is not correlated with the number of apps per category, and it is slightly correlated with the number of developers in these categories.**

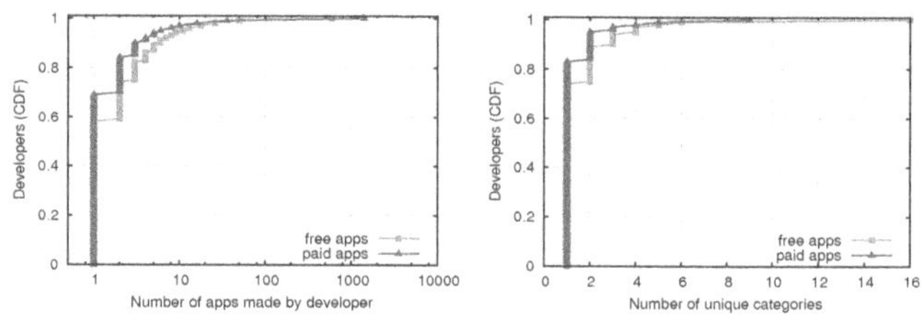

(a) Number of apps (b) Number of categories

Figure 16: ***Developers create a small number of apps focused on few categories.* CDF of the number of free and paid apps per developer shows that 95% of the developers offer less than 10 apps. CDF of the number of unique categories per developer shows that 99% of the developers focus on 1–5 categories.**

category is not related with the percentage of apps in the same category, with Pearson's correlation coefficient equal to 0.014, and it is slightly related with the percentage of developers in these categories, with correlation coefficient equal to 0.198. The percentage of apps and developers per category are more correlated, with Pearson's correlation coefficient equal to 0.378.

6.3 Revenue Stategies

In this section we set out to explore the common developers' strategies, and how these strategies may affect the developers' income (Q3). From our dataset we see that there exist 5,106 developers in the SlideMe marketplace for 22,184 applications. Thus, each developer builds 4.3 apps on average. Figure 16(a) shows the CDF of the number of free and paid apps offered by each developer. We see that 60% of the free app developers, and 70% of the paid app developers, create only a single app. Overall, 95% of the developers offer less than 10 apps. We also observe that there is a small fraction of developers that release a large number of apps, e.g., one developer with 1,402 apps and another with 592 apps. We found that these developer accounts correspond to two different companies that develop many mobile apps systematically. From these 5,106 developers we see that 75% of them offer only free apps, 15% of them offer only paid apps, while there is a 10% of developers that offer both free and paid apps. This outcome implies that most developers choose a single pricing strategy: either they offer their apps as free, aiming at income from advertisements or in-app billing, or they choose to sell their apps at a pre-defined price.

Figure 16(b) shows the CDF of the number of unique categories for which each developer create apps. We see that developers usually focus on one or just few categories: 75% of the free app developers and 85% of the paid app developers create apps belonging to a single category, while 99% of the developers in both cases focus on 1 up to 5 categories. This outcome shows that most developers are also interested in specific app categories.

In Section 6.2 we focused on the income made by paid apps in SlideMe, based on the apps' price and downloads. However, free apps also give opportunities for financial benefits to their developers, mainly due to advertisements (ads) and in-app billing. To validate this argument, we measured the percentage of free apps in SlideMe that include at least one of the 20 most popular advertising networks [33], using the *Androguard* [2] reverse engineering analysis tool, which attempts to detect advertising libraries within APK files. The results of this analysis show that 67% of the free apps in SlideMe include ads, i.e., at least one of the 20 most popular ad networks. The SlideMe web page also indicates whether each app

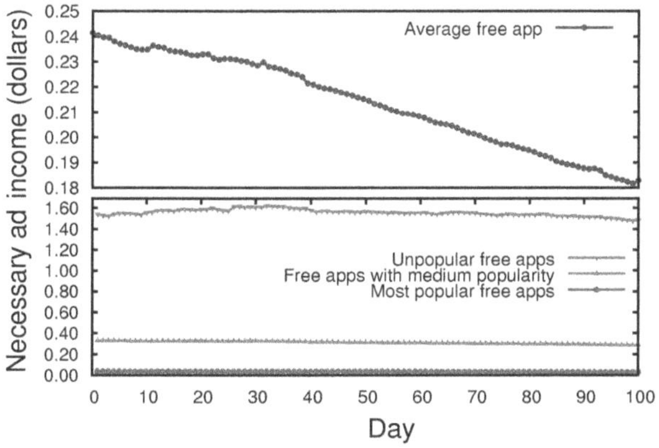

Figure 17: ***Free apps with ads may have higher financial benefits than paid apps.*** **An average free app needs about $0.21 per download to match the income of an average paid app. Break-even ad income drops over time because downloads increase faster for free apps. Popular free apps have a lower break-even ad income, thus better chances for increased revenue.**

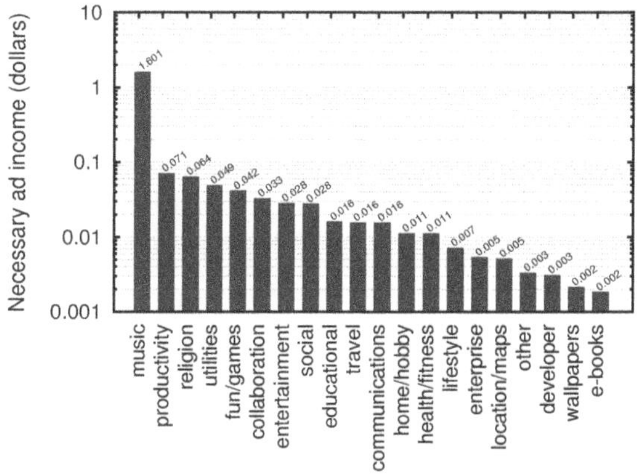

Figure 18: ***Some app categories may be more profitable for developers that focus on free apps with ads.*** **A free app in categories like wallpapers or e-books needs to make just $0.002 per download to match the income of a paid app in the same category. In contrast, free apps in the music category need to make more than $1.6 to gain a higher profit.**

(free or paid) contains ads. We observed that this information is generally true, compared with our analysis on the actual APK files for free apps, with just a few exceptions. We also observed that very few paid apps state that they use ads, which implies that there are two different revenue strategies: either paid apps with no ads, or free apps with advertisements.

Using our dataset, we evaluate the two different revenue strategies: (i) paid apps, which require a payment before downloading, and (ii) free apps using advertisements, which make profit after installation. However, we do not have any data about the usage of free apps upon installation, i.e., clicks and impressions, to approximate the actual income from those apps. Therefore, to compare the two alternative revenue strategies, we estimate the ad income that a free app needs to make per download to match the income of a paid app. We can estimate this *break-even* ad income per download for a free app based on the average number of downloads measured for free and paid apps in the SlideMe appstore, and the average price of paid apps, using the following formula:

$$Ad\,Income = \frac{\sum_{i=1}^{N_{paid}} Downloads(i) \times Price(i)/N_{paid}}{\sum_{j=1}^{N_{free}} Downloads(j)/N_{free}} \tag{7}$$

where N_{paid} and N_{free} the number of paid and free apps respectively. We consider only free apps with ads in this analysis.

Figure 17 shows the break-even ad income per download for an average free app as a function of time, for the last three months of our measurement period. We see that overall, an average free app needs to make just $0.21 per download from ads in order to match the income of an average paid app. Moreover, we see that the break-even ad income is dropping over time. This happens because the average downloads of free apps increase much faster than the average downloads of paid apps. Thus, for many apps, where users are expected to spend some time using the application, the ad-based revenue strategy seems more promising for increased income. While the paid apps collect money once per download, a free app may continue to earn money for a long period after the download, depending on app usage.

In Figure 17 we also see the break-even ad income for the most popular free apps, which are the 20% of apps with most downloads, for free apps with medium popularity, which are the next 50% of apps, and for the less popular free apps, which are the last 30% of apps with the fewer downloads. We see that a popular app needs an even lower ad income, just $0.033 per download, to outreach the income of a paid app. Even for the less popular apps, the break-even ad income is $1.56 per download, which is still 2.7 times lower than the average price of a paid app. Therefore, especially for free apps with high and medium popularity, the ad-based revenue strategy seems to be able to offer significantly higher financial benefits than asking for payment only once before downloading.

We performed the same analysis for each app category, as pricing depends on several factors that may vary across different categories. Such factors, for example, include the effort of developing an app (e.g., games in general are more complex to be developed than e-books or wallpaper apps) or the popularity of the app category. Figure 18 shows the break-even ad income per app category. We see that break-even ad income differs among categories. For instance, the highest break-even ad income, roughly $1.6, is observed for music apps, while the lowest is observed for the wallpaper and e-book categories (close to $0.002). This is because music is the dominant category of paid apps in terms of revenue, as we see in Figure 15. Moreover, it is interesting to note that a free app of the fun or games category, which is the second more lucrative category, needs to make only $0.04 per download on average to reach the revenue of a category-equivalent paid app.

7. IMPLICATIONS

We believe that our study can be useful for both appstore operators and app developers in several ways. In this section, we briefly discuss some practical implications.

New replacement policies for improved app caching. The existence of locality in user downloads, as manifested by the Pareto effect, can help appstore operators to design efficient caching mechanisms for improving the speed of app delivery to end users, e.g., by caching the most popular apps in fast memory or local network caches. To explore the benefits of this locality, we simulated a typical cache with a *Least Recently Used* (LRU) replacement pol-

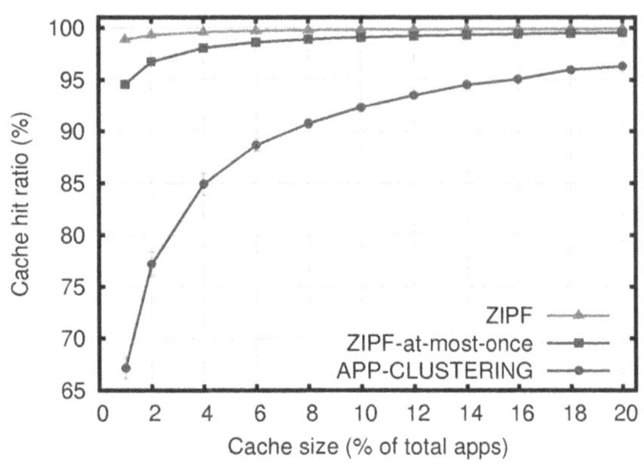

Figure 19: ***Clustering-based user behavior has a negative impact on LRU cache performance.*** **Cache hit ratio as a function of cache size for an LRU app cache. Although the LRU cache achieves a high hit ratio, APP-CLUSTERING results in a significantly lower hit ratio than ZIPF and ZIPF-at-most-once.**

icy. We varied the cache size in terms of apps, assuming that all apps have the same size. In our dataset, the average app size is 3.5 MB. For each cache size, the cache was initialized with the respective number of most popular apps. To examine the effect of the observed clustering-based user behavior on a typical LRU cache, we simulated user downloads based on the three different models: ZIPF, ZIPF-at-most-once, and APP-CLUSTERING. We simulated an appstore similar to Anzhi, i.e., with 60,000 apps divided into 30 categories, 600,000 users, and 2 million downloads. We used a ZIPF exponent $z_r = 1.7$ for overall app ranking, and a ZIPF exponent $z_c = 1.4$ for each cluster's app ranking. The percentage of downloads based on clustering was set to 90% ($p = 0.9$). In case of a cache miss, the requested app was replacing the least recently downloaded app from the cache.

Figure 19 shows the cache hit ratio as a function of cache size, which varies from 1% to 20% of the number of total apps (i.e., from 6,000 up to 120,000 apps, which roughly corresponds to 2.1–42 GB of actual cache size), when generating user downloads with each one of the three different models. In general, we see that app caching with an LRU policy achieves a high hit ratio. For example, when caching 10% of the apps, the cache hit ratio is higher than 90% for all models.

However, we see that the workload generated by the APP-CLUSTERING model, which simulates the observed clustering-based user behavior, results in a significantly reduced hit ratio compared to the other two models. While ZIPF-based workload generation (e.g., like web downloads) leads to a hit ratio higher than 99% for all cache sizes, and ZIPF-at-most-once workloads (e.g., like peer-to-peer file sharing downloads) result in a high hit ratio starting at 94.5% and exceeding 99% for cache sizes larger than 10% of the total apps, we see a significantly lower hit ratio for APP-CLUSTERING: from 67.1% up to 96.3% when the cache size varies from 1% to 20% of total apps. Thus, we conclude that although an LRU cache can exploit locality of user downloads to improve the performance of app delivery, the clustering behavior we have identified in this work has a negative effect on the performance of a typical LRU cache. To improve cache performance in the context of app delivery, we believe that new replacement policies should be used, taking into account the clustering-based user behavior.

Effective prefetching. Understanding the temporary affinity of users to app categories can help the design of more efficient prefetching methods. As we showed in Section 4, a user that downloads an app from a given category is more likely to download the next few apps from the same category. Thus, the most popular apps from this category that have not been downloaded by the user can be prefetched to a local place in order to improve user experience and app delivery performance.

Better recommendation systems. The understanding of user download patterns, like the clustering effect, can help appstore operators to design better recommendation systems, which can benefit (i) apps and developers by providing better opportunities for more suggestions and downloads, and (ii) end users by providing more useful suggestions. A recommendation system can benefit apps and developers by identifying the apps that need to be recommended to increase their popularity, and by identifying users interested in the respective app category. Also, end users can benefit from a better recommendation system by improving their user experience. A typical recommendation system follows a collaborative filtering method [18]. The main idea of this method is to find groups of users who share similar interests. These users can be determined based on their similar app downloads. If an app is downloaded by most users in a group, then it is likely to be of interest for another user in the same group that has not yet downloaded it. Thus, this is a possible suggestion from the recommendation system.

The clustering effect, however, can also suggest apps that have not necessarily been downloaded by users who share similar interests. For example, a user who downloaded an app from a given category may be interested in other popular apps of the same category. Thus, the clustering effect provides a richer set of choices than the limited choices of current recommendation systems, which are mainly based on the common apps downloaded by a set of users. Moreover, users who prefer a large variety of choices will have a better experience with recommendation systems that do not bombard them with the same set of popular apps. In addition, capitalizing on the temporal affinity of users to app categories, as we explained in Section 4, the recommendation system can suggest apps related to the most recent interests of a user, instead of apps related to older downloads.

Identify and help problematic apps. Our model of app downloads can be used by appstores to estimate future app downloads based on app popularity. This will enable appstores to pinpoint problematic apps and favor them through better recommendations.

Larger category diversity. Another possible implication of the clustering effect is that, currently, users appear to be adherent to one specific category. This may be because they were initially interested in a specific app and they ended up downloading more apps from a single category, based on appstore's suggestions. Hence, there might be a need to expose apps from more categories through recommendations. This may also incentivize developers to offer a wider set of apps across multiple categories.

Understand and improve app popularity. Understanding the parameters that affect app popularity is of high interest for developers who want to predict, understand, and most importantly, increase the popularity of their apps. To this end, we provide insights on how user behavior, app category, and other parameters affect app downloads in four popular third-party Android appstores.

Maximize income. Understanding which pricing models result in higher revenue can help developers to choose the appropriate pricing policies for increasing app popularity and, eventually, their income. To this end, we examine how cost, app popularity, and app categories affect a developer's income in our dataset. We also compare two popular revenue strategies: paid apps versus free apps with advertisements. Our results indicate that the most profitable revenue strategy depends on app popularity, app category, and ad income per download.

8. RELATED WORK

Workload Characterization. There are numerous studies focusing on the workload characterization of networks and distributed systems, aiming to improve the understanding of their complex behavior by identifying high-level trends and summarizing statistics that explain significant properties of their workloads. Many of these studies concentrate on web workloads. Breslau et al. [20] show that web requests follow a Zipf-like distribution, and propose a simple model based on this distribution to explain the observed behavior. Crovella and Bestavros [25] show that web traffic exhibits self-similar characteristics, which can be modeled using heavy-tailed distributions. Based on web workload characteristics, Barford and Crovella [19] propose a model for representative web workload generation. In a similar spirit, we show that mobile app popularity follows a Zipf-like distribution with truncated ends, and we propose a model that approximates the observed distribution.

Besides the web, there are also several studies that focus on other systems' workload characterization. Gummadi et al. [34] show that popularity distribution in peer-to-peer file sharing systems deviates from Zipf for very popular objects, which is also observed in our study, and introduce a model that explains this behavior. Cha et al. [21] study YouTube and find that the popularity distribution of user-generated video content follows power-law with an exponential cutoff, which is similar to the app popularity distribution we observe in our study. Power-law distributions with exponential cutoffs have been also identified in other networks, such as live streaming media networks [24], protein, e-mail, actor, and collaboration networks [31]. There are also many works focusing on the explanation and understanding of the power-law distributions [37,38].

Systematic studies of mobile apps. Recently, mobile systems and applications have attracted the interest of researchers that try to understand the behavior and functionality of this emerging technology. Several research efforts were made for collecting and analyzing large sets of mobile apps from multiple marketplaces. These efforts are mainly focused on security and privacy-related analysis, such as malware detection [45], malware analysis [44], overprivilege identification [30], detection of privacy leaks [26,32], malicious ad libraries [33], and vulnerability assessment [27]. In this work we collected and analyzed a similar large-scale dataset, but our analysis was focused on characterizing and modeling the workload of the monitored marketplaces.

In a work closely related to ours, Xu et al. [42] study the usage behavior of smartphone apps by analyzing IP-level traces from a tier-1 cellular network provider. Their analysis is mostly focused on spatial and temporal locality, geographic coverage, and diurnal usage patterns. On the other hand, our analysis focuses on app popularity and pricing strategies. We also use a different dataset, by systematically crawling four third-party appstores.

Other related approaches focus on mobile traffic analysis as well, but they do not study their relation with mobile applications. Maier et al. [36] perform a study of residential DSL lines of a European ISP and find that mobile devices' traffic is dominated by multimedia content and applications' downloads. Falaki et al. [28] conduct a traffic analysis on 43 different smartphones. They show that browsing contributes most of the traffic, and lower layer protocols impose high overheads due to small transfer sizes. They also study the factors that impact performance and power consumption on smartphone communications and propose improvements.

Falaki et al. [29] analyze user behavior in two different smartphone platforms in order to understand and characterize user activities and their impact on network and battery. They observe a diversity in user patterns, which implies that techniques for improving user experience or power consumption on the average case may be inefficient for a large fraction of users. Wei et al. [41] present a multi-layer system for monitoring and profiling Android apps.

Vallina-Rodriguez et al. [40] characterize the mobile ad traffic by analyzing a large network trace of mobile users. They focus on the volume, frequency, and content of the mobile ad traffic, and they show the distribution of ad traffic among the different platforms, ad networks, and mobile apps. They also study the energy implications of mobile advertising in smartphone devices. Tongaonkar et al. [39] study mobile apps' usage patterns based on mobile ad traffic found in network traces. On the other hand, we study the app download patterns, the app popularity based on the number of downloads from each marketplace, and the relation of app downloads with developers' income.

Another related work by Zhong and Michahelles [43] study app popularity patterns using data from *appaware*, an application that is optionally installed by Android users in their devices. This application captures information regarding installations, updates and removal of apps at real time. Their main outcome is that 10% of the apps account for the 90% of the total downloads, very similar to our results. Our work presents a more detailed study on app popularity distribution, along with a model for app downloads. Moreover, we gathered and analyzed data from all the apps of four different third-party Android appstores, while Zhong and Michahelles have a limited view using data only from the users that have installed the *appaware* application. To the best of our knowledge, our work is the first systematic and large-scale study that focuses on the workload characterization of mobile application marketplaces.

9. CONCLUSION

The mobile application market has recently gained increasing popularity, yet the main characteristics and parameters affecting its workload are still poorly understood. In this paper we presented a systematic study of the mobile app ecosystem by collecting and analyzing data from four popular third-party Android appstores. The analysis was focused on app popularity distribution and app pricing. We also briefly discuss possible implications of our findings.

Our results show a highly-skewed Pareto effect where 10% of the apps account for 70-90% of the total downloads. The app popularity follows a Zipf-like distribution with truncated ends, unlike web and peer-to-peer workloads, but similar to user-generated video content. We attributed the observed distribution to a new download pattern we refer to as "clustering effect." The clustering effect implies that users will download the next apps from the same categories as their previous downloads. We validated the existence of clustering effect with a user behavior study, which shows a strong temporal affinity of users to app categories. Then, we introduced a new model for app downloads based on clustering effect, and we validated with simulations that it approximates very close the actual downloads. Our model is able to approximate very well the downloads distributions of all appstores, which implies that the proposed clustering effect is a more general phenomenon rather than a random property of a single appstore.

We also studied the effect of cost on app popularity. We observed that paid apps follow a clear power law distribution, probably due to the more selective behavior of users when they are paying to download an app. We measured how the revenue of paid apps are distributed to developers. The results show that the large majority of developers have very low income, while a very small percentage of them make a significantly higher income. We also found that the number of developer's apps do not increase developer's income. Finally, we found that free apps with ads need to make just \$0.21 per download to match the income of paid apps, which seems a more promising strategy especially for popular apps.

Acknowledgements

We would like to thank our shepherd Chen-Nee Chuah and the anonymous reviewers for their valuable feedback. We would also like to thank Daniel Song for helping with the implementation of crawler prototypes for AppChina and Anzhi. This work was supported in part by the FP7 project SysSec and the FP7-PEOPLE-2009-IOF project MALCODE, funded by the European Commission under Grant Agreements No. 254116 and No. 257007. Antonis Papadogiannakis and Evangelos Markatos are also with the University of Crete.

10. REFERENCES

[1] Amazon Appstore. http://www.amazon.com/appstore/.

[2] Androguard. http://code.google.com/p/androguard/.

[3] AndroLib. http://www.androlib.com/.

[4] AppBrain. http://www.appbrain.com/.

[5] Disgo, FAQ. http://www.mydisgo.info/index.php/faq?faqid=5.

[6] Google Play. http://en.wikipedia.org/wiki/Google_Play.

[7] Google Play hits 600,000 apps, 20 billion total installs. http://www.engadget.com/2012/06/27/google-play-hits-600000-apps/.

[8] Google Says 700,000 Applications Available for Android. http://www.businessweek.com/news/2012-10-29/google-says-700-000-applications-available-for-android-devices.

[9] iOS and Android Adoption Explodes Internationally. http://blog.flurry.com/bid/88867/iOS-and-Android-Adoption-Explodes-Internationally.

[10] Scrapy framework. http://scrapy.org/.

[11] Selenium Remote Control (RC), a web application testing system. http://seleniumhq.org/projects/remote-control/.

[12] Supported locations for merchants, Google Play. https://support.google.com/googleplay/android-developer/answer/150324?hl=en&ref_topic=15867.

[13] The 1Mobile Marketplace website. http://www.1mobile.com/.

[14] The Anzhi Marketplace website. http://www.anzhi.com/.

[15] The AppChina Marketplace website. http://www.appchina.com/.

[16] The SlideMe Marketplace website. http://slideme.org/.

[17] Vodafone Egypt Ships Android Phones With SlideME App Store. http://www.distimo.com/blog/2009_11_vodafone-egypt-ships-android-phones-with-slideme-app-store/.

[18] G. Adomavicius and A. Tuzhilin. Toward the Next Generation of Recommender Systems: A Survey of the State-of-the-Art and Possible Extensions. *IEEE Transactions on Knowledge and Data Engineering*, 17(6), 2005.

[19] P. Barford and M. Crovella. Generating Representative Web Workloads for Network and Server Performance Evaluation. In *ACM International Conference on Measurement and Modeling of Computer Systems (SIGMETRICS)*, 1998.

[20] L. Breslau, P. Cao, L. Fan, G. Phillips, and S. Shenker. Web Caching and Zipf-like Distributions: Evidence and Implications. In *IEEE International Conference on Computer Communications (INFOCOM)*, 1999.

[21] M. Cha, H. Kwak, P. Rodriguez, Y.-Y. Ahn, and S. Moon. I Tube, You Tube, Everybody Tubes: Analyzing the World's largest User Generated Content Video System. In *ACM SIGCOMM Conference on Internet Measurement (IMC)*, 2007.

[22] J. Cho and S. Roy. Impact of Search Engines on Page Popularity. In *International Conference on World wide web (WWW)*, 2004.

[23] B. Chun, D. Culler, T. Roscoe, A. Bavier, L. Peterson, M. Wawrzoniak, and M. Bowman. PlanetLab: An Overlay Testbed for Broad-Coverage Services. *ACM SIGCOMM Computer Communication Review (CCR)*, 33(3), 2003.

[24] C. P. Costa, I. S. Cunha, A. Borges, C. V. Ramos, M. M. Rocha, J. M. Almeida, and B. Ribeiro-Neto. Analyzing Client Interactivity in Streaming Media. In *International Conference on World wide web (WWW)*, 2004.

[25] M. E. Crovella and A. Bestavros. Self-Similarity in World Wide Web Traffic: Evidence and Possible Causes. *IEEE/ACM Transactions on Networking*, 5(6), 1997.

[26] W. Enck, P. Gilbert, B.-G. Chun, L. P. Cox, J. Jung, P. McDaniel, and A. N. Sheth. TaintDroid: An Information-Flow Tracking System for Realtime Privacy Monitoring on Smartphones. In *USENIX Symposium on Operating System Design and Implementation (OSDI)*, 2010.

[27] W. Enck, D. Octeau, P. McDaniel, and S. Chaudhuri. A Study of Android Application Security. In *USENIX Security Symposium*, 2011.

[28] H. Falaki, D. Lymberopoulos, R. Mahajan, S. Kandula, and D. Estrin. A First Look at Traffic on Smartphones. In *ACM SIGCOMM Conference on Internet Measurement (IMC)*, 2010.

[29] H. Falaki, R. Mahajan, S. Kandula, D. Lymberopoulos, R. Govindan, and D. Estrin. Diversity in Smartphone Usage. In *ACM International Conference on Mobile Systems, Applications, and Services (MobiSys)*, 2010.

[30] A. P. Felt, E. Chin, S. Hanna, D. Song, and D. Wagner. Android Permissions Demystified. In *ACM Conference on Computer and Communications Security (CCS)*, 2011.

[31] T. Fenner, M. Levene, and G. Loizou. A Stochastic Evolutionary Model Exhibiting Power-Law Behaviour with an Exponential Cutoff. *Physica A: Statistical Mechanics and its Applications*, 355(2), 2005.

[32] M. Grace, Y. Zhou, Z. Wang, and X. Jiang. Systematic Detection of Capability Leaks in Stock Android Smartphones. In *ISOC Network and Distributed System Security Symposium (NDSS)*, 2012.

[33] M. C. Grace, W. Zhou, X. Jiang, and A.-R. Sadeghi. Unsafe Exposure Analysis of Mobile In-App Advertisements. In *ACM Conference on Security and Privacy in Wireless and Mobile Networks (WISEC)*, 2012.

[34] K. P. Gummadi, R. J. Dunn, S. Saroiu, S. D. Gribble, H. M. Levy, and J. Zahorjan. Measurement, Modeling, and Analysis of a Peer-to-Peer File-Sharing Workload. In *ACM Symposium on Operating Systems Principles (SOSP)*, pages 314–329, 2003.

[35] S. Jansen and E. Bloemendal. Defining App Stores: The Role of Curated Marketplaces in Software Ecosystems. In *International Conference on Software Business (ICSOB)*, 2013.

[36] G. Maier, F. Schneider, and A. Feldmann. A First Look at Mobile Hand-Held Device Traffic. In *International Conference on Passive and Active Measurement (PAM)*, 2010.

[37] S. Mossa, M. Barthelemy, H. E. Stanley, and L. A. N. Amaral. Truncation of Power Law Behavior in "Scale-Free" Network Models due to Information Filtering. *PHYS.REV.LETT*, 2002.

[38] M. E. J. Newman. Power Laws, Pareto Distributions and Zipf's Law. *Contemporary Physics*, 2005.

[39] A. Tongaonkar, S. Dai, A. Nucci, and D. Song. Understanding Mobile App Usage Patterns Using In-App Advertisements. In *International Conference on Passive and Active Measurement (PAM)*, 2013.

[40] N. Vallina-Rodriguez, J. Shah, A. Finamore, Y. Grunenberger, K. Papagiannaki, H. Haddadi, and J. Crowcroft. Breaking for Commercials: Characterizing Mobile Advertising. In *ACM SIGCOMM Conference on Internet Measurement (IMC)*, 2012.

[41] X. Wei, L. Gomez, I. Neamtiu, and M. Faloutsos. ProfileDroid: Multi-Layer Profiling of Android Applications. In *ACM International Conference on Mobile Computing and Networking (MobiCom)*, 2012.

[42] Q. Xu, J. Erman, A. Gerber, Z. Mao, J. Pang, and S. Venkataraman. Identifying Diverse Usage Behaviors of Smartphone Apps. In *ACM SIGCOMM Conference on Internet Measurement (IMC)*, 2011.

[43] N. Zhong and F. Michahelles. Google Play Is Not A Long Tail Market: An Empirical Analysis of App Adoption on the Google Play App Market. In *ACM Symposium on Applied Computing (SAC)*, 2013.

[44] Y. Zhou and X. Jiang. Dissecting Android Malware: Characterization and Evolution. In *IEEE Symposium on Security and Privacy*, 2012.

[45] Y. Zhou, Z. Wang, W. Zhou, and X. Jiang. Hey, You, Get Off of My Market: Detecting Malicious Apps in Official and Alternative Android Markets. In *ISOC Network and Distributed System Security Symposium (NDSS)*, 2012.

Analysis of the HTTPS Certificate Ecosystem*

Zakir Durumeric, James Kasten, Michael Bailey, J. Alex Halderman
Department of Electrical Engineering and Computer Science
University of Michigan, Ann Arbor, MI 48109, USA
{zakir, jdkasten, mibailey, jhalderm}@umich.edu

ABSTRACT

We report the results of a large-scale measurement study of the HTTPS certificate ecosystem—the public-key infrastructure that underlies nearly all secure web communications. Using data collected by performing 110 Internet-wide scans over 14 months, we gain detailed and temporally fine-grained visibility into this otherwise opaque area of security-critical infrastructure. We investigate the trust relationships among root authorities, intermediate authorities, and the leaf certificates used by web servers, ultimately identifying and classifying more than 1,800 entities that are able to issue certificates vouching for the identity of any website. We uncover practices that may put the security of the ecosystem at risk, and we identify frequent configuration problems that lead to user-facing errors and potential vulnerabilities. We conclude with lessons and recommendations to ensure the long-term health and security of the certificate ecosystem.

Categories and Subject Descriptors

C.2.2 [**Computer-Communication Networks**]: [Network Protocols]; C.2.3 [**Computer-Communication Networks**]: [Network Operations]; E.3 [**Data Encryption**]: [Public key cryptosystems, Standards]

Keywords

TLS; SSL; HTTPS; public-key infrastructure; X.509; certificates; security; measurement; Internet-wide scanning

1. INTRODUCTION

Nearly all secure web communication takes place over HTTPS including online banking, e-mail, and e-commerce transactions. HTTPS is based on the TLS encrypted transport protocol and a supporting public key infrastructure (PKI) composed of thousands of certificate authorities (CAs)—entities that are trusted by users' browsers to vouch for the identity of web servers. CAs do this by signing digital certificates that associate a site's public key with its domain name. We place our full trust in each of these CAs—in general, every CA has the ability to sign trusted certificates for *any* domain, and so the entire PKI is only as secure as the weakest CA. Nevertheless, this complex distributed infrastructure is strikingly opaque. There is no published list of signed website certificates or even of the organizations that have trusted signing ability. In this work, we attempt to rectify this and shed light on the HTTPS certificate ecosystem.

Our study is founded on what is, to the best of our knowledge, the most comprehensive dataset of the HTTPS ecosystem to date. Between June 2012 and August 2013, we completed 110 exhaustive scans of the public IPv4 address space in which we performed TLS handshakes with all hosts publicly serving HTTPS on port 443. Over the course of 14 months, we completed upwards of 400 billion SYN probes and 2.55 billion TLS handshakes, collecting and parsing 42.4 million unique X.509 certificates from 109 million hosts. On average, each of our scans included 178% more TLS hosts and 115% more certificates than were collected in earlier studies of the certificate authority ecosystem [14], and we collected 736% more unique certificates in total than any prior study of HTTPS [16].

Using this dataset, we investigate two classes of important security questions, which relate to the behavior of CAs and to site certificates.

Certificate Authorities We analyze the organizations involved in the HTTPS ecosystem and identify 1,832 CA certificates, which are controlled by 683 organizations including religious institutions, museums, libraries, and more than 130 corporations and financial institutions. We find that more than 80% of the organizations with a signing certificate are not commercial certificate authorities and further investigate the paths through which organizations are acquiring signing certificates. We investigate the constraints on these CA certificates and find that only 7 CA certificates use name constraints, and more than 40% of CA certificates have no path length constraint. We identify two sets of misissued CA certificates and discuss their impact on the security of the ecosystem.

Site Certificates We analyze leaf certificates used by websites and find that the distribution among authorities is heavily skewed towards a handful of large authorities, with three organizations controlling 75% of all trusted certificates. Disturbingly, we find that the compromise of the private key used by one particular intermediate certificate would require 26% of HTTPS websites to immediately obtain new certificates. We provide an up-to-date analysis on the keys and signatures being used to sign leaf certificates and find that half of trusted leaf certificates contain an inadequately secure 1024-bit RSA key in their trust chain and that CAs were continuing

*Permission to make digital or hard copies of part or all of this work is granted without fee provided that copies are not distributed for profit and that copies bear this notice and the full citation on the first page. Copyright is held by the authors. This more permissive statement supersedes the ACM-mandated statement below, which has no effect. Please join us in supporting open access publication.

IMC'13, October 23–25, 2013, Barcelona, Spain.
Copyright 2013 ACM 978-1-4503-1953-9/13/10 ...$15.00.
http://dx.doi.org/10.1145/2504730.2504755.

to sign certificates using MD5 as late as April 2013. We find that 5% of trusted certificates are for locally scoped names or private IP address space (and therefore do not protect against man-in-the-middle attacks) and that 12.7% of hosts serving certificates signed by trusted CAs are serving them in a manner that will cause errors in one or more modern web browsers.

Lastly, we examine adoption trends in the HTTPS ecosystem from the past year, discuss anomalies we noticed during our analysis, and provide high-level lessons and potential paths forward to improve the security of the HTTPS ecosystem security. We ultimately hope that this global perspective and our analysis will inform future decisions within the security community as we work towards a more secure PKI. In order to facilitate future research on this critical ecosystem, we are releasing our dataset to the research community, including 42 million certificates and historical records of the state of 109 million HTTPS server IP addresses. This data and up-to-date metrics can be found at https://httpsecosystem.org/.

2. BACKGROUND

In this section, we present a brief review of TLS, digital certificates and their respective roles within the HTTPS ecosystem. We recommend RFC 5280 [11] for a more in-depth overview of the TLS public key infrastructure.

Transport Layer Security (TLS) Transport Layer Security (TLS) and its predecessor Secure Sockets Layer (SSL) are cryptographic protocols that operate below the application layer and provide end-to-end cryptographic security for a large number of popular application protocols, including HTTPS, IMAPS, SMTP, and XMPP [12]. In the case of HTTPS, when a client first connects, the client and server complete a TLS handshake during which the server presents an X.509 digital certificate, which is used to help identify and authenticate the server to the client. This certificate includes the identity of the server (e.g. website domain), a temporal validity period, a public key, and a digital signature provided by a trusted third party. The client checks that the certificate's identity matches the requested domain name, that the certificate is within its validity period, and that the digital signature of the certificate is valid. The certificate's public key is then used by the client to share a session secret with the server in order to establish an end-to-end cryptographic channel.

Certificate Authorities Certificate authorities (CAs) are trusted organizations that issue digital certificates. These organizations are responsible for validating the identity of the websites for which they provide a digital certificate. They cryptographically vouch for the identity of a website by digitally signing the website's *leaf certificate* using a browser-trusted *signing certificate*. Modern operating systems and web browsers ship with a set of these trusted *signing certificates*, which we refer to as *root certificates*. In all but a small handful of cases, all CAs are trusted unequivocally: a trusted CA can sign for *any* website. For example, a certificate for `google.com` signed by a German University is technically no more or less valid than a certificate signed by Google Inc., if both organizations control a trusted signing certificate.

The set of root authorities is publicly known because it is included with the web browser or operating system. However, root authorities frequently sign *intermediate certificates*, which generally retain all of the signing privileges of root certificates. This practice not only allows root authorities to store their signing keys offline during daily operation, but also allows authorities to delegate their signing ability to other organizations. When a server presents a leaf certificate, it must include the chain of authorities linking the leaf certificate to a trusted root certificate. This bundle of certificates is referred to as a *certificate chain*. We refer to certificates that have a valid chain back to a trusted root authority as *trusted certificates*. It is important to note that while intermediate authorities provide additional flexibility, the set of intermediate authorities is not publicly known until they are found in the wild—we ultimately do not know the identity of the organizations that can sign any browser-trusted certificate.

3. RELATED WORK

Several groups have previously studied HTTPS deployment and the certificate ecosystem. Most similar to our work, Holz et al. published a study in 2011 that focused on the dynamics of leaf certificates and the distribution of certificates among IP addresses, and attempted to roughly classify the overall quality of served certificates. The study was based on regular scans of the Alexa Top 1 Million Domains [1] and through passive monitoring of TLS traffic on the Munich Scientific Research Network [17]. The group collected an average 212,000 certificates per scan and a total 554,292 unique certificates between October 2009 and March 2011, approximately 1.3% of the number we have seen in the past year. Their passive experiments resulted in an average of 130,000 unique certificates. The aggregate size across both datasets was not specified.

We are aware of two groups that have performed scans of the IPv4 address space in order to analyze aspects of the certificate ecosystem. In 2010, the Electronic Frontier Foundation (EFF) and iSEC partners performed a scan over a three-month period as part of their SSL Observatory Project [14]. The project focused on identifying which organizations controlled a valid signing certificate. The EFF provided the first recent glimpse into the HTTPS certificate ecosystem, and while their study was never formally published, we owe the inspiration for our work to their fascinating dataset. Heninger et al. later performed a scan of the IPv4 address space in 2012 as part of a global study on cryptographic keys [16]. Similarly, Yilek et al. performed daily scans of 50,000 TLS servers over several months to track the Debian weak key bug [35]. We follow up on the results provided in these earlier works, adding another data point in the study of Debian weak keys and other poorly generated keys.

Most recently, Akhawe et al. published a study focusing on the usability of TLS warnings presented by web servers, deriving the logic used by web browsers to validate certificates, and making recommendations on how to better handle these error conditions [4]. Akhawe et al. also discuss differences in how OpenSSL and Mozilla NSS validate certificates, which we arrived at simultaneously.

Our study differs from previous work in the methodology we applied, the scope of our dataset, and the focus of our questions. While Holz et al. explored several similar questions on the dynamics of leaf certificates, the dataset we consider is more than 40 times larger, which we believe provides a more comprehensive view of the certificate ecosystem. The certificates found by scanning the Alexa Top 1 Million Domains provide one perspective on the CA ecosystem that is weighted towards frequently accessed websites. However, many of the questions we address are dependent on a more comprehensive viewpoint. The CA ecosystem is equally dependent on all certificate authorities and, as such, we are interested in not only the most popular sites (which are likely to be well configured) but also the potentially less visible certificates used by smaller sites and network devices. This difference is clearly visible in the number of CA certificates seen among the Alexa Top 1 Million sites. If our study had been founded only on these domains, we would have seen less than 30% of the trusted certificate authorities we uncovered, providing us with a less accurate perspective on the state of the ecosystem. Similarly, we build on many topics touched on by the EFF study, but we present updated and revised results, finding more than 3.5 times the number of hosts serving HTTPS than were seen three years ago and a changed ecosystem. Ultimately, we consider a different set of questions that are more focused on the dynamics of CAs and the certificates they sign, using a dataset that we believe provides a more complete picture than any previous study.

4. METHODOLOGY

Our data collection (which is ongoing as this paper goes to press) involves repeatedly surveying the certificate ecosystem through comprehensive scans of the IPv4 address space conducted at regular intervals. In this section, we describe how we perform these scans, collect and validate X.509 certificates, and finally, analyze our data.

Each scan consists of three stages: (1) discovering hosts with port 443 (HTTPS) open by enumerating the public address space, (2) completing a TLS handshake with responsive addresses and collecting the presented certificate chains, and (3) performing certificate parsing and validation. The scan process requires 18 hours to complete, including flushing all changes to the backend database, and is implemented in approximately 13,000 SLOC of C. The scans in this work were conducted using the regular office network at the University of Michigan Computer Science and Engineering division, from a single Dell Precision workstation with a quad-core Intel Xeon E5520 processor and 24 GB of memory. The access layer of the building runs at 10 Gbps and the building uplink to the rest of the campus is an aggregated 2×10 gigabit port channel.

4.1 Host Discovery

In the first stage of each scan, we find hosts that accept TCP connections on port 443 (HTTPS) by performing a single-packet TCP SYN scan of the public IPv4 address space using ZMap [13]. We choose to utilize ZMap based on its performance characteristics—ZMap is capable of completing a single packet scan of the IPv4 address space on a single port in approximately 45 minutes. Using ZMap, we send a single TCP SYN packet to every public IPv4 address and add hosts that respond with a valid SYN-ACK packet to an in-memory Redis queue for further processing. Our previous work finds an approximate 2% packet drop rate when performing single packet scans on our network [13]. In order to reduce the impact of packet loss on our long-term HTTPS results, we also consider hosts that successfully completed a TLS handshake in the last 30 days for follow-up along with the hosts found during the TCP SYN scan.

4.2 Collecting TLS Certificates

In the second processing stage, we complete a TLS handshake with the hosts we identified in the first stage and retrieve the presented certificate chain. We perform these TLS handshakes in an event-driven manner using libevent and OpenSSL [24, 33]. Specifically, we utilize libevent's OpenSSL-based bufferevents, which allow us to define a callback that is invoked after a successful OpenSSL TLS negotiation. The retrieval process runs in parallel to the TCP SYN scan and maintains 2,500 concurrent TLS connections.

In order to emulate browser validation, we designed a custom validation process using the root browser stores from Apple Mac OS 10.8.2, Windows 7, and Mozilla Firefox. We find that a large number of web servers are misconfigured and present incomplete, misordered, or invalid certificate chains. OpenSSL validates certificates in a more stringent manner than most web browsers, including Mozilla Firefox and Google Chrome, which utilize Mozilla NSS [27] to perform certificate validation. To simulate the behavior of modern web browsers, we take the following corrective steps:

1. If the presented chain is invalid, we attempt to reorder the certificate chain. This resolves the situation when the correct intermediate certificates are provided, but are in the incorrect order.
2. We add previously seen intermediate authorities into OpenSSL's root store. This allows us to validate any certificate signed by a previously encountered intermediate CA regardless of the presented certificate chain.
3. Following each scan, we check certificates without a known issuer against the set of known authorities and revalidate any children for which there is a newly found issuer. This resolves the case where an intermediate is later found in a subsequent scan.

We parse collected TLS certificates using OpenSSL and maintain a PostgreSQL database of parsed data and historical host state.

4.3 Reducing Scan Impact

We recognize that our scans can inadvertently trigger intrusion detection systems and may upset some organizations. Many network administrators perceive port scans as the preliminary step in a targeted attack and in most cases are unable to recognize that their systems are not being uniquely targeted or that our research scans are not malicious in nature.

In order to minimize the impact of our scans and to avoid triggering intrusion detection systems, we scanned addresses according to a random permutation over a twelve hour period from a block of 64 sequential source IP addresses. When we perform a host discovery scan, an individual destination address receives at most one probe packet. At this scan rate, a /24-sized network receives a probe packet every 195 s, a /16 block every 0.76 s, and a /8 network block every 3 ms on average. In the certificate retrieval phase, we perform only one TLS handshake with each host that responded positively during host discovery.

In order to help users identify our intentions, we serve a simple webpage on all of the IP addresses we use for scanning that explains the purpose of our scanning and how to request that hosts be excluded from future scans. We also registered reverse DNS records that identify scanning hosts as being part of an academic research study. Throughout this study, we have coordinated with our local network administrators to promptly handle inquiries and complaints.

Over the course of 14 months, we received e-mail correspondence from 145 individuals and organizations. In most cases, notifications were informative in nature—primarily notifying us that we may have had infected machines—or were civil requests to be excluded from future scans. The vast majority of these requests were received at our institution's WHOIS abuse address or at the e-mail address published on the scanner IPs. In these cases, we responded with the purpose of our scans and excluded the sender's network from future scans upon request. Ultimately, we excluded networks belonging to 91 organizations or individuals and totaling 3,753,899 addresses (0.11% of the public IPv4 address space). Two requests originating from Internet service providers accounted for 49% of the excluded addresses. During our scans, we received 12 actively hostile responses that threatened to retaliate against our institution legally or via denial-of-service (DoS) attacks on network. In 2 cases we received retaliatory DoS traffic, which was automatically filtered by our upstream provider.

We discuss the ethical implications of performing active scanning and provide more details about the steps we take to reduce scan impact in our previous work [13].

4.4 Data Collection Results

We completed 110 successful scans of the IPv4 address space, completing 2.55 billion TLS handshakes, between June 6, 2012 and

Scan Date Completed	EFF [14] 2010-8	Ps & Qs [16] 2011-10	First 2012-6-10	Representative 2013-3-22	Latest 2013-8-4	Total Unique
Hosts with port 443 Open	16,200,000	28,923,800	31,847,635	33,078,971	36,033,088	(unknown)
Hosts serving HTTPS	7,704,837	12,828,613	18,978,040	21,427,059	24,442,824	108,801,503
Unique Certificates	4,021,766	5,758,254	7,770,385	8,387,200	9,031,798	42,382,241
Unique Trusted Certificates	1,455,391	1,956,267	2,948,397	3,230,359	3,341,637	6,931,223
Alexa Top 1 Mil. Certificates	(unknown)	89,953	116,061	141,231	143,149	261,250
Extd. Validation Certificates	33,916	71,066	89,190	103,170	104,167	186,159

Table 1: Internet-wide Scan Results— Between June 6, 2012 and August 4, 2013, we completed 110 scans of the IPv4 address space on port 443 and collected HTTPS certificates from responsive hosts.

August 4, 2013. Like to Holz et al. [17], we note that a large number of hosts on port 443 do not complete a TLS handshake. In our case we find that only 67% of hosts with port 443 open successfully complete a TLS handshake.

We retrieved an average of 8.1 million unique certificates during each scan, of which 3.2 million were browser trusted. The remaining 4.9 million untrusted certificates were a combination of self-signed certificates (48%), certificates signed by an unknown issuer (33%), and certificates signed by a known but untrusted issuer (19%). In total, we retrieved 42.4 million distinct certificates from 108.8 million unique IP addresses over the past eleven months. Of the hosts that performed complete TLS handshakes, an average of 48% presented browser-trusted X.509 certificates.

In our largest and most recent scan on August 4, 2013, we retrieved 9.0 million certificates from 24.4 million IP addresses of which 3.3 million were browser trusted. We show a comparison with previous work in Table 1. We also note that over 95% of trusted certificates and over 98% of hosts serving trusted certificates are located in only ten countries, shown in Table 2.

Country	Authorities	Certificates	Hosts
United States	30.34%	77.55%	75.63%
United Kingdom	3.27%	10.88%	18.15%
Belgium	2.67%	3.29%	1.51%
Israel	1.63%	2.56%	0.87%
Netherlands	2.18%	1.32%	0.49%
Japan	3.38%	1.06%	1.19%
Germany	21.28%	0.88%	0.35%
France	3.98%	0.38%	0.14%
Australia	0.81%	0.34%	0.11%
Korea	1.41%	0.24%	0.09%

Table 2: Top 10 Countries Serving Trusted Certificates

In this study, we choose to perform non-temporal analysis on the results from a representative scan, which took place on March 22, 2013 (highlighted column in Table 1). We choose to focus on the results from a single point-in-time instead of considering all certificates found over the past year due to varying lifespans. We find that organizations utilize certificates of differing validity periods and that in some cases, some devices have presented a different certificate in all of our scans. If we considered all certificates from the past year instead instead of what was hosted at a single point in time, these short lived certificates would impact the breakdown of several of our statistics.

4.5 Is Frequent Scanning Necessary?

Frequent repeated scans allow us to find additional certificates that would not otherwise be visible. We can illustrate this effect by considering the 36 scans we performed between January 1 and March 31, 2013 and analyzing the number of scans in which each certificate was seen. We find that 54% of browser-trusted certificates appeared in all 36 scans and that 70% of trusted certificates appear in more than 30 of our 36 scans. However, surprisingly, we find that 33% of self-signed certificates appeared in only one scan during the three month period. Many of these self-signed certificates appear to be served by embedded devices that generate new certificates on a regular basis. We found an average of 260,000 new certificates per scan during this period. The distribution is shown in Figure 1. Ultimately, we find that there are considerable advantages to scanning more frequently in obtaining a global perspective on the certificates valid at any single point in time, as well as the changing dynamics of the ecosystem over extended periods.

4.6 Server Name Indication Deployment

Both Holz [17] and Akhawe [4] cite Server Name Indication (SNI) as one of the reasons they choose to scan the Alexa Top 1 Million Domains and perform passive measurement instead of performing full IPv4 scans. Server Name Indication is a TLS extension that allows a client to specify the hostname it is attempting to connect to from the start of the TLS negotiation [9]. This allows a server to present multiple certificates on a single IP address and to ultimately host multiple HTTPS sites off of the same IP address that do not share a single certificate. Because we connect to hosts based on IP address in our scans and not by hostname, we would potentially miss any certificates that require a specific hostname.

In order to better understand the deployment of SNI and its impact on our results, we scanned the Alexa 1 Million Domains [1] using the same methodology we used for scanning the IPv4 address space. Of the Alexa Top 1 Million Domains, 323,502 successfully performed TLS handshakes and 129,695 of the domains presented browser-trusted certificates. Of the domains that completed a TLS handshake, only 0.7% presented certificates we had not previously seen in the most recent scan of the IPv4 address space. We cannot bound the number of hosts missed due to the deployment of SNI and it is clear that a small number of websites are adopting SNI, but we believe that our results are representative of certificate usage patterns. One reason SNI has not seen widespread deployment is because Internet Explorer on Windows XP does not support SNI. Although Windows XP market share is on the decline, it still represents more than a third of all operating system installations [26].

5. CERTIFICATE AUTHORITIES

The security of the HTTPS ecosystem is ultimately dependent on the set of CAs that are entrusted to sign browser-trusted certificates. Except in a small handful of cases, any organization with control of a signing certificate that chains to a browser-trusted root can sign a leaf certificate for any domain. As such, the entire ecosystem is

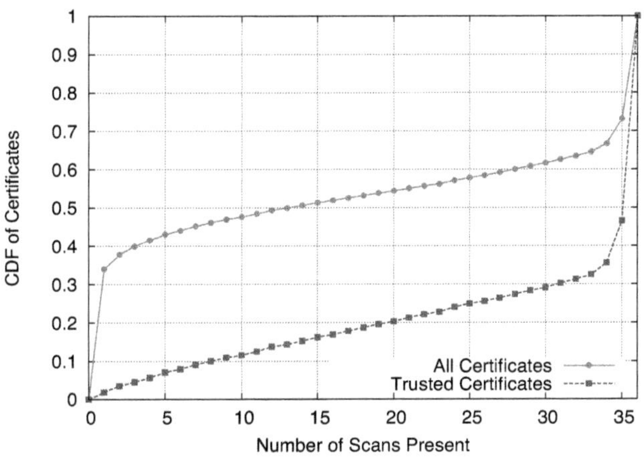

Figure 1: CDF of Scan Presence by Certificate — We performed 36 scans from 1/2013 to 3/2013. Here, we show the number of scans in which each certificate was found. We note that over 30% of self-signed certificates were only found in one scan.

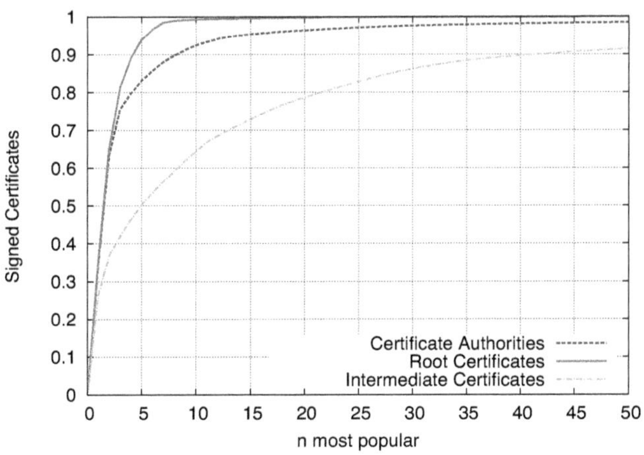

Figure 2: CDF of Leaf Certificates by CA — We find that 90% of trusted certificates are signed by 5 CAs, are descendants of 4 root certificates, and were signed by 40 intermediate certificates.

Figure 3: Validity Periods of Browser Trusted Certificates — Trusted CA certs are being issued with validity periods as long as 40 years, far beyond the predicted security of the keys they contain.

as fragile as the weakest CA. However, because there is no central, public registry of browser-trusted intermediate authorities, the organizations that control these signing certificates may be unknown until certificates they have signed are spotted in the wild. In this section, we describe the CAs we found during our scans and some of the practices they employ.

5.1 Identifying Trusted Authorities

We observed 3,788 browser-trusted signing certificates between April 2012 and August 2013 of which 1,832 were valid on March 22, 2013. All but seven of these signing certificates can sign a valid browser-trusted certificate for any domain. This is 25% more than were found by the EFF in 2010 and more than 327% more than were found by Ristic [31]. Holz et al. find 2,300 intermediate certificates in their active scanning [17]. However, this count appears to represent both browser-trusted and untrusted intermediates, of which we find 121,580 in our March 22 scan and 417,970 over the past year. While the raw number of signing certificates and HTTPS ecosystem as a whole have grown significantly over the past three years, we were encouraged to find that the number of identified organizations has not grown significantly.

These 1,832 signing certificates belong to 683 organizations and are located in 57 countries. While a large number of countries have jurisdiction over at least one trusted browser authority, 99% of the authorities are located in only 10 countries. We show the breakdown in Table 2. We classified the types of the organizations that control a CA certificate, which we show in Table 3. We were surprised to find that religious institutions, museums, libraries, and more than 130 corporations and financial institutions currently control an unrestricted CA certificate. Only 20% of organizations that control signing certificates are commercial CAs. We were unable to identify 15 signing certificates due to a lack of identification information or ambiguous naming. We also note that while there has been a 2% increase in the raw number of valid signing certificates over the past year, we have found negligible change in the number of organizations with control of a signing certificate.

5.2 Sources of Intermediates

Organizations other than commercial CAs control 1,350 of the 1,832 (74%) browser-trusted signing certificates, which raises the question of who is providing intermediate certificates to these organizations. We find that 276 of the 293 academic institutions along with all of the libraries, museums, healthcare providers, and religious institutions were signed by the German National Research and Education Network (DFN), which offers intermediate certificates to all members of the German network. DFN provided CA certificates to 311 organizations in total, close to half of the organizations we identified. While DFN has provided a large number of intermediate authorities to German institutions, we find no evidence that any are being used inappropriately. However, as we will discuss in Section 9, the attack surface of the certificate ecosystem could be greatly reduced by limiting the scope of these signing certificates.

The largest commercial provider of intermediate certificates is GTE CyberTrust Solutions, Inc., a subsidiary of Verizon Business, which has provided intermediate signing certificates to 49 third-party organizations ranging from Dell Inc. to Louisiana State University. Comodo (under the name *The USERTRUST Network*) provided intermediates to 42 organizations and GlobalSign to 20. We also saw a number of commercial authorities that provided a smaller number of certificates to seemingly unrelated entities. For example, VeriSign, Inc. provided intermediates for Oracle, Symantec, and the U.S. Government; SwissSign AG provided certificates for Nestle, Trend Micro, and other Swiss companies; StartCom Ltd.

Organization Type	Organizations		Authorities		Leaf Certificates		Hosts	
Academic Institution	273	(39.79%)	292	(15.93%)	85,277	(2.46%)	85,277	(0.92%)
Commercial CA	135	(19.67%)	819	(44.70%)	3,260,454	(94.20%)	3,260,454	(76.33%)
Government Agency	85	(12.39%)	250	(13.64%)	17,865	(0.51%)	17,865	(0.23%)
Corporation	83	(12.09%)	191	(10.42%)	30,115	(0.87%)	30,115	(4.80%)
ISP	30	(4.37%)	58	(3.16%)	8,126	(0.23%)	8,126	(1.55%)
IT/Security Consultant	29	(4.22%)	88	(4.80%)	22,568	(0.65%)	22,568	(0.98%)
Financial Institution	17	(2.47%)	49	(2.67%)	2,412	(0.06%)	2,412	(0.03%)
Unknown	*unknown*		15	(0.81%)	2,535	(0.07%)	2,535	(0.02%)
Hosting Provider	7	(1.02%)	12	(0.65%)	10,598	(0.30%)	10,598	(14.70%)
Nonprofit Org	7	(1.02%)	15	(0.81%)	11,480	(0.33%)	11,480	(0.11%)
Library	5	(0.72%)	6	(0.32%)	281	(0.00%)	281	(0.00%)
Museum	4	(0.58%)	4	(0.21%)	35	(0.00%)	35	(0.00%)
Healthcare Provider	3	(0.43%)	4	(0.21%)	173	(0.00%)	173	(0.00%)
Religious Institution	1	(0.14%)	1	(0.05%)	11	(0.00%)	11	(0.00%)
Military	1	(0.14%)	27	(1.47%)	9,017	(0.26%)	9,017	(0.27%)

Table 3: Types of Organizations with Signing Certificates — We found 1,832 valid browser-trusted signing certificates belonging to 683 organizations. We classified these organizations and find that more than 80% of the organizations that control a signing certificate are not commercial certificate authorities.

Parent Company	Signed Leaf Certificates	
Symantec	1,184,723	(34.23%)
GoDaddy.com	1,008,226	(29.13%)
Comodo	422,066	(12.19%)
GlobalSign	170, 006	(4.90%)
DigiCert Inc	145,232	(4.19%)
StartCom Ltd.	88,729	(2.56%)
Entrust, Inc.	76,990	(2.22%)
Network Solutions	62,667	(1.81%)
TERENA	42,310	(1.22%)
Verizon Business	32,127	(0.92%)

Table 4: Top Parent Companies — Major players such as Symantec, GoDaddy, and Comodo have acquired smaller CAs, leading to the 5 largest companies issuing 84.6% of all trusted certificates.

Organization	Signed Leaf Certificates	
GoDaddy.com, Inc.	913,416	(28.6%)
GeoTrust Inc.	586,376	(18.4%)
Comodo CA Limited	374,769	(11.8%)
VeriSign, Inc.	317,934	(10.0%)
Thawte, Inc.	228,779	(7.2%)
DigiCert Inc	145,232	(4.6%)
GlobalSign	117,685	(3.7%)
Starfield Technologies	94,794	(3.0%)
StartCom Ltd.	88,729	(2.8%)
Entrust, Inc.	76929	(2.4%)

Table 5: Top Certificate Authorities — The top 10 commercial certificate authorities control 92.4% of trusted certificates present in our March 22, 2013 scan.

provided certificates for The City of Osmio, Inc. and WoSign, Inc; QuoVadis Limited provided certificates for Migros and the Arab Bank Switzerland Ltd.; Entrust.net provided signing certificates to Disney, Experian PLC, and TDC Internet; and Equifax provided intermediates to Google Inc. This is not a clandestine practice, and several CAs advertise the sale of subordinate CA certificates.

Several corporations had a company authority in browser root stores. Approximately 30 of the 149 certificates in the Mozilla NSS root store belonged to institutions that we did not classify as commercial CAs, including Visa, Wells Fargo, Deutsche Telekom AG and the governments of France, Taiwan, Hong Kong, Japan, Spain, and the United States.

5.3 Distribution of Trust

While there are 683 organizations with the ability to sign browser-trusted certificates, the distribution is heavily skewed towards a small number of large commercial authorities in the United States. The security community has previously expressed concern over the sheer number of signing certificates [14], but it also worth considering the distribution of certificates among various authorities. An increasing number of signing certificates may in fact be a healthy sign if it indicates that authorities are using the new certificates in order to reduce the impact of compromise.

As shown in Figure 2, we find that more than 90% of browser-trusted certificates are signed by the 10 largest commercial CAs, are descendants of just 4 root certificates, and are directly signed by 40 intermediate certificates. Several large companies have acquired many of the smaller, previously independent commercial CAs. Symantec owns Equifax, GeoTrust, TC TrustCenter, Thawte, and VeriSign; GoDaddy owns Starfield Technologies and ValiCert; and Comodo owns AddTrust AB, eBiz Networks, Positive Software, RegisterFly, Registry Pro, The Code Project, The USERTRUST Network, WebSpace-Forum e.K., and Wotone Communications. These consolidations ultimately allow three organizations (Symantec, GoDaddy, and Comodo) to control 75% of the browser-trusted certificates seen in our study. We list the top 10 parent organizations in Table 4 and the top 10 commercial CAs in Table 5.

There is a long history of commercial CA compromise [8, 30, 32]. In each of these cases, web browsers and operating systems explicitly blacklisted the compromised signing certificate or misissued certificates [8, 28]. However, if a compromised signing certificate had signed for a substantial portion of the Internet, it would potentially be infeasible to revoke it without causing significant disruption to the HTTPS ecosystem [23]. As such, we would hope that large commercial authorities would distribute signing among a number of intermediate certificates. However, as seen in Figure 2, the exact opposite is true. More than 50% of all browser-trusted certificates have been directly signed by 5 intermediate certificates and a single intermediate certificate has signed 26% of currently valid HTTPS certs. If the private key for this intermediate authority were compromised, 26% of websites that rely on HTTPS would need to be immediately issued new certificates. Until these websites deployed the new certificates, browsers would present certificate warnings for all HTTPS communication. While it is not technically worrisome that a small number of organizations control a large percentage of the CA market, it is worrying that large CAs are not following simple precautions and are instead signing a large number of leaf certificates using a small number of intermediates.

5.4 Browser Root Certificate Stores

Microsoft, Apple, and Mozilla all maintain a distinct set of trusted signing certificates, which we refer to as root authorities. Google Chrome utilizes the OS root store in Windows and Mac OS and utilizes the root store maintained by Mozilla on Linux. Combined, the three groups trust 348 root authorities, but there are large discrepancies between the root certificates trusted by each organization. For example, as can be seen in Table 6, Windows trusts 125 additional authorities that are not present in any other OS or browser.

Systems Valid In	Roots	CAs	Signed
Windows Only	125	283	24,873
Mozilla Only	2	3	23
Apple Only	26	30	3,410
Windows & Mozilla	32	97	12,282
Windows & Apple	31	47	9,963
Mozilla & Apple	3	3	0
All Browsers	109	1,346	8,945,241

Table 6: Differences in Browser and OS Root Stores—While there are significant differences in the root certificates stores, 99.4% of trusted certificates are trusted in all major browsers.

The differences in the root stores lead to 463 partially trusted CAs. All but a small handful of the partially trusted authorities belong to government, regional, or specialty issuers. Only one of the partially trusted CAs, *ipsCA*, advertised itself as a commercial authority and sold certificates to the global market. Incidentally, the company claims to be "recognized by more than 98% of today's desktops" [2]. It fails to mention that its certificates are not trusted in Mozilla Firefox or on Mac OS.

Further investigation indicates that *ipsCA* was in the Mozilla root store in 2009, but was removed after several violations including the issuance of embedded-null prefix certificates, the unavailability of OCSP servers, and the issuance of leaf certificates with validity periods beyond the lifetime of the root CA certificate [34].

These 463 partially trusted authorities have little presence on the Internet. In total, they have signed certificates for only 51 domains in the Alexa Top 1 Million and for one domain in the Alexa Top 10,000 which belongs to *mci.ir*, an Iranian telecommunications company. Of the 348 root certificates, 121 of the authorities never signed any leaf certificates seen in our study, and 99.4% of the leaf certificates trusted by any browser are trusted in all browsers.

5.5 Name Constraints

While it is not an inherently poor idea to provide signing certificates to third-party organizations, these certificates should be restricted to a limited set of domains. Instead, all but 7 CAs in our March 22 scan can sign for any domain. X.509 Name Constraints [18] provide a technical mechanism by which parent authorities can limit the domains for which an intermediate signing certificate can sign leaf certificates. Optimally, signing certificates provided to third-party organizations, such as universities or corporations, would utilize name constraints to prevent potential abuse and to limit the potential damage if the signing certificate were compromised.

We find that only 7 trusted intermediate authorities out of 1,832 have name constraints defined, of which 3 were labeled as Comodo testing certificates. The remaining 4 are:

1. An intermediate provided by AddTrust AB to the Intel is limited to small a number of Intel owned domains.
2. An intermediate controlled by the U.S. State Department and provided by the U.S. Government root authority is prevented from signing certificates with the `.mil` top-level domain.
3. An intermediate provided to the Louisiana State University Health System is limited to a small number of affiliated domains.
4. A root certificate belonging to the Hellenic Academic and Research Institutions Certification Authority is restricted to the .gr, .eu, .edu, and .org domains.

5.6 Path Length Constraints

A signing authority can limit the number of intermediate authorities that can appear below it in a certificate chain by specifying an X.509 path length constraint [18] on the intermediate certificates that it signs. This is frequently used to prevent intermediate authorities from further delegating the ability to sign new certificates.

In our dataset, we find that 43% of signing certificates do not have any path length restriction defined. While this may not be a concern for large commercial CAs, we note that more than 80% of the intermediate authorities belonging to other types of organizations (e.g. corporations, academic, and financial institutions). While we saw little evidence of non-commercial CAs providing signing certificates to third-party organizations, we did observe governments using their intermediate authority to sign subordinate CA certificates for corporations within their country.

5.7 Authority Key Usage

All of the browser-trusted leaf certificates in our study were signed using an RSA key. As shown in Table 8, over 95% of browser trusted certificates were signed with 2048-bit RSA keys. We also note 6 browser-trusted authorities with ECDSA keys belonging to Symantec, Comodo, and Trend Micro. However, we found no trusted certificates that were signed using a ECDSA certificate.

Surprisingly, we find that 243 (13%) of the browser-trusted signing certificates were signed using a weaker key than they themselves contained. In all of these cases, the weakest key was the root authority. While only 58 (15.2%) of the 348 browser root authorities utilize 1024-bit RSA keys, these keys were used to indirectly sign 48.7% of browser-trusted certificates. In all of these cases, the CA organization also controlled a browser-trusted 2048-bit root certificate that could be used to re-sign the intermediate certificate.

NIST recommends that the public stop using 1024-bit keys in 2016 based on the expected computational power needed to compromise keys of this strength [5]. However, as seen in Figure 5, more than 70% of CA certificates using 1024-bit keys expire after this date and 57% of roots using 1024-bit RSA keys have signed children that expire after 2016. Figure 3 shows how certificate authorities are using certificates valid for up to 40 years—far beyond when their keys are expected to be compromisable. Most worryingly, it does not appear that CAs are moving from 1024-bit roots to more secure keys. As shown in Figure 4, we find only a 0.08% decrease in the number of certificates dependent on a 1024-bit root authority in the

Type	Root Authorities		Recursively Signed	
ECDSA	6	(1.8%)	0	(0%)
RSA (1024-bit)	53	(16.0%)	1,694,526	(48.6%)
RSA (2028-bit)	202	(61.0%)	1,686,814	(48.4%)
RSA (4096-bit)	70	(21.2%)	102,139	(2.9%)

Table 7: Key Distribution for Trusted Roots — The distribution of keys for root certificates shipped with major browsers and OSes.

Key Type	Authorities		Signed Leaves	
ECDSA	6	(0.3%)	0	(0%)
RSA (1024-bit)	134	(7.3%)	133,391	(4.2%)
RSA (2048-bit)	1,493	(78.9%)	3,034,751	(95.3%)
RSA (4096-bit)	198	(10.5%)	16,969	(0.5%)

Table 8: Key Distribution for Trusted Signing Certificates

past year. In 2012, 1.4 million new certificates were issued that were rooted in a 1024-bit authority, and 370,130 were issued between January and April 2013.

6. LEAF CERTIFICATES AND HOSTING

Over the last 14 months, we collected 6.93 million unique trusted certificates. In our March 22 scan, we observed 3.2 million unique trusted certificates from 21.4 million hosts. In this section, we discuss the dynamics of these trusted leaf certificates and the hosts serving them.

6.1 Keys and Signatures

Public Keys In line with previous studies, we find that over 99% of trusted leaf certificates contain RSA public keys. We provide a breakdown of leaf key types in Table 9. Over the course of the past year, we found 47 certificates that contain ECDSA public keys; none were present in our March 22 scan and none were browser trusted. Recently, Google began to use ECDSA certificates for several services. However, these sites are only accessible through the use of server name indication (SNI) and so do not appear in our dataset.

We find 2,631 browser-trusted certificates using 512-bit RSA keys, which are known to be easily factorable, and 73 certificates utilizing 768-bit keys, which have been shown to be factorable with large distributed computing efforts [20]. While a large number of these certificates were found being actively hosted, only 16 have not yet expired or been revoked. No browser-trusted authorities have signed any 512-bit RSA keys since August 27, 2012. We were further encouraged to find that less than 4% of valid trusted certificates used 1024-bit keys.

Weak Keys Previous studies have exposed the use of weak keys in the HTTPS space [16, 22, 35]. We revisit several of these measurements and provide up-to-date metrics. Following up on the study performed by Heninger et al. [16], we find that 55,451 certificates contained factorable RSA keys and are served on 63,293 hosts, a 40% decrease in the total percentage of hosts with factorable keys, but only a slight decrease (1.25%) in the raw number of hosts found using factorable keys since 2011. Three of the factorable certificates are browser trusted; the last was signed on August 9, 2012. 2,743 certificates contained a Debian weak key [7], of which 96 were browser trusted, a 34% decrease from 2011 [16]. The last browser-trusted certificate containing a Debian weak key was signed on January 25, 2012.

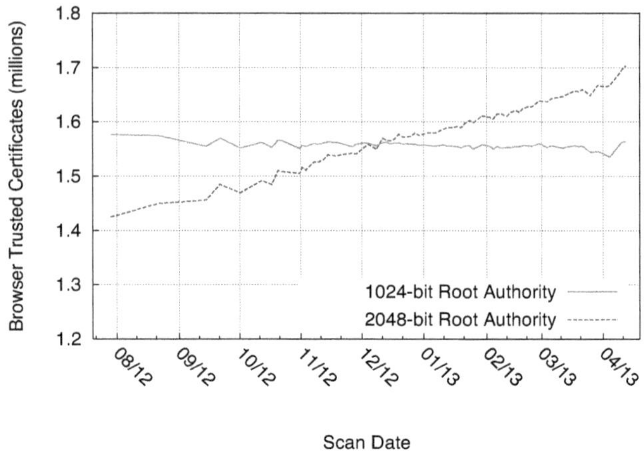

Figure 4: Temporal Trends in Root Key Size — We find that 48.7% of browser-trusted leaf certificates are dependent on 1024-bit RSA based root authorities, contrary to recommended practice [5].

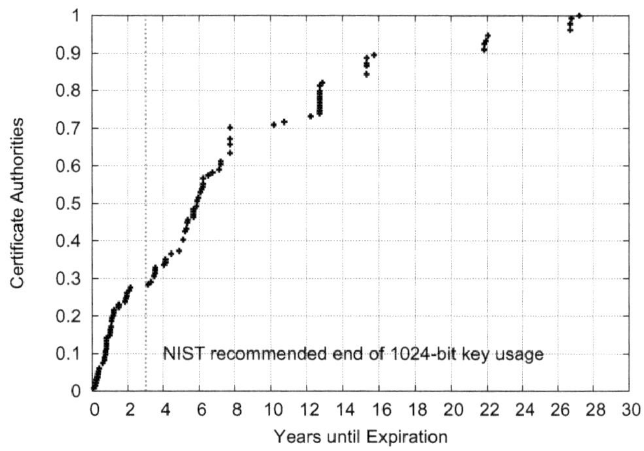

Figure 5: Expiration of 1024-bit Root Certificates — This figure shows when trusted 1024-bit RSA CA certificates expire. We note that more than 70% expire after 2016 when NIST recommends discontinuing the use of 1024-bit keys.

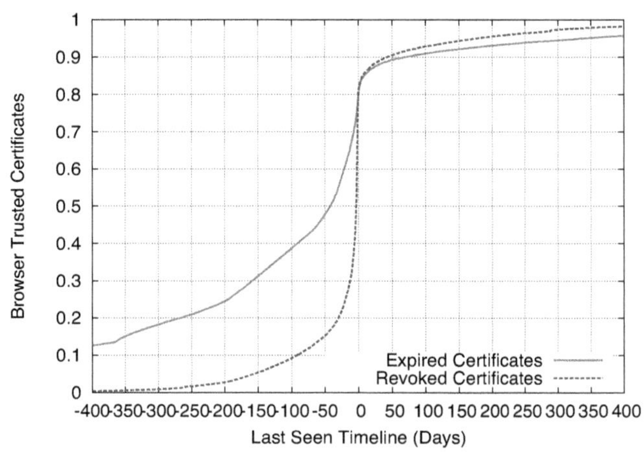

Figure 6: CDF of Certificate Removal — We find that 20% of expiring certificates and 19.5% of revoked certificates are removed retroactively (to the right of 0 days).

Key Type	All Trusted		Valid Trusted
RSA ($\leq$ 512-bit)	2,631	(0.1%)	16
RSA (768-bit)	73	(0.0%)	0
RSA (1024-bit)	341,091	(10.5%)	165,637
RSA (1032–2040-bit)	23,888	(0.7%)	105
RSA (2048-bit)	2,816,757	(86.4%)	2,545,693
RSA (2056–4088-bit)	1,006	(0.0%)	921
RSA (4096-bit)	74,014	(2.3%)	65,780
RSA (> 4096-bit)	234	(0.0%)	192
DSA (all)	17	(0.0%)	7
ECDSA (all)	0	(0.0%)	0

Table 9: Trusted Leaf Certificate Public Key Distribution

Type	Trusted Certificates	
SHA-1 with RSA Encryption	5,972,001	(98.7%)
MD5 with RSA Encryption	32,905	(0.54%)
SHA-256 with RSA Encryption	15,297	(0.25%)
SHA-512 with RSA Encryption	7	(0.00%)
MD2 with RSA Encryption	21	(0.00%)
Other	29,705	(0.49%)

Table 10: Trusted Leaf Certificate Signature Algorithms

Signature Algorithms In line with the results presented by Holz et al. [17], we find that 98.7% of browser-trusted certificates are signed using SHA-1 and RSA encryption. We find 22 trusted certificates with MD2-based signatures and 31,325 with MD5 signatures. Due to known weaknesses in these hash functions, no organizations should currently be using them to sign certificates. The last certificate signed with MD5 was issued on April 17, 2013 by Finmeccanica S.p.A., an Italian defense contractor, more than 4 years after Sotirov et al. published "MD5 considered harmful today" [32]. We provide a breakdown of leaf certificate signature types in Table 10.

Certificate Depth Similarly to the EFF and Holz et al., we find that the vast majority (98%) of leaf certificates are signed by intermediate authorities one intermediate away from a root authority. However we find that 61 root authorities directly signed 41,000 leaf certificates and that there exist leaf certificates as many as 5 intermediates away from a root authority. All but a handful of the authorities 4 or more intermediates away from a browser-trusted root belonged to agencies within the U.S. Federal Government.

We are not aware of any vulnerabilities created by having a long certificate chain. However, it is worrisome to see leaf certificates directly signed by root authorities, because this indicates that the root signing key is being actively used and may be stored in a network-attached system, raising the risk of compromise. If the signing key were to be compromised, the root certificate could not be replaced without updating all deployed browser installations. If an intermediate authority were used instead to sign these leaf certificates, then it could be replaced by the root authority without requiring browser updates, and the root could be kept offline during day-to-day operation.

6.2 Incorrectly Hosted Trusted Certificates

We find that 1.32 million hosts (12.7%) serving once-valid browser-trusted leaf certificates are misconfigured in a manner such that they are inaccessible to some clients or are being hosted beyond their validity period. We show a breakdown of reasons that certificates are invalid in Table 11. We note that Mozilla Network Security Services (NSS) [27], the certificate validation library utilized by many browsers, caches previously seen intermediates. Because of this, many certificates with invalid trust chains will appear valid in users' browsers if the intermediate authorities have previously been encountered.

Approximately 5.8% of hosts are serving now-expired certificates, which will be considered invalid by all browsers. We find that 22% of certificates are removed retroactively after their expiration and that 19.5% of revoked certificates are removed after they appear in a certificate revocation list (CRL). We show the distribution of when certificates are removed from servers in Figure 6. Another 42.2% of hosts are providing unnecessary certificates in the presented trust chain. Although this practice has no security implications, these additional certificates provide no benefit to the client and ultimately result in a slight performance degradation.

Holz et al. report that 18% of all certificates are expired. However, this statistic reflected all certificates, over 25% of which are self-signed and would already raise a browser error. We instead consider only certificates signed by browser-trusted authorities, which would otherwise be considered valid.

Status	Hosts	
Expired	595,168	(5.80%)
Not Yet Valid	1,966	(0.02%)
Revoked	28,033	(0.27%)
No Trust Chain	654,667	(6.30%)
Misordered Chain	25,667	(0.24%)
Incorrect Chain	11,761	(0.14%)
Unnecessary Root	4,365,321	(42.2%)
Optimally Configured	4,657,133	(45.0%)

Table 11: Common Server Certificate Problems — We evaluate hosts serving browser-trusted certificates and classify common certificate and server configuration errors. The number of misconfigured hosts indicates that procuring certificates and correctly configuring them on servers remains a challenge for many users.

6.3 Invalid Authority Types

We find that 47 (2.6%) of the 1,832 browser-trusted signing certificates are not denoted for signing TLS certificates for use on the web. Of these 47 signing certificates, 28 (60%) are designated for signing Microsoft or Netscape Server Gated Crypto certificates, a now obsolete cryptographic standard that was used in the 1990s in response to U.S. regulation on the export of strong cryptographic standards [29].

The remaining 19 signing certificates are designated for combinations of *Code Signing*, *E-mail Protection*, *TLS Web Client Authentication*, *Time Stamping*, and *Microsoft Encrypted File System*. These intermediate certificates were not found in any browser or operating system root stores but were found being served on public web servers. It does not appear that any of these authorities were signing certificates inappropriately; nobody was attempting to sign a TLS Web Server Authentication certificate using an authority marked for another use. Instead, we found that individuals and organizations were mistakenly using valid code signing and e-mail certificates as the TLS leaf certificate on their websites.

6.4 Certificate Revocation

Certificate authorities can denote that previously issued certificates should no longer be trusted by publishing their revocation in a public *certificate revocation list* (CRL). The location of authority CRLs are listed in each signed certificate. In order to understand why certificates are being revoked, we fetched and parsed the CRLs listed in all browser-trusted certificates. We find that 2.5% of browser-trusted certificates are eventually revoked by their authority. We present a breakdown of revocation reasons in Table 9. While RFC 5280 [11] strongly encourages issuers to provide "meaningful" reason codes for CRL entries, we find that 71.7% of issuers who revoked certificates do not provide reasons for any of their revocations.

While 2.5% of certificates are eventually revoked, we find that only 0.3% of hosts presenting certificates in our scan were revoked. We expect that this is because the site operators will request a certificate be revoked and simultaneously remove the certificate from the web server. As can be seen in Figure 6, more than 80% of certificates are removed proactively and were not seen again after the time of their revocation.

WebTrust for Certificate Authorities [3], an audit mandated by the three major root stores, requires that authorities maintain an online repository that allows clients to check for certificate revocation information. However, we find that 14 trusted signing certificates from 9 organizations fail to include revocation data in at least some of their certificates, and in 5 cases do not supply revocation data in any of their signed certificates.

7. UNEXPECTED OBSERVATIONS

We observed a variety of unexpected phenomenon during our scans over the past year. We describe these observations here.

7.1 CA Certs with Multiple Parents

Of the 1,832 browser-trusted signing certificates we found, 380 shared their subject, public key, and subject key identifier with another browser-trusted certificate forming 136 groups of "sibling" CA certificates. Because of this, leaf certificates can have more than one parent from the browsers' point of view. We find that only 37.4% of browser trusted leaf certificates have a single parent; 38.7% have two parents; 12.3% have three; 11.3% have four; and a small number have 5–9 valid parents. Depending on which parent is presented in a trust chain, the perceived validity of the leaf certificate can change. For example, if the presented intermediate certificate has expired, then the leaf certificate will be considered invalid. We note that subject key identified sometimes also specifies additional constraints such as a constraint on issuer serial number. However, we find that only a handful of certificates contain additional constraints.

In 86 of the 136 groups of sibling certificates, the signing certificates had differing validity periods. In four sets, one of the certificates was revoked, in a separate four sets, each authority was in a different browser or OS root store, and in 49 cases the authorities were signed by different parent authorities. While previous studies found evidence of this phenomenon, we were not aware of the prevalence of this behavior. We are not aware of any security vulnerabilities that are introduced by this practice, but we do find that 43,674 (1.35%) of the browser-trusted certificates are presented with the incorrect parent, which limits their perceived validity (e.g. the presented CA certificate expires earlier the leaf certificate, but another parent exists with a later expiration date).

7.2 CA Certs with Negative Path Lengths

We find that 1,395 browser-trusted CA certificates have a negative path length constraint, which renders them unable to sign any certificates due to a path length restriction earlier in the trust chain. These malformed intermediate certificates were signed by the Government of Korea and provided to educational institutions ranging

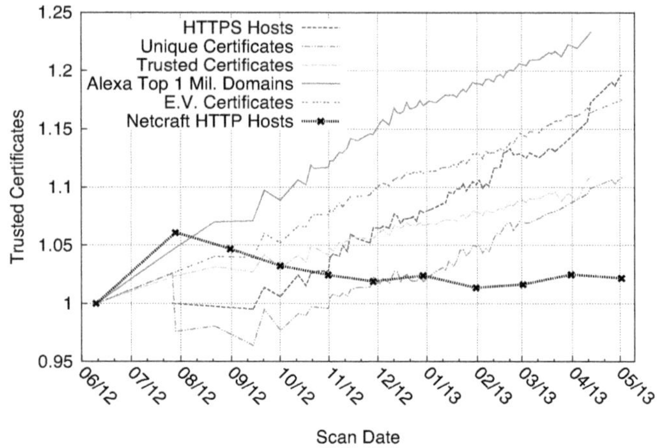

Figure 7: Growth in HTTPS Usage — Over the past 14 months, we observe between 10-25% growth of all aspects of HTTPS usage.

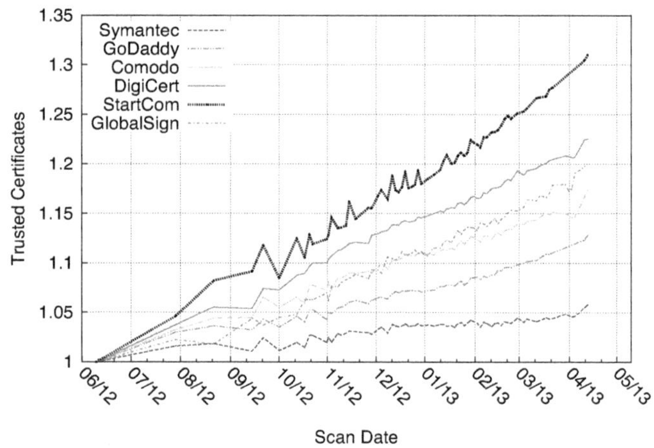

Figure 8: Change in Authority Market Share — In this figure, we should the individual growth of the top 10 most prolific certificate authorities.

Revocation Reason	Revoked Certificates	
Cessation Of Operation	101,370	(64.9%)
Not Provided	31514	(20.2%)
Affiliation Changed	7,384	(4.7%)
Privilege Withdrawn	5,525	(3.5%)
Unspecified	4,523	(2.9%)
Superseded	3,887	(2.5%)
Key Compromise	1,945	(1.2%)
Certificate Hold	45	(0.0%)
CA Compromise	2	(0.0%)
Total	**156,195**	

Figure 9: Reasons for Revocation — We find that 10,220 (2.5%) of the browser trusted certificates seen in our study were eventually revoked. Both of the "CA Compromised" revocations were due to the DigiNotar compromise [8].

from elementary schools to universities, libraries, and museums. However, because they are still technically CA certificates, web browsers including Mozilla Firefox and Google Chrome will not recognize them as valid leaf certificates.

We do not include these certificates when referring to the set of browser-trusted authorities because they are unable to sign any certificates and therefore do not have the same influence as other valid authorities. However, we note that some less common client implementations may fail to properly check the path length constraint and incorrectly treat these as valid. One of these CA certificates, issued to a Korean elementary school, was compromised by Heninger [15], who factored the 512-bit key a few hours after the certificate expired.

7.3 Mis-issued CA Certificates

We found one mis-issued signing certificate during the course of our study, which was issued for `*.EGO.GOV.TR`, by Turktrust, a small Turkish certificate authority. We found the certificate served as a leaf certificate on what appeared to be an unconfigured IIS server on a Turkish IP address. We saw 487 certificates that were signed by Turktrust over the course of our study. All were for Turkish organizations or the Turkish Government; we saw no evidence of other mis-issued certificates.

The certificate was later found by Google after being used to sign a Google wildcard certificate [21] and was revoked by Turktrust on December 26, 2012. It was last seen in our scans on December 27, 2012.

7.4 Site Certificates with Invalid Domains

We find that 4.6% (149,902) of browser-trusted certificates contain a common name (CN) or subject alternate name for a locally scoped domain or private IP address. Because these names are not fully qualified, the intended resource is ambiguous and there is no identifiable owner. As such, these local domain names frequently appear on more than one certificate. In one example, there are 1,218 browser-trusted certificates for the domain `mail` owned by organizations ranging from the U.S. Department of Defense to the Lagunitas Brewing Company.

The vast majority of certificates appear to be related to mail services. Of the 157,861 certificates with locally scoped names, 25,964 contain the name `exchange` (Microsoft Exchange Mail Server) and 99,773 contain a variation on the name `mail`. More than 100,000 of the certificates contain a domain ending in `.local`.

We suspect that certificates include these locally scoped names in order to facilitate users that are part of an Active Directory domain in connecting to their local Exchange mail server. In this scenario, the integrated DNS service in Active Directory will automatically resolve locally scoped names to the correct server on the domain. However, these clients will receive a name mismatch error if the TLS certificate presented by the Exchange Server does not match the locally scoped name that was originally resolved. Instead of requiring users to use the fully qualified domain name (FQDN) of the Exchange Server unlike other servers on the domain, certificate authorities include the local name of the Exchange server. In the case of certificates ending in `.local`, Active Directory Forests are generally rooted in an FQDN. In cases where organizations have not registered an FQDN for their forest, Active Directory elects to use the `.local` TLD.

Unfortunately, this practice does not provide security against man-in-the-middle attacks. It is trivial to procure a certificate with the same locally scoped name as another organization. Because there is no identifiable owner for the domain, both certificates are equally valid, and the subsequent certificate can be used to impersonate the original organization.

8. ADOPTION TRENDS

We observe a steady, linear increase in nearly all aspects of HTTPS adoption between June 2012 and April 2013, as shown in Figure 7. Most notably, there is a 23.0% increase in the number of Alexa Top 1 Million domains serving trusted certificates and a 10.9% increase in the number of unique browser-trusted certificates found during each scan. During this time, the Netcraft Web survey finds only a 2.2% increase in the number of active sites that respond over HTTP [25]. Based on the Netcraft Survey, we find an 8.5% increase in the number of websites utilizing HTTPS from 1.61% to 1.75%. This indicates that the increase in the number of certificates is not solely dependent on the growth of the Internet, but that there is an increase in the adoption of HTTPS in existing sites. We also note a 16.8% increase in the number of extended validation certificates, a 19.6% increase in the number of hosts serving HTTPS on port 443, and an 11.1% increase in the total number of TLS certificates over this period.

The market share of each authority did not change drastically over the past year. In terms of number of valid signed leaf certifictes, Symantec grew 6%, GoDaddy 13%, and Comodo 17%. During this time, there was a 10.9% increase in the global number of unique valid browser-trusted certificates. StartCom, a smaller authority based in Israel that offers free basic certificates, grew by 32% over the course of the year, from 2.17% to 2.56% market share. We plot the growth of the top authorities in Figure 8.

9. DISCUSSION

Analyzing the certificate authority ecosystem from a global perspective reveals several current practices that put the entire HTTPS ecosystem at risk. In this section, we discuss our observations and possible paths forward.

Ignoring Foundational Principles The security community has several widely accepted best practices such as the *principle of least privilege* and *defense in depth*. However, these guidelines are not being well applied within one of our most security critical ecosystems. For instance, there are several technical practices already at our disposal for limiting the scope of a signing certificate, including setting name or path length constraints and distributing leaf certificates among a large number intermediate certificates. There are clear cases for using these restrictions, but the vast majority of the time, CAs are not fully utilizing these options.

One example of how defense in depth successfully prevented compromise can be seen in the 1,400 signing certificates that were mis-issued to organizations in South Korea (Section 7.2). In this case, a path length constraint on a grandparent certificate prevented this error from becoming a massive vulnerability. To put this in context, if *defense in depth* had not been practiced, the erroneous action of a single certificate authority would have tripled the number of organizations controlling a valid signing certificate overnight. Unfortunately, while a path length constraint was in place for this particular situation, more than 40% of CA certificates do not have any constraints in place to prevent this type of error and only a small handful use name constraints.

In a less fortunate example, Turktrust accidentally issued a signing certificate to one of its customers that ultimately signed a valid certificate for `*.google.com` (Section 7.3). If name or path constraints had been applied to Turktrust's CA intermediate certificate, the incident could have been avoided or, at the very least, reduced in scope. In other situations, the risk associated with compromise of a single signing certificate could be decreased by simply spreading issuance across multiple certificates (Section 5.3).

Standards and Working Groups The CA/Browser Forum is a voluntary working group composed of certificate authorities and Internet browser software vendors. The group has recently attempted to resolve many of the security risks previously introduced by certificate authorities, and in November 2011, the it adopted guidelines for certificate authorities [10] that touch on many of the concerns we raise.

However with only 20% of the organizations controlling signing certificates being commercial certificate authorities and less than 25% of commercial authorities participating in the workgroup, there remains a disconnect. It is unclear how many organizations are aware of the existence of the baseline standard, but it is clear that a large number of organizations are either unaware or are choosing to ignore the forum's baseline requirements. One example of this non-adherence can be seen in the agreement to cease the issuance of certificates containing internal server names and reserved IP addresses. Despite the ratification of this policy, more than 500 certificates containing internal server names and which expire after November 1, 2015 have been issued since July, 1, 2012 by CA/B Forum members (Section 7.4).

Without any enforcement, members of the CA/Browser Forum have disregarded adopted policies and we expect that other organizations are unaware of the standards. There is still work required from the security community to reign in these additional authorities and to follow up with members that are disregarding existing policies.

Browsers to Lead the Way Web browser and operating system maintainers are in a unique position to set expectations for certificate authorities, and it is encouraging to see increasing dialogue in the CA/Browser Forum. However, browsers also have a responsibility to commit resources towards a healthier ecosystem. Many new, more secure technologies are dependent on support in common browsers and web servers. Without browser compatibility, certificate authorities lack incentive to adopt new, more secure options regardless of support from the security community.

This can immediately be seen in the deployment of name constraints. We find that the vast majority of the CA certificates issued to non-CAs are used to issue certificates to a small number of domains and, as such, could appropriately be scoped using name constraints with little impact on day-to-day operations. Restricted scopes have been shown to greatly reduce the attack surface of the CA ecosystem [19], and with 80% of existing signing certificates belonging to organizations other than commercial certificate authorities, there is a clear and present need for name constraints (Section 5). However, Safari and Google Chrome on Mac OS do not currently support the critical server name constraint extension. As a result, any certificate signed using an appropriately scoped CA certificate with the extension marked as critical will be rejected on these platforms. Therefore, while there is community consensus on the value of server name constraints, progress will be slow until all browsers support the extension.

Failing to Recognize Cryptographic Reality It is encouraging to find that over 95% of trusted leaf certificates and 95% of trusted signing certificates use NIST recommended key sizes [6]. However, more than 50 root authorities continue to use 1024-bit RSA keys, the last of which expires in 2040—more than 20 years past recommended use for a key of this size (Section 5.7). Authorities are not adequately considering long-term consequences of authority certificates and need to anticipate what the cryptographic landscape will be in the future. Many of these root certificates were signed prior to guidelines against such long-lived CA certificates. However, today, we need to be working to resolve these past errors and preparing to remove now-inappropriate root CAs from browser root stores.

10. CONCLUSION

In this work, we completed the largest known measurement study of the HTTPS certificate ecosystem by performing 110 comprehensive scans of the IPv4 HTTPS ecosystem over a 14 month period. We investigated the organizations that the HTTPS ecosystem depends on and identified several specific practices employed by certificate authorities that lead to a weakened public key infrastructure. We provided updated metrics on many aspects of HTTPS and certificate deployment along with adoption trends over the last year. Lastly, we discussed the high-level implications of our results and make several recommendations for strengthening the ecosystem. Our study shows that regular active scans provide detailed and temporally fine-grained visibility into this otherwise opaque area of security critical infrastructure. We are publishing the data from our scans at https://httpsecosystem.org/ in the hope that it will assist other researcher in further investigating the HTTPS ecosystem.

Acknowledgments

The authors thank the exceptional sysadmins at the University of Michigan for their help and support throughout this project. This research would not have been possible without Kevin Cheek, Chris Brenner, Laura Fink, Paul Howell, Don Winsor, and others from ITS, CAEN, and DCO. We thank the anonymous reviewers and our shepherd, Udi Weinsberg, for their insightful suggestions and comments. We also thank Brad Campbell, Peter Eckersley, Ralph Holz, Ben Laurie, Pat Pannuto, and Eric Wustrow. This work was supported in part by the Department of Homeland Security Science and Technology Directorate under contracts D08PC75388, FA8750-12-2-0314, and FA8750-12-2-0235; the National Science Foundation (NSF) under contracts CNS 1111699, CNS 091639, CNS 08311174, CNS 0751116, CNS 1330142, and CNS 1255153; and the Department of the Navy under contract N000.14-09-1-1042.

11. REFERENCES

[1] Alexa Top 1,000,000 Sites. http://s3.amazonaws.com/alexa-static/top-1m.csv.zip.

[2] Facts about ipsCA, April 2013. http://certs.ipsca.com/companyIPSipsCA/competitorssay.asp.

[3] WebTrust for Certification Authorities — SSL Baseline Requirements Audit Criteria v.1.1, Jan. 2013. http://www.webtrust.org/homepage-documents/item72056.pdf.

[4] D. Akhawe, B. Amann, M. Vallentin, and R. Sommer. Here's my cert, so trust me, maybe? Understanding TLS errors on the web. In *Proceedings of the 22nd international conference on the World Wide Web*, pages 59–70, 2013.

[5] E. Barker, W. Barker, W. Burr, W. Polk, and M. Smid. Recommendation for Key Management - Part 1: General (Revision 3), 2012. http://csrc.nist.gov/publications/nistpubs/800-57/sp800-57_part1_rev3_general.pdf.

[6] E. Barker and A. Roginsky. Transitions: Recommendation for Transitioning the Use of Cryptographic Algorithms and Key Lengths, Jan. 2011. http://csrc.nist.gov/publications/nistpubs/800-131A/sp800-131A.pdf.

[7] L. Bello. DSA-1571-1 OpenSSL—Predictable random number generator, 2008. Debian Security Advisory. http://www.debian.org/security/2008/dsa-1571.

[8] S. Bhat. Gmail users in Iran hit by MITM Attacks, Aug. 2011. http://techie-buzz.com/tech-news/gmail-iran-hit-mitm.html.

[9] S. Blake-Wilson, M. Nystrom, D. Hopwood, J. Mikkelsen, and T. Wright. Transport Layer Security (TLS) Extensions. RFC 3546 (Proposed Standard), June 2003.

[10] CA/Browser Forum. Baseline Requirements for the Issuance and Management of Publicly-Trusted Certificates, v.1.1, Nov. 2011. https://www.cabforum.org/Baseline_Requirements_V1_1.pdf.

[11] D. Cooper, S. Santesson, S. Farrell, S. Boeyen, R. Housley, and W. Polk. Internet X.509 Public Key Infrastructure Certificate and Certificate Revocation List (CRL) Profile. RFC 5280 (Proposed Standard), May 2008. Updated by RFC 6818.

[12] T. Dierks and E. Rescorla. The Transport Layer Security (TLS) Protocol Version 1.2. RFC 5246 (Proposed Standard), Aug. 2008. Updated by RFCs 5746, 5878, 6176.

[13] Z. Durumeric, E. Wustrow, and J. A. Halderman. ZMap: Fast Internet-wide scanning and its security applications. In *Proceedings of the 22nd USENIX Security Symposium*, Aug. 2013.

[14] P. Eckersley and J. Burns. An observatory for the SSLiverse. Talk at Defcon 18 (2010). https://www.eff.org/files/DefconSSLiverse.pdf.

[15] N. Heninger. Factoring as a service, Aug. 2013. Talk at CRYPTO Rump Session 2013. http://crypto.2013.rump.cr.yp.to/981774ce07e51813fd4466612a78601b.pdf.

[16] N. Heninger, Z. Durumeric, E. Wustrow, and J. A. Halderman. Mining your Ps and Qs: Detection of widespread weak keys in network devices. In *21st USENIX Security Symposium*, Aug. 2012.

[17] R. Holz, L. Braun, N. Kammenhuber, and G. Carle. The SSL landscape: A thorough analysis of the X.509 PKI using active and passive measurements. In *11th ACM SIGCOMM conference on Internet measurement (IMC)*, 2011.

[18] R. Housley, W. Ford, W. Polk, and D. Solo. Internet X.509 public key infrastructure certificate and CRL profile. (2459), Jan. 2009.

[19] J. Kasten, E. Wustrow, and J. A. Halderman. Cage: Taming certificate authorities by inferring restricted scopes. In *17th International Conference on Financial Cryptography and Data Security (FC)*, 2013.

[20] T. Kleinjung, K. Aoki, J. Franke, A. Lenstra, E. Thomé, J. Bos, P. Gaudry, A. Kruppa, P. Montgomery, D. Osvik, et al. Factorization of a 768-bit rsa modulus. In *Advances in Cryptology–CRYPTO 2010*, pages 333–350. Springer, 2010.

[21] A. Langley. Enhancing digital certificate security. Google Online Security Blog, http://googleonlinesecurity.blogspot.com/2013/01/enhancing-digital-certificate-security.html, Jan. 2013.

[22] A. K. Lenstra, J. P. Hughes, M. Augier, J. W. Bos, T. Kleinjung, and C. Wachter. Ron was wrong, Whit is right. *IACR Cryptology ePrint Archive*, 2012:64, 2012.

[23] M. Marlinspike. SSL and the future of authenticity, Aug. 2011. Talk at BlackHat 2011. http://www.thoughtcrime.org/blog/ssl-and-the-future-of-authenticity/.

[24] N. Mathewson and N. Provos. libevent—An event notification library. http://libevent.org.

[25] Netcraft, Ltd. Web server survey. http://news.netcraft.com/archives/2013/05/03/may-2013-web-server-survey.html, May 2013.

[26] NetMarketShare. Desktop operating system market share, Apr. 2013. http://www.netmarketshare.com/operating-system-market-share.aspx.

[27] M. D. Network. Mozilla network security services (nss). http://www.mozilla.org/projects/security/pki/nss/.

[28] J. Nightingale. Comodo Certificate Issue – Follow Up, Mar. 2011. https://blog.mozilla.org/security/2011/03/25/comodo-certificate-issue-follow-up/.

[29] E. Rescorla. *SSL and TLS: designing and building secure systems*, volume 1. Addison-Wesley Reading, 2001.

[30] R. Richmond. Comodo fraud incident, Mar. 2011. http://www.comodo.com/Comodo-Fraud-Incident-2011-03-23.html.

[31] I. Ristic. Internet SSL survey 2010. Talk at BlackHat 2010. http://media.blackhat.com/bh-ad-10/Ristic/BlackHat-AD-2010-Ristic-Qualys-SSL-Survey-HTTP-Rating-Guide-slides.pdf.

[32] A. Sotirov, M. Stevens, J. Appelbaum, A. Lenstra, D. Molnar, D. A. Osvik, and B. de Weger. MD5 considered harmful today. http://www.win.tue.nl/hashclash/rogue-ca/.

[33] J. Viega, M. Messier, and P. Chandra. *Network Security with OpenSSL: Cryptography for Secure Communications*. O'Reilly, 2002.

[34] K. Wilson. Bug 523652 - IPS action items re IPS SERVIDORES root certificate, Nov. 2009. https://bugzilla.mozilla.org/show_bug.cgi?id=523652.

[35] S. Yilek, E. Rescorla, H. Shacham, B. Enright, and S. Savage. When private keys are public: results from the 2008 Debian OpenSSL vulnerability. In *2009 ACM SIGCOMM Internet Measurement Conference*, pages 15–27.

Exploring EDNS-Client-Subnet Adopters in your Free Time*

Florian Streibelt
TU Berlin
florian@inet.tu-berlin.de

Jan Böttger
TU Berlin
jan@inet.tu-berlin.de

Nikolaos Chatzis
TU Berlin
nikolaos@inet.tu-berlin.de

Georgios Smaragdakis
T-Labs/TU Berlin
georgios@net.t-labs.tu-berlin.de

Anja Feldmann
TU Berlin
anja@inet.tu-berlin.de

ABSTRACT

The recently proposed DNS extension, EDNS-Client-Subnet (ECS), has been quickly adopted by major Internet companies such as Google to better assign user requests to their servers and improve end-user experience. In this paper, we show that the adoption of ECS also offers unique, but likely unintended, opportunities to uncover details about these companies' operational practices at almost no cost. A key observation is that ECS allows to resolve domain names of ECS adopters on behalf of any arbitrary IP/prefix in the Internet. In fact, by utilizing only a single residential vantage point and relying solely on publicly available information, we are able to (i) uncover the global footprint of ECS adopters with very little effort, (ii) infer the DNS response cacheability and end-user clustering of ECS adopters for an arbitrary network in the Internet, and (iii) capture snapshots of user to server mappings as practiced by major ECS adopters. While pointing out such new measurement opportunities, our work is also intended to make current and future ECS adopters aware of which operational information gets exposed when utilizing this recent DNS extension.

General Terms

Measurement.

Keywords

Content Delivery; DNS; CDN.

1. INTRODUCTION

In the current Internet, hostnames are typically resolved using the local resolvers provided by the respective Internet Service Provider (ISP). Unless the answer is cached, the ISP's domain name server performs a recursive lookup to receive an authoritative answer which it can then cache. Large Content Delivery Networks (CDNs) and Content Providers (CPs) use the domain name system (DNS) to map users to possible locations and consequently to appropriate servers [27, 38].

* **This work would not have been possible without the help, engagement, and commitment of Walter Willinger.**

IMC'13, October 23–25, 2013, Barcelona, Spain.

ACM 978-1-4503-1953-9/13/10 ...$15.00.
http://dx.doi.org/10.1145/2504730.2504767.

Unfortunately for the CDNs and CPs, the DNS query is not directly issued by the end-user but only by the local resolver (see [37] for details). Thus, the assumption underlying this solution is that the end-user is close to the local resolver or that a resolver serves clients that are close to each other. However, several studies [11, 26] have shown that these assumptions do not always hold which, in turn, can lead to degraded end-user experience. In particular, the introduction of third party resolvers like Google Public DNS [4] or OpenDNS [7] has exaggerated this trend as end-users, taking advantage of these as resolvers, may experience poor performance[11, 28, 32]. This empirical evidence is mainly due to the fact that these popular third-party resolvers are typically not located within the end-users' ISP and are therefore often not close to the end-user.

The solution, as proposed by Google and others to the IETF [17], is the EDNS-Client-Subnet DNS extension (ECS). While traditional DNS queries do not include the IP address of the query issuer (except via the socket information), ECS includes IP address information of the original query issuer in the query to the authoritative name server. The IP address information can then be used by the CDN or CP to improve the mapping of end-users to servers. Thus, it is not surprising that major Internet companies (e.g., Google, Edgecast, and OpenDNS) have already adopted ECS and have established the consortium "a faster Internet" [1]. The fact that ECS can indeed help improve end-user performance is highlighted by extensive active measurement studies [28, 32].

For the Internet measurement community, the adoption of ECS by some of the major Internet players turns out to offer unique but clearly unintended opportunities. To illustrate, we show in this paper how ECS can be used to uncover details of the operational practices of ECS adopters with almost no effort. Our key observation is that ECS allows anyone to issue queries on behalf of any "end-user" IP address for domains with ECS support. Thus, ECS queries can help uncovering the sophisticated techniques that CDNs and CPs use for mapping users to servers (e.g, see [24, 23, 26]). Indeed, this currently hard-to-extract information can now be collected using only a single vantage point and relying on publicly available information. In the past, to obtain similar information, network researchers had to find and use open or mis-configured resolvers [10, 22, 35], have access to a multitude of vantage points in edge networks [28, 32], rely on volunteers [11, 12], analyze proprietary data [25, 30], or resort to searching the Web [34].

In summary, the three contributions of this paper to the area of Internet measurement are:

- We show that a single vantage point combined with publicly available information is sufficient to uncover the global footprint of ECS adopters and track their expansions.
- We demonstrate how to infer the DNS cacheability and end-user clustering strategies of ECS adopters.

- We illustrate how to capture snapshots of the assignment of users to server locations performed by major ECS adopters.

At the same time, this work is also intended to increase the awareness of current and future ECS adopters about which operational information gets exposed when enabling this recent DNS extension. Despite the fact that experts in the operational community may be aware of some of the shortcomings and consequences of the ECS adoption, a systematic study is still missing. Our software and measurements are publicly available[1].

2. ECS BACKGROUND

The EDNS-Client-Subnet DNS extension [17] was introduced to tackle the problem of mis-locating the end-system which originates the DNS request. The problem is that the end-system's IP information is typically hidden from the authoritative name server. With ECS, client IP information is forwarded by all ECS-enabled resolvers to the authoritative name server in the form of network prefixes.

2.1 Protocol Specification

ECS is an EDNS0 DNS extension [36] proposed by the IETF DNS Extensions Working Group. EDNS0, which is also needed for DNSSEC, uses an ADDITIONAL section in DNS messages to transfer optional data between name servers. Since all sections from a DNS query are present in the DNS response, bidirectional data transfer is enabled as the responder can modify this section. Name servers that do not support EDNS0 either strip the EDNS0 OPTRR in the ADDITIONAL section or forward it unmodified.

An example ECS-enabled query and response is shown in Figure 1. The ADDITIONAL section includes an OPTRR resource-record containing the ECS header and data. The ECS payload consists of the address family used, i.e., IPv4 or IPv6, prefix length, scope and client prefix. To protect a client's privacy, [17] recommends to use prefixes less specific than 32. In each query the scope field must be zero and is a placeholder for the returned scope.

The response from an ECS-enabled DNS server differs in one byte, namely the scope, which is needed for DNS caching. The answer can be cached and used for any query with a client prefix that is a more specific or equal to the prefix as specified by the scope. We note that the response may contain a different scope than the query network mask, and we have indeed observed larger as well as shorter scopes than prefix length in our measurements. In the example, the query prefix length is 16 while the returned scope is 24. The scope is the essential element that allows us to infer operational practices of ECS adopters.

2.2 Challenges in Enabling ECS

While ECS is transparent to the end-user, it requires significant efforts by the DNS server operators, mainly because all involved DNS servers have to at least forward the ECS information. Among the major obstacles are: (i) ECS-support in server software is not widely available[2], (ii) all involved DNS servers need to be upgraded[3], and (iii) third-party resolvers are not necessarily sending ECS queries by default. To change the latter, an engineer of, say,

[1]http://projects.inet.tu-berlin.de/projects/ecs-adopters

[2]We find that only PowerDNS supports ECS as authoritative name-server but not as resolver. Moreover, only for some clients e.g., dig and dnspython patches are available.

[3]CDNs may internally use multiple resolution levels, e.g., Akamai [27].

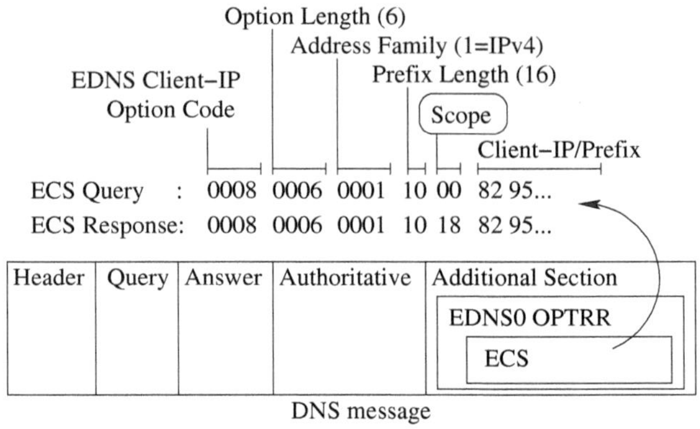

 # dig www.google.com +client=130.149.0.0/16 @ns1.google.com

Figure 1: Example of ECS query and response.

Google Public DNS or OpenDNS, has to manually check the authoritative name servers and white-list them as ECS compliant.

Moreover, appropriate cache support has to be added to the DNS resolvers. Here, ECS with its notion of scope introduces another problem. For each query, the resolver has to check if the IP address of the client lies within the scope of any cached result. If not, the query has to be relayed with the appropriate prefix information. Just imagine the extreme scenario—scope of 32. Then, the resolver should keep a separate entry per client making caching largely ineffective.

Overall, handling ECS is quite complicated as the draft requires DNS forwarders to forward the ECS information sent by the client. It may modify the prefix mask to a less specific. If no ECS information is present in the DNS request, the forwarder may add an OPTRR record based on information from the socket. This is the rule followed e.g., by Google's public DNS servers. Note, that until Google enabled EDNS0 for DNSSEC support, it stripped the ECS records. Now, this information seems to be forwarded unmodified.

3. DATASETS

The following two different kinds of datasets are used in this paper: (i) prefixes to be used as pretended "client location" for the ECS queries, and (ii) popular ECS adopters.

3.1 Network Prefixes

In principle, one list of prefixes may be considered sufficient. However, because we want to uncover the operational practices of certain CDNs and CPs with regards to client localization and clustering, we explore different prefix sets of varying scopes and magnitudes. To that end, we use both private and public sets of network prefixes.

Academic Network (UNI). This network includes a very diverse set of clients, ranging from office working spaces to student dorms and research facilities which complicates usage profiling. This network uses two /16 blocks, does not have an AS, and is localized to a single city in Europe.

Large ISP (ISP). The dataset includes more than 400 prefixes, ranging from /10 to /24, announced by a European tier-1 ISP. This ISP offers services to residential users as well as enterprise networks and also hosts CDN servers.

Large ISP, de-aggregated prefixes (ISP24). We also use the de-aggregated announced prefixes of our large ISP at the granularity of /24 blocks to investigate if the finer granularity lets us uncover additional operational details.

Popular Resolvers (PRES). This proprietary dataset consists of the 280K most popular resolver IPs that contacted a large commercial CDN. These resolvers are distributed across 21K ASes, 74K prefixes, and 230 countries.

RIPE. RIPE RIS [8] makes full BGP routing tables from a multitude of BGP peering sessions publicly available. This data includes 500K prefixes from 43K ASes.

Routeviews (RV). This is another public BGP routing table source offered by the University of Oregon [9].

3.2 Content Provider Datasets

For our experiments, we need to identify ECS adopters and the corresponding hostnames. For this purpose, we utilize Alexa [2] (April 20, 2013), a publicly available database of the top 1 Million second-level domains, as was done by Otto et al.[28]. Since the ECS extension does not allow us to directly find out if a name server is ECS enabled or not, we use the following heuristic. We re-send the same ECS query with three different prefix lengths. If the scope is non-zero for one of the replies, we annotate the server and hostname as ECS-enabled.

We obtain two disjoint groups of (domain names, name-servers) pairs. The first group fully supports ECS and accounts for 3% of the second-level domain names. The second group, about 10%, is ECS-enabled according to the IETF draft [17] but does not appear to use the additional section information for the tested domains (it may well just return a copy of the additional section). Thus, roughly 13% of the top 1 million domains may be ECS-enabled. This number is only slightly larger than what was reported in a 2012 study [28]. However, some of the big players are among the ECS adopters, including Google (and YouTube), Edgecast, CacheFly, HiCloud, and applications hosted in the cloud such as MySqueezebox.

To estimate the potential traffic affected by ECS, we use a 24 hour anonymized packet-level trace from a large European ISP. The trace is from a residential network with more than 10K active end-users and was gathered using Endace cards and analyzed with Bro [29]. It contains 20.3 million DNS requests for more than 450K unique hostnames and 83 million connections. While Alexa only includes the second-level domain names, this dataset allows us to identify full hostnames, which we use in a similar manner as above. In total, we find that roughly 30% of the traffic involves ECS adopters. This highlights that while the number of ECS adopters is relatively small (less than 3% of the authoritative name servers), it includes some of the relevant players responsible for a significant fraction of traffic.

From the set of identified ECS adopters, we select a large CDN, two smaller CDNs, and an application deployed in the cloud to explore their operational practices. In the rest of the paper we mainly focus on:

Google is a founding member of the consortium "a faster Internet" and one of the main supporters of ECS. It has adopted ECS in all their resolvers and name servers. Moreover, Google uses a sophisticated backend with many data centers, edge-servers, and Google Global Cache (GGC) servers located inside ISPs [3, 13, 19]. It is known that there can be anywhere between tens to thousands of Google servers behind a single Google IP [33].

Edgecast is a large CDN that also offers streaming solutions. It is also one of the participants in the "a faster Internet" consortium.

CacheFly is another CDN that has adopted ECS.

MySqueezebox is a Logitech product that runs on top of Amazon's Web cloud Service EC2.

4. METHOD

For our experiments, we take advantage of the ECS extension of the python DNS libraries provided by OpenDNS [7]. Based on this library, we have developed a framework which utilizes the above API to send ECS DNS queries with arbitrary ECS client subnet information to authoritative name servers. By embedding this library into our test framework, we can handle failures and retries efficiently which would have been more complicated with a standalone utility like the patched dig tool [17].

We emphasize that a single vantage point is sufficient for performing our experiments, as with ECS the answers exclusively depend on the client prefix sent. This is confirmed by synchronized measurements from two research networks (US, Germany) and a German hosting provider.

It is sufficient to use a commodity PC, issuing queries at the rate of 40 to 50 queries per second. This rate that can be achieved at a residential vantage point with no complications [11].

Scaling up the query rate is easy by using multiple vantage points in parallel, e.g., by utilizing PlanetLab nodes, but our experiments show that a simple setup serves the purpose of this study.

With regards to the queries, we use hostnames from the Alexa list and the ISP traces and the source prefixes from our prefix datasets. Note, that because a large fraction of IPv6 connectivity is still handled by 6to4 tunnels [16] and related techniques, we do not include IPv6 in this preliminary study.

For each query we issue we add an entry to our SQL database which includes all parameters including the timestamp, the returned records (answers) including TTL and returned scope. Before and after each experiment, we collect the most recent prefixes for each dataset. To speed-up the experiments, we compile a set of unique prefixes before starting an experiment.

5. EVALUATION

To evaluate the capabilities of ECS as a measurement tool, we explore how difficult it is to (i) uncover the footprint of ECS adopters, (ii) assess the effect of ECS on cacheability of DNS records, and (iii) capture snapshots of how ECS adopters assign users to server locations. All queries are sent for a single hostname (e.g., `www.google.com`) to one of the authoritative name servers of the service provider (e.g., `ns1.google.com`).

While for the RIPE, RV, ISP and ISP24 dataset we use the prefixes as announced, for the UNI dataset an ECS prefix length of 32 is chosen, as this dataset contains individual IP addresses.

5.1 Uncovering Infrastructure Footprints

We first report on our experiences with using ECS to uncover the footprint of the four selected ECS adopters. Apparently the operational community also did some investigation [5] in enumerating CDN servers using ECS.

Table 1 summarizes the number of unique server IPs, subnets, ASes, and locations. The footprint of Google is by far the most interesting one, with more than 6,300 server IPs across 166 ASes in 47 countries[4]. We also notice that GGCs are typically located in ASes that are "categorized" as enterprise customers and small transit providers [18] in both developed and developing countries. In March 2013, Google servers are found in 81 enterprise customers, 62 small transit providers, 14 content/access/hosting providers, and only 4 large transit providers (a small number of ASes that host Google server IPs do not belong to any of these categories). While

[4]For geolocation we use MaxMind [6]. We are aware that geolocation of CDN servers can be inaccurate, e.g., MaxMind maps the IPs of the main Google AS (AS15169) to California, but it is accurate on the country level for IPs that belong to ISPs [31] and thus, good enough for the purpose of this study. A more sophisticated approach of geolocating Google server IPs in the Google AS is presented in [14].

	Prefix set	Server IPs	Sub nets	ASes	Countries
Google (03/26/13)	RIPE	6,340	329	166	47
	RV	6,308	328	166	47
	PRES	6,088	313	159	46
	ISP	207	28	1	1
	ISP24	535	44	2	2
	UNI	123	13	1	1
MySqueezebox (03/26/13)	ALL \ UNI	10	7	2	2
	UNI	6	4	1	1
Edgecast (04/21/13)	RIPE/RV/PRES	4	4	1	2
	ISP/ISP24/UNI	1	1	1	1
CacheFly (04/21/13)	RIPE/RV	18	18	10	10
	PRES	21	21	11	11
	ISP	6	6	5	5
	ISP24	5	5	4	4
	UNI	1	1	1	1

Table 1: ECS adopters: Uncovered footprint.

illustrative and also informative (e.g., we uncover more locations than previously reported [12, 33]), the main and more surprising finding is the simplicity with which we can uncover this infrastructure using ECS from a single vantage point in less than 4 hours.

For validation purposes, we check each server IP—all of them serve us the Google search main page. In addition, the reverse lookup reveals that while all servers inside the official Google AS use the suffix 1e100.net [21], those deployed in third-party ASes use different hostnames (e.g., cache.google.com, or names containing the strings ggc or googlevideo.com). In some cases we observe legacy names that indicate the prior use of the IP range by the ISP. This means we cannot infer the presence of a GGC purely by looking at the reverse DNS zones.

5.1.1 *Choosing the Right Prefix Set*

Both the RIPE as well as the RV prefix sets are sufficiently complete to yield the same results. We attribute this to the fact that the advertised address space of both datasets overlaps significantly. We see around 500K announced prefixes in the data sets at various aggregation levels. Using only the most specifics without overlap this reduces to about 130K prefixes. For our experiments we decided to use the prefixes as announced. We think this corresponds to the distribution to be seen at an ECS enabled nameserver[5] and reflects the public IP-address space being used.

Next we compare our results (RIPE only) to a study of Calder et al.[14], where queries were made using /24 prefixes. We see a 94% overlap in the discovered Google server IP-addresses while issuing significantly less DNS queries in our approach.

PRES however is not sufficient to uncover the full set of Google Web servers, but yields a major fraction of them in only 55 minutes per experiment. Alternatively, one can use a subset of the RIPE/RV prefix sets. Using a random prefix from each AS reduces the number of RIPE/RV prefixes to 43,400 (8.8% of RIPE prefixes) and results in 4,120 server IPs in 130 ASes and 40 countries in 18 minutes (with 40 requests/second). By doubling the number of selected prefixes to two per AS, we uncover 4,580 server IPs in 143 ASes, and 44 countries.

When relying on the ISP, ISP24, and UNI data sets, we see the effect of mapping end-users to server IPs using ECS. In the case of Google we uncover a much smaller number of servers. However, by using the de-aggregated prefix set of the ISP (i.e., ISP24), we are able to expand the coverage from 200 to more than 500 server IPs. More than 95% of them are in the Google AS while the rest is located in a neighbor AS to that ISP. A more careful investigation reveals that the client prefixes served from the neighbor AS are from a customer of this ISP whose prefix is not announced separately but only in aggregated form (i.e., together with other prefixes of the ISP). Our conjecture is that this is due to the BGP feed sent to the GGC by the ISP [13].

[5]A study on this is currently being performed.

Date (RIPE)	IPs	Sub nets	ASes	Countries
2013-03-26	6340	329	166	47
2013-03-30	6495	332	167	47
2013-04-13	6821	331	167	46
2013-04-21	7162	346	169	46
2013-05-16	9762	485	287	55
2013-05-26	9465	471	281	52
2013-06-18	14418	703	454	91
2013-07-13	21321	1040	714	91
2013-08-08	21862	1083	761	123

Table 2: Google growth within five months.

Of the ASes uncovered by using the RIPE prefix set, only 845 and 96 server IPs are in the ASes of Google and YouTube, respectively. All the others IPs are in ASes not associated with Google. This shows the profound effect of GGCs which have been deployed to many ASes. We repeat the experiments by using the Google Public DNS server and observe that the returned answers are almost always identical (99%). This is not necessarily the case when using Google's Public DNS server for other lookups. However, we find Google's Public DNS server forwarding our ECS queries unmodified to white-listed authoritative DNS servers of other ECS adopters. Therefore, we can even (ab)use Google's Public DNS server as intermediary for measurement queries and thus (i) hide from discovery or (ii) explore if these ECS adopters use a different clustering for Google customers.

Table 1 also shows that the footprints of the other ECS adopters are "less" interesting, mainly because their footprint is not as widely distributed compared to Google. Nevertheless, we see in principle similar results. Most of the infrastructure can be uncovered with the RIPE/RV/PRES prefix sets. The ECS adopters again use clustering such that the ISP, ISP24, and UNI prefixes are all mapped to a single server IP. Note that Edgecast may use HTTP-based redirection which cannot be uncovered using only DNS. While Edgecast uses a single AS, CacheFly, and MySqueezebox are utilizing infrastructures across multiple ASes. We also observe that both players map the UNI and ISP/ISP24 prefixes to infrastructures in Europe (e.g., MySqueezebox maps them to the European facility of Amazon EC2).

5.1.2 *Tracking the Expansion of CDNs Footprints*

Our method allows us to track the expansion of ECS adopters' footprints over time. This becomes increasingly important as many CDNs continuously deploy servers at the network edges or within ISPs. Thus, one can not infer the operator of a cache by simply looking at the IP address or AS number [15]. As we show above, RIPE and RV public prefix sets uncover by far more IPs than the other prefix sets. We use the RIPE prefix set to track the expansion of ECS adopters as it is updated more frequently than RV. In Table 2 we report the rapid increase of discovered Google server IPs over a four month period (March-August 2013). We observe that the number of Google server IPs at least triples (345%), the number of ASes hosting Google infrastructure increases by 595 (458%) and the global presence at least doubles (261%). In August 2013, Google servers are found in 372 enterprise networks, 224 small transit providers, 102 content/access/hosting providers, and 11 large transit providers. Starting mid May we include the YouTube website in our measurements and notice that while the

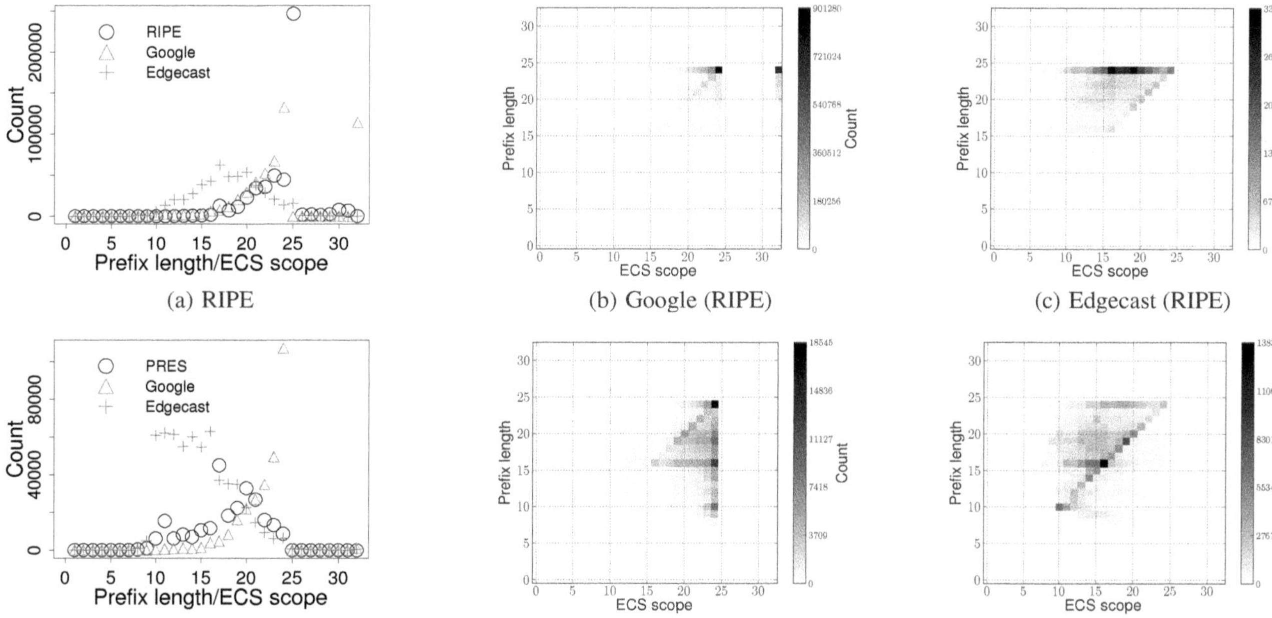

(a) RIPE (b) Google (RIPE) (c) Edgecast (RIPE)

(d) PRES (e) Google (PRES) (f) Edgecast (PRES)

Figure 2: Prefix length vs. ECS scope for RIPE and PRES (Google: March 2013, Edgecast: May 2013).

number of ASes with YouTube servers almost triples (271%) from 220 to 598, these ASes overlap with already uncovered Google infrastructure. We figure this being a result of incorporating the YouTube infrastructure into Google's global platform. By merging the sets of IP addresses for Google and YouTube, the count only increases to 24048. For an in-depth study of the expansion of Google infrastructure since November 2012 we refer to [14]. Our study did not uncover significant growth of serving infrastructure for the other ECS adopters.

5.2 Uncovering DNS Cacheability

Next, we examine the ECS specific information included in the DNS response: the scope. In principle, if the ECS information corresponds to a publicly announced prefix, one may expect that the returned scope is equal to the prefix length. However, this is not necessarily the case. Content providers often return either coarser- or finer-grained scopes e.g., they respond either with aggregated or de-aggregated prefixes. This indicates that they perform the end-user clustering for client-to-server assignment on a different granularity than the routing announcements.

We note that the scope may have a major effect on the re-usability of the DNS response i.e., the cacheability of DNS responses. While most of the responses have a non-zero TTL, a surprisingly large number have a /32 scope. An ECS scope of /32 implies that the answer is valid only for the specific client IP which issued the DNS request. In this section, we explore DNS cacheability for two ECS adopters in detail: Google and Edgecast. The others are less interesting as CacheFly always uses a /24 scope and MySqueezebox is similar to Edgecast.

Figure 2(a) shows the RIPE prefix length distribution (circles). In addition, it includes the returned scopes from using the RIPE prefixes to query our ECS adopters. We note, that the distributions vary significantly. There is massive de-aggregation by Google but massive aggregation by Edgecast which operates a smaller infrastructure.

When executing back-to-back measurements for Google (e.g., 4 queries within a second), we find that typically both the answer and scopes are consistent within the duration of the TTL (300 seconds for Google). The answer as well as the scope can change in some cases within seconds[6]. A detailed study of the temporal changes of the returned scope is part of our future work. Overall, as seen in Figure 2(a), for almost a quarter of the queries, the returned scope is 32. This indicates that currently Google severely restricts the cacheability of ECS responses or may want to restrict reuse of the answers to single client IPs. For approximately 27% of the queries prefix length and scope are identical. For 41% of the queries we see de-aggregation while there is aggregation for 31%. The difference between the announced prefix and the returned scope may also be due to the the BGP feed sent to the GGC by the ISP [13] that is not necessarily the same that is publicly announced and collected by RIPE or Routeviews. We again note, that the returned scopes for the RIPE and RV prefixes are almost identical.

Exploring the scopes returned by Edgecast may at first glance appear useless, because they only returned a single IP with a TTL of 180 seconds. However, Edgecast is using significant aggregation for all prefix lengths across all prefix sets. For example, when using the RIPE prefixes, the return scope is identical for 10.5% but less specific for 87%.

When using the ISP prefix set, the overall picture is similar even though the specific numbers vary. An initial study of the prefixes with scope 32 indicates that Google performs profiling, e.g., Google returns scope /32 for all CDN servers of a large CDN provider inside the ISP. In future work, we plan to explore if there exists a natural clustering for those responses with scope /32.

Given that the size of the UNI prefix set is limited, we issue queries from all IP addresses with prefix length 32. The returned scopes vary heavily from /32 to /15, even for neighboring IP addresses.

For the PRES prefixes, Figure 2(d) shows extreme de-aggregation. For more than 74% of the prefixes, the scope is more restric-

[6]This can be attributed to the fact that authoritative nameservers may use anycast or load balancing [11] or because the rapid increase of DNS queries (e.g., from our measurements) triggers a change on IP/prefix to server mapping.

tive than the prefix length, and in 17% they are identical. Only few returned scopes are /32s. This may indicate that Google treats popular resolvers differently than random IP addresses. Google may already be aware of the problem regarding caching DNS answers as discussed in Section 2.2. For Edgecast we see significant aggregation.

To highlight the relationship of prefix length in the query to scope in the reply, Figures 2(b) and 2(e) show heatmaps of the corresponding two-dimensional histograms. For the RIPE dataset we notice the two extreme points at scopes /24 and /32. For the PRES dataset, the heatmap highlights the de-aggregation. Figures 2(c) and 2(f) show the heatmaps for Edgecast. While for the RIPE dataset we see the effect of the extreme prefix de-aggregation for Google very clearly, the picture for Edgecast is more complicated as there is mainly aggregation. For the PRES dataset, the heatmap shows even more diversity as there is de-aggregation as well as aggregation. This results in a blob in the middle of the heatmap.

5.3 User-Server Mapping Snapshots

So far we have not yet taken advantage of the Web server IP addresses in the DNS replies. These allow us to capture snapshots of the user-to-server mapping employed by an ECS-enabled CDN or CP that can be used to shed light on CDN mapping strategies. In the following, we illustrate the measurement capabilities offered by ECS. We explore snapshots of Googles' user-to-server mappings (based on the RIPE data set) and examine how stable this mapping is.

Google returns 5 to 16 different IP addresses in each reply. Almost all responses (>90%) include either 5 or 6 different IP addresses. We do not find any correlation between the ECS prefix length or the returned scope and the number of returned IP addresses. All IP addresses from a single response always belong to the same /24 subnet (the returned IPs are not necessarily in close geographic distance to each other [20]). We also notice that typically the announced prefix length of subnets that host Google servers is /24. Thus, based on a single ECS lookup per prefix, we always find a unique mapping between query prefix and the server subnet from the DNS reply.

Next we assess the mapping consistency at AS-level. First we map all all prefixes used in the ECS queries to their corresponding AS. Then, by looking at the returned A records, we find the corresponding server ASes for each client AS.

On March 26 2013, the majority of client ASes, around 41K, was served exclusively by Google servers from a single AS. About 2K ASes were served by servers in 2 ASes, and less than 100 ASes were served by servers from more than 5 ASes. On August 8, 2013 the number of ASes that served by a single AS dropped to around 38.5K and around 5K served by 2 ASes. ASes served by a large number of server ASes typically have a global footprint. We find that client prefixes of ASes that host GGC are also served by servers in other ASes. This is to be expected as GGC capacity may not always be sufficient to handle demand and also because different prefixes within an AS, e.g., those that host the GCC servers, may be handled differently. As illustrated in Figure 5.3 a small number of ASes hosts servers that serve a large number of ASes. By far the most popular AS is the official Google AS (AS15169) that served more than 41.5K ASes in March and around 40.5K in August 2013. In the top-10 we find the YouTube AS, as well as small and large transit providers that serve their customers. There is also a small number of ASes that exclusively serve their client subnets from GGC servers they host.

From our analysis we derive some important observations. First, the Google content is not any more exclusively served by servers

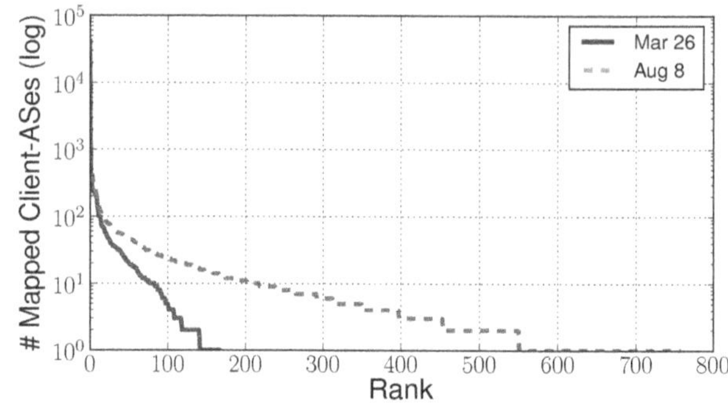

Figure 3: # ASes served by ASes with Google servers (RIPE).

in Google ASes, as was reported in [12]. Second, GCCs have been enabled in a significant number of ASes over a five months period. Third, within these five months the number of ASes that are served by GGC servers in other ASes has been significantly increased.

This trend has significant implications to caching as Google content can be available in the same or a neighboring ASes. It also has implication to peering as the presence of GGCs reduces the interdomain Google traffic and it is now possible for smaller networks to reduce their transit cost by either install GGCs or peer with ASes that host GGCs.

To assess the stability of user-server mapping over time, we analyze the returned IP addresses when asking back-to-back queries over two days (May 3-4, 2013). We found that around 35% of the prefixes are always served by a single /24 block over the 48 hours period. Given the highly distributed infrastructure of Google one may have expected larger churn. 44% of the query prefixes are mapped to two /24 and a very small percentage to more than five /24s. A possible explanation for this stable mapping is that Google uses local load-balancers [24, 33]. We leave the study of temporal dynamics in user-to-server mapping over longer periods and during flash crowds or other events as future work. Our future research agenda also includes the study of the temporal changes in user-to-server mapping not just for Google but also for other ECS adopters.

6. CONCLUSION

In this paper we show that the adoption of the EDNS-Client-Subnet DNS extension (ECS) by major Internet companies offers unique but most likely unintended measurement opportunities to uncover some of their operational practices. Using early ECS adopters like Google, Edgecast, and CacheFly as examples, our experimental study shows how simple it is (using a single vantage point as simple as a commodity PC) to (i) uncover the footprint of these CDN/CP companies, (ii) observe them clustering clients, and (iii) take snapshots of the user-to-server mappings. In addition, we point out potential implications that ECS can have on the cacheability of DNS responses by major DNS resolvers. We believe that the tools developed and the traces collected in this work, made available to the research community, shed light on the deployment and operation of CDNs given the central role they play in today's Internet. This work also highlights the need to increase the awareness among current and future ECS adopters about the consequences of enabling ECS.

Acknowledgments

We would like to thank our shepherd, Ethan Katz-Bassett, and the anonymous reviewers for their valuable feedback. This work was supported in part by the EU projects BigFoot (FP7-ICT-317858) and CHANGE (FP7-ICT-257422), EIT Knowledge and Innovation Communities program, and an IKY-DAAD award (54718944).

7. REFERENCES

[1] A Faster Internet Consortium. http://www.afasterinternet.com.

[2] Alexa top sites. http:///www.alexa.com/topsites.

[3] Google Global Cache. http://ggcadmin.google.com/ggc.

[4] Google Public DNS. https://developers.google.com/speed/public-dns.

[5] Mapping CDN domains. http://b4ldr.wordpress.com/2012/02/13/mapping-cdn-domains/.

[6] MaxMind, GeoIP databases. http://www.maxmind.com.

[7] OpenDNS. http://www.opendns.com.

[8] RIPE Routing Information Service. http://www.ripe.net/ris/.

[9] Routeviews Project, University of Oregon. http://www.routeviews.org/.

[10] V. K. Adhikari, S. Jain, Y. Chen, and Z. L. Zhang. Vivisecting YouTube: An Active Measurement Study. In *IEEE INFOCOM*, 2012.

[11] B. Ager, W. Mühlbauer, G. Smaragdakis, and S. Uhlig. Comparing DNS Resolvers in the Wild. In *ACM IMC*, 2010.

[12] B. Ager, W. Mühlbauer, G. Smaragdakis, and S. Uhlig. Web Content Cartography. In *ACM IMC*, 2011.

[13] M. Axelrod. The Value of Content Distribution Networks. AfNOG 9, 2008.

[14] M. Calder, X. Fan, Z. Hu, E. Katz-Bassett, J. Heidemann, and R. Govindan. Mapping the Expansion of Google's Serving Infrastructure. In *ACM IMC*, 2013.

[15] N. Chatzis, G. Smaragdakis, J. Boettger, T. Krenc, and A. Feldmann. On the benefits of using a large IXP as an Internet vantage point. In *ACM IMC*, 2013.

[16] L. Colitti, S. H. Gunderson, E. Kline, and T. Refice. Evaluating IPv6 adoption in the Internet. In *PAM*, 2010.

[17] C. Contavalli, W. van der Gaast, S. Leach, and E. Lewis. Client subnet in DNS requests (IETF draft). http://tools.ietf.org/html/draft-vandergaast-edns-client-subnet-01.

[18] A. Dhamdhere and C. Dovrolis. Twelve Years in the Evolution of the Internet Ecosystem. *IEEE/ACM Trans. Networking*, 19(5), 2011.

[19] T. Flach, N. Dukkipati, A. Terzis, B. Raghavan, N. Cardwell, Y. Cheng, A. Jain, S. Hao, E. Katz-Bassett, and R. Govindan. Reducing Web Latency: the Virtue of Gentle Aggression. In *ACM SIGCOMM*, 2013.

[20] M. J. Freedman, M. Vutukuru, N. Feamster, and H. Balakrishnan. Geographic Locality of IP Prefixes. In *ACM IMC*, 2005.

[21] Google. What is 1e100.net? http://support.google.com/bin/answer.py?hl=en&answer=174717.

[22] C. Huang, A. Wang, J. Li, and K. Ross. Measuring and Evaluating Large-scale CDNs. In *ACM IMC*, 2008.

[23] B. Krishnamurthy and J. Wang. On Network-aware Clustering of Web Clients. In *ACM SIGCOMM*, 2001.

[24] R. Krishnan, H. Madhyastha, S. Srinivasan, S. Jain, A. Krishnamurthy, T. Anderson, and J. Gao. Moving Beyond End-to-end Path Information to Optimize CDN Performance. In *ACM IMC*, 2009.

[25] C. Labovitz, S. Lekel-Johnson, D. McPherson, J. Oberheide, and F. Jahanian. Internet Inter-Domain Traffic. In *ACM SIGCOMM*, 2010.

[26] Z. Mao, C. Cranor, F. Douglis, M. Rabinovich, O. Spatscheck, and J. Wang. A Precise and Efficient Evaluation of the Proximity Between Web Clients and Their Local DNS Servers. In *USENIX ATC*, 2002.

[27] E. Nygren, R. K. Sitaraman, and J. Sun. The Akamai Network: A Platform for High-performance Internet Applications. *SIGOPS Oper. Syst. Rev.*, 2010.

[28] J. S. Otto, M A. Sánchez, J. P. Rula, and F. E. Bustamante. Content delivery and the natural evolution of DNS - Remote DNS Trends, Performance Issues and Alternative Solutions. In *ACM IMC*, 2012.

[29] Vern Paxson. Bro: A System for Detecting Network Intruders in Real-Time. *Com. Networks*, 31(23–24), 1999.

[30] I. Poese, B. Frank, B. Ager, G. Smaragdakis, and A. Feldmann. Improving Content Delivery using Provider-aided Distance Information. In *ACM IMC*, 2010.

[31] I. Poese, S. Uhlig, M. A. Kaafar, B. Donnet, and B. Gueye. IP Geolocation Databases: Unreliable? *ACM CCR*, 41(2), 2011.

[32] M A. Sanchez, J. .S. Otto, Z. S. Bischof, D. R. Choffnes, , F. E. Bustamante, B. Krishnamurthy, and W. Willinger. Dasu: Pushing Experiments to the Internet's Edge. In *USENIX/ACM NSDI*, 2013.

[33] M. Tariq, A. Zeitoun, V. Valancius, N. Feamster, and M. Ammar. Answering What-if Deployment and Configuration Questions with Wise. In *ACM SIGCOMM*, 2009.

[34] I. Trestian, S. Ranjan, A. Kuzmanovic, and A. Nucci. Unconstrained Endpoint Profiling (Googling the Internet). In *ACM SIGCOMM*, 2008.

[35] S. Triukose, Z. Wen, and M. Rabinovich. Measuring a Commercial Content Delivery Network. In *WWW*, 2011.

[36] P. Vixie. Extension Mechanisms for DNS (EDNS0). RFC 2671 (Proposed Standard), 1999.

[37] P. Vixie. DNS Complexity. *ACM Queue*, 5(3):24–29, 2007.

[38] P. Vixie. What DNS is Not. *Comm. ACM*, 52(12):43–47, 2009.

Mapping the Expansion of Google's Serving Infrastructure*

Matt Calder
University of Southern California

Xun Fan
USC/ISI

Zi Hu
USC/ISI

Ethan Katz-Bassett
University of Southern California

John Heidemann
USC/ISI

Ramesh Govindan
University of Southern California

ABSTRACT

Modern content-distribution networks both provide bulk content and act as "serving infrastructure" for web services in order to reduce user-perceived latency. Serving infrastructures such as Google's are now critical to the online economy, making it imperative to understand their size, geographic distribution, and growth strategies. To this end, we develop techniques that enumerate IP addresses of servers in these infrastructures, find their geographic location, and identify the association between clients and clusters of servers. While general techniques for server enumeration and geolocation can exhibit large error, our techniques exploit the design and mechanisms of serving infrastructure to improve accuracy. We use the EDNS-client-subnet DNS extension to measure which clients a service maps to which of its serving sites. We devise a novel technique that uses this mapping to geolocate servers by combining noisy information about client locations with speed-of-light constraints. We demonstrate that this technique substantially improves geolocation accuracy relative to existing approaches. We also cluster server IP addresses into physical sites by measuring RTTs and adapting the cluster thresholds dynamically. Google's serving infrastructure has grown dramatically in the ten months, and we use our methods to chart its growth and understand its content serving strategy. We find that the number of Google serving sites has increased more than sevenfold, and most of the growth has occurred by placing servers in large and small ISPs across the world, not by expanding Google's backbone.

*The U.S. Government is authorized to reproduce and distribute reprints for Governmental purposes notwithstanding any copyright notation thereon. Any opinions, findings and conclusions or recommendations expressed in this material are those of the author(s) and do not necessarily reflect the views of SSC-Pacific.

IMC'13 October 23-25, Barcelona, Spain.
Copyright 2013 ACM 978-1-4503-1953-9/13/10
http://dx.doi.org/10.1145/2504730.2504754 ...$15.00.

Categories and Subject Descriptors

C.2 [**Computer-Communication Networks**]: Network Architecture and Design; C.4 [**Performance of Systems**]: Measurement techniques

Keywords

CDN, DNS, Geolocation, Measurement

1. INTRODUCTION

Internet traffic has changed considerably in recent years, as access to content is increasingly governed by *web serving infrastructures*. These consist of decentralized *serving sites* that contain one or more *front-end* servers. Clients of these infrastructures are directed to nearby front-ends, which either directly serve static content (e.g., video or images from a content distribution network like Akamai), or use split TCP connections to relay web acccess requests to back-end datacenters (e.g., Google's search infrastructure) [7,11,28].

Web service providers employ serving infrastructures to optimize user-perceived latency [31]. They invest heavily in building out these infrastructures and develop sophisticated mapping algorithms to direct clients to nearby front-ends. In recent months, as we discuss later, Google's serving infrastructure has increased sevenfold in size. Given the increasing economic importance of these serving infrastructures, we believe it is imperative to understand the content serving strategies adopted by large web service providers, especially Google. Specifically, we are interested in the geographic and topological scope of serving infrastructures, their expansion, and how client populations impact build-out of the serving infrastructure.

Several prior studies have explored static snapshots of content-distribution networks [2, 14, 26], often focusing on bulk content delivery infrastructures [14], new mapping methodology [2], or new DNS selection methods [26]. In contrast, our work focuses on web serving infrastructures, develops more accurate methods to enumerate and locate front-ends and serving sites, and explores how one infrastructure, Google's, grows over ten months of active buildout.

The first contribution of this paper is a suite of methods to enumerate the IP addresses of front-ends, geolocate them, and cluster them into serving sites. Our methods exploit mechanisms used by serving infrastructures to optimize client-perceived latency. To enumerate the IP addresses, we use the EDNS-client-subnet prefix extension [9] that some serving infrastructures, including Google, use to more accurately direct clients to nearby front-ends. A front-end

IP address may sit in front of many physical server machines. In this work, we focus on mapping out the front-end IP addresses, but we do not attempt to determine the number of physical servers. We develop a novel geolocation technique and show that it is substantially more accurate than previously proposed approaches. Our technique, *client-centric geolocation* (CCG), exploits the sophisticated strategies providers use to map customers to their nearest serving sites. CCG geolocates a server from the geographic mean of the (possibly noisy) locations for clients associated with that server, after using speed-of-light constraints to discard misinformation. While EDNS-client-subnet has been examined before [23,26], we are the first to use EDNS-client-subnet to (1) completely enumerate a large content delivery infrastructure; (2) demonstrate its benefit over existing enumeration techniques; and (3) geolocate the infrastructure. We also cluster the front-end IP addresses into serving sites, adding dynamic thresholding and RTT-based fingerprinting to current methods. These changes provide enough resolution to distinguish different sites in the same city. These sites represent unique network locations, a view that IP addresses, prefixes, or ASes can obscure.

Our second major contribution is a detailed study of Google's web serving infrastructure and its recent expansion over the last ten months. To our knowledge, we are the first to observe rapid growth of the serving infrastructure of a major content provider. We find that Google's serving infrastructure has grown sevenfold in the number of front-end sites, with serving sites deployed in over 100 countries and in 768 new ASes. Its recent growth strategy has been to move away from serving clients from front-ends deployed on its own backbone and towards serving from front-ends deployed in lower tiers of the AS hierarchy; the number of /24 prefixes served *off* Google's network more than quadrupled during the expansion. Furthermore, these new serving sites, predictably, have narrow customer cones, serving only the customers of the AS the site is deployed in. Finally, we find that the expansion has noticeably shifted the distribution of geographic distances from the client to its nearest front-end server, and that this shift can also reduce the error in geolocating front-ends using client locations alone, but not enough to obviate the need for CCG's filtering techniques.

An explicit non-goal of this work is to estimate the increase in Google's serving capacity: in placing front-ends in ISPs around the world, Google's expansion presumably focused on improving the latency of Web accesses through split-TCP connections [7,11,28], so proximity of front-ends to clients (this paper), and good path performance between clients and front-ends (future work) were more important than capacity increases.

2. BACKGROUND

CDNs and Serving Infrastructures. Adding even a few hundreds of milliseconds to a webpage load time can cost service providers users and business [19,33], so providers seek to optimize their web serving infrastructure to deliver content quickly to clients. Whereas once a website might have been served from a single location to clients around the world, today's major services rely on much more complicated and distributed infrastructure. Providers replicate their services at serving sites around the world and try to serve a client from the closest one [17]. Content delivery networks (CDNs) initially sped delivery by caching static content and some forms of dynamic content within or near client networks.

Today, providers use this type of distributed infrastructure to speed the delivery of dynamic personalized content and responses to queries. To do so, providers direct clients to serving sites in or near the clients' networks. A client's TCP connection terminates at a front-end server in the serving site, but the front-end proxies the request back to one of the provider's large datacenters [28]. This arrangement has a number of potential advantages compared to directing the client directly to the datacenter. For example, the client's latency to the front-end is less than the client's latency to the datacenter, allowing TCP to recover faster after loss, the primary cause of suboptimal performance. Moreover, the front-end can multiplex many clients into a high throughput connection to the datacenter.

In these types of serving infrastructures, different classes of serving sites may serve different clients. Of course, the provider will still serve clients near a datacenter directly from that datacenter. But clients in networks that host a serving site are served locally. Front-ends deployed in clients' ISPs usually serve only clients of that ISP (or the ISP's customers), not clients in the ISP's providers or peers.

DNS-based Redirection. Serving infrastructures use the Domain Name System (DNS) to direct clients to appropriate serving sites and front-end servers. When a client queries DNS to resolve a name associated with a service, the service returns an IP address for a front-end it believes is near the client. Traditionally, at resolution time, however, the service only knows the IP address of the client's resolver and not of the client itself, leading to two main complications. The resolver may be far from the clients it serves, and so the server closest to the resolver may not be a good choice for the client. Existing techniques can allow many services to discover which clients use a particular resolver [22], enabling services to direct a resolver based on the clients that use it. However, some resolvers serve clients with diverse locations; for these cases no server will be well-positioned for all clients of that resolver.

To overcome this hurdle and provide quality DNS redirections for clients, a number of Internet providers and CDNs proposed EDNS-client-subnet [9]. EDNS-client-subnet is an experimental extension DNS (using its EDNS extension mechanism) allowing clients to include a portion of their IP address in their request. This information passes through possible recursive resolvers and is provided to the authoritative DNS server, allowing a service to select content servers based on the client location, rather resolver location or inferred client location.

3. GOAL AND APPROACH

Our goal is to understand content serving strategies for large IPv4-based serving infrastructures, especially that of Google. Serving strategies are defined by how many serving sites and front-end servers a serving infrastructure has, where the serving sites are located geographically and topologically (i.e., within which ISP), and which clients access which serving sites. Furthermore, services continuously evolve serving strategies, so we are also interested in measuring the evolution of serving infrastructures. Of these, Google's serving infrastructure is arguably one of the most important, so we devote significant attention to this infrastructure.

To this end, we develop novel measurement methods to enumerate front-end servers, geolocate serving sites, and cluster front-end servers into serving sites. The challenge in devising these measurement methods is that serving infrastructures are large, distributed entities, with thousands of front-end servers at hundreds of serving sites spread across dozens of countries. A brute force approach to enumerating serving sites would require perspectives from a very large number of topological locations in the Internet, much larger than the geographic distribution provided by research measurement infrastructures like PlanetLab. Moreover, existing geolocation methods that rely on DNS naming or geolocation databases do not work well on these serving infrastructures where location-based DNS naming conventions are not consistently employed.

While our measurement methods use these research infrastructures for some of their steps, the key insight in the design of the methods is to *leverage mechanisms used by serving infrastructures to serve content.* Because we design them for serving infrastructures, these mechanisms can enumerate and geolocate serving sites more accurately than existing approaches, as we discuss below.

Our method to enumerate all front-end server IP addresses within the serving infrastructure uses the EDNS-client-subnet extension. As discussed in Section 2, Google (and some other serving infrastructures) use this extension to address the problem of geographically distributed clients using a resolver that prevents the serving infrastructure from optimally directing clients to front-ends. We use this extension to enumerate front-end IP addresses of a serving infrastructure *from a single location*: this extension can emulate DNS requests coming from every active prefix in the IP address space, effectively providing a very large set of vantage points for enumerating front-end IP addresses.

To geolocate front-end servers and serving centers, we leverage another mechanism that serving infrastructures have long deployed, namely sophisticated mapping algorithms that maintain performance maps to clients with the goal of directing clients to the nearest available server. These algorithms have the property that clients that are directed to the server are likely to be topologically, and probably geographically, close to the server. We exploit this property to geolocate front-end servers: essentially, we approximate the location of a server by the geographical mean of client locations, a technique we call *client-centric geolocation* or CCG. We base our technique on this intuition, but we compensate for incorrect client locations and varying density of server deployments.

Finally, we leverage existing measurement infrastructure (PlanetLab) to cluster front-ends into serving sites. We model the relative location of a front-end server as a vector of round-trip-times to many vantage points in the measurement infrastructure, then employ standard clustering algorithms in this high-dimensional space.

Using these measurement methods over a ten month period, we are able to study Google's serving infrastructure and its evolution. Coincidentally, Google's infrastructure has increased sevenfold over this period, and we explore salient properties of this expansion: where (geographically or topologically) most of the expansion has taken place, and how it has impacted clients.

There are interesting aspects of Google's deployment that we currently lack means to measure. In particular, we do not know the query volume from different clients, and we do not know the latency from clients to servers (which may or may not correlate closely with the geographic distance that we measure). We have left exploration of these to future work. We do possess information about client *affinity* to front-end servers, and how this affinity evolves over time (this evolution is a function of improvements in mapping algorithms as well as infrastructure rollout): we have left a study of this to future work.

4. METHODOLOGY

In this section, we discuss the details of our measurement methods for enumerating front-ends, geolocating them, and clustering them into serving sites.

4.1 Enumerating Front-Ends

Our first goal is to enumerate the IP addresses of all front-ends within a serving infrastructure. We do not attempt to identify when multiple IP addresses belong to one computer, or when one address fronts for multiple physical computers. An IP addresses can front hardware from a small satellite proxy to a huge datacenter, so careful accounting of public IP addresses is not particularly meaningful.

Since most serving infrastructures use mapping algorithms and DNS redirection, one way to enumerate front-ends is to issue DNS requests from multiple vantage points. Each request returns a front-end near the querying vantage point. The completeness of this approach is a function of the number of vantage points.

We emulate access to vantage points around the world using the proposed *client-subnet* DNS extension using the EDNS extension mechanism (we call this approach EDNS-client-subnet). As of May 2013, EDNS-client-subnet is supported by Google, CacheFly, EdgeCast, ChinaCache and CDN 77. We use a patch to *dig*[1] that adds support for EDNS-client-subnet, allowing the query to specify the *client prefix*. In our measurements of Google, we issue the queries through Google Public DNS's public recursive nameservers, which passes them on to the service we are mapping. The serving infrastructure then returns a set of front-ends it believes is best suited for clients within the client prefix.

EDNS-client-subnet allows our single measurement site to solicit the recommended front-end for each specified client prefix. Using EDNS-client-subnet, we effectively get a large number of vantage points We query using client prefixes drawn from 10 million routable /24 prefixes obtained Route-Views BGP. Queries against Google using this approach take about a day to enumerate.

4.2 Client-centric Front-End Geolocation

Current geolocation approaches are designed for generality, making few or no assumptions about the target. Unfortunately, this generality results in poor performance when geolocating serving infrastructure. For example, MaxMind's free database [24] places all Google front-ends in Mountain View, the company's headquarters. (MaxMind may have more accurate locations for IPs belonging to eyeball ISPs, but IPs belonging to transit ISPs will have poor geolocation results.) General approaches such as CBG [12] work best

[1] `http://wilmer.gaa.st/edns-client-subnet/`

when vantage points are near the target [16], but front-ends in serving infrastructures are sometimes in remote locations, far from public geolocation vantage points. Techniques that use location hints in DNS names of front-ends or routers near front-ends can be incomplete [14].

Our approach combines elements of prior work, adding the observation that today's serving infrastructures use privileged data and advanced measurement techniques to try to direct clients to nearby front-ends [35]. While we borrow many previously proposed techniques, our approach is unique and yields better results.

We base our geolocation technique on two main assumptions. First, a serving infrastructure tries to direct clients to a nearby front-end, although some clients may be directed to distant front-ends, either through errors or a lack of deployment density. Second, geolocation databases have accurate locations for many clients, at least at country or city granularity, but also have poor granularity or erroneous locations for some clients.

Combining these two assumptions, our basic approach to geolocation, called *client-centric geolocation* (CCG), is to (1) enumerate the set of clients directed to a front-end, (2) query a geolocation database for the locations of those clients, and (3) assume the front-ends are located geographically close to most of the clients.

To be accurate, CCG must overcome challenges inherent in each of these three steps of our basic approach:

1. We do not know how many requests different prefixes send to a serving infrastructure. If a particular prefix does not generate much traffic, the serving infrastructure may not have the measurements necessary to direct it to a nearby front-end, and so may direct it to a distant front-end.
2. Geolocation databases are known to have problems including erroneous locations for some clients and poor location granularity for other clients.
3. Some clients are not near the front-end that serve them, for a variety of reasons. For example, some front-ends may serve only clients within certain networks, and some clients may have lower latency paths to front-ends other than the nearest ones. In other cases, a serving infrastructure may direct clients to a distant front-end to balance load or may mistakenly believe that the front-end is near the client. Or, a serving infrastructure may not have any front-ends near a particular client.

We now describe how CCG addresses these challenges.

Selecting client prefixes to geolocate a front-end. To enumerate front-ends, CCG queries EDNS using all routable /24 prefixes. However, this approach may not be accurate for geolocating front-ends, for the following reason. Although we do not know the details of how a serving infrastructure chooses which front-end to send a client to, we assume that it attempts to send a client to a nearby front-end and that the approach is more likely to be accurate for prefixes hosting clients who query the service a lot than for prefixes that do not query the service, such as IP addresses used for routers.

To identify which client prefixes can provide more accurate geolocation, CCG uses traceroutes and logs of users of a popular BitTorrent extension, Ono [8]. From the user logs we obtain a list of 2.6 million client prefixes observed to participate in BitTorrent swarms with users. We assume that a serving infrastructure is likely to also observe requests from these prefixes. We emphasize that we use Ono-derived traceroutes to obtain IP prefixes for use with EDNS-client-subnet; other methods for obtaining such prefixes would be equally applicable to our setting, and Ono itself is not necessary for CCG in the sense that we do not make use of the actual platform.

Overcoming problems with geolocation databases. CCG uses two main approaches to overcome errors and limitations of geolocation databases. First, we exclude locations that are clearly inaccurate, based on approaches described in the next paragraph. Second, we combine a large set of client locations to locate each front-end and assume that the majority of clients have correct locations that will dominate the minority of clients with incorrect locations. To generate an initial set of client locations to use, CCG uses a BGP table snapshot from RouteViews [25] to find the set of prefixes currently announced, and breaks these routable prefixes up into 10 million /24 prefixes.[2] It then queries MaxMind's GeoLiteCity database to find locations for each /24 prefix. We chose MaxMind because it is freely available and is widely used in research.

CCG prunes three types of prefix geolocations as untrustworthy. First, it excludes prefixes for which MaxMind indicates it has less than city-level accuracy. This heuristic excludes 1,966,081 of the 10 million prefixes (216,430 of the 2.6 million BitTorrent client prefixes). Second, it uses a dataset that provides coarse-grained measurement-based geolocations for every IP address to exclude prefixes that include addresses in multiple locations [13]. Third, it issues ping measurements from all PlanetLab[3] locations to five responsive addresses per prefix, and excludes any prefixes for which the MaxMind location would force one of these ping measurements to violate the speed of light. Combined, these exclude 8,396 of the 10 million prefixes (2,336 of the 2.6 million BitTorrent client prefixes).

With these problematic locations removed, and with sets of prefixes likely to include clients, CCG assumes that both MaxMind and the serving infrastructure we are mapping likely have good geolocations for most of the remaining prefixes, and that the large number of accurate client geolocations should overwhelm any remaining incorrect locations.

Dealing with clients directed to distant front-ends. Even after filtering bad geolocations, a client may be geographically distant from the front-end it is mapped to, for two reasons: the serving infrastructure may direct clients to distant front-ends for load-balancing, and in some geographical regions, the serving infrastructure deployment may be sparse so that the front-end nearest to a client may still be geographically distant.

To prune these clients, CCG first uses speed-of-light constraints, as follows. It issues pings to the front-end from all PlanetLab nodes and use the speed of light to establish loose constraints on where the front-end could possibly be [12]. When geolocating the front-end, CCG excludes any clients outside of this region. This excludes 4 million out of 10 million prefixes (1.1 million out of 2.6 million BitTorrent client prefixes). It then estimates the preliminary location for the front-end as the weighted average of the locations of

[2]In Section 5.1, we verify that /24 is often the correct prefix length to use.

[3]As we show later, we have found that PlanetLab contains a sufficient number of vantage points for speed-of-light filtering to give accurate geolocation.

	10M prefixes	2.6M prefixes
No city-level accuracy	-1.9M (19.5%)	-216K (8.1%)
Multiple locations and client location speed-of-light violations	-8K (.08%)	-2K (.08%)
Front-End location speed-of-light violations	-4M (40%)	-1.1M (41%)
Outside one standard deviation	-392K (3.9%)	-214K (8%)
Remaining	3.7M (37%)	1M (39%)

Table 1: Summary of the number of client prefixes excluded from CCG by filtering. 10M is the 10 million client prefix set and 2.6M is the 2.6 million BitTorrent client prefix set.

the remaining client prefixes, then refines this estimate by calculating the mean distance from the front-end to the remaining prefixes, and finds the standard deviation from the mean of the client-to-front-end distances. Our final filter excludes clients that are more than a standard deviation beyond the mean distance to the front-end, excluding 392,668 out of 10 million prefixes (214,097 out of 2.6 million BitTorrent client prefixes).

Putting it all together. In summary, CCG works as follows. It first lists the set of prefixes directed to a front-end, then filters out all prefixes except those observed to host BitTorrent clients. Then, it uses MaxMind to geolocate those remaining client prefixes, but excludes: prefixes without city-level MaxMind granularity; prefixes that include addresses in multiple locations; prefixes for which the MaxMind location is not in the feasible actual location based on speed-of-light measurements from PlanetLab and M-Lab; and prefixes outside the feasible location for the front-end. (Table 1 shows the number of prefixes filtered at each step.) Its preliminary estimate for the front-end location is the geographic mean of the remaining clients that it serves. Calculating the distances from remaining clients to this preliminary location, CCG further exclude any clients more than a standard deviation beyond the mean distance in order to refine our location estimate. Finally, it locates the front-end as being at the geographic mean of the remaining clients that it serves.

4.3 Clustering front-ends

As we discuss later, CCG is accurate to within 10s of kilometers. In large metro areas, some serving infrastructures may have multiple serving sites, so we develop a methodology to determine physically distinct serving sites. We cluster by embedding each front-end in a higher dimensional metric space, then clustering the front-end in that metric space. Such an approach has been proposed elsewhere [21, 27, 38] and our approach differs from prior work in using better clustering techniques and more carefully filtering outliers.

In our technique, we map each front-end to a point in high dimensional space, where the coordinates are RTTs from *landmarks* (in our case, 250 PlanetLab nodes at different geographical sites). The intuition underlying our approach is that two front-ends at the same physical location should have a small distance in the high-dimensional space.

Each coordinate is the smallest but one RTT of 8 consecutive pings (a large enough sample size to obtain a robust estimate of propagation latency), and we use the Manhattan

	IPs	/24s	ASes	Countries
Open resolver	23939	1207	753	134
EDNS-client-subnet	28793	1445	869	139
Benefit	+20%	+20%	+15%	+4%

Table 2: Comparison of Google front-ends found by EDNS and open resolver. EDNS providers significant benefit over the existing technique.

distance between two points for clustering (an exploration of other distance norms is left to future work). In computing this Manhattan distance, we (a) omit coordinates for which we received fewer than 6 responses to pings and (b) omit the highest 20% of coordinate distances to account for outliers caused by routing failures, or by RTT measurements inflated by congestion. Finally, we normalize this Manhattan distance. Despite these heuristic choices, our clustering method works well, as shown in Section 5.3.

The final step is to cluster front-ends by their pairwise normalized Manhattan distance. We use the OPTICS algorithm [3] for this. OPTICS is designed for spatial data, and, instead of explicitly clustering points, it outputs an ordering of the points that captures the density of points in the dataset. As such, OPTICS is appropriate for spatial data where there may be no a priori information about either the number of clusters or their size, as is the case for our setting. In the output ordering, each point is annotated with a *reachability distance*: when successive points have significantly different reachability distances, that is usually an indication of a cluster boundary. As we show in Section 5 this technique, which dynamically determines cluster boundaries, is essential to achieving good accuracy.

5. VALIDATION

In this section, we validate front-end enumeration, geolocation, and clustering.

5.1 Coverage of Front-End Enumeration

Using EDNS-client-subnet can improve coverage over previous methods that have relied on using fewer vantage points. We first quantify the coverage benefits of EDNS-client-subnet. We then explore the sensitivity of our results to the choice of prefix length for EDNS-client-subnet, since this choice can also affect front-end enumeration.

Open Resolver vs EDNS-client-subnet Coverage. An existing technique to enumerate front-ends for a serving infrastructure is to issue DNS queries to the infrastructure from a range of vantage points. Following previous work [14], we do so using open recursive DNS (rDNS) resolvers. We use a list of about 200,000 open resolvers[4]; each resolver is effectively a distinct vantage point. These resolvers are in 217 counties, 14,538 ASes, and 118,527 unique /24 prefixes. Enumeration of Google via rDNS takes about 40 minutes. This dataset forms our comparison point to evaluate the coverage of the EDNS-client-subnet approach we take in this paper.

Table 2 shows the added benefit over rDNS of enumerating Google front-ends using EDNS-client-subnet. Our approach uncovers at least 15-20% more Google front-end IP

[4]Used with permission from Duane Wessels, Packet Pushers Inc.

addresses, prefixes, and ASes than were visible using open resolvers. By using EDNS-client-subnet to query Google on behalf of every client prefix, we obtain a view from locations that lack open recursive resolvers. In Section 6.1, we demonstrate the benefit over time as Google evolves, and in Section 7 we describe how we might be able to use our Google results to calibrate how much we would miss using rDNS to enumerate a (possibly much larger or smaller than Google) serving infrastructure that does not support EDNS-client-subnet.

Completeness and EDNS-client-subnet Prefix Length. The choice of prefix length for EDNS-client-subnet queries can affect enumeration completeness. Prefix lengths shorter than /24 in BGP announcements can be too coarse for enumeration. We find cases of neighboring /24s within shorter BGP announcement prefixes that are directed to different serving infrastructure. For instance we observed an ISP announcing a /18 with one of its /24 subprefixes getting directed to Singapore while its neighboring prefix is directed to Hong Kong.

Our evaluations query using one IP address in each /24 block. If serving infrastructures are doing redirections at finer granularity, we might not observe some front-end IP addresses or serving sites. The reply to the EDNS-client-subnet query returns a scope, the prefix length covering the response. Thus, if a query for an IP address in a /24 block returns a scope of, say /25, it means that the corresponding redirection holds for all IP addresses in the /25 covering the query address, but not the other half of the /24. For almost 75% of our /24 queries, the returned scope was also for a /24 subnet, likely because it is the longest globally routable prefix. For most of the rest, we saw a /32 prefix length scope in the response, indicating that Google's serving infrastructure might be doing very fine-grained redirection. We refer the reader to related work for a study of the relationship between the announced BGP prefix length and the returned scope [34].

For our purposes, we use the returned scope as a basis to evaluate the completeness of our enumeration. We took half of the IPv4 address space and issued a series of queries such that their returned scopes covered all addresses in that space. For example, if a query for 1.1.1.0/24 returned a scope of /32, we would next query for 1.1.1.1/32. These brute force measurements *did not uncover any new front-end IP addresses* not seen by our /24 queries, suggesting that the /24 prefix approach in our paper likely provides complete coverage of Google's entire front-end serving infrastructure.

Enumeration Over Time. Front-ends often disappear and reappear from one day to the next across daily enumeration. Some remain active but are not returned in any EDNS-client-subnet requests, others become temporarily inactive, and some may be permanently decommissioned. To account for this variation and obtain an accurate and complete enumeration, we accumulate observations over time, but also test which servers still serve Google search on a daily basis. We check liveness by issuing daily, rate-limited, HTTP HEAD requests to the set of cumulative front-end IP addresses we observe.

The Daily row in Table 3 shows a snapshot of the number of IPs, /24s, and ASes that are observed on 2013-8-8. The Cumulative row shows the additional infrastructure observed earlier in our measurement period but not on that day, and the Inactive row indicates how many of those were not serving Google search on 2013-8-8. This shows that the front-ends that are made available through DNS on a given day is only a subset of what may be active on a given day. For example, for several consecutive days in the first week of August 2013, all our queries returned IP addresses from Google's network, suggesting a service drain of the front-ends in other networks. Our liveness probes confirmed that the majority of front-ends in other networks still actively served Google search when queried, even though no DNS queries directed to them. In the future, we will examine whether we can use our approach to infer Google maintenance periods and redirections away from outages, as well as assess whether these shifts impact performance.

	IPs	/24s	ASes
Daily	22959	1213	771
Cumulative	+5546	+219	+93
–Inactive	-538	-24	-8
Active	27967 (+22%)	1408 (+16%)	856 (+11%)

Table 3: A snapshot from 2013-8-8 showing the differences in number of IPs, /24s, and ASes observed cumulatively across time versus what can be observed within a day. Some front-end IP addresses may not be visible in a daily snapshot. However, IP addresses may be temporarily drained or become permanently inactive or be reassigned. Acquiring an accurate and complete snapshot of active serving infrastructure requires accumulating observations over time and testing which remain active.

5.2 Accuracy of Client-Centric Geolocation

Client-centric geolocation using EDNS-client-subnet shows substantial improvement over traditional ping based techniques [12], undns [32], and geolocation databases [24].

Dataset. To validate our approach, we use the subset of Google front-ends with hostnames that contain airport codes hinting at their locations. Although the airport code does not represent a precise location, we believe that it is reasonable to assume that the actual front-end is within a few 10s of kilometers of the corresponding airport. Airport codes are commonly used by network operators as a way to debug network and routing issues so having accurate airport codes is an important diagnostic tool. Previous work has show that only 0.5% of hostnames in a large ISP had misleading names [39], and so we expect that misnamed Google front-ends only minimally distort our results. A limitation of our validation is that we cannot validate against Google hosted IPs that do not have airport codes because popular geolocation databases such as MaxMind place these IPs in Mountain View, CA. Using all 550 front-ends with airport codes, we measure the error of our technique as the distance between our estimated location and the airport location from data collected on April 17, 2013.

Accuracy. Figure 1 shows the distribution of error for CCG, as well as for three traditional techniques. We compare to constraint-based geolocation (CBG), which uses latency-based constraints from a range of vantage points [12], a technique that issues traceroutes to front-ends and locates the front-ends based on geographic hints in names of nearby routers [14], and the MaxMind GeoLite Free database [24]. We offer substantial improvement over existing approaches. For example, the worst case error for CCG is 409km, whereas

CBG, the traceroute-based technique, and MaxMind have errors of over 500km for 17%, 24%, and 94% of front-ends, respectively. CBG performs well when vantage points are close to the front-end [16], but it incurs large errors for the half of the front-ends in more remote regions. The traceroute-based technique is unable to provide any location for 20% of the front-ends because there were no hops with geographic hints in their hostnames near to the front-end. The MaxMind database performs poorly because it places most front-ends belonging to Google in Mountain View, CA.

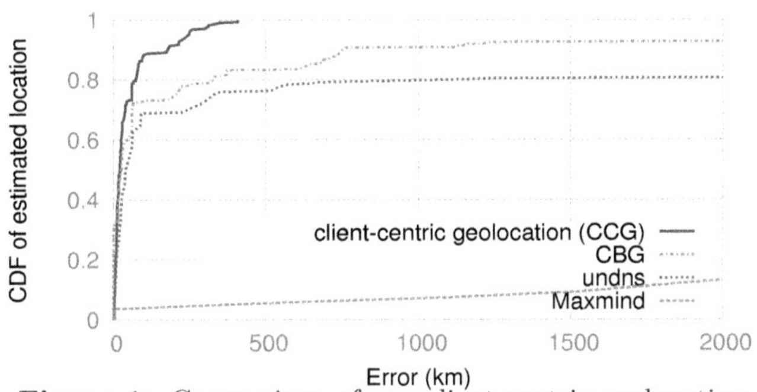

Figure 1: Comparison of our client-centric geolocation against traditional techniques, using Google front-ends with known locations as ground truth.

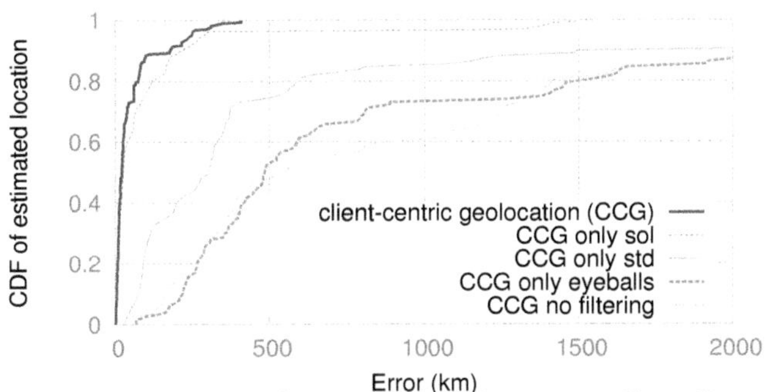

Figure 2: Impact of our various techniques to filter client locations when performing client-centric geolocation on Google front-ends with known locations.

Importance of Filtering. Figure 2 demonstrates the need for the filters we apply in CCG. The *CCG no filtering* line shows our basic technique without any filters, yielding a median error of 556km. Only considering client eyeball prefixes we observed in the BitTorrent dataset reduces the median error to 484km and increases the percentage of front-ends located with error less than 1000km from 61% to 74%. Applying our standard deviation filtering improves the median to 305km and error less than 1000km to 86%. When using speed-of-light constraints measured from PlanetLab and MLab to exclude client locations outside the feasible location for a front-end and to exclude clients with infeasible MaxMind locations, we obtain a median error of 26km, and only 10% of front-end geolocations have an error greater than 1000km. However, we obtain our best results by simultaneously applying all three filters.

Case Studies of Poor Geolocation. CCG's accuracy depends upon its ability to draw tight speed-of-light constraints, which in turn depends (in our current implementation), on Planetlab and M-Lab deployment density. We found one instance where sparse vantage point deployments affected CCG's accuracy. In this instance, we observe a set of front-ends in Stockholm, Sweden, with the *arn* airport code, serving a large group of client locations throughout Northern Europe. However, our technique locates the front-ends as being 409km southeast of Stockholm, pulled down by the large number of clients in Oslo, Copenhagen and northern Germany. Our speed of light filtering usually effectively eliminates clients far from the actual front-end. In this case, we would expect Planetlab sites in Sweden to filter out clients in Norway, Denmark and Germany. However, these sites measure latencies to the Google front-ends in the 24ms range, yielding a feasible radius of 2400km. This loose constraint results in poor geolocation for this set of front-ends.

It is well-known that Google has a large datacenter in The Dalles, Oregon, and our map (Fig. 7) does not show any sites in Oregon. In fact, we place this site 240km north, just south of Seattle, Washington. A disadvantage of our geolocation technique is that large datacenters are often hosted in remote locations, and our technique will pull them towards large population centers that they serve. In this way, the estimated location ends up giving a sort of "logical" serving center of the server, which is not always the geographic location.

We also found that there are instances where we are unable to place a front-end. In particular, we observed that occasionally when new front-ends were first observed during the expansion, there would be very few /24 client networks directed to them. These networks may not have city-level geolocation information available in MaxMind so we were unable to locate the corresponding front-ends.

5.3 Accuracy of Front-End Clustering

To validate the accuracy of our clustering method, we run clustering on three groups of nodes for which we have ground truth: 72 PlanetLab servers from 23 different sites around world; 27 servers from 6 sites all in California, USA, some of which are very close (within 10 miles) to each other; and finally, 75 Google front-end IP addresses, that have airport codes in their reverse DNS names, out of 550 (14%) having airport codes and of 8,430 (0.9%) total Google IP addresses as of Apr 16th, 2013. These three sets are of different size and geographic scope, and the last set is a subset of our target so we expect it to be most representative. In the absence of complete ground truth, we have had to rely on more approximate validation techniques: using PlanetLab, selecting a subset of front-ends with known locations, and using airport codes (we have justified this choice in Section 5.2). We also discuss below some internal consistency checks on our clustering algorithm that gives us greater confidence in our results.

The metric we use for the accuracy of clustering is the *Rand Index* [29]. The index is measured as the ratio of the sum of true positives and negatives to the ratio of the sum of these quantities *and* false positives and negatives. A Rand index equal to 1 means there are *no* false positives or false negatives.

Experiment	Rand Index	False negative	False positive
PlanetLab	0.99	1%	0
CA	0.97	0	3%
Google	0.99	1%	0

Table 4: Rand index for our nodesets. Our clustering algorithm achieves over 97% across all nodesets, indicating very few false positives or negatives.

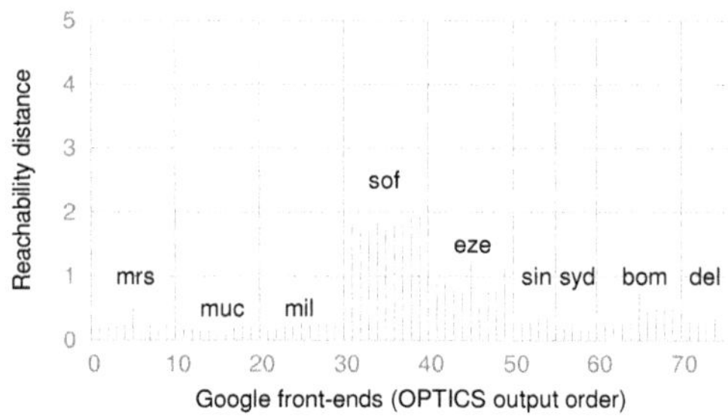

Figure 3: Distance plot of Google servers with airport codes. Servers in the same cluster have low reachability distance to each other thus are output in sequence as neighbors. Cluster boundaries are demarcated by large impulses in the reachability plot.

Table 4 shows the Rand index for the 3 node sets for which we have ground truth. We see that in each case, the Rand index is upwards of 97%. This accuracy arises from two components of the design of our clustering method: eliminating outliers which result in more accurate distance measures, and dynamically selecting the cluster boundary using our OPTICS algorithm.

Our method does have a small number of false positives and false negatives. In the California nodeset, the method fails to set apart USC/ISI nodes from nodes on the USC campus (10 miles away, but with the same upstream connectivity) which leads to 3% false positive. In the Planet lab nodeset, some clusters have low reachability distance that confuses our boundary detection method, resulting in some clusters being split into two. The Google nodeset reveals one false negative which we actually believe to be correct: the algorithm correctly identifies two distinct serving sites in `mrs`, as discussed below.

To better understand the performance of our method, Figure 3 shows the output of the OPTICS algorithm on the Google nodeset. The x-axis in this figure represents the ordered output of the OPTICS algorithm, and the y-axis the reachability distance associated with each node. Impulses in the reachability distance depict cluster boundaries, and we have verified that the nodes within the cluster all belong to the same airport code. In fact, as the figure shows, the algorithm is correctly able to identify all 9 Google sites. More interesting, it shows that, within a single airport code `mrs`, there are likely two physically distinct serving sites. We believe this to be correct, from an analysis of the DNS names associated with those front-ends: all front-ends in one serving site have a prefix `mrs02s04`, and all front-ends in the other serving site have a prefix `mrs02s05`.

In addition, Figure 4 shows the OPTICS output when using reverse-TTL (as proposed in [21]) instead of RTT for the metric embedding. This uses the same set of Google servers as in our evaluation using RTT for metric embedding. We

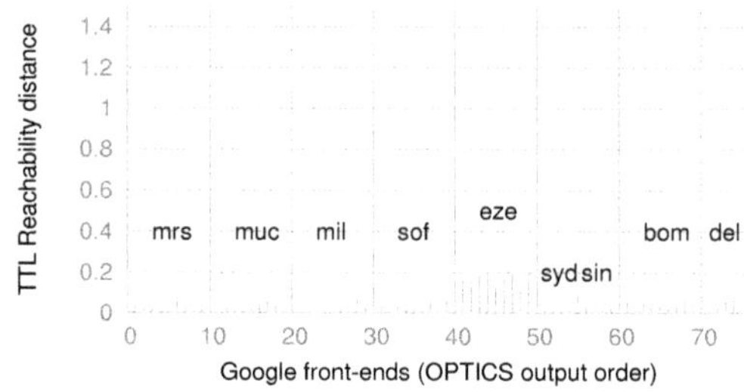

Figure 4: The output of the OPTICS clustering algorithm when reverse-TTL is used for the metric embedding. When using this metric, the clustering algorithm cannot distinguish serving sites at Bombay (`bom`) and Delhi (`del`) in India, while RTT-based clustering can.

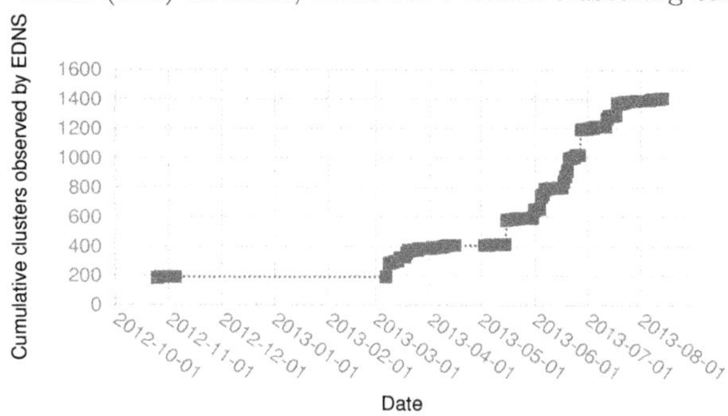

Figure 6: Growth in the number of points of presence hosting Google serving infrastructure over time.

could see that reverse-TTL based embedding performs reasonably well but results in the OPTICS algorithm being unable to distinguish between serving sites in `bom` and `del`. RTT-based clustering is able to differentiate these serving sites. Moreover, although reverse-TTL suggests the possibility of two sites in `mrs`, it mis-identifies which servers belong to which of these sites (based on reverse DNS names).

Finally, we also perform some additional consistency checks. We run our clustering algorithm against all Google front-end IPs that have airport codes (6.5%, 550 out of 8430). We find that except for the kind of false negative we mentioned above (multiple serving site within same airport code), the false positive rate of our clustering is 0, which means we never merge two different airport codes together. Furthermore, when our algorithm splits one airport code into separate clusters, the resulting clusters exhibit naming consistency — our algorithm always keeps IPs that have same hostname pattern <airport code><two digit>s<two digit>, such as `mrs02s05`, in the same cluster.

In summary, our clustering method exhibits over 97% accuracy on three different test datasets. On the Google IPs that have airport codes, our clustering show one kind of false negative that we believe to be correct and no false positive at all.

6. MAPPING GOOGLE'S EXPANSION

We present a longitudinal study of Google's serving infrastructure. Our initial dataset is from late October to early November of 2012 and our second dataset covers March through August of 2013. We are able to capture a substantial expansion of Google infrastructure.

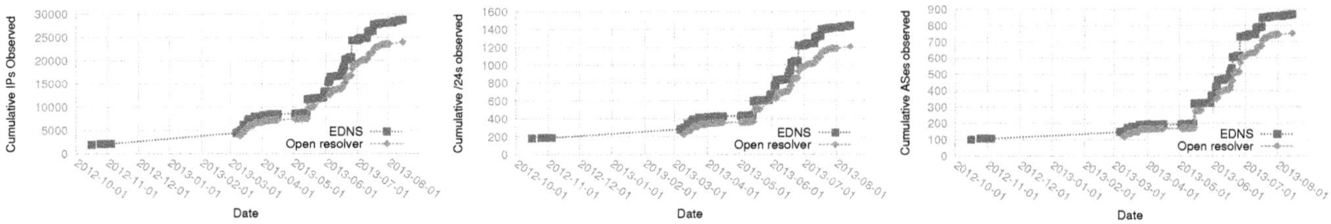

Figure 5: Growth in the number of IP addresses (a), /24 prefixes (b), and ASes/countries (c) observed to be serving Google's homepage over time. During our study, Google expanded rapidly at each of these granularities.

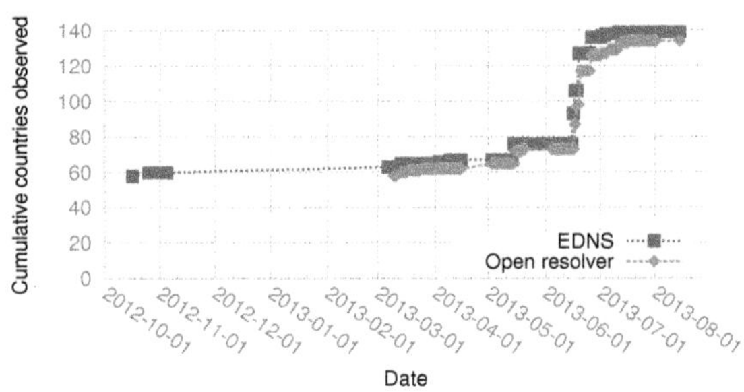

Figure 8: Number of countries hosting Google serving infrastructure over time.

6.1 Growth over time

For each snapshot that we capture, we use EDNS-client-subnet to enumerate all IP addresses returned for `www.google.com`. Figure 5(a) depicts the number of server IP addresses seen in these snapshots over time.[5] The graph shows slow growth in the cumulative number of Google IP addresses observed between November 2012 and March 2013, then a major increase in mid-March in which we saw approximately 3,000 new serving IP addresses come online. This was followed by another large jump of 3,000 in mid-May. Over the month of June, we observed 11,000 new IPs followed by an increase of 4,000 across July.

By the end of our study, the number of serving IP addresses increased sevenfold. Figure 5(b) shows this same trend in the growth of the number of /24s seen to serve Google's homepage. In Figure 5(c), we see 8X growth in the number of ASes originating these prefixes, indicating that this large growth is not just Google adding new capacity to existing serving locations. Figure 6 shows the growth in the number of distinct serving sites within those ASes.

Figure 7 shows the geographic locations of Google's serving infrastructure at the beginning of our measurements and in our most recent snapshot. We observe two types of expansion. First, we see new serving locations in remote regions of countries that already hosted servers, such as Australia and Brazil. Second, we observe Google turning up serving infrastructure in countries that previously did not appear to serve Google's homepage, such as Vietnam and Thailand. Of new front-end IP addresses that appeared during the course of our study, 95% are in ASes other than Google. Of those addresses, 13% are in the United States and 26% are in Europe, places that would appear to be well-served directly from Google's network.[6] In the future, we plan to investigate the performance impact of these front-ends. In addition, 21% are in Asia, 13% are in North America (outside the US), 11% are in South America, 8% are in Africa, and 8% are in Oceania. A link to an animation of the worldwide expansion is available at http://mappinggoogle.cs.usc.edu.

Figure 8 depicts this growth in the number of countries hosting serving infrastructure, from 58 or 60 at the beginning of our study to 139 in recent measurements.[7] We intend to continue to run these measurements indefinitely to continue to map this growth.

6.2 Characterizing the Expansion

To better understand the nature of Google's expansion, we examine the types of networks where the expansion is occurring and how many clients they serve. Table 5 classifies the number of ASes of various classes in which we observe serving infrastructure, both at the beginning and at the end of our study. It also depicts the number of /24 client prefixes (of 10 million total) served by infrastructure in each class of AS. We use AS classifications from the June 28, 2012 dataset from UCLA's Internet Topology Collection [37],[8] except that we only classify as stubs ASes with 0 customers, and we introduce a Tiny ISP class for ASes with 1-4 customers.

As seen in the table, the rapid growth in ASes that host infrastructure has mainly been occurring lower in the AS hierarchy. Although Google still directs the vast majority of client prefixes to servers in its own ASes, it has begun directing an additional 8% of them to servers off its network, representing a 393% increase in the number served from outside the network. By installing servers inside client ISPs, Google allows clients in these ISPs to terminate their TCP connections locally (likely at a satellite server that proxies requests to a datacenter [7,11,28], as it is extremely unlikely that Google has sufficient computation in these locations to provide its services). We perform reverse DNS lookups on the IP addresses of all front-ends we located outside of Google's network. More than 20% of them have hostnames that include either *ggc* or *google.cache*. These results suggest that Google is reusing infrastructure from the Google Global Cache (GGC), Google's content distribution network built primarily to cache YouTube videos near users.[9] It is

[5] It is not necessarily the case that each IP address maps to a distinct front-end.

[6] In contrast, when we submitted the paper in May, only 13% were in the US or Europe. We added in the new expansion in those regions in preparing the final version of the paper.

[7] We base our locations on our CCG approach, which may distort locations of front-ends that are far from their clients.

[8] UCLA's data processing has been broken since 2012, but we do not expect the AS topology to change rapidly.

[9] GGC documentation mentions that the servers may be used to proxy Google Search and other services.

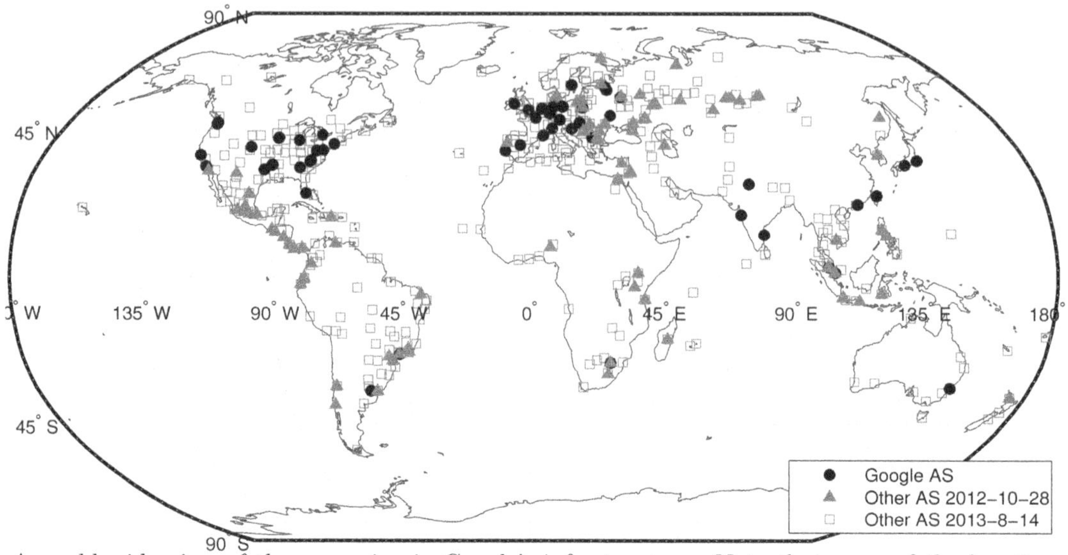

Figure 7: A world wide view of the expansion in Google's infrastructure. Note that some of the locations that appear floating in the Ocean are on small islands. These include Guam, Maldives, Seychelles, Cape Verde and Funchal.

	November 2012		May 2013				August 2013			
	ASes	Clients	ASes		Clients		ASes		Clients	
Google	2	9856K	2	(+0%)	9658K	(-2%)	2	(+0%)	9067K	(-8%)
Tier 1	2	481	2	(+0%)	201	(-58%)	4	(+100%)	35K	(+7278%)
Large	30	111K	46	(+53%)	237K	(+114%)	123	(+310%)	410K	(+270%)
Small	35	37K	64	(+83%)	63K	(+71%)	319	(+811%)	359K	(+870%)
Tiny	23	31K	41	(+78%)	57K	(+84%)	206	(+796%)	101K	(+228%)
Stub	13	21K	36	(+177%)	38K	(+81%)	201	(+1446%)	79K	(+281%)

Table 5: Classification of ASes hosting Google serving infrastructure at the beginning, middle, and end of our study. We count both the number of distinct ASes and the number of client /24 prefixes served. Growth numbers for May and August are in comparison to November. Google still directs 90% of the prefixes to servers within its own network, but it is evolving towards serving fewer clients from its own network and more clients from smaller ASes around the world.

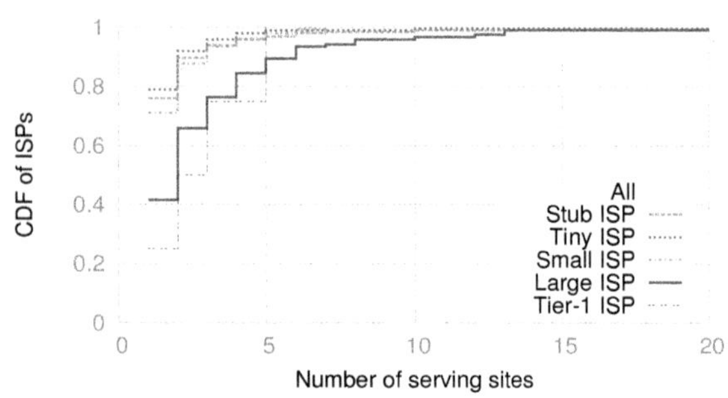

Figure 9: CDF of number of sites in different types of ISP.

possible that the servers were already in use as video caches; if so, this existing physical deployment could have enabled the rapid growth in front-ends we observed.

Figure 9 depicts a slightly different view of the Google expansion. It charts the cumulative distribution of the number of serving sites by ISP type. Overall, nearly 70% of the ISPs host only one serving site. Generally speaking, smaller ISPs host fewer serving sites than larger ISPs. The biggest exceptions are a Tiny ISP in Mexico hosting 23 serving sites consisting of hundreds of front-end IPs, and a Stub national mobile carrier with 21 sites. Befitting their role in the Internet, most Large and Tier 1 ISPs host multiple sites. For example, a Large ISP in Brazil serves from 23 sites.

Whereas Google would be willing to serve any client from a server located within the Google network, an ISP hosting a server would likely only serve its own customers. Serving its provider's other customers, for example, would require the ISP to pay its provider for the service! We check this intuition by comparing the location in the AS hierarchy of clients and the servers to which Google directs them. Of clients directed to servers outside of Google's network, 93% are located within the server's AS's customer cone (the AS itself, its customers, their customers, and so on) [20]. Since correctly inferring AS business relationship is known to be a hard problem [10], it is unclear whether the remaining 7% of clients are actually served by ISPs of which they are not customers, or (perhaps more likely) whether they represent limitations of the analysis. In fact, given that 40% of the non-customer cases stem from just 7 serving ASes, a small number of incorrect relationship or IP-to-AS inferences could explain the counter-intuitive observations.

Google's expansion of infrastructure implies that, over time, many clients should be directed to servers that are closer to them than where Google directed them at the beginning of the study. Figure 10(a) shows the distribution of the distance from a client to our estimate of the location

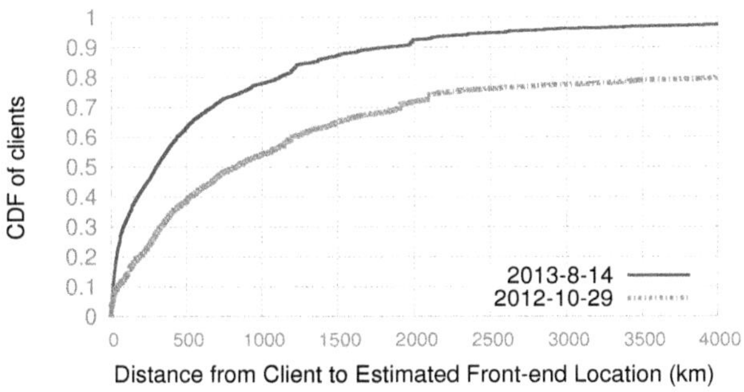

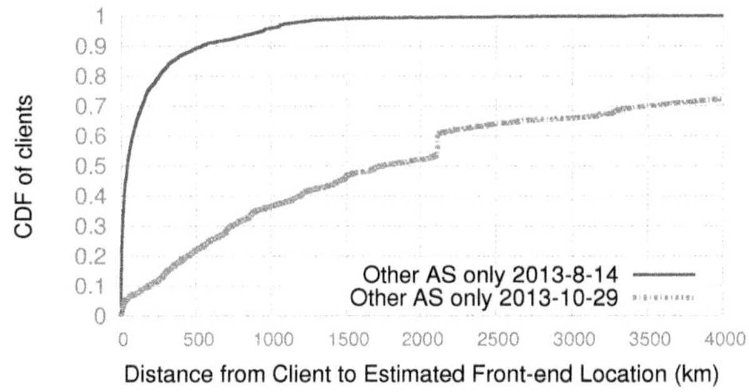

Figure 10: **(a)** Distances from all BitTorrent client prefixes to estimated front-end locations to which Google directs them. **(b)** Comparison of the distances between the set of clients served by front-ends outside of Google's network on 2013-8-14 and their estimated front-end locations on 2013-8-14 and 2012-10-29.

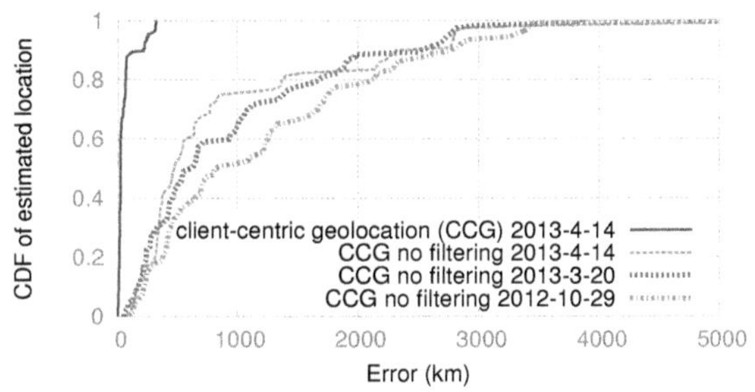

Figure 11: As Google expands, clients become closer to their front-ends, improving accuracy of filter-less client-based geolocation.

of the server serving it. We restrict the clients to those in our BitTorrent eyeball dataset (2.6 million client prefixes) and geolocate all client locations using MaxMind. Some of the very large distances shown in both curves could be accuracy limitations of the MaxMind GeoLite Free database, especially in regions outside of the United States. Overall, results show that in mid-August 2013, many clients are substantially closer to the set of servers they are directed to than in October of 2012. For example, the fraction of client prefixes within 500km of their front-ends increases from 39% to 64%, and the fraction within 1000km increases from 54% to 78%. Figure 10(b) shows the distribution of distances only for the set of client prefixes that were directed to front-ends outside of Google's network on 2013-8-14. The top curve shows the distances between the clients and front-ends on 2013-8-14 while the bottom curve shows the distances between this same set of clients and the front-ends that they were served by on 2012-10-29. The figure shows that the set of clients that have moved off of Google's network are now much closer to their front-ends in August of 2013 than in October of 2012. The fraction of client prefixes within 500km of their front-ends has increased from 21% to 89%, and the fraction within 1000km increased from 36% to 96%. Because many of the newer front-ends seem to be satellites that likely proxy traffic back to datacenters, it is hard to know the impact that decreasing the distance from client to front-end will have on application performance [28].

6.3 Impact on Geolocation Accuracy

A side-effect of Google directing more clients to front-ends closer to them is that our geolocation technique should become more accurate over time, since we base it on the assumption that front-ends are near their clients. To verify that assumption, we apply our basic geolocation approach–without any of our filters that increase accuracy–to the datasets from three points in time. We chose dates to coincide with the large jumps in Google servers that we observe in Figure 5. Using the airport code-based ground truth dataset from Section 5.2, Figure 11 shows the distribution of error in geolocation using these three datasets and, for comparison, the most recent dataset using all our filters. We can see that there is steady reduction in error over time, with median error decreasing from 817km in October 2012, to 610km in March 2013, and 475km in April 2013. However, our filters still provide substantial benefit, yielding a median error of only 22km.

7. USING OUR MAPPING

In addition to our evaluation of Google's serving infrastructure so far, our mapping is useful to the research community, for what it says about clients, and for what it can predict about other serving infrastructure. Our data is publicly available at http://mappinggoogle.cs.usc.edu.

The Need for Longitudinal Research Data. Our results show the limitations of one-off measurement studies—a snapshot of Google's serving infrastructure in October would have missed the rapid growth of their infrastructure and potentially misrepresented their strategy. We believe the research community needs long-term measurements, and we intend to refresh our maps regularly. We will make our ongoing data available to the research community, and we plan to expand coverage from Google to include other providers' serving infrastructures.

Sharing the Wealth: From Our Data to Related Data. Our mapping techniques assume the target sharing infrastructure is pervasive and carefully and correctly engineered. We assume that (a) Google directs most clients to nearby front-ends; (b) Google's redirection is carefully engineered for "eyeball" prefixes that host end-users; and (c) Google will only direct a client to a satellite front-end if the client is a customer of the front-end's AS. Google has economic incentives to ensure these assumptions. In practice, these assumptions are generally true but not always, and our design and evaluation has carefully dealt with exceptions (such as clients occasionally being directed to distant front-ends).

If we accept these assumptions, our maps allow us to exploit Google's understanding of network topology and user placement to improve other datasets. Prior work has used Akamai to chose detour routes [35]; we believe our mapping can improve geolocation, peer selection, and AS classification.

Geolocation is a much studied problem [12, 13, 16], and availability of ground truth can greatly improve results. With clients accessing Google from mobile devices and computers around the world, Google has access to ample data and measurement opportunity to gather very accurate client locations. An interesting future direction is to infer prefix location from our EDNS-client-subnet observations, and use that coarse data to re-evaluate prefixes that existing datasets (such as MaxMind) place in very different locations. The end result would be either higher accuracy geolocation or, at least, identification of prefixes with uncertain locations.

Researchers designed a BitTorrent plugin that would direct a client to peer with other users the plugin deemed to be nearby, because the potential peer received similar CDN redirections as the client's [8]. However, with the existing plugin, the client can only assess similarity of other users of the plugin who send their CDN front-end mappings. Just as we used EDNS-client-subnet to obtain mappings from arbitrary prefixes around the world, we could design a modified version of the plugin that would allow a client to assess the nearness of an arbitrary potential peer, regardless of whether the peer uses the plugin or not. By removing this barrier, the modified plugin would be much more widely applicable, and could enhance the adoption of such plugins.

Finally, in Section 6.2, we showed that 90% of prefixes served in ASes other than Google are within the customer cone of their serving AS. The remaining 10% of prefixes likely represent problems with either our IP-to-AS mapping [15] or with the customer cone dataset we used [20]. From talking to the researchers behind that work and sharing our results with them, it may be necessary to move to prefix-level cones, to accommodate the complex relationships between ASes in the Internet. The client-to-front-end data we generate could help resolve ambiguities in AS relationships and lead to better inference in the future.

Mapping Other Providers. While our techniques will apply directly for some providers, we will need to adapt them for others, and we describe the challenges and potential approaches here. Our studies of Google combine observations using EDNS-client-subnet and open recursive resolvers. EDNS-client-subnet support is increasing. However, some networks such as Akamai do not support it, and we are restricted to using open resolvers for them.

In Section 5.1, we demonstrated that even using hundreds of thousands of open DNS resolvers would miss discovering much of Google's infrastructure. Table 2 showed that EDNS-client-subnet found 20% more front-end IPs than open resolvers, but we cannot assume that ratio holds on other infrastructures. We would expect open resolvers to suffice to uncover all of a ten-front-end infrastructure, for example, but we would expect an even bigger gap on Akamai than on Google, since Akamai serves from many more locations.

We may be able to use our results from Google to project results for other providers that support only open resolvers.

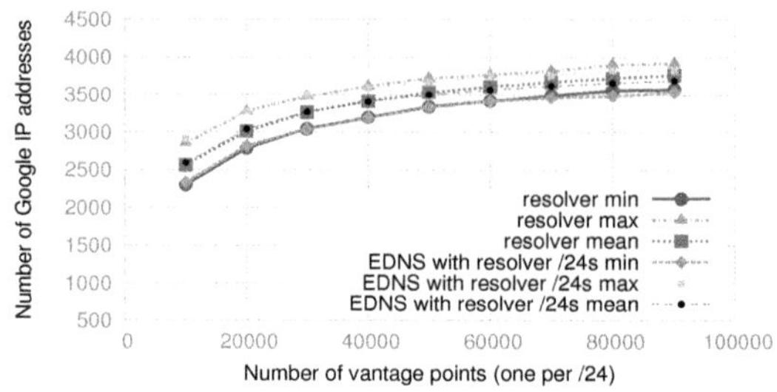

Figure 12: The relation between number of Google IP addresses discovered and the number of vantage points. Using one open resolver per /24 block and one EDNS query per /24 block.

We select one open recursive resolver from each /24 in which we know one (there are 110,000 such prefixes). Then, we select one of these /24s at a time and resolve `www.google.com` from the open resolver in the prefix and via an EDNS query for that prefix. Figure 12 depicts the growth in the number of Google front-end IP addresses discovered by the two approaches as we issue additional measurements (1000 trials). Using resolvers in a set of prefixes yields very similar results to issuing EDNS queries for that same set of prefixes, so that the benefit of EDNS is primarily that we can issue queries for many more prefixes than we have access to resolvers in.

We extrapolate these growth curves to understand the impact of having more resolvers. To test this theory, we fit power law curves to the open resolver lines ($R = 0.97$ in all cases). We project that access to resolvers in all 10M routable /24 prefixes, predicting discovery of 6990–8687 IP addresses of Google front-end servers (as of May 4th, 2013). Using EDNS-client-subnet queries for these 10M prefixes, we found 8563 IP addresses, within the range, so the extrapolation approach may be reasonable. In the future, we plan to apply it to predict the size of Akamai and other infrastructures that do not yet support EDNS-client-subnet. We can use our Google results to characterize which regions our set of open resolvers has good coverage in, in order to flag portions of other infrastructures as more or less complete.

Google lends itself to client-centric geolocation because our EDNS-client-subnet measurements uncover the client to front-end mappings, and Google's deployment is dense enough that most clients are near front-ends. We will have to adapt the strategy for deployments where one or both of those properties do not hold. Akamai uses a resolver's geolocation in mapping decisions [5], and so it may be possible to geolocate Akamai servers based on the locations of the open resolvers they serve, even though we cannot directly measure which clients they serve. We will verify the soundness of this approach by geolocating Google front-ends using resolver locations. If the approach is generally accurate, we can also use it to flag suspicious resolver locations and only use the remainder when geolocating Akamai (or other) servers.

CDNs such as Edgecast support EDNS queries to discover client-to-front-end mappings, but they lack the density of servers of Akamai and Google and so necessarily direct some clients to distant servers. Since our geolocation approach assumes front-ends are near clients, it may not be sound to assume that the front-end is at the geographic center of the clients. Edgecast publishes its geographic points of presence on its website, so we can use its deployment as ground truth to evaluate approaches to map other providers that do not publish this information. We will investigate whether our aggressive pruning of distant clients suffices for Edgecast. If not, straightforward alternate approaches may work well for these sparse deployments. For example, these small deployments tend to be at well-connected Internet exchange points, where we likely have a vantage point close enough to accurately use delay-based geolocation [12, 16].

8. RELATED WORK

Closest to our work is prior research on mapping CDN infrastructures [1,2,14,36]. Huang et al. [14] map two popular content delivery networks, Akamai and Limelight, by enumerating their front-ends using a quarter of a million open rDNS resolvers. They geolocate and cluster front-ends using a geolocation database and also use the location of penultimate hop of traceroutes to front-ends. Ager et al. [2] chart web hosting structures as a whole. They start by probing several sets of domain names from dozens of vantage points to collect service IP addresses, rely entirely on MaxMind [24] for geolocation, and use feature-based clustering where the goal of clustering is to separate front-ends belonging to different hosting infrastructures. Torres et al. [36] use a small number of vantage points in the US and Europe and constraint-based geolocation to approximately geolocate serving sites in the YouTube CDN, with the aim of understanding video server selection strategies. Finally, Adhikari et al. [1] use open resolvers to enumerate YouTube servers and geolocation databases to geolocate them, with the aim of reverse-engineering the caching hierarchy and logical organization of YouTube infrastructure using DNS namespaces.

In contrast to these pieces of work, our enumeration effectively uses many more vantage points to achieve complete coverage, our geolocation technique leverages client locations for accuracy instead of relying on geolocation databases, and our clustering technique relies on a metric embedding in high-dimensional space to differentiate between nearby sites.

In addition to this prior work, simultaneous work appearing at the same conference as this paper also used EDNS-client-subnet to expose CDN infrastructure [34]. While our work focuses on characterizing Google's rapid expansion, including geolocating and clustering front-ends, that work addresses complementary issues including measuring other EDNS-client-subnet-enabled infrastructures. Our results differ from that work, as our work exposes 30% more /24 prefixes and 12% more ASes hosting front-ends that are actively serving Google search. We believe our additional coverage results from our more frequent mapping and accumulation of servers over time, since a single snapshot may miss some infrastructure (see Table 3). Some in the operations community also independently recognized how to use EDNS-client-subnet to enumerate a CDN's servers, although these previous measurements presented just a small-scale enumeration without further investigation [23].

Several other pieces of work are tangentially related to ours. Previous work exploits the observation that two clients directed to the same or nearby front-ends are likely to be geographically close [8, 35]. Our work uses this observation to geolocate front-ends. Mao et al. [22] quantify the proximity of clients to their local DNS resolvers and find that clients in different geographic locations may use the same resolver. The EDNS-client-subnet extension we use was designed to permit serving infrastructures to more accurately direct clients to serving sites in these cases. Otto et al. [26] examine the end-to-end impact that different DNS services have on CDN performance. It is the first work to study the potential of EDNS-client-subnet to address the client CDN mapping problem, using the extension as intended, but does not repurpose EDNS to map infrastructure, as we do.

Finally, several strands of research explored complementary problems associated with serving infrastructures, including characterizing and diagnosing latency of providers [7,11,17,18,40]; geolocating ASes using client locations [30]; verifying data replication strategies for cloud providers [4]; and analyzing content usage in large CDNs [6]. Some of this research describes how providers use distributed front-ends as proxies to improve client performance [7, 11, 28]. Our work demonstrates the rapid expansion–and new strategy of front-ends in other networks–of Google's infrastructure to delivery on this approach.

9. CONCLUSIONS

As the role of interactive web applications continues to grow in our lives, and the mobile web penetrates remote regions of the world more than wired networks ever had, the Internet needs to deliver fast performance to everyone, everywhere, at all times. To serve clients around the world quickly, service providers deploy globally distributed serving infrastructure, and we must understand these infrastructures to understand how providers deliver content today. Towards that goal, we developed approaches specific to mapping these serving infrastructures. By basing our techniques around how providers architect their infrastructures and guarding our techniques against noisy data, we accurately map the geographically-distributed serving sites.

We apply our techniques to mapping Google's serving infrastructure and track its rapid expansion over the period of our measurement study. During that time, the number of serving sites grew more than sevenfold, and we see Google deploying satellite front-ends around the world, in many cases distant from any known Google datacenters. By continuing to map Google's and others' serving infrastructures, we will watch the evolution of these key enablers of today's Internet, and we expect the accurate maps to enable future work by us and others to understand and improve content delivery on a global scale.

Acknowledgments

We thank our shepherd, Aditya Akella, and the anonymous IMC reviewers for their valuable feedback. We also gratefully acknowledge Bernhard Ager, Georgios Smaragdakis, Florian Streibelt, and Nikolaos Chatzis for their feedback on earlier versions of this paper.

Xun Fan, Zi Hu, and John Heidemann are partially supported by the U.S. Department of Homeland Security Science and Technology Directorate, Cyber Security Division, via SPAWAR Systems Center Pacific under Contract No. N66001-13-C-3001. John Heidemann is also partially supported by DHS BAA 11-01-RIKA and Air Force Research Laboratory, Information Directorate under agreement number FA8750-12-2-0344. Matt Calder and Ramesh Govindan were partially supported by the U.S. National Science Foundation grant number CNS-905596.

10. REFERENCES

[1] Vijay Kumar Adhikari, Sourabh Jain, Yingying Chen, and Zhi-Li Zhang. Vivisecting YouTube: An active measurement study. In *INFOCOM*, 2012.

[2] Bernhard Ager, Wolfgang Mühlbauer, Georgios Smaragdakis, and Steve Uhlig. Web content cartography. In *IMC*, 2011.

[3] Mihael Ankerst, Markus M. Breunig, Hans-peter Kriegel, and Jörg Sander. OPTICS: Ordering points to identify the clustering structure. In *SIGMOD*, 1999.

[4] Karyn Benson, Rafael Dowsley, and Hovav Shacham. Do you know where your cloud files are? In *Cloud Computing Security Workshop*, 2011.

[5] Arthur Berger, Nicholas Weaver, Robert Beverly, and Larry Campbell. Internet nameserver IPv4 and IPv6 address relationships. In *IMC*, 2013.

[6] Meeyoung Cha, Haewoon Kwak, Pablo Rodriguez, Yong-Yeol Ahn, and Sue Moon. I Tube, You Tube, Everybody Tubes: Analyzing the World's Largest User Generated Content Video System. In *IMC*, 2007.

[7] Yingying Chen, Sourabh Jain, Vijay Kumar Adhikari, and Zhi-Li Zhang. Characterizing roles of front-end servers in end-to-end performance of dynamic content distribution. In *IMC*, 2011.

[8] David Choffnes and Fabian E. Bustamante. Taming the torrent: A practical approach to reducing cross-ISP traffic in peer-to-peer systems. In *SIGCOMM*, 2008.

[9] C. Contavalli, W. van der Gaast, S. Leach, and E. Lewis. Client subnet in DNS requests, April 2012. Work in progress (Internet draft draft-vandergaast-edns-client-subnet-01).

[10] Xenofontas Dimitropoulos, Dmitri Krioukov, Marina Fomenkov, Bradley Huffaker, Young Hyun, k. c. claffy, and George Riley. AS relationships: Inference and validation. *ACM CCR*, 37(1):29–40, January 2007.

[11] Tobias Flach, Nandita Dukkipati, Andreas Terzis, Barath Raghavan, Neal Cardwell, Yuchung Cheng, Ankur Jain, Shuai Hao, Ethan Katz-Bassett, and Ramesh Govindan. Reducing web latency: the virtue of gentle aggression. In *SIGCOMM*, 2013.

[12] Bamba Gueye, Artur Ziviani, Mark Crovella, and Serge Fdida. Constraint-based geolocation of Internet hosts. *IEEE/ACM TON*, 14(6):1219–1232, December 2006.

[13] Zi Hu and John Heidemann. Towards geolocation of millions of IP addresses. In *IMC*, 2012.

[14] Cheng Huang, Angela Wang, Jin Li, and Keith W. Ross. Measuring and evaluating large-scale CDNs. Technical Report MSR-TR-2008-106, Microsoft Research, October 2008.

[15] iPlane. `http://iplane.cs.washington.edu`.

[16] Ethan Katz-Bassett, John P. John, Arvind Krishnamurthy, David Wetherall, Thomas Anderson, and Yatin Chawathe. Towards IP geolocation using delay and topology measurements. In *IMC*, 2006.

[17] Rupa Krishnan, Harsha V. Madhyastha, Sridhar Srinivasan, Sushant Jain, Arvind Krishnamurthy, Thomas Anderson, and Jie Gao. Moving beyond end-to-end path information to optimize CDN performance. In *IMC*, pages 190–201, 2009.

[18] Ang Li, Xiaowei Yang, Srikanth Kandula, and Ming Zhang. CloudCmp: comparing public cloud providers. In *IMC*, 2010.

[19] Greg Linden. Make data useful. `http://sites.google.com/site/glinden/Home/StanfordDataMining.2006-11-28.ppt`, 2006.

[20] M. Luckie, B. Huffaker, A. Dhamdhere, V. Giotsas, and k claffy. AS relationships, customer cones, and validation. In *IMC*, 2013.

[21] Harsha V. Madhyastha, Tomas Isdal, Michael Piatek, Colin Dixon, Thomas Anderson, Arvind Krishnamurthy, and Arun Venkataramani. iPlane: An information plane for distributed services. In *OSDI*, 2006.

[22] Z. M. Mao, C. D. Cranor, F. Douglis, M. Rabinovich, O. Spatscheck, and J Wang. A precise and efficient evaluation of the proximity between web clients and their local DNS servers. In *USENIX Annual Technical Conference*, 2002.

[23] Mapping CDN domains. `http://b4ldr.wordpress.com/2012/02/13/mapping-cdn-domains/`.

[24] MaxMind. `http://www.maxmind.com/app/ip-location/`.

[25] David Meyer. RouteViews. `http://www.routeviews.org`.

[26] John S. Otto, Mario A. Sánchez, John P. Rula, and Fabián E Bustamante. Content delivery and the natural evolution of DNS. In *IMC*, 2012.

[27] Venkata N. Padmanabhan and Lakshminarayanan Subramanian. An investigation of geographic mapping techniques for Internet hosts. In *SIGCOMM*, 2001.

[28] Abhinav Pathak, Y. Angela Wang, Cheng Huang, Albert Greenberg, Y. Charlie Hu, Randy Kern, Jin Li, and Keith W. Ross. Measuring and evaluating TCP splitting for cloud services. In *PAM*, 2010.

[29] William M Rand. Objective criteria for the evaluation of clustering methods. *Journal of the American Statistical association*, 66(336):846–850, 1971.

[30] Amir H Rasti, Nazanin Magharei, Reza Rejaie, and Walter Willinger. Eyeball ASes: from geography to connectivity. In *IMC*, 2010.

[31] Steve Souders. High-performance web sites. *Communications of the ACM*, 51(12):36–41, December 2008.

[32] Neil Spring, Ratul Mahajan, and David Wetherall. Measuring ISP topologies with Rocketfuel. *ACM CCR*, 32(4):133–145, 2002.

[33] Stoyan Stefanov. Yslow 2.0. In *CSDN SD2C*, 2008.

[34] Florian Streibelt, Jan Böttger, Nikolaos Chatzis, Georgios Smaragdakis, and Anja Feldmann. Exploring EDNS-client-subnet adopters in your free time. In *IMC*, 2013.

[35] Ao-Jan Su, David R. Choffnes Aleksandar Kuzmanovic, and Fabi'an E. Bustamante. Drafting behind Akamai (Travelocity-based detouring). In *SIGCOMM*, 2006.

[36] Ruben Torres, Alessandro Finamore, Jin Ryong Kim, Marco Mellia, Maurizio M Munafo, and Sanjay Rao. Dissecting video server selection strategies in the YouTube CDN. In *ICDCS*, 2011.

[37] UCLA Internet topology collection. `http://irl.cs.ucla.edu/topology/`.

[38] Qiang Xu and Jaspal Subhlok. Automatic clustering of grid nodes. In *Proc. of 6th IEEE International Workshop on Grid Computing*, 2005.

[39] Ming Zhang, Yaoping Ruan, Vivek S Pai, and Jennifer Rexford. How DNS misnaming distorts Internet topology mapping. In *USENIX Annual Technical Conference*, 2006.

[40] Yaping Zhu, Benjamin Helsley, Jennifer Rexford, Aspi Siganporia, and Sridhar Srinivasan. LatLong: Diagnosing wide-area latency changes for CDNs. *IEEE Transactions on Network and Service Management*, 9(1), September 2012.

Indexing Million of Packets per Second using GPUs

Francesco Fusco
ETH Zurich
Gloriastrasse 35
Zurich, Switzerland
fusco@tik.ee.ethz.ch

Michail Vlachos
IBM Research - Zurich
Säumerstrasse 4
Rüshlikon, Switzerland
mvl@zurich.ibm.com

Xenofontas Dimitropoulos
ETH Zurich
Gloriastrasse 35
Zurich, Switzerland
fontas@tik.ee.ethz.ch

Luca Deri
ntop.org
Pisa, Italy
deri@ntop.org

ABSTRACT

Network traffic recorders are devices that record massive volumes of network traffic for security applications, like retrospective forensic investigations. When deployed over very high-speed networks, traffic recorders must process and store millions of packets per second. To enable interactive explorations of such large traffic archives, packet indexing mechanisms are required. Indexing packets at wire rates (10 Gbps and above) on commodity hardware imposes unparalleled requirements for high throughput index creation. Such indexing throughputs are presently untenable with modern indexing technologies and current processor architectures. In this work, we propose to intelligently offload indexing to commodity General Processing Units (GPUs). We introduce algorithms for building compressed bitmap indexes in real time on GPUs and show that we can achieve indexing throughputs of up to 185 millions records per second, which is an improvement by one order of magnitude compared to the state-of-the-art. This shows that indexing network traffic at multi-10-Gbps rates is well within reach.

Categories and Subject Descriptors

C.1.3 [**Processor Architectures**]: Other Architecture Styles—*Heterogeneous (hybrid) systems*; C.2.3 [**Network Operations**]: Network monitoring

Keywords

Indexing, packet traces, GPU

1. INTRODUCTION

The volume of data that crosses the Internet has increased rapidly in the last years and it is expected to keep increasing fast in the future. Analysis from Cisco predicts that the volume of Internet traffic will quadruple between 2011 and 2016 reaching 1.3 Zettabytes per year in 2016 [1]. This deluge of data imposes very demanding scalability requirements on network monitoring systems. In particular, a major challenge is building network traffic monitoring and archival systems that support efficient search operations over large traffic datasets. Efficiently searching traffic data is very important because it drastically increases the utility of traffic archival systems. Otherwise, traffic archives are like a world wide web without search engines.

Specifically, this is a major challenge for several network monitoring and security devices (typically called network traffic recorders or loggers in the industry) that need to efficiently process and store a recent window (e.g., the last week) of *raw* network traffic, so as to enable post mortem analyses, for example: to show the evidence of a crime, to resolve disputes of network-related performance issues (e.g., in trading environments), or to troubleshoot connectivity problems. When deployed on high-speed links, traffic recorders must be able to store millions of packets per second and several Terabytes of data per day, without losing a single packet. Recent research has shown that it is nowadays possible to process [10] and even dump on disk [4] packets at 10 Gbps using commodity hardware. In this context, implementing searches as linear scans over a storage subsystem that is constantly taxed by writing incoming new data, is not feasible. To enable efficient search operations, real-time packet indexing technologies for high-speed links are required.

Recent work has identified compressed bitmap indexes as a very effective indexing technology for network traffic data [5, 12, 13]. Bitmap indexes are more compact in size than competitive approaches, such as tree-based indexes, and provide significant speedup over complex multi-attribute queries. In addition, our previous work [6] has shown that by introducing bitmap indexing support into the de-facto packet processing library, *libpcap* [2], packet searches can be accelerated by up to 3 orders of magnitude.

The goal of this work is to enable the creation of bitmap indexes for packet data in *real-time* in the context of packet recording systems, by using solely commodity off-the-shelf hardware and without using distributed architectures. In fact, creating indexes *off-line* using distributed architectures is not desirable due to increased costs, higher complex-

IMC'13, October 23–25, 2013, Barcelona, Spain.

http://dx.doi.org/10.1145/2504730.2504756 .

ity, and physical deployment constraints (i.e., rack space). Creating bitmap indexes in real-time in very high-speed links (10 Gbps and beyond) represents a major challenge: wire-rate packet indexing poses unprecedented requirements for indexing throughput. The packet indexing throughput reported by the most related previous work is *one order of magnitude* lower than the incoming packet rate that can be observed on 10 Gbps links [6, 7]. The main obstacle to providing the required throughput is poor memory locality, which, in a packet recording context, where the same memory and cache hierarchies are constantly stressed for processing packets, can severely deteriorate system performance.

To meet our goal, we propose the adoption of GPUs as indexing coprocessors to i) expand the traffic recording system with a high-bandwidth memory subsystem dedicated to indexing, ii) entirely offload the host from the bitmap index creation, thereby saving precious computational and bandwidth resources for high-speed packet recording and, iii) achieve indexing throughputs required to index packet header data in real-time from high-speed links.

In this paper we make the following contributions:

- We introduce algorithms to build two well-known compressed bitmap indexes, namely WAH [15] and PLWAH [3], *entirely* and at *high-speed* on GPUs, thereby releasing precious resources to the host for fetching, processing and storing packets on disk.
- We build the GPU-based indexing component of a traffic recording system and show that GPUs can achieve impressive indexing throughputs of up to 185 million of records per second, which is one order of magnitude higher than the state-of-the-art.
- We compare two state-of-the-art compressed bitmap indexes and show that in the GPU space, the more complex encoding (PLWAH) results in both smaller indexes and higher throughput.
- We evaluate the indexing throughput using high-entropy data, which reflect adverse conditions resulting from attacks. We learn that the throughput on a GPU is less affected by the cardinality of the data than on a CPU. GPUs are therefore more suitable when high throughput has to be sustained under adverse conditions.

Our findings show that by using GPUs real-time packet indexing at multi-10-Gbps links is well within reach. Future work needs to assess further opportunities and challenges that will arise in the integration of our GPU-based indexing component in a complete system. GPUs have already been proposed to accelerate different networking workloads [8, 14, 11]. However, to the best of our knowledge, our work is the first to exploit GPUs for indexing in the context of high-performance packet recording systems. It makes a step forward on exploiting the parallelism of current and upcoming computing architectures for high-speed network monitoring. Our contributions are not only useful in the context of indexing network monitoring data, but also for any application that requires high-throughput creation of bitmap indexes.

2. BACKGROUND

A bitmap index is an indexing data structure for numerical records that enables expedient access to the row positions matching a given value of an attribute. More importantly, bitmap indexes corresponding to distinct attributes can be used to efficiently answer queries involving boolean operations over multiple attributes, e.g. "`SELECT` * `WHERE` $DstPort = 80$ `AND` $Proto = 17$". The bitmap index corresponding to an attribute that can assume n distinct values is a binary matrix with n columns and as many rows as the number of indexed records (as shown in the example of Figure 1).

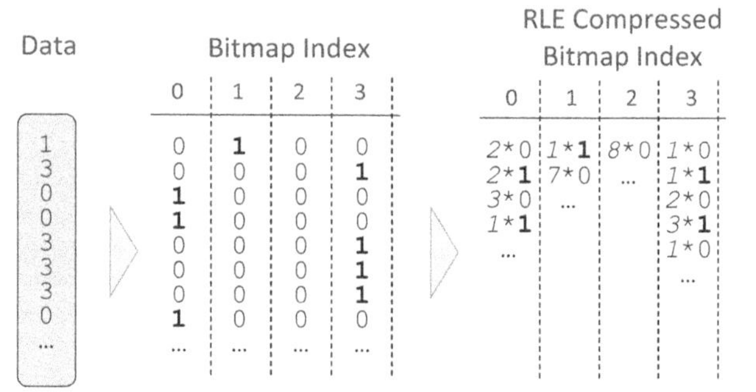

Figure 1: A bitmap index of cardinality 4.

Bitmap indexes can become very large when the number of columns (or rows) grow. Compressed bitmap indexes have been introduced to reduce the index size while preserving, or even accelerating, the index lookup time. Columns are independently compressed using light-weight compression techniques, like Run Length Encoding (RLE), that typically enable boolean operations to be performed over multiple columns in the compressed domain. Several encodings for compressing bitmap indexes have been proposed. WAH and its extension PLWAH are among the best-known compressed bitmap indexes as they stand out for their lookup performance. A thorough evaluation of the response times and compression ratios achieved by WAH and PLWAH in the context of indexing network traffic data can be found in previous work [6, 7]. Both encodings use word-aligned compression symbols.

Word Aligned Hybrid (WAH) uses a dictionary of two compression symbols: a literal `L` stores a chunk of 31 heterogeneous bits, and a fill `F` encodes a sequence of homogeneous bits. A sequence of 31 or more consecutive `0`'s is compressed using a 0-Fill symbol (`0F`), and similarly a sequence of 31 or more `1`'s is converted into a 1-Fill symbol (`1F`). The symbol type (`1F` and `0F`) is given in a 2-bit header, and a number k is recorded in the remaining 30-bits. k indicates how many $(31 \times k)$ consecutive bits of uncompressed 0's or 1's are encoded. Figure 2 provides an example of an uncompressed bitmap and its WAH-compressed counterpart.

Position Lists Word Aligned Hybrid (PLWAH) is an extension of WAH that aims at compressing sparse bitmaps better. PLWAH has the same literal `L` symbol with WAH, but introduces a different format for the 0-Fill and 1-Fill symbols. In particular, the 30-bit payload of a fill-word is used to store both the fill length k and a list of positions. The list stores as 5-bit numbers the positions of each 1 in the next literal. In this way a sparse literal can be encoded within the fill word and then suppressed to save space as shown in the bottom of Figure 2. Therefore, the maximum length that can be encoded in each fill is $31 \times (2^{31-(5i)} - 1)$, where i is the number of positions. In practice, a single 5-bit position makes PLWAH indexes half the size of WAH indexes [3].

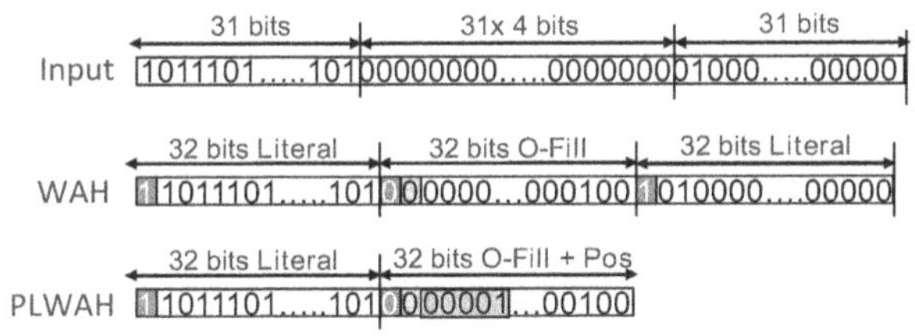

Figure 2: An uncompressed bitmap index (top) and the corresponding WAH (middle) and PLWAH (bottom) compressed bitmaps.

Given a list of input values of an attribute, the compressed bitmap can be built *incrementally*, i.e., without needing to create first the uncompressed bitmap, using the algorithm described by Lemire [9]. Input values are processed in *chunks* of 31 consecutive values. For each chunk, up to 31 literals (each corresponding to a distinct value) are created. The new literals are then appended at the end of the corresponding bitmap columns. Before appending a literal to its corresponding column, the current *chunk identifier* is compared to the identifier of the last literal appended to the column. If the difference *delta* between the current and the previous chunk identifier is greater than 1, then a 0-Fill word whose length is exactly $delta - 1$ needs to be inserted before the new literal. In this way, when an index is updated with a new chunk, only $d \leq 31$ out of the n columns have to be updated, where d is the number of *distinct* values present in the chunk.

The main obstacle to providing high-speed indexing throughput is poor memory locality, which in a packet recording context can seriously deteriorate the system performance. Intuitively, the described algorithm exhibits poor memory locality when indexing data with many distinct values. This is confirmed by our profiling measurements that show that, especially in the case of high-entropy data, cache misses are taxing the system and causing the CPU resources to be underutilized. In modern multi-core architectures, poor memory locality represents a serious performance limitation as it prevents the parallelism to be fully exploited. In fact, in multi-threaded implementations, the amount of cache *available* per thread decreases with the number of threads, making memory locality a serious problem.

3. BITMAP INDEXING ON GPUS

Modern GPUs are advanced data-parallel architectures providing hundreds of cores and an aggregated memory bandwidth that is several times higher than the bandwidth available to modern processors. In the context of packet recording, completely offloading the index creation to a GPU, removes pressure from the host's memory hierarchies, which are constantly taxed for fetching and processing packets. In contrast to CPUs, which rely on large caches to hide memory latencies, GPUs are optimized for throughput and exhibit massive data-parallelism: hundreds of hardware threads execute, in parallel, the same computation over distinct data portions. The challenge is therefore turning complex computations into sequences of simple, but highly-parallel, computing steps. In this section, we describe the steps of highly parallel computations that enable us to build compressed bitmap indexes at very high speeds directly on GPUs.

3.1 Data Flow

A given batch of numerical values of a packet header attribute (e.g., port numbers) is copied from the main memory to the GPU (see Figure 3), which computes and returns a serialized compressed bitmap index to the host memory together with metadata required to access individual index columns. The metadata consists of two parallel arrays called *keys* and *offsets*. The *keys* array is sorted and stores m distinct keys, where m is the number of distinct values present in the input data, which is smaller than the attribute cardinality (e.g., less than 65,536 for port numbers). The *offsets* array stores, for each key K_i, the offset within the index where the corresponding bitmap column can be loaded[1].

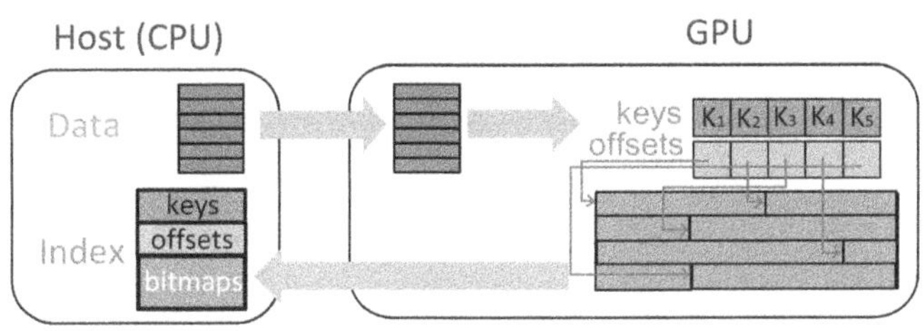

Figure 3: Data flow for indexing data on GPUs

3.2 Index creation

Exploiting the massive parallelism offered by GPUs is not trivial; it requires a complete algorithm redesign. The core idea of our approach is to exploit the high integer sorting performance provided by modern GPUs to be able to build all the bitmap index columns in parallel.

In particular, our algorithm starts with a step that associates each input value with a *row identifier (rid)*, which encodes the position of the value in the input *batch*. The input values and the corresponding rids are stored in two arrays, which are then sorted by the input values. Sorting can be performed very efficiently on GPUs. In this way, the array of rids is logically segmented into regions, one for each *distinct* input value, containing monotonically increasing identifiers. The rids array is used to produce the literal (`L`) and 0-Fill (`OF`) compression symbols. The parallelism of the GPU is further exploited by processing each individual rid on a different thread. Using a number of highly parallel refinement steps that eliminate redundant information by means of *data reductions*, the rids are turned into symbols of the compressed bitmap index.

WAH indexing. Next, we explain the steps required to build a WAH bitmap index on a GPU. Algorithm 1 shows the pseudocode of our indexing algorithm. The algorithm first copies the n input values to the array *input* in the GPU memory. Next, in line 2, it builds a second array *rids* with the raw identifiers where each value is encountered. *rids* is initialized to increasing row positions 0 to $n-1$. Subsequently, the input data and the row positions are reordered

[1]The length of the bitmap column i, expressed in number of words, can be computed as $offsets[i+1] - offsets[i]$.

Algorithm 1 GPUIndexCreate(values, n)

Input: an array *values* storing *n* input values
Output: the corresponding compressed bitmap index

```
1: input ← copyFromCPUToGPU(values,n)
2: sortRidsByValue(rid, input);
3: (chIds, lit) = produceChunkIDLiteral(rids)
4: k = mergeLitByValChID(input, chIds, lit)
5: produceFills(input, chIds, k)
6: idxLen = fuseFillsLiterals(chIds, lit, index, k)
7: keyCount = computeColumnLen(chIds, input, k)
8: copyFromGPUToCPU(keyCount keys and offsets)
9: copyFromGPUToCPU(index, idxLen)
```

in such a way that: i) the input values are sorted in ascending order, and, ii) *rids* contains the positions corresponding to the values.

Afterwards (line 3), the algorithm builds two new arrays of the same length as the input data, *chIds* and *lit*, that contain the chunk identifiers and the *partial* literals corresponding to the row identifiers. A *partial* literal is a 32-bit word with a 1-bit header and a 31-bit payload. The payload has *one* bit set to 1 as shown in Algorithm 2.

Algorithm 2 produceChunkIDLiteral(*rid*, *n*)

Input: an array *rid* of *n* row identifiers
Output: two parallel arrays of chunk identifiers and partial literals

```
for i = 0 → n − 1 do in parallel
    setBit(lit[i], rid[i] mod 31)
    setBit(lit[i], 31) //mark header as literal
    chIds[i] ← rid[i] / 31
end for
```

Next, in line 4, literals are created by merging the partial literals corresponding to the same input value and the chunk identifier. This operation, described in Algorithm 3, is a *segmented* parallel reduction. In fact, the *input* and *chIds* arrays divide *lit* into logical segments corresponding to each distinct tuple $(input[i], chIds[i])$. The logical segments carry the partial literals that need to be encoded in a single complete literal. Within each segment the values are reduced using a bitwise OR (see Figure 4). The result of this is that the three arrays (*chIds*, *input*, *lit*) are compacted and their length reduces from n to k, where k is the number of distinct $(input[i], chIds[i])$ pairs.

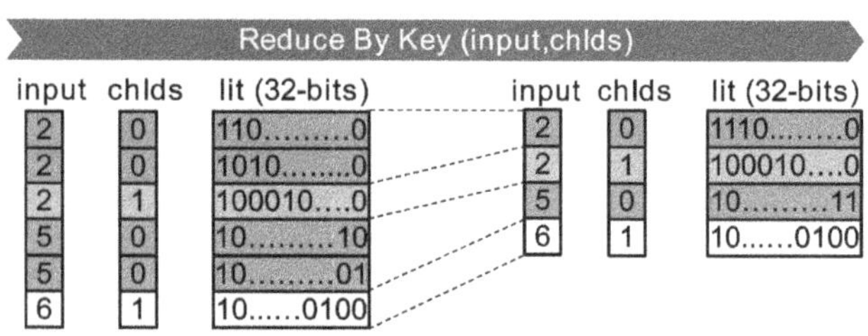

Figure 4: Literals are created by *reducing* partial literals.

The *chIds* array stores the chunk identifier corresponding to a given *literal*. The next step (line 5) is to turn the $chIds[i]$ word into the `0-Fill` symbol that precedes the literal $lit[i]$. This can be obtained by taking the difference between consecutive positions of *chIds*. If two adjacent literals belonging to the same input value are consecutive (i.e., $chIds[i] = 1 + chIds[i-1]$), the length of the 0-Fill between the two will be zero (i.e., there will not be a 0-Fill between them in the final index). It is worth to remark that this

Algorithm 3 mergeLitByValChID(*input*,*lit*,*chIds*,*n*)

Input: three arrays *input*, *lit* and *chIds* of size *n*
Output: *lit* stores complete literal symbols instead of *partial* literals

```
for i = 0 → n − 1 do in parallel
    key[i] = (chIds[i], input[i])
end for
// Merge the partial literals
k ← reduceByKey(key, lit, OP::bitwiseOR)
return k
```

operation can be performed, in parallel, for all *chIds*, which correspond to multiple keys. A corner case is represented by the first *chId* of each key. In order to distinguish this case, a parallel array called *heads* that marks the beginning of each key has to be created. In particular, $heads[i]$ is greater than 0 if $chIds[i]$ is the first *chdId* of a key and 0 otherwise. The array *heads* can be efficiently computed in parallel by performing an *adjacent difference* over the elements of the *input* array. These operations are described in Algorithm 4.

Algorithm 4 produceFills(*keys*, *chIds*, *n*)

Input: the array *chIds* of chunk indentifier
the array *keys* of values
Output: the *chIds* array stores 0-Fill symbols

```
heads ← createHeads(keys)
for i = 1 → n − 1 do in parallel
    if heads[i] == 0 then
        chIds[i] ← chIds[i] − chIds[i − 1] − 1
    else
        if chIds[i] ≠ 0 then
            chIds[i] ← chIds[i] − 1
        end if
    end if
end for
```

Finally (line 6 of Algorithm 1), the final compressed bitmap index is created as a concatenation of bitmap index columns. 0-Fill words and literal words are contained in the two parallel arrays *chIds* and *lit*. The output index is created by interleaving the *chIds* and *lit* arrays. This is accomplished by a *scatter* operation within each array in even and odd positions. There is still one step remaining: removing from the index the zero-values that are present whenever two consecutive literals are encountered. This operation is referred to as *stream compaction*. The pseudocode describing the process is shown in Algorithm 5.

Algorithm 5 fuseFillsLiterals(*chIds*, *lit*, *outindex*, *n*)

Input: the array *chIds* of chunk identifiers
the array *lit* of literals
Output: the array *outidx* stores the index

```
for i = 0 → n − 1 do in parallel
    outIndex[2 * i] = chIds[i]
end for
for i = 0 → n − 1 do in parallel
    outIndex[2 * i + 1] = literals[i]
end for
// Remove the zeros from the output
idxLen ← streamCompaction(outindex, 0)
return idxLen
```

Once the index is created we prepare the metadata, that is, the two distinct arrays *keys* and *offsets*. Recall that the input data have been sorted and compacted via the `mergeLitByValChID` step. We use a segmented reduction to find for a given key the length of the corresponding bitmap column. The length is computed by counting literals and fills, which are present in the GPU memory. The only consideration to be taken into account is that the zero elements in *chIds* have been removed from the final index and therefore do not have to be included in the bitmap column length. For that, we compute in-memory a temporary array *tmpArray* such that *tmpArray*[*i*] is 1 when *chIds*[*i*] == 0 and 2 otherwise. Finally, since we would like to compute the offsets instead of the lengths for each key, we perform an *inclusive scan*. This process is described in Algorithm 6. At this stage the *index*, the *keys* and the *offsets* are ready to be copied from the GPU to the host memory.

Algorithm 6 computeColumnLen(*chIds*, *input*, *n*)

```
Input: the two paralell arrays input and chIds of size n
Output: the array lengths stores the offsets
1: // Prepare an array for the lengths
2: for i = 0 → n − 1 do in parallel
3:     tmpArray[i] ← (1 + (chId[i] == 0 ? 0 : 1)
4: end for
5: // Compute the length of each bitmap index column
6: keycnt ← reduceByKey(input, tmpArray, OP::Sum)
7: // Transform the lengths in offsets
8: offsets ← inclusiveScan(tmpArray)
9: return keycnt
```

PLWAH indexing. PLWAH is a variant of WAH that uses an additional compression step, called `mergeFillLiteral` (Algorithm 7), which merges sparse literals with the previous 0-Fill word. This additional step is executed just after step 5 of Algorithm 1 and leverages the `popc` and `clz` instructions offered by NVIDIA GPUs to count the number of bits set to one and the leading zeros, respectively. Additionally, PLWAH requires the line 3 of Algorithm 6 to be slightly modified in order to consider the case of sparse literals that have been merged into their corresponding 0-Fill.

Algorithm 7 mergeFillLiteral(*chIds*, *lit*, *n*)

```
Input: the two parallel arrays chIds and lit of length n
Output: literals with a single bit set are merged with the previous 0-Fill
for i = 0 → n − 1 do in parallel
    if chIds[i] ≠ 0 then
        popcnt = populationCount(lit[i])
        freeBits = leadingZero(chIds[i])
        if popcnt == 1 AND freeBits ≥ 7 then
            encodePosition(chIds[i], leadingZero(lit[i]))
            lit[i] ← 0
        end if
    end if
end for
```

Limitations and considerations. WAH and PLWAH are double-sided, meaning that they can compress both sequences of 0's and sequences of 1's by using `0-Fill` and `1-Fill` words, respectively. Our algorithms do not include `1-Fill` words because this pattern, as we have shown in our previous work [7], is extremely uncommon in network traffic data. This makes the implementation simpler and more efficient.

The number of values that our GPU-implementation can index in a single batch is limited by two parameters: the maximum fill length that can be encoded by a single `0-Fill` symbol and the memory of the GPU. Our algorithm cannot create two consecutive `0-Fill` words, and, therefore, the maximum number of input values must be smaller than $31 \times ((2^{31} - 1) - 1)$ (more than 60 billions of numbers) for WAH. In a packet logging context, this number is not a practical limitation as packet traces are customarily stored in batches of Millions of packets, which usually corresponds to multi-gigabyte packet traces. A more important consideration is the available memory on the GPU. Our algorithm requires four arrays to be resident in the GPU memory for storing: the input values, the literals, the chunk identifiers, and the temporary buffers for sorting. In practice, a modern GPU with 4Gb of RAM is more than capable of indexing up to 50 Million records, which translates to traces of several Gigabytes (more than 3Gb considering the smallest packet sizes).

4. EVALUATION

We implemented our algorithms using *Thrust*, which is a C++ library provided by the NVIDIA SDK designed to enhance code productivity and more importantly performance portability across NVIDIA GPUs. To evaluate the performance of our solution, we have used similarly priced CPU and GPU: a 3.4Ghz Intel i7-2600K processor with 8 Mb of cache and a NVIDIA GTX-670 GPU fitted in a PCI-e Gen 2.0 slot.

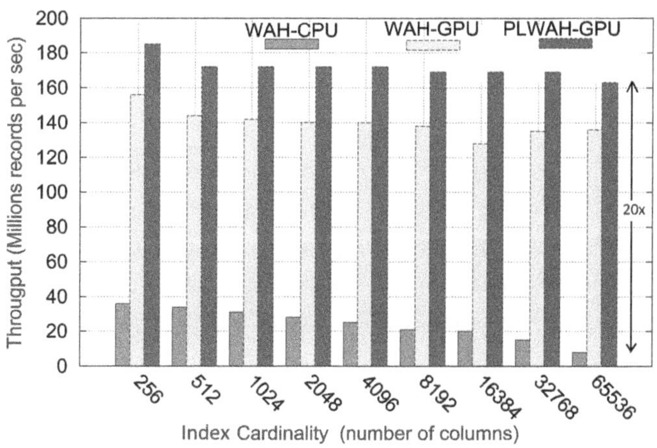

Figure 5: Indexing throughput vs cardinality for WAH on a CPU, WAH on a GPU, and PLWAH on a GPU.

Our main design goal is to enable high-speed packet indexing in the context of network traffic recording. Therefore, indexing should be able to operate flawlessly under very diverse traffic distributions, like high-entropy distributions that result from attacks. With this in mind, we evaluate how the cardinality of the index affects the indexing speed under uniformly distributed data, which is the most pessimistic scenario. We use indexes of increasing column cardinality (from 256 up to 65,536 columns) and we compare the performance obtained when indexing on a GPU using our algorithms and on a CPU using the online indexing algorithm for WAH of Lemire [9], which is the state-of-the-art. On the CPU we use a single thread implementation because it serves as a reference point that enables to estimate an upper bound on the performance that multi-core CPUs can realize. However, we highlight that the goal of this work is to show that it is feasible to build indexes entirely in a GPU without CPU intervention as in a packet recording system CPU computational and bandwidth resources are very scarce.

In Figure 5 we show the indexing throughput of WAH on a CPU and of WAH and PLWAH on a GPU. We first find that **using a GPU we achieve up to a 20-fold speedup over indexing on a CPU**. In addition, for a cardinality of 256, we reach with PLWAH a maximum speed of 185 Million records per second. With 64-byte packets, this suggests that on a GPU we can, for example, index more than 12 attributes per packet at a sustained packet rate of 10 Gbps.

Moreover, we observe that while on the CPU the throughput decreases rapidly with the cardinality of the index, **on a GPU the throughput exhibits a much better scaling behavior**. In particular, on the CPU the throughput incurs a 4.5-fold decrease when the cardinality increases from 256 to 65,536. In sharp contrast, the throughput on the GPU decreases only by a factor of 1.13 as we can effectively exploit the available parallelism. The reason for this small decrease is that the complexity of the sorting algorithm of *Thrust* depends on the actual length (in bits) of the values to be sorted.

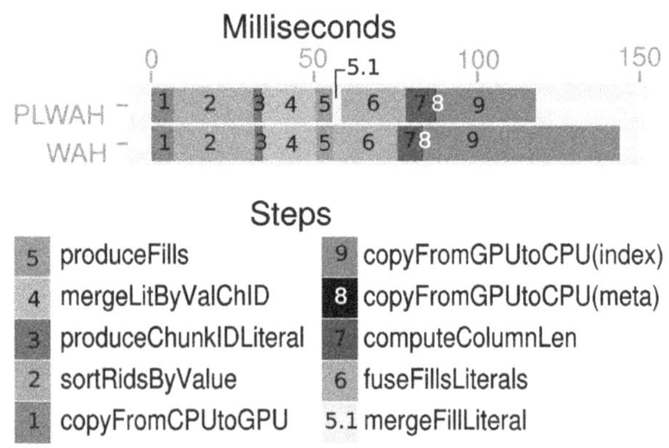

Figure 6: Time spent in different steps of our algorithm for building the WAH and PLWAH indexes on a GPU.

Furthermore, PLWAH, despite being a more complex encoding than WAH, can provide substantially higher throughputs. To better understand this point, in Figure 6 we illustrate the time spent in each step of PLWAH and WAH when indexing 20 Million random 16 bit numbers (65,536 cardinality). Recall that, compared to WAH, PLWAH uses an additional step that merges sparse literals with the previous `0-Fill` word. This step, which is indicated as 5.1 in Figure 6, is extremely fast and allows the time required to copy the index from the GPU to the host memory to be drastically reduced due to the smaller index size. From this measurement we learn that **the cost of the additional operations for building a more complex encoding in a GPU is greatly overshadowed by the savings of the more compact compression**.

5. CONCLUSION

Indexing high-speed streams of network measurement data in real-time poses significant performance challenges, especially in the context of network traffic recording, where traffic recording systems have to process packets at wire-rate without experiencing any packet loss under every traffic mix. In this paper we have shown that GPUs can provide indexing throughputs that are one order of magnitude higher than the state-of-the-art. Therefore, this work opens the path to wire-rate multi-10-Gbps packet indexing using commodity hardware.

6. REFERENCES

[1] Cisco Visual Networking Index Forecast (2011 - 2016). `http://www.cisco.com/web/solutions/sp/vni/vni_forecast_highlights/index.html`.

[2] TCPDUMP/LIBPCAP public repository. http://www.tcpdump.org/.

[3] F. Deliège and T. B. Pedersen. Position list word aligned hybrid: optimizing space and performance for compressed bitmaps. In *Proc. of the 13th Int. Conf. on Extending Database Technology*, EDBT '10, 2010.

[4] L. Deri, A. Cardigliano, and F. Fusco. 10 gbit line rate packet-to-disk using n2disk. In *Proc. of the 5th Int. Workshop on Traffic Monitoring and Analysis*, 2013.

[5] L. Deri, V. Lorenzetti, and S. Mortimer. Collection and exploration of large data monitoring sets using bitmap databases. In *Proc. of the 2nd Int. Workshop on Traffic Monitoring and Analysis*, 2010.

[6] F. Fusco, X. Dimitropoulos, M. Vlachos, and L. Deri. pcapIndex: an index for network packet traces with legacy compatibility. *SIGCOMM Computer Communication Review*, 42(1):47–53, Jan. 2012.

[7] F. Fusco, M. Vlachos, and M. Stoecklin. Real-time creation of bitmap indexes on streaming network data. *The VLDB Journal*, 21:287–307, 2012.

[8] S. Han, K. Jang, K. Park, and S. Moon. Packetshader: a gpu-accelerated software router. In *Proc. of the ACM SIGCOMM 2010 conference*, 2010.

[9] D. Lemire, O. Kaser, and K. Aouiche. Sorting improves word-aligned bitmap indexes. *CoRR*, abs/0901.3751, 2009.

[10] L. Rizzo. Netmap: a novel framework for fast packet I/O. In *Proc. of the 2012 USENIX Annual Technical Conf.*, 2012.

[11] R. Smith, N. Goyal, J. Ormont, K. Sankaralingam, and C. Estan. Evaluating GPUs for Network Packet Signature Matching. In *Proc. of the Int. Symposium on Performance Analysis of Systems and Software (ISPASS)*, 2009.

[12] K. Stockinger et al. Network traffic analysis with query driven visualization sc 2005 hpc analytics results. In *Proc. of the ACM/IEEE Conf. on Supercomputing*, 2005.

[13] T. Taylor, S. E. Coull, F. Monrose, and J. McHugh. Toward efficient querying of compressed network payloads. In *Proc. of the 2012 Usenix Annual Technical Conf.*, 2012.

[14] G. Vasiliadis, S. Antonatos, M. Polychronakis, E. P. Markatos, and S. Ioannidis. Gnort: High performance network intrusion detection using graphics processors. In *Proc. of the 11th international symposium on Recent Advances in Intrusion Detection*, 2008.

[15] K. Wu, E. J. Otoo, and A. Shoshani. Optimizing bitmap indices with efficient compression. *ACM Transactions of Database Systems*, 31:1–38, March 2006.

On the Benefits of Using a Large IXP as an Internet Vantage Point

Nikolaos Chatzis
TU Berlin
nikolaos@inet.tu-berlin.de

Georgios Smaragdakis
T-Labs/TU Berlin
georgios@inet.tu-berlin.de

Jan Böttger
TU Berlin
jan@inet.tu-berlin.de

Thomas Krenc
TU Berlin
tkrenc@inet.tu-berlin.de

Anja Feldmann
TU Berlin
anja@inet.tu-berlin.de

ABSTRACT

In the context of measuring the Internet, a long-standing question has been whether there exist well-localized physical entities in today's network where traffic from a representative cross-section of the constituents of the Internet can be observed at a fine-enough granularity to paint an accurate and informative picture of how these constituents shape and impact much of the structure and evolution of today's Internet and the actual traffic it carries.

In this paper, we first answer this question in the affirmative by mining 17 weeks of continuous sFlow data from one of the largest European IXPs. Examining these weekly snapshots, we discover a vantage point with excellent visibility into the Internet, seeing week-in and week-out traffic from all 42K+ routed ASes, almost all 450K+ routed prefixes, from close to 1.5M servers, and around a quarter billion IPs from all around the globe. Second, to show the potential of such vantage points, we analyze the server-related portion of the traffic at this IXP, identify the server IPs and cluster them according to the organizations responsible for delivering the content. In the process, we observe a clear trend among many of the critical Internet players towards network heterogenization; that is, either hosting servers of third-party networks in their own infrastructures or pursuing massive deployments of their own servers in strategically chosen third-party networks. While the latter is a well-known business strategy of companies such as Akamai, Google, and Netflix, we show in this paper the extent of network heterogenization in today's Internet and illustrate how it enriches the traditional, largely traffic-agnostic AS-level view of the Internet.

Categories and Subject Descriptors

Computer Systems Organization,Computer Communication Networks,Network Operations [**Network monitoring**]:

Keywords

Internet Exchange Points, Internet Topology, Traffic Characterization, Content Delivery

IMC'13, October 23–25, 2013, Barcelona, Spain.

ACM 978-1-4503-1953-9/13/10 ...$15.00.
http://dx.doi.org/10.1145/2504730.2504746.

Acknowledgments

This work would not have been possible without the help, engagement, and commitment of Walter Willinger.

We want to express our gratitude towards the IXP for their generous cooperation and support. Moreover, we thank the anonymous reviewers for their useful feedback. This work was supported in part by the EU projects BigFoot (FP7-ICT-317858) and CHANGE (FP7-ICT-257422), EIT Knowledge and Innovation Communities program, and an IKY-DAAD award (54718944).

1. INTRODUCTION

An ever-growing demand for Web-based traffic [30, 41] (e. g., HD video and other streaming media, e-commerce services), together with the proliferation of new Internet-enabled devices and the emergence of new content distribution models and cloud infrastructure providers are radically transforming the nature of content delivery in today's Internet. These features are also having a profound impact on how some of the main Internet players (e. g., ISPs, CDNs, Web hosting companies, and content providers) operate in such a dynamic environment and do business in an increasingly competitive marketplace. Unfortunately, carefully tracking these developments to obtain an accurate picture of how this critical cast of players shapes and impacts much of the Internet and its traffic has become an increasingly daunting task. In the past, attempts at painting such a picture had limited success because they typically relied on piecing together incomplete and often inaccurate information from many different sources of varying quality [40, 45, 50] or using various types of hard-to-get (i. e., proprietary) datasets [41] or hard-to-justify estimates of difficult-to-measure (e. g., inter-AS traffic matrix) quantities [27].

A main reason for our current inability to accurately track a constantly changing Internet has been the lack of global vantage points where traffic from a sufficiently large portion of the Internet can be observed at a granularity that is sufficiently fine-grained to discern the make up of today's Internet traffic and the interactions of the responsible parties. This raises the questions whether or not such vantage points do indeed exist in today's Internet, and if so, what exactly they enable us to discern about the Internet as a whole as well as its individual constituents?

Main contribution (part 1): The first finding reported in this paper is that some of the largest Internet Exchange Points (IXPs) in Europe (i. e., AMS-IX in Amsterdam, DE-CIX in Frankfurt, LINX in London) do indeed serve as the kind of vantage points we are looking for. In particular, our detailed analysis of 17 contiguous weeks of complete sFlow measurements from one of the largest European IXPs reveals that in addition to being a critical part of the

European portion of the Internet, this IXP also plays a global role, "seeing" traffic from a large fraction of the Internet. To highlight the kind of visibility into the Internet as a whole that is possible at these vantage points, we show that week-in and week-out, our IXP "sees" traffic from all 42K+ routed ASes, almost all 450K+ routed prefixes, from about 1.5M servers, and around a quarter billion IP addresses from all the countries around the globe. Importantly, the fact that these largest European IXPs all operate in a very similar fashion, handle comparable traffic volumes, and have similar profiles with respect to the members and range of service offerings allows us to conclude that either one of them fits the role of being a global Internet vantage point.

However, like all vantage points used in practice, visibility from these large European IXPs into the Internet is not perfect. Thus, knowing what we cannot discern about what aspects of the Internet from mining the traffic seen at one of these vantage points is as important as knowing what we can discern. To deal with this important issue, we consider a variety of different IXP-external measurements that not only complement the IXPs own data, but also enable us to either check or validate our findings that are based on the IXPs data alone or help us determine what aspects are impossible to discern from this vantage point, and why.

Main contribution (part 2): Our second main finding illustrates the new opportunities or benefits for Internet measurements that arise from having access to vantage points with such good visibility into the Internet. By squarely focusing on the analysis of the Web server-related portion of the traffic "seen" by our IXP and applying an original methodology for identifying server-based infrastructures, classifying them by ownership (e. g., company, organization), and associating traffic with them, we show that many of the major commercial Internet players are actively contributing to a clearly discernible trend towards network heterogenization. That is, many of these players' networks are undergoing major changes as a result of business decisions that either favor the hosting of servers from third-party networks within their own network infrastructures or the deployment of their own servers, often in massive numbers, in purposefully-selected third-party networks.

On the one hand, this finding simply confirms what is well-documented in press releases of some of the main commercial Internet players and technology blogs, but remains a largely under-reported issue in the networking research literature. For example, it is well-known that CDN companies such as Akamai are accelerating the deployment of their own servers in eyeball networks by forming strategic content delivery alliances with large ISPs [1, 6]. Similarly, it is also widely reported that large content providers such as Netflix are installing their own brand of single-purpose CDNs (e. g., Netflix's Open Connect) inside various regional and local ISPs for the sole purpose of enabling those ISPs to deliver Netflix video data directly to their end users [5]. Other key companies such as Google, Amazon, or Facebook have followed suit and further add to the complexities that result from this proliferation of intertwined network infrastructures and traffic.

On the other hand, by providing a methodology for discovering an organization's servers, whether they are deployed within the organization's own AS (or ASes) or inside some third-party network's infrastructure, we enable and advocate a measurement-driven approach to inferring and assessing the *extent* to which individual network infrastructures or the traffic that they carry are heterogeneous. The results of our study show that network heterogenization is wide-spread and not just confined to well-known players such as Akamai or Google. We also study the impact that this finding has on the usage of peering links at IXPs, in particular, and AS-links in the larger Internet, in general. Specifically, we show that not only is AS-link usage becoming more heterogeneous, but the task of attributing traffic to the party responsible for it faces enormous challenges in view of the complexities that result from the observed proliferation of intertwined network infrastructures and traffic. In effect, these findings argue that future attempts at accurately and meaningfully studying the business strategies of the various Internet constituents (e. g., ISPs, content providers, CDNs, IXPs, networks without an ASN, resellers, etc.) and the business relationships among them have to move beyond the traditional and largely traffic-agnostic AS-level view of the Internet. They must account for the complexities that result from today's Internet realities and are more concerned with how traffic flows across the network than with how the network is connected at the AS level.

Head-on comparison with [13]: The large European IXP considered in this paper also featured prominently in the recent work by Ager et al. [13]. However, while that study focused squarely on the discovery of a surprisingly rich peering fabric among the member ASes of that IXP, in this paper, we are mainly concerned with mining the traffic seen at this IXP to determine the IXP's visibility into the Internet. Put differently, while [13] exploited the IXP measurements to obtain an accurate picture of the "inside" of this IXP (i. e., its member ASes, their peerings, and the IXP-specific traffic matrix), this paper mines recent traffic data to obtain a view of the "outside" of the IXP; that is, the larger Internet beyond the boundary formed by the members of the IXP. In terms of results, while [13] highlighted the severe level of incompleteness of the commonly-studied AS maps of the Internet, this paper establishes and provides concrete evidence for why and in what sense this traditional AS-level view— although still useful for exploring and understanding various connectivity- or reachability-related aspects— is largely inept for accounting for critical elements of the networks that make up today's Internet. Thus, representing two largely complementary efforts, the combined findings of [13] and of this paper take the observations of the study by Labovitz et al. [41] to the next level. In the process, we identify and outline an alternative and largely orthogonal perspective to the traditional AS-level view that centers around organizations or companies and their server-based infrastructures that are spread across many networks and countries and defy traditional network and geographic boundaries.

Road-map: The remainder of the paper is organized as follows. In Section 2, we describe the available IXP measurements and report on how we extract the relevant traffic data for our study. We focus in Section 3 on our first finding that the IXP defines a vantage point that offers unprecedented visibility into the Internet, and we support this finding with concrete results based on a week's worth of traffic. Our results are complemented in Section 4 by a longitudinal analysis, and we discuss what measurements taken at this single vantage point for a 17-week long period reveal about the Internet. In Section 5, we describe our methodology for grouping an organization's servers, irrespective of their location within the Internet, and report on our second main finding; that is, evidence for and extent of network heterogenization. We continue in Section 6 with a discussion of related and future work and conclude with a summary of our main observations in Section 7.

2. IXP AS RICH DATA SOURCE

In this section, we describe the IXP measurements that are at our disposal for this study and sketch and illustrate the basic methodology we use to identify the traffic components relevant for our work. We also list and comment on the different IXP-external datasets that

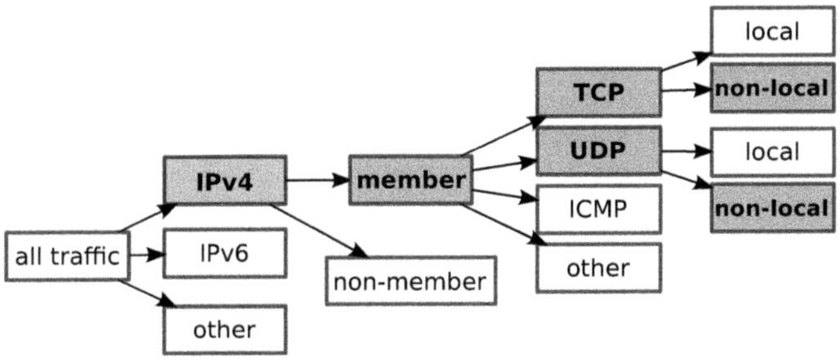

Figure 1: Traffic filtering steps

we rely on throughout this paper to show what we can and cannot discern from the IXP-internal measurements alone.[1]

2.1 Available IXP-internal datasets

The work reported in this paper is based on traffic measurements collected between August 27 (beginning of week 35) and December 23 (end of week 51) of 2012 at one of the largest IXPs in Europe. At the beginning of the measurement period in week 35, this IXP had 443 member ASes that exchanged on average some 11.9 PB of traffic per day over the IXP's public peering infrastructure (i. e., a layer-2 switching fabric distributed over a number of data centers within the city where the IXP is located). During the measurement period, the IXP added between 1-2 members per week. Specifically, the measurements we rely on consist of 17 consecutive weeks of uninterrupted anonymized sFlow records that contain Ethernet frame samples that were collected using a random sampling of 1 out of 16K. sFlow captures the first 128 bytes of each sampled frame. This implies that in the case of IPv4 packets the available information consists of the full IP and transport layer headers and 74 and 86 bytes of TCP and UDP payload, respectively. For further details about the IXP infrastructure itself as well as the collected sFlow measurements (e. g., absence of sampling bias), we refer to [13]. In the following, we use our week 45 data to illustrate our method. The other weekly snapshots produce very similar results and are discussed in more detail in Section 4.

2.2 Methods for dissecting the IXP's traffic

2.2.1 Peering traffic

Figure 1 details the filtering steps that we applied to the raw sFlow records collected at this IXP to obtain what we refer to as the "peering traffic" component of the overall traffic. As shown in Figure 1, after removing from the overall traffic, in succession, all non-IPv4 traffic (i. e., native IPv6 and other protocols; roughly 0.4% of the total traffic, most of which is native IPv6), all traffic that is either not member-to-member or stays local (e. g., IXP management traffic; about 0.6%), all member-to-member IPv4 traffic that is not TCP or UDP (i. e., ICMP and other transport protocols; less than 0.5%), this peering traffic makes up more than 98.5% of the total traffic. As an interesting by-product, we observe that 82% of the peering traffic is TCP and 18% is UDP.

2.2.2 Web server-related traffic

We next identify the portion of the peering traffic that can be unambiguously identified as Web server-related traffic. Our motivation is that Web servers are generally considered to be the engines of e-commerce, which in turn argues that Web server-related traffic is, in general, a good proxy for the commercial portion of Internet traffic. Accordingly, we focus on HTTP and HTTPS and describe the filtering steps for extracting their traffic.

To identify HTTP traffic, we rely primarily on commonly-used string-matching techniques applied to the content of the 128 bytes of each sampled frame. We use two different patterns. The first pattern matches the initial line of request and response packets and looks for HTTP method words (e. g., GET, HEAD, POST) and the words HTTP/1.{0,1}. The second pattern applies to header lines in any packet of a connection and relies on commonly used HTTP header field words as documented in the relevant RFCs and W3C specifications (e. g., Host, Server, Access-Control-Allow-Methods). Using these techniques enables us to identify which of the IP endpoints act as servers and which ones act as clients. When applied to our week 45 data, we identify about 1.3 million server IPs together with roughly 40 million client IPs. Checking the port numbers, we verify that more than 80% of the server IPs use the expected TCP ports, i. e., 80 and 8080. Some 5% of them also use 1935 (RTMP) as well as 443 (HTTPS). Note that by relying on string-matching, we miss those servers for which our sFlow records do not contain sufficient information; we also might mis-classify as clients some of those servers that "talk" with other servers and for which only their client-related activity is captured in our data.

With respect to HTTPS traffic, since we cannot use pattern matching directly due to encryption, we use a mixed passive and active measurement approach. In a first step, we use traffic on TCP port 443 to identify a candidate set of IPs of HTTPS servers. Here, we clearly miss HTTPS servers that do not use port 443, but we consider them not to be commercially relevant. However, given that TCP port 443 is commonly used to circumvent firewalls and proxy rules for other kinds of traffic (e. g., SSH servers or VPNs running TCP port 443), in a second step we rule out non-HTTPS related use by relying on active measurements. For this purpose, we crawl each IP in our candidate set for an X.509 certificate chain and check the validity of the returned X.509 certificates. For those IPs that pass the checks of the certificate, we extract the names for which the X.509 certificate is valid and the purpose for which it was issued. In particular, we check the following properties in each retrieved X.509 certificate: *(a) certificate subject*, *(b) alternative names*, *(c) key usage* (purpose), *(d) certificate chain*, *(e) validity time*, and *(f) stability over time*. If a certificate does not pass any of the tests, we do not consider it in the analysis.

We keep only the IPs that have a certificate subject and alternative names with valid domains and also valid country-code second-level domains (ccSLD) according to the definition in [35]. Next, we check if the key usage explicitly indicates a Web server role. In the certificate chain we check if the delivered certificates do really refer to each other in the right order they are listed up to the root certificate, which must be contained in the current Linux/Ubuntu white-list. Next, we verify the validity time of each certificate in the chain by comparing it to the timestamp the certificate fetching was performed. Lastly, we perform the active measurements several times and check for changes because IPs in cloud deployments can change their role very quickly and frequently. Ignoring validity time, we require that all the certificates fetched from a single IP have the same properties. In the case of our week 45 data, starting with a candidate set of approximately 1.5M IPs, some 500K respond to repeated active measurements, of which 250K are in the end identified as HTTPS server IPs.

When combined, these filtering steps yield approximately 1.5M different Web server IPs (including the 250K HTTPS server IPs). In total, these HTTP and HTTPS server IPs are responsible for or

[1]For an overview of the importance of IXPs for today's Internet, we refer to [28].

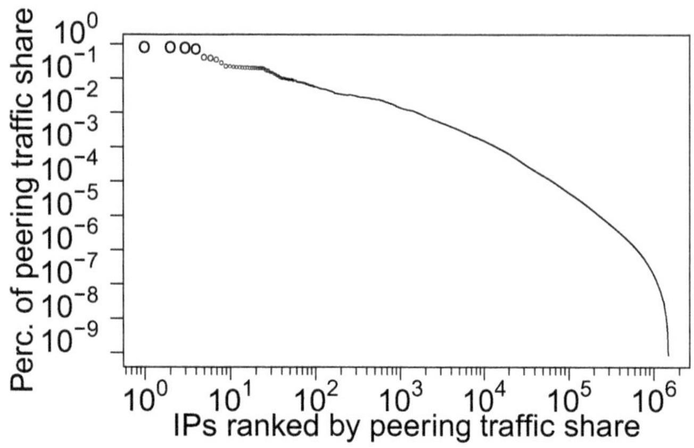

Figure 2: Traffic per server IP sorted by traffic share

"see" more than 70% of the peering traffic portion of the total traffic. Some 350K of these IP addresses appear in both sets and are examples of multi-purpose servers; that is, servers with one IP address that see activity on multiple ports. Multi-purpose servers are popular with commercial Internet players (e.g., Akamai which uses TCP port 80 (HTTP) and TCP port 1935 (RTMP)), and their presence in our data partially explains why we see a larger percentage of Web server-related traffic than what is typically reported in the literature [33, 36, 43], but is often based on a strictly port-based traffic classification [30, 41].

Among the identified HTTP and HTTPS server IPs, we find some 200K IPs that act both as servers and as clients. These are responsible for some 10% of the server-related traffic. Upon closer inspection of the top contributors in this category, we find that they typically belong to major CDNs (e. g., EdgeCast, Limelight) or network operators (e. g., Eweka). Thus, the large traffic share of these servers is not surprising and reflects typical machine-to-machine traffic associated with operating, for example, a CDN. Another class of IPs in this category are proxies or clients that are managed via a server interface (or vice versa).

In the context of this paper, it is important to clarify the notion of a server IP. Throughout this paper, a server IP is defined as a publicly routed IP address of a server. As such, it can represent many different real-world scenarios, including a single (multi-purpose) server, a rack of multiple servers, or a front-end server acting as a gateway to possibly thousands of back-end servers (e.g., an entire data center). In fact, Figure 2 shows the traffic share of each server IP seen in the week 45 data. It highlights the presence of individual server IPs that are responsible for more than 0.5% of all server–related traffic! Indeed, the top 34 server IPs are responsible for more than 6% of the overall server traffic. These server IPs cannot be single machines. Upon closer examination, they are identified as belonging to a cast of Internet players that includes CDNs, large content providers, streamers, virtual backbone providers, and resellers, and thus represent front-end servers to large data centers and/or anycast services. Henceforth, we use the term server to refer to a server IP as defined above.

2.3 Available IXP-external datasets

When appropriate and feasible, we augment our IXP-based findings with active and passive measurements that do not involve the IXP in any form or shape and are all collected in parallel to our IXP data collection. Such complementary information allows us to verify, check, or refine the IXP-based findings.

One example of a complementary IXP-external dataset is a proprietary dataset from a large European Tier-1 ISP consisting of packet-level traffic traces.[2] With the help of the network intrusion detection system Bro [47] we produce the HTTP and DNS logs, extract the Web server-related traffic and the corresponding server IPs from the logs, and rely on the resulting data in Section 3.

For another example, we use the list of the top 280K DNS recursive resolvers—as seen by one of the largest commercial CDNs—as a starting set to find a highly distributed set of DNS resolvers that are available for active measurements such as doing reverse DNS lookups or performing active DNS queries. From this initial list of DNS servers, we eliminate those that cannot be used for active measurements (i.e., those that are not open, delegate DNS resolutions to other resolvers, or provide incorrect answers) and end up with a final list of about 25K DNS resolvers in some 12K ASes that are used for active measurements in Section 3.3.

Other examples of IXP-external data we use in this work include the publicly available lists of the top-1M or top-1K popular Web sites that can be downloaded from `www.alexa.com`. We obtained these lists for each of the weeks for which we have IXP data. We also utilized blogs and technical information found on the official Web sites of the various technology companies and Internet players. In addition, we make extensive use of publicly available BGP-based data that is collected on an ongoing basis by RouteViews [8], RIPE RIS [7], Team Cymru [9], etc.

2.4 IP server meta-data

Our efforts in Section 5 rely on certain meta-data that we collect for server IPs and that is obtained from DNS information, URIs, and X.509 certificates from HTTPS servers.

Regarding DNS information, obvious meta-information is the hostname(s) of a server IP. This information is useful because large organizations [38] often follow industrial standards in their naming schema's for servers that they operate or host in their own networks. Another useful piece of meta-data is the Start of Authority (SOA) resource record which relates to the administrative authority and can be resolved iteratively. This way one can often find a common root for organizations that do not use a unified naming schema. Note that the SOA record is often present, even when there is no hostname record available or an ARPA address is returned in the reverse lookup of a server IP.

Next, the URI as well as the authority associated with the hostname give us hints regarding the organization that is responsible for the content. For example, for the URI `youtube.com`, one finds the SOA resource record `google.com` and thus can associate Youtube with Google.

Lastly, the X.509 certificates reveal several useful pieces of meta-data. First, they list the base set of URIs that can be served by the corresponding server IP. Second, some server IPs have certificates with multiple names that can be used to find additional URIs. This is typically the case for hosting companies that host multiple sites on a single server IP. In addition, it is used by CDNs that serve multiple different domains with the same physical infrastructure. Moreover, the names found in the certificates can be mapped to SOA resource records as well.

Overall, we are able to extract DNS information for 71.7%, at least one URI for 23.8%, and X.509 certificate information for 17.7% of the 1.5M server IPs that we see in our week 45 data. For 81.9% of all the server IPs, we have at least one of the three pieces of information. For example, for streamers, one typically has no

[2]For this trace we anonymized the client information before applying the analysis with the network intrusion detection system Bro. We always use a prefix preserving function when anonymizing IPs.

		week 45	educated guesses of ground-truth
Peering Traffic	IPs	232,460,635	unknown $< 2^{32}$
	#ASes	42,825	approx. 43K
	Subnets	445,051	450K+
	countries	242	250
Server Traffic	IPs	1,488,286	unknown
	#ASes	19,824	unknown
	Subnets	75,841	unknown
	Countries	200	250

Table 1: IXP summary statistics—week 45

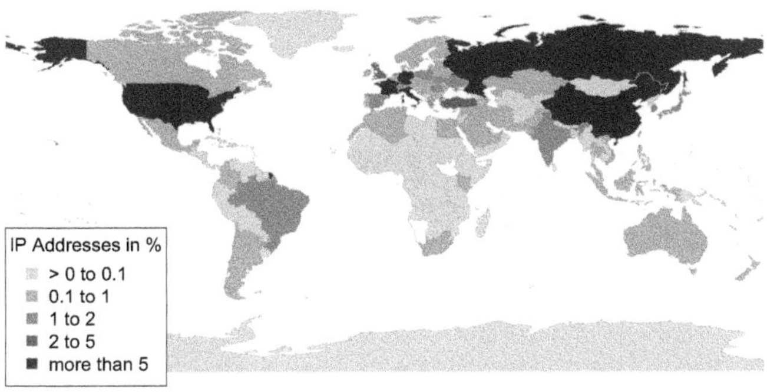

Figure 3: Percentage of IPs per country—week 45

assigned URI, but information from DNS. Before using this rich meta-data in Section 5, we clean it by removing non-valid URIs, SOA resource records of the Regional Internet Registries (RIRs) such as `ripe.net`, etc. This cleaning effort reduces the pool of server IPs by less than 3%.

3. LOCAL YET GLOBAL

The main purpose of this section is to show that our IXP represents an intriguing vantage point, with excellent visibility into the Internet as a whole. This finding of the IXP's important global role complements earlier observations that have focused on the important local role that this large European IXP plays for the greater geographic region where it is located [13], and we further elaborate here on its dual role as a local and as a global player. Importantly, we also discuss what we can and cannot discern about the Internet as a whole or its individual constituents based on measurements taken at this vantage point. The reported numbers are for the week 45 measurements when the IXP had 452 members that exchanged some 14 PB of traffic per day and are complemented by a longitudinal analysis in Section 4.

3.1 On the global role of the IXP

By providing a well-defined set of steps and requirements for establishing peering links between member networks, IXPs clearly satisfy the main reason for why they exist in the first place – keeping local traffic local. To assess the visibility into the global Internet that comes with using a large European IXP as a vantage point, we focus on the peering traffic component (see Section 2.2.1) and summarize in Table 1 the pertinent results.

First, in this single geographically well-localized facility, we observe during a one-week period approximately a quarter billion unique IPv4 addresses (recall that the portion of native IPv6 traffic seen at this IXP is negligible). While the total number of publicly routed IPv4 addresses in the Internet in any given week is unknown, it is some portion of the approximately three and a half billion allocated IPv4 addresses, which suggests that this IXP "sees" a significant fraction of the ground truth. The global role of this IXP is further illuminated by geo-locating all 230M+ IP addresses at the country-level granularity [49] and observing that this IXP "sees" traffic from every country of the world, except for places such as Western Sahara, Christmas Islands, or Cocos (Keeling) Islands. This ability to see the global Internet from this single vantage point is visualized in Figure 3, where the different countries' shades of gray indicate which percentage of IPs a given country contributes to the IPs seen at this IXP.

Second, when mapping the encountered 230M+ IP addresses to more network-specific entities such as subnets or prefixes and ASes, we confirm the IXP's ability to "see" the Internet. More precisely, in terms of subnets/prefixes, this IXP "sees" traffic from 445K subnets; that is, from essentially all actively routed prefixes. Determining the precise number of actively routed prefixes in the Internet in any given week remains an imprecise science as it depends on the publicly available BGP data that are traditionally used in this context (e.g., RouteViews, RIPE). The reported numbers vary between 450K-500K and are only slightly larger than the 445K subnets we see in this one week. With respect to ASes, the results are very similar – the IXP "sees" traffic from some 42.8K actively routed ASes, where the ground truth for the number of actively routed ASes in the Internet in any given week is around 43K [3] and varies slightly with the used BGP dataset.

Lastly, to examine the visibility that this IXP has into the more commercial-oriented Internet, we next use the Web server-related component of the IXP's peering traffic (see Section 2.2.2). Table 1 shows that this IXP "sees" server-related traffic from some 1.5M IPs that can be unambiguously identified as Web server IPs. Unfortunately, we are not aware of any numbers that can be reliably considered as ground truth of all server IPs in the Internet in any given week. Even worse, available white papers or reports that purportedly provide this information are typically very cavalier about their definition of what they consider as "Web server" and hence cannot be taken at face value [40, 50].

To indirectly assess how the roughly 1.5M Web server IPs seen at this IXP stack up against the unknown number of Web server IPs Internet-wide, we use an essentially orthogonal dataset, namely the HTTP and DNS logs from a large European Tier-1 ISP that does not exchange traffic over the public switching infrastructure of our IXP. Applying the method as described in Section 2, we extract the Web server IPs from this ISP dataset and find that of the total number of server IPs that are "seen" by this ISP, only some 45K are not seen at the IXP. Importantly, for the server IPs seen both at the IXP and the ISP, those we identified as server IPs using the IXP-internal data are confirmed to be indeed server IPs when relying on the more detailed ISP dataset. In any case, mapping the 1.5M server IPs from the IXP to prefixes, ASes, and countries shows that this IXP "sees" server-traffic from some 17% of all actively routed prefixes, from about 50% of all actively routed ASes, and from about 80% of all the countries in the world.

3.2 On the IXP's dual role

Visuals such as Figure 3 illustrate that by using this IXP as a vantage point, we are able to see peering traffic from every country and corner of the world or from almost every AS and prefix that is publicly routed. However, such figures do not show whether or not certain countries or corners and ASes or prefixes are better visible than

	rank	All IPs Country	Server IPs Country	All IPs Network	Server IPs Network
IPs	1	US	DE	Chinanet	Akamai
	2	DE	US	Vodafone/DE	1&1
	3	CN	RU	Free SAS	OVH
	4	RU	FR	Turk Telekom	Softlayer
	5	IT	GB	Telecom Italia	ThePlanet
	6	FR	CN	Liberty Global	Chinanet
	7	GB	NL	Vodafone/IT	HostEurope
	8	TR	CZ	Comnet	Strato
	9	UA	IT	Virgin Media	Webazilla
	10	JP	UA	Telefonica/DE	Plusserver
Traffic	1	DE	US	Akamai	Akamai
	2	US	DE	Google	Google
	3	RU	NL	Hetzner	Hetzner
	4	FR	RU	OVH	VKontakte
	5	GB	GB	VKontakte	Leaseweb
	6	CN	EU	Kabel Deu.	Limelight
	7	NL	FR	Leaseweb	OVH
	8	CZ	RO	Vodafone/DE	EdgeCast
	9	IT	UA	Unitymedia	Link11
	10	UA	CZ	Kyivstar	Kartina

Table 2: Top 10 contributors—week 45

		Member AS $A(L)$	Distance 1 $A(M)$	Distance > 1 $A(G)$
Peering Traffic	IPs	42.3%	45.0%	12.7%
	Prefixes	10.1%	34.1%	55.8%
	ASes	1.0%	48.9%	50.1%
	Traffic	67.3%	28.4%	4.3%
Server Traffic	IPs	52.9%	41.2%	5.9%
	Prefixes	17.2%	61.9%	20.9%
	ASes	2.2%	61.5%	36.3%
	Traffic	82.6%	17.35%	0.05%

Table 3: IXP as local yet global player—week 45

others in the sense that they are responsible for more traffic that is exchanged over the public switching fabric of the IXP. In particular, we would like to know whether the importance of the local role that this IXP plays for the larger geographic region within which it is situated is more or less recovered when considering the peering or server-related traffic that the IPs or server IPs are responsible for, respectively. To this end, we show in Table 2 the top-10 countries in terms of percentage of IP addresses (and associated traffic) and percentage of server IPs (and associated traffic). In addition, we show the top-10 networks. While the role of the IXP for the European region becomes more dominant when we change from peering to server-related traffic, there are still prominent signs of the IXP's global role, even with respect to the commercial Internet, and they reflect the relative importance of this IXP for countries such as USA, Russia, and China or ASes such as 20940 (Akamai), 15169 (Google), and 47541 (VKontakte).

For a somewhat simplified illustration of the IXP's dual role as a local as well as global player, we divide the set of all actively routed ASes into three disjoint sets, $A(L)$, $A(M)$, and $A(G)$. $A(L)$ consists of the member ASes of the IXP; $A(M)$ consists of all ASes that are distance 1 (measured in AS-hops) from a member AS; and $A(G)$ is the complement of $A(L) \cup A(M)$ and contains those ASes that are distance 2 or more from the member ASes. Intuitively, the set $A(L)$ captures the importance of the local role of the IXP, whereas the set $A(G)$ is more a reflection of the IXP's global role, with A(M) covering some middle ground. Table 3 shows the breakdown of the IPs, prefixes, and ASes for peering traffic and Web server-related traffic, respectively, for the three sets. It basically confirms our above observation that there is a general trend towards the set $A(L)$ as we move from IPs and the peering traffic they are responsible for to server IPs and their traffic. Note, while the relative importance of the IXP's local role over its global role with respect to the commercial Internet (i.e., server-related traffic) makes economic sense and is well-captured by this cartoon picture, in reality, there is potentially significant overlap between the sets $A(L)$, $A(M)$, and $A(G)$, e.g., due to remote peerings, IXP resellers, and non-European networks joining the IXP for purely economic reasons. But this is unlikely to invalidate our basic findings concerning the IXP's dual role.

3.3 On the IXP's "blind spots"

While the IXP "sees" traffic from much of the Internet, taking measurements exclusively at this single vantage point can tell us only so much about the network as a whole or its individual constituents. Hence, knowing what we can discern about the network with what sort of accuracy is as important as understanding what we cannot discern about it, and why.

We show in Section 3.1 how the use of an essentially orthogonal IXP-external dataset (i.e., the HTTP and DNS logs from the large European Tier-1 ISP) enables us to indirectly assess how the approximately 1.5M server IPs seen at the IXP in a given week compare to the unknown number of server IPs network-wide. In the following, we discuss additional examples where the use of IXP-external data, either in the form publicly available measurements, active or passive measurements, or proprietary information, enables us to check, validate, or refine what we can say with certainty when relying solely on IXP measurements.

To examine in more detail how the approximately 1.5M server IPs seen at the IXP in a given week compare to all server IPs in the Internet, we now use a more extensive combination of IXP-external measurements. To start, using the list of the top-1M Web sites available from `www.alexa.com` and based on the URIs retrieved from the limited payload part of the sampled frames at the IXP, we recover about 20% of all the second-level domains on Alexa's top-1M list of sites; this percentage increases to 63% if we consider only the top-10K list and to 80% for the top-1K. Note that many hostnames on these lists are dynamic and/or ephemeral. Next, to assess how many additional server IPs we can identify using the approximately 80% of domains we cannot recover using the URIs seen at the IXP, we rely on active measurements in the form of DNS queries to those uncovered domains using our set of 25K DNS resolvers across 12K ASes (see Section 2.3). From this pool of resolvers, we assign 100 randomly-selected resolvers to each URI. This results in approximately 600K server IPs, of which more then 360K are already seen at the IXP and identified as servers.

To provide insight into the remaining 240K server IPs that are not seen as a server at the IXP, we classify them into four distinct categories. First, there are servers of CDNs that are hosted inside an AS and serve exclusively clients in that AS ("private clusters"). These servers reply only to resolvers of that AS for content that is delivered by the global footprint of those CDNs. Traffic to these servers should not be observable at the IXP as it should stay internal to the AS. Second, there are servers of CDNs or cloud/hosting providers that are located geographically far away from the IXP. If these networks have a global footprint and distribute content in a region-aware manner, it is unlikely that these server IPs are seen at the IXP. The third group includes servers that some ASes operate for the sole purpose of handling invalid URIs. Finally, the last category contains those servers of small organizations and/or universities in parts of the world that are geographically far away from the IXP. These IPs are typically not visible at the IXP. In terms of importance, the first two categories account for more than 40% of the 240K servers not seen at the IXP.

For a concrete example for illustrating "what we know we don't know", we consider Akamai. In our week-long IXP dataset, we observe some 28K server IPs for Akamai in 278 ASes (for details, see Section 5). However, Akamai publicly states that it operates some 100K servers in more than 1K ASes [15]. The reasons why we cannot see this ground truth relying solely on our IXP-internal data are twofold and mentioned above. First Akamai is known to operate "private clusters" in many third-party networks which are generally not visible outside those ASes and therefore cannot be detected at the IXP. Second, we cannot expect to uncover Akamai's footprint in regions that are geographically far away from the IXP, mainly because Akamai uses sophisticated mechanisms to localize traffic [42, 46]. Akamai's large footprint makes discovering all of its servers difficult, but by performing our own diligently chosen IXP-external active measurements [39] that utilize the URIs collected in the IXP and the open resolvers discussed in Section 2.3, we were able to discover about 100K servers in 700 ASes. Thus, even for a challenging case like Akamai, knowing what our IXP-internal data can and cannot tell us about its many servers and understanding the underlying reasons is feasible.

Regarding our assumption that server-related traffic is a good proxy for the commercial portion of Internet traffic, there are clearly components of this commercial traffic that are not visible at the IXP. For example, the recently introduced hybrid CDNs (e. g., Akamai's NetSession [12]) serve content by servers as well as by end users that have already downloaded part of the content. Since the connections between users are not based on a HTTP/HTTPS server-client architecture but are P2P-based, we may not see them at the IXP. However, while the traffic of these hybrid CDNs is increasing (e. g., the service is mainly used for large files such as software downloads), the overall volume is still very low [31].

Lastly, by the very definition of an IXP, any traffic that does not pass through the IXP via its public-facing switching infrastructure remains entirely invisible to us. For example, this includes all traffic that traverses the IXP over private peering links. IXPs keep the private peering infrastructure separate from its public peering platform, and we are not aware of any kind of estimates of the amount of private peering traffic handled by the IXPs.

Summary: By analyzing in detail the traffic that traverses the physical infrastructure of one of the largest IXPs in Europe, we provide evidence that the large European IXPs such as AMS-IX, DE-CIX, and LINX represent global Internet vantage points that "see" week-in and week-out traffic from hundreds of millions of IPs, from almost all routed prefixes and from all routed ASes, and from essentially every country around the world. We also illustrate these IXPs' dual role as a global and a local player within the Internet's ecosystem and caution that despite their outstanding visibility into the Internet, their use as global Internet vantage points comes with caveats (e. g., having "blind spots").

4. STABLE YET CHANGING

In this section, we report on a longitudinal analysis that covers 17 consecutive weeks and describes what using our large IXP as a vantage point through time enables us to say about the network as whole, about some of its constituents, and about the traffic that these constituents are responsible for.

4.1 Stability in the face of constant growth

Publicly available data shows that during 2012, this IXP has experienced significant growth, increasing the number of member ASes by 75 and seeing the average daily traffic volume grow by 0.1%. In terms of absolute numbers, we see in week 35 a total of 443 IXP member ASes sending an average daily traffic volume of 11.9 PB over the IXP's public-facing switching infrastructure. By week 51, the member count stood at 457, and the average traffic volume went up to 14.5 PB/day. For what follows, it is important to note that these newly added member ASes are typically regional and local ISPs or organizations and small companies outside of central Europe for which membership at this IXP makes economic sense. To contrast, all the major content providers, CDNs, Web hosting companies, eyeball ASes, and Tier-1 ISPs have been members at this IXP for some time, but may have seen upgrades to higher port speeds since the time they joined.

Given our interest in the commercial Internet and knowing (see Section 2) that the server-related traffic is more than 70% of the peering traffic seen at the IXP, we focus in the rest of this paper on the server-related portion of the IXP traffic. The initial set of findings from our longitudinal analysis paints an intriguingly stable picture of the commercial Internet as seen from our vantage point. In particular, analyzing in detail each of the 17 weekly snapshots shows that during every week, we see server-related traffic at this IXP from about 20K (i. e., about half of all) actively routed ASes, some 75K or approximately 15% of all actively routed prefixes, and from a pool of server IPs whose absolute size changes only so slightly but tends to increase in the long term.

This last property is illustrated in Figure 4(a) when focusing only on the absolute heights of the different bars that represent the total number of server IPs seen in a given week. When considering the full version of this figure, including the within-bar details, Figure 4(a) visualizes the weekly churn that is inherent in the server IPs seen at the IXPs. To explain, the first bar in Figure 4(a) shows the approximately 1.4M unique server IPs that we see in week 35. The next bar shows that same quantity for week 36, but splits it into two pieces. While the lower (white) piece reflects the portion of all week 36 server IPs that were already seen during week 35, the upper (black) piece represents the set of server IPs that were seen for the first time during week 36. Starting with week 37, we show for each week $n \in \{37, 38, \ldots, 51\}$ snapshot a bar that has three pieces stacked on top of one another. While the first (bottom, white) piece represents the server IPs that were seen at the IXP in each one of the week k snapshot ($k = 35, 36, \ldots, n$), the second (grey-shaded) piece shows the server IPs that were seen at the IXP in at least one previous week k snapshot ($k = 35, 36, \ldots, n-1$), but not in all; the third (top black) piece represents all server IPs that were seen at the IXP for the first time in week n.

A key take-away from Figure 4(a) is that there is a sizable pool of server IPs that is seen at the IXP during each and every week throughout the 17-week long measurement period. In fact, this stable portion of server IPs that is seen at the IXP week-in and week-out is about 30% as can be seen by looking at the bottom (white) portion of the week 51 bar. Instead of requiring for a server IP to be seen in each and every week, we also consider a more relaxed notion of stability called recurrence. This recurrent pool of server IPs consists of all server IPs that, by week 51, have been seen at the IXP during at least one previous week (but not in each and every previous week), is represented by the grey-shaded portion of the week 51 bar, and consists of about 60% of all server IPs seen in

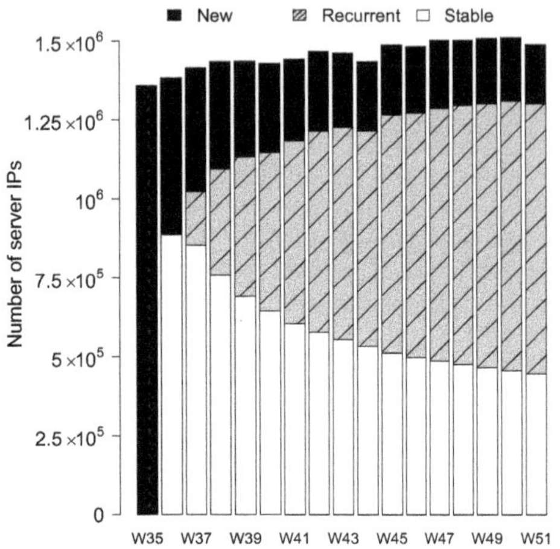

(a) Churn of server IPs

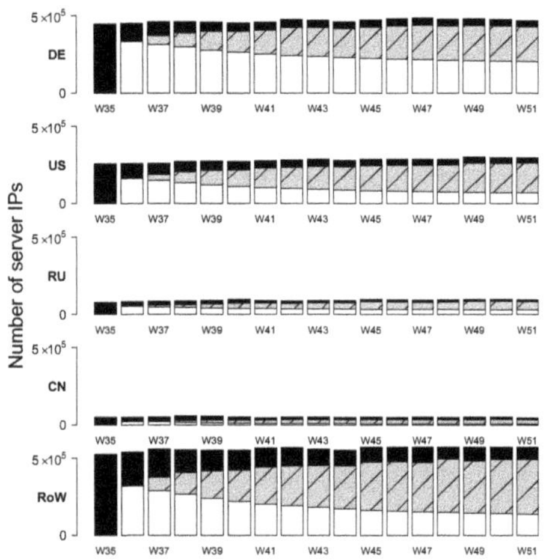

(b) Churn of server IPs per region

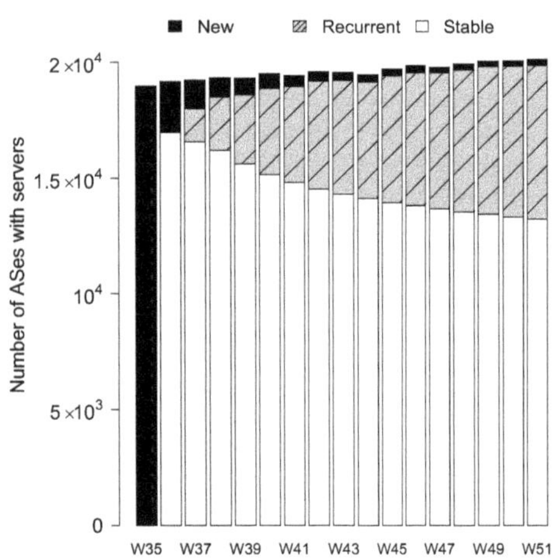

(c) Churn of ASes with servers

Figure 4: Churn of server IPs and ASes that host servers—weeks 35-51

week 51. Note that the number of server IPs seen for the first time in week n (top black portion) decreases over time and makes up just about 10% of all server IPs seen in week 51.

To look in more detail at the stable and recurrent pools of server IPs and examine their churn or evolution during the 17-week long measurement period, we rely on the GeoLite Country database [44] to geo-locate the server IPs to the country level and group them by geographic "region" as follows: DE, US, RU, CN, RoW (rest of world). Figure 4(b) is similar to Figure 4(a), but shows for each week the portions of IPs for each of these five regions and visualizes the make-up of these server IPs in the same way as we did in Figure 4(a). Note that the shown region-specific stable portions in week 51 add up to the 30% number observed in Figure 4(a), and similarly for the region-specific recurrent portions in week 51 (their sum adds up to the roughly 60% portion of the recurrent pool shown in Figure 4(a)). Interestingly, while the stable pool for DE is consistently about half of the overall stable pool of server IPs seen at the IXP, that pool is vanishing small for CN, slightly larger for RU. This is yet another indication of the important role that this IXP plays for the European part of the Internet.

An even more intriguing aspect of stability is seen when we consider the server-related traffic that the server IPs that we see at the IXP are responsible for. For one, we find that the stable pool of server IPs is consistently contributing more than 60% of the server-related traffic. That is, of the server IPs that this IXP "sees" on a weekly basis, more than 30% of them are not only seen week after week, but they are also responsible for most of the server-related traffic that traverses the IXP each week. When considering the weekly recurrent pools of server IP (grey-shaded segments in Figure 4(a)), their traffic portions keep increasing, but only to less than 30% of all server traffic. To examine the make-up of the server-related traffic attributed to the stable and recurrent pools of server IPs, respectively, Figure 5 shows for each week n three bars, each with five segments corresponding to the five regions considered earlier. The first bar is for the server-related traffic portion of all peering traffic that all server IPs see at the IXP in week n; the second bar reflects the server-related traffic portion in week n attributed to the recurrent pool of server IPs in that week, while the third bar shows the server-related traffic portion in week n that the stable pool of server IPs is responsible for. From Figure 5, we see that while the stable and recurrent pools of server IPs from China are basically invisible at the IXP in terms of their traffic, both US and Russia have the property that the stable pool of server IPs is responsible for much all the server-related traffic seen from those regions at the IXP.

In addition to examining the churn and evolution of the server IPs seen at the IXP, it is also instructive to study the temporal behavior of the subnets and ASes that the encountered server IPs map into. To illustrate, we only consider the ASes and show in Figure 4(c) for ASes what we depicted in Figure 4(b) for server IPs. The key difference between server IPs and ASes is that the stable pool of ASes represented by the white portion of the week 51 bar is about 70% compared to the 30% for the stable pool of server IPs. Thus, a majority of ASes with server IPs is seen at the IXP during each and every week, and the number of ASes that are seen for the first time becomes miniscule over time. In summary, the stable pool of server IPs (about 1/3 of all server IPs seen at the IXP) gives rise to a stable pool of ASes (about 2/3 of all ASes seen at the IXP and have server IPs) and is responsible for much of the server-related traffic seen at the IXP.

4.2 Changes in face of significant stability

One benefit of observing a significant amount of stability with respect to the server-related portion of the overall peering traffic seen at the IXP is that any weekly snapshot provides more or less the same information. At the same time, subsequent weekly snap-

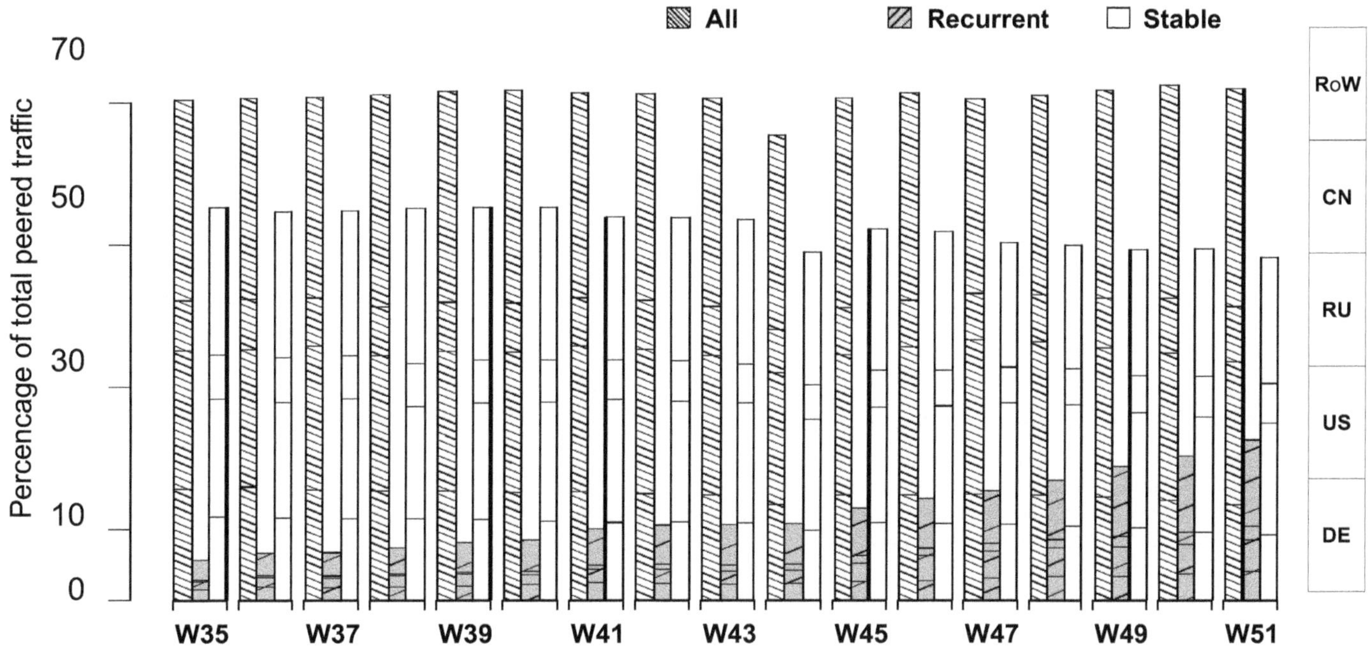

Figure 5: Churn of server traffic by region—weeks 35-51

shots that differ noticeably may be an indication of some change. Next, we briefly discuss a few examples of such changes that we can discern about the Internet as a whole and some of its individual constituents when we have the luxury to observe and measure the network at this IXP for a number of consecutive weeks.

The first example is motivated primarily by our ability described in Section 2.2.2 to specifically look for and identify HTTPS server IPs, but also by anecdotal evidence or company blogs [21, 22] that suggest that due to widespread security and privacy concerns, the use of HTTPS is steadily increasing. To examine this purported increase, we extract for each weekly snapshot all HTTPS server IPs and the traffic that they contribute. When comparing for each week the number of HTTPS server IPs relative to all server IPs seen in that week and the weekly traffic associated with HTTPS server IPs relative to all peering traffic, we indeed observe a small, yet steady increase, which confirms that the Internet landscape is gradually changing as far as the use of HTTPS is concerned.

For a different kind of example for using our IXP vantage point, we are interested in tracking the recently announced expansion of Netflix using Amazon's EC2 cloud service [10] into a number of Scandinavian countries [23]. To this end, we relied on publicly available data to obtain Amazon EC2's data center locations [16] and the corresponding IP ranges [17]. We then mined our 17 weeks worth of IXP data and observed for weeks 49, 50, and 51 a pronounced increase in the number of server IPs at Amazon EC2's Ireland location, the only data center of Amazon EC2 in Europe. This was accompanied by a significant (but still small in absolute terms) increase in Amazon EC2's traffic. All this suggests that it may be interesting to watch this traffic in the future, especially if the observed changes are in any way related to Netflix becoming available in Northern Europe towards the end of 2012.

Yet another example concerns the detection of regional or national events at this IXP. For example, considering in more detail week 44, which shows up as a clear dip in, say, Figure 4(a), we notice that this week coincides with Hurricane Sandy that had a major impact on the US East Coast region. To examine its impact, we use the IXP vantage point to discern this natural disaster from traffic that we see at the IXP from a particular Internet constituent, a major cloud provider. Using publicly available information about the cloud platform's data centers and corresponding IP ranges, we look in our data for the corresponding server IPs and find a total of about 14K. A detailed breakdown by data center location for weeks 43-45 shows a drastic reduction in the number of server IPs seen at the IXP from the US East Coast region, indicating that the platform of this major cloud provider faced serious problems in week 44, with traffic dropping close to zero. These problems made the news, and the example highlights how a geographical distant event such as a hurricane can be discerned from traffic measurements taken at this geographically distant IXP.

Lastly, we also mention that an IXP is an ideal location to monitor new players such as "resellers". Resellers are IXP member ASes, and their main business is to provide and facilitate access to the IXP for smaller companies that are typically far away geographically from the IXP. For IXPs, the emergence of resellers is beneficial as they extend the reach of the IXP into geographically distant regions and thereby the potential membership base. For example, for a particular reseller at our IXP, we observed a doubling of the server IPs from 50K to 100K in four months, suggesting that this reseller has been quite successful in attracting new networks with significant server-based infrastructures as its customers.

Summary: When concentrating on the Web server-related portion of the IXP traffic and performing a longitudinal analysis over a 17-week long period, we observe significant stability – of all the server IPs for which traffic is observed at the IXP during this 17-week period, some 30% are seen at the IXP week-in and week-out and are responsible for around 60% of all server-related traffic in each and every week. At the same time, the traffic seen at the IXP does exhibit differences from one week to the next, and we illustrate with some examples what different types of changes enable us to say about the network as a whole or some of its individual constituents. In this sense, the traffic seen at these global Internet vantage points can be used as complementary source of information for recent efforts analyzing Internet events such as large-scale outages due to censorship [32], natural disasters [29], etc.

5. BEYOND THE AS-LEVEL VIEW

To illustrate the benefits and new opportunities for Internet measurements that arise from being able to use our IXP as a vantage point with very good visibility into the Internet, we describe in this section an approach for identifying server-based network infrastructures and classifying them by ownership. In the process, we report on a clear trend towards more heterogeneous networks and network interconnections, provide concrete examples, and discuss why and how this observed network heterogenization requires moving beyond the traditional AS-level view of the Internet.

5.1 Alternative grouping of server IPs

To this point, we have followed a very traditional approach for looking at our IXP data in the sense that we measured the IXP's visibility into the Internet in terms of the number of actively routed ASes or subnets seen at the IXP. However, there exist Internet players (e. g., CDN77, a recently launched low-cost no-commitment CDN; Rapidshare, a one-click hosting service; or certain meta-hosters that utilize multiple hosters) that are not ASes in the sense that they do not have an assigned ASN. Thus, as far as the traditional AS-level view of the Internet is concerned, these players are invisible, and the traffic that they are responsible for goes unnoticed, or worse misattributed to other Internet players. Yet, being commercial entities, these companies actively advertise their services, and in the process often publish the locations and IP addresses of their servers. This then suggests an alternative approach to assessing the IXP's ability to "see" the Internet as a whole—group servers according to the organization or company that has the administrative control over the servers and is responsible for distributing the content. While this approach is easy and works to perfection for companies like CDN77 that publish all their server IPs, the question is what to do if the server IPs are not known.

Accordingly, our primary goal is to start with the server IPs seen at the IXP and cluster them so that the servers in one and the same cluster are provably under the administrative control of the same organization or company. To this end, we rely in parts on methods described by Plonka et al. [48] for traffic and host profiling, Bermudez et al. [20] for discerning content and services, and Ager et al. [14] for inferring hosting infrastructures from the content they deliver. We also take advantage of different sets of meta-data obtained from assorted active measurement efforts or available by other means as discussed in Section 2.4. Recall that this meta-data includes for every server IP seen in the IXP data the corresponding URIs, the DNS information from active measurements, and, where available, the list of X.509 certificates retrieved via active measurements. In the rest of this section the reported numbers are for week 45.

The clustering proceeds in three steps. First, we focus on those server IPs for which we have a SOA resource record and consider a first category of clusters that have the property that all server IPs assigned to a given cluster have the IP and the content managed by the same authority. We identify those clusters by grouping all server IPs where the SOA of the hostname and the authority of the URI lead to the same entry. Prominent organizations that fall into this first category are Amazon and big players like Akamai and Google when they are located in their own ASes or when they are in third-party ASes but have assigned names to their own servers. 78.7 % of all our server IPs are clustered in this first step.

In a second step, we consider clusters with the property that for the server IPs in a given cluster, most of the server IPs and most of the content are managed by the same authority. This can happen if the SOA is outsourced (e. g., to a third-party DNS provider) and is common property among hosters and domains served by virtual servers. In these cases, to group server IPs, we rely on a majority vote among the SOA resource records, where the majority vote is by (i) the number of IPs and (ii) the size of the network footprint. This heuristic enables us to group some server IPs together with organizations inferred in the previous step and also applies to meta-hosters such as Hostica. 17.4 % of all our server IPs are clustered in this second step. Lastly, for the remaining 3.9 % of server IPs that have been seen in our IXP data and have not yet been clustered, we only have partial SOA information. This situation is quite common for parts of the server infrastructure of some large content providers and CDNs such as Akamai that have servers deployed deep inside ISPs. In this case, we apply the same heuristic as in the second step, but only rely on the available subset of information.

To validate our clustering that results from this three-step process, we manually compare the results by (1) checking against the coverage of the public IP ranges that some organizations advertise (see Section 4.2), (2) utilizing the information of certificates that point to applications and services, and (3) actively downloading either the front page (e. g., in the case of Google, it is always the search engine front page) or requested content that is delivered by a CDN (e. g., in the case of Akamai, any content is delivered by any of its servers [53]). Our method manages to correctly identify and group the servers of organizations with a small false-positive rate of less than 3%. Moreover, we observe that the false-positive rate decreases with increasing size of the network footprint. However, there are false-negatives in the sense that our methodology misses some servers due to the "blind spots" discussed in Section 3.3.

5.2 New reality (I): ASes are heterogeneous

Equipped with an approach for grouping server IPs by organizations, we examine next to what extent this grouping is orthogonal to the prevailing AS-level view of the Internet. The issues are succinctly illustrated in Figure 6(a) where we augment the traditional AS-level view (i. e., a number of different ASes exchanging traffic over (public) peering links at an IXP) with new features in the form of AS-internal details (i. e., the third-party servers that the ASes host). Note that while the traditional view that makes a tacit homogeneity assumption by abstracting away any AS-internal details may have been an adequate model for understanding some aspects of the Internet and the traffic it carries at some point in the past, things have changed, and we assert that the cartoon picture in Figure 6(a) captures more accurately the current Internet reality; that is, a trend towards distributed network infrastructures that are deployed and operated by today's commercial Internet players.

To quantify how much closer the cartoon Figure 6(a) is to reality than the traditional AS-level view, we apply our clustering approach to the 1.5M server IPs seen in our week 45 IXP data and obtain some 21K clusters, henceforth referred to organizations or companies. Among them are the well-known big players like Akamai with 28K active server IPs, Google with 11.5K server IPs, and several large hosters, each with more than 50K server IPs (e. g., AS92572 with 90K+ server IPs; AS56740 and AS50099, both with more than 50K server IPs). Indeed, of the 21K identified organizations, a total of 143 organizations are associated with more than 1000 server IPs and more than 6K organizations have more than 10 servers IPs. For the latter, Figure 6(b) shows a scatter plot of the number of server IPs per organization vs. the number of ASes that they cover. More precisely, every dot in the plot is an organization, and for a given organization, we show the number of its server IPs (x-axis) and the number of ASes that host servers from

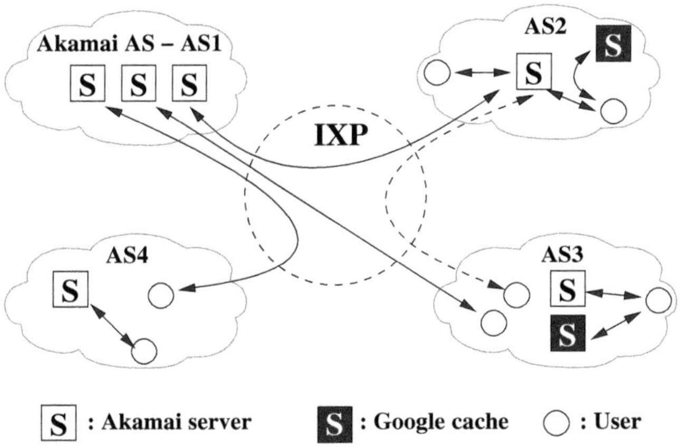

(a) Heterogeneity of ASes and AS links

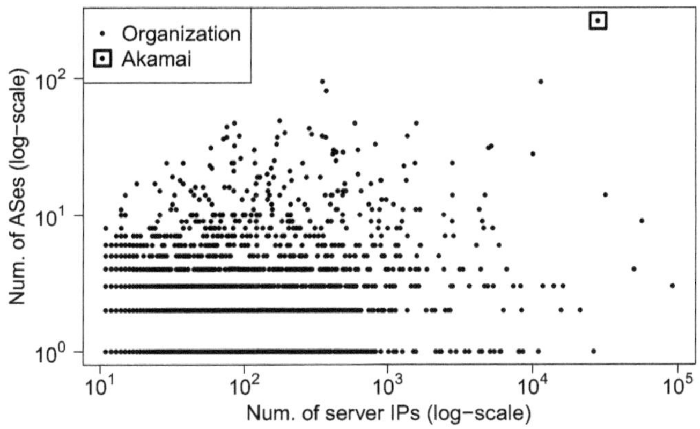

(b) Scatter plot of number of server IPs vs. the number of ASes per organization

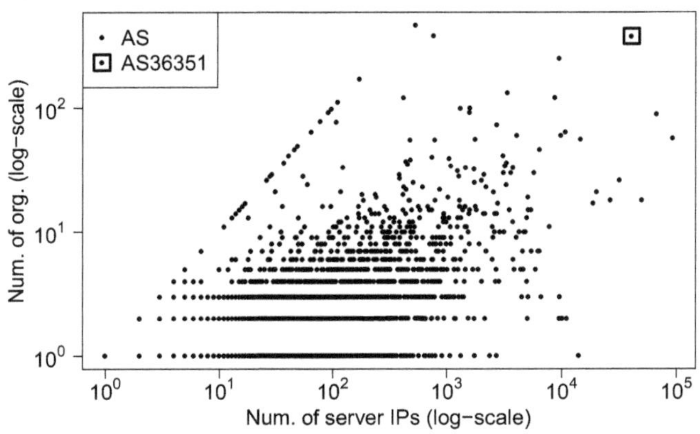

(c) Scatter plot of number of organizations vs. the number of server IPs for each AS

Figure 6: Heterogeneity of organizations and ASes

that organization (y-axis).[3] We observe that operating a highly diverse infrastructure is commonplace in today's Internet and is not limited to only the Internet's biggest players, but reporting on the bewildering array of scenarios we encountered when examining the extent of the different organizations and the networks they partner with is beyond the scope of this paper.

The realization that many organizations operate a server infrastructure that is spread across many ASes implies that the complementary view must be equally bewildering in terms of diversity or heterogeneity. This view is captured in Figure 6(a) by focusing on, say AS1, and examining how many third-party networks host some of their servers inside that AS. Thus, yet another way to quantify how much closer that cartoon figure is to reality than the traditional AS-level view with its implicit homogeneity assumption concerning the administrative authority of servers hosted within an AS is shown in Figure 6(c). Each dot in this figure represents an AS, and the number of organizations a given AS hosts is given on the y-axis while the number of identified server IPs is shown on the x-axis. As before, the figure only shows organizations with more than 10 servers. We observe that many ASes host a sizable number of server IPs that belong to many organizations; there are more than 500 ASes that host servers from more than five organizations, and more than 200 ASes that support more than 10 organizations.

Indeed, this observation is again fully consistent with public announcements [1, 6] and content providers' efforts [5] to install their own brand of single-purpose CDNs inside various ISPs. The end effect of such developments is a clear trend towards more heterogeneous eyeball ISP networks by virtue of such ASes hosting more servers from an increasing number of interested third-party networks. In view of similar announcements from key companies such as Google [51, 25, 34], Amazon [2], or Facebook [4], the challenges of studying, leave alone controlling, such increasingly intertwined networks and traffic are quickly becoming daunting. As an example, consider a large Web hosting company (AS36351), for which we identified more than 40K server IPs belonging to a total more than 350 different organizations (highlighted in Figure 6(c) with a square).

5.3 New reality (II): Links are heterogeneous

In Section 5.2, we show that organizations take advantage of network diversity and purposefully spread their infrastructure across multiple networks. This development creates very fluid and often transparent network boundaries, which in turn causes havoc when trying to attribute the right traffic to the right network. The issues are illustrated in the cartoon Figure 7(a). The figure shows the traditional AS-level perspective, whereby Akamai is a member AS (AS1) of this IXP, and so are a generic AS3 and another generic (non-Akamai) AS2, and the Akamai AS peers at this IXP with AS3 which, in turn, peers also with AS2. This traditional AS perspective is enriched with member-specific details that specify that there is an Akamai server behind/inside (non-Akamai) AS2 and behind/inside the Akamai AS. Note that in terms of the traditional AS-level view, the question of how much Akamai traffic is seen at this IXP is clear-cut and can be simply answered by measuring the traffic on the peering link between AS3 and the Akamai AS. However, when accounting for the fact that there is an Akamai server behind/inside the non-Akamai member AS2, answering that same question becomes more involved. It requires measuring the traffic on the (Akamai) peering link between AS3 and the Akamai AS as well as accounting for the Akamai traffic on the (non-Akamai) peering link between AS3 and (non-Akamai) AS2.

Clearly, for accurately attributing traffic to the responsible parties in today's network, the trend towards network heterogenization creates problems for the traditional AS-level view of the Internet. To illustrate the extent of these problems, we show in Figure 7(b) what we observe at the IXP for Akamai. Recall that Aka-

[3] While in a few isolated cases, the ASes that host servers from a given organization are part of that organization (e. g., see [24]), hand-checking the 143 organizations with more than 1000 servers confirmed that in almost all cases, these ASes are genuine third-party networks that are run and operated independently from the organization whose servers they host.

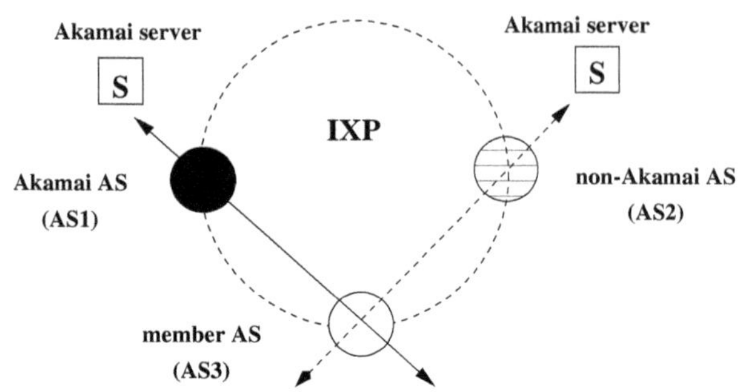

(a) Observing traffic from a direct and a non direct link of Akamai

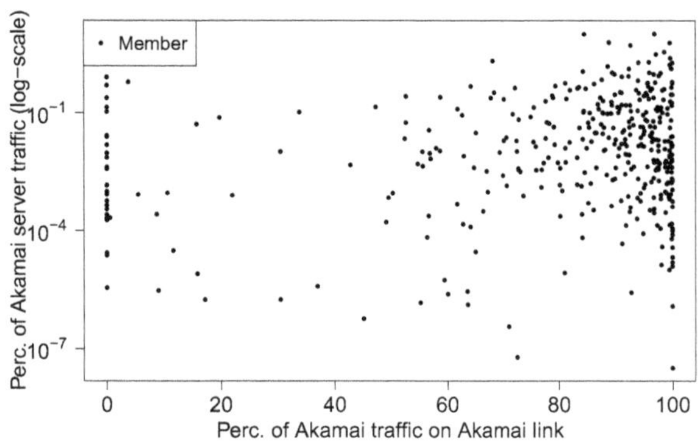

(b) Perc. of Akamai traffic vs. perc. of Akamai traffic via direct link

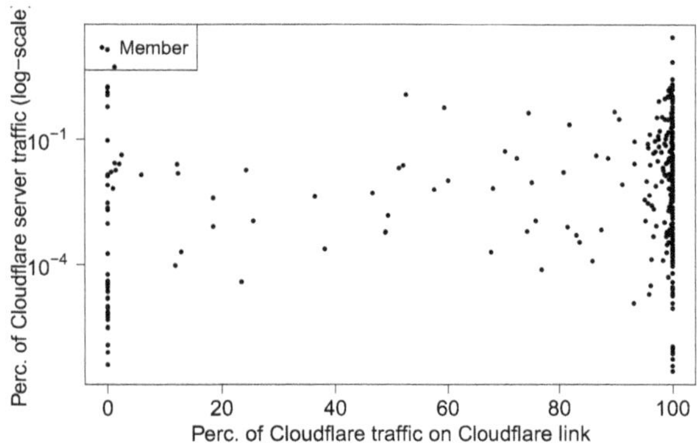

(c) Perc. of CloudFlare traffic vs. perc. of CloudFlare traffic via direct link

Figure 7: AS link heterogeneity: Traffic via direct member link relative to other member links.

mai (AS20940) is a member of the IXP and peers with some 400 other member ASes. In the traditional view, accounting for Akamai traffic traversing the IXP simply means capturing the traffic on all the peering links between Akamai and those member ASes. Unfortunately, this simple view is no longer reflecting reality when Akamai servers are hosted inside or "behind" (non-Akamai) IXP member ASes. To capture this aspect, Figure 7(b) shows for each IXP member that peers with Akamai (indicated by a dot) the percentage of Akamai traffic on the direct peering link to Akamai (x-axis) vs. the percentage of total Akamai-server traffic for this member AS (y-axis). Under the traditional assumption, all dots would be stacked up at x=100, reflecting the fact that to account for Akamai-related traffic, all that is needed is to measure the Akamai peering links. However, with Akamai servers being massively deployed in third-party networks, including many of the other member ASes of the IXP, we observe that some members get all their Akamai-related traffic from ASes other than the (member) Akamai AS (x=0), even when that traffic is sizable (y>>0). Moreover, the scattering of dots across Figure 7(b) succinctly captures the diverse spread of traffic across the direct peering link vs. the other member links. In terms of numbers, Akamai sends 11.1% of its traffic not via its peering links with the member AS. Put differently, traffic from more than 15K out of the 28K Akamai servers that we identified in our IXP data is seen at the IXP via non-IXP member links to Akamai. The same holds true for other major CDNs but also for relatively new players such as CloudFlare. Figure 7(c) shows the same kind of plot as Figure 7(b) for CloudFlare. It demonstrates that despite adhering to very different business models (i. e., Akamai deploys servers inside ISPs vs. CloudFlare operates its own data centers), the two CDNs have similar usage patters as far as their peering links are concerned.

Looking beyond Akamai, we observe that different services from the same organization use their servers differently resulting in different usage patterns of the peering links. For example, for Amazon CloudFront, Amazon's "CDN part", almost all traffic is send via the IXP's Amazon links. However, for Amazon EC2, the "cloud part", a sizable fraction comes via other IXP peering links. We also noticed that for most cases where we see the use of the non-IXP member links, the percentage of traffic in those links increases during peak times. This may be due to reasons such as load balancing, performance improvement, or cost savings. Lastly, how our view of the usage of the IXP's public peering links is impacted by private peerings that may be in place between member ASes of the IXP remains unexplored.

Summary: To illustrate the kind of benefits that arise from having access to a global Internet vantage point in the form or our large European IXP, we confirm a feature of today's Internet that is well-known among experts but remains largely under-reported in the networking research literature—a tendency of certain Internet players to either host servers from third-party networks within their own network infrastructures or deploy their own servers in strategically-chosen third-party ASes. More importantly, we present a methodology for discovering an organization's servers, whether they are deployed within the organization's own AS (or ASes) or inside some third-party network's infrastructure, and use it to systematically assess the *extent* of this network heterogenization and study its impact on the usage of peering links at IXPs by these increasingly more heterogeneous member ASes. However, we want to stress that our AS-links usage-related findings are not IXP-specific (i. e., public peering links), but apply to any AS-link in the Internet, pointing towards serious challenges when trying to attribute the right traffic to the right party.

6. DISCUSSION AND CAVEATS

We are not the first to try and uncover the footprints of the infrastructures of commercial Internet players. One group of prior studies targets specific Internet companies (e. g., Akamai [54, 39, 52], Youtube [11, 37, 26], Netflix [10]), or one click hosters [19]). Other work is more concerned with inferring Web hosting infrastructures by relying on content only [14]. Our approach differs from these earlier works. For one, we rely on a unique vantage point in the form of one of the largest European IXPs to supply us with a weekly pool of some 230M IPs from which we diligently extract some 1.5M server IPs. Next, we rely exclusively on publicly available data[4] to group these servers by organizations that have

[4]Note that our use of the set of DNS resolvers from a large commercial CDN in Section 2.3 is a shortcut. A similar list could also

the administrative authority over them and are responsible for their content. In doing so, we are inspired by earlier studies such as [20, 48]. Lastly, the methodology we develop for grouping servers by their organization is general in the sense that it applies equally well to content providers, CDNs, hosting companies, cloud infrastructure providers, eyeball ASes, or other Internet players.

The difference in perspective between the more traditional AS-level view of the Internet and our perspective that centers around organizations and companies and their heterogeneously deployed server-based infrastructure becomes evident when comparing our approach to the recent work by Cai et al. [24] on mapping ASes to organizations. For one, the starting point for [24] is the traditional AS-level view of the Internet, and two ASes are grouped into two different organizations if neither of the organizations is a subsidiary of the other (i. e., majority-owned by the other). While such a top-down ownership-based grouping of ASes captures one aspect of how ASes are inter-related, it is oblivious to how network infrastructures get used and deployed in today's Internet. In particular, while the method described in [24] may succeed in clustering all Akamai-owned ASes under the umbrella organization Akamai, the publicly known fact that Akamai has more than 100K servers deployed in hundreds of different third-party non-Akamai ASes [46] cannot be accounted for at all by that approach.

Our work relies critically on the sFlow records provided by one of the largest IXPs in Europe, and it can be argued that for many researchers, access to such data cannot be taken for granted. However, it is important to note that some of these largest IXPs in Europe generally welcome collaborations with researchers and are supportive of research efforts that make explicit use of their data (see for instance [18]). Once access to data collected from such unique and powerful vantage points is established, the opportunities for researchers are plentiful.

After presenting evidence for the kind of visibility into the Internet that comes with using one of these largest European IXPs as a vantage point, we highlight in this paper some of the benefits that arises from having access to such a vantage point. However, despite its impressive capabilities, our IXP and the measurements it collects can only tell us so much about the network's "state", and many important issues remain concerning our knowledge about what exactly we can and cannot discern about the Internet as whole and its individual constituents. While we have identified a number of "blind spots", much remains to be done in terms of identifying and collecting IXP-external information that can be brought to the table for either checking, validating, or refining the findings obtained from the use of IXP-internal data only. The question of how to appropriately fuse selective IXP-external data with IXP-internal measurements to obtain a picture of the global network and its individual constituents that is unprecedented in terms of its accuracy, details, and insight looms as an important open research problem.

7. CONCLUSION

This paper contributes to Internet measurements by reporting on the existence of single, well-localized physical locations or vantage points within the Internet infrastructure where one can "see" much of the global Internet. Mining the data collected at one such vantage point reveals a network that teems with heterogeneity whichever way one looks. Given that economic incentives drive many of the main commercial Internet players to either host third-party servers in their own network infrastructures or deploy their own servers, often in massive numbers, in strategically selected (close to the end users) third-party networks, we expect the observed trend towards increasingly more heterogeneous networks and increasingly diverse usage of IXP peering links, in particular, and AS-links, in general, to accelerate, especially in view of the growing importance of cloud providers. As an interesting consequence of more servers being deployed close to the end users, we also expect that IXPs in the future will "see" less end user-to-server traffic but an increasing amount of server-to-server traffic.

In response to this observed heterogeneity, the paper also contributes to Internet topology research by advancing a new mental model for the Internet's ecosystem that accounts for the observed network heterogenization, points towards measurements that reveal and keep track of this ongoing heterogenization process, and is rich and flexible enough to adapt to a constantly changing Internet environment. Doing so only scratches the surface of a new and rich problem space, and our efforts reported in this paper that focus less on the Internet's connectivity structure and more on how traffic flows over this connectivity structure are just a first step towards exploring that space.

---

have been obtained by relying on publicly available data only [52, 54, 39], e. g., via active scanning or from DNS logs.

8. REFERENCES

[1] Akamai and AT&T Forge Global Strategic Alliance to Provide Content Delivery Network Solutions. http://www.akamai.com/html/about/press/releases/2012/press_120612.html.

[2] Amazon CloudFront - Amazon Web Services. http://aws.amazon.com/cloudfront/.

[3] CIDR Report. http://www.cidr-report.org/.

[4] Like Netflix, Facebook is boosting its edge network. http://gigaom.com/2012/06/21/like-netflix-facebook-is-planning-its-own-cdn/.

[5] Netflix Open Connect. https://signup.netflix.com/openconnect.

[6] Orange and Akamai form Content Delivery Strategic Alliance. http://www.akamai.com/html/about/press/releases/2012/press_112012_1.html.

[7] RIPE RIS. http://www.ripe.net/ris/.

[8] Route Views Project, University of Oregon. http://www.routeviews.org/.

[9] Team Cymru. http://www.team-cymru.org/.

[10] V. Adhikari, Y. Guo, F. Hao, M. Varvello, V. Hilt, M. Steiner, and Z.-L. Zhang. Unreeling Netflix: Understanding and Improving multi-CDN Movie Delivery. In *IEEE INFOCOM*, 2012.

[11] V. K. Adhikari, S. Jain, Y. Chen, and Z.-L. Zhang. Vivisecting YouTube: An Active Measurement Study. In *IEEE INFOCOM*, 2012.

[12] P. Aditya, M. Zhao, Y. Lin, A. Haeberlen, P. Druschel, B. Maggs, and B. Wishon. Reliable Client Accounting for Hybrid Content-Distribution Networks. In *NSDI*, 2012.

[13] B. Ager, N. Chatzis, A. Feldmann, N. Sarrar, S. Uhlig, and W. Willinger. Anatomy of a Large European IXP. In *ACM SIGCOMM*, 2012.

[14] B. Ager, W. Mühlbauer, G. Smaragdakis, and S. Uhlig. Web Content Cartography. In *ACM IMC*, 2011.

[15] Akamai. Facts and Figures: Network Deployment. http://www.akamai.com/html/about/facts_figures.html.

[16] Amazon. AWS Dashboard. http://status.aws.amazon.com/.

[17] Amazon. EC2 Public IP ranges. https://forums.aws.amazon.com/ann.jspa?annID=1701.

[18] AMS-IX. AMS-IX hosts BGP-Mux research project. https://www.ams-ix.net/newsitems/82.

[19] D. Antoniades, E. Markatos, and C. Dovrolis. One-click Hosting Services: A File-Sharing Hideout. In *ACM IMC*, 2009.

[20] I. Bermudez, M. Mellia, M. Munafà, R. Keralapura, and A. Nucci. DNS to the Rescue: Discerning Content and Services in a Tangled Web. In *ACM IMC*, 2012.

[21] Facebook blog. A Continued Commitment to Security. http://www.facebook.com/blog/blog.php?post=486790652130.

[22] Google Search Blog. Making Search More Secure. http://googleblog.blogspot.com/2011/10/making-search-more-secure.html.

[23] Netflix Nordics blog. Netflix Launches Today in Sweden, Denmark, Norway, Finland. http://nordicsblog.netflix.com/2012/10/.

[24] X. Cai, J. Heidemann, B. Krishnamurthy, and W. Willinger. Towards an AS-to-Organization Map. In *ACM IMC*, 2010.

[25] M. Calder, X. Fan, Z. Hu, E. Katz-Bassett, J. Heidemann, and R. Govindan. Mapping the Expansion of Google's Serving Infrastructure. In *ACM IMC*, 2013.

[26] M. Cha, H. Kwak, P. Rodriguez, Y. Y. Ahn, and S. Moon. I Tube, You Tube, Everybody Tubes: Analyzing the World's Largest User Generated Content Video System. In *ACM IMC*, 2008.

[27] H. Chang, S. Jamin, Z. M. Mao, and W. Willinger. An Empirical Approach to Modeling Inter-AS Traffic Matrices. In *ACM IMC*, 2005.

[28] N. Chatzis, G. Smaragdakis, and A. Feldmann. On the Importance of Internet eXchange Points for Today's Internet Ecosystem. http://arxiv-web3.library.cornell.edu/abs/1307.5264v2.

[29] K. Cho, C. Pelsser, R. Bush, and Y. Won. The Japan Earthquake: the Impact on Traffic and Routing Observed by a Local ISP. In *In ACM SWID*, 2011.

[30] Cisco. Visual Networking Index (VNI) and Forecast. http://www.cisco.com/en/US/netsol/ns827/networking_solutions_sub_solution.html.

[31] Private communication.

[32] D. Dainotti, C. Squarcella, E. Aben, K.C. Claffy, M. Chiesa, M. Russo, and A. Pescapé. Analysis of Country-Wide Internet Outages Caused by Censorship. In *ACM IMC*, 2011.

[33] J. Erman, A. Gerber, M. Hajiaghayi, D. Pei, and O. Spatscheck. Network-aware Forward Caching. In *WWW*, 2009.

[34] T. Flach, N. Dukkipati, A. Terzis, B. Raghavan, N. Cardwell, Y. Cheng, A. Jain, S. Hao, E. Katz-Bassett, and R. Govindan. Reducing Web Latency: the Virtue of Gentle Aggression. In *ACM SIGCOMM*, 2013.

[35] Mozilla Foundation. Publicsuffix.org. http://publicsuffix.org/.

[36] A. Gerber and R. Doverspike. Traffic Types and Growth in Backbone Networks. In *OFC/NFOEC*, 2011.

[37] P. Gill, M. F. Arlitt, Z. Li, and A. Mahanti. Youtube Traffic Characterization: A View From the Edge. In *ACM IMC*, 2007.

[38] Google. What is 1e100.net? http://support.google.com/bin/answer.py?hl=en&answer=174717.

[39] C. Huang, A. Wang, J. Li, and K. Ross. Measuring and Evaluating Large-scale CDNs. In *ACM IMC*, 2008.

[40] Data Center Knowledge. Who Has the Most Web Servers? http://www.datacenterknowledge.com/archives/2009/05/14/whos-got-the-most-web-servers.

[41] C. Labovitz, S. Iekel-Johnson, D. McPherson, J. Oberheide, and F. Jahanian. Internet Inter-Domain Traffic. In *ACM SIGCOMM*, 2010.

[42] T. Leighton. Improving Performance on the Internet. *Commun. ACM*, 52(2):44–51, 2009.

[43] G. Maier, A. Feldmann, V. Paxson, and M. Allman. On Dominant Characteristics of Residential Broadband Internet Traffic. In *ACM IMC*, 2009.

[44] Maxmind. GeoLite Country. http://dev.maxmind.com/geoip/legacy/geolite.

[45] Netcraft. January 2013 Web Server Survey. http://news.netcraft.com/archives/2013/01/07/january-2013-web-server-survey-2.html.

[46] E. Nygren, R. K. Sitaraman, and J. Sun. The Akamai Network: A Platform for High-performance Internet Applications. *SIGOPS Oper. Syst. Rev.*, 2010.

[47] V. Paxson. Bro: A System for Detecting Network Intruders in Real-Time. In *Usenix Security Symposium*, 1998.

[48] D. Plonka and P. Barford. Flexible Traffic and Host Profiling via DNS Rendezvous. In *SATIN*, 2011.

[49] I. Poese, S. Uhlig, M. A. Kaafar, B. Donnet, and B. Gueye. IP Geolocation Databases: Unreliable? *ACM CCR*, 2011.

[50] Sandvine. Global Internet Phenomena Report. http://www.sandvine.com/news/global_broadband_trends.asp.

[51] F. Streibelt, J. Böttger, N. Chatzis, G. Smaragdakis, and A. Feldmann. Exploring EDNS-Client-Subnet Adopters in your Free Time. In *ACM IMC*, 2013.

[52] A. Su, D. Choffnes, A. Kuzmanovic, and F. Bustamante. Drafting Behind Akamai. In *ACM SIGCOMM*, 2006.

[53] S. Triukose, Z. Al-Qudah, and M. Rabinovich. Content Delivery Networks: Protection or Threat? In *ESORICS*, 2009.

[54] S. Triukose, Z. Wen, and M. Rabinovich. Measuring a Commercial Content Delivery Network. In *WWW*, 2011.

Growth Analysis of a Large ISP

Andrew D. Ferguson
Brown University
adf@cs.brown.edu

Jordan Place
Brown University
jplace@cs.brown.edu

Rodrigo Fonseca
Brown University
rfonseca@cs.brown.edu

ABSTRACT

We present a time-series analysis of Cogent's inter-continental network. The analysis is based on descriptions of Cogent's routers and their interfaces, collected each week for more than one year. These descriptions are collected from public reverse DNS records, which we cross-validate using `iffinder`, a full Internet scan, and limited ground truth data provided by Cogent. For example, our dataset, which we make available to the research community, shows that while the number of Cogent routers grew by approximately 11.3 each week, the average number of interfaces per router, and the effective diameter of the inferred network remained stable over the same period. Our collected dataset includes information about interface types, port identifications, router locations, peer and customer attachments, and more.

Categories and Subject Descriptors

C.2.1 [**Computer-Communication Networks**]: Network Architecture and Design—*Network topology*; C.4 [**Performance of Systems**]: Measurement techniques

Keywords

Reverse DNS; Alias resolution

1. INTRODUCTION

Broadly speaking, IP addresses on the Internet fall into one of two categories – they either represent hosts or other endpoints, or router interfaces. Mapping the connections between, and properties of, the router interfaces (*e.g.*, ownership, geographic location, logical location, etc.) is important for understanding the Internet's topological structure, and has been a topic of extensive research (cf., §2). Typical mapping approaches to reconstruct the router-level topology of the Internet include data from `traceroute`-like probes [25], multicast advertisements [20], IP options probing [9, 21], and DNS records [24].

As shown below, DNS records can be a rich source of information; yet, they are potentially problematic [27], and are not used in large-scale Internet topology mapping performed by CAIDA [16].

IMC'13, October 23–25, 2013, Barcelona, Spain.

ACM 978-1-4503-1953-9/13/10 ...$15.00.
http://dx.doi.org/10.1145/2504730.2504769.

For example, there are no standards for naming interfaces (resulting in idiosyncratic rules for each ISP), and there is no requirement that an interface's DNS record remain up-to-date as interfaces are added, reconfigured, or removed. Within a single ISP, however, such difficulties may be mitigated, as organizations presumably strive for consistent administrative procedures and best practices.

We find that Cogent, one of the most connected Internet service providers [1], with large networks in both Europe and North America, is such an ISP. Cogent provides reverse DNS records for more than 99% of the 51,000+ interfaces on Cogent-owned routers we could identify. For example,

```
te2-1.ccr01.jfk01.atlas.cogentco.com
fa0-2.na01.b003070-1.sfo04.atlas.cogentco.com
```

are, respectively, the reverse DNS records for the Cogent-owned IP addresses `154.54.80.85` and `38.112.5.17` during the week of March 10, 2013.

We assume that all records under the `*.atlas.cogentco.com` DNS hierarchy are part of Cogent's infrastructure.[1] These records include four pieces of information. First, a router location (*e.g.*, `jfk01` and `sfo04`) – we find Cogent has 460 router locations, almost all of which are coded with three-letter airport codes. Second, the router within a location (*e.g.*, `ccr01` and `na01.b003070-1`) – we estimate Cogent had 4,469 routers the week of March 10, 2013. Third, the type of interface, which we infer based on Cisco naming conventions (*e.g.*, `te` for 10 Gbps Ethernet, and `fa` for 100 Mbps Ethernet). And fourth, the interface's position within the router (*e.g.*, `2-1` and `0-2`, which are, respectively, the first and second ports on their line cards).

Ideally, with such structured records, we could determine the existence of a 10 Gbps interface at position `2-2` on the `ccr01.jfk01` router with a simple DNS query. Unfortunately, Cogent only provides *reverse* DNS records. However, by issuing reverse DNS queries for *all* Cogent-owned IPv4 addresses, we find that the IP address at position `2-2` on that router is `154.54.25.17`. In addition, because of the exhaustive lookup, we find that this router appears to have 18 such 10 Gbps interfaces configured across five line cards.

Other Cogent DNS records include information about related business entities. For example, `Tetratech.demarc.cogentco.com` is the reverse DNS record for `38.112.5.18`; hence, we infer that Tetratech is connected to Cogent with up to 100 Mbps of available bandwidth at a router near San Francisco, based on the information about `38.112.5.17` (the other usable address in the `38.112.5.16/30` subnet) inferred above.

To capitalize on this wealth of information, we have issued reverse DNS queries each week for more than 17 million Cogent-owned IPv4 addresses (now more than 20 million, see §4.3), start-

[1]Excluding approximately a dozen mis-named addresses such as `fixme_please.atlas.cogentco.com`.

ing the week of January 22, 2012. These weekly snapshots allow us to analyze the growth of – and change in – Cogent's network at the router-level.

This dataset, which we release to the research community, has several interesting features:

- Extensive records of the evolution of a large ISP, providing a platform for future network research – either directly using the dataset, or by offering improvements to existing topology generators [26]
- Novel information about interface types and positions
- Novel estimates of router, module, and interface growth rates for a large ISP
- A new dataset for evaluating methods to de-alias router interfaces, which are used when discovering Internet topologies using `traceroute`-like measurements (§2)
- Results from more than one billion DNS queries issued from approximately 100 globally-distributed vantage points, including more than 100,000 anomalies (*e.g.*, ID mismatches, replies from unexpected sources, corrupt responses, etc.)
- Validity and coverage-rate established through comparison with `iffinder`, public ground truth, and a complete set of IPv4 reverse DNS records

The rest of this paper proceeds as follows: first, we provide context for our study in the space of related work (§2); second, we describe and validate the approach used to build this dataset (§3, §4); next, we conduct an initial time-series analysis of this data (§5); and finally, conclude with potential avenues for further research (§6).

2. RELATED WORK

Constructing router-level Internet topologies has been a project of the networking research community for more than 10 years [14]. A common approach is to use `traceroute`-like probes with successively increasing TTL values. This approach was made scalable by targeting probes more efficiently with Rocketfuel [25], more transparent to network middleboxes through the use of TCP Sidecar [23], and has been augmented with information gathered by the IP Record Route option [22]. At their core, these `traceroute`-like approaches provide a list of router IP addresses which can be viewed as *aliases* of a single router, to be determined [14].

Therefore, numerous solutions to the *alias resolution* problem have been developed including: examining IP ID values [9, 17, 25], using prespecified IP timestamps [21], detecting variants in the source address of a probe's response [14], applying graph analysis techniques [15], and, as in this work, by examining reverse DNS lookups [24].

In this work, however, reverse DNS lookups are the *only* method for discovering router interfaces – we do not send any TTL-limited active probes. Other techniques for topological discovery without `traceroute`-like probes include inference from passive measurements [13], and gathering data with MPLS ICMP extensions [23] and IGMP messages [20].

Using reverse DNS records for this application is not without risks, however. Previous work has shown that using out-of-date and other incorrect reverse DNS records can have a disproportionately negative effect on POP-level path reconstruction [27]. In this work, by contrast, we primarily focus on inferring Cogent's router organization and interface properties, and their change over time. To the best of our knowledge, this information is only publicly available from DNS records; therefore, such inference requires careful validation of our DNS-based mapping, as we show in §4.

Perhaps the most closely related work is CAIDA's "IPv4 Routed /24 DNS Names Dataset" [7]. This dataset consists of reverse DNS records for router interfaces discovered by `traceroute`-like active probes. CAIDA's probes are sent weekly to a random IP address in every Internet-routed `/24` subnet. This measurement naturally aims for *breadth* of coverage. Our work, by contrast, aims to achieve *depth* – complete coverage of a single ISP, as we show in our validation (§4).

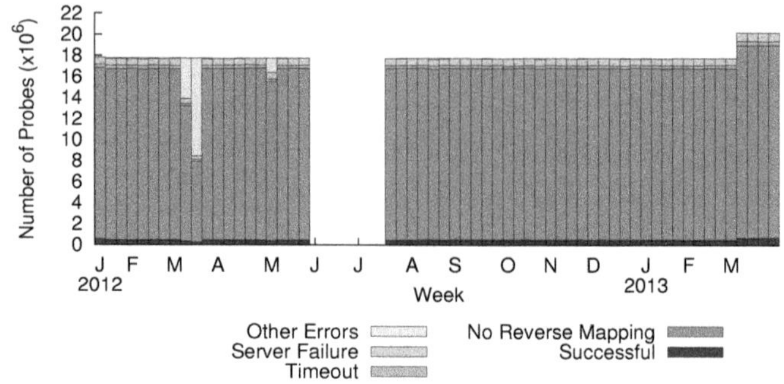

(a) Breakdown of all DNS probes we sent.

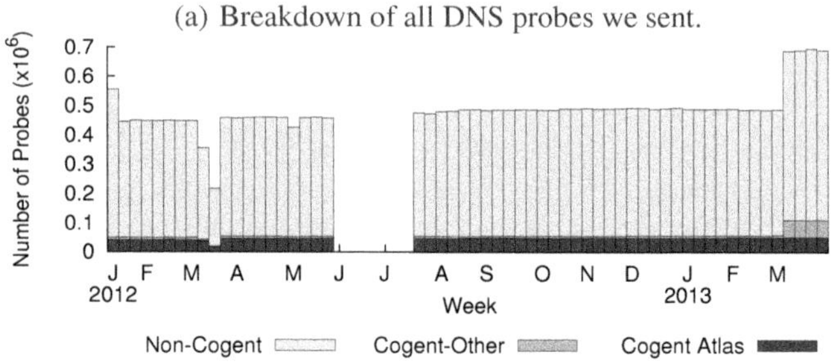

(b) Breakdown of successful DNS probes

Figure 1: Responses to weekly DNS probes.

3. METHODOLOGY

This paper analyzes weekly snapshots of Cogent's router organization, built from publicly available reverse DNS records. As described above, we systematically issue reverse DNS queries for each Cogent-owned IP address, allowing us to discover all of the corresponding interface names. This initially required more than 17 million weekly DNS queries; we now issue more than 20 million each week.

To minimize our load on the DNS infrastructure, we globally distributed our queries at 90-100 sites using PlanetLab [12]. Worker processes at each site issue queries for all IP addresses in a block no larger than a `/19` subnet (8,192 addresses), at a rate of approximately one query per second using the Linux `host` command. Between assignments, workers pause for a random sleep of between 10 to 20 minutes. Workers notify our master server every 256 queries (allowing us to detect and re-assign incomplete blocks), and upload a log when finished. With this approach, we can successfully query millions of DNS records each week.

Figure 1 provides an overview of our DNS queries' responses. During the weeks of March 11 and 18, 2012, our master server experienced data loss. In addition, our measurement infrastructure was unavailable for seven weeks (from the week of June 3, 2012

Code	Type	Class
et	10 Mbps Ethernet	Physical
fa	100 Mbps Ethernet	Physical
gi	1 Gbps Ethernet	Physical
te	10 Gbps Ethernet	Physical
se	Serial link	Physical
pos	Packet-over-SONET	Physical
ism	Integrated Services Module	Physical
lo	Loopback	Virtual
mul	Multilink	Virtual
tu	Tunnel	Virtual
vl	VLAN	Virtual

Table 1: Interface types observed in Cogent's network.

until the week of July 22, 2012, and partially during the week of May 6, 2012) due to hardware failures affecting the master server.

We also run `iffinder` [5] each week on the list of interface IP addresses discovered by the previous week's DNS queries – that is, all of the IP addresses with reverse DNS records under the `*.atlas.cogentco.com` hierarchy. In the first week, this was 42,100 interfaces (62,906 probes); as of the week of April 28, 2013, it is now 53,457 interfaces (81,736 probes). These probes are not distributed, and currently complete in approx. 38 hours (up from approx. 29 hours in the first weeks). The weekly `iffinder` data is used to validate our grouping of interfaces into routers (§4.1).

We group interfaces into routers based on the DNS records; generalizing from the examples in §1, we consider Cogent's reverse DNS records to consist of three fields:
`(interface).(router).(location).atlas.cogentco.com`, where the router field may include one or more levels of the DNS hierarchy. Additionally, we infer interface types using the Cisco naming conventions in Table 1.

Finally, to account for transient DNS failures, we smooth our weekly dataset based on surrounding weeks according to the following rule: if an interface is missing in Week N, yet present in Weeks $(N-1)$ and $(N+1)$ with the same corresponding IP address, we consider its absence in week N to be accidental. Excluding the weeks of March 11 and 18, 2012, this smoothing process increased the number of interfaces each week by 0.18% on average. By this process, an interface not present for two consecutive weeks is considered to be removed.

All of our code for measurement, parsing, smoothing, graphing, and analysis is publicly available.[2]

4. VALIDATION

Internet topographers are faced with two challenges in their work. First, because most Internet maps are built by inference, they must asses a map's validity, comparing it with maps built with other techniques, or by comparing with the limited ground-truth data available. Second, they must determine the completeness of their coverage. In this section, we address these challenges through comparison with three additional datasets: router aliases determined with `iffinder` [5], public information provided by Cogent, and a complete set of reverse DNS records collected by an anonymous "Internet Census" project [6].

4.1 Validity of router de-aliasing

As previously discussed, ISPs are not required to maintain consistency between a router interface's true location and its reverse DNS record. This makes any effort to group interfaces into routers by using DNS records potentially problematic. Therefore, to double-check our efforts, we ran `iffinder` [5], a traditional solution to the alias resolution problem, each week on the interfaces discovered in the previous week.

The `iffinder` tool works in the following manner: for each interface, it sends one or more UDP packets to high-numbered ports; these packets are designed to elicit ICMP Port Unreachable messages in response. If received, the source address of any ICMP message is assumed to also be an interface on the same router, assuming this source address is different from the destination address of the original probe [14]. This technique produces a list of IP address pairs which `iffinder` infers are aliases of the same router. By taking the transitive closure of these pairs, we produce a candidate set of router aliases (*e.g.*, if we see pairs $(A,B),(B,C),(D,C)$, we infer a single router with interfaces $\{A,B,C,D\}$).

The `iffinder` approach naturally leads to a higher rate of false negatives (failing to infer two interfaces are on the same router) than false positives (inaccurately inferring two interfaces are on the same router). Therefore, to validate our DNS-based grouping, we search for instances in which our DNS-based approach infers two or more routers for a set of interfaces, yet `iffinder` infers only one. If such instances occurred frequently and persistently, it would suggest that Cogent fails to keep their interface's reverse DNS records consistent with reality.

Our analysis implies that Cogent maintains their interface's DNS records consistently. In each week, less than 1% of the candidate routers inferred by `iffinder` contained IP address with reverse DNS records suggesting multiple routers. Furthermore, 95.8% of these discrepancies last for one week or less, and could be due to the delay between our platform's DNS queries and `iffinder` probes. We find that only 1.7% of discrepancies persist for more than two weeks, affecting just 28 interfaces (0.053% of all interfaces).

Finally, we note that `iffinder`'s technique also discovers new router interfaces, not in our DNS-based dataset. On average, these interfaces, which lack reverse DNS records, accounted for 0.86% of the total number of interfaces discovered by either approach.

4.2 Comparison with public information

Cogent provides a graphical network overview on their public website [4]. This map is very coarse, unfortunately, and only contains a single point for each of the 192 cities in which Cogent maintains a presence. Furthermore, this public graph only contains edges between geographically neighboring cities. Nevertheless, this graph provides a public source of ground truth about Cogent's network.

To compare, we extracted the list of 187 airport-like codes discovered in our dataset (*e.g.*, `jfk`, `sfo`, `fco`), and plotted each inferred location on a map. Through manual inspection, we determined that our dataset is missing only nine cities (4.7%) – three in the US, and six in Europe. In addition, our dataset contains airport codes for four cities not shown on the published map – one in the US, and three in Europe. `traceroute` probes to interfaces we believe are located in these four cities revealed IP paths consistent with the new cities' presumed locations.

While not conclusive, we believe the close similarity between our map and Cogent's suggests our DNS record-based dataset covers around 95% of the cities in Cogent's network.

In addition, Cogent's 10-K Annual Report provides public declarations about their network [2]. This legal document describes the services Cogent provides to its customers, which are consistent with the list of inferred interface types given in Table 1. The annual report also states that their primary service is provided at 100 Mbps,

[2] `http://github.com/brownsys/pl-mapping/`

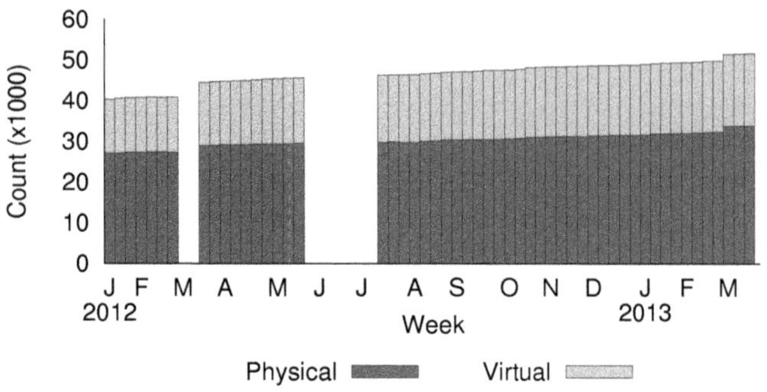

Figure 2: Count of physical and virtual interfaces in Cogent's network (stacked to show total).

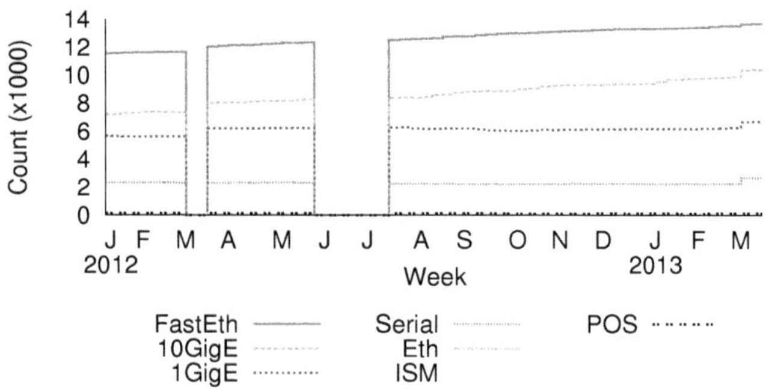

Figure 3: Weekly count of physical interfaces by type.

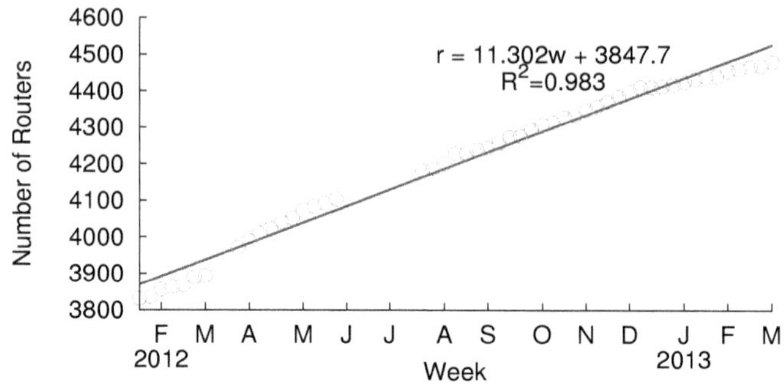

Figure 4: Number of routers over time.

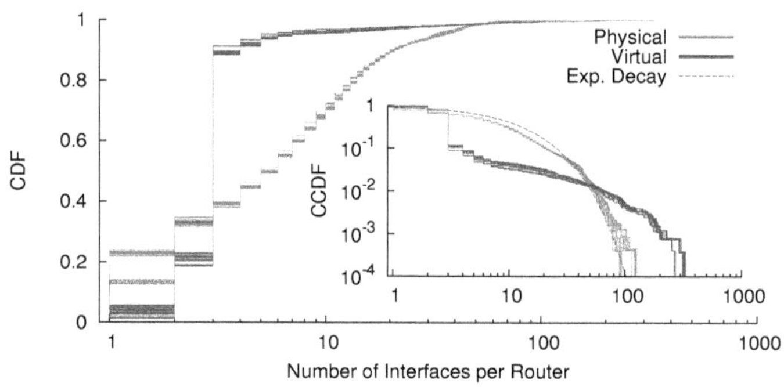

Figure 5: CDF and complementary-CDF of the number of physical and virtual interfaces per router for all weeks.

which matches the composition of physical interfaces we observed, as shown in Figure 3.

4.3 Reverse DNS coverage

The initial list of IP addresses for which we issue reverse DNS queries each week was chosen based on IP addresses observed in select `traceroute` probes. With these addresses, we identified the corresponding Cogent-owned CIDR address blocks using the ARIN and RIPE registry databases. This list contained 17,731,584 IPv4 addresses, and was used through the week of March 3, 2013.

Using data collected by a recent "Internet Census" [6], which issued multiple reverse DNS queries for the entire IPv4 address space, we identified an additional 2,426,624 Cogent-owned IP addresses which could potentially contain `*.cogentco.com` reverse DNS records. While our original query list contained just 88% of the expanded list, we found the number of `*.atlas.cogentco.com` records only increased from 50,981 to 52,643 (a 3.3% increase, cf. Figure 1(b)). Therefore, as with the map comparison described above, we believe this comparison suggests our targeted DNS-based mapping well covers Cogent's network.

5. EXPLORATION

Having established the validity and coverage of our data, we now conduct an initial time-series exploration of Cogent's network. Our analysis proceeds at three levels: first, considering the interfaces, independent of the routers; second, considering the routers, independent of their connections; and third, considering the inferred network graph.

5.1 Interface evolution

First, we consider Cogent's interfaces independently of their associated routers. In Figure 2, we see that a majority of interfaces are physical interfaces, which we further breakdown in Figure 3. The virtual interfaces are predominantly VLAN interfaces, plus loopback interfaces for each router. Based on our dataset, we infer that the three most common types of physical interfaces in Cogent's network are 100 Mbps Ethernet, 10 Gbps Ethernet, and 1 Gbps Ethernet, respectively.

We find that the number of interfaces grew linearly over the period of our data collection. We infer that Cogent adds an average of approximately 153 new interfaces each week ($R^2 = 0.92$). We also infer that this growth is not proportional to the existing distribution of interface types. Figure 3 shows that the rate of growth is highest for 10 Gbps Ethernet interfaces, followed by that for 100 Mbps Ethernet.

5.2 Router evolution

Next, we consider Cogent's routers, independent of the connections between them. In Figure 4, we plot the number of inferred Cogent routers over time, and find that Cogent adds an average of approximately 11 new routers per week. We note that the apparent recent dip in growth rate occurs at the start of 2013.

We find that the distribution of the number of interfaces per router remains relatively stable over the course of our data collection. The average number of interfaces only rises from 10.7 per router to 11.4, while the median remains six. In Figure 5, we separate the interfaces into physical and virtual interfaces (see Table 1), and find that the weekly distributions remain stable throughout the study. The number of physical interfaces decays as an exponential

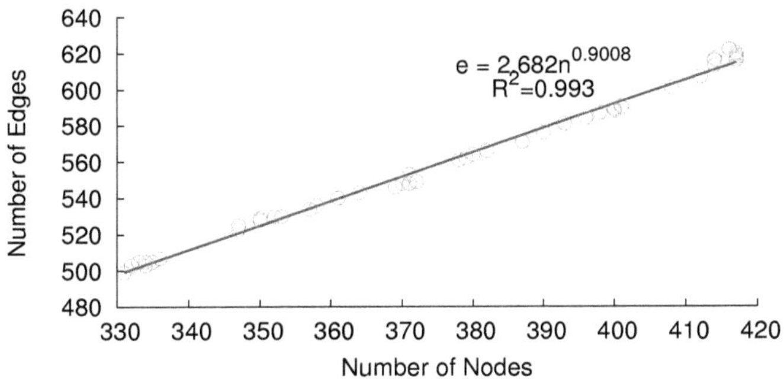

Figure 7: Number of nodes versus the number of edges of the inferred network topology with one point per week.

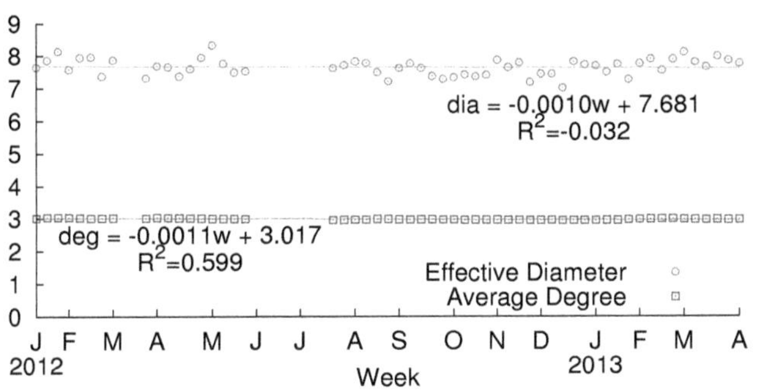

Figure 8: Evolution of the effective diameter and average degree of the inferred network topology. Both quantities remained fairly constant in the measurement period.

distribution, while the number of virtual interfaces is heavily concentrated around 3, and has a heavier tail.

Cogent's physical interface names also contain line card and port positions. Examining data for the week of April 14, 2013, we find that routers have 1.56 line cards on average, with an average port density per line card of 4.21. The maximum number of physical ports we observe on a single router is 90, and three routers appear to have nine line cards configured (the maximum we observed). The maximum number of configured ports we observe on a single line card is 43, with 1 Gbps Ethernet interfaces; the highest port number we record on such line cards is 48. For 10 Gbps Ethernet interfaces, the highest port number we record is eight.

5.3 Network evolution

Finally, we analyze our inferred graph of Cogent's network. While passively collecting Cogent's reverse DNS records each week provides us with a detailed list of interfaces, the records provide no explicit information about connections between routers. Therefore, we use the following procedure to infer a graph of their network. First, we observe that connected routers must each have an interface on a shared subnet. Thus, as in Sidecar [23], we collect candidate pairs of interfaces whose IP addresses appear to share a `/30` subnet (addresses must be off-by-one, and the inferred network and broadcast addresses must be valid and not assigned to other interfaces). Second, we conservatively consider only candidate pairs for which both are physical interfaces, and of the same type. Finally, we consult Cogent's BGP looking glass server [3], and discard any pairs where the corresponding prefix is larger than `/30`.

Figure 6 shows a visualization of the inferred network for the week of April 7, 2013, where we have grouped together all routers belonging to the same site. The graph, produced using Gephi [8], is colored according to a community detection algorithm [10], and the size of the nodes is proportional to their betweenness centrality, *i.e.*, related to the number of shortest paths the node is part of. Even though the node positions resemble geographical positions, they are computed by a force-directed layout algorithm with no geographic information. This is a further indication that the inferred network is related to the real one.

We constructed an equivalent graph for each valid week in the dataset, and now look into the evolution of a few important graph metrics. Leskovec *et al.* [18] examined the evolution of several real networks, such as the AS graph and the arXiv citation network, and found two phenomena: densification, and shrinking diameters. Densification states that the number of edges $e(t)$, and the number of nodes $n(t)$, over time follow the relation $e(t) \propto n(t)^{\alpha}$, with $1 < \alpha < 2$. This implies that the average degree increases over time. They also found that the effective diameter of the network shrinks over time.[3] We found neither of these phenomena to be significant in the evolution of the inferred Cogent graph.

Figure 7 shows a scatterplot of the number of nodes versus the number of edges for the inferred network graph. The relation is very close to linear, but the exponent of the densification law is 0.9. Correspondingly, the bottom curve in Figure 8 shows that the average degree actually decreases, with a small negative slope of -0.0011 in a linear fit. The top curve in Figure 8 shows the evolution of the effective diameter of the graph. The diameter remains nearly constant, with a negative slope of -0.001 in a linear fit.

Since our collection period of slightly more than one year is relatively short compared to the analysis in [18], it remains to be seen if these trends continue as we collect more data.

6. CONCLUSION

As noted by previous researches, DNS queries are a potentially problematic source of topological information; we find this is not the case for Cogent's network. We were lucky that Cogent's interface naming scheme was both rich with data and obvious to parse. Finding other ISPs with similar naming schemes and sensibilities is simply a matter of chance; if even feasible, it would require human intervention to build a database of rules, similar to Rocketfuel's `undns` tool, which attempts to map routers to physical locations based on DNS records [25].

Fortunately, Chabarek and Barford are currently developing such a database [11]. Using a combination of machine learning-based clustering and hand-crafted regular expressions, they have partially discovered interface speeds, equipment types, and router functions from the DNS addresses of approximately 26,000 organizations. While their initial study used only the DNS records in the CAIDA dataset previously mentioned [7], the resulting rule database could be used to expand the approach taken in this work to other ISPs.

Unfortunately, the future of performing reverse DNS queries on a large-scale looks hazy. The simple approach taken here of issuing queries at a low rate from hosts at around 100 PlanetLab locations, will not scale as ISP networks transition to IPv6. Therefore, it is important for the research community to measure as many network properties as possible while the scale of IP address blocks is still relatively small.

[3]From [18], the effective diameter is the 90th percentile of the continuous interpolation of the node distance cumulative distribution.

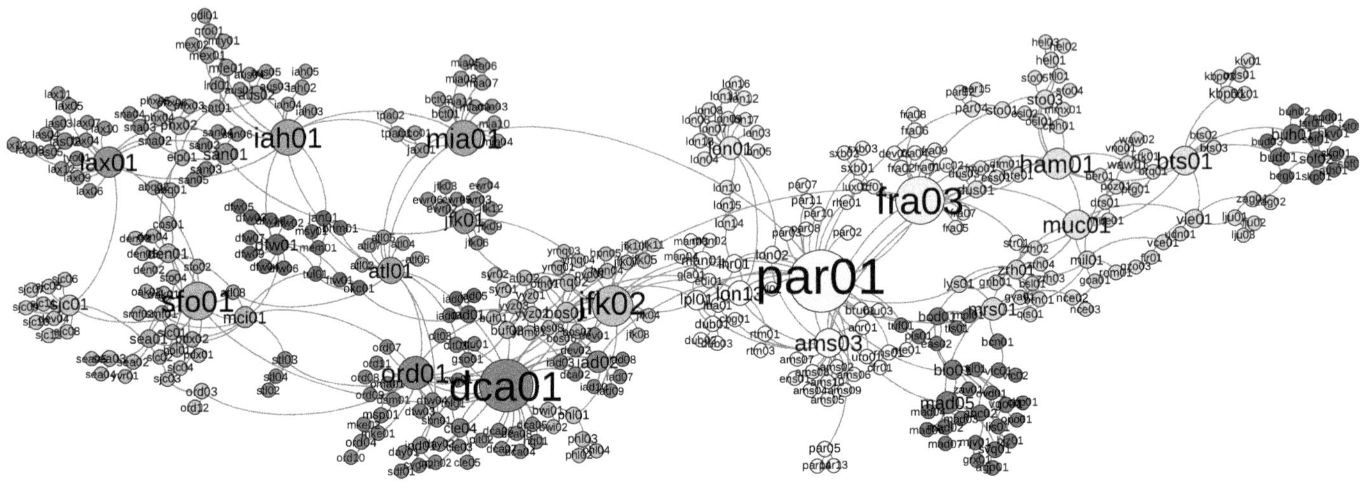

Figure 6: Visualization of paths in Cogent's network based on data from the week of April 7, 2013; nodes represent routers, edges link routers sharing the same IP subnet, and nodes are scaled to represent *betweenness* – larger nodes have a greater number of paths passing through them. The layout is force-directed, with no geographical information.

We hope that releasing the complete record of our weekly probes will be interesting and relevant to the research community. While this paper provides an extensive verification of our measurement approach, and an initial analysis of the dynamics within Cogent's own routers, we suspect additional analysis – such as of Cogent's peers and customers, or of the occasional DNS anomalies experienced by our more than one billion queries – could be possible. In addition, combining this dataset with others, such as those gathered by the iPlane project [19] or CAIDA, could be fruitful avenues of further research.

Acknowledgments

The authors thank David Trejo for plotting Cogent's routers on a physical map, and the staff of the Planet Lab Consortium for technical support. We also wish to thank our reviewers and shepherd, kc claffy, for their many helpful comments. This work was partially supported by NSF grant 1012060. Andrew Ferguson is supported by an NDSEG fellowship.

7. REFERENCES

[1] AS Rank: AS Ranking, 2013. `http://as-rank.caida.org`.

[2] Cogent Communications Group, Inc. - SEC Form 10-K Annual Report, 2012. `http://www.cogentco.com/files/docs/about_cogent/investor_relations/reports/10k_report_2012.pdf`.

[3] Cogent: Looking Glass, 2013. `http://www.cogentco.com/en/network/looking-glass`.

[4] Cogent: Network Map, 2013. `http://cogentco.com/en/network/network-map`.

[5] iffinder Alias Resolution Tool, 2012. `http://www.caida.org/tools/measurement/iffinder/`.

[6] Internet Census 2012. `http://internetcensus2012.github.io/InternetCensus2012/`.

[7] The CAIDA UCSD IPv4 Routed /24 DNS Names Dataset. `http://www.caida.org/data/active/ipv4_dnsnames_dataset.xml`.

[8] M. Bastian, S. Heymann, and M. Jacomy. Gephi: An Open Source Software for Exploring and Manipulating Networks. In *International AAAI Conference on Weblogs and Social Media*, 2009.

[9] A. Bender, R. Sherwood, and N. Spring. Fixing Ally's Growing Pains with Velocity Modeling. In *IMC '08*.

[10] V. D. Blondel, J.-L. Guillaume, R. Lambiotte, and E. Lefebvre. Fast unfolding of communities in large networks. *Journal of Statistical Mechanics: Theory and Experiment*, October 2008.

[11] J. Chabarek and P. Barford. WhatâĂŹs in a Name? Decoding Router Interface Names. In *HotPlanet '13*.

[12] B. Chun, D. Culler, T. Roscoe, A. Bavier, L. Peterson, M. Wawrzoniak, and M. Bowman. PlanetLab: An Overlay Testbed for Broad-Coverage Services. *SIGCOMM CCR*, July 2003.

[13] B. Eriksson, P. Barford, R. Nowak, and M. Crovella. Learning Network Structure from Passive Measurements. In *IMC '07*.

[14] R. Govindan and H. Tangmunarunkit. Heuristics for Internet Map Discovery. In *INFOCOM '00*.

[15] M. Gunes and K. Sarac. Analytical IP Alias Resolution. In *IEEE International Conference on Communications (ICC 2006)*.

[16] K. Keys. Internet-Scale IP Alias Resolution Techniques. *SIGCOMM CCR*, Jan. 2010.

[17] K. Keys, Y. Hyun, M. Luckie, and k. claffy. Internet-Scale IPv4 Alias Resolution with MIDAR. *IEEE/ACM Transactions on Networking*, PP(99), May 2012.

[18] J. Leskovec, J. Kleinberg, and C. Faloutsos. Graph evolution: Densification and shrinking diameters. *ACM Trans. Knowl. Discov. Data*, 1(1), Mar. 2007.

[19] H. V. Madhyastha, T. Isdal, M. Piatek, C. Dixon, T. Anderson, A. Krishnamurthy, and A. Venkataramani. iPlane: An Information Plane for Distributed Services. In *OSDI '06*.

[20] P. Mérindol, V. V. den Schrieck, B. Donnet, O. Bonaventure, and J.-J. Pansiot. Quantifying ASes Multiconnectivity Using Multicast Information. In *IMC '09*.

[21] J. Sherry, E. Katz-Bassett, M. Pimenova, H. V. Madhyastha, T. Anderson, and A. Krishnamurthy. Resolving IP Aliases with Prespecified Timestamps. In *IMC '10*.

[22] R. Sherwood, A. Bender, and N. Spring. DisCarte: A Disjunctive Internet Cartographer. In *SIGCOMM '08*.

[23] R. Sherwood and N. Spring. Touring the Internet in a TCP Sidecar. In *IMC '06*.

[24] N. Spring, M. Dontcheva, M. Rodrig, and D. Wetherall. How to Resolve IP Aliases. Technical Report 04-05-04, UW CSE, 2004.

[25] N. Spring, R. Mahajan, and D. Wetherall. Measuring ISP Topologies with Rocketfuel. In *SIGCOMM '02*.

[26] H. Tangmunarunkit, R. Govindan, S. Jamin, and S. Shenker. Network Topology Generators: Degree-Based vs. Structural. In *SIGCOMM '02*.

[27] M. Zhang, Y. Ruan, V. Pai, and J. Rexford. How DNS Misnaming Distorts Internet Topology Mapping. In *USENIX ATC '06*.

Understanding the Super-sized traffic of the Super Bowl

Jeffrey Erman, K.K. Ramakrishnan
AT&T Labs Research, New Jersey, USA
{erman,kkrama}@research.att.com

ABSTRACT

Large events like the Super Bowl, where almost 75K attendees congegrate for several hours, poses a significant challenge in the planning, design and deployment of wireless networks. This was one of the first events where the LTE cellular network was available widely, in addition to almost 700 WiFi free hotspots. The Super Bowl in 2013 was also unprecedented because of a stadium-wide power outage for over half an hour. This study is the first to look in-depth at the user behaviours and traffic demand of a large ISP's celluar network at such an unique event.

The findings of this study can be used to guide the design of the communication networks of large venues in the future. There are several key insights from our study of the data collected. First, LTE speeds enable subscribers at venues to stream high-quality video and this can be a signficant source of traffic. Second, the configuration of the uplink for such events is key, and a thoughtful approach to the design of applications that use the cloud for storing user data can substantially mitigate the congestion on the resource constrained uplink. Further, while it is tempting to take advantage of multicast on the cellular network (e.g., deploying technologies such as eMBMS in a venue), our results indicate that there is a need to combine multicast with caching to remove the strict requirement of overlap of requests from users to derive that benefit.

Categories and Subject Descriptors

C.2.3 [**Computer System Organization**]: Computer Communication Networks—*Network Operations*

General Terms

Cellular Networks; Large Venues; Characterization

1. INTRODUCTION

Cellular Data traffic has been growing rapidly, at well over 80% growth in total volume year over year, for the last 2-3 years, with the advent of smartphones [1, 2], tablets and other devices. What was mainly a network that was designed for telephony has now become a major carrier of data traffic. One of the characteristics that provides relief is that the number of users simultaneously using a particular cell sector and channel is relatively small (in the few hundreds) at a typical cell site. However, a major challenge for cellular service providers is to manage the traffic demands at special events where several tens of thousands of users congregate at a given time. A salient example is the annual Super Bowl football game in the United States, where approximately 75K attendees descend on a sports stadium for about half a day.

The 2013 Superbowl in Febrary at the New Orleans Superdome is one of the first events to have the unique characteristics of a large number of users accessing a LTE cellular network deployed using a Distributed Antenna System, and combined with a stadium-wide deployment of WiFi hotspots. As reported by one cellular operator, the amount of data carried on the cellular network at the 2013 Super Bowl was 80% more than the previous year, with about 388 GBytes transferred [4]. During a long uprecedented power outage, users 'consumed approximately 10 GB more data than they did during any other hour' of the game [4].

Our in-depth study of the traffic characteristics of LTE cellular network of a large ISP at a large venue sheds light into the differences in usage from a typical cell site. Our results show access to web content (text, images) is still dominant. A major distinguishing factor of the traffic we observed is the amount of uplink data traffic - uplink data almost matched the volume of downlink data traffic. This is driven by the use of applications such as photo and video synching to cloud-based storage and multimedia messaging between users. We also observed that video consumption uses a significant share of the downlink data volume, because of the high bitrates at which video is being streamed to mobile devices despite having only a small number of subscribers concurrently consuming video.

This work can be used to influence future design of communication networks for large venues. Applications are changing how they use the network in dramatic ways - going from being predominantly downstream, to having a comparable amount of upstream traffic (nearly 1:1). This has important consequences in terms of configuration of the uplink for events. By formulating an optimization problem, we are able to show that having these applications becoming delay tolerant, even to a limited extent, can substantially reduce the amount of uplink capacity that needs to be provisioned (by almost a factor of two). Further, one would expect significant concurrency in accessing information across users, with such a large number of people being in one area and being interested in a common theme - Super Bowl information and related media streams. Our observation is that a straightforward deployment of multicast on the cellular network (such as eMBMS), even at a venue like the Super Bowl may not yield substantial benefits. We propose an intelligent approach to combining multicast with caching to remove the

IMC'13, October 23–25, 2013, Barcelona, Spain.

strict dependency on the temporal overlap of requests from users. This helps us to get the benefit of multicast in the cellular network. We also observe large shifts in data volume at cell nodes in various parts of the venue: entrances first; then the seating areas. An intelligent self-organizing network could potentially re-allocate resources and power, depending on the phases of the event at a venue, to dynamically increase capacity to match the changing demand.

2. RELATED WORK

There have been many studies that have focused on understanding and characterizing the usage of smartphone traffic [7–9, 12, 14–16]. In many of these studies the focus has been on the characterisation of 3G traffic. However, a difference is our focus on large venues where LTE is available. Large venues are a unique consideration when the planning and operating wireless networks as the large number of people in the venue places an immense demand on resources. With LTE available, these venues are now capable of supporting even more traffic demanding applications which have a unique usage patterns due to the live nature of the event.

Most related to this work is the recent study by Shafiq et. al. [13] that looks at the performance of the 3G cellular network at two large venues hosting events. They found significant voice and data degradation. They found that due to the high demand for radio resources, pre-connection failures increase 100 to 5000 times compared to before the event. In addition, there are large increases in packet loss and round-trip times for user sessions. In terms of application usage, they found that there is an increased use of social networking. Due to demand on radio resources, they propose a connection sharing method to help aggregate demand and potentially improve performance. A key difference of our work is that we analyze a venue with a LTE network that was deployed, with significantly higher capacity. With LTE, several of the RRC state machine bottlenecks observed earlier are no longer as significant, allowing for more user sessions and higher traffic demands. For instance, we find a high percentage of the traffic is from streaming video with sustained bitrates over 1 Mbps. Another key difference is our focus on studying in-depth the user applications and traffic demands in relation to the events of the game (e.g., during the power outage) and where they take place within the stadium. In part, we find there is a significant demand from photo syncing to the cloud. Especially in the context of the available uplink capacity of cellular networks, we examine the effectiveness of optimizing this type of usage. We propose smoothing the syncing of these so as to significantly reduce traffic peaks which occur during breaks in the game.

3. METHODOLOGY

We first describe the data set collected and analyzed.

3.1 Venue

The New Orleans Superdome was setup with a permanent, high capacity Carrier Neutral Distributed Antenna System (DAS). The DAS system provides 4G LTE coverage with a collection of many strategically placed antennas, to maximize the radio coverage for all areas of the stadium - starting from the concourses, to the seating areas, etc. The DAS is organized as a set of non-overlapping cells to maximize the wireless capacity available in the stadium [4, 5].

In addition to DAS-based LTE coverage, the Superdome also had over 700 WiFi access points fully deployed to provide significant capacity for offloading from the cell networks. The network supported 802.11n, 802.11a, b, and g in the 2.4 GHz and 5GHz bands. According to a report [6], the average signal strength was -60 dB in the seating areas.

3.2 Dataset and Analysis

For this study, we passively measured the LTE traffic from the Superdome of a large US-based wireless provider. While we would have liked to also measure the traffic of the WiFi network to compare the usage of both cellular and WiFi, we were unable to do this and hope to do so in future efforts.

The data collection point was at the S1-U interface between the Evolved Node B (eNodeB) and the Serving Gateway (S-GW) for all eNodeB's serving traffic at the venue. The S1-U interface carries all the user plane traffic between the User Device (UE) and the cellular network for LTE. At the GPRS Tunneling Protocol (GTP) layer, each eNodeB can be identified specifically by an IP address. Different UE sessions can be distinguished using the separate Mobile Subscriber IP (MSIP) address assigned to each GTP session. Session terminations and hand-offs can be identified when the GTP tunnel identifiers for a specific MSIP change. While it can be used to differentiate unique UE sessions and count the number of simultaneous subscribers accessing specific data, the MSIP address cannot be used to map back to a specific subscriber or device, thus preserving user privacy.

We analyzed the HTTP header information of each request and correlated this together with flow records. The HTTP headers (and lower layer protocol headers) were collected for every request and response, without resorting to any sampling. For flow records of other protocols, in particular HTTPS, the DNS responses providing the IP addresses associated with each request/response were used to identify the content provider.

The privacy of subscribers was preserved as the study focused on aggregate statistics across all devices.

3.3 Identification of Upstream Applications

As we see in the subsequent sections, there is a significant amount of upstream traffic at the venue. It is useful to understand the particular applications that generate this traffic.

The multimedia messaging service (MMS) protocol makes use of HTTP(s) protocols to send and receive messages. These flows can be identified by the specific Hostname, and the Content-Type identifiers associated with the MMS service. Based on these signatures, we counted the total number of overall messages sent and received.

Traffic associated with Photo and Document synchronization to the cloud was also identified during the course of our analysis. Based on IP addresses and the associated DNS hostnames, we found these specific HTTPS flows going to subdomains at 'amazonaws.com' and 'windows.net' associated with the Photo and Document cloud sync service.

4. RESULTS

We present in this section an in-depth characterization of the traffic we measured at the Super Bowl.

4.1 Traffic Volumes

The overall traffic volume of the LTE traffic before, during and after the Super bowl is shown in Figure 1. For proprietary reasons, absolute values have been replaced with relative measures on the y-axis.

During the 2.5 hours before the start of the event, traffic volume steadily increases. Once the game began, traffic volume partially subsides, but picks up again towards the end of the second quarter of the game. During the half-time show, there is a substantial

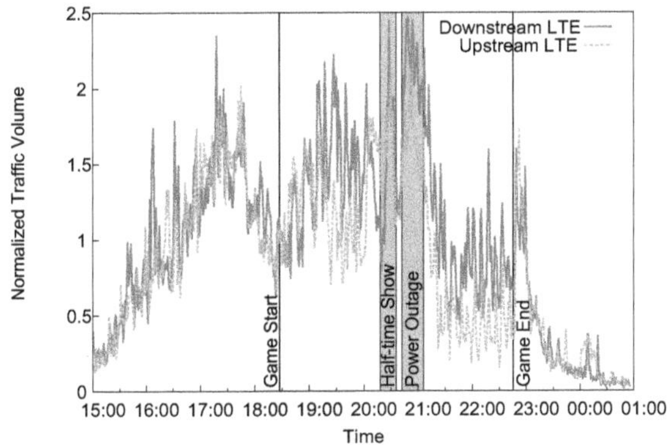

Figure 1: **LTE Traffic volumes at Super bowl**

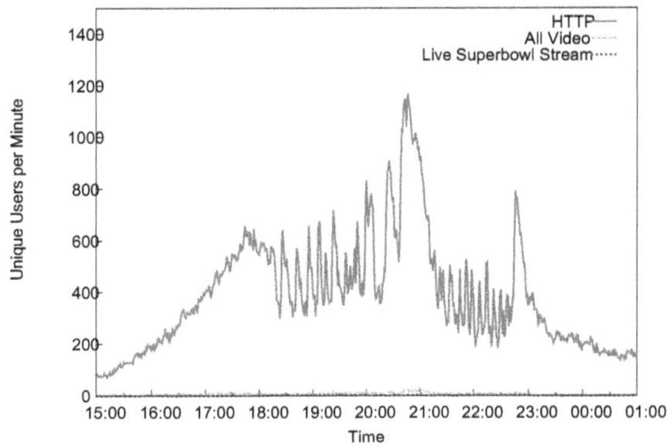

Figure 2: **Number of HTTP users per minute**

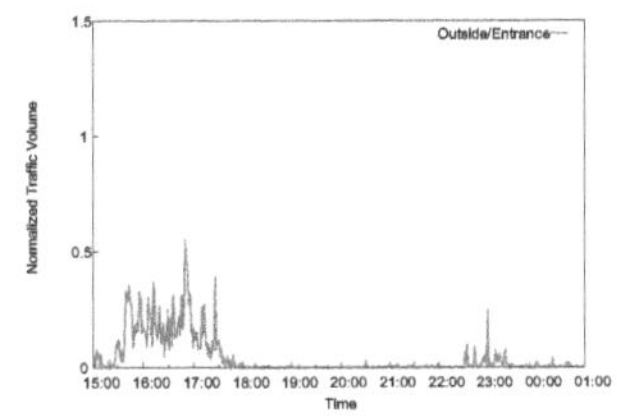

(a) **Outdoor and Entrance**

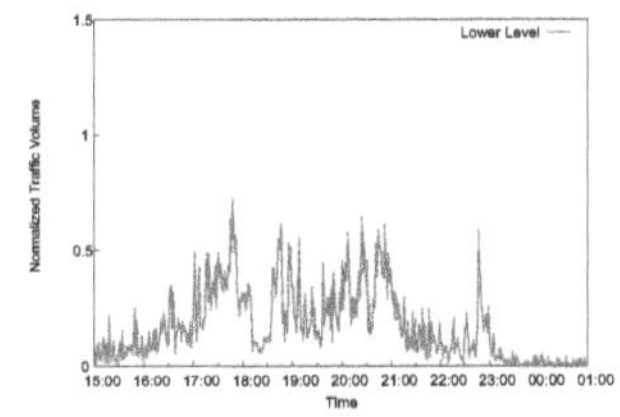

(b) **Lower Level Sections**

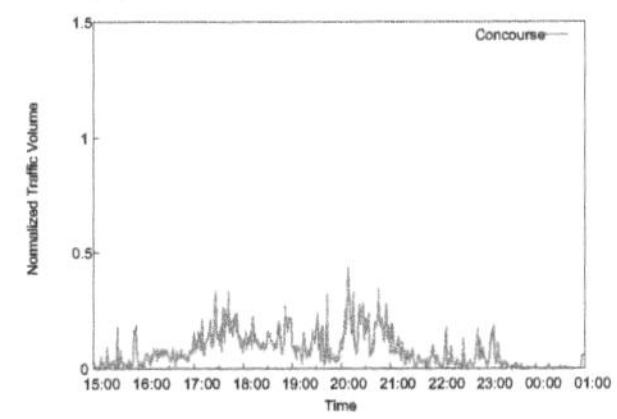

(c) **Concourse**

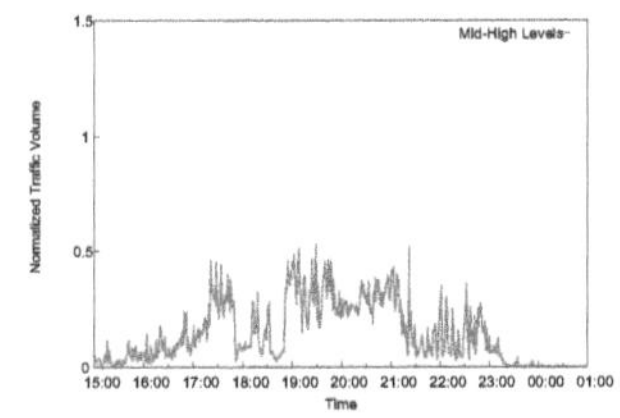

(d) **Middle/Upper Level Sections**

Figure 3: **eNodeB Volumes**

spike in usage, subsiding again at the start of the 3rd quarter. But, just after the beginning of the 3rd quarter, there was a partial power outage in the stadium that lasted 34 minutes. The interval of power outage (which did not affect the cellular infrastructure) saw the traffic volume peak, with the long break in play. At the peak usage, the data volume is 7 times the volume before the game. After the power outage was over, the game resumed. Due to the excitement of the game in the 3rd quarter, we see that traffic usage drops off substantially. Finally, the traffic builds again at the end of the game.

Figure 2 shows the total number of unique UE devices active during each minute. An interesting observation is the number of users still accessing the cellular network even with the in-building WiFi network being available. In this figure, we can also more clearly discern the individual breaks in play for television timeouts etc. (such as at 18:45).

One immediate observation is that the traffic volumes and especially the number of active users varies widely with the interest in the game at hand. This leaves many peaks and valleys over short periods of time (i.e., over a couple minutes time period). The peak-to-valley ratio over the whole game was 6.7. Even just considering the 1st and 2nd quarters, the peak-to-valley ratio was 3.1. This could be taken advantage of when scheduling uploads of images, messages or downloads of content. Having such applications capable of tolerating delays of a small number of minutes can substantially enhance system capacity. Concomitant with this is the need for the network to provide the necessary information to such delay tolerant applications to take advantages of uncongested periods in the network over short time scales.

4.2 eNodeb Volumes

In Figure 3 the traffic volume is shown for selected eNodeB's which cover (primarily) the different areas of the stadium. The traffic usage in the different areas as expected is not uniform over time. For instance, the entrances and concourses experience different traffic patterns than cells covering the seating sections of the game. This has strong implications on how DAS networks are designed, with LTE self-organizing networks [3]. The radio power and code allocations can be dynamically adjusted for each of the sectors covering the different sections based on this change in usage patterns to optimize overall resource utilization in the network (we do not attempt to cover the specifics of how the physical layer is managed in this paper).

An interesting distinction between subfigures (b) and (d) is the level shift in the traffic volumes for the eNodeB that cover the Middle and Upper sections of the stadium seating area. This level shift is due to the streaming video generated by an individual session. An important take-away is that even in LTE cell networks that have higher aggregate capacity for an individual cell site than the previous generation 3G networks, a small number of high bandwidth flows can consume a substantial portion of that capacity over short time scales. Therefore, the impact of such flows on the other users needs to be carefully considered.

4.3 Application Mix at Venues

We next look at which applications and content providers were used by subscribers. In Table 1 we find the main applications being used are HTTP-based web browsing, streaming video over HTTP and email. This is not wholly unexpected based on the plethora of other studies that report the same characteristics of smartphone traffic.

Table 2 shows which content providers were most accessed. We found surprisingly two cloud providers account for over 22.1% of the overall traffic. Upon further investigation, these were providing photo and document syncing to popular cloud services. The second largest provider is a sports website that provided a live video stream of the Super Bowl (discussed more below). Social networking and photo sharing sites were also popular. It is interesting that when summing over the top 20 providers, over 5% of the traffic was related to downloads for speed tests. In comparision to Shafiq *et. al* [13], there is a substantial difference in usage between the previous 3G results and our LTE results. Both syncing to the cloud and the live streaming were not previously observed.

We have not shown the content provider time series due to space considerations, but during the power outage, in additon to uplink

Table 1: Traffic by Application Class

Application	% Overall Traffic
Web Browsing (HTTP)	56.5%
Streaming (Over HTTP)	19.6%
HTTPS	13.0%
Email (SMTP(s), POP3(s), IMAP(s))	5.9%
Other (VPN, VoIP, etc)	5.0%

Table 2: Top 10 Content Providers

Content Provider	% Overall Traffic
Cloud Provider	16.6%
Sports	15.0%
MMS Message	9.6%
App Store	6.4%
Social Nework	7.8%
Cloud Provider 2	5.5%
User-Gen Video	4.7%
Email	2.3%
Search	2.3%
Speed Testing	1.6%

sources (see next section), there was a considerable increase in the use of social networking and photo sharing sites. But, there was not a corresponding increase in video traffic.

4.4 Video Consumption

We noted that video traffic accounted for 19.6% of the overall traffic at the Super bowl. We now investigate the sources, and the number of subscribers consuming video content.

Figure 4 shows the traffic volumes of the total downstream LTE traffic, the volume for all video traffic delivered over HTTP across all content providers, and the video traffic that related to a specific content provider that was providing a live stream of the Super Bowl. We can see that the live stream of the Super bowl accounts for 72% of the total video traffic delivered during the game. This live stream was using an Adaptive Bitrate Protocol (which adapts to the available capacity of the channel to the end-user) to deliver the content and was available at bitrates ranging from 50 Kbps to 2 Mbps. Table 3 shows the distribution of the bitrates that subscribers accessed. This evokes the key question of – *why would users access a live stream at the Super Bowl while they are at the Super Bowl venue?* One potential explanation would be that the live stream offers alternative views not available for the user to view on the in-stadium large monitors that display the game live. We investigated this and found that only 6.1% of the video chunks requested were for alternative views, while the remaining 93.9% were for the main television broadcast feed. Another possibility could be that these streams were delivered to users trying to get a better view of the game online. Upon futher investion of the User-Agent fields we found that over 99% of the live video stream requests were from tablet devices.

Another aspect we wanted to explore is – *due the substantial video usage during the game for the same type of content would multicast would be an appropriate solution?* An emerging capability for LTE cellular networks is eMBMS. Figure 5 shows, for both overall video and for the live Super Bowl streams, the number of simultaneous users during each minute. For video, we see that there are a maximum of 26 simultaneous users and for the Super Bowl

Table 3: Bitrates of super bowl stream (Kbps)

50K	200K	350K	550K	800K	1400K	2000K
0.0%	1.3%	0.7%	3.8%	5.1%	24.0%	65.2%

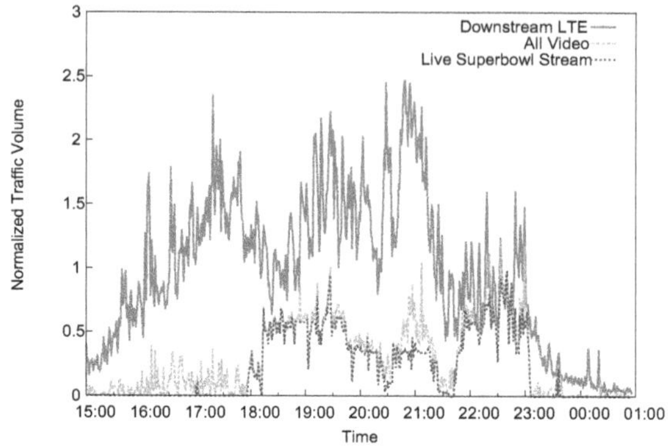

Figure 4: **Video traffic during Super bowl**

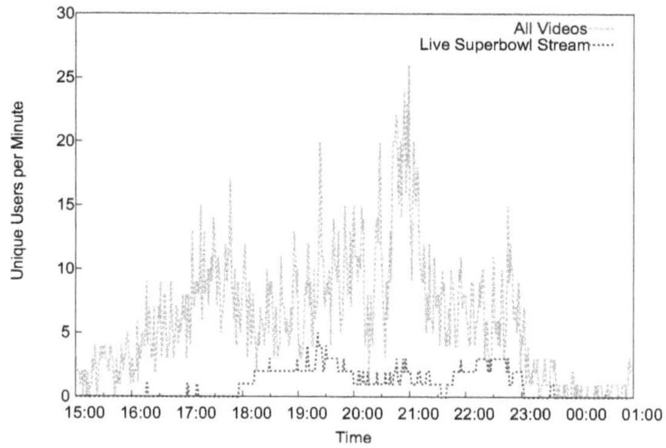

Figure 5: **Concurrent users for all video and live streams**

stream, a peak of 6 simultaneous users (on average less than 1 per cell). Thus, for the Super Bowl stream, a cellular operator would have to evaluate if it would be cost effective, both in terms of dedicating radio resources for multicast and the investment needed for deployment of the eMBMS solution, when such a small number of users concurrently access the stream.

4.5 Uplink Traffic

Access networks have traditionally seen a dominant amount of downstream traffic demand compared to the upstream demand. Currently on cellular networks, we have typically observed the ratio of downlink to uplink traffic to be in the order of 9:1. This is driven by primarily by content consumption by users. As such,the resources allocated for downstream versus upstream has also been correspondingly unbalanced. However, compared to the typical 9:1 ratio, the ratio of downstream to upstream, as observed at the Super Bowl in Figure 1 was near 1:1, which has significant implications to the cellular service provider.

The initial expectation was that the increased uplink traffic may be primiarily from social networking. However, in contrast to previous studies, we found the two largest sources of upstram traffic (which incidentally occured most during the peak demand interval that was during the power outage) was the background 'syncing' of pictures to the cloud and photo and video messaging through MMS. Demand for both of these services are highlighted in Figure 6

5. CELLULAR NETWORK CAPACITY MANAGEMENT AND SCHEDULING

The achievable aggregate capacity of radio access network (RAN) in a cellular network is determined by a large variety of parameters and configuration settings. Some of these are specific to individual vendor implementations of the RAN equipment (e.g., the base station, eNodeB, in an LTE network) and some are based on how a cellular network operator configures an individual cell site. The achievable capacity is quite different between the downlink and the uplink, because of the combination of considerations - the expected amount of downlink traffic versus the uplink traffic; the channel access protocol characteristics for uplink access for the mobile device to transmit data versus the protocol used for downlink transmissions from the eNodeB to the mobile; the overheads associated for the downlink vs. uplink protocols; the impact of contention and interference from transmissions by other mobile devices; and finally the scheduler characteristics. While a detailed treatment of each of these aspects is not feasible, we will provide a very high level overview to enable the reader to appreciate the considerations involved. In our context, it is of particular importance on how much capacity is available for the uplink versus the downlink and the overheads involved.

The first consideration is the amount of capacity that can be allocated based on the 'baseband capacity' that is available. Typically the hardware capacity sets a maximum throughput for downlink vs. uplink, and the ratio is often between 3:1 to (possibly) 4:1. This is certainly well in line with the observations of the proportion of traffic seen in a typical cell site, where there is is far more downlink traffic than uplink traffic. In addition, the cellular operator and equipment vendor may also dimension the actual amount of resources that could be allocated for the uplink. The 'physical resource blocks' (PRB) are dimensioned such that the aggregate amount of power and code resources available for all the traffic from a particular eNodeB available to be allocated to downlink and uplink traffic are managed to meet the traffic demand. Typically, the PRBs allocated also follow a ratio of near 2:1, so as to accommodate peak usage in one or the other direction.

Another important consideration is the design of the scheduler itself. Transmissions are scheduled on a 1 millisecond transmission time interval (TTI) (unlike 2 ms with 3G networks). With Orthogonal Frequency Division Multiplexing (OFDM), the radio resources are allocated for each individual flow in a manner that seeks to balance efficient usage of resources versus achieving fairness across the end user devices that are competing for resources. For each TTI period, the available PRBs along with the available capacity (e.g., downlink baseband capacity) are used by the scheduler to then schedule the transmission of data packets waiting to be sent to a particular end device (in the case of the downlink). In addition, the scheduler ensures that the end device is in a state to receive data. The frequency block that is used for transmission (e.g., downlink) may be of the order of 5 MHz or 10 MHz depending on what the cellular operator has allocated. This block is divided into subcarriers of a certain size. To avoid inter-cell interference, the frequencis selected for transmission may be selected by starting at a random subcarrier and assigning a number of subcarriers for that transmission. For downlink transmissions, only the eNodeB scheduler is involved. With LTE, Multiple Input Multiple Output (MIMO) is used on downlink transmissions. For the uplink transmissions from the mobile end device to the eNodeB, both the UE and the eNodeB are involved in the scheduling, with the buffer status information at the end device being communicated to the eNodeB. Often, on the uplink, MIMO may not be supported in current cellular networks.

Every TTI (i.e., 1 ms), the RAN scheduler determines the resources to be assigned to each end device that has data to transmit. A higher scheduling priority provided to an end device gives it a higher probability to be able to receive (from the eNodeB) or transmit data. The allocation of resources is on a per end device basis. The end device that is provided the highest priority is selected first

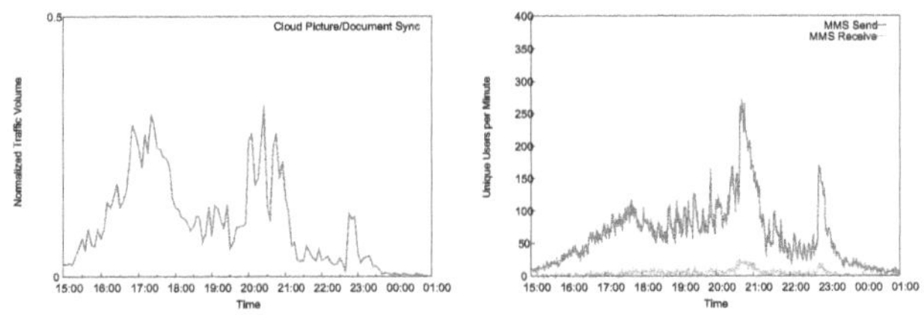

(a) **Cloud Picture/Doc Uploads** (b) **MMS Messages**

Figure 6: **Main Upstream Sources**

Table 4: Upstreaming Applications

Application	% Uplink Traffic
Photo/Document Sync to Cloud	29.2%
MMS	12.7%
Social Network	7.8%
Email 1 (HTTPS)	3.0%
Seach	2.4%
Email 2 (HTTPS)	1.3%
Others	36.1%

(ignoring issues related to the different 'bearers' associated with the end device). For the uplink, the scheduling is also done on an end device basis, with the grant provided to the end device to transmit data based on its own local scheduling policy. For both the downlink and uplink, the hybrid ARQ-based retransmissions are given higher priority over new data packet transmissions.

The cellular operator typically configures the proportion of the downlink bandwidth to be used by the downlink scheduler, which then assigns physical resource blocks in the frequency domain, on a subframe/TTI basis. This essentially determines the downstream peak throughput and capacity. Uplink transmission scheduling is slightly more complex and transmissions are managed carefully by the eNodeB upstream scheduler to avoid interference. For uplink transmissions, the end device sends a scheduling request to the scheduler in the eNodeB to indicate that it has data in its buffer and requests an opportuntiy to transmit in an upcoming subframe. When the end device is scheduled in a sub-frame, the uplink scheduler at the eNodeB transmits a scheduling grant to the end device on a control channel, indicating the resource blocks and transport format to use for uplink transmission. Together with the uplink data, the end device transmits buffer status information to the uplink scheduler which uses this information along with the channel quality information to assign an appropriate number of resource blocks to the device in the uplink.

The scheduler in the eNodeB follows a policy that balances efficiency with fairness. The fairness criterion generally used is to achieve some level of proportional fairness, with a weight used to achieve efficient use of radio resources (power and code). The weight favors those end devices at the center of the cell or at the edge of the cell depending on whether the cellular operator wishes to provide a greater weight for efficiency or fairness.

For all these reasons, we see a need for applications to be aware of their use of uplink bandwidth. We examine ways of optimizing its use for some of the applications being used in the venue setting.

6. STRATEGIES FOR BETTER CONTENT DELIVERY IN VENUES

Based on our observations in the previous section, we now discuss some possible strategies for optimizing content delivery at venues.

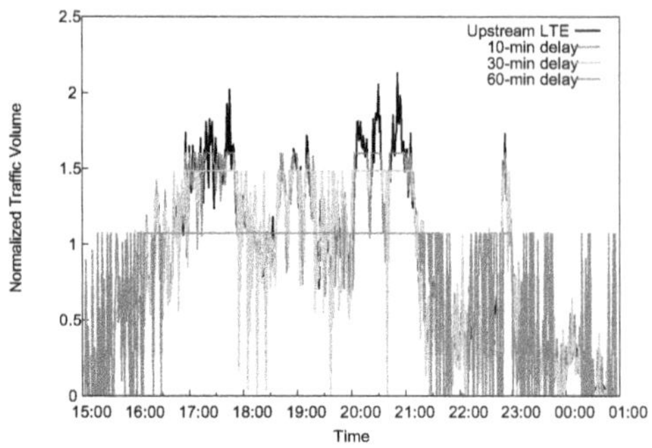

Figure 7: **Peak reduction by delaying uplink traffic during congestion**

6.1 Trading-off delay to mitigate congestion

One possible approach to mitigate the load from uplink traffic is to make applications congestion-aware and delay tolerant, so that load is shifted away from times when the network is congested. In that case, upload traffic would be only slowed under congestion.

To evaluate the benefit of having such congestion aware and delay tolerant applications, we formulated a linear program to examine the reduction in the peak uplink traffic for different amounts of delay tolerance and solved it using CPLEX. Let v_t denote the current upload rate. We define x_t as the upload rate after waiting a maximum of d. The objective is to find a solution x_t that minimizes the peak traffic during the time window T.

$$\min \max_{t \in T} x_t \tag{1}$$

$$\text{s.t.} \sum_{t \le s \le t+d} x_s - v_t \ge 1, \ \forall t \tag{2}$$

$$\sum_{t \le s \le t+d} x_s - \sum_{t \le s \le t+d} v_s \le 0, \ \forall t \tag{3}$$

$$\sum x_t - \sum v_t = 0, \ \forall t \tag{4}$$

$$0 \le x_t, \ \forall t \tag{5}$$

Constraint 2 ensures that all data was delivered within the deadline. Constraint 3 ensures that data is not delivered before it originally arrived. Constraint 4 ensures the total delayed data delivered is equal to original amount. Constraint 5 ensures x_t is a positive value.

Figure 7 shows the results of solving the LP for the peak uplink rate. The original normalized peak capacity requirement was 2.14. With just a 5-minute delay tolerance, the peak is reduced by 25% to 1.6 (not shown), with 10-minutes it reduced by 30% to 1.49, at 30-minutes by 40.1% to 1.26. Finally at 60-minutes of delay tolerance, the peak reduced by 49.7% to 1.08. Thus, with even a relatively small amount of application delay tolerance, there can be a substantial reduction in the peak capacity requirement - significantly mitigating uplink congestion at these venues.

6.2 Can we exploit multicast in LTE?

Intuition would suggest that a venue would see considerable commonality in accessing content and temporal locality in accessing that content. Thus, using multicast should be effective in saving capacity.

A proposed technology for multicast for LTE is eMBMS. Evolved Multimedia Broadcast and Multicast Services (eMBMS) is used for transmission of the same content to multiple receivers.

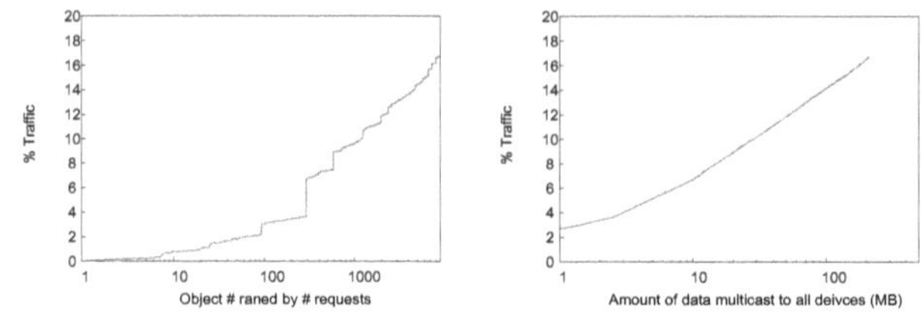

(a) **Object Rank** (b) **Bytes Saved by Multicasting**

Figure 8: **Benefit of multicasting popular content and caching**

It can be used for streaming live content or multicasting common content of interest to multiple users. It can be used across multiple cells, with what is known as a 'single frequency network' (SFN) where the transmission across cells is synchronous using a common carrier frequency. Having a single frequency network operation avoids inter-cell interference. eMBMS and unicast channels are multiplexed in the time domain, thus avoiding the long-term dedication of radio resources for multicast. Configuration of LTE cells participating in eMBMS (MBSFN areas) is determined by operations and management. The configuration of radio resources used for eMBMS can be determined dynamically, within a wide range (0.3% to 60%) of downlink unicast capacity.

Live content (e.g., live TV broadcast of the event to spectators) could be a candidate for eMBMS. But there is, on average, only one viewer of the live content per cell. The peak usage (measured over 1 minute time scales) was about 6 simultaneous viewers across all the cell sites provisioned at the stadium. Thus, one would conclude that there is not a significant benefit from multicasting the live TV broadcast to the participants at the Super Bowl.

In contrast to the viewers of live video, there were a large number of users (over 30K) accessing the network for information, with a peak number of simultaneous users of over 1K. A substantial amount of data was consumed by users at the event - especially web content. The question is: *is there temporal locality in accessing this content and can we multicast it effectively?* As one might expect, given the diversity of the content, there may not be enough web content simultaneously accessed to make multicast of such information to be effective either. There is a significant skew in popularity of information and content accessed by the users in the venue, as has been observed by others. Figure 8 (a) shows that the top 100 objects, ranked by number of requests, constitute a 2% share of the downstream bytes, and the top 1000 take up almost 10%. Previous studies have shown that, despite the lack of very tight temporal locality of access, using the end-system storage as a cache, can effectively relax the need for such tight temporal locality to deliver the information through multicast [10, 11]. By delivering the most popular content by multicast to the end-system caches (with a time to live lasting the length of the event at the venue), we can save a significant portion of the downstream bandwidth. It can also reduce the peakedness of the traffic on the downlink. Therefore, we explore how a small cache on the end-devices can save on downlink capacity, and make eMBMS-based multicast more effective. Figure 8 (b) shows that by multicasting popular content and having just a 10 Mbyte cache on the end-systems can save about 6.7% of the total downstream transfer, and a 100 Mbyte cache can save almost 14% of the transferred bytes (we need to suitably factor in applications such as "speed test", which download random bytes). In any case, we believe that multicast with eMBMS on the cellular network can be quite effective in reducing capacity, if used intelligently. It would require quickly identifying popular content and exploiting the cache on the end-systems to multicast and pre-place popular content.

7. CONCLUSIONS

Venues that host large events like the Super Bowl are a challenge to design and provision to meet user demand. Our analysis of the Super Bowl traffic indicated that with high-speed LTE there is significant traffic demand despite extensive deployment of in-stadium WiFi. Moreover, we found with the shift in application mix, uplink traffic is much more prominent (almost matching downlink). This is significant for the cellular service provider as it is more complex to provision and manage. We suggested an approach to tradeoff delay tolerance for mitigating congestion. While it is tempting to exploit cellular multicast (eMBMS), a straighforward implementation isn't enough. Our proposed approach to use end-system storage as a cache of popular content that is pre-placed through multicast can indeed help achieve the expected benefits of multicast. We also observed that video consumption, despite having only a small number of users, consumes a large share of the capacity. We believe understanding the role of providing a fair share of resources to meet the utility of all the users across the application spectrum, is important. Finally, we observed that usage changes significantly from one part of the stadium to another as the event progresses. Thus, it would be very appropriate to shift radio resources, as demand shifts from one eNodeB to another at the venue.

8. REFERENCES

[1] AT&T Press Release. http://www.att.com/gen/press-room?pid=4800&cdvn=news&newsarticleid=30527, February 2010.

[2] Cisco Visual Networking Index: Global Mobile Data Traffic Forecast Update, 2010Ű2015. http://www.cisco.com/en/US/solutions/collateral/ns341/ns525/ns537/ns705/ns827/white_paper_c11-520862.html, February 2011.

[3] 3GPP Self-Organizing Networks. http://www.3gpp.com/SON, 2013.

[4] Behind the Scenes Look at AT&TŠs Super Bowl XLVII Network Strategy. http://www.sporttechie.com/2013/04/21/behind-the-scenes-look-at-atts-super-bowl-xlvii-network-strategy/, April 2013.

[5] From party to pigskin, our network is ready for this weekendŠs fanfare. http://blogs.att.net/consumerblog/story/a7787203, February 2013.

[6] Super Bowl plans to handle 30,000 Wi-Fi users at onceŮand sniff out 'rogue devices'. http://arstechnica.com/information-technology/2013/02/super-bowl-plans-to-handle-30000-wi-fi-users-at-once-and-sniff-out-rogue-devices/, February 2013.

[7] T. M. T. Do, J. Blom, and D. Gatica-Perez. Smartphone usage in the wild: a large-scale analysis of applications and context. In *Proceedings of the 13th international conference on multimodal interfaces*, ICMI '11, pages 353–360, New York, NY, USA, 2011. ACM.

[8] H. Falaki, D. Lymberopoulos, R. Mahajan, S. Kandula, and D. Estrin. A first look at traffic on smartphones. In *Proceedings of the 10th ACM SIGCOMM conference on Internet measurement*, IMC '10, pages 281–287, New York, NY, USA, 2010. ACM.

[9] H. Falaki, R. Mahajan, S. Kandula, D. Lymberopoulos, R. Govindan, and D. Estrin. Diversity in smartphone usage. In *Proceedings of the 8th international conference on Mobile systems, applications, and services*, MobiSys '10, pages 179–194, New York, NY, USA, 2010. ACM.

[10] V. Gopalakrishnan, B. Bhattacharjee, K. K. Ramakrishnan, R. Jana, and D. Srivastava. CPM: Adaptive VoD with Cooperative Peer Assist and Multicast. In *Infocom'09*, May 2008.

[11] V. Gopalakrishnan, R. Jana, K. K. Ramakrishnan, V. Aggarwal, R. Calderbank, and F. Yu. The Effectiveness of Intelligent Scheduling for Multicast VoD. In *ACM MM'09*, October 2009.

[12] G. Maier, F. Schneider, and A. Feldmann. A first look at mobile hand-held device traffic. In *Proceedings of the 11th international conference on Passive and active measurement*, PAM'10, pages 161–170, Berlin, Heidelberg, 2010. Springer-Verlag.

[13] M. Z. Shafiq, L. Ji, A. X. Liu, J. Pang, S. Venkataraman, and J. Wang. A First Look at Cellular Network Performance during Crowded Events. In *Sigmetrics'13*, June 2013.

[14] M. Z. Shafiq, L. Ji, A. X. Liu, and J. Wang. Characterizing and modeling internet traffic dynamics of cellular devices. In *Proceedings of the ACM SIGMETRICS joint international conference on Measurement and modeling of computer systems*, pages 305–316. ACM, 2011.

[15] I. Trestian, S. Ranjan, A. Kuzmanovic, and A. Nucci. Measuring serendipity: connecting people, locations and interests in a mobile 3g network. In *Proceedings of the 9th ACM SIGCOMM conference on Internet measurement conference*, IMC '09, pages 267–279, New York, NY, USA, 2009. ACM.

[16] Q. Xu, J. Erman, A. Gerber, Z. Mao, J. Pang, and S. Venkataraman. Identifying diverse usage behaviors of smartphone apps. In *Proceedings of the 2011 ACM SIGCOMM conference on Internet measurement conference*, IMC '11, pages 329–344, New York, NY, USA, 2011. ACM.

Appraising the Delay Accuracy in Browser-based Network Measurement

Weichao Li, Ricky K. P. Mok, Rocky K. C. Chang, and Waiting W. T. Fok
Department of Computing
The Hong Kong Polytechnic University
{csweicli|cskpmok|csrchang|cswtfok}@comp.polyu.edu.hk

ABSTRACT

Conducting network measurement in a web browser (e.g., speedtest and Netalyzr) enables end users to understand their network and application performance. However, very little is known about the (in)accuracy of the various methods used in these tools. In this paper, we evaluate the accuracy of ten HTTP-based and TCP socket-based methods for measuring the round-trip time (RTT) with the five most popular browsers on Linux and Windows. Our measurement results show that the delay overheads incurred in most of the HTTP-based methods are too large to ignore. Moreover, the overheads incurred by some methods (such as Flash GET and POST) vary significantly across different browsers and systems, making it very difficult to calibrate. The socket-based methods, on the other hand, incur much smaller overhead. Another interesting and important finding is that `Date.getTime()`, a typical timing API in Java, does not provide the millisecond resolution assumed by many measurement tools on some OSes (e.g., Windows 7). This results in a serious under-estimation of RTT. On the other hand, some tools over-estimate the RTT by including the TCP handshaking phase.

Categories and Subject Descriptors

C.2.3 [**Computer-Communication Networks**]: Network Operations; C.4 [**Performance of Systems**]: Measurement Techniques

Keywords

Delay; Measurement; Accuracy; Web

1. INTRODUCTION

The accuracy of a network measurement system can be defined as how the measurement results deviate from the real network performance. Following ISO 5725 [3], a network measurement can be considered more accurate if its produced results are closer to the actual values (trueness) and are more consistent than the others (precision or repeatability). Measurement accuracy depends on a number of factors, including the correctness of adopted methodology, time resolution, system load, and so on. To ensure high accuracy, network measurement is traditionally performed in dedicated hosts with careful resource management [9, 24], and the network performance is sampled using Poisson process [4, 5, 6, 23, 30].

Recently, more measurement tools are available to end users to measure their network performance and diagnose problems. Such efforts include various speedtest services, residential broadband measurement [34], and several host-based tools [17, 32]. In particular, many of these tools, such as Netalyzr [19] and Ookla's speedtest [1], take advantage of browser's ubiquity by implementing them in browsers. These *browser-based measurement* tools usually can measure the network round-trip time (RTT) and throughput. Some can even measure packet loss and reordering rates. The effort towards this direction is recently stepped up by Fathom [11] which provides a number of APIs for network measurement functions.

Although browser-based measurement has gained popularity among end users, very little is known about the (in)accuracy of various methods used in these tools. This paper focuses on the accuracy of network delay measured by these tools, because a browser-based tool could easily inflate the network delay measurement (but not so much for loss and reordering). The delay obtained on the browser level may over-estimate (or under-estimate) the actual RTT due to a number of reasons. The inflated delay will also affect jitter, bandwidth measurement, and passive measurement methods (e.g., [13, 14]) that assume a very small inflation.

We quantify the delay inflation by investigating the *delay overhead* on the browser side, which is the difference between the value measured by browser-based tools and the actual value (calculated through packet capturing). The amount of this overhead depends on how the rendering engine (e.g., JavaScript engine) interprets the measurement code and invokes system function calls. We study ten different methods (seven based on HTTP and three on TCP sockets, including WebSocket) which are usually implemented using JavaScript (native in browsers), Flash, and Java applet. We implement these methods and experiment with the five major browsers on Windows and Ubuntu.

Our measurement results show that the socket-based methods incur much lower delay overhead than the HTTP-based methods in general. The Flash GET and POST methods are most unreliable, because their overheads are the highest among all methods, and their overhead variabilities are also the highest across different browsers and systems. WebSocket, on the other hand, provides the most accurate and consistent RTT measurement in the context of JavaScript and DOM (Document Object Model). Another interesting finding is that the typical timing API in Java, `Date.getTime()`, cannot return precise system time in some OSes (e.g., Windows 7). Although this function is supposed to provide timestamps with millisecond resolution, we find that the actual granularity is not constant. It can be one of the two values observed in our experiments: 1 ms or ~15 ms, and each possible value will

IMC'13, October 23–25, 2013, Barcelona, Spain.
Copyright 2013 ACM 978-1-4503-1953-9/13/10 ...$15.00.
http://dx.doi.org/10.1145/2504730.2504760.

last for a period of time (several minutes) before changing to other values. Consequently, the timestamps produced by this API can significantly under-estimate or fluctuate the measured RTTs.

In this paper, we report two important cases with detailed investigations. First, we discover that some HTTP-based methods over-estimate the RTT, because they include the TCP handshaking in the delay. Second, we study the effect of timing methods in the Java applet case by replacing the timing function with `System.nanoTime()`. The experiment results show that the under-estimation of RTT disappears after introducing the new timing function. Furthermore, the new implementation introduces very small and consistent delay overhead. In particular, the variation of delay overhead in the socket-based measurement can approximate to 0 ms, meaning that it can estimate the RTTs accurately as what WinDump can do.

The outline of this paper is as follows. In Section 2, we first survey the measurement methods used in browser-based network measurement tools and services. We then describe our measurement setup in Section 3, followed by a report of the results in Section 4. Based on our evaluation, we summarize several practical considerations in Section 5. After highlighting the related works in Section 6, we conclude the paper in Section 7.

2. BROWSER-BASED NETWORK MEASUREMENT

A browser-based network measurement tool can generally provide many different services. Netalyzr [19], for example, provides network-layer information (e.g., RTT and path MTU), service reachability, and DNS measurement. In this paper, we consider the accuracy of the network RTT measurement, because a browser-based tool, being operated on the application layer, may significantly inflate the actual network RTT. The inflation also affects jitter and throughput (Tput) measurement. However, we do not anticipate such impact on packet loss and reordering measurement.

We have studied the RTT measurement methods employed by a number of browser-based tools, such as Netalyzr [19], Janc's methods [16], and How's My Network (HMN) [31], and speedtest services, including Speedof.me [2] and Ookla [26, 25], by inspecting their codes and the packets exchanged between browsers and servers. Their methods comprise a preparation phase and a measurement phase, as shown in Figure 1. In the preparation phase, the browser first loads from a web server a container page containing a piece of measurement code. In the measurement phase,

1. (Send) The measurement code is executed at the browser to instantiate an object which sends a "request" message (e.g., HTTP `GET` or binary data) to the origin server or another web server to elicit a "response" message. The timestamp (t_s^B) is recorded just before sending the request message which may be sent in one IP packet (for RTT measurement) or multiple IP packets (for throughput measurement).
2. (Receive) The web server that receives the response message returns a "response" message (e.g., HTTP response message or binary data) to the browser. The timestamp (t_r^B) is recorded immediately after receiving the response message. The RTT is then estimated by $t_r^B - t_s^B$. Similar to the send case, the response message may be sent in one or more IP packets.

2.1 HTTP-based and socket-based methods

The methods for a browser to send a request message to a web server for RTT measurement can be classified into HTTP-based and socket-based. Table 1 summarizes eleven such methods and the tools that use them. The HTTP-based method could be implemented through JavaScript, Flash, or Java applet. A JavaScript code imbedded in the container page creates an XHR object and calls the `send()` function to send out an HTTP request. The object records t_s^B using the JavaScript function `Date.getTime()` and uses the `onreadystatechange` event listener to determine whether the response has been received for recording t_r^B. Another JavaScript method is based on DOM element that first records t_s^B before inserting a new DOM element to the page using a `<script>` tag or `<img>` tag. This tag points to a specified URL to download the requested object. A successful loading triggers an `onload` event which prompts the logging of t_r^B. Flash, on the other hand, provides class `URLLoader` to handle HTTP data, and Java applet offers class `URL`. Both of them provide function `Date.getTime()` to log the current timestamps, and they record t_s^B just before sending out the request. Flash detects the completion of receiving the response via function `addEventListener` for recording t_r^B. Although there is no such event listener in Java applet, the completion can be detected by reading the response content.

The socket-based method, on the other hand, establishes network connections/associations through TCP or UDP sockets for exchanging binary data. TCP socket is supported by Flash, Java applet, and WebSocket, whereas UDP socket is only supported by Java applet. Flash manipulates network socket with class `Socket`. This class also provides function `addEventListener` which detects data arrival. In Java applet, the sockets are created via class `Socket` for TCP and `DatagramSocket` for UDP. The timestamps are recorded after the receive function call. WebSocket provides its functionality through JavaScript. WebSocket is like TCP socket on the abstraction level, except that the data transmissions are based on messages. Therefore, WebSocket obtains the timestamps in a similar way as Flash and Java applet.

All the HTTP-based methods, except for DOM, suffer from the restriction imposed by the same-origin policy which prevents a browser from accessing other servers except the original one hosting the container page. However, Flash can bypass this restriction through the Flash cross-domain policy, and Java applet's approach is through a signed Java applet. On the other hand, except for Flash, the socket-based methods are not affected by the same-origin policy, but they are required to open service ports for socket connections. Another important consideration is that Flash and Java applet, as the third-party plug-ins, are not supported in mobile computing platforms. As a result, WebSocket is the remaining choice for performing socket-based measurement in both fixed and mobile network platforms.

2.2 Measuring the delay overhead

The main objective of this paper is to accurately measure the delay overhead incurred at browsers when measuring RTT. Back to Figure 1, supposing that the request and response messages are sent in one packet each, the network RTT is given by the difference

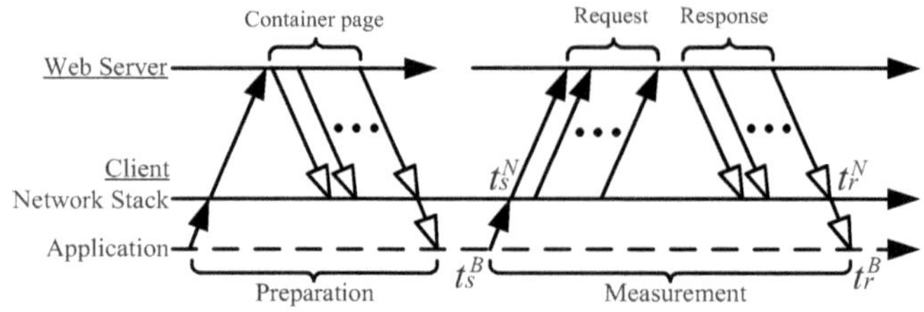

Figure 1: Two phases in browser-based network measurement.

Table 1: A summary of the browser-based network measurement methods and tools.

Approaches	Technology	Availability	Methods	Subject to the same-origin policy by default?	Measured path-quality metrics	Tools / Services
HTTP-based	XHR	Native	GET	Yes	RTT, Tput	Speedof.me [2], BandwidthPlace [21]
			POST	Yes	RTT, Tput	Janc's methods [16]
	DOM	Native	GET	No	RTT, Tput	[16], [21], Wang's method [35]
	Flash	Plug-in	GET	Yes*	RTT, Tput	Speedtest [26], AuditMyPC [7], Speedchecker [33]
			POST	Yes*	RTT, Tput	Bandwidth Meter [10], InternetFrog [15]
	Java applet	Plug-in	GET	Yes*	RTT, Tput	
			POST	Yes*	RTT, Tput	
Socket-based	WebSocket	Native	TCP	No	RTT, Tput	
	Java applet	Plug-in	TCP	No	RTT, Tput	Netalyzr [19], HMN [31], JavaNws [20],
			UDP	No	RTT, Tput, Loss	Pingtest [25], NDT [22], AuditMyPC [8]
	Flash	Plug-in	TCP	Yes*	RTT, Tput	[26]

Note: * The same-origin policy can be bypassed.

of the packet's receive and send timestamps which is measured by WinDump and tcpdump: $t_r^N - t_s^N$. Since browsers cannot access to network stack directly, the measured RTT is based on $t_r^B - t_s^B$. The time resolution for this browser-level measurement is usually assumed to be 1 ms, determined by the function `Date.getTime()` (we will discuss the real-time granularity of this function for Java applet in Section 4.2). The accuracy of the browser-level RTT measurement depends on several factors:

1. Accuracy of the timing function invoked by the adopted measurement method,
2. The delay for the browser to propagate the request message to the network stack and the delay for delivering the response message to the browser, and
3. The behavior of how the browser sends the message, for example, whether the delay includes the time for establishing a TCP connection.

To appraise the delay accuracy in browser-based network measurement, we therefore measure the delay overhead as

$$\Delta d = (t_r^B - t_s^B) - (t_r^N - t_s^N). \quad (1)$$

Besides affecting the RTT measurement, the delay overhead, if not stable enough, will also affect the jitter measurement. Moreover, the actual round-trip throughput could be seriously under-estimated by an inflated RTT.

3. EXPERIMENT SETUP

In measuring the delay overhead incurred on the RTT measurement, we consider all the HTTP/TCP measurement methods in Table 1. To make the comparison more comparable, we do not include Java's UDP socket method. Besides the ten measurement methods, we investigate the consistency of delay overhead of a given method across browsers and systems. Ideally, a browser-based tool is expected to incur similar delay overhead, regardless of which browser and system it is operated on. To this end, we consider the five major browsers on Windows 7 and Ubuntu in Table 2 with the Flash and Java applet plug-in configurations. Note that the IE and Safari versions used in the experiments do not support WebSocket. Although the latest IE 10 and Safari 6 both support WebSocket, we use IE 9 and Safari 5 instead, because IE 9 is the default browser for Windows 7 and Safari 6 is not available in Windows 7. For fair comparison, what we have tested are all 32-bit browsers, because some of the browsers do not provide 64-bit version.

We set up a testbed consisting of two machines connected to a switch by 100-Mbps Ethernet, as shown in Figure 2. Both machines have the same hardware configuration: equipped with a 1.86GHz

Table 2: Configurations of the browsers and systems used in the experiments.

OS	Browsers	Version	Flash	Java applet	Web Socket
Windows	Chrome	23.0	11.7.700	1.7.0	√
	Firefox	17.0	11.5.502	1.7.0	√
	IE	9.0.8	11.5.502	1.7.0	×
	Opera	12.11	11.5.502	1.7.0	√
	Safari	5.1.7	11.5.502	1.7.0	×
Ubuntu	Chrome	23.0	11.5.31	1.6.0	√
	Firefox	17.0	11.2.202	1.6.0	√
	Opera	12.11	11.2.202	1.6.0	√

Intel Core 2 Duo processor (E6320) and 2GB memory. One is a dual-boot system with Windows 7 and Ubuntu 12.04 LTS, and is installed with the five browsers. The other machine hosts an Apache web server version 2.2 on Ubuntu 10.04. We also introduce an additional delay of 50 ms on the server side to simulate the Internet environment. Without such delay, the link RTT (< 1 ms) is too small to sample. Beyond that, as we shall see in the next section, this delay is a major factor determining the amount of RTT inflation when a measurement method includes TCP handshaking in the delay measurement.

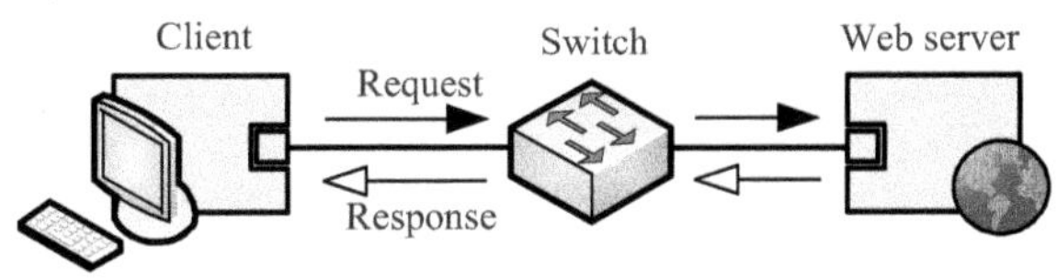

Figure 2: Testbed Setup.

We have prepared a container page using PHP or HTML for each measurement method imbedded with JavaScript code, Flash object, or Java applet[1]. The entire suite of experiments is executed automatically. Each browser program is executed on command line, and it retrieves from the server a container page for a given measurement method. When the browser renders the page, it executes the measurement code to instantiate the required object which sends a request message to the same web server which returns a reply message with the 50 ms delay. As discussed in section 2, the measurement code records t_s^B and t_r^B. At the same time, the client machine runs WinDump/tcpdump to capture t_s^N and t_r^N.

[1]Source codes are available at `http://www4.comp.polyu.edu.hk/~oneprobe/src.php`

Considering the possible impact on the browser to instantiate the object for the first RTT measurement, we conduct a second RTT measurement immediately after the first one and reusing the same object. Therefore, for each setting, we obtain two sets of delay overheads, denoted by Δd_1 and Δd_2. Moreover, we choose small request and reply messages, each of which can be sent in one packet. This setting allows us to remove other possible delay due to data segmentation, send and receive buffering, and throttling by the send window. During the measurement period, we also ensure that the network was free of cross traffic, packet loss, and retransmissions. Although the web server could bias the RTT, the bias, if any, is mitigated by the subtraction of $t_r^B - t_s^B$ and $t_r^N - t_s^N$ in the same round of measurement.

For each experiment, we run it for 50 times and compute from them useful statistics, such as minimum, median, and 25% and 75% percentiles. We do not record the system load, but we ensure that all the necessary processes (e.g., `explorer.exe` in Windows, `init` in Linux, and so on) run in the background. Besides, some other programs, such as packet capturing program and automation scripts, need to be dynamically invoked during the measurement procedure. The browsers themselves also consume resources to render the measurement objects. As a result, the delay overheads may still vary, depending on how sensitive the measurement methods are to these system loads.

4. MEASUREMENT RESULTS

We plot the ten sets of measurement results (one per measurement method) in Figure 3 using box-and-whisker plots. The first row includes the four methods using native features in browsers. The second comprises the Flash methods, and the third the Java applet methods. Each plot (except for WebSocket) includes the measurement by the eight browser-OS cases which are identified by the browser's initial (system's initial). They are then followed by Δd_1 (in red) or Δd_2 (in cyan). For example, "C (U) Δd_1" refers to Δd_1 obtained by Chrome in Ubuntu.

In each box-and-whisker plot, the top and bottom of the box are given by the 75th percentile and 25th percentile, and the mark inside is the median. The upper and lower whiskers are the maximum and minimum, respectively, after excluding the outliers. The outliers above the upper whiskers are those exceeding 1.5 of the upper quartile, and those below the minimum are less than 1.5 of the lower quartile.

Figures 3(a), 3(b), 3(c), 3(e), 3(f), 3(h), and 3(i) for the HTTP-based methods show that the delay overhead generally cannot be ignored. The XHR methods' delay overheads range from a few milliseconds to tens of milliseconds. The overheads in Flash are extremely high. The median overheads are between 20 ms and 100 ms. Even for the minimum overheads, they can reach as high as 100 ms (Δd_1 of Opera in both Windows and Ubuntu). The DOM methods achieves a better result than XHR and Flash. Most of the median overheads are smaller than 5 ms. The Java applet methods differ from the previous group in that they could (e.g., Firefox and Opera) under-estimate the RTT (i.e., negative overhead) by as much as 5 ms.

Another important result concerns the consistency of a measurement method across different browsers and systems. If the overheads are dependent on specific browsers and systems, it will make the calibration very difficult. The delay overheads for the HTTP-based methods generally see a very high variability across browsers for the Flash methods. The DOM method provides the most consistent overhead across all browsers, especially those on Ubuntu. The two Java applet methods are also quite consistent on the Ubuntu but less consistent on Windows.

On the other hand, Figures 3(d), 3(g), and 3(j) show that the delay overheads incurred by the socket-based methods are considerably small. The median overheads are mostly smaller than 1 ms. Nevertheless, the overheads for some browsers fluctuate within a range of around 10 ms (e.g., Java applet for Firefox in Windows). Overall, the WebSocket method achieves the most stable result, except for Opera (W) Δd_1. Similar to the other two Java applet methods, the Java applet socket method will under-estimate the delay, especially those in Windows.

4.1 The effect of network behavior on HTTP-based methods

The major difference between the HTTP-based and socket-based methods is that the former needs to parse the additional HTTP header. However, parsing HTTP alone cannot explain those high delay overheads. We consider some of these cases next and analyze other possible reasons responsible for the RTT inflation.

Table 3 shows the median overheads for the Flash GET and POST methods, obtained by Opera in Windows and Ubuntu. Although the data are collected from different OSes, the delay overheads behave similarly. For the GET method, O(W) and O(U) both suffer from a very large Δd_1 (> 100 ms) but a relatively small Δd_2 (< 20 ms). For the POST method, the median Δd_1 is still high, but the median Δd_2 is much larger than that for the GET method.

Table 3: Median Δd_1 and Δd_2 for the Flash HTTP methods in Opera.

		O(W)	O(U)
GET	Δd_1	101.1	105.3
	Δd_2	19.8	19.8
POST	Δd_1	100.1	105.6
	Δd_2	69.6	68.1

The packet capture files show that Opera opens a new TCP connection to handle the HTTP request issued by the Flash object for the first RTT measurement, therefore inflating the Δd_1 measurement. In the GET method, this existing connection can be reused for the second measurement. Therefore, the Δd_1 measurement excludes the TCP handshaking. However, a new connection will still be opened for the POST method. We confirm this by subtracting 50 ms, the simulated network delay, from Δd_2 in the POST method, the result ($\sim$20 ms) is almost the same as the GET method. Moreover, we compare the behavior of other browsers and find that even for the first RTT measurement they will reuse the TCP connection for downloading the container page in the preparation phase, thus resulting in a much lower overhead.

4.2 The effect of timestamp granularity

From Figure 3(h), 3(i), and 3(j), all three Java applet methods suffer from the negative delay overheads on Windows, which indicates that performing path measurement with Java applet can severely under-estimate the RTT. At the same time, significant variance can be observed. For example, Safari's overhead in Java applet socket method spans in the range of -13 ms and 13 ms, as illustrated in Figure 3(j). Due to the page limit, we only discuss the socket case for evaluation.

We show the CDFs of Δd_1 and Δd_2 of those experiments in Figure 4(a). The figure depicts that both Δd_1 and Δd_2 for Firefox and Opera, and Δd_1 for Safari have two discrete levels, whereas Δd_2 for Safari spans continuously over the range.According to [28], web browsers instantiate Java applet through Java Plug-in. In fact, an applet runs in an instance of the Java Runtime Environment (JRE) software, not within the browsers. To mitigate the influence of browsers, we directly launch the applet with `appletviewer`

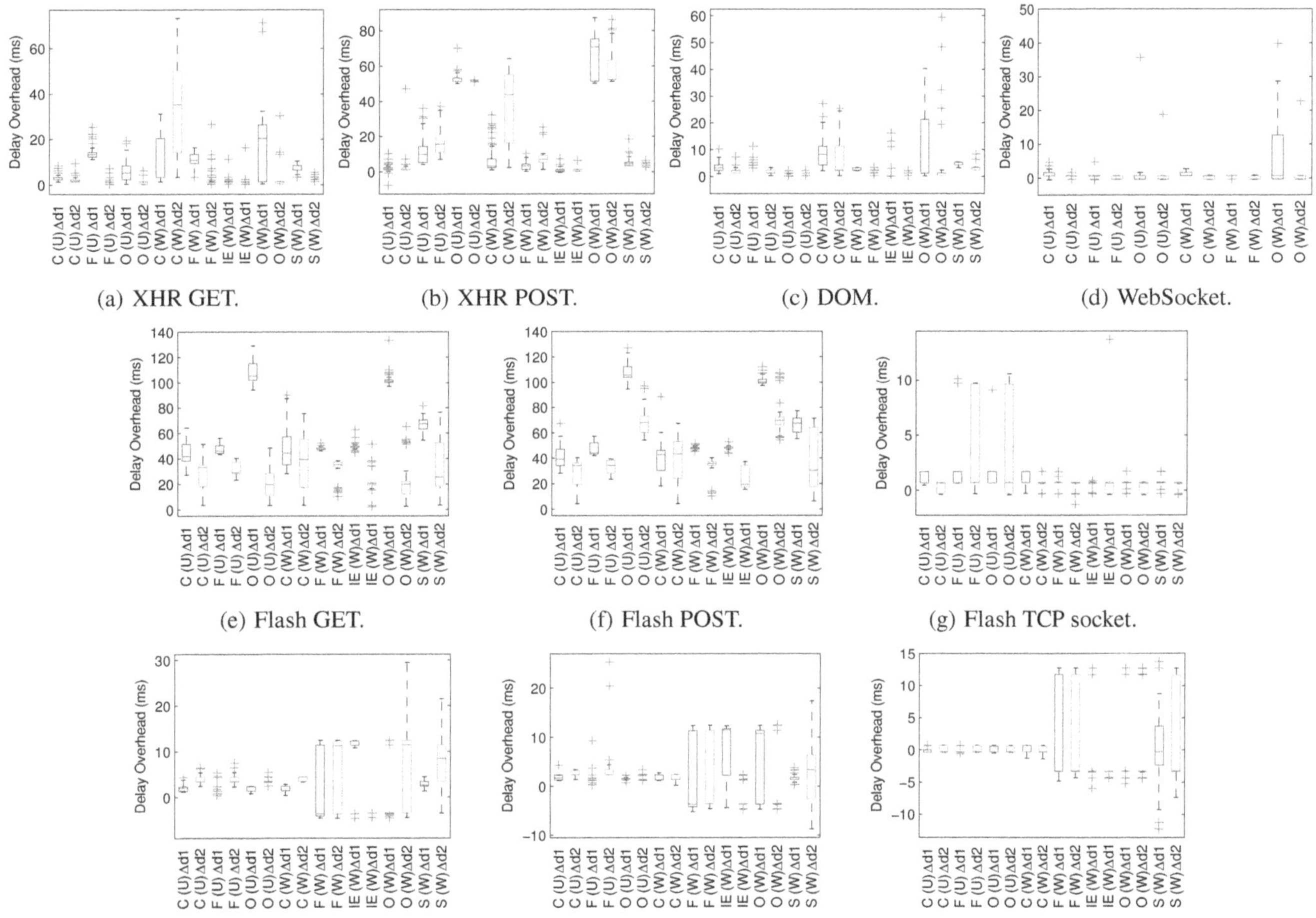

(a) XHR GET. (b) XHR POST. (c) DOM. (d) WebSocket.

(e) Flash GET. (f) Flash POST. (g) Flash TCP socket.

(h) Java applet GET. (i) Java applet POST. (j) Java applet TCP socket.

Figure 3: Box plots of the delay overheads (by methods).

provided by Oracle Java Development Kit (JDK). We plot the CDFs of Δd_1 and Δd_2 in Figure 4(b). Similar discrete levels are observed without web browser and Java Plug-in. We thereupon can rule out browsers and their corresponding Java Plug-ins being the cause of this problem.

We then focus on the JRE itself. The timing function in Java, `Date.getTime()`, is implemented with another Java function `System.currentTimeMillis()`. An Oracle's documentation warns that while the resolution of the return value is 1 ms, the granularity depends on the underlying system [29]. We test the timestamp granularity with the code shown in Figure 5. The piece of code keeps querying the timestamp with `Date.getTime()` until the current value is different from the previous one. The difference in the two timestamps is the granularity that this function can achieve. Surprisingly, we find that the granularity is not a constant value. It can be 1 ms, or ~15 ms. Each possible value will last for a period of time (several minutes) and then change to other values. While such a coarse granularity of timestamp in Windows was reported [27], it has not mentioned the non-constant granularity. Initially, we conjecture that the varying time granularity is related to the 32-bit JRE. However, we later find that 64-bit JRE also suffers from the same problem. To further validate our findings, we analyze the data obtained from the delay overhead experiments. The gap between the two significant discrete levels is about 16 ms, which concurs with one of the timestamp granularity obtained from the test codes. Hence, we believe that the coarse and instable timestamp granularity is the main reason for the bizarre behavior observed in the previous delay overhead experiments.

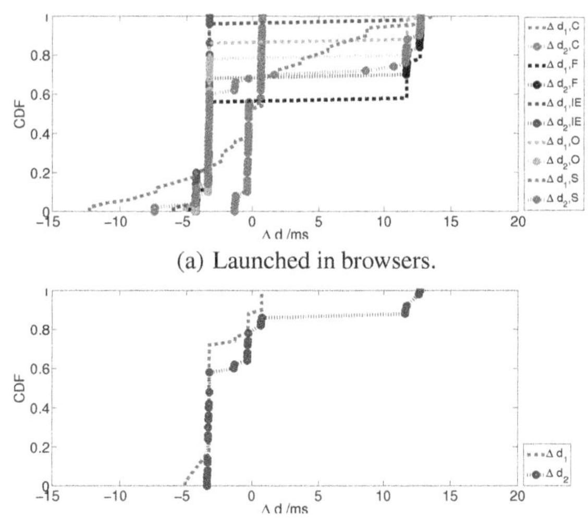

(a) Launched in browsers.

(b) Launched with appletviewer.

Figure 4: CDF plots of Δd_1 and Δd_2 using the Java applet socket in Windows.

Table 4: Delay overheads measured by Java applet methods in Windows when function `System.nanoTime()` is adopted (mean with 95% confidence interval, in ms).

Method	GET		POST		Socket	
	Δd_1	Δd_2	Δd_1	Δd_2	Δd_1	Δd_2
Chrome	2.96 ±0.02	4.80 ±0.09	2.71 ±0.03	1.84 ±0.00	0.01 ±0.00	0.07 ±0.01
Firefox	2.73 ±0.02	4.38 ±0.08	2.41 ±0.03	1.49 ±0.01	0.00 ±0.00	0.07 ±0.01
IE	2.73 ±0.03	4.56 ±0.09	2.57 ±0.09	1.49 ±0.04	0.02 ±0.01	0.06 ±0.01
Opera	2.83 ±0.03	4.46 ±0.07	2.51 ±0.03	1.57 ±0.01	0.01 ±0.00	0.06 ±0.01
Safari	1.88 ±0.05	1.52 ±0.02	1.62 ±0.07	1.42 ±0.01	0.07 ±0.00	0.13 ±0.01

We replace the timing function `Date.getTime()` with a more precise `System.nanoTime()` and then rerun the experiments with the same configurations. The measurement results are summarized in Table 4. We present the mean delay overhead as well as the 95% confidence intervals. The under-estimation and the large variation of RTTs disappears after the replacement, including the other two Java applet methods. For the GET and POST methods, the mean delay overheads range from 2 ms to 5 ms, only a little larger than the WebSocket cases. As for the socket methods, the delay overheads are trivial. Considering the accuracy of software packet capturer being larger than 0.3 ms [7], we can regard the accuracy of the Java socket method comparable to tcpdump/WinDump if `System.nanoTime()` is adopted.

```
long start = 0;
long end = 0;
while (true) {
  if (start == 0) {
    start = new Date().getTime();
  } else {
    long current = new Date().getTime();
    if (current != start) {
      end = current;
      break;
    }
  }
}
System.out.println((end - start) + "ms");
```

Figure 5: Codes for testing the timestamp granularity.

5. PRACTICAL CONSIDERATIONS

Based on the overall evaluation, the Java applet socket method is recommended if the proper timing function is applied. However, our inspection of some Java applet-based tools shows that many of them are still using `System.currentTimeMillis()` or `Date.getTime()`, such as [8, 19, 22]. Switching to the more precise function `System.nanoTime()` can greatly improve their accuracy in Windows. Based on our evaluation, the Flash GET and POST methods are not so suitable for the purpose of measurement.

For the measurements performed in Windows, Firefox is the preferred browser, whereas in Ubuntu Chrome is a better choice. We do not recommend Safari even for the Java applet socket method due to the fact that its default Java interface (`JavaPlugin.jar` and `npJavaPlugin.dll`) runs into problems easily. The measurement results obtained from Safari are much higher than the other browsers. After deleting the two files, we can force it to use the JRE provided by Oracle, and the inaccuracies are subsequently removed.

There are also issues of reusing existing connections and web objects for network measurement. The real-world applications are more complicated than our experiment settings. The browsers have to establish new connections due to the competition of downloading the other files. If a measurement object can be reused, the delay overhead can be better estimated by Δd_2 without including the TCP handshaking delay. However, some methods, as described in Section 4.1, always open new connections for measurement whether the measurement object can be reused or not. In this case, the additional delay cannot be avoided.

6. RELATED WORKS

Although browser-based network measurement tools and services have been widely deployed, only a handful of studies are devoted to appraising them. These previous works consider only a small number of methods. Janc et al. [16] proposed HTTP-based methods using JavaScript and Flash for measuring network performance, and performed control and web experiments to compare the methods. Later, Kaplan et al. [18] performed testbed experiments to investigate the delay overhead incurred by browser with four HTTP-based methods using JavaScript and Flash. Both papers concluded that JavaScript performs better than Flash for delay measurement, which is coherent with our results. However, they did not compare the HTTP-based methods with socket-based methods.

Krintz and Wolski [20] compared the performance between Java applet and C program with JavaNws, and found that Java applet is comparable with C socket. Yeboah et al. [36] performed an Internet measurement study to compare the delay measurement results from ICMP ping, King [12], Flash (socket-based), and JavaScript (HTTP-based). They found that the results from Flash socket measurement were close to ping, whereas JavaScript had an inflated delay. However, both papers did not utilize any network stack information, such as tcpdump capture, to investigate the actual overhead caused by the applications.

7. CONCLUSION

In this paper, we studied the impact of application-level delay overheads on browser-based network measurement tools. By evaluating all the HTTP/TCP methods employed by the current browser-based measurement tools and services with our carefully designed testbed experiments, we showed that both socket-based and HTTP-based methods may introduce different degrees of inaccuracy in measuring the RTT due to a number of intrinsic and system issues. Based on the results, the socket-based methods are generally more reliable than the HTTP-based methods. Although our work is done in desktop environment, the methodology can be extended to the mobile environment. Another extension is to investigate the delay overhead incurred on the server side.

Acknowledgement

We thank the four anonymous reviewers for their very useful comments and feedback for improving the paper, and our shepherd Jeffrey Pang for guiding us during the revision process. This work is partially supported by an ITSP Tier-2 project grant (ref. no. GHP/027/11) from the Innovation Technology Fund in Hong Kong.

8. REFERENCES

[1] Ookla.com. http://www.ookla.com.
[2] Speedof.me. http://speedof.me/.
[3] Accuracy (trueness and precision) of measurement methods and results – part 1: General principles and definitions. ISO 5725-1, 1994.
[4] G. Almes, S. Kalidindi, and M. Zekauskas. A one-way delay metric for IPPM. RFC 2679, IETF, Sept. 1999.
[5] G. Almes, S. Kalidindi, and M. Zekauskas. A one-way packet loss metric for IPPM. RFC 2680, IETF, Sept. 1999.
[6] G. Almes, S. Kalidindi, and M. Zekauskas. A round-trip delay metric for IPPM. RFC 2681, IETF, Sept. 1999.
[7] Audit My PC.com. AuditMyPC.com Broadband Speed Test (Flash). http://www.auditmypc.com/internet-speed-test.asp.
[8] Audit My PC.com. Internet Speed Test (Java). http://www.auditmypc.com/internet-speed-test.asp.
[9] CAIDA. Archipelago Measurement Infrastructure. http://www.caida.org/projects/ark/.
[10] cnet.com. Bandwidth Meter Online Speed Test. http://reviews.cnet.com/internet-speed-test/.
[11] M. Dhawan, J. Samuel, R. Teixeira, C. Kreibich, M. Allman, N. Weaver, and V. Paxson. Fathom: A browser-based network measurement platform. In *Proc. ACM/USENIX IMC*, 2012.
[12] K. P. Gummadi, S. Saroiu, and S. D. Gribble. King: estimating latency between arbitrary internet end hosts. In *Proc. SIGCOMM IMW*, 2002.
[13] E. Halepovic, J. Pang, and O. Spatscheck. Can you GET me now? Estimating the time-to-first-byte of HTTP transactions with passive measurements. In *Proc. ACM/USENIX IMC*, 2012.
[14] J. Huang, F. Qian, Y. Guo, Y. Zhou, Q. Xu, Z. M. Mao, S. Sen, and O. Spatscheck. An in-depth study of LTE: Effect of network protocol and application behavior on performance. In *Proc. ACM SIGCOMM*, 2013.
[15] InternetFrog.com. InternetFrog.com Speed Test. http://www.internetfrog.com/mypc/speedtest/.
[16] A. Janc, C. Wills, and M. Claypool. Network performance evaluation in a web browser. In *Proc. IASTED PDCS*, 2009.
[17] D. Joumblatt, R. Teixeira, J. Chandrashekar, and N. Taft. HostView: Annotating end-host performance measurements with user feedback. In *Proc. ACM HotMetrics*, 2010.
[18] M. Kaplan, M. Zeljkovic, M. Claypool, and C. Wills. Javascript and Flash overhead in the web browser sandbox. Tech. Rep. WPI-CS-TR-10-14, Computer Science Department, Worcester Polytechnic Institute, 2012.
[19] C. Kreibich, N. Weaver, B. Nechaev, and V. Paxson. Netalyzr: Illuminating the edge network. In *Proc. ACM/USENIX IMC*, 2010.
[20] C. Krintz and R. Wolski. Using JavaNws to compare C and Java TCP-Socket performance. *Concurrency Computat.: Pract. Exper.*, 13(8-9):815–839, 2001.
[21] S. Limited. BandwidthPlace Speed Test. http://www.bandwidthplace.com/.
[22] M-Lab. NDT (Network Diagnostic Tool). http://measurementlab.net/run-ndt.
[23] J. Mahdavi and V. Paxson. IPPM metrics for measuring connectivity. RFC 2678, IETF, Sept. 1999.
[24] D. Morato, E. Magana, M. Izal, J. Aracil, F. Naranjo, F. Astiz, U. Alonso, I. Csabai, P. Haga, G. Simon, J. Steger, and G. Vattay. The European Traffic Observatory Measurement Infraestructure (ETOMIC): A testbed for universal active and passive measurements. In *Proc. Tridentcom*, 2005.
[25] Ookla. Pingtest.net. http://www.pingtest.net/.
[26] Ookla. Speedtest.net. http://www.speedtest.net/.
[27] Oracle. Bad timing using System.currentTimeMillis() instead of System.nanoTime(). http://whileonefork.blogspot.hk/2010/12/bad-timing-using-systemcurrenttimemilli.html.
[28] Oracle. Java Plug-in and Applet Architecture. http://docs.oracle.com/javase/7/docs/technotes/guides/jweb/applet/applet_execution.html.
[29] Oracle. System. http://docs.oracle.com/javase/6/docs/api/java/lang/System.html#currentTimeMillis().
[30] V. Paxson, G. Almes, J. Mahdavi, and M. Mathis. Framework for IP performance metrics. RFC 2330, IETF, May 1998.
[31] A. Ritacco, C. Wills, and M. Claypool. How's My Network? - A Java approach to home network measurement. In *Proc. IEEE ICCCN*, 2009.
[32] M. Sánchez, J. Otto, Z. Bischof, D. Choffnes, F. Bustamante, B. Krishnamurthy, and W. Willinger. Dasu: Pushing experiments to the Internet's edge. In *Proc. USENIX NSDI*, 2013.
[33] Speedchecker Limited. Broadband Speedchecker. http://www.broadbandspeedchecker.co.uk/.
[34] S. Sundaresan, W. de Donato, N. Feamster, R. Teixeira, S. Crawford, and A. Pescape. Broadband Internet performance: A view from the gateway. In *Proc. ACM SIGCOMM*, 2011.
[35] Y. Wang, C. Huang, J. Li, and K. Ross. Estimating the performance of hypothetical cloud service deployments: A measurement-based approach. In *Proc. IEEE INFOCOM*, 2011.
[36] Y. Yeboah Jr., R. Nketia, and X. Hei. A measurement study of application layer latency. Technical report, Huazhong University of Science and Technology, 2011.

Network Fingerprinting: TTL-Based Router Signatures

Yves Vanaubel
Université de Liège
Belgium
yves.vanaubel@ulg.ac.be

Jean-Jacques Pansiot
Université de Strasbourg
France
pansiot@unistra.fr

Pascal Mérindol
Université de Strasbourg
France
merindol@unistra.fr

Benoit Donnet
Université de Liège
Belgium
benoit.donnet@ulg.ac.be

ABSTRACT

Fingerprinting networking equipment has many potential applications and benefits in network management and security. More generally, it is useful for the understanding of network structures and their behaviors. In this paper, we describe a simple fingerprinting mechanism based on the initial TTL values used by routers to reply to various probing messages. We show that main classes obtained using this simple mechanism are meaningful to distinguish routers platforms. Besides, it comes at a very low additional cost compared to standard active topology discovery measurements. As a proof of concept, we apply our method to gain more insight on the behavior of MPLS routers and to, thus, more accurately quantify their visible/invisible deployment.

Categories and Subject Descriptors

C.2.1 [**Network Architecture and Design**]: Network topology

General Terms

Measurement

Keywords

network discovery, fingerprinting, MPLS, router signatures, initial TTL

1. INTRODUCTION

Fingerprinting [1, 2] refers to the act of dividing network equipment into disjoint classes by analyzing messages sent by that equipment, usually in response to some form of active probing. Those classes may correspond, for instance, to router operating system (OS), router brand, or router configuration. Providing such a fingerprinting is useful for several applications and studies. Indeed, for instance in network management, if the fingerprinting is based on router OS, it may help in listing the network nodes and identifying vulnerable hosts in terms of security and fault tolerance [1, 3]. It may also help in identifying which nodes have an abnormal behavior (e.g., delay, packets drop/modification, etc). In network topology discovery [4], fingerprinting could find a suitable usage to understand how various types of equipment are interconnected. Indeed, obtaining the router level map of the topology from `traceroute` data requires an additional probing intensive step: *alias resolution* [5]. Router fingerprinting may drastically speed up this step, since IP addresses belonging to different classes cannot be aliases and, so, do not require to be further probed for alias resolution. Another interesting application is to understand whether IP networks are heterogenous in terms of hardware and software at different scales (e.g., temporal to study the evolution and structural to understand internal structure of autonomous systems). Indeed, an accurate fingerprinting technique may allow one to distinguish router OS among a given brand.

However, fingerprinting can be costly and possibly intrusive as it could require many probes [1]. In this case, fingerprinting could be a time consuming process using undue network resources. Moreover, too many probes towards a network node or a subnet could be seen as remote host scanning and, consequently, be filtered.

In this paper, we present a fingerprinting method that is a companion to `traceroute`-like exploration. Our method is simple[1], requires few additional probes to `traceroute` ones, but still allows for classifying Internet routers based on their hardware and OS. Our fingerprinting method infers initial TTL values [6, 7] used by routers when building their different kinds of reply packets. We call this set of TTL values *router signatures*. Router signatures are meaningful for fingerprinting as the initial TTL values vary not only between different router platforms but also depending on the protocol and the type of message (error versus standard replies for instance). Indeed, no specific default value has been standardized for the TTL field.[2]

We consider a router signature as a n-tuple made of n initial TTL values. Those n TTL values are derived from TTL included in different types of probe replies. The number and

[1]Note that most routers do not reply to "complex" scanning tools such as `nmap` [1].

[2]It is worth to notice that RFC1700 recommends to use 64 as initial TTL value [8]. This is however not followed by most router manufacturers.

IMC'13, October 23–25, 2013, Barcelona, Spain.
Copyright 2013 ACM 978-1-4503-1953-9/13/10 ...$15.00.
http://dx.doi.org/10.1145/2504730.2504761.

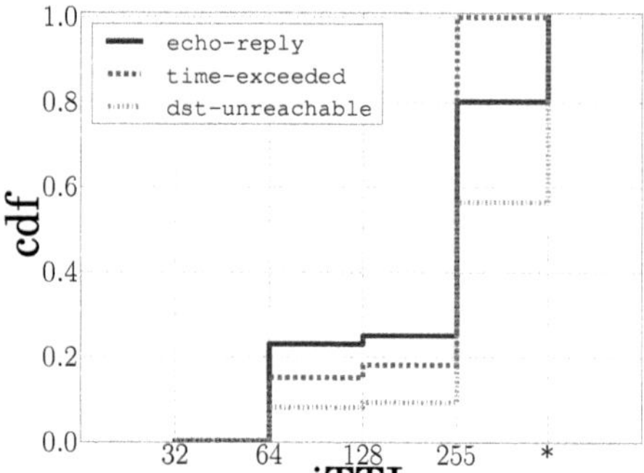

Figure 1: Initial TTL distribution (∗ refers to non-responding routers)

the variety of probes sent give the actual value of n. In this preliminary work, we focus on $n = 2$ TTL values, but we already envision longer (i.e., $n > 2$) signatures to provide better distributions among router's OS. Indeed, the more discriminating, the more meaningful the significant classes. Note that it is not that easy since the OS market is known to be not uniformly shared. Thus, for an application such as providing a pre-partition to speed up alias resolution process, the interest may be limited at the granularity of the partition.

Based on a large-scale measurement campaign, we first demonstrate that our router signatures are consistent among measurement points. After providing some general distribution results, we illustrate how it can be used in the context of topology discovery [4] or active probing in general. In particular, it can be useful to determine if measurements are biased due to router type dependency. In this paper, we focus on MPLS tunnels identification and validation [9, 10]. We try to map the behavior of several MPLS tunnel classes [10] to our set of router signatures. We are thus able to improve our previous study [10] on MPLS quantification thanks to TTL-based fingerprinting. We believe that any active probing tool can take benefit from our simple fingerprinting proposal.

The remainder of this paper is organized as follows: Sec. 2 discusses our TTL-based signatures and our methodology; Sec. 3 shows how those classes can be helpful to improve our previous MPLS tunnels classification and quantification; Sec. 4 positions this paper regarding the state of the art; finally, Sec. 5 concludes this paper by providing discussions on ongoing works and perspectives for further works.

2. ROUTER SIGNATURES

This section introduces the fundamentals of our fingerprinting method. In order to obtain replies from most routers, our probing mechanism must remain as basic as possible. We thus only rely on the standard behavior of IP routers.

The IP packet header contains a *time-to-live* (TTL) field used to avoid packets looping forever when a routing loop occurs. This 8-bit field is set by the originating host/router to an *initial value* that is usually and nearly always a power of 2 in the list 32 (or 30), 64, 128, and 255. The TTL field is decremented by one at each intermediate node along the path the packet takes. When the TTL value is one, the router determines that the packet has consumed sufficient resources in the network, drops it, and informs the packet source by sending back an *Internet Control Message Protocol* (ICMP) `time-exceeded` message. `traceroute` [11] is based on this simple behavior.

In this paper, we need to determine the initial TTL ($iTTL$) of a received packet. Obviously, the (known) received value is equal to $iTTL - \#hops$ where $\#hops$ is the number of hops between the sender and the receiver. It is worth to notice that $\#hops < 30$ most of the time (99.8% of the paths, in our dataset, are less than 30 hops). Therefore, the iTTL value can be estimated as the smallest number in 32, 64, 128, 255 that is larger than the received value. In very infrequent cases, an iTTL of 64 together with a very long route ($\#hops > 32$) would give an incorrect guess of 32 instead of 64, e.g., a route of length 34 would be interpreted as a route of length 2. Those cases could be managed during a `traceroute` campaign by looking at the number of hops of the forward route. A difference between the number of forward and backward hops close to 32 would indicate that the iTTL is 64 instead of 32.

A router *signature* is made of a n-tuple of n iTTLs, those iTTLs being retrieved from different ICMP messages. Our basic pair-signature (with $n = 2$) simply uses the iTTL of two different messages: a `time-exceeded` message elicited by a `traceroute` probe, and an `echo-reply` message obtained from an `echo-request` probe. Quite surprisingly, for the same ICMP protocol, a significant proportion of nodes use two different iTTL values for these two messages, as shown on Fig. 1.[3] We also tried to add a third iTTL to our signatures: a `destination-unreachable` message elicited by a UDP probe. As shown on Fig. 1, more than 40% of routers do not respond to such probes. Mostly, our basic signatures are thus extended with an absence of response. We decided to not take the `destination-unreachable` iTTL into account in this preliminary study. However, the information it brings extends the number of possible signatures and we think it could be helpful for alias resolution in particular. In future works, we envision to consider more ICMP reply types and also different IP header fields. We already observed that the iTTL does not only depend on the reply type (error or standard replies) nor the answer origin (the central or the per interface processors).

In theory, using n probes, we may have up to $4 \times 5^{n-1}$ different signatures since we can count the absence of answer for `echo-reply` (i.e., a $*$) as a valuable pattern. It is worth to notice that the "4" before the multiplication sign is due to the fact that ICMP `time-exceeded` messages are our basic probing mechanism, i.e., `time-exceeded` messages are used to direct subsequent probes (`echo-request`, UDP packets, ...). This means that the $*$ does not count for `time-exceeded` messages and, only $|\{255,128,64,32\}|$ patterns are available for such replies.

2.1 Measurement campaign

We used Paris Traceroute [12] with ICMP `echo-request` packets to collect IP level paths. Each ICMP `time-exceeded` packet received is used to build the first component of a router signature. In addition, for each IP interface discovered, we sent 6 ICMP `echo-request` probes (in particular to ensure the robust meaning of a $*$ and help our MPLS discovery). We used the ICMP `echo-reply` packets received to complete the second component of our router signature.

[3]The methodology of our measurement campaign will be given in Sec. 2.1.

Note that, each IP address collected is pinged six times only once per vantage point (i.e., when it is discovered for the first time).

We perform our measurement study with a team of 200 randomly selected PlanetLab vantage points (VPs). Of the 200 VPs, 121 were located within the US; 10 VPs were located in Europe, and the other 69 in different countries. We randomly selected 1,000,000 destinations in the Archipelago [13] target list and evenly divided this target list among our VPs team. The dataset has been collected between January 8th, 2013 and January 10th, 2013 using scamper [14]. Once the data has been collected, we consider each IP address only once and associate this unique address to its signature. We so gathered 335,646 distinct IP addresses.

2.2 Measurement Cost

The additional overhead of a measurement campaign to fingerprint a set of routers found by a `traceroute` measurement campaign comes at a low cost: each discovered IP address must be probed with k ICMP `echo-request` messages, where k is a robustness parameter. Usually, many traces discover the same IP addresses that need to be probed only once [15]. So, at worst, this fingerprinting needs k more messages per IP address than `traceroute` only, and, on the average, much less. In our measurement campaign (where $k = 6$), 13.437.896 `traceroute` responses and 14.803.614 `ping` responses have been received. That is with our fingerprinting method, and on the average, a probed node sends about the same number of `time-exceeded` messages and `echo-reply` messages. This number could be further reduced by using a smaller robustness factor or by adding some extra cooperation between VPs in order to avoid as much as possible pinging the same IP address several times.

2.3 Signatures Consistency

The objective behind fingerprinting is to obtain a signature that depends only on the probed node. To verify that fact, we compared the signatures of IP addresses observed by at least two distinct VPs (that is through distinct `traceroute` and `ping` probes). Note that we consider only IP addresses that responded to `traceroute` probes, but some of them do not always respond to `ping` probes (i.e., the second component of the signature may take the value $*$). For the IP addresses seen from several VPs, we classify our signatures into three categories:

- *coherent*: the same signature is observed for a given router interface among measurements done by all VPs. This is the perfect case. Coherent signatures are observed in 95.92% of the cases.
- *weakly incoherent*: from some VPs, the signature is of the type $< x, y >$ while it is $< x, * >$ for some others. This concerns 3.94% of our signatures.
- *incoherent*: several different signatures are observed for a given router interface among measurements done by all VPs. This is the worst case but it is also very infrequent (0.14% of the cases).

Weakly incoherent signatures can be explained by two phenomena: some nodes may not respond to `ping` at some time, for example because of overloading, rate limiting, or filtering inducing the `echo-reply` lost on some paths [16]. For the 3.94% of weakly incoherent signatures we observed in our dataset, we decide to keep only the best signature (i.e., the complete one). We therefore replace each weakly incoherent signatures by the complete one. After this operation, around 17.5% of the entire set of IP addresses collected in our campaign were still associated to incomplete signatures (of the type $< x, * >$). Most of them (i.e., 10.19%) are seen by several VPs, while the remaining IP addresses (i.e., 7.31%) are seen by a single VP. This latter value could be further reduced by trying to `ping` those IP addresses from other VPs.

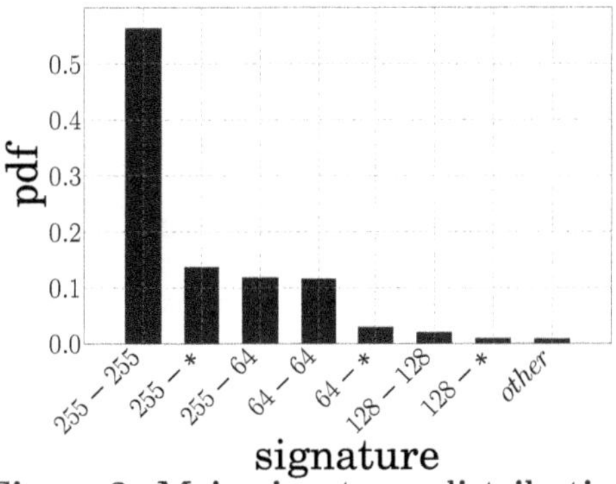

Figure 2: Main signatures distribution

Incoherent signatures may be explained by some artifacts (due to their extremely low proportion). Some middleboxes may rewrite the TTL field [17, 18, 19], or the same IP address may correspond to different nodes depending on the network location (*anycast* address). There is also the previously mentioned possible ambiguity between iTTL values 32 and 64.

2.4 Signatures Distribution

While many different platforms could correspond to the same signature, we know the signature of some well known platforms (to this purpose, we performed a bunch of tests in an emulation lab). For instance, Cisco routers generate signature $< 255, 255 >$ while, for Juniper routers, we have $< 255, 64 >$ with Junos and $< 128, 128 >$ with JunosE. Some Brocade and Alcatel equipment together with some Linux boxes result in a $< 64, 64 >$ signature. Although these signatures encompass the main router platforms, it would be very interesting to have a more complete correspondence between platforms and signatures. Obviously, when restricted to our 2-tuple, several very different platforms may have the same signature. So a more accurate signature, i.e., an n-tuple with $n > 2$, would be helpful. We already did some preliminary work analyzing signatures extended with other types of message (`destination-unreachable` in particular) or some other criterion, such as the ICMP messages size. However, since most routers come from a few major vendors, we cannot expect to partition the network nodes into a very fine-grained classification using this type of fingerprinting. This is why, in this study, we only consider this basic 2-tuple as a proof of concept that may be generalized by further study.

Fig. 2 illustrates the distribution of the main router signatures. The first class $< 255, 255 >$, that includes Cisco routers is largely dominant, corresponding to more than 50% of nodes. The fourth class $< 64, 64 >$, that includes several vendors or OSes (including Linux), and the third class $< 255, 64 >$ that includes Juniper routers running JunOS

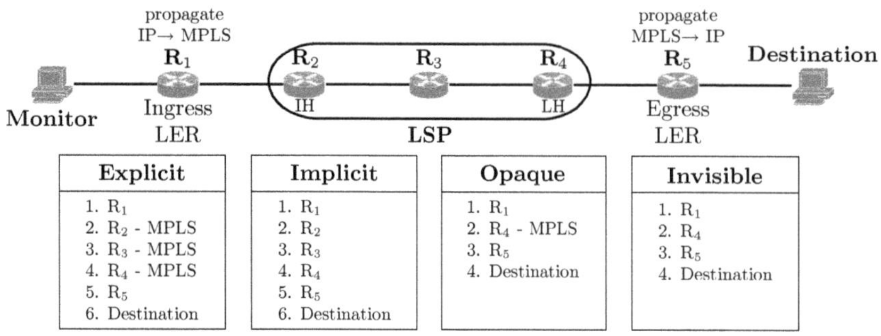

Figure 3: Example of MPLS tunnel

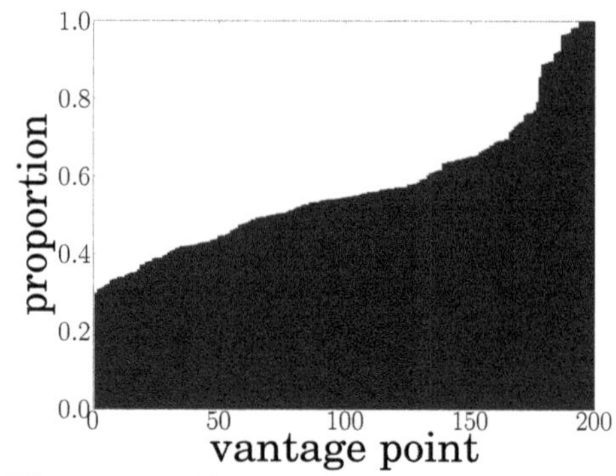

Figure 4: Proportion of paths, per VP, having at least one MPLS tunnel

have about 11% each. The second most frequent class $< 255, * >$, with about 15%, corresponds to an incomplete signature and is probably mostly made of nodes belonging, actually, to $< 255, 255 >$ or $< 255, 64 >$ but did not respond to `ping` for various reasons [16]. The class $< 128, 128 >$, including Juniper platforms running the JunosE system, is around 3% while the remaining classes are either incomplete or very rare. Therefore, at a global scale, our fingerprinting technique seems to reflect the market distribution.

To summarize, we first observe, that among different brands and OSes, routing devices use distinct iTTL values, and, second, we also notice that a single device can use multiple iTTL values (at least, this is the case for Juniper routers). We now focus on a specific use case illustrating the technical interest of a classification based on such observations.

3. MPLS USE CASE

Multiprotocol Label Switching (MPLS) [20] is increasingly deployed by ISPs to provide attractive services such as virtual private networks and traffic engineering. It is therefore interesting to have some insights on MPLS technologies in the Internet. However, MPLS tunnels may hide IP-level information by masking MPLS routers from `traceroute`. We propose to use our fingerprinting method to refine information on our previous tunnels deployment analysis [10]. We will show, using MPLS as an example, that our method could be used to determine whether a feature (here MPLS characteristics) is independent of the router type. Moreover, our fingerprinting method may also be extended to check if a given sample of routers is representative of the Internet heterogeneity.

3.1 MPLS Tunnels Signatures

The MPLS architecture is based on labels: an IP router inserts one or more 32-bit *label stack entries* (LSE – that contains a label, a TTL field called LSE-TTL, and a type-of-service field) into a packet, before the IP header, that determines the forwarding actions made by subsequent MPLS *Label Switching Routers* (LSRs) in the network. A series of LSRs connected together form a *Label Switched Path* (LSP).

In an MPLS network, packets are forwarded using an exact match lookup of the 20-bit label found in the LSE. At each MPLS hop, the label of the incoming packet is replaced by a corresponding outgoing label found in an MPLS switching table.

Fig. 3 illustrates the general behavior of an MPLS tunnel. Router R_1 is the entry of the MPLS tunnel and is the first router to *push* an MPLS label; we call this router the *ingress Label Edge Router* (LER). Router R_2 is the first LSR where the incoming packet includes a LSE; we call this router the *ingress hop* (IH). Router R_4 is the last router that *pops* the MPLS label; we call this router the *last hop* (LH). At least for Cisco routers, most of the time the LH router is located one hop before the *egress LER* due to the use of *penultimate hop popping* (PHP) [20].

Similarly to the IP-TTL, the LSE-TTL field is decremented by LSR that may send ICMP `time-exceeded` messages when the LSE-TTL expires. In order to debug networks where MPLS is deployed, routers may also implement RFC4950 [21], an extension to ICMP that specify that a LSR should embed the MPLS label stack of the incoming packet into an ICMP `time-exceeded` message. The first MPLS router of an LSP may copy the IP-TTL value to the LSE-TTL field rather than setting the LSE-TTL to an arbitrary value such as 255. That is the ingress LER uses TTL propagation. During a `traceroute`, LSRs along the LSP will reveal themselves via ICMP messages even if they do not implement RFC4950. Operators configure this action using the `ttl-propagate` option provided by the router OS.

Based on those two MPLS transparency features, we previously proposed an MPLS taxonomy made of two-by-two classes [10]. Fig. 3 illustrates those classes that are: *explicit tunnels* (i.e., `ttl-propagate` and RFC4950 are enabled), *implicit tunnels* (i.e., the router that pushes the MPLS label enables the `ttl-propagate` option but LSRs do not implement RFC4950), *opaque tunnels* (i.e., the LH implements RFC4950 but the ingress LER does not enable the `ttl-propagate` option), and, finally, *invisible tunnels* (i.e., the ingress LER does not enable the `ttl-propagate` option and RFC4950 is not implemented by the LH router). Our previous work provides MPLS signatures detection for revealing implicit and opaque tunnels based on three main patterns:

1. the quoted IP-TTL (*qTTL*) in ICMP `time-exceeded` messages[4]. A qTTL > 1 will likely reveal the `ttl-propagate` option at the ingress LER of an LSP. For each subsequent `traceroute` probe within an LSP, the

[4]These kind of replies should contain the quotation of the original IP header triggering the error message. Look at RFC 792 and 1812.

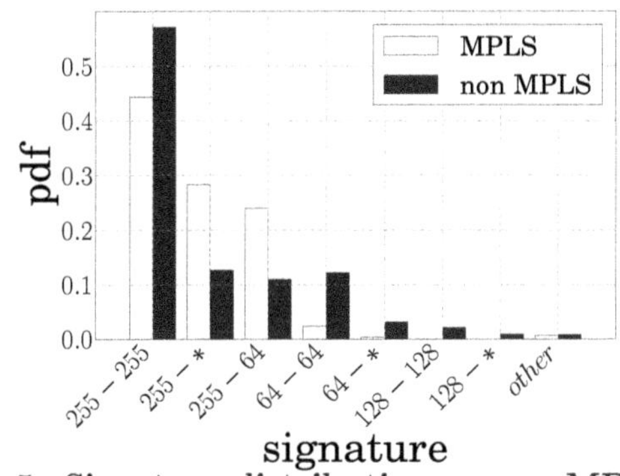

Figure 5: Signature distribution among MPLS and non MPLS routers

qTTL will be one greater resulting in an increasing sequence of qTTL values in `traceroute`;

2. #hops differences with the IP-TTL in `echo-reply` messages (*uturn*). It relies on the fact that LSRs along an LSP present an *original label stack* default routing behavior: when the LSE-TTL expires, an LSR first sends the `time-exceeded` reply to the Egress LER which then forwards the reply on its own to the probing source [5], while an LSR replies to other probes using its own IP routing table if available.

3. opaque tunnels are revealed through an *abnormal* LSE-TTL (1 <LSE-TTL< 255) returned by the LH in the `time-exceeded` reply.

Generally speaking, Fig. 4 shows that a large proportion of paths hits one or more MPLS tunnels: from about half of the VPs, at least half of the paths reveal MPLS tunnels. Explicit and implicit tunnels are by far the most frequent (respectively 46,657 and 61,054 tunnels corresponding to roughly 40% and 60% of IP addresses belonging to tunnels and, altogether, 17% of IP addresses collected). However, note that most implicit tunnels are discovered using a probing inference heuristic (uturn). This could lead to false positive or false negative tunnels. Besides, opaque tunnels are rather rare (and so subject to weak statistics – 523 opaque tunnels), and, by definition, we do not have any hints to find the invisible ones. In our previous MPLS work, we tried to extrapolate the invisible tunnels quantity using uniform linear rules over opaque and implicit ones. We made assumptions regarding RFC4950 and `ttl-propagate` independence, and did not look at any correlation between those features and the router OS. We intend here to determine how we can extend and possibly validate this work using our TTL-signatures, particularly by checking the existence of a correlation between our MPLS patterns and the router OS.

3.2 MPLS Tunnels TTL-Classification

Fig. 5 highlights the difference in frequency of our signatures between MPLS IP addresses (i.e., tagged as such by `traceroute` – it does not include implicit tunnels) and non MPLS IP addresses. The first striking difference is that the signature $< 64, 64 >$ is much less prevalent in MPLS visible networks. This could be explained by the fact that

[5]Look at the `mpls ip ttl-expiration pop` command of Cisco routers

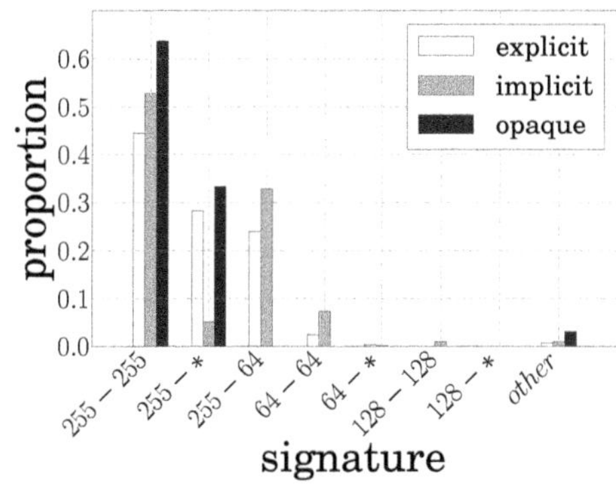

(a) Main tunnel classes

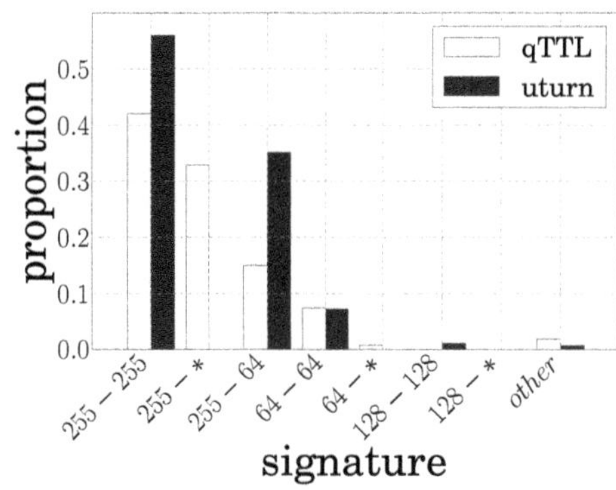

(b) Implicit sub-classes

Figure 6: Router Signature distribution among MPLS tunnel classes

this signature corresponds to a variety of middleboxes and probably less to high-end routers commonly used in MPLS networks. The second lesson is that the dominant share of $< 255, 255 >$ in non MPLS networks is less dominant for MPLS, while signatures $< 255, 64 >$ and $< 255, * >$ increase their share. The increase of $< 255, * >$ may be due to LSRs that do not have a complete IP routing table and thus cannot reply with an `echo-reply` message. Recall that, in this case, an error message such as a `time-exceeded` message is usually propagated to the end of the tunnel before being forwarded to its destination (this is the behavior captured by our uturn heuristic). The increase of $< 255, 64 >$ signatures is likely to balance the decrease of $< 255, 255 >$: it seems that $< 255, 64 >$ routers (e.g., Juniper ones) increase their market position for MPLS operations (compared to the previous ratio $< 255, 255 > / < 255, 64 >$ at a global scale).

Each of our tunnel classes exhibits a specific router signature distribution. Fig. 6(a) presents those distributions. The X-axis gives the various signatures, while the Y-axis shows the proportion of tunnels, in a given MPLS class, that exhibits a given signature. From Fig. 6(a), we see that opaque tunnels are only characterized by signatures $< 255, 255 >$ and $< 255, * >$. This property shows a bias in the linear extrapolation we used to quantify invisible tunnels [10]. We assumed that the LH router would always insert a label stack into the ICMP `time-exceeded` message if it implements RFC4950. Consequently, the difference between an opaque and an invisible tunnel was based on RFC4950 implementation on the LH router. Our new results clearly demonstrate that this is not the case (see Fig. 6(a)): if the LH does not belong to $< 255, 255 >$ class (or its incomplete companion $< 255, * >$), it will not insert a label stack in the ICMP message even if it implements RFC4950. Hence, the tunnel will actually be invisible. We verified this on a virtual testbed: considering an LSP made of Juniper OS compliant with RFC 4950 (but where the ingress LER does not propagate the IP-TTL), one may not discover any visible tunnels (there are only invisible tunnels, no opaque ones). Moreover, with Cisco OS, the same LSP will appear as opaque or invisible depending on the PHP behavior associated to the probed IP address. It seems that the opaque tunnels are more the exception and invisible tunnels the rule. This means that the ratio invisible/opaque is probably much higher than we previously expected. Thus, and unfortunately, invisible tunnels are much more common than previously stated.

A last question deserves attention: the amount of implicit tunnels being larger than the explicit one, is our uturn heuristic reliable? Indeed, this sub-mechanism is prevalent in our implicit tunnel detection. We can observe that the proportion of signature $< 255, * >$ is less prevalent in implicit tunnels (compared to other categories) and the proportion of $< 64, 64 >$ is also a bit higher (tunnels that do no implement RFC4950 are likely to be older and less mainstream). For the first fact, the reason is obvious: uturn signatures cannot result from such a $< 255, * >$ pattern. The remaining $\approx 5\%$ only comes from the qTTL technique (that is reliable by definition: it does not result from a probing heuristic). Except for these specific signatures, the distributions for implicit and explicit tunnels are relatively close. Such results tend to show that our probing heuristic to detect implicit tunnels seems quite reliable. However, the slight divergences may be due to uturn signatures that are by definition more subject to false positives than qTTL ones.

In order to understand if it is the case, Fig. 6(b) focuses on the implicit tunnels signatures to distinguish our two heuristics. The signature $< 255, * >$ only exists with the qTTL technique. The relative populations of signatures $< 255, 64 >$ and $< 255, 255 >$ balance this decrease for uturn tunnels. It confirms the robustness of our uturn technique: quantity of $< 64, 64 >$ does not move while the natural decrease of $< 255, * >$ is reported to $< 255, 64 >$ and $< 255, 255 >$ classes in the same proportion as for MPLS explicit tunnels. We can conclude that uturn is not the cause of the previous and single $< 64, 64 >$ actual difference (that seems to be induced by the RFC4950 implementation).

4. RELATED WORK

The remote identification of operating systems, also known as OS fingerprinting, aims at discovering the remote machine OS. Based on how data is acquired from the remote machine, two families of OS fingerprinting techniques are possible: *active* (that requires sending traffic towards the target) [22, 23, 24] and *passive* methods (that requires listening to communications between the target and a third-party) [25, 26]. Typically, both families investigate several fields of packet headers. In particular, it focuses on the IP and TCP headers [22, 24], or the various types of ICMP packets [23]. To the best of our knowledge, none of those solutions have explored iTTL n-tuple and applied it to router-level topology discovery.

Closer to our work, Sherry et al. [27] performs alias resolution based on signatures from IP timestamp behavior. Also, Madhyastha et al. [28] use the iTTL in order to estimate the number of hops on the reverse path back from every router to the measurement point. None of them explore iTTL n-tuples nor use signatures to determine possible measurement biases.

Recently, the deployment of MPLS started to be an active research subject. For instance, Sherwood et al. [29] investigated the presence of anonymous and hidden routers as part of DisCarte using signatures based on the IP record route option. Sommers et al. [9] examined the characteristics of MPLS tunnels that are explicitly identified using RFC4950 extensions to statistically infer non explicit ones. In the same vein, we proposed a practical taxonomy of MPLS tunnels based on RFC4950 extensions and `ttl-propagate` option [10]. We have developed techniques for revealing the presence of implicit and opaque tunnels. As demonstrated on this paper, our TTL-based fingerprinting method can be used to refine MPLS identification and quantification.

5. CONCLUSION

Router fingerprinting may help for many purposes such as detecting vulnerable routers or abnormal behaviors and alias resolution. In this paper, we proposed a lightweight router fingerprinting technique based on router signature, i.e., a n-tuple made of initial TTL values used by a router when forging ICMP reply packets. We showed that such a signature is suitable to consistently discriminate IP interfaces. Indeed, various router brands and OSes use different deterministic initial TTL values depending on the type of packet to forge.

Based on data collected during a large-scale measurement campaign, we analyzed the mapping of router OS distribution according to router signatures. As a proof of concept, we applied it on our previous work about MPLS tunnel classification and validated heuristics for revealing non explicit MPLS tunnels. At the same time, we refined our previous conclusions about the invisible MPLS tunnels quantification. More generally, our method or its extension could be used both to determine if a sample of routers is representative of the Internet router mix, and to determine whether a routing feature is independent of the router type.

As a further work, we envision to extend our basic signature. Adding new fields will enlarge the spectrum of possible classes, making them more discriminant. We will try to keep the probing overhead as low as possible while completing our n-tuple of initial TTLs with additional and possibly orthogonal features. We intend to study, among other features, the ICMP packet size, the LSE-TTL field, and the MPLS label range. In a second step, we would like to develop a new multi-probing `traceroute` tool for inferring equipment-based paths in the Internet. Generally speaking, our method can be used to understand whether IP networks are heterogeneous in terms of hardware and software and for analyzing the new OS deployment and market share evolution at different scales.

Acknowledgments

This work is partially funded by the European Commission funded mPlane ICT-318627 project.

6. REFERENCES

[1] G. F. Lyon, *Nmap Network Scanning: The Official Nmap Project Guide to Network Discovery and Security Scanning.* Nmap Project, 2009, see http://nmap.org/book/toc.html.

[2] T. Kohno, A. Broido, and k. claffy, "Remote physical device fingerprinting," *IEEE Transactions on Dependable and Secure Computing*, vol. 2, no. 2, pp. 93–108, May 2005.

[3] F. Veysset, O. Courtay, and O. Heen, "New tool and technique for remote operating system fingerprinting," April 2002, see http://www.leetupload.com/database/Misc/Papers/remote_os_detection.pdf.

[4] B. Donnet and T. Friedman, "Internet topology discovery: a survey," *IEEE Communications Surveys and Tutorials*, vol. 9, no. 4, December 2007.

[5] K. Keys, "Internet-scale IP alias resolution techniques," *ACM SIGCOMM Computer Communication Review*, vol. 40, no. 1, pp. 50–55, January 2010.

[6] N. Davis, "Initial TTL values," November 2011, see http://noahdavids.org/self_published/TTL_values.html.

[7] A. Sebastian, "Default time to live (TTL) values," December 2009, see http://www.binbert.com/blog/2009/12/default-time-to-live-ttl-values/.

[8] J. Postel, "Assigned numbers," Internet Engineering Task Force, RFC 1700, October 1994.

[9] J. Sommers, B. Eriksson, and P. Barford, "On the prevalence and characteristics of MPLS deployments in the open Internet," in *ACM SIGCOMM Internet Measurement Conference*, November 2011.

[10] B. Donnet, M. Luckie, P. Mérindol, and J.-J. Pansiot, "Revealing MPLS tunnels obscured from traceroute," *ACM SIGCOMM Computer Communication Review*, vol. 42, no. 2, pp. 87–93, April 2012.

[11] V. Jacobson et al., "traceroute," UNIX," man page, 1989, see source code: ftp://ftp.ee.lbl.gov/traceroute.tar.gz.

[12] B. Augustin, X. Cuvellier, B. Orgogozo, F. Viger, T. Friedman, M. Latapy, C. Magnien, and R. Teixeira, "Avoiding traceroute anomalies with Paris traceroute," in *Proc. ACM SIGCOMM Internet Measurement Conference (IMC)*, October 2006.

[13] k. claffy, Y. Hyun, K. Keys, M. Fomenkov, and D. Krioukov, "Internet mapping: from art to science," in *Proc. IEEE Cybersecurity Applications and Technologies Conference for Homeland Security (CATCH)*, March 2009.

[14] M. Luckie, "Scamper: a scalable and extensible packet prober for active measurement of the Internet," in *ACM SIGCOMM Internet Measurement Conference*, November 2010.

[15] B. Donnet, P. Raoult, T. Friedman, and M. Crovella, "Efficient algorithms for large-scale topology discovery," in *Proc. ACM SIGMETRICS*, June 2005.

[16] L. Jacquin, V. Roca, M. A. Kaafar, F. Schuler, and J. L. Roch, "IBTrack: an ICMP black holes tracker," in *Proc. IEEE Global Communications Conference (GLOBECOM)*, December 2012.

[17] A. Medina, M. Allman, and S. Floyd, "Measuring interactions between transport protocols and middleboxes," in *Proc. ACM SIGCOMM Internet Measurement Conference (IMC)*, October 2004.

[18] M. H. Keio, Y. Nishida, C. Raiciu, A. Greenhalgh, M. Handley, and H. Tokuda, "Is it still possible to extend TCP," in *Proc. ACM/USENIX Internet Measurement Conference (IMC)*, November 2011.

[19] G. Detal, B. Hesmans, O. Bonaventure, Y. Vanaubel, and B. Donnet, "Revealing middlebox interference with tracebox," in *Proc. ACM/USENIX Internet Measurement Conference (IMC)*, October 2013.

[20] E. Rosen, A. Viswanathan, and R. Callon, "Multiprotocol label switching architecture," Internet Engineering Task Force, RFC 3031, January 2001.

[21] R. Bonica, D. Gan, D. Tappan, and C. Pignataro, "ICMP extensions for multiprotocol label switching," Internet Engineering Task Force, RFC 4950, August 2007.

[22] Fyodor, "Remote OS detection via TCP/IP stack fingerprinting," *Phrack*, vol. 8, no. 54, October 1998, see http://nmap.org/nmap-fingerprinting-article.txt.

[23] O. Arkin, "A remote active OS fingerprinting tool using ICMP," *;login: the Magazine of USENIX and Sage*, vol. 27, no. 2, pp. 14–19, October 2002.

[24] J. Padhye and S. Floyd, "Identifying the TCP behavior of web servers," in *Proc. ACM SIGCOMM*, August 2001.

[25] C. Smith and P. Grundl, "Know your enemy: Passive fingerprinting," March 2002, see http://www.linuxvoodoo.com/resources/security/finger.

[26] M. Zalewski, "p0f," see http://lcamtuf.coredump.cx/p0f3/.

[27] J. Sherry, E. Katz-Bassett, M. Pimenova, H. V. Madhyastha, T. Anderson, and A. Krishnamurthy, "Resolving IP aliases with prespecified timestamps," in *Proc. ACM/USENIX Internet Measurement Conference (IMC)*, November 2010.

[28] H. V. Madhyastha, T. Isdal, M. Piatek, C. Dixon, T. Anderson, A. Krishnamurthy, and A. Venkataramani, "iPlane: An information plane for distributed services," in *Proc. USENIX Symposium on Operating Systems Design and Implementation (OSDI)*, November 2006.

[29] R. Sherwood, A. Bender, and N. Spring, "Discarte: a disjunctive Internet cartographer," in *ACM SIGCOMM*, August 2008.

Peeking Behind the NAT: An Empirical Study of Home Networks

Sarthak Grover, Mi Seon Park, Srikanth Sundaresan,
Sam Burnett, Hyojoon Kim, Nick Feamster
School of Computer Science, Georgia Tech

ABSTRACT

We present the first empirical study of home network availability, infrastructure, and usage, using data collected from home networks around the world. In each home, we deploy a router with custom firmware to collect information about the availability of home broadband network connectivity, the home network infrastructure (including the wireless connectivity in each home network and the number of devices connected to the network), and how people in each home network use the network. Downtime is more frequent and longer in developing countries—sometimes due to the network, and in other cases because users simply turn off their home router. We also find that some portions of the wireless spectrum are extremely crowded, that diurnal patterns are more pronounced during the week, and that most traffic in home networks is exchanged over a few connections to a small number of domains. Our study is both a preliminary view into many home networks and an illustration of how measurements from a home router can yield significant information about home networks.

Categories and Subject Descriptors

C.2.3 [**Computer-Communication Networks**]: Network Operations—*Network monitoring*

General Terms

Measurement

Keywords

BISmark, Home Networks

1. INTRODUCTION

Home broadband Internet access is ubiquitous and rapidly evolving. There are now upwards of one billion broadband Internet users worldwide [1]; much of that usage is shifting away from conventional desktops and towards mobile devices, such as laptops, smart phones, and tablets [7]. Despite their pervasiveness, little is known about most home networks or how people use them.

IMC'13, October 23–25, 2013, Barcelona, Spain.
Copyright 2013 ACM 978-1-4503-1953-9/13/10 ...$15.00.
http://dx.doi.org/10.1145/2504730.2504736 .

Indeed, to date, it has been surprisingly difficult to study home networks on a large scale, because network technologies like network address translators (NATs) present only an opaque view of the home network to the global Internet—specifically, without a monitoring device *inside* the home, traffic coming from any device in a home network appears to all be coming from a single device. This coarse granularity of visibility makes it impossible to observe the usage patterns of individual devices inside the home or observe characteristics about other parts of a home network (*e.g.*, the home wireless network). Observing home networks on a large scale requires developing—and deploying—an always-on monitoring device in the home that can capture information about individual devices, with the consent of the people that live in these homes.

To better understand home networks, we developed BISmark, a custom home router, and deployed it in more than 100 home networks in 21 countries around the world for more than one year. BISmark sits between the user's ISP access link and the rest of the home network and acts as a continuous monitoring device; as a result, it can observe all traffic entering and leaving the home network, and can attribute traffic flows to individual devices on the network. This device, if permitted, can also log other types of activity, such as the number of devices on the network at any given time and the amount of traffic that any particular device sends to a destination (*e.g.*, Google). It can also independently measure the performance of both the home wireless network and the access link. We study three aspects of home network usage:

1. *Availability.* How common are Internet connectivity outages in homes, and how reasonable is it to assume continuous connectivity?
2. *Infrastructure.* What networking technologies and devices do people use in home networks?
3. *Usage.* Is the capacity of a home network sufficient for the growing demands of users and applications? How does usage differ across individual devices in the home? What other patterns exist?

Although our study instruments a relatively small number of home networks, it nevertheless offers extensive visibility into aspects of homes that were previously opaque to researchers. Ultimately, regulators and Internet service providers may be able to use some of the techniques that we describe to perform similar studies on a larger scale. We believe that researchers, ISPs, policymakers, and users can use the home router as a measurement device to better understand various trends in availability, infrastructure, and usage. Data about availability can help regulators determine whether ISPs are delivering the service that they are promising to users. Data about infrastructure (*e.g.*, the amount of contention in the wireless spectrum) can help ISPs better understand and debug user performance, and can provide evidence for regulators to release more spectrum when it becomes appropriate to do so. Information about usage can help ISPs better provision and plan, and it can help device designers better understand how (and when) people use various devices.

The *availability* of home broadband access networks lets developers of applications running over edge networks understand the connectivity conditions of a particular environment. Our study has yielded some surprising findings. For example, although in the Western world we often think of broadband connectivity as "always on", we found examples in China and India where users only power up their home network gateway when they intend to use it. We found that trends of availability held in general: only 10% of home networks in the developed world saw connectivity interruptions of more than ten minutes more frequently than once every 10 days, but about 50% of home networks in developing countries experienced such connectivity interruptions once every 3 days. Although it is difficult from our data set to ascertain the cause for this intermittent connectivity (*i.e.*, it could result from power outages, poor connectivity, or behavioral patterns), it is clear that it is not safe to assume that Internet connectivity is highly available in certain parts of the world.

The *infrastructure* of home broadband access networks lets us understand how users construct their home networks, and what types of devices they comprise. We explore various questions relating to infrastructure, such as the number of devices on each home network, and how the number of devices on these networks varies over time with usage. We find that in today's home network, there are more wireless devices than wired devices in general and this difference is greater in the developing countries. We also find households in more developed countries tend to have more devices compared to developing countries, and those devices are more likely to remain continuously connected to the home router. Connectivity shows a diurnal pattern across a week; the number of devices on the network on weekdays typically peaks during evening hours, but on weekends device usage is more consistent throughout the day. The median number of devices on a 2.4 GHz network is about five, whereas on the 5 GHz band, the median number of devices is two.

The *usage* of home broadband Internet access can shed light on the applications and devices that people tend to use on their home network, and the overall utilization of these networks. We analyze the periodicity of usage patterns in various home networks and observe the extent to which users saturate their access link and find that most home networks are lightly used, and do not saturate their downstream or upstream link most of the time. We analyze distributions of device usage and find that users normally have a subset of devices that they prefer to use for consuming most network data. We observe the diversity of domains visited and find that about 38% of the total volume of traffic is from a single most popular domain, among 200 whitelisted domains.

The rest of the paper is organized as follows. Section 2 overviews related work. Section 3 describes the process of collecting the various types of data that we use in our study. Section 4 presents results concerning the availability of broadband access in various home networks around the world, including the duration of outages. Section 5 describes the characteristics of the infrastructure in various home networks, including the number of devices that are in the network, whether the devices are connected via wired or wireless, and to what extent devices occupy different ranges of radio spectrum (*e.g.*, 2.4 GHz and 5 GHz). Section 6 profiles the usage patterns of users in different home wireless broadband networks and explores how usage patterns differ across devices, and how download speed affects usage patterns. Section 7 describes ongoing work and extensions to this study and discusses some broader implications of our results. Section 8 concludes.

2. RELATED WORK

We briefly review related work on home broadband networks. We survey work that has performed "single shot" measurements of home broadband network performance and characteristics, Internet policy reports on performance in various regions, and qualitative studies that lend insight into how to better design home networks.

Measuring home network performance. There has been significant interest in measuring home and access networks, and many previous studies have tried to measure home networks in various ways. The studies use various methods for measuring home networks, from running measurements remotely from servers in the Internet to measure access link properties [18] to running tools on end-host devices [14, 16, 17, 25, 26, 28]. In contrast to these previous studies, we perform our measurements from gateway routers, not end-host devices, which enables *continuous* monitoring rather than one-shot measurements. Such continuous monitoring allows us to observe how usage patterns change over time, both on short and long timescales, as well as to report on other characteristics that require continuous monitoring, such as availability. Our work builds on our own previous work [32], which uses a deployment of custom home access points that conduct a unique set of performance measurements. In contrast to our previous work, this study broadly characterizes home network usage rather than focusing on access link performance.

National and regional Internet policy and measurement reports. Recently, there has been interest from national agencies to measure home networks for Internet policy and regulation purposes. The United States Federal Communications Commission, United Kingdom's Ofcom and the European Commission have all conducted large scale studies of access networks in conjunction with SamKnows [4–6]. Benkler *et al.* have a report on broadband transitions and policies around the world [10]. To date, these studies from regulatory commissions have focused exclusively on performance of the access network, rather than on properties of the home network itself or usage of the home network. The primary objective of such initiatives is to gain an understanding of access networks to enact better policies. They do not perform passive monitoring of the home network.

Qualitative design studies of home networks. There are previous studies on understanding home networks and attempts to design better systems [11, 15, 20, 21, 23, 27]. These previous studies are qualitative: they rely exclusively on human subject interviews and analysis on human interactions to identify problem areas and to suggest better designs. We offer a *quantitative* complement to these studies. We analyze passive measurement data that is automatically collected and reported, which are in turn used to derive meaningful observations about home networks that may not be obvious or even revealed through studies with human subjects. The automated nature of our data collection and monitoring allows us to observe longitudinal behavior and usage patterns, and it may in some cases result in more accurate data about human activity and network usage, since many of the questions that previous studies have asked in interviews could be more completely and accurately addressed by measuring the network traffic itself.

Previous studies have also built tools that improve interactivity and aid troubleshooting in a home network environment, for example measuring and displaying bandwidth usage and throughput in a home network [13, 14]. Our work analyzes data from *existing* networks, rather than trying to deploy new tools and observe how

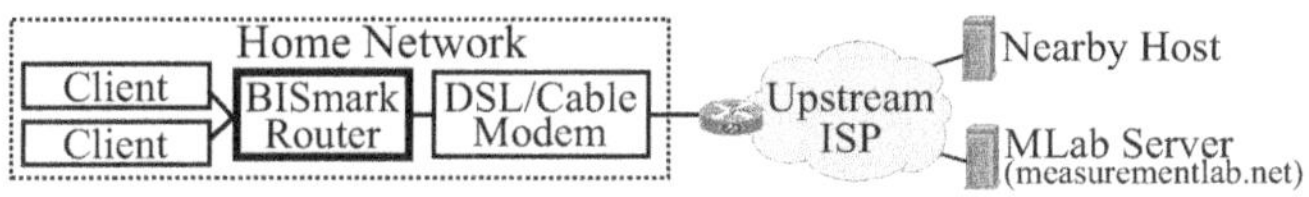

Figure 1: *The BISmark home router sits directly behind the modem in the home network. It collects both active and passive measurements.*

usage changes as a result of those tools. We analyze a wider variety of network features, including wired vs. wireless usage, number of active devices, diurnal patterns, and availability.

Behavioral studies of Internet usage in developing countries. Chen *et al.* studied the effect of sporadic and slow connectivity on user behavior and found a better Web interaction model for such environments [12]. Wyche *et al.* performed a qualitative study of how Kenyan Internet users adapt their usage behavior where Internet connectivity is a scarce resource in terms of availability, cost, and quality [33]. Smyth *et al.* performed a qualitative study on sharing and consuming entertainment media on mobile phones in urban India [31]. The data that we gathered in developing countries could help corroborate some of these studies.

3. DATA COLLECTION

Home routers can observe many aspects of home networks because typically all other devices in the home communicate both to each other and to the Internet via the router. Over the past three years, we have deployed routers in 126 homes across 19 countries. Each router measures the quality of the upstream Internet connection and collects limited information about device usage on the home network. This section introduces the router platform, the data we collect from the routers, and that data's implications for our study.

3.1 Collection Infrastructure

BISmark comprises gateways in the home, a centralized management and data collection server, and several measurement servers. We have instrumented the gateway with custom firmware that performs both passive and active measurements. Where appropriate, the firmware anonymizes certain aspects of the data before sending them back to the central repository for further analysis. Figure 1 shows a typical deployment in the home network, and how BISmark performs its measurements.

Firmware. BISmark is a custom home router firmware based on OpenWrt for Netgear WNDR3800 and WNDR3700v2 routers [2, 3]. Routers have a 450 MHz MIPs processor, 16 MB of flash storage, 64 MB of RAM, an Atheros wireless chipset, one 802.11gn radio, and one 802.11an radio. BISmark typically replaces a household's wireless access point and connects directly to the cable or DSL modem that provides Internet access to that household. Because the router sits on the path between the user's home network and the rest of the Internet, our software is uniquely positioned to capture information about both the characteristics of network connectivity and of home network usage (*e.g.*, usage patterns, applications). We expected routers to remain powered on almost all the time, since they provide the household's Internet connectivity; however, later in this paper we show that this assumption does not hold in several countries and regions.

Recruiting and deployment. Our deployment of routers across home networks has been organic: We have recruited most of our users by word-of-mouth, or through targeted advertisements for

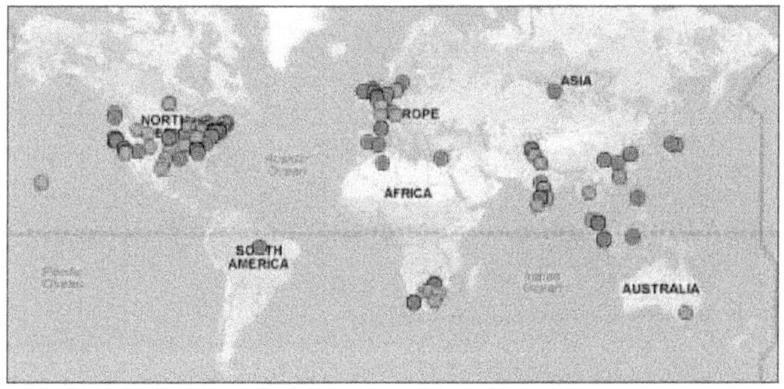

Figure 2: *The BISmark deployment as of May 2013. Each dot indicates a router. The green dots indicate routers that are currently reporting (156). Because we only use data from routers that consistently report data throughout the period of our study, we use data from 126 routers in 19 countries. The red dots include the full set of routers that have ever contributed data (295).*

Developed	Routers	Developing	Routers
Canada	2	India	12
Germany	2	Pakistan	5
France	1	Malaysia	1
United Kingdom	12	South Africa	10
Ireland	2	Mexico	2
Italy	1	China	2
Japan	2	Brazil	2
Netherlands	3	Indonesia	1
Singapore	2	Thailand	1
United States	63		
Total Routers	90	Total Routers	36

Table 1: *Classification of countries based on GDP per capita.*

specific experiments and projects that we have run as part of our research. For example, the router firmware performs continuous measurements of the performance of the home access link, which has garnered the attention of various policy and regulatory agencies. We have also performed smaller recruitment efforts in various areas for a usage cap management tool that we built on top of the firmware [24]. Depending on the experiments that different users have consented to (or not), we are able to collect different types of information. Most users have remained actively engaged in our experiments by virtue of the fact that they receive a free router as a result of their participation.

We classify the countries where we have deployed routers into two groups based on the GDP (Gross Domestic Product) per capita ranking in year 2011 [9]. We call countries for whom the per capita GDP falls within the top 50 *developed*; otherwise, we call them *developing*. Table 1 summarizes this grouping.

3.2 Data

We now summarize the data we collected from the BISmark deployment, then describe each data set in more detail. We will also highlight some factors that limit the conclusions we can (or cannot) draw from our data. Where possible, we have released the data collected from this study; the Capacity data (described below) is publicly available and is also continuously updated as the routers collect new measurements.[1] We have released all measurements that do not have personally identifying information (PII) (*i.e.*, everything except the Traffic data set).[2]

[1]http://uploads.projectbismark.net

[2]http://data.gtnoise.net/bismark/imc2013/nat

Dataset	Routers	Countries	Dates
		Active measurements	
Heartbeats	126	19	October 1, 2012–April 15, 2013
Capacity	126	19	April 1–April 15, 2013
		Passive measurements	
Uptime	113	19	March 6–April 15, 2013
Devices	113	19	March 6–April 15, 2013
WiFi	93	15	Nov. 1–Nov. 15, 2012
Traffic	25	1	April 1–April 15, 2013

Table 2: *Summary of data collected for this study. With the exception of the Traffic data set, which is subject to privacy restrictions, we will publicly release all data used in this study.*

3.2.1 Summary

Table 2 summarizes the data we collected from our deployment. BISmark routers perform both active and passive measurements. Many routers only collect performance measurements about the router's upstream Internet connection and basic diagnostic information about the number of connected devices; these measurements record no personally identifying information (PII) and, as a result, do not require written consent. In twenty-five homes where we have explicit consent, we collect additional information about the activity of users and devices on the home network; for those households we clearly explained the risks of PII exposure and obtained written consent.[3] Engineering and consent constraints dictated that we collect the data sets over different time periods. We now explain each data set in more detail.

3.2.2 Measurements

Heartbeats. Every router sends a "heartbeat" packet to the central BISmark server approximately once a minute. We use this data to measure router uptime. A heartbeat packet indicates that the router is on and online, but a lost packet could mean a router is powered off, offline, or has lossy connectivity to the server. These heartbeats can be lost, and the router makes no attempt to retransmit them. They are nonetheless frequent enough to provide reasonable confidence about the uptime of each BISmark router, which we analyze in Section 4. We consider heartbeats from 126 routers that were on for at least 25 days between October 2012 and April 2013.

Uptime. Starting in March of 2013, each router sends its uptime every twelve hours. This data distinguishes, at coarse granularity, between routers that are offline and those that are powered off.

Capacity. Every twelve hours, each router measures the capacity of its access link using ShaperProbe [30]. In Section 6.2, we jointly analyze the Capacity and Traffic data to determine the extent to which users fully utilize the capacity that their Internet service provider offers.

Devices. Every hour, most routers count the number of devices connected to their wired Ethernet ports and the number of associated clients on each wireless frequency. This data gives a broad view of users' device usage patterns, while still providing information at a coarse enough granularity to preserve user privacy. Section 5 uses this data to paint a broad picture of device usage throughout the world.

WiFi. Some routers collect data about the number of other access points (APs) in the vicinity. Each router only scans for other visible access points in the wireless channel that it is configured for; by default, the 2.4 GHz radio is configured for channel 11, and the 5 GHz radio is configured for channel 36. Each router attempts to scan for clients and access points every 10 minutes; unfortunately, the scanning process can sometimes cause wireless clients to disassociate from the router, so we reduce the scanning frequency if the router has associated clients.

Traffic. Because of potential privacy risks inherent in passively collected data, only 53 households consented to contribute detailed information about their devices and Internet activity. Of those, we consider data from 25 households that were active from April 1 to April 15 and exchanged at least 100 MB of traffic. To encourage users to consent to this data collection, we gave them access to a Web interface that allowed them to observe and manage their usage over time and across devices; this feature turns out to be quite useful for users who have Internet service plans with low data caps. We collect four types of information:

1. *Packet statistics.* We collect the size and timestamp of every packet relayed to and from the Internet. Although this data seems fairly innocuous, traffic analysis could in fact reveal very detailed information about user activity.
2. *Flow statistics.* We collect obfuscated IP addresses and MAC addresses, and application ports for a sample of Internet-bound network flows. At surface level, this data only reveals the kinds of applications participants use on their Internet-enabled devices (*e.g.*, HTTP, SMTP), but inference attacks similar to those on packet-level data are possible.
3. *DNS responses.* We collect a sample of A and CNAME records and obfuscate domain names unless they appear on a user-customizable whitelist of popular domain names; by default, the whitelist is the 200 most popular domains in the United States according to Alexa [8].
4. *MAC addresses.* We collect the MAC addresses of devices connected to the router and anonymize the lower half of each address, which allows us to identify manufacturers without identifying specific devices.

This data provides rich insights into user behavior inside the home. We quantify device ownership in Section 5.4 and characterize service usage in Section 6.

3.3 Limitations

This section discusses various limitations of our data sets.

Data collection may be interrupted. Various outages and failures—both of the routers themselves and of the collection infrastructure—introduced interruptions in our collection. Although we acknowledge that being able to collect all of our data sets over the same overlapping time period would be ideal, we needed to choose between using completely overlapping data sets from smaller time intervals or using the largest time intervals possible for each data set. As such, we used overlapping time periods where possible, and in other cases we used the largest possible time interval.

It is difficult to infer causes of downtime from Heartbeats. Although we are interested in measuring availability with the Heartbeats data, this data set really only indicates when the BISmark router is both powered up and online. Using this data to infer access link outages assumes that the BISmark router is always on, but as we will see in subsequent sections, some instances of "outages" are in fact users who power down the router for significant portions of the day. Additionally, these heartbeats are sent from

[3] Our university's Institutional Review Board (IRB) certified all aspects of our data collection and experiments.

the BISmark routers to a server at Georgia Tech only, so a loss of heartbeats might simply result from problems along the network path between the BISmark router and Georgia Tech. We assume that most persistent losses of heartbeats are due to either a failure at the access network itself, or due to the router being powered down; we are unable to distinguish these two cases. We started collecting uptime data at 12-hour intervals, but this coarse granularity means we can only confirm network outages in cases where routers are continuously powered on.

Privacy and ethics limit scalability. Although we would like to observe all passive traffic from the entire deployment, we are constrained by privacy and ethics concerns, which compel us to restrict the size of the Traffic data set and anonymize the data in ways that make certain types of analysis more difficult. For this study, we were only able to collect passive traffic traces from 25 homes in the United States; collecting these traces requires gaining institutional review board (IRB) approval, recruiting users who were willing to let us collect such traces, and obtaining consent from these users. Even for consenting users, we anonymize a significant portion of the passive traffic traces: We anonymize traffic to any domain name that is not in the Alexa top 200 or otherwise explicitly whitelisted by the user, and hash the bottom 24 bits of all MAC addresses. This anonymization prevents us from studying certain types of questions, such as the characteristics of the "tail" of user traffic volumes.

Households are not a representative population sample. Because we wished to minimize both capital risk and technical support investment, our deployment is biased toward close friends, family, colleagues, and technically-inclined volunteers in the United States and abroad. This may limit the generality of our results, particularly those drawn from only a few routers. Nonetheless, we believe our results shed light on important phenomena in home networks that could be verified in later, more targeted deployments; indeed, our ongoing research and recruitment efforts follow from data gathered on a smaller BISmark deployment.

BISmark enables its 5 GHz radio by default. Various countries have restrictions on the use of wireless spectrum; the use of the 5 GHz spectrum on wireless routers is only permitted in certain countries. For the most part, however, we do not disable the 5 GHz radio before shipping a BISmark router, and any user who flashes their own router with the firmware that we have published on the Web may have the 5 Ghz spectrum enabled by default. Therefore, although it might be interesting to explore the use of 5 GHz spectrum in countries where it is not legal, the way that we have deployed our routers necessarily biases our data set and does not allow us to answer this question accurately.

4. AVAILABILITY

We first study the extent to which Internet connectivity was available across the home broadband networks in our deployment, and whether any remarkable availability or usage patterns emerged. We observe the frequency and duration of downtime across the deployment and the extent to which these characteristics differ between home networks—we explore differences between developing and developed countries (and specifically, how downtime characteristics vary according to a country's GDP), as well as usage patterns that are unique to individual homes.

We measure the availability of Internet connectivity by recording periodic heartbeat messages which every router sends to our central server approximately once per minute. The arrival of a heartbeat signifies that the router is up and connected to the Internet. We define *downtime* as any gap in the heartbeat logs that lasts longer than ten minutes. The absence of a heartbeat could signify that the router is offline, has been shut down or rebooted, or that the heartbeat was lost. For reboots the router usually comes back up within a few minutes. In some cases, we can positively verify downtimes caused by powered off routers using the Uptime data set. All results in this section are based on the Heartbeats and Uptime data sets, as described in Section 3. Table 3 summarizes a few of the more interesting results.

Developed countries experience far less frequent extended downtime than developing countries: The median time between downtime in developed countries is more than a month while in developing countries it is less than a day.	§4.1, Fig. 3
The two countries in our deployment with the most frequent downtime are those with the lowest per-capita GDP (India and Pakistan).	§4.1, Fig. 5
In some cases in developing countries, broadband connectivity is not "always on" because users only turn on their routers to use the Internet.	§4.2, Fig. 6b

Table 3: *Highlights of Section 4 results.*

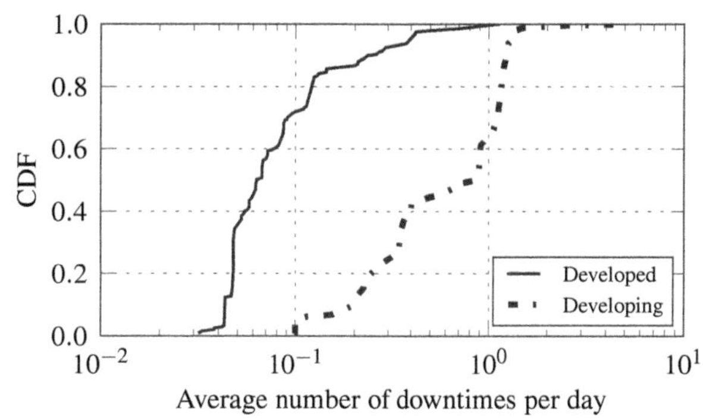

Figure 3: *Average number of downtimes per day that last at least ten minutes. Developed countries experience far fewer downtimes per day than developing countries.*

4.1 How reliable is home broadband access?

We study the "uptime" of home broadband Internet access across home networks in our deployment, in terms of the frequency and duration of downtime. We also explore the extent to which these characteristics vary by country.

Frequency of downtime. Figure 3 shows a distribution of the downtime over six months, for both developed and developing countries; we show a distribution of the average number of downtimes per day for each network, where downtime is defined as an interruption in connectivity of ten minutes or longer. As expected, the home networks in developing countries sustain substantially more downtime compared to those in developed countries. The median duration between downtimes for networks in developed countries is more than a month, whereas for developing countries, the median duration between downtimes is less than a single day.

Duration of downtime. Figure 4 shows a cumulative distribution function of the downtime durations for both developing and developed countries. The plot shows that the median downtime dura-

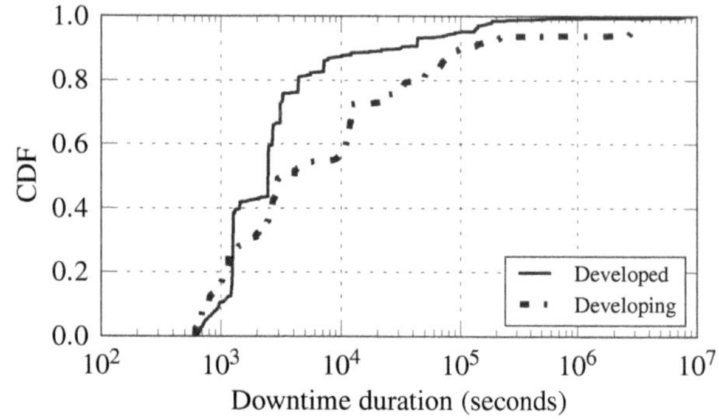

Figure 4: *Downtime duration for developing and developed countries. The median downtime duration is similar, but as we see in Figure 3, developing countries see downtime much more frequently.*

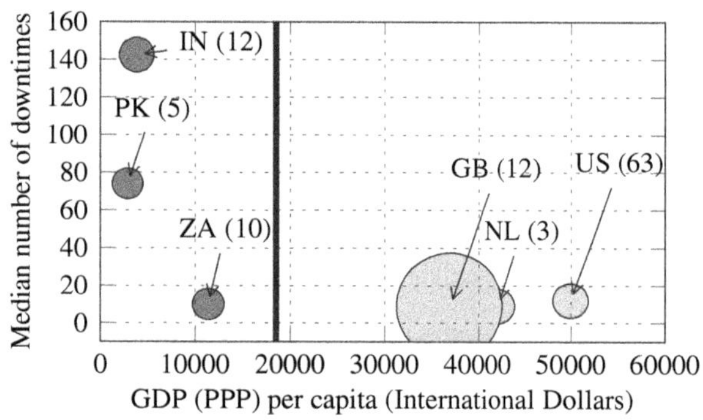

Figure 5: *The median number of downtimes across homes in each country during October 2012 – April 2013 vs. the GDP of the country where that home network was located. The marker size is proportional to the median downtime duration in that country. The vertical line separates developing and developed countries. We show only countries with at least three routers deployed.*

tion is approximately 30 minutes, and that downtime in developing countries tend to last longer. Downtime sometimes lasts several days.

Downtime characteristics vs. per-capita GDP. Figure 5 shows a scatter plot of the median number of downtimes experienced by home networks in each country vs. the *per-capita GDP* for that country in U.S. dollar equivalent (*i.e.*, the purchasing power parity) [22] for countries with at least three deployed routers. The vertical line divides nine developing from eleven developed countries. Although there is no discernible difference between any of the developing and developed countries in terms of the median number of downtimes, the two countries with the lowest per-capita GDP in our deployment—India and Pakistan—experienced significantly more downtime during October 1, 2012 – April 15, 2013. A home network in Pakistan experienced nearly two downtimes lasting at least ten minutes every day.[4]

[4]These characteristics are are based on data from about 12 routers in India and about five routers in Pakistan for October 1, 2012 – April 15, 2013. In general, some country data from this scatter plot may be inconclusive, due to the small number of countries from which we collect data, but the trend appears to hold for at least the poorest countries.

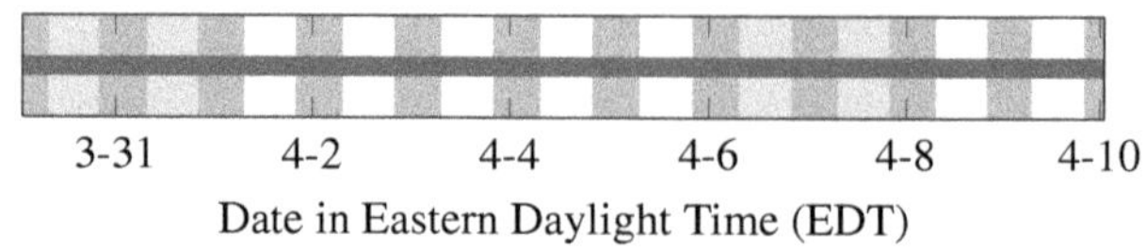

(a) *This household never intentionally turns off its router, which is typical of routers in developed countries.*

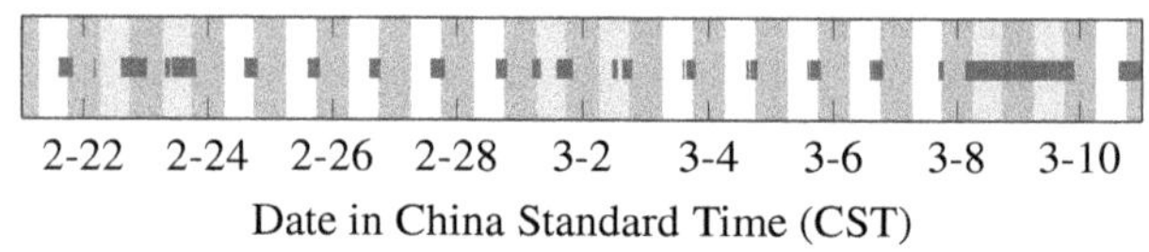

(b) *This household often turns off its router when not using it. The router is available briefly in evenings and during weekends.*

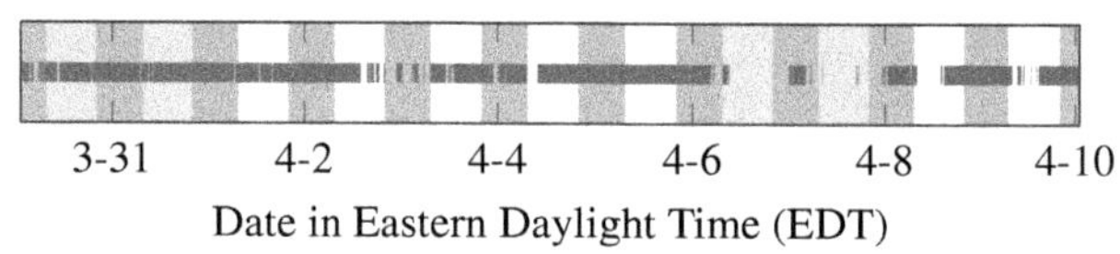

(c) *This household's access link experienced sporadic ISP outages for several days in April 2013. Although the router was continuously powered on, we label this as downtime.*

Figure 6: *Examples of different modes of router availability. The thick horizontal green lines indicate intervals when the router is* available. *For reference, dark shaded regions indicate nighttime hours and lighter shaded regions indicate weekend daylight hours.*

4.2 Case Study: Router as Home Appliance

In addition to general trends, we also discovered some interesting cases of availability and usage patterns. We observed that in the United States, most users leave their routers powered on all of the time. The median US user has his router on 98.25% of time in the measured time period. Router availability in these homes resembles Figure 6a. In contrast, *home broadband is not "always on" in the developing world.* As a comparison, median routers in India and South Africa stay on only for 76.01% and 85.57% of the time, respectively. We observed cases where users powered their router on for specific time periods when they were using the Internet, much as someone would use any other appliance. We envision multiple possible reasons for this disparity. One reason could be *behavioral patterns*: in some cases, we can observe specific patterns where users power down their router when they are not actively using it (because of data usage caps imposed by certain ISPs). For example, Figure 6b shows one Chinese household that consistently keeps its router off except during the early evening. During the weekend, the router is on for longer periods, presumably with increased activity. Another reason could be *poor connectivity*, such as high loss or network outages caused by congestion, overload, or even poor infrastructure or equipment, as is possibly the case for the home network in Figure 6c.

5. INFRASTRUCTURE

This section examines the *infrastructure* that people in home networks use to access the Internet. We look at the typical composition of devices in home networks, be they wired or wireless, and oper-

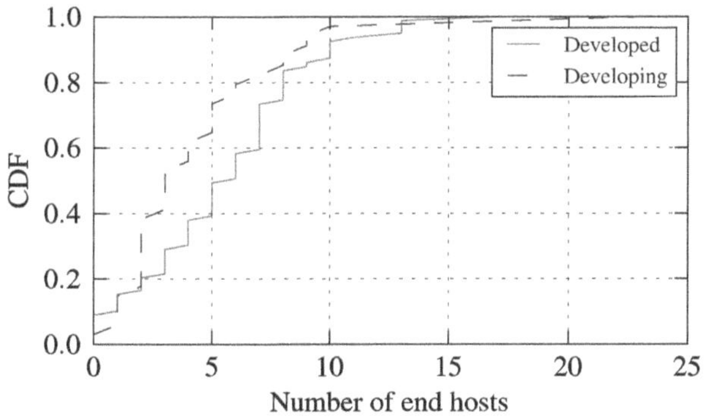

Figure 7: *Number of devices in each home network. More than half of the homes have at least five devices. Each home network has seven devices on average.*

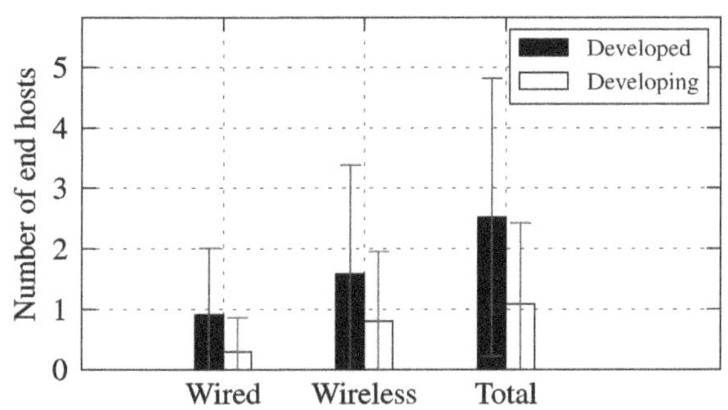

Figure 8: *Average number of devices connected to the access point at any time with error bars showing the standard deviation. We see that there are more wireless devices in both regions. Developed has more devices overall, and an even greater number of wired devices.*

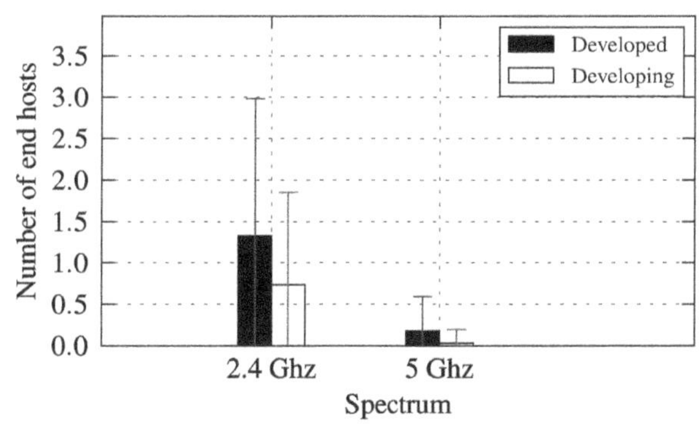

Figure 9: *Average number of wireless devices connected at any given time per spectrum with error bars showing the standard deviation. There are significantly more devices on 2.4 GHz than on 5 GHz.*

In developed countries, 43% of home networks have at least one always-on wired device; only 12% of home networks in developing countries have such as device.	§5.1, Tab. 5
The 2.4 GHz spectrum is significantly more crowded; the median number of devices seen on the 2.4 GHz spectrum is five, whereas on the 5 GHz band, the median number of devices is two.	§5.3, Fig. 10
The median number of access points seen from a home network in developed countries is about 20; in contrast, home networks in developing countries see a median of about two access points	§5.3, Fig. 11

Table 4: *Highlights of Section 5 results.*

ate either in the 2.4 GHz or the 5 GHz wireless spectrum. Table 4 summarizes the main results from this section.

5.1 How many devices?

More devices in developed countries. Figure 7 shows a CDF of the number of devices seen in each home; twenty percent of networks had at least two unique devices, and more than half of homes had at least five unique devices. Figure 8 details the number of devices for developed and developing countries. Developed countries have, on average, one more device connected to the access point at any given time than developing countries. All in all, households in countries with higher economic standards tend to have more devices in their network, and this number is more pronounced for wired devices. We assume this is because gaming consoles (*e.g.*, XBox, Playstation, Wii) or entertainment devices (*e.g.*, Apple TV, Google TV, Squeezebox) are more common in developed countries.

More "always-connected" devices in developed countries. Table 5 shows the number of households that have at least one wired or wireless device that never disconnects from the home gateway router for over five weeks and its percentage against the total number of households. The portion of households that have at least one "always-connected" device in developing countries is significantly lower than for developed countries. Media entertainment boxes are an example of a wired device that never disconnects from the router, and a wireless VoIP phone is an example of an "always-on" wireless device. Some households may never turn off their desktop or laptop. Although we do not explore the reasons for such connectivity in depth, we assume that households in developing countries tend to power off devices when not in use, possibly to minimize electricity or data usage. Unexpected and frequent power outages in these countries also affect device connectivity.

5.2 Wired or wireless?

More wireless than wired. Figure 9 shows the average number of wired and wireless devices attached to (and associated with) the home router over two weeks, measured hourly, for developed and developing router groups. There are generally more wireless devices than wired devices. Although this observation could reflect limitations of the router, which has only four available wired ports, the average number of wired ports used is less than one in both groups; this shows that many households use wireless even though wired connections generally provide better throughput, latency, and stability. This result also confirms the trend of moving away from wired communication [7] and towards primarily using wireless devices access the Internet. For many households, wireless technology has developed to the point where it is good enough for day-to-day Internet usage, and wired communication has little more to offer.

On the other hand, our results also suggest that wired devices are still in fairly widespread use in some homes. Chetty *et al.*

Group	Total houses	Houses with always-connected wired device	Houses with always-connected wireless device
developed	79	34 (43%)	16 (20%)
developing	34	4 (12%)	4 (12%)

Table 5: *Number of households that has one or more wired or wireless device which never disconnects from the home gateway router for over five weeks.*

stated that home users still desire wired communication for reliability, speed, and security [15]. Due to the physical constraint of wired communication (*i.e.*, cabling) devices using wired ports are likely stationary ones such as desktop machines, network printers or media entertainment gadgets like Apple TV. Even in homes with wired devices, our analysis suggests that a typical home gateway router could likely suffice with only two ports. Surprisingly, only a few households use all four Ethernet ports (9% for both developed and developing countries).

5.3 How much is each spectrum used?

Spectrum contention is an important problem in home wireless networks. Many devices talking to many access points in the vicinity causes contention and interference problems, which in turn reduces the available bandwidth of the wireless channel. Our results confirm that the 2.4 GHz spectrum is quite crowded, especially in developed countries, which could create bottlenecks as access link throughputs continue to increase. The 5 GHz spectrum, on the other hand, is less crowded (at least for now).

Wireless spectrum usage. Figure 9 shows that there are more devices active on the 2.4 GHz spectrum than on the 5 GHz spectrum at any given time. This phenomenon may result from the fact that dual-band devices are more expensive, and single-band devices default to the more popular 2.4 GHz spectrum. Phones are equipped almost exclusively with only 2.4 GHz radios. Figure 10 shows a CDF of the total number of *unique* devices seen per household. We see that the median number of devices on the 2.4 GHz spectrum is five, while the median number of devices on the 5 GHz spectrum is two.

We see a similar trend in the number of other access points seen on both spectrums. The median number of other access points is only about one device in the 5 GHz spectrum, while it is higher for the 2.4 GHz spectrum, as expected. Figure 11 shows a CDF of the total number of unique access points seen per household. Scanning is done only in the channel the access point is configured in (channel 11 for 2.4 GHz by default, though the user can configure it), so this does not tell us all the access points available, but it does tell us how likely it is that interference occurs due to competing access points. We see that the 2.4 GHz spectrum is more densely occupied in developed countries, and interestingly, we see that there are two modes in both sets; either there are very few access points in that channel or there are a lot (more than ten in developed and more than three in developing countries).

5.4 Which device vendors are most common?

For the 25 homes in the United States in the Traffic data set, we observed the frequency of various types of devices connected to the home network. When collecting the Traffic data set, we obfuscate the bottom 24 bits of the MAC addresses of all devices seen by the gateway. The first 24 bits allow us to look up the manufacturer, and though this does not always tell us if the device is a phone, tablet, or laptop, it still provides us enough information to distinguish network gateways from smart devices and wireless cards.

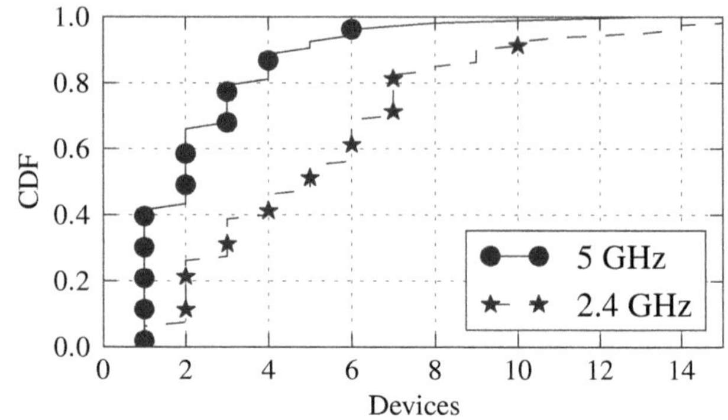

Figure 10: *Number of unique devices seen on the two wireless spectrums. The median is about five devices on 2.4 GHz and two devices on 5 GHz.*

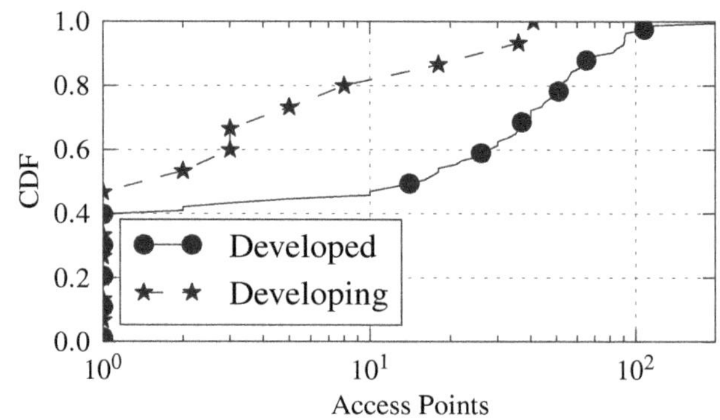

Figure 11: *Number of access points seen on the 2.4 GHz spectrum in developed and developing countries. There are many more access points visible in developed, where we see modal behavior with either very few or a lot of neighboring access points.*

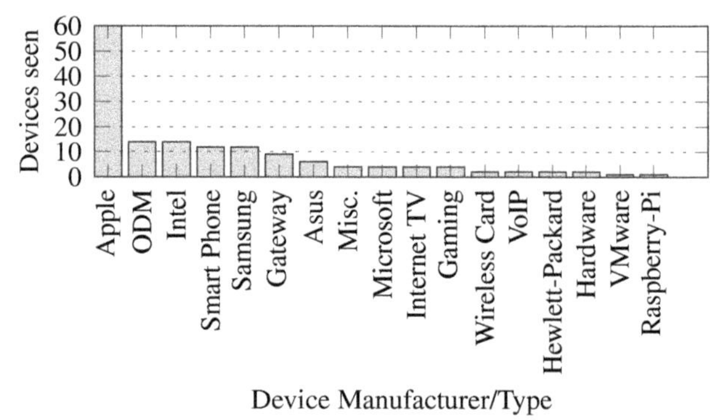

Figure 12: *The number of devices seen in the Devices data set across all homes in the Traffic data set (25 homes in the United States). We only considered devices which transferred at least 100 KB.*

Based on passive monitoring of 25 homes, Figure 12 plots the device types seen in the Traffic data set. We have removed all references to Netgear originating from our BISmark routers. The most common device was manufactured by Apple, followed by Intel. Other Samsung and smart phones were also reasonably com-

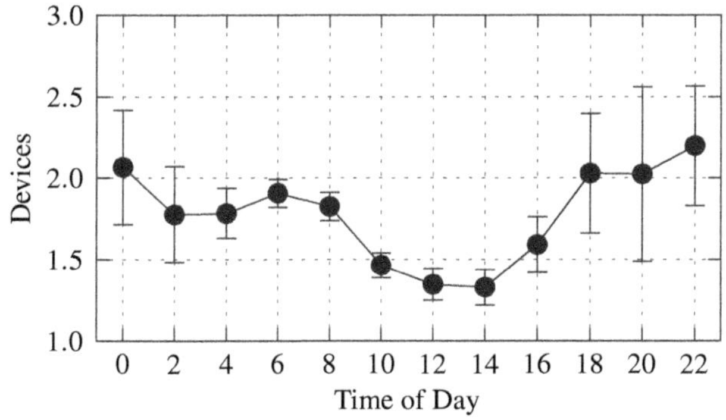

(a) *Weekday usage is diurnal.*

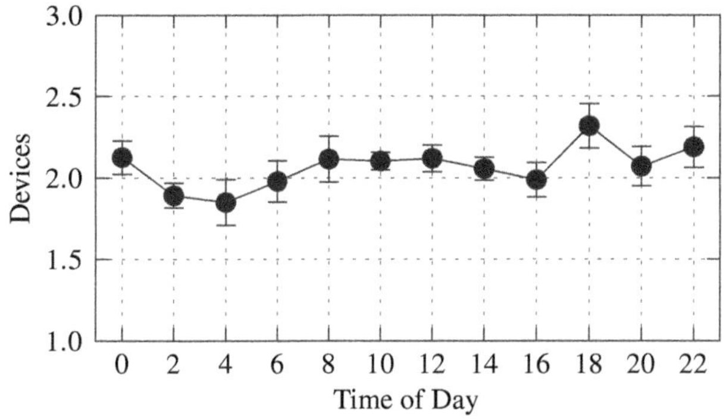

(b) *Usage on weekends is more constant.*

Figure 13: *Diurnal effect on wireless device usage. There is a clear weekday diurnal effect on the number of devices online.*

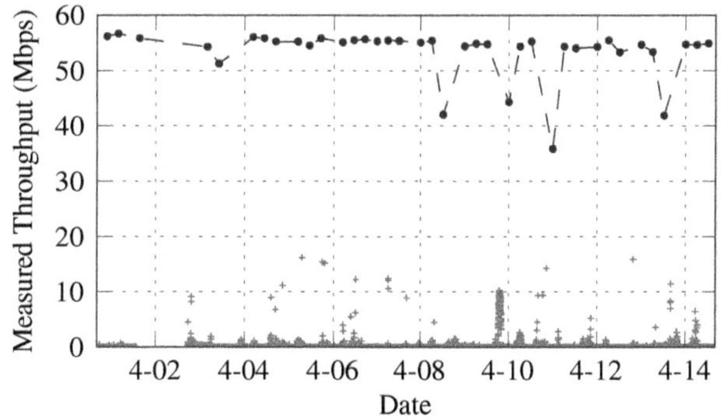

(a) *Upstream traffic, and the measured upstream capacity.*

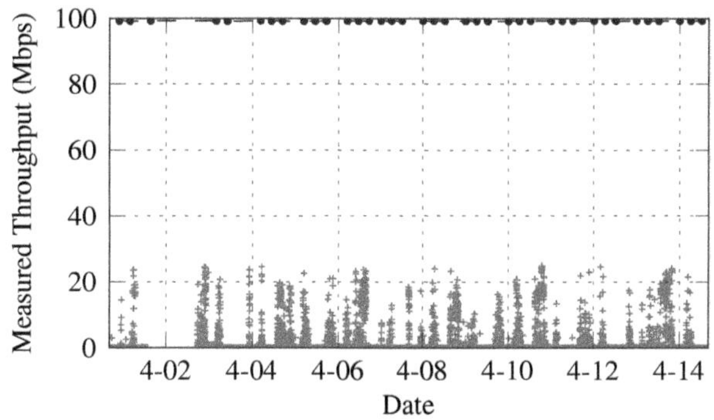

(b) *Downstream traffic, and the measured downstream capacity.*

Figure 14: *Diurnal pattern of link utilization for one home in our deployment. Capacity remains fairly constant, but utilization levels track daily cycles.*

mon.[5] We recently started gathering Traffic data in several developing countries, so we will soon be able to compare the distribution of device manufacturers in developed and developing countries.

6. USAGE CHARACTERISTICS

In this section, we identify notable characteristics of home network usage by analyzing data from the WiFi, Traffic, and Capacity data sets. Table 6 highlights our findings.

6.1 Which usage patterns are diurnal?

Figure 13 uses the WiFi data set to show the mean usage of wireless devices during each hour of the day, partitioned into weekday (Monday–Friday) and weekend. We observe a diurnal pattern in the number of unique devices at various times of day on weekdays; usage peaks during the evenings, and it is lowest during the afternoons, when users are usually at work. We see that the number of devices dips only slightly at night (compared to the dip during the day), which may result from cellular devices that remain on at night, as opposed to laptops that are more often switched off at night when users are asleep. Diurnal patterns are less pronounced on weekends.

Weekday traffic is much more diurnal than weekend traffic.	§6.1, Fig. 13
Some home networks consistently oversaturate their uplink; they are likely able to do this because of the "bufferbloat" phenomenon.	§6.2, Fig. 15
The single most usage-hungry device consumes about 65% of the total home network traffic, on average.	§6.3, Fig. 17
The most popular domain by volume in a home network is responsible, on average, for about 38% of the total wide-area traffic from that home network, but only 19% of the connections.	§6.4, Fig. 19

Table 6: *Highlights of Section 6 results.*

[5]The *Printer* manufacturer was an Epson. *Hardware* includes Giga-Byte and Microchip. *VoIP* is a UniData device. *Internet TV* includes Roku, TiVo, and ASRock home theatres. *Wireless Card* includes AzureWave and GainSpan. *Gaming* includes Nintendo and Mitsumi (which manufactures controllers for Playstations, Xbox, and Wii). Microsoft (possibly Xbox) is shown separately. Gateway includes TP-Link, Realtek, Liteon, D-Link, Cisco-Linksys, Belkin, and Askey. *Smart Phones* includes HTC, LG, Motorola, Nokia, and a confirmed Samsung Galaxy S II (Murata Inc.). Other Samsung devices, including phones and tablets, are shown separately. *Original Device Manufacturers (ODMs)* include Compal, Hon Hai Precision, Quanta, Universal Global Systems, Winstron Infocomm. Misc. includes Polycom (a telecom product manufacturer), Prolifix (which makes Internet-enabled thermostats), and Pegatron (which manufactures a variety of products including notebooks, laptops to gateways).

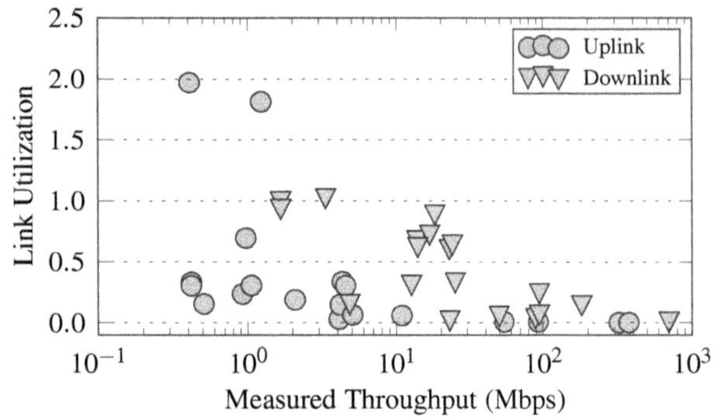

Figure 15: *Link utilization as a function of the measured throughput. Downlink saturation varies between 0 and 1. Uplink saturation is under 0.5 for most homes except for 3 cases. 2 homes over utilize their uplink*

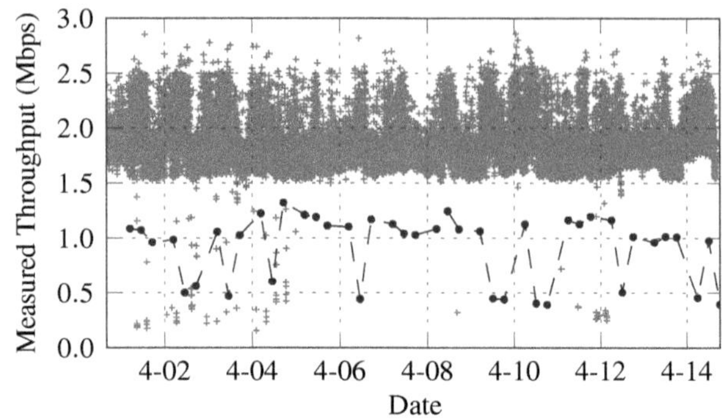

(a) *In this home, utilization always exceeds the measured upstream capacity. Upon further investigation, we discovered that this user continually uploads scientific data from his home network.*

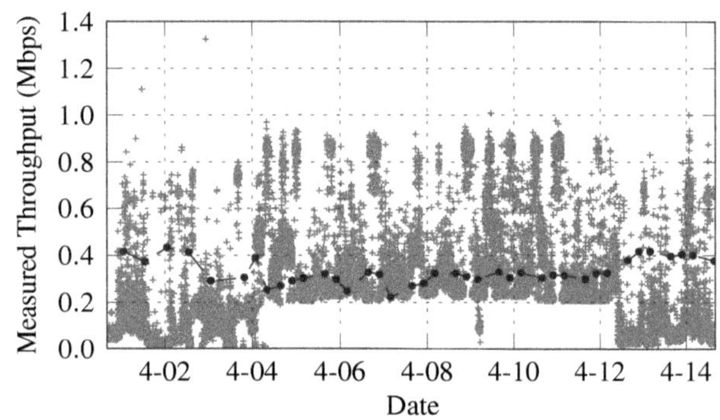

(b) *Diurnal bursts in traffic can sometimes result in utilization exceeding the network's upstream capacity.*

Figure 16: *In some cases, uplink utilization exceeds estimate of capacity. Buffering in customer premises equipment ("bufferbloat") can result in situations where utilization exceeds the measured capacity. These two homes likely experience significant latency and performance problems due to constant uplink saturation.*

Figure 14 shows an example of diurnal traffic patterns for upstream and downstream traffic from one home in the Traffic data set. Capacity measurements (shown as the dotted line at the top of each plot) remains fairly constant, while utilization follows a roughly diurnal trend. Many homes in Traffic exhibit patterns similar to those in Figure 14.

6.2 Do users saturate their access links?

Access link speeds continue to increase, but it is not known whether users actually take advantage of this additional capacity. We measure utilization by computing the maximum per-second throughput every minute for users in the Traffic data set. We then compare the utilization with the access link throughput as estimated by Capacity. We only consider instances when there is some device exchanging traffic with the Internet. Figure 15 plots 95th percentile link saturation against capacity estimates for uplink and downlink in bits per second on a log scale. In most cases there is plenty of spare capacity. At the 95th percentile, only two homes saturate the link and most homes use less than 50% of the available capacity. Thus, even when the link is used, utilization does not come close to capacity most of the time. If we include cases when the router is on and connected to the Internet but has no traffic then these numbers drop even further.

The circles on the scatterplot show the equivalent case for upstream traffic. We expect upstream usage to be less than downstream, because popular Internet services download more traffic than they upload; as expected, upstream utilization is less than downstream. Figure 15 shows that uplink utilization exceeds capacity for certain homes. Figure 16 shows a timeseries of capacity estimates and utilization for both of these homes. This user consistently saturates the uplink; when combined with "bufferbloat" problems problems endemic in home networking hardware, this behavior causes overestimation of the upstream throughput [19].

6.3 How much is each device used?

Figure 17 shows the fraction of traffic that individual devices contribute to overall home data consumption, ordered by the traffic consumption. Every household has at least three unique devices, but one dominant device typically consumes the bulk of the traffic (60% on average; the next most dominant device consumes about 20% of the traffic). Although we do not have ground truth about the types of devices in each home, it is obvious that even if people have multiple devices, they prefer to consume most data from a single device. Differentiating devices types (*e.g.*, laptops, tablets, phones, media players, etc.) from network traffic is ongoing research.

6.4 Which domains receive the most traffic?

We now examine the popular domains that users in home networks visit and how those sets of popular domains vary across different home networks. As described in Section 3, we measure statistics for network traffic to domains that match a whitelist of domain names based on the 200 most popular domain names from Alexa, plus any domains that users add to this list using a Web interface built into our router firmware [8]. The router anonymizes DNS lookups to all other domains.

Which domains are consistently popular? We first explore the domains that are the five and ten most popular domains in a significant number of home networks. Figure 18 shows this distribution; the dark bar indicates the number of times a particular domain appeared in the top five domains in a home network, and the lighter bar shows the number of home networks for which a domain appeared in the top ten. The most consistently popular domains on this list are as expected: Google, YouTube, Facebook, Amazon, Apple, and Twitter. Unsurprisingly, the tail is also quite

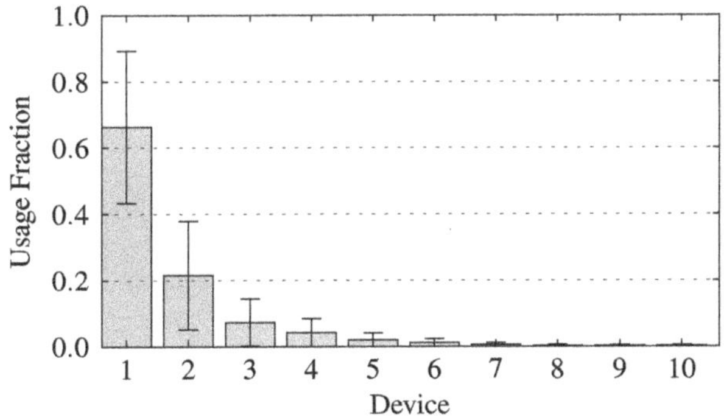

Figure 17: *Breakdown of data usage by device. We see that even in homes with multiple devices, there is usually a dominant device responsible for most of the traffic.*

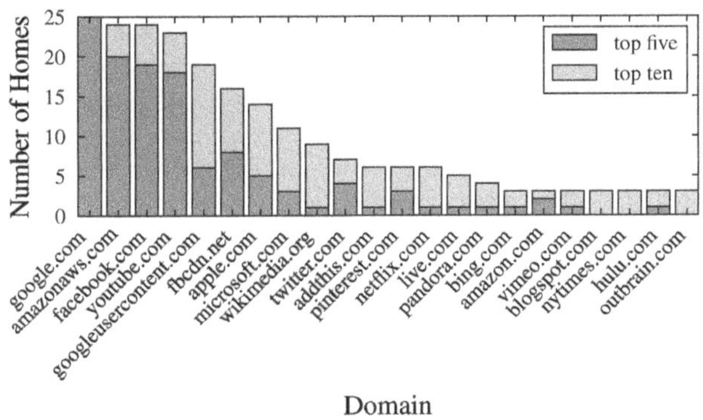

Figure 18: *The number of home networks in the Traffic data set for which a particular domain appeared in the top-five or top-ten domains, ranked by total traffic volume.*

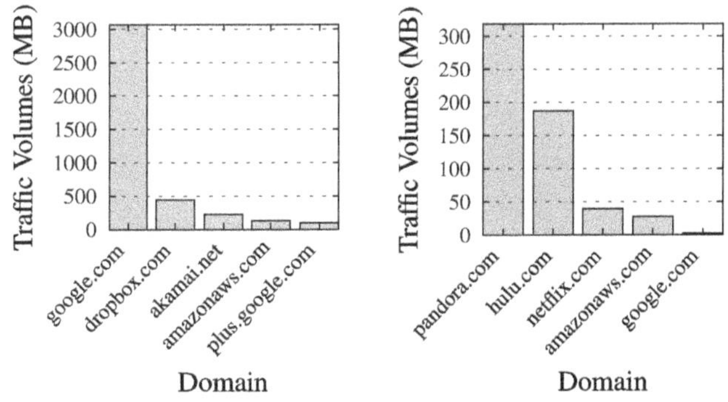

(a) *iMac (Desktop).* **(b)** *Roku box.*

Figure 20: *Traffic distribution from an Apple iMac (desktop) and a Roku streaming player. For the desktop, Dropbox creates significant traffic to* `dropbox.com` *in the process of syncing large files. The Roku is used almost exclusively for streaming, as evidenced by the large fraction of traffic to* `pandora.com`, `hulu.com`, *and* `netflix.com`.

long, with many domains being popular for just one or two homes (*e.g.*, streaming sites, news sites). This distribution confirms on a smaller scale other reports concerning the rise of "super peers" who are responsible for sending much of the content into access networks [29].

How much traffic are the most popular domains responsible for? Figure 19 shows the distribution of domains visited in terms of both total traffic volume and the number of connections made to the domain (which indicates the frequency of visits). Figure 19a shows the average volume of traffic from each home to the most popular domains in the whitelist. (We use rank indexes for domains rather than actual names, since the domain ranking is not exactly the same across all homes.)

The results show that the most popular whitelisted domain by volume on average accounts for about 38% of the total traffic volume, even though these sites are responsible for less than 14% of connections (Figure 19c); the next most popular domain accounts for about 11% of all traffic and only about 7% of all connections. This disproportionality reflects the fact that these popular domains are most likely serving streaming media content over long-running TCP connections. Hence, it is fairly safe to assume that these top two or three most popular domains by traffic volume are likely to represent streaming content, which would corroborate other reports that more than 40% of traffic into home networks is streaming video traffic. Figure 19b shows that the domain with the most number of TCP connections is responsible for about 19% of all connections on average; again, this distribution has a very long tail.

It is worth cautioning that our anonymization of some of the domains in the Traffic data set could bias some of these results. In particular, if many homes in our data set for some reason sent a significant amount of traffic to domains that were not in our whitelist (*e.g.*, domains for pornographic content, which we explicitly removed from the whitelist), our results would not reflect this phenomenon. Nevertheless, because traffic to whitelisted domains represents about 65% of all traffic volume to and from our home networks on average, we believe that we have captured a representative sample of usage. Additionally, the Traffic data set currently only represents homes in the United States; as we begin to collect this data from home networks in other countries, we will be able to compare differences in domain popularity from different home networks.

Do different devices look up different sets of domains? We also examined domain popularity for different devices in home networks, to see whether the distribution of traffic volumes to domains differed by device. Our hypothesis was that certain devices might look up considerably different sets of domains than others. For example, an Apple device might exchange more traffic with `apple.com`, a streaming set top box might exchange more traffic with `hulu.com`, and so forth. If true, such a finding could prove extremely valuable for applications and utilities inside the home that want to automatically "fingerprint" devices—typically, the manufacturer ID of a device's MAC address may narrow down the device to a manufacturer, but it is not fine-grained enough to distinguish, say, a laptop from a smart phone.

To explore this hypothesis, we surveyed users from six homes in the Traffic data set and asked them to manually identify the devices corresponding to each of the MAC addresses in their home. These labels provide ground truth identification for these devices. Here, we show an example of how different devices send different distributions of traffic volumes to various domains. Figures 20a and 20b show the distributions for an Apple iMac Desktop and a Roku Streaming Player, respectively. Whereas a device's MAC address only reveals the manufacturer, further examination of traffic behavior suggests that usage patterns may differ significantly enough across *types* of devices to serve as fingerprints for device

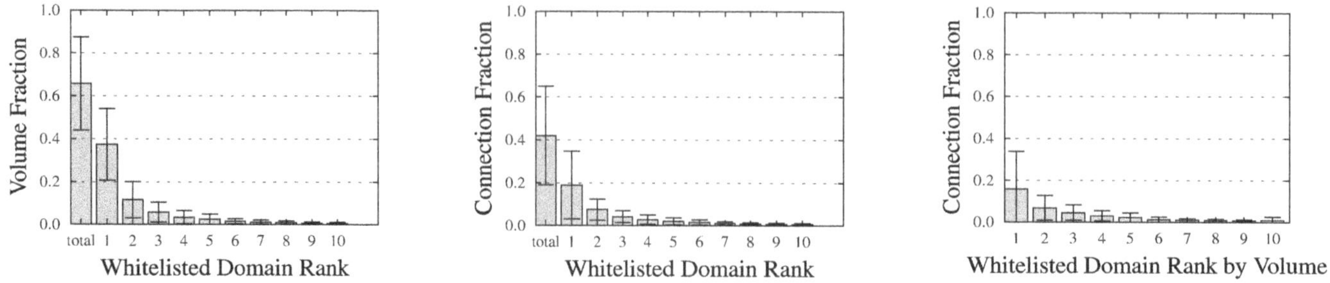

(a) *Distribution of the most popular domains by mean traffic volume.*

(b) *Distribution of the most popular domains by mean number of connections.*

(c) *Fraction of connections for the most popular domains by volume.*

Figure 19: *Breakdown of data usage by domain. The most popular domain by volume consumes about 38% of total traffic. "Total" refers to the portion of traffic to whitelisted domains (Alexa top 200, plus any domains that the user manually whitelists) and accounts for about 65% of the total traffic on average.*

identification (either automatically, or with some help from the user). Exploring how these traffic patterns can assist with device fingerprinting is an area of future work.

7. DISCUSSION

This study offers a glimpse into the characteristics of a variety of home networks; the findings in the paper suggest many avenues for future work.

Combining network measurement with qualitative studies about Internet use. Previous work in home networking has explored various characteristics of home networks via detailed user studies and interviews [13, 14]. Our results can complement these studies, which have been primarily qualitative to date. Future work might entail doing a study that jointly performs user studies in conjunction with network traffic monitoring, to determine whether users' perceptions about their network use are consistent with the reality (*e.g.*, whether people spend more or less time online than they claim).

Device fingerprinting for security alerts. Various Internet service providers offer services that alert users about possible infected devices in the home network; unfortunately, because ISPs typically cannot map offending traffic to a particular MAC address, it is difficult for them to attribute traffic to a particular device. Future work could follow up on device fingerprinting using traffic patterns to develop a system that provides more fine-grained alerts to Internet service providers about the suspicious activities of an individual device within a home.

Expanding the study of usage to more countries. Our study of home network usage focused on the United States alone. Future work could expand this part of the study to determine how usage patterns and other traffic characteristics (*e.g.*, device usage, popular domains) differ by country.

8. CONCLUSION

Despite the proliferation of home networks, very little is known about the properties of these networks, in terms of their availability, infrastructure, or usage. Although continual, longitudinal measurements of these networks can provide insight into how people build, configure, and use these networks, there has been little attempt to instrument these networks to gather such data. This paper represents the first attempt to instrument a significant number of home networks to learn about their properties. We presented the first large-scale, longitudinal measurement study of home networks, based on data from 126 homes and 19 countries. Our set of passive and active measurements allows us to characterize properties of these networks such as network availability, infrastructure, and usage. We have publicly released all data sets that do not involve personally identifying information, and we plan to continue expanding the deployment into a broader, more diverse set of environments.

Our study yields many interesting findings with respect to the availability, infrastructure, and usage of home networks that could have broader implications for ISPs, users, and policymakers. With respect to availability, we found that developing countries experience far more frequent connectivity interruptions, some of which are due to poor connectivity, but others that are due to behavioral patterns (*e.g.*, turning the router on only during times when a user wants to access the Internet). More insights into how behavioral patterns differ across countries may help both ISPs and application designers. We also found that the 2.4 GHz spectrum is significantly more crowded than the 5 GHz spectrum, both in terms of number of devices and in terms of the number of visible access points; more widespread statistics about the usage of wireless spectrum (as will hopefully be possible as we continue to expand the BISmark deployment) can ultimately help ISPs debug connectivity problems in home networks and provide policymakers important data about spectrum usage. Finally, we see that most of the traffic from homes is destined for only a few domains, and that, on average, most of the traffic originates from just a small handful of devices. These usage statistics may ultimately help ISPs with provisioning and peering decisions, and they also offer a rare picture into how people use and interact with their home networks. Although this study has offered a first glimpse into many aspects home networks around the world, we expect that more lessons will come with more experience and a broader deployment.

Acknowledgments

This research was funded in part by NSF award CNS-1059350 and a Google Focused Research Award. We thank the hundreds of BISmark users, without whom this research would not have been possible. We also thank our shepherd, Yashar Ganjali, and the anonymous reviewers for their valuable feedback.

REFERENCES

[1] Internet world stats. http://www.internetworldstats.com/.

[2] Netgear WNDR3800. http://www.netgear.com/home/products/wirelessrouters/high-performance/wndr3800.aspx.
[3] OpenWRT. http://www.openwrt.org.
[4] Reports from Federal Communications Commission. http://www.fcc.gov/reports. FCC.
[5] SamKnows & Ofcom Working together for better broadband. http://www.samknows.com/broadband/signup/ofcom.
[6] Sign up with us today to accurately measure your broadband performance. https://www.samknows.eu/.
[7] The World in 2011: ICT Facts and Figures. http://www.itu.int/ITU-D/ict/facts/2011/material/ICTFactsFigures2011.pdf. International Telecommunication Union.
[8] Top Sites in United States. http://www.alexa.com/topsites/countries/US. Alexa.
[9] The World Bank GDP per capita. http://data.worldbank.org/indicator/NY.GDP.PCAP.CD, 2011. The World Bank.
[10] Y. Benkler. Next generation connectivity: A review of broadband internet transitions and policy from around the world. Working paper 8, Regulation2point0, Oct. 2009.
[11] K. L. Calvert, W. K. Edwards, and R. E. Grinter. Moving toward the middle: The case against the end-to-end argument in home networking. In *Proc. 6th ACM Workshop on Hot Topics in Networks (Hotnets-VI), Atlanta, GA*, 2007.
[12] J. Chen, S. Amershi, A. Dhananjay, and L. Subramanian. Comparing web interaction models in developing regions. In *Proceedings of the First ACM Symposium on Computing for Development*, ACM DEV '10, pages 6:1–6:9, New York, NY, USA, 2010. ACM.
[13] M. Chetty, R. Banks, R. Harper, T. Regan, A. Sellen, C. Gkantsidis, T. Karagiannis, and P. Key. Who's hogging the bandwidth: the consequences of revealing the invisible in the home. In *Proceedings of the SIGCHI Conference on Human Factors in Computing Systems*, CHI '10, pages 659–668, New York, NY, USA, 2010. ACM.
[14] M. Chetty, D. Haslem, A. Baird, U. Ofoha, B. Sumner, and R. Grinter. Why is my internet slow?: making network speeds visible. In *Proceedings of the SIGCHI Conference on Human Factors in Computing Systems*, CHI '11, pages 1889–1898, New York, NY, USA, 2011. ACM.
[15] M. Chetty, J.-Y. Sung, and R. E. Grinter. How smart homes learn: the evolution of the networked home and household. In *Proceedings of the 9th international conference on Ubiquitous computing*, UbiComp '07, pages 127–144, Berlin, Heidelberg, 2007. Springer-Verlag.
[16] L. DiCioccio, R. Teixeira, M. May, and C. Kreibich. Probe and pray: using upnp for home network measurements. In *Proceedings of the 13th international conference on Passive and Active Measurement*, PAM'12, pages 96–105, Berlin, Heidelberg, 2012. Springer-Verlag.
[17] L. DiCioccio, R. Teixeira, and C. Rosenberg. Measuring home networks with HomeNet Profiler. In *Passive & Active Measurement (PAM)*, Hong Kong, Mar. 2013.
[18] M. Dischinger, A. Haeberlen, K. P. Gummadi, and S. Saroiu. Characterizing residential broadband networks. In *Proc. ACM SIGCOMM Internet Measurement Conference*, San Diego, CA, USA, Oct. 2007.
[19] J. Gettys. Bufferbloat. http://www.bufferbloat.net/.
[20] R. Grinter, W. Edwards, M. Chetty, E. Poole, J. Sung, J. Yang, A. Crabtree, P. Tolmie, T. Rodden, C. Greenhalgh, et al. The ins and outs of home networking: The case for useful and usable domestic networking. *ACM Transactions on Computer-Human Interaction (TOCHI)*, 16(2):1–28, 2009.
[21] R. Grinter, W. Edwards, M. Newman, and N. Ducheneaut. The work to make a home network work. In *ECSCW 2005*, pages 469–488. Springer, 2005.
[22] International Monetary Fund. World economic outlook database. http://www.imf.org/external/pubs/ft/weo/2013/01/weodata/index.aspx, Apr. 2013.
[23] W. Keith Edwards, R. Mahajan, and D. Wetherall. Advancing the state of home networking. *Communications of the ACM*, 54(6), 2011.
[24] H. Kim, S. Sundaresan, M. Chetty, N. Feamster, and W. K. Edwards. Communicating with caps: Managing usage caps in home networks. In *ACM SIGCOMM Computer Communication Review*, volume 41, pages 470–471. ACM, 2011.
[25] C. Kreibich, N. Weaver, B. Nechaev, and V. Paxson. Netalyzr: Illuminating the edge network. In *Proc. Internet Measurement Conference*, Melbourne, Australia, Nov. 2010.
[26] Netalyzr. http://netalyzr.icsi.berkeley.edu/.
[27] E. S. Poole, M. Chetty, R. E. Grinter, and W. K. Edwards. More than meets the eye: transforming the user experience of home network management. In *Proceedings of the 7th ACM conference on Designing interactive systems*, pages 455–464. ACM, 2008.
[28] M. A. Sánchez, J. S. Otto, Z. S. Bischof, and F. E. Bustamante. Trying broadband characterization at home. In *Passive & Active Measurement (PAM)*, Hong Kong, Mar. 2013.
[29] Sandvine. Global Internet Phenomena Report. http://www.sandvine.com/news/global_broadband_trends.asp, 2012.
[30] Shaperprobe. http://www.cc.gatech.edu/~partha/diffprobe/shaperprobe.html.
[31] T. N. Smyth, S. Kumar, I. Medhi, and K. Toyama. Where there's a will there's a way: mobile media sharing in urban india. In *Proceedings of the SIGCHI Conference on Human Factors in Computing Systems*, CHI '10, pages 753–762, New York, NY, USA, 2010. ACM.
[32] S. Sundaresan, W. de Donato, N. Feamster, R. Teixeira, S. Crawford, and A. Pescapè. Broadband internet performance: A view from the gateway. In *Proc. ACM SIGCOMM*, Toronto, Ontario, Canada, Aug. 2011.
[33] S. P. Wyche, T. N. Smyth, M. Chetty, P. M. Aoki, and R. E. Grinter. Deliberate interactions: characterizing technology use in nairobi, kenya. In *Proceedings of the SIGCHI Conference on Human Factors in Computing Systems*, CHI '10, pages 2593–2602, New York, NY, USA, 2010. ACM.

Identifiability of Link Metrics Based on End-to-end Path Measurements *

Liang Ma
Imperial College
London, UK
l.ma10@imperial.ac.uk

Ting He
IBM T. J. Watson Research
Yorktown, NY, USA
the@us.ibm.com

Kin K. Leung
Imperial College
London, UK
kin.leung@imperial.ac.uk

Ananthram Swami
Army Research Laboratory
Adelphi, MD, USA
a.swami@ieee.org

Don Towsley
University of Massachusetts
Amherst, MA, USA
towsley@cs.umass.edu

Abstract

We investigate the problem of identifying individual link metrics in a communication network from end-to-end path measurements, under the assumption that link metrics are additive and constant. To uniquely identify the link metrics, the number of linearly independent measurement paths must equal the number of links. Our contribution is to characterize this condition in terms of the network topology and the number/placement of monitors, under the constraint that measurement paths must be cycle-free. Our main results are: (i) it is generally impossible to identify all the link metrics by using two monitors; (ii) nevertheless, metrics of all the interior links not incident to any monitor are identifiable by two monitors if the topology satisfies a set of necessary and sufficient connectivity conditions; (iii) these conditions naturally extend to a necessary and sufficient condition for identifying all the link metrics using three or more monitors. We show that these conditions not only allow efficient identifiability tests, but also enable an efficient algorithm to place the minimum number of monitors in order to identify all link metrics. Our evaluations on both random and real topologies show that the proposed algorithm achieves identifiability using a much smaller number of monitors than a baseline solution.

*Research was partially sponsored by the U.S. Army Research Laboratory and the U.K. Ministry of Defence and was accomplished under Agreement Number W911NF-06-3-0001. The views and conclusions contained in this document are those of the authors and should not be interpreted as representing the official policies, either expressed or implied, of the U.S. Army Research Laboratory, the U.S. Government, the U.K. Ministry of Defence or the U.K. Government. The U.S. and U.K. Governments are authorized to reproduce and distribute reprints for Government purposes notwithstanding any copyright notation hereon.

IMC'13, October 23–25, 2013, Barcelona, Spain.
Copyright 2013 ACM 978-1-4503-1953-9/13/10 ...$15.00.
http://dx.doi.org/10.1145/2504730.2504738.

Categories and Subject Descriptors

C.2.3 [**Computer-communication Networks**]: Network Operations—*Network monitoring*; G.2.2 [**Discrete Mathematics**]: Graph Theory—*Network problems*

General Terms

Algorithms, Measurement, Performance, Theory

Keywords

Network Tomography; Linear Algebraic Model; Identifiability Condition; Monitor Placement

1. INTRODUCTION

Accurate and timely knowledge of the internal state of a network (e.g., delays on individual links) is essential for various network operations such as route selection, resource allocation, and fault diagnosis. Directly measuring the performance of individual network elements (e.g., nodes/links) is, however, not always feasible due to the traffic overhead of the measurement process and the lack of support at internal network elements for making such measurements [1]. These limitations motivate the need for *external* approaches, where we infer the states of internal network elements by measuring the performance along selected paths from a subset of nodes with monitoring capabilities, hereafter referred to as *monitors.*

Depending on the granularity of observations, external approaches can be classified as *hop-by-hop* approaches or *end-to-end* approaches. The former rely on special diagnostic tools such as *traceroute*, *pathchar* [2], and *Network Characterization Service (NCS)* [3] to reveal fine-grained performance metrics of individual links by sending active probes. Traceroute reports delay for each hop on the probed path by gradually increasing the time-to-live (TTL) field of probing packets. Its refinement, pathchar, returns hop-by-hop capacities, delays, and loss rates. A later advancement, NCS, also returns available capacities on each link. While providing fine-grained information, the above tools require that Internet Control Message Protocol (ICMP) be supported at each internal node. Even then, they suffer inaccuracies caused by asymmetry in routes and different priorities of ICMP and data packets. Moreover, these tools can generate a large number of probing packets, causing extra load and, potentially, congestion. In risk-sensitive applications, security policies may even block hop-by-hop measurements.

Alternatively, the end-to-end approach provides a solution that does not rely on the cooperation of internal network elements or the equal treatment of control/data packets. It relies on end-to-end performance metrics (e.g., end-to-end delays) experienced by data packets to solve for the corresponding hop-by-hop metrics using *network tomography.* Network tomography [4] refers to the methodology of inferring internal network characteristics through end-to-end measurements. Without requiring special cooperation from internal nodes, network tomography can utilize measurements from data packets to obtain path-level information [5], thus reducing the need for active probes.

In many cases, link metrics are *additive*, i.e., the combined metric over multiple links is the sum of individual link metrics. For instance, delays are additive, while a multiplicative metric (e.g., packet delivery ratio) can be expressed in an additive form by using the $\log(\cdot)$ function. For additive metrics, we can model the problem as that of solving a system of linear equations, where the unknown variables are the link metrics, and the known constants are the end-to-end path measurements, each equal to the sum of the corresponding link metrics along a path. Thus, network tomography essentially solves this linear system of equations.

Existing work on network tomography emphasizes extracting as much information about link metrics as possible from available measurements. However, past experience shows that it is frequently impossible to uniquely identify all link metrics from path measurements [6–8]. For example, if two links (not necessarily adjacent) always appear together in measurement paths, then we can at most identify their sum metric but not the individual metrics. Generally, many measurement paths are *linearly dependent* in that some paths are linear combinations of the rest, and hence their measurements do not provide new information. From the perspective of linear algebra, link metrics are uniquely identifiable if and only if the number of *linearly independent* measurement paths equals the number of links. There is, however, a lack of basic understanding of the topological conditions that ensure identifiability, even in the simplified scenario of constant link metrics.

In this paper, we consider two closely related fundamental problems: (i) Under what conditions can one uniquely identify all link metrics from end-to-end measurements; (ii) Given an arbitrary network topology, how can one place monitors to satisfy the above conditions using the minimum number of monitors? We study both problems in the context of *controllable, cycle-free* measurements, i.e., monitors can direct measurement packets to selected paths as long as they do not contain cycles. Such routing is generally supported for networks under common administration (e.g., single-ISP networks), or overlay networks formed by overlay nodes and physical paths between these nodes (modeled as overlay links), where network tomography can be applied to accurately monitor performance experienced by data traffic while reducing measurement overhead. Moreover, these assumptions capture capabilities of a new generation of networks performing *Software-Defined Networking (SDN)* [9], where monitors, in cooperation with SDN controller, can dictate paths of measurement packets in the route setup phase, while the cycle-free constraint precludes formation of endless cycles in the data forwarding phase. We assume that all link metrics are additive and constant. Our "constant" link metric refers to one that either changes slowly relative to the measurement process, or that is a statistical characteristic (e.g., mean, variance) of the link that stays constant over time[1].

Although the answer to the first question is straightforward in linear algebra (the number of linearly independent paths equals the number of links), a useful answer should be expressed in terms of externally verifiable network properties such as the network topology and the number/placement of monitors. To this end, we establish necessary and sufficient conditions on network topology and monitor placement for uniquely identifying link metrics from controllable, cycle-free measurements between the monitors. We further develop an efficient algorithm that leverages the established conditions to place monitors in a given network such that all link metrics can be uniquely identified by using the minimum number of monitors.

1.1 Further Discussions on Related Work

Based on the model of link metrics, existing work can be broadly classified as statistical and algebraic approaches. Statistical approaches model link metrics as random variables with (partially) unknown probability distributions, and apply various parametric/nonparametric techniques to estimate the link metric distributions from realizations of path metrics [1,10,11]. Algebraic approaches consider link metrics as unknown constants, and use linear algebraic techniques to compute link metrics from cumulative path metrics [6,7].

With link metrics modeled as random variables, multicast, if supported, can be exploited as a measurement method with broad coverage and low overhead [12, 13]. Sub-trees and unicast are employed in [5,14] as alternatives, due to the inflexibility of multicasting to all receivers. Employing multicast, [5, 15] derive the necessary and sufficient conditions on the multicast tree for identifying all link metric distributions. If most links do not exhibit severe losses or delays, [10] proposes algorithms to identify the worst performing links. A novel approach proposed in [8] employs the Fourier transform of the observable path metric distributions to estimate the unobservable link metric distributions. All the above methods implicitly assume the links to be identifiable, and the multicast-based methods require multiple monitors to participate in the measurement process. In contrast, we assume unicast measurements and focus on establishing topological conditions for identifying all link metrics by using the minimum number of monitors.

For constant link metrics, [7] shows that it is challenging to solve the inverse problem due to the presence of linearly dependent paths. When all but k link metrics are *zero*, compressive sensing techniques are used to identify the k non-zero link metrics [16, 17]. If all link metrics are *binary* (normal/failed), [18] proves that the network must be $(k+2)$-edge-connected to identify up to k failed links by using one monitor measuring cycles. For arbitrary valued link metrics, few positive results are known. If the network is directed (links have different metrics in different directions), [11] proves that not all link metrics are identifiable unless every non-isolated node is a monitor. Even if every

[1]In this case, end-to-end measurements are also statistical characteristics, e.g., path mean/variance. In the case of variance, we also need the independence between link qualities to make the metric additive.

node is a monitor, unique link identification is still impossible if measurement paths are constrained to cycles [6]. If the network is undirected (links have equal metrics in both directions), [19] derives the first necessary and sufficient conditions on the network topology for identifying all link metrics, given that monitors can measure cycles or paths possibly containing cycles. A similar study in [20] characterizes the minimum number of measurements needed to identify a broader set of link metrics (including both additive and nonadditive metrics), under the stronger assumption that measurement paths can contain repeated links. Since routing along cycles is typically prohibited in real networks, it remains open as to what the conditions become if only cycle-free paths can be measured. In this regard, we investigate the fundamental relationships between link identifiability, network topology, and the number/placement of monitors. Once identifiability is confirmed, a follow-up problem is to construct linearly independent paths between monitors to perform measurements, for which we have developed an efficient path construction algorithm in [21].

Little is known when it comes to placing monitors to ensure network identifiability. In [22, 23], the problem of placing the minimum number of monitors to identify all link metrics under *uncontrollable* routing is proved to be NP-hard, and the NP-hardness persists even if a subset of nodes have control over their local routing policy [24]. In contrast, we show in this paper that under *controllable* cycle-free routing, this problem can be solved optimally in linear time.

1.2 Summary of Contributions

We study here for the first time the fundamental topological conditions for identifying additive link metrics by using end-to-end measurements on cycle-free paths. Our contributions are four-fold:

1) We prove that it is generally impossible to identify all link metrics by using only two monitors, irrespective of the network topology and the placement of monitors.

2) We establish necessary and sufficient conditions for identifying the metrics of all *interior links* (links not incident to any monitor) by using two monitors: the network graph is (i) 2-edge-connected after removing any interior link and (ii) 3-vertex-connected after adding a direct link between the two monitors. These conditions are shown to be verifiable in $O(|L|(|V|+|L|))$ time, where $|V|$ is the number of nodes and $|L|$ is the number of links.

3) We transform the above result into a necessary and sufficient condition for identifying all link metrics using κ ($\kappa \geq 3$) monitors by embedding the network graph in an extended graph, with two virtual monitors connected to all the real monitors. This condition can be verified in $O(|V|+|L|)$ time.

4) We propose an algorithm to place monitors in an arbitrary network in $O(|V|+|L|)$ time, which guarantees the identifiability of all link metrics by using the minimum number of monitors. Our evaluations on both randomly-generated and real topologies show that the proposed algorithm requires a substantially smaller number of monitors than a baseline solution.

We note that our goal is to characterize identifiable scenarios for additive link metrics, and the identification of non-additive link metrics (e.g., bit error rates) is beyond the scope of this paper.

The rest of the paper is organized as follows. Section 2 formulates the problem. Section 3 summarizes our main results. Sections 4–5 present identifiability conditions for the case of two monitors, and Section 6 addresses the case of three or more monitors. Algorithms for testing network identifiability and deploying monitors are presented in Section 7. Finally, Section 8 concludes the paper.

Table 1: Notations in Graph Theory

Symbol	Meaning
$V(\mathcal{G})$, $L(\mathcal{G})$	set of nodes/links in graph $\mathcal{G}$
$\lvert\mathcal{G}\rvert$	degree of graph $\mathcal{G}$: $\lvert\mathcal{G}\rvert = \lvert V(\mathcal{G})\rvert$ (number of nodes)
$\lvert\lvert\mathcal{G}\rvert\rvert$	order of graph $\mathcal{G}$: $\lvert\lvert\mathcal{G}\rvert\rvert = \lvert L(\mathcal{G})\rvert$ (number of links)
$\mathcal{H}$	interior graph (see Definition 1)
$L(v)$	set of links incident to node v
$\mathcal{G}-l$	delete a link: $\mathcal{G}-l = (V(\mathcal{G}), L(\mathcal{G})\setminus\{l\})$, where $l \in L(\mathcal{G})$ and "\" is setminus
$\mathcal{G}+l$	add a link: $\mathcal{G}+l = (V(\mathcal{G}), L(\mathcal{G})\cup\{l\})$, where the end-points of link l are in $V(\mathcal{G})$
$\mathcal{G}-v$	delete a node: $\mathcal{G}-v = (V(\mathcal{G})\setminus\{v\}, L(\mathcal{G})\setminus L(v))$, where $v \in V(\mathcal{G})$
$\mathcal{G}_s+v$	add a node: $\mathcal{G}_s+v = (V(\mathcal{G}_s)\cup\{v\}, L(\mathcal{G}_s)\cup L_v)$, where $\mathcal{G}_s$ is a sub-graph of $\mathcal{G}$, $v \in V(\mathcal{G})\setminus V(\mathcal{G}_s)$, and L_v is the set of all links between v and nodes in $V(\mathcal{G}_s)$
$\mathcal{G}\setminus\mathcal{G}'$	From $\mathcal{G}$, delete all common nodes with $\mathcal{G}'$ and their incident links
$\mathcal{G}\cap\mathcal{G}'$	intersection of graphs: $\mathcal{G}\cap\mathcal{G}' = (V(\mathcal{G})\cap V(\mathcal{G}'), L(\mathcal{G})\cap L(\mathcal{G}'))$
$\mathcal{G}\cup\mathcal{G}'$	union of graphs: $\mathcal{G}\cup\mathcal{G}' = (V(\mathcal{G})\cup V(\mathcal{G}'), L(\mathcal{G})\cup L(\mathcal{G}'))$
$\mathcal{P}(v_0, v_k)$	simple path connecting nodes v_0 and v_k, defined as a special graph with $V(\mathcal{P}) = \{v_0, \ldots, v_k\}$ and $L(\mathcal{P}) = \{v_0v_1, v_1v_2, \ldots, v_{k-1}v_k\}$
$\mathcal{C}$	cycle: if $(v_0, \ldots, v_k)$ ($k \geq 2$) is a sequence of nodes on a simple path $\mathcal{P}$, then $\mathcal{C} = \mathcal{P} + v_kv_0$ is a *cycle*
$\mathcal{F}$	a non-separating cycle (see Definition 4)
m_i	$m_i \in V(\mathcal{G})$ is the i-th monitor in $\mathcal{G}$
W_l, $W_\mathcal{P}$	metric on link l and sum metric on path $\mathcal{P}$

2. PROBLEM FORMULATION

2.1 Models and Assumptions

We assume that the network topology is known and model it as an undirected graph[2] $\mathcal{G} = (V, L)$, where V and L are the sets of nodes and links, respectively. Note that graph $\mathcal{G}$ can represent a logical topology where each link in $\mathcal{G}$ corresponds to a combination of physical links/nodes, e.g., in an overlay network. Without loss of generality, we assume $\mathcal{G}$ is connected, as different connected components have to be monitored separately. Denote the link incident to nodes u and v by uv; links uv and vu are assumed to have the same metric. Certain nodes in V are monitors and can initiate/collect measurements. We assume that each link in $\mathcal{G}$ has two distinct end-points (i.e., no self-loop), and there is at most one link connecting a pair of nodes. Last, no link metrics in $\mathcal{G}$ are known prior to taking measurements.

[2]We use the terms *network* and *graph* interchangeably.

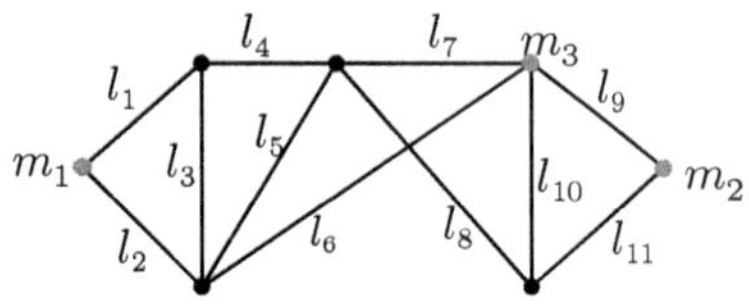

Figure 1: Sample network with three monitors: m_1, m_2, and m_3.

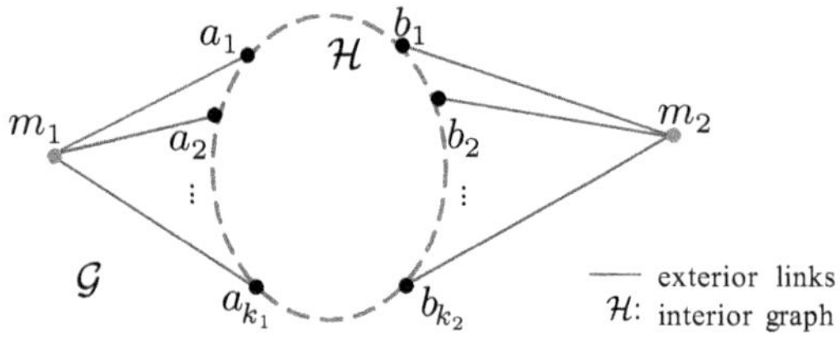

Figure 2: Reorganizing graph $\mathcal{G}$ into exterior links and interior graph ($\{a_i\}_{i=1}^{k_1}$ and $\{b_j\}_{j=1}^{k_2}$ may have overlap).

Table 1 summarizes all graph theory notations used in this paper (following the convention of [25]).

Let $n := |L|$ denote the number of links in $\mathcal{G}$, $\{l_i\}_{i=1}^{n}$ the set of links in $\mathcal{G}$, $\mathbf{w} = (W_{l_1}, \ldots, W_{l_n})^T$ the column vector of all link metrics, and $\mathbf{c} = (W_{\mathcal{P}_1}, \ldots, W_{\mathcal{P}_\gamma})^T$ the column vector of all available path measurements, where γ is the number of measurement paths and $W_{\mathcal{P}_i}$ is the sum of link metrics along measurement path $\mathcal{P}_i$. We assume that monitors can control the routing of measurement packets as long as the path starts and ends at distinct monitors and does not contain repeated nodes. In the language of graph theory, we limit measurements to *simple paths* (in contrast, a *non-simple path* may contain repeated nodes). The path measurements are expressed in terms of the unknown link metrics through the following linear system:

$$\mathbf{R}\mathbf{w} = \mathbf{c}, \qquad (1)$$

where $\mathbf{R} = (R_{ij})$ is a $\gamma \times n$ *measurement matrix*, with each entry $R_{ij} \in \{0, 1\}$ denoting whether link l_j is present on path $\mathcal{P}_i$. The network tomography problem is to invert this linear system to solve for $\mathbf{w}$ given $\mathbf{R}$ and $\mathbf{c}$.

A link is *identifiable* if the associated link metric can be uniquely determined from path measurements; network $\mathcal{G}$ is identifiable if all links in $\mathcal{G}$ are identifiable. Otherwise, the link or the network is said to be *unidentifiable.* Given the above linear system, $\mathcal{G}$ is identifiable if and only if $\mathbf{R}$ in (1) has full column rank, i.e., $\text{rank}(\mathbf{R}) = n$. In other words, to uniquely determine $\mathbf{w}$, there must be n linearly independent simple paths between monitors.

2.2 Objective

Given a network topology $\mathcal{G}$, the first objective of this paper is to derive necessary and sufficient conditions for identifying all link metrics in $\mathcal{G}$ (or certain subgraphs of $\mathcal{G}$) under a given placement of κ ($\kappa \geq 2$) monitors by solving the linear system (1). Our second objective is to compute a placement of the minimum number of monitors in $\mathcal{G}$ that enables the identification of all link metrics.

2.3 Illustrative Example

Fig. 1 displays a sample network with three monitors (m_1–m_3) and eleven links (links l_1–l_11). To identify all eleven link metrics, eleven end-to-end paths (one $m_1 \to m_2$ path, seven $m_1 \to m_3$ paths and three $m_3 \to m_2$ paths) are constructed to form the measurement matrix $\mathbf{R}$:

$$\begin{array}{l}
m_1 \to m_2: \\
\quad l_1\ l_4\ l_8\ l_{11} \\
m_1 \to m_3: \\
\quad l_1\ l_4\ l_7 \\
\quad l_2\ l_6 \\
\quad l_2\ l_3\ l_4\ l_7 \\
\quad l_2\ l_5\ l_8\ l_{10} \\
\quad l_2\ l_5\ l_7 \\
\quad l_1\ l_3\ l_6 \\
\quad l_1\ l_4\ l_5\ l_6 \\
m_3 \to m_2: \\
\quad l_9 \\
\quad l_{10}\ l_{11} \\
\quad l_6\ l_5\ l_8\ l_{11}
\end{array}
\Rightarrow \mathbf{R} = \begin{pmatrix}
1 & 0 & 0 & 1 & 0 & 0 & 0 & 1 & 0 & 0 & 1 \\
1 & 0 & 0 & 1 & 0 & 0 & 1 & 0 & 0 & 0 & 0 \\
0 & 1 & 0 & 0 & 0 & 1 & 0 & 0 & 0 & 0 & 0 \\
0 & 1 & 1 & 1 & 0 & 0 & 1 & 0 & 0 & 0 & 0 \\
0 & 1 & 0 & 0 & 1 & 0 & 0 & 1 & 0 & 1 & 0 \\
0 & 1 & 0 & 0 & 1 & 0 & 1 & 0 & 0 & 0 & 0 \\
1 & 0 & 1 & 0 & 0 & 1 & 0 & 0 & 0 & 0 & 0 \\
1 & 0 & 0 & 1 & 1 & 1 & 0 & 0 & 0 & 0 & 0 \\
0 & 0 & 0 & 0 & 0 & 0 & 0 & 0 & 1 & 0 & 0 \\
0 & 0 & 0 & 0 & 0 & 0 & 0 & 0 & 0 & 1 & 1 \\
0 & 0 & 0 & 0 & 1 & 1 & 0 & 1 & 0 & 0 & 1
\end{pmatrix},$$

where $R_{ij} = 1$ if and only if link l_j is on path $\mathcal{P}_i$. Then we have $\mathbf{R}\mathbf{w} = \mathbf{c}$, where $\mathbf{c}$ is the vector of end-to-end measurements taken at the destination monitors. In this example, $\mathbf{R}$ is invertible, and thus $\mathbf{w}$ can be uniquely identified, i.e., $\mathbf{w} = \mathbf{R}^{-1}\mathbf{c}$. In Fig. 1, other simple paths can be measured as well, although they do not provide further information since the measurement matrix already reaches full rank. However, if we remove a monitor, say m_3, then it can be verified that the remaining paths can no longer form an invertible measurement matrix. Note that a path such as $l_2l_5l_4l_3l_6l_9$ cannot be measured because it contains a cycle.

3. MAIN RESULTS

Our main contributions are a set of necessary and sufficient conditions for network identification that are explicitly expressed in terms of network topology and the number/placement of monitors (proofs of theorems can be found in Sections 4–6). To begin, we first establish a negative result that no matter where we place the monitors, we cannot identify all link metrics using only two monitors.

THEOREM 3.1. *For any given network topology $\mathcal{G}$ with $n \geq 2$ (n is the number of links), $\mathcal{G}$ is unidentifiable with two monitors, irrespective of their placement.*

Second, we examine the two-monitor case in more detail and discover that the unidentifiability issue only applies to a small subset of links, and that the majority of links can be identified under certain conditions. Specifically, given two monitors m_1 and m_2, we can reorganize $\mathcal{G}$ into two parts[3] as illustrated in Fig. 2.

DEFINITION 1.
1) *The* interior graph $\mathcal{H}$ *of* $\mathcal{G}$ *is the sub-graph obtained by removing the monitors and their incident links, i.e.,* $\mathcal{H} := (V \setminus M, L \setminus L_M)$ *for* $M = \{m_1, m_2\}$ *and* $L_M = L(m_1) \cup L(m_2)$.
2) *We refer to links incident to monitors, i.e.,* $L(m_1) \cup L(m_2)$*, as* exterior links*, and the remaining links as* interior links.

We show that the exterior links can never be identified using two monitors (see Corollary 4.1), but the interior links can be identified under the following conditions.

[3]An area with a dashed border denotes a sub-graph (nodes/links on the dashed border are also part of the sub-graph, e.g., $\{a_i\}_{i=1}^{k_1}$ and $\{b_j\}_{j=1}^{k_2}$ in Fig. 2 are part of $\mathcal{H}$), and a solid line denotes a link/path/cycle.

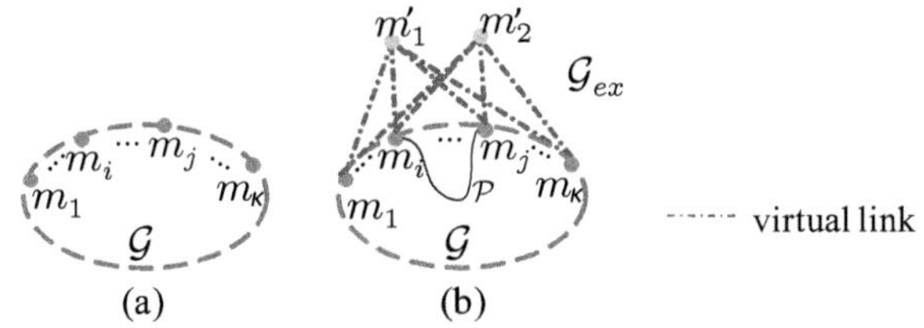

Figure 3: (a) $\mathcal{G}$ with κ ($\kappa \geq 3$) monitors; (b) $\mathcal{G}_{ex}$ with two virtual monitors.

THEOREM 3.2. *Assume that the interior graph $\mathcal{H}$ (with $||\mathcal{H}|| \geq 1$) of $\mathcal{G}$ under a given placement of two monitors (m_1 and m_2) is connected and direct link m_1m_2 (incident to m_1 and m_2) does not exist in $L(\mathcal{G})$. The necessary and sufficient conditions for identifying all link metrics in $\mathcal{H}$ are:*

① *$\mathcal{G} - l$ is 2-edge-connected for every interior link l in $\mathcal{H}$;*

② *$\mathcal{G} + m_1m_2$ is 3-vertex-connected.*

Third, we show that the above conditions can be naturally extended to a necessary and sufficient condition for identifying *all* link metrics in $\mathcal{G}$ using three or more monitors. This condition is based on an *extended graph* $\mathcal{G}_{ex}$ obtained from $\mathcal{G}$ as follows. As illustrated in Fig. 3, given a graph $\mathcal{G}$ with κ monitors, its extended graph $\mathcal{G}_{ex}$ is obtained by adding two *virtual monitors* m_1' and m_2', and 2κ *virtual links* between each pair of virtual-actual monitors. The identifiability of $\mathcal{G}$ is characterized by a simple condition on $\mathcal{G}_{ex}$ as follows.

THEOREM 3.3. *Assume that κ ($\kappa \geq 3$) monitors are used to measure simple paths. The necessary and sufficient condition on the network topology $\mathcal{G}$ for identifying all link metrics in $\mathcal{G}$ is that the associated extended graph $\mathcal{G}_{ex}$ be 3-vertex-connected.*

Finally, we develop efficient algorithms that can: (i) test whether a given placement of monitors can identify all link metrics, and (ii) compute a placement of the minimum number of monitors needed to identify all link metrics (see Section 7). Both algorithms run in linear time w.r.t. network size (i.e., $O(|V(\mathcal{G})|+|L(\mathcal{G})|)$) and hence are suitable for large networks.

4. UNIDENTIFIABILITY WITH TWO MONITORS

At least *two* monitors are required to identify link metrics through monitoring simple paths. In this section, we investigate if two monitors suffice to identify all link metrics in the network. Suppose that two distinct nodes are selected to serve as monitors. Each measurement starts at one monitor and terminates at the other via a controllable simple path. The termination node then reports the end-to-end metric, which becomes an entry in the measurement vector $\mathbf{c}$. From the perspective of graph theory, such a network can be represented as $\mathcal{G} = (\{m_1, m_2, v_0, \ldots, v_k\}, L)$, where m_1 and m_2 are the monitors, $\{v_0, \ldots, v_k\}$ are the non-monitors, and $|L| = n$. Let m_1m_2 be a direct link between m_1 and m_2 (if it exists). Since m_1m_2 can be easily identified through a one-hop measurement, we assume without loss of generality that $m_1m_2 \notin L(\mathcal{G})$ (i.e., there is no direct link) in Sections 4 and 5, where only two monitors are used.

4.1 Proof of Theorem 3.1

Any $\mathcal{G}$ with $||\mathcal{G}|| \geq 2$ can be reorganized as in[4] Fig. 2. Let $N(v)$ denote the set of neighboring nodes of node v. We define $A := \{a_1, a_2, \ldots, a_{k_1}\} = N(m_1)$ and $B := \{b_1, b_2, \ldots, b_{k_2}\} = N(m_2)$ to be the sets of neighbors of m_1 and m_2, respectively, where $k_1 := |A|$, $k_2 := |B|$ and A, B can overlap ($m_1, m_2 \notin A \cup B$).

Assuming that $\mathcal{H}$ is connected and all link metrics in $\mathcal{H}$ are known, we can reduce any equation associated with a simple path $\mathcal{P}$ between m_1 and m_2 to the form (see Table 1 for notations):

$$W_{m_1a_i} + W_{b_jm_2} = \phi_{ij} \tag{2}$$

for some $a_i \in A$ and $b_j \in B$. This is obtained by rewriting the original equation $W_{m_1a_i} + W_{\mathcal{P}'_{ij}} + W_{b_jm_2} = W_{\mathcal{P}_{ij}}$ ($\mathcal{P}'_{ij}$ is the segment of $\mathcal{P}_{ij}$ in $\mathcal{H}$) to place the unknowns on the left-hand side, and setting $\phi_{ij} := W_{\mathcal{P}_{ij}} - W_{\mathcal{P}'_{ij}}$. Thus, we obtain $k_1 \times k_2$ equations from all of the simple paths between m_1 and m_2, each corresponding to the sum of the metrics of one link incident to m_1 and one link incident to m_2. The corresponding reduced measurement matrix is (each column corresponding to an unknown link metric):

$$\mathbf{R} = \begin{array}{c} \begin{array}{cccc|cccc} W_{m_1a_1} & \cdots & & W_{m_1a_{k_1}} & W_{b_1m_2} & \cdots & & W_{b_{k_2}m_2} \end{array} \\ \left(\begin{array}{cccc|cccc} 1 & & & & 1 & & & \\ 1 & & & & & 1 & & \\ \vdots & & & & & & \ddots & \\ 1 & & & & & & & 1 \\ \hline & 1 & & & 1 & & & \\ & 1 & & & & 1 & & \\ & \vdots & & & & & \ddots & \\ & 1 & & & & & & 1 \\ \hline & & \ddots & & & & \vdots & \\ \hline & & & 1 & 1 & & & \\ & & & 1 & & 1 & & \\ & & & \vdots & & & \ddots & \\ & & & 1 & & & & 1 \end{array}\right) \end{array}, \tag{3}$$

where the blank entries are zero. We apply the following linear transformations to $\mathbf{R}$. For each $q = 1, \ldots, k_1 - 1$ and $i = 2, \ldots, k_2$, replace $\text{row}(qk_2+i)$ by $\text{row}(qk_2+i) - \text{row}(i) - \text{row}(qk_2+1) + \text{row}(1)$; it can be verified that the result is a row of zeros. Ignoring rows of zeros, $\mathbf{R}$ transforms into

$$\mathbf{R}' = \begin{array}{c} \begin{array}{cccc|cccc} W_{m_1a_1} & \cdots & & W_{m_1a_{k_1}} & W_{b_1m_2} & \cdots & & W_{b_{k_2}m_2} \end{array} \\ \left(\begin{array}{cccc|cccc} 1 & & & & 1 & & & \\ 1 & & & & & 1 & & \\ \vdots & & & & & & \ddots & \\ 1 & & & & & & & 1 \\ \hline & 1 & & & 1 & & & \\ & & 1 & & 1 & & & \\ & & & \ddots & & & & \\ & & & 1 & 1 & & & \end{array}\right) \begin{array}{l} \left.\right\} k_2 \text{ rows} \\ \left.\right\} k_1 - 1 \text{ rows} \end{array} \end{array}, \tag{4}$$

where the rows are linearly independent, and the number of rows equals $k_1 + k_2 - 1$. This transformation preserves the rank of $\mathbf{R}$ because $\mathbf{R}$ can be reconstructed from $\mathbf{R}'$ as follows: the first k_2 rows in $\mathbf{R}$ and $\mathbf{R}'$ are identical; $\text{row}(qk_2+1)$ in $\mathbf{R}$ equals $\text{row}(k_2+q)$ in $\mathbf{R}'$ ($q = 1, \ldots, k_1 - 1$); $\text{row}(qk_2+i)$

[4] If certain links in $\mathcal{G}$ cannot be included in any possible paths constructed from m_1 to m_2 in Fig. 2, then these links are unidentifiable, resulting in a disconnected or one-edge-connected interior graph $\mathcal{H}$.

in $\mathbf{R}$ equals row(i) + row$(k_2 + q)$ − row(1) in $\mathbf{R}'$ ($q = 1, \ldots, k_1 - 1$, $i = 2, \ldots, k_2$). Hence, the rank of $\mathbf{R}$ equals $k_1 + k_2 - 1$. When $\mathcal{H}$ is not connected, some rows in $\mathbf{R}$ may not exist because there is no simple path connecting the corresponding nodes in A and B, and the rank of $\mathbf{R}$ may be even smaller. Since there are $k_1 + k_2$ unknown variables $(W_{m_1 a_i})_{i=1}^{k_1}$ and $(W_{b_j m_2})_{j=1}^{k_2}$, they cannot be uniquely determined even if all link metrics in $\mathcal{H}$ are already known. Therefore, $\mathcal{G}$ with $||\mathcal{G}|| \geq 2$ is unidentifiable by using two monitors. □

In fact, we can show that none of the exterior links is identifiable because metric of any one exterior link will uniquely determine metrics of the rest; see proof in [26].

COROLLARY 4.1. *None of the exterior links (except $m_1 m_2$) can be identified with two monitors.*

4.2 Discussions on Paths with Cycles

At the end of Section III-B in [19], the authors raise the question whether or not monitoring non-simple paths (i.e., paths that may contain cycles) between two monitors suffices to identify all link metrics in the network[5]. According to Corollary 4.1, the exterior links cannot be identified even if all the interior link metrics are known; allowing cycles in the interior graph $\mathcal{H}$ provides no additional information regarding the exterior links. Consequently, the answer to that question in [19] is that monitoring (simple or non-simple) paths between two monitors is *not* sufficient to identify all link metrics.

5. IDENTIFIABILITY OF INTERIOR LINKS WITH TWO MONITORS

Network administrators are more interested in using end-to-end measurements to infer the qualities of links that are at least *one-hop away*. Therefore, in this section, we only focus on the interior graph $\mathcal{H}$ and derive necessary and sufficient conditions on the network topology $\mathcal{G}$ for identifying all links in $\mathcal{H}$ using two monitors (m_1 and m_2), under the earlier assumption that no link metrics (including those of links incident to m_1 and m_2) are known ahead of time.

Before going into details, we first point out that it is sufficient to solve the case in which $\mathcal{H}$ is a connected graph. This is because if $\mathcal{H}$ consists of K_H ($K_H \geq 2$) connected components $\mathcal{H}_i$ ($i = 1, \ldots, K_H$), we can decompose the entire graph $\mathcal{G}$ into sub-graphs $\mathcal{G}_i := \mathcal{H}_i + m_1 + m_2$, with $\mathcal{G} = \cup_{i=1}^{K_H} \mathcal{G}_i$ (see the definition of graph union in Table 1). Since none of the $m_1 \to m_2$ simple paths in $\mathcal{G}_i$ can traverse $\mathcal{G}_j$ ($i \neq j$), the identification of links within different $\mathcal{G}_i$'s is mutually independent. Therefore, in the rest of this section, we assume $\mathcal{H}$ to be connected with $||\mathcal{H}|| \geq 1$. Our result can be applied to each $\mathcal{G}_i$ separately when $\mathcal{H}$ is disconnected.

5.1 Proof of Theorem 3.2: Necessary Part

Suppose all links in $\mathcal{H}$ are identifiable. We prove the necessity of Conditions ①–② in Theorem 3.2 by contradiction.

a) Let $l_1 \in L(\mathcal{H})$ be an arbitrary interior link. If $\mathcal{G} - l_1$ is disconnected, then l_1 is a bridge[6] in $\mathcal{G}$ (shown in Fig. 4(a)). If $\mathcal{G}_1$ and $\mathcal{G}_2$ each contains a monitor, then l_1 is unidentifiable by Lemma A.1 (Appendix). If m_1 and m_2 are both in $\mathcal{G}_1$ (or $\mathcal{G}_2$), then l_1 cannot be included in any measurement path (otherwise, l_1 will be used more than once), and is thus unidentifiable. Both cases contradict the assumption that all interior links are identifiable.

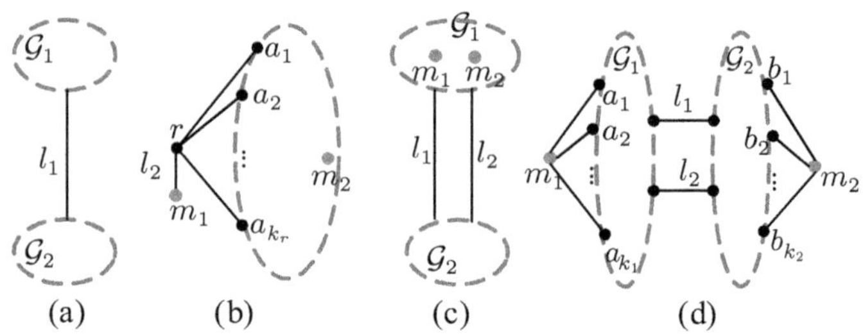

Figure 4: Illustration of Condition ①, where $\{l_1, l_2\}$ is an edge cut in (c) and (d).

b) Suppose there is a bridge l_2 in $\mathcal{G} - l_1$. If l_2 is an exterior link, as shown in Fig. 4(b), then by Lemma A.1 (Appendix), its adjacent interior links $ra_i \in L(\mathcal{H})$ are unidentifiable, contradicting the assumption that all interior links are identifiable. Thus, l_2 must be an interior link. Since by *a)*, an interior link cannot be a bridge in $\mathcal{G}$, $\{l_1, l_2\}$ must be an edge cut as shown in Fig. 4(c) and 4(d). If both m_1 and m_2 are in $\mathcal{G}_1$ as in Fig. 4(c), then all $m_1 \to m_2$ paths traversing l_1 must traverse l_2 as well. Thus we can at most identify $W_{l_1} + W_{l_2}$, but not W_{l_1} and W_{l_2} individually. If m_1 is in $\mathcal{G}_1$ and m_2 is in $\mathcal{G}_2$ as in Fig. 4(d), then all $m_1 \to m_2$ paths must traverse either l_1 or l_2, but not both. Assuming that $\mathcal{G}_1$ and $\mathcal{G}_2$ in Fig. 4(d) are connected and all link metrics in them are known, then the resulting measurement matrix $\mathbf{R}_1$ is similar to (3), except that each row in $\mathbf{R}_1$ has a new entry associated with W_{l_1} or W_{l_2}:

$$\mathbf{R}_1 = \begin{pmatrix} \overset{\textit{Exterior Links}}{\mathbf{R}} & \overset{W_{l_1}}{\mathbf{e}_1} & \overset{W_{l_2}}{} \\ \mathbf{R} & & \mathbf{e}_1 \end{pmatrix}.$$

Here blank entries correspond to zeroes, $\mathbf{R}$ is given by (3), and $\mathbf{e}_1$ is a $(k_1 \times k_2)$-element column vector of all ones. Let $\mathbf{R}_2$ and $\mathbf{R}_3$ denote the first and last $k_1 \times k_2$ rows in $\mathbf{R}_1$, respectively. Then applying the same linear transformations as applied to (3) to both $\mathbf{R}_2$ and $\mathbf{R}_3$, we can transform $\mathbf{R}_1$ into $\mathbf{R}_1'$ (ignoring rows of zeros):

$$\mathbf{R}_1' = \begin{pmatrix} \overset{\textit{Exterior Links}}{\mathbf{R}'} & \overset{W_{l_1}}{\mathbf{e}_2} & \overset{W_{l_2}}{} \\ \mathbf{R}' & & \mathbf{e}_2 \end{pmatrix},$$

where $\mathbf{R}'$ is given by (4) and $\mathbf{e}_2$ is a $(k_1 + k_2 - 1)$-element column vector of all ones. In $\mathbf{R}_1'$, for each $q = k_1 + k_2, \ldots, 2k_1 + 2k_2 - 2$, replace row$(q)$ with row(q)-row$(q - k_1 - k_2 + 1)$. Ignoring duplicate rows, $\mathbf{R}_1'$ transforms into

$$\mathbf{R}_1'' = \begin{pmatrix} \overset{\textit{Exterior Links}}{\mathbf{R}'} & \overset{W_{l_1}}{\mathbf{e}_2} & \overset{W_{l_2}}{} \\ & -1 & 1 \end{pmatrix},$$

where all rows are linearly independent. Since any subset of k ($k \geq 1$) equations in $\mathbf{R}_1''$ contains more than k unknown variables, none of these variables can be identified. When $\mathcal{G}_1$ and $\mathcal{G}_2$ are not connected, the rank of $\mathbf{R}_1''$ can be even smaller. Thus, W_{l_1} and W_{l_2} are unidentifiable, contradicting the assumption that all the interior links are identifiable.

[5]We restrict the paths from containing repeated monitors to exclude measurement of cycles, as is already solved in [19].

[6]A link whose removal will disconnect the graph is a bridge [25].

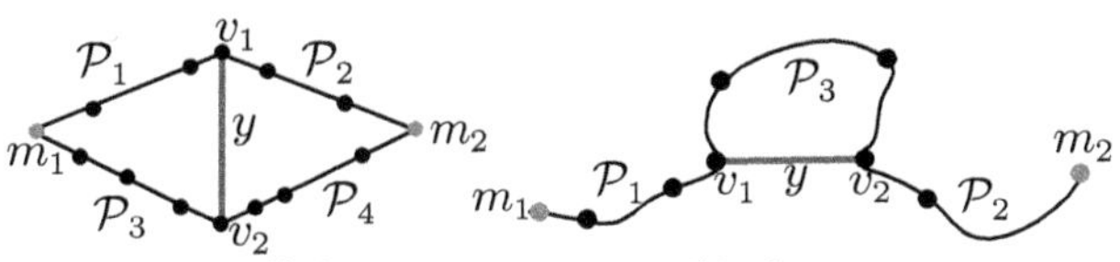

(a) cross-link y (b) shortcut y

Figure 5: Two types of identifiable links in $\mathcal{H}$.

Based on *a)* and *b)*, we see that $\mathcal{G} - l_1$ must be 2-edge-connected for any $l_1 \in L(\mathcal{H})$ (i.e., Condition ① holds).

c) We can also prove Condition ② by contradiction; see Proposition A.2 (Appendix). □

5.2 Proof of Theorem 3.2: Sufficient Part

Given Conditions ①–②, we need to show that all links in $\mathcal{H}$ are identifiable. We first introduce two types of identifiable links. The argument then consists of showing that every interior link belongs to one of these two types.

5.2.1 *Cross-link, Shortcut, and Non-separating Cycle*

We begin by introducing a few notions essential to our proof.

The first notion is a cross-link that connects nodes on two simple paths between the monitors.

Definition 2. *As illustrated in Fig. 5(a), link y is a* cross-link *if $\exists$ four $m_1 \to m_2$ paths $\mathcal{P}_A$, $\mathcal{P}_B$, $\mathcal{P}_C$, and $\mathcal{P}_D$ formed from simple paths $\mathcal{P}_1, \ldots, \mathcal{P}_4$ by:*

$$\begin{cases} \mathcal{P}_A = \mathcal{P}_1 \cup \mathcal{P}_2 \\ \mathcal{P}_B = \mathcal{P}_3 \cup \mathcal{P}_4 \end{cases}, \quad \begin{cases} \mathcal{P}_C = \mathcal{P}_1 \cup y \cup \mathcal{P}_4 \\ \mathcal{P}_D = \mathcal{P}_3 \cup y \cup \mathcal{P}_2 \end{cases}, \tag{5}$$

such that

$$\begin{cases} |\mathcal{P}_1 \cap \mathcal{P}_2| = 1 \\ |\mathcal{P}_3 \cap \mathcal{P}_4| = 1 \end{cases}, \quad \begin{cases} |\mathcal{P}_2 \cap \mathcal{P}_3| = 0 \\ |\mathcal{P}_1 \cap \mathcal{P}_4| = 0 \end{cases}. \tag{6}$$

See Table 1 for definitions of graph union/intersection and $|\cdot|$; note that paths are also graphs. The constraints in (6) are used to ensure that $\mathcal{P}_A$–$\mathcal{P}_D$ are *simple* paths, e.g., $|\mathcal{P}_1 \cap \mathcal{P}_2| = 1$ ($\mathcal{P}_1$ and $\mathcal{P}_2$ have no common node other than v_1) ensures that no cycles exist in $\mathcal{P}_A$. However, this does not require $\mathcal{P}_1$–$\mathcal{P}_4$ to be node disjoint, e.g., $\mathcal{P}_1$ and $\mathcal{P}_3$ can have common nodes. A cross-link y can then be identified by

$$W_y = \frac{1}{2}(W_{\mathcal{P}_C} + W_{\mathcal{P}_D} - W_{\mathcal{P}_A} - W_{\mathcal{P}_B}). \tag{7}$$

The second notion is a shortcut that connects the endpoints of a simple path whose metric is known.

Definition 3. *As illustrated in Fig. 5(b), link y is a* shortcut *if $\exists$ a simple path $\mathcal{P}_3$ whose metric has been identified such that the following $m_1 \to m_2$ simple paths can be formed:*

$$\mathcal{P}_A = \mathcal{P}_1 \cup y \cup \mathcal{P}_2, \quad \mathcal{P}_B = \mathcal{P}_1 \cup \mathcal{P}_3 \cup \mathcal{P}_2, \tag{8}$$

satisfying $|\mathcal{P}_1 \cap \mathcal{P}_3| = 1, |\mathcal{P}_2 \cap \mathcal{P}_3| = 1$, and $|\mathcal{P}_1 \cap \mathcal{P}_2| = 0$.

Again, the constraints are used to guarantee that $\mathcal{P}_A$ and $\mathcal{P}_B$ are simple paths. A shortcut y can be identified by

$$W_y = W_{\mathcal{P}_A} - W_{\mathcal{P}_B} + W_{\mathcal{P}_3}. \tag{9}$$

The third notion is a special kind of cycle defined as follows.

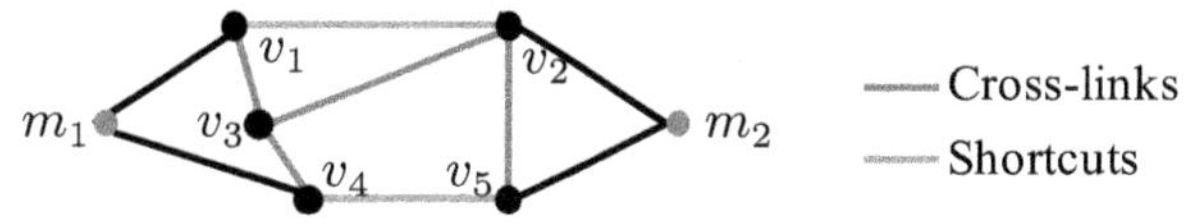

Figure 6: Sample network with identifiable interior graph.

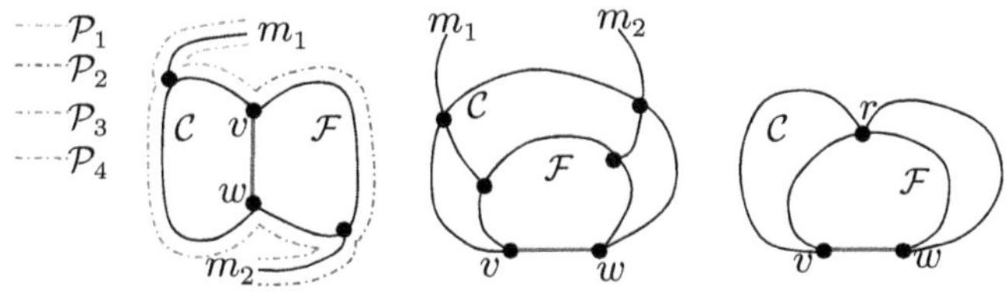

(a) (b) (c)

Figure 7: Possible cases of interior link vw: (a) Case A, (b) Case B-1, (c) Case B-2.

Definition 4. *A* non-separating cycle *in $\mathcal{G}$, denoted by $\mathcal{F}$, is an induced sub-graph[7] such that: (i) $\mathcal{F}$ is a cycle (see definition in Table 1), and (ii) $\mathcal{F}$ does not separate any node from monitors, i.e., each connected component in $\mathcal{G} \setminus \mathcal{F}$ contains at least one monitor.*

For example, there are four non-separating cycles in Fig. 6: $v_1v_2v_3v_1$, $v_4v_3v_2v_5v_4$, $m_1v_1v_3v_4m_1$, and $v_5v_2m_2v_5$. Cycle $v_4v_3v_1v_2v_5v_4$ is not a non-separating cycle as it is not induced (due to link v_2v_3), neither is $v_4m_1v_1v_2v_5v_4$ as it separates v_3 from monitors.

5.2.2 *The Proof*

The key to the sufficiency proof is to show that each interior link can be categorized as either a cross-link or a shortcut when the network satisfies Conditions ① and ②. The proof proceeds in three steps.

The *first step* is to show that under Conditions ① and ②, every interior link vw satisfies one of the three cases as shown in Fig. 7. Specifically, we have the following lemma.

Lemma 5.1. *If graph $\mathcal{G}$ satisfies Conditions ① and ②, then for any interior link vw, there exists a non-separating cycle $\mathcal{F}$ with $vw \in L(\mathcal{F})$, a cycle $\mathcal{C}$ with $vw \in L(\mathcal{C})$, a simple path $\mathcal{P}_1$ connecting one monitor with a node on $\mathcal{F} - v - w$, and a simple path $\mathcal{P}_2$ connecting the other monitor with a node on $\mathcal{C} - v - w$ such that*

(a) $\mathcal{F}$ and $\mathcal{C}$ have at most one common node other than v, w (i.e., $|V(\mathcal{F}) \cap V(\mathcal{C})| \leq 3$);

(b) $\mathcal{P}_1$ and $\mathcal{P}_2$ are disjoint, neither going through v nor w (i.e., $\mathcal{P}_1 \cap \mathcal{P}_2 = \emptyset$, $v, w \notin V(\mathcal{P}_1)$ and $v, w \notin V(\mathcal{P}_2)$);

(c) $|V(\mathcal{P}_1) \cap V(\mathcal{F})| = 1$, $|V(\mathcal{P}_2) \cap V(\mathcal{C})| = 1$.

Proof. See [26]. □

Lemma 5.1 states that there must exist two cycles sharing link vw, a non-separating cycle $\mathcal{F}$ and a (not necessarily non-separating) cycle $\mathcal{C}$ that satisfy conditions (a)–(c) in the lemma. These conditions imply three possible cases:

[7] An *induced sub-graph* $\mathcal{G}'$ of $\mathcal{G}$ is a sub-graph such that for any pair of vertices v and w in $\mathcal{G}'$, vw is an edge in $\mathcal{G}'$ if and only if vw is an edge in $\mathcal{G}$.

- *Case A (Fig. 7(a)):* $\mathcal{C}$ is also a non-separating cycle, $\mathcal{F}$ and $\mathcal{C}$ have no common node other than v and w, and $\mathcal{F}/\mathcal{C}$ each connects to a different monitor by a disjoint simple path;
- *Case B-1 (Fig. 7(b)):* any path from any node in $\mathcal{F} - v - w$ to monitors must have a common node with $\mathcal{C} - v - w$;
- *Case B-2 (Fig. 7(c)):* $\mathcal{F}$ and $\mathcal{C}$ must have at least one common node (denoted by r) other than v and w.

These cases are guaranteed to be complete by Lemma 5.1. We will show later that Case A links are cross-links and Case B (including B-1 and B-2) links are shortcuts.

The *second step* is to recognize that in Case A (Fig. 7(a)), we can construct four measurement paths $\mathcal{P}_A$–$\mathcal{P}_D$ by (5), using $\mathcal{P}_1$–$\mathcal{P}_4$ marked in the figure. Thus, a Case A link vw is a cross-link and thus can be identified as in (7). The challenge is that it is impossible to construct measurement paths as in (5) for the other two cases (Fig. 7(b) and 7(c)), since the conditions in (6) cannot be satisfied. This motivates us to explore the possibility of identifying W_{vw} in these two cases by (9), i.e., to investigate whether vw in Fig. 7(b) and 7(c) can be characterized as a shortcut.

The *third step* is to show that any link of Case B-1 or B-2 is indeed a shortcut. We prove this by showing that for any Case B link, we can find a detour path connecting its end-points such that all the links in this detour path are cross-links, and thus can be identified by (7). To this end, we show the following lemma.

LEMMA 5.2. *Let $m_1^*, m_2^* \in \{m_1, m_2\}$ with $m_1^* \neq m_2^*$. If $\mathcal{G}$ satisfies Conditions ① and ②, then*

(a) for any non-separating cycle in $\mathcal{G}$, there is at most one *Case B link in this non-separating cycle;*

(b) for any Case B link vw in the interior graph of $\mathcal{G}$, there exists a non-separating cycle $\mathcal{F}_{vw}$ with $vw \in L(\mathcal{F}_{vw})$ and $m_1, m_2 \notin V(\mathcal{F}_{vw})$. For this non-separating cycle $\mathcal{F}_{vw}$, there exist disjoint simple paths $\mathcal{P}(m_1^*, v)$ and $\mathcal{P}(m_2^*, w)$, each intersecting with $\mathcal{F}_{vw}$ only at the end-point, i.e., $V(\mathcal{P}(m_1^*, v) \cap \mathcal{F}_{vw}) = \{v\}$ and $V(\mathcal{P}(m_2^*, w) \cap \mathcal{F}_{vw}) = \{w\}$.

PROOF. See [26]. □

Lemma 5.2-(b) implies that a Case B link y must reside on a non-separating cycle $\mathcal{F}$ within the interior graph. Meanwhile, Lemma 5.2-(a) implies that all the other links on cycle $\mathcal{F}$ are cross-links, as there is at most one Case B link on each non-separating cycle. Furthermore, we show in Lemma 5.2-(b) that there exist disjoint simple paths $\mathcal{P}_1$ and $\mathcal{P}_2$ connecting the end-points of link y to different monitors, each sharing only one common node with $\mathcal{F}$ at the end-points of link y. Together, these allow us to construct two measurement paths $\mathcal{P}_A$ and $\mathcal{P}_B$ as in (8), where $\mathcal{P}_3 = \mathcal{F} - y$ consists of only cross-links whose metrics are known from (7). Thus, a Case B link y is a shortcut and can be identified by (9).

Therefore, under Conditions ① and ②, every interior link is identifiable. □

As an example, Fig. 6 displays a network satisfying Conditions ① and ②, where each interior link can be characterized as either a cross-link or a shortcut.

6. IDENTIFIABILITY WITH THREE OR MORE MONITORS

Since two monitors are not sufficient to identify all link metrics in $\mathcal{G}$, we explore in this section the case where the network contains three or more monitors.

6.1 Conversion into Two-Monitor Problem

Section 5 suggests that it is easier to identify links that are one-hop away from the monitors. This observation motivates us to construct an extended graph $\mathcal{G}_{ex}$ of $\mathcal{G}$ (see Fig. 3), so that all links of interest (actual links in $\mathcal{G}$) are at least one-hop away from virtual monitors m_1' and m_2'. This construction immediately converts the problem of identifying $\mathcal{G}$ using κ monitors to a problem of identifying the interior graph of $\mathcal{G}_{ex}$ using two monitors (again we have no prior knowledge of link metrics in $\mathcal{G}$ or $\mathcal{G}_{ex}$). Therefore, we can apply Theorem 3.2 to obtain the following result.

LEMMA 6.1. *Employing κ ($\kappa \geq 3$) monitors to measure simple paths, the necessary and sufficient condition on the network topology $\mathcal{G}$ for identifying all link metrics in $\mathcal{G}$ is that the associated extended graph $\mathcal{G}_{ex}$ has an identifiable interior graph, i.e., $\mathcal{G}_{ex}$ satisfies Conditions ① and ② in Theorem 3.2.*

PROOF. Since $\mathcal{G}$ is the interior graph of $\mathcal{G}_{ex}$, it suffices to show that the information attainable by the real monitors $m_1, \ldots, m_\kappa$ is the same as the information attainable by the virtual monitors m_1' and m_2', if the virtual monitors can make end-to-end measurements along simple paths in $\mathcal{G}_{ex}$.

First, we show that any measurement between the real monitors can be obtained from measurements between m_1' and m_2'. To this end, consider a path $m_i\mathcal{P}m_j$ ($i, j \in \{1, \ldots, \kappa\}$, $i \neq j$) in $\mathcal{G}$, as shown in Fig. 3(b). Four simple paths between m_1' and m_2' can be constructed:

$$\begin{cases} \mathcal{P}_A = m_1' m_i m_2', \\ \mathcal{P}_B = m_1' m_j m_2', \\ \mathcal{P}_C = m_1' m_i \mathcal{P} m_j m_2', \\ \mathcal{P}_D = m_1' m_j \mathcal{P} m_i m_2'. \end{cases} \quad (10)$$

Viewing $m_i\mathcal{P}m_j$ as a "cross-link", we can compute $W_{m_i\mathcal{P}m_j}$ from the measurements on these four paths via (7) (replacing W_y by $W_{m_i\mathcal{P}m_j}$).

Moreover, we show that measurements between m_1' and m_2' in $\mathcal{G}_{ex}$ do not provide extra information for identifying links in $\mathcal{G}$ compared with measurements attainable by the real monitors. This is proved by observing that for any $m_1' \rightarrow m_2'$ simple path $m_1' m_i \mathcal{P} m_j m_2'$ ($i, j \in \{1, \ldots, \kappa\}$, $i \neq j$) containing at least one link in $\mathcal{G}$, the information relevant for identifying links in $\mathcal{G}$ can be obtained by measuring its $m_i \rightarrow m_j$ sub-path $m_i\mathcal{P}m_j$, which must also be a simple path. □

6.2 Sketch of Proof for Theorem 3.3

The special structure of $\mathcal{G}_{ex}$ allows us to consolidate the two Conditions ① and ② into a single condition as stated in Theorem 3.3, based on the following arguments.

From the structure of $\mathcal{G}_{ex}$ (see Fig. 3), we can prove in Propositions A.3 and A.4 (Appendix) that $\mathcal{G}_{ex}$ satisfies Conditions ① and ② in Theorem 3.2 if and only if $\mathcal{G}_{ex}$ is both 3-edge-connected and 3-vertex-connected. According to Proposition 1.4.2 in [25], a 3-vertex-connected graph is also 3-edge-connected. Thus, the necessary and sufficient conditions in

Lemma 6.1 can be simplified to a single condition that $\mathcal{G}_{ex}$ be 3-vertex-connected. □

7. TESTING AND ENSURING IDENTIFIABILITY

The conditions we have derived have broader impact than mere theoretical interest. A major benefit of characterizing network identifiability in terms of network topology is that we can leverage existing graph-processing algorithms to efficiently test for or ensure the identifiability of a given network. In this section, we present efficient algorithms that can (i) test for the identifiability of a given network with a given monitor placement, and (ii) place the minimum number of monitors in a given network to identify all its link metrics.

7.1 Efficient Identifiability Test

The first question we want to answer is: Given a network topology $\mathcal{G}$ and a placement of $\kappa \geq 2$ monitors, how do we efficiently determine if $\mathcal{G}$ is identifiable or not? If $\kappa = 2$, then we know from Theorem 3.1 that it is impossible to identify the entire $\mathcal{G}$. Nevertheless, we can test whether the interior graph is identifiable using Conditions ① and ② in Theorem 3.2, which transform into multiple tests of edge/vertex connectivity. The problem of determining whether a given graph is k-edge/vertex-connected has been well studied. Specifically, fast algorithms have been proposed to test if a graph is: (i) 2-edge-connected [27], or (ii) 3-vertex-connected [28], both in time $O(|V|+|L|)$ ($|V|$: number of nodes; $|L|$: number of links). Using these algorithms, we can test for the identifiability of the *interior graph* of $\mathcal{G}$ as follows:

1. For each interior link l, apply the 2-edge-connectivity test in [27] to $\mathcal{G} - l$. $\mathcal{G}$ is unidentifiable if the test fails;

2. Apply the 3-vertex-connectivity test in [28] to $\mathcal{G} + m_1 m_2$. $\mathcal{G}$ is unidentifiable if the test fails.

The interior graph of $\mathcal{G}$ is identifiable if all the tests succeed. The overall complexity is $O(|L(\mathcal{G})|(|V(\mathcal{G})| + |L(\mathcal{G})|))$.

Similarly, if $\kappa \geq 3$, then we can test for the identifiability of the *entire* $\mathcal{G}$ using the condition in Theorem 3.3:

1. Construct the extended graph $\mathcal{G}_{ex}$ as in Fig. 3;

2. Apply the 3-vertex-connectivity test in [28] to $\mathcal{G}_{ex}$. $\mathcal{G}$ is identifiable if the test succeeds, and unidentifiable otherwise.

The complexity of this algorithm is $O(|V(\mathcal{G}_{ex})| + |L(\mathcal{G}_{ex})|)$, which is the same as $O(|V(\mathcal{G})| + |L(\mathcal{G})|)$.

7.2 Optimal Monitor Placement

The next question we want to answer is: Given an arbitrary topology $\mathcal{G}$, what is the minimum number of monitors needed and where should they be placed to identify all link metrics in $\mathcal{G}$? While one can enumerate all possible placements for $\kappa = 3, 4, \ldots$ monitors and test for identifiability until an identifiable placement is found, what we really want is an efficient algorithm to achieve the same. This requires a deeper understanding of the structure of an identifiable graph.

We illustrate our idea by an example in Fig. 8(a). We first consider the minimum deployment: Using fewer monitors

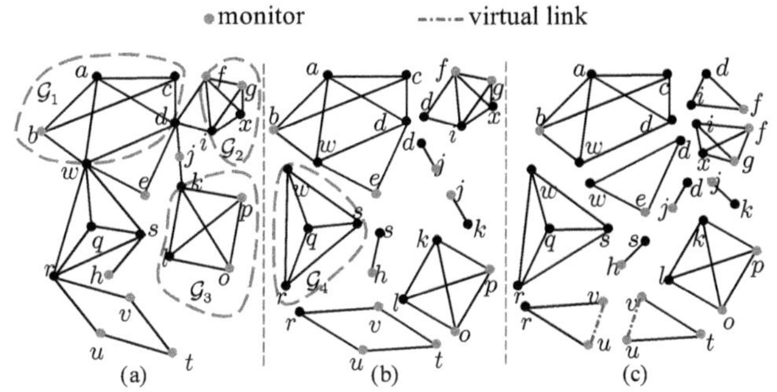

Figure 8: (a) Original graph; (b) biconnected components; (c) triconnected components.

certainly renders the network unidentifiable. This yields the following rules:

(i) *Dangling* node (e.g., h) must be a monitor, as otherwise its adjacent link cannot be measured using simple paths;

(ii) A node on a *tandem* of links (e.g., j) must be a monitor, as otherwise we can only identify the sum of its adjacent link metrics (W_{dj} and W_{jk}) and not the individual metrics;

(iii) For a sub-graph with *two cut-vertices*[8] (e.g., $\mathcal{G}_1$) or a *2-vertex cut*[9] (e.g., $\mathcal{G}_2$), at least one node other than those cuts must be a monitor, as otherwise even if all links outside this sub-graph have been identified, the vertices in the cuts (w and d for $\mathcal{G}_1$, f and i for $\mathcal{G}_2$) are effectively the two "monitors" for this sub-graph, and Theorem 3.1 states that this sub-graph cannot be identified;

(iv) Similarly, for a sub-graph with *one cut-vertex* (e.g., $\mathcal{G}_3$), at least two nodes other than the cut-vertex must be monitors.

Our strategy is to use the above four rules to deploy the necessary monitors. If we can prove that these necessary monitors are also sufficient to identify all links, then our deployment is optimal. To formally present the algorithm, we introduce the following definitions.

DEFINITION 5. *A* k-connected component *of* $\mathcal{G}$ *is a maximal sub-graph of* $\mathcal{G}$ *that is either (i)* k*-vertex-connected, or (ii) a complete graph with up to* k *vertices. The case of* $k = 2$ *is also called a* biconnected component, *and* $k = 3$ *a* triconnected component.

Intuitively, a biconnected component is a sub-graph connected to the rest of the graph by cut-vertices, and a triconnected component (within a biconnected component) is a sub-graph connected to the rest by 2-vertex cuts. For instance, Fig. 8(b) shows the biconnected components of Fig. 8(a), separated by cut-vertices d, j, k, w, s, and r. Fig. 8(c) shows the triconnected components, separated by the above cut-vertices and 2-vertex cuts $\{w, d\}$, $\{f, i\}$, and

[8]A *cut-vertex* is a vertex whose removal will disconnect the graph.

[9]A *2-vertex cut* is a set of two vertices $\{v_1, v_2\}$ such that removing v_1 or v_2 alone does not disconnect $\mathcal{G}$, but removing both disconnects $\mathcal{G}$.

Algorithm 1: Minimum Monitor Placement (MMP)

input : Connected graph $\mathcal{G}$
output: A subset of nodes in $\mathcal{G}$ as monitors
1 choose all the nodes with degree less than 3 as monitors;
2 partition $\mathcal{G}$ into biconnected components $\mathcal{B}_1, \mathcal{B}_2, \ldots$;
3 **foreach** *biconnected component* $\mathcal{B}_i$ *with* $|\mathcal{B}_i| \geq 3$ **do**
4   partition $\mathcal{B}_i$ into triconnected components $\mathcal{T}_1, \mathcal{T}_2, \ldots$;
5   **foreach** *triconnected component* $\mathcal{T}_j$ *of* $\mathcal{B}_i$ *with* $|\mathcal{T}_j| \geq 3$ **do**
6   **if** $0 < s_{\mathcal{T}_j} < 3$ ***and*** $s_{\mathcal{T}_j} + M_{\mathcal{T}_j} < 3$ **then**
7   randomly choose $3 - s_{\mathcal{T}_j} - M_{\mathcal{T}_j}$ nodes in $\mathcal{T}_j$ that are neither separation vertices nor monitors as monitors;
8   **end**
9   **end**
10   **if** $0 < c_{\mathcal{B}_i} < 3$ ***and*** $c_{\mathcal{B}_i} + M_{\mathcal{B}_i} < 3$ **then**
11   randomly choose $3 - c_{\mathcal{B}_i} - M_{\mathcal{B}_i}$ nodes in $\mathcal{B}_i$ that are neither cut-vertices nor monitors as monitors;
12   **end**
13 **end**
14 **if** *the total number of monitors* $\kappa < 3$ **then**
15   randomly choose $3 - \kappa$ non-monitor nodes as monitors;
16 **end**

$\{u, v\}$. To identify the triconnected components, we process the graph by adding *virtual links* as follows: if $\exists$ a *minimal* 2-vertex cut[10] whose vertices are not neighbors (e.g., $\{u, v\}$), connect them by a virtual link; repeat this on the resulting graph until no such cut exists. In the sequel, nodes that are cut-vertices or part of 2-vertex cuts are called *separation vertices* (e.g., w, d, f, i, j, k, s, r, u, and v).

Monitor Placement Algorithm: There exist fast algorithms to partition an arbitrary graph $\mathcal{G}$ into biconnected components [29] and then into triconnected components [28]. Note that the output of [28] is the set of triconnected components of $\mathcal{G}$ augmented with the virtual links[11]. Based on these algorithms, we propose a master algorithm, *Minimum Monitor Placement (MMP)*, to place the minimum number of monitors needed to identify $\mathcal{G}$. As shown in Algorithm 1, MMP first applies rules (i) and (ii) to select all the dangling vertices and vertices on tandems as monitors (line 1), and then applies rules (iii) and (iv) to select additional monitors in each[12] triconnected/biconnected component. For a component $\mathcal{D}$, let $s_{\mathcal{D}}$ denote the number of separation vertices, $c_{\mathcal{D}}$ the number of cut-vertices, and $M_{\mathcal{D}}$ the number of (already selected) monitors in $\mathcal{D}$. MMP goes through each triconnected and then biconnected component that contains three or more nodes to ensure that: (i) each triconnected component has at least three nodes that are either separation vertices or monitors (lines 6–8), and (ii) each biconnected component has at least three nodes that are either cut-vertices or monitors (lines 10–12). Finally, it selects additional monitors as needed to ensure that the total number of monitors is at least three (lines 14–16).

Optimality: It is easy to see from rules (i)–(iv) that MMP only deploys monitors when needed, and thus no algorithm can achieve identifiability with fewer monitors; on the other hand, we show that the monitor placement by MMP is also sufficient, i.e., all link metrics can be identified from end-to-end measurements between the selected monitors. Thus, MMP is optimal as it places the *minimum* number of monitors to identify all link metrics in $\mathcal{G}$, as stated in the following theorem.

THEOREM 7.1. *For an arbitrary connected network $\mathcal{G}$, Algorithm 1 (MMP) generates the* optimal *monitor placement in the sense that: (1) all link metrics in $\mathcal{G}$ are identifiable under this placement, and (2) no placement can identify all link metrics in $\mathcal{G}$ with a smaller number of monitors.*

PROOF. See [26]. □

Complexity: In Algorithm 1, lines 1 and 14–16 take $O(|V(\mathcal{G})|)$ time. Splitting $\mathcal{G}$ into biconnected (line 2) and then triconnected components (line 4) takes $O(V(\mathcal{G})+L(\mathcal{G}))$ time [28, 29]. Selecting monitors takes $O(1)$ time per component, and the counters ($s_{\mathcal{T}_j}$, $M_{\mathcal{T}_j}$, $c_{\mathcal{B}_i}$, and $M_{\mathcal{B}_i}$) can be computed during the splitting/selecting process. Therefore, the entire algorithm has $O(|V(\mathcal{G})|+|L(\mathcal{G})|)$ time complexity.

Example: Given the graph in Fig. 8(a) as input (totally 22 nodes), MMP selects 11 monitors, where nodes $\{h, u, v, t, j, e\}$ are selected by line 1, $\{b, g, o, p\}$ by lines 6–8, and f by lines 10–12. It can be verified that the resulting graph satisfies the identifiability condition in Theorem 3.3.

7.3 Evaluation of MMP

We evaluate MMP through a set of simulations on both randomly-generated and real network topologies. We use the following algorithm, referred to as *Random Monitor Placement (RMP)*, as a benchmark for comparison[13]: Given network $\mathcal{G}$, randomly select κ ($\kappa = 2, \cdots, |V|$) nodes as monitors and test the identifiability of the resulting network using the algorithm in Section 7.1. Generally, RMP cannot guarantee network identifiability for arbitrary $\mathcal{G}$ and κ. Therefore, we measure its performance by the fraction of random placements achieving network identifiability over multiple Monte Carlo runs.

7.3.1 Random Topologies

We first consider synthetic topologies generated according to four widely used random graph models: Erdös-Rényi (ER) graphs, Random Geometric (RG) graphs, Barabási-Albert (BA) graphs, and Random Power Law (PL) graphs. We randomly generate 100 graph realizations of each model[14], with each realization containing 150 nodes (i.e., $|V| = 150$). The generated graphs are then input to the monitor placement algorithms. We now explain the models and the corresponding results separately.

Erdös-Rényi (ER) graph: The ER graph is a simple random graph generated by independently connecting each pair of nodes by a link with a fixed probability p. The result is a purely random topology where all graphs with an equal number of links are equally likely to be selected. It is known [30] that $p_0 = \log |V|/|V|$ is a sharp threshold for the graph to be connected with high probability, which implies a minimum value of $p = 0.0334$ for $|V| = 150$.

[10] That is, neither of the vertices are cut-vertices.

[11] The algorithm in [28] does not require a separate step to add virtual links; it adds virtual links as needed in the process of graph partitioning.

[12] MMP does not depend on the order of biconnected/triconnected components being considered for monitor selection.

[13] To our knowledge, MMP is the first monitor placement algorithm for identifying additive link metrics by measuring controllable, cycle-free paths. Thus, we use random placement to represent the average performance of an arbitrary monitor placement for comparison.

[14] All realizations are guaranteed to be connected, as we discard disconnected realizations in the generation process.

Random Geometric (RG) graph: The RG graph is frequently used to model the topology of wireless ad hoc networks. It generates a random graph by first randomly distributing nodes in a unit square, and then connecting each pair of nodes by a link if their distance is no larger than a threshold d_c, which denotes node communication range. The resulting topology contains well-connected sub-graphs in densely populated areas and poorly-connected sub-graphs in sparsely populated areas. It is known that $d_c \geq \sqrt{\log|V|/(\pi|V|)}$ ensures a connected graph with high probability [31], which gives a minimum range of $d_c = 0.1031$ for $|V| = 150$.

Barabási-Albert (BA) graphs: The BA model [32] provides a random power-law graph generated by the following preferential attachment mechanism. We begin with a small connected graph $\mathcal{G}_0 := (\{v_1, v_2, v_3, v_4\}, \{v_1v_2, v_1v_3, v_1v_4\})$ and add nodes sequentially. For each new node v, we connect v to $n_{\min}$ existing nodes, where $n_{\min}$ specifies (a lower bound on) the minimum node degree, such that the probability of connecting to node w is proportional to the degree of w. If the number of existing nodes is smaller than $n_{\min}$, then v connects to all the existing nodes. The BA graph has been used to model many naturally occurring networks, e.g., Internet, citation networks, and social networks.

Random Power Law (PL) graphs: The BA model introduces an artifact that all node degrees are lower bounded by $n_{\min}$. Alternatively, the PL graph [33] provides another way of generating power-law graphs by directly specifying a sequence of expected node degrees $(d_1, ..., d_{|V|})$ according to the power law, i.e., $d_i = i^{\alpha}$ ($\alpha > 0$). The generation of a PL graph is similar to that of an ER graph, except that instead of connecting each pair of nodes with the same probability, nodes i and j in a PL graph are connected by a link with probability $p_{ij} = d_i d_j / \sum_{k=1}^{|V|} d_k$.

We conduct simulations in two scenarios, densely-connected graphs (Fig. 9 with parameter configurations: $p = 0.039$ for ER, $d_c = 0.11943$ for RG, $n_{\min} = 3$ for BA and $\alpha = 0.42$ for PL) and sparsely-connected graphs (Fig. 10 with parameter configurations: $p = 0.0253$ for ER, $n_{\min} = 2$ for BA and $\alpha = 0.32$ for PL), to evaluate how graph density affects the performance of MMP and RMP. Since the number of links n and the minimum number of monitors κ_{MMP} (computed by MMP) vary across graph realizations, we present the average values denoted by $\overline{n}$ and $\overline{\kappa}_{\text{MMP}}$ for each graph model, shown in the captions of Fig. 9 and 10. In each scenario, we have tuned parameters of each model to generate roughly the same average number of links. As RMP is a randomized algorithm, we repeat it for 2000 Monte Carlo runs to obtain the average performance for each graph realization. We then average the results over the 100 graph realizations to obtain the final results[15], shown in Fig. 9 and 10.

For densely-connected graphs (Fig. 9), the probability that RMP is able to identify all the links increases with the number of monitors κ. However, fewer than 20% of the ER, RG, and PL graphs are identifiable when $\kappa \leq 120$ (recall $|V| = 150$), whereas a careful monitor deployment in the same graphs by MMP ensures identifiability with significantly fewer monitors ($\kappa < 25$). Therefore, in most cases,

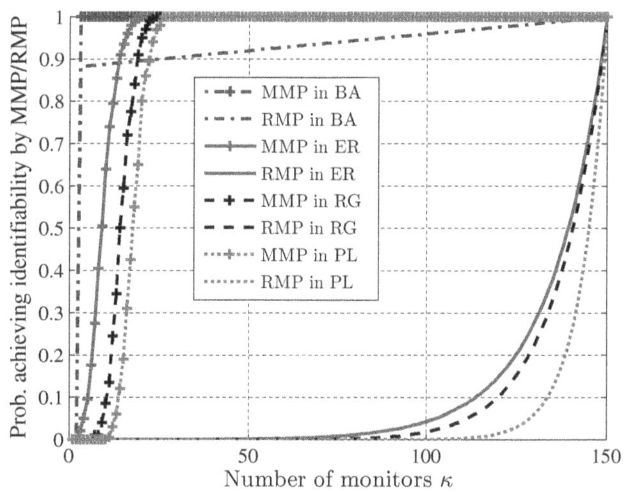

Figure 9: Comparison between RMP and MMP: densely-connected graphs ($\overline{n} = 441, \overline{\kappa}_{\text{MMP}} = 3$ for BA, $\overline{n} = 437, \overline{\kappa}_{\text{MMP}} = 9.36$ for ER, $\overline{n} = 437, \overline{\kappa}_{\text{MMP}} = 19.42$ for PL and $\overline{n} = 451, \overline{\kappa}_{\text{MMP}} = 14.52$ for RG).

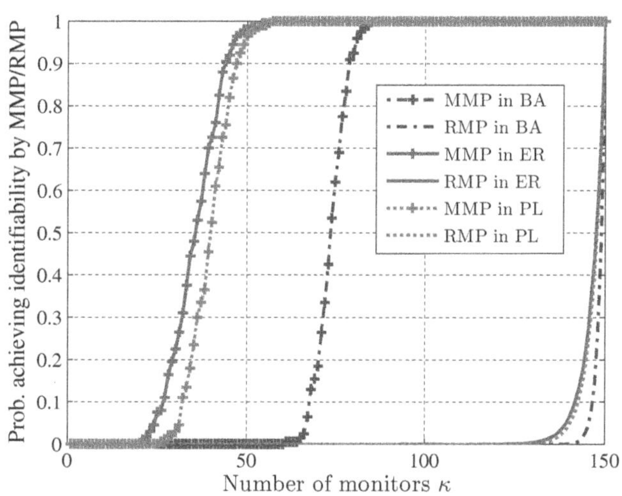

Figure 10: Comparison between RMP and MMP: sparsely-connected graphs ($\overline{n} = 295, \overline{\kappa}_{\text{MMP}} = 73.51$ for BA, $\overline{n} = 293, \overline{\kappa}_{\text{MMP}} = 36.76$ for ER and $\overline{n} = 297, \overline{\kappa}_{\text{MMP}} = 40.24$ for PL).

the proposed algorithm (MMP) substantially outperforms a randomized scheme (RMP) in the required number of monitors. One exception is the BA graphs, where RMP achieves similar performance as MMP. This can be explained as follows: When $n_{\min} = 3$, further simulations show that 87.8% of the generated BA graphs are 3-vertex-connected as each node (except the initial nodes v_2, v_3, and v_4) has at least three neighbors; according to MMP, this implies that an arbitrary placement of three monitors will achieve identifiability, and there is no need for sophisticated placement algorithms. Meanwhile, a comparison of the BA and the PL models implies that the exceptional performance of RMP in the BA model is due to the requirement that all node degrees be lower bounded by three rather than the power law distribution of node degrees, since it does not achieve the same superior performance on PL graphs. For ER, RG, and PL

[15]For each graph realization, MMP achieves identifiability with probability one for $\kappa \geq \kappa_{\text{MMP}}$ and zero for $\kappa < \kappa_{\text{MMP}}$. Therefore, the overall probability for MMP to achieve identifiability using κ monitors is computed as the fraction of graph realizations with $\kappa_{\text{MMP}} \leq \kappa$.

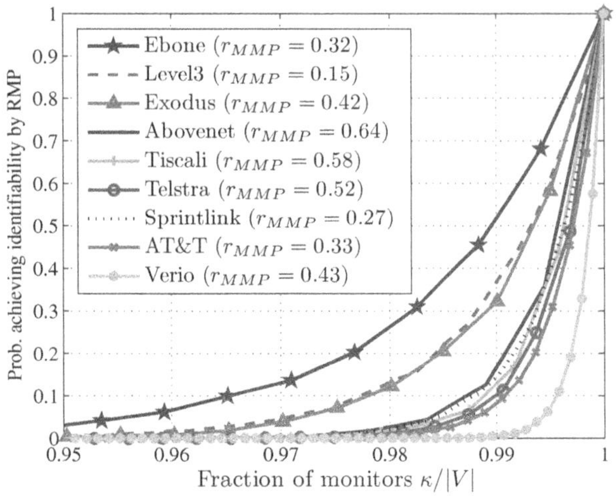

Figure 11: Comparison between RMP and MMP: ISP topologies in Rocketfuel ($15 \cdot |V|$ Monte Carlo

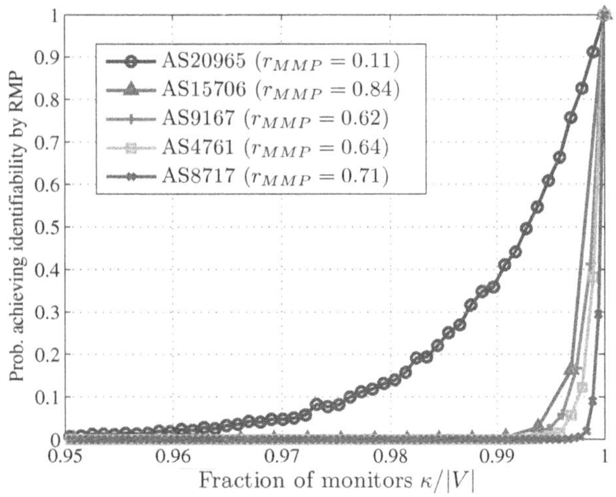

Figure 12: Comparison between RMP and MMP: AS topologies in CAIDA (3000 Monte Carlo runs, $r_{\text{MMP}} := \kappa_{\text{MMP}}/|V|$).

graphs, it is easy to form sparsely-connected subgraphs, thus requiring more monitors to guarantee identifiability. Among the four models, we observe that RMP exhibits worse performance in the model with a larger $\overline{\kappa}_{\text{MMP}}$. This is because large $\overline{\kappa}_{\text{MMP}}$ implies poor connectivity within certain subgraphs, where a considerable number of nodes have to be selected as monitors to achieve identifiability. Thus, RMP will fail to achieve identifiability if it does not select sufficient nodes in any of these subgraphs.

We perform similar simulations for sparsely-connected graphs by adjusting the parameters[16], shown in Fig. 10. In comparison with Fig. 9, both MMP and RMP perform worse in sparsely-connected graphs, requiring a larger number of monitors to achieve the same probability of identifiability. This is because sparser graphs impose more constraints on candidate measurement paths between a pair of monitors, and thus more monitors are needed to identify all links. As we compare the performance of the same graph model in Fig. 9 and 10, we observe that all models exhibit smooth transitions when we vary the average number of links $\overline{n}$ except for the BA model, which has extremely good performance for $n_{\min} = 3$ but the worst performance (except for RG) for $n_{\min} = 2$. This can again be explained by examining the 3-vertex-connectivity of the generated graph realizations. We have verified that as we reduce $n_{\min}$ from 3 to 2, the probability for BA graphs to be 3-vertex-connected suddenly drops from 87.8% to 0%, making it unlikely for an arbitrary placement to achieve identifiability. In fact, when $n_{\min} = 2$, on average 49.2% of the nodes in BA graphs have degrees less than 3, which have to be selected as monitors by rules (i) and (ii) in MMP. Therefore, RMP will fail to achieve identifiability even if it misses one of these nodes, resulting in its poor performance.

[16]To generate roughly the same number of links as in the other models, d_c for the RG graph becomes much smaller than $\sqrt{\log|V|/(\pi|V|)}$, making the probability of generating a connected RG graph very small. Thus, the RG model is omitted from Fig. 10.

Table 2: Parameters of AS Topologies in Rocketfuel

AS	ISP Name	$\|L\|$	$\|V\|$	κ_{MMP}	r_{MMP}
6461	Abovenet (US)	294	182	117	0.64
1755	Ebone (Europe)	381	172	55	0.32
3257	Tiscali (Europe)	404	240	138	0.58
3967	Exodus (US)	434	201	85	0.42
1221	Telstra (Australia)	758	318	164	0.52
7018	AT&T (US)	2078	631	208	0.33
1239	Sprintlink (US)	2268	604	163	0.27
2914	Verio (US)	2821	960	408	0.43
3356	Level3 (US)	5298	624	94	0.15

Table 3: Parameters of AS Topologies in CAIDA

AS	$\|L\|$	$\|V\|$	κ_{MMP}	r_{MMP}
15706	874	325	276	0.84
9167	1590	769	483	0.62
8717	3755	1778	1266	0.71
4761	3760	969	624	0.64
20965	8283	968	110	0.11

7.3.2 Autonomous System Topologies

We now test MMP and RMP on real network topologies. We use the *Autonomous System* (AS) topologies from both the Rocketfuel [34] and the CAIDA [35] projects, which represent IP-level connections between backbone/gateway routers of several ASes from major *Internet Service Providers (ISPs)* around the globe. The parameters of selected networks obtained from these two projects are listed in Tables 2 and 3, where we sort the networks according to their numbers of links, and $r_{\text{MMP}} := \kappa_{\text{MMP}}/|V|$ denotes the minimum fraction of monitors computed by MMP in a network with $|V|$ nodes.

1) AS topologies from Rocketfuel: As shown in Table 2, each AS in Rocketfuel corresponds to an ISP. To identify the entire network, we observe that most ISPs need a significant fraction of nodes to be monitors, ranging from around 30% (Ebone, AT&T, Sprintlink) to more than 60%

(Abovenet). This is because ISP networks contain a large number of gateway[17] routers to connect to customer networks or other ISPs, which appear as dangling nodes that have to be selected as monitors (see rule (i) in Section 7.2). We repeat RMP for $15 \cdot |V|$ Monte Carlo runs for each ISP to evaluate its average performance, measured by the fraction of Monte Carlo runs achieving identifiability, as shown in Fig. 11. To facilitate comparison, we mark the fraction of monitors r_{MMP} needed by MMP in the legends of the same plot; note that MMP guarantees identifiability for each network as long as $\kappa/|V| \geq r_{\text{MMP}}$. Here we normalize the number of monitors by the total number of nodes for the x-axis to compare networks of various sizes. Moreover, we only plot the results of RMP for $\kappa/|V| \geq 95\%$ since RMP fails to achieve identifiability in almost all the Monte Carlo runs for all the ISPs when $\kappa/|V| < 95\%$.

As in the case of synthetic graphs, we again observe a significant improvement of MMP over RMP. Specifically, RMP has at most 50% probability of identifying all the links even if 99% of the nodes are monitors, whereas MMP guarantees identifiability using at most 64% of nodes as monitors. The poor performance of RMP is due to the heterogeneous connectivity within ISP networks, which contain poorly-connected subnetworks that need a large fraction of monitors, a requirement unlikely to be fulfilled by random placement. We also observe that the relative performance of MMP and RMP varies for different networks, e.g., Level3 and Exodus experience similar performance under RMP, whereas their minimum fractions of monitors computed by MMP differ significantly (0.15 for Level3 and 0.42 for Exodus). Intuitively, this is because RMP performance is determined by the relative number of valid placements, i.e., the fraction of all the $\binom{|V|}{\kappa}$ candidate placements that achieve identifiability, whereas MMP performance is determined by the smallest κ for which this fraction is non-zero.

2) AS topologies from CAIDA: Because ISP topologies have evolved since the Rocketfuel project, we repeat the above evaluation on a recent data set obtained by the CAIDA project; see results in Table 3 and Fig. 12. Compared with the ASes in Rocketfuel data set, we notice that ASes with similar average node degrees (i.e., $2|L|/|V|$) in CAIDA data set require a larger fraction of monitors for complete identification, e.g., $r_{\text{MMP}} = 0.71$ for AS8717 with average node degree 4.2 in Table 3, whereas $r_{\text{MMP}} = 0.32$ for AS1755 (Ebone) with average node degree 4.4 in Table 2. This is because ASes in CAIDA data set tend to be more skewed in connectivity, with more densely-connected cores and a larger number of dangling nodes (likely the gateways for peer/customer connections). As all dangling nodes have to be selected as monitors, such skewed connectivity leads to a higher ratio of monitors although the average node degree is not necessarily lower. Meanwhile, comparison with RMP (3000 Monte Carlo runs), presented in Fig. 12, shows that the improvement of MMP over RMP remains significant. As in Fig. 11, RMP again exhibits poor performance for all the ASes considered in Fig. 12, which has less than 35% probability of identifying all links even if the fraction of monitors $\kappa/|V|$ is as large as 0.99. In particular, for almost all the networks (except for AS20965) in Fig. 12, RMP fails to identify all the links in more than 60% of the Monte Carlo runs even if *all but one* node are monitors. In contrast, carefully selected monitors by MMP can guarantee complete identification while substantially reducing the required number of monitors.

[17]In real networks, monitor selection may be constrained to a subset of nodes, e.g., gateways. Under such constraint, the issue of achievable number of identifiable links (i.e., partial network identifiability) is left for future work.

8. CONCLUSION

In this paper, we study the fundamental conditions on network topology and placement of monitors for identifying additive link metrics using end-to-end measurements along simple paths between monitors. We show that with two monitors, it is impossible to identify all the link metrics, but is possible to identify the metrics of interior links that are at least one hop away from the monitors, for which we derive the necessary and sufficient conditions in terms of edge/vertex connectivity of the network topology. We further study the case of three or more monitors and derive the corresponding necessary and sufficient conditions for identifying all the link metrics. We show that these conditions are not only useful for testing network identifiability under a given monitor placement, but also enable an efficient monitor placement algorithm that guarantees identifiability using the minimum number of monitors. Our evaluations on both random and real network topologies verify that the proposed algorithm significantly outperforms a baseline solution.

9. REFERENCES

[1] F. Lo Presti, N. Duffield, J. Horowitz, and D. Towsley, "Multicast-based inference of network-internal delay distributions," *IEEE/ACM Transactions on Networking*, vol. 10, no. 6, pp. 761–775, Dec. 2002.

[2] A. B. Downey, "Using pathchar to estimate internet link characteristics," in *IEEE SIGCOMM*, 1999.

[3] G. Jin, G. Yang, B. Crowley, and D. Agarwal, "Network characterization service (ncs)," in *IEEE HPDC*, 2001.

[4] M. Coates, A. O. Hero, R. Nowak, and B. Yu, "Internet tomography," *IEEE Signal Processing Magzine*, vol. 19, pp. 47–65, 2002.

[5] E. Lawrence and G. Michailidis, "Network tomography: A review and recent developments," *Frontiers in Statistics*, vol. 54, 2006.

[6] O. Gurewitz and M. Sidi, "Estimating one-way delays from cyclic-path delay measurements," in *IEEE INFOCOM*, 2001.

[7] Y. Chen, D. Bindel, and R. H. Katz, "An algebraic approach to practical and scalable overlay network monitoring," in *ACM SIGCOMM*, 2004.

[8] A. Chen, J. Cao, and T. Bu, "Network Tomography: Identifiability and Fourier domain estimation," in *IEEE INFOCOM*, 2007.

[9] "Open networking foundation." [Online]. Available: http://www.opennetworkingfoundation.org

[10] N. Duffield and F. Lo Presti, "Multicast inference of packet delay variance at interior network links," in *IEEE INFOCOM*, 2000.

[11] Y. Xia and D. Tse, "Inference of link delay in communication networks," *IEEE Journal of Selected Areas in Communications*, 2006.

[12] A. Adams, T. Bu, T. Friedman, J. Horowitz, D. Towsley, R. Caceres, N. Duffield, F. Presti, and V. Paxson, "The use of end-to-end multicast measurements for characterizing internal network behavior," *IEEE Communications Magazine*, vol. 38, no. 5, pp. 152–159, May 2000.

[13] R. Castro, M. Coates, G. Liang, R. Nowak, and B. Yu, "Network tomography: recent developments," *Statistical Science*, 2004.

[14] M.-F. Shih and A. Hero, "Unicast inference of network link delay distributions from edge measurements," in *IEEE ICASSP*, 2001.

[15] T. Bu, N. Duffield, and F. Lo Presti, "Network tomography on general topologies," in *ACM SIGMETRICS*, 2002.

[16] M. Firooz and S. Roy, "Network tomography via compressed sensing," in *IEEE GLOBECOM*, 2010.

[17] W. Xu, E. Mallada, and A. Tang, "Compressive sensing over graphs," in *IEEE INFOCOM*, 2011.

[18] S. Ahuja, S. Ramasubramanian, and M. Krunz, "SRLG failure localization in all-optical networks using monitoring cycles and paths," in *IEEE INFOCOM*, 2008.

[19] A. Gopalan and S. Ramasubramanian, "On identifying additive link metrics using linearly independent cycles and paths," *IEEE/ACM Transactions on Networking*, vol. PP, no. 99, 2011.

[20] N. Alon, Y. Emek, M. Feldman, and M. Tennenholtz, "Economical graph discovery," in *Symposium on Innovations in Computer Science*, 2011.

[21] L. Ma, T. He, K. Leung, D. Towsley, and A. Swami, "Efficient identification of additive link metrics via network tomography," in *ICDCS*, 2013.

[22] Y. Bejerano and R. Rastogi, "Robust monitoring of link delays and faults in IP networks," in *IEEE INFOCOM*, 2003.

[23] R. Kumar and J. Kaur, "Practical beacon placement for link monitoring using network tomography," *IEEE JSAC*, vol. 24, no. 12, pp. 2196–2209, 2006.

[24] J. D. Horton and A. Lopez-Ortiz, "On the number of distributed measurement points for network tomography," in *ACM/USENIX IMC*, 2003.

[25] R. Diestel, *Graph theory*. Springer-Verlag Heidelberg, New York, 2005.

[26] L. Ma, T. He, K. K. Leung, A. Swami, and D. Towsley, "Identification of additive link metrics: Proof of selected theorems," Technical Report, Imperial College, London, UK., July 2012. [Online]. Available: http://www.commsp.ee.ic.ac.uk/%7elm110/pdf/MaTechreportJul12.pdf

[27] R. E. Tarjan, "A note on finding the bridges of a graph," *Information Processing Letters*, pp. 160–161, 1974.

[28] J. E. Hopcroft and R. E. Tarjan, "Dividing a graph into triconnected components," *SIAM Journal on Computing*, vol. 2, pp. 135–158, 1973.

[29] R. Tarjan, "Depth-first search and linear graph algorithms," *SIAM Journal on Computing*, vol. 1, pp. 146–160, 1972.

[30] P. Erdös and A. Rényi, "On the evolution of random graphs," *Publications of the Mathematical Institute of the Hungarian Academy of Sciences*, vol. 5, pp. 17–61, 1960.

[31] P. Gupta and P. Kumar, "Critical power for asymptotic connectivity in wireless networks," *Stochastic Analysis, Control, Optimization and Applications*, pp. 547–566, 1999.

[32] R. Albert and A.-L. Barabási, "Statistical mechanics of complex networks," *Reviews of Modern Physics*, vol. 74, pp. 47–97, Jan. 2002.

[33] F. Chung and L. Lu, *Complex Graphs and Networks*. American Mathematical Society, 2006.

[34] "Rocketfuel: An ISP topology mapping engine," University of Washington, 2002. [Online]. Available: http://www.cs.washington.edu/research/networking/rocketfuel/

[35] "Macroscopic Internet Topology Data Kit (ITDK)," The Cooperative Association for Internet Data Analysis (CAIDA), Apr. 2013. [Online]. Available: http://www.caida.org/data/active/internet-topology-data-kit/

APPENDIX

A. LEMMAS AND PROPOSITIONS

LEMMA A.1. *Suppose two monitors are deployed in $\mathcal{G}$ to measure simple paths. If link l is a bridge in $\mathcal{G}$ with one monitor on each side, as illustrated in Fig. 13, then neither l nor its adjacent links are identifiable.*

PROOF. See [26]. □

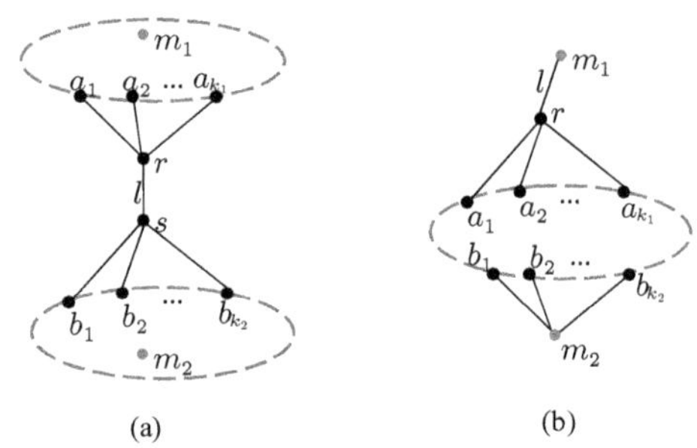

Figure 13: Two cases of bridge link l: (a) interior bridge, (b) exterior bridge.

PROPOSITION A.2. *Using two monitors measuring simple paths, if all link metrics in the interior graph of $\mathcal{G}$ are identifiable, then $\mathcal{G} + m_1m_2$ is 3-vertex-connected.*

PROOF. See [26]. □

PROPOSITION A.3. *Given a graph G employing κ ($\kappa \geq 3$) monitors, the extended graph $\mathcal{G}_{ex}$ of $\mathcal{G}$ satisfies Conditions ① (i.e., $\mathcal{G}_{ex} - l$ is 2-edge-connected for each link l in $\mathcal{G}$) if and only if $\mathcal{G}_{ex}$ is 3-edge-connected.*

PROOF. See [26]. □

PROPOSITION A.4. *Given a graph G employing κ ($\kappa \geq 3$) monitors, the extended graph $\mathcal{G}_{ex}$ of $\mathcal{G}$ satisfies Conditions ② (i.e., $\mathcal{G}_{ex} + m_1'm_2'$ is 3-vertex-connected) if and only if $\mathcal{G}_{ex}$ is 3-vertex-connected.*

PROOF. See [26]. □

Profiling High-School Students with Facebook: How Online Privacy Laws Can Actually Increase Minors' Risk

Ratan Dey
Polytechnic Institute of New York University
Brooklyn, New York
ratan@cis.poly.edu

Yuan Ding
Polytechnic Institute of New York University
Brooklyn, New York
dingyuan1987@gmail.com

Keith W. Ross
Polytechnic Institute of New York University
Brooklyn, New York
ross@poly.edu

ABSTRACT

Lawmakers, children's advocacy groups and modern society at large recognize the importance of protecting the Internet privacy of minors (under 18 years of age). Online Social Networks, in particular, take precautions to prevent third parties from using their services to discover and profile minors. These precautions include displaying only minimal information in registered minors' public profiles, not listing minors when searching for users by high school or city, and banning young children from joining altogether.

In this paper we show how an attacker can circumvent these precautions. We develop efficient crawling and data mining methodologies to discover and profile most of the high school students in a targeted high school. In particular, using Facebook and for a given target high school, the methodology finds most of the students in the school, and for each discovered student infers a profile that includes significantly more information than is available in a registered minor's public profile. Such profiles can be used for many nefarious purposes, including selling the profiles to data brokers, large-scale automated spear-phishing attacks on minors, as well as physical safety attacks such as stalking, kidnapping and arranging meetings for sexual abuse.

Ironically, the Children's Online Privacy Protection Act (COPPA), a law designed to protect the privacy of children, indirectly facilitates the approach. In order to bypass restrictions put in place due to the COPPA law, some children lie about their ages when registering, which not only increases the exposure for themselves but also for their non-lying friends. Our analysis strongly suggests there would be significantly less privacy leakage if Facebook did not have age restrictions.

Categories and Subject Descriptors

E.m [**Data**]: Miscellaneous

Keywords

Facebook; COPPA; Privacy; Minor; Policy; High School

IMC'13, October 23–25, 2013, Barcelona, Spain.

ACM 978-1-4503-1953-9/13/10 ...$15.00.
http://dx.doi.org/10.1145/2504730.2504733.

1. INTRODUCTION

It is generally recognized that protecting the Internet privacy of minors (under 18 years of age in the US) is important, with modern society manifesting this concern in many ways. The US government, through the Children's Online Privacy Protection Act (COPPA) [6] is designed to protect the privacy of children under 13 years of age. It details what a website operator must include in a privacy policy, how to seek verifiable consent from a parent, and what responsibilities an online service provider has to protect children's privacy and safety, including restrictions on the marketing to children under 13. Many consumer, privacy and child advocacy groups continue to actively lobby governments to provide better privacy protection for minors [7]. The US Congress is currently considering new bills to strengthen online safeguards for children and teens [10, 12].

Online Social Networks (OSNs) additionally take measures to protect the privacy of minors. Facebook, for example, treats minors and adults with distinctly different policies [5]. Facebook currently bans young children (under 13) from joining, does not list minors when searching for users by high school or city, and displays only minimal information in registered minors' public profiles, no matter how they configure their privacy settings.

In this paper we show how an attacker (third party) can circumvent these precautions to discover and profile most of the high-school students in a targeted geographical area. In particular, using Facebook and for a given target high school, we construct an efficient methodology which finds most of the students in the school, and for each discovered student infers a profile which includes significantly more information than is available in a registered minor's public profile. For each discovered student, the additional information minimally includes the student's current city, current high-school, graduation year, inferred birth year, and list of school friends. The generated profiles of about half of the identified minors further include varying amounts of additional information, including shared photos and wall postings. The information is collected *passively*, that is, without attempting to establish friend links with any of the students. By profiling all the high schools in a city, a third-party can discover and develop profiles for most of the minors, ages 14-17, in that city. As discussed in Section 2, the third-party could use such profiles for many nefarious purposes, including selling the profiles to data brokers, large-scale automated spear-phishing attacks on minors, as well as physical safety attacks such as prospecting candidate children for stalking, kidnapping and arranging meetings for sexual abuse.

Using off-line channels, it is difficult to obtain complete lists of students attending a given target school. For example, in the course of the research for this paper, while seeking ground-truth data, we contacted administrators of four high schools and asked them to provide us with a list of names of all students currently attending their schools, with assurances of keeping the lists entirely confidential as well as not mentioning the names of the schools in this study. But the administrations of these high schools would not provide the lists, even with such assurances, fearing potential lawsuits from parents or other legal actions. High-school websites today also do not publicly provide lists of current students.

It is also difficult to obtain complete lists of students attending a given target school directly from OSNs. As of April 2013, and documented in this paper, Facebook takes explicit actions to prevent people from obtaining school lists directly from its site. Although Facebook allows its members to search for other members who are associated with any given high school or city, *the search results returned by the service do not include registered minors*; for a high school search, they only include members who are registered as currently being 18 years or older, with the vast majority of the results being alumni of the high school. Because of this measure, it is not possible for a third party to *directly* use Facebook's search services (including Facebook's Graph Search) to collect the names of the students at any target high school and attempt to profile them. Google+ also takes similar measures to protect the privacy of minors, as described in the Appendix A of this paper.

Ironically, the third-part privacy leakages described in this paper are indirectly exacerbated by part of the COPPA law, which was designed to protect minors' privacy. As part of the COPPA law, children under thirteen are required to obtain verifiable parental consent before joining an online service. Given economic costs, social concerns, and technical issues, most online services — including Facebook and Google+ — choose to avoid this COPPA requirement by banning users younger than 13. Upon creating an account, these sites ask users for their birth date to determine if they are 13 or older. If the user indicates being under 13 years of age, the site prevents the user from creating an account. The key observations and ingredients behind our methodology are the following:

1. In order to circumvent the age restriction (due to COPPA), many under-13 users lie about their age to gain access to online social networks when creating their accounts [19]. For example, in order to gain access to Facebook, an 11-year-old boy may say he is 13 years old or may even say he is over 18 when registering.

2. Several years later, when the lying minor enters high school, his registered age very possibly will be 18 or older. The OSN will therefore consider him an adult although he is actually a minor.

3. When searching for users by high school, Facebook (and Google+) only returns members who are registered adults. But a small fraction of these registered adults will in truth be minors. A smaller fraction of these "lying" minors will indicate in their public profiles that they currently attend the target high school.

4. By identifying the minors returned by the search results, crawling their friend lists and performing statistical processing on their friend lists, we show it is possible to discover most of the students in the target high school and, for each discovered student, create a profile that contains significantly more information than should be available in a minor's public profile.

Thus, a component of the COPPA law and the fact that OSNs do not verify the age of its users have together inadvertently set the stage for widespread discovery and inference of minors' private information.

To demonstrate the feasibility of high-school profiling, we applied the methodology to one small private high school and two relatively large public high schools, located in different geographical regions in the USA. Our institution provided us with an IRB to perform the research under the condition that we keep private all collected and inferred information about individuals and only release aggregated results. For the smaller high school, we were able to obtain, through a confidential off-line channel, ground-truth information including the names of all the students in the high school and their graduating classes. For the larger high schools, we do not have complete ground-truth information to evaluate the approach. Instead, we obtain limited ground-truth information for a small set of students by scraping Facebook, and develop an evaluation methodology based on the limited ground-truth information.

We also develop a methodology to estimate how much privacy leakage would occur in a world where the OSN lets all users join, independent of age, and compare the estimate to the extent of leakage in our current world with bans on children under 13. Our results suggest that a third-party not only can discover more minors, but can also build more extensive profiles than what would be the case in a world without age restrictions. Thus, in terms of third-party privacy intrusion, this component of COPPA actually puts minors at greater risk than they would be if the law had never been enacted. We emphasize, however, that COPPA has many components, and does help to protect the privacy intrusion from first party services (such as OSNs). Although the COPPA law indirectly exacerbates the third party privacy problem for minors, we are certainly not arguing that governments should abandon enacting laws to protect the online privacy of children. We believe, however, that the laws must be carefully designed and consider leakages to third-parties as well as to first-parties.

To our knowledge, this is the first paper that (i) identifies the third-party privacy leakage problem in OSNs for minors, (ii) quantifies the extent of the privacy leakage, and (iii) using measurement and analysis, investigates and quantifies the impact of a privacy law on privacy leakage. As part of responsible disclosure, we informed both Facebook and Google about the methodology described here.

This paper is organized as follows. In Section 2 we briefly outline the consequential threats resulting from the high-school profiling. In Section 3 we provide definitions of terms used throughout the paper, discuss Facebook's policy for minors, and discuss ethical issues associated with the collection and analysis of our data. We present the details of the high-school profiling in Section 4. We evaluate the success of the attack for three high schools in Section 5. In Section 6 we investigate to what degree minors can be profiled using the attack. In Section 7 we estimate the extent of leakage that would occur in a world without COPPA. In Section 8 we consider one promising countermeasure, namely, disabling reverse lookup. In Section 9 we discuss relevant prior work, and in Section 10 we summarize our conclusions.

2. CONSEQUENTIAL THREATS

Suppose a third party, with modest crawling and computational resources, for a given target high school, is able to determine all the students in the school and profile them, with the profiles containing a varying amount of information, but minimally including full name, profile picture, gender, current city, high school name, graduation year (i.e., grade), high-school friends and inferred birth year[1]. For a given high-school, we call the collection of these pro-

[1]A public Facebook profile for a minor at most contains name, profile picture and gender. Thus the constructed profiles addition-

files the *high-school profiles*. Moreover, suppose the third party has a means to send messages directly to many of the students, and can send friend requests to all of the students. We now describe some of the consequential threats.

The first major threat is that of data brokers collecting high-school profiles and selling them to others, such as advertisers, college recruiters, and employment agencies. Because the teen market surpasses US$200 billion in the US alone, it is not surprising that data brokers are already seeking to compile dossiers on children [13, 11]. By leveraging the information in the high-school profiles, data brokers can also enhance the profiles by linking them with other personal data available online and from public records. For example, by obtaining voter registration records (which most states make available for a small fee), the data broker can use the last name and city in the high-school profiles to link the students to parents in the voter registration records, *thereby determining the street address of many of the students*. For those students with friend lists in the high-school profile, if a parent appears in the friend list, then the street-address association can be done with greater certainty.

The second major threat is that of a pedophile, who seeks to use the Internet to arrange sexual encounters with children. For example, recently a man allegedly used Facebook to arrange meetings and have indecent contact with seven different girls, ranging in age from 13 to 15. The district attorney for the case stressed the importance of minors "not sharing personal information online, like full names, ages, addresses, phone numbers and school information" [9]). A pedophile use the approach himself, using the acquired profiles to prospect for victims.

Finally, the profiles could also be used to fuel a large-scale and highly personalized spear-phishing attacks against minors. Messages could automatically be generated which mention the target students' high schools, graduation years, and friends, tricking the targets into installing malware on the family computer, for example.

3. PRELIMINARIES

Throughout this paper we define a *minor* to be any person who is currently under 18 years old. Anyone 18 years or older is said to be an *adult*. Note that most students currently attending a high school are minors. (A fraction of the final-year students may be adults, with the fraction increasing each month in the school year.) OSNs typically require users to specify their birth date (day, month, and year) when they register. As discussed in the Introduction, some users may lie about their birth dates when creating accounts in order to circumvent the minimum age requirement. A user is said to be a *registered minor* if the OSN believes the user is currently a minor based on the registered birth date. We define a *registered adult* in a similar manner. In the context of Facebook, we say a user (say, Alice) is a *stranger* to another user (say, Bob) if all the following conditions are satisfied: (*i*) Alice is not a friend of Bob; (ii) Alice is not a friend of friend of Bob (that is, Alice and Bob have no mutual friends); and (*iii*) Alice does not belong to any of Bob's school or work networks.

3.1 Facebook and Registered Minors

In Facebook, registered minors have a different experience with privacy than do registered adults. We now highlight the differences that are relevant to the current study. Table 1 shows the information about a user available to a stranger for when the user keeps the default settings and for when the user configures the setting for maximum sharing (worst case). A check in the box means the information is available to the stranger for the specific scenario. As shown in Table 1, when a stranger visits a registered minor's profile page, only a limited amount of information is available to the stranger: at most the user's name, profile photo, networks joined, and gender are available. (Typically less, depending on how the user configured her privacy settings. For example, typically less than 10% of registered minors specify network.) Further, the "Message" button will never be visible to a stranger. We say that *only minimal information is available about a user* (registered minor or adult) if a stranger, when visiting the user's public profile, sees at most name, profile photo, networks joined, and gender, and the "Message" button is not available. It follows that if a stranger visits a user's public profile and more than the minimal information is available, then the user must be a registered adult.

OSNs typically provide a friend-search feature, allowing its users to find new friends from different parts of their past and current lives, including friends from previous high schools. Facebook provides this feature in its "Find Friends Portal" [2], where a user can search for potential friends by inputting either hometown, current city, high school, mutual friend, college or university, employer, or graduate school. When a stranger does a high school search by the high school name, Facebook returns a few hundred users who are associated with the target high school. The stranger can also attempt to obtain additional users by creating additional fake accounts. We wrote a script that collects users in this manner. The script takes as input the target high school's Facebook ID, a username and password for a fake account, and outputs several hundred unique Facebook user IDs. We observed in the course of experiments that *Facebook does not return any registered minors when a stranger searches with the Find Friends Portal*. We verified this claim by carrying out an experiment with a high school for which we have the complete list of current students at the high school, as well as the complete list of recent alumni. Facebook recently introduced "Graph Search" which provides a natural way to search for content, people, pages, and so on. In particular, for a given target high school HS1, a third party can now search for users who "study at HS1 in/after/before 2013" or for "current students at HS1 who live in city1" and many other combinations. As with the Find Friends Portal, using the ground-truth data, our experiments found that *Facebook does not return registered minors when a stranger searches with Graph Search*.

In summary, in an attempt to act responsibly towards minors, Facebook takes some precautions to protect minors' privacy. We observed and verified that Facebook does not return registered minors when a stranger searches by high school. Also, when a stranger visits a registered minor's public profile page, only limited information is made available, no matter how the minor configures the privacy settings. In particular, a minor's high school, graduation year, and friend list are never directly available to a stranger. Google+ takes similar measures, as described in the Appendix A.

3.2 Legal and Ethical Considerations

To perform the research described in this paper, we implemented customized crawlers that visit public Web pages in Facebook and download the HTML source code of each Web page. Our parser then extracted relevant data from the HTML source code and stored the data in an SQL database.

Crawling data in OSNs is an ethically sensitive issue. One question that arises is if it is ethically acceptable and justifiable to conduct crawling experiments in social networks? We believe that the only way to reliably estimate success rates of the methodology in

ally contain current city, high school name, graduation year, high-school friends, inferred birth year, and for many students much more information.

Table 1: **Facebook: Default and worst-case information available to strangers**

	Default for Reg. minors	Default for Reg. Adults	Worst-case for Reg. Minors	Worst-case for Reg. Adults
Name, Gender, Networks, Profile Photo	✓	✓	✓	✓
HS, Relationship, Interested In		✓		✓
Birthday				✓
Hometown, Current City, Friendlist		✓		✓
Photos		✓		✓
Contact Information				✓
Public Search		✓		✓

the real-world is to use realistic experiments. We nevertheless took several precautions while crawling. First, we only accessed user information that was publicly available. Second, by implementing sleeping functions and limiting our study to three high schools, the crawling was not particularly aggressive and did not perturb the performance of Facebook.

We also obtained IRB approval for this work from our university. As part of responsible disclosure, we informed both Facebook and Google about the methodology in October 2012. Because of the sensitive nature of the information we gathered and inferred, we will not be making our data sets public and we will not explicitly identify the high schools involved. The data is encrypted, password protected and lies behind a firewall. In the future, we will be destroying and whitewashing all the collected data.

4. HIGH SCHOOL PROFILING

We now describe our basic version of the high-school profiling methodology. The third party begins by selecting a target high school. Let M be the set of all the students currently attending the target high school with active accounts in the OSN. The goal is to find most of the students in M and obtain (or infer) as much profile information as possible about each of those students. We do not require the third party to be an OSN friend, or a friend-of-a-friend, of any of the students in M, that is, the third party may be a stranger to all the students in the high school. With sufficient computational resources, the methodology could be applied to hundreds or even thousands of high schools.

4.1 The Basic Methodology: Exploiting Lying Minors

For any user u in the OSN, let $F(u)$ be the user's current set of friends. For some users, $F(u)$ will be visible on the user's public profile; for other users $F(u)$ will not be publicly available. The methodology in its most basic form is as follows.

1. The third party inputs the name of the target high school into the OSN's high-school search function. The search function returns a list of members who are associated with the target high school. The third party may use a script to automatically scroll down the page (thereby sending additional HTTP requests with AJAX) in order to get a longer list of members. The third party may also use multiple accounts when searching. We refer to the set of all the members found in this manner as the *seeds* and denote the set by S.

2. The third party uses a crawler to download the public profile pages for each of the seeds, parses the pages, and determines the users who indicate they currently attend the target high school (by listing their high school as the target high school and providing a graduation year that is the current year or a future year). Let C' be the subset of seeds who explicitly indicate (in their public profiles) that they are currently students in the target high school. (Most of the users in C' will be minors who, several years earlier when under 13, lied about their age during registration.) Let C be the subset of users in C' who make their friend lists public. We refer to C as the *core set*. As we will see, the number of core users is typically fairly small, on the order of 5% of the number of students in the high school. For each user in set C, we know the user's graduation class year. Assuming that the high school is a four-year school, denote C_1, C_2, C_3, and C_4, for students in the first, second, third, and fourth school years in the core set C.

3. For each student $u \in C$, the third party downloads the friend list, $F(u)$, from the OSN. Let K be the set of all friends obtained from the core users, that is,

$$K = \cup_{u \in C} F(u).$$

We refer to K as the *candidate set*. Our experiments show that the number of candidates will approximately be one order of magnitude greater than the target high school size.

4. We expect some of the users in K to be current students in the target high school. We now try to determine which ones. For each candidate $u \in K$, we use *reverse lookup* to determine its friends in the core. Specifically, for each $u \in K$, we determine the set of friends in the core set for each of the four graduation years:

$$G_i(u) = \{v \in C_i \ : \ u \in F(v)\}, \quad i = 1, 2, 3, 4. \quad (1)$$

Clearly each $G_i(u) \subseteq F(u)$. Note that to obtain the $G_i(u)$'s, the third party *does not* have to obtain the profile pages or friend lists of any of the users in the large candidate set K. In fact, user u's friend list may not even be directly available to strangers.

5. For each candidate $u \in K$, the third party calculates the fraction of users in each of the core class sets with whom the candidate is friends, and then calculates the maximum of these four fractions. Specifically, the third party calculates

$$x(u) = \max_{1 \leq i \leq 4} \frac{|G_i(u)|}{|C_i|} \quad (2)$$

6. The third party rank orders the users in K according to their $x(u)$ values, from highest to lowest. The third party chooses a threshold t in the vicinity of the total number of students attending the high school (which can typically be found from Wikipedia or some other source). The third party then considers the first t students as current students in the target high school (as well as the students in the set C'). Let T denote the set of t students and $H = T \cup C'$. The third party also classifies each such student $u \in T$ into a graduating year according to the highest $|G_i(u)|/|C_i|$ value, $i = 1, 2, 3, 4$.

At the end of these steps, the third party has a set of OSN users H believed to be students at the target high school. The third party has also classified all the students in H by graduation class year. For each student, by knowing the high school, the third party knows the current city; by knowing both the student's last name and current city, the third party can often determine the student's home address from voter registration records. The third party can also estimate birth year from the graduation year. As described in the Section 6, the third party can further determine each student's high-school Facebook friends (even though this is also not available in the public profiles), and can obtain significantly more information for about half of the high-school students.

Note that the methodology relies on the ability to obtain a small set of core users, that is, finding a set of users for whom the third party knows with certainty that the users are in the high school and knows their graduation year. Because the search function only returns registered adults who make their high school public, *a priori* the core set will have no students in the first three years of high school and few in the last year. However, because a significant high-school students lied about their birth dates when creating accounts when they were under 13 (in order to circumvent the age restriction due to the COPPA law), it is indeed possible to obtain a core set from the search function including students distributed across the four years. Also note that the methodology is passive, that is, without attempting to establish friend links with any of the students.

4.2 Performance of Methodology

The set H, and the classification of its members by graduation year, is obtained by statistical inference and therefore may contain errors. For example, some of the users in H may be false positives, that is, they are not current students at the target high school. Furthermore, H may not contain all of the students in M. Two important measures for the performance are the *fraction of students from M found*, given by $|H \cap M|/|M|$, and the *number of false positives*, given by $|H - M|$. Note that by varying the value of the threshold t we can trade off these two performance measures: increasing t should increase the fraction of students found but should also increase the number of false positives. In this paper we estimate these measures for each of the three test high schools.

4.3 Enhanced methodology

We now describe an important enhancement, which requires a relatively small amount of additional crawling. In the *enhanced methodology*, after rank ordering the $x(u)$'s and selecting a threshold t, we download the public profile pages of the first $t(1+\epsilon)$ users. (In this paper, we use $\epsilon = 1$ throughout.) Denote this set of users by $T+$. For each user u in $T+$, we then check the user's profile to see if he indicates he is currently a student in the target high school. If so, we move u from $T+$ to C, thereby increasing the size of the core set. After doing this for all $u \in T+$, we recalculate $G_i(u)$ for each $u \in T+$ and $i = 1, 2, 3, 4$, and proceed from Step 5 in the Basic Approach.

In addition to these approaches, there are many possible heuristics one may construe based on the $G_i(u)$ data. It is also possible to explore traditional machine learning approaches, use interaction graphs [26], or consider the evolution of the activity between users [25] to optimize the results. As the purpose of our research is to demonstrate the feasibility of the methodology rather than fully optimize it, we do not pursue these optimizations here.

4.4 Filtering

In order to possibly improve the performance of the basic and enhanced methodologies, we also examine filtering out some of the candidate users. This filtering variation, as with the enhanced methodology, requires the third party to download the public profiles of the first $(1+\epsilon)t$ users in the candidate set. After downloading these profiles, the third party applies filtering rules to eliminate candidates who are likely former students at the target high school (and have transferred out or have already graduated). We used the following filter rules:

- *Graduate School:* The candidate specifies a graduate school in the public profile page.
- *Different High School:* The candidate provides *one* high school and that high school is different from the target high school.
- *High school graduation year:* The candidate provides a high-school graduation year that is not in the current year or in the subsequent three years.
- *Current city:* The candidate provides a current city other than the city in which the high school resides.

4.5 Estimating the Measurement Effort

Most OSNs employ anti-crawling techniques to protect the data of their members and maintain the performance of their sites. Typically, if a member behaves suspiciously (for example, if the member tries to access many user profiles in a short time), the member's account will be temporarily, or permanently, disabled. Therefore the measurement effort is an important consideration.

For the Basic Methodology, the measurement effort has three components: (i) the number of HTTP GETs sent to obtain the IDs of the seed users S (Note that with AJAX, multiple HTTP GETs may need to be sent to get the entire page.); (ii) the number of HTTP GETs sent to obtain the public profile pages of the seed users in S; (iii) the number of HTTP GETs sent to obtain the friend lists of each of the core users (again sending multiple GETs via AJAX). The approximate number of HTTP GETs sent is therefore given by $A \cdot R + |S| + |C| \cdot f/p$, where A is the number of accounts used, R is the number of HTTP GETs sent per account when gathering the seed list, f is the average number of friends a student has, and p is the number of friends gathered with a single HTTP request. (Currently, Facebook uses $p = 20$).

For the Enhanced Methodology, we additionally (i) download the profile pages of an additional $(1+\epsilon)t$ users, where t is roughly the number of students in the target school, and (ii) download the friend lists for the augmented core set. In Section 5 we will show that the total number of requests for a typical school is small for both the basic and enhanced methodologies.

5. RESULTS FOR THREE HIGH SCHOOLS

5.1 Data Sets

In order to estimate the success of the methodologies, we applied them to three US high schools, which we refer to as HS1, HS2, and

HS3. We collected the data for HS1, HS2, and HS3 in March 2012, June 2012, and June 2012, respectively. HS1 is a small private urban high school with about 360 students. For this high school, we were able to obtain, through a confidential channel outside of Facebook, the complete student lists (segmented by graduation year) for the high school, and also complete alumni lists for recent graduation years. These lists enable us to evaluate the success of the methodologies. HS1 has a relatively high churn rate, with 10-20% of the students transferring in and out of the high school every year. Because of the high churn rate, it is a challenging problem to determine an accurate estimate of the current snapshot of the student body. However, we will see that even with this high churn rate, the basic methodology provides good results.

For the HS1 students in the 2012, 2013, 2014, and 2015 graduating classes, we were able to find the Facebook IDs and public profile pages for $|M| = 325$ students. We did this essentially by running the basic methodology on HS1, finding the users who were ranked the highest, and checking for their names in the ground truth list. We were not able to find the Facebook IDs for about 10% of the student body at HS1. Most of these remaining students most likely do not have Facebook accounts. A small number of them may have accounts with alias names that we could not match to the ground-truth list. The 325 students are roughly evenly distributed over the four years; for 112 students (34%) their friend lists are publicly available.

HS2 is a public suburban high school on the East Coast with a much larger student body of approximately 1,500 students. The school has diverse economic and racial demographics, with about 15% of the students being African-American, 10% Asian, and 10% Hispanic. HS3 is a public high school in a small city in the Midwest, also with approximately 1,500 students. Although neither for HS2 nor HS3 were we able to obtain complete ground-truth information, we develop a methodology to evaluate the approach based on partial ground-truth information mined from Facebook.

5.2 Initial Seed Set

We obtained initial seed sets from Facebook's Find Friend portal, using two accounts for the smaller HS1 and four accounts for each of the larger high schools HS2 and HS3. Table 2 provides a summary of the data collected for the three schools. As shown in Table 2, for HS1, HS2, and HS3, we found 18, 70, and 46 core users (with friend lists) and 6,282, 14,317, and 11,736 candidates, respectively. For the enhanced methodology, we obtained 22, 152, and 178 (extended) core users for each of three high schools. For each high school, the number of core users is roughly 5% of the number of students in the school.

5.3 Measurement Effort

Table 3 summarizes the approximate measurement effort required to collect the data sets for the three high schools in Table 3. Note that the effort is quite small, with the number of HTTP requests sent being about twice the number of students in the target high school for the basic methodology, and about five times the number of students in the target high school for the enhanced methodology.

5.4 Results for HS1

Recall that for HS1 there are 325 students having Facebook accounts. Also recall that we have the complete ground-truth information for HS1 (i.e., the Facebook IDs and graduation years for all of the 325 students). The results for both the basic and enhanced methodologies, with and without filtering, are shown in Table 4 for thresholds t ranging from 200 to 500. The set of users in each column includes the core users (or extended core users for the enhanced methodology). In the notation x/y, x is the number of users from the set of 325 students that are found; and y is the number of users, from the set of x users, that are classified in the correct classification year. We see for the top 200, 300, and 400 cases, the enhanced methodology with filtering gives the best results; for the top 500 case, the enhanced methodology without filtering gives somewhat better results than the enhanced methodology with filtering.

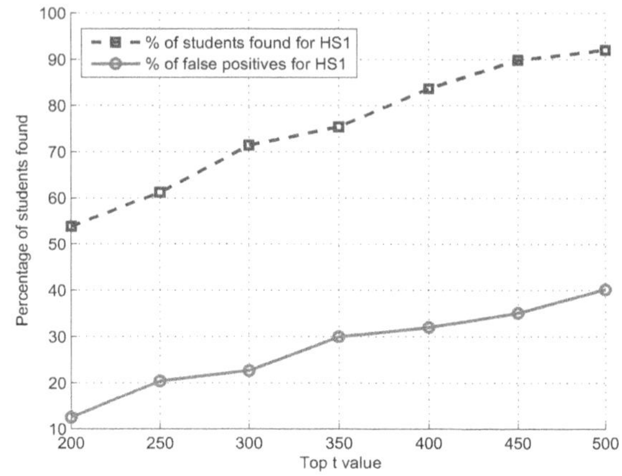

Figure 1: Overall performance of enhanced methodology for HS1

We see that the filtering indeed reduced the number of false positives for the threshold of top 200, top 300, and top 400 users. But for the larger threshold, the filtering actually increased the number of false positives. This can be explained as follows. On one hand, when we increase the threshold beyond 400, we add mostly false positives, since there are not many true positives remaining. On the other hand, the filtering also accidentally filters out some of the true positives, giving an overall decrease in performance.

As an example, let us suppose that the third party decides to use the enhanced methodology with filtering, and considers the top 400 users as students in HS1. Examining the column for 400 students in Table 4, we see that with this choice of threshold, 272 (84%) of the 325 students are included in the set. So with this threshold, the third party finds 84% of the high school student body (having Facebook accounts) with 128 false positives (32%). Moreover, of these 272 students, 250 (92%) have been classified in the correct graduation year. If the third party wants to reduce the false positives, the third party can declare only the top 200 users as students, in which case there are only 25 (13%) false positives, with 54% of the students found, of which 90% are classified in the correct graduation year. If the third party can accept a larger number of false positives, he may instead choose the top 500 students, which would include 92% of the high school student body having Facebook accounts. We show these estimates for different choices of threshold t for the enhanced methodology with filtering in Figure 1.

The results of obtaining 84% of the students in the high school, of which 92% are classified in the correct year, with 32% false positives are remarkable, particularly when considering the 10-15% annual churn rate at the high school. Many students attend HS1 for a short period of time. They make friends with the other students during their period of study, then their families move to another city. We manually inspected the 128 false positives (from the set of top 400 users) and found that about half of them were former students at HS1. For the other half of the false positives, they make very little public information available, so it is difficult to determine

Table 2: Seeds, core users, and candidates for the three high schools

High school	# of students	# of students on Facebook	# of seeds	# of core users	# of candidates	# of extended core users
HS1	362	325	352	18	6,282	22
HS2	1,500 (approx)	N/A	1,559	70	14,317	152
HS3	1,500 (approx)	N/A	1,532	46	11,736	178

Table 3: Measurement effort

	Facebook accounts used	HTTP requests for seeds	Profile pages	Requests for friend lists	Total requests for basic methodology	Total requests for enhanced methodology
HS1	2	34	352	360	746	1,576
HS2	4	101	1,559	1,400	3,060	7,700
HS3	4	90	1,532	920	2,542	8,182

if they are former students or not (although most likely are since they have a large number of friends in HS1).

5.5 Results for HS2 and HS3

For each of the two large public high schools, in order to evaluate the performance of the basic and enhanced methodologies, we collected a first set of seeds with four Facebook accounts and a second set of seeds with an additional four accounts. We use the first set of seeds in the methodologies; we use the second set for evaluation. Specifically, for HS2, from the second set of seeds we obtained 43 users who specify they are currently at HS2 and are not included in the first set of seeds. To evaluate the methodologies, we check to see which of these 43 test users are in our inferred set, and which of those are classified in the correct graduation year. For HS3, we obtained 47 such test users.

We now describe our methodology for evaluating performance with limited ground-truth information. Let x_t be the number of test users found in the top t. For the basic methodology, the set of actual high-school students discovered for a threshold t has two disjoint groups: (i) the core users; and (ii) the non-core high-school students who are discovered. The fraction of non-core high-school students who are discovered is given by $p =$ non-core HS students discovered/non-core HS students. This fraction can be estimated by $(x_t/\#\text{ test users})$. Thus, an estimate of the number of students in the high school found with a threshold t is:

$$\#\text{ of core users} + \frac{x_t}{\#\text{ test users}} \times (\text{HS size - \# of core users})$$

(For the enhanced methodology we replace the number of core users with the number of extended core users.) To estimate the percentage of high-school students found for threshold t, we divide the above by the high-school size. To estimate the number of false positives for a threshold t, we use

$$t - \frac{x_t}{\#\text{ test users}} \times (\text{HS size - \# of core users}),$$

since the false positives are those users among the top-t minus the expected number of students found in the the top-t (excluding the core users). To estimate the percentage of false positives for a threshold t, we divide the above by # of core users + t. We show these estimates for the enhanced methodology with filtering in Figure 2. For example, for HS2, the top 1,652 users ($t = 1500$ plus the extended core users), the third party can obtain 85% of all the HS2 students with 22% false positives in the set of 1,652 users. On the whole, the results in Figure 2 for HS2 and HS3 are similar to those in Figure 1 for HS1.

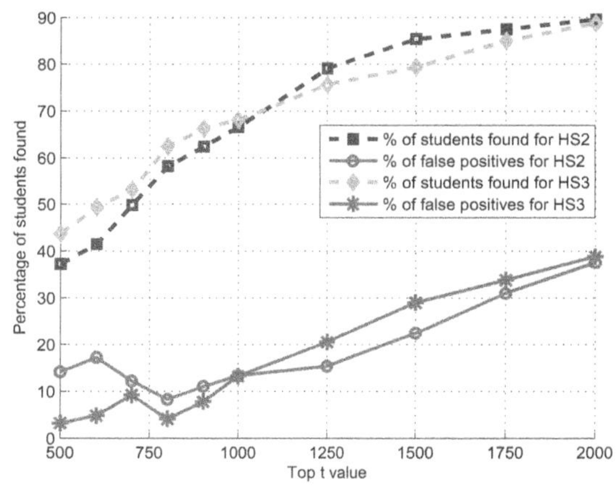

Figure 2: Overall performance of enhanced methodology for HS2 and HS3

5.6 Summary of Results

As discussed in Section 2, when using Facebook's Find Friends Portal to search for users in a target high school, Facebook takes precautions to protect minors by not returning any registered minors. We have shown that a third party, with relatively little crawling effort, can discover the majority of the students at the target high school. For example, we obtained 83%, 85% and 79% of all the students in HS1, HS2, and HS3, respectively, with false-positive rates of 32%, 22% and 29%. Moreover, for each high school student in the list, the third party can determine the student's graduation year with a high-level of accuracy. A third party can then create profiles with varying degrees of information for the high-school students, as well as a variety of means to contact the students, as described in the Appendix, our preliminary analysis indicates that the attack applies to Google+ as well.

6. EXTENDING THE PROFILES

Recall that when a stranger visits the Facebook page of a minor, in the philosophy of Facebook's current privacy policy, the stranger should see minimal information, which at most includes the minor's full name, profile photo, gender, and networks. However, due to statistical inference and many minors registering as adults, a third party can leverage OSNs to significantly extend the profiles. We now quantify the amount of additional profile information is

Table 4: Results for HS1 (which has 325 Facebook users)

	Top 200	Top 300	Top 400	Top 500
Basic methodology without filtering	140/112	206/162	271/224	301/254
Basic methodology with filtering	148/122	196/165	259/227	299/264
Enhanced methodology without filtering	169/155	231/211	261/239	304/281
Enhanced methodology with filtering	175/158	232/211	272/250	299/276

Table 5: Extending the profile for minors registered as adults

	HS1	HS2	HS3
# minors registered as adults	112	700	795
entire friend list public	73%	77%	87%
avg # of friends for users who make friend list public	405	960	908
public search enabled	71%	80%	86%
Message link	89%	86%	91%
relationship info	15%	26%	34%
interested in	13%	20%	33%
birthday	9%	4%	6%
average # of photos shared	19	51	57

readily available to the third party. We do this separately for two classes of minors: those who are registered minors, and those who are registered adults. Again, we do this for the users classified in the first three years of high school (since some of the fourth year students are adults).

6.1 Extending Profiles of Registered Minors

Suppose the attacker applies the methodologies in this paper to all the high schools in a city. Then for most of the high-school students in that city, in addition to the minimal information (full name, profile photo, gender, and occasionally networks), we have shown that a third party can infer current high school and graduation year. From the inferred high school, the third party can also infer hometown and current city, and from graduation year the third party can further estimate the minor's birth year.

Moreover, the third party can use "reverse lookup" to obtain partial friend lists of all the discovered high-school students. Specifically, after obtaining a set H of (likely) current students at the target high school, the third party downloads the friend lists for all users in H whose friend lists are publicly available. A student in H, say Alice, without a public friend list, will typically be in the friend lists of other students in H who make their friend lists public. With this information, the third party can determine at least a portion of Alice's friends. We applied reverse lookup to the registered minors in HS1 and the inferred registered minors in HS2 and HS3. For each of these minors we were able to create friend lists. In particular, we found on average 38, 141, 129 friends per registered minor in HS1, HS2, and HS3. (On average HS1 students have fewer high-school friends since it is a much smaller high school.)

In summary, for each registered minor discovered through high-school profiling, the third party can create a profile with full name, profile photo, gender, a large subset of friends, high school, graduation year, hometown, and an estimate of birth year. This is substantially more information than what Facebook makes publicly available, no matter how the registered minor configures her privacy settings. As discussed in Section 2, this information can serve as a base for creating more comprehensive profiles, by matching the information with public records and other online sources.

We briefly remark that reverse lookup will only obtain a subset of the registered minor's high school friends. In particular, it will not identify friendship relations between two registered minors, since the friend lists of both minors is unavailable to a stranger. Although not explored in this paper, it is possible to infer a friendship link between two registered minors by examining the number of common friends they have (with the common friends determined by reverse lookup). For example, for two registered minors Alice and Bob, let F_A and F_B, respectively, be their friends obtained by reverse lookup. We can then compute the Jacquard index between Alice and Bob:

$$J(A, B) = \frac{F_A \cap F_B}{F_A \cup F_B}$$

If $J(A, B)$ is high, Alice and Bob are very likely to be friends. In this way, we can also find the hidden friendship links among registered minors, and more generally between any two users for which their friend lists are not publicly available.

6.2 Extending Profiles of Minors Registered as Adults

We now examine here the additional information that a third party can obtain for a minor who is registered as an adult. In this case, significantly more information is often directly available, depending on how the user has configured her privacy settings. Possible additional information that can be collected by a stranger — beyond the information a third party can obtain and infer for a registered minor — includes shared photos, photo tags, full friend list, relationship info, interested in, wall postings, likes, favorites, political views, religious views, videos, links, website, birthday and contact info (such as personal email address, IM screen name, address, phone number). For HS1, HS2, and HS3 we determined how much additional information is available for some of these attributes. The results are shown in Table 5.

A stranger can obtain a significant amount of information about a registered minor, as we saw in the previous subsection. But the stranger can often obtain even more information for a minor registered as an adult. For example, as shown in Table 5, a third party can obtain on average over 50 shared photos in the two large high schools, and has access to the "Message" link for more than 86% of the minors registered as adults in all three high schools.

7. HOW ONLINE PRIVACY LAWS CAN ACTUALLY INCREASE MINORS' RISK

We now estimate how much privacy leakage there would be for minors in a world without the COPPA law. Without COPPA, there would be no age restrictions so that children under 13 could create accounts without having to lie about their ages. Although some children might still lie as a joke, the frequency of such occurrences would likely be much smaller. In this without-COPPA analysis, we will assume all users register with their actual birth dates. We also assume the OSN maintains the same privacy policy for minors as it does today — in particular, (i) when searching for users who attended a target high school or live in a target city, the OSN does not return registered minors; (ii) the OSN displays only minimal information on a minor's public profile page.

We now address two questions in the context of a world without COPPA. First, for a given target high school, can a third party still find a set of OSN users such that (a) most of the students in the set attend the target high school (low false positive rate), and (b) the list contains most of students attending the high school (high coverage)? Second, for the students in the set, can a third party create profiles that go significantly beyond the minimal public profiles? As we have seen, in a world with the COPPA law, the answer to both of these questions is yes. But to what extent is it also true in a world without COPPA?

In high-school profiling (with COPPA), a key component is discovering a set of "core" users who currently attend the target high school and have friend lists. Finding such a core set is facilitated by the fact that some minors are registered adults since they lied about their ages when creating accounts (when they were under 13). Because Facebook treats these minors as adults, not only are they easier to find, but their friend lists are often public, thereby also making their classmates easier to find. *However, in our modified world without COPPA, such core users become more difficult to locate, since no minors would appear in search results.*

7.1 A Natural Approach in a COPPA-less World

Nevertheless, even in a world where everyone registers with their actual birth date, it would still be possible to locate some candidate minors. Here we discuss one natural mechanism to do this. Because many young adults (18-20 years old) will likely have friends who are a few years younger than them, if the third party can find the young adults who recently graduated from the target high school and collect their friends, the third party could create a list that contains minors in the target high school. Specifically, we suppose the third party takes the following natural approach:

1. Obtain a set of users who are adults and have recently graduated from the target high school (or are adults in the last year of high school). Call the subset of these users who make their friend lists publicly available the core users.

2. Obtain the public profiles of all the friends of all the core users. Call the union of all these friends the candidate set. Most likely, the candidate set would contain many minors in the target high school.

3. All the minors (and some adults) will have minimal public profiles. To narrow down the candidate set, filter out all users who do not have minimal public profiles.

4. To further narrow down the candidate set, additionally filter out all users who have fewer than n friends in the core set. The third party then considers this filtered set H as the minors in the target high school.

7.2 Apples-to-Apples Comparison

We now evaluate how successful this approach would be for a world without COPPA, and compare the success rates with those obtained in Section 5 for the world with COPPA. One of the challenges in this evaluation is that we are not able to collect data for the world without COPPA. If we apply the above heuristic to our existing data, then the above heuristic will not find any of the minors registered as adults; however, if we were applying the heuristic to actual without-COPPA data, more minors would be found since more minors would have minimal public profiles. In order to make a mostly apples-to-apples comparison, we therefore compare the number of minimal profile students obtained by the above heuristic for the without-COPPA case with the number of minimal profile students obtained in Section 5 for the with-COPPA case. We make this comparison for HS1, for which we have ground truth information. Recall HS1 has 325 students with Facebook accounts. Of these 325 students, 148 have minimal public profiles (22, 47, 45, and 34 students in 2012, 2013, 2014, and 2015, respectively). We now investigate how many of these 148 students are discovered in the two cases.

First consider the without-COPPA case. We will use students who have graduated in 2010 and 2011 to discover students graduating in 2012-2015, using the same data we used in Section 5, which was collected in March 2012. Specifically, using the HS1 data obtained from the high-school search, we find 52 users who indicate their graduation year as either 2010 or 2011 for HS1 and publicly make available their friend lists. These 52 users become our "core set". We then apply the heuristic above. For $n = 1$, we have $|H| = 4,572$ filtered candidates and among these candidates, 92 of them are in the ground truth data set. Thus, $n = 1$ gives 62% of the minimal-profile ground-truth students with $4,480$ false positives. The results for $n = 1, 2, 3$ are shown in Figure 3.

Now consider the with-COPPA case. For any t value, we need to determine the number of minimal profile students found and the number of false positives. Let M_t be the set of top-t users from Section 5 who have minimal profiles. The number of minimal profile students, z_t, is the number of students from M_t who are in the ground-truth set. The number of false positives is given by $|M_t| - z_t$. For $t = 300$, 165 users have minimal profiles of which 95 are in the ground truth data set. Thus, $t = 300$ gives 64% of the minimal-profile ground-truth students with 70 false positives. The results for $t = 300, 400, 500$ are shown in Figure 3.

As shown in Figure 3, we see that without-COPPA, for obtaining the same number of minors as with-COPPA, the third party has *many more false positives*. For example, with-COPPA gives 64% of the HS1 students with 70 false positives; without-COPPA gives 62% of the HS1 students with $4,480$ false positives. Similarly, for the same number of false-positives, without-COPPA *finds significantly fewer students*. For example, with-COPPA gives 91% of the HS1 students with 170 false positives; without-COPPA only gives 29% of the HS1 students with 186 false positives.

7.3 Profile Creation in a COPPA-less World

Having shown that, without COPPA, the third party finds significantly fewer students for the same number of false positives, we now address the second question, namely, for the students in the guess set H, can the third party create profiles that go significantly beyond the minimal public profiles that Facebook displays for registered minors? Recall that the minimal profile at most contains name, profile picture and gender. In the without-COPPA case, using the heuristic above, the third party would be able to augment this minimal profile with high school using the target high school, although his level of confidence would be significantly less

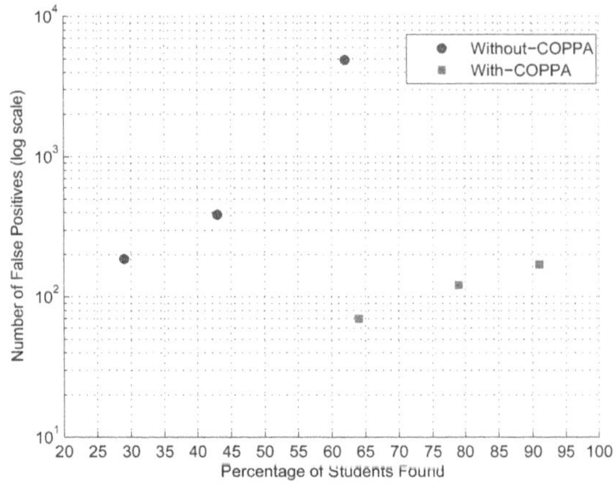

Figure 3: For HS1, False Positives Found With-COPPA vs. Without-COPPA

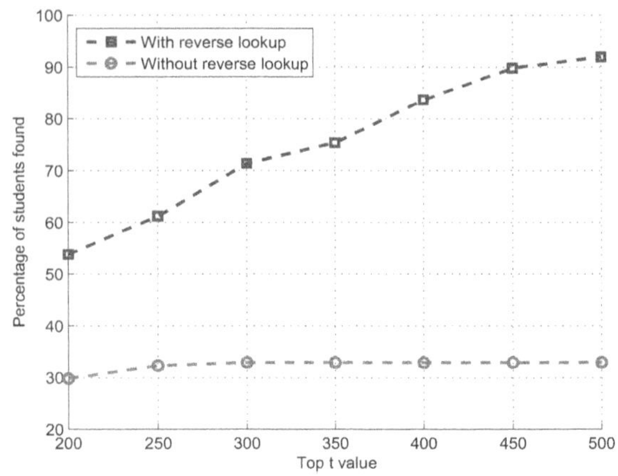

Figure 4: Percentage of HS1 students found with and without reverse lookup

because of the large number of false positives. Moreover,the third party would not be able to easily determine the student's graduation year, and the third party would not be able to create a friend list that includes students in the same year, as is the case for with-COPPA. Thus, in the without-COPPA case, using the techniques in this paper, the third party would not be able to construct a profile beyond the minimal profile plus (a low-confidence guess of) the high school. In the with-COPPA case, a third party can obtain additional profile information for all minors: specifically, graduation year and high-school friend lists for registered minors; graduation year, high-school friend lists and often much more information (e.g., complete friend lists and shared photos) for minors registered as adults. Furthermore, for the without-COPPA case, a third party would *not* be able to send Facebook messages to any of the minors (unlike the with-COPPA case).

In summary, we can conclude that an indirect result of COPPA is that a third party not only can discover more minors, but can also build much more extensive profiles than what would be the case in a world without COPPA.

8. COUNTERMEASURES

In an ideal world, policymakers would enact laws and OSNs would take measures so that (i) it would be difficult for third parties to discover minors in targeted geographical regions and construct detailed profiles of those minors; while at the same time, (ii) providing a highly usable service for minors and adults alike. Designing and evaluating all combinations of possible laws and measures is a major research problem on its own. In this paper we examine just one promising countermeasure — namely, disabling reverse lookup — and quantify the reduction in privacy leakage.

With reverse lookup disabled, if a user's friend list is hidden from strangers (either because the user has configured his friend list as such or because the user is a registered minor), then that user would not be visible to strangers in any other user's friend list. If the OSN takes this countermeasure, users with hidden friendlist will not be found using reverse lookup, thereby reducing privacy leakages. To evaluate the effectiveness of this measure, we estimate its impact on HS1, for which we have ground-truth information. Out of 325 ground-truth users of HS1, 112 of them make their friend list publicly available. For the remaining users, the friend list is not publicly available to strangers, and these users, by assumption, cannot be found via reverse lookup. So in evaluating this countermeasure, we remove these users from the candidate set and then proceed with the methodology steps.

Figure 4 shows the results of the enhanced methodology with filtering for HS1 with and without reverse lookup. From the results, it is clear that performance of high-school profiling methodology decreases significantly. For example, by removing reverse lookup, the percentage of students found in the top-500 decreases from the 92% to 33%.

9. RELATED WORK

There are several earlier studies on the usage of OSNs by minors, both for minors (under 18) and underage users (under 13). In 2010, Pew Research released a report stating that 73% of online American teens ages 12 to 17 used an OSN website [20]. In 2011, Pew released another report, with collaborators at Cable in the Classroom and the Family Online Safety Institute, where it was found that 44% of online teens admit to having lied about their age so they could access a Web site or sign up for an online account [19]. Similar results have been reported for European teens [21]. Boyd et al. [15] provided survey data showing that many parents know their underage children are on Facebook in violation of the site's restrictions, and that they are often complicit in helping their children join the site. More recently, Pew Research found that teens and adults have no significant variations for their privacy settings [22]. These reports collectively provide great insight into behavioral characteristics of minors and their parents. None of these reports, however, address automated discovery and profiling of minors. Our measurement work shows that because minors often lie to circumvent the age restriction, they put themselves and their non-lying high-school friends at risk for a variety of potential online and in-person abuses.

There is substantial previous work on using statistical inference to infer private information about OSN users. Zheleva and Getoor [28] proposed techniques to predict gender and political views of users in four real-world datasets (including Facebook) using general relational classification and group-based classification. Jernigan and Mistree [17] demonstrated a method for accurately predicting the sexual orientation of Facebook users by analyzing friendship associations. Other papers have also examined inferring private information from social networks. Thomas et al. examined scenarios where conflicting privacy settings between friends will reveal information that at least one user intending to remain private [24]. Becker and Chen [14] inferred many different attributes of Facebook users, including affiliation, age, country, degree of education, employer, high school name and grad year, political view, relationship status, university and zip code using the most popular attribute values of the user's friends. Dey et al. [16] examined a large dataset and develop a methodology to estimate ages of Facebook users. Mislove et al. [23] proposed a method of inferring user attributes by detecting communities in social networks, based on the observation that users with common attributes form dense communities. Recently Kosinski et al. [18] showed how Facebook likes can be used to predict a range of highly sensitive personal attributes automatically.

All of the above studies focus on inferring information about adults. To our knowledge, this is the first paper that identifies the privacy problem in OSNs for minors, and also the first paper to quantify the extent of the privacy leakage. The problem is challenging since, for registered minors, little information, including friend lists, is available to the third party. This is also the first paper to measure the additional third-party privacy disclosure risk for minors due to the enactment of the COPPA law.

10. CONCLUSION

In this measurement study we have shown how a privacy law for protecting children's privacy (along with the fact that OSNs do not verify users' ages) can inadvertently increase minor's exposure to third parties. Facebook and other Online Social Networks (OSNs) take precautions to prevent strangers from using their services to extensively profile minors. But because a significant fraction of minors lie about their ages, we show how many of the precautions can be circumvented, putting both lying and truthful minors at risk. For a given target high school, we described a methodology to profile the current students in the high school. The methodology finds the majority of the students in the school, and for each student builds a profile that includes information that is not normally available to strangers, including current city, current school, graduation year, high-school friends, and estimated birth year. As described in Section 6, the profiles of about half students (those who have lied about their ages) also include a varying amount of additional information, including shared photos and wall postings.

We estimated how much privacy leakage would occur in a world without an age restriction and compared the estimate to our measured results for current world with the age restriction. Our results show that a third party not only can discover more minors, but can also build more extensive profiles than what would be the case in a world without an age restriction. Thus, in terms of third-party privacy intrusion, a component of the COPPA law actually puts minors at greater risk than they would be if the law had never been enacted.

Although the age restriction in the COPPA law indirectly exacerbates the third party privacy problem for minors, we are certainly not arguing that governments should abandon enacting laws to protect the online privacy of children. We believe, however, that the laws must be carefully designed and consider leakages to third-parties as well as to first-parties.

11. ACKNOWLEDGMENT

This work was supported in part by the NSF (under grant 0966187). The views and conclusions contained in this document are those of the authors and should not be interpreted as necessarily representing the official policies, either expressed or implied, of any of the sponsors.

12. REFERENCES

[1] Age requirements on Google Accounts. http://support.google.com/accounts/bin/answer.py?hl=en&answer=1350409, accessed May 7, 2013.

[2] Find Friends Portal. https://www.facebook.com/find-friends/browser/, accessed May 7, 2013.

[3] Google+ Search by School Portal. https://plus.google.com/circles/school, accessed May 7, 2013.

[4] Google+ Teen Safety Guide - Features for teens. http://support.google.com/plus/bin/answer.py?hl=en&answer=2409072, accessed May 7, 2013.

[5] How Does Privacy Work for Minors? http://www.facebook.com/help/?page=214189648617074, accessed May 7, 2013.

[6] Children's Online Privacy Protection Act, 1998. http://www.ftc.gov/ogc/coppa1.htm, accessed May 7, 2013.

[7] Groups Make Recommendations for Kids' Facebook, Adweek, June 18, 2012. http://www.adweek.com/news/technology/groups-make-recommendations-kids-facebook-141195.

[8] Creating a Google Plus Account Now Requires You to Enter Your Birthday, August 27, 2011. http://techie-buzz.com/social-networking/google-age-restrictions.html.

[9] Attorney General Kelly announces criminal charges in elaborate "Facebook" false identity scam targeting young girls for sex, February 10, 2012. http://www.attorneygeneral.gov/press.aspx?id=6431.

[10] Do Not Track Kids Act of 2011, May 13, 2011. http://www.gpo.gov/fdsys/pkg/BILLS-112hr1895ih/pdf/BILLS-112hr1895ih.pdf.

[11] Senator Opens Investigation of Data Brokers, The New York Times, October 10, 2012. http://www.nytimes.com/2012/10/11/technology/senator-opens-investigation-of-data-brokers.html.

[12] Update Urged on Children's Online Privacy, The New York Times, September 15, 2011. http://www.nytimes.com/2011/09/16/technology/ftc-proposes-updates-to-law-on-childrens-online-privacy.html.

[13] On the Web, Children Face Intensive Tracking, The Wall Street Journal, September 17, 2010.

[14] J. Becker and H. Chen. Measuring Privacy Risk in Online Social Networks. In *Proceedings of W2SP 2009: Web 2.0 Security and Privacy*, 2009.

[15] D. Boyd, E. Hargittai, J. Schultz, and J. Palfrey. Why Parents Help Their Children Lie to Facebook: Unintended Consequences of the 'Children's Online Privacy Protection Act'. *First Monday*, 16(11), November 7, 2011.

[16] R. Dey, C. Tang, K. W. Ross, and N. Saxena. Estimating age privacy leakage in online social networks. In *Proceedings of the IEEE INFOCOM 2012, Orlando, FL, USA*, pages 2836–2840, 2012.

[17] C. Jernigan and B. F. T. Mistree. Gaydar: Facebook Friendships Expose Sexual Orientation. *First Monday*, 14(10), 2009.

[18] M. Kosinski, D. Stillwell, and T. Graepel. Private traits and attributes are predictable from digital records of human behavior. *Proceedings of the National Academy of Sciences*, 110(15):5802–5805, Apr. 2013.

Table 6: Google+: Default and worst-case information available to strangers

	Default for Reg. Minors	Default for Reg. Adults	Worst-case for Reg. Minors	Worst-case for Reg. Adults
Name, Profile Picture	✓	✓	✓	✓
Gender, Employment, HS, Hometown, Current City		✓	✓	✓
Home and Work Phone			✓	✓
Relationship, Looking			✓	✓
Birthday			✓	✓
Photos			✓	✓
Public Search		✓	✓	✓
In Your Circles		✓	✓	✓
Have You in Circles		✓	✓	✓

[19] A. Lenhart, M. Madden, A. Smith, K. Purcell, K. Zickuhr, and L. Rainie. Teens, kindness and cruelty on social network sites, Pew Internet, November 9, 2011. `http://pewinternet.org/~/media/Files/Reports/2011/PIP_Teens_Kindness_Cruelty_SNS_Report_Nov_2011_FINAL_110711.pdf`.

[20] A. Lenhart, K. Purcell, A. Smith, and K. Zickuhr. Social media and mobile Internet use among teens and young adults, Pew Internet, February 3, 2010. `http://www.pewinternet.org/~/media//Files/Reports/2010/PIP_Social_Media_and_Young_Adults_Report_Final_with_toplines.pdf`.

[21] S. Livingstone, K. Olafsson, and E. Staksrud. "Social Networking, Age and Privacy", EU Kids Online, 2010. `http://www2.lse.ac.uk/media@lse/research/EUKidsOnline/ShortSNS.pdf`.

[22] M. Madden. Privacy management on social media sites, Pew Internet, February 24, 2012. `http://www.pewinternet.org/~/media/Files/Reports/2012/PIP_Privacy_management_on_social_media_sites_022412.pdf`.

[23] A. Mislove, B. Viswanath, K. P. Gummadi, and P. Druschel. You are who you know: inferring user profiles in online social networks. In *Proceedings of the third ACM International Conference on Web Search and Data Mining*, pages 251–260, 2010.

[24] K. Thomas, C. Grier, and D. M. Nicol. Unfriendly: multi-party privacy risks in social networks. In *Proceedings of the 10th International Conference on Privacy enhancing technologies*, pages 236–252, 2010.

[25] B. Viswanath, A. Mislove, M. Cha, and K. P. Gummadi. On the evolution of user interaction in facebook. In *Proceedings of the 2nd ACM workshop on Online Social Networks*, pages 37–42, New York, NY, USA, 2009. ACM.

[26] C. Wilson, A. Sala, K. P. N. Puttaswamy, and B. Y. Zhao. Beyond social graphs: User interactions in online social networks and their implications. *ACM Trans. Web*, 6(4):17:1–17:31, Nov. 2012.

[27] X. Zhao, A. Sala, C. Wilson, X. Wang, S. Gaito, H. Zheng, and B. Y. Zhao. Multi-scale dynamics in a massive online social network. In *Proceedings of the 2012 ACM conference on Internet Measurement Conference*, pages 171–184, 2012.

[28] E. Zheleva and L. Getoor. To join or not to join: the illusion of privacy in social networks with mixed public and private user profiles. In *Proceedings of the 18th International Conference on World Wide Web*, pages 531–540, 2009.

APPENDIX

A. GOOGLE+ AND REGISTERED MINORS

Although the focus of this paper is on Facebook, we briefly mention here that Google+ is also susceptible to high-school student profiling. Like Facebook, to create a Google+ account, the user must register as 13 years or older [1, 8]. Google+ also provides a mechanism for searching for users associated with a high school [3].

Unlike Facebook, Google+, which uses circles, has asymmetric friendship links. For example, for Alice there is one set of users in her circle; and there is a second set of users who include her in their circles. Google+ also provides various safety guidelines for teens [4]. Google+ registered minors also have different default privacy settings than do registered adults, as shown in Table 6. It would also be of interest to examine the privacy settings of minors in RenRen, a large Chinese social network [27].

Demystifying Porn 2.0: A Look into a Major Adult Video Streaming Website

Gareth Tyson
Queen Mary, University of London, UK
gareth.tyson@qmul.ac.uk

Yehia Elkhatib
Lancaster University, UK
yehia@comp.lancs.ac.uk

Nishanth Sastry
King's College London, UK
nishanth.sastry@kcl.ac.uk

Steve Uhlig
Queen Mary, University of London, UK
steve@eecs.qmul.ac.uk

ABSTRACT

The Internet has evolved into a huge video delivery infrastructure, with websites such as YouTube and Netflix appearing at the top of most traffic measurement studies. However, most traffic studies have largely kept silent about an area of the Internet that (even today) is poorly understood: adult media distribution. Whereas ten years ago, such services were provided primarily via peer-to-peer file sharing and bespoke websites, recently these have converged towards what is known as "Porn 2.0". These popular web portals allow users to upload, view, rate and comment videos for free. Despite this, we still lack even a basic understanding of how users interact with these services. This paper seeks to address this gap by performing the first large-scale measurement study of one of the most popular Porn 2.0 websites: YouPorn. We have repeatedly crawled the website to collect statistics about 183k videos, witnessing over 60 billion views. Through this, we offer the first characterisation of this type of corpus, highlighting the nature of YouPorn's repository. We also inspect the popularity of objects and how they relate to other features such as the categories to which they belong. We find evidence for a high level of flexibility in the interests of its user base, manifested in the extremely rapid decay of content popularity over time, as well as high susceptibility to browsing order. Using a small-scale user study, we validate some of our findings and explore the infrastructure design and management implications of our observations.

Categories and Subject Descriptors

C.2.0 [**Computer-Communication Networks**]: General—*Data Communications*

General Terms

Measurement

Keywords

Porn 2.0; Adult websites; Video streaming; Measurements

IMC'13, October 23–25, 2013, Barcelona, Spain.
Copyright 2013 ACM 978-1-4503-1953-9/13/10 ...$15.00.
http://dx.doi.org/10.1145/2504730.2504739 .

1. INTRODUCTION

The Internet has evolved from a largely web-oriented infrastructure to a massively distributed content delivery system [27]. Video content is particularly popular: by 2016, 86% of all Internet traffic is predicted to be video [5]. This transformation has led to a multitude of research attempts to characterise key video portals and the corresponding changing consumption patterns. This includes seminal studies into user-generated content (UGC) [13], video on demand (VoD) [40], Internet TV (IPTV) [14] and catch-up TV [6, 29]. Thanks to them, our knowledge has been expanded and, in many cases, the infrastructures improved.

However, there is an elephant in the room: adult video distribution. Similar to other kinds of content, adult video consumption has been undergoing dramatic shifts. Traditionally, adult videos were distributed via pay-per-view websites and within peer-to-peer communities (e.g., one estimate found that pornography constitutes up to 18% of the files on eDonkey in some regions [35]). Recently, however, increasing amounts of traffic are being generated by emerging YouTube-like websites that provide free on-demand access to adult videos. These sites term themselves "Porn 2.0", and give users the ability to upload, view, rank and comment on videos, as well as form online profiles.

Next to nothing is known about the nature of Porn 2.0, nor the way users interact with it; little is even known (outside ISPs) about the actual amount of traffic generated by these sites. Despite this, its prominence in the Alexa rankings [1] is undeniable, with six adult websites listed in the top 100, more than any other genre of video streaming. We confirm the huge scale of adult content in this paper, where we find over 111 million requests to a single adult website in just a three day period. Considering this scale and prominence, we believe it crucial to gain a better understanding of the characteristics of Porn 2.0, and derive principles that could mitigate its impact on the network.

In this paper, we inspect one of the most popular Porn 2.0 websites: YouPorn [2]. Founded in 2006, it has quickly risen to global prominence. For the last 5 years, it has been amongst the most highly ranked sites listed in Alexa, consistently appearing in the top 100. Due to its large scale, YouPorn provides an ideal case study of the Internet's expanding adult video market.

We repeatedly crawled the YouPorn website to extract information about the videos being created and watched. The entire corpus consists of 183k videos, consisting of footage spanning in excess of 3 years. Over their lifetime, these videos collected more than 60 billion views, confirming YouPorn's huge popularity. In the last 7 days of the traces alone, 912 new videos were added and viewed over 38 million times.

Using this data, we characterise the corpus, highlighting how users interact with various aspects of the system. Further, we make a number of observations that provide evidence of its specific properties compared to other types of media. Because our data does not provide information about users' personal intentions, we further augment our data with a small scale user study (46 participants) to reflect upon the reasons behind our findings.

One running theme in many of our findings is that despite being consciously constructed as an adult site comparable to YouTube, YouPorn differs from traditional UGC sites (e.g., YouTube, Vimeo) in two key ways. First, the number of user-driven content uploads on YouPorn is comparatively low. Indeed, YouPorn itself has uploaded 36% of the overall corpus. Second, despite the lower number of videos, each video gets many more views, on average, than more mainstream UGC sites. This smaller, more popular content corpus suggests lower operating costs for such websites.

Another theme is that users appear to be flexible about which videos they consume. Whilst we verify this independently using a small scale user study, our dataset reveals that this user flexibility manifests itself in two unexpected ways, both of which point to the importance of helping users to locate content. First, although adult video content is not expected to age with time, unlike temporally-sensitive genres such as news or weather, most of the views are garnered in the first days after upload. We demonstrate that browsing order is a strong factor that affects the number of views obtained: easy to find videos collect most views. Second, we find that the number of categories a video appears in strongly correlates with the number of views it obtains. Videos which are not categorised suffer severely. We also discover that no attempt is made by YouPorn at engineering the content of individual categories: in many cases, highly populated categories have too few videos.

A list of contributions and paper roadmap follows:

1. We offer, to the best of our knowledge, the first large-scale measurement study into so-called "Porn 2.0" adult video distribution on the Internet. We present our dataset in Section 3 consisting of over 60 billion views. We will make the data publicly available.

2. We provide a detailed analysis of key characteristics of adult video content (Section 4), as well as the way in which users interact with this type of corpus and its various categories (Sections 5 and 6).

3. We explore the reasons behind our findings through discussions fuelled by a user study (Section 7). Using this, we explore potential improvements that would benefit both network operators and content providers.

2. RELATED WORK

Pornography is anecdotally the most searched for content on the Internet. Many theories exist to explain this. Cooper [16] attributes this to the Internet's "triple-A-engine": Accessibility, Affordability, Anonymity. Suler [36] expands this into 6 factors, coined as the *online disinhibition effect*. Whereas, much work has gone into looking at who engages in online sexual activities and why they do so [12, 20], little is known about about the actual engines that underpin its distribution, especially the expanding Porn 2.0 phenomenon. This has seen websites emerging (e.g., YouPorn [2]) that allow users to upload, view, rate and comment on videos for free, much like YouTube does.

Name	Period	# Vids	# Views
Snapshot	28/02/2013	183,639	61 billion
3 Day	3/03/2013	183,591	111 million
Daily	1/03 – 4/05/2013	1656	96 million

Table 1: Overview of datasets.

A few studies have provided estimates of the demand handled by these websites. For example, Ogas and Gaddam [30] mention that Porn 2.0 sites such as Pornhub, RedTube, xHamster and YouPorn can gain up to 16 million views per month. This is a very conservative estimate compared to YouPorn's report of 100 million page views a day [3]. Other estimates have suggested that sites like YouPorn have a peak traffic rate of 800 Gbps [7]. Despite all this evidence, we still have quite a rudimentary understanding of the true scale of these services. Regardless, most experts agree that Porn 2.0 is a huge emerging economy that is not, as of yet, fully understood [17, 9, 21, 39, 30].

With this in mind, it is surprising to find next to nothing reported on the (systems-level) nature and operation of online adult multimedia delivery services. Instead, various research communities have focussed on specific sub-components such as automated recognition and classification [28, 25]; pornographic practices, communities and subcultures [9]; interest recommendations [34]; security issues [39]; and illegal content dissemination [26]. To our knowledge, this paper presents the first large-scale systems-perspective study of an online adult multimedia delivery service. We believe this work to be crucial, considering the increasing prominence of video distribution [5], of which adult media will likely continue to make up a significant proportion in the future [35]. That said, there are a multitude of studies into more traditional video streaming systems that already provide some insight. These include catch-up TV [6, 29], user generated content [13, 41], VoD [40] and IPTV [14, 22, 24]. Studies such as these have provided a range of insights, including content popularity models [23], optimised caching techniques [6] and improved delivery schemes [8]. As of yet, however, we are unaware as to how these principles apply to adult media systems. The rest of this paper therefore explores this topic.

Note that we do not make a sociological statement within our work; nor do we espouse the proliferation of pornographic media. We are interested in such media's impact on the network and, as such, we believe it is important to gain a better understanding of its characteristics.

3. YOUPORN DATASET

We crawled the YouPorn website to obtain information about its corpus and user base. Each video offered is accompanied by metadata that we extract. This metadata includes the number of views, the video rating, the number of ratings received, the upload date, the user who uploaded the video, the number of comments, and any categorical information. To collect this information, we performed a number of separate crawls, embodied within three datasets, summarised in Table 1.

Our first dataset, which we term the *snapshot* trace, contains information about all videos in the corpus (183, 639), collected on the 28/02/2013. We observe over 60 billion views of videos with durations collectively spanning in excess of 3 years. To augment this, we also collected a second dataset, which we term the *3 day* trace. To obtain it, we re-crawled the same videos 3 days later (3/03/2013). It contained 183,591 videos, 48 having been removed. Using the *3 day* trace, we calculated the evolution of all quantitative metadata including popularity.

The mentioned traces provide two "snapshots" of all videos on YouPorn. This, however, does not give much insight into the temporal properties of individual videos. We have therefore also performed smaller-scale periodic crawlings to collect a time series of snapshots. The third dataset, which we term *daily*, traced 2172 videos added between the period of 1/03/2013 - 4/05/2013. For each video added, we retrieved all metadata on a daily basis to study how it evolved, offering insights into the lifetime of each video. From the full set, we filtered the entries to leave only complete videos in which we had in excess of 21 days recorded. This left 1656 videos with an accumulated set of 96 million views.

4. CHARACTERISING CONTENT CORPUS

In this section, we investigate the content corpus offered by YouPorn. We traced 183, 639 videos within the corpus dating from September 2006. This constitutes their entire video repository, as available at the time of writing.

4.1 Content duration

First, we inspect the duration of videos within YouPorn, presented as a cumulative distribution function (CDF) in Figure 1.[1] We observe from Figure 1 that most videos are rather short. About 80% are shorter than 15 minutes, with a very small fraction of them exceeding 45 minutes. If we divide them into 1 minute time ranges, the largest bucket is the 5–6 minutes, which contains 25% of all videos. This propensity could have emerged for a number of reasons. An obvious one is the presence of commercial videos that are intended to advertise content from other (e.g., pay-based) websites. Such users tend to upload short previews of longer videos in an attempt to entice users to their websites. YouPorn allows banners to be placed below videos to better enable this. It also appears that many other videos only contain relatively short scenes, without the sorts of preambles seen in other media types. Practically speaking, the corpus therefore appears very much like a convenient "pick and mix" repository where users can select snippets of videos that suit their interests rather than watching entire films. Whereas the reasons for this style of viewing could be diverse, it is important to note that Alexa reports the average viewing time on YouPorn as only ≈9 minutes [1]. With such time limitations, uploaders (particularly commercial ones) must ensure that only the most interesting elements of their films are seen by viewers. Lastly, Figure 1 also shows the duration of videos weighted by the number of times they are watched. The curves are near identical, indicating that users do not have a particular preference for one duration but, rather, watch various durations equally often.

4.2 Content injection

An extremely important component of Porn 2.0 is the injection of content by users. We therefore inspect the frequency at which videos are uploaded into the corpus. Indeed, the short durations of the videos could come with significant churn to sustain the interest of the user base. Figure 2 first provides a CDF of the number of daily video uploads. On average, only 78 videos are added per day, a surprisingly modest figure compared to sites such as YouTube [4]. This low daily injection rate therefore suggests that rapid corpus expansion is not necessarily vital for the success of this platform. As a comparison, already in 2008, YouTube was reported to have well over 140 million videos — over 700 times more than YouPorn's current corpus of 183,639 videos. Despite this, according

[1]Some videos had bogus length fields (e.g., 1000 hours). Consequently, we manually removed all entries above 3 hours (74 videos), leaving 99.99% of the videos in the trace.

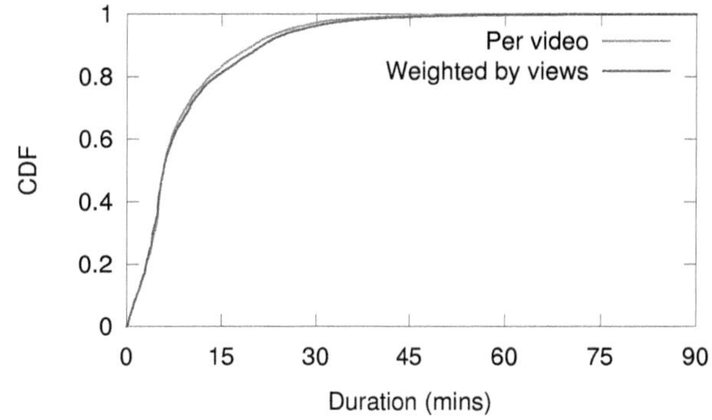

Figure 1: CDF of content duration.

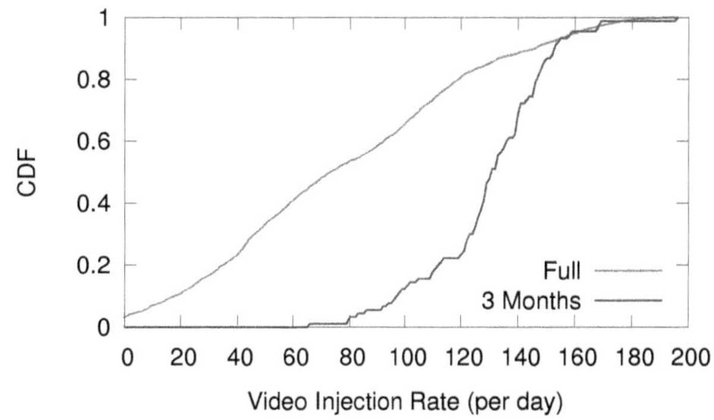

Figure 2: CDF of daily content uploads.

to Alexa, the number of pageviews for YouTube is just 100 times more than for YouPorn. This suggests that sheer volume of content is not necessary for the success of adult video streaming services. That said, Figure 2 does highlight that the number of daily uploads has increased notably over time, with an average rate of about 140 over the last 3 months of the trace.

Beyond these absolute figures, we also examine *who* uploads content. We find that only 5, 849 distinct usernames have ever uploaded over the entire 6 year history of YouPorn. Note this includes "Unknown" users with anonymous uploads (33k videos). Furthermore, as indicated in Figure 3, most users (56%) upload only a single video, with the majority (80%) uploading at most 5. Figure 3 also presents the number of submissions per user in the "am-

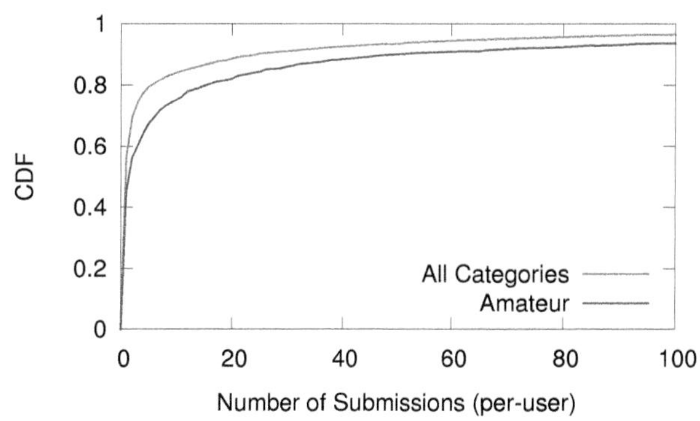

Figure 3: CDF of per user video uploads.

ateur" category, which one would initially imagine to have a far more proactive user-base. Even this category, however, shows very few uploads. In fact, overall, we observe 75 days during which no content was uploaded whatsoever.

This observation led us to perform manual inspection to better understand the nature of the uploads. We found that many uploads were actually provided by commercial producers. This observation extends to all categories, even "amateur". Figure 4 presents the daily upload rates over the entirety of YouPorn's existence. An upwards trend can be seen, suggesting an expanding base of uploaders. Investigation of these uploaders shows that 36% of the content is actually uploaded by YouPorn itself; a process that started almost 2 years after YouPorn's inception, with 39 videos, on average, being injected each day. These are all professional videos that are typically produced by a listed production studio. We conjecture that this may have been initiated, in part, to ensure a sufficient number of daily uploads. Regardless of the underlying reason, after YouPorn started uploading content, we observe that every day has new uploads, showing that YouPorn's own contributions have had a significant impact. In fact, without these contributions, the overall average daily upload rates would drop massively from 78 to 50 video per day. This can be seen in Figure 4 with extremely predictable and sustained upload rates boosting the overall uploads after year 2. Our observations therefore suggest that YouPorn is closer to a commercial platform than a user generated one.

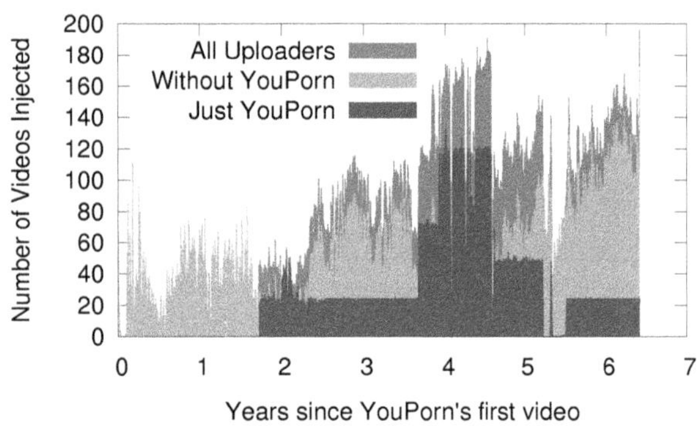

Figure 4: Breakdown for daily Upload rates (with and without YouPorn's contributions): During the first two years of YouPorn's existence, there were days without any new uploads. After this YouPorn itself has been uploading new videos, leading to a notable increase in the number of new uploads, suggesting that much of the content is not user-generated.

4.3 Content removal

So far, we have seen the number of videos added to YouPorn each day. An equally important aspect is how many videos are removed. Unlike most user generated content sites, YouPorn does not offer a straightforward way for users to remove their own content after upload. Instead, all removals must be requested — measuring removal levels therefore provides strong insight into the amount of content that deviates from YouPorn's policies (e.g., copyright issues).

YouPorn allocates each video a unique numerical identifier. These are selected from an incrementing pool of time-dependent identifiers. We surveyed a large range of the identifier space to collect the status of each video therein. We incrementally crawled all video identifiers between $7,692,093$ and $8,300,674$ in 1K blocks; this range covers March 2012–2013. Each identifier returns a status page, allowing us to ascertain the current status of each video upload.

Figure 5 shows the number of removals we observed across the measured identifier space. On average, we found that 11.7% of the content is removed. A number of notable spikes can also be seen; for example, we found that all videos were removed from a specific 1k identifier block. Manual inspection revealed many videos with production studios in their titles, suggesting possible copyright issues.

From this, one might assume that the majority of videos become active in the repository. However, we discovered other possible video statuses beyond "active" and "removed". We found a large number of videos that were classified as being "processed"[2]. This state is allocated to a video during the initial stages of its life when it is being encoded. It is therefore curious as to why many videos do not proceed beyond this state; on average, 61% of videos are still being processed even after several months of existence. We strongly suspect that some sort of (potentially manual) vetting procedure takes place. Consequently, only a minority of uploads are actually accepted for publication on YouPorn: only 18% of videos are active in the identifier range we studied. This also offers some explanation as to why the injection rates in YouPorn (particularly historic ones) are lower than could be expected for a repository of its prominence. Further, the need to vet content might also offer insight into why YouPorn started to upload a large number of its own videos.

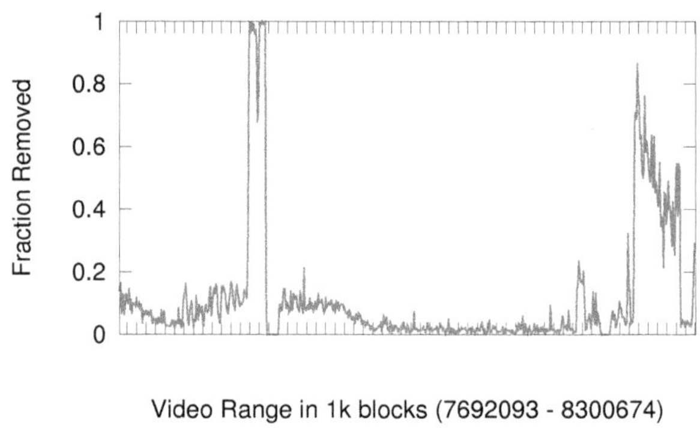

Figure 5: Removal rate of content.

4.4 Summary

We conclude that the users of such services do not particularly require huge novelty from the content available to them. It seems that a small number of new videos will still satisfy the demand. However, from the daily video uploads, it seems that the current user base requires new content to be available every day, forcing YouPorn to ensure a steady flow. Amongst the uploaded videos, only a limited fraction become available eventually with $\approx 10\%$ removed.

5. CONTENT POPULARITY

We have seen that YouPorn is a constantly expanding repository, with new (typically short) videos being uploaded on a daily basis. Next, it is important to understand the way in which users interact with this corpus. Particularly, we are interested in seeing the pop-

[2]We also note 8.6% of videos in other miscellaneous states, i.e., "failed" or "not available".

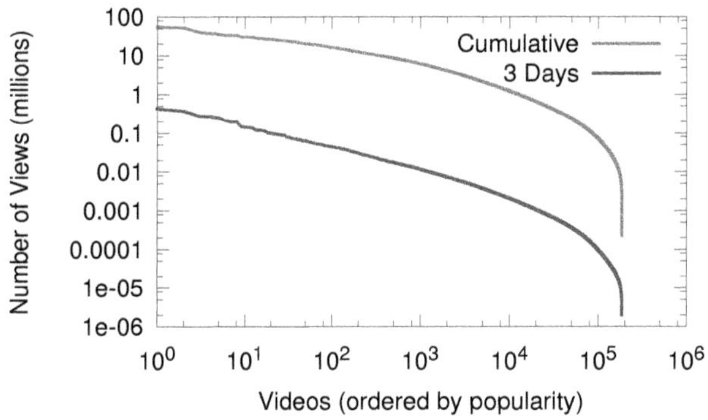

Figure 6: Number of views per video (log-log).

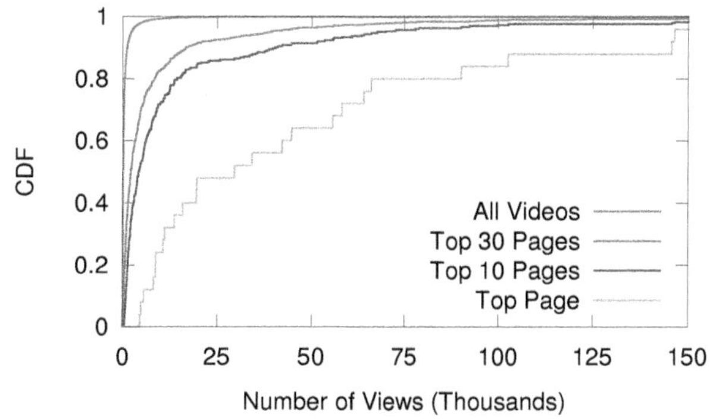

Figure 7: CDF of number of views per video.

ularity of individual objects, as indicated by the number of views they receive, and their respective importance in YouPorn.

5.1 Popularity: I'll take anything you've got

We begin by looking at the popularity of all videos taken within our traces. We rely on two different time windows: (*i*) the entirety of YouPorn's existence (cumulative) and (*ii*) a three day period.

One recurrent property that has been observed across many types of content repositories is a Zipf-like popularity distribution, evidenced by a straight line on a log-log plot. Figure 6 presents the number of views per video, on a log-log plot (ordered by rank) for both time windows. We observe a distinctive popularity skew, but not a straight line as one would expect from a Zipf distribution.

We make two complementary observations from Figure 6. First, the skew towards the "head" (or popular part) of the corpus is far less than has been previously observed in other UGC corpora. Specifically, the top 10% of YouPorn videos receive only 65% of the views. In comparison, the top 10% of videos generate 80% of views on YouTube [13], and 82% of views on Vimeo [33]. Second, the "tail" (or unpopular part) are correspondingly more popular. Nearly 93% of YouPorn's videos receive at least 10k views over their lifetime when inspecting the *snapshot* trace. In comparison, only 1.9% of videos on Vimeo generate more than 10k views. Further into the "tail", all videos in the YouPorn catalogue have at least 226 views, whereas fewer than 47% of Vimeo videos have at least 200 views.

Two explanations are possible. One possibility is that videos uploaded to YouPorn are generally of a higher quality than on other UGC sites; indeed, manual inspection reveals a wealth of professionally produced content. As such, a higher quality could encourage users to view a more diverse body of content. A second possibility is that users have a greater flexibility in their content selection requirements, i.e., users are not particularly selective in what they choose to watch, thereby resulting in views being more evenly distributed. Our user study (Section 7) suggests that the latter may well be true, with many users having far looser interest constraints than traditionally understood. For example, in mainstream VoD services, users often have relatively tight constraints on what they wish to watch. This might be a certain programme, a serialised TV show, or a particular genre [29]. Without these constraints, however, much larger sets of objects become acceptable for consumption, leading to a lesser skew in the popularity.

That said, flexibility does not explain the skew - if content selection were entirely flexible, why do some objects gain more views? One cause could be the way viewers discover content to watch. For instance, users of other user-generated video corpora such as YouTube may have particular videos in mind, driven by URL links from other websites, such as social networks. It is believed that up to 45% of requests to YouTube come from social sources [38]. Similarly, Borghol *et al.* [10] found that an uploader's social network (on YouTube) is one of the strongest predictors of video popularity. In contrast, users are less likely to share YouPorn links on social networks such as Facebook, or even discuss specific videos with friends. We conjecture that a lack of external referrals from other websites helps create an information bottleneck that prevents users from discovering the exact URLs corresponding to individual videos, thereby forcing most viewers to find videos through YouPorn's built-in facilities (like browsing or search). When combined with the inherent user flexibility, this likely predisposes any "generic" user to retrieve content from the easiest source possible, e.g., front-page listings.

To verify the above assertions, we correlate the number of views a video receives with the default front page browsing order. Figure 7 presents the outputs of this analysis for the *3 day* trace. We observe that the majority of views do, indeed, come from easy to access items. On average, videos on the front page[3] achieve 55k views, compared to an average of 9k for the top 30 pages. These can then be both contrasted with the overall average of just 603 views per video.

Our observations reflect well the type of behaviour one would expect from such a content repository. With a corpus in which it is difficult to differentiate objects, it is likely that only the most dedicated viewers (e.g., ones with special interests) would take the effort to find particular items of interest. More generic viewers seek easy access content, which, of course, creates a certain level of skew because all users are presented with the *same* easy access content items. However, due to the churn of the content, these objects are quickly pushed from the front pages, thereby flattening the popularity distribution into the one shown in Figure 6.

5.2 Popularity: But now I've changed my mind

Next, we look at how video popularity evolves over time, driven by regular content injection (Section 4.2) and what appears to be a largely flexible and browsing-driven user base (Section 5.1).

To gain insight into how videos accumulate views over time, we look at the distribution of views based on a content item's age. Figure 8 presents a log-log plot of the number of views per video, ranked by popularity. Each curve shows the distribution of videos with a given age (note that the tails are different due to a varying number of videos being uploaded on those individual days). We

[3]This is a conservative estimate as we do not include "featured" videos, which receive a more prominent status on the front page.

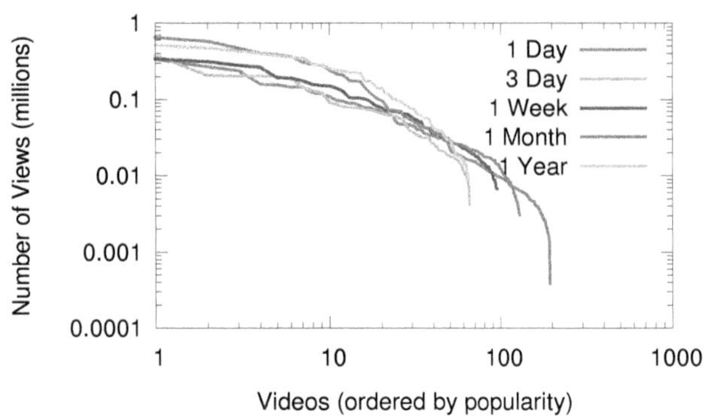

Figure 8: Number of views per video (log-log), for different time windows.

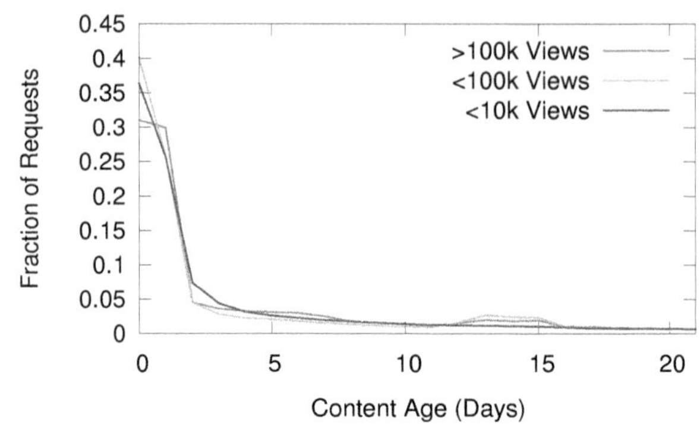

Figure 9: Evolution of number of views over time (per video).

find that videos uploaded a long time (e.g., a year) ago have not received particularly more views than recently uploaded ones. This is in stark contrast to prior UGC studies (e.g., [13, 37]) that show far greater cumulative views for older videos.

To explore this, we inspect the *3 days traces* to ascertain the most popular content ages during this short period. There is a distinct preference for recently uploaded videos. Content that was uploaded on the same day as the *snapshot* trace had collected on average 28k views, in contrast to an average of only 584 views for all other content ages. That said, we find notable exceptions: the content age with the third highest average number of views is 6 years, suggesting that there is no inherent reason why older content would not be suitable for viewing today. Note that browsing options (e.g., "most viewed") make such videos easy to find.

To understand how the characteristics of particular videos affect this rapid aging process, we inspect the *daily* traces, which show how the popularity of individual videos evolve over a more extended period of time. First, we partition videos into popularity groups based on the number of views they receive during their first day. We then average the number of views per day received by each video, and normalise that as a fraction of their total view count. Figure 9 presents the results. We observe a sharp decline in the number of views per day across all popularity groups, with the biggest decrease occurring after the second day.

We now draw a conclusion. Continuing from the discussions in Section 5.1, we see that the previously discussed user flexibility and browsing behaviour has a direct (and perhaps damaging) effect on temporal trends. YouPorn displays content on its front page in order of upload date (and then rating), thereby making more recent content easiest to find. Accessing content older than one day requires browsing through $\approx$4–5 pages of listings, a process which many users may find cumbersome.

Only the most popular videos ($>$ 100k views) can resist this decay, with similar viewing figures being recorded on the first and second day.[4] After the third day of their publication, however, even extremely popular videos are likely to be pushed down by $\approx$10 pages, making it significantly harder for users to discover them. Thus, on the third day, they immediately begin to exhibit the traits of their less popular counterparts, as their viewing figures plummet. Future views are then limited to users who are prepared to more proactively seek content of interest. Relating this to traditional UGC, Crane and Sornette [18] provide a classification of video types (memoryless, viral, junk and quality). This would place typical YouPorn videos into the category of junk. These are videos that experience a short burst of activity, followed by a popularity collapse. In comparison, such videos belong to the smallest category of YouTube videos [18, 32].

Therefore, YouPorn videos seem to have developed temporal properties similar to news and weather shows [6], which are highly temporally dependent (e.g., weather forecasts from the previous day are rarely of interest). However, contrary to news and weather content, there is no temporal dependency in adult content — videos created a year ago would still seem to be suitable for viewing today. Instead, it seems that this behaviour is formed from user flexibility: many videos meet the content consumption requirements of most users and, hence, are readily satisfied with the age-based listing on the front page.

5.3 Summary

We find that video popularity in YouPorn follows a far less skewed distribution than traditionally understood. The reason lies in the way users discover content, relying heavily on front page browsing. Due to the non-interest-specific nature of this default browsing, we conclude that most users have quite loose interest constraints, allowing them to be satisfied by a potentially large portion of the corpus. This results in a rapid decline in the number of page views; most videos die out quickly as they get pushed down the browsing order by newer published items. Consequently, we deduce that the level of skew observed is actually largely an artifact of the way content is presented to users, rather than any inherent aspect of the video content itself.

6. CATEGORY ANALYSIS

The previous sections have looked at the corpus as a single collection. However, videos within the corpus can also be listed under one or more category pages. Although these categories do not offer definitive information on the semantic nature of the videos, they allow us to inspect more targeted groups of content and their role in helping users to discover content of interest.

6.1 Category primer

In total, 62 categories[5] are available on YouPorn, spanning a range of interests. For each video, an initial category is chosen at upload time. Videos can also later be categorised further by other users once the content is published. Whilst this community-driven nature of categories means that some videos could be incorrectly

[4] Highly rated videos will appear at the top of the browsing list for the previous day.

[5] In fact, 63 exist but one was not populated; it had only been created a few days before the crawl and therefore we excluded it.

classified, category-specific web pages offer an additional mechanism by which users can browse content of a particular type; a mechanism that many users seem to find helpful (Section 7). We emphasise that categories on YouPorn are not free-form tags similar to folksonomies found on other Web 2.0 websites. In contrast to folksonomies, user choice is restricted to the well defined terms allowed by YouPorn.

We first inspect the number of videos in each category, shown in Figure 10. Due to their explicit nature, the categories have been pseudo-anonymised using their first two letters.[6] We observe a significant skew: the top 20% of genres contain 57% of the videos, whilst the bottom 20% contains less than 2%. In fact, only 11% of content belongs to the bottom 50%. YouPorn's categories therefore consist of a much longer tail than traditionally seen in UGC services [15], with far more categories for users to choose from.

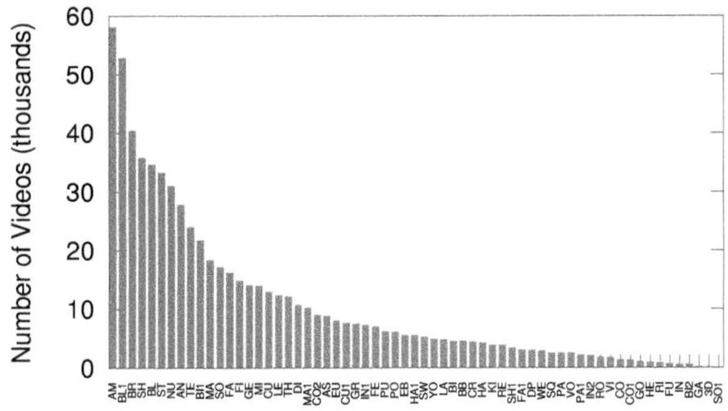

Figure 10: Number of videos per category (ordered by number of videos in the category).

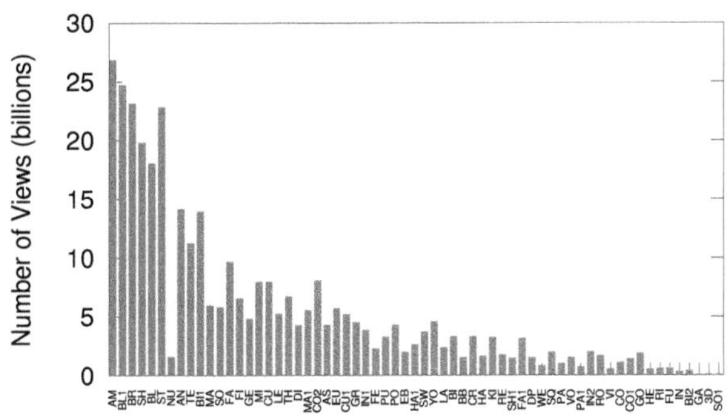

Figure 11: Number of views per Category (ordered by number of videos in the category).

We also inspect the collective popularity of these various categories. Figure 11 presents the accumulated views for each category. We observe a trend similar to Figure 10, with well populated categories receiving many views. The most notable exception is "NU" (videos without a category), which does extremely poorly in relation to its size in the corpus. Whereas 17% of the corpus has no category, these videos only collect 2% of the views. Table 2 provides an overview of the top 20 categories, ranked by size.

6.2 Efficiency of categories

We have seen that categories play an extremely important role in discovering content in YouPorn, and that not participating in this process has dire consequences in terms of views for uncategorised videos. However, categories offer insight into the interests of both uploaders and users, as well as their relationship. In a sense, Porn 2.0 sites could be considered as a form of marketplace where uploaders present their videos for consumption, competing for audience views. One should therefore strive for a marketplace in which the supply for a category exactly matches its demand. We capture this principle through the concept of corpus *efficiency* (or, more accurately, *inefficiency*). An efficient corpus is one in which the fraction of views for a category exactly matches the fraction of the corpus that the category constitutes. We measure the inefficiency, $\mathcal{I}$, for each category as:

$$\mathcal{I} = \begin{cases} \frac{V}{C} - 1, & \text{if } V > C. \\ -(\frac{C}{V}) + 1, & \text{otherwise.} \end{cases} \quad (1)$$

where V is the fraction of views that the category receives, and C is the fraction of the corpus that the category constitutes. As a video can have multiple categories tagged to it, we utilise two ways of calculating these fractions. The first approach,[7] termed *inefficiency*, attributes one view to each category that the video is part of; consequently, a video with two categories, "BL" and "AM", will have one view allocated to each. Obviously, this first approach will also artificially inflate the corpus size. The second approach, which we term *weighted inefficiency*, splits the views of a video equally between all categories it belongs to. Specifically, the number of the video's views attributed to that category are factored by $\frac{1}{\kappa}$, where κ represents the number of categories a video has. In this case, the number of videos attributed to the category are similarly factored down by $\frac{1}{\kappa}$.

For both weighted and unweighted inefficiency, if the value of $\mathcal{I}$ is above 0, it means that a category receives a disproportionately large share of the views, whilst a value below 0 indicates that a category receives disproportionately fewer views than would be

	Videos	Views (bn)	Inefficiency	Colocation
AM	58114	26.82	-0.11	5.69
BL1	52814	24.69	-0.10	6.37
BR	40447	23.14	0.12	6.79
SH	35815	19.81	0.08	7.44
BL	34607	18.04	0.02	6.67
ST	33259	22.81	0.34	7.10
NU	31004	1.59	-8.97	1.00
AN	27832	14.13	-0.01	5.65
TE	23999	11.24	-0.09	6.61
BI1	21667	13.94	0.26	6.57
MA	18348	5.96	-0.58	5.74
SO	17204	5.81	-0.52	5.63
FA	16240	9.66	0.16	7.64
FI	14844	6.55	-0.16	6.83
GE	14093	4.84	-0.49	5.44
MI	13944	7.96	0.11	6.74
CU	12959	7.98	0.20	7.46
LE	12315	5.21	-0.21	4.67
TH	12097	6.71	0.08	6.07
DI	10660	4.29	-0.27	6.33

Table 2: Category rankings ordered by number of videos. Categories appearing in other top 20 rankings (e.g. inefficiency) are not necessarily captured in this table.

[6]We make mappings available online at `http://www.eecs.qmul.ac.uk/~tysong/yp/mappings.txt`

[7]Unless otherwise stated, this calculation of inefficiency is used throughout the rest of this section.

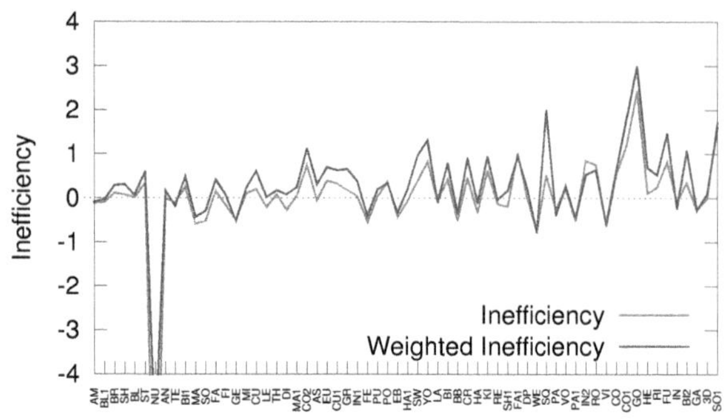

Figure 12: Inefficiency value for each category (ordered by number of videos). For null, $\mathcal{I} = -8.96$ and weighted $\mathcal{I} = -5.51$ (this is cut-off to improve readability).

expected. More generally, a value above 0 represents a category in which "demand outweighs supply" (popular), and a value below 0 represents a category in which "supply outstrips demand" (unpopular). This provides a normalised view of popularity, in contrast to the absolute one given in Figure 11.

Figure 12 presents the inefficiency levels for all categories, with both measures of inefficiency showing very similar trends. First, we observe that using the absolute number of views a category receives is somewhat misleading. The category with the highest viewing figures ("AM") actually receives fewer views than could be expected from its size in the corpus ($\mathcal{I} = -0.11$). It seems that this category collects views through its dominance in the corpus, rather than through an excessive demand for the genre. This lack of efficiency is observable in all other categories too — several unexpected genres have a disproportionately large number of views, whereas other genres have too many videos and too few views. 27 categories have a disproportionately large number of videos in comparison to the views received ($\mathcal{I} < 0$), whereas 35 categories are disproportionately popular compared to their size in the corpus ($\mathcal{I} > 0$).[8] No categories were found to be truly market efficient with "BL" coming closest at 0.016, alongside 14 others that fall between -0.1 and 0.1.

6.3 Category Colocation

The previous subsection has shown that there are some notable market inefficiencies in YouPorn's corpus. These inefficiencies could offer a significant opportunity for uploaders. For example, theorists believe that users constantly seek out new forms of visual stimulation [31]. Therefore, some less populated categories would be suitable for targeted content injections as their demand outstrips supply.

However, the ability to allocate a video to multiple categories (i.e., category colocation), could undermine the independence of the samples — a video in multiple categories will be far more visible through category-based browsing. To investigate this, Figure 13 re-plots Figure 12 whilst also presenting the average number of colocations for each category. For example, Figure 13 shows that "MA1" is, on average, tagged in a video alongside 6 other categories. We observe a strong correlation between inefficiency[9] and colocation, with a correlation coefficient of 0.66. For instance, the "GO" category gets 3 times as many views as could be expected from its proportion of the corpus. However, it is by far the most colocated category. On average, videos categorised as "GO" are also placed in 10.36 other categories. We find that 4 out of the top 10 categories, ranked by the colocation level, are also in the top 10 ranked by normalised popularity. This confirms our suspicion (backed by the small-scale user study; see Section 7) that category-based browsing is an intensively used tool.

[8] Interestingly, many of the more unusual niche categories (e.g. "GO", "IN2", "FA1") fall in this area.

[9] Note, inefficiency also offers a measure of normalised popularity.

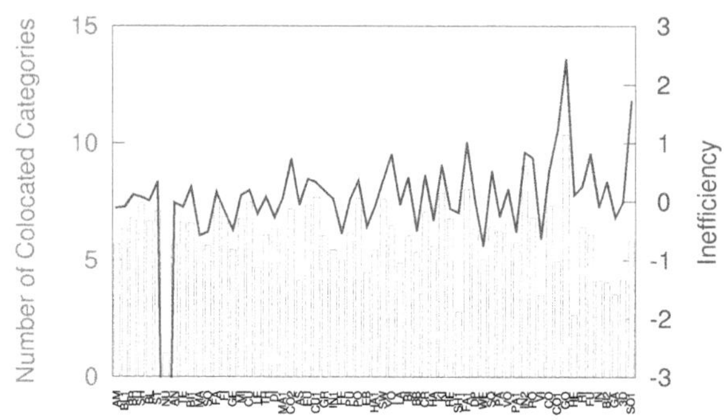

Figure 13: Number of colocated categories (ordered by number of videos in the category).

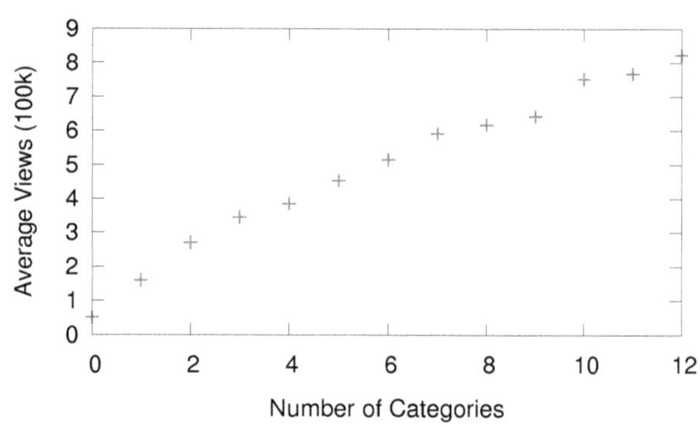

Figure 14: Number of views correlated with number of categories allocated to video.

To further validate the impact of colocation, Figure 14 presents the average number of views against the number of categories a video belongs to. We observe an almost linear trend in which videos belonging to multiple categories get more views. On average, videos without any category receive just 51k views, compared to 452k for those with 5 categories. We conclude that category tags appear to be a significant factor that contributes to views. It is quite possible that uploaders, particularly commercial ones, might exploit this observation. In fact, not being aware of the importance of categories can have dire consequences for video popularity. We observe that uncategorised videos appear in the bottom 20 most unpopular categories ranked by absolute viewing figures (and the least popular measured by normalised popularity).

6.4 Summary

We conclude that users in YouPorn rely heavily on category information for discovering content of interest. This appears to be primarily driven by category-based browsing; this observation is best highlighted by the almost linear relationship between the number of views a video receives and the number of categories it is listed in. Obviously, this raises questions about exactly how inherently important categories are, as the tagging of a video in as many as 10 categories suggests a low level of accuracy in many cases. Instead, it seems probable that many users use categories as a very coarse way of targeting interest groups. Once again, this suggests a level of flexibility that is far less prevalent in traditional media types. We also find that this information is not being exploited well in YouPorn, with a poor level of market efficiency being shown in the corpus (i.e., often uploaders do not target their content well).

7. ELASTICITY IN CONTENT CONSUMPTION

Our results have highlighted a number of characteristics that might be collectively taken as implying that users do not visit YouPorn with specific videos in mind: duration does not matter (Figure 1); users tend to simply go for the most easily accessible videos (Figure 7); the number of views depends largely on the video being listed on the front page (Figure 9); and the number of views is correlated with the number of categories a video is listed in (Figure 14). These observations lead us to hypothesise that a significant portion of users are therefore quite flexible in what they watch.

To confirm this apparent elasticity in users' content consumption requirements (and to verify other findings), we performed a small-scale user study, recruiting 46 respondents over social networks and mailing lists. Consistent with our expectations, we find that 85% of users find it easy or just slightly difficult to find content of interest, with 15% saying they found it difficult. 43% of survey respondents also said that over $3/5$ of the videos they found match their interests.

We believe that this type of flexibility sheds light on some of the results obtained in the previous sections. Confirming our earlier suspicions, the survey shows that the observed findings do, indeed, seem to arise from users' dependencies on the order in which content is displayed on the default front page, and on category-specific pages: when asked what characteristics they use to find content (multiple answers were allowed), we found that only 22% of users ever visit the site with a pre-determined video in mind. Instead, a large share of the respondents appear to utilise what we have previously termed "flexible" ways to discover content: 63% rely on browsing the front page, 59% use category-based browsing, and 50% utilise the search functionality. Further, in-line with our earlier conjecture, we found that only 9% visit YouPorn through links from other sites. This is unlike the behavior of YouTube users, for instance, who rely more on web search engines [19] and external links [38], rather than browsing. It is also unlike other types of repositories, where users primarily visit to watch specific videos (e.g., sports games [11]).

When combining the above findings, it becomes likely that the more flexible users could all be satisfied with a relatively small set of videos taken from a large range of acceptable ones. We argue that this flexibility should therefore be leveraged by the content distribution infrastructure. Specifically, where many videos could satisfy the user, we posit that the content distribution infrastructure should guide users towards those particular ones that also have a low network cost (e.g., available nearby). This could improve user quality of experience and reduce network overhead, which benefits other users as well as ISPs. Considering users' predisposition towards browsing the front page, this could be done easily: instead of ordering videos by recency of upload (a common design pattern), the different browsing pages generated by the web front-end could also take into account which videos are available near to the viewer. Most simply, nearby videos that match a user's interests could be placed at the top of the front page.

Our user survey indicates that only a small amount of shared content would be required: 87% of users watch under 10 videos a session, while 43% watch 3 or less. Assuming a large intersection between these flexible users' interests, a relatively small amount of (generic) content would likely satisfy the demands of many viewers. This suggests the approach would be highly feasible in this domain. However, it must be ensured that optimising the delivery infrastructure is not done at the expense of a user's quality of experience. A key challenge here would be to ensure that this small amount of content is kept sufficiently "fresh". Only 24% of our survey respondents stated that they do not get bored easily and would watch a video multiple times. Thus, it is important that users are given sufficient choice to ensure that they are provided with novel items they would wish to watch.

8. SUMMARY AND FUTURE WORK

This paper presented the first detailed measurement study of Internet adult media distribution, focussing on the YouPorn website. Three key aspects of this system have been inspected: the corpus, the nature of content popularity and the impact of categories. We found that YouPorn is a hugely popular service with over 60 billion views recorded from a corpus of 183k videos. Unlike traditional UGC websites, there is an extremely prominent commercial element to its content, as well as a seemingly well managed vetting procedure. We observed a number of other interesting properties, particularly relating to the rapid decay of content popularity as measured from the number of views, as well as users' dependency on category metadata to find content that matches their interests. Further investigation uncovered the main reason behind these observations: the predominant use of YouPorn's browsing options. Particularly, this is driven by the apparent flexibility that most users have when accessing adult media: they do not seek a specific video, rather, they search for *any* video that falls with certain (broad) interest constraints. We posit that this is a characteristic that likely exists more generally in other multimedia repositories, but to varying extents. We therefore propose to exploit this observation by shaping users' browsing behaviour towards videos with a low network cost. In fact, this could be done with the intention of optimising any metric. The constantly expanding size and popularity of these repositories means that this is an approach that may become increasingly necessary to scale content delivery.

Due to its infancy, there is a significant amount of future work that could focus on adult video streaming. The dataset presented in this paper has focussed on aggregated system-level and video-level information. Whereas this offers insights into various corpus and popularity aspects, it does not provide user-level analysis. The next stage of our work will therefore focus on this type of data to understand exactly how individual users interact with such websites. This will capture their behaviour (e.g., skipping), as well as things like regional differences between user groups. Although not explored in this paper, our survey indicates that these elements are potentially quite different from traditional media. Such data will also allow us to gain a better understanding of things like traffic volumes and cacheability. We also intend to further develop the ideas explored in Section 7. Through user-level data, for example, we will be able to understand the current intersection of user interests and requests. More extensive user testing will also complement this. Beyond these targeted avenues of study, there are more general topics of interest, including social networking aspects and deeper analysis of the "2.0" elements of these services (e.g., ratings, comments, and recommendations).

9. REFERENCES

[1] Alexa. http://www.alexa.com/.

[2] Youporn. http://www.youporn.com.

[3] Youporn.com is now a 100% redis site. https://groups.google.com/forum/?fromgroups=#!topic/redis-db/d4QcWV0p-YM.

[4] Youtube statistics. http://www.youtube.com/yt/press/en-GB/statistics.html.

[5] Cisco visual networking index: Forecast and methodology, 2011-2016, 2012.

[6] ABRAHAMSSON, H., AND NORDMARK, M. Program popularity and viewer behaviour in a large TV-on-demand system. In *Proc. ACM IMC* (2012).

[7] ANTHONY, S. Just how big are porn sites? http://www.extremetech.com/computing/123929-just-how-big-are-porn-sites.

[8] APOSTOLOPOULOS, J. G., TAN, W.-T., AND WEE, S. J. Video streaming: Concepts, algorithms, and systems. *HP Laboratories, report HPL-2002-260* (2002).

[9] ATTWOOD, F. *Porn.com: Making sense of online pornography*, vol. 48. Peter Lang, 2010.

[10] BORGHOL, Y., ARDON, S., CARLSSON, N., EAGER, D., AND MAHANTI, A. The untold story of the clones: Content-agnostic factors that impact YouTube video popularity. In *Proc. of ACM SIGKDD* (2012).

[11] BRAMPTON, A., MACQUIRE, A., FRY, M., RAI, I. A., RACE, N. J., AND MATHY, L. Characterising and exploiting workloads of highly interactive video-on-demand. *Multimedia systems 15*, 1 (2009), 3–17.

[12] CARROLL, J. S., PADILLA-WALKER, L. M., NELSON, L. J., OLSON, C. D., BARRY, C. M., AND MADSEN, S. D. Generation XXX: Pornography acceptance and use among emerging adults. *Journal of adolescent research 23*, 1 (2008), 6–30.

[13] CHA, M., KWAK, H., RODRIGUEZ, P., AHN, Y.-Y., AND MOON, S. Analyzing the Video Popularity Characteristics of Large-scale User Generated Content Systems. *IEEE/ACM Trans. Netw. 17*, 5 (2009), 1357–1370.

[14] CHA, M., RODRIGUEZ, P., CROWCROFT, J., MOON, S., AND AMATRIAIN, X. Watching television over an IP network. In *Proc. ACM IMC* (2008).

[15] CHENG, X., DALE, C., AND LIU, J. Statistics and social network of YouTube videos. In *Proc. IEEE IWQoS* (2008).

[16] COOPER, A. Sexuality and the internet: Surfing into the new millennium. *CyberPsychology & Behavior 1*, 2 (1998), 187–193.

[17] COOPERSMITH, J. Does your mother know what you really do? The changing nature and image of computer-based pornography. *History and Technology 22*, 1 (2006), 1–25.

[18] CRANE, R., AND SORNETTE, D. Robust dynamic classes revealed by measuring the response function of a social system. *Proceedings of The National Academy of Sciences 105*, 41 (2008), 15649–15653.

[19] CUNNINGHAM, S. J., AND NICHOLS, D. M. How people find videos. In *Proc. ACM/IEEE JCDL* (2008).

[20] DANEBACK, K., SEVCIKOVA, A., MÅNSSON, S.-A., AND ROSS, M. W. Outcomes of using the internet for sexual purposes: Fulfilment of sexual desires. *Sexual Health 10* (2012), 26–31.

[21] DINES, G. *Pornland: How Porn Has Hijacked Our Sexuality*. Beacon Press, 2010.

[22] GAO, P., LIU, T., CHEN, Y., WU, X., ELKHATIB, Y., AND EDWARDS, C. The measurement and modeling of a P2P streaming video service. In *GridNets* (2008).

[23] GUO, L., TAN, E., CHEN, S., XIAO, Z., AND ZHANG, X. The stretched exponential distribution of internet media access patterns. In *Proc. ACM PODC* (2008).

[24] HEI, X., LIANG, C., LIANG, J., LIU, Y., AND ROSS, K. W. A measurement study of a large-scale P2P IPTV system. *IEEE Trans. Multimedia 9*, 8 (2007), 1672–1687.

[25] HU, W., WU, O., CHEN, Z., FU, Z., AND MAYBANK, S. Recognition of pornographic web pages by classifying texts and images. *IEEE Trans. Pattern Analysis and Machine Intelligence 29*, 6 (2007), 1019–1034.

[26] HURLEY, R., PRUSTY, S., SOROUSH, H., WALLS, R. J., ALBRECHT, J., CECCHET, E., LEVINE, B. N., LIBERATORE, M., LYNN, B., AND WOLAK, J. Measurement and analysis of child pornography trafficking on P2P networks. In *Proc. WWW* (2013).

[27] LABOVITZ, C., LEKEL-JOHNSON, S., MCPHERSON, D., OBERHEIDE, J., AND JAHANIAN, F. Internet inter-domain traffic. In *Proc. SIGCOMM* (2010).

[28] MEHTA, M. D., AND PLAZA, D. Content analysis of pornographic images available on the internet. *The Information Society 13*, 2 (1997), 153–161.

[29] NENCIONI, G., SASTRY, N., CHANDARIA, J., AND CROWCROFT, J. Understanding and decreasing the network footprint of over-the-top on-demand delivery of TV content. In *Proc. WWW* (2013).

[30] OGAS, O., AND GADDAM, S. *A billion wicked thoughts: what the world's largest experiment reveals about human desire*. Dutton, 2011.

[31] PAASONEN, S. *Carnal Resonance: Affect and Online Pornography*. MIT Press, 2011.

[32] PINTO, H., ALMEIDA, J. M., AND GONÇALVES, M. A. Using early view patterns to predict the popularity of YouTube videos. In *Proc. ACM WSDM* (2013).

[33] SASTRY, N. How to tell head from tail in user-generated content corpora. In *Proc. ICWSM* (2012).

[34] SCHUHMACHER, M., ZIRN, C., AND VÖLKER, J. Exploring YouPorn categories, tags, and nicknames for pleasant recommendations. In *Proc. SEXI* (2013).

[35] SCHULZE, H., AND MOCHALSKI, K. Internet study 2007-2009. ipoque Report, 2009.

[36] SULER, J. The online disinhibition effect. *Cyberpsychology & Behavior 7*, 3 (2004), 321–326.

[37] SZABO, G., AND HUBERMAN, B. A. Predicting the popularity of online content. *CACM 53*, 8 (2010), 80–88.

[38] WATTENHOFER, M., INTERIAN, Y., VAVER, J., AND BROXTON, T. Catching a viral video. In *Proc. Workshop on Social Interaction Analysis and Service Providers* (2010).

[39] WONDRACEK, G., HOLZ, T., PLATZER, C., KIRDA, E., AND KRUEGEL, C. Is the internet for porn? An insight into the online adult industry. In *Proc. Workshop on Economics of Information Security* (2010).

[40] YU, H., ZHENG, D., ZHAO, B. Y., AND ZHENG, W. Understanding user behavior in large-scale video-on-demand systems. *ACM SIGOPS Operating Systems Review 40*, 4 (2006), 333–344.

[41] ZINK, M., SUH, K., GU, Y., AND KUROSE, J. Characteristics of youtube network traffic at a campus network–measurements, models, and implications. *Computer Networks 53*, 4 (2009), 501–514.

From Paris to Tokyo: On the Suitability of ping to Measure Latency

Cristel Pelsser
Internet Initiative Japan
Tokyo, Japan
cristel@iij.ad.jp

Luca Cittadini
Roma Tre University
Rome, Italy
ratm@dia.uniroma3.it

Stefano Vissicchio
Universite catholique de Louvain
Louvain-la-Neuve, Belgium
stefano.vissicchio@uclouvain.be

Randy Bush
Internet Initiative Japan
Tokyo, Japan
randy@psg.com

ABSTRACT

Monitoring Internet performance and measuring user quality of experience are drawing increased attention from both research and industry. To match this interest, large-scale measurement infrastructures have been constructed. We believe that this effort must be combined with a critical review and calibrarion of the tools being used to measure performance.

In this paper, we analyze the suitability of `ping` for delay measurement. By performing several experiments on different source and destination pairs, we found cases in which ping gave very poor estimates of delay and jitter as they might be experienced by an application. In those cases, delay was heavily dependent on the flow identifier, even if only one IP path was used. For accurate delay measurement we propose to replace the ping tool with an adaptation of `paris-traceroute` which supports delay and jitter estimation, without being biased by per-flow network load balancing.

Categories and Subject Descriptors

C.2.3 [**Computer-Communication Networks**]: Network Operations—*Network monitoring*; C.4 [**Performance of Systems**]: Measurement techniques

General Terms

Measurement, Performance

Keywords

Ping; delay; jitter; load-balancing

IMC'13, October 23–25, 2013, Barcelona, Spain.

http://dx.doi.org/10.1145/2504730.2504765.

1. INTRODUCTION

With the Internet carrying more and more critical traffic, network performance becomes ever more important. Hence, network operators need to constantly measure their networks in order to detect and troubleshoot performance degradation which can be experienced by users and applications.

Growing interest in network performance measurement has translated into the deployment of a number of large-scale end-to-end measurement infrastructures such as the RIPE Atlas [13], RIPE TTM [14], BISmark [19] and M-Lab projects [7], and infrastructures such as the one of SamKnows probes [17]. Those infrastructures make the issues of how we measure Internet performance even more significant. For example, few basic measurement tools, like `ping`, `traceroute`, and `paris-traceroute`, can be used in performance measurements from Atlas probes.

We believe that it is imperative to calibrate these basic tools to ensure accurate characterization of Internet performance. We focus on ping, one of the most commonly used tools to measure delay and jitter.

By running a few manual experiments with ping, we discovered an unexpectedly high variance in the measurements even when they were conducted within a single ISP. Hence, we decided to take a more rigorous approach to understand whether such a surprising delay variability depended on some specific features of the network, on some bias of ping itself, or both.

In this paper, we assume that a set of fields, identifying the flow to which a packet belongs, is typically used by network devices to perform load-balancing. We rely on Augustin et al. [1] definition's of flow. We discovered that most of the delay variability that ping reported was due to ping sending probes belonging to different flows. This variance is likely due to diversity and redundancy of paths at different layers. In contrast, the delay variability was much less for probes belonging to the same flow. From an application perspective, this means that delay and jitter can vary from flow to flow, that is, the network may not perform as expected from ping results on specific flows. More importantly, applications that use several transport channels (e.g., to transport different audio, video, and data streams as in videoconferencing) should not assume that delay is consistent across channels.

The remainder of the paper is structured as follows. We cover background information and illustrate our measurement methodology in Section 2. We describe the results of our experiments in Section 3. We compare to related work in Section 4. Finally, we discuss the implications of our findings in Section 5.

2. MEASURING PER-FLOW DELAY

In this section, we describe some background, introduce the `tokyo-ping` tool that we developed and refined based on the work of paris-traceroute [1], and we detail our measurement methods.

2.1 Background

Tuples of source IP address, source port, destination IP address, and destination port are used to identify TCP flows. Load-balancing and redundancy mechanisms, such as *Equal Cost Multi-Path (ECMP)* and *Link Aggregation Group (LAG)*, commonly rely on hashes over these tuples to map an incoming packet to an outgoing physical interface. Routers performing layer-4 hashing often use bytes 12-19 of the IP header and bytes 1-4 of the IP payload [1]. In the following, we refer to a single combination of those twelve bytes as a *flow-id*. Note that the flow-id of an ICMP packet is composed of the type, code, and checksum.

Source port	**Destination port**
Length	Checksum

Figure 1: UDP header [15]. Fields in bold are part of the flow-id.

Type	**Code**	**Checksum**
Identifier		Sequence Number

Figure 2: ICMP echo message [16]. Echo request messages have type=8 and code=0. Echo reply messages have type=0 and code=0.

Type	**Code**	**Checksum**
unused (zero)		
IP Header + 64 bits of payload		

Figure 3: ICMP port unreachable message [16]. Type and code fields are both set to 3.

In our experiments, we used both UDP and ICMP probes. Figs. 1 and 2 show the structure of a UDP and an ICMP probe, respectively. When replying to an ICMP probe, the target host simply echoes the ICMP payload back in an echo reply message, which looks exactly the same as the probe except the type field is set to 8 instead of 0 (Fig. 2). When replying to a UDP probe, a target host generates an ICMP port unreachable message (Fig. 3) including the offending IP header and the first eight bytes of the offending IP payload, which map to the UDP header. Classic ping and traceroute emit probes that do not keep the flow-id constant, so their output is affected by the presence of load balancing. Paris-traceroute [1] is a traceroute-like tool which overcomes this limitation by keeping the fields that contribute to the flow-id (i.e., the fields in bold in Figs. 1 and 2) set to user-specified constants.

2.2 Adapting Paris-Traceroute

To isolate delay behavior of different flows, we used a modified version of paris-traceroute, which we called `tokyo-ping` [5]. The tokyo-ping tool reports delay as the Round-Trip Time (RTT) between a given source-destination pair using a user-specified flow-id. The main difference from paris-traceroute is that our tool keeps the flow-id of the return path constant when probing servers. Tokyo-ping supports both UDP and ICMP probes, and can be configured to emit probes with the same length as ping probes.

To measure RTT, tokyo-ping considers the flow-id of both the probes and the responses. For ICMP probes, responses are automatically guaranteed to keep a constant flow-id. In fact, a response to an ICMP probe contains the same payload as the probe, but has a different type value, hence a different checksum (Fig. 2). The return flow-id cannot be controlled by the probe source, making it impossible to explore the return paths. However, there is a one-to-one mapping between the flow-id of the probe and the flow-id of the response.

In general, the same does not hold for UDP probes. For UDP probes, the flow-id of the response depends on the payload of the ICMP error message (see Fig. 3), which is the IP header followed by the first eight bytes of the probe, i.e., the UDP header (Fig.1). Note that the UDP payload influences the UDP checksum, which in turn influences the ICMP checksum in the response. The original paris-traceroute only supports control of the return flow-id when targeting routers. We extend the technique in [1] to predict the ICMP message generated at a destination host (rather than an intermediate router) and then craft the UDP payload of the probe to keep the UDP checksum constant, yielding a constant return flow-id.

Further, using UDP probes with tokyo-ping, we were able to isolate the separate contributions of the forward and return paths to the RTT variability. This has been done by comparing the RTT on paths with the same forward path and on paths with the same return path (see Section 3.4).

Unfortunately, tokyo-ping is unable to control the return flow-id when targeting some operating systems (e.g., Linux) that include the full IP payload in ICMP error messages [2]. In this case, crafting the UDP payload makes little sense because the sum of the UDP data and UDP checksum is constant, so we cannot control the flow-id of the response. In such cases, we resorted to ICMP probes.

2.3 Measurement Methodology

We used tokyo-ping, experimenting with both ICMP and UDP probes, to measure different flows between source-destination pairs. Probes were sent with a TTL value large enough not to expire before reaching the target host.

During each run, we sent probes with 100ms spacing in order to reduce the likelihood of ICMP rate limiting at the destination. For each run, we sent 100 sequential classic pings followed by 100 probes for each different flow-id to be tested. We repeated this procedure 100 times. The interleaving of probes reduced the risk of having specific flow-ids biased by temporary network events during the experiment (e.g., routing changes). In such cases multiple or all flow-ids were likely to be affected by the event. Additionally, running the experiment 100 times improved statistical significance. Finally, we compared the distribution of RTTs returned by normal ping with the distribution of RTTs obtained for each

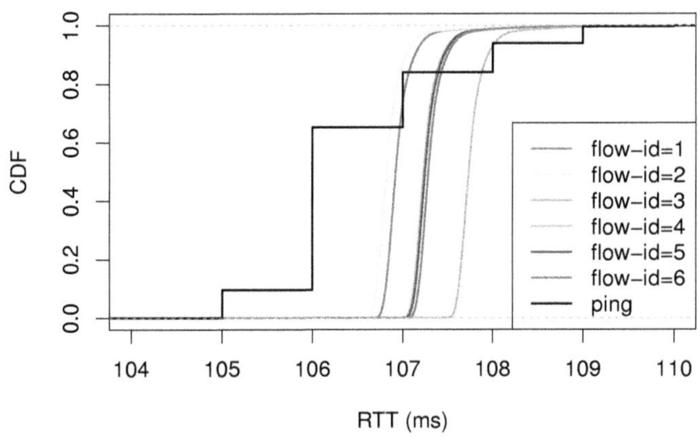

Figure 4: Per-flow and ping measured RTT from a source in Italy to a destination in the US.

distinct value of flow-id. Each experiment was repeated several times, on different days, and at different times of day, to avoid bias due to timing and traffic patterns.

Our study differs from [1] in the following aspects. First, we focused on RTT rather than on IP-level topology discovery. We made no attempt to discover paths to intermediate routers. Second, we targeted destination hosts instead of tuning the TTL to expire at the last router. This allowed us to be much more confident of the distribution of RTTs, as we were immune to the very common ICMP throttling by routers. Further, as ICMP TTL expired message generation is done in software, the load of the destination router strongly influences the RTT, adding to the variability of the distribution. This was not the case with our method. Third, we did not assume a one-to-one mapping of flow-id to IP path, in fact, the opposite. We probed different flow-ids even when the IP-level path was exactly the same. Our experiments showed that, in some cases, a single IP-level path could exhibit significantly different per-flow RTT distributions. Finally, we avoided the use of virtual machines as sources and destinations, to avoid virtualization overhead's effect on fine grained timing.

3. PING, RTTS, AND JITTER

In this section we report results of our methods when applied to measure different source-destination pairs. First, we performed measurement in controlled environments, where we had ground truth knowledge of the traversed paths. Then, we conducted larger-scale experiments. We found that differences in performance between different flow-ids can be significant. As a consequence, ping is in general a mediocre estimator for RTTs and heavily overestimates jitter.

3.1 From Italy to the US

Our first experiment ran tokyo-ping from a server in Italy to a destination in the US, using 6 different flow-id values. Results are depicted in Fig. 4 where each curve represents a Cumulative Distribution Function (CDF). The black staircase is the CDF of RTTs as measured by ping. Each data point (x, y) indicates that a y-fraction of ping probes observed an RTT of at most x milliseconds. The ping CDF is quantized because the Linux version of ping imposes a three digit precision on the reported RTTs. Each colored curve represents the CDF of RTTs measured for different flow-ids. Note that the RTT range between different flow-ids is small (4ms). The same does not always hold in the experiments we performed.

We stress that the RTT variability measured within each individual flow-id is quite low, especially compared to the variability measured by ping. In particular, ping reports jitter approximately five times greater than the largest per flow-id jitter. The apparent discrepancy of ping measuring lower RTTs than the minimum observed by setting the flow-ids is due to the fact that the six flow-id values did not cover the full range of treatment that the flows might experience. Repeating the experiment with 32 flow-ids resulted in the ping RTTs being in the same range as the RTTs measured setting the flow-ids.

Seeing this difference in performance among different flow-ids, we decided to use paris-traceroute to enumerate the IP-level paths between the two hosts. We found a surprisingly high number of IP paths, mainly due to Equal Cost Multi-Path (ECMP) configured over transoceanic links by an intermediate Tier-1 ISP.

3.2 Crossing the US using a single ISP

The above experiment showed that, in the presence of different IP paths, there may be differences in the RTT observed by packets of different flows. To ensure we completely understood what was happening, we decided to perform an even more controlled experiment. We sent ICMP probes from a server in Dallas to a server in Ashburn. The probes crossed a single IP path in a single ISP.

Fig. 5 shows the results of this experiment. In this case, the CDF for ping is not quantized because the source is a FreeBSD host running a version of ping that does not round RTT to three digits. In addition to the black staircase showing the CDF of RTT as measured by ping, we plot another staircase (shown in red) which is obtained by merging all of the RTT measures with different flow-ids and applying the same rounding. The red CDF is a very good approximation of the black one. This shows that the RTT distribution of ping is actually a sample from the collection of all distributions for different RTTs. The slight differences between the red and the black staircases are likely because our merged distribution assumes that each flow-id contributes equally to the sample, which might not be the case with ping. Moreover, 32 flow-ids may not be enough to capture the full variability observed by ping.

Looking at the per flow-id curves, we see that the difference between the RTTs of the flows with highest and lowest RTTs is even larger than in the first experiment, while we again observe low variability within each flow-id. Traditional ping can reliably estimate the upper and lower bounds of the distribution, but substantially overestimates jitter.

This result puzzled us. Thanks to the operator, we looked at the router configurations. Our probes crossed three lagged hops, one within the ingress Point-of-Presence (PoP), one across the long-haul core, and the last in the egress PoP. Each bundle was composed of slightly less than ten links. Could LAG cause flows to experience such different RTTs? Experiments between Dallas and Seattle with both ECMP and LAG showed similar behavior. We then ran two experiments with sources and destinations within the same PoP. In the first, the source and destination hosts were both connected to the same router. For the second, one LAG was used between routers in the PoP. Neither of these tests

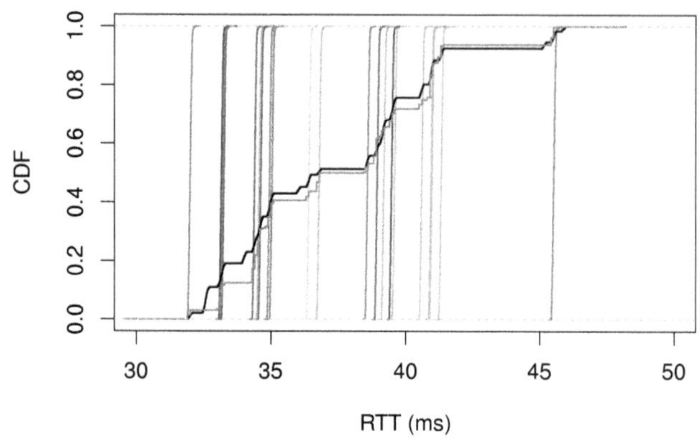

Figure 5: Experiment 2 - Performance of probes with and without fixed flow-id on an single IP path from Dallas to Ashburn.

showed any RTT difference for different flow IDs. This made us suspect that something special happened on the long-haul inter-PoP LAG.

3.3 Pruning out some potential causes

We could see a few potential culprits for the per-flow performance behavior, namely (1) the use of ICMP probes, (2) the traffic load carried by the network, (3) synchronization effects due to the interleaving of probes, (4) MPLS settings, (5) the configuration of hashing functions and hash keys, (6) the diversity of links being bundled, or (7) the LAG vendor implementation. To test whether ICMP probes were the culprit, we sent UDP probes from Ashburn to Dallas. We set the header fields in such a way as to control both the forward and the return path flow-ids. We used 6 different values for the forward flow-id and 6 different values for the return flow-id, resulting in 36 different RTT distributions. In order to quantify the contribution of the forward and return flow-id separately, we normalized the data across forward flow-ids by taking the difference with respect to the minimum RTT value measured with that forward flow-id (and across return flow-id). Fig. 6 shows the CDFs of the RTT differences, where each color represents a different value of the return flow-id. Observe that the distribution of the RTT difference is consistent across different forward flow-ids, indicated by the fact that the distributions for the same return flow-id (i.e., same color) are not scattered around the plot. We perform a similar analysis to isolate the contribution of the forward flow-id, shown in Fig. 7. The ability to clearly isolate the contributions of forward and return flow-ids also indicates that the RTT differences are not measurement artifacts.

Cross-traffic cannot be the culprit for the RTT differences either. Running the Dallas - Ashburn experiment at different times of the day, different days of the week, and for different durations led to the same graphs, with the specific flow-ids always mapping to the corresponding RTT distribution. Discussion with the operator also confirmed that the cross-traffic was very low, as the traffic load never exceeded 50% of link capacity during our experiments. With respect to synchronization effects, we repeated the experiment using a different inter-probe spacing of 157 ms, i.e., a prime number reasonably far from multiples of 100 ms (used in all our experiments), and obtained identical results. We

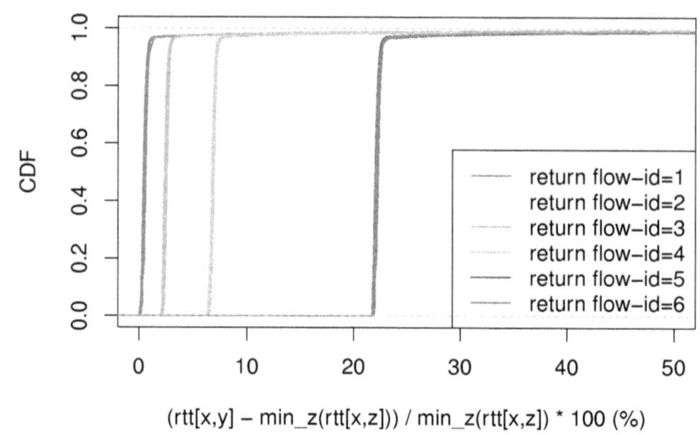

Figure 6: Contribution of return paths. Each color represents a different return flow-id. Data are normalized based on the minimum RTT experienced for a single forward flow-id.

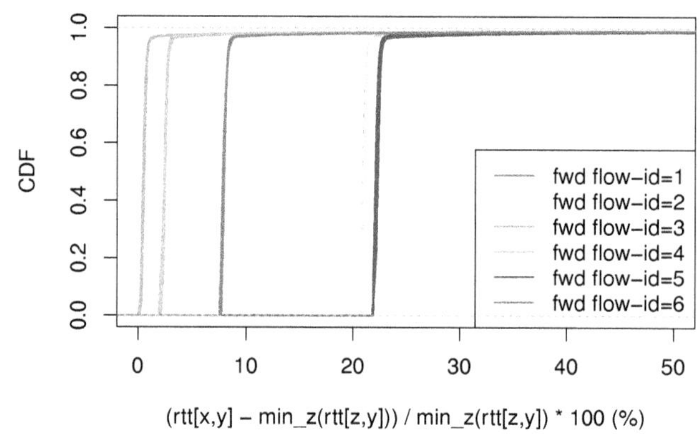

Figure 7: Contribution of forward paths. Each color represents a different forward flow-id. Data are normalized based on the minimum RTT experienced for a single return flow-id.

excluded MPLS settings and hashing specifics by checking router configurations in collaboration with network operators. This left us with LAG bundle physical link path diversity, LAG vendor implementation, or more obscure reasons as potential causes.

Despite our precautions to avoid VMs and routers as endpoints, and to cross networks for which we could get ground truth, we have not been able to pinpoint the exact causes of per-flow behavior. We know two major causes, LAG and ECMP. The ECMP issue is obvious, different path lengths, equipment, ... LAG is more subtle, and can be any combination of varied hashing algorithms on line cards (for resilience, operators usually use multiple line cards on a single LAG), varied circuit paths, etc. And serious diagnosis of LAG variance is severely hampered by lack of vendor instrumentation, e.g. one can not look into the indvidual circuits' queues.

3.4 Collecting More Evidence

To ensure that our experiments did not just discover a few corner cases, we ran ping and tokyo-ping on a larger number of Internet-wide source-destination pairs. Our sources were FreeBSD servers in Dallas, Ashburn and Seattle, plus a Linux server in Rome. As destinations, we used a subset

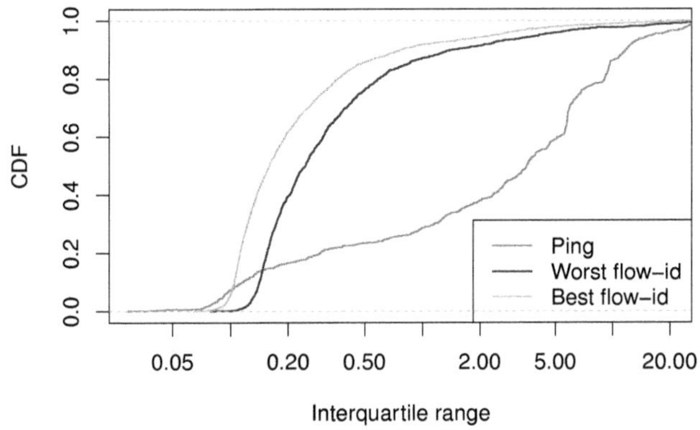

Figure 8: RTT variance with ping and tokyo-ping from a single source to 850 destinations

of the Google servers discovered by [3]. As our goal was to check the generality of the per-flow RTT behavior, we targeted distributed destinations selecting one IP per Autonomous System (AS) in this dataset. This resulted in 850 destinations. We used tokyo-ping to send ICMP probes with 16 different flow-ids. We sent ten probes for each flow-id and ten ping probes. We repeated this experiment 20 times.

Fig. 8 depicts the CDF of the inter-quantile ranges of RTT measurements that we observed using Ashburn as the source. The green curve (on the left) and the blue curve (in the middle) show the lowest and highest per-flow-id inter-quantile ranges, while the red curve shows the inter-quantile range for ping. Note that the variability of the distribution of RTTs reported by ping is systematically higher (with very few exceptions) than the variation of the most variable flow-id. In particular, for 40% of the destinations, the worst per-flow inter-quantile range is above 0.3 ms while for ping is above 5.2 ms. For 15 destinations, ping experienced lower RTT variability than the per-flow measurements (in the bottom-left). The lack of ground knowledge of router configurations and circuit paths in these larger-scale experiments prevented us from finding clear explanations.

We observed a similar behavior for all sources. We also performed experiments toward Alexa's top 100 sites and obtained very similar results.

Which portion of the RTT distribution exhibits per-flow behavior? When extending the range to incorporate 90% of the RTT distribution (the 95th-5th percentile range), instead of the 50% for the inter-quantile, the figure changes. The per-flow variance increases. For most destinations (90%) the worse per-flow variance is higher than the ping variance. This is likely a sign that while there are specific per-flow behaviors, other factors are also at play. Slightly reducing the portion of the RTT distribution we consider is enough to reflect per-flow behavior. From our source in Ashburn, 90% of the destinations have an RTT distribution with 90th-10th range lower with the flow id fixed than for ping. This shows that in general 80% of the flow observations are consistent.

4. RELATED WORK

Traceroute is renown to be error prone in load-balanced networks [1]. In [1], the authors propose a replacement for traceroute, called paris-traceroute, which takes into account path diversity at the IP layer. By measuring the minimum RTT across 100 measurements per destination and iterating over multiple flow identifiers, the authors conclude that, for most paths, there is no significant RTT difference among flow identifiers. This paper is close in spirit and complementary to [1], as we show that ping results are also biased by per-flow load-balancing techniques. We extend [1] in two ways. First, we show that IP is not the only layer to be considered in load-balanced networks (see Section 3). Path diversity may be present at lower layers given LAG or MPLS. Second, by relying on the RTT distribution instead of the minimum observation, we are able to show that ping is a bad estimator for any metric related to the RTT. Essentially, ping systematically overestimates RTT variability, which is significantly lower when measured for individual flow identifiers.

Previous efforts were devoted to better implementation of per-flow load balancing. For example, the MPLS entropy label [10] is intended to avoid routers going through deep packet inspection to perform per-flow balancing, which enables support of high traffic rates in core routers. [20] highlights the difficulties in hashing encapsulated traffic.

The effect of using different hash functions to balance traffic on multiple links is studied in [4], and best practices for optimal LAG/ECMP component link utilization while using hash-based techniques are described in [11]. In [21], the use of a given path in data centers, e.g., to avoid congestion, is achieved by modifying packet headers on the basis of traceroute-like results.

We show that predictability is a key feature for new load balancing methods, especially to ease diagnosis. From this perspective, we find interesting the load balancing technique proposed in [6]. Work on balancing traffic is of major importance as it is commonly used in ISP networks [1, 8] as well as in data centers [9, 12].

5. LESSONS LEARNED

We have shown that using ping for delay measurement may be biased if one ignores flow-based load balancing. This bias is intrinsic to ping's design, hence predictable *a priori*. In carefully crafted measurements, the dispersion reported by ping can be up to 40% of the RTT experienced by the flow with lowest latency. In other words, when we observe high variability in the delay measurements of ping, it is likely a measurement artifact of the tool itself.

This observation has several consequences.

1. **Ping is unfit to measure RTT distributions.** The distribution measured by ping is often a sample from a wider set of per-flow distributions. While this can identify upper and lower bounds for the delay with good approximation, it provides a mediocre estimate for delay. It overestimates jitter (or any other metric measuring the variability of the distribution). For this reason, it cannot reliably represent the performance experienced by applications. This should sound a warning both for researchers studying end-to-end Internet performance, and operators using ping for measurement or debugging purposes. We suggest that tokyo-ping, an adaptation of paris-traceroute, be deployed on large-scale measurement infrastructures.

2. **The importance of the flow identifier.** That a significant difference in latency may exist between flows for the same source and destination pair represents both a danger and an opportunity for applications. On the one hand, applications using multiple transport channels, e.g., the con-

trol, video, audio and data channels found in videoconferencing and streaming, cannot assume that network performance is consistent across channels. This implies that multi-channel applications are advised not to rely on a single control channel to accurately estimate delay and jitter of all opened TCP connections. If the application needs consistency across channels (e.g. to keep the lip sync in video streaming), SCTP [18] is a good alternative as it is able to multiplex streams while keeping a constant flow identifier. On the other hand, applications might experience better performance by carefully selecting the source and destination ports, e.g., during an initial negotiation phase. Moreover, our findings suggest that accurately monitoring per-channel performance from outside the application is harder than is commonly believed. Indeed, the performance that a monitoring tool (e.g., ping, IP-SLA, etc.) measures is not necessarily representative of the performance experienced by specific applications.

3. **Impact on common wisdom and prior work.** Our findings show how reality is often more complex than expected. Technologies and configurations at different layers of the protocol stack often interact in unexpected ways. Understanding these interactions and the behavior of different vendor implementations is difficult. This can frustrate or make inaccurate the modeling effort of research. Our experiments show that, at least in some cases, latency over a network path is not a well-defined concept, and we should more precisely define latency over a transport session. Generally speaking, we recommend researchers be cautious when drawing conclusions from experiments based solely on ping results.

Acknowledgements

We thank Olivier Bonaventure and Jean Lorchat for their insightful comments. We are very grateful to several network operators without whom this work would not have been possible. We are indebted to our shepherd Ethan Katz-Bassett for his guidance in producing the camera-ready. This work is partially supported by the European Commission's Seventh Framework Programme (FP7/2007-2013) Grant No. 317647 (Leone).

6. REFERENCES

[1] B. Augustin, T. Friedman, and R. Teixeira. Measuring load-balanced paths in the internet. In *ACM Internet Measurement Conference (IMC 2007)*, 2007.

[2] F. Baker, 1995. Internet Engineering Task Force (IETF) , RFC 1812.

[3] Matt Calder, Zi Hu Xun Fan, Ethan Katz-Bassett, John Heidemann, and Ramesh Govindan. Mapping the Expansion of Google's Serving Infrastructure (To Appear). In *Proceedings of the ACM Internet Measurement Conference (IMC '13)*, October 2013.

[4] Z. Cao, Z. Wang, and E. Zegura. Performance of hashing-based schemes for Internet load balancing. In *INFOCOM*, pages 332–341, 2000.

[5] Luca Cittadini. Tokyo-ping. `http://psg.com/tokyo-ping-v2.tar.gz`.

[6] Gregory Detal, Christoph Paasch, Simon van der Linden, Pascal MÃl'rindol, Gildas Avoine, and Olivier Bonaventure. Revisiting flow-based load balancing: Stateless path selection in data center networks. *Computer Networks*, 57(5):1204–1216, April 2013.

[7] C. Dovrolis, K. Gummadi, A. Kuzmanovic, and S. D. Meinrath. Measurement Lab: Overview and an Invitation to the Research Community. *SIGCOMM CCR 2010*, 2010.

[8] T. Flach, E. Katz-Bassett, and R. Govindan. Quantifying violations of destination-based forwarding on the Internet. In *ACM Internet Measurement Conference (IMC 2012)*, 2012.

[9] A. Greenberg, J. R. Hamilton, N. Jain, S. Kandula, C. Kim, P. Lahiri, D. A. Maltz, P. Patel, and S. Sengupta. VL2: a scalable and flexible data center network. In *ACM SIGCOMM*, 2009.

[10] K. Kompella, J. Drake, S. Amante, W. Henderickx, and L. Yong. The Use of Entropy Labels in MPLS Forwarding, November 2012. Internet Engineering Task Force (IETF), RFC 6790.

[11] R. Krishnan, S. Khanna, L. Yong, A. Ghanwani, Ning So, and B. Khasnabish. Mechanisms for optimal LAG/ECMP component link utilization in networks, April 2013. draft-krishnan-opsawg-large-flow-load-balancing-08.txt, work in progress.

[12] J. Mudigonda, P. Yalagandula, M. Al-Fares, and J. C. Mogul. Spain: Cots data-center ethernet for multipathing over arbitrary topologies. In *NSDI*, 2010.

[13] RIPE NCC. RIPE Atlas. `https://atlas.ripe.net`.

[14] RIPE NCC. RIPE Test Traffic Measurement Service. `https://atlas.ripe.net`.

[15] J. Postel. User Datagram Protocol, 1980. Internet Engineering Task Force (IETF) , RFC 768.

[16] J. Postel. Internet Control Message Protocol, 1981. Internet Engineering Task Force (IETF) , RFC 792.

[17] SamKnows. Samknows. `http://www.samknows.com`.

[18] R. Stewart. Stream Control Transmission Protocol, 2007. Internet Engineering Task Force (IETF) , RFC 4960.

[19] Georgia Tech et al. Project BISmark. `http://projectbismark.net`.

[20] Jeff Wheeler and Job Snijders. Understanding MPLS hashing. NANOG 57, February 2013.

[21] K. Xi, Y. Liu, and J. Chao. Enabling flow-based routing control in data center networks using probe and ECMP. In *INFOCOM Workshop on cloud computing (2011)*, page 614âĂŞ619, 2001.

A Comparison of Syslog and IS-IS for Network Failure Analysis

Daniel Turner, Kirill Levchenko, Stefan Savage, and Alex C. Snoeren
{djturner, klevchen, savage, snoeren}@cs.ucsd.edu

Department of Computer Science and Engineering
University of California, San Diego

ABSTRACT

Accurate reporting and analysis of network failures has historically required instrumentation (e.g., dedicated tracing of routing protocol state) that is rarely available in practice. In previous work, our group has proposed that a combination of common data sources could be substituted instead. In particular, by opportunistically stitching together data from router configuration logs and syslog messages, we demonstrated that a granular picture of network failures could be resolved and verified with human trouble tickets. In this paper, we more fully evaluate the fidelity of this approach, by comparing with high-quality "ground truth" data derived from an analysis of contemporaneous IS-IS routing protocol messages. We identify areas of agreement and disparity between these data sources, as well as potential ways to correct disparities when possible.

Categories and Subject Descriptors

C.2.3 [**Computer-Communication Networks**]: Network Operations

Keywords

Measurement; Reliability; Syslog; IS-IS

1. INTRODUCTION

Reliability and availability are among the most important qualities of a network and must be ensured both through careful design (e.g., deploying physically redundant devices and logically tolerant protocols to mask failures) and diligent operational practices (e.g., responding to failures that cannot be masked). To inform such efforts, there is broad interest in tracking network failures, their durations and their causes. Unfortunately, the Internet architecture does not include comprehensive failure measurement as a first-class capability and thus failure analysis inevitably involves pressing a range of other tools into this service: syslog, routing protocol monitoring, SNMP, human trouble tickets, active probes and so on. However, it is not well understood how these different techniques differ in their ability to capture and characterize availability failures.

In previous work we developed a methodology to analyze network failures based upon readily available router log messages (i.e., syslog) and used it to analyze over five years of failure events in the CENIC regional network [17]. Our original study used operator e-mails and active probing as sources of ground truth to validate the results of our method. However, both data sources provide only sparse coverage of the failures identified in our study and their own fidelity is known to be imperfect as well (e.g., operators do not record short-lived failures in trouble tickets). The "gold standard" for identifying downtime is via high-fidelity logs of link-state router messages. Configuring and deploying an IGP listener to record such logs is neither technologically difficult nor novel [9]. However, an active listener carries the risk of disrupting network operations in the event of a catastrophic malfunction or compromise. As a result such datasets are rarely available in operational networks and were not available when we first analyzed the CENIC network. Thus, in many cases, including our own previous work, network analysis is conducted using syslog data [4, 10, 14, 15, 21]. Worryingly, it remains unknown what sacrifices a syslog-based approach makes in terms of accuracy when compared to the ground truth revealed via routing protocol messages.

In this paper, we provide the first analysis of this trade-off by comparing the results of analyzing contemporaneous network-wide router syslog data and real-time ISIS routing protocol updates over a 13-month period in the CENIC network. We find significant disparities between the failure traces computed from the syslog and IS-IS data sources: the former does not capture 20% of the failures identified by the latter. Nevertheless, the statistical distribution of the failure traces is consistent for some metrics (e.g., failures per link and link downtime) but clearly distinct for others (e.g., failure duration). At a qualitative level, the importance of these differences depends greatly upon the use of the data: if an operator is merely attempting to identify aggregate link availability, syslog-based approaches seem adequate. If, on the other hand, the analysis is being conducted in order to determine more involved metrics, like identifying periods of complete isolation for portions of the network, higher fidelity data sources may be required.

In general, we find that syslog-based analyses provide reasonable approximations of those based upon routing protocol data, but with three important caveats:

1. Syslog frequently fails to accurately reflect link state during periods of flapping (i.e., rapid state transitions).

2. Long-lasting failures (e.g., over 24 hours) should be manually verified as they are frequently false positives due to lost syslog messages.

IMC'13, October 23–25, 2013, Barcelona, Spain.

http://dx.doi.org/10.1145/2504730.2504766.

3. Attempting to model link state over time through syslog occasionally results in nonsensical state changes (e.g., syslog reports that a currently operational link just came up). We find the best approach is to assume that the offending state change message is a spurious retransmission and leave the link state unmodified.

2. RELATED WORK

A large number of efforts have attempted to quantify the amount, types, and causes of failure in wide-area networks. The vast majority of these studies follow a tomographic approach, where measurements collected at the edges of networks are used to infer the causes of disruptions in end-to-end traffic flow [1, 2, 3, 5, 6, 11, 18, 22]. It is well known, however, that such approaches are not as accurate as measurement from within the network itself [5].

Direct measurements are much more complicated and costly to obtain, resulting in a dearth of such studies. One general approach taps into the interior gateway protocol (IGP) messages employed by the network under consideration to monitor how the routing protocol behaves, as route updates typically indicate connectivity changes. Two previous studies monitored OSPF networks: Shaikh *et al.* [16] studied OSPF behavior in a large enterprise network, and Watson, Jahanian and Labovitz [19] studied a network of fifty routers, including internal and customer links, over the course of one year. Markopoulou *et al.* [12], on the other hand, studied six months of IS-IS routing protocol messages collected from hundreds of nodes in the Sprint backbone. All of these studies, while valuable in providing insight into the behavior of real networks, use methodologies and hardware that is often not practical for many network operators.

In contrast, in our own previous work, we considered whether lower-quality data sources, namely syslog and operator emails, could be used instead [17]. Others have used similar approaches: Gill *et al.* used syslog to analyze failures in a data center network [4]; Labovitz *et al.* combine SNMP queries with operational logs to analyze failures in the backbone of a regional service provider [7], and Xu *et al.* parse syslog records to identify anomalies in data center operations [20]. While each of these efforts provided some form of validation against various forms of "ground truth," none directly compare their results to a contemporaneous study based upon IGP data. To the best of our knowledge, our study represents the first head-to-head comparison of the results of high-fidelity IS-IS monitoring to "lower quality" methods that employ only syslog or data sources.

3. BACKGROUND

Network failures can be categorized by many attributes including duration, cause, impact, and frequency. While no attribute is most important, some attributes are more relevant for particular purposes than others: a network engineer trying to improve reliability is likely to be concerned with cause and impact while a researcher developing a new routing protocol is likely to more interested in frequency and duration.

On the other hand, different actors have different resources available to them, and some may not be able to obtain the same quality of information with which to conduct their analyses. Ideally, analyses conducted with the most easily available data would be sufficiently accurate to be suitable for all purposes. Clearly such data sources are unlikely to provide exact failure-for-failure accounting; we seek to understand which—if any—statistical properties are similar, and to what degree.

Table 1: Summary of data used in the study.

Parameter	Value
Period	Oct. 20, 2010 – Nov. 11, 2011
Routers	60 Core and 175 CPE
Router Config Files	11,623
IS-IS links	84 Core and 215 CPE
Syslog messages	47,371
IS-IS updates	11,095,550
Syslog message types	`%CLNS-5-ADJCHANGE` `%ROUTING-ISIS-4-ADJCHANGE`

IS-IS LSP field types	`LSP ID`
	`Host Name`
	`Extended IS Reachability`
	`Extended IP Reachability`

Before delving into the details of our findings, this section provides basic information about CENIC, the network that forms the basis of our study, as well as the various data sources and methods used in our analysis.

3.1 CENIC

CENIC is a regional ISP in California that provides network connectivity to over 120 non-profit educational institutions. The CENIC network consists of 60 backbone routers connected by 10 GBit/s links as well as 175 routers on customer premises. We refer to the former as *Core* routers and the latter as *CPE* (customer premises equipment) routers. The network uses the IS-IS routing protocol on the Core and CPE devices, organized as a single IS-IS network, described next. (A more detailed description of CENIC's topology and structure is available elsewhere [17].)

3.2 IS-IS

The routing state of a network is commonly regarded as ground truth because if the routing protocol (IS-IS in the case of CENIC) declares a link is down, then for all practical intents and purposes it is down since no traffic will be directed to it. Similarly, if IS-IS declares a link to be up, then the link is at least capable of hearing and answering IS-IS "hello" packets, which is in most cases evidence enough that a link is functioning.

We capture CENIC routing state using a server running a lightly-modified version of Richard Mortier's Python Routing Toolkit [13] to act as a router participating in the IS-IS network. Since IS-IS is a link-state routing protocol each router periodically floods its current adjacencies to the rest of the network in a link state packet (LSP). Adjacencies correspond to physical links between routers; it is possible for neighboring routers to have more than one adjacency.

Each LSP advertisement is encoded as a series of type/length/value (TLV) fields. Table 1 lists the TLV fields we use. The first field, `LSP ID`, is the unique OSI identifier for each router. The second field, `Host Name`, is a human readable hostname. The `Extended IS Reachability` field contains a list of tuples. Each tuple contains the OSI identifier for a device directly connected to the router as well as the link weight (routing metric); larger weights are less preferred paths. These weights are configured by operators.

In addition to router adjacencies, LSPs also contain information about which IP networks are directly reachable from the router. `IP Reachability` is derived from interfaces that are configured with IP addresses and from statically configured information. The set of IP ranges known to IS-IS does not include customer addresses, which are handled by BGP. Therefore, almost all of the subnets advertised are those of the point-to-point links that make up the CENIC backbone and links to CPE devices.

For every LSP we receive we first extract the sender's OSI ID. If this is the first LSP from the sender we record its host name in our mapping of OSI IDs to hostnames and record its IS-IS neighbors and IP reachability. Subsequently, for each new LSP received from the node, we compare the advertised IS-IS adjacencies and IP reachability to adjacencies and IP reachability advertised previously. If any new adjacencies or IP space has been formed or lost we attempt to determine, with the help of the mined configuration files, to which link(s) this adjacency or IP space corresponds.

3.3 Syslog

Network operators often use syslog [8] to obtain diagnostic information. Its popularity is likely do to its ability to expose a wealth of diagnostic in human-readable text strings and ease of configuration. Syslog messages are nothing more than plain text strings that are transmitted via UDP to a central logging server. The convention followed by the Cisco routers in our study ensures that each syslog message has a similar format: timestamp, name of router and process generating the message, and specific diagnostic message.

Every router in the CENIC network is configured to send syslog messages to a central logging facility. We were provided access to the subset of these messages that pertain to the link, link protocol, and IS-IS routing protocol of the router. (Table 1 lists statistics about the syslog data.) Because syslog messages are transmitted via UDP and the syslog process runs with low priority, message generation and delivery is far from certain.

3.4 Matching

Our goal is to determine the relative accuracy of historical routing state, i.e., periods of link up and downtime, extracted from syslog messages. In particular, we seek to compare the failures extracted from syslog messages to those extracted from IS-IS LSPs. Making such a comparison requires the ability to extract failures from both data sources, find a common naming convention, and have a precise definition of when two failures are a match.

Determining a link's state via syslog is straightforward. A link transitions states whenever a syslog packet says such a transition has occurred. However, we do observe cases where we receive two down state transitions without an intervening up transition and vice versa. We consider the state of the link between two down/up state transitions to be ambiguous. (In contrast, in our previous work we removed such events from the data set [17].)

Determining a link's state according to IS-IS is similar. A link is in the "up" state as long as the adjacency or IP space is listed in the appropriate LSP packets, e.g. "down" transitions occur when a previously listed adjacency or IP space is no longer advertised and "up" transition occurs when it is re-advertised.

Syslog and IS-IS LSPs use different naming conventions (hostnames vs. OSI IDs). To overcome the inability to directly compare router names in LSPs and syslog messages we develop a simple method to map both to a common naming convention, a *link:* `(host name 1:port on host 1, host name 2:port on host 2)`. In order to perform this mapping we determine all of the links in the network by mining an archive of configuration files.

We consider an IS-IS failure event (i.e., a down transition followed by an up transition) and a syslog failure event to be matched if both are on the same link, their start times are within ten seconds, and their end times are within ten seconds. We choose a window size of ten seconds because there is a clear knee at ten seconds when examining the graph of window size to percent of downtime matched (omitted for space). We also find it useful to compare transitions individually; state transitions are similarly considered to match if they occur with ten seconds of each other on the same link.

Table 2: Percentage of state transitions matching syslog messages by IS or IP reachability of IS-IS LSP messages

Syslog Type	IS reachability	IP reachability
IS-IS Down	82%	25%
IS-IS Up	85%	23%
physical media Down	31%	52%
physical media Up	34%	53%

IS reachability vs. IP reachability IS-IS LSPs contain two fields that can be used to infer link state: IS reachability and IP reachability. We therefore have to choose which of the two fields two use. If we choose to use the IS reachability field there is a limitation that it is not always possible to differentiate between one or multiple physical links between two routers[1]. In the CENIC network, 26 device pairs have such multi-link adjacencies. We omit multi-link adjacencies from our analysis because, unlike all other links in the network, their state is actually function of n-physical links.

Router interfaces that form links in the CENIC network are given IP addresses in unique /31 subnets. This means that the IP reachability field can uniquely identify every link. As a result it initially appears that using IP reachability to determine link state would be superior since it does not ignore 20% of all links.

Table 2 shows what percentage of all state changes, as observed by either IS or IP reachability, match syslog state state changes that refer to IS-IS connectivity or the status of the underlying physical media. The IS reachability matches three times more syslog state transitions than IP reachability and we expect syslog to reasonably reflect ground truth. Therefore, even though IS reachability is blind to 20% of physical links it is still preferable to using IP reachability field to detect link state changes.

At the same time, IP reachability matches 20% more physical media state changes than IS reachability. Hence, we conclude that IP reachability reflects physical media state. Therefore, IP reachability must be formed in order for IS reachability to be established, but it is not sufficient to establish IS reachability. Hence, we consider state changes only from IS reachability for the remainder of this paper.

4. COMPARATIVE ANALYSIS

Our comparison of syslog to IS-IS is intended to be both descriptive and prescriptive. Ideally, syslog would provide failure-for-failure accounting and thus be usable for any purpose. However, in Section 4.1 we show that there is significant disagreement in state transitions. As a result, there is a bias in metrics having to do with link failures. Section 4.2 shows that some statistical properties are preserved, however. Section 4.3 shows how to filter the data to remove false positives and short failure bias in order to maximize the utility of syslog-based analyses. Finally, in Section 4.4 we look at a high-level metric, customer availability, as one real-world use case.

[1]RFC 5305 provides an extension to the IS-IS protocol to enable differentiation in IP networks, but it is not running on most devices in the CENIC network.

Table 3: Number of IS-IS state transitions by type (UP or DOWN) and number of Sylog messages matching.

IS-IS transition	Router Syslog messages		
	None	One	Both
DOWN	2,022 18%	4,512 39%	4,962 43%
UP	1,696 15%	5,432 48%	4,168 37%

4.1 Analyzing Link State Changes

We begin by examining the accuracy of state transitions since it is simple and straightforward. Moreover, if such a fine-grained measure were accurate, all higher-level metrics would also be accurate.

During the 13-month measurement period, our IS-IS listener recorded 22,792 adjacency state transitions: 11,496 withdrawing a previously advertised adjacency, and 11,296 introducing a new adjacency. We refer to the former as a *DOWN event*, and the latter as an *UP event*, the two events together constituting a *failure*.

Under ideal conditions, each link failure would manifest itself in syslog as a pair of messages—one from each router on either end of the link—reporting the adjacency status change (DOWN) at the start of a failure, and another pair of messages at the end of the failure (UP). Under less than ideal conditions, some or all of these four messages may be lost.

Using the procedure described in Section 3.4, we attempt to match each syslog message (generated by the router's IS-IS process) to an IS-IS listener-reported event. Syslog-reported IS-IS adjacency "Down" messages are matched to DOWN events, "Up" messages to UP events.

Table 3 shows the results of the matching. The DOWN and UP rows show the number of IS-IS listener-reported transitions with the number of Syslog-reported "Down" and "Up" messages matched to each. In the *None* column are transitions with no matching Syslog messages, in the *One* column are transitions where only one router sent a matching message, and in the *Both* column are transitions where both routers sent matching Syslog messages.

The majority of UP transitions are captured by syslog: only 15% do not have a matching syslog message from either router. The majority of DOWN transitions are also matched, but a slightly larger fraction—18%—are missed. The majority of unmatched transitions, 67% for DOWN and 61% for UP, occur during periods of link flapping. Further investigation shows that than less than half of all syslog state transitions are matched during periods of link flapping. In keeping with previous work we consider two or more consecutive failures on the same link separated by less than 10 minutes part of a flapping episode [17]. We therefore conclude that syslog does not accurately describe link state during flapping.

4.2 Analyzing Link Failures

Network operators are typically concerned with metrics like link downtime that are calculated from individual link failure events. This is concerning because our failure reconstruction methodology relies on a DOWN and UP state transition to make a failure. Thus if more than 15% of DOWN as well as UP transitions do not match IS-IS, it is possible that a syslog-based analysis might miss more than 30% of all failures. We find, however, that the unmatched state transitions predominately impact syslog's ability to capture short failures and have limited impact on most statistical properties.

The results of performing failure reconstruction and sanitation are presented in Table 4. Sanitization consists of removing failures that span periods when the IS-IS listener was offline as well as manually verifying the 25 syslog failures that lasted more than 24 hours. Manual verification primarily consists of cross-checking failures with network trouble tickets. Since one of the primary purposes of network trouble tickets is to document network events, we can reasonably expect (very) long lasting failures to be chronicled. While manual verification of long failures is time consuming, it is also critical since doing so removes 6,000 hours of spurious downtime which is almost twice the number of actual downtime hours.

Table 4: Number and hours of downtime as reported by IS-IS and syslog after basic data cleaning was performed.

	IS-IS	Syslog	Overlap
Failure Count	11,213	11,738	9,298
Downtime (Hours)	3,648	2,714	2,331

Table 5: Statistics for syslog-inferred failures and IS-IS listener-reported failures.

	Core		CPE	
Statistic	Syslog	IS-IS	Syslog	IS-IS
Annualized Failures per link				
Median	5.7	6.6	11.3	12.3
Average	14.2	16.1	49.1	45.5
95%	46.2	46.2	249	253
Failure duration (seconds)				
Median	52	42	10	12
Average	1078	1527	814	1140
95%	6318	6683	665	825
Time between failures (hours)				
Median	0.2	0.2	0.01	0.03
Average	343	347	116	136
95%	2014	2147	673	845
Annualized Link downtime (hours)				
Median	0.6	0.8	1.9	2.4
Average	4	7	11	14
95%	24	26	49	51

At first glance, concern about lost syslog messages appears unfounded since syslog reports 500 (5%) more failures than IS-IS. However, syslog reports 934 fewer hours of downtime, 25% less than IS-IS. Moreover, 20% of all individual failure instances (not shown) are false positives, i.e., they do not appear in IS-IS.

Table 5 shows key statistics for the syslog failure reconstruction technique and for IS-IS listener-reported failures. The numbers are given in annualized form by normalizing the number of failures to link lifetime. Here we break down the data according to whether the link in question belongs to the network backbone (Core) or is connected to an edge router on the customer premises (CPE). We present results for Core and CPE links separately since their different use, equipment types, and importance, suggests that they will have different statistics. The median number of failures per link is lower by about one per year in syslog-inferred data than in IS-IS listener data in both cases.

Core failure durations are higher using syslog data—52 seconds versus 42 seconds. With CPE links, it is the opposite. Median failure duration is 10 seconds for syslog-reconstructed failures, and 12 seconds for IS-IS listener-reported failures. This unusual reversal of syslog-inferred and IS-IS-reported data is most evident in the annualized link downtime. The median Core link downtime is 36

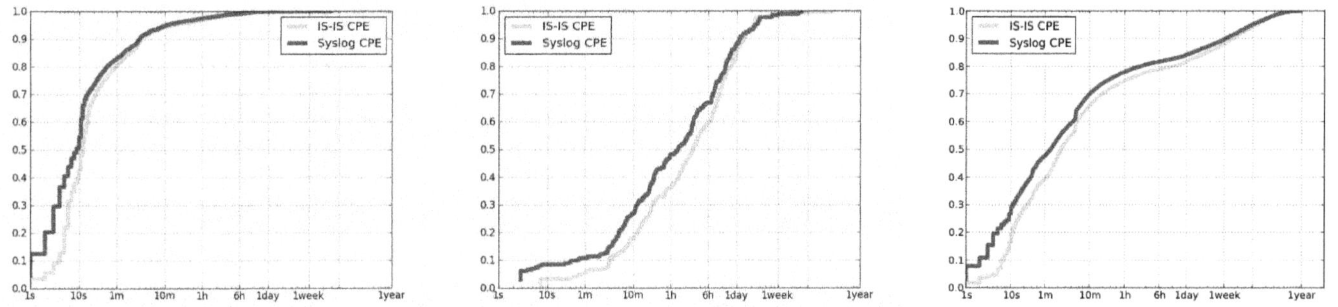

(a) Failure Duration

(b) Annualized Link Downtime

(c) Time Between Failures

Figure 1: Syslog-inferred and IS-IS listener-reported cumulative distributions for CPE links.

minutes per year using syslog data, and 48 minutes per year using IS-IS listener data. On the other hand, for CPE links, IS-IS data gives a median link downtime of 2.4 hours, compared to 1.9 hours with syslog data.

To better illustrate these differences, Figure 1 shows the cumulative failure duration distribution, the cumulative annualized link downtime distribution, and the cumulative distribution of time between failures for CPE links.

The IS-IS and Syslog distributions of failure duration for Core links track each other closely, with most of the differences attributable to short failures (less than 10 seconds): 1-second failures are more common in the IS-IS data, while 3-5 seconds failures are slightly more common in syslog data.

Among CPE links, Figure 1a , the differences between the two distributions arise in the relative frequencies of short-duration failures. Syslog-inferred failures are more frequent in the 1-4 second range, while IS-IS listener-inferred failures are more prevalent in the 5-7 second range. Ultimately, syslog contains more 1-second failures, which cause the discrepancy observed. One explanation for this finding is that syslog is capturing sub-second pseudo-failures that signal a connection reset, as we explore in Section 4.3.

From examining descriptive statistics and graphical plots, both syslog-inferred and IS-IS listener-reported failures exhibit similar characteristics. The differences stem from certain classes of failures—most notably short failures—which are poorly captured by syslog. Moreover, when we compare distributions for goodness of fit (using the two-tailed Kolmogorov-Smirnov statistic, or KS test) we find that syslog and IS-IS produce consistent data for failures per link as well as link downtime, but not failure duration.

Given that Syslog misses 20% of all failures and 25% of all downtime, it is not suitable for those who require failure-for-failure accounting. At the same time, our results indicate that using syslog to determine link state information may be sufficient for those whose applications only require the reconstructed link state to have the same gross statistical properties as those directly reported by the IS-IS listener.

4.3 Syslog's False Positives

Most of the statistical properties about failures reported by syslog closely track those reported by IS-IS, but a few—like individual failure duration—do not. In this section we examine the causes and enumerate which data filtering mechanisms can be successfully applied in an effort to increase the number of statistics syslog can accurately convey.

Table 6: Absolute count of ambiguous state changes by cause and state change direction.

Cause	Down	Up
Lost Message	194	174
Spurious Retransmission	240	28
Unknown	27	0
Total	461	202

When comparing syslog failures to IS-IS listener-reported failures, we find that syslog reports 2,440 failures (21% of all syslog-reported failures) and 17.5 hours that were not observed by the IS-IS listener[2]. These failures are actually false positives, i.e. failures that seemingly did not impact traffic.

Short failures, ten seconds or less, make up 83% of all false positives. These failures, however, lead to less than an hour of downtime. On the other hand, 94% of the false positive downtime belongs to the remaining 373 failures. Interestingly, all but 19 failures greater than ten seconds—a full 15.1 hours worth of downtime—occur during periods of flapping, when a link fails multiple times in rapid succession.

False positives occur for a number of reasons. One issue, which produces very short duration false positives, one second or less, is an aborted IS-IS three-way handshake. A second issue which also causes very short failure, one second or less, is an adjacency being reset which often occurs immediately after a longer failure without an LSP being generated and, thus, is not seen by the IS-IS listener. A reset adjacency failure is differentiated from a subsequent link failure by the type of syslog message being sent. Further complicating the issue is the fact that, as highlighted in Section 4.1, syslog message generation reliability is significantly impacted during periods of link flapping.

While there are many different causes of very short failures, we are aware of only one cause of long false positives. These occur when both an "Up" and then a subsequent "Down" message are lost such that two short failures become one long failure.

Ambiguous state changes

A failure in syslog is defined by a "Down" message followed by an "Up" message. However we find that there are 461 down messages that are preceded by an other down message and 202 up messages

[2]Table 4 implies that Syslog has 383 hours of false positive downtime, however, 365.5 hours belong to failures that only partially overlap with failures seen by the IS-IS listener.

preceded by an up message. The link state between repeated messages is ambiguous because we cannot determine if a message was lost or if the message was a spurious reminder of link state. In aggregate, these ambiguous periods between double down and up messages account for 7.8% of the measurement period across all links.

Testing if a double up/down has occurred due to a missing syslog message is straightforward with IS-IS data. A message has been lost if both syslog state change messages correspond to the correct state change as seen by IS-IS. We find that 42% of all double down periods are caused by a lost syslog up message while 86% of all double up periods are caused by a lost down message, see Table 6 . In total, lost packets explain 56% of all double up and down periods.

Next, we test if the remaining unexplained nonsensical state changes are due to spurious retransmission. To do this we check the remaining double down and up messages to see if they occurred while the link was in the same state. In fact 52% of all double down message—91% of those not explained by a lost syslog up—occur during a failure according to IS-IS and 14% of all double ups—all of those not explained by a lost syslog down—during up time. Interestingly 99% of spurious down messages are reporting the same failure as the previously received state change message; this is true for only 48% of the double ups.

We now turn from investigating the causes of the nonsensical state transitions to how to correct for them. Previous work ignored the time periods between these transitions, but with the help of IS-IS control data as ground truth, we can explore better strategies. We believe there are three potential options: assume the link is down, assume the link is up, or assume the link is in the previous state. After examining the three strategies we find that assuming the link remains in the previous state pushes link downtime as seen by syslog closest to matching link downtime as seen by IS-IS.

4.4 Isolating Failures

The statistical similarity of individual failure events according to syslog and IS-IS is one thing, but many real-world metrics are aggregates of multiple events. Hence, any error in reconstruction has the potential to be magnified when focusing on a high-level metric, such as customer availability.

We highlight the amplification issue with regards to customer availability since CENIC's primary value as an ISP is in providing connectivity to its customers. Therefore, reliability is best gauged not from statics about individual network failures, but instead through customer availability. Because most customers are multi-homed and CENIC has rings in its topology, detecting connectivity losses require accurate state information about multiple links simultaneously.

CENIC advertises a single /16 block into BGP for all of its customers, so we cannot use BGP monitors to give us insight or confirmation when a customer has been isolated. To determine when customers become isolated, we use the network topology (reconstructed from router configuration files) to identify the set of links that would isolate a customer.

During our study period, there are 1,401 failure events observed by IS-IS that isolate a customer. Here an event is one or more overlapping link failures. These isolating events affect 74 distinct customers and result in a combined total of 26 days of isolation; see Table 7. In syslog-reconstructed failures, there are 1,060 distinct isolating events affecting 67 customer sites resulting in 22.4 days of downtime. Syslog-reconstructed failure events are not a perfect subset of IS-IS events, however: There are 58 events reported by syslog which are not observed in the IS-IS data.

Table 7: Number and duration of failures in which at least one CENIC customer was isolated from the backbone, as reconstructed from syslog and IS-IS.

Data Source	Isolating Events	Sites Impacted	Downtime (days)
IS-IS	1,401	74	26.3
Syslog	1,060	67	22.3
Intersection	1,002	66	19.8

Of these 58 unmatched events, 12 have no IS-IS-reported failures on the affected links during the event, while the remaining 46 intersect (but do not match perfectly) some IS-IS failures on the affected links. There are also two particularly egregious "matches." In one case a site is isolated for 7 hours; syslog, however, only detects the isolation nine seconds before the isolation ended. In a second case, syslog believes a site isolated for 17 hours; the site was actually isolated for less than one minute according to IS-IS.

There were 399 events—corresponding to 6.5 days of downtime—reported by IS-IS that did not match an event reconstructed from syslog. Of these, 82 were a result of syslog missing a single state change message. These 82 events account for 2.1 days (32%) of downtime. Furthermore, 99 of the remaining missed isolating events *partially* matched a syslog-reconstructed event.[3] These 99 events account for 0.7 days (11%) of downtime. The remaining 218 unmatched isolating events had no related (or potentially related) Syslog messages.

5. CONCLUSION

This study represents the first attempt to compare the failure patterns reported by syslog-based analyses to those extracted through direct IGP monitoring. We find that there is significant disagreement between the two sources, with roughly one quarter of all events reported by one data source not appearing in the other. Clearly, IS-IS monitoring is more accurate, as traffic shares fate with the routing protocol. That said, our analysis indicates that syslog's omissions are heavily biased toward short failures, and that many of the larger statistical properties of the network obtained through analyzing syslog, e.g., annualized downtime, number of failures, and time to repair, are reasonably accurate. Still, one must be careful in drawing high-level conclusions; for example syslog has a significantly different view of customer isolation than that of IS-IS.

In sum, syslog-based analyses may be useful for capturing aggregate failure characteristics where IGP data is not available. It is less well suited to situations requiring more precise failure-for-failure accounting.

Acknowledgments

This work was supported in part by the UCSD Center for Networked Systems and the National Science Foundation through grant CNS-1116904. The authors would like to thank Brian Court, Darrell Newcomb, Jim Madden, Erick Sizelove, and our shepherd, Theophilus Benson, for their advice and suggestions.

6. REFERENCES

[1] COATES, M., CASTRO, R., AND NOWAK, R. Maximum likelihood network topology identification from edge-based

[3] A partial event match occurs when an IS-IS and syslog failure intersect, but do not match on start and end time exactly.

unicast measurements. In *Proceedings of ACM SIGMETRICS* (June 2002).

[2] DHAMDHERE, A., TEIXEIRA, R., DOVROLIS, C., AND DIOT, C. NetDiagnoser: Troubleshooting network unreachabilities using end-to-end probes and routing data. In *Proceedings of ACM CoNEXT* (Dec. 2007).

[3] DUFFIELD, N. Network tomography of binary network performance characteristics. *IEEE Transactions on Information Theory* (Dec. 2006).

[4] GILL, P., JAIN, N., AND NAGAPPAN, N. Understanding network failures in data centers: Measurement, analysis, and implications. In *Proceedings of ACM SIGCOMM* (Aug. 2011).

[5] HUANG, Y., FEAMSTER, N., AND TEIXEIRA, R. Practical issues with using network tomography for fault diagnosis. *Computer Communication Review* (October 2008).

[6] KOMPELLA, R. R., YATES, J., GREENBERG, A., AND SNOEREN, A. C. Detection and localization of network black holes. In *Proceedings of IEEE INFOCOM* (May 2007).

[7] LABOVITZ, C., AHUJA, A., AND JAHANIAN, F. Experimental study of Internet stability and backbone failures. In *Proceedings of FTCS* (June 1999).

[8] LONVICK, C. The BSD syslog protocol. RFC 3164, August 2001.

[9] MAHIMKAR, A., YATES, J., ZHANG, Y., SHAIKH, A., WANG, J., GE, Z., AND EE, C. T. Troubleshooting chronic conditions in large IP networks. In *Proceedings of ACM CoNEXT* (Dec. 2008).

[10] MAHIMKAR, A. A., GE, Z., SHAIKH, A., WANG, J., YATES, J., ZHANG, Y., AND ZHAO, Q. Towards automated performance diagnosis in a large iptv network. In *Proceedings of the ACM SIGCOMM* (Aug. 2009).

[11] MAO, Y., JAMJOOM, H., TAO, S., AND SMITH, J. M. NetworkMD: Topology inference and failure diagnosis in the last mile. In *Proceedings of ACM IMC* (Oct. 2007).

[12] MARKOPOULOU, A., IANNACCONE, G., BHATTACHARYYA, S., CHUAH, C.-N., GANJALI, Y., AND DIOT, C. Characterization of failures in an operational IP backbone network. *Transactions on Networking* (Aug. 2008).

[13] MORTIER, R. PyRT: Python routeing toolkit. `https://github.com/mor1/pyrt`.

[14] POTHARAJU, R., AND JAIN, N. An empirical analysis of intra- and inter-datacenter network failures for geo-distributed services. In *Proceedings of ACM SIGMETRICS* (June 2013).

[15] QIU, T., GE, Z., PEI, D., WANG, J., AND XU, J. What happened in my network: mining network events from router syslogs. In *Proceedings of ACM IMC* (Nov. 2010).

[16] SHAIKH, A., ISETT, C., GREENBERG, A., ROUGHAN, M., AND GOTTLIEB, J. A case study of OSPF behavior in a large enterprise network. In *Proceedings of ACM IMC* (Nov. 2002).

[17] TURNER, D., LEVCHENKO, K., SNOEREN, A. C., AND SAVAGE, S. California fault lines: Understanding the causes and impact of network failures. In *Proceedings of ACM SIGCOMM* (Aug. 2010).

[18] WANG, F., MAO, Z. M., WANG, J., GAO, L., AND BUSH, R. A measurement study on the impact of routing events on end-to-end Internet path performance. In *Proceedings of ACM SIGCOMM* (Sept. 2006).

[19] WATSON, D., JAHANIAN, F., AND LABOVITZ, C. Experiences with monitoring OSPF on a regional service provider network. In *Proceedings IEEE ICDCS* (2003).

[20] XU, W., HUANG, L., FOX, A., PATERSON, D., AND JORDAN, M. Detecting large-scale system problems by mining console logs. In *Proceedings of ACM SOSP* (Oct. 2009).

[21] YAMANISHI, K., AND MARUYAMA, Y. Dynamic syslog mining for network failure monitoring. In *Proceedings of ACM SIGKDD* (Aug. 2005).

[22] ZHANG, M., ZHANG, C., PAI, V., PETERSON, L., AND WANG, R. PlanetSeer: Internet path failure monitoring and characterization in wide-area services. In *Procedings of USENIX OSDI* (Dec. 2004).

Scap: Stream-Oriented Network Traffic Capture and Analysis for High-Speed Networks

Antonis Papadogiannakis
FORTH-ICS, Greece
papadog@ics.forth.gr

Michalis Polychronakis
Columbia University, USA
mikepo@cs.columbia.edu

Evangelos P. Markatos
FORTH-ICS, Greece
markatos@ics.forth.gr

ABSTRACT

Many network monitoring applications must analyze traffic beyond the network layer to allow for connection-oriented analysis, and achieve resilience to evasion attempts based on TCP segmentation. However, existing network traffic capture frameworks provide applications with just raw packets, and leave complex operations like flow tracking and TCP stream reassembly to application developers. This gap leads to increased application complexity, longer development time, and most importantly, reduced performance due to excessive data copies between the packet capture subsystem and the stream processing module.

This paper presents the *Stream capture library (Scap)*, a network monitoring framework built from the ground up for stream-oriented traffic processing. Based on a kernel module that directly handles flow tracking and TCP stream reassembly, Scap delivers to user-level applications flow-level statistics and reassembled streams by minimizing data movement operations and discarding uninteresting traffic at early stages, while it inherently supports parallel processing on multi-core architectures, and uses advanced capabilities of modern network cards. Our experimental evaluation shows that Scap can capture all streams for traffic rates two times higher than other stream reassembly libraries, and can process more than five times higher traffic loads when eight cores are used for parallel stream processing in a pattern matching application.

Categories and Subject Descriptors

C.2.3 [**Computer-Communication Networks**]: Network Operations—*Network Monitoring*

Keywords

Traffic Monitoring; Stream Reassembly; Packet Capturing; Packet Filtering; Overload Control; Performance

1. INTRODUCTION

Passive network monitoring is an indispensable mechanism for increasing the security and understanding the performance of modern networks. For example, Network-level Intrusion Detection Systems (NIDS) inspect network traffic to detect attacks [36, 40] and pinpoint compromised computers [18, 43]. Similarly, traffic classification tools inspect traffic to identify different communication patterns and spot potentially undesirable traffic [1, 24]. To make meaningful decisions, these monitoring applications usually analyze network traffic at the transport layer and above. For instance, NIDSs reconstruct the transport-layer data streams to detect attack vectors spanning multiple packets, and perform traffic normalization to avoid evasion attacks [14, 19, 38].

Unfortunately, there is a *gap between monitoring applications and underlying traffic capture tools*: Applications increasingly need to reason about higher-level entities and constructs such as TCP flows, HTTP headers, SQL arguments, email messages, and so on, while traffic capture frameworks still operate at the lowest possible level: they provide the raw—possibly duplicate, out-of-order, or overlapping—and in some cases even irrelevant packets that reach the monitoring interface [11, 28, 29]. Upon receiving the captured packets at user space, monitoring applications usually perform TCP stream reassembly using an existing library such as Libnids [2] or a custom stream reconstruction engine [36, 40]. This results in additional memory copy operations for extracting the payloads of TCP segments and merging them into larger stream "chunks" in contiguous memory. Moreover, it misses several optimization opportunities, such as the early discarding of uninteresting packets before system resources are spent to move them to user level, and assigning different priorities to transport-layer flows so that they can be handled appropriately at lower system layers.

To bridge this gap and address the above concerns, in this paper we present the *Stream capture library (Scap)*, a unified passive network monitoring framework built around the abstraction of the *Stream*. Designed from the beginning for stream-oriented network monitoring, Scap (i) provides the high-level functionality needed by monitoring applications, and (ii) implements this functionality at the most appropriate place: at user level, at kernel level, or even at the network interface card.

To enable aggressive optimizations, we introduce the notion of *stream capture*: that is, we elevate the *Stream* into a first-class object that is captured by Scap and handled by user applications. Although previous work treats TCP stream reassembly as a necessary evil [50], used mostly to avoid evasion attacks against intrusion detection and other monitoring systems, we view streams as the fundamental abstraction that should be exported to network monitoring applications, and as the right vehicle for the monitoring system to implement aggressive optimizations all the way down to the operating system kernel and network interface card.

To reduce the overhead of unneeded packets, Scap introduces the notion of *subzero packet copy*. Inspired by zero-copy approaches that avoid copying packets from one main memory location to an-

IMC'13, October 23–25, 2013, Barcelona, Spain.
Copyright 2013 ACM 978-1-4503-1953-9/13/10 ...$15.00.
http://dx.doi.org/10.1145/2504730.2504750.

other, Scap not only avoids redundant packet copies, but also avoids bringing some packets in main memory in the first place. We show several cases of applications that are simply not interested in some packets, such as the tails of large flows [9, 26, 27, 33]. Subzero packet copy identifies these packets and does not bring them in main memory at all: they are dropped by the network interface card (NIC) *before* reaching the main memory.

To accommodate heavy loads, Scap introduces the notion of *prioritized packet loss* (PPL). Under heavy load, traditional monitoring systems usually drop arriving packets in a random way, severely affecting any following stream reassembly process. However, these dropped packets and affected streams may be important for the monitoring application, as they may contain an attack or other critical information. Even carefully provisioned systems that are capable of handling full line-rate traffic can be overloaded, e.g., by a sophisticated attacker that sends adversarial traffic to exploit an algorithmic complexity vulnerability and intentionally overload the system [34,45]. Scap allows applications to (i) define different priorities for different streams and (ii) configure threshold mechanisms that give priority to new and small streams.

Scap provides a flexible and expressive Application Programming Interface (API) that allows programmers to configure all aspects of the stream capture process, perform complex per-stream processing, and gather per-flow statistics with a few lines of code. Our design introduces two novel features: (i) it enables the early discarding of uninteresting traffic, such as the tails of long-lived connections that belong to large file transfers, and (ii) it offers more control for tolerating packet loss under high load through stream priorities and best-effort reassembly. Scap also avoids the overhead of extra memory copies by optimally placing TCP segments into stream-specific memory regions, and supports multi-core systems and network adapters with receive-side scaling [22] for transparent parallelization of stream processing.

We have evaluated Scap in a 10GbE environment using real traffic and showed that it outperforms existing alternatives like Libnids [2] and Snort's stream reassembly [40] in a variety of scenarios. For instance, our results demonstrate that Scap can capture and deliver all streams with low CPU utilization for rates up to 5.5 Gbit/s using a single core, while Libnids and Snort start dropping packets at 2.5 Gbit/s due to increased CPU utilization for stream reassembly at user level. A single-threaded Scap pattern matching application can handle 33% higher traffic rates than Snort and Libnids, and can process three times more traffic at 6 Gbit/s. When eight cores are used for parallel stream processing, Scap can process 5.5 times higher rates with no packet loss.

The main contributions of this paper are:

1. We introduce the notion of *stream capture*, and present the design, implementation, and evaluation of *Scap* , a stream-oriented network traffic processing framework. Scap provides a flexible and expressive API that elevates streams to first-class objects, and uses aggressive optimizations that allows it to deliver transport-layer streams for two times higher traffic rates than previous approaches.

2. We introduce *subzero packet copy*, a technique that takes advantage of filtering capabilities of commodity NICs to not only avoid copying uninteresting packets (such as the long tails of large flows) across different memory areas, but to avoid bringing them in main memory altogether.

3. We introduce *prioritized packet loss*, a technique that enables graceful adaptation to overload conditions by dropping packets of lower priority streams, and favoring packets that belong to recent and shorter streams.

2. DESIGN AND FEATURES

The design of Scap is driven by two key objectives: programming expressiveness and runtime performance. In this section, we introduce the main aspects of Scap across these two dimensions.

2.1 Subzero-Copy Packet Transfer

Several network monitoring applications [9, 26, 27, 33] are interested in analyzing only the first bytes of each connection, especially under high traffic load. In this way, they analyze the more useful (for them) part of each stream and discard a significant percentage of the total traffic [27]. For such applications, Scap has incorporated the use of a *cutoff* threshold that truncates streams to a user-specified size, and discards the rest of the stream (and the respective packets) within the OS kernel or even the NIC, avoiding unnecessary data transfers to user space. Applications can dynamically adjust the cutoff size *per stream*, or set a different cutoff for each stream direction, allowing for greater flexibility.

Besides a stream cutoff size, monitoring applications may be interested in efficiently discarding other types of less interesting traffic. Many applications often use a BPF filter [28] to define which streams they want to process, while discarding the rest. In case of an overload, applications may want to discard traffic from low priority streams or define a stream *overload cutoff* [26, 33]. Also, depending on the stream reassembly mode used by an application, packets belonging to non-established TCP connections or duplicate packets may be discarded. In all such cases, Scap can discard the appropriate packets at an early stage within the kernel, while in many cases packets can be discarded even earlier at the NIC.

To achieve this, Scap capitalizes on modern network interfaces that provide filtering facilities directly in hardware. For example, Intel's 82599 10G interface [21] supports up to 8K perfect match and 32K signature (hash-based) Flow Director filters (FDIR). These filters can be added and removed dynamically, within no more than 10 microseconds, and can match a packet's source and destination IP addresses, source and destination port numbers, protocol, and a flexible 2-byte tuple anywhere within the first 64 bytes of the packet. Packets that match an FDIR filter are directed to the hardware queue specified by the filter. If this hardware queue is not used by the system, the packets will be just dropped at the NIC layer, and they will never be copied to the system's main memory [13]. When available, Scap uses FDIR filters to implement all above mentioned cases of early packet discarding. Else, the uninteresting packets are dropped within the OS kernel.

2.2 Prioritized Packet Loss

Scap introduces *Prioritized Packet Loss* (PPL) to enable the system to invest its resources effectively during overload. This is necessary because sudden traffic bursts or overload conditions may force the packet capturing subsystem to fill up its buffers and randomly drop packets in a haphazard manner. Even worse, attackers may intentionally overload the monitoring system while an attack is in progress so as to evade detection. Previous research in NIDSs has shown that being able to handle different flows [16, 25, 34], or different parts of each flow [26,33], in different ways can enable the system to invest its resources more effectively and significantly improve detection accuracy. PPL is a priority assignment technique that enables user applications to define the priority of each stream so that in case of overload, packets from low-priority streams are the first ones to go. User applications can also define a threshold for the maximum stream size under overload (*overload_cutoff*). Then, packets situated beyond this threshold are the ones to be dropped.

As long as the percentage of used memory is below a user-defined threshold (called $base\_threshold$), PPL drops no packets. When, however, the used memory exceeds the $base\_threshold$, PPL kicks in: it first divides the memory above $base\_threshold$ into n (equal to the number of used priorities) regions using $n+1$ equally spaced watermarks (i.e., $watermark_0$, $watermark_1$, ..., $watermark_n$), where $watermark_0 = base\_threshold$ and $watermark_n = memory\_size$. When a packet belonging to a stream with the i_{th} priority level arrives, PPL checks the percentage of memory used by Scap at that time. If it is above $watermark_i$, the packet is dropped. Otherwise, if the percentage of memory used is between $watermark_i$ and $watermark_{i-1}$, PPL makes use of the *overload_cutoff*, if it has been defined by the user. Then, if the packet is located in its stream beyond the *overload_cutoff* byte, it is dropped. In this way, high priority streams, as well as newly created and short streams if an *overload_cutoff* is defined, will be accommodated with higher probability.

2.3 Flexible Stream Reassembly

To support monitoring at the transport layer, Scap provides different modes of TCP stream reassembly. The two main objectives of stream reassembly in Scap are: (i) to provide transport-layer reassembled chunks in continuous memory regions, which facilitates stream processing operations, and (ii) to perform protocol normalization [19, 51]. Scap currently supports two different modes of TCP stream reassembly: `SCAP_TCP_STRICT` and `SCAP_TCP_FAST`. In the strict mode, streams are reassembled according to existing guidelines [14,51], offering protection against evasion attempts based on IP/TCP fragmentation. In the fast mode, streams are reassembled in a *best-effort* way, offering resilience against packet loss caused in case of overloads. In this mode, Scap follows the semantics of the strict mode as closely as possible, e.g., by handling TCP retransmissions, out-of-order packets, and overlapping segments. However, to accommodate for lost segments, stream data is written without waiting for the correct next sequence number to arrive. In that case, Scap sets a flag to report that errors occurred during the reassembly of a particular chunk.

Scap uses target-based stream reassembly to implement different TCP reassembly policies according to different operating systems. Scap applications can set a different reassembly policy per each stream. This is motivated by previous work, which has shown that stream reassembly performed in a NIDS may not be accurate [38]. For instance, the reconstructed data stream may differ from the actual data stream observed by the destination. This is due to the different TCP reassembly policies implemented by different operating systems, e.g., when handling overlapping segments. Thus, an attacker can exploit such differences to evade detection. Shankar and Paxson [42] developed an active mapping solution to determine what reassembly policy a NIDS should follow for each stream. Similarly to Scap, Snort uses target-based stream reassembly [32] to define the reassembly policy per host or subnet.

Scap also supports UDP: a UDP stream consists of the concatenation of the payloads of the arriving packets of the respective UDP flow. For other protocols without sequenced delivery, Scap return each packet for processing without reassembly.

2.4 Parallel Processing and Locality

Scap has inherent support for multi-core systems, hiding from the programmer the complexity of creating and managing multiple processes or threads. This is achieved by transparently creating a number of worker threads for user-level stream processing (typically) equal to the number of the available cores. Using affinity calls, the mapping of threads to CPU cores is practically one-to-one. Scap also dedicates a kernel thread on each core for handling packet reception and stream reassembly. The kernel and worker threads running on the same core process the same streams. As each stream is assigned to only one kernel and worker thread, all processing of a particular stream is done on the same core, reducing, in this way, context switches, cache misses [15, 37], and inter-thread synchronization operations. The kernel and worker threads on each core communicate through shared memory and events: a new event for a stream is created by the kernel thread and is handled by the worker thread using a user-defined callback function for stream processing.

To balance the network traffic load across multiple NIC queues and cores, Scap uses both static hash-based approaches, such as Receive Side Scaling (RSS) [22], and dynamic load balancing approaches, such as flow director filters (FDIR) [21]. This provides resiliency to short-term load imbalance that could adversely affect application performance. First, Scap detects a load imbalance when one of the cores is assigned a portion of the total streams larger than a threshold. Then, subsequent streams assigned by RSS to this core are re-directed with an FDIR to the core that handles the lowest number of streams at the time.

2.5 Performance Optimizations

In case that multiple applications running on the same host monitor the same traffic, Scap provides all of them with a shared copy of each stream. Thus, the stream reassembly operation is performed only once within the kernel, instead of multiple times for each user-level application. If applications have different configurations, e.g., for stream size cutoff or BPF filters, the capture system takes a best effort approach to satisfy all requirements. For instance, it sets the largest among the cutoff sizes for all streams, and keeps streams that match at least one of the filters, marking the applications that should receive each stream and their cutoff.

Performing stream reassembly in the kernel also offers significant advantages in terms of cache locality. Existing user-level TCP stream reassembly implementations receive packets of different flows highly interleaved, which results in poor cache locality [35]. In contrast, Scap provides user-level applications with reassembled streams instead of randomly interleaved packets, allowing for improved memory locality and reduced cache misses.

3. SCAP API

The main functions of the Scap API are listed in Table 1.

3.1 Initialization

An Scap program begins with the creation of an Scap socket using `scap_create()`, which specifies the interface to be monitored. Upon successful creation, the returned `scap_t` descriptor is used for all subsequent configuration operations. These include setting a BPF filter [28] to receive a subset of the traffic, cutoff values for different stream classes or stream directions, the number of worker threads for balancing stream processing among the available cores, the chunk size, the overlap size between subsequent chunks, and an optional timeout for delivering the next chunk for processing. The `overlap` argument is used when some of the last bytes of the previous chunk are also needed in the beginning of the next chunk, e.g., for matching a pattern that might span consecutive chunks. The `flush_timeout` parameter can be used to deliver for processing a chunk smaller than the chunk size when this timeout passes, in case the user needs to ensure timely processing.

3.2 Stream Processing

Scap allows programmers to write and register callback functions for three different types of events: stream creation, the availability of new stream data, and stream termination. Each callback

Scap Function Prototype	Description
`scap_t *scap_create(const char *device, int memory_size, int reassembly_mode, int need_pkts)`	Creates an Scap socket
`int scap_set_filter(scap_t *sc, char *bpf_filter)`	Applies a BPF filter to an Scap socket
`int scap_set_cutoff(scap_t *sc, int cutoff)`	Changes the default stream cutoff value
`int scap_add_cutoff_direction(scap_t *sc, int cutoff, int direction)`	Sets a different cutoff value for each direction
`int scap_add_cutoff_class(scap_t *sc, int cutoff, char* bpf_filter)`	Sets a different cutoff value for a subset of the traffic
`int scap_set_worker_threads(scap_t *sc, int thread_num)`	Sets the number of threads for stream processing
`int scap_set_parameter(scap_t *sc, int parameter, int value)`	Changes defaults: inactivity_timeout, chunk_size, overlap_size, flush_timeout, base_threshold, overload_cutoff
`int scap_dispatch_creation(scap_t *sc, void (*handler)(stream_t *sd))`	Registers a callback routine for handling stream creation events
`int scap_dispatch_data(scap_t *sc, void (*handler)(stream_t *sd))`	Registers a callback routine for processing newly arriving stream data
`int scap_dispatch_termination(scap_t *sc, void (*handler)(stream_t *sd))`	Registers a callback routine for handling stream termination events
`int scap_start_capture(scap_t *sc)`	Begins stream processing
`void scap_discard_stream(scap_t *sc, stream_t *sd)`	Discards the rest of a stream's traffic
`int scap_set_stream_cutoff(scap_t *sc, stream_t sd, int cutoff)`	Sets the cutoff value of a stream
`int scap_set_stream_priority(scap_t *sc, stream_t *sd, int priority)`	Sets the priority of a stream
`int scap_set_stream_parameter(scap_t *sc, stream_t *sd, int parameter, int value)`	Sets a stream's parameter: inactivity_timeout, chunk_size, overlap_size, flush_timeout, reassembly_mode
`int scap_keep_stream_chunk(scap_t *sc, stream_t *sd)`	Keeps the last chunk of a stream in memory
`char *scap_next_stream_packet(stream_t *sd, struct scap_pkthdr *h)`	Returns the next packet of a stream
`int scap_get_stats(scap_t *sc, scap_stats_t *stats)`	Reads overall statistics for all streams seen so far
`void scap_close(scap_t *sc)`	Closes an Scap socket

Table 1: The main functions of the Scap API.

function takes as a single argument a `stream_t` descriptor `sd`, which corresponds to the stream that triggered the event. This descriptor provides access to detailed information about the stream, such as the stream's IP addresses, port numbers, protocol, and direction, as well as useful statistics such as byte and packet counters for all, dropped, discarded, and captured packets, and the timestamps of the first and last packet of the stream. Among the rest of the fields, the `sd->status` field indicates whether the stream is active or closed (by TCP FIN/RST or by inactivity timeout), or if its stream cutoff has been exceeded, and the `sd->error` field indicates stream reassembly errors, such as incomplete TCP handshake or invalid sequence numbers. There is also a pointer to the `stream_t` in the opposite direction, and stream's properties like cutoff, priority, and chunk size.

The stream processing callback can access the last chunk's data and its size through the `sd->data` and `sd->data_len` fields. In case no more data is needed, `scap_discard_stream()` can notify the Scap core to stop collecting data for this stream. Chunks can be efficiently merged with following ones using `scap_keep_chunk()`. In the next invocation, the callback will receive a larger chunk consisting of both the previous and the new one. Using the stream descriptor, the application is able to set the stream's priority, cutoff, and other parameters like stream's chunk size, overlap size, flush timeout, and reassembly mode.

In case they are needed by an application, individual packets can be delivered using `scap_next_stream_packet()`. Packet delivery is based on the chunk's data and metadata kept by Scap's packet capture subsystem for each packet. Based on this metadata, even reordered, duplicate, or packets with overlapping sequence numbers can be delivered in the same order as captured. This allows Scap to support packet-based processing along with stream-based processing, e.g., to allow the detection of TCP attacks such as ACK splitting [41]. In Section 6.5.3 we show that packet delivery does not affect the performance of Scap-based applications. The only difference between Scap's packet delivery and packet-based capturing systems is that packets from the same stream are processed together, due to the chunk-based delivery. As an added benefit, such flow-based packet reordering has been found to significantly improve cache locality [35].

The stream's processing time and the total number of processed chunks are available through the `sd->processing_time` and `sd->chunks` fields. This enables the identification of streams that are processed with very slow rates and delay the application, e.g., due to algorithmic complexity attacks [34, 45]. Upon the detection of such a stream, the application can handle it appropriately, e.g., by discarding it or reducing its priority, to ensure that this adversarial traffic will not affect the application's correct operation.

3.3 Use Cases

We now show two simple applications written with Scap.

3.3.1 Flow-Based Statistics Export

The following listing shows the code of an Scap application for gathering and exporting per-flow statistics. Scap already gathers these statistics and stores them in the `stream_t` structure of each stream, so there is no need to receive any stream data. Thus, the stream cutoff can be set to zero, to efficiently discard all data. All the required statistics for each stream can be retrieved upon stream termination by registering a callback function.

```
scap_t *sc = scap_create("eth0", SCAP_DEFAULT,
    SCAP_TCP_FAST, 0);
scap_set_cutoff(sc, 0);
scap_dispatch_termination(sc, stream_close);
scap_start_capture(sc);

void stream_close(stream_t *sd) {
  export(sd->hdr.src_ip, sd->hdr.dst_ip,
    sd->hdr.src_port, sd->hdr.dst_port,
    sd->stats.bytes, sd->stats.pkts,
    sd->stats.start, sd->stats.end);
}
```

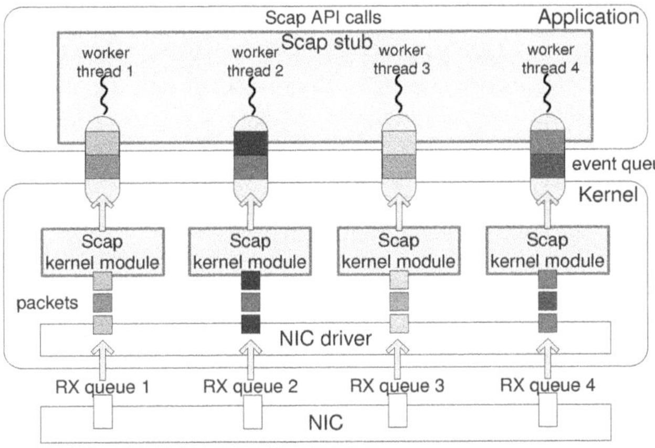

Figure 1: Overview of Scap's architecture.

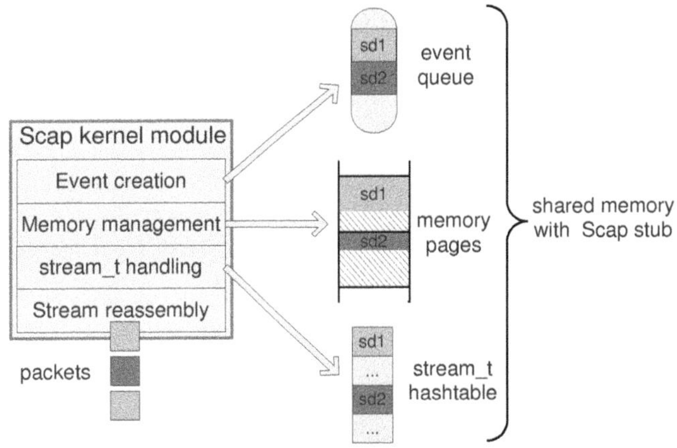

Figure 2: The operation of the Scap kernel module.

In line 1 we create a new Scap socket for capturing streams from the `eth0` interface. Then, we set the stream cutoff to zero (line 3) for discarding all stream data, we set the `stream_close()` as a callback function to be called upon stream termination (line 4), and finally we start the capturing process (line 5). The `stream_close()` function (lines 7–12) exports the statistics of the stream through the `sd` descriptor that is passed as its argument.

3.3.2 Pattern Matching

The following listing shows the few lines of code that are required using Scap for an application that searches for a set of known patterns in the captured reassembled TCP streams.

```
1  scap_t *sc = scap_create("eth0", 512M,
2       SCAP_TCP_FAST, 0);
3  scap_set_worker_threads(sc, 8);
4  scap_dispatch_data(sc, stream_process);
5  scap_start_capture(sc);
6
7  void stream_process(stream_t *sd) {
8   search(patterns, sd->data, sd->len, MatchFound);
9  }
```

We begin by creating an Scap socket without setting a cutoff, so that all traffic is captured and processed (lines 1–2). Then, we configure Scap with eight worker threads, each pinned to a single CPU core (assuming a machine with eight cores), to speed up pattern matching with parallel stream processing. Finally, we register `stream_process()` as the callback function for processing stream chunks (line 4) and start the capturing process (line 5). The `search()` function looks for the set of known patterns within `sd->len` bytes starting from the `sd->data` pointer, and calls the `MatchFound()` function in case of a match.

4. ARCHITECTURE

This section describes the architecture of the Scap monitoring framework for stream-oriented traffic capturing and processing.

4.1 Kernel-level and User-level Support

Scap consists of two main components: a loadable kernel module and a user-level API stub, as shown in Figure 1. Applications communicate through the Scap API stub with the kernel module to configure the capture process and receive monitoring data. Configuration parameters are passed to the kernel through the Scap socket interface. Accesses to `stream_t` records, events, and actual stream data are handled through shared memory. For user-level stream processing, the stub receives events from the kernel module and calls the respective callback function for each event.

The overall operation of the Scap kernel module is depicted in Figure 2. Its core is a software interrupt handler that receives packets from the network device. For each packet, it locates the respective `stream_t` record through a hash table and updates all relevant fields (`stream_t` handling). If a packet belongs to a new stream, a new `stream_t` record is created and added into the hash table. Then, it extracts the actual data from each TCP segment, by removing the protocol headers, and stores it in the appropriate memory page, depending on the stream in which it belongs (memory management). Whenever a new stream is created or terminated, or a sufficient amount of data has been gathered, the kernel module generates a respective event and enqueues it to an event queue (event creation).

4.2 Parallel Packet and Stream Processing

To scale performance, Scap uses all available cores in the system. To efficiently utilize multi-core architectures, modern network interfaces can distribute incoming packets into multiple hardware receive queues. To balance the network traffic load across the available queues and cores, Scap uses both RSS [22], which uses a hash function based on the packets' 5-tuple, and dynamic load balancing, using flow director filters [21], to deal with short-term load imbalance. To map the two different streams of each bi-directional TCP connection to the same core, we modify the RSS seeds as proposed by Woo and Park [52].

Each core runs a separate instance of the NIC driver and Scap kernel module to handle interrupts and packets from the respective hardware queue. Thus, each Scap instance running on each core will receive a different subset of network streams, as shown in Figure 1. Consequently, the stream reassembly process is distributed across all the available cores. To match the level of parallelism provided by the Scap kernel module, the Scap's user-level stub creates as many worker threads as the available cores, hiding from the programmer the complexity of creating and managing multiple processes or threads. Each worker thread processes the streams delivered to its core by its kernel-level counterpart. This collocation of user-level and kernel-level threads that work on the same data maximizes locality of reference and cache affinity, reducing, in this way, context switches, cache misses [15,37], and inter-thread synchronization. Each worker thread polls a separate event queue for events created by the kernel Scap thread running on the same core, and calls the respective callback function registered by the application to process each event.

5. IMPLEMENTATION

We now give more details on the implementation of the Scap monitoring framework.

5.1 Scap Kernel Module

The Scap kernel module implements a new network protocol for receiving packets from network devices, and a new socket class, `PF_SCAP`, for communication between the Scap stub and the kernel module. Packets are transferred to memory through DMA, and the driver schedules them for processing within the software interrupt handler—the Scap's protocol handler in our case.

5.2 Fast TCP Reassembly

For each packet, the Scap kernel module finds and updates its respective `stream_t` record, or creates a new one. For fast lookup, we use a hash table by randomly choosing a hash function during initialization. Based on the transport-layer protocol headers, Scap extracts the packet's data and writes them directly to the current memory offset indicated in the `stream_t` record. Packets belonging to streams that exceed their cutoff value, as well as duplicate or overlapping TCP segments, are discarded immediately without unnecessarily spending further CPU and memory resources for them. Streams can expire explicitly (e.g., via TCP FIN/RST), or implicitly, due to an inactivity timeout. For the latter, Scap maintains an *access list* with the active streams sorted by their last access time. Upon packet reception, the respective `stream_t` record is simply placed at the beginning of the access list, to keep it sorted. Periodically, starting from the end of the list, the kernel module compares the last access time of each stream with the current time, and expires all streams for which no packet was received within the specified period by creating stream termination events.

5.3 Memory Management

Reassembled streams are stored in a large memory buffer allocated by the kernel module and mapped in user level by the Scap stub. For each stream, a contiguous memory block is allocated (by our own memory allocator) according to the stream's chunk size. When this block fills up, the chunk is delivered for processing (by creating a respective event) and a new block is allocated for the next chunk. The Scap stub has access to this block through memory mapping, so an offset is enough for locating each stored chunk. To avoid dynamic allocation overhead, a large number of `stream_t` records are pre-allocated during initialization, and are memory-mapped by the Scap stub. More records are allocated dynamically as needed. Thus, the number of streams that can be tracked concurrently is not limited by Scap.

5.4 Event Creation

A new event is triggered on stream creation, stream termination, and whenever stream data is available for processing. A data event can be triggered for one of the following reasons: (i) a memory chunk fills up, (ii) a flush timeout is passed, (iii) a cutoff value is exceeded, or (iv) a stream is terminated. When a stream's cutoff threshold is reached, Scap creates a final data processing event for its last chunk. However, its `stream_t` record remains in the hash table and in the access list, so that monitoring continues throughout its whole lifetime. This is required for gathering flow statistics and generating the appropriate termination event.

To avoid contention when the Scap kernel module runs in parallel across several cores, each core inserts events in a separate queue. When a new event is added into a queue, the `sk_data_ready()` function is called to wake up the corresponding worker thread, which calls `poll()` whenever its event queue is empty. Along with each event, the Scap stub receives and forwards to the user-level application a pointer to the respective `stream_t` record. To avoid race conditions between the Scap kernel module and the application, Scap maintains a second instance of each `stream_t` record. The first copy is updated within the kernel, while the second is read by the user-level application. The kernel module updates the necessary fields of the second `stream_t` instance right before a new event for this stream is enqueued.

5.5 Hardware Filters

Packets taking part in the TCP three-way handshake are always captured. When the cutoff threshold is triggered for a stream, Scap adds dynamically the necessary FDIR filters to drop at the NIC layer all subsequent packets belonging to this stream. Note that although packets are dropped before they reach main memory, Scap needs to know when a stream ends. For this reason, we add filters to drop only packets that contain actual data segments (or TCP acknowledgements), and still allow Scap to receive TCP RST or FIN packets that may terminate a stream.

This is achieved using the flexible 2-byte tuple option of FDIR filters. We have modified the NIC driver to allow for matching the offset, reserved, and TCP flags 2-byte tuple in the TCP header. Using this option, we add two filters for each stream: the first matches and drops TCP packets for which only the ACK flag is set, and the second matches and drops TCP packets for which only the ACK and PSH flags are set. The rest of the filter fields are based on each stream's 5-tuple. Thus, only TCP packets with RST or FIN flag will be forwarded to Scap kernel module for stream termination.

Streams may also be terminated based on an inactivity timeout. For this reason Scap associates a timeout with each filter, and keeps a list with all filters sorted by their timeout values. Thus, an FDIR filter is removed (i) when a TCP RST or FIN packet arrives for a given stream, or (ii) when the timeout associated with a filter expires. Note that in the second case the stream may still be active, so if a packet of this stream arrives upon the removal of its filter, Scap will immediately re-install the filter. This is because the cutoff of this stream has exceeded and the stream is still active. To handle long running streams, re-installed filters get a timeout twice as large as before. In this way, long-running flows will only be evicted a logarithmic number of times from NIC's filters. If there is no space left on the NIC to accommodate a new filter, a filter with a small timeout is evicted, as it does not correspond to a long-lived stream.

Scap needs to provide accurate flow statistics upon the termination of streams that had exceeded their cutoff, even if most of their packets were discarded at the NIC. Unfortunately, existing NICs provide only aggregate statistics for packets across all filters—not per each filter. However, Scap is able to estimate accurate per-flow statistics, such as flow size and flow duration, based on the TCP sequence numbers of the RST/FIN packets. Also, by removing the NIC filters when their timeout expires, Scap receives packets from these streams periodically and updates their statistics.

Our implementation is based on the Intel 82599 NIC [21], which supports RSS and flow director filters. Similarly to this card, most modern 10GbE NICs such as Solarflare [46], SMC [44], Chelsio [10], and Myricom [30], also support RSS and filtering capabilities, so Scap can be effectively used with these NICs as well.

5.6 Handling Multiple Applications

Multiple applications can use Scap concurrently on the same machine. Given that monitoring applications require only read access to the stream data, there is room for stream sharing to avoid multiple copies and improve overall performance. To this end, all Scap sockets share a single memory buffer for stream data and

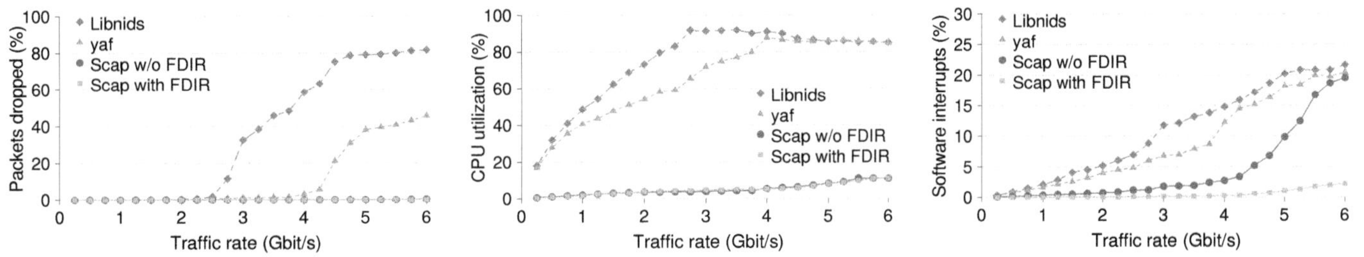

(a) Packet loss (b) CPU utilization (c) Software interrupt load

Figure 3: Performance comparison of flow-based statistics export for YAF, Libnids, and Scap, for varying traffic rates.

stream_t records. As applications have different requirements, Scap tries to combine and generalize all requirements at kernel level, and apply application-specific configurations at user level.

5.7 Packet Delivery

An application may be interested in receiving both reassembled streams, as well as their individual packets, e.g., to detect TCP-level attacks [41]. Scap supports the delivery of the original packets as captured from the network, if an application indicates that it needs them. Then, Scap internally uses another memory-mapped buffer that contains records for each packet of a stream. Each record contains a packet header with the timestamp and capture length, and a pointer to the original packet payload in the stream.

5.8 API Stub

The Scap API stub uses `setsockopt()` to pass parameters to the kernel module for handling API calls. When `scap_start_capture()` is called, each worker thread runs an event-dispatch loop that polls its corresponding event queue, reads the next available event, and executes the registered callback function for the event (if any). The event queues contain `stream_t` objects, which have an `event` field and a pointer to the next `stream_t` object in the event queue. If this pointer is NULL, then there is no event in the queue, and the stub calls `poll()` to wait for future events.

6. EXPERIMENTAL EVALUATION

We experimentally evaluate the performance of Scap, comparing it to other stream reassembly libraries, for common monitoring tasks, such as flow statistics export and pattern matching, while replaying a trace of real network traffic at different rates.

6.1 Experimental Environment

The hardware.

We use a testbed comprising two PCs interconnected through a 10 GbE switch. The first, equipped with two dual-core Intel Xeon 2.66 GHz CPUs with 4MB L2 cache, 4GB RAM, and an Intel 82599EB 10GbE NIC, is used for traffic generation. The second, used as a monitoring sensor, is equipped with two quad-core Intel Xeon 2.00 GHz CPUs with 6MB L2 cache, 4GB RAM, and an Intel 82599EB 10GbE NIC used for stream capture. Both PCs run 64-bit Ubuntu Linux (kernel version 2.6.32).

The trace.

To evaluate stream reassembly implementations with real traffic, we replay a one-hour long full-payload trace captured at the access link that connects to the Internet a University campus with thousands of hosts. The trace contains 58,714,906 packets and 1,493,032 flows, totaling more than 46GB, 95.4% of which is TCP traffic. To achieve high replay rates (up to 6 Gbit/s) we split the trace in smaller parts of 1GB that fit into main memory, and replay each part 10 times while the next part is being loaded in memory.

The parameters.

We compare the following systems: (i) Scap, (ii) Libnids v1.24 [2], (iii) YAF v2.1.1 [20], a Libpcap-based flow export tool, and (iv) the Stream5 preprocessor of Snort v2.8.3.2 [40]. YAF, Libnids and Snort rely on Libpcap [29], which uses the `PF_PACKET` socket for packet capture on Linux. Similarly to Scap's kernel module, the `PF_PACKET` kernel module runs as a software interrupt handler that stores incoming packets to a memory-mapped buffer, shared with Libpcap's user-level stub. In our experiments, the size of this buffer is set to 512MB, and the buffer size for reassembled streams is set to 1GB for Scap, Libnids, and Snort. We use a chunk size of 16KB, the `SCAP_TCP_FAST` reassembly mode, and an inactivity timeout of 10 seconds. The majority of TCP streams terminate explicitly with TCP FIN or RST packet, but we also use an inactivity timeout to expire UDP and TCP flows that do not close normally. As we replay the trace at much higher rates than its actual capture rate, an inactivity timeout of 10 seconds is a reasonable choice.

6.2 Flow-Based Statistics Export: Drop Anything Not Needed

In our first experiment we evaluate the performance of Scap for exporting flow statistics, comparing with YAF and with a Libnids-based program that receives reassembled flows. By setting the stream cutoff value to zero, Scap discards all stream data after updating stream statistics. When Scap is configured to use the FDIR filters, the NIC discards all packets of a flow after TCP connection establishment, except from the TCP FIN/RST packets, which are used by Scap for flow termination. Although Scap can use all eight available cores, for a fair comparison, we configure it to use a single worker thread, as YAF and Libnids are single-threaded. However, for all tools, interrupt handling for packet processing in the kernel takes advantage of all cores, utilizing NIC's multiple queues.

Figures 3(a), 3(b), and 3(c) present the percentage of dropped packets, the average CPU utilization of the monitoring application on a single core, and the software interrupt load while varying the traffic rate from 250 Mbit/s to 6 Gbit/s. We see that Libnids starts losing packets when the traffic rate exceeds 2 Gbit/s. The reason can be seen in Figures 3(b) and 3(c), where the total CPU utilization of Libnids exceeds 90% at 2.5 Gbit/s. YAF performs slightly better than Libnids, but when the traffic reaches 4 Gbit/s, it also drives CPU utilization to 100% and starts losing packets as well. This is because both YAF and Libnids receive all packets in user space and then drop them, as the packets themselves are not needed.

(a) Packet loss (b) CPU utilization (c) Software interrupt load

Figure 4: Performance comparison of stream delivery for Snort, Libnids, and Scap, for varying traffic rates.

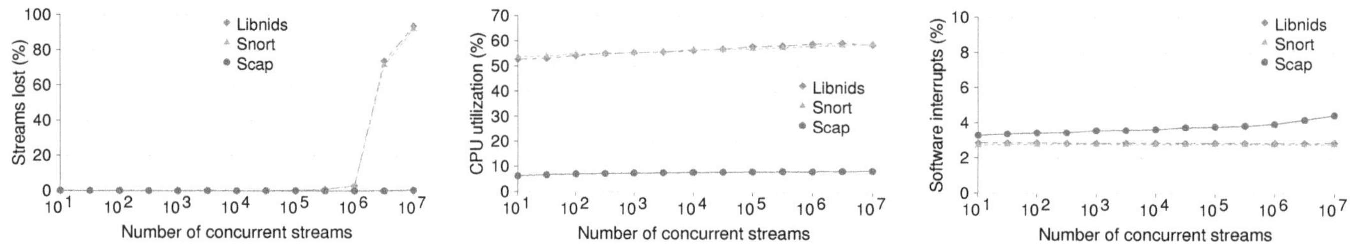

(a) Lost streams (b) CPU utilization (c) Software interrupt load

Figure 5: Performance comparison of Snort, Libnids, and Scap, for a varying number of concurrent streams.

Scap processes all packets even at 6 Gbit/s load. As shown in Figure 3(b), the CPU utilization of the Scap application is always less than 10%, as it practically does not do any work at all. All the work has already been done by Scap's kernel module. One would expect the overhead of this module (shown in Figure 3(c)) to be relatively high. Fortunately, however, the software interrupt load of Scap is even lower compared to YAF and Libnids, even when FDIR filters are not used, because Scap does not copy the incoming packets around: as soon as a packet arrives, the kernel module accesses only the needed information from its headers, updates the respective *stream_t*, and just drops it. In contrast, Libnids and YAF receive all packets to user space, resulting in much higher overhead. YAF performs better than Libnids because it receives only the first 96 bytes of each packet and it does not perform stream reassembly.

When Scap uses FDIR filters to discard the majority of the packets at NIC layer it achieves even better performance. Figure 3(c) shows that the software interrupt load is significantly lower with FDIR filters: as little as 2% for 6 Gbit/s. Indeed, Scap with FDIR brings into main memory as little as 3% of the total packets—just the packets involved in TCP session creation and termination.

6.3 Delivering Streams to User Level: The Cost of an Extra Memory Copy

In this experiment, we explore the performance of Scap, Snort, and Libnids when delivering reassembled streams without any further processing. The Scap application receives all data from all streams with no cutoff, and runs as a single thread. Snort is configured with only the Stream5 preprocessor enabled, without any rules. Figure 4(a) shows the percentage of dropped packets as a function of the traffic rate. Scap delivers all steams without any packet loss for rates up to 5.5 Gbit/s. On the other hand, Libnids starts dropping packets at 2.5 Gbit/s (drop rate: 1.4%) and Snort at 2.75 Gbit/s (drop rate: 0.7%). Thus, Scap is able to deliver reassembled streams to the monitoring applications for more than two times higher traffic rates. When the input traffic reaches 6 Gbit/s, Libnids drops 81.2% and Snort 79.5% of the total packets received.

The reason for this performance difference lies in the extra memory copy operations needed for stream reassembly at user level. When a packet arrives for Libnids and Snort, the kernel writes it in the next available location in a common ring buffer. When performing stream reassembly, Libnids and Snort may have to *copy* each packet's payload from the ring buffer to a memory buffer allocated specifically for this packet's stream. Scap avoids this extra copy operation because the kernel module copies the packet's data *not* to a common buffer, but directly to a memory buffer allocated specifically for this packet's stream. Figure 4(b) shows that the CPU utilization of the Scap user-level application is considerably lower than the utilization of Libnids and Snort, which at 3 Gbit/s exceeds 90%, saturating the processor. In contrast, the CPU utilization for the Scap application is less then 60% even for speeds up to 6 Gbit/s, as the user application does very little work: all the stream reassembly is performed in the kernel module, which increases the software interrupt load, as can be seen in Figure 4(c).

6.4 Concurrent Streams

An attacker could try to saturate the flow table of a stream reassembly library by creating a large number of established TCP flows, so that a subsequent malicious flow cannot be stored. In this experiment, we evaluate the ability of Scap, Libnids, and Snort to handle such cases while increasing the number of concurrent TCP streams up to 10 million. Each stream consists of 100 packets with the maximum TCP payload, and streams are multiplexed so that the desirable number of concurrent streams is achieved. For each case, we create a respective packet trace and then replay it at a constant rate of 1 Gbit/s, as we want to evaluate the effect of concurrent streams without increasing the traffic rate. As in the previous experiment, the application uses a single thread and receives all streams at user level, without performing any further processing.

Figure 5 shows that Scap scales well with the number of concurrent streams: as we see in Figure 5(a), no stream is lost even for 10 million concurrent TCP streams. Also, Figures 5(b) and 5(c) show that the CPU utilization and software interrupt load of Scap

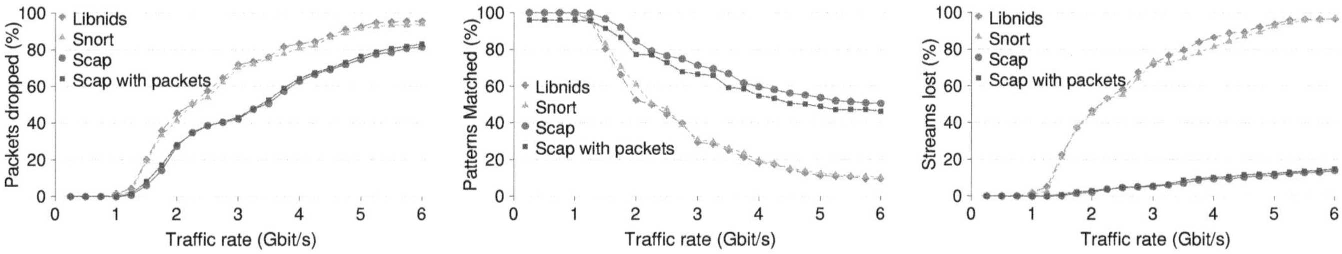

(a) Packet loss (b) Patterns Successfully Matched (c) Lost streams

Figure 6: Performance comparison of pattern matching for Snort, Libnids, and Scap, for varying traffic rates.

slightly increase with the number of concurrent streams, as the traffic rate remains constant. On the other hand, Snort and Libnids cannot handle more than one million concurrent streams, even though they can handle 1 Gbit/s traffic with less than 60% CPU utilization. This is due to internal limits that these libraries have for the number of flows they can store in their data structures. In contrast, Scap does not have to set such limits because it uses a dynamic memory management approach: when more memory is needed for storing `stream_t` records, Scap allocates dynamically the necessary memory pools to capture all streams. In case an attacker tries to overwhelm the Scap flow table, Scap will use all the available memory for `stream_t` records. When there is no more free memory, Scap's policy is to always store newer streams by removing from the flow table the older ones, i.e., streams with the highest inactivity time based on the access list.

6.5 Pattern Matching

In the following experiments, we measure the performance of Scap with an application that receives all streams and searches for a set of patterns. We do not apply any cutoff so that all traffic is delivered to the application, and a single worker thread is used. Pattern matching is performed using the Aho-Corasik algorithm [5]. We extracted 2,120 strings based on the `content` field of the "web attack" rules from the official VRT Snort rule set [4], and use them as our patterns. These strings resulted in 223,514 matches in our trace. We compare Scap with Snort and Libnids using the same string matching algorithm and set of patterns in all three cases. To ensure a fair comparison, Snort is configured only with the Stream5 preprocessor enabled, using a separate Snort rule for each of the 2,120 patterns, applied to all traffic, so that all tools end up using the same automaton. The Scap and Libnids programs load the 2,120 patterns from a file, build the respective DFA, and start receiving streams. We use the same chunk size of 16KB for all tools.

Figure 6(a) shows the percentage of dropped packets for each application as a function of the traffic rate. We see that Snort and Libnids process traffic rates of up to 750 Mbit/s without dropping any packets, while Scap processes up to 1 Gbit/s traffic with no packet loss with one worker thread. The main reasons for the improved performance of Scap are the improved cache locality when grouping multiple packets into their respective transport-layer streams, and the reduced memory copies during stream reassembly.

Moreover, Scap drops significantly fewer packets than Snort and Libnids, e.g., at 6 Gbit/s it processes three times more traffic. This behavior has a positive effect on the number of matches. As shown in Figure 6(b), under the high load of 6 Gbit/s, Snort and Libnids match less than 10% of the patterns, while Scap matches five times as many: 50.34%. Although the percentage of missed matches for Snort and Libnids is proportional to the percentage of dropped packets, the accuracy of the Scap application is affected less from

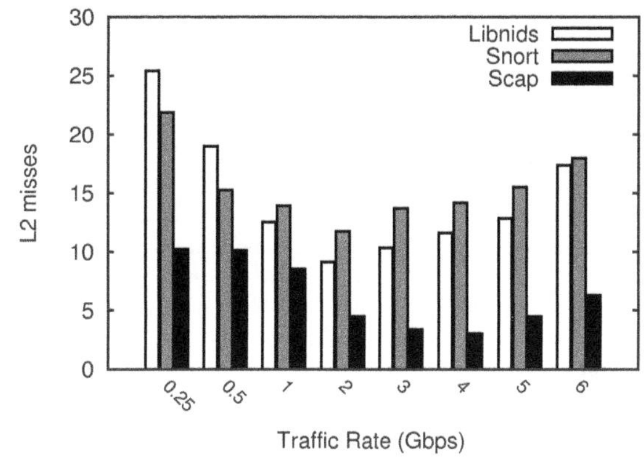

Figure 7: L2 cache misses of pattern matching using Snort, Libnids, and Scap, for varying traffic rates.

high packet loss rates. This is because Scap under overload tends to retain more packets towards the beginning of each stream. As we use patterns from web attack signatures, they are usually found within the first few bytes of HTTP requests or responses. Also, Scap tries to deliver contiguous chunks, which improves the detection abilities compared to delivery of chunks with random holes.

6.5.1 Favoring Recent and Short Streams

We turn our attention now to see how dropped packets affect the different stream reassembly approaches followed by Scap, Libnids, and Snort. While Libnids and Snort drop packets randomly under overload, Scap is able to (i) assign more memory to new or small streams, (ii) cut the long tails of large streams, and (iii) deliver more streams intact when the available memory is limited. Moreover, the Scap kernel module always receives and processes all important protocol packets during the TCP handshake. In contrast, when a packet capture library drops these packets due to overload, the user-level stream reassembly library will not be able to reassemble the respective streams. Indeed, Figure 6(c) shows that the percentage of lost streams in Snort and Libnids is proportional to the packet loss rate. In contrast, Scap loses significantly less streams than the corresponding packet loss ratio. Even for 81.2% packet loss at 6 Gbit/s, only 14% of the total streams are lost.

6.5.2 Locality

Let's now turn our attention to see how different choices made by different tools impact locality of reference and, in the end, determine application performance. For the previous experiment, we also measure the number of L2 cache misses as a function of the traffic rate (Figure 7), using the processor's performance counters [3]. We see that when the input traffic is about 0.25 Gbit/s,

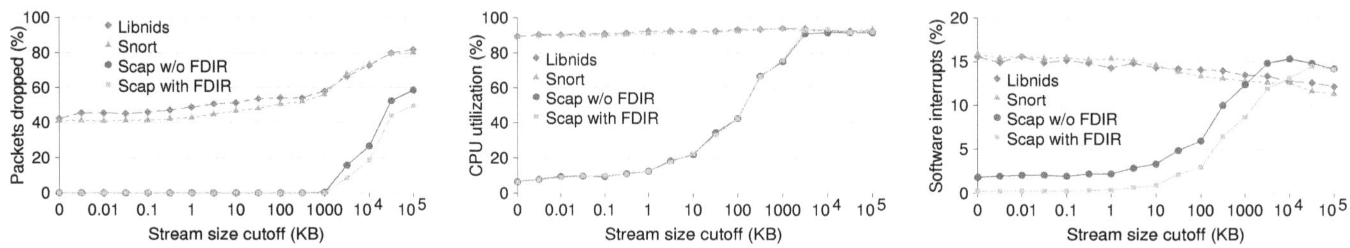

(a) Packet loss (b) CPU utilization (c) Software interrupt load

Figure 8: Performance comparison of Snort, Libnids, and Scap, for varying stream size cutoff values at 4 Gbit/s rate.

Snort experiences about 25 misses per packet, Libnids about 21, while Scap experiences *half* of them: just 10.2 misses per packet. We have to underline that at this low traffic rate none of the three tools misses any packets, and we know that none of the tools is stressed, so they all operate in their comfort zone. The reason that Lidnids and Snort have twice as many cache misses as Scap can be traced to the better locality of reference of the Scap approach. By reassembling packets into streams from the moment they arrive, packets are not copied around: consecutive segments are stored together, and are consumed together. On the contrary, Libnids and Snort perform packet reassembly too late: the segments have been stored in (practically) random locations all over the main memory.

6.5.3 Packet Delivery

To evaluate the packet delivery performance of Scap, we ran the same application when Scap was configured with packet support, and pattern matching was performed on the delivered packet payloads. The results are shown in Figure 6 as well. We see that the performance of Scap remains the same when the pattern matching application operates on each packet, i.e., the percentages of dropped packets and lost streams do not change. We just observe a slight decrease in the number of successful matches, which is due to missed matches for patterns spanning the payloads of multiple successive packets.

6.6 Cutoff Points: Discarding Less Interesting Packets Before It Is Too Late

Several network monitoring applications need to receive only the initial part of each flow [26, 33]. Other systems, such as Time Machine [27], elevate the ability to store only the beginning of each flow into one of their fundamental properties. In this experiment, we set out to explore the effectiveness of Libnids, Snort, and Scap when implementing cutoff points. For Snort, we modified Stream5 to discard packets from streams that exceed a given cutoff value. Similarly, when the size of a stream reaches the cutoff value, Libnids stops the collection of data for this stream. In Scap, we just call the `scap_set_cutoff()` function in program's preamble using the desirable cutoff. We also compare Scap with and without using FDIR filters. The applications search for the same set of patterns as in the previous experiment.

Figures 8(a), 8(b), and 8(c) show the packet loss, CPU utilization, and software interrupt load as a function of the cutoff for a fixed traffic rate of 4 Gbit/s. Interestingly, even for a zero cutoff size, i.e., when all data of each flow is discarded, both Snort and Libnids experience as much as 40% packet loss, as shown in the left part of Figure 8(a). This is because Snort and Libnids first bring *all* packets to user space, and then discard the bytes they do not need. Indeed, Figures 8(b) and 8(c) show that the total CPU utilization of Libnids and Snort is always close to 100% at this traffic rate irrespectively of the cutoff point.

In contrast, for cutoff points smaller than 1MB, Scap has no packet loss and very small CPU utilization. For instance, when Scap uses a 10KB cutoff, the CPU load is reduced from 97% to just 21.9%, as 97.6% of the total traffic is efficiently discarded. At the same time, 83.6% of the matches are still found, and no stream is lost. This outcome demonstrates how the stream cutoff, when implemented efficiently, can improve performance by cutting the long tails of large flows, and allows applications to keep monitoring the first bytes of each stream at high speeds. When the cutoff point increases beyond 1MB, CPU utilization reaches saturation and even Scap starts dropping packets. Enhancing Scap with hardware filters reduces the software interrupt load, and thus reduces the packet loss for cutoff values larger than 1MB.

6.7 Stream Priorities: Less Interesting Packets Are The First Ones To Go

To experimentally evaluate the effectiveness of Prioritized Packet Loss (PPL), we ran the same pattern matching application using a single worker thread while setting two priority classes. As an example, we set a higher priority to all streams with source or destination port 80, which correspond to 8.4% of the total packets in our trace. The rest of the streams have the same (low) priority. Figure 9 shows the percentage of dropped packets for high-priority and low-priority streams as a function of the traffic rate. When the traffic rate exceeds 1 Gbit/s, the single-threaded pattern matching application cannot process all incoming traffic, resulting in a fraction of dropped packets that increases with higher traffic rates. However, we see that no high-priority packet is dropped for traffic rates up to 5.5 Gbit/s, while a significant number of low-priority packets are dropped at these rates—up to 85.7% at 5.5 Gbit/s. At the traffic rate of 6 Gbit/s, we see a small packet loss of 2.3% for high-priority packets out of the total 81.5% of dropped packets.

6.8 Using Multiple CPU Cores

In all previous experiments the Scap application ran on a single thread, to allow for a fair comparison with Snort and Libnids, which are single-threaded. However, Scap is naturally parallel and can easily use a larger number of cores. In this experiment, we explore how Scap scales with the number of cores. We use the same pattern matching application as previously, without any cutoff, and configure it to use from one up to eight worker threads. Our system has eight cores, and each worker thread is pinned to one core.

Figure 10(a) shows the packet loss rate as a function of the number of worker threads, for three different traffic rates. When using a single thread, Scap processes about 1 Gbit/s of traffic without packet loss. When using seven threads, Scap processes all traffic at 4 Gbit/s with no packet loss. Figure 10(b) shows the maximum

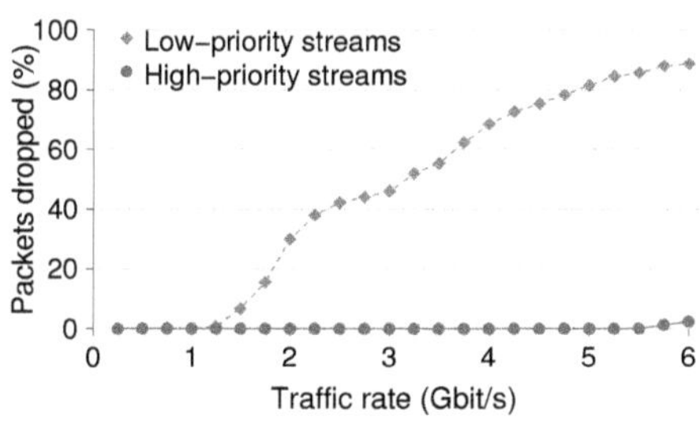

Figure 9: Packet loss for high- and low-priority streams, for varying traffic rates.

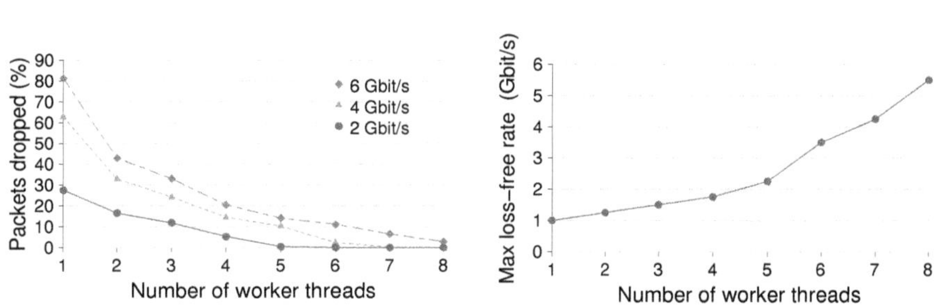

(a) Packet loss

(b) Speedup

Figure 10: Performance of an Scap pattern matching application for a varying number of worker threads.

loss-free rate achieved by the application as a function of the number of threads. We see that performance improves linearly with the number of threads, starting at about 1 Gbit/s for one worker thread and going all the way to 5.5 Gbit/s for eight threads.

The reason that we do not see a speedup of eight when using eight worker threads is the following: even though we restrict the user application to run on a limited number of cores, equal to the number of worker threads, the operating system kernel runs always on all the available cores of the processor. Therefore, when Scap creates less than eight worker threads, it is only the user-level application that runs on these cores. The underlying operating system and Scap kernel module runs on all cores.

7. ANALYSIS

In this section, we analyze the performance of Prioritized Packet Loss (PPL) under heavy load, aiming to explore at what point PPL should start dropping low-priority packets so that high priority ones do not have to be dropped. For simplicity lets assume that we have two priorities: low and $high$. We define N to be $(memory\_size - base\_threshold)/2$. If the used memory exceeds N, then PPL will start dropping low priority packets. Given that N is finite, we would like to explore what is the probability that N will fill up and we will have to drop high-priority packets. To calculate this probability we need to make a few more assumptions. Assume that high-priority packet arrivals follow a Poisson distribution with a rate of λ, and that queued packets are consumed by the user level application. We assume that the service times for packets follow an exponential distribution with parameter μ. Then, the whole system can be modeled as an $M/M/1/N$ queue. The probability that all the memory will fill up is:

$$P_{full} = \frac{1-\rho}{1-\rho^{N+1}}\rho^N \quad (1)$$

where $\rho = \lambda/\mu$. Due to the PASTA property of the Poisson processes, this is exactly the probability of packet loss: $P_{loss} = P_{full}$.

Figure 11 plots the packet loss probability for high-priority packets as a function of N. We see that a memory size of a few tens of packet slots are enough to reduce the probability that a high-priority packet is lost to 10^{-8}. We note, however, that the speed with which the probability is reduced depends on ρ: the fraction of the high-priority packets over all traffic which can be served by the full capacity of the system. We see that when ρ is 0.1, that is, when only 10% of the packets are high-priority ones, then less than 10 slots are more than enough to guarantee that there will be practically no packet loss. When ρ is 0.5 (i.e., 50% of the traffic is high-priority), then a little more than 20 packet slots are enough, while when ρ is 0.9, then about 150 packet slots are enough.

The analysis can be extended to more priority levels as well. Assume, for example, that we have three priority levels: low, $medium$, and $high$, that $N = (memory\_size - base\_threshold)/3$, that medium-priority packet arrivals follow a Poisson distribution with a rate of λ_1, and that high-priority packet arrivals follow a Poisson distribution with a rate of λ_2. As previously, assume that the service times for packets follow an exponential distribution with parameter μ. Then, the system can be described as a Markov chain with $2N$ nodes:

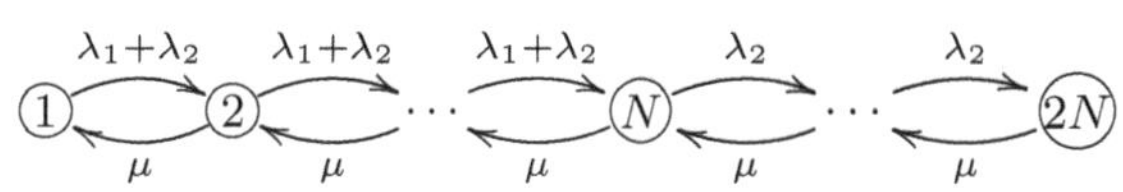

The packet loss probability for high-priority packets is:

$$P_{loss} = \rho_1^N \rho_2^N p_0 \quad (2)$$

where $\rho_1 = (\lambda_1 + \lambda_2)/\mu$, $\rho_2 = \lambda_2/\mu$, and

$$p_0 = 1/(\frac{1-\rho_1^{N+1}}{1-\rho_1} + \rho_1^{N/3}\frac{1-\rho_2^{N+1}}{1-\rho_2})$$

The packet loss probability for medium-priority packets remains:

$$P_{loss} = \frac{1-\rho_1}{1-\rho_1{}^{N+1}}\rho_1{}^N \quad (3)$$

Figure 12 plots the packet loss probability for high-priority and medium-priority packets as a function of N. We assume that $\rho_1 = \rho_2 = 0.3$. We see that a few tens of packet slots are enough to reduce the packet loss probability for both high-priority and medium-priority packets to practically zero. Thus, we believe that PPL provides an effective mechanism for preventing uncontrolled loss of important packets in network monitoring systems.

8. RELATED WORK

In this section we review prior work related to Scap.

8.1 Improving Packet Capture

Several techniques have been proposed to reduce the kernel overhead and the number of memory copies for delivering packets to the application [8, 11, 31, 39]. Scap can also use such techniques to improve its performance. The main difference, however, is that all these approaches operate at the network layer. Thus, monitoring applications that require transport-layer streams should implement stream reassembly, or use a separate user-level library, resulting in reduced performance and increased application complexity. In contrast, Scap operates at the transport layer and directly assembles incoming packets to streams in the kernel, offering the opportunity for a wide variety of performance optimizations and many features.

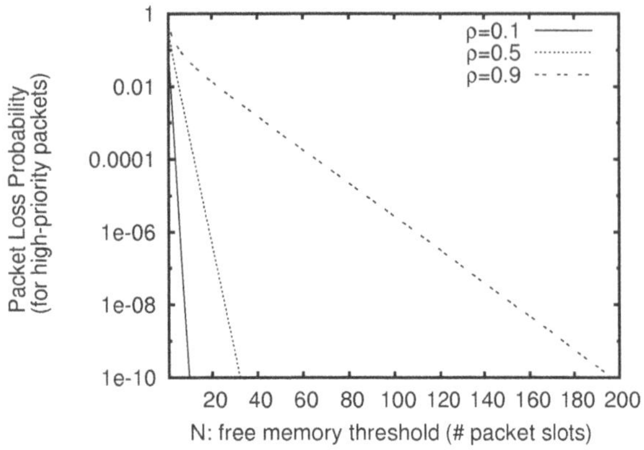

Figure 11: Packet loss probability for high-priority packets as a function of N.

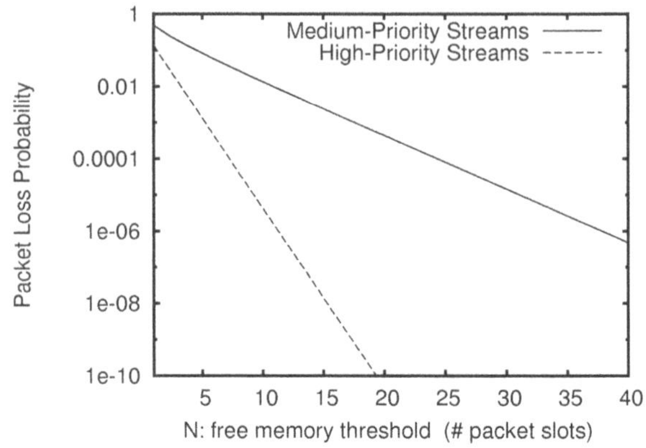

Figure 12: Packet loss probability for high-priority and medium-priority packets as a function of N.

Papadogiannakis et al. [35] show that memory access locality in passive network monitoring applications can be improved when reordering the packet stream based on source and destination port numbers. Scap also improves memory access locality and cache usage in a similar manner when grouping packets into streams.

8.2 Taking Advantage of Multi-core Systems

Fusco and Deri [17] utilize the receive-side scaling feature of modern NICs in conjunction with multi-core systems to improve packet capture performance. Sommer et al. [47] take advantage of multi-core processors to parallelize event-based intrusion prevention systems using multiple event queues that collect semantically related events for in-order execution. Storing related events in a single queue localizes memory access to shared state by the same thread. Pesterev et al. [37] improve TCP connection locality in multicore servers using the flow director filters to optimally balance the TCP packets among the available cores. We view these works as orthogonal to Scap: such advances in multi-core systems can be easily used by Scap.

8.3 Packet Filtering

Dynamic packet filtering reduces the cost of adding and removing filters at runtime [12,49,53]. Deri et al. [13] propose to use the flow director filters for common filtering needs. Other approaches allow applications to move simple tasks to the kernel packet filter to improve performance [6,8,23]. Scap suggests a relatively different approach: applications empowered with a *Stream* abstraction can communicate their stream-oriented filtering and processing needs to the underlying kernel module at runtime through the Scap API, to achieve lower complexity and better performance. For instance, Scap is able to filter packets within the kernel or at the NIC layer based on a flow size cutoff limit, allowing to set dynamically different cutoff values per-stream, while the existing packet filtering systems are not able to support a similar functionality.

8.4 TCP Stream Reassembly

Libnids [2] is a user-level library on top of Libpcap for TCP stream reassembly based on the emulation of a Linux network stack. Similarly, the Stream5 [32] preprocessor, part of Snort NIDS [40], performs TCP stream reassembly at user level, emulating the network stacks of various operating systems. Scap shares similar goals with Libnids and Stream5. However, previous works treat TCP stream reassembly as a necessity [50], mostly for the avoidance of evasion attacks against intrusion detection systems [14, 19, 51]. On the contrary, Scap views transport-layer streams as the fundamental abstraction that is exported to network monitoring applications, and as the right vehicle to implement aggressive optimizations.

8.5 Per-flow Cutoff

The Time Machine network traffic recording system [27] exploits the heavy-tailed nature of Internet traffic to reduce the number of packets stored on disk for retrospective analysis, by applying a per-flow cutoff. Limiting the size of flows can also improve the performance of intrusion detection systems under load [26, 33], by focusing detection on the beginning of each connection. Canini et al. [9] propose a similar scheme for traffic classification, by sampling more packets from the beginning of each flow. Scap shares a similar approach with these works, but implements it within a general framework for fast and efficient network traffic monitoring, using the *Stream* abstraction to enable the implementation of performance improvements at the most appropriate level. For instance, Scap implements the per-flow cutoff inside the kernel or at the NIC layer, while previous approaches have to implement it in user space. As a result, they first receive *all* packets from kernel in user space, and then discard those that are not needed.

8.6 Overload Control

Load shedding is proposed as a defense against overload attacks in Bro [36], whereby the NIDS operator is responsible for defining a discarding strategy. Barlet-Ros et al. [7] also propose a load shedding technique using an on-line prediction model for query resource requirements, so that the monitoring system sheds load under conditions of excessive traffic using uniform packet and flow sampling. Dreger et al. [16] deal with packet drops due to overloads in a NIDS using load levels, which are precompiled sets of filters that correspond to different subsets of traffic enabled by the NIDS depending on the workload.

8.7 Summary

To place our work in context, Figure 13 categorizes Scap and related works along two dimensions: the main abstraction provided to applications, i.e., packet, set of packets, or stream, and the level at which this abstraction is implemented, i.e., user or kernel level. Traditional systems such as Libpcap [29] use the *packet* as basic abstraction and are implemented in user level. More sophisticated systems such as netmap [39], FLAME [6], and PF_RING [11] also use the packet as basic abstraction, but are implemented in kernel and deliver better performance. MAPI [48] and FFPF [8] use higher

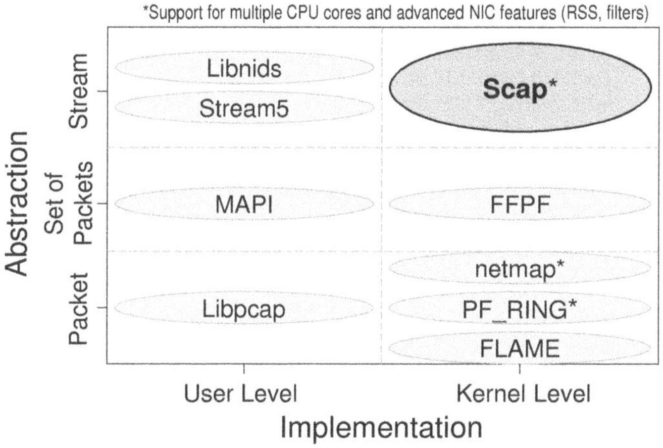

Figure 13: Categorization of network monitoring tools and systems that support commodity NICs.

level abstractions such as the *set of packets*. Libnids and Stream5 provide the transport-layer *Stream* as their basic abstraction, but operate at user level and thus achieve poor performance and miss several opportunities of efficiently implementing this abstraction. We see Scap as the only system that provides a high-level abstraction, and at the same time implements it at the appropriate level, enabling a wide range of performance optimizations and features.

9. CONCLUSION

In this paper, we have identified a gap in network traffic monitoring: applications usually need to express their monitoring requirements at a high level, using notions from the transport layer or even higher, while most monitoring tools still operate at the network layer. To bridge this gap, we have presented the design, implementation, and evaluation of Scap, a network monitoring framework that offers an expressive API and significant performance improvements for applications that process traffic at the transport layer and beyond. Scap gives the stream abstraction a first-class status, and provides an OS subsystem for capturing transport-layer streams while minimizing data copy operations by optimally placing network data into stream-specific memory regions.

The results of our experimental evaluation demonstrate that Scap is able to deliver all streams for rates up to 5.5 Gbit/s using a single core, two times higher than the other existing approaches. An Scap-based application for pattern matching handles 33% higher traffic rates and processes three times more traffic at 6 Gbit/s than Snort and Libnids. Moreover, we observe that user-level implementations of per-flow cutoff just reduce the packet loss rate, while Scap's kernel-level implementation and subzero copy eliminate completely packet loss for stream cutoff values of up to 1MB when performing pattern matching operations at 4 Gbit/s. This outcome demonstrates that cutting the long tails of large flows can be extremely beneficial when traffic is discarded at early stages, i.e., within the kernel or even better at the NIC, in order to spend the minimum possible number of CPU cycles for uninteresting packets. When eight cores are used for parallel stream processing, Scap is able to process 5.5 times higher traffic rates with no packet loss.

As networks are getting increasingly faster and network monitoring applications are getting more sophisticated, we believe that approaches like Scap, which enable aggressive optimizations at kernel-level or even at the NIC level, will become increasingly more important in the future.

Acknowledgements

We would like to thank our shepherd Katerina Argyraki, the anonymous reviewers, and Periklis Akritidis for their valuable feedback. This research was performed with the financial support of the Prevention of and Fight against Crime Programme of the European Commission – Directorate-General Home Affairs (project GCC). This work was also supported in part by the FP7 project SysSec and the FP7-PEOPLE-2009-IOF project MALCODE, funded by the European Commission under Grant Agreements No. 254116 and No. 257007. This publication reflects the views only of the authors, and the Commission cannot be held responsible for any use which may be made of the information contained therein. Antonis Papadogiannakis and Evangelos Markatos are also with the University of Crete.

10. REFERENCES

[1] Application Layer Packet Classifier for Linux (L7-filter). http://l7-filter.sourceforge.net/.

[2] Libnids. http://libnids.sourceforge.net/.

[3] Performance application programming interface. http://icl.cs.utk.edu/papi/.

[4] Sourcefire vulnerability research team (vrt). http://www.snort.org/vrt/.

[5] A. V. Aho and M. J. Corasick. Efficient String Matching: An Aid to Bibliographic Search. *Communications of the ACM*, 18, 1975.

[6] K. G. Anagnostakis, S. Ioannidis, S. Miltchev, J. Ioannidis, M. B. Greenwald, and J. M. Smith. Efficient Packet Monitoring for Network Management. In *IFIP/IEEE Network Operations and Management Symposium (NOMS)*, 2002.

[7] P. Barlet-Ros, G. Iannaccone, J. Sanjuàs-Cuxart, D. Amores-López, and J. Solé-Pareta. Load Shedding in Network Monitoring Applications. In *USENIX Annual Technical Conference (ATC)*, 2007.

[8] H. Bos, W. de Bruijn, M. Cristea, T. Nguyen, and G. Portokalidis. FFPF: Fairly Fast Packet Filters. In *USENIX Symposium on Operating System Design and Implementation (OSDI)*, 2004.

[9] M. Canini, D. Fay, D. J. Miller, A. W. Moore, and R. Bolla. Per Flow Packet Sampling for High-Speed Network Monitoring. In *International Conference on Communication Systems and Networks (COMSNETS)*, 2009.

[10] Chelsio Communications. T4 unified wire adapters. http://www.chelsio.com/adapters/t4_unified_wire_adapters.

[11] L. Deri. Improving Passive Packet Capture: Beyond Device Polling. In *International System Administration and Network Engineering Conference (SANE)*, 2004.

[12] L. Deri. High-Speed Dynamic Packet Filtering. *Journal of Network and Systems Management*, 15(3), 2007.

[13] L. Deri, J. Gasparakis, P. Waskiewicz, and F. Fusco. Wire-Speed Hardware-Assisted Traffic Filtering with Mainstream Network Adapters. *Advances in Network-Embedded Management and Applications*, 2011.

[14] S. Dharmapurikar and V. Paxson. Robust TCP Stream Reassembly in the Presence of Adversaries. In *USENIX Security Symposium*, 2005.

[15] M. Dobrescu, N. Egi, K. Argyraki, B.-G. Chun, K. Fall, G. Iannaccone, A. Knies, M. Manesh, and S. Ratnasamy. RouteBricks: Exploiting Parallelism to Scale Software Routers. In *ACM SIGOPS Symposium on Operating Systems Principles (SOSP)*, 2009.

[16] H. Dreger, A. Feldmann, V. Paxson, and R. Sommer. Operational Experiences with High-Volume Network Intrusion Detection. In *ACM Conference on Computer and Communications Security (CCS)*, 2004.

[17] F. Fusco and L. Deri. High Speed Network Traffic Analysis with Commodity Multi-core Systems. In *ACM SIGCOMM Conference on Internet Measurement (IMC)*, 2010.

[18] G. Gu, P. Porras, V. Yegneswaran, M. Fong, and W. Lee. BotHunter: Detecting Malware Infection Through IDS-Driven Dialog Correlation. In *USENIX Security Symposium*, 2007.

[19] M. Handley, V. Paxson, and C. Kreibich. Network Intrusion Detection: Evasion, Traffic Normalization, and End-to-End Protocol Semantics. In *USENIX Security Symposium*, 2001.

[20] C. M. Inacio and B. Trammell. YAF: Yet Another Flowmeter. In *USENIX Large Installation System Administration Conference (LISA)*, 2010.

[21] Intel. 82599 10 GbE Controller Datasheet. `http://download.intel.com/design/network/datashts/82599_datasheet.pdf`.

[22] Intel Server Adapters. Receive Side Scaling on Intel Network Adapters. `http://www.intel.com/support/network/adapter/pro100/sb/cs-027574.htm`.

[23] S. Ioannidis, K. G. Anagnostakis, J. Ioannidis, and A. D. Keromytis. xPF: Packet Filtering for Low-Cost Network Monitoring. In *IEEE Workshop on High-Performance Switching and Routing (HPSR)*, 2002.

[24] T. Karagiannis, A. Broido, M. Faloutsos, and K. claffy. Transport Layer Identification of P2P Traffic. In *ACM SIGCOMM Conference on Internet Measurement (IMC)*, 2004.

[25] W. Lee, J. B. D. Cabrera, A. Thomas, N. Balwalli, S. Saluja, and Y. Zhang. Performance Adaptation in Real-Time Intrusion Detection Systems. In *International Symposium on Recent Advances in Intrusion Detection (RAID)*, 2002.

[26] T. Limmer and F. Dressler. Improving the Performance of Intrusion Detection using Dialog-based Payload Aggregation. In *IEEE Global Internet Symposium (GI)*, 2011.

[27] G. Maier, R. Sommer, H. Dreger, A. Feldmann, V. Paxson, and F. Schneider. Enriching Network Security Analysis with Time Travel. In *ACM SIGCOMM Conference on Data Communication*, 2008.

[28] S. McCanne and V. Jacobson. The BSD Packet Filter: A New Architecture for User-level Packet Capture. In *Winter USENIX Conference*, 1993.

[29] S. McCanne, C. Leres, and V. Jacobson. Libpcap. `http://www.tcpdump.org/`. Lawrence Berkeley Laboratory.

[30] Myricom. 10G-PCIE-8B-S Single-Port 10-Gigabit Ethernet Network Adapters. `https://www.myricom.com/images/stories/10G-PCIE-8B-S.pdf`.

[31] Myricom. Myricom Sniffer10G. `http://www.myricom.com/scs/SNF/doc/`, 2010.

[32] J. Novak and S. Sturges. Target-Based TCP Stream Reassembly. `http://assets.sourcefire.com/snort/developmentpapers/stream5-model-Aug032007.pdf`, 2007.

[33] A. Papadogiannakis, M. Polychronakis, and E. P. Markatos. Improving the Accuracy of Network Intrusion Detection Systems Under Load Using Selective Packet Discarding. In *ACM European Workshop on System Security (EUROSEC)*, 2010.

[34] A. Papadogiannakis, M. Polychronakis, and E. P. Markatos. Tolerating Overload Attacks Against Packet Capturing Systems. In *USENIX Annual Technical Conference (ATC)*, 2012.

[35] A. Papadogiannakis, G. Vasiliadis, D. Antoniades, M. Polychronakis, and E. P. Markatos. Improving the Performance of Passive Network Monitoring Applications with Memory Locality Enhancements. *Computer Communications*, 35(1), 2012.

[36] V. Paxson. Bro: A System for Detecting Network Intruders in Real-Time. *Computer Networks*, 31(23-24), 1999.

[37] A. Pesterev, J. Strauss, N. Zeldovich, and R. T. Morris. Improving Network Connection Locality on Multicore Systems. In *ACM European Conference on Computer Systems (EuroSys)*, 2012.

[38] T. H. Ptacek and T. N. Newsham. Insertion, Evasion, and Denial of Service: Eluding Network Intrusion Detection. Technical report, Secure Networks, Inc., 1998.

[39] L. Rizzo. netmap: A Novel Framework for Fast Packet I/O. In *USENIX Annual Technical Conference (ATC)*, 2012.

[40] M. Roesch. Snort: Lightweight Intrusion Detection for Networks. In *USENIX Large Installation System Administration Conference (LISA)*, 1999.

[41] S. Savage, N. Cardwell, D. Wetherall, and T. Anderson. TCP Congestion Control with a Misbehaving Receiver. *ACM SIGCOMM Computer Communication Review*, 29(5), 1999.

[42] U. Shankar and V. Paxson. Active Mapping: Resisting NIDS Evasion without Altering Traffic. In *IEEE Symposium on Security and Privacy*, 2003.

[43] S. Singh, C. Estan, G. Varghese, and S. Savage. Automated worm fingerprinting. In *USENIX Symposium on Operating System Design and Implementation (OSDI)*, 2004.

[44] SMC Networks. SMC10GPCIe-XFP Tiger Card 10G PCIe 10GbE XFP Server Adapter. `http://www.smc.com/files/AF/ds_SMC10GPCIe_XFP.pdf`.

[45] R. Smith, C. Estan, and S. Jha. Backtracking Algorithmic Complexity Attacks Against a NIDS. In *Annual Computer Security Applications Conference (ACSAC)*, 2006.

[46] Solarfrare. 10GbE LOM/Controller Family. `http://www.solarflare.com/Content/UserFiles/Documents/Solarflare_SFC9000_10GbE_Controller_Brief.pdf`.

[47] R. Sommer, V. Paxson, and N. Weaver. An Architecture for Exploiting Multi-Core Processors to Parallelize Network Intrusion Prevention. *Concurrency and Computation: Practice and Experience*, 21(10), 2009.

[48] P. Trimintzios, M. Polychronakis, A. Papadogiannakis, M. Foukarakis, E. P. Markatos, and A. Øslebø. DiMAPI: An Application Programming Interface for Distributed Network Monitoring. In *IFIP/IEEE Network Operations and Management Symposium (NOMS)*, 2006.

[49] J. Van Der Merwe, R. Caceres, Y. Chu, and C. Sreenan. mmdump: A Tool for Monitoring Internet Multimedia Traffic. *ACM SIGCOMM CCR*, 30(5), 2000.

[50] G. Varghese, J. A. Fingerhut, and F. Bonomi. Detecting Evasion Attacks at High Speeds without Reassembly. In *ACM SIGCOMM Conference on Data Communication*, 2006.

[51] M. Vutukuru, H. Balakrishnan, and V. Paxson. Efficient and Robust TCP Stream Normalization. In *IEEE Symposium on Security and Privacy*, 2008.

[52] S. Woo and K. Park. Scalable TCP Session Monitoring with Symmetric Receive-side Scaling. Technical report, Technical report, KAIST, 2012.

[53] Z. Wu, M. Xie, and H. Wang. Swift: A Fast Dynamic Packet Filter. In *USENIX Symposium on Networked Systems Design and Implementation (NSDI)*, 2008.

A Measurement-based Study of MultiPath TCP Performance over Wireless Networks

Yung-Chih Chen
School of Computer Science
University of Massachusetts
Amherst, MA USA
yungchih@cs.umass.edu

Yeon-sup Lim
School of Computer Science
University of Massachusetts
Amherst, MA USA
ylim@cs.umass.edu

Richard J. Gibbens
Computer Laboratory
University of Cambridge
Cambridge, UK
richard.gibbens@cl.cam.ac.uk

Erich M. Nahum
IBM Thomas J. Watson
Research Center
Yorktown Heights, NY USA
nahum@us.ibm.com

Ramin Khalili
T-Labs, Deutsche Telekom
Berlin, Germany
ramin@net.t-labs.tu-berlin.de

Don Towsley
School of Computer Science
University of Massachusetts
Amherst, MA USA
towsley@cs.umass.edu

ABSTRACT

With the popularity of mobile devices and the pervasive use of cellular technology, there is widespread interest in hybrid networks and on how to achieve robustness and good performance from them. As most smart phones and mobile devices are equipped with dual interfaces (WiFi and 3G/4G), a promising approach is through the use of multi-path TCP, which leverages path diversity to improve performance and provide robust data transfers. In this paper we explore the performance of multi-path TCP in the wild, focusing on simple 2-path multi-path TCP scenarios. We seek to answer the following questions: How much can a user benefit from using multi-path TCP over cellular and WiFi relative to using the either interface alone? What is the impact of flow size on average latency? What is the effect of the rate/route control algorithm on performance? We are especially interested in understanding how application level performance is affected when path characteristics (e.g., round trip times and loss rates) are diverse. We address these questions by conducting measurements using one commercial Internet service provider and three major cellular carriers in the US.

Categories and Subject Descriptors

C.2 [**Computer-communication Networks**]: Network Protocols; C.2.1 [**Network Architecture and Design**]: Wireless communication; C.4 [**Performance of System**]: Measurement techniques, Performance attributes

General Terms

Experimentation; Measurement; Performance

IMC'13, October 23–25, 2013, Barcelona, Spain.

http://dx.doi.org/10.1145/2504730.2504751.

Keywords

Multi-Path TCP; MPTCP; Congestion Control; Measurements; Wireless; Cellular Networks; 4G; LTE; 3G; CDMA

1. INTRODUCTION

Many users with mobile devices can access the Internet through both WiFi and cellular networks. Typically, these users only utilize one technology at a time: WiFi when it is available, and cellular otherwise. Research has also focused on the development of mechanisms that switch between cellular and WiFi as the quality of the latter improves and degrades. This results in a quality of service that is quite variable over time. As data downloads (e.g., Web objects, video streaming, etc.) are dominant in the mobile environment, this can result in highly variable download latencies.

In this paper we explore the use of a promising recent development, multi-path rate/route control, as a mechanism for providing robustness by reducing the variability in download latencies. Multi-path rate/route control was first suggested by Kelly [17]. Key et al. [18] showed how multi-path rate/route control provides load balancing in networks. Han et al. [10] and Kelly & Voice [16] developed theoretically grounded controllers that have since been adapted into Multipath TCP (MPTCP) [8], which is currently being standardized by the IETF.

Numerous studies, both theoretical and experimental, have focused on the benefits that MPTCP bring to long-lived flows. These studies have resulted in a number of changes in the controller [14,19,32], all in an attempt to provide better fairness and better throughput in the presence of fairness constraints. However, to date, these studies have ignored the effect of multi-path on finite duration flows. It is well known that most Web downloads are of objects no more than one MB in size, although the tail of the size distribution is large. Moreover, online video streaming to mobile devices is growing in popularity and, although it is typically thought of as a download of a single large object, usually consists of a sequence of smaller data downloads (500 KB - 4 MB) [27]. Thus it important to understand how the use of MPTCP might benefit such applications.

In this paper we evaluate how MPTCP performs in the wild with a common wireless environment, namely using both WiFi and cellular simultaneously. We conduct a range of experiments varying over time, space, and download size. We utilize three different cellular providers (two 4G LTEs, one 3G CMDA) and one WiFi provider, covering a broad range of network characteristics in terms of bandwidth, packet loss, and round-trip time. To assess how effectively MPTCP behaves, we report not only multi-path results, but also single-path results using the WiFi and cellular networks in isolation. We report standard networking metrics (download time, RTT, loss) as well as MPTCP specific ones (e.g., share of traffic sent over one path, packet reordering delay). We also examine several potential optimizations to multi-path, such as simultaneous SYNs, different congestion controllers, and using larger numbers of paths.

This paper makes the following contributions:

- We find that MPTCP is robust in achieving performance at least close to the best single-path performance, across a wide range of network environments. For large transfers, performance is better than the best single path, except in cases with poor cellular networks.
- Download size is a key factor in how MPTCP performs, since it determines whether a subflow can get out of slow start. It also affects how quickly MPTCP can establish and utilize a second path. For short transfers (i.e., less than 64 KB), performance is determined by the round-trip time (RTT) of the best path, typically WiFi in our environment. In these cases, flows never leave slow start and are limited by the RTT. For larger transfers, in the case of LTE, as download size increases, MPTCP achieves significantly improved download times by leveraging both paths simultaneously, despite varying path characteristics.
- Round trip times over the cellular networks can be very large and exhibit large variability, which causes significant additional delay due to reordering out-of-order segments from different paths. This is particularly pronounced on the 3G network we tested. This impacts how well MPTCP can support multimedia applications such as video.
- Using multiple flows improves performance across download sizes. For small transfers, this is because more flows allow more opportunity to exploit slow start. For large transfers, this is due to utilizing the available network bandwidth in a more efficient way. Connecting multiple flows simultaneously, rather than serially, only improves performance for small transfers, which are most sensitive to RTT. Different congestion controllers do not appear to have a significant impact on performance for small file transfers. For larger file transfers, we observe that the default congestion controller of MPTCP (coupled [24]) does not perform as well as its alternative, olia [19].

The remainder of this paper is organized as follows: Section 2 provides some background on Cellular networks and MPTCP. We describe our experimental methodology in Section 3. Section 4 presents an overview of our results, and Section 5 looks at latency in detail. We discuss our some implications in Section 6, discuss about related work in Section 7, and conclude in Section 8.

2. BACKGROUND

This section provides background and basic characteristics of cellular data and WiFi networks, and MPTCP control mechanisms needed for the rest of the paper.

2.1 Cellular data and WiFi networks

With the emerging population of smart phones and mobile devices, to cope with the tremendous traffic growth, cellular operators have been upgrading their access technologies from the third generation (3G) to the fourth generation (4G) networks. 3G Services are required to satisfy the standards of providing a peak data rate of at least 200 K bits per second (bps). The specified peak speed for 4G services is 100 Mbps for high mobility communication, and 1 Gbps for low mobility communication. In western Massachusetts, where we perform our measurements, AT&T and Verizon networks have their 4G Long Term Evolution (LTE) widely deployed, while Sprint only has 3G Evolution-Data Optimized (EVDO) available.

Cellular data networks differ from WiFi networks in that they provide broader signal coverage and more reliable connectivity under mobility. Furthermore, since wireless link losses result in poor TCP throughput and are regarded as congestion by TCP, cellular carriers have augmented their systems with extensive local retransmission mechanisms [3], transparent to TCP, which mitigate TCP retransmissions and reduce the waste of precious resources in cellular networks. Although these mechanisms reduce the impact of losses dramatically and improves TCP throughput, they come at the cost of increased delay and rate variability.

On the other hand, WiFi networks provide shorter packet round trip times (RTTs) but higher loss rates. Throughout our measurements, we observe that the loss rates over 3G/4G networks are generally lower than 0.1%, while those of WiFi vary from 1% to 3%. From our observations, the average RTT for WiFi networks is about 30 ms, while that of 4G cellular carriers usually has base RTTs of 60 ms, and can increase by four to ten fold in a single 4G connection (depending on the carrier and the flow sizes, see Section 5), and 20-fold in 3G networks. We note that, although cellular networks in general have larger packet RTTs, in many of our measurements, WiFi is no longer faster than 4G LTE, and this provides greater incentive to use multi-path TCP for robust data transport and better throughput.

2.2 MPTCP

We discuss how the current MPTCP protocol establishes a connection and describe the different type of congestion controllers used by MPTCP.

2.2.1 *Connection and Subflow Establishment*

Once an MPTCP connection is initiated and the first flow is established, each end host knows one of its peer's IP addresses. When the client has an additional interface, for example, a 3G/4G interface, it will first notify the server its additional IP address with an *Add Address* option over the established subflow and send another SYN packet with a *JOIN* option to the server's known IP address. With this MPTCP-JOIN option, this subflow will be associated with a previously established MPTCP connection. As many of the mobile clients are behind Network Address Translations (NATs), when the server has an additional interface, it is difficult for the server to directly communicate with the mobile client as the NATs usually filter out unidentified packets [26]. The server thus sends an *Add Address* option on the established subflow, notifying the client its additional interface. As soon as the client receives it, it sends out another SYN packet with *JOIN* option to the server's newly notified IP address, together with the exchanged hashed key for this MPTCP connection, and initiates a new subflow [8].

2.2.2 Congestion Controller

As each MPTCP subflow behaves as a legacy New Reno TCP flow except for the congestion control algorithms, after the 3-way handshake, each subflow maintains its own congestion window and retransmission scheme during data transfer, and begins with a slow-start phase that doubles the window per RTT [2] before entering the congestion avoidance phase.

We briefly describe the different congestion avoidance algorithms that have been proposed for MPTCP. Let us denote by w_i and rtt_i the congestion window size and round trip time of subflow i, and denote by w the total congestion window size over all the subflows. Also, let $\mathcal{R}$ be the set of all subflows.

Uncoupled TCP Reno (reno): The simplest algorithm that one can imagine is to use TCP New Reno over each of the subflows:

- For each ACK on flow i: $w_i = w_i + \frac{1}{w_i}$
- For each loss on flow i: $w_i = \frac{w_i}{2}$.

This does not satisfy the design goal of MPTCP [24], as it fails to provide congestion balancing in the network. We use this algorithm as the baseline and refer to it as reno.

Coupled: The coupled congestion control algorithm was introduced in [32] and is the default congestion controller of MPTCP [8, 24]. It couples the increases and uses the unmodified behavior of TCP in the case of a loss. The coupled congestion control algorithm works as follows:

- For each ACK on flow i: $w_i = w_i + \min(\frac{a}{w}, \frac{1}{w_i})$
- For each loss on flow i: $w_i = \frac{w_i}{2}$

a is a function of w_i and rtt_i for all $i \in \mathcal{R}$. As discussed in [19], this algorithm fails to fully satisfy the design goal of MPTCP but provides better congestion balancing than reno.

OLIA: An opportunistic link increase algorithm has been proposed by Khalili et al. [19] as an alternative to the coupled algorithm:

- For each ACK on flow i: $w_i = w_i + \frac{w_i/\mathrm{rtt}_i^2}{(\sum_{p \in \mathcal{R}} w_p/\mathrm{rtt}_p)^2} + \frac{\alpha_i}{w_i}$
- For each loss on flow i: $w_i = \frac{w_i}{2}$

where α_i is a function of w_i and rtt_i for all $i \in \mathcal{R}$. OLIA satisfies the design goals of MPTCP and provides a better congestion balancing than the coupled algorithm [19].

3. MEASUREMENT METHODOLOGY

In this section, we describe our experimental setup and discuss our methodology. Note that all measurements were performed during March 20 to May 7 in three different towns (Sunderland, Amherst, and Hadley) in western Massachusetts. These towns are approximately 10 miles away from each other.

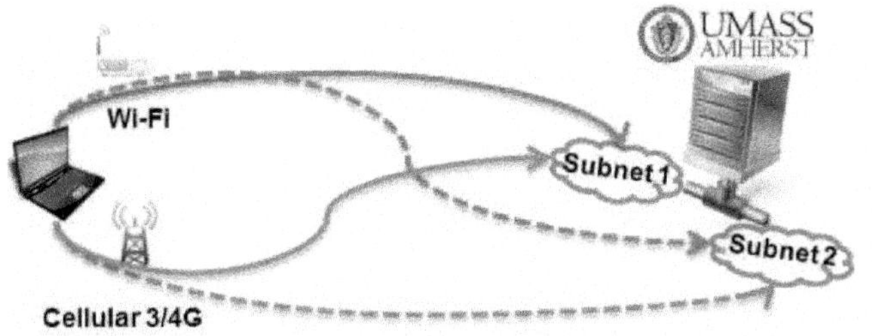

Figure 1: For 2-path MPTCP experiments, only solid-line paths are used. The additional dashed-line paths are included for the 4-path MPTCP experiments.

3.1 Experiment Setup

Figure 1 illustrates our testbed. It consists of a wired server, residing at the University of Massachusetts Amherst (UMass) and a mobile client. For most of the measurements, we focus on the 2-path scenarios (solid lines), where the client has two interfaces activated while the server has only interface in operation. A second interface is only active for performance comparisons between two flows and four flows.

Our server is configured as a multi-homed host, connecting via two Intel Gigabit Ethernet interfaces to two subnets (LANs) of the UMass network. Each Ethernet interface is assigned a public IP address and connected to the LAN via a 1 Gigabit Ethernet cable. The mobile client is a Lenovo X220 laptop and has a built-in 802.11 a/b/g/n WiFi interface. Here we consider two types of WiFi networks: private home WiFi networks and public WiFi hotspots. The home WiFi network is accessed by associating the WiFi interface to a D-Link WBR-1310 a/b/g wireless router connected to a private home network in a residential area. The home network traffic to the Internet is provided by Comcast network which serves users in the same residential community with a maximum download rate of up to 25 Mbps. Note that the actual WiFi download speed varies according to backhaul traffic load, types of home APs used, and users' wireless interfaces [29]. Unless otherwise stated, we refer to a private home network as a WiFi network. The mobile client has three additional cellular broadband data interfaces listed in Table 1, and only uses them one at a time.

Table 1: Cellular devices used for each carrier

Carrier	Device Name	Technology
AT&T	Elevate mobile hotspot	4G LTE
Verizon	LTE USB modem 551L	4G LTE
Sprint	OverdrivePro mobile hotspot	3G EVDO

Both the server and the client are running Ubuntu Linux 12.10 with Kernel version 3.5.7 using the stable release of the MPTCP Kernel implementation [21] version v0.86. The UMass server is configured as an HTTP server. It runs Apache2 on port 8080, as AT&T has a Web proxy running on port 80 which removes all the MPTCP option fields and thus does not allow MPTCP connections. The client uses *wget* to retrieve Web objects of different sizes via all the available paths.

To reduce potential WiFi interference to the working wireless interface, we disable the functionality of WiFi bandwidth sharing on both the AT&T and Sprint devices. Furthermore, though all devices run at different frequencies, to avoid possible interference between these electronic devices, we use USB cables to extend cellular dongles, and use the WiFi and only one cellular device at a time. Therefore, we assume interference among the devices is negligible. Throughout the measurements, cellular reception signals of different carriers (over different places) are in the range between -60dBm and -102dBm, which covers good and weak signals.

Connection parameters.
The default Linux TCP uses an initial slow start threshold value (*ssthresh*) of infinity, and caches parameters for per-destination TCP connections [28]. When losses occur, the *ssthresh* value will be reset and cached for initialization of future TCP connections to the same destination. However, this is shown to be harmful for short flows [13] if an earlier connection to a particular destination encounters a sequence of losses. This is because *ssthresh* will be set to a small value and all the subsequent newly open flows to that destination will have the same small *ssthresh*. Hence, we configure our server such that no parameters of previously closed TCP connections to any destination are cached. Moreover, as we are using cellular networks in nearly loss-free environments (as will be discussed later), a *ssthresh* value of infinity will lead to the case where the cellular path never leaves slow start. The congestion window of the cellular path could then become extremely large and hence suffer severe RTT inflation [3, 15], which can degrade the performance of MPTCP. Therefore, we set the default value of *ssthresh* to 64KB for fair comparisons among different configurations and file sizes, and to mitigate the impact of RTT inflation described above. We use Linux's default initial window size of 10 packets and apply TCP Selective Acknowledgement (SACK) [7].

Receive memory allocation.
As MPTCP requires a larger receive buffer than single-path TCP for out-of-order packets from different paths and uses a shared receive buffer, there is a potential performance degradation if the assigned buffer is too small [26, 32]. To avoid such events during our measurements, we set the maximum receive buffer to 8 MB.

No subflow penalty.
Throughout our experiments, we observe that the current MPTCP implementation by default monitors each flow's bandwidth delay product (BDP). If a particular flow has contributed too many out-of-order packets to the receive buffer, it penalizes that flow by reducing its congestion window by half [26], even though no loss has occurred. In our experiments, as the receive memory is always large enough, this penalization mechanism can only degrade the performance of MPTCP connections. To measure the true performance of MPTCP connections, we remove the penalization scheme from the implementation.

3.2 Experiment Methodology

As the UMass server has two physical interfaces, and the client has a built-in WiFi interface and broadband devices from three different cellular carriers, we conduct measurements of the following configurations:

- Single-path TCP: the UMass server activates its primary interface, and the client enables only one interface (WiFi or cellular). Thus, there are four configurations in this scenario: single path WiFi TCP or single path cellular TCP (through AT&T, Verizon, or Sprint).
- 2-path MPTCP: the UMass server activates its primary interface, while the client enables WiFi and a cellular device. For each configuration, we run back to back measurements of different congestion controllers described in Section 2.2. There are nine configurations in this scenario: client's three settings of two interfaces enabled (WiFi/AT&T, WiFi/Verizon, and WiFi/Sprint) to the server's primary interface with three congestion controller settings.
- 4-path MPTCP: for comparison purposes, we enable the server's secondary interface connected to a different subnet, as illustrated in Figure 1. There are also in total nine different configurations in this scenario.

As Web traffic can be short-lived or long-lived, for each configuration, the client downloads files of different sizes from the server via HTTP. As there is no clear distinction between short flows and long flows, in our measurements, we consider files of sizes 8 KB, 64 KB, 512 KB, and 4 MB as small flows. For large flows, we consider file of sizes 8 MB, 16 MB, and 32 MB. We also consider infinite backlog file transfers for performance purposes (see Section 4.2), and here file downloads are of size 512 MB.

Since network traffic might have dependencies and/or correlation from time to time, and from size to size, in each round of measurements, we *randomize* the sequence of configurations. That is, we randomize the order of file sizes, carriers, the choices of congestion controllers, single-path and multi-path TCP. To capture temporal effects, for each scenario, we conduct measurements for multiple days. To mitigate possible spatial factors, measurements were also performed at multiple locations in the same town, and at different towns in western Massachusetts. Note that we divide a day into four periods: night (0-6 AM), morning (6-12 AM), afternoon (12-6 PM), and evening (6-12 PM). For each period of time at each location, we perform 20 measurements for each configuration.

Furthermore, since cellular 3G/4G antennas have state machines for radio resources allocation and management of energy consumption, the state promotion delay (the time duration required to bring the antenna to ready state) is often longer than packet RTTs [11, 12] and might significantly impact our short flow measurements. Therefore, to avoid this impact, we send two ICMP ping packets to our server before each measurement, and start the measurements immediately after the ping responses are correctly received to ensure that the cellular antenna is in the ready state.

We collect packet traces from both the UMass server and the client using *tcpdump* [30], and use *tcptrace* [31] to analyze the collected traces at both sides.

3.3 Performance Metrics

We are interested in the following performance metrics related to MPTCP and single-path TCP:

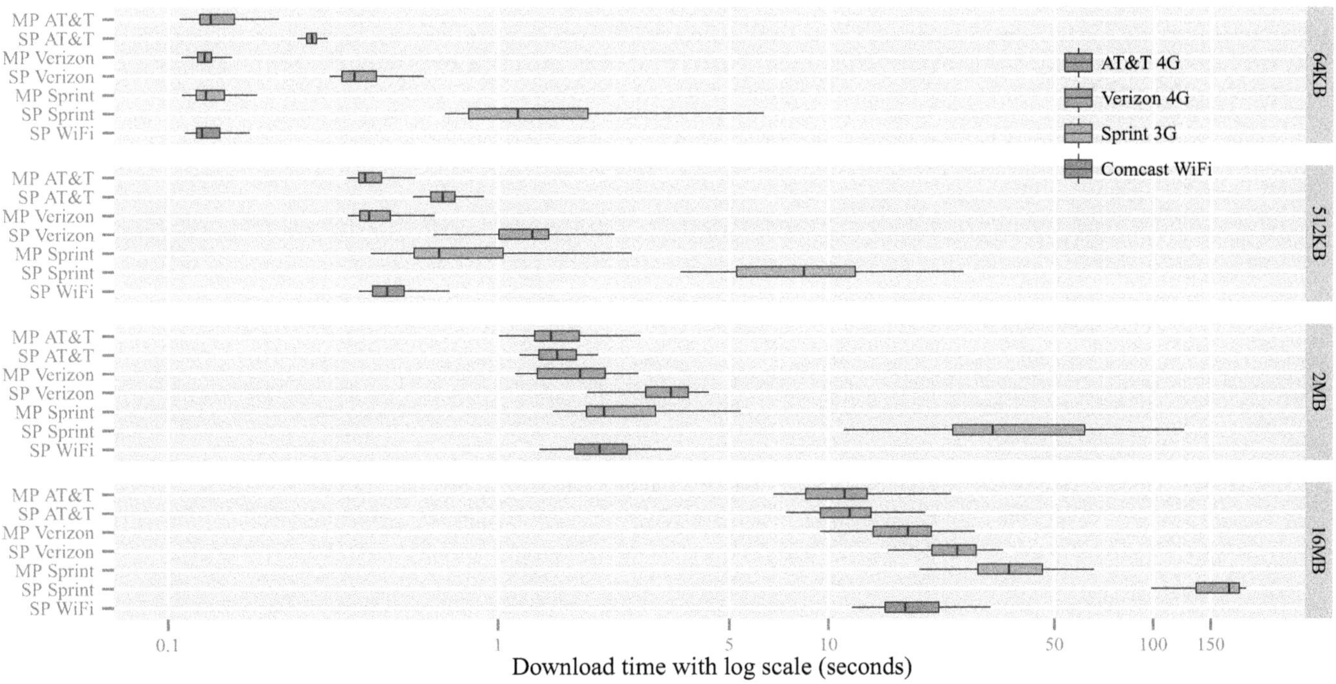

Figure 2: Baseline Download Time: MPTCP and single-path TCP connections for different carriers. The measurements were performed over the course of 24 hours for multiple days.

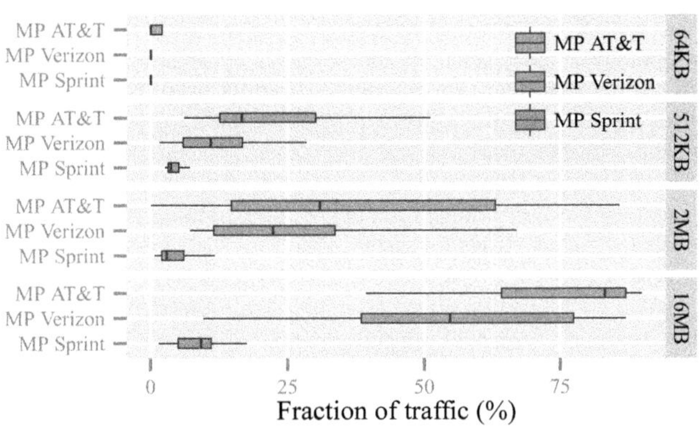

Figure 3: Baseline: faction of traffic carried by each cellular carrier in MPTCP connections.

Download time: As our goal is to understand how much gain mobile users obtain from using MPTCP, for both small flows and large flows, we focus on measuring the download time rather than the bandwidth and speed of each cellular technology. We define the download time as the duration from when the client sends out the *first SYN* to the server to the time it receives the *last data packet* from the server. We measure download time of a file using MPTCP and compare it with what we get if we use a single-path TCP over the available WiFi or 3G/4G paths.

Loss rate: The loss rate is measured on a per-subflow basis. It is calculated as the total number of retransmitted data packets divided by the total number of data packets sent by the server on the flow. We show the average loss rate by aggregating all the measurement results of the same configuration.

Round trip time (RTT): We measure RTTs on a per-subflow basis. Denote by T_r the server's receive time of an ACK packet for the previous packet sent from the server at time T_s over a subflow. RTT is measured as the difference between the time when a packet is sent by the server to the time the ACK for that packet is received (i.e., $RTT = T_r - T_s$), such that the ACK number is larger than the last sequence number of the packet and the packet is not a retransmission [31].

Out-of-order delay: MPTCP maintains two sequence numbers for each packet, a data (global) sequence number for the MPTCP connection and a subflow (local) sequence number for each TCP subflow. In-order packets arriving from the same subflow may wait in the receive buffer before their data sequence numbers become in-order. This could be due to late arrivals of packets from other paths. Therefore, a key performance metric of using MPTCP is to measure packet out-of-order delay at the receive buffer before packets are ready for delivery to the application layer. Out-of-order delay is defined to be the time difference between when a packet arrives at the receive buffer to when its data sequence number is in-order.

4. BASELINE MEASUREMENTS

Figure 2 presents the download times of different size files over different WiFi/cellular carriers using single-path or MPTCP. We show results for file sizes of 64 KB, 512 KB, 2 MB, and 16 MB. We perform our measurements over each of these four time periods in a day described in Section 3.2 and show the aggregate results in Figure 2. We use the default coupled congestion controller as the congestion control

Table 2: **Baseline path characteristics: loss rates and RTTs (sample mean ± standard error) of single-path TCP on a per connection basis across file sizes. Note that Sprint has a particularly high loss rate on 512 KB downloads. Note that ∼ represents for negligible values (< 0.03%).**

	File size			
	64 KB	512 KB	2 MB	16 MB
Loss (%)				
AT&T	0·03±0.03	0·04±0.01	0·06±0.03	0·31±0.12
Verizon	∼	∼	0·31±0.13	1·75±0.20
Sprint	0·37±0.16	8·76±4.8	3·93±0.34	1·64±0.01
Comcast	0·43±0.16	0·20±0.04	2·02±0.42	0·68±0.07
RTT(ms)				
AT&T	70·06±2.78	104·89±3.32	138·20±5.09	126·01±5.37
Verizon	92·41±13.23	204·65±20.45	422·56±28.34	624·66±54.55
Sprint	381·29±50.80	972·4 ±84.08	1209·81±178.68	703·81±81.96
Comcast	26·81±0.43	53·08±2.20	56·83±5.71	32·65±2.05

algorithm. We use box and whisker plots to summarize our measurement results. The line inside each box is the second quantile (median), the top and the bottom of each box are the first and the third quantiles (25% and 75%), and the ends of the whiskers are the minimum and maximum values.

MP-carrier refers to a 2-path MPTCP connection using a particular 3G/4G cellular network and a WiFi network. *SP-carrier* refers to a single-path TCP connection over a particular WiFi/3G/4G network.

For all file sizes, we observe that the download times for a file using MPTCP is almost the same as those using the best single-path TCP connection available to the user. Sometimes MPTCP outperforms the best path alone. MPTCP initiates the connection over using the WiFi network (i.e., the WiFi path is the default path).

For small flows, i.e., file sizes of 64 KB or smaller, single-path TCP over WiFi performs the best, and MPTCP does not provide much gain over using the cellular path. This is because WiFi connections have smaller RTTs (around 30 ms) than the 3G/4G cellular connections (60-80 ms for 4G, and 300 ms for 3G). Thus, in most small flow cases the file transfer is complete before the cellular paths can complete their 3-way handshakes. For slightly larger flows, we observe that single-path over WiFi is no longer guaranteed to be the best path (in terms of download times). Instead, single-path TCP over 4G LTE is the best choice in many instances. This is because, as can be seen in Table 2, the cellular networks (especially the 4G LTE networks) provide almost loss free paths, as opposed to WiFi's roughly 1.6% loss rate. Figure 3 shows the fraction of traffic offloaded to the cellular path from the data in Figure 2. We observe that MPTCP manages to offload traffic from the *fast but lossy* WiFi paths to the *not-so-fast but loss-free* cellular paths. Therefore, when the file size is not too small, MPTCP connections gain more by leveraging its cellular paths. Table 2 provides the loss rates and RTTs (averages and standard errors) for the measurements in Figure 2.

We observe that 3G networks tend to have slightly higher loss rates than 4G, much larger minimum RTTs (200 ms), and severe RTT variations (300-800 ms). Thus, for small flows, most packets in MPTCP-Sprint connections are delivered via WiFi. When the file sizes are large and a fraction of packets have initially been scheduled through the 3G path, it takes much longer for those packets to reach the client. In the case where the RTT variation is large over 3G paths (up to 8-10 times greater than its 3-way handshake RTT), and a packet is identified as lost and retransmitted, it can take a few seconds for a packet to be delivered and results in reduced performance. Section 5.2 analyzes this out-of-order delay in more detail.

In the rest of this section, we provide a more detailed analysis of the performance of MPTCP using different congestion controllers and different file sizes. For simplicity, we focus on one cellular carrier, AT&T 4G LTE, since it exhibits the lowest RTT variability and the most stable performance. We also utilize different WiFi networks at different locations.

4.1 Small Flow Measurements

We start by analyzing MPTCP measurements using small flows. We chose four different file sizes here (8 KB, 64 KB, 512 KB, and 4 MB) as representative of small flow measurements. For simplicity, we focus on one cellular carrier, AT&T 4G LTE, with Comcast WiFi as the default path. Our goal is 1) to understand how 2-path MPTCP performs in the wild, and 2) to understand the impact of different MPTCP congestion controllers on connection performance. For comparison purposes, we also seek 3) to understand how much more one can get when having 4-path MPTCP instead of 2-path MPTCP in the context of small file downloads.

Figure 4 shows our measurements of small flows. MP-4 and MP-2 represent MPTCP connections consisting of four and two subflows, while the congestion controller in parentheses indicates which congestion controller is used at the server. As an overview of baseline small flow measurements, a clear trend is, when file size increases, 4-path MPTCP performs better than 2-path MPTCP, which performs better than single-path TCP.

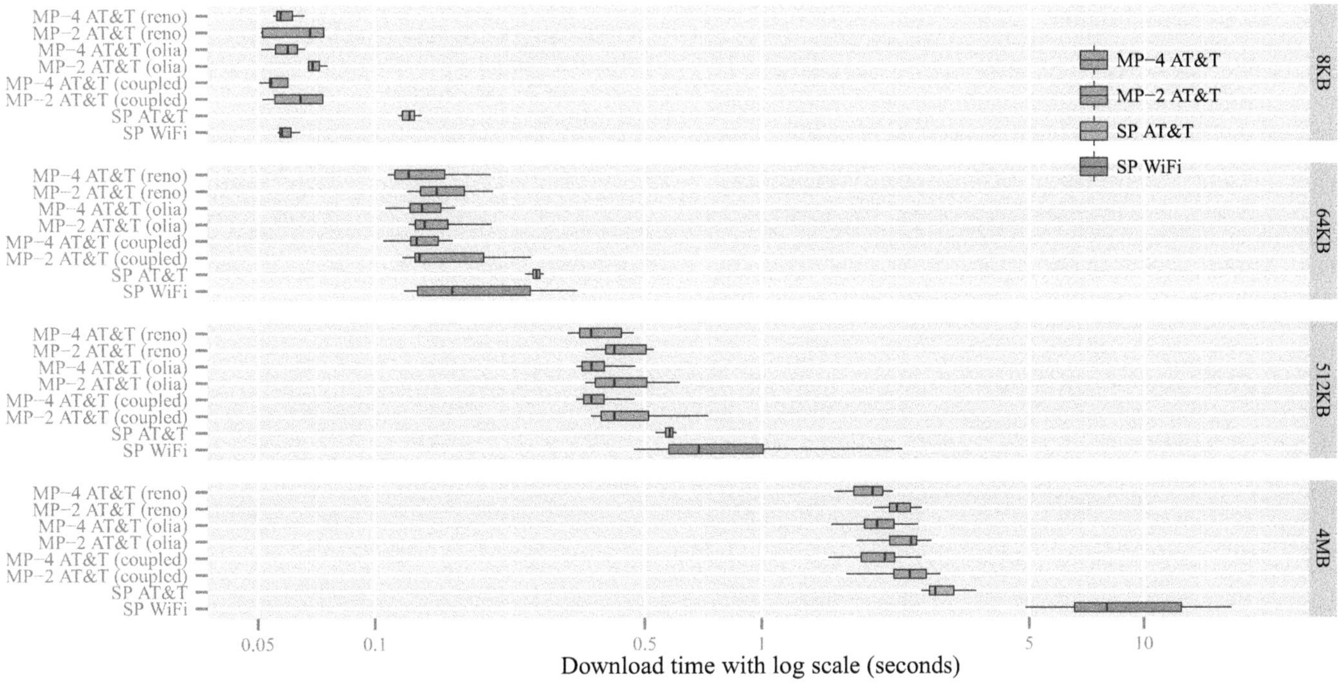

Figure 4: Small Flow Download Time: MP-4 and MP-2 represent for 4-path and 2-path MPTCP connections, and reno represents uncoupled New Reno multi-path TCP connections.

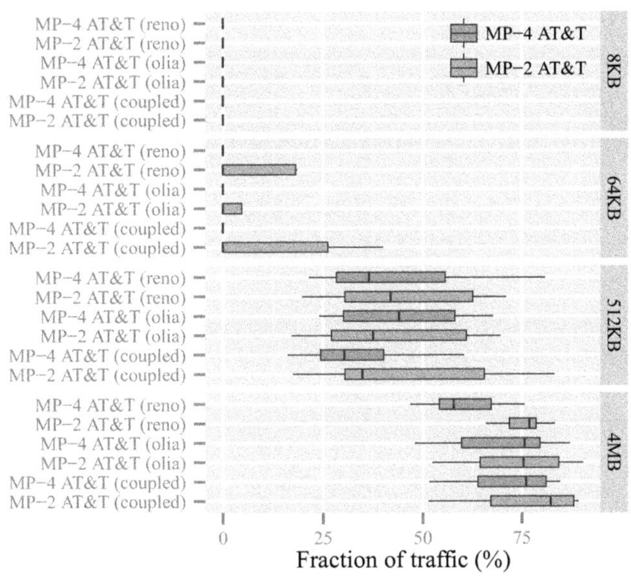

Figure 5: Small Flows: fraction of traffic carried by the cellular path for different file sizes.

4.1.1 Results at a glance

From our observations, in the case of single-path TCP, AT&T performs the worst when the file size is small (e.g., 8 KB). This is because the 4G network has a much larger minimum RTT, and the file download time over single-path WiFi is smaller than 4G's RTT of 60 ms (see Table 3). Hence, when the file sizes are as small as 8 KB, MPTCP can perform just as well as single-path TCP over WiFi (SP WiFi), regardless of the number of subflows - as most of the subflows are not utilized. Figure 5 presents the fraction of traffic carried by the cellular path in MPTCP connections over different file sizes. For file sizes smaller than 64 KB, 4-path MPTCP never utilizes the cellular path to deliver traffic, while 2-path MPTCP occasionally utilizes the cellular path.

For 4-path MPTCP, since both WiFi subflows have RTTs one half or one third of those of the cellular subflows, the two WiFi subflows can quickly complete the download of 64 KB within 2 RTTs (when no loss occurs), and the file transaction completes before the cellular paths are able to contribute. Given that the WiFi paths exhibit roughly 1.6% loss rates, in the 64 KB single-path TCP case, when a loss occurs, the cellular subflow of the 2-path MPTCP connection is able to carry some traffic.

When the flow size increases to 512 KB, we observe that WiFi is no longer the best path. Its download time is slightly larger than that of single-path TCP over AT&T LTE and has high variability. Although WiFi is characterized by small RTTs, it exhibits much larger loss rates compared to the cellular network, as shown in Table 3. When the download time spans several RTTs and the cellular path is able to contribute, the fraction of traffic carried by the cellular subflow(s) surpasses that of the WiFi flow(s). In Figure 5, we see a clear trend that the fraction of packets carried by the cellular flows reaches 50% and starts to dominate the packet delivery when the file size is 4MB. Note that by replacing the WiFi AP with a newer standard, such as 802.11n, the WiFi loss rates can be reduced because of more advanced technologies. In separate measurements, the flow loss rate of 802.11n WiFi home network is reduced but still much larger than that exhibited by cellular.

Effect of subflow number.

For each file size, we see a clear trend that 4-path MPTCP outperforms 2-path MPTCP. This result is more prominent as the file size increases. The main reason is that when a MPTCP connection starts four subflows for small file downloads (suppose all the subflows are utilized and no loss occurs), all subflows can still be in their slow-start phases before the download is complete. Therefore, the 4-path MTPCP for small file transfers in principal leverages 4 slow-start phases simultaneously to fetch the one file. This may cause some fairness issues for other users sharing the same bottlenecks as MPTCP subflows.

Effect of congestion controllers.

In terms of different MPTCP congestion controllers, we do not see much difference between coupled, olia, and reno for small flows (except for 4 MB). This is likely due to the fact that most of time the connection terminates during the slow-start phase(s) if no loss occurs and the congestion controllers do not begin to operate.

Effect of background traffic.

Figure 6 shows the measurement results performed in a public WiFi hotspot offered by a coffee shop in downtown Amherst on a Friday afternoon, where the traffic load is high over the WiFi path, and we also used WiFi as the default path. During the measurements, there were on average 15 to 20 customers connecting to the WiFi hotspot with their laptops, iPads, and smart phones. For the sake of time, we did not measure the performance of olia. We observe from the results that (1): WiFi is unreliable and does not always provide the best path, (2): MPTCP performs close to the best available path. Figure 12 depicts the fraction of traffic carried over the cellular path in MPTCP connections for different file sizes. Compared to the previous results (Figure 5), we observe that more traffic is transmitted over the cellular network. This is because the WiFi path is very unreliable and lossy and, hence, MPTCP offloads the traffic to the more reliable cellular connection. These results show that MPTCP performs resonably well even in an extreme situation. Note that for 8 KB file size, we observe that MPTCP performs better than single-path TCP over WiFi even if MPTCP sends no traffic over cellular. This is because the WiFi path exhibits very large RTT variability and we did not have enough measurement samples to provide statistically meaningful results for the 8 KB case. Table 4 shows the average loss rates and RTTs over WiFi and AT&T connections.

4.1.2 *Simultaneous SYNs*

Current MPTCP implementations require a first flow to be established for information exchange (i.e., sender/client key and interface information) before adding a second flow. The approach of delaying the SYN packet for the second flow exhibits the following benefits: 1) it is safe and easier to fall back on legacy TCP if the other end does not speak MPTCP, and 2) it provides a higher level of connection security with key exchange. However, if the servers are known to be MPTCP-capable and the connections have been authorized, this delayed-SYN procedure postpones the usage of the second path and hence increases the download time, especially for small flows.

Table 3: Small flow path characteristics: loss rates and RTTs (sample mean ±standard error) for single-path TCP connections. Note that $\sim$ represents for negligible values ($< 0.03\%$).

	File size			
	8 KB	64 KB	512 KB	4 MB
Loss(%)				
WiFi	1·0±0.5	1·6±0.4	1·4±0.2	2·1±0.2
AT&T	~	~	~	~
RTT(ms)				
WiFi	22·3±0.2	38·7±6.9	33·9±2.7	23·9±0.3
AT&T	60·8±0.5	64·9±0.5	73·2±2.1	140·9±1.1

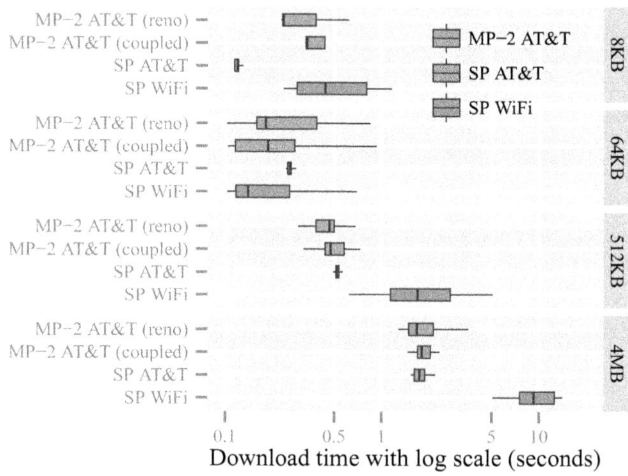

Figure 6: Amherst coffee shop: public free WiFi through Comcast business network.

Table 4: Path characteristics of Amherst coffee shop: cellular network and public WiFi hotspot. Note that $\sim$ represents for negligible values ($< 0.03\%$).

	File size			
	8 KB	64 KB	512 KB	4 MB
Loss(%)				
WiFi	5·3±1.6	3·1±0.6	4·1±0.3	2·9±0.4
AT&T	~	~	~	0·1±0.1
RTT (ms)				
WiFi	44·2±7.0	26·0±1.8	21·9±0.5	21·3±0.4
AT&T	62·4±0.6	63·4±0.4	61·4±0.4	80·8±1.8

For performance purposes, we modify the current MPTCP implementation to allow the client to send SYN packets simultaneously over each of its available paths to the server. In principle, this can allow the user to establish both its paths simultaneously and will reduce the download time of the file. This can also improve the performance of MPTCP

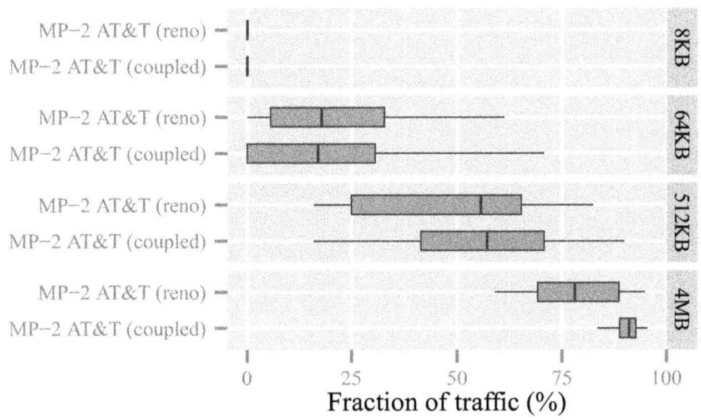

Figure 7: Amherst coffee shop: fraction of traffic carried by the cellular path. With MPTCP-coupled and uncoupled New Reno TCPs, where MPTCP is in favor of the cellular path when the file size increases.

in cases where the default path (WiFi in our case) is very lossy or has a large RTT.

Figure 8 shows that based on our measurements, even with large average RTT ratios, the simultaneous-SYN MPTCP on average reduces the download time by 14% for 512 KB files and 5% for 2 MB files, respectively. There could be even greater benefit if the RTTs of the paths are similar, especially for small downloads. Note that simultaneous SYN and delayed SYN might not differ much for very small size files since most of the packets can be delivered through the first path (as the initial congestion window is 10 packets).

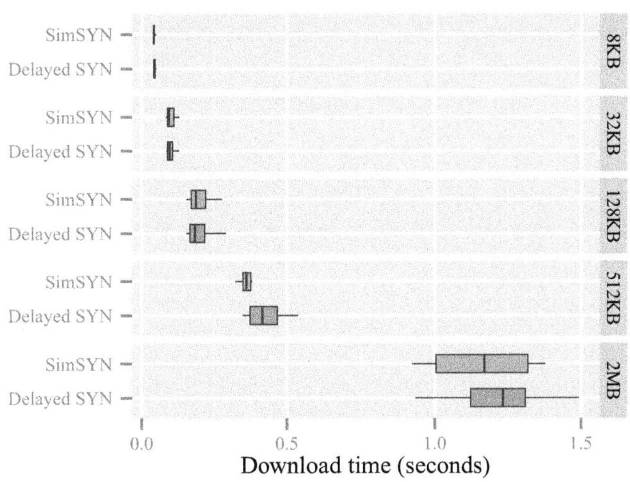

Figure 8: Small Flows: download time for simultaneous SYN and the default delayed SYN approach.

4.2 Large Flow Measurements

In this section, we present results for larger file sizes (e.g., 8 MB, 16 MB, and 32 MB). For comparison purposes, we also include 4 MB downloads with the other three large file sizes made during the day of our measurements. Our goal is to evaluate the behavior of MPTCP when subflows leave their slow start phases, and the MPTCP congestion controller takes over the connection and performs congestion control with load balancing. Our results show how current MPTCP congestion controllers (coupled and olia) perform in the wild, rather than in the environments where most of the traffic is well-controlled [19,32]. We compare the results to a baseline where we use uncoupled New Reno (reno) as the congestion controller.

Figure 9 presents the results. We observe that: (1) WiFi is no longer the best path and MPTCP always outperforms the best single-path TCP, (2) 4-path MPTCP always outperforms its 2-path counterpart, (3) MPTCP-olia consistently performs slightly better than MPTCP-coupled. In particular, we observe that MPTCP-olia performs similarly to MPTCP-coupled for file size of 4 MB, and reduces the download latencies of files of sizes 8 MB, 16 MB, and 32 MB by 5%, 6%, and 10%, respectively, in both 2-path and 4-path scenarios). TCP New Reno performs better because it is more aggressive and not fair to other users. In contrast, olia's better performance (compared to coupled) is due to its better load balancing in the network [19].

Figure 10 shows that in all configurations, over 50% of traffic is now routed through the cellular path instead of WiFi. This is because, in large flow downloads, the cellular path's very low loss rate compensates for its much larger RTTs. Table 5 lists the RTTs and loss rates seen by the subflows on a per connection average. We see from this table that WiFi loss rates varies from 1.6% to 2.1%, while 4G LTE provides very consistent and low loss rate of 0.01%, and the per connection average RTTs are more stable (i.e., have much lower variability).

To exclude the possibility that the 4-path performance gain is due solely to the benefits of having multiple slow-start phases, we also performed measurements of transferring extremely large files of size 512 MB separately to approximate infinite backlog traffic. We performed the measurements for 2-path and 4-path MPTCP using coupled and uncoupled New Reno as congestion controller with 10 iterations each (results of olia are omitted for lack of space). Figure 11 shows that the download time is around 6-7 minutes, hence the effect of slow starts should be negligible. The results of 4-path MPTCP confirms the results in Figure 9 as we observe that 4-path MPTCP slightly outperforms 2-path MPTCP.

Table 5: Large flow path characteristics: loss rates and RTTs (sample mean $\pm$standard error) of single-path TCP on per connection average. Note that $\sim$ represents for negligible values ($< 0.03\%$).

	File size			
	4 MB	8 MB	16 MB	32 MB
Loss(%)				
WiFi	2·1±0.4	1·6±0.3	1·9±0.3	2·0±0.3
AT&T	0·1±0.1	~	~	~
RTT(ms)				
WiFi	26·2±0.9	25·9±0.5	24·9±0.4	23·5±0.3
AT&T	133·1±4.4	154·5±2.7	144·5±4.1	146·4±4.3

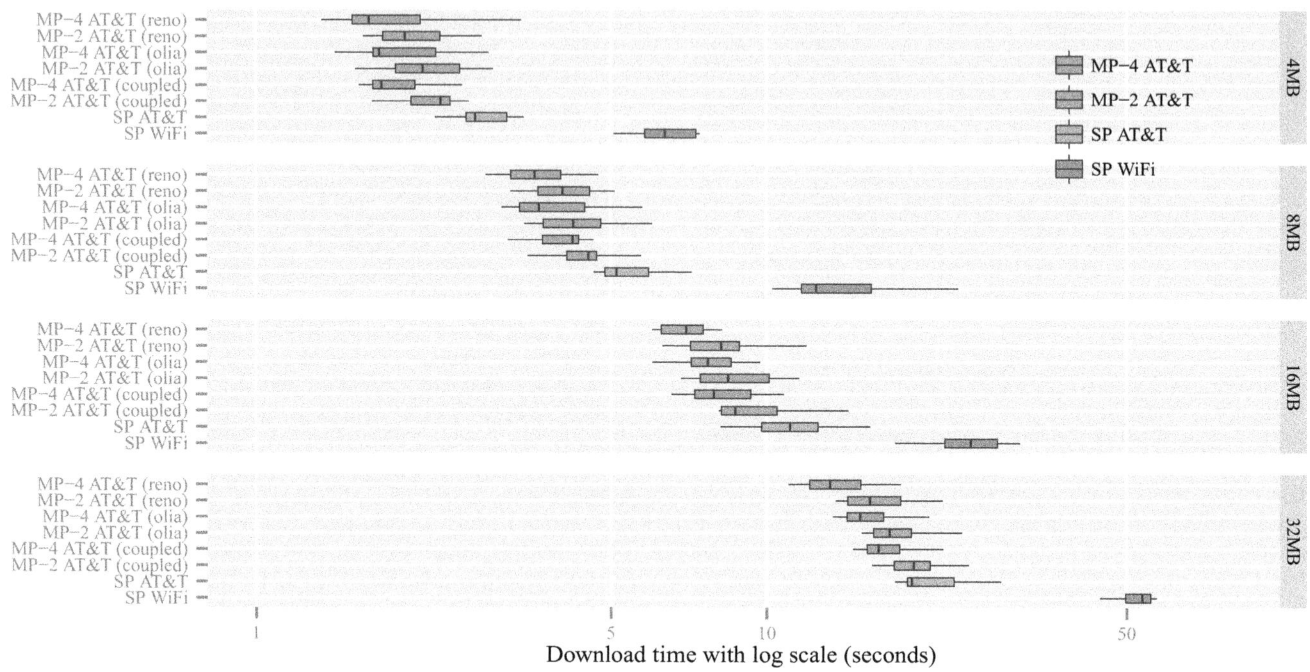

Figure 9: Large Flow Download Time: MP-4 and MP-2 represent for 4-path and 2-path MPTCP connections, and reno represents uncoupled New Reno multi-path TCP connections.

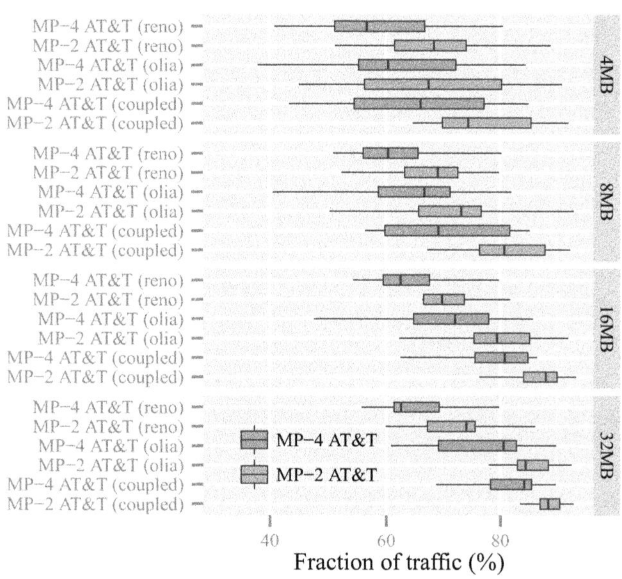

Figure 10: Large Flows: fraction of traffic carried by the cellular path for different file sizes.

5. LATENCY DISTRIBUTION

In previous sections, we focused mainly on the performance of MPTCP in terms of download times. For mobile users, however, low download time does not necessarily guarantee a high quality of experience. When using the Internet, users do more than simply fetching and viewing Web pages. Users often consume real-time applications, such as video streaming (e.g., Youtube, Netflix) or interactive services (e.g., Facetime, Skype). These applications require stable network service, i.e., low variability and jitter.

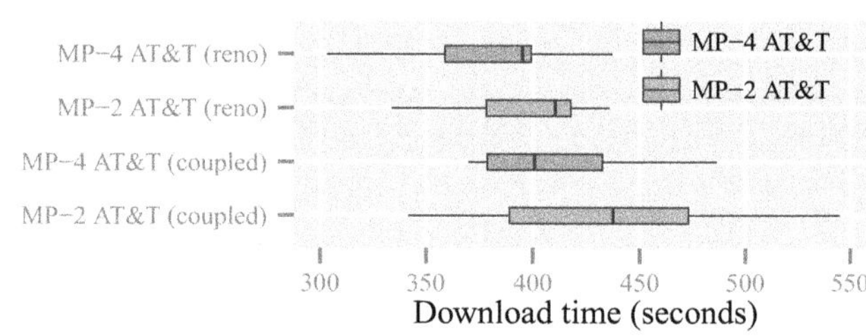

Figure 11: Large Flows: download time of infinite backlog (file size 512 MB) for uncoupled New Reno/coupled MPTCP connections with four/two flows.

Although MPTCP provides robustness against time-varying path quality, the impact to MPTCP connection quality remains unclear when another cellular/WiFi path is being exploited for MPTCP. In the following sections, we first characterize path latency (in terms of packet round trip times) of each cellular carrier and the Internet service provider, and try to understand the impact of using heterogeneous networks. More importantly, we investigate how leveraging path diversity might introduce latency to application performance, which can directly affect user experience.

5.1 Packet Round Trip Times

We reported average RTTs (and their standard errors) of single-path TCP connections over cellular and WiFi paths as indications of path quality in previous sections. Here, we investigate RTTs at a finer granularity by focusing on the distributions of packet RTT for each file download size, and

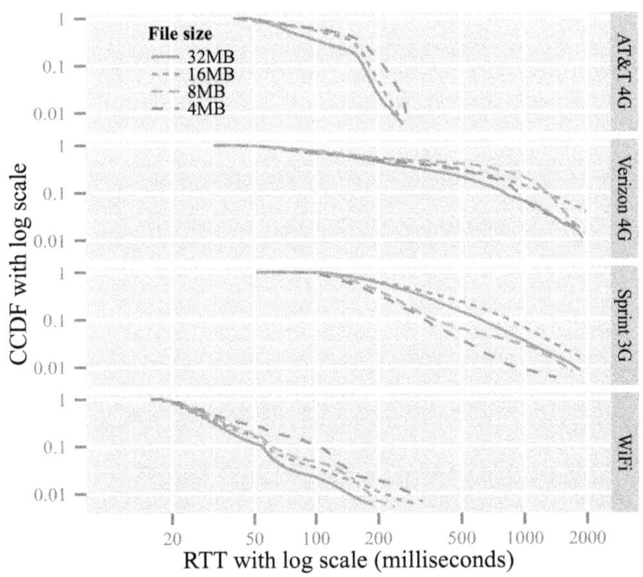

Figure 12: Packet RTT distributions of MPTCP connections using WiFi and one of the three cellular paths.

the RTT measurements are on a per-flow basis. The RTT is calculated as defined in Section 3.3. For each MPTCP connection, we record the RTT value of each packet if an ACK is received by the server for a particular packet, excluding retransmitted and timed out packets.

Note that the RTT traces are collected from the measurements described in Section 4, where the default coupled congestion controller is used. We then aggregate all the packet RTT traces over the course of 24 hours, and group them by interfaces (cellular and WiFi) and file sizes. In addition, we only report on flow sizes larger than 512KB, as some carriers have large RTTs and hence the cellular path does not carry any traffic when file sizes are smaller than 512KB.

Figure 12 presents the Complementary CDF (CCDF) plot of flow RTTs for different transfer sizes carried via different cellular/WiFi providers across all MPTCP connections. Note the the figure is in log-log scale to better visualize the tails.

Two clear behaviours are observed here. The WiFi path, on average, has lower and less variable RTTs than cellular paths. The minimum WiFi RTTs across different file sizes are about 15 ms, while 90% of packet RTTs are less than 50 ms for file sizes larger than 4 MB.

Cellular networks, on the other hand, have quite different RTT patterns than the WiFi network. The AT&T LTE path exhibits a minimum RTT of about 40 ms, and more than 70% of the RTT samples lie between 50 and 200 ms. The Sprint 3G network, on the other hand, has a minimum RTT of about 50 ms, but with more than 98% of the RTT samples larger than 100 ms, and the value could five-fold large when file sizes are 4-8 MB. If the transferred file size is as large as 16 or 32 MB, packet RTTs can be as large as 2 seconds.

Despite being based on LTE, the Verizon network, has an RTT distribution pattern that lies in between the patterns of both AT&T and Sprint. Its minimum RTT is 32 ms, which is smaller than AT&T's, but the RTT value can extend up to two seconds.

In all, packet RTTs over cellular networks have quite different patterns than conventional WiFi networks. Cellular networks exhibit larger minimum RTTs and higher RTT variability. The phenomenon of having inflated and varying RTTs over cellular networks is commonly termed as *bufferbloat* [9], and the root cause of this issue is the presence of huge buffers in the networks (routers at edge networks or in the cellular networks). Our measurements confirm results from previous studies by Allman [1] and Jiang et al. [15], which show that bufferbloat is less prominent in residential/non-residential networks (ex: private/public WiFi networks), and can be very severe in 3G/4G cellular networks.

When a MPTCP connection includes a path that has highly variable RTTs, that path can affect the overall MPTCP performance. This is mainly because for large RTT values, if the RTT values increases over time, it takes longer for the MPTCP congestion controller to update its estimated RTT and will delay the congestion controller's response to the large latency. The MPTCP congestion controller can hence underestimate the targeted throughput and lead to performance degradation. Since this issue is more related to path characteristics, we leave this for future work.

5.2 Out-of-order Delay

Our results in Section 4 show that MPTCP performs comparably to its best single-path TCP counterparts over any of the available paths, and sometimes performs slightly better. We measured the download time of a file and showed the results for different file sizes. However, in practice many applications are sensitive to the network quality (e.g., low RTT or jitter variation) rather than download time or throughput (as long as it satisfies the operational conditions). When the path characteristics (e.g., loss rate or RTT) are diverse, reordering delay becomes crucial as packets arriving early from one path need to wait for packets arriving late from another path. From our measurements, this happens very often when the paths have very different RTTs. In this case, the fraction of the traffic carried by the slow path (e.g., a 3G path) is very small, while the majority of packets arrive over the fast path, but are out-of-order in data sequence number. These packets arrive at the receive buffer as a burst, but will not be delivered to the application until the packets arrive from the slow path. In our testbed, the receive buffer is configured to be large enough so that there is no limitation due to the receive window, and thus we can measure the exact delay caused by reordering.

Figure 13 shows CCDFs of out-of-order delay using three different MPTCP configurations: AT&T/WiFi, Verizon/WiFi, and Sprint/WiFi. Note the time axis in the figure is in log scale so as to better visualize the tail. Table 6 shows the average and standard errors for RTTs and out-of-order delay of MPTCP connections.

MPTCP with AT&T 4G, and MPTCP with Verizon 4G in general do not suffer much from out-of-order packets. 75% of the packets are delivered in order (in terms of global data sequence numbers). However, transfers of of smaller files (4MB and 8MB) tend to exhibit larger out-of-order delay. This might be explained by their RTT distributions, where 4MB and 8MB flows tend to have higher RTTs. Thus, when a packet is out-of-order, it needs to wait for the later arriv-

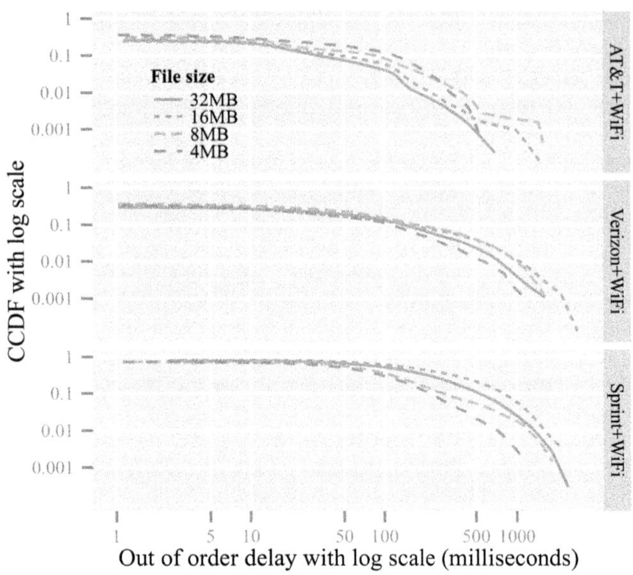

Figure 13: Out-of-order delay distributions of MPTCP connections using WiFi and one of the three cellular paths.

ing packets from the slow path (in this case, the cellular network).

MPTCP with Sprint 3G exhibits a different pattern. 75% of the packets are out-of-order when they arrive at the receive buffer. Note that the out-of-order delay might not be very important for user's Web browsing, but it is significant in the context of real-time traffic. For example, in Facetime or Skype, the maximum tolerable end-to-end latency is considered to be about 150 ms (one-way network delay plus the out-of-order delay). Here, we see more than 20% of the packets have out-of-order delay larger than 150 ms, even without including the one-way network delay. That is, given that Sprint 3G's average RTT is about 200 ms, if we consider the one-way delay to be half of the RTT, its overall end-to-end delay (prior to be available to associated application) is $(200/2)+100 = 200$ ms, which is much larger than the duration that most modern real time applications can tolerate.

6. DISCUSSION

As mobile devices and smart phones are now equipped with two interfaces (WiFi and 3G/4G), they provide natural platforms on which to use MPTCP. We have shown how applicable MPTCP is for mobile devices where multiple paths are available. We demonstrated the performance of MPTCP on file transfers of small and large flows, from 8 KB to 32 MB.

Web traffic contributes a large fraction of today's Internet traffic [4, 20], and cellular networks have also experienced tremendous HTTP traffic growth from mobile devices [5]. Although it has been reported that most Web traffic to mobile devices are flows smaller than 1 MB to 2 MB [6], online video streaming contributes the majority of the traffic to mobile devices [5], which has long been thought of as downloading a large single object from the server.

Table 6: Statistics on MPTCP RTT (flow mean ±standard errors) and out-of-order (OFO) delay (connection mean ±standard errors) over different carriers.

	File size			
	4 MB	8 MB	16 MB	32 MB
RTT(ms)				
AT&T	110.0±6.7	102.0±6.4	114.1±7.5	99.6±6.5
Verizon	228.0±26.9	399.2±46.1	360.4±44.3	296.1±31.7
Sprint	202.9±14.4	262.5±24.6	480.4±40.6	346.2±28.1
WiFi	56.2±6.7	43.4±6.4	29.4±7.5	30.0±6.5
OFO(ms)				
AT&T	30.9±3.2	26.8±4.0	16.7±1.4	13.1±1.6
Verizon	36.7±5.6	67.7±11.7	61.3±12.9	50.2±8.9
Sprint	91.3±12.6	126.9±29.9	301.7±44.3	204.5±29.8

A previous study [27] shows that, for modern online video streaming applications, such as Youtube or Netflix, transfers usually begin with a prefetching/buffering phase consisting of a large data download, followed by a sequence of periodic smaller data downloads. Table 7 summarizes the measurements we performed on two popular mobile devices when playing Netflix movies, whereas Youtube in general prefetches less aggressively by 10MB to 15MB and transfers blocks periodically of size 64 KB and 512 KB.

Table 7: Summary of Netflix video streaming

	Prefetch (MB)	Block (MB)	Period (sec)
Android	40·6±0.9	5·2±0.2	72·0±10.1
iPad	15·0±2.6	1·8±0.5	10·2±2.7

Our MPTCP measurements shed light on how MPTCP can be utilized not only for Web browsing, but also for online video streaming. We have demonstrated the utility of MPTCP for conventional Web object downloads by our small flow measurements. We show that small flows benefit from using MPTCP with multiple slow starts and by using multiple flows. When the file size is really small, say 8KB or 16KB, a fewer than a dozen of packets are required, which can be easily transmitted through the first flow within one or two RTTs. In this case, MPTCP behaves like single-path TCP and does not harm other TCP users.

In the future, when online video streaming servers are MPTCP-capable, our measurements provide some insights for understanding how well the long prefetching process and the short periodic transfers can be achieved. Furthermore, it can greatly reduce the download time without having the viewers waiting for too long and breaking the connection, even though they are mobile.

In the context of mobility, when using single-path TCP, users move from one access point to another, changing their IP address and forcing the on-going connections to be either stalled or reset. In addition, all the previously downloaded data in the stalled connections not yet delivered to the application would be wasted. In contrast, MPTCP not only leverages multiple paths simultaneously and performs traffic offloading on the fly. It also provides robust data transport in a dynamically changing environment and can support mobility without wasting bandwidth in reset connections.

An alternative to MPTCP is to identify the best network among all available ones, and maintain a single flow over that network without worrying switching among them. We argue against this option because it could be very costly or almost impossible to decide which network is the real winning network as it depends on the loss rates and RTTs over each path, as well as the file sizes. Most of this information is not available a priori at the client, and the loss rates and RTTs can also vary over time. MPTCP, on the other hand, has been shown to be responsive to changes in the networks by performing congestion balancing across different paths/networks [19, 32] and can use the best path without any of this information in advance.

Finally, as one benefits from using MPTCP by utilizing an additional interface, a natural question is energy consumption. By adding another cellular path to an MPTCP connection, there will be an additional energy cost for activating and using the antenna. We have ported the current Linux MPTCP kernel to Android phones so as to better understand the relationship between the desired MPTCP performance gain and the additional energy cost. We leave this as future work.

7. RELATED WORK

MPTCP is a set of extensions to regular TCP, which allows users to spread their traffic across potentially disjoint paths [8]. The general design of MPTCP has been inspired by the early work of Han et al. [10] and Kelly & Voice [16] that developed theoretically grounded controllers for a multipath transport protocol. Numerous studies have recently been published that discuss performance issues with current MPTCP implementations. These studies have resulted in a number of changes in the congestion controller [14, 19, 32] in an attempt to provide better fairness and throughput.

Although MPTCP is being standardized by IETF, little is understood about how well it performs in dynamic environments such as wireless networks. Raiciu et al. [23, 32] showed that MPTCP outperforms standard TCP when path diversity is available in a data center network as well as in very simple wireless settings. Paasch et al. [22] studied mobile/WiFi handover performance with MPTCP. The authors investigated the impact of handover on MPTCP connections using different modes such as full-MPTCP mode (where all potential subflows are used to transmit packets) and backup mode (where only a subset of subflows are used). They showed that MPTCP can utilize other available subflows when WiFi is disconnected but did not explore how quickly MPTCP can re-use re-established WiFi. In [25], Raiciu et al. also studied mobility with MPTCP. They examined a mobile MPTCP architecture consisting of a mobile host, an optional MPTCP proxy, and a remote host. While it shows MPTCP outperforms standard TCP in a mobile scenario, it does not examine full end-to-end MPTCP or the delayed re-use problem.

All these studies have ignored the effect of multi-path on finite size flows. Moreover, they have studied the performance of MPTCP through analysis, by simulations, or by measurement in environments where all the traffic is well controlled. In contrast, we study the performance of MPTCP in the wild, with real wireless settings and background traffic, and focuses on finite size data objects that better represent real world traffic.

8. SUMMARY AND CONCLUSION

In this paper, we reported latency measurements made for different file sizes using multi-path over WiFi and one of three different cellular providers, and compared them to the latencies using only one of either the WiFi or cellular provider. Two of the providers use LTE, and for these we observed the latencies are smaller using them exclusively except for very small files. The third provider uses a CDMA-based 3G technology and we find that using WiFi significantly reduces download latency. However, in all cases, MPTCP generates latencies that are comparable to or nearly comparable to the smallest latency produced by either WiFi or cellular. We also studied how latencies are affected by load on the WiFi path, the congestion controller design in MPTCP, the number of paths, and whether data flows are started simultaneously or in a staggered manner (as stipulated by MPTCP). In all, we conclude from our results that MPTCP provides a robust data transport and reduces the variability in download latencies.

9. ACKNOWLEDGEMENTS

This research was sponsored by US Army Research laboratory and the UK Ministry of Defense under Agreement Number W911NF-06-3-0001. The views and conclusions contained in this document are those of the authors and should not be interpreted as representing the official policies, either expressed or implied, of the US Army Research Laboratory, the U.S. Government, the UK Ministry of Defense, or the UK Government. The US and UK Governments are authorized to reproduce and distribute reprints for Government purposes notwithstanding any copyright notation hereon. This material is also based upon work supported by the National Science Foundation under Grant No. CNS-1040781 and was supported in part by the EU project CHANGE (FP7-ICT-257422).

10. REFERENCES

[1] M. Allman. Comments on bufferbloat. *ACM SIGCOMM Computer Communication Review*, 43(1):30–37, 2012.

[2] M. Allman, V. Paxson, and E. Blanton. RFC 5681: TCP congestion control, 2009.

[3] M. C. Chan and R. Ramjee. TCP/IP performance over 3G wireless links with rate and delay variation. *Wireless Networks*, 11(1-2):81–97, 2005.

[4] J. Erman, A. Gerber, M. T. Hajiaghayi, D. Pei, and O. Spatscheck. Network-aware forward caching. In *Proceedings of the 18th International Conference on World Wide Web (WWW)*, 2009.

[5] J. Erman, A. Gerber, K. Ramadrishnan, S. Sen, and O. Spatscheck. Over the top video: the gorilla in cellular networks. In *Proceedings of the 2011 ACM SIGCOMM conference on Internet Measurement Conference (IMC)*, 2011.

[6] H. Falaki, D. Lymberopoulos, R. Mahajan, S. Kandula, and D. Estrin. A first look at traffic on smartphones. In *Proceedings of the 10th ACM*

SIGCOMM conference on Internet Measurement Conference (IMC), 2010.

[7] S. Floyd, J. Mahdavi, M. Mathis, and M. Podolsky. RFC 2883: An extension to the selective acknowledgement (SACK) option for TCP, 2000.

[8] A. Ford, C. Raiciu, M. Handley, and O. Bonaventure. RFC 6824: TCP extensions for multipath operation with multiple addresses, 2013.

[9] J. Gettys and K. Nichols. Bufferbloat: Dark buffers in the Internet. *Communications of the ACM*, 55(1):57–65, 2012.

[10] H. Han, S. Shakkottai, C. V. Hollot, R. Srikant, and D. Towsley. Multi-path TCP: A joint congestion control and routing scheme to exploit path diversity in the Internet. *IEEE/ACM Transactions on Networking*, 14:1260–1271, December 2006.

[11] J. Huang, Q. Feng, A. Gerber, Z. M. Mao, S. Sen, and O. Spatscheck. A close examination of performance and power characteristics of 4G LTE networks. In *Proceedings of the 8th International Conference on Mobile Systems, Applications, and Services (MobiSys)*, 2012.

[12] J. Huang, Q. Xu, B. Tiwana, Z. M. Mao, M. Zhang, and P. Bahl. Anatomizing application performance differences on smartphones. In *Proceedings of the 8th international Conference on Mobile Systems, Applications, and Services (MobiSys)*, 2010.

[13] P. Hurtig and A. Brunstrom. Enhanced metric caching for short TCP flows. In *Proceedings of IEEE International Conference on Communications (ICC)*, 2012.

[14] B. Jiang, Y. Cai, and D. Towsley. On the resource utilization and traffic distribution of multipath transmission control. *Perform. Eval.*, 68(11):1175–1192, Nov. 2011.

[15] H. Jiang, Y. Wang, K. Lee, and I. Rhee. Tackling bufferbloat in 3G/4G networks. In *Proceedings of the 2012 ACM SIGCOMM conference on Internet Measurement Conference (IMC)*, 2012.

[16] F. Kelly and T. Voice. Stability of end-to-end algorithms for joint routing and rate control. *SIGCOMM Computer Communications Review*, 35(2):5–12, Apr. 2005.

[17] F. P. Kelly, A. K. Maulloo, and D. K. Tan. Rate control for communication networks: shadow prices, proportional fairness and stability. *Journal of the Operational Research society*, 49(3):237–252, 1998.

[18] P. Key, L. Massoulié, and D. Towsley. Combining multipath routing and congestion control for robustness. In *Proceedings of the 40th IEEE Conference on Information Sciences and Systems (CISS)*, 2006.

[19] R. Khalili, N. Gast, M. Popovic, U. Upadhyay, and J.-Y. Le Boudec. MPTCP is not pareto-optimal: Performance issues and a possible solution. In *Proceedings of the 8th International Conference on Emerging Networking Experiments and Technologies (CoNEXT)*, 2012.

[20] G. Maier, A. Feldmann, V. Paxson, and M. Allman. On dominant characteristics of residential broadband Internet traffic. In *Proceedings of the 9th ACM SIGCOMM conference on Internet Measurement Conference (IMC)*, 2009.

[21] MultiPath TCP Linux kernel implementation. http://mptcp.info.ucl.ac.be/.

[22] C. Paasch, G. Detal, F. Duchene, C. Raiciu, and O. Bonaventure. Exploring mobile/WiFi handover with multipath TCP. In *Proceedings of ACM SIGCOMM Workshop on Cellular Networks (CellNet)*, 2012.

[23] C. Raiciu, S. Barre, C. Pluntke, A. Greenhalgh, D. Wischik, and M. Handley. Improving datacenter performance and robustness with multipath TCP. In *ACM SIGCOMM Computer Communication Review*, volume 41, pages 266–277, 2011.

[24] C. Raiciu, M. Handly, and D. Wischik. RFC 6356: Coupled congestion control for multipath transport protocols, 2011.

[25] C. Raiciu, D. Niculescu, M. Bagnulo, and M. J. Handley. Opportunistic mobility with multipath TCP. In *Proceedings of the 6th ACM Workshop on Mobility in the Evolving Internet Architecture (MobiArch)*, 2011.

[26] C. Raiciu, C. Paasch, S. Barre, A. Ford, M. Honda, F. Duchene, O. Bonaventure, and M. Handley. How hard can it be? Designing and implementing a deployable multipath TCP. In *Proceedings of the 9th USENIX Conference on Networked Systems Design and Implementation (NSDI)*, 2012.

[27] A. Rao, A. Legout, Y.-s. Lim, D. Towsley, C. Barakat, and W. Dabbous. Network characteristics of video streaming traffic. In *Proceedings of the 7th Conference on Emerging Networking Experiments and Technologies (CoNEXT)*, 2011.

[28] P. Sarolahti and A. Kuznetsov. Congestion control in Linux TCP. In *Proceedings of the USENIX Annual Technical Conference (ATC)*, 2002.

[29] V. Shrivastava, S. Rayanchu, J. Yoonj, and S. Banerjee. 802.11n under the microscope. In *Proceedings of the 8th ACM SIGCOMM conference on Internet Measurement Conference (IMC)*, 2008.

[30] tcpdump. http://www.tcpdump.org.

[31] tcptrace. http://www.tcptrace.org.

[32] D. Wischik, C. Raiciu, A. Greenhalgh, and M. Handley. Design, implementation and evaluation of congestion control for multipath TCP. In *Proceedings of the 8th USENIX conference on Networked Systems Design and Implementation (NSDI)*, 2011.

Author Index

www.ingramcontent.com/pod-product-compliance
Ingram Content Group UK Ltd.
Pitfield, Milton Keynes, MK11 3LW, UK
UKHW051413290926
15471UKWH00009B/1586

9 781450 326797